INDIAN NATIONAL ARMY

A Documentary Study

(In 5 Volumes)

Volume-V

(1944-1945)

T. R. SAREEN

GYAN PUBLISHING HOUSE
NEW DELHI - 110002

INDIAN NATIONAL ARMY—A DOCUMENTARY STUDY

Rs. 4,500/-

ISBN : 81-212-0833-5 (Set)
ISBN : 81-212-0848-3 (Vol-5)

Published in 2004 in India by
Gyan Publishing House
5, Ansari Road, Daryaganj
New Delhi-110 002
Phones-23282060, 23261060, Fax-23285914
Email : gyanbook@vsnl.com
Visit our Website at : http//www.gyanbooks.com

Lasertype Setting by: Tact Computer Graphics, Delhi
Printed at: Chawla Offset Press, Delhi

To
Anuradha

List of Documents

Introduction

Volume V of the document deal with the last phase of the Indian National Army after they were brought back to India from South East Asia. British officers of the Indian army were keen that the I.N.A. men should be treated as traitors and adequately punished for breaking their oath of allegiance to the King Emperor. In their view they were also guilty of joining hands with the enemies of the Raj. Under pressure the government agreed to prosecute them now that the war was over. Surprisingly during the war the I.N.A. Soldiers who were captured during the Imphal campaign, were not punished or treated harshly. They were merely classified as 'White' 'Black' or 'Grey' according to the degree of their involvement with the Japanese. They were treated secretly and kept away from the public and even from their families. The idea was that no one should know about the existence of the I.N.A. After the war the situatiion had become different and had raised very difficult problems.The government was at a loss to decide as to how to deal with more than twenty thousands of them.

The problem had become more difficult on account of the facts, which had come to light after interrogating them. Earlier they were treated as deserters and traitors. But now it was known that they had collaborated with the enemies of the Raj for the liberation of their motherland and that they were not the puppet of the Japanese. It was further revealed that they had become nationalists in their outlook and were not now willing to serve under the British government as they were bound to the oath of loyalty, which they had taken in the I.N.A. after joining it. As regards the oath taken when they were in the British army earlier, their argument was that it was automatically annulled at the time of Singapore surrender and their being handed over the Japanese. [Document No. 4].

Even after knowing the above details, the British officers still considered them as traitors, though it was reluctantly conceded that the membership of the I.N.A. had made a deep impression on all those who joined it and they had still persevered their belief in the ideals of Subhas

Chandra Bose; that they were proud of Bose; of the I.N.A. and of their own efforts to free India. Keeping this in view, the higher authorities both in India and England decided to prosecute only those who were the worst offenders and those who were guilty of brutal behaviour towards some members of the Indian army who had refused to join the I.N.A. The British policy towards the I.N.A. had to be changed due to the political pressure and the mass upsurge in the favour of the I.N.A[Document No4, 6, 110.

All the political parties began to take deep interest in the fate of the I.N.A. soldiers, who became as Nehru puts it as 'a symbol of India's fighting for Independence'. The Indian National Congress, who had earlier denounced the creed of violence now came forward to defend the I.N.A. A Defence Committee was formed, who immediately urged the Viceroy that the trials be either postponed or abandoned until after the formation of the interim government at the centre and the functioning of the Provincial Governments' [Document No. 3]

The British government had no wish to postpone the trial. However keeping in view the mounting public demonstration in favour of these men, it was decided to put on trial only three officers of the I.N.A. in the first instance. It had become more or less a question of prestige for the British, as was reported by the American intelligence agency[Document No.9]. The trials began on 5 November1945. Soon after the authorities were faced with unprecedented, widespread popular demonstration in favour of the I.N.A. The reports came from the Director of the Criminal Intelligence that there had 'seldom been a matter which has attracted so much' attention of the public, and public sympathy as the I.N.A. isssue [Document No. 8]. Nehru warned the government that 'it would be very grave error leading to far reaching consequences if these men were treated as ordinary criminals' and the 'punishment given to them would be in effect be punishment to all India and Indians'. Other political parties also came forward to defend the I.N.A. men.

The Defense Committee of the Congress under the able guidance of Bhulabhai Desai fought the case. Desai spoke in their defense for nearly eight hours. He quoted precedent after precedent from international law in support of their actions. The main thrust of Desai's argument was that these men had the legitimate right to fight for the liberation of their motherland. He tried to prove that the Azad Hind Government was a recognized government and the I.N.A. was operating under the legitimate rules framed by this government. [Document No. 13]. The prosecution council, however did not accept the; pleadings of Desai [Document No. 14] As such all the three officers were convicted by the British and found guilty. They were sentenced to cashiering and transportation for life. During the trial the government had come to know that the punishment given to these officers by the court would be impossible to carry out in view of the strong public sympathy. As such the Viceroy issued an ordinance equipping the C-in-C with an authority of commuting the sentences of death or transportation for life just a week before the trial ended on 31 December 1945. Under this the C-in-C formerly decided to free the three I.N.A. officers only with cashiering and forfeiture of pay and allowances. [Document No 13].

In order to pacify the feelings of the British officers the C-in-C sent a memorandum saying that the 'confirmation of the sentences would have resulted in violent internal conflict, in India. As such he had taken a lenient view of their case and had commuted the sentences of all the three officers. [Document No. 18] With the above decision by the C-in-C, Shah Nawaz, P.K. Saghal, and G.S. Dhillon were released. Their release gave a fresh turn to the national movment in India, which made it difficult for the British to rely on the Indian Armed forces for the maintenance of their rule any longer.

Many are still alive, who joined the I.N.A. and there are others who were an eyewitness to the frenzied adulation of the Indian people for the I.N.A. soldiers. The author of these volumes belong to the second category who still remembers the heroic welcome given by the people to Shah Nwaz. Dhillion and Sahgal when they visited Lahore in 1946 after their release. This is evident from the report of the press included here. [Document no 16] It is interesting to note as to how the Congress afterwards under Nehru's leadership changed its policy towards the I.N.A. Some indication of this change in policy became apparent after the Congress came into power in 1946. This is evident from the record of the interview between Nehru and Lord Wavell, [Document no 19].

As mentioned earlier, the British Intelligence had closely kept an eye on the activities of the I.N.A. and detailed reports were prepared by the C.S.D.I.C., which was located at Red Fort. All their reports are not available at one place Some of these could be located in the I.N.A. papers, while others are available in the War Office papers at the Public Record Office, London. A few of these have been included in the earlier volumes, and a some are given in this volume. These reports are very informative especially the one on the Hikari Kikan, and the report containing the break up account of the soldiers of the British Indian Army who joined the I.N.A. after the fall of Singapore. Another report deal with the fighting capabilities of the I.N.A. on the Burma front.[Document No. 15,18,22]

This volume also contain a detailed report by a British agent who remained in Singapore. This report gives us a close view of many aspects of the I.N.A., not available anywhere else. The British Agent was in the special branch of the Police department at Singapore. [Document No. 10] However, it must be clarified that the reports of the Military Intelligence and the agents should not be taken at their face value. It is necessary to verify them with other evidence from the private and official records.

Death of Bose in the plane crash is still an unsolved mystery and an another commission of enquiry is looking into it at present. In this volume, only a few reports dealing with the last days of Bose are included which were prepared by the military intelligence. [Document No. 2,7.] Only one report deals with the death of Bose which was given by the Japanese doctor Tenneyashi Yoshimi, who attended him when Bose was brought to the hospital after the plane crash. Dr. Yoshimi has confirmed that Bose died of third degree burns. [Document No. 23]. Doubts have been voiced by many associates of Bose about these reports. They have never accepted the death of Bose in the plane crash. Initial doubts were circulated by Deb Nath Das who was very close to Bose. [Appendix III.] It was on account of these doubts that the Government had appointed various commissions to enquire into the mystery from time to time. It would be interesting to read the account given by John Figges, who submitted a report to the British Government on Bose more than fifty years back. In a recent book, he recalls his meeting with Habib-ur-Rehman, who was with Bose at the time of latter's death. He writes that Rehman whose left 'arm was heavily bandaged told me that after the Japanese army plane in which they were travelling crashed on take off at Taipei airport and burst into flames, he and the Japanese officers with them had great difficulty in getting Bose out of the wreckage because he was so corpulent. His clothes were on fire and he was badly burnt and died of his injuries in an hospital in Tapei a day or two later. The pilot of the aircraft also died. I could see no reason to doubt this story, which was later confirmed by G.H.Q. SCAP after detailed interrogation of the surviving Japanese officers concerned and signaled H.Q.S.A.CS.E.A. accordingly."[see Hugh Cortazzi, Post war Japan through British Eyes, Surry, 2001,p.9]

The appendices in this volume include mostly the memoirs of those who were very close to Bose, especially important is the account compiled by A.M. Sahey, who served as an interpreter to Bose when he was dealing with the Japanese. His recording of the Japanese policy towards the I.N.A. and other matters is very important in view of the absence of any Japanese records of what took place in these negotiations. Sahey's account can be further corroborated with the interrogation report included here. Another account of Bose included here is by Col. Yamamoto, who was with him in Germany and subsequently in Japan. Fujiwara's brief account is very important to understand the Japanese view of the I.N.A. and the personality of Bose. [Appendix I,II,IV]

Like the previous volumes, the documents included here were collected from different archival repositories in India and abroad and as far as possible these have been reproduced as they were found with hardly any change. I am thankful to these institutions for their help, but I am especially grateful to A.M. Sahey for giving me the copy of his memoris when I met him at Baghalpur. As I have pointed out earlier that the documents regarding the I.N.A. and other revolutionaries are lying scattered at different places. In order to understand the real contribution of those who fought for Indian's liberation from abroad, it will be essential to bring all these documents at one place. I am sure this task will be taken up by the National Archives of India for the benefit of research students.

T.R. Sareen

B-402, Kaveri Apartment,
Alaknanda,
New Delhi-110019

1

Circular Announcing the Termination of the War and Discontinuance of the Activities of the I.N.A [1]

6 September, 1945

To all Members of the Indian Independence League in Thailand, Comrades,

Jai Hind,

I have the melancholy privilege to inform you that your Azad Hind Fauj has been compelled to lay down its arms before the victorious army of occupation superior in number and superior in equipment. The Azad Hind Fauj has had to take this painful decision under the force of circumstances. This army of liberation has never thought of sparing its blood and as you all are aware, the Azad Hind Fauj has merited records of sacrifice, gallantry and chivalry second to none. Our fight was meant for liberation of India and on India frontiers and not abroad. Hence the decision to lay down arms and avoid unnecessary blood-shed and disturbance of public peace. At this fateful moment, I like to give you a few points of warning :

1. With the laying down of arms by the Azad Hind Fauj our armed struggle discontinues.
2. We must take our defeat in the coolest and most sporting manner.
3. Do not harbour any malice or hatred towards the Army of occupation, because we are vanquished today.
4. Be perfectly law-abiding, strictly disciplined and dignified in all your behaviour.
5. Avoid all possibilities of clashes with troops and one of the best means is to avoid trespassing the army camps and vicinity. Do not enter into unnecessary discussions or say or do anything likely to result in unpleasantness.

---

1. K.S. Giani, *op.cit.* pp 160-161.

6. Remember : (a) Your goal : "Independence of India."

(b) Your motto : "Unity, Faith and Sacrifice."

Remember always that with the discontinuance of armed struggle, the fight for India's freedom does not cease. We must and will continue our struggle till our goal of complete independence is achieved. Our countrymen inside India under the lead of the Indian National Congress are working with full determination to liberate India. We must be ready to do our mite in that struggle and for the sacrifices that will free India. when the call comes.

India is bound to be free and before long.

Jai Hind,

(Sd.) Parmanand,
Officer-in-Charge, Indian Independence League
Headquarters, East Asia.

2

Military Intellegence note on Last Movement of S.C. Bose[1]

10 September, 1945

S.C. Bose and his party left Rangoon on 24 April 1945 and reached Bangkok on 14 May. The party, at the time of leaving Rangoon, had in its possession gold, gold ornaments and diamonds contained in 4 boxes of varying sizes ranging between 9" × 9" × 4"and 6" × 4" × 2". An additional quantity of gold was purchased on the way at Moulmein to the extent of Rs. 700,000 drawn by S.C. Bose from Yokohama Special Bank, Moulmein Branch.

While at Bangkok several meetings of the Cabinet Ministers of the PGI were held between 18 May to 14 June, the object of which was to decide as to the future course of action so far as the existence of the PGI was concerned. No decision could be arrived at as S.C. Bose had to leave for Singapore in order to carry out his propaganda over the radio against the acceptance of "Wavell Proposal". In course of these meetings Lt. Col. (Maj-Gen) Chatterjee suggested that a nucleus of the PGI should be shifted to Yunnan Province in order to contact the communists who had more influence in that part of China, and through their help to contact the Soviet authorities in Siberia. At the same time it was thought desirable to leave behind certain Cabinet Ministers and high ranking I.N.A. officers to carry on the fight with HQ at Bangkok and Singapore. The following were the officers present in these meetings–

1. S.C. Bose.
2. Lt. Col (Maj-Gen) Bhonsle
3. Lt. Col (Maj-Gen) Chatterjee
4. Lt. Col (Maj-Gen) Kiani
5. Capt (Col) Gulzara Singh
6. Iyer[2]
7. A.M. Sahai

1. W.O.n 208/863, P.R.O.
2. S.A. Iyer.

7. A.M. Sahai
8. A.N. Sarkar
9. Isar Singh Gen. Secretary IIL Bangkok
10. Paramanand
11. D.M. Khan
12. Deb Nath Das
13. Karim Ghani (also attended the last meeting).

After the 2nd meeting (exact dates not remembered) Kiani left for Singapore to arrange accommodation for the Rani of Jhansi girls numbering about 120 who were at that time at Bangkok. At about the same time Chatterjee, Iyer and A.M. Sahai left for Saigon – Chatterjee to establish the site for the PGI, Iyer for broadcasting work and Sahai on a special mission at Hanoi not known to B1189.

On 16 Aug 1945 S.C. Bose came to Bangkok by a special Jap Bomber chartered for him, accompanied by Iyer and Capt (Col) Habib ur Rahman and Capt (Lt. Col) Pritam Singh. On 17 Aug 0700 hrs (Tokyo Time) Bose left Bangkok for Saigon accompanied by the following additional personnel of the PGI and I.N.A.:—

1. Gulzara Singh
2. "Maj" Hassan
3. Deb Nath Das

Lt. Gen. ISODA and two other H. Kikan personnel accompanied Bose and the party in a separate aircraft.

According to B1189's information received from H. Kikan and other sources, Bose and the parties reached Saigon on the same day (17 Aug). On the following day (18 Aug) S.C. Bose accompanied by Capt (Col) Habib ur Rahman left for Tokyo in a plane originally meant for the conveyance of some high ranking officials of Mori Butaui as placing of the special bomber at his disposal was no longer possible. The rest of Bose's party remained behind at Saigon where at that time Chatterjee and Sahai were also staying. ISODA who happened to be present at the Saigon aerodrome to see the party off, said that Bose took his seat in the passage of aircraft between the pilot and the tail and as such could not be seen to wave goodbye when the plane took off. According to the estimation of B1189, the remainder of the party at Saigon named above might have moved into any of the following places, as these were the names of the places suggested by various members in the Cabinet meetings mentioned before–

1. Yunnan Province
2. Hanoi
3. Shanghai
4. Harbin

In course of talk with ISODA on 21 Aug 1945 B1189 heard that the plane carrying Bose and the party landed at Taihoku (Formosa) at 1300 hrs (Tokyo Time) on 18th, and after about an hour's halt was taking off at 1400 hrs when the right engine failed resulting in the crash of the plane. The crew and the Chief of Staff Mori Butai were killed instantaneously, and Bose with Habib ur Rahman and 4 other Japanese officials were seriously injured. Bose and other injured persons were removed to an eye hospital at Taihoku where he died at 2400 hrs on the night of 18/19 Aug 1945 without regaining consciousness. No information about Habib ur Rahman could be obtained owing to restrictions put by the Allies on Jap communication. B1189 requested ISODA to keep photographs of Bose's funeral and other rites as well as his remains. No photographs or further information was received by B1189.

B1189 does not know whether Chatterjee ever met any of the nationalist Annamite leaders in course of his movements in French Indo-China. About Annamite leaders B1189 only knows that S.C. Bose on his way to Tokyo in Dec 1943 was prevented by the Japanese from meeting some of them who were eager to meet him (S.C. Bose) at Saigon.

B1189 has no direct information regarding the gold mentioned above. His own impression is, that a major portion of the gold was taken by S.C. Bose while the remainder was left with the rest of his party.

3

Representation from Defence Committee of the Indian National Congress to the Viceroy Requesting Him to Postpone the Court-Martial of the Officers of the INA[1]

15 October, 1 945

1. On behalf of the Committee appointed by the Working Committee of the Indian National Congress we make the following representation for your Government's consideration.

2. This Defence Committee consists of the following members:

   (a) The Rt. Hon'ble Sir Tej Bahadur Sapru, R.C. K.C.S.I.

   (b) Pandit Jawaharlal Nehru, Member, Congress Working Committee, Bar-at-Law.

   (c) Shri Bhulabhai Desai, Advocate.

   (d) Dr. K.N. Katju, M.A.L.D., Advocate.

   (e) Shri Raghunandan Saran.

   (f) Rai Bahadur Badri Das, Advocate.

   (g) M. Asaf Ali Esq., Member, Congress Working Committee Bar-at- law (Convenor).

   On the 22nd September 1945 the Working Committee of the Congress, having regard to the profound interest and anxiety felt throughout India in the fate and future of the officers and men of the Indian National Army now held as prisoners of the British Government, appointed this Committee to take necessary steps for their defence.

3. At present three officers namely, Shah Nawaz Khan, Sahgal and Dhillon have been formally charged with the offence of waging war against the King and other offences arising out of their activities as Officers of the INA. on active service. The 5th November 1945 has been fixed for their trial before a Court-Martial. These officers have

1. I.N.A. relief and enquiry committee file pertaining to I.N.A. trials.

formally entrusted their defence before the Court-Martial to the above mentioned Defence Committee.

4. According to press reports, trials of other officers and men for similar or cognate offences are likely to follow in the near future.

5. These trials raise questions of such grave public importance that the Committee considers it imperatively necessary to address your Government on the matter at once.

6. The circumstances which led to the formation of an Indian National Army are now common knowledge all over India. It is no exaggeration to say that while some may doubt the propriety of the policies which led to the establishment of such an Army as an independent military organisation under the command of its own officers, Indians of all communities, and persuasions and of all schools of political thought recognise and appreciate the selfless patriotism which actuated those who took part in this movement.

7. After the conquest by Japan of the French and Dutch possessions in South East Asia and the fall of Burma, Malaya and Singapore there arose a great desire in the minds of Indian inhabitants of these countries to organize not only for their own defence and protection, but also for active participation in the movement for the liberation of their home country from foreign rule. Rapid movement of events throughout the World led to the further intensification of this resolve and they appear to have determined to make a bold and resolute bid for the achievement of the Independence of India.Independence Leagues were established throughout the length and breadth of these countries and Provisional Government of Free India is reported to have been eventually set up, and a well-organized, well-trained and well-disciplined Indian National Army operated under its control. According to accounts available, this Government was not a mere puppet Government under Japanese control, but was an independent Government with a definite international status.

8. It is understood that in addition to a large number of Indian Civilians residing in the locality, numerous officers and men of the Indian Army, who had been surrendered by the British to the enemy, joined the Indian National Army.

9. We do not propose to enter here into any discussion about the legal status of the officers or men of the INA. and it would also be

inappropriate to discuss here the question whether they can be said to be guilty of any offence. The only question at this stage is whether it would not be contrary to public interest to bring them to trial and assuming that it is not so, when and by whom such a decision should be taken.

10. These men of the INA are virtually being charged with having endeavoured to enter India with armed force to liberate it from British domination. That alleged offence primarily concerns the Indian people, and the more so as the British Government have publicly announced that India will have the right to secede from the British Commonwealth if.the Indian people so desire. So far back as 1924 the then Secretary of State for India, Mr. Wedgwood Benn, speaking on behalf of H.M.G. in the House of Commons said that whatever may be the deficiency in theory India already enjoyed "Dominion status in action". The first privilege of that status "in action" is that in a matter like this which vitally affects the lives and liberties of a large number of Indians drawn from all parts and principal communities of India, the wishes of the people of India should be ascertained and given effect to. Judging by the trend of public opinion in the country, this committee urges that this matter of the trial of the INA. should not be pursued any further.

11. At this juncture the Central Legislative Assembly and the provincial Legislative Assemblies have been dissolved. But by the middle of December, 1945, the Central Legislative Assembly will have been re-elected and by the month of March 1946 general elections in all the British Indian Provinces will have been held and the British Government expects that soon thereafter ministries in Provinces will be formed to undertake the task of Government in their respective spheres. H.E. The Governor General has also announced his intention to reconstitute his Executive Council soon after the general elections so that it may be representative of popular opinion in the country. All these constitutional events are due to take place in the next few months.

12. The Defence Committee believes that the Governor General with his reconstituted Executive Council will be in a much better position to gauge public opinion in this matter. Representatives of the people will also have opportunity to express their opinion upon it in the newly elected Central and Provincial Legislative assemblies, All the

Provinces are interested in the Indian National Army because men from every province have contributed to its personnel. The new Government will be able to arrive at a proper decision whether the intended trial of the INA should take place at all and if so when and how.

13. The Defence Committee therefore earnestly urges that the trial fixed for the 5th Nov. 1945 and all other contemplated trials should, if not abandoned, be at least postponed and the whole question relating to the INA. be examined afresh after the Governor General's Executive Council has been reconstituted and the ministries in the Provinces have begun to function.

14. The Defence Committee is convinced that it would be a tragedy if this matter were approached and disposed of in a narrow, technical and legalistic spirit. Unprecedented issues of this nature require to be decided in a broad and statesman-like spirit. There are various aspects of these issues of great public and political importance and hasty decisions not in consonance with popular will and sentiment, will have far reaching repercussions throughout the length and breadth of India, so deep and widespread is the appreciation of the motives and aims of the movement of which the Indian National Army was an expression.

The Defence Committee requests that the matter of the trials of the INA. by Courts-Martial be abandoned, or that in any event no proceedings before any Court-Martial be commenced until after the formation of the Interim Government at the centre and the functioning of Provincial Governments on the completion of the ensuing election, and all necessary directions may be given to the authorities concerned.

4

British Intelligence Assessment of the Feelings of the I.N.A. Soldiers in Malaya After their Surrender[1]

26 October, 1945

Japanese Indian Fifth Column[2]

Attiutde of the I.N.A. In Malaya

1. A report from Kuala Lumpur states that, of some 370 members of the I.N.A. who have been interrogated, 5% have categorically stated that they are unwilling, whatever is decided about their future, to continue to serve in the Indian Army. Two reasons are given for this attitude; firstly, that they feel strongly bound in their loyalty to the I.N.A. and are unwilling to break their I.N.A. oath and, secondly, that they have irrevocably spoilt their army records and also those of their families who have been connected with the Indian Army, with the result that it is not worth their while to carry on.

2. The emphases laid on the "I.N.A. oath" is interesting in view of the argument put forward by so many I.N.A. officers and men that their oath of allegiance to the British was automactically annulled at the time of the Singapore surrender and their being handed over to the Japanese.

Rani of Jhansi Regiment

1. It is estimated that the Rani of Jhansi Regt. reached, at its peak, a total strength of approximately 600 in Burma and Malaya. The leader of this unit, Dr. Lakshmi Swaminathan, is still in Rangoon (at liberty) and has set up a private medical practice. According to the Press, on 21 Oct 1945 she addressed a crowd of 3000 Indians gathered in Rangoon to celebrate Provisional Government Day. Her speech was

---

1. W.O. 208/804 Public Record Office London
2. This was the name used for the I.N.A. by the British.

an exhortation to remember their pledge to "Netaji" and to return home to fight the second round of the battle for freedom. This was greeted by cries of "blood, blood, blood" from the audience.

2. Of the other prominent members of the Regt. there is little of interest to report, except that Miss Gauri Bhattacharya, who is a medical student, has made her way by air to India in order to continue her studies. Her departure from Rangoon was unauthorised and irregular and her present whereabouts in India are not yet known.

3. Although most of the Amazons are not of Indian domicile there is an undoubted tendency amongst some of them to wish to go to India, about which they have been told so much by Bose's propaganda. Moreover, some of the more intellectual who find no facilities for studying in countries recently freed from enemy occupation may, like Miss Bhattacharya, turn for further education to India.

I.N.A. In India

1. Evidence of the dangerous state of mind of certain I.N.A. military personnel at present in India is found in a letter addressed to the Punjab Provincial Congress Committee by a "faithful soldier of the I.N.A." at present in Multan Holiday Camp. This soldier takes exception to Congress leaders' repeated assertions that Subhas Bose and his followers were "misguided" in seeding Japanese aid. He quotes from Bose's speeches and private conversations, and describes various episodes in Bose's career in the Far East to prove his point that his "Netaji", far from being a Japanese puppet, was merely using the Japanese as his tools, just as the British employ coloured troops to fight their battles for them.

2. Apart from these facts, he provides much authentic inside information about the I.N.A. for the Congress propaganda mill. Everything said by this man indicates the depth and determination of his devotion to "Netaji" and the goal he has given his followers. Particularly significant is his conviction that Subhas Bose is not dead but will return to lead his army at the opportune moment, and his belief that I.N.A. personnel who returned to India are biding their time until they rise against the British : "We are his time-bomb, and will burst when the right time comes.Our Leader will return to lead us."

Reactions to News of the I.N.A.

1. With reference to para 3 of F.S.I.S. No. 5 dated 12 Oct. 1945. public reactions to the I.N.A. and the proposed trials of I.N.A. officers have crystallized during the past fortnight. There has been an increasing volume of comment from the nationalist Press and spokesmen of all political parties. The almost universally expressed view has been that Bose and his I.N.A., although misguided in hoping to obtain freedom through Japanese help, acted with the highest motives of patriotism and the desire to free their country. From this follows on an equally widespread demand, supported by almost all shades of Indian opinion (though differing in the expression given to it), for extreme leniency on the part of Government in their treatment of the I.N.A.

2. Congress has been particularly vociferous in support of this campaign, which it started. The Congress I.N.A. Defence Committee has been very active in interviewing the three accused in the first court martial to take place early next month, and in providing and briefing counsel for the defence. There is evidence that an increasing number of relatives of Indian soldiers, if they know or suspect that the latter have joined the I.N.A., are approaching the Defence Committee for information as to their whereabouts and probable fate as well as for legal aid if they are put on trial. There is little doubt that this is drawing numbers of hitherto loyal families into the Congress net.

3. A noticeable feature of the whole of this Congree-sponsored campaign (aimed at increasing Congress' prestige and winning additional votes in the approaching elections, and emulated by the other political parties for the same reasons), is that very few references have been made in the Press or by political speakers to the fact that any member of the I.N.A. is accused of any crime other than treason. No mention has been made of the torture and oppression used to induce P.W. to join the I.N.A.' of the forcible collection of money from civilians for I.N.A. funds; or of the various other persecutions at which Bose and the Jif leaders connived when they did not themselves instigate them.

I.N.A.

1. In almost every Security Intelligence Report for Sep., views have been expressed on the treatment which should be given to members of the I.N.A. and these have varied according to the degree of

knowledge of units. These views may be summarized as follows :-

(a) By a few, who believe that men were tortured into joining no punishment.

(b) By some, who have heard of the ill treatment of loyal P.W. by Jifs, but who had not met the I.N.A. in the field : those guilty of ill treatment to be punished and the remainder treated generously.

(c) By many: that officers who joined are particularly guilty.

(d) The majority view, however, is that they are all traitors. There is also indignation at the championship of the I.N.A. by Indian politicians.

2. British troops are also indignant, but in their case more emphasis is laid on the sympathy, both real and feigned, expressed by Indian politicians and press on the death of Subhas Chandra Bose.

5

Auchinleck appreciation of the I.N.A. Trials; explains the attitude of the British officers of the Indian Army towards the I.N.A.[1]

31 October, 1945

1. Of the 20,000 military personnel who joined the I.N.A., a large proportion became traitors,

    (a) To avoid brutal treatment;

    (b) To secure better living conditions;

    (c) As result of persuasion by their seniors.

    Mass trials being clearly impossible because of the obvious desirability of disposing of cases as quickly as possible, it was decided to bring only the worst offenders to trial and these were grouped into the following categories:-

    (a) Officers of the I.A.

    (b) VCOs who became officers in INA.

    (c) VCOs who joined 950 Regiment.

    (d) Those who initially deserted from our lines as opposed to being taken prisoner.

    (e) IORs who became officers or under-officers in 950 Regiment.

    (f) Those instrumental in causing the death of any British or Allies subject, whether in or out of battle.

    (g) Those guilty of brutal conduct either to fellow JIFs/HIFs or to members of the Allied Forces.

    (h) Those who took part in the capture and handing over to the enemy of and British or Allied subject.

1. Military Department No. L/WS/1/1577. I.O.L. Record London.

(i) IORs who became officers in INA and took a leading part against us in battle, including front line intelligence duties.

(j) Fujiwara volunteers.

It was estimated that six permanent Courts Martial in continuous session could complete some 300-350 trials only in one year.

Subsequently, as a result of the tense political situation, it was decided to concentrate in the first instance on the trial of those guilty of murder or gross brutality. The first trial of this kind is due to open on Nov 5.

2. As soon as it became known to the public that trials were about to commence, all the main political parties, and especially Congress, made the I.N.A. a prominent political issue. The Indian Press is full of articles extolling the I.N.A. as heroes. This, together with the fact that popular ministries will be set up in the Provinces by April, make it highly desirable, if not essential, to dispose of the I.N.A. problem during the next six months.

It was therefore decided to bring to trial those included in the following categories only:-

(i) Any person actively instrumental in causing the death of any British or Allied subject, whether in or out of battle.

(ii) Any person responsible for the brutal treatment of any British or Allied subject.

(iii) Any person taking a responsible part in the capture and handing over to the enemy of any British or Allied subject.

(iv) Officers, VCOs and IORs who became officers in the I.N.A. and 950 Regiment and took a leading part against us.

(v) Fujiwara volunteers.

No person will be charged with "waging war against the King" unless he can also be charged with other crimes so that there will be no convictions solely on the charge of "waging war".

Men who deserted to the enemy, but do not also come into one of the above categories, will be tried solely for desertion.

All Blacks who are brought to trial by Court Martial will be dismissed by the end of April.

3. It is estimated that the number of offenders to be tried under the various heads will be:-

(a) 15 to 20

(b) 20 to 30

(c) 10 to 15

(d) 20 to 30

(d) 20 to 30

The intention is to complete the trials by the end of April but delaying tactics by defence counsel may retard this.

All sentences other than death will be confirmed.

It is probable that a proportion of the sentences of transportation will be commuted to shorter terms of imprisonment.

A rough estimate of the number in each category for which the death sentence is likely to be imposed, is :-

Offences in category

(i) 10 to 15.

(ii) 15 to 20.

Offences in categories (iii), (iv) and (v) 5 to 10.

On the assumption that approximately 120 persons are brought to trial, it is estimated that not more than twenty death sentences are likely to be confirmed, but it is not possible for obvious reasons to give a definite figure at this stage.

4. It has now been possible to assess the views held throughout the Indian Army regarding members of the INA and 950 Regiment. These vary according to the degree of knowledge available in different units but may bc farily summarised thus:-

(a) a few, who believe that the men were tortured into joined consider no punishment should be inflicted;

(b) some, who have heard of the ill-treatment of loyal prisoners of war by members of the INA but who had not met that force in the field, think that those guilty of brutality should be punished and the remainder treated generously;

(c) many consider that officers who joined are particularly guilty;

(d) the majority view, however, is that they are all traitors and should be treated as such, though it is realised that it is not practicable to put all on trial.

5. I consider that, although the majority opinion is in favour of strong action, the Army as a whole will accept the policy of limited trials,

dismissals (Blacks) and discharges (Greys). I am strongly of the opinion that, although men may be tried for other crimes, the general feeling throughout the Army would be that they must be tried as traitors also. I feel even more strongly that the Army would strongly resent any measure which would allow any member of the INA or of 950 Regiment, who has not proved himself to be "White", to remain in the Army.

6

Home Department Memorandum on Policy towards I.N.A.

1 November, 1945

1. Since the conference with provincial representatives in the middle of August it has been necessary to give a great deal of further thought to this problem, and there have been various developments on which it is desirable to consult Provincial Governments. There are also points in the provincial replies to the Home Department letter of the 3rd September which could be settled more satisfactorily by personal discussion.

2. The governing factor, which accounts for the exceptional difficulty of the whole problem and the force of which must unfortunately be admitted, is that the Government in India, unlike the Government in any other country, cannot rely on public opinion to support – much less to press for- any action against "traitors" in the commonly accepted sense of that term. The most that political opinion will concede is that such persons are "mistaken patriots", but always with much more emphasis on the patriotism than on the mistake. It is now quite clear that Congress (followed willingly or otherwise by every other political party) is determined ot exploit the matter to the utmost and make a first class political issue of it.

3. The persons to be dealt with fall into two classes–

   (a) those subject to military law who, in addition to anything else they may have done, have broken their oath of allegiance; and

   (b) those not subject to military law who have broken no oath, but who have voluntarily helped the enemy either by joining the I.N.A. or in other ways.

   Certain general considerations are common to both classes. In the first place it is necessary to rule out any wide or sustained use of

---

1. Home Political Departments proceedings. The above memorandum by the Home Department was prepared after consulting the Provisional Government.

(a) the war time powers of restriction and detention without trial, or

(b) the powers of military custody pending enquiry which militry law provides but which cannot be used for more than a limited period. Secondly, it is necessary to discard the possibility of holding trials in camera (e.g. under the Enemy Agents Ordinance). It has been decided for good reasons to hold military trials by court martial in public.

It follows therefore that there is no half-way house between

(a) bringing the persons concerned to open trial and

(b) ignoring them or releasing those who are in custody.

4. The arguement in favour of trials are :-

(a) It is normal and right that the law should take its course; and not to set it in motion would betray weakness and a lack of courage which would react adversely on the ability of Government to govern successfully.

(b) There are some persons at least whom it would be repugnant to ignore or leave unpunished.

(c) To take no action against persons subject to military law who had committed one of the worst offences of which a soldier is capable might seriously impair the discipline of the whole Army.

The arguments against trials are–

(a) The numbers involved are in any case too great to make any complete solution on these lines practicable; and there is always a certain measure of amnesty by the victorious side on the termination of a successful war.

(b) Trials would be prolonged by every device known to the law; they could provide wide opportunities for anti-Government propaganda; and they would greatly increase the importance of the accused who might otherwise remain in obscurity.

(c) There would be little chance of obtaining convictions in civil trials unless the witnesses were thoroughly reliable or could be effectively protected against intimidation.

(d) There would be even less chance of enforcing capital sentences, if obtained, or even of maintaining sentences of imprisonment after a popular Government had come into power, unless the accused could be convicted of really heinous crimes abhorrent to popular sentiment, in addition to "treachery" or "waging war against the King."

On these premises the conclusion reaches is that it would do Government more harm than good to attempt prosecutions on any large scale and therefore that only a small number of the very worst cases should be selected for trial.

5. If the above conclusion is accepted, it will mean that a large number of disloyal persons must be ignored or released and the main problem will be the manner in which this should be done. The objects in view must be to face the resulting threat to law and order and reduce it to the smallest possible dimensions.

One possibility would be an immediate and complete amnesty for all except the few selected for prosecution. The opposite course would be the fullest possible examination of each case, either in India or abroad, with a view to assessing the risks that the freedom of each individual would entail and of delaying for as long as possible the release or return to India of those considered most dangerous.

However much there may be to be said for the first of these courses, it would mean throwing simultaneously on the countryside a large number of potentially dangerous and ill-disposed persons, quite a number of whom may have had previous terrorist associations or have received training in guerilla warfare and the methods of espionage (including the use of wireless). The strain on Provinces would probably be too great. The second course, or the other hand, would involve a very great deal of work it would take many months to complete the process: in the interval new Governments may come into existence, both at the Centre and in the Provinces which would take a different view of the whole matter; and the whole business would tend to become a running sore of which ever-increasing use would be made by the opponents of Government. In fact, under delay would merely intensify the dangers and aggravate the security problem.

6. The prevailing view therefore favours an intermediate course of action which would aim at the liquidation of the problem by stages within as short a time as possible in the hope that the persons concerned, if left alone abroad or widely disparsed to their villages in India and deprived of some of their most important leaders, would

be absorbed in the normal life of the country before they can be organised for dangerous political purposes. Such a course would have the additional advantages (a) of reducing the volume of agitation, much of which now comes from the relatives of I.N.A. men anxious to know their fate, and (b) of giving the Provinces early experience of the practical nature of the problem in the light of which the Future treatment of it may be guided.

So far as persons now in custody in India are concerned this would mean 'staggared' releases spread over a period of, say, six months. So far as persons outside India are concerned, it would involve arrangements (if the countries concerned can be induced to agree) to avoid the compulsory repatriation of ill-disposed Indians to this country, except for military parsonnel and the very few civilians who might be specifically wanted for trial, and to delay for a reasonable peroid the voluntary return of certain dangerous persons who might wish to come back and could not be indefinitaly prevented from doing so in view of their Indian nationality and domicile.

7. If these two conclusions are accepted, namely, (a) that the number of trials should be strictly limited and (b) that the process of releases etc. should be expedited, the resulting position as it affects the two classes mentioned in paragraph 3 may be presented as in the following paragraphs.

8. Persons subject to military law - that is to say, military members of the I.N.A. and 950 regiment.

(a) The Commander-in-Chief has decided to revise the order of the categories to be selected for prosecution, putting first those who may be charged not noly with waging war against, the King, but also with murder or other brutal conduct, etc., and leaving for trial later those who deserve prosecution on account of the rank and position that they held in the I.N.A.

(b) Three officers have been selected for trial by Court Martial in Delhi on charges that include the commission of certain atrocities as well as waging war against the King. Full publicity will be allowed to the trial and further action may depend upon its result; but it is provisionally proposed to bring about another 75 to 100 persons to trial and this numbers might be increased to 350.

(c) This will leave about 5,500 military 'Blacks' to be released after holding Courts of Enquiry and dismissing them from the Army. Of these about 3580 are already in India. The Courts of Enquiry can dispose of these cases expeditiously by releasing them in batches. As soon as an order of dismissal has been passed, there will be no legal authority for holding the person in military custody or escorting him in such custody to his home.

(d) The military authorities are anxious to release the 5500 'Blacks' at the rate of roughly 1000 a month, starting as soon as possible and maintaining a steady flow of releases throughout the month so as to avoid returning large batches at any one time to their Provinces. They propose to send the names and records of each batch to the Provincial Government concerned with the intimation that it had been decided to hold a Court of Enquiry on that batch by a given date thirty days in advance and that, if as was expected, the Court of Enquiry found that prosecution Ws not advisable, the men would then have to be released. The first lists are likely to be sent to Provinces in the near future.

(e) The whole process is likely to be delayed if Provinces make any extensive use of the right of consultation and interview as set forth in paragraph 3 of the Home Department letter of the 3rd September. The question therefore is what practical advantages are to be gained from this procedure and whether Provinces would agree to forgeing or restricting its use. It must be borne in mind that the action of the military authorities must be determined by what each individual had done as a member of the I.N.A. They cannot be expected to alter their decision in the light of the general character of an individual, which in any case had been "verified" by the provincial authorities before recuritmnet, or of how he is likely to behave in future. In fact, once the inevitability of large scale releases is recognised, it must be doubtful Whether detailed information about each man will be necessary or indeed readily obtainable and whether a rough and ready classification would not suffice, supplemented by such information as may be available regarding any particular man whose record and specialized training in the Army or the I.N.A. would suggest that he requires particular attention.

(f) The military authorities are prepared to release last those men who prove recalcitrant while in military custody and also to prosecute those whose breaches of discipline while in military custody justify such action.

(g) The number of military 'Grey' now in India is about 8000, to which must be added an indefinite number amounting perharps to over 5000, who may be sent back from occupied territories in future. The procedure in their case, as soon as they have been finally classified, is to send them to their regimental centres where they will come before Courts of Enquiry in bathces and they be discharged. Commanding Officers will send their names and a summary of each man's record to the Provinces concerned as far as possible in advance of actual release; but privinces cannot expect to be consulted further.. All these people will remain under military discipline until the expiry of their 42 days leave.

(h) All released military 'Blacks' and 'Greys' will be provided by the military authorities with railway tickets to their homes on dismissal or discharge. To send them in military custody would be difficult or impossible; but in view of the importance that some Provinces attach to this point, the military authorities would be prepared to discuss means of securing as far as possible that they travel straight to their destination- e.g. by limiting the time for which their tickets will be valid.

9. Persons not subject to military law, i.e.

(a) civilian members of the I.N.A. or 950 regiment and

(b) other civilian suspects or collaborators.

As regards (a) above the same general considerations apply as in the case of military members of the I.N.A. There are at present about 1150 civilian members of the I.N.A. in military custody in this country, whom about 230 are likely to be classified as 'Black' and the remainder as 'Grey'. There are known to be many more in Burma and Malaya but many of these may be presumed to belong to those countries and not to possess Indian domiciles. The following special points requirec notice:-

(a) The Military authorities regard all civilian members of the I.N.A. as a civil responsibility.

(b) The number likely to qualify for prosecution on the standards applied to military personnel all probably be very small.

(c) The Government of India have made it clear both to S.E.A.C. and the Government of Burma that, while they have no objection to the release in Burma or Malaya of civilian members of the I.N.A. whom it has been found unnecessary to prosecute on the spot for soecific offences, they are strongly opposed to the return of any of them in military custody to India. They would prefer them to remain where they are and this applies particularly to women who joined the Ranee of Jhansi Regiment. It has also been made clear that the Government of India realise that some of these people may have families and domiciles in India and cannot be prevented after release from eventually returning to this country, if they wish to do so. The request has therefore been made that the Government of India, or preferably Provincial Governments directs should be supplied with such information relating to 'Black' and 'Grey' civilian members of the I.N.A. as their interrogation and classification may have revealed.

(d) The immediate problem, is how to dispose of the 1550 persons now in India. The legal authority for holding these persons in the military camps where they now are is even more doubtful than in the case of military personnel who may be brought before military Courts of Enquiry. The desirability of dispersing them expeditiously to their Provinces is therefore even greater.

(e) As regards civilian 'Blacks' (apart from the few who may have to be prosecuted) the consideration mentioned in paragraph 8(e) apply with equal force. Before the problem attained its present dimensions, the cases of civilians members of the I.N.A. came to the Government of India after classification as 'Black' or 'Grey' by the combined DMI-DIB Section; the 'Black' were detained under Ordinance IV; and the Home Department passed temporary restriction orders on the 'Greys' and had them sent to their Provinces. A comparatively small number of such 'Grey' cases have been kept pending during the last few months; but these are now being disposed of by informing the Provinces concerned and asking them to take the men over without restriction orders. In future the cases of 'Greys' will not come to the Government of India at all and it is proposed to adopt the same procedure for 'Blacks'. This procedure would be for the various Commandants of the Camps concerned to inform Provinces direct of the names, classification and records of these take people and ask them to thank them over as quickly as possible. It will be for the Provinces to arrange for their reception in direct consultation with the Camp Commandants.

(f) The arrangements for securing that these people reach their destinations will be more difficult than in the case of military personnel, since the military authorities cannot undertake to provide them with tickets to their homes and have no other means of control over them. It might however, be possible for Provinces to send police parties to escort batches back to their Provinces.

10. As regards the other civilian suspects or collaborators mentioned at the beginning of paragraph 9, there are two classes to be considered.

(a) The first class consists of civilians hithereto detained by orders under Ordinances IV in the interest of "military safety". (Some of these may be members of the I.N.A.). The military authorities have recently informed the Home Department that they no longer consider it necessary to detain a number of these people. The number with which Provinces are concerned is about 115; and it is understood that provincial Criminal Investigation Department already posses full information with regards to them. Most of them were arrested while attempting to across the land frontier between Burma and India and were detained as suspected spies or as persons who knew too much about our military dispositions. Provinces have been addressed separately by the Home Department about these people.

(b) The second class referred to above consists of a number of persons, from Subhas Chander Bose downwards, who were known to have assisted the enemy abroad either in Europe or in Asia. Many months ago the Intelligence Bureau started making lists of these people and divided them into two categories:-

(i) persons whose surrender might be asked for on the terminations of hostilities with a view to prosecution and

(ii) Persons whose return to India might be required, even if it were found impossible to prosecute them.

On the termination of hostilities the western and eastern surrender lists contained the name of 13 and 12 Indian civilians, while the corresponding list of collaborators not actually earmarked for surrender contained 29 and 75 names respectively. The whole list of 129 names has been carefully examined and, for the general reasons set forth in the opening paragraph of this note, the conclusion has been reached that, with a few possible exception, it would be useless to have any of them compulsorily repatriated to India and that it would be better to leave them where they are, even at the long–term risk of their becoming centres of disaffection abroad. It is realised that some of them may eventually wish to return to India of their own accord and cannot be prevented from doing so indefinitely if they possess Indian nationality. Many of them, however, are comparatively old persons and some of them have married wives or established other connections in the countries concerned. Nearly all of them are comparatively unkown in Indian. Their importance would be greatly increased by bringing them back and attempting to prosecute them. Few, if any of them, have committed crimes, the punishment of which would command any degree of popular support. The possible exceptions referred to above are S.C. Bose himself; two persons (Nambiar and Habibur Rahman) who have broadcast for the Germans; and six persons (Hari Singh, M.G. Swami, Baba Amar Singh, N.K. Banerjee, C.B. Bhattachariya and S. Roy) who were prominent spy trainers under the aegis of the Japanese. It may be presumed that S.C. Bose is dead. The other eight parsons are hardly of sufficient importance to make their trial worth while.

The policy of leaving all these persons where they are and resisting their compulsory repatriation to India has been placed before the Secretary of State and awaited his orders. The implementation of the policy will, of course, require the cooperation of the military and other authorities now responsible for the government of the countries in which these people now are.

7

Note by the Military Intelligence on the Last Days of Subhas Chandra Bose[1]

6 November, 1945

Subject—Subhas Chandra Bose

The following information has been elicited from the conversations with the staff officers of the Japanese Army HQ. Saigon :-

1. In December 1944, Subhas Chandra Bose suggested that it would be expedient for the Japanese Government to come to terms with Chiang-Kai-Shek and further seek friendship with Russia. Bose's theory was that China would only too gladly accept a suggestion which would extract her from the convulsions of a long and weary war. In regard to Russia, he explained that he was convinced that the Russian alliance with Great Britain and America was brought about by force of circumstances and that with the completion of German defeat, Russian will repudiate her present mask of friendship and will openly revert to her well known hostile status towards Great Britain and U.S.A.

2. The Japs were in favour of such a move as they realized that their defeat was inevitable unless a paramount political event of this nature occurred. But they were doubtful if Bose was capable of procuring this new tripartite alliance. The Japanese therefore rejected this offer and conventionally reiterated their belief in their eventual victory as they intended to produce a large scale counter, attack which would turn the tide of war in their favour.

   There are indications that the Japanese Government evinced a keen interest when Bose put forth these suggestions and in fact plausible as these looked to them; it was in this connection that Bose visited Tokyo on Dec. 1944. But his preliminary effort to explore the possibilities and hence the Japanese rejections of the proposals.

1. W.O. 208/808. Public Record Office London

3. In June, 1945 while in Singapore, Subhas Chandra Bose, forseeing that the defeat of the Japanese was a matter of time only requested the Japs for permission to move his provisional Government and a part of the INA. to Japan proper or China, Southern Army, HQ passed this in turn to Tokyo. It is said that Lt. General Shidei, Vice Chief of Staff, Southern Army HQ opposed this permission on the ground that without Bose the INA in Malaya and Siam will not only disintegrate but become an administrative embarrassment at a juncture when it was least desired.

4. Again in July as the situation was fast deteriorating for the Japanese, Bose sought permission, this time to enter U.S.S.R. via Manchuria with a few selected members of his movement. No formal reply was made to this but Bose was advised to proceed to Tokyo in view of his request. Col. Yano Chief of the 2nd Sec. Southern Army HQ has been interrogated at some length on this point. He is emphatic that the Japanese decision to respect Bose's views does not denote that the Japanese Government had sought or received willingness from the Russians to accept Bose to go underground in their country.

On the contrary, he believes that the Japanese Government was then approaching Russia to sue for peace and could not at this stage allow any complication which must have arisen from Bose's admission.

5. In the absence of any specific answer from Tokyo, Bose intended to give himself up to Chinese or American forces, if on his arrival in Tokyo, the Japanese Government did not permit him to enter Soviet Russia. But the fact remains that from Saigon Bose actually travelled in a plane which was taking Lt. Gen. Shidei to Manchuria via Japan where the latter had been posted after the surrender.

Another source contends that there was no need for the Japanese to ask the Russians for Bose's entry because Bose wanted to go to Manchuria from where he thought he would be able to get in touch with the Russian forces and obtain necessary admission independently.

6. It was in view of this that S.C. Bose had left Singapore on 16 Aug. On his way, he stopped at Bangkok where he took a formal farewell of everybody. He arrived in Saigon at 1200 hrs on 17 August, 1945. Lt. Gen. ISODA had come from Bangkok to bid Bose farewell and the former returned after two or three days.

7. After the accident at Taihoku on 18 Aug. Bose and Habib- In-Rehman were admitted into military hospital where Bose died the same night.

Habib-ur-Rehman after his recovery left for Tokyo on 5 Sep. 1945 with ashes of Bose. Formosan Army informs that Habib-ur-Rehman took with him a package containing photographs taken at the time of Bose's death and also the jewellery that Bose was carrying with him.

8. It is generally recognized here that Subhas Chandra Bose had actually died. Also it is beyond doubt that he had plans to go underground together with a number of selected friends of his movement. There is nothing further by way of details or documentary evidence that can be obtained from Southern Army HQ. In the absence of substantial proof, it is still difficult to state conclusively the fate of Bose but the belief that he is dead is growing stronger and widespread.

Further investigntions are being conducted on the following lines :

(a) Allied HQ Tokyo has been requested to fly Staff Officer TADA to Saigon for examination.

(b) Interrogation Report on "Col" Habib-ur-Rehman is on the way to this H.Q. and the details of it will be checked at this end.

(c) The photographs will probably furnish best proof of his death.

8

Note by the Intelligence Bureau on the Public Reaction to the British Policy Towards INA.[1]

24 November, 1945

Reactions in India to the INA

1. There has seldom been a matter which has attracted so much Indian public interest and, it is safe to say, sympathy as the fate of the I.N.A. Public feeling is based on political, racial and sentimental considerations, and has been very greatly influenced by the Press and platform propaganda of political leaders and organisations. Generally, the nationalist Press and the politicians have spoken with one voice, and this Press campaign has had an undoubted effect, for many of the papers in question are most popular and widely read. The general theme of the nationalist case is that the men of the I.N.A. were actuated by patriotic motives. The demand is therefore made that none shall be punished, coupled with the statement that punishment would result in racial bitterness which would continue down the ages. The emphasis of current nationalist propaganda is on the treason aspect of the I.N.A. trials, and other crimes are ignored. There is no doubt that this campaign has largely captured the ear of the Indian public, to the exclusion of the other side of the case.

2. Congress has led this outcry since its commencement and continues to do so. Whatever its motives, it is certain that it attaches great importance to this matter, and there is so far nothing to suggest that its efforts will be reduced or that Congress will allow itself to be diverted from its present course without complete acceptance by Government of the demands put forward. On the contrary, there is every indication that Congress will use all available means to create still greater countrywide interest and to inflame public opinion in

1. W.O. 208/761. Public Record Office, London.

support of its demands, pursuing this line with determination throughout the election period and beyond, as long as events serve its purpose. The election campaign now in progress provides convenient platforms and growing audiences. Demands for no action against the I.N.A. have been constant at the many Congress political meetings all over the country during October and November.

3. Other political parties have followed the Congress lead, some of them with marked determination, as in the case of the Sikhs and the Hindu Mahasabha. The influence of the Sikhs in the Central Punjab rural recruiting areas needs no emphasis. The Hindu Mahasabha lacks the rural influence of the Sikhs, but their strongly worded appeals have had effect. The Muslim League also has sided with the I.N.A., but there is some reason to believe that in this, as a party, it is less earnest than others. Nevertheless, the trials of Muslims may make their effect increasingly felt on the Muslim public and the League alike, particularly now that the Muslim League I.N.A. Defence Committee has been approached to undertake his defence by a Muslim officer who is to appear before the next Court Martial.

4. The effect of all this propaganda for the I.N.A. is seen in reports which state that growing enthusiasm was obvious at meetings held in connection with I.N.A. Weeks and I.N.A. Days and that this is not only true of the towns but also of the villages. Indeed, it was recently stated that politicians engaged in their election campaign had to speak of the I.N.A. in appreciative terms to interest their audiences. This was attributed partly to a wave of anti-British feeling which is now being deliberately fostered, and partly to a genuine sympathy for the I.N.A. This report also stated that the licence apparently permitted to speakers about the I.N.A. had given rise to the feeling that anything could be said with impunity, and had its effect on those who might otherwise have supported the Government view openly, but now feel that silence is their best policy.

5. It is clear that sympathy for the I.N.A. is not confined to those who are ordinarily against Government. It is equally clear that this sympathy cuts across communal barriers. This is partly explained by the fact that the thousands in the I.N.A. have many thousands of relations who are anxious about their fate. A considerable measure of support is therefore found for the political bodies who are helping the I.N.A. and is accompanied by a growing general bitterness. There

is already evidence of some rather surprising approaches to Congress for assistance and the effect of the open association of ex-judges of the High Courts and gentlemen with titles in the defence of such cases is not negligible. Indication of any public appreciation of Government's position or responsibility for taking action are rare.

6. So far, the campaign in favour of the INA has not resulted in any overt action against Indian Armymen or Europeans. There has been no hint of social boycott of the former, for instance, and apparently nothings of this kind is intended.In respect of Europeans, however, threatening posters have appeared in towns. Although the experience of earlier terrorist movements in India justfies respect for anonymous warnings of this character, it is unnecessary to take the matter too seriously at this stage.

7. There have been numberous reports that military personnel and particularly returned prisoners-of-war, feel very bitterly about the attitude the country and its politicians have adopted, and that their animosity towards the INA is deep-seated. On the other hand, a recent informal sounding of military opinion shows a rather different picture. While animosity does exist among Armymen who have fought against the INA or have suffered at their hands as prisoners of war, the wartime Indian soldier in India usually takes a more lenient view, depending on the extent of his knowledge. He feels that members of the INA should be removed from the Indian Army, but that in general stern action is neither necessary nor desirable, for he finds extenuation in the circumstances which prevailed under Japanese occupation. The offence of the INA, in his opinion, was not so much treason as foolishness and weakness. It seems that this leniency does not extend, however, to INA personnel who were guilty of atrocities against Allied personnel. Some support for this reading of Indian Army sentiment is found in donations to INA Defence Funds by men of several Army and Royal Indian Air Force units.

8. On the whole, nationalist leaders have prudently avoided making public any plans they may have for the future use of INA personnel. There is, however, ample evidence of the interest of Congress, at least, in the men of the INA as well as in its propaganda value. It is interesting to note that in some of his speeches in Bombay earlier this month, Vallabhbhai Patel declared that Government ought to make the INA the nucleus of a new Indian Army. Similarly, Nehru,who

has publicly referred to the INA as the soldiers of independence, has been credited with ideas of using INA men as instructors in volunteer bodies: indeed, an INA officer has already been to train the Congress volunteers in Allahabad. Another report states that a Sabha is being formed in the north of India, with the object of contacting released INA officers and men in order to enrol them as members and train them, in the expectation that they will be of use to Congress in its day-to-day activities and in time of emergency. It appears that the Congress offices in the Punjab have an arrangement of advance warning of the arrival of discharged INA personnel going home and several cases have been reported of sepoys being immediately contacted by Congress officials while passing through Lahore. From these men enquiries are made, in accordance with the terms of a circular from the Congress High Command, about the locations, members and strength of INA holding camps in India, particulars of their class composition and of the officers in charge, and the names, addresses and INA histories of individual soldiers. In both the Punjab and other provinces, reports also state that in some instances the discharged soldiery contact Congress on their own initiative, offering their services and full information about the INA. A batch who visited a Congress office in Lahore were described as being "as zealous as soldier meeting their officers after having done a deed of exceptional valour in the course for their duty". INA men such as these give credit to the Congress for their release. The dangerous possibilities inherent in the mutual attraction and interest for each other of Congress and the INA merit very careful attention.

9. Briefly, the conclusions to which the information set out in this note leads are, *firstly*, that public feeling is generally sympathetic towards the INA while genuine disapproval of its conduct is lacking, *secondly*, that this sympathy is substantial and widespread, being confined neihter to the towns nor to any particular community and that it is being intensified by the day-to-day campaign of nationalist speakers and the nationalist Press; *thirdly*, that there is here a threat to the security of the Indian Army itself; and *fourthly*, that there exists the real possibility that this agitation, with its accompanying personal interest in INA members, may develop in dangerous directions.

9

OSS Report on the Feelings of Different Indian Groups Regarding the Trial of I.N.A.[1]

25 November, 1945

1. The current Indian uprising among students are sympathetic demonstration in protest against the trials of members of the Indian National Army. These outbreaks cannot be regarded as symptomatic of any revolutionary trend.

2. Many Indians feel that the members of the Indian Nationa Army who are now on trial will be convicted and then freed and on the whole programme of trials and publicity is an effort to restore British prestige, and that the anticipated releases will be intended to win the favour of the people.

3. The Muslim community and Army personnel look on the trial with tolerance, and do not wish those on trial to suffer any with punishment although they are not in sympathy with the INA program.

4. Hindu Army officers are strongly critical of the Government of these trials. According to one informant the feeling among thepeople is that they will stage uprising if the men on trial are executed.

5. The bulk of the Hindu population in general; and particularly in the Punjab are fully aware of these trials, and are strong opposed to any punishment of members of the INA. Defense have been set up, and in the Punjab more than a lakh of rupees has been given to aid the work of these groups. Signs have been erected and badges are being worn which claim that the men on trial are patriots and not traitors.

6. The Hindu Mahasabha is strongest in defense of the INA, but Communitst Party has taken a neutral position in the matter. It is claimed that the Congress is active in defense merely reasons of

---

1. Office of the Strategic Services, Record Group No.226 U.S. National Archives, Maryland, U.S.A.

publicity, and the Muslim organizations have maintaind a discreet silence on the subject.

7. At date of report there were no signs of an imminent uprising in Delhi.

10

Report by a British Agent on the Indian Independence Movement in East Asia (Extract)[1]

25 November, 1945

The Indian Independence Movement was planned by the Japanese, before the European War, with a view to creating disturbances amongst the Indians in India as well as outside and thus hampering the war efforts of the British in the event of war against Japan.

After hostilities broke out between Germany and the Allies, Japan encouraged the movement through her agencies employing Indians in the Far East for propaganda amongst Indians in countries under the government of the Allies.

Amongst others, one Hari Singh Osman, who, I am told was a member of the *Kamagata Maru* and was implicated in the Budge Budge incident and who was living in Batavia, Java, under the name of Osman Khan and had married a Malay, was taken to Shanghai where he was secretly working for the Japanese under the Japanese Navy.

Similarly Pritam Singh was another employee of theirs who was deputed for propaganda in Siam.

After the landing of the Japanese in Siam and when they were advancing towards Malaya they came across the British Indian Troops who had advanced into Siam.

The Japanese forces captured the Commanding Officer, Capt. Mohan Singh and Lieut. Mohamed Akram Khan of 1/14 Punjab Regiment at the outset.

Major Fujiwara, Officer in charge of the (Fujiwara Kikan) the Japanese political propaganda party who was following the advanced parties contacted Capt. Mohan Singh and Lieut.Mohamed Akram Khan and started negotiating with them through his agent Pritam Singh.

1. I.N.A. papers F.No. 164/I.N.A. This report was prepared by N.A.K. Mufti, Special Branch, Police, Singapore.

Capt. Mohan Singh, who in the past had anti-British inclinations, asked for the release of the Indian soldiers taken prisoners by the Japanese forces.The discussions were held in Alor Star and it was decided that the Indian Soldiers who had been taken prisoners and were kept in Alor Star Jail be released and Capt. Mohan Singh would make use of them for Fifth Column and propaganda work by sending them into the lines of the retreating army. Batches of the Indian Soldiers were sent to join the retreating Indian Soldiers, and propaganda which was of assistance to the Japanese commenced. The Nationalistic feelings of the Indian soldiers were roused and communications were cut, thus causing disturbances in the Indian Army.

Pritam Singh was responsible for propaganda and the Civilians of the occupied areas and the formation of the Indian Independence League.

After the occupation of Penang by the Japanese Military, Pritam Singh arrived in Penang and came into contact with Dr. Jagat Singh and then with N. Raghavan and Dr. Menon.

N. Raghavan in concert with Dr. Jagat Singh arranged for a general meeting of the Indians.

I personally did not attend the meeting but I was told that N. Raghavan and his party and the Sikh Community with few exceptions took a prominent part. Pritam Singh, in his address to the gathering, praised the Japanese power and sincerity in the cause of delivering the Asiatics from the clutches of the European and American powers and exhorted the Indians to cooperate wholeheartedly with the Japanese.

Muslims of Penang in general neither attended the meeting nor came forward in support of the movement *firstly* because they were anti-Indian National Congress party and *secondly* because there was no Indian Muslim propagandist with the Japanese to influence the Indian Muslims.

On the suggestion of Pritam Singh, N. Raghavan and Dr. Menon decided to change the name of the Indian Association of Penang to the Independence League of India (as the movement was called Indian Independence Movement) with the same office bearers to carry out the programme. Later the name was changed to Indian Independence League.

Sikhs and Hindus in general supported the movement wholeheartedly. The following were the leading figures at the commencement :

N. Raghavan, Dr. Menon amongst the South Indian Hindus, Dr. Jagat Singh, a Sikh who was the Secretary of the Sikh Temple whose name I have forgotten amongst the Sikh Community and another Gujarati or Marwari Hindu Makan Lal amongst the Northern Hindus.

Lawyer Gurcharan Singh was very anxious to take a prominent part but had no open support against Dr. Jagat Singh.

Gurcharan Singh got in touch with the Japanese Gestapo and worked as their informer. He endeavoured to cause Dr. Raghavan and his party and Dr. Jagat Singh to lose favour with the Japanese. He was instrumental in the arrest of H.H. Abdul Kader and Saravana Muthu of Penang.

The Indian Independence League, Penang Branch, started functioning under the presidentship of Dr. N.K. Menon.

The League succeeded in taking over the essential foodstuff, etc. from the Japanese authorities for sale to the Indian Community and appointed Abdul Kader of R.E. Mohamed Kasaim to take charge.

The League refused to sell the foodstuff etc. to those Indians who did join as Dollar members of the League.This policy helped the League to collect money and swell its membership. Many poor Indians who had little money and were not in a position to spare a dollar or who had no hope of any income in the near future underwent hardships from hunger.

The Muslim Community who were against joining the League faced the same situation. In addition they could not obtain passes to leave Penang in search of work or business, etc. as these passes were in the beginning issued by the Indian Independence League.

Hafiz Ghulam Sarwar M.C.S. retired District Judge attempted to take up the matter with the officials of the Indian Independence League but he did not receive satisfaction from Dr. Menon who refused to consider any amendments or change of their policy in this connection.

Some of the Pathans approached me for advice and I advised them to try to join the Malay Association which would solve their problem. I myself used to get rice, sugar or anythings I needed from my Chinese friends.

Seeing all these difficulties confronting the Indians especially the Indian Muslim Community of Penang and the high handedness of the Indian Independence League Officials, Hafiz Ghulam Sarwar and several other Indian Muslims decided to approach the Japanese authorities to express the difficulties of the Indian Muslims who were not willing to join the League and to request for separate arrangements to be made for the supply of foodstuffs to them. As no one was allowed to approach (personally or through the Japanese authorities in any other way than through the Japanese Association or his own Communal Association,they decided to forward an application to the Japanese Governor of Penang requesting him for an interview, through the Chairman of the Indian

Independence League. But the application was turned down by the president (Dr. Menon) of the League.

Hafiz Ghulam Sarwar then went personally to see Dr. Menon requesting him to forward the application for an interview Dr. Menon demanded the objects of the interview and when a position was explained to him, he nevertheless turned the request down.

Then a few Muslims held a private meeting and decided that, as the Japanese did not permit the formation of any other society of Indians but the Indians Independence they should approach the authorities for permission to form an Indian Commercial Association through which they would be able to solve the problems of all Muslims.

They proposed that I be on the Committee but I refused as I was not a businessman but I was persuaded to be one of the delegates to approach the authorities which they decided to arrange through the president of the Japanese Association.

Learning of the Muslim party's opposition to the Indian Independence League with whose officials he was at loggerheads, and being anxious to become a leader of Indians, Gurcharan Singh expressed his sympathies to a couple of Muslim Members, but later withdraw on finding that president of the Japanese Association by saying that the Muslim wished to create a split in the Indian Community. The President of the Japanese Association had at first intimated to some of the Indian Muslims that he would lead the Indian delegates to the Japanese Governor for the purpose of forming the Commercial Association.

Gurcharan Singh wanted me to support him and indirectly wanted me to recommend him for the leadership of the Muslim Commercial Party but I wanted the Muslim members against him. During my stay in Penang, knowing Gurcharan Singh's connection with the Japanese Gestapo I kept him under the impression that I was his supporter.

As the Japanese troops advanced to Malaya Fujiwara Kikan (the Japanese Political Department) alongwith its Indian propagandists followed them and contacted the political minded Indians on the way and formed Indian Independence Leagues in the important cities. Many Indians offered their services to help the Japanese forces, to do sabotage work or propaganda.

One Hari Chandaran of Ipoh followed the Japanese troops. On reaching Singapore he offered his further services in the Andamans and Nicobars and he was taken there.

Similarly a members of the military personal Alla Dutta who was a V.C.O. in the British Indian Army helped the Japanese and it is from his own lips that I heard that he was the first Indian to offer his services alongwith his party, to cross the straits of Johore. He was an important figure in the beginning and was considered second to Capt. Mohan Singh and was given the rank of Captain.

Prince Rawthore was another important figure in those days. He met the Japanese somewhere in Malaya, and expressing his anti-British views and professing himself a Prince followed them. He used to carry revolver and was a prominent figure in Singapore carrying out Japanese propaganda. He tried to pose as a leader and got Japanese support. The Japanese realizing that he was a quarrelsome person and had no standing here took away the privileges they had given him. Later on he was involved in a connected case of being in possession of parts of arms and taken into custody for a few days. He was then released. He then adopted the role of a Sanyasi—a holy man-–a fakir—and took his shelter in the Sikh Temple off the Singapore Railway Station. He went upcountry and was last heard of in K.L. or Malacca.

After the surrender of Singapore on 15 February 1942, the British Indian troops were separated from the British and Australian Troops and they were ordered to collect in Farrer park. On the Second Day of the surrender they were addressed by Major Fujiwara, Capt. Mohan Singh and Pritam Singh. Their speeches emphasised the sincerity of Japanese and their offer to help Indians to gain Independence of their country. Taking advantage of the emotional nature of Indians and the suffering they had endured during their retreat and emphasising the fact of the Japanese over-whelming military power in success in Malaya within such a short period, they asked the Indian prisoners of war whether they were ready to fight for their country, all the gathering unanimously raised their hands and shouted yes. But soon after the majority of them, especially the officers, realised their hasty action and regretted it. Major Fujiwara also told them that they will not be considered as prisoners of war and they will be separated under Capt. Mohan Singh.

Similarly the Japanese of the Fujiwara Kikan contacted the civilians. On the second day of surrender they interviewed Dr.K.P.K. Menon and discussed with him the same subject of Indian Independence and Japanese assistance and continued interviewing him now and then. They requested Mr. K.P.K.Menon to broadcast a speech to the Indians explaining the sincerity of the Japanese for the cause of Independence of India but he kept putting them off and refused to commit himself.

Mr. S.C. Goho was also approached by the Hikari Kikan and he and Raja Ram were taken to Saigon by aeroplane.

Pritam Singh and the party also addressed the civilian population of Indians and the Indian Independence League (Singapore Branch) was formed with Mr. S.C. Goho was the president. On the premises of the old Anzac Club in Waterloo Street as established the office of the Indian Independence League (Singapore).

About a month after the fall of Singapore an Indian Independence Conference was arranged by the Hikari Kikan to take place in Tokyo (Japan) and the following representatives of the Indians of Malaya attended it:

1. Mr. N. Raghavan, 2. Mr. K.P.K. Menon, 3. Mr. S.C. Gobo, 4. Capt. Mohan Singh, (5) Lt. Col. N.S. Gill—members of the goodwill mission from Malaya. Messrs Pritam Singh, Satyanand Puri of Thailand, Lt. M. Akram and Nilakanta Ayer of Malaya who were to attend this conference met with a fatal accident on their way to Tokyo.

The conference was also held under the chairmanship of the late Rash Behari Bose and lasted for three days from 28th to 30th March 1942 at Nanno Hotel,Tokyo.

The conference was also attended by Col. Iwagaro, Chief Officer in charge of Hikari Kikan, representing the Government of Japan.After welcoming the members of the Conference, he, on behalf of the Imperial Government of Japan expressed whole hearted support to the conference in its noble effort to achieve Independence of India.

The main idea of Rash Behari Bose and the Japanese was that the conference should elect Rash Behari Bose as a dictator with full power to deal with the situation. Mr. K.P.K. Menon opposed it and he was supported by other members of the Malayan Party.

Mr. K.P.K. Menon, who was against a dictatorial organisation and wanted the movement to run on democratic lines, opposed some of the items of the constitution which were put up by the Japanese through Deshpande. He was against the movement being under the control of one person and stated that as the representation at the conference was very poor,decision could not be binding on the Indians of Malaya and that a more representative conference of Indians of various parts of East Asia should be held at Rangoon or some other place at the earliest opportunity.

The conference appointed Mr. Rash Behari Bose as Interim President of the Council of Action.

The conference was of the opinion that the movement for the complete Independence of India be started immediately.It adopted as its motto Unity/Faith/Sacrifice.

After the return of the Goodwill Mission Delegates from Tokyo, Messrs S.C. Goho and K.P.K. Menon started reforming the Indian Independence League, Syonan and appointed a Representative Council consisting of 75 members.

On 31st May 1942, a meeting of the Representatives was called. Some of the nominees did not attend. An objection was raised that the number of Muslims on the Representative Committee was too small upon which some of the Hindu members present objected on the ground that the communal question should not be brought in. Mr. K.P.K. Menon suggested that as they had directly appointed members and had decided not to increase the number of members to more than 75, it would be difficult to deal with any adjustment then but agreed that the Muslims should be given 1/3 seats as soon as vacancies occured.

This agreement was verbal. On the same basis election of office bearers and the numbers of the working committee would be made.Before the election of office bearers and the members of the working committee. Muslim members present asked that the President or Vice-President and one of the other 3 office bearers and 5 out of the 15 of the committee members be Muslims but Mr. S.C. Goho pointed out that the Japanese required him and Mr. K.P.K. Menon to be President and Vice-President in the Committee. It was then decided to elect a Muslim as a second Vice-President. It was decided that the Committee of the Indian Independence League (Singapore) should side by side with political work carry out social and welfare work under the name of Indian Community. This committee assisted by purchasing foodstuff from the Japanese and selling it to the members at fixed prices. It also repatriated displaced and homeless persons from Singapore.

At this time another body composed of Indian Muslims was formed under the name of "All India Muslim Club" under the presidentship of K.S. Anwari which was sponsored by Japanese.

After the formation of the Representative Council and the Working Committee of the Indian Independence League, Syonan Branch, Messrs S.C. Goho, K.P.K. Menon, Amir Mohammad Khan, B.A. Mallal, Hardit Singh as nominees of the Indian Independence League, Syonan Branch Left for the Bangkok Conference on or about 6th of June 1942.

There were about 30 nominees from the officers of the Indian National Army some of whom were Capt.Mohan Singh, Lt. Col. Gill, Lt. Col.Gillani, Capt. Jahangir, Capt. Malik of Bhawalpur, Capt. Burhanuddin, Lt. Col.Aziz, Capt. Inayat Kiani, Capt. Parkash, Capt. Arshad, Capt. Patnack, Capt. Hussain and Major Brar.

H.H. Abdool Cadar of Penang was also representative for the Bangkok Conference for his own safety as he thought that he was suspected by the Japanese, and had just come out of prison.

An open session of the Bangkok Conference took place at the Silapakaram Theatre Hall under the chairmanship of Rash Behari Bose on the 15th June 1942. Representatives of Thailand, Japan, Italy and Germany also attended.

After the singing of Bande Mataram (National Anthem) and silent prayer for the martyrs in the cause of India's freedom the Conference commenced with a message from H.E. the Premier of Thailand read by a Thai girl in which he praying for the success of the Conference said that it was auspicious occasion in which all the Asiatic people may collaborate as one in doing away with the hardship imposed on them by the oppressive rule of alien races and as Japan had taken the lead to liberate Asia it was an opportunity for all Asiatics to unite and join with Japan for the accomplishment of the task.

Mr. Debnath Dass of Bangkok, Chairman of the Reception Committee welcoming the delegates said "India is passing through a most crucial period in her history of the struggle for freedom which has now become the world struggle. Indians who meet today under the able guidance of Rash Behari Bose the pioneer of our movement for Freedom in East Asia should now make their decision that they will accelerate the creation of a free happy united India."

Mr. Rash Behari Bose in his presidential address thanked the delegates for his election as the President of the Conference. After narrating the incidents leading to Bangkok Conference he said "Let us all fully realise our responsibility towards our land of birth and let us realise well that our down trodden country cannot afford to lose this golden opportunity that comes only once in centuries. Our brothers and sisters have suffered and sacrificed for more than a century so that our country may be once more free. Let us rise to the occasion in order to please the soul of the Martyrs and act so that the great preparations that Mahatma Gandhi has made may bear fruit." He also impressed on the Indians that they should not doubt their friends otherwise the world will go on and they will be left behind and they will regret it.

Then Mr. N. Raghavan addressing the Conference said, "For a hundred years, we fought the British in India inch by inch and it took them till 1857 a full hundred years before they could say that India was theirs. We have since been fighting in various other ways. Today we are fighting for our independence again. But with a little difference. For well over a century we have been trying to convince the world that the agonies of India will one day be the agonies of the world. We condemned the British at the bar of public opinion of the world. That is the change that has come in the independence movement of our nation. Until now we have been struggling all alone. Today we are getting international cooperation not in a diplomatic sense but in practical language. Never before India has been able to achieve this purpose and that is the reorientation of the movement that has come about today."

Referring to assistance from foreign powers he said, "It is said that we may be asking assistance from others, but what objection can there be if that assistance is forthcoming from other nations who have condemned Britain? What objection can there be if the hand extended to us from across the Seas is in the full conviction that the problem of India is the problem of the World". Making an appeal to Indians he continued "After all the greatest Dharma we believe in is the Dharma to our own Mother. Our Mother is calling with her dishevelled, hair, dress torn, tears streaming down her eyes. She is calling her sons abroad. She is saying 'how long more is my agony to continue'? Have I not forth nearly 400,000,000 sons and daughters, and can they not raise their little fingers in answer to my call?" Are we going to ignore the call? Are we not going to say we are coming. Yes mother we are coming, we are coming. We will act now and shall always be by your side. We are going to free you from your shackles. That will be our answer. Yes we are coming and that answer will reverberate through our hearts and throughout the world. Let us go forward at this opportunity not because our enemy is in difficulty but because our enemy stands condemned before the world opinion and because we after 39 years of development of soul force by our great leader, Mahatma Gandhi, are ready to strike for our liberty and to raise our flag of freedom."

Mr. Sahay, Capt. Mohan Singh and Col. Gill also delivered speeches on the occasion. The Japanese Ambassador of Thailand read his congratulatory message.

Messages from Subhas Chandra Bose, General Tojo and the Foreign Minister of Japan, and from the Friends of India Society, Italy were read.

The Japanese Ambassador to the Court of Thailand the Italian and German Ministers in their congratulatory speeches said that it is their intention to make it clear to the Indians that they will be backed up by joint strong support of Japan, Germany and Italy. It was also said that the war which the Tripartite powers were victoriously waging against India's oppressor was destined to create a new order in contrast with the old one ruled by Anglo Saxon selfishness and abuse and that they have no territorial interest whatsoever in India but have one desire that India and her people are set free.

After two days of general discussion and the deliberation of the subject committee, the full conference *in camera* adopted various resolutions.

It was decided to take immediate steps for achieving the object of the movement for which a Council of Action consisting of Rash Behari Bose as President and Messrs N. Raghavan, K.P.K. Menon, Capt. Mohan Singh and Col. G.Q. Gilani as members were elected.

Unity/Faith and Sacrifice was adopted as the motto of the Indian Independence Movement and that all its activity would always be on a national and not a sectional or communal basis. It was also resolved that India should be considered as one and indivisible and the programme and plan of action of the movement should, in general be to supplement from outside the valiant efforts that India's National Leaders have been making within India to achieve complete and immediate independence free from foreign domination, control or interference of whatever nature.

They also adopted the resolution requesting the Imperial Government of Japan to make a formal declaration that Japan shall respect the territorial integrity and the full sovereignty of India free of any foreign influence control or interference of a Political, Military or Economic nature on the severance of India from the British Empire and that it will also exercise its influence with other friendly powers in inducing them to recognise National Independence and absolute sovereignty of India.

It was also decided that the copy of the resolutions adopted be sent to the Imperial Government of Japan for its acceptance and the resolutions were forwarded to Col. Iwakuro for favour of transmission to the Imperial Government of Japan.In order to take the public into confidence regarding the Conference the President of the Council of Action permitted delegates to show some of the resolutions.

After the Conference the delegates waited at Bangkok for a few days—in the hope of receiving reply from the Government of Japan to their request for acceptance of the Bangkok Conference Resolutions but later on they were given to understand verbally by the Iwakuro Kikan that the Bangkok Resolutions had been sent to Tokyo and that on receiving the reply it would be transmitted to the Council of Action.

The delegates then decided to disperse but agreed that the movement should go on in the meantime with the proviso that vital and important steps should be taken only after the receipt of a reply from Tokyo.

Rash Behari Bose stayed at Bangkok where the Headquarters of the Indian Independence League was formed.

The delegates of Malaya returned. Mr. K.P.K. Menon was placed in charge of propaganda, Mr. N. Raghavan of Education and Welfare and Capt.Mohan Singh of the Military.

The delegates of Malaya also received a complaint against Dr. D.M. Khan, a delegate from Hongkong.This man became a prominent figure in the movement.

The Indian Community, Committee of the Indian Independence League (Singapore) felt the urgent need for relief. To meet these needs a Distress Relief Committee was formed under the Chairmanship of B.A. Mullal. The instructions to this Sub-Committee were to pay their full attention towards relief work only, the object of which were

1. To feed and clothe the Indian destitutes from up-country who had come to Singapore prior to its fall, and the local Indian destitutes who were homeless as a result of bombing and the destruction caused in Singapore.

2. To assist the clerical classes who were badly off and without jobs, with money to feed themselves and their families.

3. To provide medical attention to the sick and ailing destitutes.

This sub-committee opened a Distress Relief Camp at Waterloo Street to accommodate the homeless Indians to feed them and to give them medical attention.

Funds were raised by Voluntary public subscriptions and by contributions made by the Singapore Branch of the League. Some merchants gave food-stuff. Old clothing was collected and distributed to the destitute. Non-Indians such as Malayans were also received in the Camp.

Shortly after the Bangkok Conference N. Raghavan took over the portfolio of Education and Welfare and organised amongst others a school known as "Swaraj Institute" in Penang where pupils were trained for fifth column work in India.

Mr. K.P.K. Menon who was appointed as head of the department of propaganda resigned from the Vice-Presidency of the Indian Independence

League. Syonan Branch and M.V. Pillai was elected in his place. He was working as a District Judge then.

Mr. K.P.K. Menon started a Broadcast section for Indian Propaganda from the Syonan Station under the Directorship of Capt. Jahangir, Civil and Military personnel were employed for different jobs. Hikari Kikan had appointed one Ishikawa as a censor and the verbal understanding between Hikari Kikan and Menon was that the Indian Broadcasting Propaganda and its personnel will be under his direct control and that the Japanese could have nothing to do except the censoring.

He also intended to take over the Indian papers, one in Hindustani and the other in Tamil and third in Malayan which were then run by the *Syonan Times* edited by Raja Ram and V.P. Abdulllah respectively, after completing the broadcasting arrangements.

A leaflet committee was also formed for preparing propaganda leaflets in different languages and cartoons were prepared for despatch into India by aeroplanes, Mr. K.P.K. Menon was its Chairman. Some members of this committee were civilians and the others the majority officers of the Indian National Army. A Japanese officer attached to Hikari Kikan used to attend the meetings. The Japanese were not satisfied with the wording of the leaflets and wanted stronger words (abusive language) to be used. But Mr. K.P.K. Menon opposed their wishes.

Indian Independence League Headquarters in Bangkok also started Indian Broadcasting. Indian propaganda was also broad cast from Saigon by the Indian Miliatary officers amongst whom were Lt. Col. Nagar and Capt. Irshad I.M.S.

N. Raghavan implementing the Constitution passed at Bangkok converted the Central Indian Association of Malaya into Indian Independence League Malaya Branch, with himself as the President and the same office bearers as before. Although his highhanded action in thus appointing this body was criticised, Raghavan paid no heed. Mr. B.K. Das who was the Secretary of Indian Independence League of Malaya, later became the Secretary of Indian Independence League, South East Asia.

Capt. Mohan Singh, who was given full power over the Indian Military irrespective of whether or not they had joined the movement, had given 400 A.A. unit personnel to the Japanese Authorities before he left for Tokyo. One hundred persons of this unit were sent to Cebu by the Japanese without consulting Mohan Singh.

Captain Mohan Singh then started organising the Indian National Army, with the assistance of Major M.Z. Kiyani. He also started propaganda for which Major Barar was appointed and Capt. Patnaik was deputed officer in charge of the Welfare Department. Propaganda was started amongst the Indian National Army through different agents and a great amount of money as well as persuasion and force was used.

One Capt. Shingara Singh together with Lt. Fateh Khan and some others of the Indian National Army were appointed as Military police. Shingara Singh was known as a terror of the Indian National Army. These people did not hesitate to shoot non-volunteers. In Kranji Indian soldiers were fired upon by members of the Indian National Army and similarly up-country at Kuala Lumpur.

Shingara Singh was later on transferred and Major (Capt.) Rashid Khan was appointed as Chief of the Military Police.

He was equal to Shingara Singh in all respects when torturing and threatening the non-volunteers.

On one occasion some members of Non-Volunteer officers were rounded up. Their belongings were looted and they were put in a separate concentration camp. They were later taken to another area and were put under the charge of Col. Aziz of Kapurthala Regiment.

These officers were ordered to salute the Indian National Army sentries and to be their scavangers. They were given uncooked rice mixed with sand for their consumption and had to cook themselves in garbage tins etc. as they had not been provided with cooking utensils. My nephew Lt. Ismail Khan of 2/10 Baluch Regiment and many of my friends were in this group of non-volunteers.

A few of them who could not bear the hardships agreed to join the movement but most of them stuck on. Later on when some objections were raised in the Council of Action these officers were released.

In 1941 I had made a report against Capt. Mohan Singh's cousin who was also a Captain in the same Regiment as Mohan Singh then stationed at Alor Star for his anti-British views and his efforts to incite the soldiers of his regiment against the British. He was later sent back to India after a long corresponence between (I.G.P.) the then security officers and the Military Department. The said Captain whose name I have forgotten and with whom I had no acquaintance visited me in Penang on his way to India and from his talk I gather that he had some knowledge of the report against him and that he suspected the informer who was my friend and was an officer in his platoon.

I feared that Capt. Mohan Singh might suspect me of being involved in this matter and I consequently kept friendly with him. For the same reason my friend who had given me the information agreed to join the Indian National Army when he was taken to Alor Star from Taiping (where he was in hiding) by the Late Lt. Mohamed Akram Khan in the beginning.

A.S.P. Mr. Finch then in charge of Special Branch Penang knew of this fact and we had discussions on the matter with the Commanding Officer of the said regiment then. Capt. Mohan Singh who was given the rank of G.O.C. by the Japanese was negotiating directly with the Japanese authorities in the formation of the Indian National Army and drew up a scheme for the Indian National Army organisation without submitting the Scheme to the Council of Action for its approval. He was also taking unconditional pledges from the volunteers to support him as the general officer commanding and started giving promotions. He used to receive $225,000 per month from the Japanese directly for the upkeep of the Army in addition to rations.

The Japanese policy was to keep the Indian National Army separate and away from the influence of the Indian Independence League or its Council of Action. They supported Capt. Mohan Singh in his resolve to deal with the Army personally, as they had great faith in him after his conduct in the Malayan Campaign.

At the end of November the surplus volunteers and the non-volunteers who were under the control of Capt. Mohan Singh and the supervision of Hikari Kikan were taken by Beppon Department (P.O.W. Department).

Capt. Mohan Singh played into the hands of the Japanese. He later sent Rahman to Burma without informing or obtaining permission from the Council of Action. It had been decided that the Army was to be under the directions of the Council of Action and that no move was to be made before acceptance of the Bangkok Conference resolutions by the Japanese Government.

After the Bangkok Conference, the Indian National Army was formed with 12,000 men and officers and although Hikari Kikan had agreed to the further enlistment of 3,000 civil volunteers this did not materialise. Mohan Singh became the G.O.C., Col. Gilani holding no portfolio. A scheme was drafted by Lt. Col. Kagawa. Later on Mohan Singh wanted to raise the forces by enlisting 10,000 more soldiers but the surplus volunteers were not allowed to be taken into the Indian National Army.

On one occasion the Indian Independence League requested the Indians of Singapore to hoist the Indian National Congress Flag (Tricolour flag) and Hinomaru (the Japanese flag—the Rising Sun) but the majority of the Muslims hoisted the Muslim Flag (Crescent and Star) and Hinomaru. Some of the Tamil Hindus objected to the hoisting of the Muslim flag instead of the Congress flag and broke into a Muslim shop in Serangoon Road and also started trouble in Arab Street by pulling down one of the Muslim Flags and treading upon it. A fight ensued but police and Japanese intervened. In the meanwhile K.P.K. Menon went to a shop in Arab Street in order to negotiate with T.A.M. Abdul Aziz and to request the Muslim but on his coming out of the shop he was slapped by the Japanese and then taken to the M.P. Station at Y.M.C.A. Later he was set free.

Mr. Rash Behari Bose came to Syonan (Singapore) via Penang from Bangkok in the end of August 1942 and brought with him a letter sent by Col.H. Iwakuro, Head of the Hikari Kikan of the Japanese Imperial Army expressing wholehearted support of the Japanese Government as evident from General Tojo's statement, etc.

The letter was produced by the President (Rash Behari Bose) in the meeting of Council of Action in or about September 1942 and N. Raghavan was of the opinion that the reply was unsatisfactory and the Council decided to write again. This reply, copy of which is attached was sent but subsequently withdrawn on the ground that the letter was more or less a declaration of the no confidence as was indicated by Col. Iwakuro in his conversation with the President.It was pointed out to Rash Behari Bose by Col. Iwakuro that the receipt of that letter would be deemed to be a declaration of non-confidence in the Japanese Imperial Government. Rash Behari Bose explained the attitude the Japanese would take to the Council of Action and suggested that it be withdrawn. The Council of Action withdrew it, Raghavan not being present.

Meanwhile as stated above Syonan Broadcasting Station was in charge of K.P.K. Menon who made appointments and set out programme.

Without consulting or informing K.P.K. Menon,Capt. Arshad was appointed Director by Capt. Mohan Singh in consultation with Hikari Kikan. Capt. Arshad I.M.S. who was formerly in Saigon Broadcasting Station had great influence with the Japanese Authorities and refused to obey K.P.K. Menon's directions. The Japanese started appointing new hands and revised the scale of salary and in some cases refused to employ Menon's appointees.

Ishikawa who was appointed as a Censor (Officer) by the Hikari Kikan started altering the message, etc. to suit Japanese propaganda.

Col. Iwakuru and Major Ogawa were approached but with no result.

In connection with the Press Hikari Kikan was insisting in July and August 1942 that Menon should take up the Indian Press but Menon held to the view that he would take it over after he had set up the Broadcasting Station. In October Kikan intimated that the press would not be handed over to K.P.K. Menon.

Japanese Authorities employed various channels for infiltration into India. This infiltration campaign was known to members of the Council of Action but the details were not known. The following methods were employed

(a) Infiltration work by Indian National Army.

(b) Infiltration work by Ram Swarup's Party in Burma.

(c) Swarajia Institute Penang from where some students were taken away for infiltration.

(d) Osman (Hari Singh) infiltration group which was recruited by Amir Mohammed Khan,carpet dealer of Singapore. Osman was doing it for the Japanese Navy and he had no connection with the Indian Independence League although he was using the League name.

The Indians in general experiencing and hearing of the atrocities of the Japanese and being humiliated again and again by slaps and beatings for no apparent reason, lost all enthusiasm.

The anxiety amongst the educated Indians increased at receiving no satisfactory reply from the leaders of the movement who in turn had received no reply from the Japanese Imperial Government.

In addition, relations between Captain Mohan Singh, G.O.C. and Mr. Raghavan took an unpleasant turn due to Mr. Raghavan challenging Mohan Singh's power and criticising his actions in connection with the Indian National Army.

The anxiety turned into suspicion when no satisfactory reply to the letter and resolutions of the Bangkok Conference came.

In the meantime Capt. Mohan Singh who was playing in the hands of the Hikari Kikan had agreed to send the personnel of the Indian National Army to Burma and had requested the Kikan to arrange passage for them without referring this matter to the Council of Action became suspicious. Lt. Col. Gill who had come from Burma gave many stories connected with Burmese Kikan and their opinion about the movement and the Council of Action. He reported the full text of conversations that had taken place between Lt. Col. Kitabe, Captain Tsuchi and Yutani's of Iwakuro Kikan and Desh Pande and Mr. Parshad, in which the Political Officers were of the opinion that, as the Bangkok. Resolutions were not accepted and there had been no announcement by the Japanese Government, the Japanese Government has not recognised the Council of Action and any its orders or decisions were worthless and that Indian Independence League not being an independent body had to obey the orders of the Commander in Chief of the territory concerned.

Captain Mohan Singh who was very much impressed by the frankness of K.P.K. Menon was on close terms with him.

Mr. K.P.K. Menon's influence and knowledge of political matters and Col. Gill's information in connection with his suspicions against the Japanese opened the eyes of Capt. Mohan Singh and he in turn began to suspect the Japanese.

During the sittings of the Council of Action from 26th November to 5th of December 1942 members of Council put forward their complaints in connection with mistakes made by individual members and resolved to follow decisions made in the sittings and also disclosed to failure of Japanese Authorities to fulfil promises in connection with the Indian Military and Civil Volunteers.

Council also decided to and did send a further letter to Col. Iwakuro asking for a formal reply to the Bangkok Resolutions, Col. Iwakuro on receiving the letter called a joint Conference of the Members of the Council of Action and the Japanese on 1st December 1942 and expressed his inability for the reasons given to forward the letter mentioned above to Tokyo Government.

Mohan Singh, on receiving instructions from Major Ogawa to send 900 Indian National Army to Burma on the 5th of December, in spite of his previous request for transport, refused to send the Indian National Army to Burma and brought the matter to the notice of the Council of Action on 2nd December,1942. Capt. Mohan Singh (G.O.C.) was interrogated on the night of 1/2 December 1942 by Lt. Kunizuka who had been sent by Col. Iwakuro to find out the reasons for Mohan Singh's sudden loss of confidence in the Japanese.

On the evening of 2nd December 1942 Major Ogawa discussed with Captain Mohan Singh his refusal to send personnel to Burma.

Soon after Col. Iwakuro tried to bring round Mohan Singh as the thought that Mohan Singh had been influenced against Japanese.

Next day Major Fujiwara had a discussion with Mohan Singh, and explained his sincerity, trying to persuade Mohan Singh to send the 900 men of Indian National Army but with no success. Major Fujiwara also met Raghavan and Rash Behari Bose in the same connection and said that if the transport were refused it would jeopardise Indo-Nippon friendship. Rash Behari Bose and Raghavan were inclined to send the soldiers but Mohan Singh and Col. Gilani strongly opposed.

Next day in the Council Rash Behari Bose stated that Col. Iwakuro had promised that he would try his best to get a satisfactory reply from Tokyo on the point raised by Council of Action and said that his impression was that Col. Iwakuro was genuine. K.P.K. Menon and Mohan Singh requested that Col. Iwakuro should promise in writing to send the letter dated 29th November to Tokyo failing which they would have no alternative but to resign. The President said that this could not be done.

Raghavan tried to persuade them to give time and suggested that the President should take up the matter with Tokyo Government if necessary but K.P.K. Menon, Mohan Singh and Col. Gilani said that the position was just as unsatisfactory and after some discussion stated that unless Col. Iwakuro gave an assurance that he would forward the letter to Tokyo and that the reply would be given on or before 1st January, and no major action would be taken regarding Indian National Army etc. the three of them would resign. The President said that he would place these matters before Col. Iwakuro and would obtain his views.

The President of Council of Action induced them, not to do so until he had further discussed the matter with Col. Iwakuro.

On the morning of 8th December, Col. Gill was taken away by the Japanese Military Police without the knowledge of the members of the Council of Action. This enraged Mohan Singh, K.P.K. Menon and Col. Gilani who on receiving the message of President's failure in his talks with Col. Iwakuro, sent in their resignations from membership of the Council of Action. The president accepted their resignations.

On 7 Dec. 1942, the eve of 1st anniversary of Japan's entering into this war, N. Raghavan, Goho and others gave statements to Domai agencies.

Raghavan also submitted his resignation but separately.

The President informed Iwakuro Kikan about the resignation of the members of Council of Action and his acceptance of it. He also informed K.P.K. Menon and others about the acceptance of the resignation on 9th December.

On the 8th morning Major Fujiwara and Senda met Mohan Singh in Senda's house where Fujiwara brought in the subject of Col. Gill's arrest and explained the charges against him, he was a British espionage agent and that he was responsible for sending 6 officers 2 of whom succeeded in crossing to India to convey to the British Government of India information about events in the Far East. He also said that the Japanese authorities had come to know about Gill's being a British agent from 6 Parachutists who landed in Pegu in November 1942 and by deciphering a British Code letter.

Captain Mohan Singh asked Major Fujiwara for an interview with the parachutists and Col. Gill but was refused.

Capt. Mohan Singh (G.O.C.) not believing Fujiwara's story about Gill said that "In 1939 after the outbreak of the European War certain officers (Sikhs) planned to capture Punjab. It was then we decided to put up the claim of Maharaja of Patiala and one senior officer amongst us took the scheme to Col. Gill at Army Headquarters, Simla. Col. Gill kept that secret to this date. He advised us to wait as it was not the proper time."

I cannot say whether or Mohan Singh was telling the truth and Col. Gill was consulted/connected with the above mentioned conspiracy but judging from Mohan Singh's activities and his cousin's views already mentioned there may be something in it. I have no proof or witness to the effect.

N. Raghavan who did not resign from the post of the President of Malaya Branch and seeing the crisis facing the Council of Action called a meeting of the Presidents of the State Branches at Syonan to (Singapore) which was held at the Headquarters of the Malaya Branch on the 8th and 9th December. The idea behind it was to get the support of the Presidents of the Branches for Rash Behari Bose and the carrying on of the movement.

It is interesting to note that N. Raghavan gave as his reason for resigning from the Council of Action the arrest of Col. Gill whereas the rest of the members did so on the ground that the Japanese Government would not clarify the position of Indepenence Movement and further it was not possible or desirable to go on with it.

On 10th October 1942 the President of Council of Action Rash Behari Bose gave out a written statement. In this statement he expressed his regret at the resignation of the members of the Council of Action and his acceptance of it and expressed that they should not have resigned at all and thus precipitated a crisis and a deadlock which would result in hardship misunderstandings and unhappiness and damage to the cause. He further declared that he had taken control of the movement on 9th December 1942 in order to save the movement from collapsing and appealed to the Indians to continue to render him and the movement their support and cooperation.

In general the Indian public had no faith in Rash Behari Bose and considered him a Japanese Puppet and a mouthpiece. The resignation of the members of the Council and his persistence confirmed the opinion of the general public as mentioned above, but some who were paid by him especially his lieutenants like Linghan and D.M. Khan and similarly men from Indian National Army and the Bengali Hindus either from civil life or Indian National Army started propaganda for him and worked as informers for him.

On the 11th December Rash Behari Bose asked Mohan Singh (G.O.C.) Indian National Army to arrange for an interview with some high ranking officers of the Indian National Army upon which Mohan Singh challenged his authority and refused to obey him which enraged Rash Behari Bose. He purported to remove Mohan Singh from the post of G.O.C. of Indian National Army and to dismiss him from the membership of the Indian National Army.

Mohan Singh sensing trouble called a private meeting of the High ranking officers of the Indian National Army. Mohan Singh G.O.C. Indian National Army issued a special order stating that the Indian National Army would be dissolved shortly as it was impossible for the Indian National Army to achieve its goal, and that a confirmatory order would be issued as soon as arrangemens with the Japanese were completed. He added that in the events of his being taken before such confirmation the dissolution would take place automatically and immediately and that the members of the Indian National Army would be released from all their obligations and undertakings to him and the Indian National Army. On the same date he issued the order of immediate Dissolution of Indian National Army. Later on Mohan Singh was taken to some neighbouring island alongwith Lt. Ratan Singh, his A.D.C. and Lt. Iqual. They were provided with boarding and lodging. Mohan Singh was not allowed to communicate with any civilian or military personnel.

Mr. Rash Behari Bose issued another statement addressed to the Civilian and Military in which he criticised Capt. Mohan Singh for his activities in connection with the Indian National Army and the Indian Prisoners of War and blamed him for the crisis.

It was followed by a statement issued by the Chief of Iwakuro Kikan explaining the circumstances leading upto his dismissal.

There was no doubt that Mohan Singh was responsible for the organisation of the Indian National Army and helped in making the movement a success and was ultimately responsible for the atrocities committed against the Indian prisoners of War with a view to forcing them to join the movement. He lost his head somewhat in trying to be the sole master of Indian National Army, a belief encouraged by the Japanese as well as members of the Council of Action who did not object or check him at the beginning. Similarly the Iwakuro Kikan did not question his authority or the power of Council of Action until they found that he, having became suspicious, started opposing their plan.

This crisis created a deadlock amongst the supporters of the Indian Independence Movement, and was a blow to the Sikh Community, as they considered themselves very important in view of the presence of Capt. Mohan Singh as G.O.C. of the Indian National Army and the helpful activities of the late Pritam Singh in support of the Japanese. The Sikh community in general wholeheartedly supported the Japanese and the movement and even went out of their way to please the Japanese by adopting a harsh and severe attitude towards the internes and prisoners of War. The removal of Mohan Singh shattered their hopes.

Shortly after the arrest of Mohan Singh, opinion was divided amongst the members of Indian National Army. Some claimed that it was dissolved,others that it was not. A questionnaire was issued to the officers of the Indian National Army.

On 13.12.1943 Rash Behari Bose issued a circular touching upon the replies to the questionnaire.

Col. Bhonsle was now appointed Director of Indian National Army Bureau, which meant that he was in virtual Command of Indian National Army which was reorganised by him.

Some of the Indian officers who had joined the Indian National Army as a result of persuasion and some who had joined under pressure, did not rejoin the Indian National Army on its reorganisation. Some also refused to rejoin as they were strong supporters of Mohan Singh. All these were sent to Prisoner of War Camps.

After a short time about 7 officers were separated on the charge of propagating views unfavourable to the reformation of the Indian National Army. They were kept in Hill Street Police Station lock up for about 6 months. They were released some time after the arrival of Subhas Chandra Bose and were sent to the Prisoner of War Camp.

Rash Behari Bose asked Raghavan the President of the Malaya Branch of the Indian Independence League to take over the Department of Publicity and Information and Civil Volunteering. N. Raghavan delegated his power to two members of the executive Council of the Malaya Branch. S.C. Goho was entrusted with the Department of Publicity and Information and Dr. Lukhshimayah with Department of Civil Volunteering. Mr. Dalal was appointed as a Chief Executive Officer under S.C. Goho.

Criticism was now levelled against Rash Behari Bose for not withdrawing from the Presidentship and against Raghavan for not sending in his resignation jointly with K.P.K. Menon, Capt. Mohan Singh and Col. Gilani.

The Japanese appreciating the unpopularity of Rash Behari Bose wanted to set up another organisation under the name of the Youth Movement being of the opinion that if the Indian Independence League movement ceased they would be able to pull strings through that organisation.

Raja Ram who was employed as a publisher of the Indian Press and was in League with the Japanese was taken into confidence of the promoter of the Indian Youth Organisation. One Mr. Mizumo got in touch with Raja Ram, K.R. Menon and Narayanasamy who were members of the former Indian Youth League and Indian Passive Defence and started encouraging them to start the Indian Youth Movements. I believe a large sum of money was given to them for expenses.

On the other hand Rash Behari Bose was trying to become a dictator and his Lieutenants V.C. Linghan, Desh Pandey and Dewan Das were busy doing propaganda for him.

Mr. Goho learning about the Japanese intentions to start the Youth Movement tried to stop it on the ground that was an understanding with the Japanese that no other political organisation would be allowed to function other than the Indian Independence League, but without success. He suggested that the organisation be run under the Indian Independence League and wanted to consult N.Raghavan and promulgate a scheme for it.

N. Raghavan seeing that he had become unpopular with the public and fearful of losing the support of the Japanese,who were instrumental in the formation of Youth Movement, called a meeting of the Territorial Committee at Penang. The Territorial Committee met from 18th to 21st February 1943 and discussed the Japanese policy, cooperation between the civilian and military side of the movement, reorganisation of the Indian National Army and liaison between them, direct dealing between the Japanese and the workers and members of the League and Indian Youth Movement, help to be extended to the League in matters of communal questions and collections and few other subjects, and passed some resolutions, and also decided to send a memorandum to Rash Behari Bose, President of the Council of Action with a request to solve the difficulties which confronted them.

In this meeting resolutions were passed in which Dictatorial Powers were given to the President of Malaya Branch and the Presidents of other Branches with the President of the Malaya Branch for removing and appointing President of any Branch or sub-Branch and its members.

The said memorandum was brought by S.C. Goho on 22/2/1943 as Raghavan was not well and sent to Mr. Rash Behari Bose through Mr. Watan be of Iwakuro Kikan.

Two days after his return Goho met Rash Behari Bose.

At the instigation of Raja Ram, K.R. Menon, and Narayanasamy the organisers of the Youth Movement, Japanese M.P. sent for S.C. Goho and warned him against hindering the formation of the Youth Movement.

Next day, S.C. Goho was asked to resign from the Presidentship of the Indian Independence League, Syonan (Singapore) Branch and Rash Behari Bose also told him to tell N. Raghavan to resign from the Presidentship of the Malaya Branch of the Indian Independence League.

On 7/3/43 S.C. Goho sent in his resignation from the Presidentship of the Singapore Branch of the Indian Independence League.

The Representative Council of the Singapore Branch after accepting Goho's resignation elected Mr. Yellappa as the President. Mr. S.C. Goho after handing in his resignation requested Raghavan to tender his resignation by telegram through him,where upon Raghavan also sent his resignation from the Presidentship of the Malaya Branch of Indian Independence League.

On 8th March 1943 a body of Indians mostly composed of the coolies from Seleter were taken round the town in lorries carrying Indian Congress Flag and shouting slogan, and then collected at Victoria Memorial Hall, Singapore. Kumarasamy of Singapore Traction Company presided, the meeting organised an Indian Youth Movement. The people who went to attend the meeting were asked to sign forms before entering.

In the meeting they condemned and impeached the office bearers and the members of the Indian Independence League and passed a resolution to the effect that they have organised the movement in order to get rid of the pro-British elements and those who are hindrance to the Independence Movement.

They again held a meeting in the Capital. Theatre where officers of the Indian National Army were also present and in that meeting Raja Ram blamed the leaders of the Indian Independence League movement and their committee and called them British fifth columnists without mentioning names. They expressed their full faith in A. Yellappa the then President of the Indian Independence League, Singapore Branch. They also exhorted the people to support the movement and have full faith in the Japanese and Mr. Rash Behari Bose their leader.

A. Yellappa was also responsible for this impeachment as he was against Mr. S.C. Goho and wanted him discredited. The reasons for sponsoring this Youth Movement by the Japanese were firstly to revive enthusiasm which had lagged as a result of the crisis that arose and secondly to stop the pressure that the leaders of the Independence League were bringing for a declaration of Japanese policy towards India by the Japanese Government which the Japanese found inconvenient to comply with. Sometime later, this Youth Movement was absorbed by the Indian Independence League. Later on Youth Sections were opened in all the places under the name of Independence League Youth Section.

The Territorial Committee held meetings from 16/3/1943 to 18/3/1943 in Singapore under the Chairmanship of Dr. M.M. Lukshmeyan. In these meetings resignation of Mr. N. Raghavan from the Presidentship of the Malaya Branch and S.C. Goho from the membership of the Territorial Committee were accepted.

Dr. M.K. Lukshimeyeh was elected President of the Malaya Branch.

Mr. Thivy stated that objectionable speeches were made by the Youth Movement members impeaching the leaders of the Indian Independence League movement and calling them fifth columnists and suggested to the President of the Malaya Branch to approach the President of the Council of Action and requested him to take action to have such statements withdrawn and apologies tendered.

Mr. A. Yellappa was of the opinion that they should ignore the incident as the Youths had been silent and inactive and he thought that the speeches must have been scrutinised by Rash Behari Bose before they were delivered as he had directed the Indian National Army officers to be present at the meeting. But it was decided that the President of the League Malaya Branch should take up the matter with Rash Behari Bose President of the Council of Action.

The President met Rash Behari Bose who was of the opinion that the incidents should be ignored in view of the fact that the Youth Movement would cause under the Singapore Branch League (as a Section) and it should be left to the President of the said Branch to deal with this matter.

The weekly journal in English *New Light* edited by Raja Ram stopped publication and it was replaced by another weekly journal in English called *Young India* after the organisation of the Youth Movement.

A.Yellappa suggested that a band of young men be sent on tour in Malaya to rouse up the public as in Syonan (Singapore) the public spirit was lagging behind and it was necessary to whip up their enthusiasm and set the movement on progressive lines.

Dr. Lukshimeyah the president moved a resolution in Territorial Committee reaffirming its confidence in the sincerity of Japan which was unanimously carried. K.A. Narayanasamy moved many resolutions.

During these days a women's section was created in the Indian Independence League, Singapore Branch. On the refusal of Mrs. Davies and Dr. Lakshmi to become the Chairman Mrs.Chidambaram was elected. Dr.Lakshmi agreed to be Vice-Chairman and Miss S.N. Saraswathi Secretary.

Similar sections were opened in the other places of Malaya. Beside these sections a school for the training of fifty young Indians was also opened in Singapore on 20th April 1943 under the name of "Azad School." The students were given revolutionary training and Raja Ram was incharge.

I am attaching a rough translation* of Hindustani speech of one Jai Ram Bali of the Indian Army delivered to the personnel of the Indian National Army, in the Headquarters of Hind Field Force, Biddadari on 9th April, 1943. The speaker was captured by the Japanese troops in Burma. He also delivered the same speech on 13th April 1943 at a Mass Meeting on the occasion of Jallianwala Bagh Day.

At the meeting of the Representative Council of the Indian Independence League Singapore Branch held on 16/4/43 at which Yellappa presided, it was decided to appoint a sub-committee to arrange for the celebration of Tantryo Batau (Tenno Heika's Birthday) on 29th April 1943. The sub-committee decided to release $20,000 out of which $10,000 were to be given to Nippon Red Cross Society for the benefit of the Japanese soldiers and at the second meeting held on 23rd April under the Chairmanship of Mr. M.V. Pillai it was reported that $10,000 had been collected upon which the Chairman said that the amount will not meet with the expenses of the celebration and at least $15,000 had to be collected.

It was decided to spend not more than $2,000 on decoration feeding and other incidental expenses and $3,000 to be set aside for donation to the Indian sick soldiers.

A Committee was nominated for handing over $10,000 to Mr. Shinozaki for the Nippon Red Cross Society.

The president authorised Udharam Manager of Chotirmall and Co., to fix up an appointment with Mr. Shinozaki.

During this period an Officers Training School was also opened at Neesoon with Lt. Col. Habib and Major Dara of the Indian National Army as supervisors.

After acquiring control of the Civil and Military (Indian National Army) organisations Rash Behari Bose, the president of the Council of Action, tried to change the constitution framed in Bangkok Conference, and in order to assume dictatorial powers (which he was already in fact practising) invited Indian Representatives from the different places in East Asia to hold the Indian Independence League Conference of Delegates at Singapore on 27 April 1943.

A Reception Committee was formed from the members of the Representative Council of the Indian Independence League Singapore on the instructions of Rash Behari Bose. Programme of the Conference and arrangements in connection therewith were prepared in consultation with Col. Chatterjee by the various sub-committee appointed.

Representatives from Java, Sumatra, Hong kong, Manila, Burma, Thailand and Malaya including persons from the Indian National Army attended Conference which was held in Singapore Branch of Indian Independence League for 5 days from 27th April under the presidentship of Rash Behari Bose.

Besides the representatives in the list of the subject committee Dwarka Dass from Java and Amar Singh and Moulvi from Bangkok, one Banerjee from Burma and many others from Indian National Army, and other delegates appeared for the Conference.

The following persons were nominated by the President as the Members of Council of Action who according to the rules formed could function only in an advisory capacity and then only when their advice was asked for by the President.

1. Rash Behari Bose, President
2. A. Yellappa.
3. J.A. Thivy.
4. Lt. Col. Bhonsle of the Indian National Army.
5. Lt. Col. Zaman Kiani of the Indian National Army.

The word President was only used for the President of the Indian Independence League and the other Presidents of the Branches were designated as Chairman.

Many changes in the way of organisation in the League Headquarters as well as branches took place.

The following departments were formed and were run by the secretaries deputed.

1.	Secretary General		Lt. Col.Chatterjee
2.	"	Finance	"
3.	"	Supply	Hardial Singh
4.	"	Recuriting	Lt. Col. Gilani
5.	"	Training	Lt.Col.Ihsan Kadir
6.	"	Health and Social Welfare	D.M. Khan of Hong Kong
7.	"	Housing Deptt.	-do-
8.	"	Transport	-do-
9.	"	Education and Culture	Mr. Thivy
10.	"	Reconstruction	Mr. Sarkar
11.	"	Propaganda	Iyer of Bangkok
12.	Members Overseas Deptt.		A.M. Sahai
13.	Director of Military Bureau		Lt.Col. J.K. Bhonsle.

The President appointed Mr. Yellappa the Chairman of the Singapore Branch of Indian Independence League and the following amongst others were chosen to look after the various affairs, beside their names:

1. Maganlal of Maganlan Nagindas, Treasurer or Finance Officer.
2. G. Sarangapany in charge of Propaganda and Publicity.
3. Dr. P.T. Nathan in charge of Social Welfare.

During the open session of Bangkok Conference one person went to the stage and protested that they have been played with by the leaders who had given the impression that Subhas Chandra Bose will be coming and he will lead the movement but to his surprise he was not there. He started blaming the leaders present there. He was removed from the stage by force on the ground that he was mentally affected.

One of the resolutions of the Bangkok Conference was to request S.C. Bose to come to East Asia and an appeal was made to the Japanese Government to obtain permission from the German Government to enable Subhas Chandra Bose to come to East Asia.

The Japanese who had fully realised the unpopularity of Rash Behari Bose, whom the Indian public in India as well as outside in general thought to be a tool in the hands of the Japanese, and realising the need for Indian propaganda to support them in causing disturbances in India had no alternative but to bring Subhas Chandra Bose from Germany to East Asia. As he was then of no practical value to Germany who had failed in her advance towards Persia and was then in retreat. They were able to persuade the German Government to send him out to the Far East.

Subhas Chandra Bose was taken to Japan from Germany where he stayed for sometime on account of his health. Rash Behari Bose was taken to Japan to meet Subhas Chandra Bose.Thereafter Subhas Chandra Bose was brought to Malaya by aeroplane accompanied by Rash Behari Bose and reached Singapore on 2nd July, 1943.

They were received at Singapore Airport by Indian National Army and Indian Independence League representatives. The prominent figure were Lt. Col. J.K. Bhonsle, Lt. Col. Zaman Kiani, Lt. Col. Raju of Indian National Army, A. Yellappa, Amir Mohamad Khan and others.

Subhas Chandra Bose was provided with a guard of honour from the Indian National Army after which he was taken to a residence near Katong Park which was fully guarded by the Indian National Army slodiers. Japanese in plain clothes were also on duty there.

On 4th July, 1943 a Conference of the Indian Independence League Delegates from East Asia was held at Dai Toa Gekijo (Cathey Cinema) where admission was by tickets issued by the Chairman of the Indian Independence League Syonan Branch (Singapore). Besides the Military and Malayan representatives the following represented the places mentioned against their names:-

1. Daswani	2. Daljit Singh	—Manila
3. Dewarka Dass	4. Tejunal	—Java
5. Matani	6. Ibrahim	—Sumatra
7. Mr. Karkata	8. Matani	—Bangkok
9. D.M. Khan		—Hang Kong

Rash Behari Bose in his Presidential address after explaining the then war situation and the sincerity of Japan towards India and Indians gave up his presidentship and appointed Subhas Chandra Bose as the Leader of the Independence Movement, Mr. J.A. Thivy, Chairman of the Malai Branch in his address welcoming Subhas Chandra Bose said that the Indians in Malaya will show their faith and trust in him as their leader.

Lt. Col. J.K. Bhonsle D.M.B. (Director of Military Bureau) welcoming Subhas Chandra Bose on behalf of the Indian National Army said they had placed their lives and the destiny of India in his hands. He added that he was certain that they will meet the enemy in the field and destroy him there and rid India from the evil influence of Anglo-American Imperialism forever.

Subhas Chandra Bose before starting his address praised Rash Behari Bose for his services to his country. He also expressed his desire that Rash Behari Bose should continue his activities as his Supreme Adviser.

Subhas Chandra Bose in his address asked the Indian gathering to line up in one solid flank under one Leadership and prepare themselves for action and the fight that lay ahead of them. He expressed that the final victory will be won by the Tripartite Powers and their allies. He added that if anyone had still any doubt about Japanese intentions to help in the liberation of the Asiatic Nations, he should place his trust in him. He also indicated that he intended organizsing a Provisional Government of Free India to lead the Indian Revolution to a successful conclusion and to prepare the Indian people for an armed struggle.

A Resolution was passed thanking General Tojo for his congratulatory message.

On 5th July, 1943 a Military (Indian National Army) review was arranged on the field opposite the Municipal Office. Subhas Chandra Bose after inspection gave a speech to the Officers and men of the Indian National Army expressing full faith in their victory and said that battle cry would be "To Delhi" "To Delhi" and the ceremony ended after the March Past.

On 6th July a review of the Indian National Army was again held in the same place in honour of General Tojo who had come to Singapore on 5th instant.

Mass Rally of Indians in Singapore was held on July 9th on the Padang opposite Municipal Offices in honour of Subhas Chandra Bose. Men, women and Indian youths participated in great numbers.

Subhas Chandra Bose addressed the audience in a speech in which he gave reasons for running away from India and his experience and faith in the victory of the Axis Powers. He asked for total mobilisation and money and manpower. He expected to enrol at least three hundred thousand soldiers and collect thirty million dollars. Addressing the women he said that he wanted a death defying regiment of women.

The title Netaji was conferred upon Subhas Chandra Bose by public acclamation. Netaji means the leader.

A mass meeting of Indian women of Singapore was organised under the auspices of the women section of the Indian Independence League, and the Supreme Commander of the Indian National Army on 19th July, 1943.

Subhas Chandra Bose after inspection of the guard of honour composed of 40 women with fixed bayonet addressed the gathering and exhorted them to sacrifice for the freedom of their country and called for volunteers for the "Rani of Jhansi Regiment".

Indian Independence League East Asia appointed recruiting officers for Singapore and applications were invited on the understanding that they would have to parade in the evening at the different centres and they would be sent for when required.

Subhas Chandra Bose contacted some of the Senior Indian Officers of the prisoners of war to find out their reasons for not joining the Indian National Army and also to hear their complaints regarding the atrocities committeed on those who did not want to join during Capt. Mohan Singh regime.

I understand that amongst them was Lt. Col. Choudhari I.M.S. a Bengali who told Subhas Chandra Bose that as he had pledged to serve the King Emperor he could not break that pledge but would have no objection to join if he was absolved by the British Government from oath.

Subhas Chandra Bose also visited the Macpherson Road Camp where the Indian Prisoners of War were present. There, after delivering the lecture which was not well received he asked those who wanted to join the movement to collect under the Indian National Flag (Congress Flag) which was then hoisted up. Only one soldier who has gone there from the Changi guard stood under the flag. Subhas Chandra Bose called the Indian Prisoners of War British dogs. The Prisoners of War were highly insulted by this remark of his.

Subhas Chandra Bose took the command of the Indian National Army in his own hands on 8th August, 1943 and designated himself the Supreme Commander of the Indian National Army and the Director of Military Bureau (Lt. Col. Bhonsle) became Chief of Staff of the Indian National Army.

Sometime later Rash Behari went back to Japan accompanied by his A.D.C. V.C. Lingan, sometime in August 1944. Rash Behari Bose died in January, 1945.

Desh Pande the other Lieutenant of Rash Behari Bose who had a Japanese wife in Japan was in the independence Movement. He, in the beginning had great faith in the Japanese but some time after the crisis started suspecting the Japanese. He was frank in his talks and views and aired them daringly. The Japanese began to suspect him after his conversation, with the officer in charge of the Hikari Kikan Burma. He was sent back to Singapore from Burma and was just passing his days in silence.

He was allowed to go to Japan to see his family but met with sudden death on board the Ship Awa Maru on 1st April 1945.

I am told that Subhas Chandra Bose met Mohan Singh and had talk with him about the movement but Mohan Singh did not agree with Subhas Chandra Bose's views and expressed in strong terms his complete lack of faith in the Japanese.

After sometime Mohan Singh was sent by air to Sumatra as he was run down in health and Lt. Ratan Singh followed him by boat.

Lt.Iqbal who remained behind was sent to a Prisoner of War Camp in Singapore.

On the representation of the Ceylonese a Ceylonese Department was also started in the Indian Independence League Headquarters. Hotchawala became the Secretary. Similar sub-branch of the Ceylonese was also started in the Indian Independence League Syonan Branch under the Chairmanship of M.V. Pillay.

At its inception the Indian Independence League then known as Indian League of Independence Syonan Branch had S.C. Goho as its President and Kanan Pillay as the Secretary of the Syonan Branch League.

After Goho's return from the Tokyo Conference, Kanan Pillay who was suspected of selling League Newspaper and pocketing the money and misappropriating other things, e.g., foodstuffs, papers, etc., to the Malaya Branch as Secretary by arrangements between Raghavan and S.C. Goho who did not wish to take drastic steps as he was one of their staunch supporters.

On the transfer of Kanan Pillay, Muthiah and Kadar were elected Assistant Secretaries of the Singapore Branch of the League.

The Education Department was under the Municipality and Muthiah who was by profession a teacher found it difficult to discharge his job as a teacher. The Municipality raised objections and requested the League to release both Bhag Singh and Muthiah from their posts in the League so that they may attend regularly to their duties as teachers. Bhag Singh resigned from the League and Muthiah from the school becoming a full time paid General Secretary of the Singapore Branch of the League.

In February 1942 Mr. S.C. Goho was not available to attend to some Japanese celebration and the address which he had to read was passed on to Muthiah to give to Mr. M.V. Pillay to deliver. M.V. Pillay found himself in an awkward position when the leaders of the other communities brought properly drafted and decorated addresses whereas the one he had to read was not.

Mr. Pillay got very annoyed about this and Mr. Muthiah on learning that the Mayor had felt that there was neglect on the part of the Indians went to see Shinozaki and apologise for such neglect.

Mr. Pillay who was not on good terms with Mr. S.C. Goho the President thought that the Secretary Mr. Muthiah who was henchman must have played with him and let him down in the eyes of Japanese, strongly protested against the Secretary's slackness in the meeting of Representative Council and demanded Muthiah's resignation or alternatively offered his resignation from the Committee. Mr. Muthiah realising the seriousness of the situation and also feeling that Mr. Yellappa who was against Mr. Goho and his elique had been elected as President of the League, resigned from the post of secretaryship of the Indian Independence League.

K.R. Menon took over the Secretaryship temporarily and during this time the post was advertised and applicants called for. I was served with a notice from K.R. Menon the Hon. Secretary on the instruction of the President A. Yellappa informing me that I had ceased to be a member of the working committee as well as a member of the Representative Council for not attending meetings. After sometime one K.R. Ramanathan was taken in as the paid secretary of the Indian Independence League in the middle of April 1943. Later on there were misappropriations from the monies donated and loss of jewellery received from the public for the League and Rani of Jhansi Regiment. Ramanathan, A. yellappa President and Chidambaram were suspected of having a hand in the losses.

On enquiry Ramanathan was held responsible as the person whose duty it was to issue receipts for money and jewellery received. Yellappa and Chidambaram were trying to hush up the matter but public criticism was loud against them and at last the matter was referred to the Police and Ramanathan was charged and convicted. He was recently released on 11/45 when the convicts were released from Jail.

After the Sohan Singh who was very friendly with the high officers of the Indian National Army and Indian Independence League and helping them by supplying various articles was given the post of Secretary as one who could be relied upon.

When Subhas Chandra Bose came to Singapore he was not in favour of wasting time and energy in looking after the sick or poor Indians and expressed that as they were in the midst of a war they could not pay any attention to the sickly and the dying.

Those who were very sick were removed from the Camp established by the Distress Relief Committee to Pungol with no proper arrangement and the others were sent away from the camp. Distress Relief Committee ceased to function furthermore its funds were exhausted.

This camp became the headquarters of the Rani of Jhansi Regiment, with Captain Lakshmi as its Commanding Officer.

In 1944 when the question of providing rice for the Indian sick and destitutes who were housed at Pungol arose Municipal Authorities were approached. They refused to give rice but Shinozaki of the Municipal Department suggested that it will be helpful to Indians if they were to start Indian Welfare Association under the (Tokubetu Si) Municipality similar to the Associations formed by Eurasians, Malaya and Arabs.

The members of the social welfare branch of the Indian Independence League Singapore agreed to it. The Indian Welfare Association started to function under the Chairmanship of Mr. M. V. Pillay and used to meet at Indian Independence League, Singapore Branch premises. Amongst others were Balbir Singh, Dr. Nathan, Maganlal, Paul, Sammy, Rev. Handy, Davies, Anwari.

The Indian Welfare Association, which had no connection with the Indian Independence League, utilised the premises of the Indian Independence League, Singapore Branch, for its purposes, and began to collect donations from the public independently for the support of the Indian destitutes and bulit huts behind the Indian Independence League, Singapore Branch, Waterloo Street.

Mr. N. Raghawan who had rejoined the Indian Independence League Movement and was Minister of Finance in the Azad Hind Government did not approve of this formation of the Welfare Association probably for personal reasons. Nor did Subhas Chandra Bose approve of the Association, as the Indian Independence League had no control over it.

A meeting was called by the Indian Welfare Association at Jalan Bazar for collection of money, and during the opening address by M.V. Pillay, objections were raised for omitting to Sing at the outset "Bande Mataram". Heckling and disorder prevailed. I am informed that soldiers of the Indian National Army and the members of Azad School Singapore were sent in plain clothes to create confusion at the meeting.

Subhas Chandra Bose on the advice of N. Raghavan made strong protests to the Japanese against this organisation on the ground that no other body outside the Indian Independence League should be formed in connection with Indian affairs and it was later dissolved.

In order to carry on the work of Indian Independence League and to support the Indian Independence Army, Subhas Chandra Bose made an appeal to Indians for funds which appeal met with a good response especially from the Hindus of the United Provinces. Contributions from the rich class were not so satisfactory and questionnaires were issued by the League Headquarters to individuals known to be well off calling for information regarding their income and wealth. This scheme did not succeed as many did not return the questionnaire forms at all.

On the instructions of the Indian Independence League Headquarters the local League Branch issued a circular to members of the Representative Council to help the persons nominated to collect statistics of Indians residing in Singapore in every way possible.

Most of the Muslims either did not join the League or did not cooperate whole-heartedly on the ground that they did not approve of the Indian National Congress and the singing of "Bande Mataram". Nor did the leaders who were mostly Hindus care for the feelings of Muslims. This attitude of the Muslims offended the Leaders of the Indian Independence League.

Non-Muslims especially Hindus started a propaganda to the effect that Muslims were pro-British and anti-Japanese. They did not trust the Muslims who were in the movement whether they were members of the Indian Independence Army or the Indian Independence League.

During the time of Rash Behari Bose, A. Yellappa the President of the Indian Independence League, Singapore Branch sent for T.A.M. Abdul Aziz who was a representative of the South Indian Muslims along with Haji A. Mohammed Hussain, B. Mohammed Ibrahim, and few others and hold a meeting in which Rash Behari, A. Yellappa, Lt. Col. Bhonsle, Lt. Col. Z. Kiyani, Lt. Col. Chatterjee, Lt. Col. Ihsan Kadir, M.V. Pillay were present. Col. Chatterjee accused the Muslims of lack of cooperation and non-participation in the movement calling them enemies of India, and warned them that unless they changed they will be the sufferers. On the objection raised by Muslims regarding the singing of "Bande Mataram"and the Congress Flag Col. Chatterjee replied that the League will not stop the singing of"Bande Mataram" and will continue the use of the Indian National Flag. Lt. Col. Ihsan Kadir and Lt. Col. Bhonsle supported Col. Chatterjee and also used harsh and threatening words. Lt. Col. Zaman Kiani dealt leniently with them and suggested that the League should give some privilege to the Muslims and consider their objections.

Sometime after his arrival Subhas Chandra Bose called at his house, Abdul Aziz and a few others Muslims. Lt. Col. Chatterjee and M. K. Chidambaram were present. Subhas Chandra Bose asked the Muslims the reasons for not coming forward for the Independence of their country upon which the representatives said that they objected to the song "Bande

Mataram", the Congress Flag and that as they were followers of the Muslims League of India which is also fighting for the Independence of India and as they were unaware of its policy and attitude towards the Indian Independence League they could not participate in the Movement. Subhas Chandra Bose told then that he will consider their objections but that they should participate in the movement.

Under the persistant threats of A. Yellappa who had asked for $ 250000 from Indian Muslims only $ 130000 was collected and given to Subhas Chandra Bose.

The Muslim objection against *Bande Mataram* was that it formed part of a song written by a Hindu Bengalee, to excite the Hindu population in Bengal against the Muslim rulers of Bengal. It contains many objectionable references to Muslims and although these references do not appear in the stanzas which form the supposed national song, yet the implication is there. Subhas Chandra Bose ordered the substitution of another song for *Bande Mataram* but in practice *Bande Mataram* used to be sung at meetings.

After sometime A. Yellappa took T. A. M. Abdul Aziz to Penang with him in order to persuade the Penang Muslims to participate in the movement and make contributions. T. A. M. Abdul Aziz at a meeting in Penang asked the Muslims to join and contribute. Thereafter a Committee of Muslims under the Chairmanship of Abdul Wahab of Penang was formed to collect money. Although Muslims were not willing but not desiring to bring trouble on themselves collected about $ 5,000.

After a speech made by Subhas Chandra Bose (soon after his arrival) circulars for total mobilisation were issued to the members of the Representative Committees by the League Branches asking them to exert and try their best to raise volunteers for the Indian National Army.

On 21st October 1943 the fifth Conferences of the Indian Independence League in which delegates from all the centres of the East Asia including Malaya participated was held at Dai Toa Gekijyo (Cathay Cinema) Singapore.

M. K. Ramachandran read an address welcoming the delegates which was followed by a report on the working of the League, by the General Secretary Lt. Col. A.C. Chatterjee.

After that Subhas Chandra Bose delivered an address in which he dealt with all aspects of the current world situation with particular reference to India. He also declared that the formation of the Provisional Government had become a necessity for the final fight for freedom.

The Conference reassembled in the afternoon. Subhas Chandra Bose appeared at the Conference accompanied by Col. Yamamoto the then chief of the Hikari Kikan. Before proclaiming the inauguration of the Provisional Government of Free India Subhas Chandra Bose read two messages of congratulations he had sent to Burma and Philippines and another to the Japanese Government expressing the thanks and gratitude of the Indians for their kind help in the movement. The message were adopted by the Conference.

Subhas Chandra Bose announced the composition of the Provisional Government comprising a cabinet of ministers consisting of the representatives of the Indian National Army and a body of advisers.

Subhas Chandra Bose then made a statement in Hindustani explaining the significance of the extablishment of the Provisional Government which was translated into Tamil by Mr. M. K. Chidambaram.

Then Subhas Chandra Bose the Head of the State and Prime Minister took the following oath:

"In the name of God I take this sacred oath that to liberate India and the 38 crores of my countrymen I Subhas Chandra Bose, will continue the sacred war of freedom till the last breath of my life. I shall remain always a servant of India and to look after the welfare of 38 crores of my Indian brothers and sisters shall be for my highest duty. Even after winning freedom, I shall always be prepared to shed even the last drop of my blood for the preservation of India's Freedom".

This was followed by the oath taking ceremony of the members of the Government. The oath ran as follows

"In the name of God I take this holy oath that to liberate India and the 38 crores of my countrymen I will be absolutely faithful to my Leader Subhas Chandra Bose and shall be always prepared to sacrifice my life and all I have for fulfilling this pledge."

Subhas Chandra Bose shook hands with each member and this was followed by the Proclamation of the Provisional Government of Free India which was read in Hindustani by Mr. A.M. Sahay, in Tamil by Mr. M.K. Chidambaram and in English by Subhas Chandra Bose.

A luncheon party was given by the Indian Independence League in honour of the delegates at the Indian Independence League organisation of East Asia at Cricket Club, Singapore. Lt. Col. Mitabe of the Hikari Kikan Burma was also present. Subhas Chandra Bose spoke on that occasion and said that all arrangements necessary for a revolution were completed and that they should be ready for the last phase of struggle. He appealed to the rich Indians to sacrifice whatever they possess.

On 22nd October 1943 Birthday of Rani Lakshmi Bai of Jhansi and the opening ceremony of the "Rani of Jhansi Regiment Training Camp" was celebrated at the Indian Independence League, Singapore Branch, Waterloo Street. Subhas Chandra Bose was received by Mrs. M.K. Chidambaram the President of the Women Section Syonan. Mr. Bose then inspected the guard of honour presented by an armed unit of the Rani of Jhansi Regiment in company of Capt. Dr. Lakshmi.

Subhas Chandra Bose in his speech said "It was not merely political movement but on the other hand it was engaged in the great task of regenerating the nation. He added that India has a glorious tradition of producing brave women like Rani of Jhansi and others and it did produce a Lakshmi Bai today for the war of Independence of India. He further said that the women of India have not only taken part in the Passive Resistance Movement but in the history of the Revolutionary party also there are many examples of the Indian women. He gave a short history of Rani of Jhansi and her fight against the British for freedom of Jhansi. He added that 156 Indian women are going to start their training in the Central camp but hoped that the numbers in Syonan (Singapore) will reach to 1000 and added that Training Camps for women had also started in Thailand and Burma and declared the Rani of Jhansi Camp Syonan opened. The first meeting of the Council of Ministers of the Azad Hind (Free India) met at the residence of Subhas Chandra Bose at 9.00 p.m. on 22/10/43.

On the night of 23rd and 24th October the Provisional Government of *Azad Hind* declared a war on Britain and the United States of America.

On 24 Oct. 1943 a military parade of the members of the *Azad Hind Fauz* (Indian Independence Army) was held in the playing ground in front of the Municipal Building, Singapore and Subhas Chandra Bose after inspecting the Indian National Army gave a speech to the members of the Army.

On 24 Oct. 1943 Provisional Government of Free India was host to a Banquet to high ranking Japanese Army and Navy officers as well as prominent Japanese civilians at Japanese Army Officers' Club. Subhas Chandra Bose gave a short speech in which he said that since the war broke out in Europe in 1939 Britain and her Allies professed that they are fighting for democracy in the world and similarly the United States of America has repeated it after joining in the War but the truth can be judged by the refusal to apply the Atlantic Charter wherever any suppressed nation asked for it. The domination of India by the British is by itself a proof of this false declaration. Praising the Axis Powers he said that they are fighting on the Principle of Justice and Right. Japanese Air Commander and High Ranking Officers of the Burmese Army also spoke.

A general meeting of Businessmen and Chettiars for collection of funds was held at Jalan Bazar Stadium on 25/10/1943 in which Subhas Chandra Bose demanded money for carrying on of the movement. Nearly 7 million dollars were promised. On 26th at another meeting held at the Indian Independence League, Singapore Branch Office, about six million dollars in promise were added to the above contribution.

A gold plated silver Charkha (Spinning wheel) was bought by the Chettiar (Nagarathers) of Negri Awmbilan for a sum of $ 500000 at the auction.

The general procedure in these collections was that some important figure such as A. Yellappa the President of the Singapore Indian Independence League, Branch Singapore, Mr. M.K. Chidambaram or Udha Ram of Chotirmall & Co. used to tax the people in whatever amount they thought best and a garland was sold for so many dollars to such a person who had no option but to accept it and pay the sum specified.

Furthermore people were summoned to the League Headquarters and the Singapore Indian Independence League Branch where they were compelled to agree and pay the amount at which they were assessed. The collection was made by threat of confiscation of all one's money and property or handing one over to Japanese Military Police and calling one Pro-British. Men responsible for these extortions were A. Yellappa, M. K. Chidambaram, Udha Ram and Magan Lal and in the case of wealthy persons, Subhas Chandra Bose, Raghawan, Thivy and Dr. Lakshmeyah used to interview and force contribution out of them.

Many cases have occurred wherein persons who could not afford to pay the amount demanded or were not willing to pay were taken by the Japanese M.P.'s.

Besides the above mentioned extortions the Manager of the Indian Overseas Bank Mr. Jagathesan was giving them full information about the account of deposits of individuals in his bank or their other businesses. After the formation of the Provisional Government of Free India a fresh oath of allegiance and pledge were asked to be taken by the Indians and the old membership card of the Indian Independence League was cancelled and a new card issued.

The Provisional Government of Free India was officially recognised by the following countries.

Japanese Government recognised the Provisional Government of Free India on 23rd October 1943.

German Foreign Minister Her Von Ribbentrop officially notifying Subhas Chandra Bose, by telegram that the Reich Government extended the recognition to the newly formed Provisional Government of Azad Hind Fauj (Free India).

On 25th October, 1943 information was received in Syonan that the Independence State of Burma had recognised the Provisional Government of Azad Hind.

The Philippine Republic's recognition of the Provisional Government of Azad Hind was conveyed to Subhas Chandra Bose, Head of the Provisional Government of the Free India by Jose P. Laurel, President of the Republic of the Philippines.

Croates extended its formal recognition to the Provisional Government of Free India on October 27, 1943.

On November 1st, 1943 Nanking Government of China officially announced its recognition of the Provisional Government of Free India.

Manchouko Government as announced on 1st November 1943 in Hainking that Manchouko formerly recognises the Provisional Government of Free India.

Fascist Republic of Italy recognised the Provisional Government of Free India on November 9th, 1943.

On November 18th 1943 Bangkok Radio announced the recognition of the Provisional Government of Free India by the Government of Thailand.

Central Bureau of Free India Berlin issued a declaration.

A few days after the formation of the Provisional Government of Free India Subhas Chandra Bose alongwith Lt. Col. Bhonsle, Lt. Col. Raju, I.M.S., A.M. Sahai and Mr. Hassan who was his Private Secretary and hand followed him from Germany flew to Japan and on arrival at Tokyo on November 1st, 1943 was officially received by the Government of Japan as the Head of the Provisional Government of Free India to attend the East Asia Conference as an observer.

General Hideki Tojo Premier of Japan in response to a speech made by Subhas Chandra Bose at the Assembly of Greater East Asiatic Nations on 6th November 1943 made a declaration transferring the Andaman and Nicobar Islands to the Provisional Government of Free India headed by Subhas Chandra Bose.

Nippon Territorial Committee of the Indian Independence League entertained Subhas Chandra Bose at a Tea Party at the Imperial Hotel on

11th November 1943 and also a Rally was held jointly sponsored by the Taisei Yokusankai and the Japan Indian Society at the Hibiya Public Hall on November 14th, 1943 where Subhas Chandra Bose gave speeches.

Subhas Chandra Bose also made Radio speeches from Tokyo to his compatriots in Germany and other places in Europe on 16th November, 1943 and on 17th to the people of India.

On his way back to Malaya Subhas Chandra Bose visited Philippines and Nanking in China where a welcome Rally was held in his honour on November 19, 1943. There in his speech he called upon Chiang Kai Shek and other leaders to shake off Anglo-American influence and do the utmost for the unification of China and stress that India and China should both fight for freedom and liberation of Greater East Asia. The intention of the Provisional Government of Free India was to establish its Government at Andamans so that they may have their own territory but it was not agreed to by the Japanese *firstly* because in handing over the Islands to the Provisional Government the interests of Japanese who were defernding the place and were in full control would have clashed with that of the Provisional Indian Government. *Secondly* in Japan there was public criticism of the action of the Prime Minister. *Thirdly* the Japanese wanted to strengthen the Burma front and furthermore Subhas Chandra Bose wished to be on the borderline of India for opportune moment to enter India.

A suicide squad of selected volunteers from the Azad Hind Forces (Indian National Army) was formed under the Command of Lt. Col. Shah Nawaz (formerly Captain of 1/14 Punjab Regiment) who had offered himself and the personnel of this squad signed an agreement with their blood and they were moved to Burma. At the same time the 1st Division of the Indian National Army under the Command of Col. M.Z. Kiyani also left for the Burma front. Subhas Chandra Bose on his return from Japan addressed a gathering in front of the Municipality on 2nd December 1943 to celebrate the Andamans and Nicobar Day.

Subhas Chandra Bose visited Sumatra, Borneo and Java on a four days tour where he delivered lectures and collected money. I was told by Lt. Col. Giani who was there that the Japanese did not allow the Indian National Congress Flag to be put on Subhas Chandra Bose's car and also the lecture in Batavia was arranged in a hall where only Indians and some Japanese were present. He further told me that the President of Java was the only Javanese who was invited but was not allowed to enter. The reason for this restriction was, he said, that Japanese did not want the Indian Independence movement to come openly as the Indonesian may start demanding their freedom too.

After that Subhas Chandra Bose visited Andamans and Nicobar Islands which were renamed as Shaheed (Island of Martyr) and Swaraj (Independence) Islands respectively on 30th December 1913 and hoisted the Indian Tricolour Congress Flag.

During this time arrangement were made for transferring Headquarters of the Provisional Government of Free India and the Supreme Command of the Indian National Army to Burma. Subhas Chandra Bose reached Burma on 7th January, 1944, Rear Headquarteres were left in Singapore under the control of Col. Chatterjee.

Colonel (later on Major General) Loganathan who was the Minister of State was appointed the first Chief Commissioner of the Shaheed and Swaraj (Andaman and Nicobar) Islands where he went with one Capt. Alwi his private secretary. Col. Loganathan was just a nominal figure and his work consisted at looking after the Indian Independence Movement there.

Long before Subhas Chandra Bose departed to Burma arrangements were made to send some of the Indian boys for higher military training to Japan and for that purpose Dr. N. K. Menon brought his son from Penang for an interview and later on Mr. Gurcharan Singh of Penang also came down with his son, Menon's son and two sons of Gurcharan Singh were selected for training and were sent to Japan and are still there with some others.

Two months after the transfer of Headquarters of Azad Hind Provisional Government and the Azad Hind Army to Burma Lt. Col. Chatterjee the Secretary-in-General of the Rear Headquarters was also called there and Lt. Col. Alagapan was appointed in his place.

Lt. Co. Bhonsle Chief of the Staff of the Indian National Army who had also gone was replaced by Lt. Col. Nagar in the Rear Headquarters as acting Chief of Staff. By this time the 2nd Division of the Indian National Army also left Singapore on its way to Burma under the Command of Lt. Col. Bhagat Lt. Col. Nagar was also appointed the commander of 3rd Division formed with the Malayan recruits in the main.

A. Yellappa, Chairman of the Indian Independence League, Singapore Branch and the adviser of the Azad Hind Government also went to Burma and M.V. Pillay was appointed to act as Chairman in his place.

Azad Hind Government in the official announcement declared 21st March to be observed as Azad Hind Day, and that the 21st Day of every month shall be observed as Azad Hind Day.

A public meeting of the Indians was held in the playing field of Waterloo Street on 21st March for the celebration of Azad Hind Day and the victories on the Arakan Front and Indo-Burma Front.

Indians of Johors also held a meeting on the 21st under the Chairmanship of Major Dara.

Lt. Col. A.C. Chatterjee the Finance Minister of the Provisional Government of Azad Hind was appointed as Governor of Liberated Areas of India Azad Hind 22/3/44.

A public procession and Mass Rally was organised by the Indian Independence League. Singapore Branch to celebrate the entry of Indian National Army into India and the Bhagat Singh Day in which Lt. Col. Alagappan and Lt. Col. G.R. Nagar were speakers and resolutions were passed.

At a meeting for the celebration of Azad Hind Government Day in Burma Major I.S. Misra of the Indian National Army was personally garlanded by Subhas Chandra Bose and was awarded the Sardar-E-Jung for his meritorious services in the Akyab Sector, Subhas Chandra Bose the Head of the Government of Azad Hind issued citations and awards to 15 members of the Indian National Army including Major I.S. Misra for the act of gallantry during the Arakan operation in February 1944.

A ceremony was held on 30th March 1944 at Waterloo Street playing ground on the occasion of Passing out Parade of the first batch of volunteers of the Rani of Jhansi Regiment in which Lt. Col. Bhonsle, Chief of Staff of the Indian National Army and Capt. Lakshmi, Minister and Commandant of Rani of Jhansi Regiment, Syonan (Singapore) spoke. Most of the members who were willing to go to Burma were sent there.

The following Lt. Colonels were promoted to the rank of Colonels:—

1. A.C. Chatterjee, Administrative General of Free India from 28th March 1944.
2. J.K. Bhonsle, Chief of Staff, Indian National Army from 28th March, 1944.
3. A.D. Loganathan, High Commissioner of Andaman & Nicobar from 31st March 1944.
4. M.Z. Kiyani, 1st Division Indian National Army Commander from 1st April 1944.

In Indian National Army the Muslims units refused to sing the *Bande Mataram* and were singing Iqbal's Poem *"Sare Jahan se Achcha Hindustan Hamara"* (Our India is far better than the rest of the world) which was generally not taken up by the Hindus as it was a composition of a Muslim poet, although Iqbal's song was the only one sung by the Indian National Army during Mohan Singh's regime.

The translation of Tagore's poem and also the songs of Jai Hind and "On to Delhi" were composed by Syed Mumtaz Hussain on the instructions of Col. Chatterjee. The songs are in Hindustani and besides these many songs in Tamil and Hindustani languages were composed by different people which I have lost.

On April 1944 Provisional Azad Hind Government opened the Azad Hind Government Bank in Burma.

Although the arrival of Subhas Chandra Bose put fresh enthusiasm in the hearts of the members of Indian Independence League yet most of the educated classes still had doubts about the Japanese intentions and deplored the Japanese behaviour towards the Indian labourers and employers.

The news of the Indian National Army's entry into Indian territory shook the determination of most of them and fearful at losing the chance of becoming great men they joined the movement. Enlistment in the Indian National Army and other Schools and organisations of the Indian Independence League started again. On the other hand the poorer class of people were dying of hunger and the wages paid were not sufficient to support them owing to high prices prevailing of food stuffs and the difficulty of procuring food and also the ill-treatment of their Japanese employers had forced them into the arms of the Indian National Army.

Mr. N. Raghavan had expressed his willingness to Subhas Chandra Bose in his first interview to rejoin the movement. Subhas Chandra Bose wanted him to go to Burma but he was not willing to do on the pretext that he was ill.

After learning of the favourable turn in the fighting in Burma was taking and of the successes of the Indian National Army and the Japanese entry into India he expressed his willingness to go to Burma and work there. Subhas Chandra Bose sent for him and N. Raghavan took along with him, some of his followers to Burma.

N. Raghavan was then made Minister in the Azad Hind Government and was later given the Portfolio of Finance.

In compliance with the appeal made by Subhas Chandra Bose on 29th March 1944, National Liberation Week was celebrated in remembrance of Jallianwalla Bagh, Amritsar incident of 1919 in Singapore from the 7th to 13th April 1944. The programme for the celebration is attached.

Special prayers for the success of the Indian National Army and Liberation of India were offered in Temples and Rama Krishna Mission on 7th April.

On 8th a public meeting of Indian women was held in the Indian Independence League, Singapore Branch and Mrs. M.K. Chidambaram. Members in charge of the women section of the Indian Independence League made the presentation of $ 6500 collected by the women section of the Indian Independence League, Singapore Branch for the Rani of Jhansi Regiment.

On 9th April Indian National School Children held a Mass Rally which was attended by Lt. Col. S.C. Alagappan, Minister of State and Secretary General, Rear Headquarters, Brahmachari Kailasam, Principal of the Indian National School and Mr. S. Raja Ram representing the Indian Independence League Rear Headquarters and several others. Lt. Col. Alagappan gave a short speech.

A mass meeting was held under the chairmanship of J.A. Thivy the General Secretary of the Rear Headquarters in place of Lt. Col. Alagappan (who had left for Burma) at the Waterloo Street Playing Ground on 13 April 1944. The Chariman addressed the meeting and Major A.S. Dara of Indian National Army also spoke. It was also announced by Mr. M.V. Pillay acting Chairman of the Indian National League, Singapore Branch that seven hundred and fifty dollars were donated by the Indians during the week.

Sikhs of Singapore also had a prayer meeting at Queen Street Sikh Temple, Singapore in observance of "Jallianwallah Day" on the13 April 1944 in which Sohan Singh sports dealer the General Secretary of the Indian Independence League, Singapore Branch exhorted them to follow the example set by Udham Singh who assassinated Michael O' Dwyer who was responsible for the incident and slaughter of Indian people at Amritsar.

Penang Indians under the auspices of the Indian Independence League, Penang Branch held a route march headed by Dr. R.K. Menon the Chairman of the Indian Independence League, Penang in commemoration of the Indian Liberation Week on 9th April 1944. At the close of the march Dr. N.K. Menon urged the gathering to exert greater efforts for their fight for freedom.

On an appeal made by Subhas Chandra Bose a Youth Corps of Indians was formed in order to be instructed in political matters and to imbibe the love of their country. A children's group under the name of "Balak Sena"(Youth Corps) was formed in Singapore and their Headquarters were in the Indian National School No. 9 Morris Road, Singapore. Similar parties of children, girls and boys, were formed in Johore and other parties. A weekly organ was also started under the name of "Balak-E-Hind".

On 21st April 1944 Azad Hind Day was celebrated in Singapore by a free Cinema show at Dai Tea Gekijo (Cathey Cinema) and lectures by M. Siva Ram, Director of Indo Shimbum Sha (Newspaper) and the spokesman of the Provisional Government of Azad Hind and Lt. Col. Kaslival of the Indian National Army.

On 22 April 19444 the Provisional Government of Azad Hind announced the appointment of 5 new Ministers:-

1	A. Yellappa	formerly the advisers to the Provisional
2.	Ishar Singh	Government of Azad Hind and S.B. Basir of Rangoon was appointed advisor.
3.	N. Raghavan	
4.	Lt. Col. G.R. Nagar	
5.	Lt. Col. Habibur Rahaman	

Lt. Col. Alagappan who was Minister without portfolio was appointed as Minister I/C of Supplies in addition to his other duties.

As usual Indians, with other communities took part in the Tenchu Satau (Tenno Heika Birthday) celebrations on 29th April 1944 and the leaders of the communities of Singapore renewed their pledge of loyalty to the Japanese Government. T.A.M. Abdul Aziz representing the Indians.

On 10th May, 1944 "First War of Independence Day" was celeberated by the Indians under the auspices of Indian Independence League in Singapore. By this was meant the Indian Mutiny of 1857 on which occasion Mr. J. Thivy and Lt. Col. Nagar spoke.

On 21st May "Azad Hind Day" and the victories on the Indo-Burma Front were celebrated by holding mass meetings and small group meetings at Indian Independence League, Singapore Branch Waterloo Street, Ramakrishna Mission, Indian Chamber of Commerce and 976 Geylang Road in which (1) Mr. M.V. Pillai, J.Thivy, (2) Brahma Chari Kailasam, (3) G. Maganlal, (4) M.K. Chidambaram spoke respectively and resolutions were passed.

The Civilian Police Training Centre was opened on 3rd June 1944 in Singapore by the Indian Independence League Rear Headquarters under its Reconstruction Department known as "Azad Hind Dal" and this centre formed are of sub-branches of Reconstruction Department. The object was to train policemen for the liberated areas of India.

On 13 June 1944 "Udham Singh Day" in commemoration of the fourth anniversary of the execution by the British of Udham Singh for assassinating Sir Michael O'Dwyer at a meeting of the East India Association in Caxtion Hall, London was celebrated as by the Indians under the auspices of the Indian independence League, Singapore Branch. A meeting was arranged at "Dai Toa Gekijyo" (Cathay Cinema Hall) in which J. Thivy, Lt. Malik of Indian National Army, M.M. Pavalliar and A.M. Nair spoke.

As usual Azad Hind Day was celebrated on 21st June 1944 in which Lt. Col. Gilani of the Indian National Army and Dr. R.T. Nathan spoke at a meeting held in the Indian Independence League, Singapore Branch, Waterloo Street.

Under the instructions of the Provisional Government of Azad Hind issued on 27th June 1944 Netaji Week was celebrated from July 4th to 10th by the Indians in East Asia by displaying Indian Tricolour Flags on houses and holding flag hoisting ceremonies and processions and public meetings under the auspices of the Indian Independence League branches in order to commemorate the taking over of the Leadership by Subhas Chandra Bose in June 1943 as the President of the Indian Independence League of East Asia and Supreme Commander of the Azad Hind Fauz (Indian National Army).

On July 4th a mass rally of Indians after a march in procession from Bidadari was held in the Padang opposite Municipal Building under the Chairmanship of J.A. Thivy. Messers. J.A. Thivy, M.K. Chindambaram and Lt. Malik of Indian National Army spoke.

On 9th July Open Air Cinema shows depicting the events connected with the Independence Movement since the arrival of Subhas Chandra Bose and the formation of the Indian National Army into India were shown in front of the Indian Independence League office, Singapore Branch. A meeting of women was also held in the preeincts of the Indian Independence League, Singapore Branch, on 8th July in which Mrs. Davies, Mrs. Subramaniam Ayer, and Lakshmi Devi Raida of the Rani of Jhansi Regiment expressed their gratitude to Subhas Chandra Bose for having allowed them to form the Jhansi Regiment for the emancipation of their motherland.

A training camp for civil administrations and labour agencies was inaugurated at Bidadari Camp by the Reconstruction Section of the Azad Hind Government by Mr. Thivy., Lt. Col. Gilani, Secretary of Reconstruction Department spoke briefly of the work to be done by the organisation. The trainees were to be sent to the liberated areas to run the affairs of the Provisional Government.

On 21st July "Azad Hind Day" was celebrated as usual by hoisting flags on the Indian Houses and holding a meeting at the Indian

Independence League, Singapore Branch. The meeting was addressed by J.A. Thivy, Daljit Singh of Manila and G. Sarangapani.

Towards the end of July 1944 the Provisional Government of Azad Hind created a new department known as "Man Power" with A.N. Sircar the former legal adviser as its head (Minister of Man Power).

Karim Ghani of Burma was appointed Minister of State. N. Raghavan who was Minister of State took over the portfolio of flnance from Col. A.C. Chatterjee and in addition to his duties as Minister of Finance he was placed on special duty to undertake the task of National Planning for a Free India. Col. Chatterjee continued holding the rank of Minister without portfolio.

Mrs. M.K. Chidambaram was appointed as Deputy Minister of the women's organisation.

Besides helping the Jhansi Regiment and the Training of Nurses the women section of the Indian Independence League, Singapore Branch used to treat now and then sick soldiers of the Indian National Army Camp Bidadari, Singapore to parties. Later in August 1944 it organised charity concerts to collect funds for the comfort of the front line soldiers and for the Health and Social Welfare section of the Local League Branch. A Committee of the following women was formed and authorised to collect money. Dr. Narula (Convenor), Mrs. Davies, Mrs. Jamnadas, Mrs. P.C. Nair, Mrs. Doshi, Mrs. Chatterjee, Mrs. Issac, Mrs. Subramanian Iyer, Miss. S.N. Saraswathi.

Indian Independence League, Singapore Branch, also arranged Boxing matches in aid of charity the proceeds being given to Health and Social Welfare work among Indians.

On 21/8/44 Azad Hind Day was celebrated as usual, Mr. Thivy and 2 others spoke at the meeting.

In or about 8th September 1944 Mr. M.K. Chidambaram was appointed acting Chairman of the Singapore Indian Independence League Branch in place of M.V. Pillay who resigned. Mr. M.V. Pillay continued to serve as a Chairman of the (Singapore) Syonan Indo-Jin Kosei Kyokai Singapore Welfare Association.

On 21st September " Martyrs Day" was observed by the Indians on the instructions of the Indian Independence League. The Indian Tricolour Flag draped in black was flown at half mast side by side with Himomaru (Japanese Flag).

A public meeting was held at Dai Toa Gekijyo (Cathay Cinema) the same evening. Lt. Col. G.Q. Gilani, the acting General Secretary of the Rear

Headquarters, Indian Independence League, presided at the meeting. Lt. Col. Gilani, M.K. Chidambaram, acting Chairman of the Independence League, Singapore Branch and Lt. Col. Hassan of Indian National Army spoke. This celeberation was observed in memory of 5 Indians who were employed for fifth column work and had gone to India where they were executed.

On 2nd October 1944 "Gandhi's Birthday" was celebrated by hoisting Indian Tricolour Flags and Himomaru on most of the shops and houses of the Indians and free food was distributed at some places. A meeting was held under the auspices of the Indian Independence League, Singapore Branch the same evening at Waterloo Street playing ground under the Chairmanship of M.K. Chidambaram.

Mr. Chidambaram and Lt. Col. Alagappan spoke on the life of Mahatma Gandhi.

Azad Hind Government anniversary week was celebrated from the 18th to 24th October 1944 throughout East Asia by the Indian Independence League Branches.

In Singapore on 18th October the Army Day in memory of those who sacrificed their lives for the cause of India's Freedom was celebrated.

Flags were hoisted at the Indian Independence League Rear Headquarters and Singapore Branch. In the afternoon a meeting was called at the Indian Independence League, Singapore Branch premises, Waterloo Street where the pictures of Messrs. Agail Singh and T.P. Kumaran Nair, which were available out of the five who had gone to India as advance agents and were executed in India, were unveiled by Col. J.K. Bhonsle.

Col. Bhonsle, J.A. Thivy, Lt. Col. S.C. Alagappan and Mrs. Sinha spoke on that occasion.

Indian National Army Hospital and Training Camp were visited, speeches to the Indian National Army and lectures were given exhorting them to place their services at the disposal of their country. 21st October was celebrated as Anniversary of formation of the Provisional Government of Azad Hind by holding a military parade at Bidadari Camp and Mass meeting at Cathay Cinema under the Chairmanship of Lt. Col. G.Q. Gilani who spoke and was followed by Mr. Chidambaram.

Lectures were given to the students of the "Azad Hind Dal" (Free India Reconstruction School) by Lt. Col. Gilani and J.A. Thivy on 22/10/44.

On 24th October a State Luncheon Party was given by J.A. Thivy Vice-President of the Indian Independence League Rear Headquarters as a round off to the anniversary celebrations of the Azad Hind Government in which representatives of the Nippon Army and Navy, prominent officials of the Indian Independence League and Indian National Army and other well known Indians were invited.

On 26th October 1944 passing out ceremony of Second Batch of Jhansi Volonteers which was scheduled for 23rd was held at Waterloo Street playing field. A batch of about 180 graduated, Mrs. Thavar and Col. Bhonsle spoke on the occasion.

The creation of a War Council Cabinet proposed by Subhas Chandra Bose to consider all problems concerning the war, its future development and speeding up of war efforts was approved by the Minister and advisers of the Azad Hind Government on 19th October 1944. The following Military and Civil personnel were appointed:

Col. J.K. Bhonsle, Chief of staff, Col. M.Z. Kiani, Col. Aziz Ahmed, Divisional Commander, Lt. Col. Ihsan Kadir, the Minister of Man Power, N. Raghavan Finance Minster, S.A. Ayer, Propaganda Minister, Parmanand, Deputy Minister of Supplies, Col. A.C. Chatterjee, Governor of liberated area, Lt. Col. Galzara Singh, Regimental Commander, A. Yellappa. Transport Officer and Lt. Col. Habib Rahman.

At the end of October 1944 a new Ministry known as Revenue Ministry was formed in order to exercise general supervision over the Income and to exploit all possibilities of increasing the income of the Azad Hind Government in close cooperation with the Finance Ministry. A.N. Sircar took over the Revenue portfolio.

Early in November 1944 Subhas Chandra Bose alongwith Lt. Col. Chatterjee, Col M.Z. Kiani, Lt. Col. Habibur Rahman went to Japan to attend the first anniversary of the Joint Declaration adopted at the Greater East Asia Assembly at Tokyo which had taken place on November 6th 1943.

In order to celebrate Joint Declaration Day a meeting of the Indians was arranged at the premises of the Indian Independence League, Singapore Branch on 6th November under the Chairmanship of J.A. Thivy., M.K. Chidambaram, Dr. H.H. Moonshi and Brahma Chari Kailasam were the speakers.

Mrs. Krishna Gouri Jamnadas who had been taking an active interest in the women section of the Indian Independence League, Singapore Branch was elected by the committee as its member in charge in place of Mrs. M.K. Chidambaram who went to Burma for special duty.

Indian Independence League, Local Branch had appointed Committee for Local Affairs in the Seven Police Divisions of the island under seven divisional chiefs with ward representatives on line similar to the Japanese

Auxilary Police Organisation. These appointments of committees were made in the middle of August 1944 with S.G. Sarangapani (Chief of publicity) as the head for the purpose of giving publicity to news among the Indians in their respective areas and to help obtain recruits for Indian National Army and to assist the league in any other matter concerning Indians.

This committee held its first meeting on the 5th of November 1944 at the local League premises under the Chairmanship of J.A. Thivy and unanimously decided that it was essential in the battle for Liberation of India that propaganda relating to the work and activities of the Indian Independence movement must be carried out.

The usual monthly meeting for celebrations of Azad Hind Day was held under the auspices of the local Indian Independence League at its premises on 21st November under the Chairmanship of Lt. Col. Gilani, R.S. Naidu, and G. Maganlal were the speakers.

J.A. Thivy General Secretary of the Rear Headquarters of Independence League was transferred to Burma and Dr. Lakshimayah who had gone to and returned from Burma advance headquarters in the middle of May 1944 took over the General Secretaryship of the Rear Headquarters from him.

Indian National School, Singapore entertained Mr. & Mrs. Thivy at a farewell Tea Party at Ramakrishna Mission Hall on 27th November, Brahmachari Kailasam, Principal of the Indian National School praised Thivy for his untiring service in the Movement and help and interest in the working of the Indian National School and the "Balak Sena Corps".

Indian Independence League, Singapore Branch also gave a farewell party to Thivy and welcomed Lakshimayah at the Nanno Hotel on 1st December 1944. Dr. Chidambaram who presided at the functions lauded the services of Mr. Thivy and extended a cordial welcome to Dr. Lakshimayah.

On 5/12/44 the Christening ceremony of the 14 aeroplanes ten of which were given by Subhas Chandra Bose and 4 by the Chinese, Malays and Eurasian Committees to the Japanese Air Force, was held at Kallang Airport.

Mr. M.K. Lakshimayah, Secretary-General of Indian Independence League Rear Headquarters represented the Indian Independence League, Azad Hind Fauj (Indian National Army) being represented by Lt. Col. J.K. Bhonsle, Chief of Staff Col. Loganathan, Lt. Col Alagappan.

The third anniversary of the Dai Toa Senso (Greater East Asia War) was celebrated by Indians of Singapore at a meeting at Theatre Royal Hall on 10th

December under the Chairmanship of M.V. Pillai. After M.V. Pillai's Presidential address M.M. Pavallar, Bashista Raj and M.K. Chidambaram spoke.

Subhas Chandra Bose visited Singapore on his return from Japan where he had gone to attend the first anniversary of the Joint Declaration adopted at the Greater East Asia Assembly. A meeting was arranged by the Indian Independence League, Local Branch at the Waterloo Street, playing ground on 17th December, Subhas Chandra Bose gave a speech in which he expresed the firm determination of the Indian National Army to fight to the end and said that people should not lose heart and slacken their enthusiasm for the failure to capture Imphal, which he said was due mainly to the setting in of Rainy Season. He threatened those who were carrying on anti-League propaganda by spreading false rumours. Large contributions were made to him.

Another mass meeting was organised on 24th December in which he, amongst other things expressed the certainlty of the Axis victory in the War.

Subhas Chandra Bose on his way to Burma toured Malaya and at different places delivered lectures and collected money for the League.

On 27th March 1945 Martyr's Day was observed and a meeting was arranged by the Indian Independence League, Singapore Branch on the same evening in which M.Raghavan the Finance Minister of the Provisional Government of Azad Hind delivered a speech.

"National Liberation Week" was observed by Indians in Singapore by hoisting Tricolour Flags and Hinomaru, by a drive for recruiting and collection of funds by the Local Branch League, by a meeting of the Indian women on 8th March, by a rally of children at which Raja Ram and Sarangapany spoke and comfort visits to the Japanese wounded soldiers hospital and by special treats to the inmates of the Indian Distress Relief Camp and Rama Krishna Orphanage, and by a meeting on 13th April at the Branch premises, Waterloo Street. Dr. M.K. Lakshimayah, Secretary General of the Rear Headquarters of the Indian Independence League addressed the gathering. As usual Azad Hind Day was celebrated on 21st April, 1945 by holding a meeting in the premises of the Indian independence League, Singapore Branch. Col. S.C. Alagappan addressed the gathering on the significance of the day.

On 10th May, 1945 "First War of Indian Independence" was Commemorated by the Indian Independence League, Singapore in which speeches were made in remembrance of the mutiny of 1857.

By this time the British offensive in Burma was progressing favourable and the Japanese Army was retreating from their advance positions. Subhas Chandra Bose left Rangoon for Bangkok and formed his headquarters there. He then came down to Singapore on 18th June 1945 and kept himself busy broadcasting to Indians in India and to the Congress Leaders to reject Lord Wavell's offer.

Furthermore, collections were made and meetings and lectures were delivered and sports and show were held in order to keep up the morale of the populace who had also heard of the fall of Germany and of defeat and retreats of Japan in other places.

On 30th July 1945 a united mass meeting of communities sponsored by the Indian Welfare Association at Dai Toa Gekijyo (Cathey Cinema) under the Chairmanship of M.V. Pillai was held to pledge wholehearted cooperation of the various sections of the local populace to the Japanese Military administration and the Japanese Forces in the defence measures against any attack.

"Netaji Week" was celebrated. During this week mass meetings were held, sports and parties and dramatic shows were given. Collections were made. On 8th of July 1945 Subhas Chandra Bose laid the foundation stone for a Memorial to Heroes who had lost their lives in the Battle of Freedom at the water front at Connaught Drive; Subhas Chandra Bose addressed the gathering comprising Azad Hind Fauj (Indian National Army) Volunteers of the Jhansi Regiment, the Balak Sena Unit, high ranking Japanese Officers, high officials of the Azad Hind Government, Community Leaders and leading members of the Indian public. Wreaths were placed.

The opening ceremony of this memorial took place in the end of August 1945. Major General M. Z. Kiani who was the highest officer of the Indian National Army present in Singapore organised a rally for the opening ceremony. Indian public and officers and personnel of the Indian National Army attended the parade.

This memorial was blown up on September 1945 on the re-occupation of Singapore[2].

Many changes in the Ministry and ranks of the Indian National Army had taken place by this time. Col. A.C. Chatterjee later Foreign Minister along with S.A. Ayer the Propaganda Minister had gone to Saigon to raise funds and also to obtain the cooperation of Indians there.

The Japanese seeing the imminent danger of war coming to Malaya specially Singapore pressed the evacuation of the necessary part of the population to camps up country.

The Japanese and Indian National Army retreated from Burma and by the end of July 1945 Subhas Chandra Bose went to Bangkok. He, soon after peace was declared and the cease fire given left by plane with Col. Habibur Rehman for Tokyo after issuing an order of the day praising the Indian National Army for its brave fight against great odds and said that their fight was not over yet.

It is reported that the plane in which Subhas Chandra Bose was flying met with an accident and Subhas Chandra Bose succumbed to the injuries suffered and Habibur Rehman, although injured, survived.

There are two different views held by the Indian Public in Singapore regarding the death of Subhas Chandra Bose. One view is that the news of his death is genuine and that he was deliberately killed by the Japanese. The other view is that Subhas Chandra Bose is still alive and is probably hiding in Russia and awaiting for an opportune movement to start the Independence Movement again.

The desertion of Subhas Chandra Bose is criticised by some Indians who are of the opinion that he should have faced the situation and shared with his troops the trials consequent upon the re-occupation of Malaya by the British.

I attach printed copies of the Indian Independence Movement in East Asia and also speeches and writings of Subhas Chandra Bose from the time of appearance composed and edited by Narayan Menon in Bangkok named "On to Delhi" and also a copy of discourses on cultural and national subjects published by Indian Independence League Headquarters, Singapore.[2]

These documents which I have attached are mostly taken from Mr. B. A. Mallal whom I had asked to collect as I was afraid to do myself being under suspicion of the Japanese.

I was arrested by the Japanese on 22nd April 1944 and released on the 20th August, 1945. I was during this period not in a position to follow the political situation but I have endeavoured to collect the information from my friends and others.

This report has taken some time to prepare as I have been recovering gradually from the effects of my incarceration in prison and I have found it painful to exert my mind continuously. Nor I had any facilities or assistance in its preparation with the result that it has taken longer than I expected.

2. Not included

11

Viceroy to the Secretary of State for India Regarding the Revised Policy towards I.N.A.[1]

1 December, 1945

No.13860. Our telegram No.13814, November 30th. Follwing is the tesxt of press communique put out last night and published this mornings:—

Begins. Since there is clearly much misconception regarding the policy that has been adopted towards the officers and men of the Indian Army who joined the so-called I.N.A., It will be useful to summarise the intntions of Governemnt and the various communiques which have appeared. It will be appreciated that fresh evidence come to light almost daily, and it is therefore now possible to give more information than when the communique of 27th August was issued.

Of the 60,000 men of the Indian Army who were taken prisoner, some 40,000 stood firm to their oath of allegiance, resisting throughout the period of their captivity the propaganda to which they were subjected and in some their captivity the propaganda to which they were subjected and in some cases also facing starvation and torture, thus setting and example of soldierly qualitites and steadfastness in endurance worthy of the highest praise. There were, however, 20,000 who joined the I.N.A. who joined the I.N.A. Of these rather more than 5,000 have yet to reach Indian while less than 1,000 are still untraced. Of the 14,000 in India, some 2,500 have been exonerated of having intended at any time to aid the enemy and will rejoin their units in the same way as other prisoners of war.

Of the remaining 11,500 some 6,000 are men who are believed to have joined the I.N.A. because they were persuaded eirhter by enemy propaganda or by threats or torture that it was in their best interest to do so. In dealing with these men, the Government of India took into account the conditions in which the founded themeselves, at a time when it appeared that the enemy's arms were successful on all fronts, and when

1. L/8/0/10/25, India Office Library and Records, London.

they had no access to any news, except enemy propagands. In spite of the serious nature of their offence, which in ordinary circumstances is punishable by death under the laws of all countries, the Government of India decided from the beginning to treat these men with clemency and generosity, and this was announced on August 27th. Throughout the time that they were in arms against the forces of the Allies, their families continued to be in recipt of their family allotmetns as though no change had taken place in their status as ordinary prisoners of war of the Japanese; and thesee allotments are not to be forfeited. They will also be given pay from the date of their recovery from enemy hands and 42 day's leave with pay in order to enable them to settle down in their villages or to find employment. They are being realsed as fast as Court of Enquirey can settle their case.

There remain some 5,500 of these, the examination of some 1,700 is still in an early stage, while 3,800 are believed to have gone over to the enemy with the clear intention of helping the Japanese in an invasion of India, which would, if successful, have led to her subjegation by the Japanese. Many of them were captured with armsin their hands against their fellow contrymen, whose lives they were endeavouring to take. Nevertheless it is believed that although they were fuly aware of wath they were doing, a large number(though by no means all) were genuinely misled and had no realisation of the bloodshed and misery that would have resxulted to theri fellow countrymen from a Japanese conquest of India. The Government of Inda therefore decided from the begining to extend clemency to the grat majority of theis category also. Such men will be dismissed from the army and will forefeit their pay, but their families will keep the allotments paid in full while they where supposed to be prisoners of war and no further caction will be taken against them.

There is evidence, however, that of these men a small number have committed acts of gross brutality, resulting in some cases in death, upon their fellow countrymen who wre prosoners of war or members of the I.N.A. Crimes of this nature are abhorrent to all civilised peoples, and it would be worng for the government to refrain from bringing to trial men against whom therre is prima facie evidence that they have committed such offences. Trial by court-material of such persons, and of no others, will therefore take place, and Government are confident theat public opinion will support them in this decision.

In reviewing any sentences which may be passed by Courts-Martial, whether in the present or any future trial, the competent authorities will have regards to the extent to which the acts proved offend against the canons of civilised behaviour.

In order to relieve the anxiety of the men and their relatives and friends, decisions not to bring to trial will be intimated as soon as they are reached and the men concerned will be given facilities to communicate with their relations.

The name of persons whom it is intended to bring to trial will be published as soon as the decisions are reached.

The Government of India wish to take this opportunity of pointing out that they have refrained from publishing in advance the allegations made against the accused because such allegations migh have prejudiced the accused in their defence. All possible steps have neen and will continued to be taken to afford every facility to the defence and to ensure a fair trial. They would also point out.that in no case is the finding of a court of justice a foregone conclusion. They would therefore urge persons of all shades of 0opinion to refrain from forming concllusion until the facts of each case have been brouught in evidence in the course of the trial, and until the court has reached its findings.

Until all investigations are complete, it is not possible to state the number who will be brought to trial but the total is unlikely to be as many as fifty and may be as few as twenty: and, as explained above, trials will be limted to those against whom brutality is alleged.

12

Commander-in-Chief Remission of Life Sentences Awarded to I.N.A. officers at Red Fort Trial[1]

1 January, 1946

Captain Shah Nawaz Khan, Captain Sahgal and Lieut. Dhillon have stood their trial by Court-Martial on charges against all three of waging war against the King Emperor; Lt. Dhillon being also charged with murder and the other two with abetment of murder. The findings of the court are that all three are guilty of the charge of waging war, while Captain Shah Nawaz Khan is also convicted of the charge of abetment of murder. Lt. Dhillon is acquitted of the charge of murder and Captain Sahgal of the charge of abetment of murder.

Having found the accused guilty of the charge of waging war, the court was bound to sentence the accused either to death or to transportation for life. No lesser sentence was permissible under the law. The sentence of the court on all three accused is transportation for life, cashiering and forfeiture of arrears of pay and allowances.

No finding or sentence by Court-Martial is complete until confirmed. The confirming officer in this case, the Commander-in-Chief, is satisfied that the findings of the court are in each instance in conformity with the evidence and he has, therefore, confirmed them.

The confirming officer is, however, competent to mitigate, commute or remit the sentences. As already stated in the press, it is the policy of the Government of India to bring to trial in future only such persons as are alleged, in addition to waging war against the state, to have committed acts of gross brutality, and it has been announced that in reviewing sentences in any trials, the competent authority will have regard to the extent to which the acts proved offend against the canons of civilised behaviour.

Lieut. Dhillon and Captain Sahgal have been acquitted of the charges of murder and abetment of murder and it has not been alleged that they

1. *Tribune*, 3 January, 1946.

were guilty of other acts of brutality. Although Captain Shah Nawaz Khan has neen found guilty of abetment of murder and the acts proved against him were harsh, the prevailing circumstances have been taken into account by the confirming officer.

The Commander-in-Chief has decided, therefore, to treat all three accused in the same way in the matter of sentence and to remit the sentences of transportation for life against all three accused. He has, however, confirmed the sentences of cashiering and forfeiture of arrears of pay and allowances since it is in all circumstances a most serious crime for an officer or solider to throw off his allegiance and wage war against the state. This is a principle which it is essential to uphold in the interests of the stability of any Government by law established, present or future.

12

I.N.A. Defence By Bhulabhai Desai[1]

1 December, 1946

During the last many days, you have heard evidence on the two charges with which my clients, the accused before you, have been arraigned. Shortly stated, the two charges are waging war against the King and, without detailing anything, murder and abetment of murder, in that certain deserters were tried and ordered to be shot. My submission to the Court is that substantially there is really one charge before the Court, because in so far as the charge of murder is concerned it is a part of the first charge; and I say so for this reason that it would be quite possible in the case of a charge of waging war against the King, to be able to charge every single act of firing a shot, which would be, I think, *reducio ad absurdem;* and therefore it will be my duty later on to point out to the Court that really and truly there is only one charge before the Court and that is waging war against the King. Evidence has been admitted on other matters to which I do not wish at this stage to refer, so that for the moment, I will occupy the time of the Court for the purpose of considering what facts have been established in support of the first charge, namely, waging war against the King; and in due course it will also be my duty to point out to the Court that in so far as the second charge is concerned, there is no foundation fact for it except to this extent that in reference to the four persons who are alleged to have been shot there is on record evidence that they were tried and sentence passed. In reference to Mohammed Hussian, there is nothing on record to show that any sentence was passed. In all these cases it will be my duty to submit that on the evidnece the Court is bound to come to the conclusion that though sentence was passed in one case and not at all passed in

1. I. N. A. Trial Papers. See also Bhulabhai J. Desai, *I. N. A. Defence* (Delhi 1946) This booklet containing the address by Desai was published separately also.

the other, none of these sentences was actually carried out. That is the nature of the examination on facts which will be necessary for me to place before this Honourable Court.

There are one or two matters which I am bound to mention to the Court before I come to the actual facts of the case. This case raises issues which are not of the normal type which a Court Martial is called upon to decide, because most, if not all, of such cases are generally cases of individual dereliction of duty or individual offences. Here is a case in which, I venture to say—and the evidence supports it—that it is not at all a case of what you might call three individuals waging war against the King. The evidence amply bears out the fact that these men charged before you were a part of an organised army which waged war against the King even according to the prosecution. Therefore the case before the Court is not a personal case of any kind or sort. The honour and the law of the Indian National Army are on trial before this Court. What is now on trial before the Court is the right to wage war with immunity on the part of a subject race for their liberation. I shall be able to cite authorities on International Law that a nation or part of a nation does reach a stage where it is entitled to wage war for tits liberation, and I shall be able to prove that point to your Honours' satisfaction.

There is another thing I wish to say, and I say it with a certain degree of earnestness. This case has naturally aroused a considerable amount of public interest. It is not for me to say whether it is right or not but the fact remains that it is so, and opinions have been expressed from the point of view of the public and from the point of view of what I might call 'official sources' beginning with the Viceroy of India. You, Sir, having sworn to do justice to these men on the evidence before you will, I have not the smallest doubt, come to your own decision guided by your conscience and entirely unaffected by oipinions for or against them. For in all trials of this kind—and in a few of them I have had the honour to be engaged—it is very difficult for the human mind to maintain that detachment which justice requires. In the case of Juries I have had to caution them against the use or abuse of the effect of public expressions of opinions on matters which it is for them to decide. In this case what I wish to say is this. Having studied the rules which guide the proceedings before this Court I find that you, Sirs, are the judges both of law and of fact. I am aware that the Judge-Advocate who is your adviser, will take care to do justice to everything that myself or my learned friend on the other side will place before you on questions of law and fact, and while you will very seriously regard his advice in the end, the final decision is your privilege and your responsibility. Therefore what I might have done in another place I do not do before you and that is, I cannot say that I will address the Judge on law and the Jury on the facts. There it is an easier process because I must confess that before a trained Judge it is easier to deal with the question of law than before a tribunal of this character. At the same time I have this consolation that sometimes of the law is plain—as I submit it is in this case, it will probably be much easier, appealing to commonsense, to establish the law on which I rely, and I desire to ask your indulgence and your attention in the somewhat difficult task which I am undertaking.

My next submission to the Court is that I desire, as far as possible, to state categorically the conclusions of fact which are established in this case. Having done that I will proceed to deal with the law applicable to them. In dealing with any single item, should any doubt arise in the Court's mind, I trust that you will be pleased to tell me, so that, if it is necessary, I will go into the details of evidence, because as at present advised, I do not desire, unless there is a real doubt about it, to weary you with reading over 250 pages of evidence and about 150 pages of exhibits, which are before the Court. A few important ones I will certainly read where necessary. Having regard to the attention which the Court has paid to the evidence as it was recorded, I will avoid reading them in extenso.

With these remarks I now proceed to place before the Court what I submit are the conclusions of fact justified by evidence. Before I do that, I will give you a few important events. In the month of December 1941, war was declared by Japan against Britain and America. Then followed certain events which are the subject-matter of controversy to a certain extent before this Court. The next event of importance is the surrender of the British Indian forces at Singapore, which took place on the 15th February, and then the most important material event took place on the 17th February at Farrar Park.

The next event of importance, after that which the Court will have to bear in mind, is the formation of what I shall shortly describe as the first Indian National Army in the month of September 1942. The next event of importance is the dissolution of that Army in the month of December 1942 and the arrest of Capt. Mohan Singh. The next important events thereafter are the efforts which were being made for the formation of the second Indian National Army. On 2nd July 1943, Sri Subhas Chandra Bose arrived in Singapore. He later took command of the Indian National Army and there was a conference of what is called Greater East Asia, attended by Indians, with delegates belonging to the Indian Independence League from different parts of the Far Eastern countries. One of the resolutions at that Conference was that a Provisional Government of Free India should be established. The next event of importance is that on the 21st October 1943 there was proclaimed a provisional Government of Free India which for brevity I will call "Provisional Government". That Proclamation is one to which I shall refer later, but now I will try to give the Court events of importance which the Court will have to bear in mind. On the Proclamation of that Government the different Ministers concerned with the functions of the State took Oath of Allegiance, of course headed by Nataji Subhas Chandra Bose as the Head of the State. The next event of importance is the Declaration of War by that Government on Britain and America. The next event of importance thereafter is that so far as the I.N.A. was concerned, it began to carry out its functions under the orders of the new State. Thereafter the events of importance so far as the actual facts are concerned, are only three : the movement of this Government from Singapore to Rangoon; the movement of the Indian National Army from Burma into, beyond and within the territories of India right up to Kohima; and the rest, dealing with the retreat of that Army back again until the event which took place at Rangoon slightly before, at the time, and slightly after the occupation of Burma by the British Forces. These, Sirs, are the main undisputed events with which the Court is concerned. Bearing in mind these events, I shall now place before the Court the conclusions of facts which we submit have been established either in cross-examination of the evidence of the prosecution or in the affirmative evidence which we have called in defence.

The first conclusion of fact which we ask this Court to accept is that the Provisional Government of Free India was formally established and proclaimed. I submit, Sirs, there can be no doubt about this event and no cross-examination of withesses who have been called to prove that event, as far as I can see, has been seriously attempted. You have to remember, Sirs, the picture of the Proclamation of that Governemnt and Exhibits put in on that point. Before I proceed any further, I wish to call attention to that proclamation. It is Exhibit FFFF[2] before this Court. I do not wish to read the whole of that document; the only passages

2. These exhibits were placed before the court. Some of the relevant ones have been produced in these volumes. For the rest, see the Trial Papers at National Archives of India, New Delhi.

which I wish to read are passages which bear on the issue before this Court.

Reads the following from the document:

"Forcibly disarmed by the British after 1857 and subjected to terror and brutality, the Indian people lay prostrate for a while—but with the birth of the Indian National Congress in 1885 till the end of the last World War, the Indian people, in their endeavour to recover their lost liberty tried all possible methods—namely, agitation and propaganda, boycott of British goods, terrorism and sabotage—and finally, armed revolution. But all these efforts failed for a time. Ultimately in 1920, when the Indian people haunted by a sense of failure, were groping for new methods, Mahatma Gandhi came forward with the new weapon of non-cooperation and civil-disobedience.

"Thus, on the eve of the present World War, the stage was set for the final struggle for India's liberation. During the course of this war, Germany, with the help of her allies, has dealt shattering blows to our enemy in Europe—while Nippon, with the help of her allies has inflicted a knockout blow to our enemy in East Asia. Favoured by a most happy combination of circumstances, the Indian people today have a wonderful opportunity for achieving their national emancipation.

"For the first time in recent history, Indians abroad have also been politically roused and united in one organization. They are not only thinking and feeling in tune with their countrymen at home, but are also marching in step with them along the path to freedom, In East Asia in particular, over two million Indians are now organized as one solid phalanx, inspired by the slogan of "Total Mobilisation",

I stop here to submit to the Court that evidence have been adduced as to the numbers of Indians in East Asia and the figure mentioned here is more or less what is borne out before this Court.

"Having goaded Indians to desperation by its hypocrisy, and having driven them to starvation and death by plunder and loot, British rule in India has forfeited the good-will of the Indian people altogether, and is now living a precarious existence.

"It will be the task of the Provisional Government to launch and to conduct the struggle that will bring about the expulsion of the British and of her allies from the soil of India. It will then be the task of the Provisional Government to bring about the establishment of a permanent National Government of Azad Hind constituted in accordance with the will of the Indian people and enjoying their confidence. After the British and their allies are overthrown, and until a permanent National

Government of Azad Hind is set up in Indian soil, the Provisional Government will administer the affairs of the country in trust for the Indian people.

"The Provisional Government is entitled to and hereby claims, the allegiance of every Indian. It guarantees religious liberty, as well as equal rights and equal opportunities to all its citizens. It declares its firm resolve to pursue the happiness and prosperity of the whole nation and of all its parts, cherishing all the children of the nation equally and transcending all the differences cunningly fostered by an alien government in the past.

"In the name of God, in the name of bygone generations who have welded the Indian people into one nation, and in the name of the dead heroes who have bequeted a tradition of heroism; and self-sacrifice, we call upon the Indian people to rally a round our banner, and to strike for India's freedom."

Then follows the signature of the members of the Government. The reason why I called attention to this document is the purpose for which the Provisional Government was formed, and the means by which that Provisional Government intended to carry out its purpose. The fact that it failed to achieve its purpose is entirely irrelevant to the issue before this Court.That is the first fact which we say has been established. The second fact which we say has been established is that is was an organised Government. It does not require many words to establish that proposition. Witnesses have spoken before the Court as to the allocation of duties which appear at the end of the document which I have just read to the Court, and it is also in evidence before the Court that the Indian Independence League became the executive of the Provisional Government which organized, so far as it was possible to do in those warlike conditions, the care of the people who owed allegiance to it. In the month of June 1944, as the evidence is quite clear—it is also in the Exhibit—in Malaya alone, 2,30,000 persons actually took written Oathş of Allegiance to the Government. That was in June 1944, and it is in evidence that thereafter the process continued. The object of stating the figures is that is was not a case of a Government of what you may call, or what somebody being my opponent may facetiously call, a set of rebels, a desultory sort of crowd of no consequence. I wish to give a lie to that kind of suggestion, and that is the reason why I suggest that the provisional Government was an organized Government to whom the whole of the two million odd people owed allegiance, and out of whom 2,30,000 persons actually took the Oath of Allegiance in Malaya.

Then, Sir the next fact which I submit is established before the Court is that this Government was recognized by the Axis powers. I use that expression briefly because it is quite unnecessary either in law or in fact to prove that the recognition must be by a particular number of Government or by a particular class of Government. The recognition is proof and more than proof that it had the right to declare war for the purpose for which it intended to fight, and having the right to declare war in so far as its armies were concerned they became subject to the international laws of war.

On the question of recognition, I wish to call attention to certain cross-examination by my learned friend. Of course in so far as recognition by Germany or Italy was concerned there could be no cross-examination and none was attempted. But with reference to certain East Asia matters in those days, a suggestion was made that those Government were under the control of Japan. I for my part, with very great respect, fail to understand the significance of the suggestion. Supposing Japan had an empire, that is to say succeeded in keeping the territories it conquered without giving them liberty, the recognition would be nonetheless effective because it makes no difference whether and which Government recognised this particular Government of Free India. The point still remains, and I assert that the recognition is but a proof of what I may call a statehood which gives it the capacity of declaring and making war for the liberation of its own countryment. The material point therefore is whether it had attained that degree of statehood which gave it that power. Once you have a State which can and is entitled to declare war, the war itself is its own justification. There is no question that any two independent States have a right to declare war. Any, act done in the prosecution of that war is justified by the mere fact of the war itself. Barring this, it may be asked why trials are going on in parts of Asia and elsewhere, and in Germany. In fact they themselves emphasize the truth of the correctness of the proposition that any act done in due prosecution of war cannot be the subject of any municipal court by way of examination. What has happended is that in addition to the due prosecution of war according to civilised laws, individuals have been guilty of acts outside the pale of civilized warfare, which we popularly call now war crimes. But the very fact that you can only deal with and do deal with war crimes, emphatically and clearly proves that in so far as the normal civilised conduct of war is concerned including the use of an atomic bomb, is outside the pale of examination by way of right or wrong by any municipal tribunal.

Then, Sirs, the next fact which I submit is established is that this State had an army which was properly organised, having its own distinctive badges and emblems, functioning under regularly appointed officers. I am obliged to the prosecution in this matter for I was spared the necessity of having to prove this proposition. They put in document after document to show that the Indian National Army was properly organised. First, that it was regulated by an Indian National Army Act. The only point as far as I could see from the cross-examination which was made was with reference to certain items of corporal punishment. On that it is necessary to point out to the Court that for the moment those who pursue that course forget the course of legislation in British India itself. It is true that Liet. Nag told the Court that apart from the Indian Army Act certain provisions relating to corporal punishment were incorporated in the Indian National Army Act. It was probably forgotten that a little while before, in the Indian Army Act were incorporated provisions in Section 45 of the that Act, headed "Corporal Punishment". I am reading from Section 45 of the Indian Army Act of 1911:

"Where any person subject to this Act, and under the rank of warrant officer—

(a) on active service, is guilty of any offence; or (b) at any time is guilty of the offence specified in clause (c) of Section 31 or (d) at any time is guilty of a civil offence which would be punishable with whipping under the law of British India, and is triable by court-martial under this Act,

it shall be lawful for a court-martial to award for that offence corporal punishment not exceeding thirty lashes."

It is true that about the time of this war this particular provision was omitted. But it is a mistake to think that a similar provision in the Indian Statute Law did not exist. As a matter of fact, in so far as the Defence of India Act and certain Ordinances are concerned, the provision was definitely made, making corporal punishment as part of the punishment applicable to the personnel of the Indian Army. Ordinance 37 of 1943 practically replaced the provisions of the Indian Army Act which were not found in it; a certian amount of effort was made as if under an Act governing a civilised army corporal punishment was not permissible as against the provisions which were to be found in the Indian National Army Act. I am quite certain that it was done under misapprehension.

The Military Operation Areas Special Powers Ordinance, Part II, Sections 22 and 23 read :

"Sec. 22 : Whoever commits an offence punishable under Section 121-A, 122, 125 or 131 of the Indian Penal Code (XLV of 1860) may, in lieu of any punishment to which he is liable under the said code be punished with death.

"Sec. 23: Whoever contravenes any of the provisions of Rule 36 of the Defence of India Rules or is deemed under the provisions of the said Rules to have contravened such provision, may, in lieu of any punishment to which he is liable under the said Ruled, be punished with death, or with whipping, in addition to any punishment to which he is liable under the said Rules. I will be able if necessary to read out all the Rules which clearly show that under the Indian Law, taken as a whole, the punishment with reference to whipping exists, such as the provision which was made in the Indian Army Act. I have got, Sirs, a *summary* made out of the provision with reference to *whipping which I shall afterwards hand over to the Court.* Shorlty stated, my submission to the Court is this that the only attack made by the Advocate-General on the making and framing of the Indian National Army Act, was the provision with reference to whipping, and I submit to the Court that that was done under a misapprehension, got it is as much a part, though not technically quite, in the Indian Army Act but in the defence of India Rules and the Ordinance. It makes no difference. But taking in the aggregate, Indian legislation does sanction corporal punishment throughout the period with which we are concerned and therefore it is that I say and submit to the Court that this was a properly organised army, having a code of its own, which for all practical purposes is the Indian Army Act and any condemnation of the rules under which that army functioned is a condemnation of the Indian Army Act itself, which I submit is not the purpose of the prosecution in this case. Therefore, we come back, Sirs, to this point that this was an organized army functioning under a civilised code. As regards the appointment of officers and the regular method by which it was done, as regards the different branches and the functions, you, Sirs, are more competent than myself to judge from the documents which have been placed before you. They are in the shape of army orders or orders of the day and so on, which have been placed before the Court. On a question of fact we have arrived so far that there was a state which declared war for the purpose of fighting for the liberation of the country and it had an organised army organised under a code which for all practical, substantial purposes, accorded with the aggregate law on the same subject prevailing in British India. I use the word aggregate, because I must bring in the other laws also which provided for and permitted the infliction of corposal punishment in all these cases. The next fact whch is established beyond all dispute was that the object of the declaration of war by the Provisional Government of Free India was the liberation of India.

The next important fact which I think must be mentioned is that the Indian National Army was formed with two purposes. The main purpose was the securing the liberation of India and no doubt, Sirs, from the most important witness that the prosecution called, it has never been difficult to establish that that was the object with which that Army was formed and that was the object with which the individuals who joined it. The other object also was which was somewhat subordinate, but useful purpose, the protection such as could be afforded to the Indian inhabitants of Burma and Malaya, particularly during the days when law and order in those parts of the country was poorly looked after, the lives and the honour and the property of the people was not quite so easily protected. The first object is the one which the army was called upon to fulfil as a part of its duties. Again taking the evidence as a whole, I submit it has been amply proved before this Court that the I.N.A. was formed with the object of fighting for the liberation of India and also with the object of protecting the lives, honour and property of people residing in East Asia at that time.

The next point which is established, I submit, is this—though I speak with less confidence because I do not see it admitted—but the fact has been proved and it is my duty to examine the evidence on it, is that the Japanese Government or the Nippon Government as it is called, ceded to the new Indian State the islands of Nicobar and Andamans, that the Indian State acquired territory in the form of Ziawadi, which was about fifty square miles in area, and that it administered for a period of four to six months the Manipur and Vishnupur areas.

As regards the first, in so far as Lieut. Nag was concerned, he has given definite evidence that the two islands were ceded. The evidence falls under three parts : the first is a declaration to that effect by the Japanese Government, announced by a document which has been proved before this Court. That document is a statement by General Tojo that they were about to concede the islands of Andamans and Nicobar to the Free Indian Government. That document is UUUU. (Counsel reads relevant portions of the document). This was on the 5th November 1943.

Statement by Prime Minsiter General Hideki Tojo regarding the Independence of India

(Delivered before the Assembly of Greater East Asiatic Nations, November 6, 1943)

"Not only India but all Greater East Asia was, without doubt, highly invigorated by the speech just given by His Excellency the Head of the Provisional Government of Azad Hind, in which His Excellency made it clear that the Indian people under the Provisional Government, with the future destiny of India and of Asia at heart, have risen resolutely to realise their long cherished aspiration to regain Indian's freedom, independence and prosperity.

As has been reiterated in the various statements already issued, the Empire of Japan means to give India every possible aid so that she may free herself from the American and British yoke and attain her long-cherished ambition. Now that the foundation of the Provisional Government of Azad Hind has been solidified still further and the Indian patriots under the same Government, bound in close units as never before, are firmly determined to accomplish their steadfast aim, I take this occasion to declare that the Imperial Government of Japan is ready shortly to place the Andaman and Nicobar Islands, Indian territory now under the occupation of the Imperial Japanese Forces, under the jurisdiction of the Provisional Government of Azad Hind, as the initial evidence of her readiness to help in India's struggle for independence.

The lofty ideal that guided Japan's national founding of enabling all peoples to have each its proper status and to enjoy well-being has been and is being steadily carried out. The Japanese Empire today has been strengthened further in its determination to extend all-out co-operation to India in her fight for freedom. Japan is anxious that the Indians on their part shall extend redoubled efforts in that direction.

From the spirited utterances by Their Excellencies the representatives of various countries of East Asia at yesterday's and today's sessions of this Assembly, I note with assurence and satisfaction that these countries, in concert with Japan, are extending every support to the cause of India's independence. I trust and hope that they will give even greater support to- that cause in the future."

Then followed events which clearly, showed that that purpose was carried out. You have in evidence that the declaration was made and that the new Indian state was called upon to administer it by means of a Commissioner, that a commissioner was in fact appointed, that the Commissioner in fact went, and you have evidence of a definite ceremony at which the naval and military authorities then in charge handed over the islands to the Commissioner on behalf of the Indian State at Port Blair. These are points on which, as far as I am able to see the evidence, very little criticism has been made by way of croos-examination.

The point on which there has been a difference between the prosecution and ourselves is the actual form and extent of the administaration of the islands. But it is clearly a misconception to confuse the ceding of a territory and taking over every item of administration of that territory, particularly under the conditions then prevailing. The fact and it is commonsense I submit-that a house might well be sold and completely sold, sold outright and yet possession for time may not be wholly given. It is a familiar illustration I am giving, so that it is easy to appreciate. In the somewhat elaborate cross-examination for this purpose of Col. Loganadan, it was intended merely to point out that the whole of the administration was not taken over-which is not dnied-he said it over and over again; and I think It is established and I ask the Court to hold it is estalbished that he went for the purpose of taking over the administration. It is true that he did not take over more than two items-one, education and the fact that the area was small and the people ignorant is hardly an argument that he had not taken ove the administeration daresax in other countries where the standard of Literacy is something like 99 per cent, ther eare may more shcools than in this unfortunate country whre the standard of literacy is probably 15 per cent. Therefore the argument that schools were few and the expenditure was so little I think there is very little point in the cross examination on this matter. I did enter a protest but it was overruled and it is not for me to say anything more about it. but you do not detract form the cession of a territory in quantity or tie by pointing out that hte whole of the administaration was not and vcould no be taken over. Colonel Logandan told the Court again and again—almost painfully over again—of the fact that until he got complete control of the police in the matter of spies (which seemed to be a sore point with the local inhabitants), he was not prepared to take over any other part of the administration. But there is one significant thing that my learned friend got out of Colonel Loganadan, and that is that one of the officers who went with him, administered what you may call very elementary justice which it was possible to do in the conditions then revailing in the islands. So much so that having asked it and got it, he tried to shake it off but he could. not, and it was proved to the hilt that Justice and Education were taken over. True, police was not taken over because the Japanese from the point of view of defence wre keen on retaining control over what you may call the spy population of these islands. But one thing remains and that is the most significant fact, and that is the renaming, of the islands. So that any amount of examination as to why or how month by month or day by day further acts of administration were not made, cannot possibly get rid of three important facts : first, the clear solemn declaration that the islands would be handed shortly. A suggestion was made—it remained at a suggestion only—that they would be handed over after the war. Where my friend got the words "after the war" I do not know. I hope he will point it out and that is why I read out this document. The document clearly shows that they were to be very shortly handed over.

The second fact was that it was to be administered through a Commissioner, which was a definite proposition made at that time. A Commissioner was in fact nominated by the Provisional Government and the Commissioner in fact reached there and began to function. No doubt, as in every case of this kind, I presume this Court will take almost judicial notice of the fact as to how Germany and other countries are being administered today. No doubt the man will be qualified, and he may be the best educated man from amongst his staff, and he may hope that hte local machinery would soon adapt itself for the purpose of continuing the administration, because it is unthinkable that you can transfer quickly and at one stroke the whole administrative machinery from one country to another. Anybody who is familiar with the administration fo this very country, is aware that Britain administers this country through practically the entire machinery of the Indian people themselves. So that the number of men and all the rest of it, I submit, is so much, without any disrespect, hot air. The real point is, were or were not the islands ceded? And I say there is so much evidence that they were.

The last point is the renaming of the islands : Shahid and Swaraj.

I submit that it is clearly established on the evidence before this Court that though by reason of the exigencies of the situation, it may not have been possible to take over the complete administration, in law and in fact the islands were given over to the Indian State, or to what I would call the Provisional Government.

Next I deal with the question of Ziawadi. The position is this, accordance to the evidence on the record : that this was property, about 50 sq. miles in area, with 15,000 inhabitants who were Indians. It had on it a sugar factory and various other means of production, agricultural or otherwise and every branch of administration of that territory was carried out by men appointed by the Indian National Army and belonging to the *Azad Hind Dal*.

My learned friend did not even venture, in the course of cross-examination, to challenge the truth of the statements made before this Court by witness Shiv Singh and Arshad on this head. Shiv Singh said that every branch of administration was taken over. He gave the name of the person who was the officer in charge of every branch of administration, Revenue, Police, P.W.D., Justice, both civil and criminal. Under these circumstances, the legal position is simple. I shall come to it in greater detail afterwards. Japan conquered Burma. By right of conquest it was in a position to dispose as it liked of the whole or any portion of any territory and as the witness told you clearly, by reasons of the agreement between the Provisional Government and the Nippon Government this territory was handed over as a part of the liberated territory to the I.N.A. and the Azad Hind Dal. At this stage let me point out to the Court that the Azad Hind Dal, it has been proved, was an organisation of men trained for the purpose of administering areas as soon as they came under the control or occupation of the I.N.A. or as soon as they were handed over to them. I must also remind the Court that it has been proved beyond question—because as far as I see there was no cross-examination or effective cross-examination any way, that as soon as the I.N.A. crossed the borders of Burma into India a proclamation was issued in two parts, one signed by the Head of the Indian State and the other signed by General Kawabe under the orders of the South Eastern Command. In that it was distinctly stated that any part of the Indian territory which would be acquired by conquest or otherwise by the Japanese Army whould be handed ober to the I.N.A. for the purpose of forming part of the liberated territory and to be administered by them. That is the history of the ceding.

Then we come to Manipur and Vishnupur areas. Evidence has been given before the Court without any reasonable demur to the effect that during the time, the Japanese and the I.N.A. were operating, those portions of India were in fact adminsitered by the I.N.A. through its organisation, the Azad Hind Dal, and the area was 150,000 square miles. The duration, of administration has no bearing on this issue, for indeed it can happen, as it did happen in this war, that territories were as easily acquired as lost. This Court is not concerned with the question of duration. I would ask the Court to hold that the two islands, Andamans and Nicobar, were in fact ceded, that Ziawadi became a part of liberated Indian territory, and that, though for a short period of time, Manipur and Vishnupur areas were exactly in the same position.

The next point to which I wish to refer is the resources of the State. I order to judge the existence of the State the resources of the State is also one of the matters to be considered. It has been proved before the Court that some 30 crores of rupees were in fact donated to the State, out of which was maintained the civil government and the army. Dina Nath, who impressed this Court, gave extremely clear evidence on this head. He was one of the Directors of the Azad Hind Bank and he told the Court that between Burma and Malaya, during that short period of time, the State had resources to the tune of 20 crores of rupees, in addition to the produce of Ziawadi. It is a remarkable thing to notice that on the reoccupation of Burma and Malaya every single document which was in the possession of this Indian State was found intact. It was amazing. See the monthly reports which the Prosecution was able to produce with reference tot he administration of the Andamans and Nicobars! It only emphasizes—and I wish to make a point of this—that there was a complete organization, and that organisation was as good as could reasonably be expected. That alone accounts for half the documents which my learned friend was able to produce.

The point is that we were a little handicapped owing to the lack of certain documents. As the evidence before the Court shows, this Bank was closed after the occupation of Rangon, and in fact it is in evidence that some 35 lakhs worth of property was sequestered. I am not complaining of the sequestration. That I think was the right of the conquerors. What I am saying is that in so far as the resources of the State were concerned, they were full and adequate for the purposes which the new State had then in view.

Here I wish to refer to a bulletin. It is not what I might call technical evidence before the Court by it may be my duty to submit that it is a document of which the Court should take judicial notice. The document is dated the 10th November 1945 and called Stamp Collecting.

Mr. N.P. Engineer : My learned friend is reading from a document which as not been accepted.

Mr. Desai : I am only making a submission to the Court. Is it my friend's contention that if I read a book on law, it should be put in as an exhibit?

Judge-Advocate : The document itself cannot be admitted at this stage.

Mr. Desai : All I am doing now is to make a submission to the Court Section 57 says :

"The Court shall take judicial notice of the following facts:

"In all these cases and also in all matters of published history, literature, science or art the Court may resort for help to appropriate books or documents of reference"

And if the learned Advocate General solemnly suggests that every single book of history, literature, science, and art is to be an exhibit before it can be refered to, I am very sorry that it is a statement which defeats itself.

Judge-Advocate : Mr. Desai, will you read out what you want the Court to take judicial notice of ?

Mr. Desai: May I not apply that the Court may consider it ? And I am asking is that this application be considered. Of course the Court may reject it; I am not suggesting that the Court is bound to accept it. My submission is that under Section 57 it may be taken as judicial notice.

I was referring to an issue of November 10, 1945, of a weekly publication called "Stamp Collecting" Published in London and edited by Douglas Armstrong, a well-known philatelist. In that issue at page 136, column 1, the following appears :

"Imphal Stamp that failed.

"So confident were the Japs that they would occupy Imphal, when they invaded Southern Assam that they actually prepared a special issue of stamps for use there . Needless to say these stamps failed to materialise, but our correspondent, Flying Officer T.A. Broomhead, informs us that he has seen proof impressions in the hands of the man who was responsible for the printing (in Rangoon). Two denominations appear to have been prepared, viz., 3 pice plum and 1 anna red, both in the same design and roughly perforated 11½ x9½ (approx.). The subject of the vignette (illustrated is the old Moghul Fortress at Old Delhi accompanied by the slogan "On to Delhi". Bi-lingual inscription reads "PROVISIONAL GOVERNMENT OF FREE INDIA". When it becameevident that the Imphal stamps would not be required, the dies were destroyed and the bulk supply of sheets printed in readiness was burnt with the exception of a small quantity salvaged by the printer."

At the top corner on the left-hand side is a facsimile of the stamp referred to in the above quotation.

It is submitted that this document should be taken judicial notice of in support *inter alia* of proof that the Provisional Government of Free India had got prepared, issued or were about to issue postal stamps of that character. As appears from the above quotation, the dies were prepared under the direction of the Japanese.

Counsel for the Prosecution: I submit................

Judge-Advocate : Would it not be more convenient to deal with this point in your arguments, and so shall I. There is no point, when the document is read whether the Court accepts it or not.

Mr. Desai : I frankly submit to the Court that it is not a matter of such importance, but as the document was brought to my notice I thought it was my duty to put it before the Court. Nobody should question books of history, science, literature and art. It is a very accepted magazine in England 'ealing with this subject, edited by a very well-known man indeed.

Then, Sir, it appears from the evidence that this Indian State had a

Civil, and what I may call, an Army Gazette of its own. That is also established before this Court.

On these facts, Sir, the first question of law which I wish to raise is this: Having regard to the condition in which this Free Government of India had been formed and was functioning, it was entitled to make war and it did make war for the purpose of liberating this country. That is the first and the main issue before the Court. This Court is trying civil offences under the Indian Penal Code, and there are two ways of looking at this question. One is that when two States declare a war—and I may assume for the purpose of this argument, because I cannot do more than place evidence before this Court for its acceptance, that the condition in which the new Indian State found itself, it was in a position to declare war—and having declared war, in so far as any acts in the prosecution of that war are concerned, they are outside the pale of municipal law. I will tell you, Sir, what I mean because I will elaborate this sufficiently to make myself understood by the Court. Supposing a German during the prosecution of the war had shot two or three or ten Britishers in England and was found in England, the question is, could he be charged with having committed murder. I submit never, for the simple reason that those acts were done during the due prosecution of the war which, unfortunately, in the present world of infirmities the International Law accepts. That is to say, what International Law accepts is that two independent countries or two States, as they are called, may make war on each other, and those who carry out any action in due prosecution of the war (apart from war criminals) is outside the pale of municipal law. Alternatively, if that is not sufficient for this Court (though I submit it should be in view of what I am going to read to you from accepted authorities on International Law) under Section 79 of the Indian Penal Code the acts done in due prosecution of the war were not offences. Section 79 of the Indian Penal Code reads thus:

"Nothing is an offence which is done by any person who is justified by law.........." And my submission to the Court is that under the term 'law' is covered 'International Law', and for that reason in so far that German—continuing the example which I was giving—who was arrested in England was concerned, his defence would be :

"My country, my State, was at war with your States. Under the orders of my State, and in due prosecution of the war, I did the acts which under ordinary normal circumstances might be offences, but which having regard to the circumstances are no offences at all."

Sir, it is unthinkable that any member of any organized army could be charged with an offence merely because he fought one or ten or a million men belonging to an army of the State with which he is at war. It is perfectly obvious to anybody that during the prosecution of the war, the municipal law relating to that country does not apply, except, I quite agree, when one soldier steals the pocket-book of another soldier. That I appreciate. But the question which we have got to bear in mind is the very important distinction. Was that act done in due prosecution of the war which one State declared upon another.

Once you get to that state, it is perfectly obvious that that municipal law must and is bound to remain in abeyance. It is impossible to arraign any individual for carrying out as a matter of duty acts which might otherwise be offences—killing a man every day, destroying property every day. In fact it is a very part of the war itself. Therefore the agreement is twofold. The alternatives are either that any act done in due prosecution of war is outside the pale of municipal law—that is why I pointed out to you in the commencement that the charge against these young men before you is not as if they had committed an act of private murder by reason of some private quarrel. The documents accepted by the prosecution clearly bear out that whatever they did, they did as part of the prosecution of war. Remember that always, because without that the law cannot be appreciated with reference to the facts in issue.

But there is another way of looking at it, if you must. That is whether the exception provided by Section 79 is not equally applicable to the case. My submission to the Court is that whether you accept the one or the other makes no difference to the decision that I am asking for as to the immunity from those acts being offences at all ; because the very language of Section 79 is : "Nothing is an offence which is justified by law." The Section assumes that in private life it might otherwise have been an offence. If you, gentlemen, in the due prosecution of war committed murders, could be civil laws as propounded by the other side be put into action against you, when in all honour you acted in prosecution of your duties as members of an organised army of a State that had declared war ? It stands to reason—and it must—that any act done by a member of an organised army fighting under the order of one State against another State between which war exists, is an act entirely outside municipal law. But assuming for the purpose of argument the Court requires some nearer justification. In the eye of the Court in so far as the administration by this Court is concerned, it is fortunate that I am able to find the exception in the Indian Penal Code itself, because the young men are being charged either under Section 121 or Section 302 of the Indian Penal Code and I am relying on

Section 79 of the same Code which says in terms that it is not an offence. Supposing war was declared between two States and when peace time returned every individual soldier is called upon to say whether he killed so and so. I am quite sure that as I am addressing men of commonsense, you would laugh at the idea. But then quite agree that I would have to satisfy you that the new Indian State that declared war was entitled to do it in the sense of international law.

And now I will proceed to quote from books of international law on the question of right to make war. I am reading to you Vol. II of Dick Corbett's Cases of International Law under the heading of "War", 1937 Edition.

"International war is a contest carried on by an armed force either between States or between a State and some community or body which is treated as a State for the purpose of the conduct of hostilities. International war differs from other kinds of war in that it has the effect of setting up a new relation in law both as between the belligerents themselves and as between each of them and the other States. As between the belligerents, the State of war although it departs from normal relations, is nevertheless a State of regulated violence in which the conduct of hostilities is governed by certain principles and rules which rest part on custom and part on convention, and which are sanctioned in the last resort by the action of international society however uncertain may be their operation."

I next call attention to Wheaton's International Law. I am reading Wheaton's "International Law", 1945 edition, Vol. II, page 98:

"War in the absence of any international authority competent to suppress effectively international wrongs has always been held legal by international law."

Remember that as a definite proposition that so long as there are two states, if they declare war against each other, there is no justification required for it. And once you have a war, any person being a member of an organised army or one of the warring States, cannot be called upon individually to account for the acts, which in civil matters or normal times if done individually in a private capacity for private motive, be considered to be an offence.

"War, in the absence of any international authority competent to suppress effectively international wrongs, has always been held legal by international law.... Even the creation of the League of Nations leaves war in certain cases legal, there is now on record the unanimous. Assembly condemnation of aggressive war. War is essentially a struggle between States, involving the application of force. Mere armed occupation, as in the seizure of Strassburg by Louis XIV in 1680-81 or as in that of Corfu by Italy in 1913, is not war unless the State affected declares it so, and similarly, as regards pacific blockade. The States need not necessarily be fully sovereign: in 1876, Serbia and Montenegro warred on Turkey through vassal States: in 1877... Rumania followed suit. In 1855, Bulgaria warred on Serbia, then fully sovereign, and in the treaty of peace of March 8, 1886, though Turkey as suzerain took part, Bulgaria appeared independently as a party. So the South African Republic warred on the United Kingdom in 1899.

So, the first step in the argument is that the State which declares war is and must be in a position to do it. But once it declares war against any other State, then there can be no question of its propriety, or right. In the particular case before the Court, and not with standing their territories which were occupied, I do say that this war at all events was completely a justified war. International law in the question of war is not static. It is law that has grown from time to time with the progress of civilization.

Therefore, the question really is, once it comes to war, there is no question of justification. But hitherto at all events now in the global war a great many events have occurred of which international conscience takes note. I will read out to you two passages, one from Mr. Winston Churchill from the Hansard and another from Mr. Eden. The position now is that international law has reached this stage that if liberty and democracy are to have any meaning all over the world, and not merely just for a part of it, and this is not politics, it is law—any war made for the purpose of liberating oneself from foreign yoke is completely justified by modern international law. And it will be travesty of justice if we were to be told as the result of any decision arrived at here or otherwise, that the Indian may go as soldier and fight for the freedom of England against Germany, for England against Italy, for England against Japan, and yet a stage may not be reached when a free Indian State may not wish to free itself from any country, including England itself. We maintain that this particular war, according to the decisions, requires no justification. If one State can declare war, then the other State can also declare war and fight, and anything done in its due prosecution has no civil consequences of any kind. In other words, not one of these men now charged before you can be called upon to account for his actions. We can show that they have done nothing outside the scope of the due prosecution of war on a civilized basis. That is an emphasis which I always wish to put. It is not alleged against these men that there was any question about the acts with which they are charged. They were acts carried out in due prosecution of the war, under what you may call civilised rules. Therefore the question before the Court is a very narrow one.

To continue what I was reading :

"A civil war between different members of the same society is, what Grotius calls, a mixed war. It is according to him public on the side of the established Government and private on the part of people resisting its authority. The general usage of nations is as regards such a war as entitling both the contending parties to all the rights of war as against each other and even as respects neutral nations. It seems to be now settled that it is unnecessary in order to constitute war that both parties should be acknowledged as independent nations or sovereign States."

There was at one time the old idea that you had to be an independent State or a sovereign State in order to be able to declare war. Of course that created a vicious circle, that a subject race will remain in perpetuity a subject race. It can never make a legitimate war for the purpose of liberating itself. Hence modern international law has now recognised the right of subject races which are not for the time being or at the moment independent, to be so organized, and if they are organised and fight an organized war through an organised army, the individual members of that army are unanswerable before any municipal court for what was done in due prosecution of that war.

It seems to be now settled that it is unnecessary in order to constitute a war that both parties should be acknowledged as independent nations or sovereign States. A war may certainly exist between a State and its suzerain as in the Boer War. May I appeal to this Court and all of you are familiar with British history—what about Charles I and his death? What about the Magna Charta? What about James II? It is all recorded in history. In other words, you do reach a stage where the organisation, call it rebel if you like, call it insurgent;—insurgents or rebels may reach a stage of organisation for the purpose of liberating themselves when what they do after declaring war is subject to the laws of war.

"A war may certainly exist between a State and a suzerain as in the Boer War. Moreover, a war may exist where one of the billigerents claims sovereign rights as against the other, whether in a federal or a unitary States......."

But it is quite an unnecessary requisite. If ever a subject race finds itself in a position where its organisation is able to declare war, then acts done by the armies on either side come under this. I put a very simple question: What about the acts of those who fought on the side of the British in this War? They killed lots of people. Would they be put up before this Court under Section 302? Most amazing! It was a properly fought war, no doubt as in order wars one or the other side lost, and the fact that a war is lost has no effect on the immunity from the consequences in acts done in due prosecution of the war. He says further :

"Whether the struggle is a war or not is to be determined, not from the relation of the combatants to each other, but from the mode in which it is carried on. The Government of the State may recognize its subjects as belligerents, in which case other States will normally but need not follow the same course. Or other States may recognize belligerency, in which case the parent State will all but certainly follow suit."

That is the crux of the matter. I quite agree that if ten persons in a village declare war. British, they are rebels, and I am not here to justify it. What I am saying is this that struggle between two organizations a stage must be reached where the organisation of the State and the organisation of the army are such that it is a war recognised by civilised nations; and if it is once recognised, then the immunity follows. As the books point out, we had the instance of the war between the South and North of America and you have a declaration from Abraham Lincoln downwards that it was a proper war and there was nothing more to be said about it as soon as the hostilities ceased. It goes on to say :

"Among the tests are the existence of a de facto political organization of the insurgents sufficient in character, population and resources to constitute it, if left to itself, a State among nations capable of discharging the duties of a State; the actual employment of military forces on each side acting in accordance with the rules and customs of war..... If all these elements exist, the condition of things is undoubtedly war; and it may be war before they are all ripened into activity."

Therefore what I wish to say is this : that the test by which you will judge this case is, have we or have we not proved the existence of a *de facto* political organization of insurgents? I do not deny that they wree insurgents. Apart from the other question to which I shall come presently, I will assume against myself that the people who declared war and who declared the Provisional Government of Free India were a set of insurgents, a set of rebels—I will assume that against myself.

"As President Grant said in his message of June 13, 1870 : 'The question of belligerency is one of fact not to be decided by sympathies for or prejudices against either party. The relations between the parent State and insurgents must amount, in fact, to war in the sense of international law".

I call upon you to do the same. It is not a question of prejudice; it is not a question of prestige or what happens to the Army, to this or the other person. Please remember that you are here as judges; you are not politicians, I agree, and I do not want you to be such. If you find that there is a *de facto* political organization sufficient in numbers, sufficient in character and sufficient in resources to constitute itself capable of declaring and making war with an organised army, your verdict must be in favour of these men—no more and no less than the verdict on your own men for killing others, of which act you are justly proud.

That is the position in law.

Then I wish to call attention to another book on International Law—an accepted book and what is more it is borne out by all the earlier cases in which war was waged by what you may call insurgents against their own sovereign, if you must use that expression. This book is by Lawrence—page 309. The whole question before the Court under this particular head is whether or not there was a properly declared war in presecution of which the accused before you did the acts which they did. And if they did that in due prosecution of that war, then there can be no question of any civil offence, as I think all of you in your own person will easily realise. I am not obliged in my civil life to kill anybody except on pain of conviction, but you are.

Lawrence says :

"War may be defined as a contest carried on by public force between States, or between States and communities having with regard to the contest the rights of States, the parties to it having the intention of ending peaceful relations, and substituting for them those of hostility with all the legal incidents thereof".

These were no private acts done with a private motive or done for private individual benefit. They came to be done by them as members of an organised army, having declared war and the law says to them that no such consequences as the government demands can arise. Lawrence goes on:

"It is true that two States are said to be at war as soon as one of them has received a declaration of war from the other."

Here there was in fact a formal declaration of war. Then I call attention to a well-known work of Oppenheim on International Law. Oppenheim was Professor of International Law at Cambridge University. He says this—(Vol. II, page 166):

"War is a contention between two or more armed States through their armed forces for the purpose of overpowering each other.... War is a fact recognised, and with regard to many points, regulated but not established by International Law."

Once you get to the stage of war, naturally it is the primary purpose of each party to overpower the other. Therefore in due prosecution of it, acts which might be called offences under civil law are not offences : the very purpose is to destroy men and property : the very thing which would otherwise be unlawful becomes right, becomes patriotic, becomes a duty.

"In any case it is universally recognised that war is a contention, i.e., a violent struggle through the application of armed force......

To be war, the contention must be between States...... On the other hand, to an armed contention between a suzerain and its vassal State the character of war ought not to be denied, for both parties are States, although the action of the vassal may, from the standpoint of constitutional law, be rebellion." (Para 56)

I have already said that States are those which have the right to make war *like States.*

The first proposition for which I stand before this Court is this, that the two States sufficient in number, in organisation and in resources may make war against each other. That is the proposition to which I stand, and if they made war against each other, then there is complete immunity for what might otherwise be a private offence. That must necessarily follow from the acceptance of war as a necessary evil in this infirm world, and no individual member can be called upon to answer for the consequences of his acts so long as it is a properly declared war. I shall call the Court's attention to Mr. Hyde's book on 'International Law', Vol. III, page 1792, para 648.

"So soon as a man is armed by a sovereign government and takes the soldier's oath of fidelity, he is a belligerent; his killing, wounding or other war-like acts are not individual crimes or offences. No belligerent has a right to declare that enemies of a certain class, colour or condition, when properly organised as soldiers, will not be treated by him as public enemies."

In other words the position is simple. Any act done by members of an armed force against any opponent, which in ordinary times in a personal case would be a civil offence, ceases to be an offence altogether. Otherwise, war and recognition is not a possibility.

There is a very important decision of the Federal Court of the United States expressing the same thing. I may be pardoned for multiplying authorities, but I do so because I feel that instead of paraphrasing the idea myself, if I do it through the medium of an accepted authority, I might be able to carry better conviction. It is Vol. 168 United States Reports, page 250. It is the case of *Underhill* v. *Hernandez*. I am reading the judgement of Chief Justice Fuller. The opinion of the Court is as follows :

"Nor can the principle be confined to lawful or recognised Governments or to cases where redress can manifestly be had through public channels. The immunity of individuals from suits brought in foreign tribunals for acts done within their own States in the exercise of Governmental authority, whether as civil officers or as military commanders must necessarily extend to the agents of governments ruling by paramount force as a matter of fact. Where a civil war prevails, that is, where the people of a country are divided into two hostile parties, who take up arms and oppose one another by military force, generally speaking, foreign nations do not assume to judge of the merits of the quarrel. If the party seeking to dislodge the existing government succeeds, and the independence of the government it has set up is recognised, then the acts of such government from the commencement of its existence are regarded as those of an independent nation. If the political revolt fails of success, still if actual war has been waged, acts of legitimate warfare cannot be made the basis of individual liability."

Chief Justice Fuller was deciding the case arising out of the war between the North and the South. A war might exist between what you might call an existing State and insurgents, and yet the insurgents, as they were called by the Federal Government, may have such organisation, force and strength that the relation between the two parties is one of the existence of war. Once the war exists, what is the legal position? If the party seeking to dislodge the existing Government succeeds, it is now accepted law that a successful rebellion is a Government established by law. The question is—what is the position in case of an unsuccessful rebellion. The law is, I submit, that if the stage is reached where the rebels or insurgents are sufficiently organised and are sufficiently resourceful to make war, then it is entitled to be regarded as war, and there will be no individual consequences to persons who take part in it. If actual war has been waged, and my learned friend himself was at pains to prove that a regular war was being waged, and he put forward document after document to prove it, then the question is: What is the distinction between a private individual waging war on his own and his waging war as a member of a force or organized State. That is the real distinction which makes one immune from the consequences. If actual war has been waged, then acts of legitimate warfare cannot be made the basis of individual liability.

There is another case belonging to the same period. It is *Ford* v. *Surget,* 97 United States Reports, page 594, (equal to 24 Law F.D.).

"The Confederate Government can be regarded by the Courts in no other light than as simply the military representative of the insurrection against the military authority of the United States.

"To the Confederate Army was however conceded, in the interest of humanity and to prevent the cruelties of reprisals and retaliation, such belligerent rights as belonged, under the laws of nations, to the armies of independent Governments engaged in war against each other; that concession placing the soldiers and officers of the rebel army, as to all matters directly connected with the mode of prosecuting the war on the footing of those engaged in lawful war and exempting them from liability for acts of legitimate warfare."

The first proposition is this that in view of the fact that a state of war existed between the Provisional Government of Azad Hind and the British, any act done in prosecution of that war has not the consequences which the Crown claims or might have claimed in the case of a private individual.

In International Law it is permissible for those who are subject to a foreign authority to organize themselves, and having reached that stage of organisation and having an organized army to fight for liberation, whether it is successful or not, during the process while the war is being carried on, there is immunity, so far as individual members of the organized army are concerned for all acts done in due prosecution of war on a civilized basis (other than war crimes like those which are the subject of trial now in different parts of the world). That being so, my submission is that the accused men before you are entitled to be declared innocent in that there is no civil or criminal responsibility for those acts. In terms of the language of the books on law, the liability is on the State under whose direction they fought, and such liability in international law on the cessation of hostilities does not exist. Of course if a rebellion is successful, then it becomes a new Government, and there is the end of it and there will be no tribunals, but it is only in a case in which it is not successful that the question arises and the answer is given in my clients' favour by International Law.

The next point to which I wish to advert is the alternative point which I made under Section 79 of the Indian Penal Code. The issue which arises, apart from the Indian Penal Code, is an issue of great international importance. It has arisen, if I may say so, in its actual form for the first time though the authorities directly or indirectly support the principles on which my contention is based. At the same time, appearing before this Tribunal, it becomes my duty to justify it on what I may call a narrower ground to the extent to which it is necesary, for I do feel that before a Tribunal constituted as this is, it is equally important that I should put myself within the narrow sphere of the Indian Statute itself. Then I submit, assuming my submissions are correct and accepted, the hands of the Tribunal are fairly strengthened. The words which I referred to in Section 79 of the Indian Penal Code are 'justified by law'. The question is what is the meaning of the word 'law' appearing in Section 79 of the Indian Penal Code. If I can satisfy this Court that the law there comprehends and includes international law, I submit my Honourable Friend on the other side would have hardly any case to present to the Court at all. If the word 'law' in Section 79 includes International Law so far as the immunity which I have described before is concerned, then I submit the three men at your bar are entitled to plead that they were so justified in the actions which in ordinary private personal life might have been offences under the Indian Penal Code. I wish to call your attention to a certain number of authorities on the question. The first authority to which I call your attention is Blackstone's Commentaries in Book IV, but it is volume II in this binding. It is accepted at all events by British lawyers that Blackstone's Commentaries are the fountain-source of Common Law of England and it is a matter which I wish to particularly assert before this Court. The page that I am reading is 2237 (Vol. II, edited by W.C. Jones). Most of us who are not lawyers are familiar with Blackstone's Commentaries and know that he is father, to a very large extent, of Common Law. Blackston's Commentaries are relied upon in British Courts as a very authoritative exposition of the law on the particular question which he has dealt with.

"In arbitrary States this law, wherever it contradicts or is not provided for by the municipal law of the country, is enforced by royal power; but since in England no royal power can introduce a new law, or suspend the execution of the old, therefore the law of nations (wherever any question arises which is properly the object of its jurisdiction) is here adopted in its full extent by the common law, and is held to be a part of the law of the land."

So that, as soon as the Court has ascertained what is the International law on a particular point before the Court, it is the bounden duty of the Court to administer that part of International Law as a part of the law of the land, and hence it is that I am submitting to the Court that the word 'law' in Section 79 should be given that extensive meaning which the law has by the Common Law of England.

The next work on which I rely for the purpose of the meaning of the word 'law', meaning thereby that 'nothing is an offence which is justified by law', is Oppenheim's International Law. The question is what is law, and it is in support of that I am submitting next Oppenheim's International Law Vol. I, Fifth Edition, page 36, article 21a :

"In view of this wide divergence of doctrine it is necessary to inquire into the actual legal position in the principal countries in the matter of International Law and Municipal Law.

(I) As regards Great Britain, the following points must be noted :

(a) all such rules of customary International Law as are either universally recognised or have at any rate received the assent of this country are *per se* part of the law of the land. To that extent there is still valid in England the Common Law doctrine to which Blackstone gave expression in a striking passage, that the Law of Nations is part of the law of the land. It has repeatedly been acted upon by Courts. Apart from isolated *obiter dicta* it has never been denied by judges. The unshaken continuity of its observance suffered a reverse as the result of the *dicta* of some judges in The Franconia Case in 1876, but *West Rand Central Gold Mining* Co. v. *The King* decided in 1905, must be regarded as a reaffirmation of the classical doctrine."

So that ever since the time of Blackstone, untile the last edition of Oppenheim, which belongs to the year 1937, there has never been any question that on any issue in which the doctrine of international law is accepted to be the international law it becomes a part of the law of the land, law of the land in England, and law of the land here.

Next, I call attention to the work of an American Jurist Hershey on International Public Law and Organisation, page 14, 1927 Edition.

"International Law is a part of our law, and must be ascertained and admitted by the Court of Justice of appropriate jurisdiction as often as questions of right depending upon it are duly presented for their determination. For this purpose, where there is no treaty and no controlling executive or legislative act or judicial decision, resort must be had to the custom and usages of civilized nations, and, as evidence of these, to the works of jurists and commentators who, by years of labour, research, and experience, have made themselves peculiarly well-acquainted with the subjects of which they treat. Such works are resorted to by judicial tribunals, not for the speculations of their authors concerning what the law ought to be, but for trustworthy evidence of what the law really is."

So, you will see from this quotation which has come from Justice Gray in the case which is cited—195 United States Reports, page 113 at page

163, that it has been accepted that while administering justice it is your bounden duty to find out, recognise and apply the principles of international law where a person at your bar seeks justice on the ground that the act with which he is charged is an act justified by law and that for the purpose of ascertaining it you may have resort as it is stated by the learned Judge himself to "the usages and customs of civilized nations, and as evidence to this to the work of jurists, commentators, who by years of labours, research and experience have made themselves peculiarly well-acquainted with the subject of which they treat."

Therefore, I plead that when the time comes for your deliberation you will carefully, of which I have no doubt, and diligently, of which I am perfectly conscious, study and apply your mind to the citations which I have already given and which I am about to give. Because, according to the well-accepted canons, the commentators who by years of labour, research and experience have made themselves peculiarly well-acquainted with the subjects of which they treat, and such works are resorted to and have to be resorted to by judicial tribunals. I have got, Sirs, the original judgment from which this quotation is given. The judgment is reported in 175 United States Report in the judgment at page 700. The case is Paquet Habana, Appeals from the District Courts of the United States for Southern Districts of Florida. The judgment of Mr. Justice Gray on this question is to be found at page 700. I do not wish to read it again, because I have already read it from the textbook in which it is now accepted. At the same time I may be pardoned for pressing this point upon the Court because then the issue before this Court becomes exceedingly narrow. If I am able to presuade this Court, as I submit I hope to do, that in administering the law you are bound to have regard to international law, there will be no difficulty whatever in the way of the defence which I am presenting. Then the Statute law has made it incumbent upon you, and in fact has declared that nothing is an offence which is justified by law. If therefore the acts which are said to be offences are declared not to be offences, and if I am able to show that the law so declares them, then it will be your duty to declare that, notwithstanding apparent confusion of thought, words like treason and so on, will have no value.

The law of treason in India is codified. It is to be found in Chapter VI of the I .P.C. (Offences against the State) in Sec. 121 and following Sections. Therefore let me caution the Court against the general use of words like "treason". The question is whether my clients who have been charged under Sections 121 and 302 have or have not, in doing those acts, been justified by law, i.e., the law of nations, and if they are so justified the law of this country declares that it is not an offence. In other words the law of this country recognises that there may be acts which if done in private life for private motive might be an offence but which in public life or public duty are not an offence. A judge is not liable as an abettor of murder because he orders a man to be hung, because he is justified by law. Similarly and equally, if not more emphatically, the member of an armed force having declared war, if during the state of that war he has committed acts which in private life might be offences, the law says nothing shall be an offence. Therefore, I do wish in so far as in me lies, to press this point upon your attention, because the first line of argument which I submitted to the Court stands, and I submit to the Court that is the law. In other words the law is that in the prosecution of war the acts which take place are beyond municipal law. But assuming for the purpose of argument, I have to take my stand on a narrower ground. Then the law of this country, the Indian Statute Law itself enjoins upon you that if I can show justification by means of international law for those acts, then my clients are entitled to a verdict in their favour. I say this to you in the language of one of your greatest poets that if in so far as God grants me the tongue of persuastion and you the ears of hearing, I have not the least doubt that when you have considered the cases before you, you will have no difficulty or hesitation to decide in my favour on that narrow ground.

The next point to which I wish to call attention is Moore's International Law and Digest page 2, Vol. I, and this is how it is stated :

"It is thus apparent than from the beginning the scene in question denoted something more that the positive legislation of independent States and the term international law which has in recent times so generally superseded the earlier titles served to emphasize his fact. It denotes a body of obligations which is in a sense independent of and superior to such legislation. The Government of the United States has on various occasions announced the principle that international law as a system is binding upon nations, not merely as something which they may be tacitly assumed to agree but also as a fundamental condition for their admission to the full and equal participation in the intercourse of civilised nations."

I therefore cannot more emphatically assert than the ground on which I appear before the Court and I have no doubt that it will rise superior (in the language of one of the cases that I read) to all question of prejudice and come to the right conclusion in considering Section 79 and the immunity granted by it.

Just one more passage to which I wish to call attention. It is the judgment of the Privy Council on this question. The last under these heads is a judgment of Their Lordships of the Privy Council, reported in a recent number, 1939 appeal cases, page 168. There a question of international law arose. The name of the case is Chang Chi Chu. It was a case of murder committed on a Chinese ship and that is how the question arose of the liability of the prisoner to be tried. And the question arose to what extent in international law it was necessary to consider whether the prisoner was liable. The contention shortly stated was that the Chinese ship was so much floating Chinese territory. That was the claim made under the international law. Their Lordships of the Privy Council held that under international law it is probably not correct to say that a floating ship of foreign power is so much, what you may call, island foreign territory. But they have ruled by reason of the respect accorded to comity of nations, that anything that occurs on a foreign ship is not within the authority or jurisdiction of municipal law. In this particular case what they held was that in as much as the ship itself accepted the authority of the power which was exercising authority in those waters, they held it became an exception. But in considering the applicability of international law to the question whether or not the Court had jurisdiction to try this particular Chinaman, the question arose to what extent international law has to be considered and the judgment of Their Lordships delivered by Lord Aitkins is very important from this point of view. I would not enter into the question of details which arose in that case though by themselves they are interesting enough. But I may say this that the observations which I propose to read are necessary and essential because the whole defence to the charge of murder, and the want of jurisdiction of the Court, were based on the ground that under international law the Court had no jurisdiction and for that purpose the Court went into the question of what was the appropriate international law on the question. Their Lordships said with reference to the necessity of the application, or rather with reference to the obligation to ascertain and apply international law ourselves was a part of the law. That is how that part of the case is stated.

Page 167 : "Their Lordships entertain no doubt that the law is the correct conclusion, namely, that a ship is not so much floating part of a foreign territory, but that immunity is granted for whatever happens in that ship in so far as jurisdiction is concerned. It more accurately and logically represents the agreement of nations which constitute international law, and alone is consistent with the paramount necessity expressed in general terms for each nation to protect itself from internal disorder by trying and punishing offenders within its boundaries."

It must always be remembered that in so far as, at any rate, the courts of this country are concerned, international law has validity in so far its principles are accepted and adopted by domestic law. There is no external power that imposes its rules upon our code of substantive law or procedure The Court acknowledge the existence of a body of rules which nations accept among themselves. On any judicial issue they seek to ascertain what the relevant rule is, and having found it, they will treat it as incorporated into the domestic law so far as it is not inconsistent with the rules enacted by any Statute or finally declared by their tribunals. What then are the immunities of public ships of other nations accepted by our courts and on what principle? I say that in this particular case not only there is no Statute to the contrary, but in fact the Statute imposes that obligation, coming back to the action of Section 79, *viz.*, nothing is an offence which is justified by law. Therefore what you have got to do, Sirs, is to ascertain the relevant body of international law, and having done so, apply it to what is described as domestic law. Therefore there can be no reasonable doubt that in the construction and application and application of Section 79 the submission which I have already made on the immunity of individual members of an armed force fighting in a war properly declared, that immunity is a part of international law and therefore is a part of national law. And I submit that your own experience whenever emergencies of war have arisen should bear ample testimony to that position. Each time a soldier fights under the orders of a state in a war properly declared, if he were to consider what would be his liabilities, I am afraid the efficiency of war would be a very difficult process indeed. It is an assumed part of the law of nations that once you become a member of a fighting force of a properly qualified State entitled to make a war, there is an end of all individual liability for the acts which if they were private acts for a private purpose might be an offence within the law. Though according to may submission the first is an essentially correct ground, in any case the justification by law is a sure ground on which I stand before this Court. Hence I submit that nothing is an offence which is justified by law, and I therefore say that the acts with which the accused are charged before the Court are justified by law, that is to say by the international law, and therefore, there can be no question of a personal or individual liability.

This questions has been considered in a different from or perhaps in different language because I wish to point out to you, as you have seen in the earlier works to which I referred, the law of war is often described as the law of belligerency. I wish to point out to the Court, as I shall presently do, what is the law of belligerency ; in other words, who are entitled to be treated as billigerents in the light of international, and what I may call, municipal or domestic law.

For that purpose I wish to call attention to the authorities which clearly show where and how the law of belligerency rests. I again refer you to Oppenheim on International Law, 1944 edition, Vol. II : he was professor of international law at Cambridge and falls within the description which I gave of men who have by their labour and research and experience and knowledge, contributed to the formulation of international law on many questions. The present question is dealt with on page 200—Article 76 A :

"Recognition of belligerents by other States is not as a rule binding upon the State. Notwithstanding such recognition, it is entitled to treat the insurgents as traitors ; but the position is controversial with regard to recognition as a belligerent power granted to separate armies which comprise subjects of the enemy who are fighting to free their nation from this rule and which are responsible to an authority recognised as representing the nation in question."

That really epitomises the whole of the issue—"but the position is controversial with regard to the recognition as a belligerent power granted to separate armies which comprise subjects of the enemy who are fighting to free their nation from this rule and which are responsible to an authority recognised as representing the nation in question."

To translate it according to law, the accused before you were members of an army responsible to the Provisional Government of Free India, fighting to liberate themselves from the rule of the army of those who were fighting against them, and I submit that is precisely the case before us. The author goes on and gives instances of cases of that kind, and I want to draw your particular attention to those historical instances which fortunately have occurred before, so that I stand before you on much more solid ground than if this were perhaps actually the first instance:

"Thus, in the year 1918, during the world war, Great Britain, France Italy and the United States of America recognised Czecho-Slovaks as co-belligerents. Similar recognition was granted in the year 1917 to the Polish National Army, composed to a substantial degree of the subjects of the enemy powers. It has been maintained that as in the case of insurgents in a civil war—(quotations of which I have already given)—the enemy is entitled to disregard such recognition and treat the members of the insurgent army when they fall into his hands, in accordance with the provisions of the criminal law. The better opinion is probably that when such recognition is granted by and adversely to large bodies of men effectively organised on foreign soil in anticipation of independent nationahood, a point is reached at which the belligerents, confronted with disaffection and desertion of a considerable number of his subjects engaged in hostilities against him, can no longer, without exposing himself to justifiable retaliation, assert the provisions of his own criminal law as the only legally element in the situation."

I want to draw your attention pointedly to the conditions which are here laid down and which, I submit, we have more than amply fulfilled. I ask this Court to declare that is the better opinion, and I do say that we have reached a stage far in advance of the illustration given by Oppenheim. In this case not merely men were effectively organised, but there was a regularly organised army. This has been amply proved by the Prosecution—thanks to them for that. They have amply proved that there was a regular army, a properly organised army—on foreign soil it is true—but with this added qualification in my favour, that Indians residing in places where the army was organised, numbering not a few hundreds, even a few thousands, but two million men and women and children, through 230,000 adult men and women swearing allegiance to that Provisional Government, for the purpose of liberating their country—which unfortunately failed, but nonetheless the condition required that you may at your peril call to aid the criminal law of the country against such an organisation—effectively organised on soil in anticipation of an independent nationhood. It is true—and that is why I read the Proclamation to this court—I read it with a view to show to you that the object with which on foreign soil an independent government was formed was the liberation of their country : It was undoubtedly in anticipation of independent statehood ; and of course if the independent state had been established by the successful prosecution of force, as I said, this tribunal would not have been there to try them. It was because it was done in anticipation, which failed, and which does not detract from the point, that a stage is reached in which a belligerent confronted with the disaffection and desertion of a considerable number of his subjects engaged in hostilities against him, can no longer assert the provisions of his own criminal law as the only legally relevant element in this situation. In other words, the legally relevant element in this situation is that we, meaning the two armies, had reached a stage where, having reached a stage of war—there can be no question at all that under Section 79 we are entitled to the justification which the laws of war give to belligerent armies. And that no acts done during the course of the prosecution of the war are matters of what you may call domestic law, pure and simple ; which would be as if any one of these three accused went and did any of these acts out of private motive. Therefore, it is essential to remember that in all these cases the substance of the law is this : two independent States can always make war and the members of their combatant forces are unanswerable for their acts. Only the question, or the intermediate stage arises, whether without having reached the stage of independent statehood (to take the words of Oppenheim) you have attained a stage, and whether having founded a state for the purpose of liberating your own country, you are so organised, both the state and the army, that it assumes the proportions of a state and as a result of the war-as much a war between two independent states. I am pleading before you that we have proved before this court, and the documents which otherwise we would not have had the benefit of and have generously been produced by the prosecution all of them distinctly and clearly showed that we had reached that stage and this court would not only be justified, but, I submit, bound in law and in consciences to regard the accused as belonging to that organisation, and as member of such a belligerent army they are entitled to all the privileges of the laws of war. In other words, immunity for personal acts carried out in due prosecution of the war, as you yourself in your own person would claim.

The next book to which I call attention is the British Year Book of International Law, 1937, page 18. It says:

"What we call belligerent recognition is not so much recognition, even temporary and provisional, of a new government, so the recognition of the existence of awar."

I may explain what is meant here, because the recognition comes as a stage when it has not yet succeeded in establishing its own government. Of course, if for instance perchance this very army had succeeded in its aim, as the maxim of international law is, the successful revolution is the government established by law. But earlier than that there is the stage at which it is in a state of war and that is all that is necessary for the purposes of my case. If I can establish that they were making war, which is regarded as a stage of belligerency by international law, they are entitled to the same privileges and immunities as would be accorded to the armies of two independent nations. It continues :

"The existence of war is purely a question of fact; but if we recognise the fact that a war is being carried on, then the recognition of the insurgent government follows as a necessary consequence. Wars can only be carried on by governments, and there must be at least two parties to every war. Much of the confusion which obscures the current discussion of the Spanish problem arises form the failure to observe this correct logical consequence. The true doctrine is that recognition of the insurgent government is the necessary and logical consequence of recognising the fact of war."

Therefore I submit that once you recognise, as I submit this court is bound to do on the evidence before it, that there was a regular properly declared and properly prosecuted war, then I submit there can be no question that the acts of these men, done in due prosecution of that war, are completely justified by international law and therefore by law.

The instances are given in the Year Book of International Law. This is what it says :

"Lets this should seem to be merely doctrinaires, that is the kind of criticism with which we people are sometimes apt to run away-and theoretical opinion, I shall try to fortify my doctrine by authority. In 1828 Don Miguel, the Pretender to the throne of Portugal, was carrying on war by sea and land against his niece and nominal fiancee the child-Queen Donna Maria, who was recognised by Great Britain and other powers as the legitimate Sovereign of Portugal. At no time during the struggle was Don Miguel recognised by Great Britain under any form *de jure or de facto*. In 1828 he proclaimed naval blockades of Opor to and of the Azores. These blockades were notified to the British Government which published the notices in the London Gazette and communicated them to the committee of loyd's. The king's advocate Sir herbert Jenner advised the British Government that the blockades, if effectively maintained, might be recognised as valid, although no form of recognition had at any time been conceded to Don Miguel."

In other words the distinction that is sought to be made is that you may recognise the state of belligerency without necessarilly recognising the state.

Refusal to recognise the blockade, so Jenner advised, would be a departure from the neutrality which this country had professed in the civil war. Twenty years later the Palmerston Government, following the advice of Sir John Dodson- and I hope that Judge Advocate will advise you accordingly-then the Queen's Advocate decided to recognise the blockade of Trieste by the Italian insurgents during the Revolution of 1843, although there had been no other act of recognition of the insurgent government.

The point I am trying to emphasize is this that you need not necessarily recognise you opponent as a government, and yet during the course of the war, once you recognise that it was a proper state of belligerency, then the immunities and privileges which I described before follow, because the men, and in modern times the women, who are fighting for the insurgent government, are recognised for the purpose of these immunities. It goes on :

"Upon the point which we are now discussing Dodson's opinion is very clear. 'It is sufficient he says to justify a blockade if duly maintained that a *de facto* war is carried on by Sardinia and Venice on one side and Austria on the other'."

Even more clear is the opinion of a later Queen's Advocate Sir John Harding when advising the Government in 1860 upon the question raised by Garibaldi's rebellion. This is perhaps nearer in its application. This is he quotation from the opinion of Harding:

"If Her Majesty's Government considers that a civil war actually exists between the dictatorial Government of southern Italy ad that of is Majesty the King of the two Silicious in which Great Britain is to be strictly natural and that the dictatorial government has in fact attained (howsoever) an independent and sovereign existence and governs de facto a portio of the Neapolitan dominions, then Her Majesty's Government may without violating or disregarding the law of Nations and without encouraging piracy, so far recognise the acts of this de facto government as to admit the validity of an effective blockade, maintained by a competent naval force acting under its orders, for to acquiesce in the capture and condemnation buy it of articles of contraband of war designed for use of the King of the two Sicilies."

The belligerency which existed was between what you might call the King of Italy and the insurgents, and the advice of Sir John Harding was that if there was a de facto war between the two, then the rights of the belligerencts should be accepted and acknowledged. In other words, supposing they took as prize of war ships belonging to what you might call the constituted King of Italy, it would still be a perfectly good prize.

In the course of the same opinion, Harding pointed out that Garibaldi and his officers could not possibly be regarded as pirates, since they were carrying on war in a regular manner and had been dealt with on equal terms by British naval officers. The three opinions which I have just cited are those of British law officers ranging over the period from 1828 to 1860.

Without further multiplying citations, I will therefore summarise their effect by saying that what we recognise in these cases is the existence of war. The recognition of the insurgent government is merely incidental or consequential since a war implies the existence of some independent authority which carries on the war.

The next thing to which I wish to call your attention is the recognition this matter has received from the British Government through the then Foreign Secretary, Mr. Eden. I am reading from the Hansard which is the recognised report of the Debates of the House of Commons. I am reading from the debates of the 14th April 1937, page 113. This is what I have here :

"The leader of the opposition spoke earlier today as though the Government had given something up in this case. Of Course, we have not given anything up, because you can never grant belligerent rights to one side only; they must be granted to both sides, if they are granted at all."

This issue arose on the question of the Spanish war.

"The Honourable Gentleman remarked that he thought that never in history had there been any question of granting belligerent rights early in a dispute. As a matter of fact, in the American Civil War we did grant belligerent rights within six weeks of the outbreak of the Civil War."

"Mr. Noel Baker said : The Government themselves declared a blockade, which, as all international lawyers will agree, comples them to grant belligerent rights to both sides."

"Mr. Eden: We ourselves made, in point of fact, a declaration of neutrality out to which arose the granting of belligerent rights to both sides. That is what we did in the American Civil War. Of course, that does not stand alone. It is not the only example. The Honourable Gentleman is probably familiar, I think, as I know something of his associations in this respect, with the Greek rebellion against Turkey in 1821-25. At that time also—remember that in each case these were insurgents against their parent State fighting for their liberation, and it was during the course of that struggle that the rights of belligerents were granted by Britain. At that time also, belligerent rights were granted and His Majesty's Government voiced this opinion to which I would draw the attention of the House; the character of belligerency was not so much a principle as a fact that a certain degree of force and consistency acquired by any mass of population engaged in war entitled that population to be treated as a belligerent and even if this title were questionable, rendered in the interest well-understood of all civilised nations so to treat them."

The position of British politicians and British law on the question of the recognition of belligerency even as between what I might call the parent State and the rebel States has always been recognition of belligerency.

At that time Canning was the Foreign Secretary of this country and Professor Philips in his History of Europe deals with this very interesting chapter of modern Greek independence. He says :

"Curiously enough as in the affairs of Spain, so now his (Canning's) attitude was frankly based upon the interests of England. The interests of England in his opinion demanded peace ...... The recognition of the belligerent character of the Greeks was necessitated by the impossibility of treating as pirates a population of a million souls and of bringing within the bounds of civilised war a contest which had been marked at the outset on both sides, by disgusting barbarities.

"Those were both cases in which belligerent rights were granted. A third and perhaps, in a way, even more remarkable case, was the revolt of the Spanish Americans Colonies against the Spanish Government, from which resulted the establishment of the South Ameracan independent Republics as we know them today."

So that you have instances on both sides of the line. You have instances where those who rebelled against a State for their own independence ultimately succeeded, but while they were in a state of war both were recognized as belligerents. Those others in which they did not succeed but nonetheless during the interval of the struggle, they were both recognized as belligerents.

"A third, and perhaps, in a way, even more remarkable case was the revolt of the Spanish American Colonies against the Spanish Government, from which resulted the establishment of the South American independent Republics as we know them today. In that dispute we recognized the rights of the belligerent colonies..."

People were actually revolting against their own Government for their own freedom, and one need not be apologetic in this period of world history to say that the subject race may free itself.

"In that dispute we recognized the rights of the belligerent colonies long before we recognised them in any other way, and, when I heard the Right Hon. Gentleman below the Gangway speaking earlier this afternoon, I bethought me that he might well have remembered the enthusiasm shown by the Liberal Party of that day for those new State across the Atlantic to whom we accorded belligerent rights, though they were rebels against their own mother country."

Sir, I say that I could not quote a stronger authority for your adoption than the action of the British Government as stated authoritatively by the Foreign Secretary of Britain and I would like to read it again in order that I may not miss the point:

"I bethought me that the might well have remembered the enthusiasm shown by the Liberal Party of that day for those new States across the Atlantic to whom we accorded belligerent rights, though they were rebels against their own mother country."

And I say that the same point arises for you. It is true that those who fought were rebels from the point of view of constitutional law as against their own King—and later on I will come to the question of zallegiance it will be my duty to analyse before you what that means, though it is irrelevant to the issue as I shall point out. The very fact that those colonies were fighting against their mother country as it is called, shows that at that time there was what you may call 'legal allegiance', but legal allegiance cannot be a matter of perpetuity because if it becomes a matter of perpetuity no subject race will ever attain freedom. For the moment, the point with which we are concerned is merely this : that while in a state of belligerencey Britain recognized the rebels as proper belligerents, those who were fighting against their mother country, and if that belligerency is recognized, I venture to submit it will be far too much to ask this court to refuse it to this Provisional Government of Free Inda and the Armies fighting under them. Mr. Eden goes on—because he wanted to make the point that the State will be recognized not only when it comes into existence, but while still the struggle goes on. New I read :

"What I wish to deduce from these three examples is that the natural thing, ..." mark the words—

'........ when a struggle has reached the large dimensions of the present war in Spain, would have been to recognise its belligerent character, and for States whose maritime interests are involved, as ours are, to grant belligerent rights to both sides."

In other words, as he put it before, it is essentially a matter of fact. If we find that the struggle, - call it rebellion, call it what you like—has reached such proportions that you connot control it by normal means, then you must recognize that it is a state of war, and once you recognize that it is a state of war, those who fight in pursuance of the declaration of war and in prosecution of it are entitled to all the rights of belligerency. Then he goes on :

"That would have been the natural thing to do. Recognition of belligerencey is, of course, quite distinct from recognising anyone to whom you give belligerent rights as being the legitimate Government of the country."

And that is what I want to impress upon you, that if it is asserted on the other side that it is required for the purpose of immunity from all acts done in due prosecution of the war that the Provisional Government should have been recognized by Britain, it is a completely futile argument. In fact, the very hypothesis cannot exist. The hypothesis is this: The rebels as I have called them—I do not mind it—are fighting for their freedom against another country. If they succeed, the Government will be recognized, but, in the meantime, during the course of fighting, the Government won't be recognized, but what is recognised is belligerency. I shall presently point out what it involves,—immunity from all acts done in due prosecution of the war.

"Recognition of belligerency is, of course, quite distinct from recognising anyone to whom you give belligerent rights as being the legitimate Government of the country.'

It is a fact that the Provisional Government was not then and did not become the actual Gvoernment of India, but that does not matter at all. What are the rights and privileges during the course of the struggle, and if I am right in my submission to the Court, there can be no doubt that during the course of struggle there was only one duty owed by men like the accused before you, and that is to prosecute that war under the orders of the Provisional Government,—and anything that they did by way of prosecuting that war gives them complete immunity.

"It has nothing to do with it. It is a conception simply concerned with granting belligerent rights which are of convenience to the donor as much as they are to the recipients. I will not go into the reasons, but for a variety of reasons in the present dispute we are not granting belligerent rights."

So that you have here recognition of an adoption of the principle supported by precedents as stated by the Foreign Secretary of that day.

Then there is a quotation from Mr. Churchill's speech during the course of the same discussion to which I wish to call your attention. That is on the 14th of April 1937, page 1068:

"When I hear my Right Hon. friend opposite speak of rebels, I must remind him that, sitting there as he does in the seat of the Whigs, he is departing from Whig principles. The saered rights of rebellion was one of their first doctrines. In regard to liberal statesmen, there the Right Hon. Gentleman sits, the successor to Mr. Gladstone, striving to uphold the great principles for which his party stands. But what was Mr. Gladstone's record? He was a stong supporter of rebles. He was a strong supporter of the rebels in the war of American secession. There, we had a civil war in which the rebels were not only rebels but slave owners. Mr. Gladstone went about the country, and in a famous speech either at New Castle or Hull proclaimed that the Confederate States (i.e., the Southern States had not only founded an army, but that they had founded a navy, they had founded a Government, and more than that, they had founded a nation. (An Hon. Member :"He was a Tory then.") He was not a Tory then. Therefore before one takes the view that rebels are like mad dogs to be put down and shot at sight, we should remember these things."

In other words, in that debate the Government of the day in England recognized that while a rebellion may or may not be successful, while it had attained a stage of war, you must recognize and give immunity to those people who fight on either side, for what justification is there on the part of one set of them to fight and claim immunity as against the other side? If the I.N.A. shot, I daresay the British Indian Army equally shot from the other side. The justification is equal in both cases in so far as this particular struggle is concerned. Mr. Churchill goes on :

"If we search the history of the 19th century we shall find many cases where the British Government have actually espoused the cause of rebels. The Hon. Member (Mr. Maxton), the leader of the Glydeside party, with this customary candour and frankness, made no bones about supporting rebels. He declared that the question was whether or not they were rebelling for the thing you wanted."

I am quite certain that we have proved to the hilt that they were rebelling for a thing they wanted which is fully approved of by any civilised human being. There cannot be two different laws for two different sets of people. "Everyone will support rebels who are fighting for the things of which they approve and they will criticise the Government which is for the things which they dislike. Therefore do not let us have too much of an attempt to make out that the Government in Spain have all the right on their side and the rebels none."

The Court will appreciate that I am pleading for a very limited right. I am not here before this Court on the question of the recognition or non-recognition of the unfortunate failure of the Provisional Government to obtain the independence of India. That is not the issue. There is a very narrow issue. It is this. While they were fighting and struggling, were they or were they not entitled to the rights of belligerents.

Mr Churchill goes on : "Therefore do not let us have too much of an attempt to make out that the Government in Spain have all the right on their side and the rebels none. It is one of the most evenly balanced struggles and one of the most unpleasant and certainly it is the least cause for us to espouse. If we were to take the course which is recommended by the Right Honourable gentleman and to break the blockade, if we throw the might of the British Navy into the scale, could he guarantee or could he be sure that we might not provoke that very alignment and crystallisation in Europe along those unnatural and idiotic—perhaps I had better say ideological—lines which it is our whole message and mission to rupture, or least to avoid. "So that Sir, even up to the very last war, up to the year 1937, just on the eve of the last war, it is perfectly obvious that a distinction has been maintained, a distinction which I cannot too often insist upon between a state of belligerency which may be recognised and the rights accorded without the ultimate success of those who fought for the cause for which they could fight. They may fail but nonetheless in the interval they are entitled to the rights of belligerency."

Then, Sirs, there is a further point and I tell the Court that it is a question of fact. This Court should find that this Provisional Government had ceded to it the territories which I have described. But while insisting on that finding of fact, because we submit that it was a fact, I wish to point out to you that from the point of view of belligerency it is quite unnecessary that the particular government for the time being need have any territory in its possession at all, and for that purpose, I wish to give you illustrations in history. Take Belgium in the last war and all the emgre Governments residing in London during the last but one war and the last war, what were those emigre Governments? Not an inch of territory which they could call their won at that time and yet who ventures to say before this Court that a member of the Dutch Army or for that matter the Polish or the French or the Yugoslavian Army may not fight to liberate its own country and not have the right to claim, even if they failed, all the rights and immunities as far as their soldiers are concerned of belligerencey. I think, Sirs, the last war has illustrated more than any other that some of these old principles may be overdone and that it is quite unneccessary in order that you may have a state of war, that country that is fighting a war on one side need not necessarily at that time have, what I may call in the common English parlance, a local habitation though it may have a name. Many of these emigre Governments were deprived of their territory and the fact that they were deprived of their territory temporarily, or the fact that the Indians were deprived of their territories for 150 years, makes, not the slightest difference to the point that we are submitting to the Court. What we submit to the Court is this. They were all liberating armies, trying to liberate their country and therefore were entitled to the immunities of those who were fighting. The next question before you, Sirs, is this. There is no such thing as the law of limitations in dealing with nations so that if either the Dutch or the French or anybody else was trying to fight for the liberation of their country while having lost their territory to the enemy, can it ever be argued in a British Court that those who were fighting to liberate their country were not fighting a struggle where they there entitled to the rights of belligerents. Supposing any one of them failed, is it to be said in a British Court that they were not fighting a struggle to which all the laws of immunities and privileges of a fighting army exist? I therefore urge upon you not to take the instance that you have before you as any different because we happen to be Indians. Remember that. They were trying to liberate their country. I am not here to espouse the cause of the Provisional Government. I am pleading for men who fought under the orders of their Government for the liberation of their own country. If therefore they were entitled to fight for their own county. Country for the purpose of liberating their country, I am centitled to tell this Court that they are entitled to hte privileges of belligerency. One more instance on which there was a certain amount of struggle in proving the facts is the case of the Maquis in France. Remember the facts. At the time when the Maquis were fighting, the *de facto* and the *de jure* Government in France was Marshal Petain's Goverrnment and the latter were allied witht Germany. The Maquis were fighting in order to release France from their own French Government which was allied with Germany, and what did Eisenhower say? I am going to read that to you because it is a very short document and it is very important. At that time it was apprehended that the Maquis might be dealt with unjustly by the then French Government, because it was the *de jure* Government of the time and would shoot as rebels, very much the same as the Advocate-General will later on argue to say about the persons who took part in the Indain National Army. But you have the Pronouncement of no less a person as Field Marshal Eisenhower that that shall not be. In other words, if persons with a view to liberate their Government fight against their own Govrnment, they are entitled to the rights of belligerents. That was the reason why I was very anxious that I should be able to prove that statement. Sirs, this is the statement which has been proved and I army incidentally agree to what my learned friend insisted upon That I should put in also the German view of the matter. If he prefers that it is his look-out. I do not. I prefer the American and the British view.

"There is conclusive evidence that the German forces in France are—(I am obliged to my honourable friend for saying that he does not doubt the authenticity of the source, meaning that it came from General Eisenhower. Of course, he insisted that I should put in the second passage and I leave it to you to judge which of the two you should prefer, with the submission that you should prefer Eisenhower to General Keitell.

"Now recruiting members of the French resistance group as France Tireurs and today an announcement from SHEAF in the name of General

Eisenhower makes these four points :

1. That the French forces of the interior constitute a combatant force commanded by General Koeniggaud forming an integral part of the Allied Expeditionary Force.
2. That the French Forces of the interior in the Maquis bear arms openly against the enemy and are instructed to observe the rules of war they are provided with a distinctive emblem and regarded by General Eisenhower as an Army under his command.
3. Reprisals against resistance groups violate the rules of war by which Germany is bound."

This is what I ask you to do : that anything done against the members of the Indian National Army fighting for their freedom according to the rules of war—I submit that any action taken against them is a breach of international law.

4. "Every effort will be made to trace the authors of any atrocities against members of the forces under General Eisenhower's command. Steps to this end are already being taken."

Then the rest reads :

"General Eisenhower in a declaration broadcast to the B.B.C. tried to legalise the French partisans as a fighting force ...."

The question that arose was somewhat delicate from a constitutional point of view, because for the time being the then French Government was still under the thumb of Germany. The people of France for the time being fighting against their Government which was pro-Germany were undoubtedly guilty of fighting against their won Government, but the ground of immunity accorded was that they were fighting alongside the allies for the purpose of freeing France. What is the distinction, I ask, between those who fought on the side of, even if we say Japan, for the purpose of freeing their own country? With very great respect it is difficult to understand any distinction. In other words, if the Maquis were entitled to all the privileges and immunities of a good fighting force for liberating their own country, I cannot see how you can fail to accord a similar treatment to those standing in the position of the Indian National Army.

Then, I read on:-

"General Eisenhower in a declaration broadcast by the B.B.C. tried to legalise the French partisans as a fighting force. From responsible circles in the Wilhelmstrasse the following statement has been given out :

"This attempt by the Allied High Command is unjustified. French partisans revolt against the legal French Government and violate the French laws, which enforce capital punishment for such violations."

Now you are asked solemnly to adopt what the Germans said in a similar situation. With what face could ever such an argument be presented to a British Court?

"The activities of the French partisans do not constitute regular war conduct ...."

(Precisely the kind of argument that is likely to be advanced).

"The activities of the partisans do not constitute regular war conduct but a malicious system of ambush fighting against the occupation power. Thus the partisans have forfeited the right to be treated as regular troops."

I submit that the view put forward by General Eisenhower is the more correct of the two. But the other view clearly shows what I have to establish before you in order to claim immunity, namely, that it is a regular organised army, fighting according to the laws of war, and not guilty of any personal atrocity beyond and outside merely fighting a regular war, and it is fortunate in this case, the first test of its kind, because the issue is neat. There is not even a charge of any personal atrocity. My submission to the Court is that the British, and I mean no empty compliment, civilised instinct has recognised that if a struggle for freedom is waged, then if it reaches a stage at which there is an organised Government and an organised army, it must be accorded all the rights, privileges and immunities of fighting army, and that is what I plead for.

The question which arises under Section 79 of the Indian Penal Code is that by all rules of civilised warfare what you claim for yourself you must accord to your opponents, even though you may have succeeded in defeating them. You are entitled to come to your own conclusion on the merits of the controversy at issue before you. But the Government says this:

"The policy of the Government of India is, however, that only these cases will be brought to trial where there are serious charges, apart from that of waging war against the King."

As I said it is not law and in no manner binds you. I must frankly confess that much, because it must not be said that I was trying to take refuge behind any executive statements. But the fact remains that behind that statement is almost a reluctant admission that waging war is in this case not an offence, or at least seriously treated as an offence. That is perfectly obvious, not because waging war per se not an offence, but because in the circumstances of the case, where, with an organised government and an organised army, a war was carried on, then waging that kind of war is not an offence. I am not denying that if ten individuals in India collected arms and began to fight the Government of India, waging war is not or would not be an offence. But what is meant is that waging war, meaning the prosecution of war in the circumstances of the case, namely, of the Indian National Army under the Provisional Government that is not an offence. But it is a matter which I want to be judged entirely on the merits of the legal and factual submissions which I have made.

The next issue which really, I submit, does not arise, but inasmuch as I have only one address before this Court I must try and anticipate things and answer them,—sometimes it is unjust to one's self, because one may raise more things than the opponent is likely to think of and I may make a present of an argument to him—but having regard to the rules of this Court, I am obliged to resort to that course—it cannot be helped; otherwise I should have preferred to have a short reply to any new point which may be raised by my learned friend on the other side. The short way to deal with the issue is this: the cases which I have cited and the authoritative works which I have quoted to the Court, clearly show that in judging this case, no question of allegiance arises. All insurgents, while they are fighting, are still held by allegiance, and all the books which I have read will be worth nothing if the question of allegiance had been raised,—because until you successfully throw it off, the *prima facie* allegiance, if I may so call it, exists; and nonetheless while it is not successfully thrown off, while it is in that ambulatory stage, the rights of fighting and the rights of war, if it is a properly declared war and a properly conducted war (I will not repeat that qualification again, you will assume it from me that when I talk of the rights of war, I am talking of a properly declared war and a properly prosecuted war as to which I have made my submission)—in such a case *ex hypothec* the allegiance exists. They want to throw off the foreign yoke, and the rest is that undoubtedly if the question of allegiance arose or had everyone's , no grant of immunity to insurgents fighting for liberty against the parent State would have ever arisen; but the fact remains that notwithstanding the fact of allegiance remaining , the right and freedom to liberate their own country being recognised at the same time, it is given effect to by recognising belligerency; that is to say, when an organised force is fighting under an organised government for its own freedom, while they have not completely succeeded and taken allegiance remains, they are still entitled to fight. That is recognised by the law of nations. But should such a question ever be raised by my learned friend—which I submit is irrelevant—I have important submissions to make. First, that on the events which took place at Farrar Park on 17th February, there was no allegiance left and hence it is very important that I try to concentrate my attention on what occurred at that meeting.

The fact, which probably may remain unnoticed, but which was most important, was that the British officers and British other ranks were separated from Indian officers and Indian ranks. It is an extremely important fact to remember, in order to be able to appreciate the events and the occurrences of that day. They having been separated, the Indian officers and ranks, numbering anything between 30,000 to 45,000, were all asked to assemble at Farrar Park —Colonel Hunt made a short statement or speech, saying that he was handing them over on behalf of the British Government to the representative of the Japanese Government, Colonel Fujiwara. Colonel Fujiwara then made a speech in Japanese which, as the evidence now show, was translated both in English and in Hindustani; and the statement of Col. Fujiwara amounted to this—using my own language—that those of the Indian prisoners of war who wanted to join an army for the purpose of liberation of their own country were free to do so, and handed them over to Captain Mohan Singh. Captain Mohan Singh then addressed them saying that he was prepared to organise the Indian National Army for the purpose of fighting for the liberation of India; and we had the evidence—uncontradicted—that he was acclaimed by the whole of the Indian prisoners of war present. I wish even at the risk of repetition to submit that when an insurgent fights against the then constituted government to free his own people and his own country from the alien, the question of allegiance does not arise. I want in that connection to take the statement of Captain Arshad —it is a most emphatic statement he made.

"We believed that the only allegiance we owe is allegiance to our country." I cannot describe better than in his words the result of that day's proceedings.

That brings me up to a somewhat difficult subject like the case of any subject people, in particular India. All of you are aware that every charge of treason in England is a charge of working against the King and the country. The last one is the reported case of John Amery. In the situation in which an Indian finds himself, the question is under what circumstances and to what extent this question of allegiance can be raised at all, because once you divide the King from the country, it becomes a very difficult issue altogether for any human being to decide, and hence I would prefer to rest my argument on the occurrences of 17th February. The position of an Indian in a case of this kind is difficult and I am going to submit to the Court on first principles what its true solution is. Where the King and the country coincide there is no question of an alternative. If you fight against the King and also fight against the interest of your own country, the question does not arise, but the question does arise where there is a fight for freedom, and I propose to read passages to show to what extent the world has progressed in the matter of the recognition of human rights. When you are nominally fighting against the King but really fighting to liberate the country, then the point is whether the question of allegiance can arise at all. Unless you sell your own soul, how can you ever say that when you are fighting to liberate your own country there is some other allegiance which prevents you from so doing. That means that if that happens there is nothing but permanent slavery.

Therefore, it is that I submit that in the circumstances of this case a choice was presented by the force of circumstances to those prisoners of war who were surrendered by Britain—I do not say wrongly—because there are reverses in the fortunes of war. Who am I to say whether it is rightly or wrongly done? At the same time you cannot disregard this most important fact that for the time being by reason of the exigencies of the war Britain found itself unable to give any protection to her soldiers to fight for the country and that being so, they found themselves in a very unenviable position. My learned friend may say : "you ought to have remained prisoners of war, and he may argue that they may do anything under the circumstances short of making war. I concede that proposition where allegiance to the King and country coincide, but where the two do not coincide, a different situation arises altogether. My learned friend may say that they were fighting on behalf of a puppet Government or they allowed themselves to be used as stooges of the Japanese. Even accepting this somewhat unenviable expression of stooges or otherwise, the question is one of fact, namely, whether or not it was a regular army honestly believing that it is fighting for the freedom of its country. The question of a bad name that may be given has really no relevancy to the legal issue by inasmuch as a great deal of dirt has been thrown by expressions of this character—puppet Government and puppet army and words to that effect—and the question of the strength of—that army may be raised, it is my duty to tell the Court how the evidence stands on record. The evidence that stands on record is that the No. 1. I.N.A. was formed and was dissolved in December. I shall forget that for the purposes of this case, because waging war which is the subject of the argument applies to what you might call I.N.A. No. 2. I have attempted to prove that I have established that the I.N.A., though small in numbers, was fighting as allies of the Japanese Army and there is no ignominy in admitting that or in doing that, because the objective at that time of both the armies was undoubtedly to free India from Britain. The objective was no more and no less than that of the allies in fighting to free France or Belgium or any other country, and if in that process there was a unified command or a single strategy, you, Sirs, will not say with your knowledge of military affairs that makes one army the stooge of the other. It is a phrase with which my learned friend will not be able to walk away if he uses it, and that is why I want to tie his legs, if I can. If the British and the American armies fought under the command of General Eisenhower, Britain may not be called the stooge of the Americans, and I hope my learned friend will not descend to the level of calling the I.N.A stooges of the Japanese. The evidence given by Lt. Nag is very important from this point of view. He was extremely prolific in the results and he came to prove at the instance of the prosecution that there was a very organised regular army, and that a big war was fought. My submission is that he was hoisted with his own petard. If he proved that a regular war was fought that is precisely my defence. He was qualified to speak about it. He was legal adviser of the I.N.A. and he told this court in effect—I am quoting his words —that the two armies fought as Allies. Whether the alliance was right or wrong is not before this Court. The only thing that is before this Court is whether or not this army fought as an organised army. My learned friend will not be able to support any allegation that they fought for any other objective except the liberation of India. If an allegation of that kind is made, it is a false allegation, and we have given a complete lie to it. The prosecution witnesses from beginning to end admitted that the object of the I.N.A. was to fight for the liberation of India, and everyone, whether volunteer or non-volunteer, willing or unwilling, has admitted that they had no other objective except the liberation of their own country. That being so, my submission to the Court is that in so far as any allegation is made to the contrary it is only put forward as a point of prejudice, and I had to meet it with a view to remove the prejudice, because as I said it is not in human hands to choose your allies under the circumstances which may be forced upon you. And whether you fight with the aid of X, Y or Z for the purpose of liberation of your own country, the fact that Y was otherwise a bad person has got nothing to do with the case. But in all human discussions there is always an argument at a tangent; many human minds confuse the issue, and hence it is that I have attempted to cross-examine, at all events in the briefest possible way, to make this point clear. The point that I tried to bring out was that the I.N.A. was, though small, a very organised army, inspired by the best of motives, and fought for that purpose, though unsuccessful for the time being.

There is one other thing which I ought to have mentioned and I regret I omitted it while I was talking on the first issue. That was with reference to the Minister sent by Japan to the Government of Azad Hind. I ought to have stated earlier, because the points which I have mentioned were proclamation, recognition, declaration of war, followed by possession of territory, and also the Minister of the Nippon Government accredited to this Government. The last is not essential, but still in point of fact it was alleged, and I will state how the facts stand under that head. The fact is that a Minister was sent in fact. No less a person than Mr. Sawada of the Foreign Office told the Court that it was decided to send a Minister to the Provisional Government of Azad Hind, while he was the Vice-Foreign Minister and he was competent to speak about their decision that a Minister in fact was sent. As it happened he came without letters of credit or his credentials, and as if it mattered the whole argument was to show that a Minister ceases to exist because he did not bring the papers. Supposing one of you, Sirs, sent me your agent, and I choose not to demand from him his letter of authority and I accept him, it is a most extraordinary argument that the agent ceases to exist. That is a sort of logic which my learned friend wishes to apply to this case. But a good reason was given founded on diplomatic practice which you should accept. The evidence says that being a Provisional Government, in accordance with the dignity of nations, or comity of nations, no credentials are required. In other words, the important point is whether the man came and was recognized by the person for whom he was intended. During the evidence, my learned friend got an answer from one of the witnesses to the effect that the head of the State, Netaji Subhas Chandra Bose, did not receive him. But there is further evidence which really destroys any other points on this question : Thereafter credentials were asked for, the head of the State according to his conception required it, and you have the evidence that credentials were prepared and that they were signed by the Japanese Emperor and were despatched but the then conditions of war they did not reach. But because the Japanese Minister was duly accredited I submit it is a reinforcing argument in my favour. When he came, the two Governments—meaning the Provisional Government of Azad Hind and the Japanese Government-took a different view of what you may call diplomatic practice, but that does not affect the issue. The sending Government in the end, when so required, actually sent letters of credit, and the fact that it reached or did not reach does not affect the issue: at all events it completely cured such defect or deficiency as there was in the procedure. And in point of fact I ask the Court to hold that there was a duly appointed Minister, which is all that arises here. The reason why we brought in the evidence was among other things that the Provisional Government of Azad Hind was a properly organized Government, and accepted, and the acceptance does not require necessarily the sending of an envoy, or an ambassador, or a Minister, or whatever the position or the relation between the Governments may be.

What is it that the I.N.A. embarked upon in collaboration with the Japanese? According to their agreement which I submit I have proved, any part of Indian territory which may be liberated would be immediately. handed over to the I.N.A. If you, as men of affairs, understand things rightly, it is the only thing to do. Where is the question of being an instrument. If, however, there was any instrument, it was the Japanese, because it is they who wee assisting in liberating India, with a view that the liberated parts of India would be handed back to the I.N.A. The facts of the case are that two proclamations were issued by the representatives of both the Governments—Gen. Kewabe on behalf of the Japanese Government and Mr. Subhas Chandra Bose on behalf of his Government. You may say nobody fights a philanthropic war. But whether or not it was philanthropic remains to be seen. I can well understand, and I submit it for your consideration, that Japan, as indeed one of the witnesses said, that the East would be better protected by a free India or that they might have better prospects of trade which is their only means of maintaining their standard of life, which incidentally is also the means of Britain. It was not a philanthropic war at all. So far as the freedom of India was concerned, it was, I submit, the object of that war, and you have it in evidence on oath before the Court. It may well be, I presume it was, that a free India might better be able to assist by means of trade and otherwise to enable the Japanese to maintain their high standard of life. Therefore, it is idle, unless people appreciate the true issue for them, to say that unless you conquered territory there can be no other object in assisting in getting its freedom. It is that idle argument which I wish to meet before this Court. But we are not left to speculation. My learned friend cross-examined one of the witnesses. He said, Oh yes, you are assisting the Indian National Army with a view to attain your Japanese war aims, and he thought he had got away with it. But when we asked what were the war aims, then I am afraid all this cross-examination fell to the ground. He said it was with a view to assist war aims which was to free India. There may be many who doubt promises in this country but I am not one of them. I am one who looks on the brighter side of life and believes that if India could be freed in that way, why honest men should not believe it, it is difficult to understand. The question before the Court shortly is this. What were the relations between the I.N.A. and the Japanese Army. That is the short point. It is a point of prejudice and yet it is my duty in defence of the honour of those whom I am defending and the group to which they belong that they were not the stooges of the Japanese, as cheaply might be said by the opponents. That is the short history of the position of the I.N.A. vis-a-vis the Japanese Army. I was speaking about the quality of allegiance, and I submitted to the Court that in a case of this kind where you have got to administer the law as a matter of justice, equity and good conscience, you may have a case where the country and the King do not coincide and where there is an imposed allegiance on a subject people; and I am not talking merely as a matter of theory. I am going to give you an instance of a case of this kind which has occurred in the days when the British Commonwealth was called the British Empire; and the statement that I wish to read is the Declaration of Independence by the United States of America on the Declaration of war and before they had attained any statehood, as it is called in the cases which I have given. I am reading from a book called "Speeches and Documents on Colonial Policy", edited by Keith and published by the Oxford University Press in London. It is at page 70. It says :

"When in the course of human events, it becomes necessary for one people to dissolve the political bonds which have connected them with another, and to assume, among the powers of the earth the separate and equal station to which the laws of nature and of nature's God entitled them, a decent respect to the opinions of mankind requires that they should declare the causes which impel them to the separation.

We hold these truths to be self-evident, that all men are created equal, that they are endowed by their Creator with certain inalienable rights; that among these are life, liberty, and the pursuit of happiness"—(and here I would like to point out that the recent pronouncement of Mr. Truman and of Mr. Churchill are to the same effect)—

"that, to secure these rights, governments are instituted among men, deriving their just powers from the consent of the governed, that, whenever any form of government becomes destructive of these ends, it is the rights of the people to alter or to abolish it, and to institute new government, laying its foundation on such principles, and organizing its powers in such form, as to them shall seem most likely to effect their safety and happiness. Prudence, indeed, will dictate that governments long established should not be changed for light and transient causes; and accordingly all experience hath shown, that mankind are more disposed to suffer while evils are sufferable, than to right themselves by abolishing the forms to which they are accustomed. But, when a long train of abuses and usurpations, pursuing invariably the same object, evinces a sign to reduce them under absolute despotism, it is their right, it is their duty, to throw off such government and to provide new guards for their future security. Such has been the patient sufferance of these colonies, and such is now the necessity which constrains them to alter their former systems of government. The history of the present King of Great Britain is a history of repeated injuries and usurpations, all having, in direct object, the establishment of an absolute tyranny over these estates. To prove this, let facts be submitted to a candid world:"

(Then they cite the grievances—I will not read them at all). Then the statement says :

"Nor have we been wanting in attention to our British brethren. We have warned them, from time to time, of attempts made by their legislature to extend an unwarrantable jurisdiction over us. We have reminded them of the circumstances of our emigration and settlement here. We have appealed to their native justice and magnanimity, and we have conjured them, by the ties of our common kindred, to disavow these usurpations, which would inevitably interrupt our connections and correspondence. They too have been deaf to the voice of justice and of consanguinity. We must, therefore, acquiesce in the necessity which denounces our separation, and hold them, as we hold the rest of mankind, enemies in war,—in peace, friends. We, therefore, the representatives of the United States of America, in General Congress assembled, appealing to the Supreme Judge of the World for the rectitude of our intentions, do, in the name and by the authority of the good people of these colonies, solemnly, publish and declare"—(and this is the point)—"That these United Colonies are, and of right ought to be, Free and Independent States;"—(and then comes the important sentence)—"That they are absolved from all allegiance to the British Crown, and that all political connection between them and the State of Great Britain is, and ought to be, totally dissolved; and that , as Free and Independent States they have full power to levy war, include peace, contract alliances. Establish commerce, and to do all other acts and things which Independent States may of right do. And for the support of this declaration, with a firm reliance on the protection of Divine Providence, we mutually pledge to each other, our lives, our fortunes and our sacred honour."

Here you have a case in which this quality of allegiance came to a test. They owed allegiance in the familiar sense to the King of England. They owed allegiance to their own country, and they realised that the time had arrived when the question became one of conflict between the allegiance to the King and the allegiance to the country. So that in accepted history, we have got a classical instance of a case where the choice between allegiance to the King and the allegiance to the country was presented to the world, and men of honour chose allegiance to their own country to the imposed allegiance to a foreign king. Therefore I venture to stand before this Court today with the most classical illustration, the illustration of a race, of a country, that has saved the world today, and in the last war and did marvels in the cause of civilization; and if that illustration is not going to be respected, I submit justice would be denied completely. I submit that what happened at Farrar Park, by reason of the actual state of events in this country, was perfectly legitimate, and indeed legitimised by what I may call the course of history. Indeed it is amazing how from the year 1776 to today the words are as true as they were then :

"We hold these truths to be self-evident that all men are created equal, that they are endowed by their Creator with certain unalienable rights; that among these are life, liberty, and the pursuit of happiness."

And I commend this to you, Sirs, in order that you in your wisdom will consider it just, if ever any question arises. This declaration took place on the 4th July, 1776; and ultimately a war was fought, which resulted in 1781 in establishing what is today the United States of America as an independent republic of the world. I venture to submit this a historical instance, important in its character, valuable as showing the way in which the world has functioned. I want to call attention to the oath of allegiance to the Provisional Government of Azad Hind and its context, for it is important that you should know it.

"Indians in East Asia today are not more the subjects of an alien power; they are the proud citizens of the Provisional Government of Azad Hind. To bring this home to the mind of every Indian in Malaya and to rouse our community to a full realisation of the responsibilities of the new status, it has been decided to ask each member of the Indian Independence League to take an oath of allegiance to the Provisional Government of Azad Hind. Detailed directions regarding this have already been sent to all the State branches along with the form of the oath. Each member, on taking the oath, will be given 'oath of allegiance card', and the "Indian Independence League membership card " he or she now holds will be taken back by the officer administering the oath and destroyed. The privilege of owing allegiance to our government will be extended only to members of the Indian Independence League as any Indian who is not a member of the League cannot be considered as a true Indian. As Netaji said in his speech in Syonan on 25th October 'we will not treat them as Indians or friends. There is no place for them in India."

What I wish to point out is that in so far as these documents are concerned they evince the same interest as was evinced by those who issued the Proclamation of Independence of the United States of America.

The next point to which I wish to call attention in this context is the law of treason with reference to India. So far as India is concerned, it is a loose expresssion. The whole of the law on this subject has been codified in the Indian Panal Code and I call attention to Chapter VI of the Indian Penal Code—Offences against the State. There you find codified what is the law of treason in other countries. Section 121 is waging or attempting to wage war against the Queen, 121A is conspiracy to commit offences punishable by 121,122 is collecting arms; 123 is concealing with intent to facilitate design to wage war; 124 is assaulting Governor-General, etc., 124A is sedition; 125 is waging war against any Asiatic power in alliance with the Queen, 126 is committing depredation on territories of a power at peace with the Queen; and 127 is receiving property taken by war or depredation mentioned in Sections 125 and 126; 128 is public servant voluntarily allowing prisoner of State or war to escape; 129 refers to a public servant negligently suffering such prisoner to escape. These are the offences against the State.

My submission to the Court is this. In so far as the question of the law of treason is concerned in this country, my learned friend cannot talk of treason. For what would be called treason in the common law of England, my learned friend would have to look to the language of Chapter VI of the Indian Penal Code. In other words my submission to the Court is this—that generally speaking, apart from Section 121, my learned friend will not and has no right to resort to what he calls the principles of treason.

The next point to which I shall call attention is a classic book on the Law of England written in the old English. I have got a transcript of it here. It is on page 95:-

When a nation has placed itself under the protection of another that is more powerful, or has even entered into subjection to it with a view to receiving its protection—if the latter does not effectually protect the other in case of need, it is manifest that, by failing in its engagements, it loses all the rights it had acquired by the convention, and that the other being disengaged from the obligation it had contracted, re-enters into the possession of all its rights, and recovers its independence or its liberty. It is to be observed that this takes place even in cases where the protector does not fail in his engagements through a want of good faith but merely through inability. For the weaker nation having submitted only for the sake of obtaining protection—if the other proves unable to fulfil that essential condition, the compact is dissolved—the weaker resumes its right, and may, if it thinks proper, have recourse to a more effectual protection. Thus the Dukes of Austria, who had acquired a right of protection and in some sort a sovereignty over the City of Lucerne being unwilling or unable to protect it effectually, that city concluded an alliance with the three first cantons; and the Dukes having carried their complaint to the Emperor, the inhabitants of Lucerne replied "that they had used the natural right common to all men by which everyone is permitted to endeavour to procure his own safety when he is abandoned by those who are obliged to grant him assistance."

This is the law which has been enunciated and accepted in England ever since. This was in 1797.

My submission is that the insurgents are in the position of rebles up to a stage, but a stage is reached where if the State has an organised army it becomes possessed of the right of belligerency, even though they may ultimately fail. The question of allegiance does not arise then, but I would not be surprised if with a view to divert the discussion into a wrong channel any such statement is made.

Before I go further, I wish to make quite clear a point about the prisoners of war. The prisoners of war may submit even to the extent of assisting the enemy—that is passive assistance up to the point of labour. You will find in the same books that they may not actually join the enemy and in this connection I wish to submit to the Court what was the relation of the I.N.A. to the Japanese. You belong to the profession of arms and will appreciate what I am submitting to you. I have stated the position as much against myself as possible. I am now assuming the events which took place at Farrar Park did not take place. I am assuming against myself that they were just prisoners of war. The question still remains what it is that they did. The question arises whether they ever allowed themselves to be used as what I might call tools of the enemy or any other instruments, whatever the phrase used. Having been surrendered as prisoners of war, if the Japanese chose to leave the Indians to secure their liberty—I am willing to agree that it suited them—that by itself does not bring the I.N.A. and the accused before us within the prohibition imposed upon the prisoners of war. It is a point that I wish to elaborate up to a stage. I wish to state that there is no obligation whatever which prevents a person who is a prisoner of war from fighting on his own for the liberty of his own country. I submit that my learned friend will not be able to controvert that, and therefore I wish to make it quite plain that the question of the relation between the Japanese Army and the I.N.A., the question of the Objective of the Japanese Army and the I.N.A., the question of the objective of the

Japanese as regards India—these points have got to be re-emphasized before this Court. Unless they are borne in mind, the Court may easily go into a wrong track.

The point is this. I quite agree that the Court or any member of it may say: "They were fools in believing the Japanese". That has nothing to do with the case. Other men may have been wiser. The question is whether those who formed the I.N.A. did believe in a *bona fide* manner that they would be able to secure the freedom of the country. If they *bona fide* believed it, the fact that there are wiser men on earth does not alter the issue so far as the renouncement of the guilt of that army fighting for the liberation of India is concerned. Hence it is that I wish to submit that the evidence which I submitted yesterday and a few more passages to which I wish to call attention today is relevant for that purpose. You have it in evidence and it is a matter again in which the question is of one's own belief. The question is not whether that belief was something which probably the Court or any member of it may think was of very credulous people. That has nothing to do with the point. You have it definitely in evidence before this Court, in the evidence of prosecution witnesses, that if any nation or any race or any class came into being to oppose the independence of India, they were prepared to fight that, including the Japanese. That is why I was very anxious to point out that it is only when a story is completely pieced up and comes before the Court that its significance can be appreciated. The whole point of it is that the question is not so much as to whether you or I or anybody else would have relied upon it as a promise. From that point of view probably we are a credulous race. We have relied on many promises of others and of Japanese also. But that has nothing to do with the point. The point is that if these people honestly believed, as I say they did, that they were securing the independence of India, then the question of what a prisoner of war cannot do, does not actually arise and will not arise.

In this connection I would like to read the evidence of Nag. The question that I put to him was: Do you remember ever attending a meeting in Singapore at which Capt. Mohan Singh told the prisoners of war that if need be they would fight the Japanese in addition to the British? He said he would fight anybody who stood in his way even if it were the Japanese or anybody else. The next is P.W. 9 Havildar Sucha Singh, and this is the passage to which I wish to refer: "He said that the I.N.A. has already been started in Singapore and a good many people had joined it; and the I.N.A. will only fight for the freedom of India and for no other cause. If we go to India the Japanese go with us, we are equipped with arms, and we will fight the Japanese if they turn round against us. This is a golden chance for us and we may not get such a chance again." The next witness is P.W. 18. He said: "After I was posted to Bose Brigade, Captain Shah Nawaz Khan delivered a lecture which I heard. He said that the Bose Brigade which was formed was to go first of all to the front, and this Brigade is composed of picked officers and men." And then the passage goes on: "He also said that if and when we fight with our allies the Japanese nations, it should not happen that we remain as second rate in the fight and thus disgrace our nation. When we reach India we shall meet Indian men and women, and those who are elders to us we should consider them as mothers and those who are younger we should consider them as our daughters and sisters, and if anybody will not obey these instructions he will be shot dead; and if and when India is freed and the Japanese who are now helping us tried to subdue us, we shall even fight them. He also said that even now if a Japanese gives you one slap, you should give him three in return, because our Government is parallel to their Japanese Government, and we are in no way subservient to them, and that when we reach India, if we notice any Japanese maltreating an Indian lady he should be first warned by word of mouth not to do so, but if he continued to do so, we were at liberty to use force and even shoot him in order to prevent it, because the fight which we are making now is for the freedom and well-being of India and not for the benefit of the Japanese. This lecture was delivered in Taiping." Then, I come to P.W. 19. He said : "I was aware of the declaration of the Provisional Government of Free India. Prior to my joining the I.N.A. I was in a prisoner of war camp." Then I came to the other passage which is relevant for the purpose. "I knew after joining the army that the sole ambition of the I.N.A. was to fight for the freedom of India against any army in the world, but my own idea was not to fight but escape. By 'any army in the world' is meant also the Japanese." Then I come to P.W. 24. He said : "In August 1943 I was in Neesoon Camp. Captain Shah Nawaz came to address the Heavy Gun Battalion there. He said that the I.N.A. had been formed for the liberation of India and it would fight not only British Imperialism but also those would put obstacles in the way of India's freedom or any other party which wished to subjugate India."

I had hitherto avoided reading any evidence because there was no substantial contest as to the facts which have been proved. The record of evidence clearly shows that in so far as the I.N.A. was concerned, they acted on their own. No doubt, they accepted the alliance with Japan on promises which they, at all events, honestly and sincerely believed, and if they believed them, I submit there can be no question of any obligation.

There are so many matters which have been gone into and which in patience we suffered in the belief that there was no relevancy to the charges before the Court. But now that they are before the Court, I must separate them as best as I can and, while separating them, give answer to every single suggestion that was made or is likely to be made. Hence it is that I am here before the Court to point out that in doing what the I.N.A. did, there was no question of any breach of any obligation or the prisoner of war obligations or duties, remembering the extreme obligation, which, I submit, I have stated as strongly against myself as it is possible to do.

The next point to which I wish to call attention is this. In addition, there is the evidence of the last witness, P.W.12, and that sets out more or less fully the point of view of those who honestly believed in doing what they did. I am not saying that the Court is not called upon to examine the matter in its own light. At the same time, the Court has got to see not so much what any individual member might have done as that whether you believe what they said before this Court and that was their object.

This witness said: "My reasons for joining I.N.A. were many. I admit that it was a difficult question to decide whether I should join the I.N.A. or not, because there were many factors which I had to consider. It was a momentous decision. Uptil that time I was not greatly interested in politics or the political welfare of India because I was educated that way, and moreover when I joined the Indian Army in 1936, I felt that politics was not encouraged in the Indian Army and hence I stayed away, but when the question of I.N.A. arose and we had to decide whether we should join it or not, I had to think deep, but it was such a big question that I could not make a decision myself."

The reason why I am reading this to the Court is this. He was a witness of truth and the very fact that they had a conflict in their minds is illustrative of the extreme *bonafides* of the men who chose to take the course which they did. Hence it is that I shall read a few more lines of that evidence: "I remember sometime in the beginning of July 1942, when we were being asked whether we were going to volunteer for the I.N.A. or not, I was staying at Mount Pleasant, Singapore, where Capt. Mohan Singh had his Headquarters. I know Capt. Sahgal for the last 12 or 13 years; we were in College together and we were friends there. I felt that if I had a discussion with him along with a few other officers, we may come to some decision regarding volunteering for the I.N.A. So in the beginning of July, he and two or three other officers came to my bungalow at Mount Pleasant and we went through this question of joining the I.N.A. We discussed all the pros and cons. We unanimously decided that under the circumstances we all owed our allegiance to our country.

"We also felt and agreed upon that so far concerning our career in the Indian Army, there had been distinctions between the British Officers and the Indian Commissioned Officers. The Indian Commissioned Officers had not been treated as well as our English comrades or brother officers. We also felt that if the senior officers present in Singapore or in Malaya did not join the I.N.A., it was quite possible that the Japanese would exploit the Indian prisoners of war, because then the Indian prisoners of war would be split up into small groups. Some people would join and some would not, and the Japanese would take advantage of that and enrole people from amongst the prisoners of war who would be willing to do any service for them. We felt that that would be a disgrace to Indians. We agreed that if the senior officers joined the I.N.A. and formed a strong party and organised the I.N.A. as a regular army and fought the Japanese on every point regarding the army, we would have a far stronger position with the Japanese than otherwise. We also felt that if we created an army of our own, we may be able to establish a certain amount of standing with the Japanese, and by doing that we may be able to stop the Japanese from committing any atrocities on the Indians in Malaya. We had seen what the Japanese were doing to the Chinese and Anglo-Indians and the Malayans. They were not treating them very well. Certain atrocities had been committed on the Chinese and also on the Eurasian community, and we thought that if the Indians refused to join the I.N.A., it was quite possible that the whole of the Indian community in Singapore or in Malaya might suffer. So we had a discussion on all these points. But then arose the question that if we did join the Indian National Army, what would be the reaction of our people in India?"

My suggestion to the Court is this that, apart from the process, the thought which the last witness brought to bear upon it and the discussions which he had with other people, clearly show that they did not take the steps either dishonestly or hastily. They took this step after taking into account the whole of the situation in existence at that time, and the future as they saw it.

And if that is the condition in which they did it, I ask the Court to hold that they honestly believed in the propriety of the step they took and the justice of the cause for which they took it. And hence it is that I wish to point out to the Court that it was not a case, as the text-books say, of a prisoner of war joining the enemy in order to fight his battle. That, I quite agree, according to the text-books, he may not do. But where a prisoner of war already of war released, as I have told you earlier, finds himself in the situation in which he did and then fights for himself and for his own country, being prepared to fight against the Japanese themselves if they ever became untrue to them, in such circumstances, I submit, there was no question and there could be no question of the Indian National Army being guilty and of those who joined that army being guilty of any act which may be regarded as contrary even to what you may call the code of duties imposed upon a prisoner of war. I have already submitted and at the risk of repetition I will say, that it is entirely irrelevant and there is no such thing as a charge against these men before you of a breach of duty as prisoners of war. In fact there is no such charge in the Indian Penal Code, so far as I can see. There may be a charge under the Indian Army Act but no such charge is at present before you. There is not even a charge of desertion and indeed there cannot be, for when the prisoners of war were surrendered there was no occasion for desertion. So let us not be carried away by what you may call the popular language of desertion, breach of duty and all the rest of it. Let us concentrate, and I ask the Court so to do, on the charge on which the accused are on trial before the Court, and on that only. The rest is a matter of prejudice; and if one has a complete answer even on a matter of prejudice, it is a matter of satisfaction. It is a matter which I understand—and I appreciate— that tribunals of this kind are likely to take account of, namely, that general *bonafide,* honestly and integrity all goes to the credit of individuals who are on trial as so much in their favour.

Then, Sir, there is one piece of evidence in so far as this particular matter is concerned, a piece of evidence of extreme importance, and that is how the first I.N.A. broke up. As to how it broke up you have evidence before the Court and it is unanimous as to the reasons for which that event occurred. Rash Behari Bose was for many years in Japan and he was too easily inclined—to put it most mildly—to believe in the Japanese. Mohan Singh on the other hand was very cautious. Mohan Singh in fact has himself evinced by his conduct that should anything happen to him, that is to say, if he is arrested or removed, the army should be dissolved. And the real reason is this, that while on the one hand Mohan Singh was anxious that there should be an army formed for the liberation of India, at the same time he was equally anxious that the army should not serve as a mere instrument of Japan. And it is because he had his suspicions, is because—of the Resolutions in the Bangkok Conference with regard to making clear the aims of the Japanese for the purpose of fighting the war so far as India was concerned—that Mohan Singh began to lose faith in the promises of the Japanese. And as soon as the Japanese realised that through the agency of Rash Behari Bose—and you have picturesque evidence here—Rash Behari Bose came along, collected all the senior officers and declared that Mohan Singh had been removed. I could not quite appreciate, with all the throught that I devoted to it, the point that my learned friend made or attempted to make as to whether he was actually removed by Rash Behari Bose or by the Japanese. For my own part I do not mind the suggestion that my learned friend made that the Japanese arrested him. That is precisely the point, that the first I.N.A. was at a stage at which there was a trial of strength between those Indian National Army and those who were likely or wanting to join it were not prepared to become tools in their hands, that there was a break, and hence when you come to the second I.N.A., when Subhas Chandre Bose took command of the Indian National Army, the second time you find an association between the two armies—may be very unwilling on the part of the Japanese. Very often one has to make a choice when one finds strong man on the otherside; and hence it is that I wish to insist before this Court that throughout the dealings between the I.N.A. and the Head of the Provisional Government of Free India at the time, the position taken up by them was not an instrument of the Japanese, but a body formed with the object of liberating themselves, no doubt getting all the assistance that they could from the Japanese as an allied army. And that, I submit, is the key to the *bonafide* of the belief of every individual man who at all events thinkingly—if I may use that expression—joined the I.N.A. I dare say it often happens in the world that once you find a thinking and leading man taking a course, other people *bonafide* believe it to be the true course and join it. Therefore I submit there is ample evidence on record, evidence emanating from witnesses which in ordinary courts and tribunals is the best to be relied upon by the defence, evidence from prosecution witnesses, not all willingly given, that they fought their own ground, they fought their own cause, and therefore there was no question whatsoever of their breaking any duties which they owed as prisoners of war. But you have to remember to all the time and again and again that there is no such charge in the trial before you. There are only two charges before you which I need not repeat. But I want to be quite careful because it will be my duty to deal with the material, lest it might be suggested that I did not deal with it, and I wish to point out its relevancy and its significance to the extent to which these points bear on the conduct of the men on trial before you. I have no desire to shirk an inquiry; in fact I am here as far as I can—apart from any question of private opinions on political issues—to impress upon you the truth, integrity and sincerity of men, which after all is a bigger asset sometimes than the legal technical issue. There is also the evidence of Lt.-Col. Loganadan, D.W.7 with reference to the question; and I am obliged to refer to it particularly because of the pamphlet called " Our Struggle" which was placed before you. There is just one point which I must make before I read the evidence, that all that is proved is that the pamphlet was issued. But I hope and trust that my learned friend will not suggest that the mere fact that a pamphlet is issued, that by itself proves the truth of the statements made therein. Let me therefore begin by saying that I am not obliged to explain why Rash Behari Bose said what he did. It will be an error on the part of the Court to say that because Rash Behari Bose said something about Mohan Singh, therefore it is true. At the same time I wish to call attention to this evidence with a view of pointing out the terms on which Mohan Singh and Rash Behari Bose stood, with a view to point out that any allegations emanating from the disappointed Rash Behari Bose at that time are not to be taken as words of truth. Secondly, in any case an allegation made by A against B, neither of whom has appeared in Court as a witness, is no proof of the allegation made by him.

With this observation I now call attention to the evidence of D.W.7 (Lt.-Col. Loganadan).

"I know Captain Mohan Singh. When I joined the Indian National Army, he was G.O.C. The relations between Captain Mohan Singh and Rash Behari Bose were not very happy. Of my own personal knowledge I knew that Rash Behari Bose, having lived so long with the Japanese, was inclined to be guided and controlled by them. Whereas Mohan Singh said he felt that the Japanese should be dealt with a firmer hand than what Rash Behari would be able to do."

I then come to P. W.12 (Captain Arshad). The passage to which I call attention is this:-

" I was in the first Indian National Army Headquarters, they as General Staff Office in 'G' Branch. The first I.N.A. was dissolved in December 1942. The I.N.A. had been raised after the Bangkok resolutions were forwarded for ratification to the Japanese Government. The Bangkok resolutions were the result of a Conference held in Bangkok in June. There were many resolutions in that and they were passed by the Conference and then sent to the Japanese Government for ratification, and we hoped that the ratification would come quickly; but as the days went by, Captain Mohan Singh, who was then G. O. C. of the Indian National Army, felt that the Japanese were delaying the ratification of the Bangkok resolutions and he asked the Japanese liaison body which was attached to us, called the Iwakuru Kikan to expedite the ratification of the resolutions. They were not very clear in their replies. They tried to delay them as much as possible. I was present. Captain Mohan Singh kept his Headquarters informed of all the correspondence and the arguments which he was having with the Japanese. Captain Mohan Singh told us his doubts of the intentions of the Japanese. He said that he noticed that the Japanese were not playing the game, and he said that if the Japanese continued with that attitude of theirs he would dissolve the Indians National Army, and we all agreed with him because we felt that unless and until there was a clear understanding between the I.N.A. and the Japanese we would not continue the Indian National Army. Besides that, there was another main point of dissension between the Japanese and Captain Mohan Singh. At the Farrar Park meeting the Japanese had handed over all the Indian prisoners of war to Captain Mohan Singh. Until that time the members of the I.N.A. as well as those prisoners of war who had not joined the I.N.A. were under the command of Captain Mohan Singh. But in December the Japanese wanted to take those people away from Captain Mohan Singh who had not joined the I.N.A. Captain Mohan Singh felt that the Japanese were not keeping to their word and he refused to part with the prisoners of war. These main reasons as well as the other minor reasons forced us to dissolve the I.N.A.

And, Sir, the Bangkok Resolution No.13 which is referred to, reads thus :

"(13) Resolved that the Indian National Army shall be made use of only.

(a) For operations against the British or other foreign powers in India.

(b) For the purpose of securing and safeguarding Indian National Independence, and

(c) For such other purpose as may assist the achievement of the object, viz., Indian Independence."

Lt. Nag (P.W.1) refers to the same subject in these terms :

"Capt. Mohan Singh left written instructions that if he was arrested, the I.N.A. should be dissolved. 'In the event of my arrest the I.N.A. will be dissolved and all the I.N.A. badges of rank and records will be destroyed.' There was a general feeling from the beginning that the I.N.A. should not be subordinated to the Japanese and that we would not allow it to be subordinated to the Japanese. There was no question of dissolving it at any time during those days. The predominant motive was to free India for the sake of Indians.

"After the 2nd I.N.A. was formed the same feeling was there, untill Subhas Chandra Bose arrived in July 1943. After that everybody thought that they had got a leader who could guide them on proper lines without being subordinated to the Japanese. Thereafter the two armies fought as Allies, i.e., the Indian National Army and, the Japanese."

This, Sir, is the evidence which has been placed before this Court. As I said, my submission before the Court is that it was when the I.N.A., which was formed on the second occasion, felt confident that they would not be subordinated to the Japanese that they really fought as Allies. And hence it is that I submit to the Court that in so far as relations between the I.N.A. and the Japanese Army were concerned, it has been established by evidence that they were of the character which I claim for them, namely as allies. So far as the I.N.A. was concerned, it was actuated by only motive and one business, and that was to secure the freedom of India. That is the issue, which as I have said, does not actually arise, but was bearing on the integrity of purpose of those who are on trial as members of the Indian National Army.

Then the next point of which I wish to call attention is the evidence before the Court that the Indian National Army was completely officered by Indian officers. True, an attempt was made by my learned friend in cross-examination as to the question of the High Command. I do not deny for a moment, though I do not understand or profess to understand very much the organisation of armies when they fight together for apparently the same purpose in any case, but knowing what you do about the last but one war and the last war, when any question arises of unified command it serves very little purpose to suggest that in so far as the higher strategy is concerned, it was no doubt in the hands of the Japanese. No doubt probably they claimed at all events that they understood the art of war better, and that after all the Indian National Army consisted of men of not that standing. But apart from accepting better judgment on what should be the proper strategy, when it came to a question of internal administration of the I.N.A., it has been amply proved before the Court that the I.N.A. was entirely independent in its composition, including every officer. The evidence of Lt. Nag is in these terms:

"The whole of the Indian National Army was trained by Indian Officers and not by the Japanese. It was entirely and throughout officered by Indian officers and not by Japanese officers.

The colours of the Indian National Army were the Indian National Congress colours, i.e., saffron, white and green. Their badges were distinct from the Japanese badges."

And then he answered other questions which are immaterial, namely, that among the colours in the middle of one of the badges there was a brown star and it was resented by the personnel of the I.N.A. as it might be mistaken for the Rising Sun.

P. W. 19 gave the following evidence:

"So far as I am concerned, I took instructions from our own Indian officer a only and not from the Japanese. As far as I am aware, there were no Japanese in command in our area or otherwise in the I.N.A. I was Assistant to Lt. Abdur Rehman who was left in charge of the rations at Falam. There was a long carry of 48 miles for rations. The rations consisted of rice, salt, oil and sugar. Sugar was very scarce. The rations were very short consisting of rice, salt and a little oil. The Indian National Army was fighting under great hardship on that front. Whilst I was in the I.N.A., I carried out my duties faithfully."

The next point which I wish to make is that apart from what you may call the general higher strategy, the Indian National Army was completely independent. And through I am not anticipating a point which it will be my duty to argue, namely, whether or not the question arose that people joined the I.N.A. because they might be worse off as prisoner of war, the less said about it the better. The evidence clearly shows that the only ration that the I.N.A. had, apart from sugar and oil which was nominal, was rice, and that was the luxury which attracted men to the I.N.A. My learned friend will consider twice over before trying any such argument. The question really is that one set of men believed in a cause and the other set of men either from supineness or otherwise did not, and nobody ever gave thought to the question as to whether one would be better off or not. One thing is quite certain: that apart from what actually happened by the Japanese, those who joined the I.N.A. were certainly facing the possibilities which every soldier has to face, unless he wishes to avoid it, which prisoners of war could, namely, fighting with the opponent army. And, therefore, my submission to the Court is that this idea of contrasting the comforts of the I.N.A. and the comforts of the prisoners of war under the Japanese, is entirely overdone. It is entirely a question as to what points of view appealed to one or the other sets of men, and therefore, Sir, my submission is that in so far as that is concerned, we have now been able to place before the Court the actual evidence on the question.

The next point is that the I.N.A. was a purely voluntary army, and notwithstanding the attempt made, the Prosecution entirely failed to prove that it was not voluntary, because from time to time it has been proved before this Court by the speeches made by the accused and Sri Subhas Chandra Bose, which indicate that at every stage opportunity was given to every member of the I.N.A. to withdraw if he chose to do so. But the strongest evidence is this: It is common ground, apart from actual principles which have not been accurately proved, that only a portion of the volunteers could be armed, equipped and trained, because of the paucity of material, and that there was a large number of people who could not be trained and could not be armed for want of resources—what is called the surplus volunteers. But I put it to you, Sir, as men of commonsense that it would require very much effort on the part of my learned friend to say that when they had more than enough men already, that they coerced more people to join the I.N.A. Or, in the language of Lord Shaw, I think it is a statement that stultifies itself because it is stated that 'we have enough men and we cannot arm them,' and yet it is alleged that you go on coercing people to join. I think it is a folly of which no decent human being would be guilty if he had a grain of commonsense. What has actually happened is that people have been punished for crime of their own, and in order to appear glorious before this Court, they attributed it to pressure by the I.N.A. It is a very clever half-truth, which is not uncommon.

You get a fact which occurred. Then in order to appear virtuous he would say that he was punished to be coerced to join the I.N.A. A more ludicrous story could not have been presented to the Court, because in one case the witness admitted the reason why that took place. They were sent to the Detention Camp Having been sent there, they were asked to surrender their ringleaders. When they did not, ten people came and there was a free fight—300 on one side and 10 on the other. And for the Government to put forward this sort of half-backed story in order that the Court may swallow it passes one's understanding.

This is Lt. Nag : "I heard Subhas Chandra Bose state at a meeting held soon after the meeting of the 21st October, 1943, that anyone who wished to leave the I.N.A. was permitted to do so."

P.W.5: "Prior to my arrival at Port Doxon in Kuala Lumpur—at that time I was in the custody of the Japanese-the bad conditions were due to the Japanese. In January—February 1943, I saw Capt. Shah Nawaz for the first time when he came to collect volunteers. I am quite clear that Capt. Shah Nawaz Khan left it open to everybody to join the I.N.A. or not as they chose. I remember that he wanted staunch men who were prepared to lay down their lives for the freedom of India. I never saw Capt. Shah Nawaz after that lecture."

P.W.24: "I reached Popa on the 25th or 26th February. Col. Sahgal said at Popa that those who did not wish to stay in the I.N.A. and wished to gooverto the enemy should tell him today. He will then makearrangements to send them in one party to the enemy, but they will not be permitted to take any arms or papers with them. 'I do not want that men should desert in driblets.' As far as I understand it was Sahgal's intention that after the party went over, men should not go over on driblets and so cause demoralisation,"

P.W.6: "The recruitment was absolutely voluntary. We had surplus volunteers whom we could not train or arm."

P.W.7: "The Indian National Army was purely voluntary. As far as I am aware no coercives methods were used in recruiting. I am aware as a member of the Provisional Government that we declared war on Britain and America."

Then, Sir, there is one more statement referring to Lt. Dhillion, to which I wish to call attention. My submission to the Court is that in so far as the accused before the Court are concerned, they by their open speeches gave everybody to understand that it was entirely their own choice whether to join the I.N.A. or not.

That brings me next to the evidence about the alleged coercion for the purpose of compelling men or inducing men to join the I.N.A. The position, Sir, is this with reference to that. At the time when the question arose as to the admissibility of the evidence, it was candidly stated by the Advocate-General that he did not rely on Sec. 10 but the way in which it is sought to make it relevant is this. He said that the accused did not participate in it, did not do it, did not encourage it. But that they knew about it.

The matter did not rest there. When they asked other people to join the I.N.A., they gave a veiled threat : "Remember if you do not join, what hardships exist." And the matter was further strained before this Court bu saying—meaning thereby among other things— that there would be personal coercion. It was on that statement that this honourable Court was pleased to admit the evidence. Thc attempt was made to show that the accused made this veiled suggestion. That attempt has completely failed because Capt. Dhargalkar who was called to give evidence in support of this, fell through. I shall read that part of his evidence to show that he completely collapsed on what he came to prove. He came to prove that the three caused, or some of them, went with the other officers. He came to support what the Advocate-General was instructed to put forward, namely, that he was given the alleged veiled threat. When we came to cross-examine Capt. Dhargalkar, he said : "I was never asked by anybody. I was never addressed by anybody" and the more significant thing is, he ended by saying : "I cannot state to the Court who said what to anyone." The net result of his evidence amounts to this that the Government having undertaken to this Court to prove that the veiled threat was given in that form, and that meant evidence possible relevant in the eyes of the court, the evidence was allowed to be given. But in the light of the evidence of Capt. Dhargalkar, there is none in which any allegation of veiled threat exists. I therefore ask the Court to hold that evidence as completely irrelevant because it was admitted on this provisional promise, namely, that it would be proved that there was a veiled threat given by the accused, because there is no other way in which it could be made relevant. There is no charge against the accused of any personal cruelty of any kind. There was no charge that they encouraged it, and the mere fact that they had knowledge would not be anything—even that, they have failed to prove. When I pointed out that mere knowledge was not enough, my learned friend added a further point, which I presume induced the Court to allow that and that is when they used the words which they are alleged to have used- "If you do not join remember the hardships"—meaning thereby that inasmuch as they knew that wrong methods were being adopted, they threatened the men by saying wrong methods would be adopted in their case. That I submit is the only process of reasoning by which he attempted to make his evidence relevant. My learned.friend has completely failed to establish either the knowledge or alleged threat and for these reasons, Sirs, I submit that this evidence should not be excluded, and I have prepared a petition so that it may remain on record for my submission.

The learned Judge-Advocate told the Court on the occasion of the question of admission of the evidence:

The learned Advocate-General really bases his case on the speeches of the accused which he will prove showing, as he says, that the accused referred to the hardships which would be inflicted on prisoners of war unless they joined, and thereby implying that they had knowledge of the methods by which he alleges that recruiting for the I.N.A. was being carried on.

At the same time, now we have arrived at a stage when I respectfully ask that the Court should rule that that evidence should be entirely disregarded, because there is no proof of the promise on which that evidence was submitted. That is the formal application I make to the Court.

Judge Advocate : Do you mean that you are asking us to make a decision on this now?

Counsel for Defence : On this point.

Judge Advocate : I am afraid it is not at all the procedure to make piecemeal decision on parts of the case, without hearing the learned Advocate-General and without hearing me. That decision will be made in due course, but I must ask the Court that they should go on now without making any piecemeal decision at this present stage.

Sri Desai : I shall leave it at that. I thought that I would save the Court, and perhaps incidentally myself, the necessity of having to go through that evidence, to show how utterly useless it is. But that being the view of the Court, I will not pursue it.

That brings me to the next question. My submission is that the basis on which that evidence was admitted has completely disappeared; and inasmuch as it has disappeared it should not be taken into considered in this case at all.

The only reason why I thought it my duty to call the attention of the Court at this stage was that you might have to go through the evidence and think if it is relevant.

The first witness, to whose evidence I think it necessary to call the attention of the Court, is Capt. Dhargalkar. This is what Captain Dhargalkar said in his examination in chief:

"I do not remember Lt. Dhillion being there, but I remember Capt. Shah Nawaz Khan and Capt. Sahgal coming there. I recognise both these officers as accused before the Court. Neither of the two accused ever spoke to me, but discussions usually took place and nearly all the discussions were concerned with our joining the I.N.A. I was present at these discussions. It is very difficult for me to quote the exact word which Capt. Sahgal and Capt. Shah Nawaz Khan said, but the gist of the thing was : 'Why don't you all join the I.N.A. rather than waste yourselves living under these conditions'."

That is really the whole point. Let me examine whether the promise is fulfilled even in the examination-in-chief. If "conditions" merely meant conditions as prisoners of war, whether for the time being under the I.N.A. or the Japanese, that is not a matter of charging the accused. But I suppose my learned friend will use the word "conditions" to mean almost anything, meaning thereby that "some people did something to somebody else and that will be your condition." I submit it does not carry the matter far enough.

I would then call attention to the cross-examination of this witness. He says:

"I saw all the three accused on several occasions. I saw them anything between 20 to 50 times. I only spoke to Capt. Sahgal a couple of times; I do not remember having spoken to Capt. Shah Nawaz Khan or Lt. Dhillon. I spoke to Capt. Sahgal in Col. Bhonsle's house. I cannot remember any other occasion. I was present at fifteen occasions at which discussions took place. Capt. Shah Nawaz may have been present about twice and Capt. Sahgal was present about the same number of times. This was in a

Separation Camp at Bidadari. There was one huge Camp at Bidadari and also a Separation camp. I was in the Separation Camp. The whole of the Bidadari Camp was the Indian National Army Camp. We were taken by Capt. Mohan Singh. There were about sixteen of us living in the room. I did not take part in the discussion nor was I addressed by Capt. Shah Nawaz or Capt. Sahgal. That is all that happened during the discussion."

Then he goes on to say:

"Capt. Shah Nawaz Khan came there, but I do not know whether he came to see Capt. Sher Dil Khan. I was not invited to a discussion, I was living in the room and I overheard certain conversations. I cannot remember the words of these discussions accurately but I remember the gist of them. The gist of the conversation included many other subjects other than the Indian National Army. I was addressed but not by any of the officers present there. Capt. Shah Nawaz Khan was speaking to 16 other people. The gist of his conversation was : "Why do you join the Indian National Army?" I remember that occasion to the best of my knowledge. It may have been any time in that month. I cannot remember all that he said. I cannot say exactly what he said."

(You will see, Sirs, a change in the gist. There was no question of what consequences would follow.)

"I cannot remember exactly what he said. I cannot single out from the others what Capt. Shah Nawaz Khan said. My answer is the same with regard to Capt. Sahgal. What I told the Court is the generel impression without knowing who said what."

This is the evidence of Capt. Dhargalkar, and I respectfully and emphatically submit to the Court that the promise on which that evidence was admitted remains unfulfilled: and inasmuch as it remains unfulfilled, my submission is that the evidence should be disregarded completely.

Now, with that submission and in view of the record, it is my duty very briefly to examine the evidence which has actually been given, and I will preface the examination with this remark. This is a case where in some instances what is called a half-truth implies an untruth : e.g., there was a Detention Camp where people were taken if they were guilty of acts of insubordination or any other act contrary to the discipline of an army. Having been taken there, there was no doubt a certain amount of tasks and fatigues they were asked to do. That is perfectly true, but that having been done, the man wants to make a martrydom of it. I will tell you why. He says he was taken there and he was asked to join the I.N.A. It is all, I submit, embroidery of the case, and I will ask the Court to examine that evidence in that light, and in one or two instances I shall be able to show that reluctantly he almost admitted the case I put to him, that he was sent there because he was guilty of insubordination. People very picturesquely said they were asked to pick up one end of a pole and every time a man followed them or hit them—I think the very exaggeration defeated its own purpose. I do not think any Court will believe such an absurd story. True, he was taken there, and no doubt he had to do a certain amount of fatigue. No doubt it may be that a noncommissioned officer thought it was below his dignity to pick up things which were necessary. In fact you might remember with what amount of reluctance the witnesses gave the kind of evidence before the Court—I would recall a picture of one of the witnesses when I told him that this was only for the purposes of manure and there was the evidence of a garden—it almist taxed one's patience to be able to get out of him that evidence, and get him to admit those facts; and even then he kept on saying "Oh, there was a road there and in between there was something and if you call it a garden it is wrong and so on". The fact remains that the witness was taken there for some act of insubordination; he was put to a certain amount of task, but then in order to glorify himself as a martyr, he now comes forward before this Court and says "I was taken there because I did not join the I.N.A." And when I cross-examined him as to what distinguished career he had, he ultimately collapses and admits he was an ordinary soldier. To think therefore that stories of this kind would pass muster before a Court composed of men of affairs and experience, I submit, will not do.

I call attention first to Wolit Bahadur, P.W. 14. The kind of picture he gave—this method of carrying baskets at the end of a pole—I do not suppose it is any great innovation or torture, unknown in India. The way in which he described it, and if he was not giving evidence before men of experience in this country, was almost insulting to one's intelligence. After all it is common method of carrying a load on bars with a man at each end; and if he objects to carring a load like that I am very sorry for him: but I am afraid he has to labour, and if he has to work, he has to work ; and the more we learn to do manual labour, I think, the better for men of my country.

And then he said—it was a ridiculous story—he carried out the order and picked up the cow-dung. There came a road. There were six men who stood just for the purpose of giving a stroke as he lifted the load. That I submit defeats itself. In cross-examination—that is where I wish to call attention to a few passages—this is what he says : "He said that we had now fallen from the English into the Japanese hands and we have to carry out their orders and do their fatigues. He told us that the British had run away and left us there. He said that our home was in India and we have to join with other Indians to fight for India. He also said that for this reason we should join the I.N.A. He also said that the I.N.A. was being formed to set India free. He said that for this reason we should join the I.N.A. About one or two men said that they did not know anything about the I.N.A. and they were not going to join it. At that time we did not know what this I.N.A. was. I know Jamadar Til Bahadur Adhikari." This is a very important thing. They are the people who are said to have come in this party to attack this gentleman and his friends in order that they may be coerced to join the I.N.A. It would be fortunate if one can think a little in advance. He admitted that every single one of them who took part in this raid to induce this gentleman and his friends to join the I.N.A. were all men respected in their Regiment and respected in the parts of the country from which they came. If he had only realised what it involved, he would probably not have admitted it. "I came to know that the I.N.A. was being formed. I knew Jamadar Til Bahadur Adhikari. Jamadar Puran Singh Khawas was a man who was respected by our unit and so was Jamadar Til Bahadur Adhikari. Jamadar Til Bahadur delivered only one lecture at which I was present. He also told us about the object of the I.N.A. which was the same as Puran Singh had told us. When Til Bahadur delivered the lecture there were about 600 men present." He admitted to me that they were being asked in the ordinary course to join the I.N.A., asked by people whom he admitted to be respectable and the point in asking for the admission is this, that those were among the people who came armed with a view to attack these innocent men in order that they may join the I.N.A. I make a present of that kind of story for your acceptance.

Then, Sir, comes in very common parlance the cat out of the bag. "Those who did not join the I.N.A. were required to do fatigues for the Japanese. Those who joined the I.N.A. were not required to do fatigues for the Japanese."

Prosecution Counsel: I am afraid my learned friend is under a misapprehension. He gave no names.

Defence Counsel: In his examination-in-chief he gave the names of the people who formed the party of attackers. It comes in cross-examination.

Prosecution Counsel: He does not say that these were the people who came to assault him. I know my learned friend put those names to him. No such questions were asked that these were the people who were in the firing party.

Judge Advocate: That certainly was not said, Mr. Desai.

Mr. Desai: The point of the argument will be perceived, name or no name.

"Those who did not join the I.N.A. were required to do fatigue for the Japanese. There was dispute when we refused to do fatigue duties for the Japanese. The leaders whom I have named told us not to object to the fatigue. In spite of their persuasion some of us did not obey. We reported that we will do fatigues for the Japanese but we have nothing to do with the I.N.A. The guard was sent because some of us did not obey". That is the point. The point is that it was not because they were to be persuaded to join the I.N.A. that the guard was sent. On his own admission they did not obey to do the task they were sent on and that destroys the whole of that evidence, names or no names. His whole purpose was that these people came on their own with a view just to educate them, because they would not join the I.N.A. If my learned friend will follow the process of cross-examination and the admission made by Wolit Bahadur, I only point out that it was up to the witness to say that they were not in the firing party.

Judge Advocate: It is you here who is in the wrong. You have said that these men were in the firing party, whereas it was pointed out that they were not.

Mr. Desai: There is the evidence in chief. I took the names from the summary of evidence. Because of that ruling the names were not allowed to be given. Whether the witness proved or failed to prove that the attack took place, because they would not join the I.N.A. that is the true issue, and remembering that to be the true issue, I beg leave to read where I left, and that is this: "There was a dispute when we refused to do fatigue duties for the Japanese. The leaders whom I have named told us not to object to do fatigue. In spite of their persuasion some of us did not obey. We reported that we will do fatigues for the Japanese but we have nothing to do with the I.N.A. The guard was sent (that is the material point) because some of us did not obey." You cannot get out of that. In other words the story that the guard was sent with a view to shoot them because they did not join the I.N.A., is entirely destroyed by this evidence. "The guard was sent because some of us did not obey. The guard came to seize the ring-leaders." That is precisely my point. I said they were all guilty of one or other offence against discipline, and hence action was taken against them, and this is the best illustration. Of course people get warned: after one man has been cross-examined you may not get the same type of actual admission. But here you have the clearest possible admission, the negation, the complete negation that any attack was made on them, because they did not join the I.N.A. Of course, they always repeat like parrots, when it becomes necessary : that is what happens. But occasionally there are lapses. "The guard was sent because some of us did not obey. The guard came to arrest the ring-leaders. We were about 550 men. Some of the men had a dispute with the guard stopped us from doing this and then fired in the air." What possible course forsooth—it was sent for the purpose of asking them to join the I.N.A. and they should have fired in the air! The whole point is that these were recalcitrants, a disobedient crowd. They were asked to surrender. As a warning they fired in the air. They would not obey. Of course the trouble took place. "When we did not obey the order of the guard, they fired. The guard did not prevent us from young fatigue but they spoke to us about I. N. A. which we did not obey." All this rubbish is difficult to understand. "First they fired in the air, and when we did not obey ultimately they fired at us. About two or three men were injured after the firing. Then we pursued the guard. The dispute between the guard and ourselves was that we resented the appearance of the guard during the lecture time." I do not know what it means. Whatever that means, they know better. As I said here, it is a complete demolition and the best illustration of how the false is mixed up with the true. There is no doubt that there was a scuffle. That is not denied. But they want to annex the scuffle to something else. That is a piece with all the evidence with which I am familiar. You get hold of a known fact which is not disputed, and then put it on to something else. My submission to the Court is that this evidence alone is sufficient to discredit the kind of evidence the Government has put forward with a view to show that atrocities were inflicted for the purpose of joining the I.N.A. As to the tortures, they were of two kinds. Regarding one, I have got definitely out of the mouth of the witness himself that they objected to the fatigue. They were persuaded not to do it. The very leaders whom they respected, persuaded them not to object to do fatigue. They were again asked to surrender their ring-leaders. These people would not. They fired in the air and ultimately they fired at us. Three people died and there were 550 of them. Such evidence, can my learned friend or any gentleman in his very high position ever place before the Court, name or no name?

Prosecution Counsel: I only corrected a statement which was not justified by the record.

Mr. Desai: I admit that I was in the wrong. I say the point of the argument is really this that the witness who came to swear false to the fact that the party was sent armed with a view to fire at them in order to compel them to join the I.N.A., here stands on his own evidence self-condemned. He admits that the purpose was different. The occasion was difficult, and that disobedience was the only cause. My case is that the cases which they have selected are cases of a similar kind where people undoubtedly were dealt with for breach of discipline, but which they now attribute to a false cause, namely, their refusal to join the I.N.A. The next is the case of Mohammed Hayat. That is the case in which we said that because they killed some cows, a quarrel arose and hence a scuffle. It is true a scuffle took place. The question is—was it with a view to compel them to join the I.N.A. That is where I say they get hold of an admitted event, or a more or less admitted event, and annex it to a false cause. He said:

"The Camp Commandant was Captain M.Z. Kyani, who was succeeded by Col. Shah Nawaz Khan. I heard Col. Shah Nawaz Khan lecturing to the Camp. I was not present at the lecture he delivered in the camp, but I was present at the lecture he delivered in the mosque. He said that Sikhs and Hindus have already volunteered, and that the Mussulmans should also join." He said: " Muslims must join the I.N.A. because when the Hindus and Sikhs go, they will trouble you in your homes in India. He did not threaten us with force but he said that we ought to join the I.N.A. He did not say that he only wanted sincere men. He said: 'I will not give any sort of trouble to you, but you should volunteer. I want true volunteers. After *Dua Khair,* we said that we will not join the I.N.A. We meant by that that none of us who were present there had a right to join the I.N.A. There was no charge against the men of my unit of having committed theft of seven cows belonging to civilians, and of having slaughtered and eaten them. I deny that. That charge is a lie and that the cows were eaten is also a lie. I am shows my additional statement in the summary of evidence I admit that I said in the summary of evidence that Major Aziz Ahmed told us that we were to go to the Concentration Camp because we had killed a cow."

That was at the time they were sent. Remember what was the contemporaneous statement made. I want you to remember that. The Court would have no doubt that that was the real cause of the dispute, and that joining the I.N.A. or not joining the I.N.A. was not the cause.

"No skins or bones were found, and no investigation was made. I never volunteered for the I.N.A. The Bidadari camp was a mixed Camp of volunteers and non-volunteers in July 1942. Neesoon Camp was also a mixed camp...... There was no difference in rations for the volunteers and non-volunteers. In July 1942 there was no separate treatment for volunteers in the Bidadari Camp. I was carrying on anti-I.N.A. propaganda. There was no charge against me of killing or stealing a cow when I was removed from the Bidadari Camp to the Concentration Camp. Aziz Ahmed never told us that we were being sent to the Concentration Camp because we had killed a cow. I am again shown my statement in the summary of evidence. I signed my statement. It was read over to me. I made this statement about Major Aziz Ahmed having told us that we were all to go to the Concentration Camp because we had killed a cow."

In other words, at the time when he was taken, it was proved from his own mouth that he was definitely told that the reason for his being sent was the killing of the cow.

"On the day I went to the Concentration Camp there were approximately 60 or 70 men there....... I said that after two or three days men of my unit were sent away from the Concentration Camp. I and11 other men were kept there. After our people went away, there were approximately 60 or 70 people left. They were all non-volunteers. I am talking of the month of July 1942."

Then comes the most tell-tale thing which any man of commonsense will understand:

"I was released from the Concentration Camp after 21 days because I had become very weak."

The whole point is this. Any man reading between the lines will be able to see that these people were taken to the Concentration Camp because they were charged with having stolen and killed a cow. He himself admits that it was a charge made at the time. Major Aziz Ahmed said 'you have to go to the camp, because this is the charge against you'. After investigation, he was released after 21 days. Is that the real story, or what he now says is the real story? It does not show that they were oppressed or coerced to join the I.N.A.

There is one ordinary canon of reasoning and commonsense. Is the court to accept the story he said at that time or is it to accept the story told now? I submit that at that time nobody imagined that anybody was going to make anything out of this incident for the trial against some people in future. The question is, which of the two stories is likely to be true, and I respectfully submit to the Court that there can be only one conclusion. The story he told then is the true story, and not the story he tells now. That is my submission with respect to this witness.

The next witness I take is Ahmed Nawaz, P.W.10. Every man has to undergo some sort of punishment for an offence. This witness is taking the story as it occurred, and adding to it so as to make out that what was done to him was a punishment to induce him to join the I.N.A. The only grievance of this gentleman is that he was asked to carry cow-dung. It was not after all such a serious punishment as he tried to make out. When I asked him whether he was asked to mix cow-dung with soda-ash, he said that in his part of the country they did not do so. The time has not yet come in this country for the use of every kind of mineral manure, of any other kind of manure except cow-dung. I asked him whether it was not intended to be used for the purpose of manuring the garden, and it took a very long time before we could get anything at all from this witness. The demeanour of this witness and his behaviour to the Court stands condemned.

I am now reading part of the cross-examination.

"I do not know what the cow-dung was taken for. I only know we were made to take it as a punishment. We stacked the cow-dung near a road in the camp and on both sides of the road was the garden. We were never told to powder the cow-dung for manure. It is correct that we mixed ash with the cow-dung but I do not know for what purpose it was used. I only did as a punishment."

To this man everything is a punishment. When this gentleman was asked to mix some soda-ash with cow-dung for manure, he thinks it is by way of punishment. He is indignant when he is asked to do something and thinks he was asked to do it as a punishment. He says :

"As a farmer, in our own home, we only use cow-dung as manure and we do not mix ash with it. Only for three hours on the first day I did this work of carrying cow-dung and stacking it near the garden. It was stacked at a distance of about 10 or 12 yards from the garden. For the remaining five days we were digging and levelling earth and preparing garden plots."

When you come to analyses the facts, the indignity this witness comes to nothing. He was asked to do the ordinary work of preparing garden beds for the vegetable garden and mixing some manure. So far as the manuring is concerned, it only lasted three hours of his life time. If this is what is called an atrocity, I submit to the Court, it is a ridiculous type of atrocity. A man is asked to make beds in a garden and prepare some manure, and he imagines it to be a punishment. He may think so, but it is for the Court to say whether it is so. Does the Court believe that it was an ordinary piece of work, or it was an oppression, coercive methods, and I do not know what other language is used to describe it. Is it a torture to prepare beds and to prepare manure? I submit with great respect it is a ridiculous kind of evidence which is put forward as an item of torture, and for what purpose?—for the purpose of making this gentleman join the I.N.A.! Does this stand to reason and commonsense? I submit with great respect that, in spite of the picturesque language used, the Court will not accept the version of the witness. It is a ridiculous thing. He was asked to do ordinary fatigue. This is legitimate work which ought to have been done willingly and it is ridiculous to suggest that this was a kind of torture used to induce or coerce the witness to join the I.N.A. That, Sirs, is the evidence of Ahmad Nawaz.

Then, take the next witness, Havidar Mohammed Sarwar. He said : "Every—body refused to join the I.N.A. The *Jamadar* and Subedar were armed with pistols and they took them out and started firing on us, and ordered the guard also to fire on us. The guard consisted of approximately 14 men. They started firing. Two of us were killed ..... Everybody said Allah-o-Akbar." Now I will read from the cross-examination of this gentleman. He said : "I was for three weeks in No. 4 hospital. It was a very big hospital. There were patients of all kinds there. I was taken to the hospital. I do not know who took me, because I was unconscious. There was an officer to whom I said that I was willing to join the I.N.A. The only force that made me join the I.N.A was that I wanted to escape this bad treatment and bad food. When I joined the I.N.A., I came to know that they were trying to free India. "And this is the gentleman who says that there was a regular firing in order to make him join the I.N.A. He goes on : "I knew I was expected to go and might. I knew it was a question of life and death. I thought that death was better than these troubles. I had no faith that they would set India free. I had every faith that if I went to the front, I might be able to go to the other side, because we had so many hardship otherwise. At the place where we were first, there were numerous other people besides the 300. I do not know the Camp Commander's name. The Unit Commander was Lt. Purshotam Dass. That was the Japanese Prisoners of War Camp. We were split up into parties for the purpose of fatigues. On the day prior to the firing accident, we were not divided into parties of 323 for fatigue purposes. We were not asked to form a party of 323 men. We were not given an order. I do not know anything about being asked to surrender our leaders. I never heard of it. It is not true that Lt. Purshotam Dass advised us not to resist. In the party which came to the Camp there was one Mohammedan Jamadar. He was second-in-command of the guard. There was a scuffle between the men of my unit and the guard after the firing had taken place. Only one man of the guard was killed. The guard consisted of about 300. The name of the guard who was killed was Sardar Singh, who belonged to the Kapurthala Regiment. "That will show who attacked first. I leave it to you, Gentlemen, to judge who was the attacker and who was the attacked. And remember this that they were in a party of a few hundred, whereas the guard consisted, as he puts it, of 300 men. "Because we refused to join the I.N.A., they started firing." That is the picture which we are asked to accept. I submit with very great respect that the story is a most incredible story. There was no conversation and they at once started firing!

Now, Sirs, that is the story which is presented to you for acceptance, and I ask the Court not to accept it because it is a ridiculous story. What is the idea of firing at the men whom they ask to join the I.N.A.? What do you gain by it? You gain this kind of soldiers with a view to fight! My submission to the Court is that there was this scuffle which he reluctantly admits, and evidently they were the first attackers. But they have employed a little story by means of which they say that there was firing on them. If the Counsel thinks that he can walk away with this story, I submit he is mistaken. But when you come to torture, I ask, is it supposed to be a torture? It was an ordinary fatigue duty. In this connection, I would like to call the attention of the Court to the Geneva Conventions, Articles 27 to 34, with reference to the work of the prisoners of war on page 298. I am talking of 1929. "They should be kept according to their rank and if they are physically fit they may be employed by private individuals, but the captors must assume entire responsibility for their maintenance."

Prosecution Counsel : I am afraid I must interrupt. The evidence is not as my learned friend reads it. The evidence is not that the guard was killed first.

Mr. Desai : What he said was : "The name of the guard who was killed was Sardara Singh. There was no other member of the guard who died before Sardara Singh was killed." I had not the least doubt about it.

The point that I submit to the Court is this. The witnesses fall into three types of classes. The first category belongs to the cow-killing incident. The second that the incident was with reference to refusal to do fatigues. The third relates to the incident of refusing to form parties for fatigues as required by the Japanese, whose prisoners they were. As a result of these three incidents, certain accidents occurred. I submit to the Court that the Government had definitely failed to prove any torture for the purpose of joining the I.N.A. Each of these accidents is attributable—in two cases almost—to an admitted fact. In one case it is due to the form which the attack took. With reference to the other witnesses, the less said the better. All that they have said was that they were asked to do certain duties which they thought was an indignity, which they were asked to do, which, I submit, is ordinary decent labour. I know many men of higher rank who do gardening as a matter of honourable occupation, and as a change of occupation from ordinary work. What these gentlemen were really asked to do was gardening, and they seriously come here and say what an indignity it was to ask a soldier to do gardening. And that is why he refused to join the I.N.A. The Counsel has entirely failed to prove what he set out to prove, and I feel the Court should hold if it were necessary—according to my submission it is not necessary at all—that it has not been proved, apart from what is read or stated or alleged, beyond any reasonable doubt, that any torture was inflicted in order to join the I.N.A. That, Sir is my submission on that count.

That is all that I wish to say about the evidence on the subject of atrocities alleged to have been committed on these men to join the I.N.A. With reference to the point that I mentioned in the morning as regards cases which might possibly be relied on, I will give you a list of the three cases which may be relied upon and give you my remarks on them. Before that I wish to make a submission. I will make a request at a later stage but I wish to mention to the Court in so far as any new authority is cited by my learned friend I do not want a general right of reply but I will ask the Court in the end that on any new law that may be cited I may be allowed to give a reply because I could have no opportunity even by anticipation of doing it. I will make that request more formally towards the end. The three cases which may be relied upon are Regina vs. Lynch (1903) I King's Bench Regina vs. Jaegrae (1907) Appeal Cases. p. 346 and Regina vs. Casement (1917) I King's Bench. I do not wish to address you as if you were a high court, and therefore what I will do is this. There are two points which distinguish these cases which I will briefly state. They are cases of an individual being charged under the English law for an act of treason; they were not cases of men who were members of an organized army and of an organized Government. The second distinguishing ground is that in these cases there was no question of what I have submitted shortly as double allegiance. Therefore my submission will be that if these cases are relied upon this is the answer that I have got with reference to them. I will now go on with the regular trend of my argument.

The next point which I have to deal with before the Court is the evidence relating to the charges of murder, but I will take them all together without attempting to distinguish them. But I distinguish them under two heads : one is with reference to the four persons alleged to have been shot on one occasion and Mohammed Hussian, the person shot on the second occasion. I will first briefly state the case as I desire to present to the Court, and then deal with the evidence. It is a matter in which with due submission I probably will call attention in some greater detail to the evidence of three or four witnesses. As to the others, I will only make a submission as to what they said.

The position with reference to that is this. As regards the four persons there is a crime report and therefore up to the point of punishment there is evidence before the Court. As regards Mohammed Husain there is no crime report. In fact as regards Mohammed Husain there is no document whatever relating either to the sentence being passed or the sentence being carried out. Further, there is not even a casualty record in either case that I find on the record. As to Mohammed Husain the only answer given by one of the witnesses as to why a casualty report was not made was that they were moving from Popa that day, and then when I further cros—examined him which you will find in the cross—examination when I come to it—he has given no adequate explanation for the absence of the casualty report. There is this further evidence—I am only anticipating it that in the case of Mohammed Husain there are three persons who are alleged to have shot—Jagiri Ram and two others, whom Jagiri Ram himself did not know. I do not wish to enter into details at this moment except when I read it, but I wish to point out the salient features. It is said in the evidence that Mohammed Husain had three shots on his heart or near thereabout. It is further said in the evidence—he said this—that there was a tear in the shirt; and further in answer to the Court, which is most material point, he said there was no blood of any kind or sort. That is the state of evidence with reference to Mohammed Husain.

And now I will deal with the two sets of cases. There is one other ruling which I should have mentioned and that is that there is in evidence before the Court that Lt. Dhillon who is said to have signed and watched the sentence carried out was in a state of complete collapse of health and on that the document before the Court is Exhibit VVV. And the date of that document is 6th March 1945, the date on which it is alleged this execution was carried out. I am reading this relevant part of that document which is at the bottom.

"Jai Hind—I think most of your queries have been answered in this order. Others I will answer when I come tomorrow. I ought to have come today but last night I went to check certain defences and on my arrival back I felt very weak, so weak that I have never felt before throughout my life. Major Shankar gave me an injection today though for a complete course I must get 12 here when there are none available. I will get one tomorrow."

My case is that so far as carrying out the sentence on the four persons is concerned, though in fact the order was passed, it was never carried out. Not only that, but I will be able to point out from the evidence on record that there are many other similar instances, sworn to and admitted by the witnesses for the Prosecution. That is in outline why I submit that the case in so far as the execution of the sentence is concerned, is no proved. I may go a little further and state to the Court that there is no presumption that because sentences were passed they were therefore carried out. The charge of murder has got to be proved by proving completely what is called the *corpus delicti* of that particular person. And I will say that if there is a reasonable doubt in your mind that the prosecution has failed to prove the actual execution of the sentence, my clients are entitled to the benefit of that doubt.

That is the position with reference to the executions. There are four witnesses with reference to Mohammed Husain. As regards the first witness Havildar Ghulam Mohammed the evidence need not be read to the Court because all that he says is that he was brought up before Capt. Shah Nawaz, which in fact is not denied. There is this in Ghulam Mohammed's evidence:

"I know Havildar Ganga Saran. The first Battalion Commander reported that he (Ganga Saran) had refused to obey his orders. He was a sub-officer in the I.N.A. He was prodiced before Col. Sahgal for this offence and was tried and sentenced to death. He was afterwards pardoned and released." Havildar Ganga Saran himself in his cross-examination has admitted that as a fact.

The next witness is Sepoy Allah Ditta (P.W. 24). He deals with the earlier part of the story, namely, his intention to desert. This is what he says:

"Mohammed Husain said : 'I had a few difficulties and therefore I intended to desert'. But no inquiries were made into his complaints. Mohammed Husain was told by Col. Shah Nawaz : 'You are sentenced to death by shooting because you intended to desert yourself and were persuading others to do the same. Therefore you are not pardoned.' I heard Col. Shah Nawaz say : 'Put off the case to the Regimental Commander'. (Note by Court : Witness used the words in English). Then we all three of us were sent out. I recognise Col. Shah Nawaz Khan as an accused before the Court. We waited there for ten minutes and were brought back to Brigade Headquarters. Mohammed Husain, Jagiri Ram and myself came together back to Brigade Headquarters. Mohammed Husain and myself were put back in the same cell in which we were before and Khazin Shah took away Jagiri Ram. The same day at about 5 p.m. Sardar Mohammed, Adjutant of our Battalion and Aya Singh took away Mohammed Husain. I have never seen Mohammed Husain since then."

Then, Sir, in cross-examination he said :

"No decision was arrived at either in my case or in the case of Jagiri Ram."

The Court will remember that there were three people, and it is common ground that as regards two the sentence was not carried out.

It is true that all that Col. Shah Nawaz Khan said was : 'You deserve to be shot.' Col. Shah Nawaz Khan said that rebels like you will be sentenced to death by shooting. Col. Shah Nawaz Khan told Mohammed Husain: 'You yourself wanted to escape; secondly, you have tried to persuade others to escape; therefore, you are a rebel to the I.N.A. and sentenced to death by shooting.' 'I saw Col. Shah Nawaz Khan write something on the crime report. How could I read the crime report without picking it up from the table. I do not understand English.'

I come to the part of the story which in itself has not the same importance as what it indicates, showing that the witness was a completely factual witness. The man does not know English and yet he says "he was writing a crime report", and the object of the cross-examination is to show that he told a set story which he himself could not have possibly seen or done, and that is the kind of witness he is. That is the object of that part of the cross-examination.

"I saw Col. says he does not know what is crime, but he was told what is a crime report. Yet he is asked to tell a set story that there was a crime report which Col. Shah Nawaz Khan was actually writing, because he was called upon to prove that it was a crime report and sentence was written on it.

"I saw Col. Shah Nawaz Khan write something on the crime report. How could I read the crime report without picking it up from the table? I do not understand English. I do not know what he wrote and where, because I do not know English and I was not reading the crime report at that time."

And the only re-examination is :

"The crime reports were lying on the table and Col. Shah Nawaz Khan read them out as he spoke to us individually. He wrote on the crime report which had already been drawn up."

That is his part of the story. Then we come to the actual evidences of persons by whom sentence is said to be carried out—Jagiri Ram. You have seen him in the witness box. He is in the Nursing Department. He admitted to the Court that he had never handled a gun in his life, or a rifle, or any shooting instrument. But in order to give the colour of truth, Jagiri Ram is made to say this : "I was unwilling; I do not know how to shoot; I have never handled a shooting instrument, but a gun was put on my shoulder..." I ask you, Sirs, to give me the benefit of any description on his part rather than attempt to construct the story for him as if he did so. Then he put the gun here and the trigger was pulled and it seems that this untutored rifleman was extraordinarily accurate, that along with the others all the three shots lodged in the chest of the deceased. Sirs, it will be for you to judge the story. I am going to read out only that part of it which is material:

"I knew Mohammed Husain and Allah Ditta. Mohammed Husain, myself and a Garhwali talked about escape when we were in Popa Hill area. While we were talking of escape, Khazin Shah sent an orderly and ordered us to report to Battalion Headquarters.

Mohammed Hussain said that he had mentioned to Jagiri Ram and Alla Ditta jokingly about an escape. Khazin Shah questioned me and asked if they mentioned this jokingly. I replied that I had no proof of his intention to escape, but he mentioned it jokingly to me. Mohd. Husain and myself were tied to a tree near the Battalion Headquarters, while Khazin Shah was questioning us. Khazin Shah questioned me as to who was trying to escape and I said that I did not know the name of any one who was trying to escape. Then Mohd. Husain was questioned. He also said that he did not know anything. After sunset Khazin Shah took Mohd. Husain and myself to Brigade Headquarters. When I was taken to Brigade Headquarters, Mohd. Husain, Khazin Shah and one sentry were with me. Brigade Headquarters were near a nullah. On arrival at Brigade Headquarters, Khazin Shah went to a telephone and after that Allah Ditta also arrived at the nullah. After that all three of us, Mohd. Husain, Allah Ditta and myself, were put in the Quarter Guard and our hands were tied. On the following day, we were brought before Col. Sahgal. Col. Sahgal questioned me as to whether I intended to escape. I said "no". I did not intend to escape. During this conversion with Col. Sahgal, other people present were Major Negi and Khazin Shah. Col. Sahgal asked me if I had reported to any one after Mohd. Husain had mentioned to me about escape. I said I did not know anything about Mohd. Husain, and I did not reply to any N.C.O. I worked with my Medical Officer. Then we came out of the room and went back to the Quarter Guard. Then Lt. Aya Singh of Brigade Headquarters gave each one of us a beating and said that he would release us if we would tell him the names of the people who intended to escape. I continued to say that I did not know. Next day we were taken to Divisional Commander, Shah Nawaz Khan. We were accompanied by Major Negi, Khazin Shah and a sentry. All three of us, myself (Jagiri Ram), Allah Ditta and Mohd. Husain were lined up before the Divisional Commander. The Divisional Commander asked me to speak the truth whether I intended to escape. I said "no". I did not intend to escape. Capt. Shah Nawaz Khan asked up why we did not report the matter. I said that I did not know anything about it, and I did not intend to escape. He asked if there was any officer or N.C.O. near me. I said no, I was working with my medical officer. Then Captain Shah Nawaz Khan asked Allah Ditta: "When Mohammed Husain had talked to you about escaping, did you report to any one ?" Allah Ditta said : 'I do not know anything about Mohd. Husain's escape; I thought it was a joke, I do not know anything about it. " Capt. Shah Nawaz Khan then said to Allah Ditta : "You are an N.C.O. Why did not report?" Allah Ditta begged his pardon and said that he did not know anything about Mohd. Husain. Then Capt. Shah Nawaz Khan questioned Mohd. Husain, and Mohd. Husain replied that he was in difficulties and that the intended to escape and asked to be forgiven. Capt. Shah Nawaz Khan then told him: "You are not for our country; you are our enemy. I will give you death by shooting." Then Mohd. Husain asked for forgiveness and said that he was prepared to go anywhere he was ordered. Capt. Shah Nawaz said nothing to this.

The whole importance of the question is, whether in fact any sentence was actually pronounced. But, whether or not it was pronouned, the ultimate issue is, whether it was carried out. Like the case of the other two cō-accused—Jagiri Ram and the other man—he said that nothing was decided, and "all three of us were then sent out, and taken to Brigade Headquarters accompanied by Major Negi and Khazin Shah."

I need not read the rest of it.

Then comes the next material part of the story :

I moved towards the Battalion with Khazin Shah and Sub-Officer Barfi Singh. When I reached Battalion Headquarters, Khazin Shah told Barfi Singh to take me to Company Headquarters. In the evening an ordeal took me to Battalion Headquarters. Mohd. Husain was there. Khazin Shah and Aya Singh were also there when I arrived."

The most important point is—and which appears from the evidence of witness—that both Khazin Shah and Aya Singh are alive, and they are the only real proper witnesses to that particular transaction. Neither of them has been produced. The story continues:

"Khazin Shah told me, 'You will shoot Mohd. Husain, because you are one of the men who were trying to escape with him'. I declined and said I will not shoot him....."

I have understood many psychological problems but this particular one is curious, namely, that a who does not know how to shoot and cannot shoot, is made to shoot just as a sort of punishment, which I do not understand, and which I trust you will not be able to understand even if you set a problem to yourself.

Khazin Shah told me: "You will shoot Mohammed Husain, because you are one of the men who were trying to escape with him." I declined and said I will not shoot him and that I did not know how to fire a rifle. Khazin Shah told me again : "If you do not shoot Mohammed Husain, you will be shot yourself. I still refused and he drew his pistol."

I can only express my inability to understand this particular psychology except a very foolish invention.

"I refused again and Aya Singh get hold of a rifle. He put the rifle to my shoulder and put my finger round the trigger. Khazin Shah told Aya Singh to give the order to fire. Ther were three of us, one Singh, one Tamil and myself. Mohd. Husain was blindfolded by Aya Singh he was made to sit on the ground with his back against a tree stump and his hands were tied behind his back. Aya Singh ordered me to fire and all three fired. Mohammed Husain died there. Khazin Shah ordered Aya Singh to give the order to fire and Aya Singh gave it. Khazin Shah told me to report to my company and not to come to the Battalion Headquarters. That evening we marched off to Logyi. Then we stayed at Logyi two or three days. Then I went over to the British".

The cross-examination is further continued:

"After I had made the statement it was read over to me and I was asked whether it was the correct version of my statement and I said : 'Yes,' it was. I was again shown my statement day before yesterday and I was asked if the contents were correct and I said : 'Yes.' It was translated to me in Hindustani and read over to me, and I also repeated my statement once again and they both tallied. I have had no training in the use of weapons. I joined the army, I worked as a servant and a labourer. On joining hospital, I was trained in the work of bandaging patients and making their beds. I had nothing to do with the fighting part of the army. Except when the patients were sent to the hospital I had nothing to do with the men of the fighting units....."

The point which I wish to make is that not one of the persons is able to identify any of them by even the remotest possible description, and you cannot prove the death of "A" by saying that I saw somebody shoot someone whom I cannot identify. Continuing be said :

"Mohd. Husain and the Garhwali I have referred to were members of the fighting units. At that time of the conversation they were not sick. I did not know them before the conversation, but they were living in the same company. I had no talk with them before, but when they came to my company I was in company headquarters. When this conversation took place I was in Popa Camp. I had never been to Burma before. Before joining the I.N.A., we were given very hard fatigues by the Japanese in connection with the loading of coal at the ports day and night... I do not know the name of the Garhwali to whom I have referred."

The test is whether the other alleged conspirators were known to him.

"I know he was a Garhwali because he lived with us and he spoke Garhwali. I had never talked either to the Garhwali or to Mohammed Husain before the day Mohd. Husain joined company headquarters. I had never spoken to the Garhwali before that day in the nullah; and from that day's conversation I say that he was a Garhwali. I do not know any language or dialect beyond the dialect which I speak.

"I came to know Mohammed Husain in company. He used to live with me at headquarters. He used to sit in my company. I know he was a Mohammedan. I do not know anything more about him. He used to speak in Punjabi with me. He used to live with me, surely I knew him. I cannot give a long description of him except his physical description. I do not know anything else about him. It was by chance that Mohd. Husain and I got together and the Garhwali arrived in the meantime.....

"When I was arrested I said that I never intended to run away because I would have been also shot otherwise. I knew Lt. Aya Singh because he was in my company. I know he is alive. I saw him in Jigargacha and Chittagong. The last time I saw him was at Chittagong where he arrived two or three days after my arrival there in about May last.

"I saw Capt. Shah Nawaz Khan at Divisional Headquarters. There were other orderlies and sepoys there. I do not remember having seen any officers other than Capt. Shah Nawaz Khan. I do not know the English word "crime" I know the word "report" in the sense of making a report to somebody. I do not understand the words "crime report' which are written on a piece of paper now shown to me. There was no need for anybody to teach me the meaning of crime report when I was about to be produced."

I put it to him to ascertain if he understands the explanation. There cannot be any other explanation except tutoring.

"I was told that a crime report would be put up against me and that we three men would be brought before Capt. Shah Nawaz Khan. No announcement was made before me in respect of anybody except Mohd. Husain being ordered to be shot. Capt. Shah Nawaz Khan did not say anything about myself and Allah Ditta. Allah Ditta was not present with us when we conferred in the nullah...

"Mohd. Husain admitted that he had intended to run away; that he wanted to run away because he was in trouble; and asked to be forgiven and said that he was prepared to go anywhere that he was ordered to. After that Capt. Shah Nawaz Khan said that he (Mohd. Husain) was not for his country: that he was an enemy, and that he would give him death by shooting. We were then marched out. I am quite clear that nothing else happened.

"I was given a rifle at the time of the shooting of Mohd. Husain. I do not know any weapons other than a rifle was put on my shoulder in the aiming position by Aya Singh. I do not know the names of the Tamil and the Sikh who were present at the shooting of Mohd. Husain, but they were both present on the scene when I arrived. I do not know anything else about them or what they did. I do not know their names but I have seen them in Battalion Headquarters. I cannot say anything more about them than what I have said. I was not myself then. The rifle was put into position and I was told to hold it. I held it with the help of Aya Singh. The rifle was pointing to Mohd. Husain. He was sitting on the ground about five yards away. I pressed the trigger when one, two, three was said. Three shots were fired but I do not know which shot shots him down. I did not go to Mohd. Husain's body to see how many shots had penetrated it. I did not go near Mohd. Husain's body after the firing. The last time I saw it, it was lying there."

This is the account given by Jagiri Ram and the most important points are these : First, that he did not know his fellow shooters and he cannot identify them. Secondly, he admits that Khazin Shah and Aya Singh are both alive. The third thing that he says is that I do not know Mohammed Husain and there is no intelligible ground given why a man who did not know how to shoot was made to go through this process and it is for the Court to give some explanation. I can only submit that I can find none, and under these circumstances, I ask you to say that this witness's evidence is evidence which falls short of proof of the death of a particular individual otherwise not described, and in the absence of two persons who have not been produced before this Court.

Then, Sir, there is one more witness on this point, and that is witness L/Naik Sardar Mohammed. I will read the evidence which relates to this matter.

"I knew Mohammed Husain. On the 27th March, Lt. Khanzin Shah sent for the runners. On arrival of the runners he ordered them to bring the following men to the Battalion Headquarters : Sepoy Mohammed Husain, Lance Naik Alla Ditta, Lance Naik Mohammed Shafi, Sepoy Jagiri Ram and Sepoy Gobbru Singh... Khazin Shah told me that these men intended to run away. He further told me that he was going to Brigade Headquarters that evening to talk about these men, and he went away... I met Lt. Khazin Shah on the way and I handed over these men to his charge. He let off Lance Naik Mohammed Shafi on the spot, because his platoon commander had recommended him, and I came back. He said that Mohammed Husain had been sentenced to be shot."

I submit with due respect that it is not good evidence.

To be shot : Nothing was said about others, but Jagiri Ram was with him at the time. He asked me to go to Ghulam Mohammed, the Brigade Adjutant and ask him whether Mohammed Husain was to be shot under Battalion arrangements or Brigade arrangements .... I was also asked to bring sepoy Mohammed Ibrahim who had been released from the quarter guard. I received instructions that Mohd. Husain was to be shot under Battalion arrangements and on the same day. I brought him back with me to Battalion Headquarters..... I conveyed these orders to Lt. Khazin Shah. Lt. Khazin Shah then ordered me to arrange for the execution of Mohammed Husain ... He asked me to detail to men with pickaxes and shovels. I detailed these men to dig a grave. I know that a grave was dug. I was then ordered by Lt. Khazin Shah to take Mohammed Husain to the edge of a nullah. Mohammed Husain was taken to edge of the nullah, Lt. Khazin Shah, 2nd Lt. Aya Singh and Havildar-Major Govind Singh, some sepoys and myself went with Mohammed Husain to the nullah. Lt. Khazin Shah ordered Mohammed Husain to be tied to a tree and also ordered that he should be blindfolded. I passed on the orders to Sub-Officer Govind Singh who carried them out with the help of two other sepoys. After this Lt. Khazin Shah called two men out of the fatigue party to shoot Mohammed Husain. They were both sepoy, one was a Tamil and the other was a Sikh. After the arrival of these men, Khazin Shah ordered that Jagiri Ram would also fire on Mohammed Husain. The three men stood in a line facing Mohammed Husain and Khazin Shah told Aya Singh to give the order to fire. Aya Singh gave the order, "Kneeling Fire." All the three sepoys fired a round each on Mohammed Husain. Mohammed Husain was killed. His body rolled over sideways. Khazin Shah then ordered me to send Abdul Hakim to arrange for his burial.... No casualty report was sent. The sending of a casualty report was part of my duties. I did not make a casualty report because night had fallen and we had to march the same night. On the 3rd April I escaped and reported to the allied forces....

"The night that Mohammed Husain was shot we moved to Logyi. That was on the 29th March, 1945.

That question was put with a view to find out the connection between that day and the day of escape.

".... I did not have the time to prepare a casualty report of Mohammed Husain's death. On the 1st April 1945, I did not take a casualty report to Capt. Sahgal. I do know if any was sent. I knew Jagiri Ram from the day he was arrested and taken to Brigade H.Q. I had been posted to the regiment only three or four days previously, and that is why I did not know Jagiri Ram. I knew that he was a non-combatant nursing orderly. Aya Singh was helping Jagiri Ram to fire the rifle. He was standing near him. Jagiri Ram fired with help. Lt. Khazin Shah ordered that Jagiri Ram will also be one of the firing squad. I could not see very well but the firing squad had been ordered to adopt the kneeling position and they did kneel a bit. I do not remember whether jagiri Ram was standing or in the kneeling position. I was between 12 or 15 yards away when Mohd. Husain fell. I went away after giving orders to Abdul Hakim. I went near Mohd. Husain and found that he was dead. He had three shots in him. The shirt covering his left breast was torn and from the amount of tear I considered there were three shots. I was not present at his burial.

(Question by the Judge-Advocate) :

"When I found that three shots had gone into him and that he was lying on a side I inferred that he was dead. The firing was about 8 to 10 yards away from Mohd. Husain. The shooting of Mohd. Husain occurred at about dusk. I did not see any blood on Mohd. Husain.'

This is the whole of the evidence that you have before the Court and with the absence of Khazin Shah and Aya Singh, with the inexplicable alleged joining of Jagiri Ram, with the complete unidentification of the other two persons who joined in the shooting, and with the most extraordinary story of three shots having gone into the body of this man in one and the same place and not a single drop of blood was found, I submit to the Court that the evidence falls short of any proof of the execution of this sentence.

Though it is a small point Jagiri Ram himself said that he fired the rifle standing and I have a vivid recollection that later on, when he was asked to say where his muzzle was pointing he was completely at sixes and sevens to answer the question or to explain the position, or to answer where and how he held the riffle and where he aimed and how he shot. That is the position in so far as the record is concerned.

Then to the evidence relating to the alleged shooting of the four persons. The first and the most important point in reference to that shooting is the exhibit 3V which I have read to the Court. If you had such clear evidence it is obvious that the other evidence must be rejected. You have the evidence about the condition in which Lt. Dhillon then was. The submission I am making to the Court is that this event did not take place because the whole of the story hinges around order after order being given by Lt. Dhillon. I am able to show, as I submit I am able to show, that document was written at a time when there was not the remotest occasion of making up any document whatsoever as to the condition of his health. But the fact remains that the previous night he had gone out on reconnoitering and he came back, and I ask you to pay attention, 'in a condition so weak that he had never felt like that in his life before.' He was actually given an injection by the doctor, that 11 more had to be given, and it was difficult to find any more medicine. For that reason alone, if there were no either reason, the picturesque account given by the two witnesses, whose evidence I am going to read as to the company being called out and Lt. Dhillon standing and giving orders and calling each man, is a story entirely untrue. More than that, the story of the location of it all seems to be completely upsetting.

As to one of the two witnesses a comment is necessary. He had no intelligible reason to be there; and he had medicines to give as I shall presently point out. He also happens to be one of the members of the nursing staff and he said he had no reason to remain there. But the still more important thing is that the second person says—his evidence shows—that the first witness was not there. What do you make of that?

Counsel for the Prosecution : He does not say that he was not there. He only says, "I did not see any other man.

Mr. Desai : I say that the true inference is that he was not there, because he said he saw nobody, no stranger. The evidence suffers from such grievous infirmities; first, the practical improbability of the person who gave orders for shooting being there. Of course one can disregard anything; but after all you are to judge by human standards and not by possibilities. In fact, I do go as far as this : supposing a charge of his kind had been brought—apart from a trial of this kind– and evidence had been given as to the improbability of the person who is alleged to have given orders for shooting being there, no jury would ever venture to convict him. You may say : "Oh, yes the man was ill but we still believe he went there." Of course you are entitled to do so; you are judges; I do not deny that. But I ask you to be judges on material before you; and the material before you is such that as judges of fact it is impossible at all events, as I respectfully put it then and put it now—if you had a reasonable doubt that Lt. Dhillon could not have been there that day, I submit there is an end of the case. Any other picturesque description in immaterial. What is material is that the man who is alleged to have given orders for the shooting was not there and whether he was there or not depends on the state of his health, as to which there is a contemporaneous report; and I submit to the Court that it would be highly dangerous to accept, in the state of that man's health, the story of these two men. As to both of them I will be able to point out inherently from their own evidence that they are not witnesses of truth; and that you prefer that evidence and act on your own peril. I submit that is the real issue before the Court. I will read the evidence of the other two persons who said they were there.

There is another point which also comes out. There is no identification of the persons alleged to have been shot with the persons mentioned in the crime report. I do submit to the Court that if you find a Crime Report and on the strength of that document it is quite easy to have two willing witnesses of this kind—people who, I submit on their own confession (and I can show it by examination of their evidence) ought not to be believed. I say the strongest piece of evidence in my clients' favour is the evidence of his state of health that day, and you cannot disregard it. You can say : "Oh, no; never mind how his health was; we still believe he was there". But I submit that that is a process of reasoning which is not, what I may call, founded on justice or will be accepted by this Court. I will read the evidence of the first witness on this point :

"One day I was carrying a patient and saw four men near a nullah whose hands were ties behind their backs and who were escorted by two sentries. When I was coming back after leaving the patient in hospital, I noticed some men assembled near the nullah. Seeing this assembly of men, I went up there. When I reached there, one company was fallen in, and a trench had been dug there. The four men were made to sit in the trench. Then Major Dhillon asked for volunteers to shoot these men. Two men from that company and one man from Brigade H.Q. came up. Their names were Naik Sher Singh, Kalu Ram and Hidayatullah. Two carried rifles and one a pistol : Sher Singh had the pistol. Then Major Dhillon called out the name of one of the four men in the trench. Major Dhillon told the Company present that these four men had gone over to the enemy and had been caught, and therefore their punishment would be death. Then Major Dhillon ordered Hidayatullah to shoot the prisoner who had been called out to the trench first. But this time this prisoner had come out of the trench. He was standing on the edge of the trench. This prisoner was then shot by Hidayatullah and he fell down. The prisoner was not blind-folded. He was about 20 yards from Hidayatullah when fired upon."

Then there is the description about the other three men in the same way. Then he says :

"I did not see them moving after Sher Singh had fired. Then I saw Capt. Lee, the Medical Officer of the Battalion examine them. Capt. Lee said something to Major Dhillon."

Capt. Lee is another witness who should have been called to prove this :

"Afterwards Major Dhillon ordered the dead bodies to be buried. I did not see them being buried .... I went over to the Gurkha Regiment a fortnight after these men were shot. These four men who were shot were Jats. I know nothing else about them."

It is most extraordinary. You have A, B, C and D condemned to death, and you are asked to believe the one man who did not know who they were. In a trial for murder, if you are told that A was ordered to be shot and some one says: "I saw somebody shot and therefore I come to the conclusion that A was shot," I think one would be shocked to hear such a thing. I submit we have made our points quite clear in cross-examination. This witness said :

"I have never seen these men before. I did not know where they had come from."

It is not the charge at all that any four men were shot for any other crime or for no reason whatever. You are not called upon to say whether some other men were shot or why they were shot. That is not the charge.

Having dealt with the first part, which I do not want to repeat again, you will see how many infirmities are there. First, the improbability of Lt. Dhillon being there, according to the description in the sick report : next, no identification of any of the four man, never having been seen by these two men before. I do not say merely the cumulative effect of the whole thing—but even if any one of them was wanting you cannot say it is proved.

Then I have tried to prove from this evidence as far as it is possible to do so, as to whether or not he was required to go back to his duties, and he ultimately had to admit that he could not be there in the proper discharge of his duties; and after all the way in which you will judge a man is not by merely saying what they did, but by the probabilities of circumstances. If a man is expected to be on duty, and he says he stayed away out of sheer curiosity, would you rather prefer to believe that he went to his duty and was not there, or are you prepared to say, just because he said so, that he was there ? He says further :

"I stopped there for about half an hour." It is rather important from the point of view which I submit is of a man in that condition which as I said, is a fact which you cannot possibly disregard. In that condition, according to him, this process took half an hour. Then he says:

"I had nothing to do with either the men who were present there or the incident which took place there. I cannot tell the date or the week or the month on which this incident happened. I went over to the Gurkha Regiment which was in nearby village, the name of which I do not know. The incident to which I referred happened in 1945. I did not mention this incident at all in the Gurkha Regiment. I did not talk to anybody out to the assembly in the *nullah.* The company assembled in the nullah was about 100 strong."

The next witness will tell you there were about 25 men there :

"I did not see any outsider apart from the officers, the company and myself."

If in the teeth of that, the Advocate-General still insists that my interpretation of the evidence of the other man that he was no stranger is not correct, I ask the Court not to accept such an argument, because he may be plain and tell us who were there. I cross-examined the other witness and asked him whether besides the officers and the Company there was any stranger, and he said 'No'; and if after that I am to be told that I have not proved from the mouth of the other witness that the first witness was not there, it is an untrue interpretation of the evidence. He further says :

"I knew the names of Hidayatullah, Sepoy Kalu Ram and Naik Sher Singh because they belonged to my Battalion. My duty was to render first-aid. I never preferred first-aid to the three men I have mentioned. While at Popa, the Battalion consisted of 200 to 250 men. The three men do not come from the same place in India as I do. Ido not know where they come from. I had no personal contact with these three men before that date. I had nothing to do with them after the incident."

I say the probability is one in a thousand—the man knows nothing before, knows nothing afterwards; does not shoot and does not know how to shoot; has no business to be there; and yet you are asked to believe that the shooting took place. I submit it is a story which men of reason, just as we have on this tribunal, will not accept. The evidence goes on—

"They used to be in my Battalion ad I knew them. I cannot give the nominal roll of all the men of the Battalion. I knew the names of some but not of all men in the Battalion. I can give the names of 10 or 12 people in the Battalion ...... I did not talk to any of these men before that date. I have never seen these three men since."—(that is with reference to the person alleged to have been shot).

"I was 10 or 12 yards away form Major Dhillon. Nobody asked me why I was standing there. I had nothing to do with what Major Dhillon said on that occasion. I am not a poet. I am not a writer either. I swear and say to the Court that I remember every detail of what I have told the Court. I remember very well that none of the first men nor any of the other men were blindfolded. I omitted this detail in my evidence because I was not asked. I said that three volunteered to shoot these four men. The whole Company was armed. Most of them had rifles and a few of them had not. I knew at that time the name of the man whom Major Dhillon selected to shoot first. I do not know the names of any of the four men who were shot nor do I know their identity. After the shooting, Major Dhillon went away and so I went away as well. At the beginning I did not know what was happening there, but when I came to know what was happening there, I stayed on to see the end. I was 12 to 13 yards away from the place where these men fell. This occurred at about 4 o'clock in the afternoon. I did not have a watch."

The next improbability is that at the time there were sudden air raids, and this process which , according to the witness went on for half an hour is a matter for you to consider. But the important points are those which I mentioned first. This witness himself says:

"The place was subject to air attacks during those days..... Aeroplanes used to come over us frequently. There were trenches about and the nullah was a sheltered area. I do not know the persons who chose the *nullah*.... I am shown my statement of the Summary of Evidence. I signed that statement and identify my signature. It was read over to me before I signed it. My attention is drawn to the passage. As far as I remember, I said that Major Dhillon had ordered Sher Singh to fire a pistol, but it was not taken down."

I mean, he is quite willing to improve on any story so long as you ask him to do so.

"I was not interested in Captain Lee's examination or his Report. I was not interested in their burial either. Darbans Singh gave orders for their burial in my presence."

Questioned by the Court he said :

"This Company in the *nullah* was properly fallen in. These men were in front of the Company. The Company was about 10 or 12 yards from these men and I stood near the Company on one side. Major Dhillon gave orders for the fourth man to be shot."

Sepoy Gian Singh : "I remember four men being shot there. At about 4 o'clock one evening our Company got orders to fall in a *nullah*. On arrival there I saw four men whose hands were tied behind their backs. They were in a trench. Major Dhillon said that these four men had tried to go over to the British and so they were sentenced to death." Then he gives the names and details of the shooting of each man. "These four men who were killed were Jats. I do not know anything more about them . " For all I care any four Jats were killed, that would be the proof. That this particular sentence was carried out would be, I submit, the height of improbability, and unless there is definite evidence that the four particular individuals named in the crime report were shot, as having been identified as having been shot, I submit to the Court that you cannot possibly hold that these particular four persons were shot. The charge is aiding or abetting or the committing of the crime of shooting, and by proving that a Jat was shot, I submit with very great respect, nothing is proved. My case is honestly and deliberately that this is a false story. The sentence was not carried out. But taking everything against myself, and standing before a Court of law I say you do not establish a charge of shooting A by saying that you shot a Hindu. A Hindu may have been shot for all I know one same day.

Then, Sir, we come to the cross-examination of this witness. "The nullah to which I have referred was about five feet wide." Imagine the picture as this man gives, and of course it cannot possibly agree with the other picture. The other picture was one hundred people were present. This man's picture is that "from where I stood to where the trench was, it was about 25 feet, 20 feet deep and five feet wide." Few would believe that the company had fallen in such a place for such a purpose. I cannot imagine that a company would be asked to fall into a kind of well as this gentleman has described. Then he says that the height of the room was about 20 feet. "There were about 30 men in this space. Such men of the company as were in the lines were present there. Some men had gone out on fatigue. The trench was dug at one end of the nullah. I do not remember how many officers were there. Capt. Dhillon was in front of the company. The trench was below the nullah bed. I did not see the depth of the trench. The trench was between 20 and 25 yards from where the company had fallen in. A person in the trench could hear what was said from the place where the company was, if it was spoken loud enough to be hard. In that narrow space it is impossible to suppose that the other gentleman if he was there could ever have escaped detection. The man says that the whole process took half an hour, and hence the value of the submission that I make. "I do not remember any person not belonging to the company being there." I say that it requires a lot of conviction to submit to a court of law that this does not prove what I say it proves, namely that the first witness is proved by the second witness not to have been there. After all he said that there were thirty people. He knew that they were members of his company. Others had gone out on fatigue duty. This man says definitely : "I do not remember any person not belonging to the company being there." I submit with great respect that it has only one and one result, and that is that at all event the second witness says that the first witness was not there at all. Remember that within that five feet space you could not escape noticing any man. You could not help it if he was there. "We were standing in a place like this room except that it was not so broad. At some places it was wider but the place where we were standing in the nullah was about 5 feet broad. Of these three men who volunteered to do the shooting, two belonged to the company and one to Brigade Headquarters Police. Those three men who did the shooting were fallen in with the rest of the company when they volunteered to shoot. Because of air raids men used to go and hide themselves in the nullah bed and Naik Sher Singh was hiding in the nullah at the time. At that time there were constant apprehensions of air raids. The trench was about 20 yards away from where I was standing. The trench was at right angles to the bed of the nullah. I did not notice at the time what the length of the trench was. I did not notice whether the nullah was any wider at the point where the trench was. We were standing in two lines in the nullah facing the end of the nullah and I was in the middle of the company. All the men were facing towards where the men were shot. The men were in two groups. Major Dhillon was standing in front of the two groups, about 2 paces away from me. I heard Major Dhillon order the four men out one by one. I do not know their names. I had been in the company for a long time and that is how I knew the names of Kalu Ram and Hidayatullah." I submit that this again falls completely short of the proof of anything whatever like the death of an individual with whose death a man is accused. Remember that you have got to be satisfied, not in a vague sort of way, that some people were ordered to be shot, that some people were shot and those who were shot were those who were ordered to be shot. It is a process of absolutely vicious reasoning which I hope will not be resorted to or made use of by the Prosecution. Merely because the names of four persons whom you say were shot were there, you cannot prove that they were shot by saying that some people were shot.

Therefore, to summarise the evidence, it suffers from the worst infirmities, and much more so in a case where a man is charged with murder. First, it is improbable that the person who is alleged to have given orders was there or could have been there. It is improbable that in that state of health he could have been there for the period of time alleged for the process. Next, neither of the two witnesses is able to identify in the least degree who was shot. Then, the second witness say that the first witness was not there, and the second witness gives a picture which it is for you to believe to what extent it is correct. And then in addition to that, I am going to call attention to the evidence of witnesses, where in many instances of that kind, people were sort of sentenced but the sentence was never carried out.

The evidence to which I am referring is the evidence of P.W. 5 and it belongs to the same period to which this particular alleged shooting refers. The evidence of P.W. 5 in cross-examination is :" I know Captain Rab Nawaz. He was the commander of one of the P.O.W.'s Camps at Port Dixon, and the other camp was commanded by Capt. Karam Chand Bias of the first Bahawalpur Infantry. Capt. Rab Nawaz did not volunteer for the I.N.A. nor did Captain Bias. After Capt. Sahgal's conference on the 1st of March, within the next two weeks, there were several people arrested. After investigation all were released except Capt. Bedi. The reason for my remembering the date on which Capt .Sahgal commanded No. 2 Division was that on 28 February 1946 five officers deserted and on that occasion Capt. Sahgal arrested Captain Bedi. Captain Sahgal arrested Captian Bedi on the 1st or 2nd of March 1945 as a Divisional Commander. I do not remember the exact date on which Capt. Sahgal began to act as Divisional Commander."

Then, Sir, you have then the evidence of Gangasaran, to which I have already called attention, and this belongs to the same period as the date of the alleged execution of this sentence. Considering the evidence on record, I would submit to the Court that there is such a lacuna of evidence of identity, of improbability, that the Court should hold that there is at least a reasonable doubt whether this particular event took place. I of course put it more affirmatively myself, but feeling as I do in a case of this kind, it is my duty to put the case at the very lowest, and I say that there is want of evidence that is sufficient for my purpose. It is not enough that A should have been ordered to be shot, that by any process of reasoning therefore he must have been shot. That is a process which I submit is wrong and not permissible. The actual execution of the sentence has got to be proved with complete identity between those against whom the sentence was passed and those whom it is alleged were shot on this occasion. The thing has got to be proved by affirmative evidence and the burden of proof is completely on the Prosecution, hundred witnesses notwithstanding. In this case there are only two. One of them says that the other was not there. The point really is not how the deficiency of evidence arises. The question really is that the burden of proof being on the Prosecution to show that a definite person, A, B, C or D was killed, and died as a result of the action of a person who ordered the shooting is a fact, which must be proved.

All that is proved is, taking the allegation at its face value, that four shots were fired, and the identity of the persons shot is not known. My submission to the Court on that is that the evidence on this point suffers from infirmities which I have detailed to the Court in dealing with the evidence.

Therefore, with reference to this charge dealing with murder, my submission is that the Prosecution has entirely failed to prove the charges. The alternative submission is, assuming that the Court agrees with me that this was done in due course of the execution of the duty of an office in the I.N.A. governed by its own code, there is no question of any liability.

I say that Kalu Ram and Sher Singh who are said to have fired the shots are alive, and there is not that sufficiency of evidence either on facts or identity. Therefore I ask the Court not to run away with the idea that a sentence was passed on A, B, C and D, some people were shot on that day, and thereof the persons shot were those identical persons. This is a point which I cannot too often submit for the consideration of the Court. To say that A was shot because some persons were shot, is indeed a piece of logic which ought not to be allowed in a case of this grave magnitude. It is not permissible even in an ordinary case. The question says : Did you see A? The answer is : I do not know, but I saw somebody going into the fort and he was expected to go there. In a case of his kind, to say that he did go, would be the height of wrong reasoning. That is all I have got to say on the question of the sentence.

I submitted in the beginning of this case that this army of the I.N.A. was an organised army. The actual sections of the I.N.A. Act have been cited, as the Court will see from the crime report, and the Court will see that there can be no liability for any acts done in due prosecution of the war in the execution by officers of their respective duties. That of course is a complete answer. I was submit that even if the case is laid against A as a private individual, even then the evidence on the subject of having caused death, falls short.

Then there is a small point. I come to the evidence of Col. Kitson and Ghulam Mohammed with reference to the circumstances of Captain Sahgal's surrender. It is a point of substance, because under the terms of the surrender which were offered and accepted, the accused are entitled to all the privileges of prisoners of war on the cessation of hostilities. I shall now read the evidence of Col. Kitson, P.W. 29. He says:

"I then went forward myself up to the east corner of his village, when I met my leading Company Commander together with Captain Sahgal, the accused. With him were a number of other officers of the Indian National Army and approximately a hundred Indian troops of the I.N.A. at that particular time. More appeared late. My leading Company Commander handed me a note which he had received from a surrender party under a white flag. I am afraid I have not preserved the note. I destroyed it about two months later when I was going through some papers, and I am afraid I saw no importance of this note which I threw away. The note was addressed to the Commander of the British Forces, or may have been addressed to the Allied Forces, and it said that approximately 30 officers and 500 troops of the I.N.A. wish to surrender as prisoners of war. I then talked to Captain Sahgal, and he gave me his name and his regiment. He said 'I am Captain Sahgal', and I asked him what his unit was both in the I.N.A. and in the Indian Army, and he told me then that he had been in the 5/10th Baluch and that he was then commanding a regiment of the I.N.A., and that he had with him there at his Regimental Headquarters a 1st Aid attachment and one Battalion of his Regiment. I then made arrangements for the collecting of all the arms of the prisoners and arranged with Captain Sahgal about their feeding. We had no food for them."

You have to read this evidence in the light of what Ghulam Muhammad said. He has given evidence before you to this effect that all non-commissioned officers collected together, they were give an hour's time to consider the question of surrender as prisoners of war, and that if that was not accepted they were prepared to fight. A letter to that effect was written and despatched, and you have the evidence of Col. Kitson as to what happened. Under these circumstances I submit that in so far as the surrender of Captain Sahgal is concerned, it has been on the terms on which the offer was made, and I submit he is entitled to be released.

There are one or two small matters which I should like to deal with before I raise three points of law. You must have heard the evidence of the last defence witness, Captain Arshad. He gives you a truthful account of what occurred prior to the surrender of Rangoon, and the reoccupation of Rangoon. I have produced four documents which clearly show the recognition on the part of the British officers of the existence of an organised army called the I.N.A. The men in charge have been addressed by their proper designation and they have been entrusted with definite duties, and there is ample evidence to prove that the I.N.A. was an organised army, and it was treated as an organised army . I would draw your attention to Exhibits 5 Us. 5Vs. and Ws. You will find instructions there regarding the address of officers. This includes a document by Brigadier Lauder.

So, I submit that right up to the time of the surrender there has been recognition on the part of the opposition armies, that the I.N.A. was an organised army and it was so referred to an addressed through its proper officers. They were also recognised as officers for the time being. That, Sir, is practically the whole of the case regarding the documents and the recorded evidence.

I now come to certain submissions regarding further points of law. They are three in number and they are founded on a true interpretation of the Indian Army Act and of the rules thereunder. Under Section 41, this Court is authorised and is given jurisdiction to try among others civil offences.

The word 'civil offence' is defined in the Act itself. Section 7, Sub-section (18) reads : "A civil offence means an offence which, if committed in British India, would be triable by a Criminal Court." The question really depends on the true construction of the words 'triable by a Criminal court.' I know and I am fully aware that the Criminal Procedure Code has not been applied to the proceedings of this Court. But that is irrelevant to the issue that I am now going to submit to the Court. If, by the definition under Sub-Section (18) you have to find out what is triable by a Criminal Court, you cannot just do it in the air. I defy my honourable friend, or anybody else, to say what it is unless you go to the appropriate Act which shows what things are triable by a Criminal Court. That is not saying that the Criminal Procedure Code is applied here. That is where there is a likelihood of false reasoning. The point is this. In order to understand one statute, and where the statute expressly refers to what is triable by a Criminal Court, you must go to the statute which defines what is triable by a Criminal Court. It would be an extraordinary thing if the whole thing were left in the. Therefore, if there is another statute which shows what is triable by a Criminal Court, you have got to go to it, notwithstanding that the statute is not applicable to the proceedings of this Court. What I do say is this. If you have to find out what is triable by a Criminal Court, you must go to the statute which shows what is triable by a Criminal Court, and that Statute, so far as one is aware, is the Criminal Procedure Code. On that two points arise. One is that under Section 196 of the Criminal Procedure Code it is laid down as follows :

"No court (meaning no criminal court) shall take cognizance of any offence punishable under Chapter VI (which is this offence) unless upon the complaint made by the order or under the authority of the Provincial Government or some officer empowered by the Provincial Government in this behalf." If merely for the purpose of finding out what is it that is given to you for trial you have to go to another statute, then it is a wrong argument to say that you will not. Let me put it in plainer language. When you say that my terms of engagement are the same as those of Major Preetam Singh's, it is not enough. I must ascertain my terms from the contract. That is the simple illustration which will bring home to even a layman's mind the point that I am intending to make. The point that I am making is this that the civil offences which are committed to you for trial are those which will be triable by a Criminal Court. Therefore, my first submission is that what offences are triable by a Criminal Court you can only discover by looking at another law which is appropriate to the purpose and not by shutting your eyes to it. When you go and look into that law, what do you find? That law requires that that offence would not be triable by that Criminal Court except upon the complaint of an officer of the Local Government, etc. It has nothing to do with Captain Mead's case or any other case. That was a case of Section 270 of the Government of India Act and has got no bearing on the question. The point is this : How do you discover or where do you discover that the offence is triable by a Criminal Court. That you must discover because you cannot say that anything that is brought to you for trial, you will try. You will yourself ask : "What is it that I am entitled to try and if I am only entitled to try that which is triable by a Criminal Court, I must necessarily go to the statute which gives me that power." My submission to the court is that by reason of Section 196, no complaint having been made by a Local Government or an officer in that behalf appointed by them, this Court may not try an offence under Section 121, Chapter VI. My next point is again a point of construction, a point which, I submit, is of commonsense. If I am given a power to try offences within a certain limit, then I must find out what is being triable by a Criminal Court. If I find that a Criminal Court is incapable of trying an offence, then you must come to the conclusion that a Criminal Court of its own motion and of its own authority is incapable of trying that offence. If a Criminal Court is incapable without more of trying the offence, equally this Court is incapable of trying the offence. In other words, there are two alternative arguments before the Court. One is that within this sphere of the offences triable by this Court, this particular offence does not fall, in that it is not triable by a Criminal Court without more. In other words, a Criminal Court of its own motion could not possibly take cognizane this charge. Until the Local Government by itself or through its proper officer, does not move, the Criminal Court is incapable of trying it. Therefore, the question is two-fold. Firstly, that the Criminal Court being incapable of trying, this Court is also incapable of trying it. Secondly, if you put the point that the Criminal Court is capable of trying, but with a condition satisfied. There fore, in either view of the case, this Court is not competent to try the charge before it. My submission is that, in so far as the charge of alleged murder by Shah Nawaz or Dhillon are concerned, they are really part of it and nothing else. It is not suggested on the record that either of them wanted to shoot anybody for personal enmity or for any other cause of any other kind. It is patent on the face of the record that they were part of the actions which they took as officers of the I.N.A. Therefore, my submission is that the Court is not competent to try the two sets of offenses before it. *Per contra* if the Court is of opinion or hould it come to be of opinion that the charges of murder or abetment of murder are independent charges, then my submission to the Court is that under Rule 24 of the rules of conduct of trial in this court, the joint trial is completely illegal on a decision of the Privy Council in Indian Law Reports, 25 Madras, Subramaniam's case. (Rule 24 was read out and the Judge Advocate pointed out the amendment to it). That does not fall within the Rule because as to the murder and abetment of Mohanmmed Husain all the persons are not there. So that whether you call up this rule or any other rule, that is what you my call in the plain language of the section, a complete misjoinder of the charges and of the accused. Shah Nawaz has nothing to do with the alleged murder nor has Dhillon anything to do with the murder of Mohammed Husain. I submit to the Court confidently that if you treat the second set of charges as independent charges, this trial is wholly illegal.

I will now give to the Court the judgement of the Privy Council in Law Report 25 Madras, on page 61.

"The appellant was tried at the Criminal Session of the High Court, and convicted on an indictment the first count of which contravened the provisions of Sections 233 and 234 of the Code of Criminal Procedure (which proved that every separate offence shall be charged and tried separately, except that three offences of the same kind may be tried together in one charge if committed within the period of one year), and did not fall within the provisions of section 235 (I) which provides that if, in one series of acts so connected together as to form the same transaction, more offences than one are committed by the same person, he may be charged with and tried at one trial for every such offence. On a case certified under article 26 of the Letters Patent and heard by the Full Court, it was held by the majority of the Court that the union of the first count with the others made the whole indictment bad for misjoinder, but that it was open to them to strike out the first count, rejecting the evidence with regard to it, and deal with the evidence as to the remaining counts of the indictment. This was done with the result that the conviction was upheld on one count only, the sentence being reduced:

Held, by the Judicial that the disregard of an express provision of law as to the mode of trial was not a mere irregularity such as could be remedied by Section 537 of the Criminal Procedure Code. Such a phrase as 'irregularity' is not appropriate to the illegality of trying an accused person for more different offences at the same time, and those offences being spread over a longer period than by law could have been joined together in one indictment.

"Nor could such illegal procedure be amended by arranging afterwards what might or might not have been properly submitted to the jury. To fallow this would leave to the Court the functions of the jury, and the accused would never have been really tried at all upon the charge afterwards arranged by the Court. The trial having been conducted in a manner prohibited by law, was held to be altogether illegal and the conviction was set aside."

The judgement of the Lord Chancellor is on P. 96.

"In this case the appellant was tried on an indictment in which he was charged with no less than forty-one acts, these acts extending over a period of two years. This was plainly in contravention of the Code of Criminal Procedure, Section 234, which provides that a person may only be tried for three offences of the same kind if committed within a period of twelve months. The reason for such a provision, which is analogous to our own provisions in respect of embezzlement, is obviously in order that the jury may not be prejudiced by the multitude of charges and the inconvenience of hearing together such a number of instances of culpability and the consequent embarrassment both to judges and accused. It is likely to cause confusion and to interfere with the definite proof of a distinct offence which it is the object of all criminal procedure to obtain. The policy of such a provision is manifest and the necessity of a system of written accusation specifying a definite criminal offence is of the essence of Criminal Procedure. Their Lordships think that the course pursued and which was plainly illegal cannot be amended by arranging afterwards what might or might not have been properly submitted to the jury."

It means that it is too late for even this Court to say, " We will either strike out the charge of waging war or strike out the charges of murder and abetment of murder in which some of the persons are uninterested and not charged with reference to offences charged against others."

Then the judgment proceeds—

"Upon the assumptions that the trial was illegally conducted it is idle to suggest"—I am glad I am not using those words by the Lord Chancellor uses them—"that there is enough left upon the indictment upon which a conviction might have been supported if the accused had been properly tried. The mischief sought to be avoided by the Statute has been done. The effect of the multitude of charges before the jury has not been averted by dissecting the verdict afterwards and appropriating the finding of guilty only to such parts of the written accusation as ought to have been submitted to the jury.

"It would in the first place leave to the Court the functions of the jury and the accused would never have really been tried at all upon the charge arranged afterwards by the Court.

"Their Lordship cannot regard this as cured by Section 537."

They do not say that any irregularity has not caused injustice and so does not matter. But even that does not exist, because he must be held to the consequence in both ways. My learned friend says that the Criminal Procedure Code does not apply, and as such we proceed. So he cannot have resort to Section 537. And then you get back to a very narrow point that the trial, as I submit, is clearly in contravention of Rule 24 of the Rules of Procedure. It is a complete irregularity and there is no way of curing it. Their Lordships proceed :-

"Their Lordships are unable to regard the disobedience to an express provision as to a mode of trial as a mere irregularity."

In other words, you cannot in one trial charge people collectively unless they have committed all the offences collectively, which admittedly they have not done. Even on the extended words which the judge-Advocate read they would not apply because one thing is quite clear in relation to the charges and that is this, that some of accused are not in any manner liable for the offences alleged to have been committed by others. Therefore, I submit that this trial is wholly illegal. The judgment proceeds:-

"Such a phrase as irregularity is not appropriate to the illegality of trying an accused person for many different offences at the same time and those offences being spread over a longer period than by law could have been joined together in one indictment. The illustration to the section itself sufficiently shows what was meant."

The remedying of mere irregularities is familiar in most systems of jurisprudence, but it would be an extraordinary extension of such a branch of administering the Criminal Law to say that when the Code positively enacts that such a trial as that which has taken place here shall not be permitted that this contravention of the Code comes with in the description of error, omission or irregularity.

"Some pertinent observations are made upon the subject by Lord Herschell and Lord Russel of Killowen in *Smurthwaite* vs. *Hannay*, where in a civil case several causes of action were joined. Lord Herschell says that 'If unwarranted by any enactment or rule it is much more than an irregularity', and Lord Russell of Killowen in the same case says, 'Such a joinder of plaintiffs is more than an irregularity; it is the constitution of a suit in a way not authorized by law and the rules applicable to procedure.'

With all respect to Sir Francis Maclean and the other Judges who agreed with him in the case of In the Matter of Abdur Rahman, he appears to have fallen into a very manifest logical error in arguing that because al irregularities are illegal, that therefore all things that may in his view be called illegal are therefore by that one adjective applied to them become equal in importance and are susceptible of being treated alike. But the trial was prohibited in the mode in which it was conducted, and their Lordships will humbly advise His Majesty that the conviction should be set aside."

And I submit it does not require much argument. It is therefore wrong on the face of the charges with which these men are charged, and I submit that this trial is wholly illegal and I ask you to hold it so.

That is as far as I will go on the record on the points which arise for your decision, and there are very few points indeed. I will plainly and briefly state to the Court the points on which I really, so that there may be no room for mistake or equivocation about it. I say that this is a case of men not acting on their own in any struggle or waging war at all. This is a case of men as part of a regular organized army, accepted as such by their opponents, fighting a war under the directions of a regularly formed Government. That being so, I submit that they are subject to the ordinary laws of war with which I have troubled you at some length, namely, they are entitled to all the rights and immunities of belligerents. My submission is that to the extent to which this is a matter pertaining to war and the conduct of war it is outside the municipal law. But I am afraid sometimes in the narrow precincts of a Court like this, one may say : "What have I got to do with international law ?" But fortunately for myself I am fortified in this case so that I can fall within the four corners of the Indian enactment, i.e., Sec. 79. I say that if my first submission as to the jurisdiction or municipal law and its non-application is not upheld by this Court—though I submit is should be—I say that within the meaning of Sec.79 it is quite plain—you are bound to give effect to it and I have submitted authorities—that the word "law" as ministered in Britain and Indian recognises the principles of international law. And therefore , if a thing is justified by law, I can plead justification before this Court under Sec. 79. That is my first point.

My second point before the Court is that as regards questions which were incidental, I do not wish to repeat them here, though I wish to submit to the Court that the question of allegiance is irrelevant to the issue, but to the extent to which it is relevant I have already submitted that when the time arrives in relations between the Crown and the Colonies, the Colonies are entitled to throw off their allegiance on the outbreak of war for the purpose of their liberation. And I have given you the most classical instance of those who are now the friends of Britain and , if I may say so, their warmest and greatest supporters in the task of saving civilization. You could not have a stronger instance than that.

Then the next point which I ask the Court to hold is that on a question of fact entirely, in so far as the Indian National Army was concerned, it was voluntary organisation. Even if there were conscription, it does not make any difference in this case, because there are countries where there is conscription and punishment attached to it even today. But it has become fashionable to says : "Oh, there was torture and coercion" and all the rest of it, and I ask the Court to hold that it was entirely free from any such complaint. At all events, apart from any hearsay, on the evidence recorded before this Court, I have already submitted that the people who complain of torture fall into four classes : there were those who prove that in two cases it was for reasons which are self-confessed in one case and practically admitted in the second case. The first was refusing to do fatigue and the second case was cow-killing. As to the other cases of an isolated character, they are exaggerated, and deserve nothing else but contempt at your hands. If men were asked to do fatigue duty, merely because they have to carry baskets or make beds for the purpose of sowing vegetables, if they say it was torture, I hope my learned friend will not use that word in connection with that conduct.

Then I ask the Court to hold that in any event this evidence is totally irrelevant for the purpose of this case, for the reasons which I have submitted, namely, that the ground on which that evidence was attempted is entirely proved not to exist.

The next thing that I submit to the Court is that the evidence with reference to the alleged charges of murder would be really covered, if I am right in my first submission, by the fact that they are part of the prosecution of the war, in that these people were sentenced by Court Martial to be shot under the proper law. The next thing I ask the Court to hold is that there was an organised Government, that a very large number of Indians in the

Far East owned allegiance to this Government, which was recognised, having had ceded to it territories which are mentioned, and it was by this Government that war was declared, and the Indian National Army fought this campaign.

I will hand over to the learned Judge Advocate the list which I offered to give him yesterday on the point which my learned friend on the other side attempts to make, in that as if there was some provision as to flogging, intending possibly thereby to argue that the whole of that Code was an uncivilised Code. I think he was snatching at a complete straw, because as to the rest of the Act he admitted that it was in consonance with the Indian Army Act. And the only thing that he referred to is corporal punishment. I am therefore handing to the Judge Advocate provisions of the law in which the same thing appears under a different head, in force when the Indian Army Act was in operation.

Judge Advocate : Are you referring to Sec. 22 of the Indian Army Act?

Mr. Desai: My learned friend tried to make out as if whipping was a punishment which was abolished with reference to the army in this country, and I submit that he was entirely mistaken.

Judge Advocate : The very first sentence in writing that you have given is wrong. You have got flogging under the Act as it stands. Punishment of whipping can be inflicted on menial servants up to a maximum of 20 scores—that is what is written here, and the correct thing is 12 strokes on active service.

Mr. Desai : If I am wrong, I must correct myself.

Judge Advocate : I have corrected it now.

Mr. Desai : The point, Sirs, which I am trying to labour before the Court is this : In addition to the provisions in the Indian Army Act, there are provisions under the Defence of India Act and in the Ordinances. All of them have got to be taken together to see whether or not, and what punishment is permissible.

By Ordinance 3 of 1942—if necessary we will produce the actual copy of the Ordinance before you —whipping was ordered as a punishment.

Let me get back to the point : The point really is that in so far as the governance of the Army is concerned, it was governed by an Act which except for the purpose of whipping, has been practically or tacitly admitted to be the Indian Army Act. As regards whipping, I submit to the Court that that kind of punishment exists, though not in the Army Act wholly, in the there ordinances which are reproduced. Supposing to the extent to which there was an excess of the number of strokes, I submit with very great respect that it is not going to make an uncivilised Army because of that. Therefore, substantially the point is, there is an army governed by a Code which is substantially, if not actually, word for word, the same as the Indian Army Act.

I next come to the question that, in fact, the alleged atrocities—that is the mildest word that can be used from the point of view of my learned friend—which are said to have been exercised for the purpose of getting enrolment to the I.N.A. are in fact not true. The accused are not charged with it, nor have they anything to do with it. They neither did it, nor permitted it, nor encouraged it, nor have they any knowledge of it. That, Sir, is the actual position so far as that charge is concerned.

Then, coming to the alleged charge of murder and abetment, I have dealt with that and I have satisfied that Court that the execution of the sentences has not been proved.

My next submission to the Court is that this trial is wholly illegal.

My next submission to the Court is that so far as the construction of the words 'offences triable by a Criminal Court' is concerned, the Court must have reference to the only enactment which says what are the offences triable by the Court, and you cannot do by saying that the Criminal Procedure Code is not applicable—and if it has to be resorted to, then it has to be stated : First, this charge is not triable at all. Alternatively, in any case, this charge is not triable except on the complaint of a Local Government or an officer authorized in that behalf, and such a complaint does not exist. And for this reason my clients should be declared innocent of the charges against them.

The last thing that I wish to say is that if any new or fresh authority is cited by my learned friend which I had no opportunity of meeting, I should be permitted to hand in a very short statement, covering a single page, as to why those authorities if they are relied upon are not applicable to the facts of this case or to the decision in this case.

Finally, Sirs, I acknowledge with appreciation the courtesy and attention that has been given to us, and I hope that when I hand over a signed transcript to each member of the Court, it will receive such attention as it may deserve.

Judge Advocate : With regard to your last submission, under what rule are you applying to make another address?

Mr. Desai : I do not pretend that there is a rule. It is a matter of common Justice. If any authority is cited by one side which the other side has never had any opportunity of seeing or meeting, with the best of imagination he could not possibly deal with it. Therefore, common fairness demands that he should be given a chance to explain. All that is forbidden is an address to the Court. But surely for your own assistance, if we may pretend that we are able to give any assistance, if anything is cited by the other side which is not seen by me, surely I should be allowed to present to the Court a very short resume of my grounds on which it is not applicable.

Judge-Advocate : Would that not apply to any case in which your opponent had the last word?

Mr. Desai : Then the law is accepted. My learned friend will not contradict it. Even when a man has no right of reply and a fresh authority is cited, he has a right to answer. I hope my learned friend will agree with me there. It is a rule of common fairness. You do not need a rule for this: that a thing which is never urged before this Court, is urged before this Court, and no reply is allowed.

Judge-Advocate: As I have often told you, gentlemen, a Court Martial is bound by very rigid rules outside which they cannot go. The rule is laid down for your strict obedience by the Indian Legislature, and whether rightly or wrongly you cannot go outside that rule. Rule 48 of the Indian Army Act is the only rule I know with regard to the right of address, and it reads as follows.

(Reads Rule 48 of the Indian Army Act).

That rigid rule is for your strict compliance.

Mr. Desai : There is one point I would like to urge. The words are : "The Prosecutor may reply." If the Prosecutor confines himself to merely replying to what I have said, I have nothing to say. Let him be confined completely to what I have argued by way of reply, and I am quite content. I am glad that thought the ruling is partly against me, it is partly in my favour also. Let that ruling be strictly followed, namely that it will be enjoined on the Prosecution that he does nothing more than reply to what I have argued. Then I am quite content.

Judge-Advocate : The Court regret they are unable to permit a further address by the Counsel for the Defence after the address of the Counsel for the Prosecution.

Mr. Desai : Would the Court direct that the Prosecutor would only reply what I have argued and nothing more? You cannot have it both ways.

Council for the Prosecution : That is not the meaning of the word 'reply', I submit.

Mr. Desai : If my friend thinks that he is supporting the cause of justice by saying that I cannot reply to a new matter in case law, that is a new law. Unless he is prepared to submit to this restriction, I submit the law lays on him the duty merely to reply to what I have said. I have nothing more to say, justice or no justice. I hope my learned friend cited nothing that is not strictly relevant to what I have said.

Counsel for the Prosecution : My submission is that it is not replying to what you have said but it means addressing the Court on the case. I ask for an adjournment for my address and I have to ask for an adjournment up to Saturday. What I intend to do is to give my address in writing, if not the whole of it, at least the largest part of it.

President : The whole of your address on Saturday?

Counsel for the Prosecution : I think so. But I would suggest that an extra hour might be thrown in. If I have in writing, it will not take so long.

Mr. Desai : I have no objection.

The case was adjourned to December 22.

13

Prosecution Address at I.N.A. Trial, Red Fort[1]

22 December, 1945

Mr. President and Members of this Honourable Court :

I will first deal with the charge relating to the waging of war. The evidence shows that all the accused recruited men for the I.N.A., took part in the organization of the I.N.A. gave directions and orders for fighting against His Majesty's Forces and themselves fought against them. Capt. Shah Nawaz Khan was promoted to the rank of 2nd Lieutenant in the I.N.A. with effect from September 1, 1942, On September 9, 1942, he was made a Major with effect from September 10, 1942. On October 15, 1942, he was promoted to be Lieutenant Colonel. On November 30, 1942, he was appointed to be Officer Commanding Cadets Training School with effect from November 26,1942. On April 10,1943, he was transferred from Reinforcement Group to the Office of Directorate of Military Bureau. On April 17,1943, he was appointed Chief of General Staff. In February 1945 he was promoted to be Colonel in the I.N.A. Capt. Sahgal was made a 2nd Lieutenant in the I.N.A. on September 1, 1942, and he was promoted to be Captain with effect from November 10, 1942. On October 15, 1943, he was promoted to be a Mahor. On October 10, 1943, Capt. Sahgal was transferred form the Headquarters of Hind Field Force, G.P. to the D.M.B's office with effect from February 26, 1943. On April 17, 1944, he was posted as Military Secretary. Lt. Dhillon was appointed 2nd Lieutenant in the I.N.A. on September 1, 1942. He was promoted to be a captain with effect from September 10, 1942. On October 15, 1942 he was promoted to be a Major. On April 17, 1943, he was posted to "O" Branch as Deputy Quarter Master General.

---

1. *Ibid.*, The above address was delivered by Sir. N.P. Engineer, Advocate-General of India, Council for the Prosecution.

The evidence establishes beyond doubt not only that all the three accused joined the I.N.A. immediately after the fall of Singapore but that they also tried, by means of lectures, to make other prisoners of war forsake their allegiance to the Crown Capt. Shah Nawaz Khan lectured in March 1942 when he was in the Neesoon Camp to all the V.C.Os. and N.C.Os. who were collected for the purpose.

This is provided by the evidence of Subedar Major Baburam. Witness Jemadar Mohammed Hayat also deposes to Capt. Shah Nawaz Khan having given lectures in Neesoon Camp after the fall of Singapore. Witness Jemadar Iltaf Razak desposes to the fact that Capt. Shah Nawaz Khan went to Port Dickson in January or February 1943 and gave a lecture there to the Indian Officers asking them to join the I.N.A. Witness Nayak Santok Singh says in his evidence that Capt. Shah Nawaz Khan lectured in April 1943 in Saletar Camp which was for non-volunteers, saying that it was the duty of every Indian to join the new I.N.A. Witness Lance-Naik Gangaram says in his evidence that he saw Capt. Shah Nawaz Khan in port Swettenham at the end of April or beginning of May 1943 and that he delivered a lecture to the prisoners of war in the camp.

Witness Naik Santok Singh says in his evidence that Capt. Sahgal in January 1943 came to the men of No. 1 Signal Company and told them that the I.N.A. which was going to be formed would be the new Indian National Army and that every Indian should join it.

Subedar Major Baburam in his evidence says that at the end of February or the beginning of March, 1942, Lt. Dhillon delivered a lecture at Neesoon Camp to the V.C.Os. and N.C.Os. and to the men of the Battalion; asking every one to join the I.N.A. Witness Subedar Asal Nur Khan says that he saw Lt. Dhillon in Neesoon Camp at the end of February or the beginning of March 1942, and he delivered a lecture asking the prisoners of war to co-operate with the Japanese. Witness Havildar Suah Singh says that in June 1942, Lt. Dhillon came to Jitra accompanied by Major Dhara and that Major Dhara delivered a lecture asking the prisoners of war to join the I.N.A. Lt. Dhillon spoke after Major Dhara and asked them to join the I.N.A. Witness Sepoy Kaka Singh said in his evidence that Lt. Dhillon delivered a lecture in Taiping in March 1943 to the prisoners of war who were there, asking them to join the I.N.A.

All the accused admit having fought against the Forces of His Majesty the King. In view of that admission, it is not necessary to deal at length with the evidence establishing that fact. The entries in the diaries of Capt. Shah Nawaz and Capt. Sahgal are themselves sufficient to prove the part which they took in the fighting. Witness Sepoy Dilasa Khan who was in the Third Battalion Bose Brigade commanded by Capt. Shah Nawaz deposes to the fighting on the Falam Haka Front. He was instructed to try to contact with a company of Punjabi Mussalmans. In a scuffle which took place, his company captured a party of Chin Levies. Witness Havildar Nawaz Khan who was attached to No. 1 Guerilla Regiment, deposes to Capt. Shah Nawaz giving directions for the fighting in April 1944.

Witness Hanuman Prasad who was in the Seventh Battalion Nehru Regiment, which was commanded by Lt. Dhillon, deposes to the fighting which took place on March 16, 1945, when some Gurkha troops attacked his Regiment at Myingan. Witness Gunner Bhal Singh who was in the First Battalion of the Fifth Guerilla Regiment deposes to the encounter with an Allied Patrol on March 3, 1945, near Popa Hill. That was an encounter when two Allied soldiers were killed and two jeeps were captured with a wireless set by the I.N.A. Battalion, One of these Jeeps was in fact, thereafter, used by Capt. Shah Nawaz Khan. An entry in the diary of Capt. Shah Nawaz corroborates this incident.

Witness Sepoy Sadullah Khan who was in the seventh Battalion of the Nehru Brigade deposes to the fighting near Popa Hill under the command of Lt. Dhillon. Witness Lance Naik Mohammed said who was in the Fifth Guerilla Regiment, which was afterwards called the Second Infantry Regiment, deposes to Capt. Sahgal taking over the command in December 1944 and to the attack on Pyinbin and to the fighting near Legyi village at the end of March 1945. Witness Havildar Ghulam Mohammed was posted to No. 2 Battalion as adjutant. Lt. Dhillon was second in command. The Regiment Commander was Capt. Sahgal and the Divisional Commander was Capt. Shah Nawaz. This witness desposes to the fighting with the Allied patrol on the occasion when the two jeeps were captured by the Battalion. The witness also deposes to the fighting which took place immediately before the surrender of Capt. Sahgal on April 28, 1945.

As regards the Defence application to exclude the evidence of coercion, it is submitted that no such application can be entertained. The Prosecution tendered this evidence on the ground that the Prosecution was entitled to show that the accused tried to win over other prisoners of war from their allegiance to the Crown in order to join them in waging war against His Majesty the King and to show the conditions under which they did this recruiting work. It is true that the Prosecution case is that in the speeches which the accused made they referred to the conditions prevailing and to the hardships which they were undergoing and they held out promises that, if the prisoners of war did join the I.N.A., they would avoid those hardships and the treatment and that the accused also held out various threats as to what happen if they did not join the I.N.A. This, however, is by no means essential to make the evidence relevant. As I said, when I argued the question of the relevancy and admissibility of this evidence, "it will be sufficient for my case to show that atrocities were committed openly and notoriously and that they (the accused) were aware of them, and with knowledge of that they continued to press the Indian prisoners of war to join the I.N.A." Of course, it will be for the Court to decide after considering the whole evidence :—

(a) whether in fact atrocities were committed in order to make the prisoners of war join the I.N.A.;

(b) whether the accused to press the Indian prisoners of war to join the I.N.A.; and

(c) whether they held out veiled threats as to what would happen if they did not join the I.N.A.

The Court will come to its own conclusions on these questions, at the proper time ; but the question of excluding the evidence cannot arise and the application cannot be entertained.

There is ample evidence to prove that not only men of Indian Army but the officers also were brutally treated if they refused to join the I.N.A. Several witnesses despised to the fact that while they were being tortured they were told that they would continue to be tortured unless and until they joined the I.N.A. Capt. Dhargalkar in his evidence deposed to his experiences in the concentration camp in August 1942. He says that the conditions were very bad and he was not treated as an officer. For the first seven days he and others with him were kept in a tent which was full of white-ants. They were then removed from the tent to a hut about 500 yards away. They had to fall in with the other prisoners to collect their food. There was a lot of wire fences in which lots of Indian ranks used to be kept throughout rain and sun. On several occasions he saw a good number of Indian ranks being beaten. He and others with him had to salute the I.N.A. sentries and if they did not wear head gear they had to bow to them. When he developed some sort of body rash and went to the hospital and asked for medicine, he was told that he could not have any.

Jemadar Mohammed Nawaz deposes to the treatment which he and his companions received in the concentration camp on September 13, 1942. According to this witness, they were first deprived of all their belongings and then they were taken to a tent which was surrounded by barbed wiring and guarded by an armed sentry. They were told that as they were undergoing troubles and were educated people, it was better for them to volunteer for the I.N.A. They were also told that they had been asking Mussalmans not to join the I.N.A. This witness was asked to join the I.N.A. but he refused. The next day all those who refused to join the I.N.A. were made to fall in and they were asked to double march. They were then beaten with lathis and made to do fatigue work consisting of carrying dung heaps. While carrying them, were beaten by the sentries who were with them. He further deposes to the fact that there was a roll call every evening and if anybody reported sick and the doctor said that he was not sick, he would be given 12 strokes by the cane. He deposed to having seen while he and his companions were doing fatigue a man clad in khaki uniform whose hands were tied to a stick and his feet to iron pegs from behind and two sepoys were beating him. He further deposes to the fact that at the roll call every evening they were told that they were foolish people because the Japanese had promised that they would hand over India to Indians after conquering it. This witness in his evidence said that he never joined the I.N.A.

Capt. Arshad, one of the witnesses for the defence, said in his evidence that sometimes in October or November 1942 he was sent for by the V.C.O.s. of his unit who had volunteered and the V.C.Os., including Jemadar Mohammed Nawaz and about 400 other ranks, signed their names on the form. When Jemadar Mohammed Nawaz was in the witness box this was never put to him. The summary of evidence of Jemadar Mohammed Nawaz was furnished to the defence a long time before the trial commenced and the defence had also interviewed Capt. Arshad as a contemplated witness on their behalf.

Capt. Arshad also in his evidence said that Subedar Ahmed Khan had been arrested and taken to the detention camp for stealing, and that there was a protest against his arrest. Jemadar Mohammed Nawaz and a few other V.C.Os. also went to the detention camp.

According to Capt. Arshad he was instrumental in getting them out of the detention camp. It is submitted that this version of the story cannot be accepted. It is impossible to conceive that the Commander of the concentration camp would admit into it all these people simply because they wanted to go in. The evidence of Capt. Arshad on this point, it is submitted, is very unsatisfactory. He himself cannot explain how it was possible that these people could have been taken in. He did not go into the alleged charge of theft which, according to him, was preferred against Subedar Ahmed Khan, and it is difficult to accept the statement that without making any enquiries into the matter he could have asked for the release of these persons.

Witness Havildar Mohammed Sarwar deposes to the incident of the firing in Kranji Camp. According to him, he and the Punjab Mussalmans refused to join the I.N.A. One day a Jemadar and a Subedar with a guard came to them and the Jamadar delivered a lecture asking them to join the I.N.A. All of them refused to do so and the guard then started firing on them and two of the prisoners of war were killed. Thereupon, the prisoners of war attacked the guard and the guard continued firing on them and many of them were wounded. One of the guards was killed on the spot.

Later on, some Japanese officers accompanied by I.N.A. officers came and the witness and his companions were told by the Japanese officer that if they continued behaving like that they would be all killed. The Japanese officer told them that if they killed one I.N.A. man they would kill a hundred of them in return. The witness and his companions were then taken to the concentration camp and they were beaten with canes. The witness was rendered unconscious and taken to hospital. He remained in hospital for approximately three weeks. When he was discharged from hospital he was taken to Kranji Camp. After that he joined the I.N.A. because of those troubles. But he had made up his mind that when he was detailed to the fron the would desert.

In the cross-examination of this witness, it was suggested that all this treatment was given to them because on the previous day they refused to obey an order to be divided into parties of 323 for fatigue purposes. The evidence of this witness remained unshaken and it is submitted that there is no reason why this evidence should not be accepted.

Jemadar Mohamad Hayat said in his evidence that the Mussalmans of his Battalion did not join the I.N.A. The Hindus and Sikhs of the Battalion joined it and a few Mussalmans also. He was ordered to join the I.N.A. but he refused. He was of the idea that he should not join the I.N.A. He always told his officers and his soldiers that they should not join the I.N.A. and he always carried on propaganda against the I.N.A.

In July 1942, the unit of this witness was at Bidadari Camp. In that month he was taken with 500 men of his unit to the concentration camp. They were stripped of their belonging and they were ordered to take off their Indian Army badges. The officers, N.C.Os and sepoys were then taken separately to separate places and imprisoned in separate cages. Among the prisoners there were four I.C.Os. and 12 V.C.Os. The witness then describes the beating given on the next day to 12 of them, the witness being one of them. They were made to lie flat on the ground and beaten with sticks five feet long and two inches thick. Witness became unconscious by reason of the beating. The other 11 men were also injured by the beating. They were then made to do fatigue consisting of carrying sacks filled with earth. While they were doing this, they were beaten by the sentries who were posted along the way. At night they were not allowed to sleep. One after another of the inmates of the cage had to do duty as sentry in the cage and every five minutes a report was called for by the I.N.A. sentry outside. The inmates of this concentration camp were made to salute every member of the I.N.A. including sweepers. The food which was given to them was absolutely bad.

The witness and his companions complained to the Camp Commandant but he replied that they would continue receiving the same type of food. The wetness then told him to shoot him but the Camp Commandant replied that he would not be shot, but that he should volunteer for the I.N.A. He said that if they volunteered they would be taken out of the concentration camp and all good things given to them. He further said that if they did not volunteer they would continue to be beaten like that until they died.

They remained in the concentration camp for 17 days on that occasion. After that they were taken to Saletar Camp. There they were repeatedly given lectures urging them to join the I.N.A. The witness did not join the I.N.A. and carried on propaganda against it. They were then put in an enclosure which was enclosed with barbed wire and after that sent back to the concentration camp, after being in Saletar Camp for about 15 or 20 days. The same 11 men were taken with the witness to the concentration camp and they were given the same treatment as before. On the day following that on which they were taken to the concentration camp they were asked by the Camp Commandant to volunteer saying that, if they did not volunteer, they would get the same treatment as before. The witness and his companions refused to volunteer. The same fatigue was given to them as before. This time they were in the concentration camp for 21 days. They were beaten and no medical treatment was given to them. On one occasion when the witness asked for a drink of water he and another companion of his were given 18 strokes. When they called upon God and his Prophet, the persons torturing them replied that the Prophet and God were not present in those enclosures. They added: "If there is a God he is outside these enclosures ; inside the enclosures the concentration camp authorities rule".

This time they were in the concentration camp for 21 days and then they were sent to Saletar Camp. They were kept in the portion called D. I which was for non-volunteers. From there witness was taken to the hospital. He remained in the hospital for seven or eight days. In the hospital volunteers and non-volunteers were kept separate. Some fruit used to come from the Supreme Headquarters and it was given only to volunteers.

The non-volunteers did not get anything. From the hospital he was again taken to Saletar Camp. He was again asked to join the I.N.A. but he and his party refused to do so and they were kept in the D. I Camp for about one month. They were then sent to the concentration camp where also they were lectured to join the I.N.A. For a third time they were sent to the concentration camp where again they received the same treatment as before.

The witness then describes an incident which he saw of two Sikhs close by being beaten. They were beaten from 9 p.m. to 1 a.m. and then they were put in the hospital closeby and the sweeper who was there was told to report to them if the two persons died. The next morning the witness saw them in the hospital tent lying with their faces to the ground and fetters on their legs. This time they were kept in the concentration camp for 24 days, after which they were again taken to the D.I camp at Saletar.

Ultimately, the witness and his party were sent to New Guinea on May 1, 1943. There were about 2,400 persons who went with the witness to New Guinea. The witness never joined the I.N.A.

In his cross-examination the witness related an incident of a lecture given by Capt. Shah Nawaz Khan in a mosque. He said that Capt. Shah Nawaz Khan did not treat them with force, but said that they ought to join the I.N.A. He said : "I will not give any sort of trouble to you but you should volunteer".

He further said : "I do not want to press the men, but I want true volunteers". After that 11 Mussalmans said "Dua Khair" and decided in the "Dua Khair" that they would not join the I.N.A. It was suggested in the cross-examination that there was a charge against the men of this unit of having committed theft of seven cows belonging to civilians and of having slaughtered and eaten them.

It was put to the witness that in his summary of evidence he said that Major Aziz Ahmad told them that they were to go to the concentration camp because they had killed a cow. Even if that be so, it was merely an excuse for sending them to the concentration camp. Witness denied that any skin or bones were found and denied that any investigation was made.

The fact that the witness and his companions were taken to the concentration camp on three different occasions as stated by him in his evidence refutes the suggestion made in the cross-examination of the witness. Obviously, the witness and his companions were tortured in the camp for several days at a time and then taken back to Saletar Camp and again taken to the concentration camp because such a course was likely to weaken the resolution of the witness and his companions not to volunteer.

The evidence of this witness also should, it is submitted, be accepted as true.

The next witness was Havildar Wolit Bahadur. He related the incident which happened in Bidadari Camp on September 24, 1942. Prior to that the witness and his companions had been exhorted to join the I.N.A. They had often been told that they should join the I.N.A., otherwise it would have bad results for them. Subsequently about 14 officers and N.C.Os from the unit of the witness were taken to the concentration camp. The witness and his companions were told that if they did not volunteer it would have bad consequences for them.

The incident which happened on September 24, 1942, was, according to him, as follows : An I.N.A. officer delivered a lecture and said? "We have already informed you about the I.N.A. You people have not accepted what we said in the lectures. With reference to this I am going to show you one result of your conduct".

The witness belonged to the 2/9th Gurkha Rifles but the followers of this unit were Indians. The followers were asked whether they were prepared to join the I.N.A. They, however, said that they would stick to their unit and would not join the I.N.A. The followers were then cruelly beaten. Thereafter the I.N.A. officer called out six or seven people by name from among the men of the unit. He said that they were the ringleaders who did not allow the 2/9th Gurkha Rifles to volunteer for the I.N.A. He then ordered two I.N.A. men to beat those six or seven people and one of them fell down. Thereupon the unit stood up to protest and said : "Even if you beat us like this we are not going to join the I.N.A. but we are ready to do fatigues for the Japanese".

One of the I.N.A. officers then said : "Whilst you were gathered at this meeting on whose orders did you stand up?" The men from the unit replied that they were not getting justice and they stood up to make a report. Thereupon one of the I.N.A. officers ordered the guard to fire. At first they fired in the air. Another I.N.A. Officer said : "Are these Gurkhas your fathers that you are not shooting them?" The Gurkhas then started moving forward. The guard fired on them and one or two of the Gurkhas fell on the ground. The witness himself received a bullet in his left knee and fell down. Nine people were wounded, eight by rifle fires and one by being struck by a lathi. The unit was then made to fall in and march off. The witness was taken to the hospital. According to the witness, I.N.A. officers came to him in the hospital several times and they told him to sign in the I.N.A. books. They said : "If sign the I.N.A. books, you will get good medicines and the bullet will be taken out from your left knee". The witness, however, did not agree to volunteer for the I.N.A. The witness remained in the hospital for about five months. Witness never joined the I.N.A.

In the cross-examination of this witness, it was put to the witness that there was a dispute about fatigues and that they were required to do fatigues for the Japanese. The suggestion was that the firing was done because the unit refused to do fatigue duty. If the passage relating to this point in the cross-examination is taken as a whole, it becomes clear that the attitude of the witness and his unit was that they were prepared to do fatigues for the Japanese, but would have nothing to do with the I.N.A. The whole of the relevant cross-examination on this point is as follows : "There was a dispute about the fatigues, that they were required to do fatigues for the Japanese. Those who did not join the I.N.A. were required to do fatigues for the Japanese. There was a dispute when we refused to do fatigues for the Japanese. The leader whom I have named told us not to object to the fatigue. In spite of their persuasion, some of us did not obey. We reported that we will do fatigues for the Japanese but we have nothing to do with the I.N.A.". The interpretation of the question put to the witness and answers given by him were not quite satisfactory and at this stage Major Pritam Singh was sworn as interpreter. The answers in further cross-examination were as follows : "The guard was sent because some of us did not obey. The guard came to arrest the ringleaders. We were about 550 men. Some of the men had a dispute with the guard. The guard stopped us from doing this and then fired in the air. When we did not obey the order of the guard, they fired. The guard did not prevent us from doing fatigue but they spoke to us about the I.N.A. which we did not obey. First they fired in the air and when we did not obey ultimately they fired at us. About two or three men were injured by the firing. Then we pursued the guard". In his re-examination the witness said that the dispute between the guard and him was that they resented the appearance of the guard during lecture time. In answer to a question by the Court witness said that the bullet was taken out of his knee after one or one and a half months.

The next witness Rifleman Rabilal also deposes to the same incident. He mentions the lectures in the Bidadari Camp in which it was said that those who did not join the I.N.A. would be put in danger later on. Witness further said that an I.N.A. officer told him that if he did not join the I.N.A. he would be sent to the concentration camp and would be given a beating. It was thereafter that the V.C.Os. and N.C.Os. were taken away to the concentration camp. This witness also describes the incident of the firing. Witness said that before this firing took place some men in the Bidadari Camp were doing fatigues for the I.N.A. and others being ill-treated.

Witness said that he never refused to do this fatigue work and he was certain that none of this company refused. This witness was one of those who were taken to the concentration camp after the firing and he describes the hardship and torture suffered by them there. According to this witness, an officer in charge of the concentration camp separated 14 men from the party saying that they were doing propaganda against the I.N.A. and stopping the personnel from joining the I.N.A. The rest of the party were sent back to Bidadari camp. Thereafter, the battalion to was sent for a second time to the concentration camp. Witness went along with them. On the day following their arrival in the concentration camp the I.N.A. guard there started beating them and making them do fatigues. This continued for five days. After five days they were sent back to Bidadari camp. The witness was then taken to hospital and ultimately he and his unit were taken to River Valley Camp and the Japanese kept them for digging trenches in the jungle. The witness and his party were released from the Rivery Valley Camp when the British Army arrived there. There is nothing in the cross-examination of this witness to throw any doubt on the veracity of the deposition. It is submitted that there is no reason why this evidence should not be accepted by the Court as true.

Another witness examined on this point was Subedar Ram Sarup. According to this witness, as he refused to volunteer he was taken in about July 1942 to the concentration camp with five other men. He was told that he was doing anti-I.N.A. propaganda and that was why he was there and that he would now suffer the consequences. He then gave the details of the cruel beating given to him by an I.N.A. man following the instructions given to him by one of the camp staff in Punjabi in these words: "Guests have come, given them a good reception". The witness became unconscious by the beating. The next morning he and several others were made to do fatigue. In the evening one of the camp staff officers with another man came and asked him how he was. The witness replied he was all right. The officer then asked him if he was willing to volunteer to which the witness replied that he had already suffered and was ready to suffer more, but he was not going to volunteer under those conditions. Thereupon the officer abused him and told the other fellow to show him how they treated those who did not agree to volunteer. They then tied hands of the witness at his back, gave him a blow on the face, kicked him and beat him with a stick. Witness again became unconscious. When he regained consciousness the other fellow asked him whether he was still unwilling to volunteer. This time he gave his consent under the impression that it was better to become a volunteer than to die there of beating etc. In the cross-examination of this witness it was suggested that he had invented this story in order to save his skin when he went back to the Indian Army. It was put to the witness that under the instructions of Capt. S.A. Malik, he infiltrated into India and that on his arrival in India he reported to his Depot. It is submitted that there is no substance in the suggestion made in the cross-examination. On the contrary if a man was forced to join the I.N.A. under circumstances related by the, witness, it is quite natural that at the first opportunity he would report back to the authorities of the Indian Army. The numerous desertions which took place in the I.N.A. are very significant. As soon as men and even officers of the I.N.A. got an opportunity to leave the I.N.A. they did so and reported to their authorities. It is submitted that the inference to be drawn from these significant desertions is that a large part of the I.N.A. had been made to join the Army under compulsion.

Lance Naik Fitter Mohinder Singh originally volunteered for the I.N.A. in the Saletar Camp in September 1942. After the December crisis, he did not volunteer and he also communicated his ideas to his companions. Sometimes afterwards he and two of his communions were taken to the concentration camp where he was beaten. Before he was beaten, he was informed the beating was given to him because he had done anti-I.N.A. propaganda. After the beating he was put into a barbed wire cage six feet long and three feet wide and he was kept in the cage for 15 days. From the third day he was made to do fatigues. The rice which was given to him and his communions was mixed with lime and grit. He became very weak. He enquired from the sentry how he could escape from there. The sentry advised him not to do propaganda against the I.N.A. but to volunteer. He then became a volunteer. In March 1944, witness was sent to the front. He was detailed to bring rations from a nearby hill. When he went there he found a British Regiment to whom he surrendered. I may add, the evidence given by Col. Loganadan in which he says that one case that one case of atrocity came to his notice when a man with gangarene was admitted to the hospital. Col. Loganadan made a report about it but received no reply.

It is submitted that there is ample and trustworthy evidence in support of the fact that gross atrocities were perpetrated by the officers and men of the I.N.A. who were in charge of the concentration camp in order to make persons who were unwilling to join the I.N.A. and those who were advising others not to join the I.N.A. to change their minds and to compel them to join the I.N.A.

A very significant corroboration of this fact appears in the leaflet styled. Our Struggle (Exhibit 5C) by Rash Behari Bose. The relevant paragraph in this pamphlet is as follows: "Prior to election, Mr. Mohan Singh in his speech made statements which now appear to be misrepresentation of facts because he solemnly gave us to understand that the majority of the Indian Army personnel were prepared to join this movement without any threat or force and that they had acclaimed him as their military leader. I was horrified at a later date to learn of the atrocities meted out to officers and men of the Indian Army for which the blame naturally falls on Capt. Mohan Singh. Many of our poor brethren were shot while many were tortured, humiliated or sent to concentration camp and thus by sheer threat and violence he demoralized the majority of officers and men and compelled them to become volunteers, which is against our principle. I for one will be the last man to see my countrymen shot in cold blood. This is what we are fighting for against the British and I personally cannot afford to see Indians tortured in this manner".

The document was published under the authority of the Indian Independence League. That this pamphlet was widely circulated is borne out be the fact that an Urdu translation of this pamphlet was also published at the same time by the Indian Independence League. The profession made in this pamphlet that the same thing was not going to happen as regards the Second I.N.A. is to be taken for what it is worth. Even as regards the First I.N.A. several witnesses said that those who made speeches for recruitment said that they did not intend to use force or coercion. The question, however, is not what was said but what was done. Mr. Ayyar who was in charge of the Publicity Department of the Headquarters of the Indian Independence League in East Asia asserted that the Army ws raised voluntarily. When confronted with this pamphlet he said that he did not remember having read this passage and that he might not have read the whole of this pamphlet but might just have seen it. He also said that he did not remember whether the pamphlet was published in Urdu. He, however, admitted that he had no reason to doubt that the pamphlet was published by the Indian Independence League Headquarters at Singapore. In the evidence of Capt. Arshad, he said that the relations between Mr. Rash Bihari Bose and Capt. Mohan Singh were not too cordial. The suggestion was that Mr. Rash Behari Bose in this pamphlet made allegations against Mohan Singh which were not true. Mr. Ayyar, however, admitted that so far as he knew no protest was made against this passage by anybody. The evidence makes it clear that Mohan Singh had a large number of friends and followers in the I.N.A. It is impossible to conceive that, if this passage contained an allegation which was not true, no protest should have been made by any of Mohan Singh's friends.

In view of the above facts, the statements made by the defence witnesses that no compulsion was used to make prisoners of war join the I.N.A. cannot be accepted as correct. It was not part of the Prosecution case that the accused themselves committed or helped to commit any atrocities on prisoners of war; but it was the case of the Prosecution that the accused held out veiled threats meaning thereby that the threats convoyed were that, unless the prisoners of war joined the I.N.A., they might have to suffer tortures and be the victims of atrocities.

As Counsel for the Crown, it is my duty to concede and I concede, that the evidence does not support this averment. The question, however, remains whether the accused themselves had knowledge of any atrocities that were committed in the concentration camp. The duty of proving this is on the Prosecution. It has to prove it beyond reasonable doubt. There can, of course, be no presumption that the accused had any such knowledge; but knowledge might be inferred from such evidence as there is on record. If the Court comes to the conclusion that the atrocities were committed and that such atrocities were a matter of public notoriety, and that the accused could not have been ignorant of them, the Court may come to the conclusion that they had no knowledge of such atrocities. On the other hand, there is a considerable body of evidence to show that while delivering lectures in order to persuade prisoners of war to join the Indian National Army the accused said that they did not want anybody to join the Indian National Army. It is for you, Sirs, to arrive at your conclusion on the evidence before you.

There is no doubt, and in fact it has not been attempted to deny, that the accused recruited men for the Indian National Army by delivering lectures asking them to join it. The further fact as to whether they did it with knowledge of any atrocities that might have been perpetrated can only be a matter of aggravation.

International law does not come into this case at all either as regards the jurisdiction of the Court or as regards the law to be administered by it. The question is between the State and its subject. The accused hold commissions in the Indian Army as Indian Commissioned Officers. They became subject to the Indian Army Act and they remain subject to that Act under Section 2 until duly retired, discharged, cashiered, removed or dismissed from service. They have not so retired or been discharged, cashiered, removed or dismissed from service. In fact, there is evidence which I will point later to show that the officers and men of the Indian Army who, when they were prisoners of war, joined the Indian National Army at first but subsequently did not agree to continue in it after December

1942 were to revert to their position as prisoners of war. The argument for the Defence amounts to this that Section 121 (a) of the Indian Penal Code must bear different meanings where the offender is an Indian and where he is not an Indian. They want to read into the section a proviso that waging war against His Majesty the King is not an offence if it is accompanied by a declaration of Provisional Government and a declaration of war with Great Britain. In fact, a declaration of Provisional Government is itself an offence and such an act cannot give immunity to the offender. The object with which the war is waged is entirely immaterial. The act is an offence, whatever the motive for it may have been.

In Halsbury's Laws of England (second edition), Volume 6, page 504, paragraph 623, the following propositions are laid down: "The rules of international law are part of the law of England, but only in so far as they can be proved by legislation, judicial decision; or established usage to have been received into English law. A consensus of international jurists even if unanimous does not make a rule of international law a part of the law of England. To the extent that rules of international law are part of English law, they are applied by municipal courts so long as they are not in conflict with an Act of Parliament or a rule of common law; but the Courts have no jurisdiction over acts of State. "In Halsbury (second edition), Volume 31, page 509, paragraph 959, we have the following proposition of law: "Statutes are to be interpreted provided that their language admits so as not to be inconsistent with the comity of nations. International law, however, being mainly conventional can, it seems, only be administered by the courts when it forms part of the law of this country. If, therefore, statutory enactments are clearly inconsistent with international law, they must be so construed, whatever the effect upon the rights of aliens not within the jurisdiction may be". In footnote (s) at page 504 of Volume 6 of Halsbury, after mentioning that the wider view concerning the incorporation of international law in the law of England is seen expressed in the cases mentioned there, it is stated that it was also the view of Blackstone, and that the modern more limited view was first enunciated clearly by the majority of the judges in R. Vs. Keyn, 2 Ex. D., page 63, at page 202 and though the Territorial Waters Jurisdiction Act which gave effect to the opinion of the minority was declaratory in form, the view of the majority has since been upheld in West Rand Central Gold Mining Company Vs. R. (1995) 2 K.B., page 391. In that case, at page 408, it is stated as follows: "The expression the law of nations forms part of the law of England ought not to be construed so as to include as part of the law of England opinions of text writers upon a question as to which there is no evidence that Great

Britain has ever assented and *a fortiori* if they are contrary to the principles of her laws as declared by her courts!"

In the Zamora (1916), 2 Appeal Cases, the Privy Council in giving the judgment stated as follows: "A court which administers municipal law is bound by and gives effect to the law as laid down by the Sovereign State which calls it into being. It needs to inquire only that law is; but a court which administers international law must ascertain and give effect to a law which is not laid down by any particular State, but originates in the practice and usage long observed by civilized nations in their relations towards each other or in express international agreements".

This court is not sitting as an international court. It has not to decide questions between different States or between one State and a subject of another State. In Pitt Cobbett, Volume I, page 4, international law is described as the sum of the rules accepted by civilized States as determining their conduct towards each other and towards each other's subjects, and in the footnote it is stated that this definition save for its concluding words is virtually that put forward by Lord Russell of Killowen in 1896 which was judicially adopted in the West Rand Central Gold Mining Company V. Rex (1905) 2 K.B., page 391.

This court is sitting as a court duly constituted under the Indian Army Act to try persons who are subject to the Indian Army Act for offences which are made punishable under the Indian Army Act and the Indian Penal Code.

It was then argued that the word 'law' in Section 79 of the Indian Penal Code includes international law. My submission is that the term 'law' in Section 79 means a law in force in British India. In this connection, reference may be made to the definition of special and local law in Sections 41 and 42 as follows: "A special law is a law applicable to a particular subject"; and "a local law is a law applicable only to a particular part of British India".

There is a decision of the Bombay High Court which reports my submission. In re Ram Bharashi (I.L.R. 47 Bom. 907), Section 191 of the Indian Penal Code which gives the definition of giving false evidence is in these terms: "Whoever being bound by a rule or by an express provision of law to state the truth or being bound by law to make a declaration upon any subject makes any statement which is false and which he either knows or believes to be false or does not believe to be true is said to give false evidence".

The charge against the accused in that case was under Section 193 for giving false evidence, and in delivering the judgment the court said as follows: "As regards the offence under Section 193, India Penal Code, it is not suggested that the accused was legally bound by oath, that his oath was administered under the provisions of law in force in British Indian or by any express provision of law that is law in force in British India to state the truth before the Vyara court". In that case, the change was for giving false evidence in a court in Baroda territory.

While repeating the submission that no question of international law can or does arise in this case, it is further submitted that even according to principles of international law there is no obligation on the part of a State to give recognition of belligerency to insurgents. Unless such recognition is given by the State itself, there is no immunity for the persons taking part in the insurgence. Further, the recognition of insurgence by another State does not affect in any way the parent State so far as its own subjects who are insurgents are concerned.

I will cite only a few passages from Oppenheim's International Law, sixth edition, Vol. II, at page 173, paragraph 59, we have the following statement:

"In the proper sense of the term a civil war exists when two opposing parties within a State have recourse to arms for the purpose of obtaining power in the State or when a large portion of the population of the State rises in arms against the legimate Government. As war is an armed contention between States, such a civil war would not be war from the beginning nor become war at all in the technical sense of the term. But it may become war through the recognition of the contending parties or of the insurgents as a belligerent power. Through such recognition a body of individuals receives an international position in so far as it is for some parts and in some points is treated as though it were a subject of international law. Such recognition may be granted by the lawful Government and the other States will, in most cases, although they need not, likewise recognize a state of war as existing and assume duties of neutrality. But it may happen that other States recognize insurgents as billigerents power before the State on whose territory the insurrection broke out recognises them. In such a case, the insurrection is war in the eyes of these other States, but not in the eyes of the legitimate Government".

At page 197, Par. 76, we have the following passage: "The distinction between legal qualification and actual power to make war explains the fact that insurgents may become a belligerent power through recognition. The principles governing recognition of belligerency are essentially the same as those relating to the recognition of States and Governments. Certain condition of facts, not stigmatized as unlawful by International Law—the law of nations does not treat civil war as illegal—create for other States the right and the duty to grant recognition of belligerency. These conditions of fact are the existence of a civil war accompanied by a state of general hostility: occupation and a measure of orderly administration of a substantial part of national territory by the insurgents; observance of the rules of warfare on the part of the insurgent forces acting under a responsible authority; the practical necessity for a third State to define its attitude to the civil war. Without the latter requirement recognition of belligerency might be open to abuse for the purpose of gratuitous manifestation of sympathy with the cause of the insurgents. In the absence of these conditions recognition of belligerency constitutes illicit interference in the affairs of the State affected by civil disorders—an international wrong analogous to the premature recognition of a State or a Government. Refusal to recognize belligerent status, notwithstanding the existence of these conditions, must be deemed contrary to sound principle and precedent".

In Oppenheim's International Law, sixth edition, Volume II, at page 200, in footnote (2), it is stated as follows : "See also case concerning certain German interests in Polish Upper Sillies where the Permanent Court held in regard to claims put forward by Poland under the Armistice Agreement that the recognition by the principal Allied powers of the Polish Armed Forces as an allied, autonomous and co-belligerent army could not be relied on as against Germany which had not granted such recognition".

The next passage which I will refer to is that which has already been cited by learned counsel for defence. That is Para. 76a at page 200. The passage runs as follows: "Recognition by a third State is not as a rule binding on the parent State. Notwithstanding such recognition, it is entitled to treat insurgents as traitors. But the position is controversial with regard to recognition as a belligerent power granted to separate armies which comprise subjects of the enemy who are fighting to free their nation from his rule and which are responsible to an authority recognised as representing the nation in question. It has been maintained that as in the case of insurgents in a civil war the enemy is entitled to disregard such recognition and to treat the members of the insurgent army when they fall into his hands in accordance with the provisions of his criminal law. The better opinion is probably that when such recognition is granted by the adversary to large bodies of men effectively organized on foreign soil in anticipation of independent statehood a point is reached at which the belligerent confronted with the disaffection and desertion of a considerable number of his subjects engaged in hostilities against him can no longer, without exposing himself to justifiable retaliation, assert the provisions of his own criminal law as the only legally relevant element in the situation". This passage does not mean that it is obligatory upon a parent State to grant recognition to the insurgents because the State which was at war with it granted recognition to the insurgents as a belligerent power.

The passage in question refers to the position as between the parent State and the State at war with it, and not the position as between the parent State and the insurgents who are fighting on the side of the enemy State. Further, the only effect of the parent State not granting recognition would be that it might expose itself to justifiable retaliation. There is one more passage to which I will refer on the point of recognition as a State. I refer to the first volume of Oppenheim, page 125, paragraph 74: "Recognition is of special importance in those cases where a new State tries to establish itself by breaking off from an existing State in the course of a revolution. And here the question is material whether a new State has really already safely and permanently established itself or only makes efforts to this end without having already succeed. That in every case of civil war a foreign State can recognize the insurgents as a belligerent power if they succeed in keeping a part of the country in their hands, set up a Government of their own, and conduct their military operations according to the laws of war. But between this recognition as a belligerent power and the recognition of these insurgents and their part of the country as a new State, there is a broad and deep gluf. The question is precisely at what exact time recognition as a new State may be given instead of the recognition as a belligerent power. For an untimely and precipitate recognition as a new State is a violation of the dignity of the mother State, to which the latter need not patiently submit. It is frequently maintained that such untimely recognition comprises an intervention. This is, as a rule, not correct, unless such recognition is accompanied by active assistance rendered to the rebellious party.

"In spite of the importance of the question, no hard and fast rule can be laid down as regards the time when it can be said that a State created by revolution has established itself safely and permanently. Indication of such safe and permanent establishment may be found either in the fact that the revolutionary State has utterly defeated the mother State, or that the mother State has ceased to make efforts to subdue the revolutionary State or even that the mother State, in spite of its efforts, is apparently incapable of bringing the revolutionary back under its way. Of course, as soon as the mother State itself recognizes the new State, there is no reason for other States to withhold their recognition any longer, although they have even then no legal obligation to grant it".

This passage deals with the right of recognition by a third State of a revolutionary State which tries to break off from the parent State. So far as the parent State itself is concerned, unless recognition is granted by the parent State to the insurgents, no belligerent rights accrue to the insurgents.

Further in the present case there was no revolutionary State and no civil war. There was no contention between two States. There was no recognition by the parent Government of the insurgents as a belligerent State or as having belligerent rights. There was no war in the eyes of the legitimate Government. There was no occupation of national territory by the insurgents, no administration by them of a substantial or indeed of any part of national territory. No part of the country was in their hands which they could call their part of the country. There was no revolutionary State, much less any safe and permanent establishment of any such State. The so-called revolutionary State did not defeat, much less utterly defeat the mother State, nor can it be said that the mother State ceased to make efforts to subdue the revolutionary State or that the mother State was incapable of bringing the revolutionary State back under its sway.

As regards the authorities cited by learned counsel for the Defence, most of them are American authorities. This court is not concerned with what the law in America is or even with the view of the American courts on questions of international law. In fact, the law in America is different from that in England. The law in America is that international law overrides previous municipal law of a State. In America there is a digest of the International Law of the United States consisting of documents relating to that subject issued by Presidents and Secretaries of State, of the decisions of Federal Courts and of the opinions of Attorneys-General.

The propositions laid down in those volumes have all been accepted by the American Federal Government. One of the propositions there laid down is "the law of nations is part of the municipal law of separate States. The intercourse of the United States with foreign nations and the policy in regard to them being placed by the constitution in the hands of the Federal Government, its decisions upon these subjects are by universally acknowledged principles of international law obligatory on everybody. The law of nations unlike foreign municipal law does not have to be proved as a fact. The law of nations makes an integral part of the laws of the land".

The above appears from Maine's International Law, published in 1888 at page 36. Again, at page 37, the author says : "Here you see that according to American doctrine international law has precedence both of Federal and of municipal law, unless in the exceptional case where Federal law has deliberately departed from it".

The authorities I have cited above show clearly the great difference between the law in America and the law in England. All American authorities whether in text-books or in decided cases are, therefore, irrelevant.

I will, however, deal briefly with the authorities cited for the defence. A passage in Pitt Cobbett's Cases on International Law was cited in connection with the case of the Paquete Haband which case is reported in 175 U.S. Reports, page 677. It was laid down in that case that international law formed part of the law of the United States and must be ascertained and administered by courts of justice of appropriate jurisdiction as often as any question of right dependent on it duly presented itself for determination, and for this purpose where there was no treaty and no controlling executive act or judicial decision, resort must be had to the custom and usages of civilized nations.

As a matter of fact that case was one in a Prize Court. Prize Courts are those set up by the respective different States in which they exist and they administer international law. No question of administering municipal law arises in those cases. But even as regards Prize Courts, it has been held in England that if there is a statute which lays down a principle of law in contravention of international law that statute must be given effect to. In the present case, the court which has been duly constituted according to the law of this country, namely, the Indian Army Act, is trying persons who are subject to that Act, and no question of international law arises.

While dealing with this authority, it may be pointed out that at page 21 in Volume I of Pitt Cobbett, it is stated, while dealing with the relation of international law to English law, that notwithstanding some statements to that effect made by text-writers, and some dicta to be found in the decisions, it can scarcely be said that the law of nations is adopted in its full extent by the common law, or that it is deemed to be part of the law of England. It may also be pointed out that at page 61 of the same volume (Vol. I of Pitt Cobbett's Cases on International Law) in connection with recognition by a third State of the belligerent character of the subjects of another State, that the question whether such recognition should be accorded or not is a question for the political or executive department of Government, by whose action the courts will be bound. It goes on to say : "It would seem that such recognition cannot be demanded as of right for the reason that it is strictly a question of policy and not of law".

The question in the present case is as to whether the British Government recognized the belligerency of the insurgents. As submitted above, the parent State is not affected at all by the recognition of belligerency by other States. At page 246 of Vol. II of Pitt Cobbett, while dealing with Prize Courts, the decision in the Zamora, which has been cited above is given as regards the international character of Prize Courts and the fact that what it administers is international law.

Wheaton's International Law, Vol. II, was also cited by the learned Counsel for the Defence and the passage at page 101 on civil war was referred to. It may be pointed out that the question between a State and its suzerain is entirely different from the question between a State and its subjects. The passage cited expressly states that the Government of the State may recognize its subjects as belligerents in which case other States do normally but need not follow the same course. I submit that it is clear that there is no obligation on the part of the parent State to recognize insurgents as belligerents and there is no right on the part of the insurgents to claim such recognition. The passage goes on to say that the rule of General Grant that the question is one of fact is opposed by the doctrine that the matter is one of unfettered discretion.

The next authority cited was Lawrence on International Law, page 309. The passage in question deals with contests between States or between States and communities having with regard to the contest the rights of States. In the same passage it is stated : "War is a contest, not a condition; and moreover, it is restricted to contest carried on under State authority directly or indirectly given". Then follows the sentence : "Private war has long ago disappeared from civilized societies". But the author goes on to say : "If individuals now attempt to redress their real or fancied wrongs by the might of their own hands, they are regarded by the law as disturbers of the public peace, and their act is an offence in itself, however gross may have been the injury that brought it about". At page 310, after saying that all war is now public war, the author goes on to say : "Even the military and naval operations of revolted provinces or colonies have a public character impressed upon them by the process known as recognition of belligerency". It is clear that the public character impressed upon such a contest is by reason of recognition of belligerency".

The really relevant passage in this book is at page 328, Par. 141 : "Every independent State decides for itself whether it shall make war or remain at peace. If it resorts to hostilities it obtains as a matter of course all the rights of a belligerent. Other States have no power to give or to withhold them. But the case is very different with regard to such communities as are not already States in the eye of international law, though they are striving to become independent, and to have their independence recognized by other powers. Technically they from portions of old-established States. Practically, each is in revolt against the State organisation to which it belongs in law, and is endeavouring to set up a separate State organization for itself or to gain control of the existing organisation. By the municipal law of the country of which the community is still legally a part its members are traitors and liable to punishment as such. Yet they are carrying on open war under the orders of authorities analogous to those of recognized States. How then are they to be treated? International law gives no answer to this question as far as the Government against which they are in revolt is concerned. Questions between it and its rebels are domestic questions to be resolved by internal authority".

Moore's Digest of International Law, Volume I, which was cited is, as the title of the book says, a Digest of International Law as embodied in diplomatic discussions, treaties and other international agreements, international awards, the decisions of municipal courts, and the writings of jurists and especially in documents—published and unpublished, issued by Presidents and Secretaries of State of the United States, the opinions of the Attorneys-General and the decisions of courts, Federal and State. The passage cited at page 2 in fact expressly states that "the Government of the United States has, on various occasions, announced the principle that international law as a system is binding upon the nations not merely as something to which they may be tacitly assumed to have agreed but also as a fundamental condition of their admission to full and equal participation in the intercourse of civilized States." I have pointed out above the difference between the doctrine prevailing in America and that prevailing in England. I have cited authorities which, I submit, are conclusive on the question of the relation of international law of England.

As regards Oppenheim, I have already referred to the relevant passages.

Hyde on International Law was next cited. The title of the book is "International Law chiefly as interpreted and applied by the United States". The passage refers to a man being armed by a sovereign State. It has no relevance at all to the question as to whether the subjects of a State taking up arms against the State have any right of belligerency.

The case of *Underhill* vs. *Hernandez*, United States Supreme Court Reports, Volume 168, page 250, was cited and an isolated passage was read which says that whether the political revolt fails or succeeds, still effectual war has been waged and acts of legitimate warfare cannot be make the basis of individual liability. Apart from its being an American authority, and having no relevance to the question before the Court, it is necessary to consider what the case was and some salient facts thereof. The third headnote of that case is as follows : "This court is bound to take judicial notice of the facts that flagrant civil war existed in another country, that the revolution was successful, and that the revolutionary Government was recognized by the United States as the Government of the country and for information as to those facts this court may consult the Department of State". The action was brought to recover damages for the detention caused to the plaintiff by reason of the refusal to grant a passport and for the alleged confinement of the plaintiff to his own house. The case was tried in the Circuit Court of the United States for the Eastern District of New York. The acts which were alleged to have been wrongful had taken place in Venezuela.

The facts stated above are sufficient to show how irrelevant the authority is to the present question. There was no question in that case as between a State and its subjects. The second paragraph of the headnote of the case of Ford vs. *Surget,* 97 United States Reports, 594, is as follows: "destruction of cotton under the orders of the Confederate military authorities for the purpose of preventing it from falling into the hands of the Federal Army was an act of war upon the part of the military forces of the rebellion for which the person executing such orders was relieved from civil responsibility at the suit of the owner voluntarily residing at the time within the lines of the insurrection." The defence was that at and before the time the alleged trespasses were committed, the people of Mississippi and of Virginia, North Carolina and South Carolina, Floria, etc., had confederated together for revolt against the United States and within their territorial limits, had entirely subverted the Government of the United States and in place thereof and within and for their territory and people had created a new and separate Government called the Confederate States of America having executive, legislative and judicial departments. From pages 605 611 of the Report it appears that to the Confederate Army was conceded in the interests of humanity and to prevent the cruelties of reprisals and retaliation such belligerent rights as belonged under the laws of nations to the armies of independent Governments engaged in war against each other. This is sufficient to show how irrelevant this case is to the question now before the Court. Further, as stated above, the Court is not concerned with what the law is in America. Reference has already been made to authorities and textbooks showing what the law is in England.

Blackston's Commentaries, Volume II, were then cited. As regards this, it is sufficient to point out that in Halsbury, Second Edition, Volume 6, page 504 in footnote(s), dealing with the statement of law set out in paragraph 623, it is mentioned that there was a wider view held originallv concerning the incorporation of international law in the law of England and that such was also the view of Blackstones; but the modern more limited view was enunciated in *Reginas* vs. *Keyn,* and the view of the majority has since been upheld in *West Rand Central Gold Mining Co.* vs. *R*: (1905), 2 K.B. 301, which has already been cited above.

Hershey, which has also been cited, is also an American authority. The more appropriate reference should, I submit, be to the English authorities on the point which have already been cited. 159 U.S. Reports, page 113, stands on the same footing. The case reported in 1939 Appeal Cases page 160, is really not against the Prosecution. The passage cited from the judgment is as follows; "It must be always remembered that so far at any rate as courts in this country are concerned, international law has no validity save in so far as its principles are accepted and adoppted by our domestic law. There is no external power that imposes its rules upon our own code of substantial law and procedure. The courts acknowledge the existence of a body of rules which nations accept among themselves. on every judicial issue, they seek to ascertain what the relevant rule is and having found it they will treat it as having been incorporated into the domestic law so far as it is not inconsistent with the rules enacted by statute." This enunciation of law is in no way different from the propositions laid down in the authorities I have already cited.

The British Year Book of International Law, 1937, page 18, contains an article on some problems of the Spanish Civil War. It deals with the recognition by a third state of belligerent rights of insurgents and their parent state. Whatever the views of the author of this article may be, I have mentioned above the authorities on the question. It is submitted that it is beyond dispute that the recognition by a third State of belligerent rights in a conflict between a parent State and its insurgents is :-

(a) a matter of policy; and

(b) does not affect the parent State at all.

The quotations from "Hansard" of the speeches made by various English politicians on the occasion of recognizing the belligerent rights of insurgents in other countries are not authorities on the point. If, as submitted by me, recognition by a third State is a matter of policy, the recognition by England of belligerent rights on the part of its insurgents against their own parent country does not affect the question whether, without such recognition the insurgents are entitled to any immunities. In fact, in some of the speeches it was actually stated that the act of recognition by England was based upon the interests of England and was necessitated by the impossiblity of treating the insurgents as pirates. It is entirely incorrect to say that the same point arises for decision by this court. It is incorrect to say that it is not necessary that the Provisional Government of Free India should have been recognized by Great Britain. A third State may find it necessary or may choose to grant belligerent rights to the parent state as well as to the insurgents; but that does not mean that the insurgents are entitled to any immunity for their acts, so far as the parent State is concerned, unless the parent State has recognized or granted such rights. The illustrations given of Belgium and other countries are entirely out of place. Those countries were in military occupation. So too as regards France. There was a Free French State which refused to recognize the Petain Government. The proclamation of Eisenhower was directed against Germany and not against France. The Berlin reply is relevant to show that the recognition by other states is not binding upon a State which considered itself a parent State. It is not correct to say that the Prosecution asks the Court to adopt the view of Germany on the point. In any event, no such prodlamatiou affects the rights of a parent State against its insurgents if the parent state has not granted belligerent rights to the insurgents or has not recognized a Government formed in opposition to itself . The communique published by the Government of India and the statement made in the House of Commons are absolutely irrelevant to the question. Even if they were relevant, they do not amount to an admission of justification as regards the conduct of those who joined the I.N.A.

Many, if not most, of the considerations urged on behalf of the defence may be appropriate to be urged before a legislative body which enacts legislation, but are entirely irrelevant before a court administering law.

Learned Counsel for the accused referred to the *communique* published by the Government of India and the statement in the House of Commons. This is not evidence in the case, but since mention has been made of it, I may be permitted to mention that, according to another statement made by His Excellency the Viceroy, 45,000 Indian Prisoners of war did not join the Indian National Army and out of those 45,000, 11,000 lost their lives as a result of disease, starvation and murder. Twenty thousand prisoners of war joined the Indian National Army and the casualties from that Army were only about 1,500—of course, all these considerations are irrelevant in this trial.

Much has been said on behalf of the accused as regards the activities of the Provisional Government of Free India. The defence witness, Mr. S.A. Ayyar, who was in the Publicity Department of the Headquarters of the Indian Independence League in East Asia, said in his evidence that the Provisional Government used the machinery of the Indian

Independence League as its own executive. This statement is by itself significant. He then goes on to say that the Provisional Government collected donations from Indians throughout East Asia and that in Burma the Provisional Government opened a National Bank of Azad Hind. The position occupied by Mr. Subhas Chandra Bose was that of the President of the Indian Independence League and he took over the command of the I.N.A. Mr. Ayyar then states that there was a school for training civil administrators. He further said that the Azad Hind Government in Malaya and Burma took care of social welfare through the Indian Independence League branches in the matter of education, medical and other relief and relief of air-raid victims. As regards himself, he said that he was appointed to take charge of the Publicity Department in July 1942. and that later he become a Minister of the Provisional Government. As regards his own duties as a Minister of the Provisional Government, he said in his cross-examination that they were to give publicity to the activities of the Provisional Government and of the I.N.A. and to carry on propagand directed to the people in India through the short wave radio, to arrange public meetings with the help of the machinery of the Indian Independence League and generally to do the publicity and propagand activities of the Provisional Government. In further cross-examination he said; "The Indian Independence League had various departments and the Provisional Government got its policy executed through the staff and the other machinery of the Indian Independence League. The Indian Independence league had various department which were in the charge of secretaries—these were secretaries of departments—and whatever policy was laid down by the Provisional Government was put into actual execution by the secretary with his staff. From time to the instructions were sent from the Headquarters of the Provisional Government to the secretaries of the Indian Independence League branches. By policy I mean any decision taken by the Provisional government; it was immediately communicated to the secretaries of the departments concerned by the minister and they put it into execution. In my own department, apart from the ministry of Publicity and Propaganda, there was a Press Publicity and Propaganda Department of the Indian Independence League which was in the charge of a secretary and whatever we decided about propagand, for instance of starting a new broadcast or a newspaper, was communicated to the secretary of the League and he took the necessary measures to carry out that decision. As an instance, in Burma when we decided to have an additional broadcast on the short wave radio, I communicated the decision of the ministry to the secretary of the Propaganda Department and he arranged for the additional broadcast session. I know instances relating to my own department and I know other Ministers did the same. I cannot give you instances relating to other Ministries. "In regard to my own Ministry, I can give other instances, Secretary of Publicity Department of the League communicated to the secretaries in the branches of the League about carrying on propaganda in their territories. That is a typical example. Another instance was when we decided to hold a celebration of Netaji Bose Week, that is, on the arrival of Netaji Subhas Chandra Bose in in Singapore and his taking over the presidentship of the Indian Independence League. The Ministry communicated to the secretaries of the Publicity and Propaganda Department of the League and we issued instructions to the Secretary and he communicated these instructions to the League branches throughout Burma to observe that week. Similarly, the decision about the celebration of the first anniversary of the Provisional Government of Azad Hind in October 1944 was communicated to the secretaries, on the lines of the instructions given by the Ministry through the Secretary of the Propaganda Department. Similarly, when we celebrated February 4, 1944, when the I.N.A first went into Indian on the Arakan Front, instructions were issued in the same way. I cannot think of any other decision as much immediately as far as the Propaganda Department was concerned." The above evidence is sufficient to give an idea of the scope and extent of the functions of he Provisional Government of Free India.

This witness also purported to say in his evidence-in-chief that he heard about the famine in Bengal and that Netaji Subhas Chandra Bose offered 100,000 tons of rice for relief of the famine in Bengal and that it was not accepted. In his cross-examination, he said that the offer to send rice to Bengal was made through the radio to the people of India for information and to the British authorities in India so that they could consider the offer. This broadcast was, I believe, made either in July or August 1943. The offer was made by broadcast from Singapore. Rice was to be sent from any port in Burma, I believe. I could not tell you whether it was said on the radio that the rice was to be sent from any port in Burma but I believe that it could be sent from any port in Burma if the British authorities in India could vouchsafe safe conduct. The people of Burma were not starving for want of rice ". This evidence is extremely unsatisfactory and by no means proves the allegation made: but even if it be true, it does not advance the defence case any further.

Col. Loganadan in his evidence-in-chief said that he was present when the Provisional Government of Azad Hind was formed, that he was one of the Cabinet Ministers and that he was also the Director of Medical

Services, I.N.A. In his cross-examination, he said : "On the day on which exhibit 4 F was proclaimed the functions of officers were as stated in the proclamation. I was the Director of Medical Services of the Provisional Government form the time the Government was formed until I left for the Andamans. Each officer performed his duties as laid down. As D.M.S. I carried out my functions in the Provisional Government. We held Cabinet meetings. Various details were discussed, e.g., about the National flag, the National Song, Marching Songs, Declaration of War, language to be used in the I.N.A., various things concerning the Indian Independence League branches and their functions, the recruitment of the Army, training and such other subjects. The subjects were inter-linked."

Mr. Dina Nath said in his evidence-in-chief : "I was a member of the Indian Independence League, Rangoon Branch. I know of the formation of the Provisional Government of Azad Hind. There was an Azad Hind Bank. I was one of the Directors of that Bank. " Further on in his evidence-in-chief he said : "There were branches of the Indian independence League all over East Asia. The activities of the Indian Independence League so far as I personally know of them are these : they worked as an executive body to carry out the instructions of the Provisional Government of Azad Hind. Each branch had various departments dealing with various activities. For example, it had a Finance Department, a Recruiting Department, Training Department, Propaganda Department, Welfare Department, A.R.P. Section, Women's Section, and Boys Scouts Section. The League branches looked after the interests of the Indians and one of the main functions in this respect was to look after the absentee-Indian properties, to provide relief to the suffering people to do A.R.P. Service and each branch had also opened schools for the education of children". In cross-examination, he said; "When I mentioned recruiting, I meant recruiting for the I.N.A. by propaganda I meant propaganda for the Provisional Government of Free India and I.N.A When I mention protection, I meant protection against air attacks and helping the victims. When I mentioned women's section, I meant an organisation of women who gave their support to the movement and used to collect funds for the movement and enlist ladies for the Rani of Jhansi Regiment. The main job of Boys Scouts used to be welfare work during air-raids and other periods.'

One may ask oneself the question as to what it was that the Provisional Government of Free India governed. It did not own nor was it in occupation of an inch of territory. Not a pie of tax or revenue was recovered. It was supposed to be a Provisional Government of Free India. Such activities, there fore, if any, as it pursued in Malaya cannot be said to be in exercise of any function as regards the Government of Free India. In fact, as the name itself indicates, it was supposed to come into existence as a Government if and when the Japanese, after conquering India, handed it over to the Indians. It was a Government only on paper. There was in fact no Government.

As regards the defence application to the court to take judicial notice of a magazine called "Stamp Collecting" published in London by a philatelist, it is submitted that the application cannot be entertained. Section 57 of the Indian Evidence Act says that the court shall take judicatio notice of certain facts. The defence asks the court to take judicial notice of this magazine. There is no provision in the section for this. The document in question cannot be brought within any of the 13 items in Section 57. It is only if a fact of which judicial notice is requested to be taken comes within any of the 13 items and further on all matters of public history, literature, science or art the court may resort to appropriate books or documents of reference. Further, the magazine in question is not an appropriate book or document of reference. Moreover, the application itself shows that what the defence want to do is to prove that the Provisional Government of Free India had got prepared to issue and were about to issue postal stamps of a particular character and that the designs were prepared under the direction of the Japanese. There is this further objection against the defence application and that is that the evidence, if admitted, would be hearsay of the worst character. The magazine says that its correspondent informs them that he has seen proof of impressions in the hands of the man who was responsible for the printing in Rangoon. If this is not hearsay, it is difficult to imagine what is hearsay evidence.

As regards the recognition of the Provisional Government of Free India by Japan and her allies, the evidence clearly establishes that the recognition by Japan was for its own object in order to enable it to win the war. It was Japan who made arrangements with Germany for getting Mr. Subhas Chandra Bose to come from Germany to Malaya. Mr. Shunichi Matsumoto in his cross-examination says as follows : "Japan made arrangement with the German Government and he (Mr. Subhas Chandra Bose) was sent to Japan. He was asked because they knew that he was working for the independence of India and he thought that it would help Japan's war aims and at the same time Japan wanted to help this man to obtain independence for India. The Japan Government did this at its own instance. It was done to help the Japanese war aims. As far as I am concerned, I understand that Mr. Subhas Chandra Bose came to Japan in about April 1943. I heard of the intended Provisional Government of Free India in or April 1943. I think Mr. Subhas Chandra Bose remained in Japan for about one month on that occasion. I knew officially that the Indian National Government was going to be formed and that Mr. Subhas Chandra Bose was to be the head of it and that Japan would recognize and help that Government. I think the only reason why the Japanese Government wanted to recognize the Provisional Government of Free India was to help the Japanese war efforts. Japan had asked all her allies to recognize the Provisional Government of Free India and they did recognize it." Later on, the witness said that Mr. Bose asked Japan's allies through the Japanese Government to recognize the Provisional Government of Free India. He, however, could not mention any document containing such a request. But whether it be so or not, there is no doubt that it was Japan who got her allies to recognize the Provisional Government of Free India. He further says : "I think that Japan recognized the Provisional Government because she thought that it was going to help her war effort. I think that Japan asked all her allies to recognize it because she thought that it would be a good thing for Japan." In the re-examination of this witness, he said that Japan's war aim as regards India was to make it independent. This statement is, of course, to be taken for what it is worth. Japan had to win the war first and defeat Great Britain and her allies. The professed desire of Japan to hand over of the estate was donated India to the Indians after it was conquered has also to be taken for what it is worth. It may be pointed out here that Mr. Ayyar who was the Publicity Officer says : "I am not aware that the Japanese ever made a formal clarification of the attitude of Japan towards India". What the Japanese did in countries conquered by them is a matter of history. As regards the other countries which are said to have recognized the Provisional Government of Free India, he had to admit and it is an undisputed fact that they were all in the Military occupation of Japan. The witness, of course, said that the countries were independent and not under Japanese control. He had to admit, however, that Japanese troops were in all these countries but he said they were not in occupation.

As regards Japan sending her Minister to the Provisional Government of Free India, he said that the decision to appoint a Minister was taken in November 1944 and that Mr. Hachiya was appointed Minister and that he arrived at Rangoon in March 1945. In cross-examination this witness admitted that no letters or credentials were given to Mr. Hachiya when he went to Rangoon. The credentials were not issued solely because the Government was Provisional. He went on to say that at the instance of Mr. Bose a decision was arrived at to issue credentials and they were issued and sent to Mr. Hachiya about the middle of May. In fact, no credentials ever reached Mr. Hachiya. The witness further said in his cross-examination that Mr. Hachiya actually acted as Minister in this sense that he paid an official visit to the Foreign Minister of the Provisional Government and the Foreign Minister paid a return call to him. He admitted, however, that Mr. Bose refused to have anything to do with Mr. Hachiya because he had no credentials.

Mr. Hachiya himself in his evidence said that he did not bring any credentials when he went to Rangoon and that he never received any credentials; but that he received a telegram stating that the credentials had been sent. According to this witness, he saw Col. Chatterji twice or thrice and he saw Mr. Ayyar once. He also admitted that Mr. Bose refused to see him because he had no credentials. He said that he sent a telegram to Tokyo asking for his credential because he was told to do so by the request of Mr. Subhash Chandra Bose which was conveyed to him through Col. Chatterji.

As regards the alleged administration of liberated territory, the defence tried to make out in the evidence-in-chief of Lt.-Col. Loganadan that the Andaman and Nicobar Islands had been ceded by Japan to the Provisional Government of Free India. The version given by Col. Loganadan in his evidence-in-chief was deliberately misleading. His own documents put to him in cross-examination showed how far from true were the statements made by him in his examination-in-chief. He said in his evidence-in-chief: "In the Far Eastern Asiatic Conference, the Andaman and Nicobar Islands were ceded to the Provisional Government. On February 17, 1944, I went to Port Blair. After I had been there two to three weeks we had a ceremony at the Indian Independence League Headquarters at Port Blair. The Rear Admiral in charge as well as the Army Commander there, one Major-General, attended the function and the Andaman and Nicobar Islands were handed over to me as Chief Commissioner. Mr. Subhas Chandra Bose appointed me Chief Commissioner.... I took charge of the Administration two or three weeks later at the time of the function which I have described. Major Alvi was in charge of the Education Department in the Andaman and Nicobar Islands. Lt. Subha Singh was in charge of Revenue and Finance and Lt. Iqbal was in charge of Police. With the help of the local administration, I began to administer these Islands. I administered these islands as long as I was there, that is, until September 1944, when I returned to Singapore."

In cross-examination, when it was put to him that the only department which was handed over to him was the Education Department, he tried to make out that it was because he refused to take over the other departments, unless the police Department was also handed over to him. He admitted that the authority for the Statement that the Andaman and Nicobar Islands were ceded to the Provisional Government of Azad Hind was a broadcast from Tokyo; but he did not remember the exact wording of the broadcast. Mr. Subhas Chandra Bose gave a letter to this witness (Exhibit 5 B) appointing him Chief Commissioner, dated January 6, 1944. At the same time he gave him a letter dated November 16, 1943, from the Japanese Vice-Admiral to Mr. Subhas Chandra Bose. In this letter (G5 E) it was stated as follows : "We are already going ahead with preparatory measures necessary for a speedy and smooth transfer of the Islands. In accordance with a statement made by the Prime Minister, a Governor is to be appointed after completion of the transfer. It is to be understood that pending completion of the transfer an official of the Provisional Government bearing some such title as the Chief Commissioner for the Andaman and Nicobar Islands should be despatched to co-operate fully in the military administration of the Islands, under the direction of the Naval Commandant there". When confronted with this letter, Col. Loganadan said that certain verbal instructions were given by Mr. Bose to him. When asked what those instructions were, he said that they were that consistent with the local difficulties he should as soon as possible take over the whole of the islands. Later on, in his cross-examination, Col. Loganadan said as follows: "The word 'minsimu' means civil administration. The head of this was Jochi. The military and naval administration was in the hands of the Rear Admiral. As regards the self-sufficiency programme, I went to the villages and gave lectures. Apart from running schools and the self-sufficiency programme, my administration comprised nothing else. The Education Department consisted of running schools; that is all. There were about 30 or 33 schools. We had our own funds for running these schools. The funds for running the schools were issued by the Japanese to me. All these sums were not repaid by the time I left. I have not worked out how much this sum would come to per month. I never knew what it cost to run these schools. Teachers were there and they continued to work; if a vacancy arose, I filled it. Regarding the self-sufficiency programme, I went about from village to village urging the peasants to grow more food. I did nothing else specially. I was interesting myself in other departments, if you put that way, that is, taking charge of departments. That was the extent of my administration." He admitted that except for domestic purposes, the Provisional Government of Azad Hind incurred no expenses with regard to the administration of these islands, and that other than the loans received from the Japanese, there was no other expenditure by the

Provisional Government of Azad Hind.

The reports made by the witness to Mr. Subhas Chandra Bose from time to time show that it was not true that the other deparments were not taken up because the Police Department was not transferred.

The witness also admitted that the Administrative and Consultative Committees were in existence when he came. He also admitted that the Japanese had a Supply Department and that the self-sufficiency programme was carried out under instructions of the Japanese Supply Department. The witness also admitted that, if he wrote anything which was unpalatable to the Japanese in any of his letters, they would either suppress it or ask him to alter it. He admitted that when he was in the Andamans gross atrocities were committed by the Japanese in spy cases. He said he was aware of that but he was unable to remedy the matter.

The witness admitted that it was true as a general statement that civilians feared to come near any of them and they were not anxious to expose themselves to be seen with them.

When Col. Loganadan left the Andaman Islands, Major Alvi wrote a letter to him (Ex.5/c) in which he stated, among other things, as follows : "I do not know how I can maintain the prestige of the Provisional Government here without either commanding the least respect or confidence of the people or being able to render any co-operation to the Government; for it I cannot help the people in the least in their misfortunes. I cannot expect to work them into patriotic frenzy and make them go all out to help the Government war effort." He also stated that there was absolute insecurity of life and liberty and that if the Provisional Government was merely to watch but not to open its mouth where the question of spying was concerned, he could not stick to a place where he was expected to watch without emotion and without powers of interference in the execution of men whom he believed to be innocent.

In the report which Col. Loganadan made to Mr. Subbas Chandra Bose (Ex. 5/c), he stated, among other things, that the propaganda required by the Japanese Government was carried out and that any propaganda for the Independence movement was ineffective. It further said that the total amount of work done by the staff was so little that their absence would not be missed. "The higher authorities say that we have been helpful but to what extent I cannot conceive. The subordinates think and feel and say that we are a hindrance to their work. This is applicable chiefly to the Police Department. The public have lost confidence in us as we failed to lessen their sufferings. The public feel that the withdrawal of the Provisional Government may improve their lot as its intervention, if any, is likely to stiffen the attitude of the local authorities."

This report, according to the witness, was handed over by him to Mr. Subhas Chandra Bose in December 1944.

The witness was asked whether, before he left the Andamans, he did not tell the Vice-Admiral and the Civil Administrator that he was going to recommend the withdrawal of the Provisional Government from the islands. He denied it. He also denied that he sent any telegram himself to Mr. Subhas Chandra Bose after his arrival in Singapore recommending the withdrawal of the Provisional Government from the Andaman and Nicobar Islands.

He was then confronted with an entry in his diary (Ex. 5.c) under the date, October 25, 1944, in which he had made a copy of the telegram sent by Col. Bhonsle to Mr. Bose to the effect that Col. Loganadan was strongly of opinion that the entire Provisional Government staff should be withdrawn from the Andaman Islands as they had not got any useful work to do there. Col. Loganadan then said that a copy of the telegram was shown to him by Col. Bhonsle after the telegram had been despatched, and that he did not quite approve of the wording of the telegram and that he would have sent it differently. He said that it was not correct that he caused the telegram to be sent. He said that the words which he did not approve of were, "as they have not got any useful work to do here." He added that he did not think it worthwhile taking steps to correct the false impression on a telegram which had already been sent.

It was argued on behalf of the defence that Col. Loganadan in his evidence said that he had re-named the Andaman and Nicobar Islands and that he was not cross-examined on this point. Surely, it was not necessary to cross-examine the witness on a statement made by him which is contradicted by the documents produced by him. All the reports which Col. Loganadan made from the time of his arrival in the islands up to the time of his departure from that place are signed by him as Chief Commissioner of the Andaman and Nicobar Islands. The report which he made on December 23, 1944, also refers in terms to the Andaman Islands and is signed by him as Chief Commissioner of the Andaman and Nicobar Islands.

My submission is that it is abundantly proved that Japan never ceded the Andaman and Nicobar Islands or indeed an inch of any other territory to the Provisional Government of Free India, nor did Col. Loganadan or anybody else on behalf of the Provisional Government of Free India administer it. As a matter of fact, Japan had no right to cede any territory, even if it wanted to. The rights of an army inoccupation are thus set out in Oppenheim's International Law, Vol. II, Page 341, Par. 169 : "As the occupant actually exercises authority and as the legitimate government is prevented from exercising its authority, the occupant acquired a temporary right of administration over the territory and the inhabitants; and all legitimate steps taken by the exercise of rights must be recognized by the legitimate government after occupation has ceased. But as the right of an occupant in occupied territory is merely a right of administration, he may neither annex it while the war continues, nor set it up as an independent State, nor divide it into two administrative districts for political purposes. Moreover, the administration of the occupant is in no wise to be compared with ordinary administration, for it is distinctly and precisely military administration. In carrying it out the occupant is totally independent of the constitution and the laws of the territory, since the occupation is an aim of warfare, and the maintenance and safety of his forces and the purpose of war stand in the foreground of his interest and must be promoted under all circumstances and conditions. But although as regards the safety of his army and purpose of war the occupant is vested with an almost absolute power, as he is not the sovereign of the territory he has no right to make changes in the laws or in the adminsitration, other than those which are temporarily necessitated by his interest in the maintenance and safety of his army and the realisation of the propose of war. On the contrary, he has the duty of administering the country according to the existing laws and the existing rules of administration; he must ensure public order and safety, must respect family honour and rights, private property, religion and liberty. It is clear that these and other obligations of the occupations of the occupant cannot be avoided by dint of the additional illegality of prematurely annexing the occupied territory".

As regards the evidence given by Col. Loganadan, he could not have forgotten the substance of the various reports which he made and the contents of the letter which Major Alvi wrote to him, and the report which he made to Mr. Subhas Chandra Bose in December 1944. He attempted to give an entirely misleading impression to the court in his evidence-in-chief about the administrations of the Andaman and Nicobar Islands by him. His attempt to get out of the fact that the letter of the Japanese Minister to Mr. Subhas Chandra Bose definitely stated that in accordance with a statement made by the Prime Minister a Governor was to be appointed after the completion of the transfer and that it was to be understood that pending completion of the transfer an official of the Provisional Government bearing some such title as Chief Commissioner for the Andaman and Nicobar Islands should be despatched to co-operate fully in the Military administration of the Islands under the direction of the Navāl Commandant there was futile.

He attempted to make out that Mr. Bose actually gave him greater authority than what was contained in the letter of the Japanese Minister. Ultimately, however, when asked what those instructions were, he said that the instructions given by Mr. Bose were that consistent with the local difficulties, he should as soon as possible take over the whole of the islands and that the full instructions were to take over the Islands as soon as possible. The witness in his evidence-in-chief tried to make out that his reports were not censored by the Japanese and that he gave them in sealed covers to the Japanese authorities for being transmitted to Mr. Subhas Chandra Bose. He had subsequently to admit that all his reports were seen and that if they contained any passages which were not palatable to the Japanese they would either withhold the report or ask him to alter the objectionable passage. He admitted that, in fact, from one of the reports a paragraph had to be deleted and that that paragraph was never communicated to Mr. Bose. His statement that he refused to take over the other departments unless the Police Department was transferred to him is also shown to be incorrect by the report which he himself made. He denied in the first instance about a telegram having been caused to be sent by him to Mr. Subhas Chandra Bose for withdrawing the so-called Provisional Government from the Andaman and Nicobar Islands. When confronted with the entry in his diary all the explanation that he could give was that he did not quite approve of the wording of the telegram and that he would have sent it differently. He said that the words of which he did not approve were "as they have not got any useful work to do there!" He said that he did not think it was worthwhile taking steps to correct the false impression on a telegram which had already been sent.

The story of the Andaman Islands having been ceded by the Japanese to the Provisional Government of Free India and having been administered by the latter having been exploded, the defence next tried to make out that the Provisional Government of Free India administered a portion of Burmese territory known as Ziawadi Estate. The two witnesses called in connection with this part of the case were Mr. Dina Nath and Mr. Shiv Singh. According to Mr. Dina Nath, this estate was handed over to the Provisional Government of Azad Hind and their representative administered it. In his evidence-in-chief this witness said : "This representative was appointed by the Revenue Ministry of the Azad Hind Government. There was one big sugar factory on the estate. There were yarn factories, blanket making factories, gunny-making factories, hospitals, and in addition to them cultivation was being carried out there. The population was about 15,000 mainly consisting of Indians. The Indian National Army had a base there. They had hospitals and these factories were also being run by the Indian National Army there. They had training camps also there. The produce was all handed over to the Provisional Government to be utilized by them in the manner they thought best." In cross-examination, he said that the estate belonged to a man named Mr. Parmanand, but he did not know personally who was the owner of that estate, and that it was handed over to the representative of the Provisional Government of Azad Hind by Mr. Parmanand. He said that at a public meeting at which Mr. Subhas Chandra Bose spoke and appealed for funds, Mr. Parmanand came up and announced: "I formally hand over the estate to the Provisional Government of Free India today". Mr. Parmanand was Minister of supplies. He added that after this announcement the products from that area were going to the Provisional Government only and the factories there were also run under the control of the Indian National Army. He admitted that the estate was in Burmese territory and he said that the estate was handed over as well as its revenue, income from factories, etc. He understood that it was handed over for the purposes of administration and for looking after the production. He wound up by saying : "All that the I.N.A. did was to sell the produce and whatever produce there was they sold it. The I.N.A. also arranged for further production. As I have said before, factories were also set up and they administered that area. I have no personal knowledge of the administration of that area."

There is nothing to prove that even the estate itself was handed over to the Provisional Government of Free India. What really happened was that the income to the fund of the Provisional Government of Free India, but even if the estate itself was handed over, it did not amount to an administration of liberated territory by the Provisional Government of Free India. The witness, Mr. Dina Nath, said that he did not know what happened to the estate afterwards.

The next witness called on this point was Mr. Shiv Singh. He put forward a ridiculous story of the estate having been occupied by the Provisional Government of Free India and having been administered by it. According to him, there had been agreement between the Japanese Government and the Provisional Government of Free India that the Provisional Government of Free India was to be the master of all that property which belonged to other owners who were not present. Apart from the inherent absurdity of this story and its being contrary to the version given by Mr. Dina Nath, the evidence of this witness is of no value at all. He said that he volunteered to fight for the Provisional Government of Free India in August 1942. He said that when he went to the Bangkok conference he belonged to the Indian National Army. Later on he tried to show that he joined the Indian National Army from the time the Japanese recognized the I.N.A. and the Provisional Government of Free India, and that that was in September 1943. He admitted that he was in the I.N.A. even before also but that he did not start work till September 1943. He further admitted that he went to Rangoon in September 1942 as one of a special party who were sent under Col, Gill, and that he actually proceeded to Arakan to reconnoitre and that he returned and made his report. This witness after joining the Indian National Army gave information about it to the British Army as regards the whereabouts of the I.N.A. He made a flimsy effort to wriggle out of this by saying that in so doing he did a trick to save the Ziawadi estate, the I.N.A. and the Provisional Government. It would be a waste of time and energy to say anything more about the evidence of this palpably false witness.

It was then attempted to show that when the I.N.A. entered Indian territory they administered the area occupied by them. The area referred to is the portion of the Manipur State which is on the border of Burma. The source of information of this witness, viz., Capt. R.M. Irshad, is according to him, reports from Vishnpore area which was commanded by Capt. S.A. Malik.

If the defence wanted to prove this fact they could have called better evidence than the evidence of a witness who deposes to facts from his recollection of certain reports which he saw. The declaration which he deposes to having been seen by him only stated that the administration in the liberated areas would be carried out under the head of the Provisional Government of Azad Hind. All that he says in his evidence-in-chief about the alleged administration of the area is that he came across official documents about the administration carried out on the Manipur Front and that at the time when operations were being carried on in Manipur Area, the administration of the liberated area was being carried on by Major M. Kiani, No. I Division Commander, that there were also units of Azad Hind Dal at More hand that these units came under the orders of No. I Division Camp. He further said that in his official capacity as G.I. He received reports from Vishnupore area which was commanded by Capt. S.A. Malik who came under the command of No. I Division Camp, about the administration carried out by him and by units of the Azad Hind Dal in Vishnupore sector.

In cross-examination, the witness could give only two instances of the administration about which he deposed. He said that Capt. Kiani operating on the left of the road had to settle some land dispute among the Manipuris in that particular area. As regards the other incident, all that the witness said was that he remembered the instructions given to the Azad Hind Dal Unit for collection of supplies, giving medical aid, etc., to the villagers. The witness admitted that at the time when Palel was besieged there were British troops in the operational areas of Manipur and that fighting had never ceased in Manipur and that the areas which had been liberated from Moreh to Chimol—a little this side of Palel—were administered by the I.N.A. He said that there were certain areas where operations had not actually been carried out; there were certain areas where operations had been or were being carried out and there were certain areas where operations had ceased. In other words, where Japanese and the I.N.A. were in military occupation. He added : "That is what I meant by liberated areas. " Finally, he said : " There was, as, I have said before, military administration in those particular parts of Manipur and Vishnupore area where the I.N.A were operating. " As a matter of fact, the Azad Hind Dal, which consisted of a small body of persons trained for civil administration, was, according to the prosecution case, never in Manipur and never went beyond the limits of Burma. Proof of this fact appears in Exhibit 5-L which is a letter dated June 21, 1944, by Subhas Chandra Bose to Col. Loganadan. Paragraph of the letter is as follows : "We have started a new organisation called the Azad Hind Dal. It is a semi-military organisation consisting of civilians and administrators who will be going to India in the wake of our victorious armies. " This letter clearly shows that up to June 21, 1944, the Azad Hind Dal had not gone into India. It will be recollected that from about the end of June or beginning of July, 1944, the Japanese and the units of hc I.N.A. that were there began to retreat from the Manipur area.

The evidence given by Capt. Irshad is coloured by a desire to make it favourable to the defence. In his evidence-in-chief he said that Col. Hunt had said : "From now on you belong to the Japanese Army and you will obey their orders as you have been obeying our orders." In cross-examination he admitted that those were not the words used by Col. Hunt and that in the statement which he made to the defence what he said was : "Now you are prisoners of war and I hand you over to the Japanese authorities." His statement about having heard that the Congress was hostile to the Japanese is also without foundation. His statement about Capt. Sahgal having joined the I.N.A. in August 1942 is also not correct. There is abundant evidence to show that Capt. Sahgal joined the I.N.A. long before August 1942 and actually made speeches persuading other prisoners of war to join the I.N.A. He stated that he was not aware of any coercive methods used in making prisoners of war join the I.N.A. This is entirely inconsistent with another statement in his evidence-in-chief to the following effect :" It was also decided that the recruitment for the 2nd I.N.A. should be entirely voluntary." He could not explain why such a decision should be taken if previously the recruitment was voluntary. The explanation which he attempted to give is lacking in sincerity. He admitted that the alternatives before the Indian soldiers who were prisoners of war were either to join the I.N.A. or to be treated as prisoners of war. He however would not admit that the treatment by the Japanese of prisoners of war was brutal. He would not go beyond stating that the treatment was unsatisfactory and that the Japanese were not treating the prisoners of war according to international rules and regulations. He admitted that in February officers were separated from the men but he suggested that he did not know the object of doing so. He denied having seen the pamphlet "Our Struggle" (Exhibit 5A). His statement that he did not know what happened to Capt. Mohan Singh after he was arrested can hardly be accepted. The statements, therefore, of this witness even as far as they go can hardly be taken as carrying any weight.

It was then attempted to show that there was something like a State Bank called the Nationl Bank of Azad Hind. In cross-examination, witness (Mr. Dina Nath) stated that the bank was registered in Rangoon like any other public bank and that there were shareholders in the bank. The capital of the bank was Rs. 50 lakhs. He further stated that the bank acted as the bankers to the Provisional Government just as it acted for its other constituents. He also said that all the money was in Japanese occupancy notes and that there was only about Rs. 50 to 60 thousand in British currency.

An attempt was made to rely on the evidence of Col. Kitson and Ghulam Mohammed in support of the contention that Capt. Sahgal sent a note saying that he and his party wished to surrender as prisoners of war and that as this offer was accepted, there was a recognition of belligerency so far as he is concerned and he is not liable to be tried for the offence of waging war against the King. So far as the evidence of Col Kitson is concerned, it is quite clear that in the conversation which he had with Capt. Sahgal, Capt. Shahg told him that he had fought for what he considered to be right and that now that he had lost he was preprared to take the consequences. Col. Kitson then told him that he would be marched off to Brigade Headquarters on the morrow and that he would be sent back and disposed of by Brigade or Division but that his disposal had nothing to do with him after he had sent him off. In any event, it cannot be suggested that the leading Company Commander to whom Capt. Sahgal surrendered had or could have any authority either to grant belligerency or to recognize belligerent rights. So far as the evidence of Havildar Ghulam Mohammed is concerned , it was suggested in his cross-examination that there was something more written in the letter. No such suggestion was made to Col. Ketson and he was not cross-examined by Counsel for the defence. As a matter of fact, according to the evidence of Ghulamna Mohammed after Capt. Sahgal and his party had decided to surrender and before they actually surrendered, Capt. Sahgal asked the officers to communicate to all the men about the decision which had been taken and ordered the pickets on the hills to withdraw.

An attempt was also made to rely upon what happened in Rangoon when the British Army entered it in the beginning of May, 1945, in support of the defence plea of recognition. It is difficult to see how any such contention can be urged. It was admitted that some days before the British entered Rangoon the Japanese Army had evacuated Rangoon and it is in evidence that Mr. Subhas Chandra Bose, while leaving Rangoon, told Capt. Irshad and Col. Loganadan that he was leaving the Indian Army in Rangoon for the sole purpose of looking after Indian civilians in Rangoon. There was no question of resisting the British entry. The evidence also makes it clear that, when the Japanese evacuated Rangoon, they withdrew the sentries from the prison in which the British prisoners of war were kept and according tot he evidence of Capt.. Irshad and the documents put in during his examination, Wing-Commander Hudson, who was the senior officer among the Allied prisoners of war there, gave him certain orders and Capt. Arshad implemented those orders but before the orders were carried out, the British Army arrived in Rangoon. In fact, according to Capt. Irshad himself, Brig. Lander said that he was not in a position to accept Capt. Irshad and the other I.N.A. troops as prisoners of war.

In the statements made by accused, an attempt has been made to give an explanation of their conduct in joining the I.N.A. and waging war against His Majesty the King. Waging war against His Majesty the King is an offence on the part of a person even if he is compelled to do so by threats. Section 94 of the Indian Penal Code which creates a general exception in respect of an act to which a person is compelled by threats excludes murder and offences against the State from this general exception. Waging war against His Majesty the King which is an offence under

Section 121 of the Indian Penal Code is an offence against the State. There might conceivably be circumstances in the commission of an offence, which may be a palliative of the offence but if war has been waged in terms of the section, no reason or explanation can be a defence to the charge under Section 121. In the statements of all the accused it is attempted to be made out that the Indian prisoners of war were left in the lurch to face the consequences of the surrender by themselves. This is not true. It was under the orders of the Japanese authorities that the British prisoners of war were separated from the Indian prisoners of war, it is not suggested and it cannot be suggested that the British prisoners of war expected to receive or in fact received better treatment from the Japanese than the Indian prisoners of war. The statements of the accused attempt to suggest that they were freed from their allegiance to the Crown by reason of what happened at the Farrier Park meeting. As Capt. Shah Nawaz Khan says in his statement, Col. Hunt on that occasion said : "Today I on behalf of the British Government hand you over to the Japanese Government whose orders you will obey as you have done ours." Of course, Col. Hunt said this under the orders of the Japanese authorities : It is difficult to conceive what else could have been said on an occasion like this, When the Singapore army surrendered the whole army came under the orders of the Japanese Government and all the prisoners of war had to obey the orders of the Japanese authorities from that time. Even if no statement had been made by Col. Hunt, the consequences and the result of the surrender would have been exactly the same. There is no justification for saying that the Indian prisoners of war were handed over like cattle by the British to the Japanese. The British prisoners of war were similarly surrendered.

The very fact that immediately after the surrender they were asked to join the I.N.A. shows that the idea of making the Indian prisoners of war to fight against the British as members of the I.N.A. had been conceived and put into train before they fall of Singapore. The evidence shows that at the meeting at Farrar Park there were Indian prisoners of war wearing arm bands with the letter F on them : F stands for Fujiwara Kikan. Capt. Shah Nawaz Khan says in his statement that up to the end of May 1942 he was against the idea of the organization of the I.N.A. coming into existence. This is in consistent with the evidence for the prosecution which is to the effect that Capt. Shah Navaz delivered lectures even before April 1942 asking other prisoners of war to join the I.N.A. Capt. Shah Nawaz Khan further says that from June 1942 to July 1943 he decided in the interests of his men to volunteer for the I.N.A. with full determination that he would do everything possible to break it or to sabotage it from within as soon as he felt that it would submit to Japanese exploitation. This is also inconsistent with the proved facts that Capt. Shah Nawaz Khan took an active part in winning other prisoners of war from their allegiance to the Crown. Capt. Sahgal says in his statement that he joined the I.N.A. in August 1942 and that up to that time he was in the non-volunteer camp in Tangan aerodrome. No question was put to any of the prosecution witnesses suggesting this.

Lt. Dhillon admits that he co-operated with Mohan Singh in the organisation of the I.N.A. till June 29, 1942, when he became ill and had to go to the hospitals. He says that on receiving the assurance that Netaji Subhas Chandra Bose would come to lead the movement, he decided to continue in the second I.N.A. after December 1942.

It is also suggested in the statements of the accused that their object in joining the I.N.A. was that they did not wish indiscriminate looting and raping taking place in India as had happened in Malaya after the Japanese entered the country. The evidence, however clearly establishes the fact that all the accused did everything they could to enable the Japanese to conquer India. In fact, they insisted on the Japanese authorities giving them an active part in the fight at the front. It is also significant that, even after the Japanese began to retreat from Manipur and Kohima, the accused kept on fighting in Burma and in fact were anxious that the Japanese should overrun India.

The explanations sought to be given of their conduct in their statements are inconsistent with their own case that the I.N.A. was raised in order to drive the British out of India; in other words, to help the Japanese to conquer India. The entries in the diaries of Capt. Shah Nawaz and Capt. Sahgal are significant on this point. They have been read to the Court more than once and I will not read them again.

It was argued that, so far as the accused are concerned, there was a question of duel allegiance. This argument overlooks the wording of Section 121. The offence mentioned in that section is that of waging war against the Queen. The word "Queen" is defined in Section 13 of the Indian Penal Code as denoting the Sovereign for the time being of the United Kingdom of Great Britain and Ireland. The cases of the King Vs. Casement (1917) 1 K.B. 98, and the King vs. Lynch (1903) 1 K.B. 444, give a complete answer to this contention. The case of Jeager the Attorney-General for Natal (1907) Appeal Cases, 326, is a complete answer to the contention that the accused no longer owed allegiance because the Crown failed to protect them. As a matter of fact, the British Government did succeed in protecting India against the Japanese. The fact that up to a certain stage the fortunes of war were against Great Britain can make no difference in the question. It is relevant to point out in this connection that the officers and the men of the Indian Army who, when they were prisoners of war, joined the Indian National Army at first, but subsequently did not agree to continue in it after December 1942, were to revert to their positions as prisoners of war. Not only that, but even as regards those men who were willing to join the Indian National Army but who were in the category of B and C men who could not be absorbed in the Indian Natinal Army, it was announced that they would be reverted to prisoners of war and sent to those camps . I am referring to exhibit SS which is a document signed by Capt. Shah Nawaz Khan and addressed to the Headquarters, Indian National Army, and is dated May 27, 1943. It states, *inter alia,* as follows:

"Besides this, the Indian National Army has approximately 2,000 men under-strength and up to date it has been found very difficult to fill up this large gap. All Unit and Formation Commands are, therefore, requested to give their best co-operation and support in overcoming this difficulty .... There is also a likelihood that all category B and C men who can not be absorbed in the Indian National Army will be reverted to prisoners of war and sent to those camps. It is fully realized that it is a very hard and regrettable decision; nevertheless, it may have to be resorted to."

In exhibit which is a document from Mr. Rash Behari Bose, President of the Council of Action, and addressed to officers and men of the Indian National Army, it is stated as follows : "Some of you many be anxious to know what will happen to those rejected from the Indian National Army. Unfortunately, I shall have no control over those who deliberately chose to quit the Indian National Army at the present juncture. I cannot speak for the Japanese, nor say in what manner or at what place they will be employed by the Powers whose prisoners they choose to be". It is also interesting to know that in Exhibit AA which is a Special Order dated September 1, 1942, and refers to the promotion *inter alia* of the accused, their old rank and unit is mentioned. Even as late as March 26, 1944, in a document signed by Capt. Shah Nawaz Khan headed 'security' and which gave the allotment of personal numbers to the officers, the Indian Army Units of the officers are also mentioned.

As regards the contention of the accused that they were entitled to throw off their allegiance to the Crown and that they were justified in doing so, because they were fighting for the freedom of their country, it is relevant to consider some cases which throw light on the subject. In King vs. Casement (1917) 1 K.B. page 98, the report of the case shows that Sir Roger Casement circulated a leaflet which said as follows : "Irishmen! Here is a chance for you to fight for Ireland. You have fought for England, your country's hereditary enemy. You have fought for Belgium in England's interest, though it was no more to you than the Fiji Islands. Are you willing to fight for your own country with a view to securing the national freedom of Ireland? With the moral and material assistance of the German Government, an Irish Brigade is being formed. The object of the Irish Brigade shall to be fight solely for the cause of Ireland and under no circumstances shall it be directed to any German end. The Irish Brigade shall be formed and shall fight under the Irish flag alone. The men shall wear a specially distinct Irish uniform and have Irish officers. The Irish Brigade shall be clothed, fed and efficiently equipped with arms and ammunitions by the German Government. It is to be stationed near Berlin and be treated as guests of the German Government. At the end of the war, the German Government undertakes to send each member of the Brigade who may so desire to the United States of America with necessary means to land. The Irishmen in America are collecting money for the brigade. Those men who do not join the Irish Brigade will be removed from Lumburg and distributed among other camps. If interested, see your company commanders. Join the Irish Brigade and win Ireland's independence". Sir Roger Casement circulated the said leaflet among British subjects who were prisoners of war of the Germans. In delivering judgment Chief Justice Lord Reading referred to the case of William Caundell which was decided in 1812. It was the case of persons who were confined in the Isle of France and who had there fore saken their allegiance to the King and transferred it to the French. In that case a number of British sailors and marines were confined as prisoners of war in the Isle of France. The prison being much crowded was greatly incommoded with dirt and vermin and there being no way of escaping from such inconvenience but that of desertion every art was practised by their keepers to induce the unhappy prisoners to enter the French service. Fifty men among whom were Cundell and Smith had not virtue enough to resist the temptation on the one hand, and the hope of escaping from distress and filth on the other. They forgot their country and their allegiance and put on the enemy uniform acting as sentinels over those who were so recently their companions in captivity. The traitors continued to do the duty with the French until the surrender of the Island to the British forces when Cundell and Smith with ten others positively refused to accompany the ememy and threw themselves upon the mercy of their country, having immediately surrendered to the English, while 38 others marched off to old France. These culprits were then transmitted to England and a Special Commission was issued for their trial. They were convicted and hanged. The Chief Justice, in giving his judgment, said : "I cannot doubt that before the statute, it was treason in a British subject to join the force of an enemy abroad, and that if a British subject had joined the forces of an enemy abroad at war with the country and he afterwards returned or was brought back to the country he could be tried here for that offence. When one has regard to the nature of the offence of high treason I think it is obvious, it must have been so. Foster in his Crown Law page 183 thus describes the offence of high treason: "High treason being an offence committed against the duty of allegiance it may be proper to consider from whom and to whom allegiance is due. With regard to natural born subjects, there can be no doubt they owe allegiance to the Crown at all times and in all circumstances. This is what we call natural allegiance in contradistinction to that which is local. Natural allegiance is found in the relation every man standeth in to the Crown, considered as the head of the society whereof he is born a member and on the peculiar privileges he derives from the relation, which are, with great propriety called his birth-right. This birth right nothing but his own demerit can deprive him of; it is indefeasible and perpetual; and, consequently the duty of allegiance which arises out of it and is inseparably connected with it is in consideration of law likewise inalienable and perpetual." Justice Darling in his judgment after referring to Cundell's case said that he had violated his allegiance which followed him, which remained with him wherever he might be outside the King's dominion, and by which he was bounden even when he was a prisoner of war. In King versus Lynch (1903) I K8. page 444, the accused was a British subject born in Australia. During the Boer War he made a declaration of willingness to take up arms for the South African Republic where he was residing in order to maintain and defend its independence and he became a fully enfranchised burgher of the South African Republic. On March 22, 1900, he published an address to Irishmen inciting them to assist the enemy and he commanded an armed body of men called the second Irish Brigade with intent to co-operate with the military forces of the enemy. He actually fought on behalf of the enemy against the British troops. The defence was that he had transferred his allegiance during the war by becoming naturalised in an enemy country. It was held that he could not do so during the time of war. In his judgment, Justice Wills said at page 459 : "With regard to the rest of this case it is sufficient for me to say that throughout the argument I have never been able to comprehend how an act of treason could give any sort of rights or could exempt a person from criminal responsibility for subsequent acts of treason. If Mr. Sheeny's argument was sound, an army might, if each member of it were individually to accept letters of naturalisation from the enemy, desert in the hour of battle without rendering any of its members liable to the penalties of treason. So extravagant a conclusion shows conclusively that the contention cannot be supported."

In Jaeger vs. Attorney General of Natal (1907) Appeal cases 326, the defence against a charge of treason which was sought to be raised was that when the protection of the State ceased its counterpart, namely, the duty of allegiance ceased also. This was a case of a resident alien within British territory owing allegiance to the Crown. He was a burgher of the South African Republic and when the British forces had retired from Waschbank to Ladysmith and the Boer forces occupied that part of Natal in which Waschbank was situated, he joined the Boer Forces and aided and assisted them both as Commandant and as a Commissioner and Justice of Peace. In giving judgment their Lordships of the Judicial Committee of the Privy Council said : "Their Lordships are of opinion that there is no ground for this contention. The protection of a State does not cease merely because the State Forces for strategical or other reasons are temporarily withdrawn, so that the enemy for the time exercises the right of an army in occupation. On the contrary when such territory reverts to the control of its rightful sovereign, wrongs done during the foreign occupation are cognisable by the ordinary courts. The protection of the sovereign has not ceased. It is continuous though the actual redress of what has been done amiss may be necessarily postponed until the enemy forces have been expelled."

Learned Counsel for the Defence put forward two points of distinction : (I) That they were cases of individuals charged with treason under the English law and that they were not members of an organized body; and (2) that in those cases there was no question of double allegiance. I have dealt with both these points in my address. It was further contended that in India there is no such thing as treason and that the whole law is codified in the Indian Penal Code. Treason, never the-less, is an offence against the State. High treason has been defined as an offence committed against the duty of allegiance. The essence of waging war against the King is that the offence is against the duty of allegiance. It is an offence against the State. The principles laid down in the cases which I have cited are applicable to the cases of waging war against the King.

The only other case to which I wish to refer on this subject is Aung Hla vs. King Emperor, I.L.R. 9 Rangoon 494. That was a case where the accused was charged with the offence of waging war against the King. In delivering the judgment, Chief Justice Page at page 413 said : "We propose, therefore, to make clear what is meant by the word 'wage war' in Section 121 of the Indian Penal Code". In his judgment, he quoted from 21 State trials pages 644, 645, from the charge of Chief Justice Mansfield to the jury which deals with two kinds of waging war, one against the person of the King and the other against the Majesty of the King: in other words, against him in his Regal capacity, where it was pointed out that it was treason to attempt to attain by force and violence any object of a general public nature. The learned Judge then quotes from the charge of Lord President Hope in Rex vs. Wilson, 21 St. Tr. 1353. If they rise to effect a general public purpose by force and numbers that object renders the rising treason, be the numbers great or small. The learned Judge then quoted from the charge of Justice Tindal in R. Vs. Frost, 4 St. Tr. at page 93. An assembly of men armed and arrayed in a warlike manner with any treasonable purpose is a levying of war although no blow be struck. And enlisting and drilling and marching bodies of men are sufficient overt acts of that treason, without coming to a battle or action. And if this be the case, the actual conflict between such a body and the Queen's forces must beyond all doubt amount to levying war against the Queen—not necessarily that it should be accompanied with the pomp and pageantry of war. The learned Judge then quotes from page 216 of Foster's Crown cases that joining with rebels in an act of rebellion or with enemies in acts of hostility will make a man traitor.

It is submitted that, notwithstanding all that has been said about the formation of Provisional Government and the immunity which it is supposed to have given to the accused what the accused did was nothing else than joining the enemy in act of hostility against His Majesty the King.

It was argued that there was no charge of desertion or any breach of duty on the part of the accused as prisoners of war. It is submitted that it was not necessary to have any separate charge of desertion. Desertion was the first step taken by them in connection with the offence of waging war against His Majesty the King. Not only did they desert the army, but they actually waged war against the King.

It must be remembered that the accused were not merely civil subjects but Indian Commissioned Officers in the Indian Army. If they waged war against His Majesty the King, it necessarily implies previous desertion by them from the army. They could not have fought against His Majesty's forces without first deserting the army in which they held commissions.

As regards the contention that this court-martial has no authority to try the case because of Section 196 of the Criminal Procedure Code, it is not denied by the defence that the Criminal Procedure Code is not applicable to these proceedings. Section 41 of the Indian Army Act provides that every person subject to this Act who either within British India or at any place beyond British India commits any civil offence shall be deemed to be guilty of an offence against military law and if charged therewith under this section shall, subject to the provisions of this Act, be liable to be tried for the same by court-martial and on conviction be punished. It will be noticed that the section itself gives jurisdiction to the court-martial to try the offence. It is contended that by Section 7 (18) civil offence is defined as an offence which if committed in British India would be triable by a criminal court and it is argued that it cannot be left in the air as to which criminal court is to try the offence. The answer to this has already been given, namely, that Section 41 itself says that the person shall be liable to be tried for the same by court-martial. It was contended that we must go to an appropriate Act to show what is triable. It is submitted that the appropriate Act is the Indian Army Act itself. The Criminal Procedure Code is a Code of Procedure. All offences under the Indian Penal Code are triable by some criminal court or other. The Criminal Procedure Code lays down which particular court shall try which particular offences. In dealing with this procedure, Section 196 of the Criminal Procedure Code says that no court shall take cognisance of an offence punishable under Chapter VI unless upon complaint made by order of or under authority from the Provincial Government or some officer empowered by the Provincial Government in this behalf. The words "no court" in this section, of course, mean no court under the Criminal Procedure Code. There is no prohibition either in the Indian Army Act or in the rules under the Indian Army Act of a nature similar to that contained in Section 196 of the Criminal Procedure Code. It is submitted that the attempt to bring in Section 196 by the back-door is futile.

As regards the contention that the trial is illegal by reason of Rule 24 of the rules under the Indian Army Act, it is submitted that this contention is also unfounded. Rule 24 deals with the joint trial of several accused persons. If that is an offence which is charged to have been committed collectively by more than one person and they are tried together, there is no provision in the rules to prevent separate charges being brought against one or other of the accused and tried at the same trial along with the joint charge. Rule 18 says that a charge sheet may contain one charge or several charges. This is in marked contrast to the provision in Section 233 of the Criminal Procedure Code that for every distinct offence of which any person is accused there shall be a separate charge and that every such charge shall be tried separately except in the cases mentioned in Sections 234, 235, 236 and 239. Rule 39 provides that the accused when required to plead to any charge may object to the charge on the ground *inter alia* that it is not in accordance with the rules. Rule 68, sub-rule (e), says: "Where a charge-sheet contains more than one charge, the accused may before pleading claim to be tried separately in respect of any charge or charges in that charge-sheet on the ground that he will be embarrassed in his defence if he is not so tried separately and in such a case the court, unless they think his claim unreasonable, shall arraign and try the accused in like manner as if the convening officer had inserted the said charge or charges in different charge-sheets. No such objection was taken. It was only in the closing address of counsel for the accused that the objection was taken. Rule 135 of the Indian Army Act Rules provides for validating irregular procedure in certain cases and, omitting the unnecessary part, says that the finding and sentence of a court-martial may be confirmed and shall, if so confirmed and in all cases where confirmation is not necessary, be valid notwithstanding any deviation from these rules, or notwithstanding any defect or objection, technical or other, unless it appears that any injustice has been done to the offender. The case of Subramania vs. the King-Emperor, I. L. R. 25 Madras, page 61, cited by Counsel for the Defence has no relevance in this case.

The tenth charge against Capt. Shah Nawaz is of abetment of the murder near Popa Hill on or about March 29, 1945, of sepoy Mohammed Husain, by Khazin Shah and Aya Singh. The witnesses who disposes to this incident are Havildar Ghulam Mohammed, Alla Ditta, Jagiri Ram and Lance Naik Sardar Mohammed. Hav. Ghulam Mohammed in his evidence said that on or about March 26 or 27 he received the report that three men from No. I Battalian had been placed in quarter guard and he gave the name of one of these three men as sepoy Mohammed Husain. The witness was told that these men had tried to desert and therefore had been placed under orders in the quarter guard. According to this witness, on the evening of March 28 when Capt. Shah Nawaz Khan returned from his duty the Commander of No. 1 Battalion brought these three men before him. Capt. Sahgal interrogated them and Mohammed Husain admitted his guilt and the other two pleaded not guilty. The witness was told by Capt. Shah Nawaz to ask the officer to investigate the case. According to the witness, on the morning of March 29 the three accused were again brought up. He says in his evidence : "On the morning of March 29 these three accused were again brought up. The Battalion Commander read out the same charges to them and Col. Sahgal asked them whether they pleaded guilty to the charge or not. Mohammed Husain pleaded guilty, the other two pleaded not guilty. Three separate charge-sheets were prepared. I read all the three; then these men were sent back to the Divisional Headquarters. I was present at the office and saw them go out accompanied by the regimental second in command and the Battalion Commander. Between 2 and 3 p.m. I was in my hut when the regimental second in command and the Battalion Commander came back. Their names were Major Negi, and Lt. Khazin Shah. They they went away. I saw Mohammed Husain in the evening at about 4 or 5 o'clock when he passed in front of my room. He was accompanied by 2nd Lt. Sardar Mohammed, Adjutant of No. I Battalion, and 2nd Lt. Aya Singh". It will be noticed that this witness was not cross-examined on the statement which he made that three separate charge-sheets were prepared and that he read all the three.

The next witness Alla Ditta said in his evidence that he knew sepoy Mohammed Husain who belonged to a British regiment before. Witness belonged to the "C" Company and Mohammed Husain to Headquarters "C" Company. Witness also said that he knew Jagiri Ram who was also in "C" Company of his battalion. The witness then said that on March 26, 1945, between 2 and 3 p.m. Mohammed Husain came to him and told him that he intended to desert that day. The witness told him that that day was not suitable for escaping and that some other day would be more suitable. He went back. The same day at sunset witness was called to battalion headquarters where he saw Jagiri Ram, Mohammed Husain and Khazin Shah. The further evidence of this witness is in these words. "After that Khazin Shah gave me a beating and told me that I was disloyal to the I.N.A. and that I was one of the men who intended to escape and said : Mussalmans like you betrayed even Turks. Then I was shut up in the quarter guard and taken to headquarters. The next day I was brought before Col. Sahgal and statements were taken individually. Col. Sahgal asked me if I intended to escape. I said "no," I did not intend to escape'. I mentioned to him about Mohammed Husain's visit to me regarding his intended escape. Then I was sent out. Khazin Shah ordered Ghulam Mohammed, the Brigade Adjutant, to inquire and question Alla Ditta and others who wished to escape. Ghulam Mohammed detailed Aya Singh to beat us and question Alla Ditta and others who intended to escape. Ghulam Mohammed told Aya Singh to find out from Alla Ditta regarding the six other persons who intended to escape. On March 25, 1945, I was beaten and interrogated by Aya Singh. I stayed there on March 27 and 28. On March 28, our battalion was to move to Legyi village. Khazin Shah told

Ghulam Mohammed to inform Capt. Sahgal that if these men were not punished he would give up the command of the battalion. I was present then. On March 29, Major Negi and Khazin Shah took me before Col. Shah Nawaz to the Divisional Headquarters. I was put before Col. Shah Nawaz. Three of us were present : myself, Jagiri Ram and Mohammed Husain, besides Col. Shah Nawaz, Major Negi, Khazin Shah and two other sentries stayed out and were sent in.

I saw that three different crime reports had already been made regarding us. Major Negi took the crime reports and handed them to Col. Shah Nawaz who read them out separately to each one of us. First, Jagiri Ram was questioned by Col. Shah Nawaz. There myself and Jagiri Ram were present at the same time. Col. Shah Nawaz inquired from Jagiri Ram if he had intended to desert. He replied "no." I did not inquired from Jagiri Ram if the had intended to desert. He replied "no". I did not intend to desert. I was questioned next and I told that I did not intend to desert. Then Col. Shah Nawaz said that I was an N.C.O. and Mohammed Husain had approached me and I had not reported the matter. I said that it was my fault. Then he questioned Mohammed Husain as follows : Did you intend to desert or make others to desert with you ? Mohammed Husain replied "No". I did not intend to desert. Col. Shah Nawaz told : "speak the truth." Mohammed Husain said : "I had a few difficulties and, therefore, I intended to desert. But no inqueries were made into his complaints. Mohammed Husain was told by Col. Shah Nawaz : 'You are sentenced to death by shooting because you intended to desert yourself and were persuading others to do the same. Therefore you are not pardoned. I heard Col. Shah Nawaz saying put off the case to the Regimental Commander. Then we all three of us were sent out. I recognize Col. Shah Nawaz as the accused before the Court. We waited there for to minutes, and were brought back to Brigade Headquarters. Mohammed Husain, Jagiri Ram and myself came together back to Brigade Headquarters. Mohammed Husain and myself were put back in the same cell in which we were before and Khazin Shah took away Jagiri Ram. The same day at about 5 p.m. Sardar Mohammed, adjustant of our battalion, and Aya Singh took away Mohammed Husain. I have never seen Mohammed Husain since then."As regards the witness himself, he says that he did quarter quard for three or four days; then he was produced before Major Negi. He was reduced in rank and Major Negi said : "You will have to go to Rangoon.." This witness was taken to a concentration camp in Popa and on April 7, 1945, along with 16 other men he was despatched to Rangoon by march route.

In the cross-examination of this witness, it was attempted to be made out that Capt. Shah Nawaz did not sentence Mohammed Husain to be shot. The whole or the cross-examination is as follows : "No decision was arrived at either in my case or in the case of Jagiri Ram. It is true that all that Col. Shah Nawaz said was that you deserve to be shot. Col. Shah Nawaz said that persons like you will be sentenced to death by shooting. Col. Shah Nawaz told Mohammed Husain.: 'You yourself wanted to escape ; secondly, you have tried to persuade others to escape. Therefore you are a rebel to the I.N.A. and should be sentenced to death by shooting.' I saw Col. Shah Nawaz write something on the crime report. How could I read the crime report without picking it up from the table? I do not understand English. I do not know what he wrote there and I do not know English and I had not read what was written in the crime report at that time." In his re-examination , witness said that the crime reports were lying on the table and Col. Shah Nawaz read them out as he spoke to us individually. He wrote on the crime report which had already been drawn up.

It is submitted that this cross-examination does not help the defence in any way. Reading the cross-examination as a whole, it is submitted that, according to the evidence of this witness, Capt. Shah Nawaz sentenced Mohammed Husain to death by shooting. The previous witness deposed to three crime reports having been prepared and his having read them ; the fact that the witness did not know English does not detract from his evidence on this point. In fact, as noted by the Court, the witness used the word 'Put off the case to the Regimental Commander' in English. Even a sepoy who does not know English knows what a crime report is and from the fact that Major Negi gave the papers to Col. Shah Nawaz and he read them out separately to each of the three accused, witness can certainly say that they were crime reports. The questions put by Capt. Shah Nawaz to the accused from the papers before him were sufficient to convey to the witness the fact that the papers were crime reports.

The next witness on this point was Jagiri Ram. He says that he knew Mohammed Husain and Alla Ditta and that Mohammed Husain himself and a Garhwali talked about escape when they were in Popa Hill area. He also deposes to the inquiry made by Khazin Shah in the matter and that Khazin Shah allowed the Garhwali to go. He gives the details of the inquiry by Khazi Shah. Witness then deposes to the fact that at sunset Khazin Shah took Mohammed Husain and the witness to Brigade Headquarters. Alla Ditta arrived later. After that all the three of them, Mohammed Husain, Alla Ditta and the witness were put into the quarter guard and their hands were tied. On the following day they were brought before Col. Sahgal who interrogated them. Major Negi and Khazin Shah were present. Witness then deposes to the fact that Lt. Aya Singh gave each of them a beating and said that he would release them if they would tell the names of the people who intended to escape. Witness continued to say that he did not know.

The further evidence of the witness is in these terms. "Next day We were taken to the Divisional Commander, Col. Shah Nawaz. We were accompanied by Major Negi, Khazin Shah and the sentry. All three of us, myself, Alla Ditta and Mohammed Husain were produce before the Divisional Commander. The Divisional Commander asked me to speak the truth. He asked whether I intended to escape. I said no, I did "not" intend to escape! Capt. Shah Nawaz asked us why we did not report the matter. I said that I did not know anything about it and If did not intend to escape. He asked me if there was any officer or N.C.O. near me, I said No, " I was working with my medical officer! Then Capt. Shah Nawaz asked Alla Ditta : 'When Mohammed Husain talked to you about escaping did you report to any one? Alla Ditta said : I do not know anything about Mohammed Husain's escape. I thought it was a joke. I do not know anything about it.

Capt. Shah Nawaz then said to Alla Ditta " 'you are an N.C. O. Why did you not report ? Alla Ditta begged his pardon and said that he did not know anything about Mohammed Husain. Then Capt. Shah Nawaz questioned Mohammed Husain and Mohammed Husain replied that he was in difficulties and that he intended to escape and asked to be forgiven. Capt. Shah Nawaz then told him : 'You are not for our country; you are our enemy. I will give you death by shooting. Then Mohammed Husain asked for forgiveness and said that he was prepared to go anywhere he was ordered. Capt. Shah Nawaz said nothing to this. All the three of us were then sent out and we were taken to Brigade Headquarters accompanied by Major Negi and Khazin Shah. I moved towards the battalion with Khazin Shah and sub-officer Barfi Singh. When I reached the Battalion Headquarters, Khazin Shah told Barfi Singh to take me to Company Headquarters. In the evening an orderly took me to Battalion Headquarters. Mohammed Husain was there. Khazin Shah and Aya Singh were also there when I arrived. Khazin Shah told me :"Your will shoot Mohammed Husain because you are one of the men who were trying to escape with him ! I declined and said : I will not shoot him and that I did not know how to fire a rifle. Khazin Shah told me again : "If you do not shoot Mohammed Husain, you will be shot yourself." I still refused and he drew his pistol. I refused again and Aya Singh got hold of a rifle. He put the rifle to my shoulder and put my finger round the trigger. Khazin Shah told Aya Singh to give the order to fire. There were three of us, one Sikh, one Tamil and myself. Mohammed Husain was blindfolded by Aya Singh. He was made to sit on the ground with his back against a tree. His hands were tied behind him. Aya Singh ordered me to fire and so I did. Mohammed Husain died there. Khazin Shah ordered Aya Singh to give the order to fire and Aya Singh gave it. Khazin Shah told me to report to my company and not to come to the Battalion Headquarters. That evening we marched off to Legyi. Then we stayed at Legyi for two or three days. Then I went over to the British."

In the cross-examination of this witness, it was suggested that the witness could not know that a man was a Garhwali because the witness did not know the Garhwali language. Surely a man can know that another man is a Garhwali even if the first man does not know the Garhwali language. Witness said that he knew that he was a Garhwali because he lived with him and he spoke Garhwali. Witness further said that he came to know Mohammed Husain in the company. He used to live with him at headquarters. He used to sit in his company. He knew that he was a Mohmmedan and he did not know anything more about him. Witness said : "He used to live with me. Surely I knew him. I cannot give a long description of him except his physical description. I do not know anything else about him." The suggestion in the cross-examination was that the witness did not know Mohammed Husain. But the answers of the witness are, it is submitted, abundantly clear to show that the witness knew Mohammed Husain. The witness was not asked to give a physical descriptio of Mohammed Husain. A man may definitely know many persons by sight and by name without knowing anything more about them. In fact, witness knew Mohammed Husain more than merely by name and by sight as his evidence shows. It was then attempted to shake the evidence of this witness by showing that he did not know the English word crime. Witness said that he knew the word report in the sense of making a report to somebody. Witness was given slip of paper on which the words "crime report" were written and he was asked whether he understood the words written on the piece of paper. Of course, the witness said no. Witness never suggested that he could read English. As stated above, the phrase 'crime report' would be known even to Indian sepoys who do not understand English. In fact, it would be surprising if they did not know the phrase. Witness further said in his cross-examination that Capt. Shah Nawaz said that he (meaning Mohammed Husain) was not for his country, that he was an enemy and that he would give him death by shooting. It was contended on behalf of the defence that no reason has been given why Lt. Khazin Shah ordered Jagiri Ram to be one of the shooting party. The reason has been given by Jagiri Ram in his evidence when he said:

"Lt. Khazin Shah told me : 'You will shoot Mohammed Husain because you are one on the men who were trying to escape with him'. Obviously, this was Lt. Khazin Shah's idea of 'nemesis'. It was also suggested in the closing address of Counsel for the Defence that Jagiri Ram's evidence was to the effect that nothing was decided 'in our' case. The attempt was to read the words 'in our case' as meaning in the case of all the three of them. But if the whole passage is read, it is clear that the witness meant in the case of himself and Alla Ditta. He had already deposed to the fact of Mohammed Husain having been sentenced to death. Then he goes on to say "nothing was decided in our case" meaning thereby in the case of himself and Alla Ditta. The next witness on this point was Lance Naik Sardar Mohammad. He was the Adjutant of the First Battalion. According to his evidence, on March 27, Lt. Khazin Shah sent for the runners. On arrival of the runners he ordered them to bring the following men to the Battalion Headquarters, sepoy Mohammed Husain, Lance Naik Alla Ditta, Lance Naik Mohammed Shah, sepoy Jagiri Ram and sepoy Gobru Singh. Witness said that Mohammed Husain was a sepoy in the Indain Army before he joined the I.N.A. and that he knew it from his own knowledge. Witness said that when he brought him from Brigade Headquarters he asked him what he was in the Indian Army and to what unit he belonged. He said : "I am a sepoy of the H.K.S.R. A. Witness then deposed to the interrogation of the men by Khazin Shah. Lt. Khazin Shah told the witness that he was going to Brigade Headquarters that evening to talk about those and then he went away. Lt. Khazin Shah then ordered him to take those men to Brigade Headquarters. Witness and a sub-officer took them there . Witness met Lt.. Khazin Shah on the way and he handed over those men to his charge. He let off Lance Naik Mohammad Shafi on the spot because his Platoon Commander recommended him and he came there. He said that Mohammed Husain had been sentenced to be shot. Nothing was said about the others, but Jagiri Ram was with him at the time. Lt. Khazin Shah asked the witness to go to Ghulam Mohammad, the Brigade Adjutant, and ask him whether Mohammad hussain was to be shot under battalion arrangements or brigade arrangements.

The further evidence of this witness is in the following terms : "If the orders were for Mohammed Husain to be shot under battalion arrangements, I was to bring back Mohammed Husain with me. I was also asked to bring sepoy Mohammad Ibrahim who had been released from the quarter guard. I received instructions that Mohammed Husain was to be shot under battalion arrangements on the same day. I brought him back with me to Battalion Headquarters. I also brought back sepoy Mohammed Ibrahim and Aya Singh came with me. I conveyed these orders to Lt. Khazin Shah. He then ordered me to arrange for the execution of Mohammed Husain. I then asked him what arrangements I should make. He asked me to detail 10 men with pick axes and shovels. I detailed those men and a grave was dug. I was then ordered by Lt. Khazin Shah to take Mohammed Husain to the edge of a nullah. Mohammed Husain was taken to the edge of the nullah. Lt. Khazin Shah, 2nd Lt. Aya Singh and Havildar Major Gobind Singh, some sepoys and myself went with Mohammed Husain to the nullah. Lt. Khazin Shah ordered Mohammed Husain to be tied to a tree and also ordered that he should be blindfolded. I passed on the orders to sub-officer Gobind Singh who carried them out with the help of two other sepoys. After this Lt. Khazin Shah called two men out of the fatigue party to shoot Mohammad Hussain. They were both sepoys : one was a Tamil and the other was a Sikh. After the arrival of these men Lt. Khazin Shah ordered that Jagiri Ram would also fire on Mohammed Husain. The three men stood in a line facing Mohammed Husain and Khazin Shah told Aya Singh to give the order to fire. Aya Singh hesitated. Khazin Shah once again told him to give the order to fire. Aya Singh gave the order. All the three sepoys fired a round each on Mohammed Husain. Mohammed Husain was killed. His body rolled over sidewards. Lt. Khazin Shah then ordered me to send Abdul Hakim to arrange of his burial. I passed on these orders to Abdul Hakim. The battalion was to move the same day on an operational role and it did so. No casualty report was sent. The sending of a casualty report was part of my duties. I did not make a casualty report because night had fallen and we had to march the same night. On April 3, I escaped and reported to the Allied forces. I escaped from Legyi village."

In cross-examination it was suggested to the witness that on April I, he took a casualty report to Capt. Sahgal. Witness denied this. Witness said that he did not know if any casualty report was sent. No evidence was called by the defence to support this suggestion. Witness said in his cross-examination that he was between 12 and 15 yards away when Mohammed Husain fell. He said that he went near Mohammed Husain and found that he was dead, with three shots in him, 'The shirt covering his breast was torn and from the amount of tear I considered there were three shots." Witness was not present at his burial. In answer to the Judge Advocate the witness said that when he found the three shots had gone into him and he was lying on a side, he inferred he was dead. The firing was about eight to ten yards away from Mohammed Husain. The shooting of Mohammed Husain occurred at about dusk. Witness did not see any blood on Mohammed Husain.

In the statement of Capt Shah Nawaz it is stated that it is in fact wrong that he sentenced Mohammed Husain to death or that he was shot in execution of a sentence passed by him. According to the witness' statement, Mohammed Husain and his companions were only informally produced before him, there being no crime report drawn up. Capt. Shah Nawaz said that he only very strongly admonished Mohammed Husain and told him that he had committed an offence for which he could and should be shot. Capt. Shah Nawaz says that he left the matter there and asked the case to be put up again before him or the regimental commander, who had in the meanwhile been vested with the power to try such cases if the men concerned attempted to misbehaviour a second time and that the case never came up before him, presumably because the contingency never arose.

It is submitted that the evidence clearly shows that Mohammed Husain was sentenced to death by Capt. Shah Nawaz, that the sentence was to be carried out under battalion arrangement and that Lt. Khazin Shah as the battalion commandant ordered Aya Singh to give the order for firing and that Mohammed Husain was shot dead pursuant to such order. It is submitted that the evidence leaves no doubt as to the identity of Mohammed Husain. It is also submitted that as the result of the shooting Mohammed Husain died. The detailed evidence of the prosecution on this point is more than sufficient to prove the above facts. Havildar Gulam Mohammad who was the adjustant actually saw the crime reports, and the statement of Capt. Shah Nawaz that no crime reports were drawn up cannot be accepted as correct. Havildar Ghulam Mohammad's statements that the crime reports were drawn up and that he read them was not challenged in his cross-examination. The fact of the shooting is, it is submitted, also proved beyond doubt. As also the fact that Mohammed Hussain died as the result of the shooting. The evidence shows that a grave was dug for Mohammed Husain before the sentence was carried out and after he was shot orders were given for him to be buried. It is submitted that the proof of death is beyond reasonable doubt; but even if there is any doubt left in the mind of the court, the only consequence would be that the conviction of Capt. Shah Nawaz would be that of abetment of an attempt to murder instead of abetment of murder.

I will now deal with the charges two to nine which are against Capt. Sahgal and Lt. Dhillon, of the murder, as far as Lt. Dhillon is concerned, of the four sepoys and abetment of murder, so far as Capt. Sahgal is concerned, of the four sepoys. So far as these charges are concerned, there is documentary evidence which, it is submitted, is conclusive. There are two crime reports both dated March 6, 1945, exhibits K K K and W W W. We do not know why and how there came to be two such reports. They are identical except that in exhibit W W W the service is stated to be "years 3," whereas in exhibit K K K the servioce is stated to be " years 4-8 months." The only differsnce therefore is that in exhibit W W W the figure "4" before the letters "years" is omitted, but both these documents are original crime reports and the evidence as regards these documents which has not been challenged in cross-examination is that given by Lt. Nag. He says : "The words remanded for Divisional Commander's trial' under the column punishment awarded are in the handwriting of Lt. Dhillon and the signature below it is that of Lt. Dhillon. The words "sentenced to death": are in the handwriting of Capt. Sahgal and there is the Signature of Capt. Sahgal under the column by who awarded and date and at the bottom of the crime report there is the signature of Lt. G.S. Dhillon as "Commander of Unit No. 420.' He could not recognize the handwriting of the words after the words 'sentenced to death' which is before the signature of P.K. Shagal. As regards exhibit W W W, witness says "under the column head punishment awarded. The words ":remanded and signed by him. the words sentenced to death' are in the handwriting of Capt. Sahgal and signed by him. At the bottom of the crime reports conclusively prove that Capt. Sahgal passed the sentence of death on these four persons. In the statenebt of Capt. Sahgal he admits that they found guilty and sentenced to death, but he says that the sentence was not carried out, and the convicts like many others who were similarly tried and sentenced about the time had been pardoned on their expressing regret and giving an assurance not to misbehave in future. He says that the fact of a sentence having been passed was used for its propaganda value in order detector others from deserting. Lt. Dhillon in his statement says : "It is true that I committed four men for trial witht the charge of desertion and attempt to communicate with the enemy. It is, however, quite untrue that these men were shot at my instance or under my orders. On the day and at the time they are said to have been shot, I was confined to bed and unable to move. In fact, the sentences of death passed on these men were subsequently remitted by the Divisional Commander and were never executed." In making this statement both Capt. Sahgal and Lt Dhillon seem to have overlooked exhibit W W which is a special order of the day dated March 19, 1945, signed by Capt. Shah Nawaz Khan who was the Divisional Commander. This document was also not referred to by Counsel for the Defence in his address. This document has also been proved by the evidence of Lt. Nag which has not been challenged in cross-examination . In this document it is clearly stated as follows : "The sentence of death was carried out at 19-00 hours on March 6, 1945, and then goes on to say : "This order will be read out to all troops."

As regards the actual shooting of the four sepoys we have the evidence of Nursing Sepoy Abdul Hafeez Khan. He says in his evidence as follows: "After I came back from Rangoon I saw four men being shot. They belonged to No. 8 Battalion. There was a company fallen in to witness this shooting. This Company belonged to No. 7 Battalion. One day I was carrying a patient and saw four men near the nullah whose hands were tied behind their backs and who were escorted by two sentries. When I was coming back after leaving the patient in hospital I noticed some men assembled near the nullah. Seeing this assembly of men I went up there. When I reached there one company was fallen in and a trench had been dug there. The accused Major Dhillon and a few other officers were collected there. The four men were made to sit in the trench. Then Major Dhillon asked for volunteers to shoot these men. Two men from that company and one man from Brigade Headquarters came up. Their names were Nayak Sher Singh, Kalu Ram and Hidayatullah. Two carried rifles and one a pistol; Sher Singh had the pistol. Then Major Dhillon called out the name of one of the four men in the trench. Major Dhillon told the Company present that these four men had gone over to the enemy and had been caught and, therefore, their punishment would be death. "Then Major Dhillon ordered Hidayatullah to shoot the person who had been called out of the trench first. By this time this person had come out of the trench. He was standing on the edge of the trench. This person was then shot by Hidayatullah and he fell down. The person was not blindfold. He was about 20 yards from Hidayatullah when fired upon. Then Major Dhillon called out the name of another person who also came out of the trench. As in the first case, this person was also told his punishment and this person also was shot by Hidayatullah. Then Major Dhillon called out the name of the third man who was also told his sentance like the previous ones and Kalu Ram shot him under Major Dhillon's orders. Major Dhillon then similarly called to the fourth man and this man was also shot by Kalu Ram. I saw the four persons after they had been shot. They where not dead because I saw them move. Major Dhillon then ordered Naik Sher Singh to put one or two bullets into those who had not died . Sher Singh then went up to them and fired putting one or two bullets into each one of them. I did not see them moving , after Sher Singh had fired. Then I saw Capt. lee, the medical officer of the service battalion, examine them. Capt Lee said something to Major Dhillon. Capt. Lee told Major Dhillon that these men were dead. Afterwards Major Dhillon ordered the dead bodies to be buried. I did not see them being buried. I then came away from the scene."

In the cross-examination of this witness it was suggested that his conduct in stopping to see what was happening was extraordinary, and that instead of waiting to see what was happening he should have gone back straight to his unit after admitting the patient. It is submitted that there is nothing unnatural in the witness stopping to see what was happening. It was only human and natural on his part to stop and see the tragedy. It was then suggested in the cross-examination that he could not have known the names of Hidayatullah, sepoy Kalu Ram and Naik Sher Singh because he never rendered first-aid to these three persons. The witness said that he knew them because they belonged to his battalion. He was, of course, attached to No. 7 battalion hospital. That, however, does not mean that for that reason he could not have known them. It was also put to the witness and the witness admitted that he had no personal contact with these three men before that day and he had nothing to do with them after the incident. But he added : "They used to be in my battalion and I knew them." He also said : "It was part of my duty to know the names of as many men as I could in the battalion. When a few men live together they know the names of each other. I had not talked to any of these men before that day. I have never seen these three men since. Witness said that he was 10 to 12 yards away from Major Dhillon at the time and that he remembered every detail of what he had told the Court. He said he did not know the names of any of the four men who were shot nor their identity. It was then put to him in cross-examination that in the summary of evidence which he gave he did not say that Major Dhillon had ordered Sher Singh to fire a pistol. The answer of the witness was that as far as he remembered he said that Major Dhillon had ordered Sher Singh to fire a pistol, but that it was not taken down. In answer to the Court the witness said: "This company in the nullah was properly fallen in. These man were in front of the company. The company was about 10 to 12 yards for the men and I stood near the company on one side. Major Dhillon gave orders for the fourth man to be shot."

The next witness examined on this point was sepoy Gian Singh. He corroborated the version given by the previous witness including the firing and said that Major Dhillon ordered Sher Singh to shoot and finish off those of the four who were not dead and then Sher Singh fired an all the four with a pistol from a distance of about five yards. He further said : "Before Naik Sher Singh had fired on them, they were shrieking but I do not see them. They were lying near the nullah. Mjor Dhillon then said that anybody who did what these men had done would be dealt with similarly. The four bodies were buried in a trench. I saw them being buried. These four men who were killed were Jats. I do not know anything more about them." The witness was cross-examined in detail as regards the size of the nullah and the position of the four sepoys and of the persons who were present there. It is submitted that the answers given in the cross-examination, throw no doubt on the veracity of his evidence. The statements made by him in cross-examination did not show that there was anything improbable or inconsistent in the evidence given by him. Even if there is any ambiguity, it was completely removed in the answers which he gave to the Court at the end. Witness also stated to the Court that Maj. Dhillon read out that these men were Jats from No. 8 Battalion.

On behalf of Lt. Dhillon it was argued by counsel that he was ill on the date in question, namely, March 6, 1945, and that he could not have been present at the shooting as deposed to by the witnesses for the prosecution. For this reliance is placed on exhibit V V V which is an operation order signed by Lt. Dhillon and dated March 6, 1945. What is relied upon is the letter at the foot of this operation order in which Lt. Dhillon says that the previous night he had gone to check certain defence and on his arrival back he felt very weak, so weak as he had never felt before throughout his life, and that Shankar gave him an injection that day and that he would get one the next day. But the same letter says as follows : "I hope most of your queries have been answered in this order, others I will answer when I come tomorrow." I submit it is not possible from this document to come to the conclusion that Lt. Dhillon could not have been present at the shooting as deposed to by the prosecution witnesses.

It was further contended that there was no proof of identity of the four persons who were shot. I submit that hte identity has been sufficiently established by the two crime reports exhibits K K K and W W W and by the special order of the day dated March 19, 1945, exhibit W W W There is the further fact that according to the prosecution evidence, Lt. Dhillon stated at the time of the execution that these men had attempted to desert and they were, therefore, being shot.

It was also contended on behalf of the defence that the fact of nursing sepoy Abdul Hafiz Khan having been present at the incident has been contradicted by the next witness (Sepoy Gian Singh) because Gian Singh said : "I do not remember any person not belonging to the company being there." This is entirely incorrect. It is not the second witness Gian Singh who says that he first witness nursing sepoy was not there. The answer in question was given by nursing sepoy Abdul Hafiz Khan and not by the second witness Gian Singh. What nursing sepoy Abdul Hafiz Khan said is as follows : "I did not see any outsiders apart from the officers of the company and myself ."

But even if the answer had been given by the several witnesses as stated by Counsel for the defence and not by the first witness as appears from the record of the evidence it does not follow that a person could not have been there because somebody else did not see him there.

There is, therefore, nothing in the point sought to be made by my learned friend.

Section 302 of the Indian Penal Code provides the punishment for murder. According to Section 299 of the Indian Penal Code, whoever causes the death by doing an act with the intention of causing death commits the offence of culpable homicide. Section 300 provides that except in the cases therein excepted culpable homicide is murder if the act by which the death is caused is done with the intention of causing death. The exceptions mentioned in that section have no relevance to the present case. Section 109 of the Indian Penal Code provides for the punishment of abetment if the act abetted i committed in consequence. Section 107 of the Indian Penal Code says that person abets the doing of a thing who, among other things, instigates any person to do that thing or intentionally aids by any act or illegal omission to the doing of that thing. As Capt. Sahgal was not present when the four sepoys were shot, he is charged only with abetting their murder and not with the murders itself. Section 144 of the Indian Penal Code says "whenever any person who is absent would be liable to be punished as an abettor is present when the act or offence for which he would be punishable in consequence of the abetment is committed, he shall be deemed to have committed such act or offence." As he was not present at the shooting, he can only be charged with abetment of the offence. For the same reason as Captain Shah Nawaz Khan was not present at the shooting of Mohammed Husain, he is charged with offences of abetment of murder.

It has been contended that there is only one charge, namely, that of waging war because murder is a part of the first charge. I was argued that the first charge would cover every charge of firing a second shot. It issubmitted that this contention is not correct. The prosecution has not charged the accused with more than one charge in respect of waging the war. The charge of murder is distinct and separate from that of waging war because waging war involves fighting against and it might be killing the persons in the opposing army. Waging the war does not necessarily involve killing a man who is on the same side as the person charged with the offence.

If it is conteneded that the accused were justified in passing the sentence of death and in shooting the persons mentioned in the charges because they were authorised under the Indian National Army Act which is said to have been passed under the authority of the Provisional Government of Free India, the answer to the ergument is that the Provisinal Government of Free India was itself and illegal body an the formation of that body was itself an offence against the State and neither that body nor any tribunal constituted under it nor any order or authority derived from such a body can be recognised by this court, all of them being unlawful. In the case of R. Maguire and O'Sheil reported in 1923 second Irish Reports, King's Bench Division, page 58, the question of such a body and authority derived under it came up for consideration. The question arose on an application for a writ of *certiorari.* Certain persons in Ireland were attempted to be deprived of their land under certain orders or judgements of the judges and commissioners of Land Court and Land Settlement Commission of Dail Eireann. Jurisdiction of those courts was said to be derived from a decreed of An Dail. In dealing with the question, Justice Molony at page 63 said : "In the present case, far from there being any right or duty in the tribunal to decide the matter, their assumption of authority was illegal from the beginning and consequently they are not subject to the writ of *certiorari*. "In further dealing with the point, he said : "The answer is that this court while it prohibits and quashes the orders of inferior tribunals which exceed their jurisdiction does not take notice of bodies which act openly and avowedly in defiance of the law. The court has never issued a writ of prohibition of *certiorari* to an illegal body which challenges the authority of the Government and with which it is the duty of the Government to deal. "Justice Dodd said : " I extract from all the authorities that the only courts that can be restrained by prohibition are courts established by the Legislature who are usurping a jurisdiction of a judicial character not within or in excess of powers conferred upon them by the Legislature.... I do not ground my decision on the proclamation: I base it upon the fact that the courts were not established under any legislative enactment. Their orders are without sanction. They cannot protect any sheriff, jailor or other officer acting upon them.":

Justice Samuels in his judgement at page 66 said: "These tribunals whether of first instance or of appeal were not courts in any sense known to the law. They had no jurisdiction either by common law or by statute to sit, decide or decree. Further they purported to act as tribunals of a Republic claiming to have been established in Ireland within a Dominion of His Majesty the king. At common law and by the statute law of the Realm, those who instigated or took part in the proceedings of this court were themselves liable to indictment." Further on at page 69 the learned Judge said: "The so-called court that we have to consider, however, never had any legal powers and was never entrusted with any jurisdiction which it might exceed. It operations were not merely extra-legal, but anti-legal." At page 70 the learned judge said : "The tribunal we have to consider in the case was not so created. It acknowledged no such authority. It was not a court within the British constitution. It was set up as the court of a Republic and in repudiate of any such allegiance as is inherent in all court hitherto known as court within the King's Realm."

My submission is that charges two to nine have been proved beyond any reasonable doubt.

In conclusion, I submit that all the charges against all the accused have been proved beyond any reasonable doubt. There is no defence in law to the charges against the accused. There is a good deal of evidence to the effect that what the accused did was done by them not with any mercenary motive, but out of what the accused *bona fide* consider to be patriotic motives and impelled by a sense, whether wise or misguided, of doing service to India. This, while not affording any defence to the accused in law, may legitimately be taken into consideration on the question of punishment, if the court's findings on the charges are against the accused. So far as the court is concerned, its hands are tied in the matter of punishment. The minimum punishment which this court can give is transportation for life. If the court's finding is against the accused, but the court feels on the evidence before it that the case is fit one for mitigation of punishment, it is open to the court to add a rider to its finding and sentence to that effect for the consideration of the confirming officer.

The court reopens : the accused is brought before the court. Counsel for the prosecution addresses the court. Transcript of his address is marked 6 A, signed by the President and attached to the proceedings.

Note by the Court

The Judge -Advocate requests an adjournment until December 29, to enable him to prepare his summing up. The court grants this application.

At .... hours the court adjourned until 10 a.m. on Saturday, December 29.

15

Report by Military Intelligence on Hikari Kikan, Japanese Liaison Agency Dealing with I.N.A.[1]

2 January, 1946

1. **Introduction**—The Hikari Kikan was the Indian Affairs of the earlier Fujiwara and Iwakuro Kikans. The Fujuwara Kikan itself had its roots in No. 8 Sec of the Second Bureau (M. I. Dte) at Imperial H. Q. Tokio where its Commander Major Fujiwara was working for some years before the war.

   The name Hikari was selected for in Sanskrit its means "Help". Relations, however, between Indians and Japanese were by no means as good as the choice of nomenclature would suggest, and the history of the Kikan is one which they sought to control. The attitude of the I. N. A. towards the Hikari Kikan is well illustrated by the nickname which they give to it MURGHI (Chicken) Butai, for its propensity for assimilating the rations intended for its "allies".

2. **Sources of Interrogation**—The sources available for interrogation in Rangoon arc on thc whole disappointing. None had any connection with the Kikan before the end of the 1943, during the interesting period of the despatch of agents by the land route into Indian and the arguments over the control of such organisations as the S.Y.T.I. All were posted away by the beginning of 1945. This has rendered interrogation on stay behind activities completely inconclusive. The whole of the Hikari Kikan as constituted in 1945 evacuated to Bangkok where the most interesting personalities such as Lt. Gen Isoda, Col. Kagawa, Lt. Kunizuka and the earlier Chief Col. Kitabe were recovered at the time of the Japanese surrender.

   The following should, however, in the opinion of the interrogators be despatched to S'Pore for D. I.

1. War Office, 203/808. P.R.O.

Col. Kadomatsu	–	for his pre war work in No. 8 Sec, Second at Burma.
Col. Komtasubara	–	for his connections with the Spy-schools at Penang
Capt (now Major) Kawaji	–	who is co-operative under i nterrogation.
Major Fumio Miura	–	Evasive under interrogation. It is considered that under D.I. he might part with more information.

3. **Pre-War Jiffery**—Col Kadomatsu, although head of Chinese intelligence before the war was also a member of No. 8 Sec (Co-ordination) under Col Nishi in the Second Bureau. In the same section were working Maj Fujiwara and Major Ozeki (Both in Japan at the end of the war) who concentrated on Indian affairs.

The organisation of Lt. Gen Arisue's Second Bureau has already been given in detail in Kadomatsu's preliminary interrogation issued separately. The various Secs were organised on regional basis e.g. Intelligence on China, Intelligence on Russia, Anglo-American intelligence, Southern Regions intelligence, Kadomatsu was, however, very vague about the demarcation between Southern Regions and Anglo-American intelligence with reference to Siam, Malaya, Burma and India, claiming that he himself was only interested in the China Section.

Sources of intelligence were

(a) M. I. Channels which fed the appropriate Sec of the Second Bureau.

(b) Naval Intelligence,.There was in Naval H.Q. a parallel organisation to the Second Bureau. Copies of Intelligence summaries were exchanged and weekly conferences of Army-Navy opposite numbers were held to ensure liaison.

(c) The Deptt. of Foreign Affairs which received intelligence through diplomatic channels,. Col. Kadomatsu opines that pre-war agents were sent out to contact Indians by the Military Intelligence Bureau. Information and dealings with Indians in countries like Siam, Malaya etc. would be the responsibility of the local consuls. Copies of Intelligence reports were sent by the Foreign Affairs to the Military Intelligence Bureau but NOT vice versa.

When questioned about the responsibility for the organisation of puppet movements to support Mily oprations (such as that of Wang Ching Wei in China), Col Kadomatsu stated that to the best of his knowledge this belonged to the Mily Affairs Bureau of the War Ministry.

This Mily Affairs Bureau was divided into 2 main Secs.

Gumo – Dealing with political movements and agitation.

Gunji – Dealing with the 'Q' side of local suppllies and requisitioning of food and material from the local population.

Both these Secs were divided into a number of Sub Secs on a regional basis comparable to the Second between the Second Bureau and the Mily Affairs Deptt of the war Ministry by the replacement of Maj Fujiwara by Col Iwaguro in May 42.

4. **The Fujiwara Kikan**—Major Fujiwara had been dealing with Indian Affairs from the Mily-Intelligence angle in No. 8 Sec of the Second Bureau. Just before the outbreak of war he was summoned to a direct interview with the Chief of Staff who briefed him personally for his mission to Bangkok and despatched him to work under the command of H.Q. 15th Army. Fujiwara himself was responsible for the selection of Lt. Kunijuka as his deputy and for the formation of his Kikan which included about 10 Ind Agents from Bangkok. Col Kadomatsu believes that Fujiwara's aim was striclty limited and tactical in scope-fifth column activity to aid the Japanese advance and ensure co-operation from Indians residents. to Malaya for the occupying troops. Branches of the I.I.L. were formed during the advance probably with this latter end in view on the Japanese side rather than with any ideas of harassing the Indian population for a large scale mobilisation to achieve Indian Independence. It was only after the Fujiwara Kikan's initial outstanding success, the capture of Captain Mohan Singh, his discussions with Major Fujiwara and the really spontaneous welcome which the Indian population gave in the first few days at least of their "liberation" that the larger air took shape.

It was at this stage that the War Ministry took a hand and Col. Iwaguro who was head of the "Adjutant Sec" of the Ministry was deputed to attend the TOKIO conference in Mar 42. He was afterwards removed from his former post and transferred to work directly under the Chief of Staff in the formation of the Iwaguro Kikan which took over from the Fujiwara Kikan the organisation of Indians throughout E. Asia. Iwaguro set up his H. Q. in Bangkok and the famous Bangkok Conference was one of the first results of his activities.

5. **Indian in Prewar Japan**—As regards Indians who co-operated with the Japanese before the war, Col Kadomatsu remembers only 3

(a) Rash Behari Bose. The Japanese had implicit faith in him and regarded him as "a Japanese amongst Indians" unlike A. M. Sahay whom they regarded with some suspicion as an "Indian amongst Japanese" who might learn their secrets and later betray them. Col Kadomatsu himself saw R. B. Bose in the 8 Sec office a number of occasions before the War - he used to attend conferences (matter under discussion unknown) with Major Fujiwara and with a Lt. Col. Kato from the Anglo-American Sections of the Ministry of War. This officer is now in Tokyo. Kadomatsu impression is that R. B. Bose was not in the regulars pay of the Japanese but was advanced money on an "as required" basis for propaganda and publishing work. He heard that Bose was a close friend of Toyama, the old statesman from the Black Dragan Society.

(b) A. M. Sahay—A free-lance amateur who was well known in with the monied classes.

(c) Baba Osman[2]— Col. Kadomatsu remembers hearing "vaguely" of the San Francisco Party. In his work on Chinese Intelligence he came across Osman's name. Osman, however was not working directly under the Second Bureau but under a Commander Hidaka of the China Intelligence Sec. of the Japanese Navy in Shanghai Hidaka's present whereabouts unknown.

None of the officers or men in the Jail know anything of the Pre-war activities of Giani Pritam Singh, Baba Amar Singh, Deb Nath Das, Endo etc. etc.

---

2. Baba Hari Singh alies Osman khan has an old revolutionary, who worked with the Germans during the first world war for India's freedom. After the war lived in Indonisia before joining the Japanese Intelligency agency in China

Col. Kadomatsu has denied the story of G. A. Qureishi (vide C.S.D.I.C. (I) No. 2 Sec Report No. 1053). He states he has never heard of Qureishi, knows of no Indian answering to his desciption and never had anything to do with the briefing of Ind agents for Bangkok. He claims that Qureshi may have mistaken him for another Col possibly Iwaguro whom he resembles. This is a point of considerable importance. If Qureshi's story is true Col Kadomatsu was himself directly involved in Indian affairs before the war and will be able to furnish even more important information. Kadomatsu should be subjected to D.I. on this question and if necessary confronted with Qureshi (Now in Delhi).

6. **Tokyo Foreign Languages School**—Both Cols. Kadomatsu and Komatsubara (himself a student of Russian) remember a Tokio Foreign Languages School before the War which was attended yearly by 10 officers selected by the personnel Sec (Honinka) of the Imperial H.Q. No knowledge of any officers who studied Hindustani.

7. **Iwaguro and Hikari Kikan in Burma Prior to move of HQ to Rangoon**—No information worth recording. None of the sources came to Burma before the end of 1943 and even their hearsay is limited to well known facts such as the arrival of Capt Tsumimuchi with his Kikan on the heels of the adv tps, the early quarrels with Indians in Burma the friction between Col Kitabe and the INA/IIL and his replacement by Col Yamamoto.

8. **Organisation of Hikari Kikan-Jan 44**—As below, the organisation was believed to be slightly different in Dec 44 but the differences are not known to the sources present in RGN Central Jail.

H. Q. Hikari Kikan
Staff Deptt. Mily Affairs Deptt. Political Deptt. Admin Deptt.
Finance Deptt. Ordnance Section. Medical Sec. Sigs Sec.
In addition there were "agencies" at Kalewa, Homalin, Myiktyina, Maymyo and Akyab of which more hereafter.

Staff of the various deptts are listed at Appendix "A".[3] The functions of each Deppt are in most cases self-explanatory, with the notable exception of the Staff deptt which from the names of some of its more well-known members would appear to cover a multitude of aims.

9. **Chain of Command**—H. Q. Hikari Kikan come directly under H. Q. Burma Area Army and through them under Jap H. Q. at Shonan.

3. Not printed

There was no direct contact with the Second Bureau in Tokio and no and no references were ever made to Tokio.

10. **Hikari Kikan as an Intelligence organisation**—The sources deny that there was any regularly Joho Han (Intelligence Section) in Burma or that the Hikari Kikan was anything but a purely liaison "organisation". They plead ignorance of the Tokumu Han. Their contention is that strategic infiltration of agents into India was an extremely high level affair organised by Neta ji Chandra Bose himself in direct contact with the Penang Branch of the Hikari Kikan. Local tactical intelligence was the responsibility of the I. N. A. Intelligence and Bahadur Groups and although Hikari Kikan personnel were attached to their parties, the Hikari Kikan did not organise or control the work of the parties, this being responsibility of the local Commanders INA or Japanese. The Hikari Kikan attached staff were responsible for (1) Liaison with Japanese Units. (2) Reporting of information received by Indian intelligence parties to the local Jap Commander just as HQ Hikari Kikan in RGN was responsible for passing all "Indian" information of military intelligence value to the Intelligence Branch of H. Q. Burma Area Army. (3) Supply of rations (I.O.'s Comment:— This state of affairs although certainly not true of 1942-1943. I find more acceptable when applied to 1944. The earlier situation whereby Tsuchimuchi could direct the operations of Ram Sarup, Tsukamoto organised separate W/T courses in conjuction with G. S. Pardesi and Awata sent away trainees from the S.Y.T.I. to Japanese forwarding agencies at Sagaing, Monywa etc in rather amateurish attempts at infiltration into India had by then been largely resolved by the establishment of the P. G. A. H. in RGN and the insistence by Bose of Indian control over Indian affairs.

Capt Kawaji who was in the political Deptt from Feb. 44 - Dec. 44 states that the administration regarding the despatch of agents, if any, would be done by the Staff Deptt. He and all others in the Jail plead ignorance on the subject of the "Bats" dropped by parachute in Assam.

11. **Political Deptt.**—The Political Deptt besides being responsible for liaison with the P. G. A. H. on important issues between the Japs and the Indians also dealt with propaganda. This was confined to the provision of paper, priniting and propaganda facilities to the P.G.A. H. whose publicity branch under S.A. Ayyar actually issued all propaganda. Propaganda lines and thesis were sometimes supplied

with relevant extracts from Domei News to this Deptt but actual commentaries were always written by Indians.

There had formerely been pre-censorship by the Hikari Kikan but after a vigorous protest from Subhas Chandra Bose a tacit arrangement (Not a formal agreement) was Subhas Chandra Bose copies of all publications were sent to the Kikan. Capt Kawaji knows of no instances where the Kikan had occasion to suppress or alter any articles. He remembers an incident which took place in early 44. Some person or persons unknown on the Japanese side had on their own an initiative printed propaganda leaflets directed at Indian tps describing Subhas Chandra Bose and his movement and asking the I.N.A. to join them. These leaflets were signed by the local Japanese Commander and never submitted to Netaji for approval. When a copy finally found its way into his hands, he collared the unfortunate, Gen, Isoda who had recently arrived in Maymyo and indignantly demanded an explanation saying that the pamphlet being signed by a Japanese would have exactly the opposite to the desired effect upon the I.A.

12. **Komura Kikan**—An offshot of the political deptt was the Komura Kikan. Function - liaison with the local administration in the occupied areas of India. The Kikan moved from Rangoon to Maymyo in Apr., to Tamu in July and thence retreated via Shwegyin. Sources think that it worked in close liaison with the Azad Hind Dal but never had an opportunity to function. Capt Kawaji met (Lt Col) Ehsan Qadir in Maymyo and describes him as a "man of soldier bearing". He did not know of Ehsan's reputation with the rest of the INA.

Officers of Komura Kikan
Major (now Lt.–Col) Komura
Lt. Komohara
Lt. Nishiyama

The Mily Affairs Deptt was a straightforward liaison organisation to ensure adequate co-operation between the Japanese Army and the I. N. A. in the field. Notes on the activities of individual Hikari Kikan personnel attached to INA Units are attached in Appendix "B".

Unions of INA and P.G.A.H.

The general Hikari Kikan impression of the I. N. A. was that it was not up to much . Chandra Bose, as they call him, obviously impressed them a great deal and they speak with considerable respect of him and of a few of his subordinates including let it be said Shah Niwaz who had such a tussle with them in the Manipur Campaign. I. N. A. Div they considered not all bad; of 2 Div (apart from its Commanders) they had a very low opinion. At that stage of the Campaign as one officer put it "INA" meant only one thing "Hands up". The incident which stuck most in their minds was the surrender of such a large body of men under the Bde Comd (Lt Col) S. M. Hussain at Magwe without fight.

None of the sources would volunteer any opinion on why 1 INA Div whose morale and discipline they admitted was high on the Indian frontier. They pleaded surprise when told of the tenor of Shah Niwaz famous letter to Netaji from his Bde. H. Q. at Myittha Haka complaining that the I. N. A. was being treated as a labour Corps.

Col. Komatsubara opined that had the invasion been successful, Indian would have been given her "independence important communications." The other sources merely replied that it was a question of high policy to be decided between Chandra Bose and the Imperial Govt in Tokyo. It is perhaps significant that they all refer to negotiations with "Chandra Bose" and do not with the Provisional Govt of Azad Hind.

The only names in the Provisional Govt which excited any comment were,

(a) 'Maj–Gen' Bhonsle—for his corpulence.

(b) A.M. Sahay – who was considered to have made an unmitigated nuisance of himself over building material for barracks in Thingangyun.

(c) One O-Rakshmi San commanding a "Strange" (source Capt Kawaji) organisation known as the Jhansi Butai, This lady and/or her Butai in one of their more plighty moments also caused much heartburning over their insistance that a Ry should shift out of its quarters to make room for them. The Ry Regt finally shifted!

Finance Dept.—My Miura has been interrogated at some length on the distribution of "M.I. Funds". He disclaims all knowlege of these, a disclaimer which coming from a man in his position. I find extemely difficult to accept especially considering the fact that numbers of

Indian agents despatched from Burma have been arrested with counterfelt Indian Currency in their possession. He first for feigned surprise when confronted with this fact but later suggested that one of his officers Lt. Miyake, Gintaro now believed to be in Rankok was actually in charge of the distribution of funds and might be able to elucidate.

O.C. of the Finance Deptt, Hikari Kikan in S'PO was Lt. Col Murata, Maki, present wehreabouts unknown and under him were two officers - one a Lt. Koga: One of his own officers from RGN Capt Unoki, Taro he now believes to be in Bangkok.

Other Deptts.—The Admin Deptt, the ordanance and Med Secs were internal organisations served Hikari Kikan personnel only and had no dealing with Indians.

O. C. of the Med Sec was a Maj Kochi who was transferred to S'pore in 1944 and relieved by Maj Kawamura. Sources impact that this Maj Kawamura's activities were purely medical.

None of the sources was ever in the Sigs Sec and can give no information about it.

15. **Homalin & Myiktyina Agencies.**—There are in RGN Jail 3 men who were attached to agencies.

Homalin—Med orderly, Civ Ujino Tokiyoshi. Arrived Homalin Dec 43. Found that the agency was an intelligence Unit of 20 Men. A Lt Kubo form HQ Hikari Kikan, RGN was L. O. At this time there was no "Indian" activity as the agency was employed on the collection of rations for Retsu Butai then moving up for the attack on Manipur. After a visit to Maymyo as med orderly to Lt. Kaneko he retuned to Homalin found that the agency had moved so followed it up to join 58 Inf Regt with in the Kohima Ops. Knows nothing about (Lt) N. D. Sinha, the hoisting of the Indian National Flag or the capture of the B. C. R." who is alleged to have broadcast propaganda after capture.

Myiktyina.

Sgt–Maj	Kamezawa Shoichi
Sgt	Satake Tsuzuku

Object of Myiktyina agency liaison between 18 Div and local Indians. In Myiktyina there were 20-30 INA Sikhs and Gurkhas under (Capt) Harka Singh Bahadur. One of them name unknown, could speak Japanese. Their activities were recruitment for INA and supply of rice to Indians. There was a fwd post at Sinkaling Hkamti which sources heard was visited by an Indian name Durga Mali into organised at 1(S) F.I.C. No infiltration parties despathced to India. Agency retreated 25 Mar 44 to Mogaung and to Hopin 20 June 44. The 'Nippon Guerrilas' were caught by the Chindit Ops in the ry-corridor and only 3 eventually reached Maymyo. Sources do not have a high opinion of them. Disclaim any knowledge of espionage activities by these Gurkhas against Chindit Columns.[4]

---

4. This note was prepared by the Forward Interrogation unit after interrogating many Japanese officers, who were available in Rangoon at that time.

16

Reception to the I.N.A. Officers at Lahore after their Release[1]

5 January, 1946

We have no words to describe adequately and fully the scene that we, along with over a lakh of people, witnessed at the Lahore Railway Station on the arrival of Col. Shah Nawaz, Col. Prem Sahgal and Col. Gurbakhsh Singh Dhillon here to day. The least that one can say is that Lahore has never seen ever before such crowds, bubbling with enthusiasm.

The Frontier Mail, by which the three I.N.A. officers arrived was late by about three and a half hours. At every stoppage of the train from Delhi to Lahore, there were crowds shouting "Jai Hind" and "Shah Nawaz, Sahgal and Dhillon Zindabad".

Crowds at the Lahore railway station, which began gathering from early morning, even before the dawn, continued expressing their joy by raising slogans of "Jai Hind" "Sanghal Dhillon Shahnawaz Lal Qila se ho gai Azad". But what was even more exciting was the enthusiasm among the students. They sang and danced. There were students "Bhangra" parties and one cannot do full justice to the enthusiasm that prevailed by trying to describe it. These dances and singing of songs went on outside the railway station and on the station platform itself.

All roads, that lead to the railway station premises were full, and while pedestrians began to march their way to every available space at the railway station, traffic remained almost suspended for over four hours so far as going to the railway station was concerned.

In spite of the best efforts of the railway authorities, which gave their full co-operation to the Lahore District Congress Committee, which organised the reception, thousands—and their number cannot be mentioned correctly—secured entry into the railway station and occupied

1. *Tribune*, 6 Junuary, 1946

every available space on the station platforms, and on the bridge. Outside the railway station every inch of space within the area surrounded by the octroi posts was occupied and the whole area looked like a seething mass of humanity.

The Qaumi Sewa Dal volunteers of the District Congress committee, the volunteers of the Azad Hind Fauj Brigade of the Lahore Students' Congress, the Khaksars in their characteristic dresses, the scouts, the Patel Sewa Samti volunteers and the Police did their utmost to keep the crowds under control and regulated entry to the premises of the railway station. But it required yeoman's effort to keep such tumultuous crowd under control for about five hours and naturally therefore these control arrangements collapsed towards the end. The volunteers of all the organisations and the Police did their utmost to maintain order.

The one flag at the occasion which was seen being waved at hundreds of places, was the National flag and the one slogan that people were not tired of raising over and over again was "Jai Hind" when a special train carrying soldiers passed through Mughalpura the crowd which had gathered there shouted "Jai Hind" and this was enthusiastically responded to by many of the young and enthusiastic officers and men in the train who shouted "Jai Hind" and waved their hands to the crowd at the platform.

Outside the Lahore Station the District Congress Committee had provided an improvised platform on a lorry from where speeches continued to be made by Shrimati Amar Kaur, Mr. Ram Nath and others to keep the people busy.

The organisers succeeded in maintaining secrecy about their plans and in order to avoid any mishap at the Lahore Station and the "mobbing" by people of their heroes they detrained Shah Nawaz, Prem Saighal and Dhillon at the Mughalpura railway station and then brought them by motor cars to the lawn outside the Lahore Railway Station.

While the crowd at the Lahore railway station kept waiting for the Frontier Mail to come the organisers with the co-operation of the Railway authorities had the train stopped at Moghulpura railway station where Col. Shah Nawaz, Col. Dhillon were detrained. At Moghulpura the three were received by Prem Sehgal's father, Mr. Justice Acchru Ram and Mrs. Acchru Ram, Mr. Amrik Lal Budhwar, his brother-in-law, Raizada Hans Raj, M.L.A.(Central), Maulana Daud Ghaznavi, President P.P.C.C., Dr. Gopi Chand, Lala Bhim Sain Sachar,. M.L.A., Mr. Virendra, M.L.A., Mr. Ram Krishan Secretary , P.P.C.C. Maulana Habib-ur-Rehman, Malik Jeewan Lal Kapur, Comrade Ram Chandra, President and Mr. Hem Raj, General Secretary of the Lahore District Congress Committee.

In spite of the fact that this arrangement was kept a close secret about 500 people gathered at the Moghulpura station also getting their clue from the presence of the Congress leaders there. As the train stopped Shah Nawaz, Sehgal and Dhillon were greeted with slogan of "Jai Hind" as they appeared at the door of their compartment which was loaded with garlands and flowers which had been offered to them the whole way long from Delhi. The three jumped out of the compartment on being told that they were to be detrained there and they bowed to the mother of Prem Sehgal who blessed them and Prem's sister applied 'Tilak' on the foreheads of the three, a ceremony which in ancient Indian history used to be performed by the sisters when their brothers came back victorious from the battlefield. Maulana Daud Ghaznavi, on behalf of the Provincial Congress Committee, garlanded the three I.N.A. officers whom Mr. Justice Acchru Ram embraced in paternal affection.

The train steamed off to Lahore and as it entered the distant signal at the Lahore Railway Station rows of men standing along the whole route from the distant signal to the other end of the platform No. 2 where the Frontier Mail was specially taken, cheered and raised slogans of "Jai Hind."

From platform No. 1 to platform No. 2 there was hardly any space left vacant by men who were eager to have a look at the heroes. But they were all disappointed when they were told by men in the train that the three had been detrained at Moghalpura. The crowds, however, rushed out to the open space outside the station where the three I.N.A. officers were brought by cars from Mogulpura.

There was an outburst of "madness" as Shah Nawaz, Sahgal and Dhillon standing on the roof of the car appeared before the multitude. There were deafening cheers and sky-rending slogans of "Jai Hind" and "Zindabad" as they approached the improvised platform on the lorry to which place they were taken up from the car. They stood saluting the mass of humanity sitting and standing around them in the area that looked like a vast ocean of human heads. Joyous outburst and gladness of heart found expression in slogans being raised and "Jai Hind" being shouted. Shrimati Shanno Devi, Shrimati Amar Kaur and some other lady workers applied 'Tilak' on the foreheads of the three as they stood on the lorry saluting the crowds.

After silence had been restored as a result of appeals made by Prem Sahgal himself, the three addressed the gathering and were heard with the utmost respect and attention which they deserved.

Col. Prem Sahgal said that he wanted to reiterate the pledge that he and his comrades gave to Netaji, that pledge being that they shall consider no prize too big for the freedom of their country. He said that he and his comrades stand by that pledge even today. Amidst deafening cheers Prem Sahgal said, "Let me assure my countrymen that every man and officer of the I.N.A., including my comrades and myself, will be prepared to shed the very last drop of blood in us for the freedom of our motherland. The struggle for freedom which commenced in the Far East has not ended. Under the guidance of the Congress leaders we will now continue the struggle for the freedom of India and her teeming millions up to the time there is even one drop of blood left in us."

Thanking for the honor which the people had done to his comrades and to himself Prem Sehgal said: "Let me say that this honour which you has done us is the honour done to our Netaji who had nothing nearer to his heart than the freedom of India."

Col. Shah Nawaz, who received a warm ovation, said that he was glad that every organisation and community, including the Congress and the Muslim League, the Hindus, the Muslims and the Sikhs, Jains, Christians and others had demanded their release with one voice. He wanted to thank every body not for the fact that he and his two comrades had come out alive but for the fact that British imperialism had for the first time yielded to pressure of public opinion. Amidst prolonged cheers Shah Nawaz added : "Let me say to you and to the people of India that it is wrong that Netaji Subhas Chandra Bose ever thought of helping any foreign power to come and invade India.

Netaji's Last Message

With a voice full of feelings Shah Nawaz referred to what he described as Netaji's last message, given to the Indian people through Col. Habib-ur-Rehman who, he said, was unfortunately still behind the stony walls of the Red Fort. Shah Nawaz mentioned how at the time of the crash of the plane in which Subhas Chandra Bose travelling along with Col. Habib-ur-Rehman, Netaji received five serious injuries on his head and Col. Habib-ur-Rehman, got burns on his forehead and arms. Col. Habib-ur-Rehman at great risk to his own life succeed in extricating Netaji from the plane which had caught fire. It was at this time that Netaji asked Col. Habib-ur-Rehman to convey his message to his countrymen. Netaji's message was:

> "I have been injured rather seriously and I do not know if I will survive these injuries. Let my countrymen however know that I have fought upto the last minute of my life for the freedom of my Motherland and I want them to continue that fight till India is free."

Shah Nawaz commending the message of Netaji to the people exhorted them to continue that struggle for the freedom of India.

Lt. Col. Dhillon speaking said that they were being honoured for the brave and courageous acts of the men of the I.N.A. who were lying dead, cold in the battlefields of Far East where India's battle for freedom was fought. He was sorry that the fathers, mothers and the sisters of those brave men would never see their faces but all honour to them who laid down their lives in that heroic manner. He said that after the speech of Major-General Shah Nawaz and Prem Sahgal he as their junior officer had nothing further to add. He, however, said "Let me request you, my countrymen, whether you are Hindus, Muslims, Sikhs or member of any other community you should all regard me as your humble servant and my life is at your disposal in the service of mother India. I only appeal to you to learn discipline : for discipline and sacrifice combined can result in great achievements."

A touching scene was witnessed when the old father of Lt. Col. Dhillon came up and embraced his own son and two comrades and patted them on their backs with tears of joy in his eyes.

17

Note by C.S.D.I.C. Red Fort, Delhi on the Number of Indian PW who Joined the INA[1]

8 January 1946

1. This report is an attempt to give statistical information regarding the number of Ind PW who, on the one hand volunteered for the INA., or on the other resisted its propaganda.

2. A clear distinction must be made between the first and the second INA. While there was much spontaneous enrolment in the first INA., there was also considerable compulsion. In this connection, the words of Mohan Singh, the founder of the whole movement, are considered substantially correct. (CSDIC(I) 'S' Sec Report 1007, Appx B para 7 on Capt. Mohan Singh)[2]

   "Of about 55,000 Indian prisoners of war, about 45,000 voluntered for India's cause, although the Japanese did not allow me to raise an army of more than 20,000. (CSDIC (I) Note: 15,000 only). These volunteers included men from all classes recruited into the Indian Army, including a large number of Gurkhas as well. Out of the remaining 10,000 nearly half were such who were prepared for India's cause, but who did not trust the Japanese".

3. Thus of the original 55,000 PW,

15,000	were enrolled in the first INA. Of these about 4000 resigned, became ex-volunteers, and were sent to the South West Pacific.
25/30,000	were 'surplus' volunteers.
15/10,000	were non-volunteers.
55,000	

---

1. W.O. 208/818. P.R.O. See also F. No. 601/13097/H.S.
2. These reports are available with the I.N.A. Papers in the National Archieves of India and some amogest the War office at the Public Record office, London.

4. The 25/30,000 'surplus' or unabsorbed volunteers were in 1942 administered by the Japanese and not by HQ I.N.A. The 'surplus' volunteers received treatment little better than that of the non-volunteers and were employed on fatigues. The Japanese organised many of these surplus volunteers into Fatigue Parties (including the well-known 323 parties), which were sent to various places on the Malaya mainland and elsewhere (Sumatra etc). The remainder of the 'surplus' volunteers were kept in Singapore. In Jan 43, the 'surplus' volunteers reverted to genuine PW status but about 20 per cent (approx) later volunteered for the second I.N.A. A large number of these original 'surplus' volunteers have returned to India as RAPWI. (See also the Note on page 9 of this Report).

5. In the second I.N.A., the element of compulsion was very largely removed, and large number of civilians were recruited to reinforce the depleted ranks of the I.N.A., and later served to make possible the raising of 2 and 3 Div. I.N.A.

6. The information is based on interrogation and should be assessed accordingly. The degree of reliability with which the information given should be accepted is shown in the first column, thus:—

   (a) Reliable: generally provided by KCOs.The following units fall into this category:—

      (i) 3 Cav

      (ii) HKSRA (Singapore only)

      (iii) Inf units

      (iv) Mil Accts Dept

   (b) Fairly reliable

   (c) Uncertain. Requires Confirmation from other sources.

7. The information given is incomplete. Of the 55,000 Indian PW captured in Malaya, it has been possible to obtain figures for only approx 31,000. The statistics cover infantry units only and a few units of other arms.

8. As sub-units in the RIASC/IACC/IE/IAMC, etc. were mostly small, figures for these arms of the service are very incomplete. It is well known that the Japanese desired troops from combatant units to form the backbone of the early I.N.A., and such units were therefore

subjected to much more persistent propaganda than the "non-fighting" troops such as RIASC/IACC/IE/IAMC etc. of which only a very small number were selected for the first I.N.A., and then mostly for Bahadur and Intelligence Groups. The bulk of the remainder served as surplus volunteers during 1942, and large numbers reverted to PW status from 1943 onwards.

9. More exact details of non-volunteers, volunteers and surplus-volunteers from non-combatant units might be available or obtainable from the Depots of these respective arms of the service.

For the following arms of the service, only partially complete figures are available :—

RIASC	Figures are available only for :
	12 SPC Coy
	8 IBT Coy
I.E.	Figures are available only for :
	46 Army Tps Coy, Madras S &M
	6 Bdg Sec Madras S &M
	14 Bdg Sec Madras S &M
	13 Fd Coy Madras S &M
	15 Fd Coy Madras S &M
	23 Fd Coy, Royal Bombay S & M
	17 Fd Coy, Royal Bombay S & M
	19 Fd Coy, Royal Bombay S & M
	22 Fd Coy, Royal Bombay S & M
	42 Fd Pk Coy " "
	45 Army Tps Coy " "
	3 Fd Coy, Bengal S & M
	43 Fd Park Coy " "
	54 Eng Sec " "
IMS/IAMC/IHC	Figures are available only for :
	19 IGH
	5 CCS
IAOC	No reliable figures available.

Unit and degree of reliabilty	FIRST I.N.A.												SECOND I.N.A.									No. of RAPWI up to 10 Dec 45 (through Madras only) all rank.
	No of man alive on 15 Feb 42			Vol in First INA			Surpluse Vols in First INA			Non-Vols in First INA			Vols in Second INA			Non-Vols & Ex Vols sent to SW Pacific			Ex Vols Ex Surp Vols/Non-Vols Sent to PW Camps in Malaya Singapore			
	ICO.	VCO.	IOR.	ICO.	VCO.	IOR.	ICO	VCO.	IOR.	ICO.	VCO.	IOR.	ICO.	VCO.	IOR.	ICO.	VCO.	IOR.	ICO.	VCO.	IOR.	
(d) 6/1 Punjab	Total 900 all ranks			Total 900 all ranks						NIL			810-Jat & Sikh Coys			Total 90 all ranks			Jat & Sikh Coys (whereabouts after Jul 42 not know)			391
(A) 5/2 Punjab	11	23	1400	9	10	450	0	12	700	2	1	250	6	6	250							208
(A) 1/8 Punjab	6	27	1250	4	2	20	0	12	650	2	13	580	3	12	550	2	11	550	1	4	140	329
(A) 7/8 Punjab	2	19	800	1	8	420	0	1	20	1	10	360	0	5	330	0	4	110	2	10	360	
(A) 2/9 Jat 4/9 Jat	7	35	1100	6	2C	600	0	1	50	1	14	450	5	15	750	0	9	220	0	11	130	138
(A) 2/10 Baluch	7	28	1320	3	0	10	0	2	90	4	26	1220	4	0	30	1	2	80	2	26	1210	133
(A) 5/22 Sikh	5	0	750	3	0	350	0	0	30	2	0	100	2	0	400	0	0	275	3	0	75	228
(A) 2/12 FFR	2	28	1125	2	16	515	0	0	50	0	12	660	0	3	288	1	16	484	1	9	235	236

Unit and degree of reliabilty	FIRST I.N.A.												SECOND I.N.A.									
	No of man alive on 15 Feb 42			Vol in First INA			Surpluse Vols in First INA			Non-Vols in First INA			Vols in Second INA			Non-Vols & Ex Vols sent to SW Pacific			Ex Vols Ex Surp Vols/Non-Vols Sent to PW Camps in Malaya Singapore			No. of RAPWI up to 10 Dec 45 (through Madras only all rank.
	ICO.	VCO.	IOR.	ICO.	VCO.	IOR.	ICO.	VCO.	IOR.	ICO.	VCO.	IOR.	ICO.	VCO.	IOR.	ICO.	VCO.	IOR.	ICO.	VCO.	IOR.	
(A) 1/13 FF Rif	3	54	1300	1	16	600	0	4	100	1	14	600	1	4	200	0	20	800	0	10	300	267
(A) 1/14 Punjab	8	21	650	8	15	600	0	0	10	0	6	40	8	9	480	Officers Nil, VCOS 12, IORs 170						1718
(A) 5/14 Punjab	1	23	750	1	8	300	0	12	350	0	3	100	0	8	100	1	6	350	0	9	300	
(A) 6/14 Punjab	3	19	650	3	13	350	0	6	300	Nil			1	7	100	1	6	300	1	6	250	
2/15 Punjab	1	18	750	9 VCOs, 225 IORs Stayed in Balikpapan/Kuching/Miri. 25 IORs sent to unknown destination. 1 Offr, 9 VCOs, 441 IROs brought to Singapore—details as under																		357
				1	0	10	0	4	240	0	5	190	1	0	235	0	0	148	0	0	.57	
(A) 2/16 Punjab 3/16 Punjab	8	36	1350	5	10	550	0	0	175	3	26	625	4	3	150	0	17	700	3	16	500	610
(A) 2/17 Dogra 3/17 Dogra	6	48	2600	5	33	1390	0	15	100	1	0	110	1	10	1000	3	29	950	2	9	650	514
(A) 2/18 R Garh Rif 5/18 R Garh Rif	5	45	1850	5	30	1375	0	10	200	0	5	275	5	30	1375	0	5	425	0	10	50	149

Unit and degree of reliabilty	FIRST I.N.A.												SECOND I.N.A.									
	No of man alive on 15 Feb 42			Vol in First INA			Surpluse Vols in First INA			Non-Vols in First INA			Vols in Second INA			Non-Vols & Ex Vols sent to SW Pacific			Ex Vols Ex Surp Vols/Non-Vols Sent to PW Camps in Malaya Singapore			No. of RAPWI up to 10 Dec 45 (through Madras only) all rank.
	ICO.	VCO.	IOR.	ICO.	VCO.	IOR.	ICO.	VCO.	IOR.	ICO.	VCO.	IOR.	ICO.	VCO.	IOR.	ICO.	VCO.	IOR.	ICO.	VCO.	IOR.	
(A) 4/19 Kumaon	7	20	1000	6	9	650	0	5	225	1	6	125	3	6	650	1	3	4	3	10	340	373
(A) 1 Bahawalpur Inf	13	19	900	11	10	200		Offrs 2, VCOs 9, IORs 700					5	6	100	2	6	180	6	7	620	322
(A) Kapurthala Inf	12	18	698	10	18	612	0	0	40	2	0	46	11	17	290	0	1	340	1	0	68	16
(B) 1 Mysore Inf			700*			50*			500*			150*			50*			107*			543*	405
(B) 1 Hybad Inf			650*		Nil			Nil				650*		Nil				650*		Nil		489
(B) Jind Inf			650*		Nil			Nil				650*		Nil			Nil				350*	592
(A) S Cav	2	19	606	0	5	140		Nil		2	14	466	0	5	295	0	3	64	2	10	247	99
(A) BKSRA			4240*		1300* (jats)			*400 (PMs)			* 2540 (PMs)			1450* (1300 Jats, 150 (PMs)			*375 (PMs)			*2415 (PMs)		2078

* All ranks

	FIRST I.N.A.				SECOND I.N.A.			
Unit and degree of reliabilty	No of man alive on 15 Feb 42	Vol in First INA	Surpluse Vols in First INA	Non-Vols in First INA	Vols in Second INA	Non-Vols & Ex Vols sent to SW Pacific	Ex Vols Ex Surp Vols/Non-Vols Sent to PW Camps in Malaya Singapore	No. of RAPWI up to 10 Dec 45 (through Madras only) all rank.
	ICO. VCO. IOR.	ICO. VCO. IOR.	ICO. VCO. IOR.	ICO. VCO. IOR.	ICO. VCO. IOR.	ICO. VCO. IOR.	ICO. VCO. IOR.	
HONG KONG	4700 ?	Exact figure for HKSRA Hong Kong are not known.						
HKSRA		Volunteers for Gd duties Hongkong /Swatow etc				600		
		Semi-Volunteers (Hainan Islands etc)				800		
		Joined INA at Singapore Jan 44				1300		
		Non- Volunteers				?	(Depend on total strength of Hong Kong HKSFA which is not known)	
		If has not been possible so far to make any reliable assessment of the figures for HKSRA (HONG KONG) because						
		(a) Exact degree of collaboration of the Hainan and other "Gurard parties is not known.						
		(b) The only men who actually volunteered for service in the INA (about 1000) were shipped to Singapore in Jan 44 after the recruiting tour by Lt. Col Loganadan to Hong Kong/Shanghai etc. They were posted to Rft Gp at Jobore Bahru from where they were allotted to INA units. Mostly units of 3 Div.						
		(c) Total strength of HKSRA (Hong Kong) is not known at CSDIC (i).						

18

General Auchinleck to Army Commanders Explaining the Reasons for Changing the Policv Towards I.N.A.[1]

12 February, 1946

1. I have now been able to study a large number of reports from higher and unit commanders and other sources on the effect of the action taken in respect of the first "I.N.A." trial on the Indian Army as a whole.

   It is most important that we should study and analyse carefully these effects, as they may influence very greatly our ability to maintain the solidarity and reliability for the Indian Army in the difficult times which undoubtedly lie ahead of us. It is for this reason that I am writing this letter to you. I have considered the desirability of making a personal public statement in explanation of my action in commuting the sentences of transportation passed by the Court on the first three accused, but I have decided that this would not be in the best interests of discipline or the maintenance of my influence and authority as commander-in-chief.

   I feel, however, that we should do all we can to remove the feelings of doubt, resentment and even disgusts which appear to exist in the mind of quit a number of British officers, who have not the knowledge or the imagination to be able to view the situation as a whole or to understand the present state of feeling in India.

2. As I see it, the commutation of the sentences of transportation on Shah Nawaz, Dillon and Sahgal has had the following effect in India :

   (a) *On the general public, moderate as well as extremist, Muslim as well as Hindu*

---

1. Aruchinleck Papers. The above memorandum was sent to all the senior British officers, who were deadly against the I.N.A. and wanted that they should be punished.

Pleasure and intense relief born of the conviction that confirmation of the sentences would have result in violent internal conflict.

This feeling does not, in my opinion, spring universally from the idea that the covicted officers were trying to rid India of the British and, therefore, to be applauded, whatever crimes they might commit, by from a generally genuine feeling that they were patriot and nationalist and that, therefore, even if they were misled they should be treated with clemency, as ture sons of India. In this connection, it should be remembered, I think that every Indian worthy of the name is today a "Nationalist", though this does not mean that he is necessarily "anti British". All the same, where Indian and her independence are concerned, there are no "pro-British" Indians.

Every Indian Commissioned Officers is a Nationalist and rightly so, provided he hopes to attain independence for India by constitutional means–

(b) *On the Indian officer of the Indian Army*

Except for a few recovered prisoners of war who have suffered much at the hands of their fellow countrymen who joined the so-called "I.N.A.", the vast majority, almost without exception, however much they may like and respect the British, are glad and relieved because of the result to the trial. Most of them admit the gravity to the offence and do not condone it, but practically all are sure that any attempt to enforce the sentence would have led to choose in the country at large and probably to mutiny and dissension in the Army culminating in its dissolution, probably on communal lines.

The more senior and intelligent undoubtedly realize the implications of our having established in Principle the seriousness of the crime of forsaking one's allegiance and the wisdom of meeting it with a heavy banishment such as "Cashiering" which carries with it the stigma of disgrace.

They realize that their future is to be at all secure, discipline and loyalty must be maintained, but they, too, are nationalists and their feelings are much the same as those of the public at large.

(c) *On the V.C.Os.* and rank and file of the Indian Army

In very many units apparently little interest was displayed in the "I.N.A." trials, especially in the more illiterate and educationally backward arms of the service, such as the infantry and artillery.

In the technical units and amongst clerks, etd., however, interest was keen and widespread.

Some of the V.C.Os. and rank and file had suffered like their officers at the hands of their former comrades who joined the "I.N.A." and perhaps feel correspondingly bitter and disgusted at the leniency shown. This is inevitable and cannot be helped, regrettable though it may be. This section of opinion is relatively small.

The great majority are, I think, pleased that leniency has been shown for a variety of reasons.

Many of them have relations and friends from the same villages amongst the "I.N.A." Many think that, as the war is over, bygones should be bygones and a fresh start made.

Others are genuinely nationalistic in outlook and have been affected by agitation and propaganda. The great majority feel, I think, that the whole episode is unpleasant and discreditable to them as a class and to the Army as a whole, and would wish it forgotten and decently buried as soon as possible.

Under all this, there is, I think, an uneasy feeling as to the future and doubt as to whether their interests will be as well watched in the days to come as they have been in the past.

(d) *on the British officers of the Indian Army*

As I have already said, the effect on many British officers has been bad, and has led to public criticism, which has not been in accordance with the traditional locality I am entitled to expect. To these officers, perhaps not always very perceptive or imaginative, an officer is an officer, whether he be Indian or British, and they make no allowance for birth or political aspirations or upbringing, nor do they begin to realize the great political stresses and strains now affecting this country. They are unable to differentiate between the British and Indian points of view.

Moreover, they forget, if they ever knew, the great bitterness bred in the minds of many Indian officers in the early days of "Idealization" by th discrimination, often very real, exercised against them and the discourteous, contemptuous treatment meted out to them by many British officers who shold have known better.

These facts constitute the background against which the decisions should be judged, always keeping before one the object, which is to preserve by all possible means in our power the solidarity of the Indian Army, and of the R.I.N. and the R.I.A.F. as well. I have not specifically mentioned the two younger services, but everything I have said in this letter applies to them just as much as to the Army, and perhaps more so, as the ratings or other ranks of these services are better educated and perhaps more politically minded than those of the Army.

3. I would like you also to consider and to impress on others, especially those British officer who have been upset by the result of the first "I.N.A." trial, the effect of the capitulation of Singapore on the Indian troops involved in it, from amongst whom the "I.N.A." was subsequently formed.

Those who have served for many years with Indian troops, as I have done, have always recognized that the loyalty of our men was really to the officer of the regiment or unit, and that although there may have been some abstract sentiments of loyalty and patriotism to the Government and to the King, the men's allegiance for all practical purpose was focused depended for the (i) welfare, advancement and future prospects.

In these officers, their faith and trust was almost childlike, as events have proved time and time again. It is true to say that in almost every case of serious discontent or indiscipline, and there have been remarkable few of them, which has occurred in the past fifty years, the cause could be traced to indifferent officers and bad man-management.

4. The terrible tragedy of Singapore following on the fall of Hong Kong must have seemed to the great majority of the V.C.Os. and rank and file to be the end of all things, and certainly of the British "Raj" to whom the Army had been used for so many years of war and peace to look to as its universal provider and protector, acting through their own regimental officers.

Their British officers were at once taken from them and they were at once assailed by traitors who had been kept in readiness by the Japanese to seduce them from their allegiance. Their Indian officers in many instances proved false to their trust and used their influence to suborn their own men, skillfully aided and encouraged by the Japanese.

The strain and pressure to which these men, the majority of whom were simple peasant farmers with no cultural or educational background, were subjected is very difficult for any British officer, however experienced, to visualize. Nevertheless it is quite impossible for any British officer to judge them fairly unless he does try to visualize it and realize what these men must have thought and felt.

It is quite wrong to adopt the attitude that because these men had taken service in a British controlled Indian Army that therefore their loyalties must be the same as those of British soliders. As I have tried to explain, they had no real loyalty or patriotism towards Britain as Britain, not as we understand loyalty.

5. So much for the rank and file. The officers who went over present a much more difficult problem. Owing to their presumably superior education, knowledge of the world and experience generally, it is not possible to apply the same reasoning to them, except possible to the vary junior and to those who had been promoted from the ranks, whose background was more limited and whose knowledge was less.

There is no excuse for the regular officers who went over, beyond the fact that the early stages of "Indianisation" from its inception to the beginning of the late war were badly mismanaged by the British Government of India, and this prepared the ground for disloyalty when the opportunity came.

There is little doubt that "Indianisation" was at its inception looked on as a political expedient which was bound to fail militarily. There is no doubt also that many senior British officers believed and even hoped that it would fail.

The policy of segregation of Indian officers into separate units, the differential treatment in respect of pay and terms of service as compared with the British officer, and the prejudice and lack of manners of some—by no means all- British officers and their wives, all went to produce a very deep and bitter feeling of racial discrimination in the minds of the most intelligent and progressive of the Indian officers, who were naturally nationalists, keen to see Indian standing on her won legs and not to be rules from Whitehall for ever.

It is no use shutting one's eyes to the fact that any Indian officers worth his salt is a Nationalist, though this does not mean, as I have said before, that he is necessarily anti-British. If he is an anti-British this is as often as not due to his faulty handling and treatment by his British officer comrades.

It is essential for the preservation of future unity that this fact should be fully understood by all British officers.

No Indian officers must be regarded as suspect and disloyal merely because he is what is called a "Nationalist" or in other words—a good Indian!

6. This aspect of the business, though it cannot excuse the action of those officers in going over to the enemy, must be considered as it does provide the background against which we must view the present and the future.

We have very full evidence of the mental processes which these officers went through and many of them hesitated for a long time before they finally succumbed to circumstances and the persuasion of the Japanese and their extremist fellow-country men. Many of them having joined the first so-called "I.N.A." under Mohan Singh refused to join the second under Bose and spent the next three years as prisoners of war in the islands of the Pacific. This does not excuse their original lapse but does show that they were subjected to conflicting stresses and strains mentally.

7. There remains the matter of the decision to commute the sentences of the first three officers (Sahgal, Dhillon and Shah Nawaz) from "Transportation" to "Cashiering". If, as we have admitted, they were guilty of the worst crime a soldier can commit, then it may well be asked—"why be lenient with them?"

In taking the decision to show clemency, the whole circumstances past, present and future had to be considered and was (were) so considered most carefully and over a long period.

The overriding object is to maintain the stability, reliability and efficiency of the Indian army so that it may remain in the future a trustworthy weapon for use in the defence of India and, we hope, of the Commonwealth as a whole.

It was essential to establish the principle that falseness to his allegiance is a crime which cannot be countenanced in any officer under whatever Government he may be serving. By confirming the finding of the Court and the sentence of "Cashiering" which carries with it the highest degree of disgrace to an officer, we have done this. To have added imprisonment to the sentence would not in any way have helped to emphasise the principle we were concerned to preserve.

On the other hand, having considered all the evidence and appreciated the best of my ability the general trend of Indian public opinion and of the felling in the Indian Army, I have no doubt to all that to have confirmed the sentence of imprisonment solely on the charge of "waging war against the King" would have had disastrous result, in that it would have probably precipitated violent outbreak throughout the country, and have created active and widespread disaffection in the Army, especially amongst the Indian officers and the more highly educated rank and file. To have taken this risk would have been seriously to jeopardise our object.

Always keeping before one the difference in outlook between British and Indian, which I have tried to explain in this letter, I decided, therefore, that in the interests of the future of both India and British and because of the unprecedented circumstances of the case, the only proper course to pursue was to confirm the finding and so establish the principle but to show clemency in respect of the sentence. Some bewilderment has been caused, I believe, by the fact that Shah Nawaz who was found guilty of "abetment of murder" as well as of "waging war" received the same treatment as the other two accused who were found guilty of "waging war" only. Shah Nawaz's offence, which was committed by him as an officer of the "I.N.A." in the alleged execution of his duty, in that he ordered a sentence authorised by a higher I.N.A. authority to be carried out, did, in the circumstance, flow from his basic offence of "waging war" as a member of the I.N.A. The punishment for this—the principle offence—Was "Cashiering" in the case of all three officers. Shah Nawaz did not himself commit any brutal or violent act against any person, but passed on the orders of a superior authority which he claims to have believed to have been properly constituted.

It is necessary also to remember that some 20,00 officers and men joined the so-called "I.N.A." and that, even if it were desirable, it would have been a physical impossibility to bring all these men to trail within anything approaching a reasonable period of time.

8. The situation now is that the principle that the for sake of his allegiance by a soldier is a crime in any circumstances has been established, and that no further trials on this account alone will be held. Those against whom there is adequate evidence of murder and brutality will be tried and punished in the ordinary way.

In the second, third and fourth trials the charge of "waging war" has been included in addition to the other charges because trials were commenced before the finding of the Court in the first trial was known. If the accused in these three trials are found guilty on this charge the court will pass the sentence of "Transportation of life" which is the minimum admissible under the Army Act for the offence of "waging war".

When it comes to confirmation of the sentence, however, the facts in respect of the other charges of brutality will be the guiding factor.

In any subsequent trials, the charge of "waging war" will be omitted as our object is now to punish those who may have been guilty of brutal acts towards their former comrades.

9. As to the great mass of rank and file of the so-called "I.N.A.", these are now being examined by Courts of Inquiry as rapidly as possible with a view of finding out whether they are to be classified as "White", "Grey" or "Black". I realise very well and so does everyone else at G.H.Q. and in the War Department, the urgent need for disposing of these men at the earlier possible moment, so that the whole affair may have a reasonable change of being forgotten, which is I am sure the ardent desire of the Army as a whole. At the same time, it is quite certain from the evidence at our disposal that if this enquiry is not carried out with reasonable thoroughness, great injustice may be done to innocent men. The temptation, therefore, to discharge or dismiss all and sundry summarily and without more ado must be resisted.

10. There is one other criticism which is often made. If is said that we ought to have dealt with the accused summarily in forward areas; that if the men were to be brought to India we should have avoided

publicity, and in particular trial in the Red Fort; and that we ought to have put out counter-publicity from the start. The answer to the first point is that we had to deal with 45000 men, in one instance a whole I.N.A. division surrendering without firing a shot. It was obviously impracticable for forward areas to deal with men on this scale summarily and it was the obvious course to send them back to India where the records and Intelligence organisation existed for interrogation. As to publicity, I am sure it was right to decide not to hold trials in secret because it would have been thought that the men were not getting a fair trial. Once it was decided that the trials could not he held in secret, it would have been wrong to tuck them away somewhere where defence counsel, relations, etc., could not conveniently attend; and the Red Fort was the most convenient place from nearly every point of view. We avoided counter-publicity because it was practically certain that a big publicity drive would be represented as prejudicing the accused in their trial; but in any event it is not possible for us to force papers to publish anything which they regard as propaganda and with which they do not agree. We have no control over them in this respect.

11. This letter has become very lengthy, but I make no apology for this as I consider it essential that the full facts of this sad business should be put before you, so that you in your turn can put them before the officers serving under you, as and when it appears necessary to you.

You should not, in explaining the matter to your officers, quote me as Commander-in-Chief but should use the material I have tried to give you in this letter in any way you think suitable to the purpose as if it came from yourself.

12. Finally let me again state the object : it is to maintain the reliability, stability and efficiency of the Indian Army for the future, whatever Government may be set up in India.

This can be done only if the British and Indian officers of the Army trust and respect each other and continue to work wholeheartedly together for the common cause as they have done in war.

It is your task to do your utmost to bring this about and I am sure you will ? You have excellent material on which to work.

13. If your are still in doubt on any point or have any suggestions to make in furtherance of our common object, I will be glad if you will let me or the Adjutant-General know.

C.J. Auchinleck,
General

19

Wavell's Report of his Interview with Jawaherlal Nehru Regarding I.N.A.

2 May, 1946

1. I had asked Nehru to come and see me because of letter he had written to the Commander-in-Chief about certain proposed I.N.A. trials. I told him that after discussion with the Commander-in-Chief and consideration of the evidence, we had decided that these particular men would not be tried. I asked him not to make public the fact that he had written to the Commander-in-Chief and sought to influence him in the matter, as it would cause the Commander-in-Chief some embarrassment. He promised not to do so, but said he could not entirely guarantee that the Press might some embarrassment. He promised not to do so, but said he could not entirely guarantee that the Press might not attribute the matter to his intervention.

2. I then told him my views on the I.N.A.; and that I thought it was an act of folly on the part of the political parties to have glorified the I.N.A. men, who were for the most part the weakling and softlings of the prisoners of war in Malaya; by far the greater percentage of them had joined to obtain better treatment and rations or to avoid hardship. The real heroes were the 45,000 men who had remained staunch; in spite of starvation, ill-treatment, and torture; 15,000 of them had perished as result of this, while the casualties of the I.N.A. had been relatively very small, and they had done little real fighting.

   Nehru listened quite quietly, and said that any body of men were a mixture; but that while he realised that some of the I.N.A. men had not joined from the best of motives and were not the best type of men, he had met many of them who were of a good type. He said that the attitude taken by the Congress Party towards the I.N.A. trials

1. Wavell Papers. Indian office Library & Records. London.

was not simply from political motives but in response to the real feeling in the country. I said that the feeling in the country had been largely worked up by agitation in the press and on the platform. He said that nevertheless the feeling was a very genuine one. He said there was no intention to withhold admiration from the regular Indian Army, though they had hitherto felt that this was a foreign instrument of repression.

I think, from what he said, that Congress has begun to realise that the I.N.A. is not entirely a creditable asset.

Nehru to Claude Auchnileck Pleading for Leniency Towards the I.N.A. Soldiers[1]

4 May, 1946

Dear Sir Clude,

I want to think you for your decision to withdraw all trial of I.N.A. personnel. I am sure this decision will be widely welcomed and will help in producing an atmosphere which we all desire.

It has been said sometimes that the regular Indian army has been largely ignored while the members of the I.N.A. have been lionised. To some extent this may be true, but I do not think it is fundamentally true. All Indians are proud of the courage and capacity of the Indian army. They are splendid material, but inevitably they have been looked upon in the past as agents of foreign authority and so long as political conditions in India do not change completely, this approach will remain. As a matter of fact do not change completely, this approach will remain. As a matter of fact various factors during the past few months have gone towards breaking down, or at any rate lessening, the barriers between the army and the civil population. This is all to the good. Nevertheless the final barrier will remain till the army can consider itself, and is in fact, a real national army. I hope the day is not distant when this will happen. You must know that most of us have friends and relatives in the Army, the Navy and the Air Force and so, apart from wider national considerations, even personal factors make us interested in the future of the defence services.

We know that large numbers of officers and men of the Indian army, who were taken prisoners by the Japanes in Malaya, suffered terribly. Thousands did not survive this ordeal. Those who underwent this suffering certainly deserve our full sympathy. We know also that every person who joined the I.N.A. did not necessarily do so for patriotic motives, but, having personally come across a fairly large number of I.N.A. officers and

1. Nehru Papers, Nehru Memorial Museum and Liberary, New Delhi. Also Printed in Auchinleck (London, 1959) pp. 817-819, by John Connell.

men, I must say that I have been struck by the high calibre of many of them. I have no doubt that basic motive for many of them was patriotic and the desire to help in achieving India's freedom.

It is sometimes said that we have exploited this I.N.A. situation for political purposes. Almost everything in India fits in somewhere into the political picture because the fact of India's subjection dominates life here. But I can say with some confidence that there was no desire or even thought of exploiting the I.N.A. issue for political purposes when this matter first came before the public. I believe I was the first person to mention it is public. The sole thought before me was that thousands of my countrymen, whom I believed to be patriotic, were in grave danger. I did not then know the full story of the I.N.A., but knowing my countrymen fairly well I could understand how they must have felt in a difficult situation. I realised also the repercussions on them of events in India. I had not appreciated the political and international approach of some of the leaders of the Indian independence movement in South East Asia. I had differed from them in the past on international and national issues. Nevertheless I felt kinship and sympathy for these people and I knew well what the reaction of the public mind in India would be. The possibility that some swift action by courts martial might be taken against large numbers of them filled me with apprehension not only because of the persons involved, but also because of the inevitable consequences in India. Sensing all this I made my first public reference to the I.N.A. and followed this up with subsequent reference. It did not strike me at all at the time that political advantage could be taken of this affair. Then a strange and surprising thing happened, not strange in itself but very surprising because of its depth and extent. Though I had sensed the mood of the Indian people, I had not fully realised how far it went in the direction. Within a few weeks the story of the I.N.A. had percolated to the remotest villages in India and everywhere there was admiration for them and apprehension as to their possible fate. No political organisation, however strong and efficient, could have produced this enormous reaction in India. It was one of those rare things which just fit into the mood of the people, reflect, as it were, and provide an opportunity for the public to give expression to that mood. The reason for this was obvious. Individuals were not known nor were many facts known to the public. The story as it developed seemed to the people just another aspect of India's struggle for independence and the individuals concerned became symbols in the republic mind. Whether one agrees with this or not, one should at least understand how things happen and what forces lie behind them. The widespread popular enthusiasm was surprising enough, but even more surprising was a similar reaction of a very large number of regular Indian army officers and men. Something had touched them deeply. This kind of thing is not done and cannot be done by politicians or agitators or the like. It is the fundamental aspect of the I.N.A. question that has to be borne in mind. All other aspects, however important, are secondary.

I suppose everyone who has given thought to the matter realises fully that it is a dangerous and risky business to break the disciplines of an army. It would obviously be harmful to do any injury to a fine instrument like the Indian army, and yet at every step, till major changes take place converting it into a real national army, we have to face the political issue which governs every aspect of Indian life today. Risks have to be taken sometimes, more especially when existing conditions are felt to be intolerable. You will forgive me for writing this rather long letter. It was my intention only to think you; but then I felt that I should say something also on this subject, something that might give you a glimpse into my own mind.

Sincerely yours,
Jawaharlal Nehru

21

Note by the C.S.D.I.C. (I). on the Part Played by the INA in Active Operations Against Allied Forces[1]

12 May, 1946

Note: This Note has been prepared at 12 hours notice and does not purport to be either an exact or a comprehensive account of the subject dealt with.

1. **The First INA, 1942—**

The INA of Mohan Singh comprised of

16000 Absorbed volunteers.

30000 Surplus volunteers.

The maximum allowed by the Japanese.

Men who had signed volunteer forms but who could not be absorbed into Mohan Singh's organisation. The Japanese declared on 1/1/42 that all surplus volunteers would thenseforth be regarded as PW/- itself a sign that the Japanese did not intend to allow the INA to become too strong.

The first INA was organised, trained and disbanded in Singapore. Its officials life was from 1 Sep. 42 to 28 Dec. 42. 400 men left Singapore for Burma in Nov. 42 as an Advance Guard.

In Burma in 1942 a group of about 400 men captured during the Burma Campaign volunteered for 5th Column tasks, were taken from Rangoon Jail and trained by Capt. L.S. Misra 5/17 Dogra and Jem Ram Sarup. These 400 men were trained in line contact work and propaganda.

2. **1943, The Second INA**—The INA in Singapore languished after Mohan Singh's arrest, when R.B. Bose announced that in future only willing and enthusiastic volunteers were required. 4000 men resigned from the INA, leaving only 12000 members. The DMB took

1. W.O. 208/868. P.R.O.

charge until S.C. Bose arrived in July 43 from Germany to infuse new life into the moribund INA. The Japanese, however, knew exactly how they intended to use the INA, and pushed ahead with the training of the SS (Bahadur), Intelligence and Reinforcement Groups. These units were intended to spearhead the Japanese invasion of India, and they moved to Burma in Sept./Oct. 1943 to link up with the other large group of trained saboteurs and fifth columnists under Jem Ram Sarup and Capt Misra.

S.C. Bose immediately reorganised the INA, secured an unlimited ceiling for recruitment, and initiated a large programme of training schools for civilians. Thousands of civilians flocked to join the Training Centre and the OTS 1943 was thus the year of training for the INA, whose strength was then about :-

Military	-	15000
Civilians	-	5000
		20000

Towards the end of the year, the INA units began to move to Burma (1,2,3,4, Guerrilla Regts) in anticipation of the forthcoming Japanese all out offensive of early 1944.

In Burma, throughout 1943, there was nothing but frontier patrolling and skirmishing. Small Groups of trained JIFS from Rangoon were sent to numerous towards posts (Paungbyin, Kalewa, Mawlaik, Homalin etc.) to carry out recces for Japanese units and to disseminated propaganda leaflets. There was however no real fighting and a large numbers of these JIFS seized the opportunity to return to India and surrender.

3. **1944.**

1944 was the year planned for the Japanese all-out offensive. Unfortunately for them, owing to the earlier crisis in the INA, the INA was still an embryo organisation and though the training schools were full of recruits and cadets. Only No 1 Div (Comd M. Z. Kiani) of the INA was fully trained by early 1944 and sent to Burma. Its composition was:-

1 Guerrilla Regt (Bose Regt)	–	2000 men
Guerrilla Regt (Gandhi Regt)	–	2000 men
2 Guerrilla Regt (Azad Regt)	–	2000 men
2 Guerrilla Regt (Nehru Regt)	–	2000 men

HQ 1 Div	-	400 men
HT Coys	-	800 men
SS Gp	-	600 men
"I" Gp	-	400 men
Rft Gp	-	400 men
Rear details/L of C	-	2000 men
	Approx.	12600 men

The above force was purely a Guerrilla Force, lightly armed and really intended as skirmishers for the Japanese Divisions. The INA force had no aircraft, no artillery, no heavy mortars, no tanks or AFV's. They were equipped with British rifles and equipment of 1941 issue, and were consequently outmoded and out-weaponed.

4. **The Kohima/Imphal Campaign of 1944**

(a) **General**—The massive Japanese offensive opened with the unsuccessful drive in the Arakan, followed in March by the advances on Kohima, Imphal and Tiddim These advances were made by purely Japanese forces to which had been allotted a quota of trained JIFS of Bahadur and "I" Gp. Thus, during the early and sweeping phases of the advances many reports were received of JIF activity, particularly in the Sangshak fighting and the siege of Kohima when broadcast exhortations were made to subvert British/Indian troops. In the wider picture of INA history, however, the activities of these small bands of specialist JIFS can be disregarded as they were essentially part of the enemy "I" offensive and not part of his armed offensive. The JIF Sector or Butai Commanders were:-

Capt	Maghar Singh	(Imphal Area)
Lt.	Ajmer Sing	(Kohima Area)
Capt.	S.A. Malik	(Imphal/Tiddim Area)

The first two met with practically no success in their attempts to subvert Allied personnel. Capt S.A. Malik enjoyed a certain measure of suceess, mainly because much larger numbers of Allied PW and Stragglers were captured in his Sector.

(b) **The Guerrilla Regts in Action**—The INA Guerrilla Regts followed up behind the Japanese thrust which was levelled at Imphal along the Term/lale Rd. Whereas the siege of Kohima took place in Apr 44, it was early. May before the leading Grla Regt (Ghandhi) arrived in the Tamu area. After much argument, the Japanese agreed to allow the Regts of 1 Div INA to operations Regts and not as sub-units of Japanese formations. Gandhi Regt was ordered to pursue allegedly retreating British elements along the Tamu/Palel road. Flushed with enthusiasm but without adequate reconnaissance, a special raiding force of about 20 men under Lt Pritam Singh (Kapurthala Inf), set out on the night of 2/3 May to capture the Palel Landing Strip. Unbeknown to this force, path of advance, on a hill near Litan village (Point RK 4018 1/4" map. Five miles from Palel and three miles north of Purum Khulan). This Gurkh a picquet was No. 11 platoon of 'B' Coy 4/10 Gurkhas (10 Ind Inf Bde), and comprised 26 men commanded by Jem Bharta Singh Rai. At 2230 hrs the INA force was discerned approaching, talking and smoking. It was allowed to proceed into an ambush position before fire was opened upon it. During the next hour seven separate attacks were made on the Gurkha picquet position, but each attacks was repulsed. The INA force then withdrew in disorder having suffered considerable câsualties. The Gurkha picquet lost only two men killed.

The above action was the first recorded and concerted action undertaken by INA troops under their own commanders. Its utter defeat and discomfiture must have spread incalculable pessimism and defeatism amongst the INA troops then massing in the Tamu area. The action served to remind the INA troops who had fed on stories of mutiny and disintegration in the Allied forces that:-

(a) British/Indian troops would not hesitate to shoot on the INA

(b) British/Indian troops would not throw down their arms when attacked by INA.

(c) British defences were soundly organised, with overwhelming fire-power support.

After the above action, operations became largely static owing to the monsoon. There were no pitched battles but a certain number of patrol clashes. 2 Guerrilla (Gandhi) Regt (Comd Capt I.J. Kiani) was deployed on either side of the Tamu Palel road. 3 Guerrilla (Azad) Regt (Comd Capt Gulzara Singh) was deployed north of the road in the Mintha/Narum area. Malaria and sickness took heavy toll and when the Japanese supply system broke down, starvation and disease overtook the Japanese and the INA. Of the 6000 INA troops on the Tamu front.

250 were killed in action/by bombing
1000 died form starvation/disease
600 deserted to join the British.

1. **Guerrilla (Bose) Regt was known as the "Crack" Regt.**

In Mar 44 one of the Batallions moved via Prome to the Arakan, under Lt P.S. Raturi, whilst the other two Batallions moved via Kalewa/Myittha Haka to the Chin Hills above Falam.

The Bn in the Arakan operated on the Kaladan against west African troops and took part in about a dozen patrol clashes. The West Africa forces withdrew during the monsoon and the INA force advanced to occupy Mowdok at the head of the Sangu River - just inside the Indian frontier. This advance was extensively used in Japanese/INA propaganda but at the end of the monsoon the West Africans advanced again and the INA force retraced its steps to Paletwa and eventually to Myohaung. In INA circles 1 Bn Bose Regt was reputed to have put up one of the best performances against Allied troops, for the return to Rangoon in Nov 44 it was earmarked to become No 1 Bn of a new unit known as "X" Regt.

2 and 3 Bns Bose Regt under Capt Shah Niwaz (Comd Bose Regt) moved to the Falam area of the Chin Hills and remained there from March to June doing nothing but patrols and keeping its L of C (via Kalewa/Natchaung) in repair. In Mar the famous "Manning Incident" took place when 20 British Chin levies were captured by a ruse: this was followed by the abortive attack on Klang Klang. Decimated by malaria and disease 2 and 3 Bns Bose Regt were moved up in June 44 to the Ukhrul/Humine area, to assist in the extrication of Japanese/INA remnants from the Kohima/Imphal disasters.

From July onward the Japanese/INA withdrawal degenerated into a route. Thousands of Japanese and hundreds of INA perished en route from Tamu to Kalewa. Throughout the campaign (March-July 44) after the first fiasco at Palel the INA was never again entrusted with any really independent combat task. Its strength was dissipated by patrol actions, the maintenance of a precarious L of C, and the constant loses caused by sickness, disease, starvation and desertion.

Of the total of 8000 INA troops who crossed the Chindwin

300	-	were killed in action
600	-	deserted to the British
1000	-	were captured or picked up by the Advancing British Forces.
1500	-	died of sickness or starvation.
3400	-	(Figures approx. only).

It is to be noted here that 4 Guerrilla (Nehru) Regt never moved North of Mandalay as it arrived too late to take part in the Imphal operations.

The failure of the INA in the 1944 campaign sent S.C.Bose to Tokyo to secure greater independence and autonomy in the INA Command, and freedom from Hikari Kikan. This bore fruit in the campaign of 1945 when INA Regt took orders only from HQ Supreme Comd and from INA Div HQ and when INA Regt 1/Bn Commanders were authorised to exercise initiative and independent command within the areas allotted to them. In 1945 the INA became more of a fighting force and fought more as Allies of the Japanese rather than as an appendage of the Japanese Army.

It was to rely more on its own strength of arms and military virtue than on hopes that the British /Indian forces would crumble at the first shout of front-line propagandists. It is indicative of the campaign of 1945 that the sedulously trained men of Bahadur and SS Groups (whose work in 1944 had been zealous but fruitless) were sent to the rear and never used. For the 1945 campaign propaganda was abandoned as a weapon - perhaps because it was appreciated that propaganda has less affect on an advancing than on a retreating enemy.

The INA failed in 1944 because

(a) It grossly underestimated the strength and determination of Allied resistance, and sadly overestimated the military efficiency of the Japanese Army.

(b) It had beguiled itself by its own propaganda, and thought it could win battles by propaganda alone. It relied on the Japanese to win battles and territory and its own intended task was to consolidate the territory so won.

(c) It was not present in sufficient numerical strength to make any real impression on the Allied Forces opposed to it.

(d) It was outdated in its weapons and its tactics. It was David against Goliath but a David without a sling. It had enthusiasm and revolutionary ardour, but locked most of the other military requisites. S.C. Bose devoted too much of his energies to delivering propaganda lectures, rather than insisting on better military equipment etc.

(e) Its "commisariat" was part of the Japanese "Q" organisation-which failed radically, and was one of the chief reasons for the Japanese defeat.

The actual fighting performed by the INA in the 1944 campaign was negligible. It spent the bulk of its time fighting hunger and disease and the inefficiency or inadequacy of its own organisation. Even as a propaganda weapon it was over-rated because it achieved practically nothing. In every recorded clash between British and INA troops the latter were worsted. From the sorry tale of the 1944 campign there emerges no name from the petty hierarchy of INA Commanders which can be said to be even mediocre, let alone great.

5. **The Pause between The Campaigns**—From July 1944 to Feb 45 the INA was withdrawing and reorganising and practically all contact with it was lost. The remnants of 1 Div 1, 2 and 3 Grla Regts (about 4000 men) were finally sent back to Zeyawaddy Rest Camp. Meantime units of 2 Div INA were being hurriedly brought up from Malaya. These units were :-

5 Guerrilla Regt (later named 2 Inf Regt)	2000 men
Hind Fd Force (later named 1 Inf Regt)	2000 men
HQ 2 Div	400 men
Miscellaneous units	2000 men
INA AA Coy (5) stationed in southern Burma and Siam	1000 men

To the above fresh troops were added the 1000 men of 4 Guerrilla (Nehru) Regt of 1 Dev, which had not been committed in the 44 fighting. Thus in early Feb 45 the INA front-line set-up was : -

4 Guerril la (Nehru) Regt	- South bank of Irrawaddy between Nyaungu and Pagan.
2. Inf Regt	- Moving up to Mt Popa/ Kyaukpadaung area.
1 Inf Regt	- Movilng up to Magwe area.
Remnats 1 Div	- Zeyawaddy (Toungoo)

By the begining of Feb 45 the Allied Divisions had advanced through Shwebo, Monywa, Sagaing and Pakokku and stood poised for the assault on Mandalay and for the thrust across the Irrawaddy. The ensueing period 15 Feb to 30 April was a period of heavy and constant fighting and these 2/1 months include the entire INA 1945 campaign of front-line fighting. The period opens with the British thrust across the Irrawaddy at Nyaungu and ends with the total disentegration of all INA forces.

6. **Outstanding Events of the 1945 Campaign**

(a) On 15 Feb 45 British forces in the Pakokku area opened there attack on the INA forces (1000 men of Nehru Regt) who lined the Southern bank of the Irrawaddy in the Nyaungu/Pagan area. The weight of the Allied bombing, mortaring and shelling demoralised the INA defenders and on 18 Feb over 300 men of Nehru Regt surrendered voluntarily to British forces. The remaining 700 men under Regt Comd Lt G.S. Dhillon retreated in disorderly confusion to the Mount Popa area. By that time however, the 2000 men of 2 Inf Regt under Capt. P.K. Sahgal had reached the vital Mount Popa positions and entrenched themselves there where they were to remain for the next six weeks. Shortly after Nehru Regt had settled down at Popa the British airborne landing at Meiktila was flown in and the British bridgehead forces at Nyaungu/Nyingyan moved across country to link up with the Meiktila garrison. These moves brought the British bridgehead forces into contact with the Screen of INA positions covering the northern approaches to Mount Popa. A number of hard-fought engagements resulted, in which for the first time INA troops fought with mettle and determination.

(b) By the end of Feb 45, HQ 2 Div INA had set up its HQ MT Pop,. Within a few days of arrival, and by means of a brilliant subterfuge, four of the five staff officers of HQ 2 Div deserted and escaped to the British lines. This joint desertion severely rattled the INA High Command and S.C. Bose was obliged to inaugurate a "hate campaign" against all traitors. The gaps in th staff of HQ 2 Div were filled by second rate officers.

(c) The remnants of Nehru Regt were allotted the defence of an area between the Irrawaddy and Mt Popa, and were based on Kyaukpadaung. On 15 March 45 a newly arrived company of reinforcements under "Lt" Gian Singh (and comprising 75% civilians) moved forward to village Kunywa (or Kazaung) and took up position inside a dry water tank. This position was attacked by Gurkha troops and British tanks. The INA Coy stood its ground, and after 45 men had been killed the remainder surrendered. "Lt" Gain Singh was killed. This action was made much of by the INA Rangoon propagandists and a newsheet was published called : "The Charge of the Immortals" which was an idealised version of the action referred to above.

(d) On the 10th March 45 all Bns of 2 Inf Regt were in position et Mt Popa. Capt Shah Niwaz had taken over command of 2 Div and capt. P.K. Sahgal reverted to Comd 2 Inf Regt. To cover an intended move by Japanese forces under General YAMAMOTO up the Irrawaddy, 2 Inf Regt under Sahgal made a night attack on 15/16 March on the village of Pyinbyin, but withdrew to its positions at Popa when met by Allied MG fire.

(e) On 16 March a coy of INA troops of 2 Inf Regt, under Sub Khan Mohd attacked Sade Village and fierce hand-to-hand fighting took place, the INA troops fighting well.

(f) On 25 March a second attack was made on Pyinbyin Village by 2 Inf Regt, in conjunction with Japanese troops. This operation was intended to assist Japanese troops at Maiktila who were counter attacking the British.

(g) From 26/31 Mar 2 Inf Regt was ordered to attack northwards to assist the Japanese counter offensive towards Myingyan/ Mandalay. Moving from Popa to Seiktein with 1 Bn 2 Inf Regt Capt P.K. Sahgal was rambushed and narrowly escaped and drew back to Legyi to dig in.

(h) One the three Bns of 2 Inf Regt were in position at Legyi on 30 March, there developed the biggest pitched battle of the campaign. For four days the INA positions were shelled and mortared and attacked by Allied troops, but the INA stood their ground well. Capt. P.K. Sahgal wrote a long appreciation of this battle and named Nk (2/Lt) Kanwal Singh as a men who distinguished himself. However, men were deserting every day, and by 4 April over 400 men had deserted, mostly in large groups led by officers. Heavy casualties had also been suffered and 2 Inf Regt (which had fought extremely well, mostly due to Sahgal's leadership) withdrew and gradually disintegrated. Nehru Regt and 2 Inf Regt joined their depleted forces on 8 April but by then British tanks were forging ahead towards Magwe, from Meiktila. The INA in the Popa area therefore withdrew via Yenangyaung to Magwe. There were no more pitched battles. The INA in Burma had shot its bolt.

(i) During the period 15 Feb-8 April 45 there was a constant stream of desertions from the INA and it was this flow of desertions which weakened and disorganised 2 Inf Regt and rendered it incapable of further effective resistance. Many of the desertions were assisted by the dropping of Allied surrender leaflets singed by the recently escaped Staff Officers of HQ 2 Div.

(j) The three battalions of 1 Inf Regt (previously Hind Fd Force) under Capt S.M. Hussain were stationed in the Magwa area in an anti-paratroop role. 2 Bn (650 men) were at Megwa and when British Tanks arrived (650 men) were at Magwe and when British tanks arrived on 19 April 45 the 650 men surrendered without firing a shot. 1 and 3 Bns disintegrated on contact with British forces and surrendered in numerous parties, some large some small. Only a small number of die-hards attempted to make their way across country to Pegu and thence to Siam. In the end, only one party led by Lt. S.N. Gupta finally reached Bangkok.

(k) Thus the Fiercest resistance by INA troops was put up by 2 Inf Regt under P.K. Sahgal, but ever his men deserted him. Eventually Sahgal himself was compelled to surrender near Allanmyo with 600 of his men, when overtaken and surrounded. Comparatively, Nehru Regt and 1 Inf Regt offered no resistance whatsoever to Allied troops.

(1) Meantime, S.C.Bose had formed "X" Regt under Capt Thakar Singh, Kapurthala Inf from amongst the fit personnel of 1 Div INA from Zeyawaddy Rest Camp. Three Bns were formed.

No 1 under "Capt" Suraj Mal	(from 1 Bn Bose ex-Arakan)
No 2 Lt Ran Singh	(600 men)
No 3 Civ (Major) Abid Hussan	(600 men)

2 and 3 moved forward from Zeyawaddy but disintegrated at first contact with Allied forces. They moved eastwards from Tougoo/Mawchi/Papun/Moulmein/Bangkok, disdaining even to join combat with the small parties of Forces 136 guerrillas which occasionally tried to bar their way and the bulk of the men reached Bangkok - the only formed bodies of INA troops to do so.

(m) Thus the story of the INA 1945 campaign in Burma is one of half-hearted resistance and constant surrenders relieved only by the few battles fought with determination by 2 Inf Regt. The reasons are many, and include general demoralisations, superior to Allied weapons, tactics, air-power etc. But one of the reasons is also the poor leadership exhibited by the great majority of INA officers - with one or two notable exceptions only. The INA lacked real officers: it had a number of good Nks - cum- Lieuts, the majority of INA officers though suitable for propaganda parades, were not suitable for the battle field. The INA had an excellent paper organisation but its foundations were inherently weak and insubstantial. There were thousands of INA troops in Rangoon in April 45 but they all surrendered without firing a shot.

(n) the following points emerge from the INA's 1945 campign :-

(i) It fought as an ally of the Japanese to hold Burma for the Nippon Empire. It on longer fought as the Indian Army of liberations. Inspite of this, S.C. Bose by his propaganda and personality kept alive in the minds of the INA the illusion that they were fighting for the freedom of India.

(ii) 2 Inf Regt fought with courage and determination from 15 March 45 to 15 April 45, inspired by the personal example and leadership of capt. P.K. Sahgal. All other INA unit collapsed at first contact with British forces and mass surrenders followed. First contact was joined on 15 Feb 45 and during the next two months over 3000 "fighting troops" of the INA surrendered.

(iii) With one or two notable exceptions, the INA officers proved poor leaders. The "Officers" who distinguished themselves were mostly ex-NCOs. The bulk of NCIO/IECO officers in the INA retained jobs on the L of C and in rear areas, and hoped for a comfortable journey from Rangoon to Delhi.

(iv) INA medical and evacuation arrangements were rudimentary. There was an ample supply of doctors but organisation was poor because the senior IMS officers discarded medicine for politics.(Lt Col Chatterjee, Lt-Col Loganadan, Lt Col Alagappan etc), and left medical organisation in the hands of men of mediocre ability.

(v) On Paper, the INA had an impressive organisation, but when this was reduced to terms of fighting potential, the inherent feebleness of the INA was revealed. At no time was the INA properly equipped to wage war on modern lines.

(vi) Though as a fighting force the INA was a negligible factor it cannot be denied that the political (or spiritual - as it was called) indoctrination given to the troops had a more potent and lasting effect. The patent sincerity of S.C. Bose was made clear to all ranks for Bose shared the dangers of the battle fields with them.

7. **The INA in Burma**—Thus, in the two campaigns of 1944 and 1945, a total of approx 15000 men served with the INA in Burma.

Of those :-

750	were killed	}	
1500	died of disease	}	Figures
2000	escaped to Bangkok	}	
3000	"Surrendered"	}	approx
7000	"captured"	}	only

8. **The INA in Malaya (3 DIV)**—Malaya remained the Trg ground for the INA. Strengths in Malaya in Aug 45 were :-

HQ 3 DIV	800
3 Inf Regt (6 Grla)	2250
7, 8, 9 Grla Regts	6000
AHF Trg Centres	3000
AFV Bn	1000
Pack Tpt Unit	1000
Animal Tpt Unit	1400
Rft Gp	1000
Miscellaneous	2200
	19000

(* About 60% Civilians). The above men all surrendered without firing a shot, after S.C. Bose had instructed "Maj Gen" M.Z. Kiani to order capitulation.

The total strength of the INA in 1944/45 was from 35000 to 40000 of whom about 20000 were ex-military and 20000 were civilians. Of those 40000 only about 10000 were ever engaged on active operations against Allied Forces, and on not more than 10 or 12 occasions were pitched battles fought. The INA was 95 per cent "ballyhoo" and 5 per cent "Serious business". In 1944 it failed as a propaganda weapon, and in 1945 it failed as a fighting weapon. It was never a cause of real trouble or annoyance to the Allies: the most trouble it ever gave was in giving the British the problem of handling thousands of its men as recovered PW when the Allied L of C in Burma was littered by thousands of surrendered JIFS.

Note—The above does not purport in any way to be a complete or meticulously accurate statement of the case. Most of the paragraphs could be amplified and much additional material introduced.

22

Fujiwara's Observations on INA. and Subhas Chandra Bose[1]

9 July, 1946

My experience of the INA. is limited to the main force of I Div.[2] which took part in the Imphal operations. It cannot be positive or accurate judgement.

1. **General Observation**—As a revolutionary army, its morale was high and it was quite well organised. But the standard of its tactics, training and leadership was low. These together with other shortcomings and weaknesses mentioned below contributed to make the fighting strength of the INA. not what it might have been. It lacked in particular offensive strength and tenacity.

2. **Morale of the INA.**—The revolutionary spirit, organisation and discipline which was the foundation of the INA. morale, was low and maintained by all officers and men of the INA. on their enthusiastic respect and pledge of loyalty to Subhas Chandra Bose. Had they not had Mr. Bose as their leader, their morale certainly would have been considerably lower than it was and during a crisis when they would have been shaken and divided. During the most distressing and difficult period of the Imphal operations about June and July 1944, the great majority of the I.N.A. answered the urgent appeals of Mr. Bose and followed the leadership of their superiors maintaining discipline and otherwise carrying out their respective duties. Even during the retreat they overcame overwhelming difficulties and retreated in an orderly fashion. This won for them the admiration even of the Japanese army.

3 **Leadership**—The leaders were quick to observe enemy intentions and generally speaking they were competent in their leadership. But with the Div. as the strategic unit of operations, they lacked experi-

1. S.E.A.T.I.C. Bulletin No 240. This Bulletin consists of the translation of essays written by Fujiwara on various topics when he was in prison in Singapore in 1946.
2. Col. M.Z. Kiani was commander of this Division.

ence and training and not infrequently they failed to see the picture in its correct prospective. I have the impression that the officers were incompetent when faced with unforeseen difficulties, but this can be attributed to their lack of experience.

4. **Technical Training**—Technical training of INA. troops in jungle and mountain warfare was lacking and they had little imagination or experience in the construction or fortification. As a result when faced by Allied forces superior in equipment and numbers although they pushed ahead ferociously, if those advances met a counter off sure they were unnecessarily heavy. Having once suffered a set-back the psychological effect was great and they were always inclined to on the defensive.

5. Other than the attempted advance made by the INA. to the area south of Palel, they did not participate in any major battle. Their main job was to guard the flank of the Yamamato Force and prevent the Indian Army from outflanking this unit i.e., their job was a defensive one.

Difficulties met by INA Division

(a) Civil volunteers were mixed with military and they lacked the proper housing.

(b) Personnel arrived piecemeal and had to be employed separately for instance I infantry Regiment arrived in Haka and Falam in March 1944 as 2 Inl. arrived at Palel front in April whereas the 3 Int. did not arrive until June 1944.

(c) They were short of equipment especially guns.

(d) They lacked organisation and means of supply and during the monsoon season, when supply lines were cut, they had to rely on manpower alone for movement of supplies.

(e) The Chins and Shans on the frontier were not sympathetic to the Indians.

On S. C. Bose

I would like it to be mentioned that what I shall state below is from my observations not very profound. Bose was a man who fought body and soul for independence. He was by nature a revolutionary. He had a zealous fighting spirit, though in outward appearance, he was very gentle. His earnest and precise mind, his vigorous actions, and his initiative together with his love for the masses showing no discrimination between classes won him the respect which was later transformed into reverence from all those who came into contact with him.

As a revolutionary, his political abilities were great as his record from July 43 shows, but he had not the capacity for constructive political projects.

When contacting the Japanese, it was his policy to give as his motto "Freedom and Equality" when and if there was any fear of being apprehensive of the Japanese taking advantage of him, he was quick to refuse, however, slight the matter may have been.

As a leader of the Army, he became the fountain head of spiritual strength and was the pivot of the INA. organisation. However, the standard of operational tactics was, it must be said with regret, low. He was inclined to be idealistic and not realistic. For instance, without being familiar with the actual fighting power of the INA., he was always demanding that the INA. be employed in a separate and decisive operation on Imphal front, and in July 1944, when the tide of battle had turned and the Japanese Army had retreated, he urged that although the Japanese might retreat the INA. should continue to confront the Allies until their aim was attained. He was temperamental and had strong likes and dislikes. It is also said that although stubborn he would adhere strongly to his arguments on matters which were slight in importance. This is so and it cannot be said that he possessed an extraordinary magnanimity of mind or very tolerance for the opinion of others.

23

Statement of Yoshimi Taneyoshi, Captain (Medical) of the Imperial Japanese Army regarding the death of Subhas Chandra Bose in the Air-crash

19 October, 1946

Taneyoshi Yoshimi, Captain (Medical) of the Imperial Japanese Army at present at Stanley Gaol, Hong Kong, having observed a statement in a Japanese newspaper, requesting information regarding the death of Chandra Bose, wish of my own free will to place any knowledge I have of this matter at the disposal of the Authorities requiring it. To the best of my ability and memory I hear state the events surrounding the death of Chandra Bose.

In August, 1945, I was the Senior Officer at the Nanmon Military Hospital, Taihoku, Formosa. At about 1700 hrs on the 18th day of August, 1945, a truck driven up before the hospital contained several men who had been injured in an aeroplane crash. Two of the men were Indians, and the remainder, about five or six in number were Japanese. One of the Japanese, a Staff Officer with the rank of Lt-Colonel whose name I cannot properly recall but believe was Ishii-something, informed me that one of the Indians, pointing him out, was Chandra Bose and that I was not to spare myself and must give him very best of treatment. I immediately gave instructions for some medical orderlies to go and prepare a bed, and for other to carry in the injured man.

When he was laid on the bed, I personally cleaned his injuries with oils and dressed them. He was suffering from extensive burns over the whole of his body, though the most serious were those on his head, chest and thighs. There was very little left on his head in the way of hair or other identification marks. During the first four hours he was semi-conscious, and practically normal, speaking quite a good deal. The first words I remember him speaking were in Japanese, when he made a request for

1. W.O. 208/3812. Public Record office London

water, which had to be fed to him through a hospital cup with a spout. As most of his speaking was in English, a request for an interpreter was made, and one was sent from the Civil Government Offices named Nakamura. He informed me that he had very often interpreted for Chandra Bose and had many conversations with him. He appeared to have no doubt that the man he was speaking was Chandra Bose. During the treating of his injuries, I twice inquired of Chandra Bose if he was in any pain and neither time did he make any answer. After about four hours, I inquired whether there was any statement, will, or such matter he wished to make. He answered "Nothing". After the fourth hour he appeared to be sinking into unconsciousness. He murmured, and muttered in his state of coma, but never regained consciousness. At about 2300 hrs. he died. There was apart from the injuries mentioned above, abrasions on his elbows and knees. There were no fractures.

The other Indian was Chandra Bose's Adjutant, a Colonel of the Indian National Army, who was suffering from burns to the sides of his head, arms, hands and knees. I do not remember this man's name, but recall that it was a very long one. He was a very tall man, about six feet or over, medium build, and clean shaven.

It was the wish of this Colonel, and also that of the authorities that the remains of Chandra Bose should be transported to Tokyo, and to facilitate this I injected Formalin into the body, and also had the coffin partly filled with lime. The whole was put in a box, and on the 20th August, was taken to Taihoku airport for transporting to Japan, in charge of Warrant Officer Nishi. W.O. Nishi returned later and informed me that the body could for some unknown reason, not be taken to Japan, and was to be sent to the crematorium for cremation. I therefore made out a Death Certificate, stating the cause of death to be extensive burning and shock. The orders for this change of plans came from the Adjutant's Department, Taiwan Army.

On the morning of the 19th August, Colonel Miyata, Staff Officer of General Ando came to the hospital to express mourning on behalf of General Ando and his staff, and as is our custom brought gifts of flowers, fruits and cakes for the deceased. The news of the death of Chandra Bose was kept a secret, and I and my staff were warned not to divulge that we know who it was that had died.

Statement of Yoshimi Taneyoshi Continued

From the other passengers of the aircraft I have some direct and some information which was told to me. As far as I could make out, the aircraft, carrying Chandra Bose, his Adjutant and about ten or twelve others (Japanese), took off from the Taihoku Air Port, and after rising to a height of about thirty feet, suddenly burst into flames and crashed to the ground. A Major-General Shidei and two others escaped or were rescued, and were brought to Nanmon Hospital. The two pilots, Warrant Officer (later 2/Lt.) Adyagi and a Sergeant Major, were both burned, but after remaining in my care for about two or three weeks had practically recovered and were transferred to the Hokuto-Military Hospital here. I later heard they had died, about three weeks after admittance.

The Indian Colonel, Adjutant to Chandra Bose, remained in my care for about 10 days, and was then sent to the Hokuto Military Hospital. The interpreter Nakamura went up there with him, and I have no knowledge of what became of either of them. I do know, however, that the ashes of Chandra Bose were handed over to the Indian Colonel.

There is nothing more I can remember of this matter, at the present, but will give thought to it, and anything of importance I later remember I will disclose. Signed at Stanley Gaol, this 19th Day of October, 1946.

Yoshimi Taneyoshi.

Certificate of Interpreter

I, Hanagaki Yoshio, state that I truly and correctly translated the above statement made by Yoshimi Taneyoshi, into English, and saw it taken down by Captain A.R. Turner. I later read over the whole of the above statement in the Japanese language, and Yoshimi Taneyoshi agreed and then signed the above statement. Signed at Stanley Gaol, this 19th Day of October, 1946.

Hanagaki Yoshio.

I, Alfred Raymond Turner took the above statement of Yoshimi Taneyoshi, with regard to the death of Chandra Bose, and the Certificate of the Interpreter Hanagaki Yoshio at Stanley Goal, this 19th day of October, 1946, duly witnessing their signatures.

Captain,
A.R. Turner.
War Crimes Liaison Section (Formosa).

Appendix-I

Memoirs of Anand Mohan Sahay Regarding his Activities in Japan and his Role in the Indian Independence Movement

Early in 1923, when the Gaya Session (1922) of the Indian National Congress, held under the Presidentship of Desbbandu Chitranjan Das, could not offer any dynamic programme resulting in an atmosphere of uncertainty regarding the future of Gandhiji's Non-violent Non-Co-operations Movement, I decided to leave for U.S.A. to complete my study of Medicine there and then return to continue my part in the struggle for Indian's freedom. I did not get a passport for U.S.A. from the Government of Bihar and, after consulting my well wishers, decided to proceed to Japan. I sailed from Calcutta for Japan by an Indo-China steam Navigation Company's ship, KUMSANG, on 6th May, 1923, with the blessings of Deshratna Rajendra Prasad and Deshbandhu Chitranjan Das.

I landed in Kobe, an international port in Central Japan, where a large number of Indian merchants were settled in export and import trade, just Rs. 75/- (Seventy-five) in my pocket and without any letter of introduction for any one except one from Prof. Pearson of Santiniketan of Dr. Rabindra Nath Tagore, for a Japanese Christian Social worker of Tokyo, Mr. Ogawa. Being interested in politics of my country, I naturally wanted to know if there was any awakening among the Indians in Japan regarding our freedom struggle at home. To my great disappointment, I found that although most of the Indian merchants in Kobe were from Bombay and Gujarat, they did not take any interest in Indian politics. I learnt that they were keeping aloof from Politics out of the incurring the displeasure of the local representatives of the British Government who might have cancelled their passport.

I learnt that the Indian revolutionary, Rash Bihari Bose, of 1912 Delhi Lord Hardinge Bomb Case fame, was living in Tokyo in exile under the protection of famous Black Dragon Society leader, Toyama Misturu of Japan, Toyama had saved him from being handed over to the British

Embassy by the then Japanese Government. Those were the days of Anglo-Japanese Alliance and Treaty of Friendship. Most of the Japanese political leaders of intelligentia class were under the influence of Western Political Schools.

I failed to obtain a passport for U.S.A. from the Consul of Britain even in Japan. Thus, I had no choice but to return home or to continue to stay in Japan and do some publicity work for Indian independence movement there. I consulted Pandit Jawaharlal Nehru, Deshratna Rajendra Prasad and some other leaders who knew me. They encouraged me to stay on in Japan and work as I suggested. However, to do publicity work for our freedom movement in Japan in those days was not any easy job. No Japanese newspaper would accept any materials that would openly or directly speak of British aggression in India, however truthful the story might have been. I had to be contented with within about the life history of various nationalist Indian leaders like Mahatma Gandhi, Rajendra Prased, Deshbandhu Chit Ranjan Das or Jawaharlal Nehru.

Rash Bihari Bose visited Kobe early in 1925, with Toyama Mitsuru, to see off the great Chinese revolutionary leader, Dr. Sun Yat Sen, known as the father of the Chinese Republic. I met Rash Bihari Bose in the Oriental Hotel and he introduced me to Toyama and Sun Yat Sen and invited me to join the banquet given in honour of the Chinese leader. Later, we had extensive discussions about some work in Japan for Indian independence. He informed me that Indians in Japan would not even invite him to visit them or dine with them due to British influence and no political activities on behalf of the Indian National Congress against British would be tolerated by the Japanese authorities that time.

Same year, later, Raja Mahender Pratap, well known Indian revolutionary, who had attempted to liberate India during the first World War of 1914-18, by organising the first free India Government in Exile with the help of Germany, Turkey and visited Japan as an Afghan national and with an Afghan passport. I met him when he came to Kobe. He was staying in a Buddhist Temple called Gokurakuji, in Kobe. Ostensibly, he was more interested in his World Federation Movement. However, I found in him the fire of Indian patriotism very much burning. Later, we become very good friends and whenever he visited Japan and came to Kobe, stayed with me. My relations with Rash Bihari Bose was also very close and whenever I visited Tokyo, I invariable stayed with him.

I realised by coming in close contact with Rash Bihari Bose that, being completely cut off from Indian scene for such a long time, he had no idea, much less appreciation, of the great mass upheaval in India after the

Jallianwala Bagh tragedy of 1919. Being active in secret societies revolutionary movements, he did have the opportunity to work in a mass struggle and could not imagine how the peaceful and non-violent movement of Mahatma Gandhi could be helpful in driving the powerful British Raj from India. Naturally, he did not support the N.C.O. Movement of the Indian National Congress. Being in Japan and living and moving in the circle of feudal politicians, who protected him from the arm of the British agents, he was largely influenced by the type of feudal politics of Black Dragon Society of Toyama Misturu, known as Robin Hood of Japan.

I, therefore, felt an urge to do something to primarily make the Indians in Japan conscious of their duty towards their motherland. I worked in Indian firms, as assistant, to come in close touch with the youthful assistants and gradually impressed them of the need to study India's N.C.O. Movement and the happenings there through Indian newspapers. I also came in contact with the young Japanese students and youth through the local Y.M.C.A. where I had established friendly relations with the Secretary, Mr. R Okumura, and had rented a room for my abode in its dormitary. I also secured a job as English teacher in the night school of the same Y.M.C.A. that offered me golden opportunity to come in close contact with the young men. Gradually both Indian Assistants of Indian firms and the Japanese students become more and more interested in India's Gandhiji and his unique non-violent struggle. Young assistant of Indian firms and another reason close to me. They were treated not too well by their bosses who did not permit them even to go to Indian Club and mix with them even socially.

In August 1926, some prominent Japanese politicians in cooperation with Rash Bihari Bose and myself, organised an Asian Youth Conference in Nagasaki, Southern Japan. Some Indian friends of Rash Bihari Bose like K.R. Sabarwal and Vidyadhar Bakshi also attended the Conference. Raja Mahendra Pratap, who was then touring North China and Manchuria, rushed to Nagasaki to attend the Conference. I believe, he was invited by some Japanese friends-organisers of the Conference. But, when the ship arrived, the Japanese authorities did not permit him to land although he held valid Afghan passport. Perhaps he did not have proper entry or landing visa on the passport. We felt much disappointed; but, the Port Police of Nagasaki said they had orders form Tokyo and they were helpless. The ship carrying Rajaji proceeded further to Osaka, its destination. We learnt later that the British Embassy in Tokyo had brought pressure on the Japanese Foreign Office to prevent him from attending the Conference.

However, through the efforts of the Japanese friend, Rajaji was allowed to land in Osaka and remain there so long as the ship remained in the port. He was lodged in a hotel but not allowed to go out. In the meantime, after the conclusion of the Nagasaki Conference, Rash Bihari Babu and myself reached Osaka and met Rajaji. Efforts were made to secure the permission of the Japanese Foreign Officer to enable Rajaji to stay on. But we did not succeed. When time come for the ship to leave the port on return journey, the police asked Rajaji to return to the ship. But, he refused to leave the hotel and claimed that he was a follower of Mahatma Gandhi and would not obey unjust orders. The police had to physically remove Rajaji from the hotel and carry him on their shoulders to the waiting car and thence to the ship.

When the ship arrived at Kobe Port, where I resided, some Japanese young men came to me and expressed resentment at their Governments timidity and for the refusal of permission to Rajaji to stay in Japan due to British pressure. They asked me to persuade him to accompany them to a waiting launch and they would escort him to a safe place and would not allow the Police to find out. I did not like the ideas, but on their pressure told Rajaji about their plan. Rajaji did not comply. He was, he said, not prepared to run away and hide like a thief. The ship sailed back to North China with Rajaji, to our great regret. But, before the ship sailed I got plenty of Indian delicacies prepared by my Sindhi and Gujarati merchant friends for him so that he could have them on the way.

At Nagasaki Conference important secret plans were prepared to organise the youth of enslaved Asian countries for revolt. It was decided that, as I held a valid passport for East Asian countries, I undertake a tour of these countries and meet nationalist youth and establish contact for further activities. To do this secretly, I had to travel in the guise of the trader. I organised an Export/Import concern and named it "International Traders", collected varieties of textile and other kinds of samples that Japan was exporting to East Asian countries at that time, collected some addresses of traders of different countries, wrote to them informing them that I was visiting their respective, centres to establish business relationship and negotiate business. All this done, I started on my adventure by sea route on 6th November, 1926. I visited Hong Kong, Canton, Saigon, Thailand, Malaya, Singapore, Sumatra, Colombo and then crossed over to South India, staying in each place for a week or less according to need. I arrived in Calcutta towards the end of December or early in January, 1927, when the Gauhati Session of the Indian National Congress was in progress.

I was tempted but decided to keep away from anything that might have created suspicion in the mind of the Indian Government about my political intention. I remained in India for several months and also got married in Calcutta with Sm. Sati Devi, niece of Deshbandhu Chittaranjan Das and daughter of Smt. Urmila Devi, well known woman leader of Bengal Congress. I visited other parts of the country to meet some of the revolutionary leaders, like Jawaharlal Nehru, Maulana Azad, and others.

On the eve of my departure for Japan, with my wife, in September 1927, I learnt that Subhas Chandra Bose had been released from Mandalay jail and was brought to Calcutta in a very bad state of health. I learnt that doctor did not allow any one to meet him. Yet, I with my wife called at his home and when he was told about me he immediately called us and we had about fifteen minutes to talk when I confided in him the real purpose of my tour. He expressed great satisfaction at my plan and asked me to keep in touch with him and keep him informed about our efforts.

On our way back, we had to change ships at Singapore. We stayed with a South Indian friend, Mr. Dharma Rajah, during the sojourn. During our sojourn, the Indian Association of Singapore came to know about us and its Secretary, Shri Abid Ali, invited me to an Association Meeting and dinner. At that meeting I spoke on duty of Indians towards their motherland. Unconsciously, having forgotten that I was visiting Singapore as a merchant, I put myself in a trap that might have undone all my plan, because next day I had to go to the Police Commissioner's office and face prolonged interrogation. They had asked me to leave Singapore only after informing them. However, by sheer luck, I managed to escape from Singapore with my wife on a French ship within a few days after the investigation.

Back in Japan, I met Rash Bihari Babu and the Japanese leaders and reported the result of the tour. I also told them about my meeting with Subhas Chandra Bose in Calcutta and other leaders like Jawaharlal Nehru and Maulana Azad, who had directed me to establish a Congress branch in Japan. I set about organising the Congress Committee. But in this I did not receive any co-operation either from Rash Behari Bose or from those Japanese leaders who had helped and sponsored the Nagasaki Conference. They were rather opposed to the propagation of the ideals of non-violent NCO. However, when Raja Mahendera Pratap visited Japan, I received wholehearted cooperation from him at the India Club, I proposed the formation of the Congress Committee, with the support of some young Sindhi and Gujarati merchants. Rajaji himself offered to become its member and the resolution was passed.

In 1930, I started publishing a monthly journal by the name of the "Voice of India", in English with Japanese translation side by side, for publicising the Congress struggle at home. The publication proved very popular among the college and University students because it helped them in learning English, I also started a home for Indian students coming from Indian for educational purpose. This proved very useful for accommodating such Indian revolutionaries who escaped from India and needed safe shelter. It was called "India Lodge". Simultaneously, Rash Bihari Bose had also started a similar home in Tokyo, calling it ASIA JIKU, where our youngmen stayed when going to Tokyo for similar purposes. Gradually, several Indo-Japanese Youth Associations, Indo-Japanese Buddhist Associations and Indo-Japanese Students Associations were also formed in various parts of Japan; and, I regularly visited those centers and gave talk on India's struggle for freedom Large gatherings of students heard such speeches with keen interest and offered moral support to the cause.

In due course these activities gave satisfactory dividend. The younger generations, particularly University students and members of the Buddhist Associations became considerably interested in our struggle at home. On the other hand, trade rivalry between the British and Japanese industries in Indian Market, and imperial perference to British goods, encourged discontent among the Japanese commercial community in Japan and the Indian exporters in Japan found a common ground for them because their trade was equally affected. This helped us in encouraging anti-British sentiment among the Japanese.

I had kept Subhas Babu constantly acquainted with these developments, and our plan to take advantage of the situation if and when the opportunity came, through letters carried by same Indian crew of the British Indian Steam Navigation Co. ships that plied between Calcutta and Japan. I sent my wife to Calcutta with more important secret informations regarding Japanese preparations in Feb. 1939, declaring that she had returned home separated from me, due to serious differences, and she was in Calcutta when Subhas planned SATYAGRAHA at Holwell Monument on 3rd April, 1940 and was arrested and imprisoned. When our emissary, Atul Sen, was sent to Bombay with some secret documents to meet the Indian leaders, Subhas was in prison and Sen contacted him there with the help of a relative, Bela Bose.

Soon after the declaration of War in Europeon 1st September 39, in consultation with Raja Mahendra Pratap and Rash Behari Bose, a Council of Action was formed to prepare for active support to our struggle in

India. I had long considered Thailand to be the only country from where external aid to Indian could be possible. I had some young. Indian merchants there who were prepared to co-operate. We, therefore, decided to send my nearest intimate colleague, Deb Nath Das, to Bangkok to organise a centre there. Funds were collected from Indian merchants. I was already in contact with the Japanese Army Headquarters (ASMBO-HAMBU) through Captain (now a Retired General I. Fujiwara). They were helpful in sending Das to Bangkok with plans and documents, and Atul Sen to Bombay.

In 1935, due to some foreign branch of the Congress having acted against the creed of the Congress, the working Committee decided to withdraw recognition to all foreign branches. I received a letter from Jawaharlal Nehru informing me that, as our Japan branch has been working in line with Congress creed, we should continue our activities as usual, though we could no longer claim to be an official branch. After that we decided to change the name of our organisation to "Indian National Association of Japan" from the "Indian National Congress Committee of Japan". As the Indians in Shanghai had expressed their desire to work for the country under our organisation, when I visited Shanghai in 1933. I started an organisation known as the "Indian National Association of China". Shanghai, in pre-War days had a large Indian population. The Shanghai British Police Force consisted mostly of Sikha. There were some Pathans also. And, there was an Indian Mercantile community consisting of Sindhis, Punjabis, Gujaratis and Parsis. I enrolled a large number of members from all sections of Indians. Sikhs of the Police Force were particularly enthusiastic to join the Association, but, I explained to them the implication that because they were in the British Police Force, the British authorities would immediately take steps against them. They were ready to risk that but agreed to wait till time for their open co-operation came. However, our meetings were generally held in the Gurdwara.

In December, 1941, when Japan declared War, and when Rash Behari Bose was declared President of the Movement, it was necessary to bring all Indian national activities under one organisation. Rash Behari Bose had already started his Indian Independence League. I therefore decided to abolish the branches of Indian National Association both in Japan and China and let all Indians join the League. This was also desirable from another point of view. Indian National Association, although no more a branch of the Congress, was still considered as an associate organisation I did not want to betray the trust of the Congress leaders and misuse that name. I consulted my colleagues and decided to declare that Congress had nothing to do with the new movement.

When Subhas Bose disappeared from his home and arrived at Kabul, he informed me through Japanese Embassy there. Captain Fujiwara informed me that Mr. Bose wanted to go to Japan. But, he told me, Japanese High Command were not prepared for that because they were afraid that his arrival in Japan would make the British suspicious of Japan's war intentions. After Netaji's arrival in Germany, in October, 1941, the German Embassy informed me that Netaji wanted me to proceed to Germany for consultations. The Ambassador told me that I could go on a Japanese ship to Brazil, as a Japanese citizen with Japanese passport, and thence I could fly to Germany by air. The preparations were under way, when on 8th December 1941, Japan attacked Pearl Harbour and Malay Peninsula and declared War against the Western Powers.

For some time I was feeling that Japanese did not like my contact with the Germans. I had lent the services of some Indian youngmen in Shanghai for German Broadcasting in Indian languages, who were paid by them. I had also got them publish Will Durant's well known, "CASE FOR INDIA", for free distribution among the English knowing people in China and Japan. I did not consider anything undesirable in such activities because we were fighting a common enemy . But, the Japanese wanted me to be exclusively in their camp and I was not prepared to mortgage my liberty of action, or to follow their dictate. The Japanese Kempaitai (Gestapo) interrogated me for hours to fine out I had any financial transaction with the Germans. When I told them frankly and they realised that neither from them nor from the Germans I received any funds either for the Indian freedom movement or for an personally, they left me alone. But, since then, I decided not to cooperate with them more than absolutely necessary to avoid a break and unpleasantness.

When, on 8th December, 1941, Japan declared War, we had to organise our active efforts and select a leader, I knew, the Japanese wanted Rash Bihari Bose to be the leader because he was a naturalised Japanese national and would be more amiable to their ideas and plans. When they consulted me, I promptly suggested Rash Behari Bose on the ground that he was senior to me; and I assured them of my co-operation wherever necessary. I considered that period to be a temporary phase because I had in mind the ultimate leadership of Netaji Subhas Chandra Bose. Raja Mahendra Pratap did not join. I had constantly kept Netaji informed of these developments through the German Embassy in Tokyo.

Rash Behari Bose was a revolutionary of old days when our activities consisted of secret sabotage and sporadic attack on British and pro-British Indian officials. With all his zeal to serve the cause of freedom he could not have been expected to lead a mass struggle during a war in 1942. Much less control or command a regular army. Our armed forces of ex-British Indian Army were well-trained and well-disciplined hardened soldiers and they would not have liked to fight under a virtual Japanese command. Japanese Army Officers, generally speaking, were of medieval mentality. They were brave fighters and commanders but they had very little knowledge of the training land habits of our soldiers of British Army. They were devoted to their Emperor and were ready to die for him because he was the symbol of their country and God. Japanese Naval officers were somewhat different in the scheme of War except where Naval warfare was concerned.

Japan High Command, i.e. the Japanese Army wanted to control and guide our freedom's fight. Naturally, they welcomed Rash Behari Bose with open arms. I considered it necessary in the interest of our struggle to continue to cooperate with the Japanese sponsored set up. After the British surrender at Singapore on 15th Feb. 1942, a preliminary conference of some Indian officers of surrenedered British Indian Army and Indian civilians of different East Asian regions was held in Tokyo from 28th to 30th March, 1942. I kept out of it to the great relief of the Japanese. But, most of the delegates expressed their astonishment at my absence. They came for lunch at my residence and I explained to them Why I did not attend. Then Mohan Singh secretly gave me a letter form one Swami Satyanand Puri, a devoted Indian revolutionary who was residing in Thailand and who was one of the delegates to Tokyo Conference. The plane carrying him and other two delegates (Capt. Akram and Sardar Pritam Singh) from Shanghai, was reported crashed in a mountain in south Japan, in danger and that he would explain everything when he met me. He never met me. I have a copy of terms and conditions on which I had offered to co-operate with the Japanese and of which one copy was forwarded to Netaji and other Indian leaders through Atul Sen, to Mr. Raghavan.

Tokyo Conference decided, among other things, to hold a larger conference in Bangkok in June, 1942. When Lt. Col. Kadomatsu, the Japanese incharge of Indian Affairs, came to request me to accompany Japan's Indian delegation to Bangkok, as its leader, I agreed in order to avoid bitterness and with future plan in view. Rash Behari Bose was to be the President and the leader of the whole conference. Debnath Das was already in Bangkok and was the Chairman of the Reception Committee of Bangkok branch of the Indian Independence League, and with the help of Mr. Raghavan of Penang, we got a resolution passed at the Conference, requesting Netaji to visit East and asking the Japanese and German Governments to facilitate his journey. This was not liked by the Japanese and the Rash Behari group of Tokyo Indians. No steps were taken to implement the resolution. I had already informed Netaji through German sources about the resolution. I, later, learnt that the Germans had consulted to send Netaji to Japan. But, the Japanese, reportedly, replied that as there was already a revolutionary Indian leader in the East, there was no need for another.

Japanese attitude in this matter was intelligible. They wanted a leader who would be guided and controlled by them and would not create any problem for them. They were aware of Netaji Subhas Chandra Bose's calibre. When Netaji defeated official candidates of the Congress for Presidentship and defied even Mahatma Gandhi, I had written in my paper, VOICE OF INDIA, "Subhas would gladly give his life but would not submit to any suggestion of compromise on the question of Indian independence, not even to Mahatma Gandhi, whom he respects as his father-"Japanese knew that they would not be able to control him, and they could not tolerate defiance of their operation. However, after the Bangkok Conference when the Council of Action was formed and the Headquarters moved to Singapore, within a short period it was clear that Rash Behari Bose could neither impress his colleagues in the Council nor the Indians of East Asia as a leader. There were constant differences between the Army officer and civilian wings of the council and neither of them respected President's opinion. Mohan Singh , who was designated as General and was Commander-in-Chief of Armed Forces, and his own ideas and ambitions. At last the climax came in January 1943 and the I.N.A. broke up and Gen. Mohan Singh was arrested. Japanese High Command at last realised that it was a folly to depend on such a leader and to conduct a war depending on the Indian Army of liberation that they could not control. And then they agreed to approach the Germans to arrange for Netaji to go to the East. When Netaji returned form Rangoon to Bangkok withdrawing his Head Quarters towards the end to the war, I told him that it was my greatest regret that, due to the folly of the Japanese, we could not secure his presence in th East before "QUIT INDIA" declaration of the Congress on 9th August 1942. Had the Japanese agreed to invite Netaji to go to Japan directly from Kabul or even a little later, and had we been able to enter

India with I.N.A. Forces simultaneously in August or September, 1942, the history of Indian freedom might have been written differently. That opportunity was lost due to the narrow minded and selfish attitude of the Japanese.

However, only after the collapse of the first I.NA. in January 1943, the Japanese realised that they had to request Netaji to visit East and take over the leadership of the I.N.A. They approached the Germans and the latter arranged for the hazardous journey of Netaji to the east by submarine. German sources informed me about Netaji's departure though they would not tell me the means of journey. The Japanese kept mum. At last, about the middle of June, I learnt that Netaji had arrived in Tokyo. My wife had met him. I heard his voice on Radio Tokyo, perhaps, on 21st June, 1943, I felt Japanese had deliberately kept me out of picture because they were afraid that, if I met Netaji before reaching Tokyo, I might have poisoned his mind by giving him facts of past developments. Or, perhaps, they were ashamed that they could not manage the things without Netaji, and had kept him out against our wishes.

Netaji arrive at Singapore on 2nd July, 1943. I was one of the first Indians to be with him at tea on arrival at his residence. He wanted to know facts about the happenings during the past months. We discussed various problems including our approach to Mahatma Gandhi, Jawaharlal Nehru and the Indian National Congress as a whole. We discussed our programme and plan for future move. He told me he heard everything from my wife in Tokyo regarding Japanese treatment to me and added, "they were sadly mistaken if they thought they could mislead me. I have seen enough of such games in the past in my life". He also told me about his plan to form a Provisional Government of Free India as soon as possible and to reorganise the I.N.A. and the India Independence League on modern lines. I promised him whole hearted co-operation under all circumstances. and dedicated myself to the cause under his leadership. I enjoyed his confidence to the last.

Rash Behari Bose handed over the leadership of the Movement to Netaji Subhas Chandra Bose formally on 4th July, 1943, at a conference of the Indians of East Asia, at the Cathay building of Singapore. Netaji, assuming the leadership, made a very impressive and emotional speech that touched the heart of the audience. The next day, 5th July, 1943, Netaji addressed the I.N.A. jawans and officers and again on 6th July, Netaji addressed them in the presence of Gen. Tojo. His talk to the jawans impressed rank and file of the I.N.A. as deeply as Gen. Tojo himself. The officers of the fauj regained their self-confidence and the civilians realised that atlast they have found a leader in which they could place their confidence unreservedly. Indian merchants all over East Asia began contributing to Azad Hind Fund liberally . Young Indians started pouring in to enrol as volunteers.

At the very first Press Conference arranged by the Japanese, when the Japanese Army Chief of Press Bureau welcomed Netaji, he assured him of all out Japanese aid to I.N.A., and asked him to let them know what help would be expected from them . Netaji with his usual politeness expressed his gratitude for the offer of help that he said was necessary and indispensible for the fight and said "For the present I want to make one request and that is that not to give us any help so long as we did not ask for it. I request that no propaganda or publicity be done on our behalf. We know that mind of our people and we shall address them ourselves in a way that would be conducive to our mutual interest I know, you need publicity for Japan to be directed to India. For this I would lend you some young men who would speak on your behalf as you desire. That would be your voice not ours. When we need your help I will certainly not hesitate to ask for it...." Language may not be exactly as mentioned. But, in substance that is what he said. And, the Japanese had no difficulty in realising the calibre of the leader they had to deal with.

Japanese had taught the Indian volunteers to salute their superiors in Japanese fashion, i.e. by taking off their cap and bowing. Netaji told the Japanese that the Indians had bowed to their alien rulers for centuries. "I want them now to learn to stand erect and look straight into the face of the officers when saluting and not top take off their head gear." Japanese agreed. Netaji gave us a new way of greetings, "Jai Hind". He gave the Azad Hind Fauj a new slogan, "Chalo Delhi" just as the old French Forces were given "Al Sa Ce Lauran" of German slogan "on to Paris".

All preparations complete, the Provisional Government of Azad Hind was formed on 21st October, 1943. And, at a very impressive ceremony in the same spacious hall of the Cathay Mansion of Singapore, in the presence of a large gathering of the representatives of Indians of different regions of East Asia, Netaji declared the establishment of the *Arazi Hukumate* Azad Hind, and took Oath of Allegiance and Loyalty to India and the cause of Indian fight for freedom. All the members of the Cabinet, then, took Oath of Allegiance, one by one, to Netaji under whom they promised to fight for the freedom of India. Besides being the Secretary to the Azad Hind Government, due to my knowledge and close contact with the Indians in East Asia, I was also later appointed Minister of Revenue and Man Power.

We needed both men and money and I had to tour all the countries east of Thailand where Indians were residing. I visited the territorial branches of the Indian Independence League; sent written appeal for men and appointed influential Indians 33 in each region to take up the work earnestly. The response was spontaneous and very encouraging. Even young women volunteered to be enrolled in Rani of Jhansi Regiment. Shanghai had a large population of Punjabis and in recruitment both men and women vied with each other.

At the very first meeting of the Cabinet on 21st October; 1943; we declared war against the Anglo-American Allies. Some members were of opinion that; as India was only under British domination, we should declare war only against the British. Netaji told them that "all those powers who were working for the helping our enemies were our enemies and we must declare war against all of them : He said "Our enemy's friends were our enemies. Our enemy's were our friends." The same evening it was also decided that a delegation of our Government should attend the GREATER EAST ASIA CONFERENCE in Tokyo in November, to which we were invited. Our delegation consisted of Netaji, the leader, Maj. Gen. J.K. Bhonsle, the chief of staff and, A.M. Sahay, Secretary to Netaji and Lt. Col Dr. D.S. Raja, Personal Physician to Netaji, were the two personal staff of Netaji.

In reply to the proposal that we should attend as full-fledged Delegation of the Greater East Asia Co-Prosperity Sphere Conference, as the Japanese called it, Netaji made it clear to the hosts that India was not yet independent land we had no territory of our own. Ours was a Government in Exile, and it was a Provisional Government. To join the Co-Prosperity Sphere or not could be decided only by the people of India when India was free. The Japanese appreciated our contention and we attended as Observers, although the Indian Delegation was given all honour and were treated at par with other delegations. In fact Netaji received much greater attention and commanded much greater respect than other leaders of the Conference, both by the Government and the people of Japan, almost to the point of Netaji becoming an object of envy.

The Conference being over, we sat down for business negotiations. We had quite a few important subjects to discuss and secure Japanese concurrence. Most important of them all was the transfer of Andaman and Nicobar groups of islands to our Government. We had to face certain difficulties in achieving this. The islands were, naturally, under Naval Command, They were very important because they were the first line of defence against any attack from Indian mainland. We had no Navy of our own . Thus, clearly, the presence of Japanese Navy was unavoidable in our mutual interest. Another difficulty was that the Burmese Government claimed it as their territory because the islands were far separated from India, were straight sougth of Burma, and there was a sizable population of Burmese settled there. We had prolonged discussions with Admiral Yamamoto, the Navy Minister of Japan. However, our contention was that for India it was impossible and totally unacceptable any party's claim on those islands because they were the symbols of our very struggle for freedom, Netaji told them that hundreds of our patriots were sent to the islands as political convicts for the fault of their love for India. Many of them died there. For those who were fighting for freedom, Andamans was symbolic of a shrine as Yasukuni or Ise Shrines were for the Japanese. This immediately touched Japanese sentiment and they agreed to our demand. However, we had to agree that we could not undertake the defence of the islands. So an arrangement was mutually made according to which some departments of Civil Administration like, Education, Agriculture etc. were to be undertaken by our Government and Defence and allied subjects were to be under Japanese control. We were engaged in a life and death struggle on the mainland and, even if allowed, we could not have been able to spare much, either in men or in money, for the territory thus transferred to us. However, it was of great importance for our prestige in international and constitutional realm. This gave us the status of a dejure Government with our own territory. I had every reason to feel proud because I had played an important part in getting the Japanese to agree to it due to my very friendly relations with some of the Japanese Naval senior officers who were negotiating on th side of the Japanese. I had also given hint to Netaji about the sentiment of the Japanese regarding their two Shrines mentioned above and Netaji took full advantage of that. Those shrines in Japan are of Imperial ancestors of the Japanese, and they hold them in highest esteem. Even, when declaring a war, they go to those shrines to pray for their blessings, to begin with.

Other subjects we had to discuss were about the printing of our own currency. I had to stay on in Tokyo to get the designs of our currency prepared according to the direction of Netaji. I had also to get all other stationaries of the Government printed in Tokyo. In this the German Embassy in Tokyo was of great help. They introduced me to their printers who supplied very high quality of papers for the purpose and the printing was equally of very high standard. Netaji was very pleased and satisfied when I presented the currency to him at Singapore on my return. He also liked the final designs of the currency notes, of our government. It was decided in Tokyo that after returning to our Headquarters at Singapore, Netaji would visit the Andamans to formally take over the administration and to unfurl our National Flag of Free India.

Netaji returned to Singapore, after visiting the Philippines. Shanghai etc. I returned later by the end of December after finishing the work assigned to me. Immediately after my arrival I was told that we had to proceed to the Andamans on 29th December, 1943. We took off early in the morning. Besides Netaji, the party consisted of Lt. Col. D.S. Raju Personal Physician to Netaji. We arrived in the Andaman in the afternoon, and were received by a large crowd of Indians, Burmese and Japanese officials. We were received by the Naval Commander of the Islands and escorted to the palatial residence of the Chief Commissioner of British Raj of old days. At an impressive ceremony Netaji formally took over the charge of the islands of Andaman and Nicobars. The Flag of Free India, the tricolour, was unfurled by Netaji in the presence of a large gathering amidst prolonged cheers. 30th December was full of engagements. Most important one was a visit to the notorious Cellular Jail where so many of our brave patriots were detained by the alien rulers of India for their fault of loving their motherland and died as martyrs. We visited Defence establishments of the Island, agricultural farms, children school etc. addressed large public meeting where the citizens presented purse to Netaji, interviewed some prominent Indians settled there and enquired about their problems and grievances and finally discussed the details of transfer of administration with the commander of the Naval Bose. Next morning on the 31st Dec. the National Flag of India was again unfurled at the official residence of the Chief Commissioner by Netaji. And we took off for Rangoon.

The programme was to reach Rangoon and declare the establishment of Advance Headquarters of Azad Hind Government there. However, when we were nearly half way between Andaman and Rangoon, a message came by wireless that the enemy planes were invading Rumree Island near Akyab on the western coast of Burma and it was considered undesirable to proceed to Rangoon at that moment. I have a feeling that it was a preplanned thing to keep the people in Andamans under the impression that we were proceeding to Burma, while actually Netaji was to proceed to

Bangkok as the guest of the Thai Government and then to move to Rangoon after a week or so. However, Netaji ordered the plane to proceed to Bangkok where arrangements were made for us to stay at Ratua Konshin Hotel, very near the Royal Palace.

All the arrangement being ready for starting our Advance Headquarters in Burma, we flew to Rangoon and Netaji occupied as his residence an impressive building previously belonging to a Parsee High officer of British days. He was given a warm welcome both by the Burmese and the Indians on his arrival at Rangoon. Soon after his arrival Netaji started preparations for sending the I.N.A. contingents to Indo-Burma border to start the war of liberation. Major Gen. M.Z. Kiani as Commander-in-Chief of one full division, with Lt. Col. Inayat Kiani commanding a Regiment under him. Maj. General Shaw Nawaz Khan, Col. Gulzara Singh and Col. Pritam Singh, as commanders of various regiments were sent to various fronts. We had some difficulty with command of forces on battle front.

Naturally the Japanese had more senior officers than we had and according to code no senior officer could work under the command of a junior officer. Yet, it was not possible to allow I.N.A., i.e. our forces of liberation of India to serve under any foreign and, it was not possible to allow the Japanese to act independently command. That was totally unacceptable to Netaji. However, after long negotiations, it was mutually agreed that while in Burma, the fighting forces may remain under all Japanese senior officers command, after entering Indian command and the Japanese contingents under the Japanese and they would work and fight in complete co-operation, and with complete understanding. A Committee of Indian and Japanese officers was formed. The Japanese wanted that the Chairman of the Committee be a Senior Japanese Officer. But, Netaji did not agree. And this was left undecided to be settled at very meeting according to the situation.

There were some Indians in Burma who were detained in Prison because they did not abide by the decisions of the Japanese to surrender their assets to the Japanese, after the British left Burma and the Japanese occupied the territory. After Netaji's arrival, a massage reached him about these Indians. I was sent to meet them in prison. I was surprised to find my old friend, Mr. S.M. Bashir, who was my close comrade in Japan in my national congress work there. He was a staunch nationalist and I could not believe the Japanese version that he was anti-I.N.A. He had a large rubber factory in Rangoon and he had refused to hand over that to the

Japanese. There were other similar cases. In the presence of the Japanese officer who went with me, I explained the purpose and the programme of the I.N.A. and for the satisfaction of the Japanese, I rebuked them for not co-operating. Bashir got up and refuted the charge and said they were all prepared to give not only the properties but also their life for Indian's freedom. "But that must be India's freedom". I assured them that justice will be done and returned to report the whole story to Netaji".

After some discussion with Netaji, we decided that we should tell the Japanese frankly that Indians in Burma were not enemies but allies of ours. Therefore, it was wrong even according to international practice of allies. I told them that all the Indians, throughout East Asia, from Japan to Burma, were the subjects and the citizens of free India; and it was for our Government to decide things about them. They argued that to fight the war, in mutual interest, we needed material those Indians had. I agreed and told them that we would find our ways and means to achieve that end. I suggested to Netaji that in response to his appeal for total mobilisation of the resources of Indians in East Asia to fight our war of liberations. We should persuade the Indian industrialists and prosperous traders to formally surrender their concerns to the Azad Hind Government and declare so. On our part, as we had no time to take care of those establishments our agents to manage their respective concerns and supply such goods as they manufactured and as we needed for our common war efforts. Netaji promptly agreed and asked me to tackle the Indians.

I had already such an assurance from those whom I met in Jail. I told the Japanese that whatever we needed from the Indians for our war efforts, that would come through us. As raw materials were needed for manufacturing things, we asked them to help us either by importing from other territories under them or securing from the Burmese. They in response to Netaji's call all Indian factories were surrendered to Azad Hind Government and without disturbing the working capacity, as mentioned above, they were allowed to manufacture goods required by the fighting forces. We i.e. the Japanese, supplied materials as and when required and paid minimum wages to the workers through us. The largest estate of Ziawadi, of Hariji of Dumraon, that produced sugarcane and had large sugar factory, was under the management of Shri Parmanandji, who joined our struggle and took leading part in various capacities. He placed the estate at the disposal of Azad Hind Government and the management continued as it was.

A Committee to collect donations for Netaji Fund was appointed by Netaji, of which Mr. Hamid, a multimillionaire of Burma, was made the Chairman and Shri S.M. Bashir, the Vice-Chairman. Collection of funds started with a big bang. Shri Hamid had already enrolled as total mobiliser by giving away his entire huge assets to Azad Hind Govt. and enrolling himself as volunteer of the Fauj. Netaji in his speeches always asked the Indians to take : "HAMID MIXTURE" to get intoxicated with the spirit of freedom. He once said, "Some say, Hamid has gone mad. I agree. I want every one of you Indians to get mad to achieve Victory and freedom of our motherland. We need such mad men and women." He declared more than once that he was not going to ask the Japanese allies for financial help before the Indians have given for the fight all they have. He said "We are fighting for Indians. We can ask others to help only when our own resources have exhausted. There can be no justification to beg from others before that." And the Indians wholeheartedly responded, irrespective of social, religious or another distinctions. Volunteers poured in for recruitment. Camp were started and the training started. Women vied with men and joined Rani Jhansi Camp as cadets and volunteers. Materials like textiles, medicines and grains were donated so liberally that, Gen, Takhin Aung San, the Prime Minister of Burma , once told me at a dinner in Delta area, that I gave in his honour while visiting the area at the same time, that he wondered whether Burma was the island of Burmese or of Indians. He said, "While we are unable to meet the expenses of even administration from taxes and Burmese contributions you just make and appeal and millions of rupees, hundreds of tons of rice, gold medicines etc. in large quantities pour in." They were openly jealous of our position and popularity of Netaji. Another friend of mine in Burma's Government, Takhin Tan Tun, a communist and Minister of Agriculture, came to me and asked me to help him in collecting funds for his government. Takhin U Nu, Prime Minister of Burma after the War, was very friendly with us and was always prepared to co-operate whenever I approached.

By the end of 1944 our Azad Hind Fauj Jawans were already fighting on different front, inside India, and had liberated some parts of our motherland. Netaji wanted our Headquarters to move forward. Azad Hind Dal was organised to prepare the administrative wing of our government to take over the responsibility of civil administration in liberated areas. Netaji appointed. Lt Col. Ehsan Qadir as the leader and myself as the Deputy leader of Azad Hind Dal and asked us to proceed to Maymyo. We had to travel in coal loaded wagons. Netaji himself was present at the railway platform of Rangoon to send us off. At night our train was attacked by enemy planes, but we escaped any casualty. The bomb fell just outside the railway station by the side of the line and made more than 10 feel deep ditch. In the morning we were received at the Ziawadi railway station by Shri Parmanandji and we were escorted to his residence where we had a rest and lunch.

Immediately after the establishment of our Headquarters in Rangoon was announced, Netaji addressed himself to get our forces ready to march towards Indo-Burma border. Vigorous training of our Jawans in various types of Guerilla warfare and jungle operations were undertaken in various camps. Units of Rani Jhansi Regiment also started vigorous practice. As October approached we also decided to celebrate the first anniversary of the formation of the Azad Hind Government on an impressive scale. Apart from other programme one particular event must remain memorable for all those who participated in it. On 18th Oct. 1944, at about 10 a.m. a grand parade of a full regiment was arranged at the parade ground outside Rangoon, when all the minister present in Rangoon, all the officer of the I.N.A and a large number of High officers of the Japanese Army in Rangoon were invited and were present. Netaji was to address the contingent.

The programme started exactly in time. After preliminaries. Netaji went to the rostrum to receive the salute and march past started. Just then an AcAc shell burst hitting a Jawan and blowing off his head. We could not understand where did the shell come from. But General Shah Nawaz Khan, immediately went to Netaji and asked him to come down. Netaji unmindful of his request, remained standing. This made Gen. Shah Nawaz unhappy and he told Netaji that the danger is approaching and he would not allow him to play with the life of a full Regiment beside Netaji's himself. Other senior officer also jumped to the rostrum and strongly pleaded for that he comes down without delay. Netaji, most reluctantly came down the rostrum and the Jawans were ordered to quick march to safety in bush or barracks. We, along with Netaji hurried to a nearby bamboo bush and took shelter there. Within seconds after that more than twenty enemy fighter planes swooped over the ground and riddled the whole area, shelling the ground and vicinity indiscriminately for nearly twenty minutes. Very fortunately, there was not a single casualty thanks due to the thick bamboo bush and timely warning of our AcAc shell. Had we not left the place so quickly, this might have proved the greatest tragedy and might have put our whole plan of future fight to a halt. The existence of the whole Regiment of I.N.A. was at stake, besides the large number of our senior officers and

Netaji himself. His car went to another station, about fifteen miles ahead, where our train was resting for the day. We travelled only at night, to avoid enemy vigilance. Next morning, having reached Mandalay, we travelled to Maymyo the Hill station of Burma, by road and were accommodated in spacious Government English High School. Our contingent consisted of administrators, office assistant, stenographers, engineers, electricians, mechanics, some military guards and volunteers, including an unit of Rani Jhansi Regiment. Advance units of Azad Hind Dal volunteers had already gone ahead of us and were awaiting our arrival in various places on way to the Indian border.

After a few weeks Netaji also arrival from Rangoon. Advance Headquarters of Azad Hind Fauj and Government were announced to have been established there. Pending Netaji's arrival we had organised the inhabitants of Maymyo to start working for the movement. An office of the Independence League was started. Women section of the League was also organised and young Indian women enrolled to be the members of the Rani Jhansi Regiment. We were anxious to march forward. Gen Chatterjee was appointed the Governor of liberated area. We were anxiously waiting news of progress from the Front lines. But, the Japanese informed us that they were receiving no message from the fighting front. From Indian source we learnt that our forces were suffering due to shortage of food and medicines. Netaji immediately decided to send a Mission to the front to assess the situation and to carry some medicine. ration and cash for the Fauj.

In the meantime, one night, our camp was subjected to heavy bombardment by the enemies. Just after dinner, at about 9 p.m. waves of bombers carried on continuous bombing for nearly culvert and keeping them there under the bridge. About fifteen of them were in another shelter the entrance of which were completely blocked by a bomb that fell nearby throwing large chunks of earth to the entrance. After the raid, when I was going around to check the casualty, I heard some noise from one of the shelters. Volunteers were immediately called, the blocked entrance was cleared and all the Ranis were safely brought out. Very fortunately, there was no casualty in our camp in that night's raid, though most of our vehicles were damaged and the building was badly damaged. Next morning Netaji visited the camp and we were ordered to shift to other places and Gen. Chatterjee, Capt Rawat, A.D.C. to Netaji, and myself escorted the Rani to a well protected area in a thick wood by the side of I.N.A. hospital. On our way we encountered a reconnaissance enemy plane flying very low and I had to stop the truck, order the running from one tree to another to avoid the enemy's eyes. Later, he himself told me that never in his life he had run for safety like that. We ourselves moved to a Reserve forest where thatched barracks were immediately constructed for us. I got some materials collected from the fallen school building and our mechanics and carpenters built a nice little hutment with a dining-cum-sitting room and a bedroom, bath attached, within three days for me.

After a few days, according to plan, we started on our trek to the battle fronts. Gen. Alagappan, the Supply and Health Minister, Gen. Chatterjee, Minister of Finance and Governor designate for liberated area, and myself along with some of our aides and officials of India Independence League of Indo-Burmese border area, started from Mandalay in a car and a truck with loads of sweet packed in gunny bags. We had to leave the vehicles on the eastern bank of Irrawady river because the available boats could not carry them across. We unload the ration and other belongings and carried to the western coasts and therefrom we managed to secure two trucks to take us forward. It took us several days to reach More and Tamu travelling at nights and hiding in some safe bush during the days, to avoid enemy reconnaissance. The party had to face unusual hazards including some accidents and breakdown of our transport. Trucks had to pass on narrow strip of roads with high hills on one side and deep river on the other and all this in dark nights because we could not use head lights for fear of being detected by the constant enemy planes flying over head. We also met our comrades in some places, including wounded and ailing Jawan brought back from the front, parties of Azad Hind Dal etc. We distributed ration and money to our contingents according to need.

At More we found our camp on the bank of a river waiting for us to arrive and give them line clear to proceed to the liberated areas to take over the Civil Administration. Shri D.M. Khan was in command.

As it was necessary to assess situation and get first hand information before asking our administrative machinery to proceed further, we decided to visit the fighting front and see the thing for ourselves. We crossed the official border between India and Burma that was shown by a sign Board of British days. Some Japanese news men had also accompanied us and they promptly took our snaps. We met enemy planes on the way. But they could no do any harm because the mountain roads were so zigzag that by the time they located us we took another turn and went out of their sight. At last at about midnight we reached Chamol, a place where he had to leave the truck and walk down the hill to reach the underground headquarters of Gen. Kiani's Division. There I was so delighted to meet Major Hassan, Col. Pritam Singh and Col. Enayat Kiani, the latter being the commander of the contingent presently fighting very near Imphal a few miles ahead of us. They were in high spirit.

Next day we paid a visit to Gen. Yamamoto. the Div. Commander of the Japanese Army, about a mile away on the other side of hill. Gen Alagappan and myself visited him because Gen Ghatterjee met an accident just a few hours before when an enemy shell burst from the opposite hill and a splinter slightly burnt his abdomen and he was lying in the shelter. The Japanese Commander gave us the information regarding the existing position of fighting front. Although, he did not say so, I realized that they were not in a position to do much to help the fight. They were not able to supply ration to our Jawan, their transport and communication had almost broken down. Our injured and sick Jawans had neither medicine nor other aid. On the other hand the Monsoon was fast approaching and that would flood all the rivers making supply position almost impossible. And then in that condition, even withdrawal would become impracticable. I, therefore, felt that our troops had to withdraw to Rangoon and be reorganised. I was confident, after the rainy season, it would have been possible for us to return to Manipur and give a good fight. In the mean time, I felt we could collect money, materials and ration from the Indians and equip our forces sufficiently to continue the fight and liberated Eastern part of Assam, including Manipur. Although Gen. Chatterjee did not agree with me, I decided to report to Netaji on those lines after returning to our Headquarters. Having finished our work, I became anxious to return. We returned to our camp at More on the following day and an immediately started for Mandalay & Maymyo. At Yeu, our Transport Depot, we changed our means of transport and travelled by our own cars and jeeps. After a hectic journey, we reached Mandalay on 7th June, 1944, only on learn that Netaji had already left Maymyo for Rangoon and had asked us to proceed to Rangoon.

The journey to Rangoon was equally trying and we had to face the fury of unusually heavy rain during the journey. Having returned to Rangoon we met Netaji, who informed us that he had already received report about the deteriorating condition on front and had ordered for the withdrawal of troops from Imphal (Manipur) sector before the rain set in and the rivers are flooded. Work had already started in Rangoon to reorganise the Azad Hind Fauj and to improve supply and Transport condition. We needed rice, medicine and money to replenish our stocks. Netaji asked me to form a team and to tour for the purpose. The Delta area, south of Rangoon was considered the rice bowl of Burma. The area was not yet tackled. We also expected donations to our War fund from the Indians of Delta.

I organised a team consisting of my friend and industrialist, Mr. S.M. Bashir, Mr. Nachiappan, and a number of other members of the Indian Independence League who were well acquainted with that area. We requisitioned a motor boat and started on our tour, probably in the third week of June. There were a large number of Chattiar owning rice mills. There were flourishing Muslim merchants and also a large number of stockists of medicine. They all came forward and liberally contributed to our fund. Some of Indian ladies donated also their gold ornaments. We received several hundred tons of rice for our Fauj, stock of medicine and nearly two crores of rupees in cash. We had also places. Mr. Bashir was very helpful in our efforts because he knew the people of the area and was well known to them. When we returned to Rangoon and reported the result to Netaji, he was very satisfied.

In Sep 1944, Netaji asked me to proceed to the Philippines and China to collect funds and to inspect the work of the League and Azad Hind Volunteers Corps. after Saigon I had to take a seat in a bomber that took me to Shanghai after a night's halt in Hainan. Immediately on arrival at Shanghai, I started visiting various camps of the I.N.A. volunteers where the training had started by Captain B. Narain, an Ex-Army officer. I called a meeting of the Indians of Shanghai in the local Gurudwara and appealed for men and money. I also sent a representative to Tientsin and Dairen with our appeal for funds. The response was very encouraging. Volunteers also started pouring in for recruitment. Quite a number of young Sikh women enrolled themselves for training and wanted to be sent to the front as early as possible. I had also made some changes in the structure of the Indian Independence League of Shanghai. Mr. Jalal Rahman, a tried national worker of Japan and Shanghai India National Association, was made the chairman of the China Territorial Committee, Shri Nanik Ram an old merchant was nominated as the Chairman of the Shanghai branch and concurrently Treasurer of the Territorial Committee along with one Harnam Singh. In the meantime, by the end of Nov. 1944, I was informed by the Japanese Liaison Officer, that Netaji was arriving at Shanghai with his party for a short visit on his way back from Tokyo. I received them at the Air Port. The journey had to be kept a secret. The party was escorted to Cathey Hotel where a suite and about 10 other bed rooms were reserved for them. We held a number of meetings of the local Indians where Netaji spoke at length about the achievements of our Azad Hind Fauj on various fronts. He also visited the Training Camps for volunteers an also the Gurudwara where the women volunteers of Rani of Jhansi Camp presented a guard of honour. Netaji also visited Nanking where some Indians were residing. His party consisted of Gen. M.Z. Kiani, Gen. A.C. Chatterjee, Col. Habibur Rahman and his personal staff. As the birth day of Netaji was approaching, I decided to stay for the celebration in Shanghai to encourage the League and Fauj officials and Volunteers. Before leaving Shanghai, Netaji had asked me to visit Tokyo returning to Burma to attend to some pending work regarding the printing of currency notes. Actually, I felt, he wanted me to meet my family in Tokyo before returning to the front.

The celebration of Netaji's birth day was a grand function. I inspected the volunteers, hoisted national flag. I received Guard of Honour by them and Rani of Jhansi volunteers. I spoke on various functions. I distributed sweet meats among the children at Gurudwara. At the main function where I inspected the parade and guard of honour was presented to me a large number of Japanese, German and Italian high official and Army officers, besides the representatives of the Chinese Government attended the function, in spite of the biting cold. Assured of continued efforts by Rahman, Nanik Chand and Harman Singh and other members of the League office in Shanghai, I left China for Tokyo by a plane on 10th February, 1945 reaching Nagasaki after a few hours. From Nagasaki I had to travel by train, reaching Nagasaki after a few hours. From Nagasaki I had to travel by train, reaching Tokyo on 13th Feb. There my two elder daughters, Asha (Bharati) and Tulu (Razya) were on the platform to receive me besides the Japanese official, and Rama Murti, the Chairman of the Japan League.

Although I did not like it, I was detained in Japan for more than a month for want of transport facilities. The enemy reconnaissance had also increased. My wife and children wanted to go to the front and work there for the country. Taking everything in to consideration, that was not possible. My third daughter and my son, the youngest one were already in a far off forest village, sent for safety by the authorities. I found that my wife was ailing and was almost invalid due to Arthritis. I, therefore, wanted to take the two elder daughters with me. However, Japanese knew that the War was coming to an end and told me that unless I wanted my wife to be left to die unattended, I should not take away both of my grown up daughters from her. Helplessly, I had to leave the younger one (Tulu) to look after the mother. But, Asha, the eldest was determined to accompany me. She said Netaji had promised her that. I agreed and got her ready to the journey.

Our journey back was full of hazards and very exciting. We travelled by train from Tokyo to Nagasaki. From there after a few days we were flown to Taihoko (south Taiwan) in a civilian plane. On the way we encountered enemy reconnaissance plane and were asked to tighten our belt for any emergency. However, we landed at Taihoku air port safely and stayed in Railway Hotel for nearly a month, again for want of transport facilities. Every night enemy bombers dropped bombs near about the places. Then we were asked to proceed to central Taiwan (Taichu) by train. On the way at about midnight, train stopped because enemy planes had bombarded the track and train could not proceed further. Early next morning when the train started, on the way it had to pass through a tunnel up the hill. The engine failed to draw the train. We had to get down and all the passengers had actually to push the train through the tunnel. The Governor of Taichu received us at the Railway station on arrival at Taichu and escorted us to a Japanese hotel, the best of the town. We were given a suite of rooms. But, here too, every forenoon we had undesirable visitors, the enemy planes. As soon as the danger siren sounded we had to rush to a shelter by the side of a nearby canal. The fighter planers shelled the area mercilessly. One day while we were in the shelter a bullet aimed at the hotel hit its window, pierced through the paper sliding door in to my sitting room, hit the telephone and lodged on the mat there. When we returned we found it lying there.

There after authorities decided that every morning we should be escorted to a far off village temple or in some bush for safety. Thereafter our daily routine was to take our breakfast in the hotel and then rush in a car or a jeep to some far off Buddhist Temple and spend the day. Some days we spent our days in the hutment of a Formosan (Taiwanese) farmer, who would prepare rice and some vegetables for us, for our lunch. One day I asked them to get some spice like chili, garlic, onion, etc. and their cooking oil and prepared Indian curry. And we enjoyed it with rice that they used to eat. They were so happy that they wanted me to come every day. I found that they liked spiced vegetables or meat as we do.

Our departure from Taichu was again unusually delayed due to lack of transport. At last in the third week of April, our Japanese friends informed me that an Army plane was flying to Saigon that night and we may be able to take advantage of this facility. I immediately agreed. We went to the air strip at about midnight. The driver had to search in the dark for the starting point for about half an hour to locate the place. At last the Commandant of the Base addressed the crew as follows: "You are going to the south. As you know the plane is very new and you have the responsibility of carrying valuable guests of another country, you must do your duty fully conscious of your country's honour." He perhaps did not know that we could understand his language. Asha asked me if I understood what he meant. I noded, and said we have to face the situation. So we left at about 1 a.m., stopped at about 9 a.m. in a small place, pushing the plane to a hiding place under a tree and then walking about two miles to rest for the day. In the evening we again took off on our final hope arriving next morning at Saigon and thence to Bangkok airport in the afternoon. I was greatly concerned about my daughter because she was so young and this was her first experience. But, she proved courageous beyond expectation and calmly faced all that came, At Bangkok we learnt that our troops had withdrawn from Rangoon and they were coming to Bangkok with Netaji, we waited there for his arrival. He arrived after a few days with the contingent of Rani Jhansi and some officers of Azad Hind Fauj. He declared that "our fight had not ended. We lost only the first battle and our men had done marvellously well. We will reorganise our Force and march again." A camp for the training of Rani of Jhansi cadets was started and training started. My daughter Asha was admitted as a cadet. Training in other camps were started. Consultations were held for future steps. Collection of funds and materials were started. But, Netaji knew that the Japanese were not in a position to continue the fight and we had to find some other means to continue our fight on some other front if India could not achieve freedom after that war. When in Tokyo, Netaji had approached the Japanese to help him in contacting the Soviet embassy. But the Japanese did not agree. When Netaji told me about it after returning from Rangoon, I told him that there were some other ways to approach the Soviet.

Early in 1945, when it became evident that Japan may not be able to continue war for long, and when they refused to allow Netaji to contact the Soviet Embassy in Tokyo, we decided to make direct effort, secretly, to contact Communists in China. Netaji was determined to continue our fight for freedom from some other theatre. He calculated that the Anglo-Soviet friendship was a marriage of convenience and might not survive long after the war. Thus was decided to seek collaboration with U.S.S.R. in case India was not free after the war.

I informed Netaji that when I visited Yanching University in 1938, I had met a number of Chinese professors who were prominent members of the Chinese Communist Party and were friendly of India. They could be contacted through Hanoi. This had to be kept guarded secret from the

Japanese. Accordingly, Netaji sent Gen. Chatterjee and myself for collection of funds. Later I proceeded to Hanoi. ostensibly, for the same purpose. There I contacted the revolutionary Vietnamese and two trusted young men were despatched to Chungking, the Headquarters of Generallissimo Chiang Kai Sheck Government of what was called Nationalist China, to contact and negotiate with the Chinese Communist leaders to help us in surrendering to Soviet Forces in Manchuria when the Japanese surrendered to them.

I was confident that when Japan's defeat became imminent, U.S.S.R. would not leave the strategic Manchuria to be occupied by the Anglo-Americans. Unfortunately, Japan's collapse came earlier than expected, due to American atom bombing. And, our plan did not materialise. On August 17th, 1945 Gen. Chatterjee, Major Abid Hasan, John Thivy, Col. Gulzara Singh, Col. Pritam Singh and Debnath Das arrived at Hanoi, quite unexpectedly, and informed me that Netaji had left for Japan. They joined me and were accommodated in the same house where I was staying with some Japanese civilian officials. On the evening of 18th August, Tokyo Radio announced Netaji's plane crash in Taihoku, the capital of Taiwan, and his demise. We did not believe it. I thought it was a planned as camouflage to mislead the enemy.

The North Vietnam was to be occupied by the Chinese Forces and the British Forces were to occupy south of the 17th parallel latitude. This news came to us to our great relief. After a while, where the Chinese Forces arrived and occupied North Vietnam with their Headquarters at Hanoi, under the command of Gen. Lo Han, Gen. Chatterjee and myself called on him by appointment and offered to be arrested. But, he refused and asked us as to why should he arrest us. The conversation was interesting; and, if I remember correctly, it was as follows:

General Lohan	:	What have you done to be arrested?
Sahay	:	We fought against the British.
Gen.	:	Did you fight against the Chinese?
Sahay	:	Netaji asked us not to do so.
Gen.	:	But, you collaborated with our enemies no?
Sahay	:	Yes, that was the tragedy. We collaborated with your enemies and you collaborated with ours. But, neither of us fought for them, did we?

The General was silent for a moment and then he laughed and said, "You may go and live as free man or go away wherever you want. No Britisher can touch you within my territory, unless my Government ask me to hand you over to them ."

Thus, till 22nd December, 1945, we remained free men and went about as such. On 20th December, a Sindhi merchant of Hanoi, Mr. Kewal Ram, came and informed me that a British Colonel Wilson, had arrived and wanted me to go and meet him. I had already learnt that a British Military Mission under Col. Wilson had come to Hanoi and was making enquiries about us. Two days earlier, my car was removed from my gardage at midnight by some armed men, supposed to be the agents of Col. Wilson. I told Kewal Ram that I knew why I was called but I was no prepared to go. I said, "As I am a Minister of Azad Hind Government and Col. Wilson is just an Army officer, my rank was higher than that of a Colonel. If he wants to meet me, please ask him to come and see me at my residence." Kewal Ram was upset and pleaded with me saying that he can arrest me by force. I told him, "You are just a messenger and should take a message to him." Very reluctantly he went back only to return with in a short time to report that the Colonel had agreed to visit me an wanted time to be fixed.

The next day 21st of December, the monthly Azad Hind Day and I invited Col. Wilson to come and have tea with me. I had the national flag of India and that of Ho Chi Minh's Vietnam beautifully displayed on the wall of my drawing room along with the photos of Netaji and Ho Chi Minh. The Colonel stared at them rather with interest. He told us frankly that he was sent to "Collect" us. I told him equally frankly that we were prepared provided we are taken to Delhi. He said he would consult his Headquarters at Singapore and would meet again the next day.

The next day, i.e. 22nd Dec. 1945, at about 5 P.M. two cars pulled up in front of my residence to escort us, as arranged. On our way, Colonel was waiting at the pavement and entered my car and told me that, instead of meeting at the appointed place, we would proceed to his office. He told us that he had received instructions that air transport was coming to fly us on the following morning via Saigon. When we reached his office a Chinese unit formally handed us over to the British and withdrew. On our request Col. Wilson readily agreed to escort us to our residence to collect our belongings. I distributed the heavy items among my neighbours and servants and packed my bedding and suitcases to be taken with us. I had already arranged with my Vietnamese comrades to broadcast our arrests from their station the same day and they, kindly, did it.

We spent the night at the office of Col. Wilson and were next morning flown to Saigon, Where we spent the night in some barrack. On arrival at Saigon airport when our luggages were unloaded I found that one of the suitcases, containing important document, cash and clothing, was missing. Evidently, it was deliberately removed by Colonel's men. I wrote to the Colonel complaining. But, there was no reply. The next morning, on 24th. Dec. 73, we were flown to Singapore where were lodged in two different Jails-Myself, Gen. Chatterjee, John Thivy and Abid Hasan in Pearl Hill Prison and Col. Gulzara Singh and Col. Pritam Singh in notorious Changhi Prison. (Deb Nath Das had already slipped out to Thailand before our arrest). In jail we were lodged in single cells with just one wooden Chowki, two blankets and a bucket for easing. Every morning we had to carry our buckets to a ditch, empty them, clean them and bring them to our cells. After entering the prison. I took things easy and made myself at home.

I wrote to my wife in Japan to inform her about my arrest. I told her that I was prepared to face the worst gladly, and that I was proud of what I had done to serve the cause of my country's freedom. I asked her to return home and take proper care of the children. During my last visit to Tokyo, before the end of the war, I had brought my eldest daughter Asha (Bharati) with me to Bangkok and she had joined the Rani Jhansi Regiment as a Cadet and with in very short time of training she had become an officer in the rank of 2nd Lieutenant. I did not know her fate. After being detained in solitary cells for some time, we were later taken to better solitary cells, meant for European prisoners, with sanitary toilet attached. Australian soldiers, working as wardens, became friendly with me and used to bring informations regarding happenings in India. We were also allowed to spend the day time with other I.N.A. prisoners in an enclosure with in the jail. My younger brother, Satya Dev Sahay, who was incharge of Intelligence of Azad Hind Government, was in hiding in Singapore and Malaya. He contacted me with the help of Indian wardens of the Jail and used to supply Indian food every day and other needed articles through them. Later we secured permission to get our daily meals openly from Indian friends in Singapore. I became friendly with the English Jailor by helping him in translation work. Gradually, I received all amenities of life like laundry, hot water for shaving etc. with the permission of the Jailor. I was also made-in-charge of jail bakery and pantry where best of cakes and pastries of Singapore were made for white officers in the city. I enjoyed cakes and coffee every afternoon. Indian wardens of the Jail greatly respected us as patriots and were very helpful. I took to walking and running around the compound every afternoon before taking a good shower bath.

In Feb. 1946, one Rai Bahadur Bakshi Badrinath of the Intelligence Dept. of the Govt. of India, came to Singapore to Interrogate us. Gen Chatterjee and Major Abid Hasan were greatly harassed by him during the interrogation. When they told me about their experience I decided to be tough with him when my turn came. I told him at the outset that I would tell him frankly and fearlessly what I knew and what I did, if he dealt with me like a gentleman, I reply to his queries I gave a detailed factual reply at every point. I think he was convinced that I was not trying to conceal anything. I gave him more than he wanted, so much so that he once remarked that I was myself trying to put the noose round my neck. I retorted, "Rai Bahadur I know, Your British bosses know what I have during the last twenty-five years. They would not spare me if I even kept mum. I am prepared to go to gallows proudly. If I am saved. I would be certainly not due to any mercy from your bosses but only due to the strength of my countrymen"

I did not know much about the negotiations that were then going on in Delhi nor about the Great Trial of my brave comrades of the I.N.A. in Red Fort. until the Australian warden came to my cell at 10.30 P.M. and informed me that Shah Nawaz, Prem Saigal and Gurubaksh Dillon were Court Martialled, acquitted and cashiered at Red Fort and were defended by Jawaharlal Nehru and Bulabhai Desai. Later H.N. Kunzru, P.N. Sapru and Kodanda Rao visited us in Jail and told us that efforts were being made to release us. I told them that our release was not as important as the freedom of India. On 19th March 1946, Jawahar Lal Nehru visited us. I knew about his visit to Singapore a couple of days back from the Indian Warden and I had written a welcome address for him in Hindi verses. I had it written in beautiful letters. And made two copies outside the jail with the help of my brother Satya Dev Sahay. Before Jawaharlal visited us in Jail, Satya Dev, had already presented a copy to him. So when he visited us and when I presented it to him, he remarked, "I have already received it."

The Jailor informed me on 26th March, 46, that we were to be unconditionally released on 30th March, 46, because the Civil Authorities were to take over the administration of Singapore I came back to my barrack and told my comrades in a depressed tone that I had a bad news for us. Many were scared and pressed me to divulge it. Then I told them that we were to be released unconditionally; and they cursed me for frightening them. I said, my problem was that, while I was enjoying all the amenities of life in Jail, once out I did not know where were I to go and how to manage without funds. Earlier, a batch of Indian Civilian prisoners of the I.N.A.

were also brought from Bangkok, including Parmanandji, Sardar Isar Singh, Pandit Raghunath Sharma and others. They informed me that my daughter, Lt. Bharati (Asha) was safe and with the family of Pt. Raghunath Sharma. I was greatly relieved.

Eleven days after Jawaharlal Nehru came to see us, we were released on 30th March 1946, in the morning at 9 a.m. I dressed up in full I.N.A. uniform with shining top boots all complete and went to the superintendent to take leave. He looked at me, smiled and said, "It seems you are going to fight again." I replied, "Our fight is not yet over. India must win her freedom before our fight ends." And we parted. Many patriotic Indians greeted us at the gate, even garlanded us and escorted us to their respective homes. I was taken to one Major Misra's House where I stayed for nearly four months before I was permitted to return home. My daughter Lt. Bharati came and joined me there from Bangkok. Thus ended my life as a soldier of NETAJI and his Arazi Hukumate Azad Hind.

Jai Hind.

Appendix-II

Interrogative Report of Anand Mohan Sahay[1] (Extract)

Great Asia Conference

12. In about Sep 26 (1926), the Japanese organised a gathering called the "Great Asia Conference" at Nagasaki. Delegates were invited by the Reception Committeee from all over ASIA but as none could come from INDIA the following were accepted as Indian delegates :–

    (a) Rash Behari Bose

    (b) Keshio Ram Sabarawal (Punjabi) – Deported by the Japanese in 1937 on suspicion of having Russian contacts. Last seen by H/1459 at Dairen in 1937.

    (c) Vidhya Dhar Bakshi – Left JAPAN about 1926.

    The conference was also attended by representatives from China, Philippines, Java and SIAM. Resolution on Asiatic unity to accomplish the "Resurgence of ASIA" were passed. Raja Mahendra Pratap – then in Manchuria, was also to come to Japan for the Conference, but he was refused entry because he had no passport, and was returned by the same steamer to Tientsin or Dairen.

Business Trip in the Far East and Visit to India

13. In Nov 26 H/1459 went on a tour to Hong Kong, Bangkok , Malaya, Ceylon and India, for business purposes. In India he visited Dr. Rajendra Prasad, M. Gandhi, S. C. Bose and other political leaders of his acquaintance. He informed them of the ignorance of the Japanese

---

1. C.S.D.I.C. Report I.N.A. Papers: H/1459 number was allotted to Anand Mohan Sahey. Other prominal leaders of the I.N.A. Who were interogeated by the C.S.D.I.C. were allotted similar numbers. These reports of the C.S.D.I.C. which are frequently mentioned in these document are available in the National Archives of India amongest I.N.A. papers which were previously in the custody of the Historical Section of the Ministry of Defence, New Delhi. Some of these reports are available amongst the War Office Papers at the Public Record Office, London. Sahey's account is very important for understanding the Japanese Policy towards I.N.A.

about conditions, political, cultural and spiritual, in India. During this visit H/1459 married the daughter of Urmila Devi, a national worker of Calcutta and sister of the late C. R. Das. By this marriage he has 3 daughters and one son. As he had always intended to return to India he had his children registered with the British Consulate at Kobe, to ensure their Indian nationality. His eldest daughter is now in Bangkok with the family of Pt. Raghunath Sharma. The rest of his family is in Tokyo.

The Return to Japan

14. H/1459 and his wife left Calcutta in Sep 27. They broke their journey at Singapore for business reasons, and reach Kobe in October. Soon after their arrival in Japan H/1459 delivered a speech under the auspices of the India Club on the situation in India.

Raja Mahendra Pratap in Japan

15. About the end of 1927 or early 1928 Raja Mahendra Pratap visited Kobe and H/1459 arranged a public meeting of the Indian to unable Raja Mahendra Pratap to express his views. At this meeting Raja Mahendra Pratap described his own activities in Germany during the war of 1914/1918 and his subsequent work in Afghanistan, Moscow, America and China. He claimed that he had collaborated with the Germans to secure armed assistance for the liberation of India and described how later on he was received by Amir Amar Ullah in Kabul and by the Soviet leaders in Moscow. Raja Mahendra Pratap possessed a number of photographs of his visits to foreign countries which he showed to his audience.

16. The Indian National Congress Committee in Japan had the following objects:–

(a) Political and cultural propaganda in order to create better understanding and friendhsip between India and Japan.

(b) To make efforts to raise the prestige of the Indian Merchants in Japan in the eyes of the Japanese and thus to secure better facilities for trade.

(c) Helping Indian students in their higher studies.

In order to achieve this H/1459 started a monthly journal called "Voice of India" and established a boarding house called "India Lodge" in KOBE. He also made efforts to foster unity between the various Indian communities, and to develop national feelings.

National anniversaries were observed on 4 occasions in the year:–

(a) Indian Independence Day (26 January)

(b) Id

(c) Diwali

(d) Parsi New Year

Outbreak of War in Europe

17. Soon after the outbreak of War in 1939 H/1459 called a meeting of the Indians under the auspices of the Indian National Association at Kobe and after a review of the situation in India a resolution was passsed similar to that of the AICC which had protested against the Govt of India's declaration of war. More meetings were held, one of which was addressed by Raja Mahendra Pratap who said that the fullest advantage should be taken of the war to obtain freedom of India. H/1459 and Raja Mahendra Pratap teared Japan addressing meetings on the lines of Congress attitude towrads the war. H/1459 also wrote newspaper articles on the subjects, and issue pamphlets for the Indian National Association reproducing speehes and statements of Congress leaders as well as the correspondence between the Congress and the Govt of India on the India subject of the war and Congress demands. He frequently visited Shanghai in connection with this propaganda.

18. During one of these visits to Shanghai, a German journalist called on H/1459 for an interview during which H/1459 stated that India had no liking for Fascism or Nazism, and that Indians were equally against Imperialism. They would not support the British war effort because they were not convinced that the war was being fought in the cause of freedom or democracy as declared by the Allies. The German asked H/1459 to speak afterwards the German journalist asked H/1459 to introduce to him Indian announcers suitable for an Indian Session which was being introduced into the broadcast programme. H/1459 agreed on condition that nothing would be said against the Indian National Congress or its leaders in these broadcasts. H/1459 introduced to the German an educated Sikh watchman (name not remembered), who, he thinks, was evacuated by the British on the outbreak of war in the East. The description of the Sikh is:–

Height :– 5' 9"; Age :– 25 yrs;
Fair complexion; a shaven Sikh.

H/1459 as Author

19. The German Publicity Dept in Shanghai also produced WILL DURANT's book "Case for India" and asked H/1459 to write an introduction. He did so, recommending the book to those who wanted to know the facts about the British Rule in India. H/1459 had by now himself written a book in English on India. This had been translated by a publishing company under the joint names of H/1459 and T. Muto. The book was called simply "India". In 1935 H/1459 had written a small play called "In India" depicting scenes of the non-cooperation movement of 1920. He later learnt that this play had been banned by the Government of India. He wrote another booklet in English called "Coloured Ethiopia" which denounced Italian aggression against Abyssinia. He followed this is 1940 by a book in Japanese entitled "Doomsday of the British Empire", which was a denunciation of British Imperialist policy in India. H/1459 bore the expenses of all these publication from his own assets except for "Coloured Ethiopia" which he wrote for the Greater Asia Society at the request of Professor Nakatani.

Indian Political Parties Working in Japan at the Time of the Outbreak of War in Europe

20. There were three Indian Political groups in Japan which were carrying on propaganda for Indian freedom. They were:–

(a) Indian National Association–controlled by H/1459. Its represented the Indian community on various non-commercial matters and also served Indian merchats in their business affairs there being no Indian Chamber of Commerce or other similar institution. When, owing to tariff barriers imposed against Japanese goods and the retaliation of the Japanese by Tariffs on Indian raw materials, Indian merchats became commercially embarrassed, H/1459 put up to the Japanese the argument that the merchants could not held responsible for the policy of the govt of India. The Indian National Association also helped the merchants when their assets were frozen by the Japanese Govt.

(b) Raja Mahendra Pratap was the founder of the "World Federation" Movement and editor of a periodical of the same name. He did not enjoy much political following but was held in great esteem on account of his sacrifice and sufferings in the cause of India. His political ideology was unintelligible to most of the Indians and won little backing. With the help of contributions by Indians in Japan he purchased a piece of land at Kokubunji near Tokyo and built some huts where he lived and worked. His only ardent followers was a Sikh named Sohan Singh who had been living in Japan for a long time and was married to a Japanese girl.

(c) Indian Independence League–This was run by R. B. Bose who had some staungh supporters among the young Indians in Tokyo. Some of the Indian merchants in Kobe and Yokohama were his personal friends and he had a large number of intimate Japanese friends in both official and non-official circles. The following in particular were his satellities:–

(i) Desh Pande—Later went of Bangkok (believed drowned on torpedoed Japanese ship)

(ii) Miglani (Punjabi)– Was employed as an announcer at the Tokyo Broadcasting Station during the war. Still in Tokyo.

(iii) Raja Sharma –A South Indian who accompanied R. B. Bose to Bangkok; present wherabouts not known.

(iv) Gupta–Was a student in Tokyo and came to Malaya with R. B. Bose. In 1943 H/1459 saw him in Singapore, and later heard that he was working with the Japanese.

21. R. B. Bose and his associates were not very friendly with H/1459 because he was the official representative of Congress which, because of the well-known leanings of its leader Nehru, they suspected of socialism, H/1459 was on the other hand very popular among the Indians and was also respected by the Japanese intelligentsia.

Ever since the outbreak of the European War the antagonism of the IIL group towards H/1459 had been growing more acute and he found that the Japanese MP and a section of the Japanese Press were paying him some attention. An article was published in the "Nippon" of Tokyo, dannouncing H/1459 as a follower of Nehru, and at the same time R. B. Bose's grouup passed a resolution condemning the policy of the Indian National Congress. H/1459 replied with an article in the "Osaka Mainichi" repuiating the resolution and saying that it was foolish to think that a few Indians in Tokyo were wiser than the great brains of the Congress.

Differences in the Trinity

22. The unity of the 3 Indian political groups was superficial and in spite of all efforts could not last. Raja Mahendra Pratap was keen on joining hands with the Germans and Italians to which H/1459 and Bose did not agree. On one occasion BOSE suggested to H/1459 that they should obtain arms from the Japanese and send them to India. H/1459 did not agree because he did not think that arms would serve any unseful purpose under the conditions which existed in India and in the absence of any organised nation-wide revolutionary party. He argued that Congress was the only organised national body in India and that it could never welcome such a move. He told R.B. Bose that if Japan was prepared to help India with arms there must be some ulterior motive, but agree that provided Japan had no territorial or selfish design on India, and that India was in a position to sustain a nation-wide armed revolution, the proposal would bear consideration. Bose suggested that he had friends in India with whom he could communicate and whom he could interest in project. He claimed that the Japanese anthorities might also agree to give an undertaking that they had no ulterior motives in helping India. Bose refused to divluge the names of his friends in India and Japan through whom he hoped to secure all this. These discussions resulted in serious and immediate differences among the parties.

Outbreak of War in the East

23. On 8 Dec 41 H/1459 learnt that JAPAN was at war and later the same morning R. B. BOSE telephoned him calling him to a meeting in the Rainbow Restaurant to discuss the situation as it affected INDIA. H/1459 arrived at the rendezvous and found BOSE and some other Indians gathered there. He remembers the following :—

(a) R. B. Bose

(b) Desh Pande

(c) Lingam–A South Indian follower of R. B. Bose

(d) Raja Sharma

(e) Narain–A South Indian employed in some paper press.

(f) Ramamurti

(g) S. N. Sen–Bengali

(g) Rastrapal

The discussion which took place was quite informal. It was decided to call a meeting in Tokyo of Indians from all over Japan. Various suggestions for cooperation with the Japanese in order to achieve the freedom for India were also discussed. H/1459 suggested that before they obtain any help from the Japanese Govt they must have a categorical declaration that Japan had no territorial or other designs on India. H/1459 was authorised to call the meeting mentioned above.

24. H/1459 unofficially sounded his Indian friends in Kobe, Yokohama and Tokyo. He felt inwardly confused. On one hand were his staunch Congress feelings, which did not fit in with the aggressive creed of the Japanese: on the other there was the apparently excellent opportunity to liberate India which, he felt, should not be missed. He felt, however, most strongly that whatever was done, Indians should not merely exchange one master for another or become Japanese tools. He was strongly opposed to the idea of a Japanese Army invading India and after long deleberations and heart searching came to the conclusion that while the opportunity should not be missed, he personally should not accept the leadership of any movement which would be organised in Japan. He thus went against the wishes of his friends.

Indian Independence League Conference

25. The Indian conference was held in the Railway Hotel Tokyo on 26 Dec 41. R. B. Bose was elected President at the suggestion of H/1459. The following were the most prominent of the 30 Indians who attended:—

(a) S. C. Das	–	From Kobe	
(b) S. Mangan Mal	– "	"	
(c) Ramchand	–	From Yokohama	
(d) Mahtani –	"	"	
(e) D. W. Sadhani	–	"	"
(f) H. N. Khoob	–	"	"

(g) Hans Raj – from Kobe
(h) Rawal – " "
(i) Ramamurti – From Tokyo
(j) Deshpande – " "
(k) Lingam – " "
(l) Kishore – " "

Resolutions were passed:–

(a) To open branches of the IIL in Kobe and Yokohama.

(b) To call upon India to rise against the British and fight for freedom.

(c) To cooperate fully with the Japanese.

(d) To request the Japanese Govt to help India in achieving complete independence.

26. R. B. Bose took upon himself the task of negotiating with the Japanese Govt while H/1459 was entrusted with the organisational work of the IIL Branches in Japan. H/1459 consented to close down the Indian National Association in the interest of Indian unity.

Opening of IIL Branches

27. After having closed down the Indian National Association H/1459 handed over its funds (about Yen 6,000), to R. B. Bose. He then visited Kobe and Yokohama where he called public meetings of Indians and explained the significance of the war in India's fight for freedom. He explained the closing of the Indian Association and the handing of the leadership of a united movement to R. B. Bose, and advised his hearers to cooperate with the IIL. R. B. Bose had accompanied H/1459 to Kobe. At the termination of the meeting at KOBE a branch of the League was set up with the Mehta, a Punjabi businessman (Description:— about 50 yrs old, short stature, medium built, wheat complexion, wears glasses and is married to a Japanese woman) as Chairman. Mehta was told to select other office bearers himself.

28. H/1459 next opened a League branch at Yokohama. Mahtani, a Sindhi merchant (Description :— Age 50, medium height, well built, fair complexion), who was President of the Local Merchants Association, was requested to take up the work of Chairman.

29. Early in Jan 42 H/1459 accompanied by Deshpande went to Shanghai. They stopped in the Astor House Hotel and interviewed workers of

the Indian National Association. The Shanghai Indians did not agree to close down this Association immediately although they raised no objection to the opening of a branch of the IIL there. Nair, a South Indian living in Manchuria, was also on a visit to Shanghai at the instance of the Japanese. H/1459 learnt that he had already organised a local IIL with the help of Indians who were not members of the Indian National Association.

H/1459 held discussions with Nair on the subject of the IIL. (H/1459 had by this time made up his mind to agree to the continuation of the Indian National Association in Shanghai. Amongst other things he saw that the League would be considered a Japanese sponsored body and would therefore not be able to obtain relief for Indian destitues from the Swiss Consulate as the Indian Association was doint. H/1459 told Nair this, assuring him that the League and the Association would cooperate, and Nair agreed. Nair was accompanied by a Japanese officer (name not remembered) who told H/1459 to see that the Indian Independence Movement did not suffer. H/1459 assured the Japanese that to an Indian like himself the independence of India was very dear and that he would do all he could to maintain harmony and goodwill among the Indians.) (Note:— These two factions — for such they became – continued until after S. C. Bose's arrival. Loganadan (B 953) tried to solve differences in Sep 43 and the Association was finally closed by Hassan (H/1457) in Nov-Dec 43.)

30. H/1459 discovered that there were 2 other Indian groups functioning in Shanghai. One was led by Osman, a Punjabi watchmen in the service of the Japanese Navy, and the other, which had started at the outbreak of war inthe East and was called "Welfare Society" was led by Kapahi and Seth, both Pubjabi businessmen. Both these groups had Japanese backing. Osman's party was supported by the Japanese Navy. It consisted of Sikh and Pathan watchmen and had been formed sometime before the war in the East. Osman had come to Shanghai from Java with the help of the Japanese Navy after the outbreak of war in Europe. H/1459 had met him before on a couple of occasions and had found that he had not only fantastic ideas about the independence movement but that he was illiterate and completely ignorant of politics. The welfare Society under Kapahi and Seth was helped by Lt. Col. Akiyama of the Publicity Bureau of the

Japanese Army. Kapahi and Seth had lived in Japan for a number of years and knew many Japanese officers. (Note : Osman Khan, Hari Singh was still in Java in Nov 45 living near Bandoeng).

31. H/1459 met Osman, Kapahi and Seth separately. He appealed to them to unite in the interests of Indian independence and to merge their parties in the League.

All said they were ready to cooperate but insisted that as there was no capable leader for the IIL in Shanghai under whom they would come to serve, they should carry on their respective parties. Osman promised to attend any functions organised by H/1459 to show his cooperation H/1459 learnt that Kapahi, as leader of his party, was obtaining wheat flour from the Japanese and selling it at a high price to the Indians. This was the reason for his unwillingness to forego his leadership.

32. H/1459 addressed Indian gatherings at various places in Shanghai appeaiing for unity. The response was very encouraging. He then held 2 meetings on 26 Jul 42 (Indian Independence Day); there was a flag hoisting ceremony under the auspices of the IIL in the morning, and a public meeting under the auspices of the Indian National Association of China in the evening. To the flag hoisting ceremony Japanese officials and Chinese had also been invited and H/1459 hoisted the flag. He delivered a short speech on the importance of the Movement and called upon Indians to merge their differences and to rally round their flag. The public meeting in the evening was a purely Indian function and was presided over by J. Rahman. It was well attended and was addressed by H/1459. Desh Pande, Mahtani and a few others.

33. During his stay in Shanghai H/1459 also met Lt. Col Akiyama and told him that his support of Kapahi and Seth was deterimental to the Movement and should be withdrawan. Akiyama agreed. H/1459 insisted that the political work of the Indian National Association be handed over to the League. H/1459 was visited by a representative of the German Broadcasting Station, Indian Section, who complained that the Sikh announcer H/1459 had introduced previously was not efficient at his work (ref para 30). At his request H/1459 introduced 2 Punjabis, one named Kochhar and the other possibly Ram Sarup. Both had been in Japan as annoucers. These 2 worked for a time and were eventually repatriated to India during the course of the war

while H/1459 was in Bangkok. H/1459 is not aware whether they were given any instructions for secret work in India.

Mohan Singh's Goodwill Mission to Tokyo

34. About the middle of Mar 42 H/1459 visited the League Office and saw some new faces there. He had not been informed about any fresh arrivals. He was introduced to Mohan Singh (H/1050), Raghavan (H/1193), Goho (H/1357), Gill (B1190) and Menon, who informed him that they had come from Singapore buy did not disclose the object of the visit. Mohan Singh secretly gave H/1459 a letter from Swami Satianand Puri. The letter complained bitterly against Japanese behaviour and treatment. Puri expressed his desire to stay with H/1459 in Tokyo and talk over the whole matter in confidence. In talks with Mohan Singh and others H/1459 learnt the object and arrangements of the "Goodwill Mission". He decided, however, not to participate as he had not been informed of the arrival of the edelegates or of any proposed conference, and he informed Bose accordingly. Some of the delegates, however, lunched with him privately. Lingham and Nair came too, possibly to spy on the gathering. (Note: The Tokyo Conference is fully described "S" Sec Reports 1007, 1144 and 1310. Swami S. N. Puri of course was killed on the way to the Conference and thus did not stay with H/1459.)

H/1459 Rejoins R. B. Bose

35. After the delegates to the above conference dispersed in mid Apr 42, R. B. Bose summoned H/1459 to his office. Bose gave H/1459 detailed information about the conference and asked him to come to Bangkok where Bose intended to set up IIL HQ. At first H/1459 refused to accede to this request but when Bose insisted, he asked for time to think matter over. About a week later Bose invited him to a dinner arranged by some Japanese staff offers. Among these present were :—

(a) R. B. Bose

(b) Deshpande

(c) Nair

(d) Maj Ozeki

(e) Takeda

and about 5 other Japanese. H/1459 wasd formally requested by the Japanese officers to join the movement wholeheartedly. He found it difficult to refuse thus suddenly brought to bay. He wanted as far as possible to restrict Bose's power and he did not wish unnecessarily to antagonise the Japanese.

Furthermore he had recently spoken the telephone to Deb Nath Das in Bangkok. Deb Nath Das had pressed him urgently to join, for reasons which he would disclosed when they met. H/1459 accordingly agreed to join R. B. Bose.

To Bangkok

36. 11 May 42 was fixed as the day of departure from Tokyo and the following were selected to accompany Bose and H/1459 to Bangkok:—

(a) Desh Pande – Continued in the movement but was drowned when the steamer Awa Maru was torpedoed in Apr 45.

(b) Nair– Now in Japan

(c) Lingam–Now in Japan

(d) Gupta– was last seen in Singapore in 1943.

(e) Raja Sharma–Drowned in the Awa Maru.

(f) Parekh–Probably still in Malaya

(g) Ram Singh Rawal–A Punjabi merchant. Was in Bangkok at the time of surrender.

(h) Vinayaka Supanekar– A Maharathi student, joined INA.

(i) S. N. Sen– Now in Tokyo

About 7 May 42 a farewell party was given to the above by Japanese staff offrs in a restaurant near the Sanne Hotel. Almost all the Japanese officers who had attended the previous dinner were present. The Indians of Yokohama also gave a farewell party at the India Club. At this party H/1459 delivered a speech saying that if the Japanese Army wanted to go to India against the will of the Indians it would only do so by marching over his dead body.

37. On the night of 11 May 42 the party left Tokyo by rail for the Ise Shrine where it paid homage to the Japanese Gods. It was accompanied by a Japanese lieutenant (name not remembered) who remained with it throught the journey. The party sailed from Moji on

15 May 42 in a Japanese convey and disembarked at Saigon on 28 May 42. From Saigon to Bangkok it travelled on the following day by air.

In Bangkok

38. They arrived at Bangkok on 29 May 42 and were received at the aerodrome by some Japanese who took them to Renaissance Hotel, Suriwongse Road. A few days later a temporary IIL office was established and preparations were begun for the Independence Conference fixed for 15 Jun 42.

39. Deb Nath Das told H/1459 that the Indian community was extremely anti-Japanese because of arrogant Japanese behaviour towards Indians and because it was thought that Swami S. N. Puri had been murdered by the Japanese for his independent views H/1459 told Deb Nath Das of the need for the greatest caution as they could neither allow the Japanese to have their own way nor afford to antagonise them. Both agreed that their chief difficulty was the weakness of R. B. Bose's character.

40. The party left Singapore by air on 29 Oct 43 arriving at Tokyo via Manila and Fukuoka on about 1 Nov 43. Bose was received at the Haneda Aerodrome by leading Indians and high Japanese military and civil officials, and taken straight to the residence of the viscound Sibuzawa, where Bose and his personal staff were to be lodged. In the evening Bhonsle (B1189), Mak Raju (B 956) and H/1459 were moved to the Imperial Hotel.

41. On the following day all were taken to the Imperial Palace where they signed the Visitors' Book. Later they called on th Dowager Empress, Prince Chichibu and Prince Takamatsu. On this or on the next day visits were exchanged by Gen Tojo and S. C. Bose. H/1459 was present at Bose's interview with Tojo at his official residence. Bose suggested to him the handing over of the Andaman and Nicobar Islands to the PGI, and the issue of Indian National Currency. Tojo promised to consider the matters and to reply later. Bsoe also attended a press conference and expressed his views on the international situation, expanding on the formation of the PGI and on its declaration of war. The main object of Bose's visit to Tokyo was to attnd the Greater East Asia Conference. Bhonsle and H/1459 attended the Conference with him. They attended as observers and not as delegates as Bose

considered that he could not commit India, without the consent of the Indians in India, to the Co-prosperity Sphere Group sponsored by Japan. (Note :— Confirms "S" Sec Report 1407 para 24.) Maj Raju (B 956) and Hassan (H/1457) attended the Conference as visitors. The proceedings were fully published in the press.

42. On the last day of the Conference TOJO announced the decision of the Japanese Govt. to hand over the Andaman and Nicobar Islands to the PGI. The detailed plans of this handing over were discussed at a Conference at the official residence of the Navy Minister which Bose and H/1459 attended. The Navy Minister explained that the Islands were very important for strategic reasons, and that it would be difficult to hand over their defences to the PGI during the war. He agreed that the civil administration might gradually be transferred and suggested that a Conference be held between the PGI and the local Naval Command of the Islands to discuss plans of transfer. Bose suggested that Indian National Currency be issued in the Islands as soon as it was printed. The minister raised various practical objections to this although he did not object in principle. He said, when asked, that he would be unable to transport INA to the Andamans. (Note:— The document published at Appx "C" to "S" Sec Report 1407 dates these conversations as 12 Nov 43 and gives written answers to the points Bose raised.)

43. Bose accompanied by H/1459 and possibly Bhonsle also called on M. Toyoma, founder of the Black Dragon Society. This was purely social call and R. B. Bose was also present. Bose was entertained to various official and non-official dinners by Indians, Japanese and others including the German Ambassador and Toyama. Bose also addressed public meetings.

With a puse, and a meeting of Indian women. The party left the Andamans by air on 31 Dec 43 reaching Bangkok the same evening. (Note:— The above should be read in conjunction with the relevant portions of CSDIC 2 Sec Reports 956 and 978, and "S" Sec Reports 1208/and/71123/11/2).

Conference with Mutaguchi

44. After formal visits, there was a conference with Gen. Mutaguchi at which the following decisions were taken. They should be read in conjunctions with paras 28–31 of "S" Sec Report.

Appendix-III

Statement by Deb Nath Das Regarding Doubts About the Death of Bose[1]

27 March, 1953

Mothers, Sisters and Brothers of India.
Jai Hind

I am placing before you my first report on Netaji Subhas Chandra Bose, as the Ex-General Secretary, the Indian Independence League Headquarters. East Asia, and as the Special Officer entrusted with a great mission as per the order of Netaji on 17.5.45 and 16.8.45. I owe my compatriots an apology for the delay in submitting my findings; but I feel sure that considering enormous responsibility inherent in the task and the magnitude thereof, the development of a reactionary force in India-creating hostilities against the cause, the insurmountable difficulties arising out of sheer disability on the part of workers to move and work in various places of different countries, and the last but not the least, the extreme beggarly condition of the workers, you will condons this delay. Moreover, the complete disintegration of the I.N.A. and its subsequent neutralisation shattered its very foundation. The most disgraceful feature exhibited in the game of some result of some of our colleagues created no less difficulties in the way of our mission, due to difference in common outlook and doubtful co-operation almost amounting to sabotage.

The reported death of Netaji created three reactions in India :

(a) Some felt relief thinking that the greatest Indian Revolutionary Leader is gone and thus with him the stiffest resistance in their way to fame and fortunes and power.

(b) Some took it philosophically and believed that it was a call of Destiny and that Netaji died after the fulfilment of a great mission, destined as he was, in the eternal way of Eternal India.

(c) But the greater number of people believed that the 'Plane Crash' was no crash and that it was merely an item in accordance with

1. History of Freedom Movement Papers.

the Master plan, envisaged by Netaji and that the beloved Leader would appear in the historic moment in the shaping of India's destiny.

The first reaction sought to completely Quarantine Netaji's ideals; the second—typical of India's philosophic way—neutralised the very great love for Netaji by inaction and completes surrender to Fate. The third- a logical conclusion of political thinkers and workers of revolutionary faith and ideals - was ineffective, because of their differences in contents and approach, neutralising one another and thus dragging the issue in their own way rather than leading the issue to a higher plane in the true perspective, away from compartmental political gains.

The main Issue was thus sidetracked in the midst of landslides of psychological currents and cross currents.

The people of India, bereft of all guidance, looked askance to one another with a fond hope, but remained in the dark, hoping against hope, in India's way of faith in God. Netaji's ideals remained in mere story-telling and not in preaching and practising them.

Thus sandwiched between two forces, one unsympathetic and hostile and the other sympathetic but not serious to the highest pitch with a soldier's mind, we few, appointed by Netaji in his order of the Day, had therefore to gear our mind and action into two channels; firstly, to conduct in the way as was instructed by Netaji and endeavouring at the same time to contact him, and to ensure confidences in him, to keep our stature, moral and political, strictly that everything was done according to the Plan. In that process, all calmness and precision was observed with the absolute pre requiste that was needed. Secondly, we had also to investigate whether everything was also followed according to Netaji's plan since the operative part of the plan was entirely in the hands of Japanese Military Officers who took charge of him and as such the success of our mission hinged on the precision in the manner of execution of the solemn pledge undertaken by the Japanese Military Officers, concerned. We proceeded from both angles. We had to be extremely cautious and reserved since even more lapse of some words would cause still more difficulties and might jeopardise the success of the very mission. In the terrific suspense we walked on. Ours was a colossal task. Not a single Zone remained unapproached with hope and confidence in the course of the last seven years. My worthy colleagues stood all attention in their respective positions till the last moment.

Now, on a final checkup of the findings in regard to the whereabouts of Netaji Subhas Chandra Bose, we have come to the conclusion based on circumstantial evidence and individual contact that nothing whatsover was done by the operative machinery of the then Japanese Military authorities as solemnly promised as per the wish of Netaji.

According to our study through patient work into the Japanese ranks entrusted with the operative part of the Plan (First Phase) this failure on the part of the Japanese was deliberate and was attributed to the complete frustration of the defeated Japan and her anxiety to avoid, in every possible way, any further hostility of Britain (which was at that time ruling over our country) and America over the shielding of Netaji from the British clutch. Japan could not think of handing over Netaji to the British authorities as such an act would invariably mobilize Indian opinion against her, since Japan was conscious of Netaji's immense popularity in India; nor could she keep him (Netaji) underground away from British clutch, as it would, on the other hand, make the occupation forces in the South-eastern Asian region more embittered to the occupied Japan.

The Japanese Military authorities knew the mind of Netaji and had a glimpse of the Post War Revolutionary programme and the Leader's determination to form new alliance for the liberation of India and to open a new phase in India's struggle for freedom and life. The Japanese calculated that his resurgent appearance in the future would only cast doubt in Britain's mind towards Post war Japan's bonafides in her (Japan's) policy towards Britain and her Allies with whom the Post war Japan must cast her lot for many more years. Japan tried to save herself from wrath of both India and the Occupation forces in South-East Asia. At the same time an impression was created that the accident was one according to the Alternate plan apparently to cover up her defeatist mentality and frustrated stature. All this is not my hypothetical assertion–truth will come out if public investigation is made.

Now I should touch upon the plan chalked out by Netaji before he emplaned from Bangkok immediately after the termination of the South - East Asia war. As I was constantly with him in those fateful days and as I was fortunately taken into his fullest confidence, with regard to the Plan (Original and alternate) and was appointed to head the mission, I claim to speak with a certain amount of authority. From May 1945, Netaji began to think of new move because of overwhelming enemy forces. It was Netaji's plan to go to India (First Priority) and continue the country's liberation fight from some underground centre. Japan agreed to take Netaji from

Bangkok to somewhere in Bengal and agreed to take responsibility so far as the necessary transport was concerned. All other parapheranalis were made by us, from the middle of June,1945. This is known to some of my colleagues in the Cabinet of Azad Hind Government and some members of Armed Forces.

On that understanding, Netaji emplanned for Saigon, as according to the Japanese, it could have been easier him and his officers to go to India through Saigon, as there was vigilance of the Allied Forces on that route. Mr. S. A. Ayer Singh Colonel Habib-ur Rehman., Colonel Pritam Singh, Colonel Abid Hassan and myself accompanied Netaji early in the from Bangkok (Netaji arrived from Singapore on 16.8.45) morning of 17.8.45. After reaching Saigon only, the Japanese Military authorities seperated Netaji from the rest of us on the ground that there was no accommodation in the plane. Not only that, we were informed for the first time that he was to be taken towards Tokyo; nor had Netaji any idea of the whole picture.

Here I must emphasise the talk that passed on between us on one side and General Isoda, Chief of the Hikari Kikan, that was set up by the Japanese High Command to serve as the Liaison Department for conducting military affairs with the Supreme Command, I. N. A., on the other. It was 8 o'clock in the morning when we arrived at Saigon from Bangkok and we went straight from the aerodrome, to two houses for a little rest. In one house, Netaji (in one room), Colonel Habib ur Rehman and myself were accommodated; in another house, just adjacent were Mr. Ayer, Colonel Gulzara Singh, Colonel Pritam Singh and Major Hassan. Seven days and nights we had no rest we longed for it. I was first to be awakened and Netaji was found beside me. The first few words of Netaji (he spoke in Bengali) were; "You see, they are changing the Plan- I don't know why - just come and have a talk with General Isoda", I was stunned and Netaji was requested by me not to give his consent. I immediately felt a little helpless for the new move, so surprisingly made and that too at Saigon where we were placed in the most disadvantageous position having been far away from our own Armed Forces yet strong in moves and courageous in mobility. I found Netaji's face full of signs of restlessness; for the first time I found in him a little uneasiness and helplessness of a child. "Any way" hurry up, come to that room". Netaji said, I hurried up and found General Isoda and another Japanese Officer. Immediately I gave vent to my feelings that there should be no change in the plan and that Netaji must be taken to India – the only logical step for him: "Even if we are captured", I said "the people will come to know and help us". Netaji was listening - he did not utter a single word but his eyes spoke and I could understand his mind. General Isoda enumerated some difficulties; but they were minor and he suggested that the Alternate Plan be taken up. (The principal feature of the Plan was to keep Netaji safe somewhere in East Asia) and gave me an idea of bases and routes, General Isoda said, that there would be no difficulties and so long he lived, he would keep Netaji safe. I still refused to accept his suggestion. Netaji, then intervened and asked General Isoda; "Suppose I go towards Tokyo, all of them (he meant the whole party) are certainly coming with me. "Then, the other Military Officer said; "Your Excellency, there is no accommodation in the plane - we shall try to accommodate at least one officer to go with Your Excellency. "Netaji did not reply direct but turned towards General Isoda and said, "Do you think,General, they (The Party) will agree to leave me alone?" Then hurriedly he told me to call other Officers. Immediately I called Col. Habib-ur-Rehman and just told him the gist of the talk. Then I ran to the adacent house and called Sri S. A. Ayer, Col. Gulzara Singh, Col Pritam Singh and Major Hassan to hurry up and report to Netaji. They all came and all of us vehemently opposed General Isoda's idea and even questioned him about the change. All of us, including Col., Rehaman resented the idea of giving seat to one Officer only to accompany Netaji. Meanwhile, Mr. Hachiya, Japan's envoy to the Azad Hind Government joined us. Both General Isoda and Mr. Hachiya assured safety of Netaji and promised to provide conveyance to the rest of us at the earliest possible opportunity to follow Netaji. But still we argued. At this moment, another Japanese military officer came in and talked to General Isoda. The General told Netaji that just at 1 o'clock in the afternoon a plane was leaving towards Tokyo and that Netaji should hurry up–there was one seat more, he added. Yet, we all did not agree. Netaji at this moment said: "You all don't worry - General Isoda has promised to provide you all with transport within the shortest possible time", and then he turned towards General Isoda and just asked. "Could you not give one more seat? Let Das come with me - he knows the place and language and will be of some help to me." "Can't say now, Netaji", the General, said," any way, I shall try once more while we are at the aerodrome. " "Netaji, however, asked all of us to bring our kits, and said he (Netaji) would try once more in the aerodrome for giving us the facility." Well, let us try, you all come, if you don't get transport, come back, "Netaji said. And he gave some instruction with regard to steps to be followed. He looked determined, calm, and collected. It was 17th August, 1945."

We all went towards the aerodrome with our kits and three suitcases of gold ornaments and gold bars, donated by the people of East Asia towards the Netaji Fund Committee. It was only a 20 minutes' drive. When we had only a few minutes to talk, Netaji once more told General Isoda and Mr. Hachiya about the plane for us which they had promised. Meanwhile, we were anxious about the gold; when I talked to General Isoda that the treasure must go with Netaji, he told me that the plane was already overloaded and he did not know whether the pilot would agree. Netaji interrupted and told "it does not matter - these may come with you all." Immediately I submitted to Netaji : "The treasure must go with you, Sir , "And all other officers spoke in the same strain. I turned towards General Isoda and told him: "Why not ask one or two of your Japanese Officers to get down and make room for the treasure? Meanwhile, the propellor started so we did not wait for General Isoda's reply; Col. Pritam Singh, Major Hassan and myself took the three cases and just put them inside the Bomber and told Col, Habib-ur-Rehman to take care of them. Netaji embraced everyone of us and boarded the plane. We all shouted "Habib, take care of Netaji".

After three days, stay in Saigon, we were told that Netaji had gone towards Tokyo and that we were to follow him. But finally, only on 21-8-45 Mr. Ayer alone was flown to Tokyo and the rest of us were taken to Hanoi the same day, though at the time of explaining we were given no hint of our Hanoi destination. On 21-8-45 Major General A.C. Chatterji and Sri J.A. Thivy arrived at Hanoi from Singapore. They were misled too. Sri A.M. Sahay was already at Hanoi.

At Hanoi we heard of Netaji's reported demise over the Radio on 24th August 1945. On the 26th August just a week after Intellegence Department met me at Hanoi together with a Military Officer from Towloon the seat of Marshal Tarauchi's Headquarters and told me: "Netaji no Hikoki ochiru kotowa shinio shimasan. Das Sanwa Netaji no yu koto torini shitekudaisai mase," the exact translation of which as follows : "Don't believe the plane crash as a real crash, you adjust your movements and plans in accordance with the alternate plan of Netaji" (This alternate plan was to continue the freedom fight from a suitable place in East Asia, in case it was not possible for Netajhi to go inside India immediately), we consulted the plan and took note of new base. I took Col. Pritam Singh , Major Abid Hassan and Mr. J. A. Thivy into confidence and took all steps and precautions. Major General A. C. Chatterjee, Sri A, M. Sahay and Col. Gulzara Singh were all consulted. And I went ahead. My colleagues in different places in accordance with the Plan until I was arrested at Bangkok by the Occupation authorities of the Allied Powers in May, 1946 and brought to India on 30.8.46

These seven years we have worked with faith in man and God in co-operation with my trusted workers all over East Asia, in the midst of Himalayan odds and suspense. We very often had discussed the bonafides or otherwise of the Japanese Military officers who took charge of Netaji, we took the late Sri Sarat Chandra Bose into confidence. We did not, however, allow our mind to be prejudiced. The late Sri Sarat Chandra Bose gave me inspiration to proceed with my mission, since some allowances of time must be given in view of Japan's extremely delicate position, war-criminal's trial and other international complications and no less, the disguised hostility of the Power that be in Indian towards Netaji. We became very often restless though, we did not like to cast any doubt, lest that might be interpreted as a branch of faith. Moreover, so long there was the least chance of Netaji being contacted according to the alternate plan, any suspicion on our part towards the 'benefactor' would have been as if to destroy the very roof that gave him (Netaji) shelter. Hence we had to wait until Japan got rid of the occupation forces and enjoyed better channels for outside contact. Hence the delay in accordance with the strategic necessity. There was a historical necessity too, in case everything was done according to the plan, for Netaji's remaining underground for obvious reasons only to appear at the historical moment for shaping India's destiny.

We gave our last push as soon as Japan got rid of the bindings of the occupation period. Meanwhile, to our utter surprise Sri S. A. Ayer went to Japan and gave the report of his conducted tour. In his statement he did not care to go through the salient features and simply came to a conclusion of his own apparently to bury the great issue of such national importance. We were perplexed when we found to our utter surprise that he was inducing the Government of India to bring the so called ashes of Netaji. The Japanese authorities concerned, on the other hand, have been also trying to hush up the matter. The Government of India have not chosen to set up a Top-level Enquiry Commission as has been demanded by the people of India.

When all avenues to find out Netaji were exhausted and when we found after thorough investigation and minute scrutiny that nothing whatsoever was done by the Japanese military officers in matters of executing instruction to different bases, as they promised in accordance with the alternate plan, we tried our best to contact the Japanese officers concerned. Replies were available are only too vague. Most of them are dead silent.

Contact or no contact, we believe Netaji should naturally remain alive but, if Netaji is no more, we equally believe there is some foul play somewhere and that some heinous crime must have been perpetrated in our darkest moment of history. This is our charge. And the responsibility lies on those Japanese Military officers who took charge of Netaji. Those officers who are all living today can not shirk that responsibility. It is one thing if, due to changed circumstances, they failed to continue the task even though solemnly pledged but it is quite another when the life of Netaji is concerned. As one who knows Japan for the last twenty years and has worked with brave Japanese people in the making of that glorious history under the banner of Netaji my grateful heart goes to the Japanese people for all they did for us. I. N. A.'s contribution, service and sacrifice, which will remain written in golden letters, It is with that feeling I would appeal to the Japanese Government and its people to see that their fair name be not married with stigma in their relation with the I. N. A. and the Leader before the posterity. Hence I appeal to them in fairness to their love towards India to allow such enquiries vis-a-vis the reported plane crash in Taihoku on the 18.8.45 when the fate of India's most beloved son is involved.

We understand that the Government of India is making arrangements to bring Netaji's ashes to India. Why did not the Government of India form a Top Level Investigation Committee at the outset to investigate the reported death of Netaji a Committee representing all shades of Indian opinion and the public? Why did the Government choose to send just one man (Sri S. A. Ayer) to Japan for the said Investigation—a man who had been in Japan just for month or so and did not know the language and the country well and had to yield to a conducted tour? When he did know what transpired between the Japanese officers and us in the matter of the execution of the plan did not he find him in an independent position to question them for their (the Japanese officers) failures to keep up the pledge and the reason thereof. If not; why? If so, why should he choose to keep his fingings secret from us who are all piligrims to that 'journey's end'. The question of the person of Netaji is the concern of the people of the whole of India.

Now, again during all this seven-year period, the whereabouts of the gold, which rightfully belongs to the Indian Nation, has remained a mystery. I put up this matter many times in the Central I. N. A. Advisory Committee but Sri S. A. Ayer did not give any reply. It was after my interview with the United Press in Bangkok on the 23rd January this year, which we published in all major papers of Japan, Thailand and other parts of East Asia that the 'Oskan Mainichi', a leading daily of Japan came out with a three column banner that Netaji's have been found. It is also noteworthy that in that report the name of Mr. Rammurti Ex-President of the Indian Independence League, Tokyo Branch, who became multimillionaire overnight, was mentioned prominently. It is also known that Sri S. A. Ayer delivered the treasure to him. I understand Mr. Rammurti is now in India with his Japanese wife and as an old acquaintance of his, I would earnestly request him to explain to the people of India why he did not report this to the Government of India or to the I. N. A. Inquiry Committee or to the Central I. N. A. Advisory Committee al these seven years. He should also explain how he got the treasure and under what circumstances he got it. Is it a fact that he offered him service to the British Information Service in Tokyo as soon as the Occupation Troops landed in Japan?

Sri S. A. Ayer should also explain the reason of his silence over these particular points and, as one who was on the very spot at Tokyo and as one who chose only Mr. Rammurthi to deliver the sacred treasure he should explain the situation in the light of the information that might be at his disposal. It is also astonishing that inspite of repeated appeal of Indian community in Japan. India's envoys accredited in Japan did not take any action for the restoration of the national treasure from Mr. Rammurthi. Why have not the Government made any arrangements to interview and question those people whose names are prominently associated with the disappearance of the gold? The details of the treasure will be submitted to the Investigation Commision.

It is a glorious chapter of the Azad Hind Government how this national treasure voluntarily contributed by Indian mothers, sisters and brothers in East Asia to Netaji for the sacred cause was presented by loyal officers and men. Sri Yellappa, Colonel Misra, Lt. Nazir Hussain and Lieutenants Josephina and Stella (Rani Jhansi Regiment) become martyrs to protect the treasure. Our worthy colleagues Major General A. C. Chatterjee, Major General J. K. Bhonsle, Sri J.A. Thivy, Sri J. N. Bhaduri, Director Azad Hind Bank, Pandit Raghunath Sharma, Secretary, Finance Department, Indian Independence League, Thailand, Major Abid Hassan, Confidential Secretary to Netaji, SriE. Bhaskaran, confindential stenographer to Netaji, Sri U.C. Sharma and Sri C. Rai Narulla, Sri S. N. Dasgupta, Sri A.C. Das Sri P.N. Pillay - officers of the General Secretariat and Hav. Kundan Singh and Adya Prasad, personal orderlies to Netaji - to name only a few - who played a great part in protecting the treasure in toto will. I am sure, varify the details as correct.

It was the greatest moment of our life when the national treasure was delivered to Netaji's new Headquarters in full on evacuation from Rangoon. This sacred treasure belongs to the nation and anyone found guilty of appropriating so is a traitor to the country and must be punished accordingly. The findings will also throw light on the circumstances that led to the reported plane crash.

Will the people of India remain quiet and accept without any investigation the so called ashes of India's most beloved son?

It is beyond our comprehension to think why the Government of India have chosen not to set up an Investigation Commission for findings out the circumstances and evidence in connection with the reported 'Plane Crash'. A new situation has arisen by the Prime Minister's declaration for the first time in the Parliament recently that the Government of India are convinced about the death of Netaji. Why did not the Government of India take it to be a supreme moral duty to place before the people of India the reason of their conviction and the materials leading to their conviction. It is the question of life of one so dear to India and universally respected and cannot be disposed of light-heartedly. We do no know how a National Government could remain true to its character by choosing to withold publication of the materials concerning the life of India's greatest revolutionary, Could there be any relation in the policy making of the State, with the materials available at the disposal of the Government in connection with the reported 'Plane Crash' or any other incident? The people have the right to know the details and themselves to judges. We therefore appeal to the Government of India to form an Investigation Commission with the Chief Justice of India, judges of integrity and international repute like Dr. Radha Binode Pal and other distinguished citizen.

The question of bringing the 'ashes' of Netaji does not arise.

Mothers, Sisters and Brothers

We appeal to you to call upon the Government of India to take up the issue, lest the Posterity shuld blame us all of our indifference towards the fate of India's Man of Destiny.

I earnestly pray that Pandit Jawaharlal Nehru should exert his influence to order a through investigation into the issues I have raised in the report and thus satisfy the people's demand to know the real truth following the disapperance of Netaji. Let me pray the voice of millions will break the barrier of the vicious circle and reach and move the conscience of the Prime Minister of India.

I swear, in the name of God, in the name of those Martyrs who have died for our freedom and in the name of the people of India that my findings are not based on any hypothesis or imagination. If called upon by the Investigation Commission, I and my colleagues will prove what I have siad. I take the full responsibility of this Report, including the charges I have made, As a soldier, I have worked with utmost disciplines, as a solider, I submit to-day the findings to the people of India without mincing matters and as a soldiers, I will stand on duty to defend what I have said. I swear I have no political motive.

Let India take Netaji's issue- the great National Issue concerning the Life and Mission of India's greatest Revolutionary.

Let the sons and daughters of Eternal Hind remember that the deathlessness of Her Soul lies in what we do, not in what we are.

JAI HIND

N.B.
Submitted at a Press Conference
on the 27th March, 1953.[2]

(Deb Nath Das)

2. It was after this campaign that the Government of India appointed an Enquiry Commission to report on the death of S.C. Bose under Shah Nawaz Khan, in 1954.

Appendix-IV

Memoirs of Col. Yamamoto[1]

I think Mr. Subhas Chandra Bose was one of the greatest statesman who ever lived in modern India.

I, led by fate, had close relations with him from the time of his residence in Germany upto 10 months before his tragic death at Taipeh in Formosa.

There have been quite a few articles in newspapers and magazines after the termination of the War on Mr. Subhas Chandra Bose and the movement for Indian Independence. Most of them however contained many inaccuracies.

I am afraid the people of the coming generation might put undeserved blame on a number of Japanese and Indians who sacrificed themselves for Mr. Bose and Independence, and thereby might cause a breach in Indo-Japanese good relations.

I, as one of the men who worked with him for the independence of India, think it is my duty, to say what I know were the real facts.

Soon after the termination of the war, I was asked by the investigating officers of both the American and the British Armies to give whatever detailed information I had concerning the Indian Independence movement.

After interrrogation of all my subordinate officers, the investigation in respect of me was the final one to close the case.

History of Freedom Movement Records N.A.I.

I revealed all the facts known to me and, at the same time, expressed my views.

"It was wrong to call our part in aiding India to attain her independence, as a conspiracy", I stated.

"There were no instructions nor any other papers from the General Headquarter indicating any conspiracy". "It was a cooperative action

1. History of Freedom Movement Papers. Col. Yamamato was in Berlin when he met Bose. At that time he was military attacke at Japanese Embassy.

taken by the provisional Indian government and the Japanese Army" I affirmed. What I wanted to say was that the Japanese Army never made use of India to win the war.

I can recall Mr. Bose making a speech with tears in his eyes, moved by the wholehearted support shown to him by the Japanese to win Indian Independence.

I thought it was Hikari-Kikan's duty (Espionage Counter Intelligence Corps) to materialise the wishes of the Japanese people then.

It was in the spring of 1940, I remember, that Mr. Bose fled from India to live in Germany.

In the early autumn, I met him for the first time. I was then serving at the Japanese Army Office at Berlin as a Colonel and received a telegram from Tokyo instructing me to report on Mr. Bose.

For sometime after Mr. Bose's arrival in Germany, the German Ministry of Foreign Affairs somewhat suspicious about his real intentions, but upon recognizing his worth, and bona fides, they treated him as a national guest.

Seeing that it was difficult to have an interview with him, I had him invited through Ambassador Oshima and Minister of Foreign Affairs, Ribbentroppe, to the official residence of the Japanese Embassy, where I met him for the first time.

Having gained the impression that he was a man of worth, I reported it to the G. H. Q., together with information about him gathered from German sources.

After that I had many chances to have talks with him when he visited Ambassador Oshima. There was about him no 'meanness ' such as one might come across in a political refugee, nor had he any sense of egoism, Simplicity marked his character. But he was a man of dignity. Any on who came in contact with him was impressed with his fierce fighting spirit for the cause of Indian Independence. Yet his speeches and actions were marked by the stamp of great gentlemanliness.

One evening when we had a conversation, he told me how he had got out of India and came to live in Germany.

It is as follows:

"I am confident that Indian Independence will be realised only at the cost of our blood."

And there is scarcely any hope of its realization through the creed of non-violence exhorted by Gandhi.

"Luckily I have had many supporters of my view among the younger group of the Congress."

When the European war, caused by the struggle between Germany and England, began I started to make public speeches to stir anti-British feelings and emphasisings the need to resort to force, being convinced that it was a great chance for the realisation of Indian Independence.

"I dared to do it though realizing that I would be put in prison for doing so. Sure enough, I was put in Prison not long after that."

"Now I was afraid that if I were to be kept in prison the best chance would be lost. Disguised as one who might belong to the scheduled castes, I travelled by the lowest class in the train and crossed the boundary , joining a caravan heading for Kabul. At the boundary pass, I slept among my co-travellers on the bare ground of the caravan inn."

"It was snowing heavily and was so cold that I had to take some liquor-up-to when I had never touched alcoholic drinks to keep myself warm and excape death from cold."

"At Kabul, receiving indications that the Afghan police authorities were after me, I hide myself amongst one caravan now and amongst another later."

"Finally, I came to think that it was useless to continue like that, Then, I visited firstly , the Japanese Legation, a fellow Asian legation, for help, where they politely refused to see me. The Minister was supposed to be absent then."

"Then I visited the German Legation in vain."

It was at the Italian Legation that the Minister condescended to see me and at once took steps to protect me. Both Italian and German ministers in cooperation made efforts to get a passport for me to go to Soviet Russia.

Knowing that the British police authorities had located me, I thought of entering Soviet Russia without a passport. Saying that they were able to get a passport for me at last.

"Thus I came to Germany through Soviet Russia".

After coming to Germany, Mr. Bose was broadcasting to India through German and Italian propaganda radio stations.

After the end of the year of his entering Germany, the Pacific war started.

And in the following year, 1942, it was reported that the Japanese army was going to start operations in Malaya.

Mr. Bose vigorously asked the Japanese GHQ, in Tokyo for his participation in the Malayan operations with the Japanese Army saying,

"Now that the whole situation has changed, I want to fight against the British army in Asia. I cannot expect to achieve any results through broadcasting from here (Europe)".

Thinking his desire as quite reasonable, I transmitted it to Tokyo Headquarters.

We waited and waited for an answer. And at last I got it, allowing him to come over to Japan if he could manage it. Meanwhile, he met with opposition from the German side against his going over to Japan.

The reason was because German officials of the Foreign Affairs Ministry made use of him as a "living encyclopaedia" on Indian Affairs.

Everytime they got questions concerning India, they went to him for his comments, clarifications and uptodate information. Inspite of their opposition he, according to Ambassador Oshima's advice, expressed to Fuhrer his desire to go over to Japan, "You can do as you wish to" said Fuhrer Hitler, accepting his proposal willingly.

"All that I want is the realization of India's Indpendence. So if you want to go over to Japan, I will do everything in my power to help you".

This reply from Hitler terminated all oppositions arising from officials of the Ministry of Foreign affairs.

It was about the end of 1942 that they reached an understanding about this.

Now, the only question left for him to solve was how to get to Japan. First of all, submarine was considered as the means of tranportation and he negotiated with the authorities concerned in Germany and Japan. As Germany and Japan too had no long-range submarines to spare for him, he came to think of the trip by air which then was generally considered as a dangerous one.

I was ordered to accompany him on his trip.

In 1942, an air trip to Asia was planned many times in Germany and Italy; each time failing to materialise. So great was his joy everytime he was notified of such a plan that he could not contain himself. And great was his disappointment when he was notified of its failure.

At the end of the year, I was ordered to return to Japan via Russia. On my leaving Germany I promised Mr. Bose that I would make efforts for him in Tokyo.

To my great joy, I was told by the Chief of Staff of GHQ that, Mr. Bose has decided to come over to Japan by submarine".

It was on the Java Island to the North of Sumatra that Mr. Bose, accompanied by his secretary *Hasan* put his first steps on Asia in the early part of May 1943.

Great efforts on the part of both Germany and Japan, and luck, made it possible.

Submarines of both the countries were scheduled to rendezvous at a certain point off the Southern Coast and they planned to use wireless signals just once to locate each other. Their plan proved to be a success and they could meet at sea. The sea was so rough then that Mr. Bose could not be trans-shipped. Drifting along for three days, they received a light signal from the German submarine saying that owing to fuel situation they were, to their great regret, compelled to tour back the next day.

Meanwhile, the sea had become a little calm. Taking this opportunity they joined the two ships with a rope and with the aid of this rope, Mr. Bose was transhipped successfully.

Returning home, I was relieved from the job in which I had participated till then and was transferred to the Hamamatsu Air Training School.

During the later part of March, I was ordered to take over the Iwakuro Kikan (Intelligence Organization). Soon afterwards, Mr. Bose arrived at the Savan Island. With him I flew to Tokyo and was lodged at the Imperial Hotel.

He expressed his view on Indian Independence so ardently that any person who interviewed him was impressed.

With all the interviews with press reporters, and all the busy life otherwise, he had to sit up late into the night.

He made it a point to make inspection tours of industrial plants, military barracks and schools when he had no interview to give.

It seemed to me that he was trying to improve himself every minute and fit himself for the independence and the reconstruction of India.

Of the Japanese food, he liked Tempura best.

The plan for the establishment of provisional Indian Government was proposed by him on the day previous to his scheduled departure for Tokyo.

To gauge the opinion on the part of Japan to his plan, he postponed his departurte for several days.

In the plan he had proposed to fight for Indian Independence with the help of Axis powers and army in accordance with international law.

This proposal met with no opposition from any of the authorities concerned, as they knew his worth well.

In July, he was fervently welcomed by Indians in Singapore. Upto then, Rash Behari Bose was the president of the Indian Independence League and with the speech of welcome for Mr. Subhas Chandra Bose the Presidentship was handed over to the latter.

The thing which most impressed me then was Mr. Rash Behari Bose's admirable attitude. All that occupied his mind always was Indian Independence and nothing else. He never thought of anything for his own interest. I wonder if it was due to his having accepted Japanese nationality that he was called, and regarded by some Indians as that cat's paw of Japan.

All his efforts and energy were directed towards bringing the members of the Indian Independence League together for the cause of *Indian Independence* and not for Japan. Regarding his talents and the hope pinned on him by the Indian people, they were not small in comparison with those attached to Mr. Chandra Bose; great were his efforts for the independence movement in spite of his old age and poor health. In appreciation of his services and merits, Mr. Chandra Bose recommended him as the Supreme Adviser to the League. Ever since his arrival in Singapore, Mr. Chandra Bose worked and worked like a fire ball.

He slept only 2 or 3 hours a day. With constant meetings with high ranking persons of the League and the Indian Army to keep himself up-to date as to how things were going on, and with the column of writing and broadcasting he performed and, the work of inspecting the Indian Army, making speeches for the members of the League in various places, etc he had scarcely any time for rest.

He was really a revolutionary statesman, but not much of an administrator nor a cold-blooded businessman.

On many occasions the members of the Hikari-Kikan were quite at a loss as how to meet his request, as it was often made all of a sudden, without giving any time for prior arrangements.

He believed in self-help and never asked unnecessarily for aid or advice. This was probably due to some extent to his having had no competent advisers but certainly due also to his own character.

His request to the Indians went always as follows:

"We Indians should be prepared to sacrifice as much as we can for the Independence of India. If Independence is gained without any effort on our part just like a X'mas present it has no worth. Youth should offer blood and one who is rich should offer his property". And he urged Japan saying, "I want Japan to accommodate us. We will repay her when independence is realized".

The amounts needed for the monthly expenditure of the provisonal Indian Government was supplied by me in cheque to him and I received I.O.U.S. with his signature in place of a receipt."

The expenditure of the Indian National Army was added as an other item to the amount specified as owing.

Mr. Bose once said "There is no way of paying Japanese who would be killed in action fighting with the Indian Army, but we will console their souls by enshrining and paying pension to their bereaved families".

I think he knew well that the Japanese Government had no intention of demanding payments for the aid given by them to the Indian Independence movement.

Still, I am sure, he would not be satisfied with receiving "charities". He had also his own reasons to be dissatisfied with Hikari-Kikan.

The first reason was because, I believe the Japanese Government did not exchange Ambassador with them when the Provisional Government was established despite the fact that the Japanese Government approved the Indian Government.

The reason on the part of the Japanese Government might have been that there was not much necessity for a diplomatic organization approach in the southern area under a military government scheme of things.

But they sent Ambassador Swada to the Burmese Government. So he might have felt it proper to expect an ambassador or a minister assigned to his government.

The Imphal operation was not staged as a means to invade India. Mr. Bose used to exhort ever since the day of his residence in Germany that when the Japanese staged any operation on India they should find their way into India first through Chittagong. Because in and around this district was the centre of the independence movement.

Only through the occupation of this district would the decline of the British influence be achieved.

But his plan was not adopted by the Japanese Army and Navy of as it was beyond their power to carry it out.

As far as I know, the Imphal operation was staged for the purpose of defending Burma.

The preparations were started during the autumn of 1944.

Then, he proposed:

(a) I want to have as many units of the Indian Army as possible sent to the front and have some front lines assigned to them.

(b) When Imphal is occupied, I want to have the occupation administration of the area commissioned to the Indian Provisional government. These two proposals were accepted by the Japanese Army of the Burma Area but it was not easy to have them materialise.

The first step of the operation was started with the army moving from Singapore to Burma.

As all the rail facilities were utilised for the transportation of ammunition to capacity, the army moved on foot.

Thus the Provisional Government moved to Rangoon in the early part of January 1944.

The biggest difficulty about the Imphal operation lay in supply at the front. The Indian army was assigned to various divisions of the Japanese army at the front and engaged in fighting as bravely and as well as we had expected.

Especially it was the case with the division led by Col. Kiani. But the Imphal operation ended in total failure on our part. The casualities on the Indian Army side were small in comparison to those on the side of the Japanese Army.

I think some of the reasons was that the Indian army retreated several; days earlier than the Japanese Army—under the advice of the Japanese Army.

Their well maintained military discipline was another reason. From the very outset of the operations, Mr, Bose insisted on sending his provisional government as far to the front as possible. As we suffered from inadequate supply of food, fuel and insufficient transporatation facilities, we could not afford to receive a large number of guests at the front.

So Lt. Gen. Isoda, Mr. Bose and his military advisers went to the front and we had the rest of the government staff awaiting on the way.

Soon after the termination of the Imphal operations, I had a talk on the outcome of the war with him.

"The enemy front at Burma became as tough as an iron wall". I said, "I think teh old military saying that the gateway to the invasion of India was still at its western barrier" still proved a truth.

I sound his opinion.

"Judging from the information so far obtained from Russia and knowing that their interest in India was rising" I ventured to ask him and "what do you think about seeking Soviet Russia's assistance". After a while he said, "As I have always told you I never refuse to get assistance from any countries as far as they are against Britain".

"And I am sure that India will not turn 'red' if they have friendly relations with Russia", he declared.

Appendix-V

Note by Office of Strategic Service on the Rise and Fall of the Indian National Army

The virtual disintegration of Subhas Chandra Bose's Indian National Army (I.N.A.) in the general Japanese retreat from Burma marks the latest failure in Japan's attempt to exploit Indian Nationalism in her war against the Allies in Southeast Asia. In the last few months large scale surrenders, revealing a radical decline in morale have rapidly reduced I.N.A. ranks. Remaining troops have presumably retreated with the Japanese into the Shan moutains towards Thailand. Bose the I.N.A. Commander in Chief, reportedly has fled to Bangkok, from where is allegedly reorienting his propaganda to longer range objectives.

The I.N.A. was established as the military arm of the Indian Independence League which the invading Japanese had organised throughout Southeast Asia in 1942. Bose's troops, operating in conjuction with a Japanese drive into India, were intended to engage in military infiltration, espionage, and anti-British propaganda urging the Indians to work for a Japanese victory in the interests of their own future independence. Japanese anti-British propagands,with its slogan of "Asia for the Asiatics", and the policy of singling out the Indian communities for especially favourable treatment undoubtedly carried a certain appeal to Indians in Southeast Asia. Furthermore, ever since the Russo-Japanese War of 1904, Japan has enjoyed increasing prestige as the one Asiatic nation able to establish herself as an independent equal of the Western powers. In the early years of the Pacific War, Japan's position in Asia was stronger than ever, and Great Britain's defeat in India may have seemed a matter of months. Expediency appeared to many Indians to require cooperation with the Japanese.

In Burma the Indian Independence League had been concerned largely with protecting the Indian minority from Burmese hostility until

1. O.S.S. Papers. No. 31428. U.S. National Armies Marlaglaw, U.S.A.

Bose arrived in 1943 to assume its leadership and to organise the "Indian National Army". In early 1944 Burma became the headquarters of the whole movement when the I.N.A. First Division was moved up from Malaya to aid the Japanese in the Manipur campaign. Bose an energetic and persuasive speaker, was probably most popular with those Indians who had some previous contact with political agitation or who came from his own province of Bengal. There Bose had won his largest following as one of the most turbulent and conspicuous of the nationalist leaders in India. In 1938 he served as President of the All-India Congress but, when re-elected in 1939, was virtually forced to resign after a clash with Gandhi and Nehru,who both distrusted his extremism. Subsequently, Bose organised his followers into the left-wing "Forward Bloc", which functioned as an opposition party to the Congress. Already at that time Nehru recorded his fear that Bose was turning fascist. In 1941 after another arrest, Bose escaped from India and was next heard from broadcasting for the Axis from Berlin.

In Bose the Japanese found an excellent potential puppet. He had frequently been imprisoned by the British in India, and his hatred for Great Britian was violent. He had long arged that there was no hope in the policy of compromise with the British which Gandhi was following,and that Indian Independence could be achieved only be force. Until June 1943 the Japanese used another man named Bose, Rash Behari Bose, to spread the idea of winning Indian freedom with Japanese aid. Rash Behari Bose had fled to Japan after having directed terrorist activities in the Punjab during the last war. In 1931 he organised the first Indian Independence League in Japan, which announced as its objective "the attainment of independence of India by all possible means." Until Subhas Chandra Bose arrived in Japan from Germany, the elder Bose was reorganised leader of the network of Indian Independence Leagues throughout Southeast Asia. When in June 1943 the younger Bose took over completely, Rash Behari apparently retired to Japan, and has since died.

Burma succeeded Malaya as the suitable headquarters for the Japanese sponsored Indian Independence movement not only because it was to be the staging area for the military attack on India but also because after Malaya it provided the largest Indian population outside of Indian upon which to draw for membership. At the time of the Japanese invasion over a half-million Indians remained in Burma. By far the greater part of them belonged to the laboring class, but a large number of Indian merchants also had heavy financial stakes in the country, accumulated through money-lending the rice-selling. Although many of these merchants fled to India in 1942, some left representatives to protect their interests and provided Bose's movement with a source of funds. The Japanese, contrary to Burmese desires, allowed the Indian community to retain control over all Indian-held property in Burma.

Indians in Burma have long been conscious of being a minority and are jealous of their status as a separate political group. The Burmese are openly hostile toward the Indians, considering them a meance to Burma's national and economic life. As early as 1922, Indians had formed a separate electrorate which, under British auspices, was incorporated into the present constitution in the face of Burma, opposition. Most of the educated Indians in Burma sympathized with the aims of the Indian National Congress, and although the imported laborers who formed the bulk of the Indian population were politically inactive before the war, Indian National Congress propaganda may have influenced them to a certain extent before they left India.

During early 1942 the Japanese conducted a campaign to persuade Indian prisoners of war in Hong Kong, Shanghai, and Singapore that they should fight along with the Japanese for the "liberation" of India. In June the Japanese sponsored a conference in Bangkok at which the I.N.A. war formally launched, and by November the Japanese claimed that the strength of the force was 16,000 troops. Disagreement between its first leader and Rash Behari Bose ended in the temporary disbandment of the I.N.A. In June 1943 Subhas Chandra Bosc arrived from Germany and, besides taking over the Indian Independence League and the new I.N.A. as commander in Chief, became President, Premier, Foreign Secretary, and Defence Minister of the "Provisional Government of Free India". His extensive propaganda and recruiting campaign for the I.N.A. was at first conducted among Indian prisoners of War, of which about 70,000 were in Japanese hands, and among Indian rubber plantation labour in Malaya In February 1944 Bose moved I.N.A. headquarters to Rangoon and continued his recruiting from there.

Several factors aided Bose in his work. At that time British prestige was at lowest ebb. Enlistment afforded escape from POW camps, where conditions were bad, and a possible opportunity for Indians to return to their homes and families. Bose's propaganda spoke of the "the sacred soil of the mother land" and of raising the flag of free India in ever city,. town and village in India. Many Indians doubtless incerely believed that by joining the I.N.A. they would participate in achieving real Indian Independence. Furthermore, they were told that they would be welcomed by the British Indian Army, which would refuse to fight them, and that all India would rise to welcome them. Thus the general morals of the I.N.A. troops before their first engagement in Arakan was fairly high, and Japanese propaganda was able to aim at the British-Indian Army, urging desertion and telling of comrades-in-arms training outside of India to liberate their native country.

In the military engagements that followed, I.N.A. regiments were intended primarily to confuse British-Indian troops in the combat areas by shouting orders in Urdu or English, to encourage deserters, and to take full charge of fall British-Indian prisoners in order to persuade them to chage loyalties and join the I.N.A. cause. They were also used in forward reconnaissance and as screens for Japanese troops, often regarded with suspicion by the Japanese, I.N.A. forces were almost never employed as regular fighting units, and were assigned inferior equipment.

The first encounter between British-Indian and I.N.A. troops, a surprise engagement, took place a few miles north of Buthiadaung in Arakan. INA units were successful through trickery and civilian disguise in overpowering British Indian sentires and enabling the Japanese to capture a divisional headquarters. In the next encounter, however, an I.N.A. sikh, who had been encouraged to leave cover shouting slogans and invitations to desert, was riddled with British-Indian bullets.

Optimism aroused among the puppet Indians by initial military successes quickly disappeared. The ineffectiveness of the I.N.A. was clearly demonstrated at the time of the fathest Japanese advance into India in the spring of 1944. Japanese expectations had obviously been high and the British themselves had been uncertain how much confusion Bose's Indians could cause. Buit actual encounters proved that British-Indian troops would fight the enemy whether he was Indian or Japanese.

Three I.N.A. regiments, their morale evidently high, crossed the Chindwin in March 1944 for the Manipur Campaign and the much-heralded "March of Delhi". Indians trained as occupation officers for the "Indian Provisional Government" actually arrived in Tamu (on the frontier below Imphal) but were soon forced to retreat. Although the Japanese penetrated into India almost as far as Imphal, by June they were pushed back into Burma. I.N.A. troops withdrew in very poor condition. Disease swept their ranks, they were inadequately supplied and their morale fell sharply. Japanese officers in charge of I.N.A. intelligence operations in Manipur complained that while Japanese were being killed, I.N.A. men were no longer willing to die "for the cause of India's freedom".

Japanese failure in the Manipur campaign seriously impaired the strength of Bose's "Provisional Government"and dashed the Japanese hope for widespread local revolts against the British resulting from an invasion of Indian soil. Despite military reverses, however, Bose continued his propaganda. When the Gandhi-Jinnah meeting in the summer of 1944 was first scheduled , Bose urged Indians not to believe that a settlement between the Congress and the Muslim League could lead to independence. The failure of Gandhi and Jinnah to break the Indian political deadlock by a reconciliation between nationalist elements and compromise with the British restored some hopefulness to the Japanese-sponsored "Free India" movement, and in the fall of 1944 Bose talked of engaging the I.N.A. with Japanese aid in a new campaign to win Indian Independence by force.

In November 1944, in line with renewed Japanese emphasis on the Greater East Asia program, Bose visited Tokyo to establish closer relations between his "Provisional Government of India" and Japan. An exchange of diplomatic representatives was arranged in the hope of increasing collaboration and improving occasionally strained relations. In the past, members of the I.N.A. and even Bose himself had difficulties with Japanese military men in the field. Another troublesome problem had been the Burman puppet government's desire to liquidate all Indian claims to property in Burma. Also there had been conflict between Bose and the Japanese concerning propaganda directives beamed to India. With his own dilomatic representative in Tokyo, Bose may have hoped to have his India policies more effectively presented. At the same time, Tokyo's warm and impressive welcome of Bose indicated that the Japanese still considered his role important to their war effort.

Although in the 1944-45 winter operations in Burma, isolated I.N.A. units belonging to the fresh and untried second division are said to have fought with determination, the I.N.A. as a whole continued to be an ineffective device for Japanese exploitation of anti-British sentiment in India. I.N.A. strength in March 1945 was estimated to have declined to about 35,000. Since February, when at Bose's request the I.N.A. was given a defensive position on the Irrawaddy, its troops, in units varying in strength from 200 to 3000, have surrendred on a large scale.

Index

H

I

R

T

U

V

W

Y

Z

INDIAN NATIONAL ARMY
A Documentary Study

INDIAN NATIONAL ARMY

A Documentary Study

(In 5 Volumes)

Volume-III

(1943-1944)

T. R. SAREEN

GYAN PUBLISHING HOUSE

NEW DELHI - 110002

INDIAN NATIONAL ARMY—A DOCUMENTARY STUDY

Rs. 4,500/-

ISBN : 81-212-0833-5 (Set)
ISBN : 81-212-0846-7 (Vol-3)

Published in 2004 in India by
Gyan Publishing House
5, Ansari Road, Daryaganj
New Delhi-110 002
Phones-23282060, 23261060, Fax-23285914
Email : gyanbook@vsnl.com
Visit our Website at : http//www.gyanbooks.com

Lasertype Setting by: Tact Computer Graphics, Delhi
Printed at: Chawla Offset Press, Delhi

To
Dr. Lata Singh

List of Documents

Introduction

The documents in this volume deal with the most momentous events in the history of the Indian National Army (I.N.A.). They cover mainly 1944 when I.N.A. alongwith the Japanese forces crossed the Indo-Burma border and carried the armed struggle on the Indian soil.

They came very close to success. The Japanese—I.N.A. offensive consisted of two campaigns in Arakan and Imphal. Two I.N.A. battlions and two Bahadue units joined the Japanese forces from the very beginning of the campaign, two other regiments of No. 1. I.N.A. Division under Col. M.Z. Kiani joined them in April and May, 1944. Between February and May, I.N.A. fought on the Indian side in the Arakan Secter and in Imphal. The inital success in the Arakan caused much enthusiasm and Bose as the Supreme Commander of the I.N.A. in a special order of the day referred to the glorious and brilliant actions of the brave forces of "Azad Hind Fauj" (Doc. 8)

This was immediately followed by a proclamation urging the Indian people to cooperate with the I.N.A. and its allied forces for ousting the British from India (Doc. 16)

The news of the welcome by the people of Manipur and their cooperation with the I.N.A. and Japanese were not mere propaganda (Doc. 19). These were supported by the reports from the Political Agent Manipur and how the people were punished for their cooperation. The prospects of initial success made it necessary for the Provisional Government of Azad Hind to prepare for taking over the civil administration of the liberated territories. A party of civil administrators trained also in the military discipline called the Azad Hind Dal was organized. A detailed scheme was drawn up for the civil administration of the liberated areas and even proclamation was issued informing the local people about the Provisional Government of Azad Hind. They were requested to cooperate with it. Even the Japanese Prime Minister gave full promise and declared in the

Diet that the liberated areas would be placed under the Azad Hind Government (Doc. 17, 31).

British were fully aware of the activities of the I.N.A. as is clear from the notes prepared by the military intelligence. (Doc. 12, 25). On the basis of the information received from their agents, counter-measures were taken to frustrate the designs of I.N.A. These measures included strict secrecy about the I.N.A., and creation of special "Josh group". In all the official documents. I.N.A. was labelled as J.I.F. (Japanese Inspired Force). Safe conduct passes were issued to those, who were still loyal to the British army (Doc. 27.)

By press statements, interviews, promotion and even special orders of the Day, Bose kept up the spirit of the I.N.A. very high. But there were number of administrative difficulties, which the I.N.A. had to face while fighting in Imphal and Kohima sectors. These were pointed by Col. M.Z. Kiani. Steps were taken to solve these difficulties, to some extent (Docs. 45, 46)

The failure of the Imphal campaign was a very significant event for the I.N.A. It definitely minimised the chances of success for the I.N.A. to liberate India.

Bose tried to thwart British propaganda and appealed to Indian leaders and people regarding the sincerity of Japan and the need for outside help for the liberation of India (Doc. 38)

Bose went to Tokyo for exchanging views with the new Japanese Premier. His speeches and statements during the time show as to how his mind was working about the liberation of India. His speech at the Tokyo Imperial University is very important to understand his views about the fundamental problems of India.7

Bose was also aware of the fact that the congress leaders in India had written off chances of a Japanese victory after the failure of the Imphal campaign and were ready to come to terms with the British. Bose was against the partition of India and gave a warning in his broadcasts that the Indain leaders should not play into the hands of Britain.

The Appendices dealing with this period throw a good deal of light on the activities of the I.N.A. and the Provisional Government of Azad Hind. Especially important are some notes prepared by the British Military Intelligence on the training schools run by the I.N.A. British had full details about the despatch of I.N.A. agents in India and could take prompt action against them. They were aware of the working of the Hikari Kikan, the Japanese liaison agency dealing with the Indian National Army. From these documents, it is evident that the British had prior knowledge about the I.N.A.'s activities and was prepared to take adequate action on the basis of the information.

The documents are arranged in the chronological order and have been drawn from various archival repositories in India and abroad. I am specially thankful to Netaji Subas Chander Bose Academy. Japan for their help and providing me with the photocopies of documents included in this volume

T.R. Sareen

1

British Military Intelligence on Spy Training Schools of I.N.A[1].

2 January, 1944

Swaraj Young Men's Training Institute

1. This was last referred to in W.I.S. No. 95 dated 13 Aug 43, part III, para 12 (e). There is very little to add to what has already been published. The first course known to have taken place at this Institute started in Nov. 43 and consisted of some 60 students. These were disbanded and returned to their homes on the arrival of a batch of some 40 (not 96 as previously reported) students for the second course, which opened about the middle of Dec 45. Training continued at this Institute, on the lines already ascribed, until March or April 43, when the Institute was finally closed down and students who completed the course were issued with certificates. They were returned to their homes and told to be prepared to be called up at any moment. It appears that this Institute was intended chiefly to serve as a holding centre, for some of its students who were later identified at the Swaraj Young Men's Training Institute at Kanbe and Thingangyun. The need for such holding centres probably disappeared when intelligence agents under training were concentrated at Kanbe in the middle of 1943.

Biren Roy's School, Rangoon

2. This school was in the Neogy Building, Sparke Street, Rangoon, and was run by Biren Roy, an ex-detenu of Dacca and an important I.I.L.

1. British had an elobuate system of getting information from their agents. Number of Notes on the Indian National Army and its activites were prepared and circulated in weekly intelligence summary. The name I.N.A. was hardly used in these notes. I.N.A. was described as J.I.F.C. (Japanese Inspried Fifth Columnist) F. No. 601/7378/H.S. Ministry of Defence.

organizer in Burma, sometimes between the end of Aug. and Dec. 42. Roy and his assistants recruited about 32 students, all Bengalis, in various parts of Burma. There appears to have been no regular, staff apart from Roy himself, but N.K. Banerji of the Thingangyun Institute and some of the senior students delivered lectures.

3. **Training.** Instruction in the use of fire-arms was given on the roof of the building. Apart from this there was no regular syllabus and "training" was confined to informal discussions between Roy and the students on the aims and objects of the I.I.L. The main theme of these discussions was anti-British and pro-Japanese propaganda and the "liberating" role of the I.N.A. Students were strictly confined to the building and their presence there was kept secret.

4. **Instructions.** Biren Roy's professed object was to train students to cause internal chaos in India during the advance of forces. True to the Bengali terrorist tradition, N.K. Banerji instructed the students to resort to "money-actions" when in need of funds, to sabotage telegraph wires and railway lines, students were sent off for infiltration purposes in India with revolvers and small amount of cash in (forged) Indian currency notes. They were told that their arms were to be used in self defence if attempts were made to arrest them, and if arrested they were to commit suicide in order to avoid disclosing their mission.

5. **Summary.** The school is now defunct. It appears to have been more of an informal secret group rather than regular training centre, the majority of its members being diseffected Bengalis who were willing to engage in terrorist activities under Biren Roy's leadership.

Baba Amar Singh's School, Rangoon and Mawlaik

6. This was last referred to in G.H.G.W.I.S. No. 93 dated 13 Aug. 43, part III, para 12(j). Baba Amar Singh, the old Ghadrite conspirator whom the Japanese took to Burma form Bangkok to organise intelligence activities, started a training school for about 25 students in Feb. or Mar. 43. His staff seens to have consisted only of 2 "chief recruiters" named Chanda Singh and Ram Lekha. The agents he selected were of a poor type and were given little useful training. There appears to have been no particular syllabus, emphasis being laid on propaganda. Later the school was moved to Mawlaik, and there

some elementary training in bomb-making and the use of small arms was given.

7. Full details of the instructions given to agents sent from this school are not yet available, but a number of them were dispatched to Manipur State to contact the ex-Royal family on behalf of the Japanese and to engage in sabotage, espionage and propaganda against Indian troops and Government employees. As far as is known on success attended these efforts, all the agents who were sent out being arrested before they had approached their tasks. One feature peculiar to Baba Amar Singh's school is that the secret parties whom he had sent out were provided with guides, residents of the Indo-Burman frontier area, who had been through the same training as the agents themselves. Some of these guides were intended to provide the means of communication between the agents and the enemy in Burma.

2

Bose's Broadcast from Burma after Visiting Andamans, Announces the Appointment of A.D. Loganandan as Chief Commissioner of the Islands[1]

6 January, 1944

"FRIENDS! I shall now give you a very interesting peace of news-namely, that before I arrived in Burma, I was able to visit the Andaman and Nicobar Islands. You will remember that on the 6th November, 1943 at the assembly of Greater East Asiatic Nations held in Tokyo, His Excellency Premier General Hideki Tojo made an historic declaration to the effect that the Government of Nippon would transfer the Adaman and Nicobar Islands of the Provisional Government of Azad Hind. Following that declaration I had conversations with the Nippon Authorities on the subject both in Tokyo and in Shonan. After these conversations, the Nippon Authorities arranged for my visit to these islands in which I was accompanied by members of my Government and of my personal staff I have now come here after completing that trip. The object of the journey to the Andaman Islands was to discuss with the local Nippon authorities the preparatory measures necessary for effecting the transfer of the Andaman and Nicobar Islands to the Provisional Government of Azad Hind. In pursuance of the discussions that were held there, I can now announce that I have appointed Lt.-Col A.D. Loganadan, a high ranking officer of the Indian National Army, as the Chief Commissioner of the Andaman and Nicobar Islands. As soon as Transport arrangements are made, the newly appointed Chief Commissioner will proceed to the above Islands with his staff.

"During this visit, I and the other members of my party had the unique experience of our lives when we stood on the soil of free India for the first time. It was an unforgettable event for us to see our tri-colour

1. *Greater Asia*, 8 Jan, 1944. A.D. Longananden was appointed as Chief Commissioner of Andamans and Nicobar Islands. Which Japanese had accopied in 1942. Logananden was in Andamans from Feburary 1944 till September, 1944. After his departure Alvi acted as Chief Commissioner till July 1945.

national flag fluttering in the air, over the former British Chief Commissioner's residence in Rose Island. During our stay there, we occupied the former British Chief Commissioner's residence and we wonder all the time how the wheels.

History was now moving in India's favour. The sight of our national flag flying over the Chief Commissioner's house made all of us think of the day when the same flag would be hoisted over the Viceroy's house in New Delhi.

"My countrymen will remember that since August last year, I have been giving expression to my hope and belief that before the end of 1943 we would stand on the soil of Free India. That this dream has actually been fulfilled before the 31st December 1943 has given me the greatest happiness.

"While we were in the Andaman islands, we visited the notorious Cellour Jail in Port Blair and paid silent homage to those patriotic countrymen of ours who suffered indescribable persecution and torture in the past and some of whom even laid down their lives as victims of British tyranny and brutality. We were informed by the Superintendent of the Jail that the last batch of political prisoners consisting of about 200 court-martial prisoners were transported back to India along with some British officials shortly before the Nipponese occupation of the Islands.

"During my visit to the Island I was able to study conditions there and to get acquainted with the local population. I found that they were all happy that the British had been expelled from the place and their joy knew no bounds when they heard the declaration of the Government of Nippon regarding the Islands in November last. A strong national awakening was visible among the people and they were determined to become good and patriotic citizens in future.

"In the mass meeting that was held I told the people that since they had suffered so much at the lands of British Imperialism in the past, it has pleased Providence to give them the first taste of freedom and happiness. Consecuently, they should now forget their unhappy past, become worthy citizens of Free India and work hard in order to create a bright and happy future for themselves.

"From what I have seen of the Islands and of their natural resources, I am confident that as a part of Free India the Andaman and Nicobar Islands will become a place fit for free, cultured and progressive men and women to live in.

"I am sure that if, in future, the British attempted to reconquer the Islands, they will meet with the fierce and stub-born oppositiion of the people there."

3

Japanese Orders for the Treatment of I.N.A. and Handling of Indian Army Soldiers, who would Join them (Extract)

1 February, 1944

1. Policy—When handling Indian prisoners the object is to reinforce the Indian National Army and thus facilitate Japanese Army operations. Prisoners are to be won over to allegiance to the Imperial Army by concrete evidence of the sincerity of our intentions. Hence, except for those who are hostile to us, no Indian prisoner will be killed or treated harshly for any reason.

2. Procedure in handling—Indian prisoners captured at the front (including deserters) are to be separated from white prisoners and treated warmly. They are to be won over to cooperation with our army by kindling their sentiments for independence from GREAT BRITAIN and resistance against GREAT BRITAIN and the UNITED STATES.

Indian prisoners are classified into three categories based upon their military qualifications and their attitude regarding independence from GREAT BRITAIN. Methods of handling should be determined by these classifications:

Class A—	Men strongly anti-British and favouring independence, who are fit for fighting, are immediately inducted into the Indian National Army.
Class B—	Men not physically equal to those in class A, but fit for work, are inductedd into labour units.

1. South East Asia Translation and interrogation Bulletine No 23. A memographed copy of these orders was captured by the British. Though undated, these must have been issued before the I.N.A. and Japanese forces crossed the Indo-Burma, border" in Feb 1944

Class C— Men who are anti-Japanese and pro-British, or unfit for either combat or labour, are handled according to the general regulations for treatment of prisoners.

It is a basic rule that the above classification is to be done by the Replacement Department of the Indian National Army (INDOKOKUMINGUN HOJUBU); under the direction of branches of the HIKARI Agency (HIKARI KIKAN BUNHAKIKAN) as directed by Army supreme command. (TN: the HIKARI KIKAN is the special service organization of the Japanese Army in charge of espionage, propaganda and subversion in BURMA, FRENCH INDO-CHINA, PHILIPPINES and DUTCH FAST INDIES. It is now know as "Southern Area Guerrilla Unit" (NAMPO YOUGEKITAI).

The presence of subversive elements among Indian prisoners should be anticipated. Each unit will take all measures for its own security. Such prisoners should not be killed indiscriminately, but branches of the Mieari Agency or the replacement Department of the Indian National Army will take appropriate measures for their elimination.

The HIKARI Agency is to be given preference in the selection of personnel for agents.

As regards rations, Indian prisoners of even class C should be treated much better than white prisoners.

3. Reports—Reports on type and number of prisoners taken are required.

Supplement 2 Handling the ordinary Indian in the Theater of Operations.

1. Policy—The policy in treatment of the ordinary Indian in the theater of operations is to make him respect and obey the Imperial Army and cooperate in operations against INDIA.

2. Procedure in Handling—Prohibitions and precautions to be observed.

3. Reports—Reports on Indian willingness to cooperate in the theater of operations are required.

Supplement 3 Handling the Indian National Army.

1. Policy—The Indian National Army is to be inculcated with complete faith in and respect and friendliness for the Imperial

Army, and then allowed to cooperate in military activities. To this end its ambition for independence end its hostility to GREAT BRITAIN is to be encouraged, and its officers imbued with enthusiasm. The mistake must not be made at any time of adopting a superior or arrogent attitude toward it, nor will there be harsh treatment or insults in word or action.

2. Procedure—The Indian National Army will be treated as the military force of an allied nation, since it is under the jurisdiction of the Free India Provisional Government and is cooperating with the Imperial Army against a common enemy. The right of command of the Indian National Army is to be respected. When it is attached to the Japanese Army, the command will be given to a Japanese officer of a rank lower than the former Indian National Army officer, and care will be taken to preserve the original organization. Furthermore, the execution of command will be carried as much as possible through the Hikari Agency. The key to the employment of the Indian National Army is to keep firm control of its highest commander, to permit him to exert command, while retaining full responsibility ourselves, and to give him a clear and concrete mission.

   Care will be taken to see that the Indian National Army carries out its own counter espionage measures. Rewards and punishments for the Indian National Army will be promulgated by the Area Army, to whom the units will submit cases.

3. Reports—Reports are required on all aspects of the situation.

Supplement 4 Handling Indian (Soldier) Agents (INDIAN HEIKOSAKUIN)

1. "Special activities" (TOKUMU KOSAKU) (TN: espionage, propaganda; and subversive activities) against INDIA will be perfected if we develop in the Indian (soldier) agents a spirit of sacrifice for the nation which will enable them to infiltrate boldly into enemy territory and perform "special activities", and if we do everything possible to facilitate their work.

2. Procedure—Care should be taken against given away agents, indentities, and againsts maltreating or killing them on their return from enemy territory through failure to indentify them.

To prevent their revealing information to the enemy if captured or being used by the enemy against us, they will not be given information about our own troops or the Indian National Army.

Supplement— Tables of rations and clothing issued to officers and men of the Indian National Army.

Supplement— Method of Identifying the Indian National Army in Forward Areas.

1. Method of Identification during Infiltration of Enemy Territory— Until crossing the most advanced front line of our forces, an identity certificate, issued by units concerned or by the HIKARI Agency, will be carried. This will be destroyed upon crossing that line.

2. Method of Indentification at Time of Return from Enemy Territory—All persons returning from enemy territory will establish their identity by repeating "HIKARI KIKAN" (IN;HIKARI Agency) and "INDOKOKUMINGUN" (TN: Indian National Army), and by showing the "T". symbol sewn somewhere on their garments. Persons in enemy territory, such as those who, even though they are not in the Indian National Army, have received the necessary certification from the Indian National Army which has infiltrated into the area, will follow the above method of ilndetification for liaison with the Japanese Army. However, these will not show a "T" symbol. Persons returning from anemy torritory will not be harmed, but will be turned over to an official of the HIKARI Agency.

Notes—Persons wearing the uniform of the Indian National Army will not carry indentity certificates.

4

Announcement about the Advance of I.N.A. and Japanese Forces Towards Arakan[1]

7 February, 1944

The Spokesmen of the Nippon Army in the Burma sector declared a second "Tragedy of Arakan" is what lies ahead of enemy forces as a result of our new operations in the Burma-India sector launched since last Friday.

He said the present operations are featured by active participation by troops of the Indian National Army, who with their Nippon comrades-in-arms are surging ahead, with the capture of Chittagong, enemy stronghold in Bengal, as the first objective of their historic advance into Indian territory.

The Spokeman recalled that all the enemy's attempts to recapture Burma have ended in miserable failure involving heavy losses to the enemy. He pointed out that the enemy's counter offensive aimed at the recapture of Burma last spring met with disaster at the hands of our forces, resulting in what is known as "The Tragedy to Arakan".

He added that the enemy High Command made another unsuccessful attempt last Autumn to invade northern Burma from the upper reaches of the Salween River.

He pointed out that the enemy sustained crushing defeats on this occasion, after which enemy activities in this sector had been confined to defence of its positions on the eastern bank of the Salween River.

The Spokesman recalled in this connection that Chen Cheng. Commander of the Chungking forces in the Burma sector, tendered his resignation to Chiang Kaishek in protest against the Anglo-American High Command's attempt to subjugate Chungking troops following their defeat at the hands of our forces.

He futher recalled that the enemy High Command, since it was reorganized under Mountbatten, were launching yet another counter-

1. *The Syonan Shimbun 8 Feb. 1944*. This paper was started by the Japanese after occupation of Singapore.

offensive campaign against Buthidaung with the main force of the British 14th Army supported to tank and heavy artillery corps.

The spokeman pointed out that the enemy's much publicized "recapture of Maungdaw" followed only after our strategical withdrawal from that point which by that time had lost its strategic importance. He added how the enemy is capitalizing on this "recapture of Maungdaw" can be seen from being from the fact that Churchill wired Mounthatten congratulation on that intrinsically insignificant military development.

The spokesman declared that our High Command in the meantime, completed all necessary preparations for the next offensive in close concert with the Indian National Army who had been itching for action to accelerate the advent of the day of complete liberation of their motherland from Anglo-American oppression.

The fact that enemy forces were able to make an advance was the result of part of our strategy to draw the enemy forces close to our positions before dealing a decisive blow to the enemy. He declared last Friday marked the day when our forces, hand in hand with our Indian comrades-in-arms, started on their long awaited march towards India.

He revealed that this onslaught is now being pushed ahead most satisfactorily with our forces surging ahead towards the enemy base of operations in this sector, after, inflicting heavy blows on enemy units. The Spokesman pointed with complete satisfaction to the successful progress being made by units of the Indian National Army, whose first objective in the current operation is believed to be the capture of Chittagong, enemy stronghold in Bengal.

He declared that the hour of the second "tragedy of Arakan" is thus fast approaching the enemy forces, which are bound to perish in a watery grave in the Bay of Bengal. He disclosed that our force simultaneously succeeded in silencing Chungking troops which have been making, nuisance moves in the Hukawng sector in northern Burma. He declared the enemy's much vaunted attempt to reopen the Burma route to aid the isolated Chungking regime will also end in a mere propaganda campaign.

Concluding, the Spokesmen declared that the Nippon Army in the Burma sector launching the present offensive is directing its attack right at Mounthatten's headquarters, with the flag of Free India already flying over Arakan.

5

Bose Statement on the I.N.A. Penetration in Arakan to Crush the British Forces[1]

7 February, 1944

THE GREAT battle which has just begun on the Arakan front for the destruction of the Anglo American forces of aggression and the liberation of India's four hundred million people heralds the decisive phase of the Dai Toa Senso (Greater East Asia War) for the achievement of the ideal of Asia for Asiatics. In the initial stage of the war, the invincible forces of Imperial Nippon dealt the death blow on the Anglo-American-Dutch imperialism in Toa (East Asia), leading of Asiatic people. And now the campaign has started for the crowning achievement of Nippon's noble mission.

It is hardly forty-eight hours since the great news of the beginning of the offensive on the Arakan front was announced by the Imperial Headquarters: But the dispatches that have come in during these hours are extremely gratifying indeed. The joint operations launched by the Imperial Nippon Army and the Indian National Army, have been progressing most favourably. The allied forces of Nippon and Free India have already pierced the enemy lines at several points. The British forces have been pushed back all along the fighting line and their retreat is fast developing into a rout. Judging from these frontline despatches, it is apparent that the British forces are panic-stricken over the second "Arakan Disaster" that now threatens them.

The Indian campaign, now in full swing, is of tremendous significance, not only in the light of the far reaching repercussions it will have on the entire trend of the Dai Toa Senso, but also in view of the active participation in this campaign by the Indian National Army organised in Toa under the supreme command of Subhas Chandra Bose.

1. *The Syonan Shimbun 9 Feb. 1944.*

This Army of patriotic Indians in Toa (East Asia) appropriately called the Azad Hind Fauj (India's Army of Liberation)—is at the forefront of the battle, fighting shoulder to shoulder with the Imperial Nippon Army: and the presence of the Indian Army at the battle front is bound to produce the most heartening effect on the people in India, soldiers and civilians alike, Nippon and Indian forces, waging the common war, for the common cause, against the common enemy and for the common goal, have gone into action on the Arakan front, as true comrades-at-arms, grimly resolved to share the hardship and sacrifices of war and the joy of victory as well.

It is this salient aspect of the Arakan campaign which makes it the most outstanding demonstration of Asiatic unity and resolve in the war to crush the Anglo-Americans and to establish an Asia for Asiatics.

Nationalist Indians, in India and abroad, have been convinced that they must take up arms and fight the British if ever their goal of national independence is to be achieved. Free Indians in Toa, under the inspiring leadership of Subhas Chandra Bose have therefore been organising themselves for the battle against the Anglo American enemies in India; and Nippon in pursuance of her policy, has pledged all-out aid to the Indian people in their efforts to win their freedom. Nippon's war aim is a free Asia but there can be no Free Asia without Free India. The expulsion of the Anglo-American forces of aggression, now entrenched in india, is a vital necessity not only for the liberation of India, but also for the safety of Toa and the victory of Nippon and her allies in Toa.

Such is the ideal that has inspired the combined Indian and Nippon forces to battle on the Indo-Burma frontier. It is the beginning of the March to Delhi by the Indian National Army and its Nippon allies. And the outcome of this historic campaign has been best expressed by Subhas Chandra Bose, Head of the provisional Government of Free India, in the following terms:-

"We have full confidence in our own strength. We have complete faith in our allies; and we have unlimited optimism regarding national victory. We shall go on toiling and fighting till our flag is fluttering in India's metropolis."

6

Bose Statement Countering British Propaganda Against I.N.A.[1]

8 February, 1944

The following cable was sent by Netaji Subhas Chandra Bose, Supreme Commander, Indian National Army, to the officer commanding, Indian National Army, Arakan front under date February 8.

All officers and men of the Indian National Army and myself feel happy and proud over the achievements of our troops at the Arakan Front under your command. I am confident that all Freedom-Loving Indians in the world share our feelings. Please accept my warmest congratulations and convey the same to the officers and men under you.

"Since the time that the announcement regarding the formation of the Azad Hind Fauj or the Indian National Army was first made several months ago, enemy propagandists have been trying to tell the Indian people as well as Britian's Indian Army in India that the Indian National Army does not exist and that it is only a propaganda-stunt. In December last, the Headquarters of the Indian National Army opened its own broadcasting Station and from that station officers and men of the Indian National Army began to broadcast regularly in their own names. This made enemy propagandists extremely uneasy and uncomfortable and they, therefore, fell back on a new propagandastic. They put out a false story to the world that I had promised to reach Delhi with my Army before the end of 1943 and on that false story they began to issue radio commentaries everyday saying that I had failed to redeem propaganda-offensive against me was to hide Mountbatten's utter failure to start his much-advertised offensive for re-conquering Burma.

"I have already replied to enemy propagandists saying that I made no promise to them or to their masters—the British Government-and that whatever promise I made to my own countrymen either have been already

1. *Greater Asia, 10 Feb. 1944.*

redeemed or will be redeemed in the fulness of time. I have also declared to the whole world that during the last twelve months, we have been working according to plans that we have been advancing from one success to another. The only thing about which any complaint can be made is that our time-table has been slightly delayed.

When the Headquarters of the Provisional Government of Azad Hind and of the Supreme Command of the Indian National Army were removed from Shonan to Burma in the first week of January, there was nervousness and panic at Delhi. Enemy propagandists thereupon had to discover new methods for hiding their discomfiture. Not being able to deny the existence of the Indian National Army any longer, they started abusing me and my Army and began to assert again that this Army had not been able to advance towards its destination. But, he laughs best who laughs last. The announcement that is being made from Tokyo regarding the Indian National army will tell something about our activities, of the Indian National Army. I shall not say much at this stage but let events speak for themselves. I shall only say this that we are working according to plan and that in the fulness of time we shall redeem our solemn pledge to liberate our Motherland. We have full confidence in our own strength—we have complete faith in our Allies and we have unbounded optimism regarding our final victory. We shall go on toiling and fighting till the Flag that is now fluttering over the Arakan Hills flies over the Viceroy's House and the Red Fortress in India's Metropolis.

7

An Editorial on the Importance of I.N.A. : "March on to Delhi"

9 February, 1944

Free Indians, On to Delhi!

The Battle is on, Warriors of the Indian National Army are in full cry after the enemy who is already beginning to retreat in disorder on the India-Burma front. Confident of the support they will receive from the Imperial Nippon forces who have smashed previous enemy bids to launch counter-offensives in this theatre of war, soldiers of the Indian National Army are dashing forward, convinced of the success that awaits them once they enter their motherland and join forces with the disgruntled British Indian troops who are waiting to turn on the British at the opportune moment.

Today all attention is focussed on the doings of the Indian National Army. The Netaji's battle-cry of "On to Delhi" was no empty rhetoric. It is an inspired slogan, with which the Revolutionary Army will go on to tear down the British flag from the Red Fortress in Delhi and in its stead hoist the National Flag of Free India. Sympathisers with the cause of the people of India are thrilled at the way the Azad Hind Fauj has gone into battle. Everything augurs well for the future; the enemy is already hard pressed.

Already Nippon air units are paying the way for the advances of the ground forces. The enemy's plan of attack has been frustrated, nipped in the bud. Winging their war far over the Bay of Bengal, Nippon Wild Eagles have blasted enemy concentrations and installations at bases in India, dive-bombing the enemy's rear and causing havoc to his communications. A convoy in the Bay was attacked, causing severe loss to the enemy. All this is going to help the task of the Indian Nationalist Army. and hasten their entry into India.

---

1. *The Syonan Shimbun, 9 Feb. 1944.* This paper was published from Singapore and was controlled by the Japanese. Its chairman was Tashio.

Once the Indian Revolutionaries set foot on Indian soil, they will fight with renewed vigour and inspiration, for then will their goal-their long-cherished dream of an India free of alien domination, able to call her soul here own-more realistically appear within their reach. The people of Malai, together with the peoples of the rest of Dai Toa, will earnestly pray for the success of the Indians; campaign.. They have suffered long and patiently. The day of retribution is at hand. The British are on the run and must be swept out of India. There must be no halting, no respite. Free Indians, march to Delhi.

8

Special Order of the Day by Subhas Chandra Bose, Supreme Commander, Azad Hind Fauj, on the Success of I.N.A. in Arakan[1]

9 February, 1944.

The eyes of the whole world are focussed on the Arakan Front, where events of far-reaching consequences are taking place to-day. The glorious and brilliant actions of the brave units of Azad Hind Fauj working in close concert with the forces of the Imperial Nippon Army, have helped to foil attampts by the Anglo-American forces to start counter-offensive in this sector.

I am sure that the brave deeds of our comrades on the Arakan Front will be a great inspiration to all the Officers and men of the Azad Hind Fauj wherever they may be stationed at the present moment. Our long awaited march to Delhi has begun and with grim determination, we shall continue that march until the tricolour National Flag that is flying over the Arakan mountains is hoisted over the Viceregal Lodge and until we hold our victory parade at the ancient Red Fortress of Delhi.

Comrades, officers and men of India's Army of Liberation: Let there be one solemn resolve in your hearts—'Either liberty or death.' And let there be but one slogan on your lips 'Onward to Delhi.' The road to Delhi is the road to freedom. That is the road along which we must march. Victory will certainly be ours.

Inqlab Zindabad : Azad Hind Zindabad.

1. I.N.A. Trial Papers.

9

Statement of S.A. Ayer on the I.N.A.'s Success on the Arakan Front[1]

10 Feburary, 1944

Mr. S.A. Ayer, Publicity and Propaganda Minister of the Azad Hind Government comments on the Dai Honyei announcement as follows:-

"A stunning reminder to the British in India that Netaji Subhas Chandra Bose is a man of action and that he means what he says". This was the comment of Mr. S.A. Ayer, Minister of Publicity and Propaganda of the Provisional Government of Free India when a Greater Asia representative interviewed him on the historic announcement of the Dai Honyei to the effect that the Indian National Army is fighting in close unison with the Imprial Nipponese Forces in the Arakan regions, in an effort to crush the British Indian troops once again, in order to bring about the second "Arakan Debacle". This represents, no doubt, the feelings of all freedom-loving Indians in India as well as outside India who are rejoiced at the news that Netaji has at last started his offensive against the Anglo-Americans.

Continuing, the Propaganda Minister said "I would recall Netaji's first words on his arrival in East Asia eight months ago when he said : 'The enemy who has drawn the sword must be fought with the sword."

Mr. Ayer added, "Lately, the British in India have been indulging in the cheap and foolish propaganda that Netaji and his Army are idle. Well, Netaji is content to let events speak for themselves; I would add that events have begun to speak for themselves," the Propaganda Minister concluded.

In co-ordinated action with Netaji Subhas Chandra Bose, 3,000,000 Indian people residing in East Asia rose equal to the occasion to follow him toward Delhi and liberate all Indian people from British tyranny, as an opportunity like this will never come again for centuries.

---

1. *Greater Asia, 10 Feb, 1944*

9

Statement of S.A. Ayer on the I.N.A.'s Success on the Arakan Front[1]

20 February 1944

Mr. S. A. Ayer, Publicity and Propaganda Minister of the Azad Hind Government, broadcasting on the Free India Radio, commented as follows:

"A startling revelation to the people in India that Netaji Subhas Chandra Bose is a man of action and that he means what he says." This was the comment of Mr. S. A. Ayer, Minister of Publicity and Propaganda of the Provisional Government of Free India when a [illegible] representative interviewed him on the historic announcement of the [illegible] to the effect that the Indian National Army is fighting in conjunction with the Imperial Nippon Forces in the Arakan front, in an effort to [illegible] in order to [illegible] the so-called "Onward Delhi". This [illegible] to doubt the [illegible] of all freedom-loving Indians in India as well as outside India who are [illegible] that the [illegible] offensive against the Anglo-Americans.

Continuing, the Propaganda Minister said, "I would recall Netaji's [illegible] words on his [illegible] in East Asia eight months ago when he said: 'The enemy who has drawn the sword must be fought with the sword.'"

Mr. Ayer then added, "[illegible] the British in India have been [illegible] in their [illegible] propaganda that [illegible] Army [illegible] words speak [illegible] events have begun to speak for themselves," the Propaganda Minister concluded.

[illegible] Indians [illegible] in East Asia [illegible] equal to the occasion [illegible] Delhi [illegible] opportunity like this will never come again [illegible].

1. Greater Asia, [illegible] 1944.

10

Impact of I.N.A. on British Forces in Arakan[1]

21 February, 1944

February, 1944 will long remain one of the most memorable days in the annals of the Indian people—as a day of monumental importance to the Indian race heralding the coming of their national redemption. On this fateful day, the Indian National Army in cooperation with the imperial Japanese Forces began its historic march toward New Delhi over the mountains of Mayu and on the Burma-India border.

In outlining the policies of the Imperial Government, Prime Minister Hideki Tojo on January 21 declared in the Imperial Diet :

"Subhas Chandra Bose is ready to march into India at the head of his National Army. The Imperial Government will give its wholehearted assitance to his attempt to secure Indian Independence.

The Indian National Army has already begun its westward march in India's first armed contest against its hideous master-Britain. And side by side with the army stand the formidable Imperial Forces which are ready to cruch all enemy resistance in their onslught over the Burma-India frontier.

Thc Indian National Army is marching shoulder to shoulder with the Imperial Japanese Army. In its sacred mission of liberting India. It is now dealing a deadly blow on the British troops which had long been planning to launch an invasion of Burma in its for hold to recover its lost prestige in East Asia. When Mr Bose advanced to Burma at the head of his National Army, it had the effect of fundamentally shaking the very souls of the Indian populaces, who had been groaning under the terrifying mistreatment of British rule. The number of desertions among the Indian soldiers at the front increase steadily, while others will join the Indian National Army as soon as they come into contact with it, and take up arms against the British Troops.

1. *Nippion Times, 21 Feb, 1944.*

Dismayed by such stupendous effects, the British authorities in India placed a strict ban on any reports about the army and circulated the falsehood that the exitence of such an army was war propaganda. But such decription has been disproved by the actual fighting of the Indian National Army in colliboration with the Japanese troops in the persents operations around the Muyu region. When the news of this historic event is flashed over India, its people will respond in their surging enthusiaism to overcome British rule. The thick wall which the Indian people had tried vainly to break down in order to secure their freedom is at last being shattered by their brave sons who are marching over the Burma India border. India is on the eve of its emancipation.

11

Bose on the success of the I.N.A. on the battle front[1]

29 February, 1944

"The annihillation of the main fore of the British Seventh Division is really glorious news. Particularly, it is joyful to hear that the Indian National Army has scored a glorious victory in its first battle in the Arakan district, under close cooperation with the Imperial Japanese Forces.

"This fact proves, that the Burma offensive planned by Lord Louis Mountbatten is fated to end in a disastrous result. It is impossible to get around the effect the defeat at Arakan will bring on the fighting spirit of the British forces in India. The army under Lord Mountbatten has now fallen into a death pit. I am interested to learn what excuse Lord Mountbatten will make for his defeat in reporting to Churchill. Stillwell or Chiang Kai-shek.

"Probably Churchill is now regretting that he prematurely sent a telegram of congratulation to Lord Mountbatten on the victory at Maungdaw and thus made himself a laughing stock of the whole world. If he had known that the Seventh Division was unable to gain any success, beyond rushing blindly to his self-destruction, he would have recollected the ancient saying, 'silence is golden'.

"Chaing Kai-shek also must have been disappointed as he believed that the anti-Axis forces in India would gain considerable success by the next rainy season, and the Burma supply route would be reopened. Not only was the Burma route unopened, but the Mountbatten forces have received a decisive blow on the Burma front. No longer can Chiang hope for the materialization of the empty promise given him by Lord Mountbatten to send aid over the reopened Burma route. Stillwell, no doubt, is also disappointed in the strategy and fighting strength of the British troops.

---

1. *Nippion Times*, 1 March, 1944.

For Churchill there will be no further need to send congratulations to Lord Mountbatten.

"The retreat from Burma in June, 1942, the first Arakan tragedy of last spring and the present second defeat at Arakan form links in the total defeat of the British forces. It is a prelude to final collapse of Britain in India.

"The victory gained by the Indian troops on the Burma front has stirred great excitement among the officers and men of the Indian National Army and also among all the Indian residents in Greater East Asia. There is not doubt whatever that our brother in India have been greatly comforted by the fatal blow Britain has suffered on thé Burma frontier.

—

12

British Intelligence's Assessment of the I.N.A.[1]

10 March, 1944

The Indian National Army

1. Introduction—Unconfirmed reports from several sources have been received recently of the arrival of organised Jif units or formations in the Kalewa area. While little definite is known as yet about the armament, training and morale of the I.N.A. information recently received enables some amplification to be made of the tentative review given in paras 16-24 of W.I.S. part III No. 97 of 1943.

The I.N.A. in Malaya

2. To recapitulate, the first serious attempt to organise the I.N.A. were made after the Bangkok conference in June 42 and, by Nov. the approximate strength in Malaya was estimated at 24,000 concentrated in and around Singapore.

3. A Paper organisation, which may have existed on the ground, was announced as:

(a) Three Guerilla Brigades (Gandhi, Nehru and Azad).

(b) A field Group (Brigade) consisting of a Signal Coy., and Armoured unit, an Ordance unit and a Supply unit.

(c) A Special Service Group (now known as the Bahadur Group).

(d) An Intelligence Group.

(e) A Cadets Training School.

(f) A Provost Units and Detention Camp.

1. War office 203/803 Public Record office, London.

Training was elementary and armament and equipment, mostly from captured British stocks, was issued on a meagre scale.

4. In Nov. 42 a so-called "advance party of the I.N.A" of 400 men left for Burma. In Dec. a quarrel occurred, between the leaders and the Japanese, which resulted in the disarshment of the "army" by the latter. Reorganisation took place about March 43, but it was not until after Subhas Chandra Bose arrived in Malaya that serious steps were undertaken to recruit, organise and train the I.N.A.

5. Of this new "army" little definite is known. Army H.Q. is in Singapore and the following units have been reported:-

(a) A field Force (Gandhi, Nehru and Azad Bdes).

(b) A Guerilla Regiment.

(c) Ancillary Units.

(d) "Crack" Regiment.

(e) Rani of Jhansi Regiment (Women's Regt.)

(f) A Signed Coy.

(g) An I.N.A. Hospital.

6. The Bahadur (hitherto known as the Special Service Group) and Intelligence Groups, a feature of the pre-Bose I.N.A., have moved into Burma. Reports of strengths, training, organisation and morale of these units when in Malaya are still conflicting. Units which had finished their training are reported to have left for Burma on 8 Jan 44 by overland and sea routes.

The I.N.A. in Burma

7. On arrival in Burma the I.N.A. "Advance Party" consisted of 200 picked men from the Gandhi, Nehru, Azad and Field Brigades, and 200 of 'A' coy of the Bahadur Group. Throughout 1943 little was heard of this body, except that the Bahadur Group representatives were being trained as intelligence agents, had been supplemented by a new ('E') company and that many of them were despatched to the forward areas on intelligence tasks in Sep. and Oct. 43. On 29 Oct. 43, 'B', 'C', and 'D' companies of the Bhadur Group arrived in Rangoon. This confirms the forecast made in paragraph 8 of A.I.S.,

8. Simultaneously with the arrival of reinforcements for the Bahadur Group, the Intelligence Group of the I.N.A., totalling 350 men, arrived in Rangoon under the command of Copt. (I.N.A. Lt.-Col.) S.A. Malik, 1st Bahawalpur, Infantry. Since then but 70 to 80 have moved up into Arabun and about 80 (two sections) were seen at the end of Jan in transit to Myitkleyina. Three other sections are said to have moved out to an unknown destination. Personnel from this and the Bahadur Group style themselves I.N.A. They are in fact intelligency agents; the Bahadur Group is intended for deep penetration and the Intelligence Group to carry out a role similar to that of our Battalion Intelligence Sections, and also to carry out espionage tasks in plain clothes.

9. In addition to the Bahadur Group, the Intelligence Group and elements of the Field Force, unconfirmed reports speak of the arival in Rangoon of a detachment of ancillary and other units of the I.N.A. during the letter half of 1943.

Jifs in Arakan

10. The first elements of the Bahadur Group moved up to Arakan in Sep. 43, and others in late October. Captain (I.N.A. major) Misra, 5/17 Dogra Regiment, who commanded 'A' company of the Bahadur Group in Rangoon, left there in Oct. with a detachment and established his H.Q. in Buthidaung, with Lt. (I.N.A. Capt.) Mehar Dac, 3 Lt. A.A. Bty., as his 2nd in command. By 17 Dec. Misra had disposed the Bahadur Group in the Buthidaung and coastal areas. Their duties were chiefly military espionage in forward areas.

11. The Intelligence Group did not arrive in Arakan until the beginning of Feb., although captured document states that 73 men of the Group were to come under command of 55 Div. from 15 Jan. They were to operate under the orders of Capt. Misra through an officer of 143 Regiment. The latter was linked with the Akyab branch of the Hikari Kikan through a small liaison group.

12. An operational order of 20 Jan stated that, in the event of operations, most of the Hikari Kikan personnel would operate on the Buthidaung-Maungdaw front with one section in the upper regions of the Kaladan. Their tasks were "to collect intelligence necessary to conduct operations and look for deserters from British Indian Army

Kaladan. Their tasks were "to collect intelligence necessary to conduct operations and look for deserters from British Indian Army and destroy enemy installations."

13. At the beginning of Feb. all Jifs were ordered to concentrate east of the Malu Range for an operation "whose zero hour had been put forward." During the early stages of the Japanese attack they participated in raids, were used as a screen for an out flanking movement, attempted to cause confusion amongst our troops by shouting in English and Urdu, carried out espionage tasks, and acted as messengers.

14. On 10 Feb. Capt. Misra and capt. Hattori (O.C. of the Akyab branch of the Hikari Kikan) were joined by '3' section of the Intelligence Group (70 men of the 73 referred to in para 11 above) and 110 men of the field force. Personnel of both forces were lightly armed. On 11 Feb., with a detachment of 'A' Company of Bahadur Group and about 50 Japanese, this composite force moved to S.E. of Taung Bazar and dug in. From there mixed patrols of Japanese and I.N.A were sent out.

15. In addition to these purely ex P.W. bodies of Jifs, agents from the Kanbe Swaraj Training Institute also took part in the operations. In Dec. 43 their HQ known as HQ 'J' force, was well forward with a detached HQ of the Bahadur Group. Jif strengths in Arkan forward of Akyab in the latter half of Feb. were approximately:-

Bahadur Group	70
Intelligence Group	70
Field Force	110
Kanbe S.T.I Students	50
Others	110
Total	410

Jifs on other Fronts

16. There are reliable indications that Jifs on other fronts are being reinforced. On the night 2/3 Mar, about 14 miles N.E. of Tiddim, 5 out of a party of 7 Jifs voluntarily surrendered to our troops. They stated that they formed the Intelligence Group of the Nehru Brigade, and

Malik, who as mentioned in para 8 above, is believed to command the Intelligence Group of the I.N.A.

17. From this and other information it seems probable that the Japanese intend using I.N.A troops in 4 Corps area in a more active role than hitherto. The Hikari Kikan has been paying particular attention to the Manipur plain for some time. A pointer may be the recent Japanese broadcast announcing a new organ for smoother liaison in future between the I.N.A., the Japanese army and the B.T.A. "To strengthen the joint strategic operations of the three allies for frustrating the enemy guerilla attempt to re-capture Burma and to draft important offensive as well as defensive operations."

16. ... as mentioned ... is believed to command the Intelligence Group of the I.N.A.

17. From this and other information it seems probable that the Japanese intend using I.N.A. troops in [illegible] operations in a more [illegible] than hitherto. [illegible] has been paying particular attention to the Manipur plain for some time. A further [illegible] of the [illegible] Japanese [illegible] together [illegible] between the I.N.A., the Japanese army and the B.I.A. [illegible] strengthen the joint strategic operations of the three allies for breaking up the enemy guerilla attempt to recapture Burma and to [illegible] as well as defensive operation.

13

Report of A.D. Loganandan on his Taking over as Chief Commissioner of Andaman[1]

12 March, 1944

Having left Syonan on 17th Feb 2604 the party arrived at Port Blair on the 18th mid-day. We were accommodated temporarily in the bungalow of Min Sei Bu-cho (Chief of the Civil Administration). Owing to extreme congestion, with difficulty a small bungalow was ultimately found, to which we shifted on the 11th instant. On the 21st of Feb there was a rally to celebrate the first Provisional Government day, and another rally on the second Saturday to mourn the death of Srimati Kasturba Gandhi, and also to celebrate the Arakan Victory. It is hoped to set up an office a few days hence when the transference of some of the departments will be made, details of which are still under discussion. The packages have not yet arrived, may be they may not have been despatched so far from that end. Attempts may please be made to expedite despatch, as the stationery is urgently required here. Sorry to report that nothing whatever is available here locally, and hence we are seriously handicapped. Crockery and cutilery for a dozen persons if despatched will greatly be appreciated. Dysenterics, amoebic and bacillary are endemic and in equal proportion. It will greatly help if emetine or its equivalent, as much as can be spared, could be sent. There is not a grain of Mag Sulph available here. About 420 lbs. which will last about 3 months may please be also sent. All kinds of food-stuffs are scarce, and the chance of feeding the propulation with a well-balanced diet is remote. Up-to-date no communication has been received from that end, and therefore we are absolutely in the dark as to what is happening outside. Jai Hind.

(Sd.)
A.D. Loganandan, Chief Commissioner,
Admans and Nicobar.

1. I.N.A. Trial Papers.

14

Role of Indian Women in the I.N.A.[1]

12 March, 1944

SHONAN. March 12, Miss Swaminathan Lakshimi. Director of the Women's Department of the Rani of Jhansi Regiment, in an interview with a Domei correspondent yesterday, asserted that the Indian women's corps is taking an active part in the fight for the attainment of freedom Lakshimi had just returned from a two months visit to the women's corps at a certain base in Burma, and on returning to Shonan has plunged into the task of training new women recruits.

"Since the Provisional Goverment of Azad Hind took up its headquarters in Burma, a large number of Indian women in Burma have joined our ranks and are training with remarkable ardor and earnstness," remarked Miss Lakshimi. "Wonderful progress has been made by the women's corps and the members in Rangoon are all anxious to advance to the front lines. Every time we see the men of the Imperial Forces march off to the front, the women persistently ask me when they, too, will be allowed to go.

"Although frequently raided by enemy planes, Rangoon, according to members of the women's corps is on longer the line of battle. A firm determination to wrest back their motherland from fetters of British domination burns flercely in their hearts.

"Manifestations of genuine comradeship are evidemt every where between the men of the Japanese Forces and those of the Indian National Army. Once when we were advancing on X.X. a certain Japanese officer was wounded in an enemy air attack. An officer of the Indian National Army immediately carried the wounded Japanese officer on his back to the hospital When the Indian officer visited the hospital, the Japanese officer

1. *Nippon Times*, 14 March, 1944.

on the verge of death, grasped the Indian's hand firmly and with his dying breath shouted 'Jai Hind'. The Indian officer was profoundly moved and vowed that the death of his Japanese comrade would be revenged.

"The Indians who rally to our banners from the British Indian army all express amazement at how well the Provisional Government of Azad Hind and the National Army has been perfected. Also the Indian troops did not know of the famine in Bengal Province. The crafty British Propaganda had kept the Indian masses in complete ignorance."

15

Duties of I.N.A. and the Japanese Forces while Fighting together on Imphal Front[1]

21 March, 1944

1. The Indian National Army, under the leadership of the Provisional Government of Azad Hind, has now massed in force and advanced into a territory of Eastern India as the spearhead for the creation of a free India.

The Indian National Army with the help and cooperation of the Imperial Nipponese Army, has pushed into Eastern India with the object of crushing the Anglo-American forces the common enemy of East Asia: of making India really an India for Indians by liberating her from the shackles of the despotic role under which she has been groaning for ages; of bringing complete freedom and peace and order to three hundred and eighty million of our brothers and sisters in India; and also of driving away the Anglo-American menace from the borders of our neighbours the Independent Burmese.

Brothers and Sisters in India

Be engaged in your daily work without fear; gather wholeheartedly under your Tricolour Flag of Independence hoisted by the Provisional Government of Azad Hind; brace yourselves up for winning Complete Independence by retaking our Motherland from the hands of our enemies, the Anglo-Americans.

The East Indian Territory into which the Indian National Army has advanced with the powerful aid of the Imperial Nipponese Army, as well as the people thereof have now been liberated from the bondage of the Anglo-Americans. The terriroty has become the first free Indian territory on the Mainland of India under the Provisional Government and will serve as the base for liberating our Motherland. The Imperial Nipponese Army will not

1. I.N.A. Relief and Enquiry Committee Papers.

establish a military administration but will cooperate with and wholeheartedly help the Provisional Government of Azad Hind in maintaining perfect peace and order.

2. If any person fails to understand the intentions of the Provisional Government of Azad Hind and the Indian National Army, or of our Ally, the Nippon Army, and dares to commit such acts as are itemised hereunder which would hamper the sacred task of emancipating India, he shall be executed or severely punished in accordance with the Criminal Law of the Provisional Government of Azad Hind and the Indian National Army or with the Martial Law of the Nippon Army, the application of which has been agreed upon between the two allied Armies, namely the Indian National Army and its Ally, the Imperial Nipponese Army.

Punishable Acts

(i) Rebellious acts against the provisional Government of Azad Hind or the Indian National Army, or our Ally, the Nipponese Army.

(ii) Acts of spying.

(iii) Acts of stealing and taking by force, damaging and destroying war materials which are in the possession of the Provisional Government or belong to our Ally, the Nippon Army.

(iv) Acts of damaging or destroying of valuable material resources controlled or utilised by the Provisional Government of Azad Hind or by the Nippon Army under previous agreement with the Provisional Government.

(v) Acts of destroying various installations or equipment's for traffic, Communication, transportation, broadcasting etc., which are controlled or utilized by the Provisional Government of Azad Hind and the Indian National Army, or by the Nippon Army under Previous agreement with the Provisional Government utilization thereof.

(vi) Violent acts against, intimidation of, killing or wounding of, or doing other harmful acts to those who belong to the Provisional Government of Azad Hind and the Indian National Army or our Ally, the Nippon Army.

(vii) Acts of spreading enemy propaganda or wild and false rumours, and other acts of disturbing and misleading the minds of the inhabitants.

(viii) Acts of disturbing the money circulation and economic organisation or of obstructing the production and free interchange of commodities.

(ix) Any act other than those contained in the above items, that benefits the enemy or is harmful to peace and order, and the well-being of the Provisional Government of Azad Hind and the Indian National Army or our Ally, the Nippon Army.

(x) Acts of attempting, instigating and abetting those acts contained in the above items.

The trial and punishment of such criminals will entirely be at the discretion of the Provisional Government of Azad Hind except when crimes committed are of such a nature as of necessity, owing to war-time emergency, must be dealt with by the Nippon Army as agreed upon between the two Allied Armies.

III. The Nippon Army will maintain strict discipline and protect in the area into which they have advanced the lives and properties of the Indian masses who do not commit any hostile act; and due respect will be paid to the religions, customs and manners of the Indian people.

It is guaranteed that any Nippon soldier that may violate these strict injunctions shall be severely punished in accordance with the Martial Law of the Imperial Nipponese Army.

The Indian National Army will maintain strict discipline and protect, in the area into which it has advanced, the lives and properties of the Indian masses who do not commit any hostile act; and due respect will be paid to the religions, customs and manners of our countrymen.

It is guaranteed that any Indian soldiers that may violate these strict injuctions shall be severely punished in accordance with the Martial Law of the Indian National Army.

THE ABOVE IS SOLEMNLY PROCLAIMED IN THE MONTH OF MARCH IN THE YEAR 1944 BY THE SUPREME COMMANDER OF THE INDIAN NATIONAL ARMY.

16

Historic Proclamations by Bose that the Azad Hind Fauj had Crossed the Indo-Burma Frontier; Bose also called on all Indians to Extend their Help direct or Indirect to the Armies of Liberation[1]

21 March, 1944

"The Azad Hind Fauj under the leadership of the Provisional Government of Azad Hind and the Imperial Nippon Army, working in the closet co-operation, and fighting shoulder-to-shoulder, when the allied armies of India and Nippon are crossing the frontier and marching into India, the Provisional Government of Azad Hind makes the following proclamation :

"Since the bloody war of 1857 when the armies of Indian were defeated in battle by the invading forces of Britain, the Indian people have never morally surrendered to the British. In spite of inhuman persecution, and in spite of forcible disarmament, they have continued their resistance to British domination. Through propaganda and agitation, through acts of terrorism and sabotage, through armed revolution, and in recent years through satyagraha or passive resistance initiated by Mahatma Gandhi-they have not only kept up the struggle for independence but have also advanced a long way toward the goal of freedom.

"Since the outbreak of the present war, all attempts have been made by the Indian people and their leaders for the achievement of liberty through peaceful settlement with Britain. But all these attempts have failed. More over British has in the course of this war, strengthened her stranglehold over India through ruthless exploration and brutal suppression, and has converted Indian into a gigantic military base for presecuting her imperialistic war.

"In pursuance of this policy, foreign troops namely Australian, American, Chinese and Negro troops—have been imported in to India,

1. *The Syonan Shimbun*, 22 March, 1944.

and owing to the unbearable burden thrown on the shoulders of the already impoverised Indian masses, famine conditions of an unprecedented nature have broken out in large areas of the country.

"In a last desperate attempt to spare India the horrors of war. Mahatma Gandhi advised the British Government to recognise India's demand for independence and quit India. The reply of the British. Government was to throw him into prison along with hundreds of it Thousands of India's patriots. The last act of vandllam committed by the British Government was the virtual murder of Mrs. Kasturba Gandhi in British custody.

"Viewing the worsening situation to India, Indian in East Asia numbering about 3,000,000 made a solemn resolve to participate actively in the fight for the Indian people at home and their national liberation. They organised themselves politically under the Azad Hind Sangh, or Indian independence League. They organized an army and on Oct. 21, 2003 (1943), they set up the Provisional Government of Azad Hind when the Azad Hind Fauj had completed all its preparations, it lanunched the last fight for freedom of its sacred Motherland on Feb. 4. 2604 (1944) in the Arakan region of Burma.

The success achieved in this fight by the allied armies of India and Nippon has now enabled the Indian National Army to cross the frontier of India and continue its march to Delhi.

"Since the outbreak of the war in East Asia, the victories achieved by the armed forces of Nippon, which are unparalled in military history have rended it possible for Indians in East Asia to organise themselves for active participation in India's fight for freedom. The Government of Nippon has repeatedly declared before the whole world that Nippon is fighting not only for her own security but also for the destruction of Anglo-American imperialism in East Asia, and further that Nippons stands for the complete and unconditional independence of India.

"In pursuance of this policy, the Government of Nippon has repeatedly expressed its readiness to give all out aid to India in her struggle for independence—formally recognised the Provisional Government of Azad Hind has decided to hand over the Andamans and Nicobar Islands to the Provisional Government.

"Now the Azad Hind Fauj has launched its offensive and the Azad Hind, with the co-operation of the Imperial Nippon Army, is marching shoulder-to-shoulder in the common fight against the comon foe—the Anglo-American and their allies. Until these foreign armies of rigression are thrown out of India, there can be no freedom for the Indian people, there can be not freedom and security in Toa, and there can be not and to the present imperialistic war of the Anglo-Americans:-

"Nippon is therefore determind to reduces her pledge to keep the Indian people to create an India for the Indian."

"The Provisional Government of Azad Hind hereby proclaims its solemn determination to go on fighting in closet brotherhood with Nippon until India is completely liberated. We call upon Indian people who are the bone of our bone, the flesh of our flesh to ender all help—direct or indirect to our armies of liberation.

"We call upon all patriotic Indians—men, women and children, our brothers and sisters in India, to throw themselves wholeheartedly into this last fight for India's Independence. We call upon every Indian to destroy the Anglo-American war effort in India by systemic sabotage and thereby hasten the successful conclusion of the war for our country's freedom.

"We call upon our brothers, Indian soldiers and officers in Britain's army to refuse to fight any longer for their despotic rulers, and to come and actively join our ranks. We call upon Indians worring in various departments of the British service to render all possible help to us in the sacred fight.

"We solemnly ensure the Indian people our brothers and sisters. That they have nothing whatever to fear so long as they do not help the Anglo-America or their allies in India. We assure them further, that in liberated territory in India, the Provisional Government of Azad Hind will be established and that the Provisional Government will take over the administration of that territory.

We advise the Indian people, our kith and kin, to keep away from the Anglo-American armies, their munltion factorles, their harbours and mullatry inslations, and their war destroyed by us before the enemy can be defeated.

"Sisters and brothers in India! This is the golden opportunity for you to fulfil your long-cherished aspirations for freedom. If you rise to the occasion and do your duty, freedom will be yours before long. In this momentous event Indian expects every one to do his or her duty Jai Hind! Head of state of the Provisional Government of Azad Hind and Supreme Commander of the Indain National Army.

It is only natural with the advance of the Indian National Army that anti-British activities should become more intensified than over. Fearing the possible revolt of the Indian soldiers at the front, the British authorities have been resorting to various objectionable measures to cope with the situation. They recently withdrew the Gurkha soldiers who are said to the faithful watchdogs of British rule to carry out machinations among the upper classes of the Indian populase for the purpose of effecting some compromise concerning protest against British administration in the country. These soldiers are also utilized in dividing up the Indian National Congress members in order to weaken their united resistance. During the past several months, some 30,000 Indian patriots have been placed under arrest because of their alleged complications in plots against the British authorities.

"Minister of State for Indian Army recently declared that a famines no longer exists in Bengal Province because of its good crop this year amounting to 8,300,000 tons of rice. But the annual consumption by this single province is more than 11,000,000 tons.

Moreover India must supply provisions to the Anglo-American forces in that country and the British troops in Western Asia and as a results of these demands, the people are facing a still greater difficulties in securing foodsetuffs. The authorities declared recently that Britain has not been exporting food from India in recent months, but the exports of rice and other foodstuffs from India to Western Asia for the consumption of British troops there are not included in these statistics.

Moreover, Indian has been shouldering a considerable amount of Britain's war burden since the beginning of the present World War. The contribution of 2,100,400,000 rupees for the fiscal year of 1942-43 is 75 per cent of her entire revenue for that year. Britain exploitation of Indian resources has become increasingly unbearable, the total amount of goods supplied to Britain by Indian up to the end of July 1943 being estimated at the vast sum of 37,150,000,000 rupees. It is expected that further increases will be made in present war in respect to both material resources and manpower. The economic exploitation and objectionable administrative measures adopted by the British authorities have led the people of India to become more and more anti-British in their thoughts and activities.

The inactivities of Admiral Mountbatten, who is supposed to recapture Burma. and of viceroy Wavell as well as the misgovernment of Minister of State for India Army have aggravated the unrest in India. Anti-British riots, boycotts, strikes, etc. in the home front and in the industrial field have increased in both scale and internally, whole desertions in the army have been growing in numbers. So serious is the situation throughout India that in such cities as Calcutta, Bombay and Madras dire conditions are prevalent.

To make the situations still worse, friction of a most serious nature has developed among Britain, the Untied States and Chungking over the question of military command, Britian in undertaking various forms of patchwork in order to retrieve the existing situations but its success seems well nigh impossible of statement. Conditions are going from bad to worse, and soon the whole of India will be overrun by a growing anti-British agitation. It was such a situation in India that Ambassador Halifax had in mind when he recently declared in a lecture before a meeting of the National Geographic Society.

"Britain hopes India will remain in the British Commonwealth after the war, but will not block her if India desires to sever Empire connections."

But India will not be swayed by such sweet words and sugar-coated expressions. She is advancing headlong toward her prime objective—independence. Minister of State for India Amery may try to intimidate by declaring that emergency measures might be adopted against the present critical conditions, but such threats will not deviate the Indian masses from their present progress toward their "Fateful Day." The more relentless British oppression becomes the greater will be the zeal and enthusiasm of the Indian patriots to gain their coverted prize which means complete freedom.

17

Japanese Premier's Statement in the Imperial Diet Declaring to Place all Liberated areas under the administrative Control of the Provisional Government of Azad Hind[1]

21 March, 1944

Tokyo, March 22—Regarding the march on Delhi already started by the Azad Hind Fauj in cooperation with Nippon forces, Premier Hideki Tojo, addressing the Imperial Diet which reconvened today, say Nippon aims at expelling enemy influence from India and placing India completely in the hands of Indians.

"It is natural," he asserted "that all areas over which the Azad Hind Fauj marches within India must be placed completely under the administration of Provisional Government."

Premier Tojo reiterated Nippon's firm resolve to surmount all difficulties in order to prosecute the war to a victorious conclusion. He called attention to the further intensified war situation with particular reference to fierce enemy air attacks on the Marshall and Mariana Islands and urged the nation to give its all for the downfall of Britain and the United States.

"This is the only way complete victory can be attained." he declared.

The Premier praised the progress of the emergency administrative measures initiated by the Government at the bond of September last year. In that respect the Premier said the speedy strengthening of the nation's air strength was significant. He suggested importance of adopting decisive war time administrative manual as well as closer liasion between the fighting forces and the civil administration in order to cope with the present situation.

He declared that by adopting decisive wartime measures. Government aims at mobilizing national strength to the maximum extent through total concentration on bolstering the fighting strength , thus guaranteeing the

1. *The Syonan Shimbun*, 23 March, 1944.

attainment of certain victory. He praised the readiness of the Nippon nation to face any difficulty as well as its firm and immutable resolve to overcome all obstacles which, he said, will make certain that Nippon can fight its way to victory.

The Premier said that Government on the strength of the absolute trust and reliance placed in it by the people, is determined to adopt most suitable measures in future in order to ensure victory in the present war.

Commenting on developments within Dai Toa, he asserted that all nations and people of Dai Toa are closely collaborating in the face of all difficulties and marching bravely forward for the destruction of Anglo-American aggressive designs in Asia and for the construction of a new order in Toa.

High tribute was paid by the Premier to the fighting spirit and full co-operation shown by East Asia.

The Premier lauded the gallant fight carried on by Germany in the European theatre of war in the face of all difficulties and the fact that Germany is now about to launch fierce counter-attacks against the Anglo-Americans and his wishes for the success of Germany's war efforts.

Declaring that "India's Independence is the unanimous will of all Asia and the demand of the world's sense of Justice," the Premier reaffirmed Nippon's determination to spare no efforts in extending all possible assistance for India's liberation.

"Nippon's object is to crush enemy influence and leave India completely in the hands of the Indian people", he said. He added that those who, knowing the distress and suffering of India, dare to interfere with the liberation of India "cannot but be regarded as enemies of Justice."

"The Azad Hind Fauj under the command of the head of the Provisional Government of Azad Hind, Subhas Chandra Bose has in co-operation with imperial Nippon forces started its long expected advance into the Indian homeland. It is a matter for sincered congratulations that in the brief period of only half a year since the establishment of the Provisional Government, the Azad Hind forces of the National Army have vigorously embarked upon their march. The joy of the 400 million people of India who have been under in tyranny and prosecution of Britain for many years must surely be beyond our imagination.

"Nippon's object is to crush enemy influence and place India completely in the hands of the Indian people. All territories of India into which the Indian National Army advances will immediately be placed under the administration of the Provisional Government of Azad Hind. We may confidently expect that with the growing patriot fervor of the Indian people who welcome the advance of the National Army, the areas to be liberated will rapidly expand and that India's independence will ultimately be realized.

"It is not difficult," he concluded, "to imagine that the road leading to the complete liberation of India is yet rough, and I wish, therefore, to clarify at this time on behalf of the Nippon Government that while the Nippon Government will not under any circumstances grudge Indian patriots every possible support, it is sincerity hoped that Indian both soldiers and civilians united more than ever before will continue to fight to overcome all obstacles until that final victory is won and secured."

18

Assurance of Japan's Help for the I.N.A.[1]

22 March, 1944

Tokyo, March 22—Assuring that Nippon will extend all-out assistance and support to Subhas Chandra Bose and his Government, Sadao Iguchi, spokesman of Joho Kyoku (Board of Information), in a statement today, expressed the firm conviction that the Azad Hind Fauj will not lay down arms until the British are ousted from India and Indians gain complete freedom.

Mr. Iguchi's statement follows: "The Azad Hind Fauj of the Provisional Government of Azad Hind has crossed the Indo-Burma border as a result of successful joint operations with the Imperial Nippon force. This advance into the home soil of India is a matter of historical significance for the India Independence movement and gives boundless hope to its future.

"Subhas Chandra Bose has stated that India's anti-British independence movement has a long history of more than 100 years. At the time of the First World War, Britain coerced India into the war with a promise of home rule as a reward, but as soon as the war was over. Britain trampled upon her given word. Since then the independence movement has become more intensified.

"It is literally a miracle that though India has been robbed of all weapon, Gandhi and many other Indian patriots as well as a countless number of Indian people have upheld and carried on the Independence struggle in the face of many overwhelming obstacles, staking indeed their very lives, with undying faith in their ultimate victory. This struggle manifests to the world, the noble spirit of India ultimately to win over the brute forces of British injustice.

"The indomitable courage of the Indian people in resisting British pressure to enter the war, the highhanded exactions upon India's man-

1. *The Syonan Shimbun*, 23 March , 1944.

power and resources, the conversion of India into a military base and other policies of force taken by Britain since the beginning of the war contracts sharply with the severity of the Britain measures and moves to stronly. But why in spite of these heroic efforts has the movement for Indian Independence failed so far to succeed and instead has resulted in the imprisonment of Gandhi and tens of thousands of patriots? The foremost reason is to be found in the fact that the people of India have had no means to arm themselves, and thus armed force is the prime requiste in crushing British control and carrying through the independence struggle to its final goal.

"In July, 2603 (1943), three million Indians in Toa (East Asia) united under the Provisional Government of Azad Hind with Subhas Chandra Bose as his head and by creating the Azad Hind Fauj accomplished the first great step towards the arming of Indian people. Crack forces of the Independence Army which had since their formation been polishing their arms and preparing for the day of advance in their homeland, co-operated in our operation against the British in the Arakan region which began on Feb. 4 and succeeded in smashing their sworn enemy, the British army, thus giving concrete proof to their countrymen at home and to the world, of Indian armed power.

"The people of Nippon, sharing as they do the same blood as people of Asia, and fighting as they are in the same cause of crushing British imperialisms cannot withhold their unbounded joy over the reports of this splendid achievement by India's own forces. Inspired with confidence and hope by the success already achieved the Azad Hind Fauj today is on the march, fully conscious that each advance, earn piece of Indian soil they wrest back from the British., brings the Indian people nearer their ultimate goal.

"Since the attitude of India will determine Britain's doom or survival, it is to be expected that the British could not hold India as a military base. But no matter how unscrupulous the measures the British may take, one stern and immovable fact remains—the inde-structibe spirit of the Indian people for independence, and their complete distrust and enmity towards Britain. The greater the oppression the British may apply in their desperation, the greater will become the intensity of India's resistance at home and the fury of the Independence Army now knocking at the gates of India.

"The situation that has been brought about by the enhancement of the anti-British independence spirit, the decline of British military strength, intensification of military participation of the armed revolutionary power of India herself, promises, the days of British control of India will have been completely destroyed from its foundations. The Nippon Government has declared from time to time that the defense of Nippon's existence against Anglo-American control means at the same time the liberation of the people of Toa (East Asia) from the shackles of Britain and America.

"Accordingly Nippon desires to extend all her national assistance and support to Subhas Chandra Bose and his Provisional Government and the Azad Hind Fauj in the firm conviction that through this war India will surely win her freedom and national independence."

19

Welcome by the People of Manipur to the I.N.A. and Japanese Forces[1]

22 March, 1944

UNDISCLOSED BASE ON THE BURMA FRONT. March 22—Shouting "Banzai" as they welcomed the Indian heroes as they crossed the border at a point west of Myinthamin, the Manipuris residing in the Indo-Burmese border area witnessed with great astonishment and profound respect the gallant entrance of the Indian National Army into Indian territory in conjunction with the Japanese Forces.

After having cooperated with the Japanese Forces in the Kabaw Valley, the Indian National Army together with its Unit crossed the Arakan Range and penetrated the Indo-Burmese border west of Myinthamin.

As they set foot on the soil of their motherland, the India troops could hardly express their deep feelings. The Japanese, on their part, shared the joys of the Indians and re-doubled their determination to crush the Anglo-American foe. A narrow precipitous path confronted the advancing warriors. Giant teak trees deprived of their leaves stood in their way.

Laboriously and courageously struggling over the mountains and valleys, the Japanese and Indian troops arrived at a small hamlet. Though the village had been completely demolished, no British-Indian troops were to be found there, thus attesting to the hasty restart of the enemy. It was apparently a common practice of the enemy to burn all foodstuffs, buildings, and everything available before retreating.

The Manipuris and Chins who were treated most cruelly by the British-Indian troops deepened their faith in the Japanese and the Indians when they witnessed how well the latter were disciplined. As a token of hearty welcome, they brought rise, chicken and other foodstuffs to the

1. *Nippon Times*, 29 March 1944.

Japanese. Finding the Japanese very much like themselves in complexion and physique, the Manipuris immediately took to the former, offering their services as guides.

Anticipating the advance of the Japanese Forces, the British-Indian troops had ordered the native villagers to evacuate. Because of such coercive measures, the resentment of the villagers against the British was intensified. The fact was also revealed that the native youths on the border had been compulsorily requisitioned and had been trained in guerrilla warfare by the British.

As soon as they had finished their training, these native youths had been ordered to conceal themselves among the trees with light machine guns and automatic rifles and to fire on the Japanese. However, during a three-day march through the jungle, the Japanese were not attacked even once by these native youths. On the contrary, they volunteered their unlimited services to the Japanese.

Upon advancing into Indian territory, the Japanese Forces witnessed how deeply rooted the Indians' anti-British sentiment is and how ardently they are struggling for the liberation of their motherland.

20

Bose's Message Thanking the Japanese Premier for his Help[1]

27 March, 1944

A telegraph message of gratitude was received on Sunday by Prime Minister General Hideki Tojo form Subhas Chandar Bose, Head of the Provisional Government of Azad Hind and Commander-in-Chief of the Indian National Army, who is now at an undisclosed frontline base commanding the Azad Hind Fauj.

Prime Minister Tojo, sometimes ago, sent a cordial cable to the Netaji congratulating the Indian National Army on its successful drive toward the Indo-Burme border and reaffirming Japan's deterimination, to extend every possible assistance to the Netaji army of liberation until it has achieved its long cherished aspiration of freeing the Indian people from British shackles.

Commander-in-chief Bose's acknowledgement read as follows "I have been profoundly moved by Your Excellency's cordial telegraphic message in which your Excellency, evinced satisfaction over the Indian National Army's advance toward our motherland. On behalf of the Indian people and the Indian National Army. I express my deep gratitude for your Excellency confirmation that Japan is ready and willing to accord us assistance for achievement of the common objective of crushing our common enemies, American and Britain.

"I take this opportunity to express the determination of the Indian National Army to fight on until final victory has been won in close collaboration with the Imperial Japanese Army.

Subhas Chandra Bosc Head of the Provisional Government of Azad Hind and concurrently War Minister.

---

1. *Nippon Times*, 28 March 1944.

21

Statement by Capt. Lakshmi Criticising British Slanderous Propaganda against I.N.A.

28 March, 1944

Miss Lakshmi Blasts British Canards Of Impotency of Indian National Army

Miss Swaminathan Lakshmi, Director of the Women's Department of the Rani of Jhansi Regiment, rebuts the slanderous British propaganda in the capability of the Indian national Army in a memorandum entitled. **"The real power of the Indian National Army sent to the Manipur."**

Miss Lakshmi has just returned to Shonan from the Indo-Burmese front and she emphatically shatters the vile British propaganda which plays up to the world that the Indian National Army is a puerile impotent force, drawing this conclusion from the utter lack of fighting spirit and vigor on the part of the Indian troops mustered under arbitrative British coercion.

'It is a matter of boundless rejoicing to us that the Indian National Army in collaboration with the Imprial Japanese Forces should vanquish the opposing British-Indian forces on the Indo-Burmese border and firmly Imprint their foot on the sacred soil of our motherland writes Miss Lakshmi.

"The loss of India through the advance of the Indian National Army will signify that British has been overthrown for all ages to come, she continues. "British on her part is fully aware of this and for this reason will challenge us all the more persistently and stubbarnly.

"However the more objective the British opposition the more determined will be the Indian National Army, spurred on by an unquenchable order to fly the Tri-colour flag of freedom over the whole of India, and to oust the Anglo-Americans to the very last man out of the Indian territory.

1. *Nippon Times*, 29 March 1944.

"The Anglo-Americans may think that the Indian National Army is composed of a conglomeration of prejudiced fanatics, ignoble cowards and incapacltated weaklings, but such is a picture of the Indian troops as depicted under the malicious British Propaganda and scheme disseminated, under the ruthless British policy of oppression coercion, exploitation and deceit. It is a fantasy created by the Anglo-American mind that does not know the Indian National Army of today.

"The Provisional Government of Azad Hind is Indian's own government of independence. It is the hightest authority leading the Indians in their fight for independence against the British and is entrusted with all important role of completely exterminating all British American influence from Indian Government of Azad Hind that has initialed the armed resistance against the British, and the Indian National Army is the fundamental component of the bloody struggle for Indian freedom.

"Moreover. the men have been carefully selected out of the countless volunteers whose souls have been fired with intense love for the motherland and an irrepressible desire to crush the Anglo-Americans. From this alone it can be obviously seen that the men in the Indian Nation Army are diametrically different from the Indian soldiers in the British army.

"Centering around the nucleus of Indian patriots, who have vowed to sacrifice their lives for the attainment of Indian independence, the Indian National Army includes in its rank men who have been liberated from the lethargic bondage of Anglo-American oppression and have been fully reborn as true Asiatics. Therefore these inspired patroits are able to plunge into the enemy positions and courageously graple with the British forces.

"With the fighting spirit at white beat augmented by the marvellous resistance to heat and the wonderful adaptability to training, the Indian National Army commands our wholehearted confidence.

"I firmly believe that the Indian National Army will march into Delhi without fail, and we are sincerely grateful to the men of the imperial Japanese Forces, who have infused the Indian National Army with a vigorous and indomitable fighting spirit.

"During the days of army life under the British, the Indian troops only underwent a very prefunctory training of one or two hours a day but under the leadership of the Japanese Forces, the men throw themselves into hard, vigorous training beginning each day at 9.30 a.m. Truly, the fruit of such efforts must be garnered in the soil of the Indian motherland.

"I would also like to stress the fact that the Runi of Jansi Regiment, too, has advanced to the front lines and are attaining excellent results in the accuracy of bring in the background of the Indian struggle for independence, many women Indian patriots had done their share but it is to be specially noted that the Indian women's army, stripped of all disguise, is valiantily taking an active part in the fight for freedom side by side with the Indian National Army. I am firmly confident that the time will come when I can report to you the numerous brave and courageous deeds of the members of the Rant of Jhasi Regiment."

22

British Assessment of the Strength of the I.N.A.[1]

2 April, 1944

5. Of this new "army" little definite is known. Army H.Q. is in Singapore and the following units have been reported:-

   (a) A Field Force (Gandhi, Nehru and Azad Bdes)

   (b) A Guerilla Regiment.

   (c) Ancillary Units.

   (d) "Crack" Regiment.

   (e) Rani of Jhansi Regiment. (Women's Regt.).

   (f) A Signal Coy.

   (g) An I.N.A. Hospital.

6. The Bahadur (hitherto known as the Special Service Group) and Intelligence Groups, a feature of the pre-Bose I.N.A., have moved into Burma. Reports of strength, training, organization and moral of these units when in Malaya are still conflicting. Units which had finished their training are reported to have left for Burma on 8 Jan 44 by overland and sea routes.

The I.N.A. in Burma.

7. On arrival in Burma the I.N.A. "Advance Party" consisted of 200 picked men from the Gandhi, Nehru, Azad and Field Brigades, and 200 of 'A' coy. of the Bahadur Group. Throughout 1943 little was heard of this body, except that the Bahadur Group representatives were being trained as intelligence agents, had been supplemented by a new ('E') company and that many of them were dispatched to

1. W.O. 203/803, Public Record office, London.

the forward areas on intelligence tasks in Sep. and Oct. 43. on 29 Oct. 43, 'B', 'C', and 'D' companies of the Bahadur Group arrived in Rangoon. This confirms the forecast made in paragraph 8 of W.I.S., Section D, No. 122, 1944. In Dec. 43, Bahadur Group strengths were 700 in Rangoon and 170 in the forward areas.

8. Simultaneously with the arrival of reinforcements for the Bahadur Group, the Intelligence Group of the I.N.A, totalling 350 men, arrived in Rangoon under the command of Capt. (I.N.A. Lt. col.) S.A. Malik, Ist Bahawalpur Infantry. Since then about 70 to 80 have moved up into Arakan and about 80 (two sections) were seen at the end of Jan. in transit to Myitkyina. Three others sections are said to have moved out to an unknown destination. Personnel from this and the Bahadur Group style themselves I.N.A. They are in fact intelligence agents; the Bahadur Group is intended for deep penetration and the Intelligence Group to carry out a role similar to that of our Battalion Intelligence Section, and also to carry out espionage tasks in plain clothes.

9. In addition to the Bahadur Group, the Intelligence Group and elements of the Field Force, unconfirmed reports speak of the arrival in Rangoon of a detachment of artillery and other units of the I.N.A during the latter half of 1943.

Jifs in Arakan

10. The first elements of the Bahadur Group moved up to Arakan in Sep. 43 and others in late October. Captain (I.N.A. Major) Misra, 5/17 Dogra Regiment, who commanded 'A' company of the Bahadur Group in Rangoon, left there in Oct. With a detachment and established his H.Q. in Buthidaung, with Lt. (I.N.A. Capt.) Mehar Das, 3 Lt. A.A. Bty., as his 2nd in command. By 17 Dec. 43 Misra had disposed the Bahadur Group in the Buthidaung and coastal areas. Their duties were chiefly military espionage in forward areas.

11. The Intelligence Group did not arrive in Arakan untill the beginning of Feb., although a captured document states that 73 men of the Group were to come under command of 55 Div. from 15 Jan. They were to operate under the orders of Capt. Misra through an officer of 143 Regiment. The latter was linked with London the Akyab branch of the Hikari Kikan through a small liaison group.

12. An operational order of 20 Jan stated that, in the event of operations,

most of the Hikari Kakan personnel would operate of the Buthidaung-Maungdaw front with one section in the upper regions of the Kaladan. Their tasks were "to collect intelligence necessary to conduct operations and look for deserters from British Indian army and destroy enemy installations."

13. At the beginning of Feb. all Jifs were ordered to concentrate east of the Mayu Range for an operation 'Whose zero hour had been put forward." During the early stages of the Japanese attack they participated in raids, were used as a screen for an out flanking movement, attempted to cause counfusion amongst our troops by shouting in English and Urdu, carried out espionage tasks, and acted as messengers.

14. On 10 Feb. Capt. Misra and Capt. Hottori (O.C. of the Akyab branch of the Kikari Kikan) were joined by '3' section of the Intelligence Group (70 men of the 73f referred to in para 11 above) and 110 men of the Field Force. Personnel of both forces Company of Bahadur Group and about 50 Japanese, this composite force moved to S.E. of Taung Bazar and dug in. From there mixed patrols of Japanese and I,N.A. were sent out.

15. In addition to these purely ex-P.W. bodies of Jifs, agents from the Kanbe Swaraj Training Institute also took part in the operations. In Dec. 43 their H.Q., Known as H.Q. 'J' force, was well forward with a detached H.Q. of the Bahadur Group. Jif strengths in Arakan forward of Akyab in the latter half of Feb. were approximately:—

Bahadur Group	70
Intelligence Group	70
Field Force	110
Kanbe S.T.I. Students	50
Others	110
Total	410

Jifs on other Fronts

16. There are reliable indications that Jifs on other fronts are being reinforced. On the night 2/3 Mar, about 14 miles N.E. of Tiddim, 5 out of a party of 7 Jifs voluntarily surrendered to our troops. They stated that they formed the Intelligence Group of the Nehru Brigade, and that their orders were to report back to a Lt. Col., late of the Bahawalpur

State Forces. This officer is probably Captain (I.N.A., Lt. Col.) S.A. Malik, who as mentioned in para 8 above, is believed to command the Intelligence Group of the I.N.A.

17. From this and other information it seems probable that the Japanese intend using I.N.A. troops in 4 Corps area in a more active role than hitherto. The Hikari Kikan has been paying particular attention to the Manipur plain for some time. A pointer may be the recent Japanese broadcast announcing a new organ for smoother liaison in future between the I.N.A., the Japanese army and the B.T.A. "to strenghen the joint strategic operations of the three allies for frustrating the enemy guerilla attempt to re-capture Burma and to draft important offensive as well as defensive operations."

18. I.N.A. propaganda. Copies of a new I.N.A propaganda leaflet entitled "Enlistment Card" and addressed to Indian Soldiers have been applied up in the forward areas. The leaflet is printed in Engish and Roman Urdu and issued jointly by the commanders of the Japanese and Indian National Armies. Space is left at the bottom for the signature of the prospective recruit. A copy is attached as Appendix 'A'.[2]

6. I.N.A. Awards. Following on the award of Sadar-i-Jang to Captain (Jif Major) Misra (Para 7 sec W.I.S. 1.10.126) 12 other ex-P.W. member of the Bahadur Group have been decorated. The following I.N.A. awards have so far been reported in broadcasts.

Nishi (west) Kikan

7. Previous reports have suggested the existence of a "Nishi" Kikan in Burma. A Chin, recently captured distributing Jif leaflets in the Faman area, was touched to belong to this organization. He wore an arm band bearing a white patch with a red letter "N"- and Japanese characters "Nishi Kikan"

8. He also had in his possession a pass written in Japanese to the effect that the holder was a volunteer guards leaders under the Nishi Kikan, while on the bottom of two of the leaflets in his possession, in Jap writting, he was described as "a propaganda distributor of this organization". The leaflets themselves were cyclo-styled and written in Burmese and Chin. They were addressed to Chins, both military and civilian, which indicates that this Kikan may be engaged particularly in propaganda among the chin tribes.

---

2. Not Printed.

9. Reactions to Jifs. A division which has met armed Jifs cooperating with Japanese troops for the first time, in the area MS 109 Tiddim Road, reports that in spite of the usual deceptive ruses Jifs have met with no success and a number of them have been killed. Forward troops report that the majority wear British type uniform and steel helmets and as a result are difficult to distinguish from our own troops during the hours of semi-darkness. The division comments that identify slips are not a satisfactory answer to the problem of distinguishing friend from foe in these circumstances.

10. Japanese propaganda. Recent batches of propaganda leaflets found in forward areas contain some new types. Of these the most striking is a pictorial leaflet depicting the allied leaders being shattered by Tojo's declaration of independence for the Phillippines, Burma's freedom, "no obstacles to the aspirations of the Indonesians and Japan's willingness to help India in her struggle for independence". The written leaflets contain:-

(a) Declaration of war against the allies by the Provisional Government of India.

(b) An appeal to Indian soldiers to shoot their British officers and help their unarmed brothers and sisters in India, with the consolation that if some are killed their sons and grandson will be proud of their memory.

(c) An appeal to Indians to rise all over India and drive out the British, and

(d) Seven reasons why Indians should not trust the British.

Jifs in Arakan

11. Documents captured in the recent Araken operations provide interesting information on the activities of the Hikari Kikan and I.N.A. "operatives". Intelligence reports concerning strength, composition and movements of our troops and of individual officers were being submitted by Hikari Kikan agents prior to the commencement of operations. Its agents were graded according to three degrees of reliability.

12. 55 Div orders dated 21 Jan, stated that one officer and 73 men of the Intelligence Group of the I.N.A. had been placed under command. As regards the duties of Hikari Kikan personnel, the orders stated 'most of the Akyab-Han personnel will operate on the Buthidaung-

Maungdaw front and one section will operate in the upper reaches of the Kaladan river to collect intelligence necessary to the conduct of operations and look for opportunities to secure deserters from the British Indian army and destroy enemy installations. The O.C. Hikari Kikan, Akyab Branch, was included in the list of intelligence officers to be present at a meeting to be held on 24 Jan intelligence officers to be present at a meeting to be held on 24 Jan.

13. Two messages dated 2 Feb. from this officer to two Japanese controllers of Jifs in the forward areas refer to the suspension of work in the Maungdaw area and the concentration of 'agency personnel" on the left bank of the Mayu. Care and speed are heavily stressed. This obviously has reference to the order to all Jifs to concentrate east of the Mayu Range.

14. An entry dated 2 Feb. in the diary of a Japanese officer envisages the I.N.A. cooperating in attacks scheduled for 3 Feb. by staging a feint attack. This has a possible bearing on a report of Jifs being used as a screen for an out-flanking movement by Japanese troops. An entry dated 8 Feb. in a diary written east of Buthidaung describes the activity of the I.N.A. as "amazing" and on 9 Feb. describes Indian P.W. being forced to surrender and "cooperate with the Hikari Kikan organization and the I.N.A.". An entry dated 11 Feb., in the diary of the officer mentioned above, states that a "Hav. Chief Technician, 10 Signallers, and one intelligence personnel were left behind for use by the Butai." There is no clue as to the indentity or type of signallers but the presence of a "chief technician" indicates the possibility of W/T. In the same diary an entry dated 15 Feb. mentions I.N.A. personnel attached to a Bn. engaged against Indian troops, to be employed in obtaining deserters. An entry dated 26 Feb. states that operatives and tired to be of further use". The writer expresses sympathy for Indian troops and remarks that they are unable to desert "because of the strict watch kept over them by the British". This is obviously the result of letting his own side's propaganda take him in. An entry dated 15 Feb. in this diary mentions the payment of Rs. 60,000/- to I.N.A. operatives. This possibly refers to cash payments to agents infiltrating into India.

23

Proclamation issued after the I.N.A Entry into Indian Territories, Requests the Indian People to Cooperate with the Provisional Government of Azad Hind[1]

4 April, 1944

"Sisters and brothers: under the leadership of the Provisional Government of Azad Hind which was formed on October 21, 1943, at Syonan, (formerly Singapore), by the unanimous will of three million Indians of East Asia, the Indian National Army has crossed the frontier and penetrated deep into Indian territory.

The Provisional Government of Azad Hind, your own Government has only one mission to fulfil and that mission is to expel the Anglo-American armies from the sacred soil of India by armed forces and then to bring about the establishment of the permamnent National Government of Azad Hind in accordance with the will of the Indian people. The Provisional Government of Azad Hind will continue the armed struggle until the Anglo-American forces are annihilated or expelled from Indian.

"While prosecuting the struggle for the complete liberation of India, the Provisional Government of Azad Hind will push on with the work of reconstruction of liberated areas. The Provisional Government of Azad Hind is the only lawful government of the Indian people. The Provisional Government calls upon the Indian people in liberated areas to render all assistance and co-operation to the Indian National Army and to civilian official appointed by the provisional Government.

The Provisional Government guarantees the safety of life and properly of the Indian population in liberated areas, but will inflict severe punishment on those who carry on any activities which might be of help to our Anglo-American enemies or their allies or might disturb the work of reconstruction to be started by the Provisional Government. The Provisional Government calls upon the Indian people to co-operate whole

1. *The Syonan Shimlum*, 6 April, 1944.

heartedly with our Ally, the Nippon army, who is giving unstinted, unconditional assistance in defeating our enemies.

"In the last two years the British have been strongly reinforcing themselves with troops from America, Austria, Chungking, China, and East and West therefore, felt compelled to avail itself of the generous offer of all-out aid made by Nippon, whose armed forces have accorded unparalleled victories over the Anglo-Americans since the beginning of the War of East Asia. The Provisional Government of Azad Hind is supremely confident that the Indian crush the Anglo-Americans and bring about the complete liberation of India.

"The Provisional Government is fully convinced of Nippon's sincerity towards Indian. The Provisional Government is convinced that Nippon has no territorial, political, economic or military ambitions in India. The Provisional Government is convinced Nippon is interested only in destroying the Anglo-American forces in India, which are the enemies not only of India, but of Asia as well. The destruction of Anglo-American imperialism alone will terminate this war and bring peace to the world.

"In accordance with its status as an independent government the Provisional Government of Azad Hind is arranging to issue its own currency in Rupee notes of different denomination. But owing to the rapid development of the war situation culminating in our quick advance into India, it has not been possible to bring into India in time, currency of the Provisional Government. The Circumstance therefore have rendered it necessary for the Provisional Government to borrow from the Nippon Government currency (military rupee notes) already in its possession and to use that currency as a temporary measure. As soon as the Provisional Government's own currency is available, the currency borrowed from the Nippon Government will be gradually withdrawn from circulation.

"Brothers and sisters! Now that our enemies are being driven out of Indian soil, you are becoming once again what you were before-namely free men and women. Rally round your own Government of Azad Hind- and thereby help in preserving and safeguarding your newly-won liberty. Subhas Chandra Bose. Head of State of the Provisional Government of Azad Hind

24

Note by Military Intelligence on the Activities of I.N.A. in Arakan and other Place in Indian Territory

7 April, 1944

I.N.A. Activities

1. **The Bahadur Group**—A Jif, considered reliable, states that the remaining 3 coys of the Bahadur Group (paras 1-10 of Sec.D, W.I.S. No. 122 and subsequent summaries) have moved into the forward areas from Rangoon.

2. **M.T. Company**—The arrival of this unit (Para 1, Sec. D, W.I.S No. 124) in Burma is confirmed. The C.O. was in Mandalay in Jan 44. Details of strengths and vehicles are still unknown.

3. **Reinforcement Group**—This is one of the 4 group (Para 2, sec. D, W.I.S. No. 126) reported to be attached to No. 1 Div. A detachment, strength unknown, has been identified at Kalewa. The function of the Group is reliably reported to be the handling of Indian P.W. with a view to conditions them for enlistment into the I.N.A.

4. **Arakan**—According to a Jif, who states that he is a Havildar of the Intelligence Section, No.2 Bn., Bose Bde., (Para 2, Sec. D, W.I.S. No. 126) No. 1' Bn. of the Bde. was in an area 9 miles SSE of Kaladan on 31 Mar. and intended offensive action against our rear. The platoon of Jifs which attacked a scouts. position on 31 Mar. and the company later reported as engaged in hand to hand fighting With west African troops were probably from the Bde. This identification of a part of the Bde in Arakan is considered relibale in view of previous information that the Bde. had left Malaya for Burma.

---

1. F.No. 601/7378/Historical Section, Ministry of Defence, New Delhi.

5. **Chin Hills**—Unconfirmed reports from Jifs indentify a battalion of I.N.A. in Tiddim and another in the area Haka-falm and along the Falam-Natchaung L of C . These indications of I.N.A. reinforcements are considered reliable.

25

Japanese press on the entry of I.N.A into India[1]

17 April, 1944

The majority of the editorials of the leading newspaper in Tokyo devoted their columns to the progress of war in the Pacific and the great military achievements of the combined Forces of the Japanese and Indian National Armies in India, during the week beginning March 31. These comments on the war progress have been made in special reference to the general East Asia. Other important topics were the intrusion of the Chungking troops into outer Mongolla. The Palestine dispute, the political offensives of Soviet Russia in Europe the situation in Argentina and the British coal mine strike. Comparatively few comments were made on European issues being superseded by the progress of the war in East Asia and further because of the absence of any great changes on the eastern front and other parts of Europe.

Concerning the general situation of the war in the pacific, the *Mainichi*, after dwelling in detail on the latest operations, declared that the existing state of affairs had been fully anticipated. "The enemy may boast of the excellency of their military weapons," the paper continues, "but they are unable to build airplanes that cannot be build air plans that cannot be shot down, nor can they construct ships that are unsinkable. There is no reason why the bases built by the enemy will remain invisible. Moreover. our army and navy defenses are impregnable while the people of our nation have unexcelled fighting spirit that will prevail against any foe."

Turning to the great military accomplishment of the Imperial Japanese and Indian Forces in the Indian compaign, the same journal declared. "We may achieve tomorrow-this will come for it is our furm determination to achieve such war results on all fronts."

The *Asahi* dwelt on the importance of cooperation among the three nations of Japan, China and India and urges their closer collaboration in

1. *Nippon Times*, 19 April, 1944.

order to forestall the invasion of Greater East Asia by the Anglo-Americans. The paper believes that close relations between the three Asiatic nations will be the cornerstone of new Asia and that the reçent victory of the combined Japanese and Indian Armies in the Indian campaign the great reprecussions created, thereby in India and the existing strife between Chungking and the United States, indicate that Asia is entering into an era of cooperation among these leading Asiatic nations.

In an editorial entitled "War developments and the Chungking regime," the *Tokyo Shimbun* pointed to the disastrous effects on the Chungking supply routs by the advance of the Japanese and Indian troops into Indian territory. After stating that the latest developments in India pointed to the inevitable downfall of British rule in India the journal continued. "In view of the fact that Chungking's dependence on the Anglo-Americans has been increasing in proportion to the weakling of the anti-Japanese elements it can be said that the downfall of Ching's regime is only a matter of time.

Taking up the latest American offensive on Pulho in the Central Pacific in their ambition to cut the Greater East Asia into two, the same paper declared that attempt was not only completely frustrated by the determined defense of the Imperial Forces, but the American Chungking troops which were to act in concert with the American naval offensive have been rudely shaken by the attacks of the Japanese Army in Burma and that the combined troops of America and Chungking were about to become the "orphans of the Himalyas." The enemies are bound to make still further attempts but each time they will meet the same fate, the paper concluded.

After narrating the latest offensives of the American naval units in the Marshalls, Truk and Saipan in the Central Pacific and the gallant defense put up by the Imperial Forces on land and in air, the *Asahi* said, "The way to our victory cannot be always smooth and easy. The greater our difficulties, the more determined our nation will be to secure final victory for our conviction of ultimate triumph is firm and unshakable le in fact of the most severe trials."

The *Yomrui Hochi* stressed the need of assuming the offensive in the Pacific, after pointing to the latest enemy attacks on the Caroline Group. "In the central as well as in the North Pacific, the enemy may launch attacks upon our nation so that we must be prepared all the time and in fact we have perfected our defense structure against any enemy offensive," the journal asserted. "But what is important is to turn to the offensive from the defensive at the opportune moment for such is the secret of a successful campaign."

The *Tokyo Shimbun* took up the enemy's failure in the Indo Burnese operations and points to the ubiousness of their strategy as the main cause of their complete inibility to meet the attacks of the combined Forces of the Japanese and Indians. The paper also revealed the enemy's plotting against the Chungking regime and the existing friction between them and declared that their present disunity of purpose and views conclusively demonstrate that the enemy's declared object of "advance to Tokyo" was only a hazy dream detached from any real possibility. In another editorial, the same daily touched upon the advance of the combined Japanese and Indian Forces toward Imphal and Bose's second statement and urged the Indian populace to rise against the British to secure their glorious independence because, the paper said the present will be the only opportunity for them to relize their long-cherished aim.

The *Mainichi* compared the progress of the war in East Asia and Europe and concluded that although peculiarities were seen in each, the course of total war was the same for both. The same paper urged the Government to adopt drastic war measures in order to act in advance of any condition due to the progress of the war. The *Yomiuri Hochi* dwelt on the importance in wartime of the native trait of courtesy for the people of Japan stating that it was an object of admiration by Western people and urged the nation to take pride in this racial virtue. Such an editorial as this is in sharp contrast to the enemy press which endorses the inhuman acts committed by their soldiers on the field ofer battle, thereby incurring the enmity of the world.

The *Nippon Sangyo Keizai* warned the people concerning the present strategy of the Untied States naval forces in the inner South Seas, by pointing to the great speed with which the American task forces have been repenting attacks on Japanese possessions in the central Pacific in their island-to-island-strategy.

Warning the peoples of Greater East Asia against the insidious propaganda of the Anglo-Americans regarding the present Indian campaign, the *Asahi* appealed to the Astatic people to trust one another and advance to final victory until the enemy nations are completely crushed in their inordinate ambition to subjugate Asia.

In another editorial, the same journal clarified the nature of the Indian independence movement and the significance of the statement of Subhas Chandra Bose, Head of the Provisional Government of Free India. and concluded with the works, "What is paramount is that the Indians should go ahead with their program of securing independence and of recorstructing their own land. Thus, they can prove to the world that the declared purpose of the Azad Hind Fauj to advance to New Delhi is not a fairy tale," as has been claimed by the enemy. This same statement is characterized by the *Mainichi* as "A historic document of stupendous importance." Pointing to Boss's words that the Provisional Government of Azad Hind is the only lawful government of India. The journal stated that the Provisional Government, by virtue of this statement, has become a full-fledged belligerent government.

26

Military Intelligence Reporting on the I.N.A. Despatch of Agents[1]

19 April, 1944

Bose Brigade

1. The arrival of the Bose Bde. in Burma from Singapore is now confirmed. Al three Bns. arrived in Jan. 44 and were billeted in Mingaladon barracks. At the end of Jan., about 120 of the Bahadur Group were attached to the Bd. of these, 25 were allotted to No.1 Bn which left Mingaladon on 4 Feb., and travelled by train to Prome. From there part of the Bn. marched to the Kaladan area and by 1 April, the whole Bn. was concentrated around Khabaw village (South of Kaladan).

2. According to a Bahadur Group Jif who was attached to Bn. H.Q. the 'plan of operations' for the Bn. was:-

   (a) An initial recce. of our dispositions by Bahadur Group personnel dressed in civilian clothes. The recce. party to return by 2000 hrs. on 31 Mar.

   (b) two companies to take up a defensive position.

   (c) three companies to attack British positions on 1 April This plan was partly carried out.

3. No.1 Bn. moved out to the forward areas according to schedule. The other two Bns. were due to leave Rangoon on 6 Feb., No. 2 for Buthidaung and No. 3 Bn. plus Bde. H.Q. in the Chin Hills is confirmed. According to a former member of the Bn., one coy. moved from Falam to Haka on 1 Apr. and took over garrison duties from the Japanese. Previous information indicated the dispositions of 'a Bn.

1. F.No. 601/7378/H.S.

of I.N.A.' as one coy. in Haka, one in Falam and three along the Falan-Natchaung L. of C. or haka and raiam but no independent operations of Jifs have yet mixed party of Japs, Jifs and locals and killed eight.

4. The location of No. 2 Bn. is still uncertain. If the movement schedule referred to above is accurate (and two Bns. plus Bde. H.Q. are known to have arrived in their present Locations according to plan), No.2 Bn. may be in the Buthidaung-Maungdon area. Other sources have referred to "a Bn." intended for the Mayu front. Recent reports of the activities of Jifs in the Maungdaw area strengthens the possibility of No. 2 Bn. being in that area. On 7 April Japs and Jifs numbering 100 were indentified at point 904 (6 miles S.E.. of Maungdaw). On the night 9/10 April this composite force attacked our positions and inflicted casualties. Reinforcements brought the mixed enemy force up to about 400 on the 11 April Our troops report the presence of increasing numbers of fighting I.N.A. in the front line in this area.

5. The following information comes from a Jif who accompanied No.1 Bn. from Rangoon to the Kaladan. Bn organization-Bn. H.Q. and five coys, each of three pls., each of three secs. Personnel a 'Sapper" Hav., a Hav. Clerk, two runners, two nursing orderlies' and a "defence platoon." Coy. Comds are 2/Lts; Pl. Comds are Havildars. Two Japanese officers are attached to each Bn. as advisors and interpreters. The Bn. is composed of Sikhs, Jats and Dogras - all ex-P.W. The Bn. possessed no signal equipment, bicycles, or motorcycles, and only one 3-ton ration lorry. Each platoon has a mule cart which is manhandled by 6 men; these carts carry ammunition and officers' kits. There are no stretchers and there is a great shortage of bandages and iodine. Only half the Bn. possess field dressings; the majority of these are the original British issues. Each company has 6 Boyes A/Tk. fifles, 6 Bren L.M. Gs, 6 Vickers M.Gs. and 6 TSM Gs. Each man has a 303 rifle and bayonet and officers wear pistils. The Sapper Hav. at Bn. H.Q. has 6 A/Tk. mines and 6 mines used for blowing bridges. The senior representative of the Bahadur Group has a stock of British handgrenades which he issues to men going forward on duty. Some N.C.Os and men in the Bn. carry grenades. Uniform is the same as that of the Indian army with the exception of special I.N.A. badges. No. 2 and 3 Bns. are said to be similarly organized and equipped.

Strategical Offensive

6. Recent developments show that the enemy; is intensifying his efforts to introduce agents into India. Important agents for deep penetration task are likely to be introduced by submarine or aircraft rather than by the difficult frontier crossing. This intensification of the strategical offensive is co-ordinated with Japanese military operations on the Eastern frontier, probable by Bose himself. Some undetected agents are in the country already, it is certain that other can be expected in the very near future. Upcountry men and Bengalis seem likely to be particularly marked out for this work, and special attention should be paid to the indentification of strangers of these classes who come to notice in suspicious circumstances.

7. Present information suggests a uniformity of plan in respect of the secret parties which the enemy is now sending to India for deep penetration work. They are ordered to collect military economic and political intelligence to conduct propaganda against the Anglo-Americans and in favor of the enemy; to incite subversive elements to commit sabotage; to obtain money and assistance in their work from persons in this country named by Subhas Bose; to operate in pairs and transmit the intelligence they obtain by means of wireless. The invariable means of maintaining contact between different parties, and between the component groups of the same party, appears to be through regular meetings at places selected author prior to loading enemy occupied territory or before the agents separate on arrival.

8. Espionage groups which are already known have been ordered to concentrate on Bengal, Bombay, the U.P. and North India generally, but this should not be regarded as an indication of a lack of interest in South India. The correctness of this view is emphasized by the fact that a party of enemy agents has been recently landed in Ceylon. Little is yet known in regard to intelligence plans and intentions affecting South India and it is therefore necessary for strict precautionary measures to be taken, and for constant vigilance to ensure that security arrangements are maintained at the maximum pitch of efficiency

British Counter Measures to Check the Impact of I.N.A. on the Soldiers of Indian Army[1]

15 May, 1944

CONFIDENTIAL
GENERAL HEADQUARTERS (INDIA)
NEW DELHI, MAY 1944

To
All Commanding Officers of Indian Army Units

Instructions of Josh work and Josh Group Organization within Units

1. **"Josh" Vs. "Jif"**—Josh is the strongest and most effective counter propaganda method yet evolved to combat the Japanese 'I' offensive against the morale and loyalty of Indian troops. "Jif" means Japanese inspired fifth column, but it may be taken throughout these instructions to denote any pro-Japanese organization having Indian members "Josh" means "Pep", and it is the morale counter offensive weapon against those dangerous activities.

2. **Rumour as offensive propaganda**—One of thc chief weapons of the Japanese 'I' offensive against India has been and still is rumour. Rumour are spread by a variety of means : by radio, by leaflet and by agent. The essence of a rumour useful to the enemy is that however false and tendenaious it is in content, it must contain a quality which makes it likely to be believed. In India the populations largely illiterate and tends to believe starting and plausible stories which spread extremely quickly. And the Japanese have sought to make the maximum use of this type of offensive weapon of psycho logical warfare.

3. **Anti-rumour**—The weapon used so far as Indian troops are, concerned to combat these activities is also the spreading of stories

1. War Office, 203/803. Public Record office, London.

of statement, with this important difference that in the cause they are true. It is of the highest importance that they should be true and that their truth should be implicitly belived in by all who spread them. The Josh Group is told facts, in the form of stories or statements by its leader, and the task of Group members is to disseminate these in the unit by repeating them or otherwise helping in their circulation.

4. **Purpose of Josh Group**—Josh Groups are intended to : (a) build in every Indian soldier the knowledge and firm faith that the Japanese and everyone who represents the Japanese are his own personal enemies; (b) introduce stories of our victories against the Japanese and so turn the conversation round to the topic of why the Japanese are India's enemies and why and how they will be defeated; (c) introduce stories of the bravery of Indian soldiers in action and his comrade-ship-in-arms with his Allies; (d) utilize entertainment, radio, drama, information rooms, picture layouts, etc., to bring home to the sepoy, through every medium that strikes his imagination, the existence of his chief enemy-the Japanese; (e) inoculate the Indian soldier with a sound factual basis of true knowledge so that false rumours and brazen lies spread by Japanese, Jifs and Japanese agents can be easily shown to be such.

5. **Josh organization and mechanics**—It is necessary that all officers in an Indian unit should have received and fully imbibed the basic information contained in the pamphlet "Against Japan".

Officer supervising Josh work in Units—This should be a very, senior officer (either the C.O. or the second in command) working in close conjunction with the Subdar Major.

Josh group Leader—These should work on a Comapany basis and the Josh Group leader of the Company Group ought to be either the Coy. Commander or someone working closely under his direction. Men chosen for the Group should be those in whom the troops have confidence.

All members of Josh Group should know the basic fact of the four talks in Appendix 3 in the pamphlet "Against Japan."[2] They should receive in discussions with the Josh Group leader; this informaion he obtains from material countained in"Josh," the weekly Josh directive. All members should be able to hold their own indiscussions which may arise in the lines about the Japs and the Jifs; their arguments should be reinforced by fact which they have obtained as members of the Josh Group.

2. Not printed.

The Prime essential in Josh work is enthusiasm. This should be felt throughout and should filter down from the officer supervision the work to every member of every Group. In view of this fact in view of the problem of language involved, it is impossible to define the number necessary in a Josh Group, but every Group must give the widest coverage possible for all casts, languages and ranks. A suitable Company Josh Group will contain 3 representative from each platoon of infantry in addition to the Supervision Officer and or Josh Group Leader.

Josh Group Co-ordination-In a battalion, this is the responsibility of the C.O. or second in command close conjunction with the Subedar Major. In a Training centre, co-ordination of Josh Group work through Bn commanders is the responsibility of the Training Centre Commandant (or second in command) and the Subedar Major.

6. **Conclusion**—The responsibility for the success of Josh work within unit lies with the Commanding Officer. If he is fully apprised of the purpose of Josh Groups and fully enthusiastic about it, he can make his enthusiasm felt throughout the Unit. That enthusiasm can be directed towards a most useful training in knowledge of the enemy, a training which goes on after parades are over, in the "Langars," in lines, in the barracks and wherever discussions take place. If Josh work become rigid, it loses freshness and keenness and when it loses these qualities it loses its drive and strength, and a weak spot is made for easy infiltration by Japanese and Jif propaganda.

28

INA Proclamations on Entering India

20 May, 1944

I. The Indian National Army, under the leadership of the Provisional Government of Azad Hind, has now massed in force and advanced into a territory of Eastern India as the spearhead for the creation of Free India.

The Indian National Army with the help and co-operation of the Imperial Nipponese Army, has pushed into Eastern India with the object of crushing the Anglo-American forces, the common enemy of East Asia, of marking India really an India for Indians by liberating her from the shackles of the despotic rule under which she has been groaning for ages; of bringing complete freedom and peace and order to the three hundred and eighty millions of our brothers and sisters in India; and also of driving away the Anglo-American menace from the borders of our neighbours—the Independent Burmese.

Brothers and Sister in India!

Be engaged in your daily work without fear; gather whole-heartedly under your Tricolour Flag of Independence hoisted by the Provisional Governments of Azad Hind; brace yourselves up for winning Complete Independence by retaking our Motherland from the hands of our enemies, Anglo-Americans.

The East Indian Territory into which the Indian National Army has advanced with the powerful aid of the Imperial Nipponese Army, as well as the people thereof, have now been liberated from the bondage of the Anglo-Americans. This territory has become the first free Indian Territory on the Mainland of India under the Provisional Government and will serve as the base for liberating our Motherland, The Imperial Nipponese Army

1. I.N.A. Relief and Enquiry Committee papers, Darya Ganj, New Delhi. The above proclamation was issued by Bose as Supreme Commander of Azad Hind Fauj.

will not establish a military administration but will cooperate with and wholeheartedly help the Provisional Government of Azad Hind in maintaining perfect peace and order.

II. If any person fails to understand the intentions of the Provisional Government of Azad Hind and the Indian National Army, or of our Ally, the Nipponese army, and dares to commit such acts as are itemised hereunder which would hamper the sacred task of emancipating India, he shall be executed or severely punished in accordance with the Criminal Law of the Provisional Government of Azad Hind and the Indian National Army or with the Martial Law of the Nipponese Army, the application of which has been agreed upon between the two allied armies, namely, the Indian National Army and its Ally, the Imperial Nipponese Army.

Punishable Acts

1. Rebellious acts against the Provisional Government of Azad Hind or the Indian National Army, or our Ally, the Nipponese Army.
2. Acts of spying
3. Acts of stealing and taking by force, damaging and destroying war materials which are in the possession of the Provisional Government or belong to our Ally, the Nipponese Army.
4. Acts of damaging or destroying of valuable material resources controlled or utilised by the Provisional Government of Azad Hind or by the Nipponese Army under previous agreement with the Provisional Government.
5. Acts of destroying various installations or equipments for traffic, communication, transportation, broadcasting, etc. which are controlled or utilised by the Provisional Government of Azad Hind and the Indian National Army, or by the Nipponese Army under previous agreement with the Provisional Government; to acts of interference with the employment and utilisation thereof.
6. Violent acts against, intimidation of killing or wounding of, or doing other harmful acts to those who belong to the Provisional Government of Azad Hind and the Indian National Army or our Ally, the Nipponese Army.
7. Acts of spreading enemy propaganda or wild and false rumours, and other acts of distrubing and misleading the minds of the inhabitants.

8. Acts of disturbing the money circulation and economic organisation or of obstructing the production and free interchange of commodities.

9. Any act other than those contained in the above items, that benefits the enemy or is harmful to peace and order and the well-being of the Provisional Government of Azad Hind and the Indian National Army or our Ally, the Nipponese Army.

10. Acts of attempting instigating and abetting those acts contained in the above items.

The trial and punishment of such criminals will entirely be at the discretion of the Provisional Government of Azad Hind except when crime committed are of such a nature as of necessity, owing to wartime emergency, must be dealt with by the Nipponese Army as agreed upon between the two Allied Armies.

III. The Nipponese Army will maintain strict discipline and protect, in the area into which they have advanced, the lives and properties of the Indian masses who do not commit any hostile act; and due respect will be paid to the religious, customs and manners of the Indian people.

It is guaranteed that the Nipponese soldier who may violate these strict injuctions shall be severely punished in accordance with the Martial Law of the Imperial Nipponese Army.

The Indian National Army will maintain strict discipline and protect, in the area into which it has advanced, the lives and properties of the Indian masses who do not commit any hostile act; and due respect will be paid to the religions, customs and manners of our countrymen.

It is guaranteed that any Indian soldier who may violate these strict injuctions shall be severely punished in accordance with the Martial Law of the Indian National Army.

29

Impact on the National Government of China of the Advance of I.N.A. into India

27 May, 1944

In an interview which he granted to the press, immediately after the issue of his historic statement in regard to the breaking through of the indo-Burmese border by the Japanese-Indian forces, Subhas Chandra Bose, head of the Provisional Government of Free India, stressed the far-reaching effects which it would produce on the Chungking regime. He expressed the confidence that the developments of this particular campaign would compel the Chungking leaders to reconsider their attitude seriously.

As Subhas Bose pointed out, the Chungking leaders who, in defiance of the advice of their fellow Asiatics, have been adhering stubbornly to their wrongful course now find themselves in a serious quandary. Reduced to straits military and politically, they are in utter consternation and disappointment.

The very serious nature of the menace to which Chungking is exposed in the new situation is admitted by the enemy camp itself. It was broadcast from Chungking on March 24, for example, that in view of the fact that Assam is not only very important strategically but is on Joseph Stilwell's Indo Chinese air route, the Japanese army would surely attack it relentlessly with the object of severing the supply route to Chungking. The anti-Axis. Headquarters in south-eastern Asia also admitted that in the event of the loss of Imphal, the communication line of Stilwll army operating in the Fukawng Valley would be exposed to a grave menace.

Chungking's great embarrassment and consternationis regarded indifferently by Britain who is responsible for the direction of the border operations. She has already discarded the repeated slogan of the recovery of Burma in favor of that of the defense of India. In his broadcast on 20,

1. *Nippon Times*, 22 May, 1944.

Winston Churchill, the British Prime Minister, simply stated that seeing that Britain had already suffered a staggering blow at the hands of the Japanese army, her best efforts in the theater of war in India and in the Bay of Bengal would be directed to the assistance of the American force so as to realize contact between Chungking and America. This lukewarm statement has naturally served to intensify the discontent of America and Chungking with Britain. Due to the lack of unity in sentiment and policy in the Anglo American-Chungking camp, bad blood is being created between Britain, who is bent on the defense of India, and America, who is eager to secure a speedy contact between Chungking and herself in the belief that delay in aiding exhausted Chungking involves the danger of making a Badoglio of Chungking with the result that the plan to create a second front on the Chinese Continent will fall through. Antagonism is in the meantime growing between Britain and Chungking due to the latter's increasing contempt for the fomer who has betrayed her crass impotence. Futhe, it is noticed that here is a gradual estrangement of feeling between Chungking and America because the latter and her troops in china are ambitious to establish control over Chungking.

Particularly noteworthy is a marked deterloration of feeling between America and Chungking for which the anit-Axis defeat on the Indo Burmese border furnished the occasion. The failure of the Chungking army under General Wet Lihuang on the Nu River to take any positive action when Stillwell's army was threatened with isolation as the result of the advance of the japanese Indian forces across the border caused high discontent among, the Americans with Chungking, and the American press was very bitter in its critucism of Chungking. The *New Republic*, an American weekly, in its recent issue, gave free vent to its sentiment against Chungking. In an aditorial entitled "Confusion, in East Asia," the journal warned Chungking that if it is to continue its present attitude of leaving active registance against Japan in the hands of the Chinese Communist Army, itself doing nothing beyond maintaining the posture of hostillity America and Britain will have to support the Yanan regime instead of the Chungking Administration.

On the other hand, Chungking contends that although friendly relationship between America and itself is maintained on the basis of America's training of Chinese airmen, the presence in China of Brigadier-General Claire Chennault's volunteer air force, the creation of the 14th air force, training by American officers of Chungking troops in India and in China, the supply of materials to Chiang by the Indo-Chinese air route, the formation of the mixed Sino-American air force. Sino-American Cooperative campaign in Burma and America's grant of loans to Chungking. This friendship is only nominal and it does not apply to the Chinese masses. It then proceeds to demand America's faihful fulfilment of all her promises to Chungking. The Ta Kung Pao in its editorial on "Accord between America and Changking." says: "The Chungkng expeditionary army will harbor prejudice against the American army unless Stillwell's declaration finds gerneral application that the officers and ment of the American and Chaing's armies are given the same food and the same conforts and are sharing hardsips. Liaison officers and interpreters are in request inorder to remove discord and antagonism bor of the language difficulty and the sense of rcial superiority on the part of American soidiers who are generally of low educdation."

The sentiment of the Chungking expeditionary army, as pointed out is the Taung Pao, is certainly the sentiment of all in the entire area under the jurisdiction of the Chungking regime also. The reason why the paper Confined its observation to the chungking expeditionary army is presumable that consumed; as it is, with discontent with America, Chungking has to be as mealy mouthed as possible from the necessity of obtaining America's positive aid.

Many episodes that came to light on the Indo-Burmese front bespeak the cruel treatment of which the officers and men of the Chungking army are victims at the hands of Americans. The poor Chungking officers and men are told by the Americans that they are none other than what has been given over in payment of the American arms supplied to Chungking and that they would therefore be shot immediately if they dared to retreat an inch. It is said that a Chungking soldier who was taken prisoner on the Indo-Burmese border declared in a frenzied tone that it was his intention to beat America anti Britain after defeating the Japanese. The officers and men of the Chungking army who are treated so cruelly by American and British officers are witnesses of the triumph entry of the Indian National Army into India. They are also acquainted with the truth about the anti-British movement which is sweeping over India. Nor are they ignorant of the fact that, composed, as it is, of pro-British and opportunist members, the Indian Central Assembly thought fit to reject the budget for the new fiscal year introduced by the government or that the representatives of all circles in India have demanded the reiease of Mahatma Gandhi. Apprehensive of the possible secession of the Chungking army from the Anglo American camp, which they fear would produce very grave effects on the populace under the jurisdietion of the Chungking regime, the Chungking authorities are, as urged by the Ta Kung Pao, asking America to take steps to prevent prejudice against America from being created, out of their desire to maintain collaboration with America. In other words, they are striving to see that the advance of the Japanese-Indian forces into India does not produce grave millitary and political effects.

Whether is the Chungking Administrator drifting? We must try to fathaom the reason why the Chungking army is doing nothing beyond maintaining the posture of hostility against the Japanese, leaving the task of active resistance in the hands of the Communist Army and why the Yunnan army is continuing its strategic attitude of inactivity despite the demand of America. Britain and the Chinese Communist Party for action. It is also important to find out whether it was for cooperative operations with America and Britain, in the true sense of the term, that the Chungking expeditionary army was sent into India.

Chiang Kai-Shek is inwardly distrustful of America and Britain, though he is outwardly maintaining the attitude of reliance on them. He is also secretly resolved on the elimination of the Chinese Communist Party. This double-faced policy is now being exposed by America and Britain as well as by the Chinese Communist Party. It is likely that the Anglo-American Plax and sinister phases with the progress of the war situation in East Asia; while Chungking will be obliged to put an end to its double-faced policy.

Special Orders, Regarding Pay, Decorotions of the I.N.A. by Lieut-Colonel I.Z. Kiani Commander No. 10 unit Azad Hind[1]

31 May, 1944.

1. **Rates of pocket money of the Azad Hind Fauj**—To commemorate the victories entry of the Azad Hind Fauj into India, a special monthly

Rank	Present rate in Malaya	Future rate in Malaya	Present rate in Burma	Future rate in Burma
General	400	400	400	400
Lt. General	—	350		375
Major-General		300		330
Colonel	300	270	310	29
Lt. Colonel	220	220	235	235
Major	170	170	185	185
Captain	120	120	135	135
Lietu:	80	90	90	100
2/Lietu:	70	70	80	80
Sub Offr I	60	60	70	70
Sub Offr II	50	50	60	60
Havildar	20	25	24	32
Naik	16	20	19	26
L/Naik	14	18	17	23
Sepoy	18	15	15	20

(A.H.F.O. 144/44)

1. I.N.A. Trial Papers

allowance called the "AZADI ALLOWANCE" will be given to sepoys and N.C. Os. w.e.f. the Ist April, 1944. Along with a slight change will be made in the rate of pocket Money hitherto prescribed for Lieute : and Colonels. The changes introduced are laid down in the table in previous page.

2. **Decoration-recommandations for**—All units forwarding recommendations for any award or decoration shall invariably submit a detailed report about the distinguished services rendered by the individual concerned. These report will be forwarded to H.Qrs., Supreme Command through proper channels. Recommendations in respect of officers and other ranks shall be submitted separately.

Distinguished Services Rendered throughout a Campaign

1. If an individual is recommended for a decoration for distinguished services rendered during the course of operations in a particular sector, a brief summary of the activities of the individual and results achieved shall be submitted.

2. Distinguished services rendered in a particular action-When an individual is recommended for a decoration for distinguished services during a particular action, a detailed report giving date, time, place, act of bravery and results achieved shall be submitted. (A.H.F.O. 118/44)

3. **Promotion-medical Personnel**—

1. Promotion.

(a) Henceforth all Group Commanders can promote Medical personnel upto the rank of Havildar within the war Establishment on recommendations from the senior Medical officer within their own Group.

(b) Information for all such promotions will be forwarded to D.M.S. Rear HQrs. No. 2. Supreme Comd. AHF.

2. E.D. Pay-MEDICAL PERSONNEL.-All Nursing personnel in front line units are entitled to E.D. Pay, provided they are within the war Est: and recommended by the M.O.i/c., units. Units will publish in unit orders and claim such E.D. Pay henceforth.

(A.H.F.O. 144/44)

31

Detailed Scheme for the Administration of Liberated Area by Provisional Government of Azad Hind[1]

15 June, 1944

Chapter 1

For the smooth Administration of a liberated area, Provincial Government (Central Organ) will consist of a Governor, Governor's Secretariat and an Advisory Council.

Organization

1 Governor's Secretariat

(A) **Department of Internal Affairs**

(I) Police (including Fire Brigade)

(II) Inspection of Local Organizations

(III) Census

(IV) Passports

(V) Air Raid Precautions

(VI) Civil Defence Organization

(VII) Jails

(B) **Finance**

(i) Revenue

(a) Land Revenue

(b) Income Tax

1. Office of the Strategic Services, Records group 226, U.S. National Archives, Maryland. U.S.A.

(c) Excise

(d) Absentee and Enemy property

(e) Registration

(f) Customs

(ii) Expenditure

(a) Budget

(b) Audit

(c) Accounts

(iii) Banking

(C) Law

(i) Legislation

(ii) Administration of Justice-

(High, District, Sub-Divisional, Circle and Panchayat Courts)

(D) Public Enlightenment

(i) Internal Propaganda

(a) Press

(c) Theatre, Cinema, and

(d) Literature

(ii) External Propaganda: Areas still under control of the enemy

(a) Civil

(b) Army

(iii) Education

(E) Health and Social Welfare

(i) Prevention and Treatment of Diseases

(ii) Relief of destitutes, including Air Raid Victims

(iii) Supply and distribution of medicine

(F) Agriculture and Industries and Labour

(i) Agriculture

(ii) Industries

(iii) Forests

(iv) Supply and distribution of labour and matters relating to the Joint Central Labour Board

(G) Commerce

(i) Production and Collection of Commodities-Food, Clothing etc.

(ii) Distribution (including Rationing)

(iii) Price Control and matter relating to the Joint Central Purchasing Board

(H) Communication and Transport

(i) Posts, Telegraphs, Telephone and Wireless

(ii) Railways, Steamer, Motor Vehicles, Boats, Carts, Cycles,

(iii) Public Works

(I) Roads: Buildings

(ii) Water Supply and Drainage (including irrigation).

(iii) Electricity : Gas

(J) Women's Affairs

(K) Co-operation

(i) Central Purchasing

(ii) Indo-Nippon Co-operation.

Chapter II

Advisory Council—The Governor of the Province or state will constitute an Advisory Council for the Province or State, by nominating 22 members, fifty per cent of whom will be unofficial while the remaining fifty per cent will be officials. The Governor will be ex-officio, President of the Council.

Duties and Functions—The Council will render advice on such matter as are brought before it from time to time. Any member may initiate the discussion of a subject with the previous sanction of the Governor.

The functions of the Council will be purely advisory.

There will be a Secretary to the Advisory Council who will prepare agenda, issue notice of the meetings, etc.

Chapter III

Administration

(a) Organization

1. **Village**—A village will be the smallest administrative Unit.

20 Houses	-	1 Beesghara,
10 Beesgharas	-	1 Mondal (Supervisor).
10 Mondals	-	1 Pradhan or Mukhia.
1 Panchayat	-	for every village.

The Pradhan will preside over a Panchayat.

2. **Dasgaon**—(Village Union) Ordinarily 10 Villages will constitute on one Dasgaon. It will have an area of about 10 sq. miles and a populations not exceeding 15 thousand.

3. **Sarkl (Circle)**—5 to 10 Dasgaon will form a Sarkl (Cirlcle)

4. **Mahakume (Sub Division)**—5 to 10 Sarkle (Circles) will form a *Sub Division* or *Mahakuma*.

5. **Zila (District)**—3 to 5 sub Divisions (Mahakumas) will form a district.

6. **Towns** (See Appendix I.)

(b) Duties and Functions

1. **Beesghara**

   (i) Census and Information (Cattle, Poultry, Land, Houses, Education etc.).

   (ii) Birth, Death, Immigration, Emigration.

(iii) Report on Theft, Robbery, and other Crimes, Fire.

(iv) Report on suspicious movements.

(v) Transmit information, instruction and orders of the Government and Local organization to the families for execution.

(vi) Report on prevalence of epidemic diseases and damage to crops.

2. **Mondal (Supervisor)**

(i) Supervision and co-ordination of the work of Beesgharas.

(ii) Transmitting to higher authorities of information received from Beesgharas.

(iii) Transmit information, instruction, orders of the Government and local organizations to the Beesgharas for necessary action.

3. **Pradhan or Mukhia**

(i) Representative of the Government in the area for executive work.

(ii) Will preside over Panchayat.

(iii) Will enforce decision of the Panchayat.

(iv) Transmit to higher authorities of information received from Mondals.

(v) Transmit information, instructions, orders of Government to Mondals Panchayat.

4. **Panchayat (Advisory Body to Pradhan)**

Advisory (i) To render advice to the Pradhan or Mondal in matter of purely local significance.

Judicial (ii) Will have powers to try civil and criminal cases.

(a) **Civil**—Money suits not exceeding Rs. 100/- other claims (small) generally not exceeding Rs. 100/-.

Boundary disputes not exceeding Rs. 100/-

(b) **Criminal**—Petty thefts.

Damage to crops whose value does not ......(sic) power of awarding punishments.

Fine not exceeding Rs. 100/- and/or

Compulsory manual labour not exceeding three month and/or Whipping, not exceeding 10 strokes.

(c) Lawyers will not be allowed to appear for cases.

Executive Panchayats will also undertake:-

(i) Construction and maintenance of :

(a) Village roads.

(b) Village buildings.

(c) Village Wells.

(d) Tanks.

(e) Bridges.

(f) Dispensaries.

(g) Primary Schools.

A Panchayat will consist of four members and one Pradhan to be appointed by the Zila Hakim.

In case where there are no suitable men available for the Panchayat, the Mondal or Pradhan will have the powers of the Panchayat court.

The power given to the Panchayat or to the Pradhan or Mondal may be curtailed by Government to meet any emergent conditions.

5. Ilakadar

Each Dasgaon will be incharge of an Ilakadar whose functions and duties will be:

(i) Co-ordinate and supervise the activities of the Mondals and the Panchayats.

(ii) Transmit orders of the Government to the Pradhan and Mondal for necessary action.

(iii) He will transmit information received from the Pradhan, Mondals, etc., to the higher authorities for such action as they may deem necessary.

(iv) He will refer to higher authorities any case or suit which may come to his notice in which he thinks that there has been a failure of justice dealt with by the Panchayat.

6. Sarkl Hakim (Circle Officer)

(i) Representative of the Government in charge of his area.

(ii) Responsible to the Government for the efficient and economic administration of the Sarkl.

(iii) Tour round his area to see and report how far peace and order prevails, conditions of Crops and economic condition generally: prevalence of any epidemic disease.

(iv) Report suspicious movements.

(v) Transmit to higher authorities of information received from Ilakadars.

(vi) Transmit information, instructions, orders of the Government and Local organizations to the Pradhan or Mondals.

(vii) Insepct and report if necessary on the activities of the different departments of Government functioning within his area, such as police, Public Enlightenment, Health and Social Welfare, Agriculture.

(viii) Will have power to try civil and criminal cases.

(a) **Civil:**

Money suits-value not exceeding Rs. 500

Rent suits-value not exceeding Rs. 50.

(b) **Criminal:**

Grievous Hurt.

Loss or damage to property, up to the value of Rs. 2,000.00

Riot.

Wrongful confinement.

Criminal intimidation.

Power of enquiry, arrest and detention in custody.

Danger to public safety and Welfare.

(c) Power of awarding punishments:

Fine :	Rs. 2000	and/or
Imprisonment	2 Years	and/or
Whipping	20 stokes	and/or

Confiscation of Commodities in Black Market up to Value Rs. 1,000/-.

(d) As a rule trials in Sarkl Courts will be summary,

(e) Lawyers will not be allowed to appear for cases.

7. **Mahakuma Hakim (Sub Divisional Officer)**

(i) Representative of the Government in his area.

(ii) Responsible to the Government for the efficient and economic administration of the Sub Division.

(iii) Officer-in-Charge of Government treasury.

(iv) Transmit to higher authorities of information received from Sarkl Hakim.

(v) Transmit information, instruction, orders, of the Government and local organization to the Sarkl Officer.

(vi) Responsible for the execution of Government orders and instruction.

(vii) Tour round his area to see and report how far peace and order prevails, conditions of the crops and economic condition generally of the people.

(viii) Supervise and co-ordinate the activities of Sarkl officers.

(ix) Submit monthly reports to the District officer and in case of emergency immediately.

(x) Inspect and report if necessary on the activities of the different departments of government functioning within his area, such as Education, Health and Social Welfare, Public Enlightenment, Police, Agriculture & c.

(xi) Report to the District officer immediately any outbreak of epidemics, suspicious movements which may jeopardize either Indo-Japanese. relationship or prosecution of the War of Liberation.

(xii) Carry out relief measures when sanctioned by Government.

(xiii) Enforce orders and instruction of Government or higher authorities.

(xiv) Will have the powers to try both Civil and Criminal Cases.

(a) Civil—Value up to Rs. 500

(b) Criminal—Same plus

Power of Inquiry, arrest and detention.

Rape

Abduction

Kidnapping

Mischief by fire and explosive

Danger to Public safety and welfare

(c) Powers of awarding punishment:

Fine-Up to four thousand	and/or
Imprisonment 3 years	and/or
Simple and Rigorous.	
Whipping: 30 strokes	and/or
Confiscation of Commodities in Black Market	unlimited

The Governor may notify if necessary that certain types of cases have a right of appeal in the Mahakuma Hakim's Court from the Court of Sarkl Officers.

8. Zile Hakim (District Officer)

(i) Representative of the Government in the District.

(ii) Responsible to Government for the efficient and economic administration of the District.

(iii) Enforce orders and instructions of the Provincial Government.

(iv) Transmit to Provisionial Government of information received from Mahakuma.

(v) Transmit information, instruction, orders of Government and local organization to the Mahakuma.

(vi) He will have authority to inspect the activities of the various departments of the Government functioning in the District (e.g. Police, Public Enlightenment, Health and Social Welfare & c.)

(vii) Report any outbreak of epidemic diseases.

(viii) Report on suspicious Movements.

(ix) co-ordinate activities of the different Sub Divisional Officers.

(x) Investigate reports submitted to him and take necessary action or forward to Government for orders.

(xi) Responsible for the appointment, transfer or dismissal of Mukhias or Pradhan, Mondal and Beegharas.

(xii) He will perform any special duties such as Recruitment for the Armed Forces, mobilization of national resources and such other matters as the Government may entrust him with.

(xiv) Will have power to try civil and criminal cases

(a) Civil —Value unlimited

(b) Criminal—All types of cases.

(c) Power of awarding punishment:

Fine	Upto 20,000 Rupess	and/or
Imprisonment	10 Years	and/or
Whipping	50 strokes	and/or
Forfeiture of Property of		
and kind		unlimited.

Capital punishment : Death (Subject to confirmation of the High Court).

(xv) Will have power of Inquiry, arrest and detention in custody.

(xvi) Will hear final appeal of cases tried in the Mahakuma officer's Court where the punishment awarded amounts to over 75 per cent or the claim is less than 75 per cent.

9. Provincial Government or state-A number of Districts will comprise a Province, in the liberated area. The number of the Districts will depend upon the extent of the territory liberated.

Government of the Province or State

Each Province or State will be administrated by a Governor.

Duties and Functions

(i) Representative of the Provisional Government of Azad Hind.

(ii) Responsible for the efficient and economic administration of his area.

(iii) Responsible for the the promulgation of any orders and instructions received from the Azad Hind Government for his Province.

(iv) Responsible for the general welfare of the people in his Province.

(v) Responsible for the protection of life and properly of the people in Province.

(vi) All the secretaries will be responsible to the Governor for the efficient working of their respective departments.

(vii) The Governor will exercise supervision and control over the day to day working of the Departments.

(viii) The Governor is invested with powers of appointment, dismissal and transfer of all important officer of the Government and he can delegate this power for appointing, dismissing, transferring, etc. in respect of other officers to any other responsible officer by notification from time to time.

(ix) Responsible for co-ordinating the activities of the different Head of Departments of Government functioning within his province, or state.

The Provincial Government or state will have on its own initiative or reference the residuary powers to Enquirer, reduce, commute, increase or reprieve any sentence passed by any Court without assigning any reasons.

The Provincial Government or state may issue an order for the release of any person under confinement or arrest.

Chapter IV

DEPARTMENTAL ORGANIZATION

(a)	*Department of Internal Affairs*		—Secretary
	(i)	Police-Insp. Gen. Police Census.	—Assistant Secretary
	(ii)	Passport, Inspection of Local Organization.	—Assistant Secretary
	(iii)	Air Raid Precautions. Civil Defence Organization	—Assistant Secretary
	(iv)	Jails-Insp. Gen. of Prisons	—Assistant Secretary
(b)	*Finance*		
	(i)	Revenue	—Secretary
		Land Revenue	—Assistant Secretary
		Income-Tax commissioner Absentee & Enemy Property	—Assistant Secretary
		Registraion & Excise	—Assistant Secretary
	(ii)	Expenditure	
		Budget—2 Asstt. Secretary Audit—Auditor General Accounts—Accountant General	—Deputy Secretary
		Banking	—Assistant Secretary

(c) *Law* —Secretary

Legislation —Assistant Secretary

Administration of Justice- High, District, Sub-Divisional Circle & Panchayat Courts —Assistant Secretary

High Court

(i) It will be the Highest Court in the Province. It will have two or more Judges.

(ii) Power of awarding punishment. :

Forfeiture of Property of any kind	Unlimited and/or
Fine	Unlimited and/or
Imprisonment	Life and/or
Whipping	50 strokes
Capital punishment	Death

(iii) Hearing Appeals from District Courts where the punishment awarded amount to over 75 per cent or the claim allowed is less than 75 per cent.

(d) *Public Enlightment*

Internal Propaganda-Press and Publicity other than Press,Theatre, Cinema, Literature. External Propaganda Civil and Army. —Assistant Secretary

Education-Director of Public instruction. —Assistant Secretary

(e) *Health and Social Welfare*

Prevention and Treatment of Disease.	Director of Health and Social Welfare	Assistant Secretary
Relief of Destitutes including Air Raid Victims.		Assistant Secretary
Supply and Distribution Welfare of Medicines		Assistant Secretary

(f)	*Agriculture, Industries, Labour*	—Secretary
	Agriculture-Director of Agriculture Industray-Director of Industries	—Assistant Secretary
	Forests-Chief Conservator Supply and Distribution: Labour Matter relating to the Joint Cent. Lab. Board.	—Assistant Secretary
(g)	*Commerce*	
	Production and Collection of Commodities-Director of Commerce. Price Control—and matters relating to the Joint cent. Pur. Board.	—Assistant Secretary
	Distribution (including Rationing)	—Asstt Secretary
(h)	*Communication and Transports*	—Secretary
	Posts and Telegraphs, Telephone, Wireless-Director of posts and Telegraphs,	—Asstt Secretary
	Railways, Steamer, Motor Vehicles, Boats, Carts, Cycles- Director of Transport	—Asstt Secretary
(i)	*Public Works*	—Secretary
	Roads, Building, (Chief Engineer)	—Asstt Secretary
	Water Supply and Drainage (inclu- ding Irrigation) Chief Engineer. Electricity and Gas	—Asstt Secretary
(j)	*Women's Affairs*	—Secretary —Assistant Secreatry
(k)	*Co-operation.* Indo Nippon Co-operation.	—Secretary —Assistant Secreatry

Note—Necessary Technical, Ministerial and Menial Staff will be employed as and when required.

Chapter V

Relation between departments and provincial administrative organization

(i) The Administrative Organization (e.g. District officer, sub-Divisional officer & c) will have inherent rights of inspection of a general nature, over the activities of the respective departmental officers (e.g. Officers of the Health & Social welfare Department, Police, Agriculture, & v.) of the Provincial Government functioning within the respective area of each administrator.

(ii) They will bring to the notice of the department concerned any matter that may have come to their notice for necessary action.

(iii) Each Department will be responsible for the technical administration of the personnel of their respective department and the maintenance of discipline and efficiency of work.

Chapter VI

Relation between provincial Government and Local bodies (District Board, Local Board, Municipality, & c)

(i) The Local Bodies will not be elected bodies for the present but the member will be nominated by the Government.

(ii) The duties and function of the Local Bodies will be assigned from time to time by notification by the Governor.

(iii) The Provincial Government will enunciate fundamental policies and communicate them to the Local Bodies such as District Boards, Municipalities, etc.

(iv) The Provincial Government will have the residuary power of direction and instruction, and where necessary, of execution of its orders in the territory of the Local Bodies.

(v) The Local Bodies will enforce all ordinances and regulations promulgated by the Provincial Government.

(vi) The Local Bodies may ask for the help of the Provincial Government in any matter considered essential.

Chapter VII

Relationship between Provincial Government and the Provisional Government of Azad Hind.

(i) The Provisional Government will appoint the Governor of each Province or State. The Governor will be responsible to the

Provisional Government of Azad Hind for the efficient administration of his territory.

(ii) The Provisional Government can delegate any of its power to the governor.

(iii) In the first occasion, the Secretaries will be appointed by the Provisional Government of Azad Hind. Thereafter, when vacancies occur, the governor of a province will appoint, subject to the approval of the Provisional Government of Azad Hind. But the Provisional Government may not accept the proposal and may appoint another man.

(iv) The Provisional Government will enunciate the fundamental policies and will communicate the same to the Provincial Government for execution.

(v) The Provincial Government will enforce all ordinances and regulations promulgated by the Provincial Government of Azad Hind.

(vi) The Provincial Government will have the residuary power of directions and instruction and in extreme cases of execution of any of its orders in the territory of the Provincial Government when the latter has failed in the execution of orders.

(vii) The Provincial Government may ask for the help of the Provincial Government in any matter which is considered essential.

Note:—The present constitution may be modified or abrogated when necessary by the Provincial Government or the Governor when duly authorized by the Provincial Government.

Chapter VIII

General Policies and Measures of the Provincial Government of Azad Hind.

(i) To give general direction to the Provincial Government.

(ii) To use the liberated territory for organizing the next stage of the campaign.

(iii) To give necessary help to the Azad Hind Fauj and the Imperial Japanese Army in the matter of defense and future campaign.

(iv) Formation of Provinces (see Appendix III).

Chapter IX

Policies and Measures of the Provisional Government of Azad Hind for self sufficiency.

It is very necessary that self-sufficiency with regard to the requirements of the inhabitants, Azad Hind Fauj and Nippon Army should be achieved as early as possible. But it can only be done by full co-operation between the Provincial Government and the Nippon Army. In this connection three items are of Primary importance:

What the Provincial Government can do.	What is expected of the Nippon Army.
1. Food Ariticles	
(a) Commander, Ration and allot all articles of necessity.	(a) Importation of Food supply for six months recruitments, Rice, salt, sugar, Atta-Dal-Tea.
(b) Organize, encourage and provide facilities for local production as much as possible.	(b) Importation of seed cuttings for growing food crops lacally- paddy, maize, wheat, dal, tapioca, Sweet Potatoes.
(c) Recruit Kisans and Agri-cultural Experts.	
2. Medical supplies	
(a) Recruit Doctors, Dres-sers, Nurses.	(a) Quinine Tablets and Ampoules
(b) Collect and purchase Medi cines Durgs and Dressing and Anti-septics.	Anti-Cholera) Anti-Typhoid) Vaccines Lymph Vaccines
3. Clothing	
(a) Collect and Purchase Burma Khaddar (i.e. Hand Made cloth).	
4. Recruitment of Labour	

5. The quantities required should be as much as can be obtained, because as time goes on, the British are likely to destroy more and more as

they go on retreating and consequently our requirements will also be increasing. It is likely that we may be required to provide for a population of 10 millions within the next few months plus those of the Nippon Army and of the Azad Hind Fauj. And after that, we may have to provide for a population of over 70 Millions. So we should go on collection as much as is possible.

Chapter X

Policies and Measures for the Maintenance of Currency.

In order to maintain the value of currency we will have to adopt preventive as well as curative methods. The preventive method will have to be applied first; these tend to prevent inflation of currency. But later, when inflation of currency does appear, we will have to adopt additional measures which have a deflating effect by taking off from the market surplus currency, that is currency which is not covered by Goods and services and which is really the cause of inflation. The more effectively the preventive methods are applied the lesser would be the necessity to apply the curative (deflative) methods. The following measures are proposed to be applied:

(a) Preventive Methods to be Applied Immediately

(i) To control the amount of currency out in circulation, Provisional Government must be informed of the amount of new currency that the Nippon Army is bringing into the country, as well as the amount of old currencies left in the country-in Banks, Treasuries, etc.

(ii) Price Control.

(iii) Control of consumption of essential commodities and food.

(iv) Elimination of Departmental competition in purchasing materials by establishing joint central purchasing Board.

(v) Strict rationing of food and commodities.

(vi) Stern suppression of Black Market.

(vii) Prohibit the export of gold.

(viii) Prohibit private sale or transfer of gold.

(ix) Control of sale and purchase of all commodities necessary for war.

(b) Curative Methods to be adopted. Later if necessary

(i) special taxing of immovable property.

(ii) Levying of a graded tax on incomes over a certain level.

(iii) Levying a tax on amusements, narcotics, tobacco, alcoholic drinks and motor vehicles.

(iv) Organization of State Lotteries.

Chapter XI

Policies and measures of the Provisional Government of Azad Hind for controlling commodities and the restriction of Consumption

(i)	Seizing and scaling of the Commodities.	By Department of Commerce.
(ii)	Dealers, Merchants and manufacturers to be asked to declare their stocks of articles of (a) Rice, Flour, Salt, Sugar, Maize, Dal, Molasses. (b) Cloth, of all kind, including Mosquito Netting. (c) Stationery, machinery of all kinds, motor vehicles, and their spare parts. bicycles, and their spare parts, drugs, chemicals, acids, alkalies and other medicines.	By Department of Commerce.
(iii)	Rationing, Food, Cloth and essential materials (Stationery, mechanical Parts, motor vechicles, & c.)	By Department of Commerce.
(iv)	Forbidding transfer, sale and purchase of the above mentioned articles without a special order from the Provincial Government. Purchases to be Permitted only on the ration scale in case of items in (a),	By Department of Commerce.

	(b) and in very restricted quantity of (c) in sub-para (iii) above.	
(v)	Prohibition of Big Parties- not more than 10 persons and once a month and with special permission of the Rationing Board to be established under the Department of Commerce	By Department of Commerce.
(vi)	Severe Punishment for Blace Marketting-Death Sentence.	Police-Prosecution or Reference by Department of Commerce.
(vii)	No Japanese Firms to go in the country at this stage.	

Chapter XII

Administrative organization for Managing Labour controlling and distributing Commodities, Police work and Civil Defence Work.

(a) Management of Labour

(i)	Collection of Information	Beesghara
(ii)	Change of profession from Non-Essential to essential services (War Material)	Police Thana
(iii)	Supply No forcible recruitment of farm labour No separate recruitment of labor by any party	Joint Labour Board
(v)	Compulsory employment of labor	All unemployed males -18 to 40 year-fi necessary

(b) Controlling and Distribution of Commodities

(i) Seizure and Sealing of the Commodities in the premises of Merchants, Dealers and Manufacturers.

(ii) Declaration of stock by Merchants, Dealers and Manufacturers compiled in the presence of Department Inspectors.

(iii)	Census	Beesgharas.

(iv)	Census Family Ration Cards	Police Thana
(v)	Order to merchants, dealers, manufacturers, forbidding the transfer, sale or purchase of the notified commodities without a permit.	by Department of Commerce.
(vi)	Order publishing the price and scale of ration of each commodity which an adult of child is entitled per week, month, half year, or year as the case may be.	By Department of Commerce.
(vii)	Order to merchants, dealers manufacturers, to sell, or purchase, at the controlled price only or to sell only sanctioned scale and only on the production of the family census ration card where entries must be made in accordance with the articles sold.	By Department of Commerce

(c) Police Work

Inspector General of Police

Deputy Inspector General of Police — Provincial Secretariat

A.I.G.P. (Intelligence) — A.I.G.P. — A.I.G.P. (Armed Police)

Criminal Special D.S.P. — ZILA

Dy. Supdt.

I.P.

S.I.P. Thana

A.S.I.

Pradhan — Head Constable & Constable

Mondal

Beesghara

(d) Civil Defence Work—This will be organized on a voluntary basis under the leadership of Mondals and Pradhans in villges and towns. Instruction and guidance will be given by the Police and Military Authorities. People will undergo regular physical and spiritual training and military drill. It will supervised by the Mahakuma and Zila Hakim.

(e) Air Raid Precautions—This will be organized also on a voluntary basis. Doctors, Dressers, Warden, Watchers, etc., will be recruited, organized and trained under suitable leadership. Instruction and guidance will be given by the Police and military Authorities. It will be supervised by the Mahakuma and Zila Hakim.

Chapter XIII

Help wanted from Nippon Army in the matter of:

(i) Imports.

(ii) Whole-hearted co-operational Nippon Army:

(a) In the case of rationing

(b) Price Control

(c) Suppressing the Black Market

(d) Control their own M.P.

(e) Protection of women

(f) Control of sale and purchases of all commodities necessary for war.

Appendix 1

Towns

30 Families	1 Beesgara
10 Beesgharas	1 Mondal
10 Mondals	1 Mukhia or Pradhan
10 Mukhias or Pradhans	1 llakadar

The ILAKADAR will submit information received from the Pradhans to the Inspector of Police and will transmit to theMukhias orders of the government.

In a town a number of I lakas will constitute to form a Ward and a number of wards will constitute to form a District.

Relation between the town organization proposed above, and a Municipal organization will settled later on but tentatively a proposal is put forward that the Pradhans will form a town council which will be an advisory body for assisting the Mayor of the town who will be appointed by the Provincial Government.

In those places where elected Municipalities exist and are functioning well, the Provincial Government will consider the question of continuing the system.

The Mayor will have executive functions. He will be not only the Head of the Town but will be the Executive head of the town also.

Appendix II

Scale of Rations

This can only be fixed when the whole stock available can be ascertained plus the quantity that can be imported. Even then it may have to be changed if the circumstances demand. Tentatively:

(a) For those doing Hard Manual Labour:

	Man	Woman			
Rice or	10	8	Seer	(Kilo)	Per month
Maize	9	8	"		"
Salt	1/3	1/3	"		"
Sugar	3/4	1/2	"		"
Cooking oil	1	5/8	"		"

(b) For Others:

	Man	Woman	Child		M.or. F.
Rice or	6	5	3	Seer	Kili/p.m.
Maize	5.5	4.5	2	"	"
Salt	1/4	1/4	1/5	"	"
Sugar	1/2	1/2	1/4	"	"
Cooking Oil	3/4	1/2	1/4	"	"

Appendix III

Formation of Provinces

1. Any area that is liberated from the British rule and comes under the Provisional Government will be declared a Province or State as the case may be.

2. In case another area is liberated which is not contiguous to the first liberated territory and where a separate administration is necessary on account of the emergencies of the situation, the second liberated territory will also be declared a Province.

3. With the progress of the campaign when two liberated areas are joined up, the Provisional Government will consider the question whether the administration of the two territories should be combined under an unified administration.

4. Subject to the above, the Provisional Government will adhere as far as possible to the existing boundaries of the Provinces and States in India.

32

P.K. Sahgal to M.Z. Kiani Praising the Achievements of I.N.A.[1]

16 June, 1944

Sadar Dafter, Ala Kaman, Azad Hind Fauj.
(Head Quarters, Supreme Command, I.N.A.)

D.O. No. 16/2/18/ MS.

Dear Colonel,

Your report, dated the 15th of May, together with your points for Netaji were received here on the 4th June. A copy of your telegram asking for lorries, horses, sugar and oil, etc., was also received on the same day.

Major N.N. Khosla together with Rear H.Qrs. had already left. I hope the M.T. with the Rear H. Qrs would be able to relieve the transport situation to some extent. We are doing our best to buy some horses, but unfortunately most of the good horses have already raised an A.T. Platoon from among the old 3rd Cavalry personnel and as soon as we have bought 20 horses, arrangements shall be made to send them on to you.

Four thousand ground sheets have already been sent with your Rear H.Qrs. No. 2, Engineer Coy., No. 2 Hospital, No. 1 MPT. Coy. and No. 1 Mortar Coy. have already left for the front. No. 1 M-T. Coy. and No. 2 Eng. Coy. shall come under command of No. 1 Div. after they arrive in Mandalay. Although I have not been able to get the Hikari Kikan to state in absolutely concrete terms, they have given me to understand that No. 1 M.T. Coy. shall be employed to carry out the duties for no. 1 Div.

We tried to get a wagon to send some soap, gur, oil and mess tins to you but unfortunately were not successful. However, a wagon has been promised us next week when No. 4 Engineer Coy., shall leave here.

At present communications between our H. Qrs. and the front line units are most inadequate. We have started a weekly courier service

1. I.N.A. Trial Papers.

between Rangoon and Mandalay and form there the H.Qrs. in Maymyo are trying to make arrangements for D.R.L.S. to the front with the Hikari Kikan. The original objection was that our cipher was too simple, however, we produced other modified forms of our cipher which came up to their standard, but they wish to make another code based on the Nippon Army Code, for us. Even after that the question of equipment and Trinidad personnel shall still remain and we may have to fall back on using the Nippon Units to ascend our messages, In that case a code consisting of numerals alone may solve the script problems. I am at present trying to find some solution to this problem and if you can help me by some suggestions, I shall feel most grateful.

Every one hear has been most thrilled to read about the bold actions of the Init No. 24 from 24th Aprill to 6th may 1944. I shall feel very grateful if you will please convey my heartiest congratulations to Col. I.J. Kiani, Pritam Singh and the others who took part in it.

Staff Officers of the Mori Head Quarter from time to time, inform us of the very good work being done by the units under your command and the other day we were told by a senior officer of Mori H.Qrs. who has recently returned from the front line that he had met you in the front line and that all the neighbouring units spoke very highly of your brilliant leadership and the wonderful work being done by the units under your command. It is indeed a matter of pride for us all that the vanguard of the I.N.A. is creating traditions which the following units shall don well follow.

Please give very best regards to Major Hassan and other officers.

With best regards.

'Jai Hind'

Yours sincerely,

(Sd.) P.K. SAHGAL.

33

Bose to Karuppiah Encouraging him to Complete his Training in Tokyo[1]

18 June, 1944

Arzi Hukumate Azad Hind

(The Provisional Government of Free India.)

Sri N.Karuppiah.,
Tokyo.

Jai Hind.

I am extremely happy to receive your letter and to know that you are getting on very well with your studies. It gives be very great pleasure indeed to know that you are determined, to derive the maximum benefit from your stay in Nippon, and to return to free India as worthy Sons of our Motherland. You ahve gone to Nippon to undergo training which will enable you to become full-fledge soldiers who will defend Indian's Independence with the last drop of their blood. Mean while, the heroism and half-sacrifice with which officers and men of the Azad Hind Fauj are fighting on the battle fields of Arakan, Kaladan, Imphal and Kohima should serve as a shining example to you to follow all your life.

Though you are yet in your teens, you have left your homes and parents and brothers and sisters and you have travelled thousands of miles to far-off Nippon and will stay there for some yours. Though physically you are thousands or miles away from me, you are always in my thoughts.

There was much that I wanted to tell you when I addressed you in Syonan. But the thought of parting form you so overpowered we that I could hardly speak. I wanted to go back to Syonan again in March to see

1. Azad Hind Center, Kaula Lumpur. Number of Young person were sent to Tokyo for military Training. They were known as Tokyo Cadets. Sri N. Karuppiah was one of them.

you off-but I could not, owing to the military operations then going on at the Indian-Burma frontier. I future, I shall be moving further and furter from you and may not, therefore, be able to write to you. But do write to me, my dear boy, whenever you have a chance of writing. Wherever my be, I shall always think of you and pray for your success.

I hope you will continue singing the National Anthem every day during your stay in Nippon. And pray every morning and night that you may become a worthy son of Mother India.

Jai hind

34

Bose Asking Lognandan to Send a Detailed Report on the Administration of Andamans[1]

21 June, 1944

Jai Hind,

1. I was glad to receive your letter or 15th march and the 2nd April. I also received two reports through the Hikari- kikan-one on the 22nd and the other on the 15th June.

2. I am gratified to learn from different sources that you have been carrying on your duties with ability and tact. I am, however, not satisfied at the progress made in actually transferring the administration. For this, I do not blame you.

3. I am anxious to know how you have been keeping in health, because I was informed that when you left Port Blair, you were in poor health. I hope you are taking all impossible care any our healthy.

4. Please let me know by wire, if necessary if you need one money.

5. I wonder if you have in organizing a unit of the there.

6. I understanding that your are the chairman of the Civilized Administration Council of the Andaman and Nicobar Islands. I understand, further, that this Council is an Advisory Body. Is that correct.

7. Along with your letter of the 15the March I received a group photograph taken after your arrival in Port Blair.

8. I am sorry that we have not attended to your needs from this end-but we shall do so in future. Since you left Malaya, events have been moving at a break neck speed and we have all been plunged in work.

1. I.N.A. Trial Papers.

9. I note that in your first letter you wanted cutlery and crockery and also medicine. It we can arrange or the transport through the wavy, we shall send you the articles.

10. I entirely agree with you that without police powers you cannot have prestige in he eyes of the people.

11. You may tell the authorities that I dissatisfied at the progress made in the transference of the administration.

12. You must be aware that our Army is now fighting on Indian soil in Manipur and in Kohima sector (Assam). On the whole, our troops have done very well and have learned the appreciation the Nippon Army. Co. Chatterji is the Governor designate of the liberated Territory.

13. We have started a new organization called the Azad Hind Dal. It is a semi military organization consisting of civilians and administrations who will be going to India in the wake of our victorious armies.

14. I am now in Rangoon on a short visit from the front. I also paid a flying visit to woman and have just returned from there. I shall soon be moving forward again.

Hope this will find you all well. Cordial greeting to all.

Jai Hind

Signed
Subhas Chandra Bose.

35

Bose's Statement on the Reponsibilities of the Provisional Government of Azad Hind[1]

3 July, 1944

"Our activities hitherto have been confined substantially to East Asia but the situation is considerably changed now. Those areas of India which have been liberated have given rise to the problems of administration and reconstruction.

The military operations now progressing with such brilliant results have also created new problems, namely, how are these military operations to be carried farther into India and how is the Indian revolution within India to be completed.

"One year since the present struggle for the liberation of our mother country it has become necessary now to survey the past and make plans for the future.

"As a result, we have three fields of activity. The first is East Asia, which is still to be our political and strategic base. The second is the liberated territory, the problems with which we are confronted there being mainly those of administration and reconstruction and proportions for future development. The third is the rest of India now under enemy occupation. The revolution of India must be completed. For that our troops must penetrate into that territory.

"Until very recently the activities of the Provisional Government of Azad Hind had been virtually restricted to East Asia, but now that the situation has undergone a change it would be necessary to reorganize the Government and expand its activities. In other words, the Provisional Government will have to expand its three spheres of activities, namely. East Asia, the liberated zones and the enemy occupied territories. For this purpose, it will be necessary for the Government to dispose State ministers

1. *Nippon Times*, 5 July, 1944

and Advis with clear responsibility to the respective spheres. The first squad will supervise various activities in East Asia, the second one in the liberated zones while the third one will engage in its duties in the enemy occupied territories. The first squad now active in East Asia is called the east Asiatic Committee of the Cabinet, the second squad now engaged in activities in the liberated zones the Liberated Area Committee of the Cabinet, and the third squad the Wartime Committee of the Cabinet.

"The mobilization of manpower, finance and material in East Asia must be enforced more and more vigorously in the future. For this end a new administrative department should be established or the existing administrative organ expanded to meet the need. The present financial affairs department will be enlarged and its scope of activity greatly expend.

"The new administrative body under the name of 'Mobilization Department' will call for and mobilize the personnel necessary for the activities of each of such bodies as the Indian National Army, the Rant of Jhansi Regiment, the department in charge of reconstruction of the liberated areas and the affairs of the Indian Independence League.

"The recently established Supply Department will also be expend.

"Although there will be no changes in the fields of activies of the various existing organs or of those to be established, in the future the greater part of matters of importance will be entrusted to the three departments of finance, mobilization and supply.

"The East Asia Committee will be composed of a regular East Asia Minister and an Adviser, who will supervise activities in East Asia.

"There are plans ready for the administration of liberated areas and for reconstruction work therein. These will be enforced at a proper time. The personnel needed by the department dealing with reconstruction in the liberated areas has already been sent to the regions where it is required. The member of the department already are at work within India and near the border.

"The Liberated Area Committee is composed of ministers and advisers who have been selected to work in liberated areas and ministers and advisers who are on missions in various regions.

"Lastly, the Wartime Committee is made up of ministers and advisers who are qualified to deal from an expert standpoint with matters connected with military operation, propaganda, revolutionary movements, and re-examination of the existing system of administration.

"The three committees mentioned above will constitute the Cabinet, a step intended to enable it to meet the needs of the existing situation.

The Provisional Government will give every assistance to the committees. As a measure intended to help it in doing this it will be arranged for the work of the committees to be concentrated where they are functioning. The committees will be made to work so as to facilitate the achievement of the first object of the Provisional Government which is the independence of India.

36

Bose's reply to British Propaganda Against I.N.A.[1]

5 July, 1944

The formation of the Azad Hind Fauj has been a source of extreme worry and anxiety to our enemies. They tried to ignore its existence for a time, but when the news could no longer be suppressed, their organ-the anti-India Radio at Delhi-started propaganda to the effect that Indian prisoners-of-war, under Japanese control, had been coerced into joining the army. The propaganda could not, however, endure long, because the news began to infiltrate into India that large number of Indian civilians from all parts of East Asia were joining the Azad Hind Fauj. The experts of the anti-India Radio had therefore to alter their tactics. They then started fresh propaganda to the effect that Indian prisoners-of-war had refused to join the Azad Hind Fauj and that, thereupon, Indian civilians were being forced into joining that army. It did not probably strike the wiseacres at Delhi that if it was impossible to coerce prisoners-of-war into joining the army, it was even more impossible to coerce free civilians into becoming soldiers...

Anybody who has a grain of common sense will realize that though a mercenary army can be organized by coercion, a Volunteer Army can never be so organized. You can perhaps force a man to shoulder a riffle, but you can never force him to give his life for a cause which is not his own.

At an early stage our enemies used to say that the Azad Hind Fauj was not army-that it was a mere propaganda stunt-and that it would never fight. Latter on, the anti-India Radio at Delhi began to shout that the Azad Hind Fauj had not crossed the frontier of India. Now that frontier has been crossed and the battle for India's freedom is being waged on Indian soil, enemy propagandists have taken recourse to a last desperate trick. They are now inventing fictitious dated supposed to have been given out by us

1. *Greater Asia*, 8 July, 1944.

for our entry into Delhi and are abusing us for not rechange our destination according to schedule...

I have already told you that the Azad Hind Fauj is composed not only of men but also of women...

Friends, the Azad Hind Fauj is an army which is not only composed of Indian, but it has also been trained by Indian. That army is today fighting under Indian officers.

The Azad Hind Fauj is the military organ of the Provisional Government of Azad Hind. The Provisional Government and its Army are the servants of the Indian nation. Their task is to fight and liberate India. When that liberation is achieved, it will be for the Indian people to determine the form of Government that they desire. The Provisional Government will then make room for a permanent Government in Free India, which will be set up in accordance with the will of the Indian people. For that glorious day we are now toiling, sweating and fighting.

37

Heroic Deeds of the I.N.A.[1]

5 July, 1944

On the occasion of the first anniversary of the assumption by Subhas Chandra Bose of the Leadership of the Indian Independence Movement in East Asia, a mammoth parade was held yesterday morning with a large number of crack reinforcement forces of the Azad Hind Fauj participating.

In the Parade. a battalion of the Indian National Army marched past in review while Netaji Bose, Commander-in-Chief of the Azad Hind Fauj. saluted with profound confidence in his army of liberation. On the parade stand were high ranking Japanese Army officers and Renzo Sawada, Japanese Ambassador to Burma, as well as Major-General Thakin Aung Sun, Burmese Minister of Defense.

Following the parade Netaji, speaking to the officers and men of the Indian National Army from the platform which was decorated with the national flag of Azad Hind declared that crossing the frontier of India has brought about unique inspiration to the Indian National Army whose unflinching optimism and burning fighting spirit will lead the army into the very heart of India.

"No sacrifice, no hardship and no suffering." the Netaji said, "are too great for the Indians fighting for the liberation of their motherland." and asked his officers and men to throw in every ounce of energy into the struggle, for he declared that, "this war is for us a life and death struggle, and no matter what suffering and sacrifices are involved we are convinced of our final victory."

In the course of his speech, Mr Bose announced the awarding of the medal "Vir-Hind". to Lieutenant Pira Singh for his singular bravery. The Netaji commended the Lieutenant in his address, saying, "This office, who is an example to the members of Azad Hind Fauj, has won our

1. *Nippon Times*, 7 July 1944.

admiration by exhibiting a high standard of patriotism, courage and devotion to duly throughout the campaign in the Arakan area."

Lieutenant Singh distinguished himself in ecounters with the British forces during the Arakan fighting in Feburary this year in the course of which he was injured by a trench-motor and deprived of the use of both legs. When he appeared before the dails, carried by his comrades in an armchair, to receive his award a deep silence enveloped the entire parade ground. The Netaji warmly shook his hand and pinned the medal on his chest.

The ceremonial Parade was brought to a close by the singing of the national anthem. The parade ground was then cleared off for a mock battle which was staged by troops of the Rani of Jhansi Regiment which for the past year has received intense training for combat in modern warfare.

38

In a Broadcast Message to Mahatma Gandhi, Bose Tried to Convince him about the Need for Armed Struggle and Foreign help for India's Freedom[1]

6 July, 1944

Mahatmaji,

Now that your health has somewhat improved, and you are able to attend to public business to some extent, I am taking the liberty of addressing a few words to you with a view to acquainting you with the plans and the activities of patriotic Indians ouside India. Before I do so, I would like to inform you of the feelings of deep anxiety which Indians throughout the world had for several days, after your sudden release from custody on grounds of ill health. After the sad demise of Srimati Kasturbaiji in British custody, it was but natural for your countrymen to be alarmed over the state of your health. It has, however, pleased Providence to restore you to comparative health, so that 388 millions of your countrymen may still have the benefit of your guidance and advice. I should next like to say something about the attitude of your countrymen outside India towards yourself. What I shall say in this connection, is the bare truth and nothing but the truth.

There are Indians outside India, as also at home, who are convinced that Indian Independence will be won only through the historic method of struggle. These men and women honestly feel that the British Government will never surrender to persuasion or moral pressure or non-violent resistance. Nevertheless, for Indians outside India, difference in method are like domestic differences. Ever since you sponsored the Independence Resolution at the Lahore Congress in December 1929, all members of the Indian National Congress have had one common goal before them. For Indians outside India, you are the creator of the present awakening in our country. In all their propaganda before the world, they give you that

1. *Greater Asia*, 7 and 18 July, 1944.

position and the respect that due to that position. For the world public, We Indian Nationalists are all one having but one goal, ond desire and one endeavor in life.

In all the countries free from British influence that I have visited since I left India in 1941, you are held in the highest esteem, as no other Indian political leader has been, during the last century. Each nation has its own internal politics and its own attitude towards political problems. But that cannot affect a Nation's appreciation of a man who has served his people so well and has bravely fought a first-class modern power all his life. In fact, your worth and your achievements are appreciated a thousand times more in those countries that are opposed to the British Empire that in those countries that pretend to be the friends of Freedom and Democracy. The high esteem in which you are held by patriotic Indians outside India and by foreign friends of India's Freedom, was increased a hundred-fold when you bravely sponsored the "Quit India" Resolution in August, 1942.

From my experience of the British Government while I was inside India-from the secret information that I leave gathered about Britain's policy while outside India-and from what I have seen regarding Britain's aims and intentions throughout the world. I am and honestly convinced that the British Government will never recognize India's demand for Independence. Britain's one effort today is to exploit India to the fullest degree, in her territory to her enemies and another part to her friends. Even if the Allies could somehow win the war, it will be the United States of America, and not Britain that will be the top dog in future and it will mean that Britain will become a protege of the U.S.A. In such a situation the British will try to make good their present losses by exploiting India more ruthlessly than ever before. In order to do that, plans have been already thatched in London for crushing the nationalist movement in India once for all. It is because I know of these plans from secret but reliable sources that I feel it my duty to bring it to your notice.

It would be a fatal mistake on our part to make a distinction between the British Government and the British people. No doubt there is a small group of idealists in Britain-as in U.S.A.-who would like to see India free. These idealists, who are treated by their own people as cranks, form a microscopic minority. So far as India is concerned for all practical purposes, the British Government and the British people mean one and the same thing. Regarding the war aims of the U.S.A. I may say that the ruling clique at Washington is now dreaming of world domination. This ruling clique and its intellectual exponents talk openly of the "American Centurey", that is, that in the present century the U.S.A. will dominate the world. In this ruling clique, there are extremists who go so far as to call Britain the 49th State of the U.S.A.

There is no Indian, whether at home or abroad, who would not be happy if India's freedom could be won through the method that you have advocated all your life and without shedding human blood. But things being what they are, I am convinced that if we do desire freedom we must be prepared to wade through blood.

If circumstances had made it possible for us to organize an armed struggle inside India, through our own efforts and resources, that would have been the best course for us. But, Mahatmaji, you know Indian conditions perhaps better than anybody else. So far as I am concerned after twenty years experience of public service in India, I came to the conclusion that it was impossible to organize an armed resistance in the country, without some help from outside-help from our countrymen abroad, as well as from some foreign power or powers. Prior to the outbreak of the present war, it was exceedingly difficult to get help from a foreign power, or even from Indians abroad. But the outbreak of the present war threw open the possibility of obtaining aid-both political and military-from the enemies of the British Empire. Before I could expect any help from them, however, I had first to find out what their attitude was towards India's demand for freedom. British propagandists, for a number of years, had been telling the world that the Axis Powers were the enemies of Freedom and, therefore, of India's freedom. Was that a fact? I asked myself. Consequently, I had to leave India in order to find out the truth myself and as the whether the Axis Powers would be prepared to give us help and assistance in our right for freedom.

Before I finally made up my mind to leave home and home land, I had to decide whether it was right for me to take help from abroad. I had previously studied the history of revolutions all over the world, in order to discover the methods which had enabled other nations to obtain freedom. But I had not found a single instance in which an enslaved people had won freedom without foreign help of some sort. In 1940, I read my history once again and once again I came to the conclusion that history did not furnish a single instance where freedom had been won without help of some sort from abroad. As for the moral question as to whether it was right to take help, I told myself that in public, as in private life, one can always take help as a loan and rapay that loan later on. Moreover, if a powerful Empire, like British Empire, could go round the world with the begging bowl, what objection could there be to an enslaved and disarmed people like ourselves taking help as a loan from abroad. I can assure you, Mahatmaji that before I finally decided to set out on a hazardous mission, I spent days, weeks and months in carefully considering the pros and cons of the case. After having served my people so long, to the best of my ability, I could have not desired to be a traitor, or to give anyone a justification for calling me a traitor.

It was the easiest thing for me to remain at home and go on working as I had worked so long. It was also an easy thing for me to remain in an Indian prison while the War lasted. Personally, I had nothing to lose by doing so. Thanks to the generosity and to the affection of my countrymen, I had obtained the highest Honour which it was possible for any public worker in India to achieve. I had also built up a party consisting of staunch and loyal colleagues who had implicit confidence in me. By going abroad on a perilous quest, I was risking-not only my life and my whole future career-but what was more, the future of my party. If I had the slighest hope that without action from abroad we could win freedom, I would never have left India during a crisis. If I had any hope that within our lifetime we would get another chance -another golden opportunity-for wining freedom, as during the present war, I doubt if I would have set out from home. But I was convinced of two things, firstly that such a golden opportunity would not come within another century-and secondly, that without action from abroad, we would not be able to win freedom, merely through our own efforts at home. That is why I resolved to take the plunge.

Providence has been kind to me. In spite of manifold difficulties, all my plans have succeeded so far. After I got out of India, my first endeavour was to organise my countrymen, where I had happened to meet them. I am glad to say that everywhere I found them to be wide awake and anxious to do everything possible for winning freedom for India. I then approached the Governments that were at war with our enemy, in order to find out what their attitude was towards India. I found out that contrary to what British propaganda had been telling us for a number of years—the Axis Powers were now openly the friends of India's freedom. I also discovered that they were prepared to give such help as we desired, and as was within their own power.

I know the propaganda that our enemy has been carrying on against me. But I am sure that my countrymen, who know me so well will never be taken in. One who has stood for national self-respect and honour all his life and has suffered considerably in vindicating it, would be the last person in this world to give in to any other foreign power. Moreover, I have nothing to gain personally at the hands of a foreign power. Having received the highest honour possible for an Indian at the hands of my own countrymen, what is there for me to receive from a foreign power. Only that man can be a puppet who has either no sense of honour and self-respect or desires to build up a position for himself through the influence of others.

Not even my worst enemy can dare to say that I am capable of selling national honour and self-respect. And not even my worst enemy can dare to assert that I was a nobody in my own country and that I needed foreign help to secure a position for myself. In leaving India, I had to risk everything that I had including my life. But I had to take that risk because only by doing so could I help the achievement of India's freedom.

There remains but one question for me to answer with regard to the Axis Powers. Can it be possible that I have been deceived by them?

I believe it will be universally admitted that the cleverest and the most cunning politicians are to be found amongst Britishers. One who has worked with and fought British politicians all his life, cannot be deceived by any other politicians in the world. If British politicians have failed to coax or coerce me no other politician can succeed in doing so. And if the British Government, at whose hands I have suffered long imprisonment, persecution and physical assault, has been unable to demoralise me, no other power can hope to do so.

Moreover as you personally are aware, I have been a close student of international affairs. I have had personal contacts with international figures before the outbreak of this war. I am therefore no novice who could be duped by a shrewd and cunning politician. Last but not least, before forming an opinion about the attitude of the Axis Powers I established close personal contact with important leaders and personalities in the Axis countries who are responsible for their national affairs.

Consequently, I make bold to say that my countrymen can have the fullest confidence in my judgment of the international affairs. My countrymen abroad will testify to the fact that since I left India. I have never done anything could compromise in the least, either the honour or the self-respect or the interests of my country. On the contrary, whatever I have done has been for the benefit of my nation, for enhancing India's prestige before the world and for advancing the cause of India's freedom.

Mahatmaji, since the beginning of the War in East Asia our enemies have been carrying on a raging and tearing campaign against Japan. I shall, therefore, say something about Japan—particularly because at the present moment I am working in the closest co-operation with the Government, Army and people of Japan.

There was a time when Japan had an alliance with our enemy. I did not come to Japan so long as there was an Anglo-Japanese alliance. I did not come to Japan, so long as normal diplomatic relations obtained between the two countries. It was only after Japan took what I consider to be the most momentous step in her history—namely, declaration of war on Britain and America—that I decided to visit Japan of my own free will.

Like so many of my countrymen I had read anti-Japanese propaganda material for a number of years. Like so many of my countrymen. I did not understand why Japan went to war with China in 1937. And like so many of my countrymen, my sympathies in 1937 and 1938 were with Chungking. You may remember that as President of the Congress, I was responsible for sending out a medical mission to Chungking in December, 1938. But what I realised that after my visit to Japan and what many people at home do not yet realise, is that since the out-break of the war in East Asia, Japan's attitude towards the world in general, and towards Asiatic nations in particular has been completely revolutionised.

It is a change that has overtaken not merely the Government, but also the people of Japan. A new consciousness—what I may best describe as an Asiatic consciousness—has seized the souls of the people of Japan. That change explains Japan's present attitude towards the Philippines, Burma, and India. That is what explains Japan's new policy in China.

After my visit to Japan and after establishing close contact with the present day leaders of that country I was fully satisfied that Japan's present policy towards Asia was no bluff but was rooted in sincerity.

This is not the first instance in history when an entire nation has been seized with a new consciousness. We have seen instances of it before in France during the French revolution and in Russia during the Bolshevik revolution. After my second visit to Japan in November, 1943, I visited the Philippines, and met Filipino leaders there and saw things for myself. I have also been in Burma for a fairly long time and I have been able to see things with my own eyes, after the declaration of Independence. And I have been to China to find out if Japan's new policy was real or if it was a fake. The latest agreement between Japan and the National Government of China has given the Chinese people practically all that they had been demanding. Japan, under that agreement, has even agreed to withdraw her troops from China on the termination of hostilities.

What then is Chungking-China fighting for? Can one believe that Britain and America are helping Chungking-China out of purely altruistic motives? Will not Britain and America demand their pound of flesh in return for the help that they are now giving to Chungking to make her continue the fight against Japan? I clearly see that Chungking is being mortgaged to Britain and America because of past hatred and antagonism towards Japan.

So long as Japan did not initiate her present policy towards China, there might have been some justification or excuse for the Chinese to seek British and American aid for fighting Japan. But now that an entirely new chapter in Sino-Japanese relations has begun, there is not the slightest excuse for Chungking to continue her meaningless struggle against Japan. That is not good for the Chinese people; it is certainly not good for Asia.

In April, 1942, you said that if you were free to do so you would work for an understanding between China and Japan. That was an utterance of rare statesmanship. It is India's slavery that is at the bottom responsible for the chaos in China. It is because of the British hold over India that Anglo-Americans could bluff Chungking into hoping that sufficient help could be brought to Chungking to enable Chungking to continue the war against Japan. You were absolutely right in thinking, Mahatmaji, that a free India would work for peace between Japan and China. I go so far as to say that the freedom of India will automatically bring about an honourable understanding between Chungking and Japan, by opening the eyes of Chungking to the folly that she is now committing.

Since I came to East Asia and visited China, I have been able to study the Chinese question more deeply. I find that there is a dictatorship ruling in Chungking. I have no objection personally to dictatorship, if it is for a righteous cause. But the dictatorship that rules at Chungking is clearly under foreign American influence. Unfortunately, the Anglo-Americans have been able to deceive the ruling clique at Chungking into thinking that if Japan could be somehow defeated, that China would become the dominant power in Asia. The fact, however, is that if Japan were defeated by any chance, then China would certainly pass under American influence and control. That would be a tragedy for China and for the whole of Asia.

It is through this false hope of becoming the dominant power in Asia, if Japan could be somehow defeated, that the ruling clique at

Chungking has entered into an unholy alliance with the ruling clique at White House and at Whitehall. I know something of the propagandist activities of the Chungking Government in India and of its efforts to play upon the motions of the Indian people and win their sympathy. But I can honestly say that Chungking which has been mortgaged to Wall Street and Lombard Street, does not deserve the sympathy of the Indian people any longer specially after Japan has initiated her new policy towards China.

Mahatmaji, you know better than anybody else how deeply suspicious the Indian people are of mere promises. I would be the last man to be influenced by Nippon if her declarations of policy had been mere promises. But I have seen with my own eyes, how in the midst of a world war Nippon has put through revolutionary changes in countries like the Philippines, Burma and National China. In General Tojo, Nippon has a leader and a Prime Minister, who is true to his word and whose actions are in full conformity with his declarations-and a leader who, in moral stature, towers head and shoulders above contemporary statesmen.

Coming to India, I must say that Nippon has proved her sincerity by her deeds. There was a time when people used to say that Nippon had selfish intentions regarding India. If she had them, why should she recognize the Provisional Government of Free India? Why should she decide to hand over the Andaman and Nicobar Islands to the Provisional Government of Free India ? Why should there now be an Indian Chief Commissioner of the Andaman and Nicobar Islands stationed at Port Blair? Last but not least, why should Nippon unconditionally help the Indian people in East Asia in their struggle for their Independence? There are Indians all over East Asia and they have every opportunity of seeing Nippon at close quarters. Why should three million Indians distributed all over East Asia, adopt a policy of the closest co-operation with Nippon, if they had not been convinced of her bona fules and of here sincerity? You can coerce one man or coax him into doing what you want him to do. But no one can coerce three million Indians distributed all over, East Asia.

If Indians in East Asia had taken help from Nippon without putting forward them own efforts and without making the maximum sacrifice, they would have been guilty of wrong-doing. But, as an Indian, I am happy and proud to be able to say that my countrymen in East Asia are putting forware the maximum effort to mobilize men, money and materials for the struggle for India's freedom. I have had experience at home in collecting funds and materials and in recruiting men for national service for a period of twenty years. In the light of this experience, I can properly assess the worth and value of the sacrifice that our country men in East Asia are now making.

Their effort is magnificent. It is because they are putting forward a magnificent effort themselves and are prepared to make the maximum sacrifice that I see no objection to taking help from Nippon, for such necessary articles as Arms, Ammunition etc., that we ourselves cannot produce.

Mahatmaji, I should now like to say something about the Provisional Government that we have set up here. The Provisional Government of Azad Hind (or Free India) has been recognized by Nippon, Germany and seven other friendly Powers and this has given Indians a new status and a new prestige in the eyes of the whole world. The Provisional Government has, as its one objective, the liberation of India from the British yoke, through an armed struggle. Once our enemies are expelled from India and peace and order is established, the mission of the Provisional Government will be over. It will then be for the Indian people themselves to determine the form of Government that they choose, and also to decide as to who whole take charge of that Government. I can assure you, Mahatmaji, that I and all those who are working with me, regard themselves as the servants of the Indian people. The only reward that we desire for our efforts, for our suffering and for our sacrifice is the freedom of our Motherland. There are many among us who should like to retire from the political field, once India is free. The remainder will be content to take up any position in Free India, however humble it may be. The Spirit that animates all of us today is that it is more honourable to be even a sweeper in Free India, than to have the highest position under British rule. We all know that there are hundreds of thousands of able men and women at home to whom India's destiny should be entrusted, once freedom is achieved

How much help we shall need from Nippon till the last Britisher is expelled from the soil of India, will depend on the amount of cooperation that we shall receive from inside India. Nippon herself does not desire to thrust her assistance upon us. Nippon would be happy if the Indian people could liberate themselves through their own exertions. It is we who have asked for assistance from Nippon after declaring war on Britain and America, because our enemy has been seeking help from other powers. However, I have every hope that the help we shall receive from our countrymen at home will be so great that we shall need the minimum help from Nippon. Nobody would be more happy than ourselves, if by any chance our countrymen at home should succeed in liberating themselves through their own efforts, or if by any chance, the British Government accepts your Quit India Resolution and gives effect to it. We are, however proceeding on the assumption that neither of the above is possible and that an armed struggle is inevitable

Mahatmaji! There is one other matter to which I shall refer before I close and that is about the ultimate outcome of this war. I know very well the kind of propaganda that our enemies have been carrying on in order to create the impression that they are confident of victory. But I hope that my countrymen will not be duped thereby and will not think of compromising with Britain on the issue of independence, under the mistaken notion that the Anglo-Americans will win this war. Having travelled round the world under wartime conditions with my eyes open, having seen the internal weakness of the enemy on the Indo-Burma frontier and inside India, and having taken stock of our own strength and resources, I am absolutely confident of our final victory. I am not so foolish as to minimise, in the least, the strength of the enemy. I know that we have a long and hard struggle in front of us. I am aware that on the soil of India Britain wil fight bravely and fight hard in a desperate attempt to save her Empire. But I know also that however long and hard the struggle may be it can have but one outcome—namely our victory. India's last war of independence has begun. Troops of the Azad Hind Fauj are now fighting bravely on the soil of India and in spite of all difficulty and hardship they are pushing forward, slowly but steadily. This armed struggle will go on, until the last Britisher is thrown out of India and until our Tricolour National Flag proudly floats over the Viceroy's house in New Delhi.

Father of our nation! In this holy war for India's liberation, we ask for your blessings and good wishes.

Jai Hind

39

Bose's Message to I.N.A. Soliders

12 July, 1944

The ceremonial Parade was brought to a close by the singing of the national anthem. The parde ground was then cleared off for a mock battle which was staged by troops of the Rani of Jhansi Regiment which for the past year has received intenise training for combat in modern warfare.

As I study the events of 1857 and think of the atrocities perpetrated by the British after the revolution collapsed,-my blood begins to boil. If we are men, we will certainly see to it that the heroes of 1857 and after, who suffered so much from British terror and brutality, are properly avenged. India demands revenge. The British who split the blood of innocent freedom-loving Indians and tortured them in an inhuman manner—not only during the war, but after it was over—must pay for their crimes. We Indians do not hate the enemy enough. If you want your countrymen to rise to heights of superhuman courage and heroism, you must teach them not only to love their country but also to hate the enemy.

Therefore, I call for blood. It is only the blood of the enemy that can avenge his crimes of the past. But we can take blood, only if we are prepared to give blood. Consequently, your programme for the future is to give blood. The blood of our heroes in this war will wash away our sins of the past. The blood of our heroes will be the price of our liberty. The blood of our heroes—their heroism and their bravery—will secure for the Indian people the revenge that they demand of their British tyrants and oppressors.

1. *Greater Asia*, 12 July, 1944

40

Japanese View of the Provisional Government of Azad Hind and Indian National Army[1]

12 July, 1944

The Japanese Government has decided to despatch a diplomatic envoy to the Provisional Government of free India as a concrete measure of promotiing cooperation and friendly relation. This decision was made by the Japanese Government on the occasion of the recent visit here of Subhas Chandra Bose,s President of the Provisional Government. I shall take this opportunity to review the various events that have occurred since the establishment of the Indian Provisional Government on oct. 1943.on the occasion of an assembly at Shonan of East Asian delegates of the Indian Independence League in East Asia. Prior to this assembly in July the same year Bose went to Shonan to assume leadership of the Indian Independence League and the position of Commander-in-chief of the Indian National Army. At a plenary session of the assembly of the delegates of the Indian Independence League on the afternoon of Oct. 21. Bose proposed the inauguration of a Provisional Government of Free India. His motion was unanimously supported by all the delegates present and the assembly promptly elected Bose as President of the Provisional Government. After Bose had taken the oath as the head of the newly established Government its organization and other important matters were decided by the assembly and the first declaration of the Government was promulgated. Thus the Provisional Government of Free India came into being.

The declaration of the newly inauguarated government in part said "With the approach of the emancipation of our fatherland, the Indians have the task of establishing their own Government and of commanding their last fight under its direction. In view of the fact that the leader are all being imprisoned and our brethren in our native country have been

1. *Nippon Times*, 12 July 1944.

deprived of arms. It is impossible to establish a Provisional Government with in Indian territory, to direct our struggle. Thus the Indian Independence League in East Asia must take up this task with the aid of the patriots within and with out country....The task of the Provisional Government is to commence a struggle in order to bring about the complete expulsion of Britain and her allies from Indian territory and to guide this struggle. The Provisional Government also has the duty of establishing a free and permanent national government which shall be based on the will and trust of the Indian people. The Provisional Government shall carry out its national affairs with the confidence of the people until a permanent and free Indian Government is established on Indian soil." Thus, did the declaration clarify the combative and transient character of the newly established Provisional Government.

The Provisional Government of Czecho-Slovatia estatblished during the First World War. The Czecho Solvakian National Congress was orgainzed with Dr. Masaryk heading it in the early part of 1916 with its headquarters established at Paris. It appealed to the moral suppart of the world for its aspirations for the establishment of an independent Czecho-Slovakian State. The organization also created a Cecho— Slovakin army which cooperational with the Allied and Entente force on the German and Austrian fronts in summer of 1918, the Allied maltons extended to the Czecho-Slovakian. Czecho-Slovakian Nation Congress, as the supreme organ of the Czech-slovakian people and its army, as a belligerent army on the Allied side. When this National Congress created a Provisional Government at parts at the end of September the same year, and notification of the same was sent to the powers, both France and Italy formally recognized the newly created government. Another independent organ was created in Austria and Hungary and was amalgamated with the Provisional Government later on. On Nov. 14,1918 the National Parliament, convened at Prague, announced the creation of the State of Czeco-Slovakia. Masaryk was elected the first President of this nation and a formal government was then organized.

Immediately after the Japanese Government announcement of its recognition of the Provisional Government of Free India. Bose came to Tokyo on Oct. 31 to convey his gratitude for the cooperation shown his government by the Japanese Government. He attended the Assembly of East Asiatic. Nations which was held in Tokyo on Nov 5 and 6 in the capacity of an observer. At the meeting of the Assembly on the sixth, Dr Ba Maw, Burmese Prime Minister, proposed after the adoption of the Joint Declaration by the Assembly that the Assembly declare itself in favour of giving its wholehearted support to Bose in his attempt to emancipate India together with the Indian National Army as the head of Provisional Government of free India. After the adoption of this motion for support, Mr. Bose rose to thank the Assembly for his unanimous decision on this motion.

Due to this provisional nature of the Indian Government. its organization is simple. It is composed of the Military. Foreign Affairs, Finance Propaganda and Women's Affairs Departments all under the direction of the head of the Government. The direction of Military and Foreign Affairs Departments were concurrently held by the head of the Government. There are several Ministers without Portfolio and several Cabinet Advisers.

The Indian National Army was placed under the Provisional Government and the supreme direction of Bose. The Indian Independence League continued its activities in cooperation with the Government in order to stimulated the Indian National Movement. The Provisional Government was to be located within Burma.

On Oct. 23,1943, the Imperial Japanese Government announced its recognition of the newly created Provisional Government of Free India. The statement of the Japanese. Government is as follows. "Firmly beliving that the newly established Provisional Government of Free Indian with Mr. Subhas Chandra Bose as President makes a great advance towards the complete realization of an independent India which has been the aspiration of the Indians for many year we hereby announce that we shall extend recognition to the Provisional Government of Free India and to accord it all conceivable cooperation for attainment of its objects." The Board of Information also issued a statement regarding the above announcement. On the same day Burma also recognized the Provisional Government. "This was followed by the extension of recognition by Germany on Oct. 28 the Phillipine republic on Oct 29 China and Manchoukuo on Nov. 1 Italy on Nov 2, Thaliand on Nov. 17 and Croatia on Nov. 19.

Viewed from the standpoint of International Law the Provisional Government of Free India resembed the National Congress and its success.

Then, former Prime Minister general Hideki Tojo. the Japanese delegate, made the following announcement in connection with Dr. Ba Maw's motion and the speech of the head of the Provisional Government of Free India. "The imperial Japanese Government has repeatedly announced its intention of giving support to all movements for the temancipation of India from the Anglo-American yoke and for the realization of this aspiration. In view of the fact that the firm goundation of the Provisional Government of free India have been laid down and because of the growing patricle endeavors and unity of purposes on the part of the Indian who are now working towards their National Independence under the Provisional Government. I have the honor of declaring herewith that Japan is prepared to return shortly to the Provisional Government of Free India the Andaman and Nicobar Islands which are now under Japanese occupation as the first step toward the realization of India Independence.

At the time of the advance of the Japanese Force into India in the spring of 1944 the Imperial Headquarters announced on March 23 that our Army together with the Indian National army had entered Indian territory in the middle of March. Further communiques of the Imperial Headquarters on March 31 and April 8 also stated that our army together with the Indian National Army had been engaged in operations.

On the occasion of this advance into India. Bose issued a second statement on April 4 in which he declared that the Indian National Army. under the direction of the provisional Government of Free India which was established at Shonan on Oct. 21, 1943 by 3,000,000 Indians, had penetrated far into Indian territory after crossing the Indian frontier that the Provisional Government is the only legal Government requests the Indian nationals in the liberated areas to extend their cooperation and assistance to the Indian National Army and to all administrative officials appointed by the Provisional Government.

Later on Oct 15th, Prime Minister Tojo referred in his speech at the meeting of the mixed committee based on the Tripartite. Treaty among Japan Germany and Italy to the Indian problem and declared that the Japanese Army together with the Indian National Army, ahd crossed the Indian border and had marched into Indian territory and that the fact that the indian National Army, under the command of Bose, has been fighting the support of Burma and other number states of Greater East Asia. He said that with this, an opportunity for India'emancipation had presented itself and that our objective of freeing the oppressed peoples was about to be realized.

On November 1, Bose arrived in Japan in order to consolidate the close relations existing between the Provisional Government of Free India and Japan, and also to exchange views with the Japanese Government and military leaders. We have already noted, as a result of this, the Japanese Government decide to send a diplomatic envoy to the Provisional Government. Regarding this, the Board of Information issued the following statement of November 26 : "Following conversation, carried out between Subhas Chandra Bose, head of the Provisional Government of Free India, who has been staying in the capital, and the leaders of the Japanese Government, regarding the prosecution of the Greater East Asia War and means for promoting collaboration between the two governments, the Imperial Japanese Government had decided to dispatch a diplomatic envoy to the Provisional Government.

On the same day, Bose issued a statement in which he said, "It is a source of great joy for me to observe that formal diplomatic relations have been established between the Japanese Government and the Provisional Government of Free India and that the Japanese Government has decided to dispatch a diplomatic envoy to our Provisional Government."

This diplomatic envoy is to be installed by viture of Imperial decree Number 64, promulgated in 1917 which provides that, in case of the necessity of dispatching a diplomatic official abroad. In order to execute a special duty, a temporary extra-ordinary Ambassador or Minister may be installed until the execution of such duty may be completed.

41

Message by the Provisional Government of Azad Hind to the New Japanese Government[1]

27 July, 1944

On receipt of information on the formation of a new Cabinet with General Koise as Premier, Netaji Subhas Chandra Bose, Head of the State, Provisional Government of Azad Hind cabled congratulations and felicitations to General Koise and other Ministers of his Cabinet, and assured them of the determination of Indians in East Asia to continue to fight shoulder to shoulder with Nippon until victory is achieved.

His excellency Netaji Subhas Chandra Bose, Head of the State, Provisional Government of Azad Hind and Supreme Commander of the Azad Hind Fauj sent the followning message of felicitations to His Excellency Nainggandaw Adipadi Dr. Baw Maw, Head of State, Independent Burma, on the occasion of the Anniversary of Burmese Independence.

On behalf of freedom loving Indians, the Provisional Government of Free India, the I.N.A. and myself, I wish to offer my warmest congratulations to Your Excellency, to the Government and the people of Independent Burma on the occasion of the Anniversary of Burma's independence.

I wish to take this opportunity to express the heartiest thank of the Provisional Government of Free India, the Indian National Army and of myself to your Excellency to the Government and to the people of Independent Burma for all the valuable help that has been and is being rendered to us in our fight for the Independence of India.

I wish also to assure your Excellency that we, Indians, are irrevocable resolved to fight shoulder to shoulder with Independent Burma and Nippon, under all circumstances until our common enemies are curshed and our common Victory is achieved.

1. INA Trial Papers.

42

Rules of the Indian Independence League, and the Organisation of I.N.A. in Andamans[1]

30 July, 1944

Article 1—This league will be called the Indian Independence League, Andaman Branch and it will have its office at the so-Soncho's Office, Port Blair.

Article 2—This branch will be organised by Indians, residing in the South Andaman, who are fervently willing to attain the independence of India.

Article 3—This branch will maintain contact with the Headquarters of the Indian Independence League at Syonan and its chief objects will be to take measures to popularize the idea of Indian independence among the Indians in Andaman, to co-operate with the local Imperial Japanese Forces and to accelerate the independence of India.

Article 4—This branch will take undermentioned steps to execute the objects of Article 3.

(1) It will positively organise the independence movement.

(2) It will explain the real meaning of the war of Greater East Asia.

(3) It will propagate and spread the idea of Indian independence among the public.

(4) It will give mental and spiritual education to the young and adults (e.g. unity, honesty, equality etc.)

1. I.I.L. Papers. F. No. 45/3

(5) It will give relief and first aid in case of fire and air raid.

(6) It will give relief to the poor and distressed.

(7) It will enlighten the women and children..

Article 5—The undermentioned honorary officials will be appointed for the management of this branch.

President	1
Vice-President	1
Member	20 (about)

Article 6— In a public meeting, 50 candidates who have strong idea of Indian independence and who are gentlemen of judgement and nobility will be elected. Out of these 22 men will be selected and appointed as office bearers by the Minseibucho. The term of their office will be for 1 year but they can be re-elected.

Article 7—Three candidates will be elected for the post of the President from among the offcials, out of which the Minseibucho will select and appoint the President. Three candidates will be elected for the post of the Vice-President from among the officials, out of which the President will select the Vice-President and will appoint him after the approval of the Minseibucho.

Article 8—The President will manage the affairs of the league. The Vice-president will help the President in his work and will act for him in his absence. A meeting will be held once in every month when the President as a chairman will execute all the important matters. A special meeting can be called if the President thinks it necessary.

Article 9—This branch will request the following officers to act as advisors.

Minseibucho and All Kachos from Minseibu.

Assistant Commander-in-chief from Shireibu.

Shibutaicho from Army.

The advisors will give advice when consulted and thus help the President in carrying out his duties (in the management of the branch).

Article 10—The public meeting will be called twice in a year but a special meeting can be called if the President thinks it necessary.

Article 11—The expenses of the branch will be met out of the fees and contributions received from the members. The annual fee will be Rs. 1 only.

Article 12—In order to carry out the objects of articles 3 and 4 successfully the following departments will be organised. In addition to these, an Indian Independence Volunteer Corps will also be organised. The officials of the Branch will be distributed in all these departments and they will work according to the instructions from the President.

(i) General Affairs Department.

(ii) Propaganda Department.

(iii) Relief Department.

(iv) Youth Department.

(v) Women Department

Article 13—Every department will work as defined below:-

(i) General Affairs Department - The cashier will give report on the income and expenses of the branch twice a year in the public meeting.

(ii) Propaganda Department - (a) Spread the idea of Indian independence and the Japanese language.

(b) Real explanation of the East Asia co-prosperity sphere and other propaganda.

(iii) Relief Department - (a) Give relief in case of actual fighting and fina.

(b) Give relief to the poor familes in distress.

(iv) Youth Department - Start movement of the youths and adults.

(v) Females Department - Enlighten the women and children.

Article 14—The organisation of the volunteer corps will be made as follows :-

(i) This corps will be organised from those Indians of South Andaman, who are very enthusiastic about the independence of India and who are able bodied between the ages of 20 and 45.

(ii) At present about 100 men will be selected from the undermentioned villages for enrolment.

A. Abderdeen Town	25
B. „ Village	20
C. Phoenix Bay	10
D. Delaneypore	10
E. Junglighat	15
F. Deane Street	10
G. South Point	10

(iii) The leader of the corps will be selected by the President from the officials and will be appointed after the approval of the Minseibucho. Each group will contain 10 volunteers. Each group will select its own head from the group. Such 3 or 4 grcups will make a company. The head of the company will be selected by the heads of the groups mutually. Assistant heads will also be selected. They will officiate for the heads when they are absent.

(iv) The leader will get orders from the President of the League. The other heads will get their orders from their seniors and lead their subordinates.

(v) The corps will receive systematic mass training on fixed days and will mutually cultivate the unity of mind and body and discipline. It will always be prepared for the event.

(vi) Band parties will be organised in the corps

(vii) All the members of the corps will have badges.

(viii) Indian National Flag will be the flag of the volunteer corps.

Supplementary Rules—

1. January to December will be the calendar year for the above rules.
2. The term of the members for the first term will finish in the end of the year 2604.
3. The general affairs department will have the list of the members and corps always ready at the office.
4. The volunteer corps will have the list of the members always ready.
5. The organisation of the branch will be as shown in the table below.

Indian Independence League.

President Advisors.

43

Loganandan on his Position in the Andamans[1]

31 July, 1944

Your letter of the 21st June was received on the 15th instant.

1. Transference of Departments. "Minseibu" is the Department which is directly responsible for all the care of the Civilian population in Andamans; hence all my work is wholly linked up with this department.

    (i) I am the Adviser to the Head (Minseibucho);

    (ii) Captain Mr. Alvi is in charge of Education and volunteers;

    (iii) 2nd Lieutenant Subha Singh is attached to Finance and Propaganda;

    (iv) 2nd Lieutenant Iqbal is attached to the Police.

    It is hoped that each of us would not miss the opportunities placed at his disposal to make himself useful, and later indispensable. A good deal of mutual good will and cooperation is essential and this shall not be working from our side.

    Taking condition and circumstances as they stand or could be visualised in the near future, I am of opinion that transference of Departments should not be speeded up. Hence the need for further funds would not arise in a hurry.

2. Spying. As indicated in my previous reports handling of this problem is the most important as it adversely affects all our activities here. I have had detailed discussions with the Authorities, and we do hope to succeed in reducing it to the minimum, or not completely controlling it, by intensive propaganda and local executive action.

1. F. 601/7510/H.S.

I am pleased to report that the most recent case of June, wherein 37 were arrested (including witnesses) terminated in the release of all, except one who was sentenced to seven years' imprisonment.

This favourable judgement has dispelled the gloom and is bound to cheer up the people to greater war efforts.

3. Unit of INA and Azad Hind Dal. Owing to extreme shortage of labour of all kinds and greater shortage of persons of the fighting fit class raising of a Unit of the I. N. A., is out of the question. This applies equally to A. H. Dal.

The Andaman Administrative Advisory Council.

4. The members of the above council consist of ten Officials and ten non officials of all classes of interests are well represented. It is purely an advisory body with a selfimposed restriction on the freedom or speech, in spite of apparent official encouragement. They can become more useful with increase in their personal liberties.

5. Finance. Expanditure incurred up to the end of July is approximately Rs. 3,000.00. The staff has not drawn any allowance, as it is not required for use locally.

Further Funds for transferred subjected will not be required for some good time.

6. The Monthly Teachers' Conference, the Assembly Meeting and the Provisional Government Day were held as usual.

7. We are proud of the achievements of our Army earning the appreciation of the Nippon Army being in itself an achievement. The Staff and I do feel sincerely that we are left out from the more thrilling excitements of the front line.

8. Our needs are small, and we are sufficiently self contained. There is no longer any need for crockery and cutlry or medicines, as we have salvaged sufficiently for our daily needs.

9. I am writing as a separate notes to the I. I. League headquarter at Syonan to conform to the promise of a more regular despatch of newsprint, which we greatly look forward to.

10. My health has improved quite to my satisfaction. All the staff are keeping fit.

11. With the termination of the monsoon we expect to hear of something really happening up there.

44

Special Order of the Day for the Temporary Postponement of the Operation[1]

14 August, 1944

Comrades of Azad Hind Fauj,

In the middle of March this year, Advanced units of the Azad Hind Fauj, fighting shoulder to shoulder with their valiant allies, the Imperial Nippon Forces, crossed the Indo-Burma border and the fight for India's liberation thereupon commenced on Indian Soil.

The British authorities, by ruthlessly exploiting India for over a century and bringing foreign soldiers to fight their battles for them, had managed to put up a mighty force against us. After crossing the Indo-Burma border, our forces inspired by the righteousness of our cause, encountered these numerically superior and better equipped, but heterogenous and disunited forces of the enemy and defeated them in every battle.

Our units, with their better training and discipline and unshakable determination to do or die on the path of India's freedom, soon established their superiority over the enemy, whose morale deteriorated with each defeat.

Fighting under the most trying conditions, our officers and men displayed such courage and heroism that they have earned the praise of everybody. With their blood and sacrifice, these heroes have established traditions which the future soldiers of free India shall have to uphold.

All preparations had been completed and the stage had been set for the final assault on Imphal, when torrential rains overtook us and to carry Imphal by an assault was rendered a tactical impossibility.

Handicapped by the elements, we were forced to postpone our offensive. After the postponment of the offensive, it was found disadvantageous for our troops to continue to hold the line that we then

1. I.N.A. Trial Papers.

had. For securing a more favourable defensive position, it was considered advisable to withdraw our troops. In accordance with this decision, our troops have withdrawn to a more favourable defensive position. We shall now utilise the period of lull in completing our preparations, so that with the advent of better weather, we may be in a position to resume our offensive.

Having beaten the enemy once in several sectors of the front, our faith in our final victory and in the destruction of the Anglo-American forces of aggresion has increased tenfold. As soon as all our preporations are complete, we shall launch a mighty offensive against enemies once again. With the superior fighting qualities, dauntless courage and unshakable devotion to duty of our officers and men, victory shall surely be ours.

May the souls of those heroes, who have fallen in this campaign inspire us to still nobler deeds of heroism and bravery in the next phase of India's War of Liberation.

JAI HIND.

(Sd.) SUBHAS CHANDRA BOSE
Supreme Commander,
Azad Hind Fauj.
Burma

45

P. K. Sahgal to M. Z. Kiani Promising Re-inforcement[1]

20 August, 1944

I received your report , sent from Yeu, on 13rd August 1944, together with a copy of Col. Shah Nawaz's report (incidentally original of that report has never been received here yesterday) and I immediately took up the reports to Netaji. Yesterday evening Netaji had a conference with Lt. Gen. Ishoda concerning the matter mentioned in your report, I was also present during the discussion. Throughout the conference, although he promised to send telegrams here and there, it was quite apparent that either he (Gen. Ishoda) could or would do little.

Ever since, the Japanese have decided to go on the defensive, I feel a change in their attitude, which I find very difficult to explain, may be you can explain it better than I can. Anyhow, one thing is certain that we can expect little help from Nippon authorities in Rangoon. You will have to tackle Hayachi Butai to solve most of your problems. We even offered to send a steam launch from Rangoon to relieve a Nippon steam launch in the front line, which could be despathched immediately to Yirwam to evacuate the four hundred men of No, A Grla. Regiment. But even that they did not agree to.

We have managed to collect about six lorries, which are being touched up in our workhouse and as soon as they are ready, they shall be sent forward to help solve the transport problem. Another emergency hospital to function in Mandalay has also been organised and as soon as we can get some equipment from the Japanese, it shall be sent there.

Arrangements are also being made to buy enough cloth to give two sets of clothing to all our men coming back and a Boot shop is also being organised to make enough boots for whole of No. 1 Division. Our main difficulty is to get the materials, they are not available at any price. We,

1. I.N.A. Trial Papers.

here, are truing to do our best, which is mighty little, to help the people coming back. Fèeling of impotence and frustration for not being able to do anything to lessen the suffering or our comrades is terrible.

Lt. Col. Habib-ur-Rahman has gone to receive the new area where Nos. 1 and 2 Div. are going to be sent, and he is expected back here any day. As soon as he returns I shall try and move up to see if I could be of any help.

Please give my best regards to Inayat, Hassan and Arshad.

46

P. K. Sahgal to M. Z. Kiani Regarding Deployment of I. N. A. and Supply Position[1]

21 August, 1944

Comd. No. 1 Division

Sub:—Situation Report.

Reference your report, dated 13th August 1944 sent from You to rear H. Qrs. No. 1 Div.; and forwarded on to the Supreme Comd. under Rear H. Qrs. No. 1 Div. No. 77/8/44, dated 15th July, and the report submitted by Lt. Col. Shah Nawaz Khan, Comd. No. 1 Div Grla. Regt.

*1. The Supreme Commander took up the matter with the Chief of the Hikari Kikan, who has promised to take the following action in the matter:—

(a) Approach the Mori Head Qrs. to allow No. 2 M. T. Coy I. N. A. to retain their lorries until the evacuation of No. A Div. troops is completed.

(b) Send a telegram to make arrangements to supply rations to 150 men in Mawlik, if these men have not already been withdrawn.

(c) Send a telegram to Hayashi Butai to try and arrange the withdrawal of 250 men from Sittong by boats.

*2. It is not possible to send any boats from here to Tirwan and it also appears that the Yeu River is in floods and transport up-stream is most difficult, however, Chief of Hikari Kikan has promised to take up the matter with proper authorities to arrange for the evacuation of these 400 men of No. 1 Grla. Regt. in Tirawan. If it is not possible to evacuate these men at the present moment, arrangements shall be made to send ration supplies and medicines to them.

1. I. N. Trial Papers . M. Z. Kiani was Commander No. 1 Division I. N. A.

3. The Chief of Hikari Kikan pointed out that by the time reports from No. 1 Div. are received in Rangoon, it is sometimes too late to take any action, therefore, he suggested that Comd. has agreed to this suggestion and wishes Comd. No. 1 Div should stay near the H. Qrs. of Hayashi Army, who may be able to help in solving our problems. The Supreme Comd. has agreed to this suggestion and wishes Comd. No. 1 Div. to establish his H. Qrs. in the vicinity of the H. Qrs. of Hayashi Butai.

(Sd.) P. K. SAHGAL,
Lt. Col.,
for Assistant Chief of Staff.

Copy to :—
H.Qrs. Supreme Command.,
Rear H.Qrs. No. 1 Division.

* I have just been informed that the Hikari Kikan have already taken action on these points.

(Sd.) P. K. SAHGAL
Lt. Col.

47

Bose to Kiani Assuring all Help[1]

29 August, 1944

Colonel M. Z. Kiani,
Commander, No.1 Div.,
AZAD HIND FAUJ.
Jai Hind

Your telegram of the 23rd instant, brought by messenger, reached me on the 27th. I cannot say that my anxiety has been allayed. On the contrary, I am still very anxious about what is going on at Sittaung and at R. H. Tirawan.

Ever since I got your letter (along with that of Lt. Col. Shah Nawaz) from Yeu, we have left no stone unturned at this end. Lt. Colonel Habib-Ur-Rahman, who left for Mandalay on the 26th will tell you something of what we have been trying to do here. But, I am afraid, that what we have been able to do is not much. We have been able to get a few lorries but unfortunately they are not yet quite road-worthy. As soon as they are, they will be sent up to be used between Sagaing and Shewgyin. I hope to be able to get sixs in all, of which only three are now in our possession. Two motor-boats, donated by Indians, are expected tomorrow and we hope to send them up soon, if no difficulties are raised from the Japanese side. Whatever we can spare in the way of Medicine, blankets, mosquito nets, etc., have either been sent up already or will be leaving immediately. A few days ago, two wagon-loads were sent. Today, one and a half wagon loads are leaving. Mr. Paramanand, before he left for Mandalay, was fully instructed by me about purchasing any food supplies available there or anywhere within reach in North Burma.

In your telegram of the 23rd, there is a reference to the need of fresh Officers,. I would have sent up a few without further reference to you. But

1. *Ibid.*

since No. 4 Guerilla Regiment is there, as well as your Rear Headquarters, it may not be necessary to send any Officers from here at present. But if you need any, do not hesitate to ask for them and I shall gladly send as many as could be spared from here. Without any further reference to you, I am arraging to send up as many Doctors as I can from here by reducing the staff here to the very minimum. These Doctors may be used either for the new hospital in the vicinity of Mandalay or they may be sent up to Yeu, Akibono and Kalewa with medical supplies.

Priors to this, I sent Lt. Col. Rai and Lt. Col. Raju with instructions to go up as far as circumstances will permit, and render what help they can on the medical side.

Now I have sent Lt. Col. Habib-ur-Rahman with the same instructions. I hope he will be able to go up as far as Shwegyin.

With regard to front-line needs, the Indian public here is not only sympathetic but generous. Consequently, you can rest assured that whatever is possible to get, will be procured. Since our stock of Blankets had run short, we made a house to house collection and got quite a good response. Now we are trying to make a house to house collection of Tinned Milk. My only regret is that transport is the prime need today and in that we can do little.

Wishing you all the best and with the most cordial greetings.

"JAI HIND"

48

P. K. Sahgal to Hikari Kikan for Deployment of I.N.A.[1]

31 August, 1944.

No. 103/2/11/G.,
Rear "H. Qrs., II. S. C.
A. H. F. Burma

Most Secret
Immediate

To,
H. Qrs.
Hikari Kikan, Rangoon.

Sub:—Movement of troops.

Lt. Col. Takagi of H. Qrs. Hikari Kikan gave the following advance information to Lt. Col. P. K. Sahgal of Rear H. Qrs. No. 2 Supreme Command, A. H. F. on 30th August 1944:—

The H. Qrs. of the Mori Army are going to issue orders to the following effect in the near future:—

The following units of the I. N. A. at present under the command of the Hayashi Army shall revert to the command of H. Qrs.

Supreme Command, A. H. F.:—

(a) No. 1 Division less 1st Bn. of 1 Grla Regt.

(b) No. 2 Engineering Coy.

(c) No. 3 Engineering Coy.

(d) No. 1 M. T. Coy.

(e) No. 11 M. T. Coy.

(f) No. 2 Hospital

(g) No. 1 Medical Staging Section.

1. *Ibid.*

2. These units shall revert to the command of H. Qrs. Supreme Command, I. N. A. on the day of their arrival in Mandalay.

3. The future location of I. N. A. troops shall be as under:—

   (a) No. 2 Div. Will move to the Pakaku area.

   (b) Two Regiments from No. 1 Div will be in Myingyan area.

   (c) Remainder of No. 1 Division units will be in Pyinmena area.

4. Supply points for these units will be at Myingyan, Pakakku and Pyinmena.

5. The Provision of medicines and building of barracks in these areas shall be the responsibility of the Nippon Garrison Commander of Mandalay.

6. No. 2 Hospital, Menywa, as soon as situation permits, will start evacuating its patients and when all the patients have been evacuated the Hospital will leave that area and move to a place to be selected by the H. Qrs., Supreme Command, A. H. F.

7. Wherever the accommodation is not available new barracks shall be built. The H. Qrs., Mori Army takes the responsibilities of supplying the necessary materials and funds, but the construction work shall have to be carried out under the direction of Engineers of the I. N. A.

With reference to the above information, it is requested that when the final and executive orders are issued by the Mori Army, administrative details should also be worked out and special instructions issued on the subject at the same time.

It is considered most necessary that information on the following points should be included in the administrative instructions:—

(i) The method of sending supplies from the Nippon supply points to I. N. A. Units.

(ii) The amount of material that shall be provided at each place for building of barracks.

(iii) The amount of money that shall be placed at the disposal of I. N. A. for carrying out these construction works.

(iv) When will the Nos. 1, 2 and 4 Eng. Coy. of I. N. A. be available to be sent to the areas where the construction work has to be carried out.

(v) What other facilities for this construction work may be expected from the Nippon side.

(vi) What shall be the means of communication between H. Qrs. Supreme Command, I. N. A. and No. I and II Divisions of the I. N. A.

(viii) What shall be the means of communication between the troops of No. 1 Div. situated in Pyinmena area, and other troops in Myingyan area.

(Sd.) P.K. SAHGAL
Lt. Col.,
Asstt. Chief of Staff.

49

Bose to Kiani Assuring him Necessary Medical Supplies for the Wounded I. N. A. Soldiers[1]

3 September, 1944

Col. M. Z. Kiani,
Commander
No. 1 Division,
A. H. F.
Jai Hind,

Your telegram of the 7th July from Chamol, No. 078, and your telegram of the 17th July No. 082 reached me by post on the 31st August. The actual telegrams never reached me. Your telegram of the 26th August, No. 22, also reached me on the 31st August.

You have probably misunderstood my intention regarding the loacation of your Headquarters. You are the best judge as to where your Headquarters should be located for the time being. I wrote to you about remaining near the Hayashi Headquarters because in the discussions with the Hikari Kikan Headquarters here we thought that since we could do little at this end, perhaps you could do more up by remaining close to the Hayashi Headquarters. Please do not have any hesitation in establishing your Headquarters wherever you find it most suitable and beneficial to the formations under your command.

Your telegrams have been immediately attended to in the case of matters which depend on the Hikari Kikan, or on Hayashi Command or Mori command — though we have done our best to move them I cannot tell you what resutls will actually follow. In those matters which rest with us, we are doing our very best. Necessary supplies., including medical supplies, have been sent up and will continue to be sent up in future, so far as our resources permit. After reducing the medical staff here to the

1. *Ibid.*

minimum we are sending up some more Doctors. Two lorries are in stock and if and when they are made road worthy, they too will be sent at once. We hope to be able to send up two motor-boats, but I can not tell you when they will actually reach their destination. These efforts namely in the matter of supplies and transport- will continue in full swing. I hope at Tirawan is great. I am equally anxious about conditions at Sittaung. The ony relief I have is that judging from enemy news broadcasts, enemy troops are still five miles from Sittaung. I hope this will give time for our men to evacuate.

As soon as you have news about Sittaung, and Tirawan, please send me a messenger.

The lorries that we are sending today and hope to send in future are meant for front line needs. But if you find transport arragements between Ye-u and Shwegyin are perfectly satisfactory, you may divert them, to other stretches of the road. So far as these lorries are concerned, I wanted Lt. Col. Habib-Ur-Rahman to take them upto Akibobno and beyond if necessary. Consequently, if he is still in Mandalay, when the lorries reach there, it would be desirable to ask him as to how he would like to use them. I have told Lt. Col. Habib-ur-Rahman to go up as far as possible - even beyond Kalewa.

Lt. Col. Sahgal is writing to you on other points I hope that your health will now steadily improve. Please convey my most cordial greetings to the Regiments Commanders and Officers and men who are within your reach.

With the most cordial greetings,

"JAI HIND".

50

Indian Minorities in South And East Asia. The Background of the Indian Independence Movement (Extract)[1]

8 September, 1944

Table of Contents

1. The above survey report was prepared by the office of Strategic Services U.S. Government Record Group 226 U.S. National Archives, Maryland USA.

C. Indian Organizations

D. Early History of the Indian Independence League in Thailand and its Founders

III. Indians in Malaya

A. Population Statistics

B. Principal Occupations

C. Indian Associations

D. Indians under British Administration in Malaya

IV. Indians in Indochina

V. Indians in Netherlands East Indies

IV. Indians in China

A. Population Statistics

B. Indians in China and Indian Nationalism

C. Indian Organizations

VI. Indians in Japan

A. Indian Population of Japan

B. Indian Revolutionaries of Japan

1. Maulvi Mohammed Barkatulla

2. Hariharnath Thulal Atal

3. Raja Mahendra Pratap

4. Rashbehari Bose

5. Anand Mohan Sahay

C. Indian Organizations in Japan

VII. Indian National Congress and Indians overseas

Summary

The Indian Independence Leagues in South-East Asia, as far as manpower is concerned, have in several areas a large population upon which to draw for membership. Indians are most numerous in Burma and

Malaya, where they form a considerable proportion of the laboring class. There is also a fairly large group in the N.E.I. In Thailand and Indochina the Indians are a rather small, compact merchant community with the laboring class a relatively insignificant minority in the Indian group. The Indians in China are settled chiefly in Hongkong and Shanghai. Their number is small and for the most part they are former members of the police force or army who remained in China when their term of service was completed. The Indian population of Japan consisted of a small group of merchants settled in the principal cities. There were in addition a number of students and a few exiled Indian patriots

In all of these areas Indian males greatly outnumber the females, and a large proportion of them are between the ages of 15 and 35. Although the population of Indians born in the country of enumeration is increasing, Indians in all countries of South— East Asia are largely immigrants who return after a period to the country of their birth. In 1931 for example, four-fifths of the Indian population of Malaya has been born outside the country, the figure for Burma in the same year was 62 per cent. A certain index to the immigrant nature of the population, and its temporary character, is the sex ratio.

There is no indication that the majority of those Indians took any interest in Indian political problems. In Burma, before its separation from India, there was a provincial committee of the Indian National Congress. It is probable that members were drawn from the professional, educated classes among the Indians of Rangoon, and that the laborers who formed the bulk of the population had no part in the organization. On the whole, Indian organizations in Burma and Malaya had as their objective the economic and social advancement of Indians in those countries. In Thailand and Indochina, Indian societies were probably business associations or social clubs. Certainly in Thailand and perhaps in Indochina as well there were a few Indians who where interested in the Indian struggle for freedom but they seem to have made little headway among their fellow countrymen.

The situation in China seems to have been somewhat different. The Indians formed a small, compact group largely belonging to the Sikh community. A revolutionary movement, dating from the years of the last war, fed by resentment against the British and influenced by Chinese nationalist activities, in present-day Indian nationalism with its creed of nonviolence and civil-disobedience, but in the older terrorism which long ago ceased to play a part in Indian politics. In recent years, however, the activities of the Indians in Shanghai have been increasingly inspired by the Indian National Congress.

Japan has a smaller Indian population than any other country in East Asia. Nevertheless the presence in Japan of a small group of Indian revolutionaries and the fact that they have received encouragement and support from the Japanese has made Japan the center of Indian nationalist activities in eastern Asia. Several associations were devoted to the cause of Indian Independence and the degree of organization for this purpose surpassed anything achieved or attempted in other countries of Eastern Asia.

It seems clear that the Indian Independence Leagues have not been built up on the basis of pre-existing nationalist organisations in South-East Asia. Nor is it likely that there was any widespread demand on the part of Indians in this area that the war be made the occasion of obtaining India's freedom, although a few Indians in Japan, such as Rashbehari Bose, probably regard the present war as the opportunity missed in 1914-18.

The Independence Leagues are, then, the creation of the Japanese. These is very little reliable information regarding the degree to which the Japanese have been successful in enlisting the support of Indians in this movement. There were doubtless in each country a few Indians ready to respond to appeals to their patriotism. It is likely that Japanese anti-British propaganda would prove effective especially in Burma and Malaya; and "Asia for the Asiatics" is an old and attractive slogan throughout the area. Pro-Japanese sentiments dating from the Russo-Japanese war provided a basis upon which to erect Japanese aid, of national status for India. There is no reason to believe that politically intelligent Indians in the area would have had many qualms about accepting much aid, and if Japan's ultimate inentions were ever called into question, it is probable that few Indians would have been found to prefer British to Japanese domination. Furthermore, in the early years of the war Japan appeared to have established herself firmly in south Eastern Asia. Britain's defeat in Indian must have seemed to those Indians who were informed as to the course to events, a matter of months merely. Expediency demanded that they cooperate with the Japanese. It is probable also that the Japanese resorted to coercion when persuasion failed. It has been reported, for instance, that the Indian merchants in Bangkok were forced, by threat of boycott, to provide funds for the League, and there have been statements to the effect that prisoners of war volunteered for service in the Independence Army to escape torture at the hands of their captors.

A notice in the *Shanghai Times*, 22 January 1944, states "In order to make a complete official list, all Indian nationals who have not yet registered with the Indian Independence League are urgently requested to register before the end of the month, otherwise much inconvenience may arise to the defaulters." It would seem that the Indians of Shanghai have not been in a hurry to join the League and the mention of "inconvenience" suggests that enrollment is not altogether a voluntary matter.

The appearance of Subhas Bose on the scene gave a great impetus to the movement. A former Congress President with a large following in India, an able leader, widely considered to be a sincere patriot, he would have had little difficulty in persuading even the hesitant that an opportunity was at hand to drive the British from India. Generally speaking, it may be concluded that the Japanese have successful in mobilizing Indian opinion in their favor.

Indian Minorities in South and East Asia: The Background of the Indian Independence Movement

Introduction

In all countries of South and East Asia now occupied or controlled by the Japanese the Indian residents have organized Independence Leagues, the purpose of which is to free India, with the aid of the Japanese, from British domination. These Leagues were established under Japanese, from British domination. These Leagues were established under Japanese sponsorship in the early days of the war, and by June 1942, when representatives met for a conference at Bangkok, a large membership was claimed for each country. Increased activity followed the arrival of Subhas Bose a year later. Chief in importance was the formation of the Independence Army, composed of Indian volunteers.

In order to assess the potentialities of this movement, it is essential to have available the facts concerning the Indian populations of these areas: vital statistics; social and economic position; the degree to which Indians were organized before the war, and for what purpose; contacts with nationalist and other groups in India; attitudes towards Japan. The following account of Indians in South and East Asia attempts, insofar as possible, to provide the facts.

I. Indians in Burma

A. Population Statistics

Politically a part of India until 1937, Burma had a large Indian population. According to the most recent estimate available, Indians in

Burma numbered 1,017,825. The 1941 figure would be somewhat higher. Since roughly 400,000 Indians escaped from Burma at the time of the Japanese invasion, the present Indian population is probably between six and eight hundred thousand.

1. Geographic Distribution. The following account of the distribution of the Indians in Burma is taken form the 1931 census. At that time 93 per cent of the total number of Indians were concentrated in the delta, coast and center subdivisions. Forty-two per cent lived in Rangoon and Akyab district. In Rangoon, Indians formed 53 per cent of the population and in Akyab district, 33 per cent. In northern Burma the number of Indians was small except for Myitkyina district where there were 17,000; a larger number of these were Gurkhas who had settled there, and in addition there was a considerable number of Indians among the military police.

2. Racial Affiliation. The following table classifies Indian by race.

Race	*Number of persons*	*Number per thousand persons*
Bengali	65,211	64
Chittagonian	252,152	248
Hindustani	174,967	172
Tamil	149,888	147
Telugu	159,759	157
Oriya	62,585	61
Others	153,263	151

"Others" include 39,532 Gurkhas and 28,289 Punjabis.

The largest single group is the Chittagonian, of which 74 per cent were located in Akyab district. Over 50 per cent of the Indian population were from North India. Tamils and Telugus together constituted less than 33 per cent.

3. Birthplace. The majority of Indians in Burma are immigrants to the country. In 1931, 62 per cent of the total number of Indians in Burma has been born outside the country. However, the district of Akyab presents a striking contrast to conditions elsewhere in Burma: in that district only 21 per cent had been born outside Burma. There is also a considerable difference in the percentages for males and for females. For Burma as a whole 72 per cent of the males had been born outside Burma, while only 36 per cent of the Indian females were foreign born. Here again Akyab is not typical of Burma as a whole: 30 per cent of the males, and 7 per cent of the females were born outside Burma.

It is interesting to contrast the racial classification of Indian immigrants with that of the Indian population of Burma as a whole.

Race	*Persons*
Bengali	39,809
Chittagonian	83,511
Hindustani	125,054
Oriya	57,906
Tamil	84,327
Telugu	131,727
Others	107,757

It will be noted while the largest single group of Indians in Burma is composed of Chittagonians, the Telugus form the largest single group among Indian immigrants to Burma,

4. Sex and Age Grouping. The sex ratio for Indians in Burma in typical of an immigrant population. In 1931 there were 387 females per thousand males. For the Indian immigrant group considered separately the sex ratio was 191. The various racial groups among the immigrants differ considerably in this respect. The Tamils had the highest sex ratio with 43 females per 100 males; the figure for the Telugus was 21; for Bengalis 13; for Oriyas 3.

The age distribution per 10,000 Indians indicated in the following table. The district of Akyab is omitted in the calculations since "figures for the whole province would be representative neither of the Akyab district nor of the remainder of the province.

	Whole Province less Akyab district	
Age Group	*Males*	*Female*
0 5	565	1,732
5-10	535	1,292
10-15	576	1,086
15-20	1,023	1,030
20-30	3,051	2,227
30-40	2,389	1,363
40 and over	1,861	1,269

5. Religious Groups. The following table ciassifies Indians by religion.

		Actual Population		
Religion	*Persons*	*Males*	*Females*	*Per 1,000 Persons*
Hindu	565,609	425,389	140,220	556
Muslim	396,594	271,514	125,080	390

Religion	*Persons*	*Males*	*Females*	*Per 1,000 Persons*
Buddhist	12,600	9,778	2,822	12
Christian	30,135	18,015	12,120	30
Sikh	10,896	7,882	3,014	11
Others	1,991	1,333	658	2

It is important to note that over half the Indian population is Hindu by religion. Muslims form the only other large group. Another fact of some importance is the large number of female Muslims compared to the proportion of females to males in the other religious groups. It appears that this is largely due to the inclusion of Akyab district in the enumeration; in this district, where many of the Indian Muslims are permanent residents, the sex ration is 787, while it is only 246 for the rest of the country. The overall figures for Muslim female given in the table above are therefore misleading: with the exception of Akyab district the proportion among Indian Muslim is one female to every four males, while among Indian Hindus, there is one female per 3 males.

6. Occupation. The following table shows the chief occupations of Indian in Burma.

Occupations	*Indians Born in Burma*	*Indian Born Outside Burma*
Exploitation of animals and vegetation	67,366	108,842
Exploitation of minerals	402	14,350
Industry	7,178	97,489
Transport	5,510	96,020
Trade	9,151	87,060
Public Force	617	13,378
Public Administration	1,012	12,810
Professions and Liberal Arts	1,593	8,825
Persons living on their income	283	1,546
Domestic Service	2,339	21,687

The table given below brings out more clearly the difference with respect to occupation between Indians born in Burma and those born outside. The distribution by occupation of 1,000 workers is indicated.

Occupations	*Indians Born in Burma*	*Indian Born Outside Burma*
Production of raw materials	486	249
Preparation and supply of material substances	374	578

Public Administration and Liberal Arts	55	75
Miscellaneous	86	98

It is possible to make a rough classification of racial groups by occupation. Bengalis as a rule are employed in government service or work in a clerical capacity, while some are shopkeepers or traders; in addition a number of Bengalis are mechanics. The Chittagionians are engaged in small craft traffic and furnish labour for ship and launch crew; many of this group works in mills and dockyards. The Tamils are usually engaged in agriculture or work in the rice mills, but middle class members of this group are employed in various clerical activities. A small but very important minority among the Tamils are the Chettyars, the moneylenders and the principal financing agency in the country. Telugus for the most part work in mills and factories, though many are rickshaw pullers, porters and carries. Hindustanis from the United Provinces serve as watchmen and messengers, and many are petty vendors. The Oriyas work on railroads and in the Public Works Department on road construction; some are engaged in mills and dockyards. Gurkhas are generally cultivators, though some are to be found in domestic service. Punjabis work largely in railway and motor workshops, dockyards and foundries as mechanics and overseers.

7. Summary. The Indian population in Burma is largely an immigrant group composed chiefly of people from the southern and northeastern part of India. The Indians are for the most part concentrated in southern and central Burma, and nearly one half of them were in Akyab and Rangoon. Both the age grouping , which shows a majority between the age grouping, which shows a majority between the ages of 15 and 40, and the sex ratio, with a great preponderance of males, are typical of an immigrant group. Over half of the Indians are Hindus, and Muslims whom are largely located in Akyab district, are next in respect to numbers of immigrants are engaged in administrative and professional activities.

B. Relations between Burmans and Indians

A fact of outstanding importance in considering the position of Indians is Burma is the hostility of the Burmans towards the Indian immigrants and residents in the country. This hostility has an economic base and has been intensified since 1930 due largely to the economic depression and to the fact that rising Burman nationalism has tended to make capital of economic grievances and the exploitation of Burman resources by foreign elements. This hostility was never veiled and in 1938 severe riots broke out in which Indian lives and property suffered at the hands of the Burmans. The Riot Inquiry Committee in discussing the causes of the disturbances drew attention to the fact that while in 1930 Indian Chettiars occupied area in the thirteen principal rice-growing districts of Lower Burma, in 1937 they had acquired possession of 25percent. This did not take into account the areas over which the Chettiars held mortgages. The city of Rangoon and its business was to a large extent in Indian hands. Indian owners and landlord paid over 55 percent of the total taxes of the city, and all large private bazaars were Indian-owned. The depression resulted in a drain on the resources of the poorer class of Burmans who were forced to turn to industrial where Indians were already established, and this led to additional dissatisfaction.

Another grievance against the Indians was the problem created by intermarriage between Burman woman and Indian men. Objections on the part of Burmans to such marriages were based "sometimes on the ground of their race purity of the Burmese nation, sometimes on the fear that mixed marriage may tend to remove a portion of the population from Burmese nationality and from the national religion and sometimes on the ground that it results in material hardship." Under Burmese law a widow fares better than either Muslim or Hindu law. The question of the Burmans woman's status was also involved; since laws pertaining to marriage differed, a Buddhist Burman woman might consider herself a married women under Buddhist law, but would bot be so considered under either Hindu or Muslim law.

Burmese nationalism has made an issue of the position of Indians in Burma since 1916. When the separation of Burma from Indian came up for discussion in 1932-33 " the whole question of Indian in Burma was thrown into the political arena, attention became focussed upon it, and the whole question... received a prominence and a reality which is never before assumed and possibly does not deserve...... It was continuously represented as a menace to Burma's national life and even to the Buddhist religion."

Indians in Burma, and this applies to those domiciled in the country rather than to the shifting immigrant population, were conscious of being a racial minority and jealous of their status as a separate political group. Indians had formed a separate electorate as early as 1922, and at the Round Table Conference in London in 1931-32 the Indian delegates demanded that separate electorates be continued to safeguard their interests. This insistence and the separate electorate in the present constitution were contrary to Burman desires.

C. Indian Organization. It is probably a safe assumption that members of the labouring classes had few definite opinions regarding political affairs in India. The majority of the educated Indians in Burma appears to have sympathized with the aims of the Indian National Congress. With few exception the Indian owned and edited newspapers were pro-Congress Committee, the members of which were nearly all Indians, and delegates regularly attended the annual conference of the Congress. After the separation of Burma, the provincial committee was abolished and in its place the Burma Committee was set up to work for the freedom of Burma. This committee continued to elect members to the All India Congress Committee and in 1939 two Indians and one Burman, All from Rangoon, Were elected.

Other Indian organization including the All Burman Muslim league, and the Burmans Provincial Hindu Sabha, founded in 1930. It is not known whether or not these were branches of National organizations in India; the All Burman Muslim League appears to have has some connection with the All India Muslim league, but probably was not directly affiliated with it. The Young Chulia Muslim League was an organization of Tamil Muslim from Madras. Another organization was the All Burma South Indian Association. Most of the groups appear to have been concerned mainly with the advancement of Indians in Burma, and the improvement of their social and economic status.

II. Indians in Thailand

A. Population Statistics

It is impossible to state accurately the number of Indians living in Thailand. According to the 1931 Census of Thailand, Indians and Malays together numbered 379,618. Since 272,484 of these were located in Pattani circle, an area adjoining Malaya, presumably the great majority of the total number are Malays. Dr. Lanka Sundaram, who spent some time investigating the condition of Indians in Thailand, estimated that there were 100,000 in the country. His figure included Burmese Indians and Karens not even if allowance is made for a possible total of 50,000 Karens this figure seems high. A brief account of Indians in Thailand in the *Indian Review* gives 10,000 as the total Indian population. The Indian Year Book for 1940-41 states that thereare appoximately 5,000 Indians in Thailand and the some figure is given in the Indians Abroad Directory by S.A. Waiz. Some figures from the *Statistical Year Book of the Kingdom of Siam* may bee considered as evidence favoring acceptance of the last estimate as more nearly correct. The number of Indians arriving at the Port of Bangkok from 1918 to 1933 are listed in table 18. The figures vary from 708 in 1919-20 to 293 in 1919-32; generally from 300 to 500 Indians per year entered Thailand during this period. Table 19 lists departure from Bangkok during the same period. The number of Indian leaving Thailand by the port of Bangkok varied from 250 in 1927-28 to 600 in 1925-26. Table 20 lists arrivals of aliens at A Bangkok, and presumably included persons arriving overland, probably from Malaya, as well as by sea. In 1931-32 the number of Indian arrivals was 1,333; in 1932-33, 1,195. These figures do not support an estimate of 100,000 Indians resident in Thailand. Five thousand may probably be considered a reasonable minimum, with 10,000 as the outside limit.

Little can be said concerning the place of origin of these Indians. Virginia Thompson states that two-thirds of the Indian merchants were Tamils from south Indian, while the other third were speakers of Hindustani. It is evident from her account that there were also some Sikhs. Mukerjee mentions "a fair number of South Indians" and "a few Muhammadan agriculturists from eastern Bengal" who entered Thailand by way of Burma.

Of 1,333 Indians arriving in Bangkok during the year 1931-32, 894 were married males, 284 were unmarried, adult males. There were only 49 married females, and 17 unmarried females over 15 years of age. The largest number of Indian males (410) were between the ages of 25-35; 775 were between the ages of 15 and 25.There were only 19 males aged 65 and over, and children under 7 years numbered only 44. Although these data refer to only a section of the Indian population, they suggest that the average Indian immigrant is a male, that he comes to Thailand at the age of 25; and it is possible to infer from the scarcity of women and children among the immigrants that the average Indians resident of Thailand is a transient who regards India as his home and expects to return after a few years. It should be noted, however, that two Thai informants, Dang Tilaka and Tularaksa stated in conversation that Indians in Thailand regard themselves as Thai rather than as Indians and have become permanent residents of the country. It seems probable that this observation refers chiefly to second generation Indians.

B. Economic Status

The majority of the Indians in Thailand are merchants. A few, probably Sikhs, are employed in the Bangkok police force; other serve as watchmen and messenger boys. The yearbook for the Kingdom of Siam lists the occupations of 1,178 male Indians aged 15 or over who arrived in Thailand during 1931-32:

General laborers	8
Professional	57
Commercial	583
Agricultural, etc	2
Personal and Domestic	371
Theatrical, etc	7
Others	150

Some, at least, of the Indians are well to do. A.E. Nana and Bhagwan Singh are said to be among the largest landowners in Thailand. The Sikh community in 1933 spent Tcs. 80,000 ($35,200) to build a temple in Bangkok.

C. Indian Organizations

There were two Indian organizations in Thailand. The Indian Association of Siam was founded in 1930 and A.E. Nana [became its life president with Hira Lall as secretary, Baboo Chhangur Singh was president of the second organization, the Hindu Dharma Sabha (Hindu Religious Society). There was also the Thai-Indian Cultural Lodge, founded by Swami Satyananda Puri, to foster cultural relations between Thailand and India. It is doubtful whether there were any political organizations as such among the Indians prior to 1941. Messrs. Tilaka and Tularaksa have expressed the opinion that attempts to establish organizations of this type would have been discouraged and that furthermore Indians as a whole were not vitally interested in political developments in their homeland. As followers of Gandhi, Indians sympathized with the Indian National Congress, but there seems to have been no local branch of the Congress in Thailand.

D. Early History of the Indian Independence League in Thailand and its Founders

Many, if not most of the Indians probably regarded the Japanese invasion with some apprehension. Indians and other Asiatic subjects of Great Britain in Thailand were assured by the Japanese that they had nothing to fear. Nevertheless, on 14 and 15 December 1941, about 50 Indians, "including some principal agitators," tried to escape and were arrested. The Bangkok Times in a notice of this affair stated that "in view of the fact that the establishment of an Indian association is being planned to collaborate with the Japanese Army force and because some Indians are enthusiastically cooperating with the Japanese Army force, those who were arrested were especially liberated under the guarantee of the founders of the association." The notice concludes with a warning that no mercy will be granted in the future.

There were undoubtedly a few individuals in the community who were ardent nationalists with a record of participation in subversive activities in India. The end of 1941 found them eager to take the lead in organizing their countrymen behind the Japanese program. One of these was Giani Pritam Singh, who had been in Thailand since 1933. He was born in Lyallpur district in the Punjab, of a "respectable" Sikh family, and educated at a Sikh missionary college. During the years from 1920-23 he participated in the Akali movement, during the course of which Akali Sikhs came into conflict with the Government of India over questions of religious reform. When in 1930 the government fired upon the Red Shirts, a nationalist group in the North West Frontier Province, Giani Pritam Singh, together with 300 other Akalis, went to Peshawar to protest against the government's action. He was arrested in Gujarat and jailed for a year and a half. It has been stated that while in prison he came into contact with Indian nationalist leaders. In April 1933 he was invited by the Singh Sabha, a Sikh religious organization, to go to Bangkok as a "lecturer," and as far as is known he did not return to Indian.

Another Indian revolutionary in Thailand when Japan entered the war was Amar Singh. During the last war he engaged in seditious activities in India and seems to have been involved in one of the various plots to obtain Indian's freedom with German aid. The *Bangkok Times* states that "he is the person who acquired 1000,0000 rifles from Germany during the last great war." In 1917 or 1918 he was imprisoned and sent to the Andamans. After his release in 1940 he went to Thailand where he joined forces with Giani Pritam Singh. Together they started an anti-British movement in which they are said to have received help from the Japanese government. These two men probably formed the nucleus of what later became known as the Independent League of India. It is doubtful if there was any organization, properly speaking, before the end of 1941. A note in the Bangkok Times for 12 February 1942, says that the Independent League, of which Giani Pritam Singh was the leader, "though it had its origin before [the declaration of war by Japan] did not do any work openly." It is further stated that Giani Pritam Singh "had some to an understanding with the Japanese Government concerning the Independence of India." The entry of Japan in the war found these men anxious to play a more active role. On

9 December 1941, the Bangkok Times carried an advertisement signed by A Representative of the Independent League of India: "Attention all Indian residents in Thailand. All patriotic Indians who wish to serve their Motherland India are, requested to enlist their respective names at 1840 (Green House) Saphan Maha Megh." Two days later the same newspaper contained an appeal to Indians to look to Japan to free India. This was signed by "Giani Pritam Singh," very probably a garble for Giani Pritam Singh.

A third Indian who achieved considerable prominence in the early days of the war with Japan was Swami Satyananda Puri. Profulla Kumar Sen, as he was named, was born in 1902 in Bengal. He was educated at Calcutta University where he obtained the degree of M.A. During his student days he was a member of Anushilan Samiti, a society for the promotion of culture and training, which, however, functioned chiefly as an organization "to arouse public opinion against the Government by circulating seditious literature, popularizing revolutionary songs, and organizing secret associations." His connections with this group landed him in jail. While still a young man he became a follower of Tagore and Gandhi. He decided to become a sannyasi (holy man), and having made over his entire property to the National Congress, wandered about in India for four years and spent another three years meditating in the Himalayas. He was afterwards appointed Professor of Oriental Philosophy at Calcutta University and held this post for two years, during which time he founded the Society of Oriental Culture. In 1932 Tagore was requested by the Royal Family of Thailand to send an Indian as unofficial cultural ambassador to Thailand. Tagore selected Swami Satyananda. While in Thailand, the Swami wrote several books on Indian history, philosophy, etc., as well as a biography of Gandhi in the Thai language. There is no indication that he had any dealings with the Japanese prior to December 1941 nor does he seem to have been associated with Amar Singh and Giani Pritam Singh. On 22 December 1941, Swami Satyanada gave notice in the *Bangkok Times* of a meeting to inaugurate an Indian National Council for the Freedom of India. The council was formed several days later and the Swami became its president with Debnath Das as secretary.

For some time the two groups, the Independent League of India and the National Council for the Freedom of India, continued as separate organizations. The first appears to have been the more active. Some of its members, including S. Kishan Singh, Babu Sudarshan Aouja, and Bhagwan

Singh went to Malaya in December 1941, to do propaganda work among the soldiers of the British Indian army. They apparently met with a certain amount of success, but an article in the *Bangkok Times* comments that some of the soldiers "it seemed, had lost their sense of reason and stayed where they were." Giani Pritam Singh went to Malaya shortly after its fall and was instrumental in founding branches of the League in that country.

Towards the end of March 1942, Swami Satyananda Puri and Giani Pritam Singh were killed en route by air to Japan. In May 1942 the Indian National Council and the Independent League merged; the union is reported to have been brought about by Colonel Gill, "a very senior officer," formerly of the army in Malaya. Debnath Das became general secretary and Amar Singh was made a patron.

Such information as is available indicates a general lack of enthusiasm on the part of the Indian community for this Japanese-sponsored organization. It is said that the merchants of Thailand are forced by threat of boycott to become members of the League and to contribute to its funds. Many of them apparently are becoming Thai citizens in order to avoid this pressure.

III. Indians in Malaya

A. Population Statistics

Indian emigration to Malaya in modern times dates from beginning of the nineteenth century. Today Indians form over 12 per cent of the total population of the country 754,849. Detailed information relating to the Indian population, however, is taken from the 1931 Census of British Malaya when the total number of Indians was 624,0009. The following table shows the distribution of Indians in the political subdivisions of Malaya:

Singapore	51,019
Penang	58,020
Malacca	23,238
Straits Settlements	132,277
Perak	159,152
Selangor	155,924
Negri Sembilan	50,100
Pahang	14,820
Federated Malay States	379,996

Johore	51,038
Kehad	50,824
Perlis	966
Kelantan	6,752
Trengganu	1,371
Brunei	377
Unlocated	408

Following is the Indian population of the principal towns.

	Total Population	*Indian Population*
Singapore	445,719	51,019
Kuala Lumpur	111,738	25,342
Alor Star	11,596	2,746
Penang	149,408	58,020
Taiping	31,881	7,726
Seremban	21,650	4,087
Johore Bahru	21,777	3,220
Ipoh	53,183	12,301

About five-sixths of the total Indian population are Tamils from South India. The Following is a tabulation according to sectional groups of the Indians in Malaya;.

Tamil	514,959
Telugu	32,541
Malayali	35,125
Punjabi, etc.	31,001
United Provinces	1,898
Bengal, etc.	1,833
Burmese	1,160
Bombay, etc.	1,388
Bihar and Orissa	219
Nepal	490
Other and unidentified	3,395

As regards religion, the great majority are Hindus, as might be expected considering the great preponderance of Tamils in the population. The Mohammedans are also chiefly from southern India, especially the Malabar coast, but in addition there is a number of Pathans, Punjabis, and natives of Bombay and Bengal in the Muslim group. The following table lists Indians by religion.

	British Malaya	*Straits Settlements*	*F.M.S.*
Hindus	509,202	93,793	322,272
Mohammedans	56,506	24,797	20,184
Sikhs	18,180	4,326	12,117
Christians	36,614	8,507	23,787
Buddists	1,204	398	562
Others	2,303	456	973

The following table showing age distribution per 1,000 Indians indicates clearly the immigrant nature of the population.

Age	Male	Female
0-10	136	279
10-20	124	178
20-30	312	290
30-40	275	162
40-50	138	78
Over 55	15	13

As in almost all countries where Indian immigrants are found, the number of males is greatly in excess of the number of females. In 1931 there were 421,0028 males and 2002,981 females. The several racial groups, however, show wide variation in the sex ratio. Among the Tamils there were 514 females per 1,000 males; for the Telugu, the figure was 717; for the Malayali, 2009; for the Punjabi, 263.

In British Malaya as a whole, about one-fifth of the Indian population is Malaya born. It has been reliably estimated that the "average duration of the southern Indian's continuous stay in Malaya is under three years." As the following figures show, there is little variation between different areas with regard to the number of Indians born in Malaya and those born elsewhere.

	Indian born in Malaya		Indian Born elsewhere	
	Number	*Percent of total Indian population*	*Number*	*Percent of total Indian population*
Straits settlements	30,236	23	101,974	77
F.M.S.	84,036	22	295,903	78
	131,505	21	491,919	79

It should be noted that between 1921 and 1931 the percentage of Indians born in Malaya greatly increased. For British Malaya as a whole in 1921 only 12.4 per cent of the total population was born in Malaya, while 87.6 per cent were born elsewhere. Presumbly this tendancy has continued and the 1931 figures therefore cannot be considered typical of conditions today. Lennor A. Mills, writing in 1942, remarked that Indian labor in Malaya is now in a transitional stage. "Formerly the labourer migrated to Mayala for two or three years and then returned to India with his earnings. Today the majority still return to their villages, but increasingly they come back to Malaya, often accompanied by relatives and friends, and even more important, wives... During the past decade the number who have been in Malaya and regard it and not India as their home has been growing...On a few on the older plantations the majority of the labourers have been born on the estate."

B. Principal Occupations

In British Malaya (exclusive of Brunei) 189,998 Indians including men and women, were engaged in the cultivation of rubber. Of these 101 were estate owners, managers, and assistants. The 42,650 Indians employed in commerce included proprietors and managers of businesses, salesmen, shop assistants, peddlers, moneylenders, etc. Most of the 25,595 Indians occupied in transport and communication were railway laborers, drivers of vehicles, bullock cart owner and drivers; in the Straits Settlements a large number worked as dock laborers, boatmen and lightermen. Only in the Federated Malaya States was there a large number of Indians in the mining industry. The total number was 6,189 and over half of these were in Perak. Laborers general and indeterminate, numbered 61,237; 3,712 were in the police force, most of these in the Straits Settlements and Federated Malay States. In the unfederated states the total number of Indians in the police was 266. With the exception of four commissioned officers and inspectors among the Indian police, all were in the ranks; these four were in Singapore municipality. Of the 920 Indians in the army, 736 were in the Federated Malay States, with 94 in the Straits Settlements and 70 in Johore. One in Singapore and six in the Federated Malay States were commissioned officers.

Broadly speaking sectional groups are associated with occupational divisions. Thus the Tamils, Telugus, and Malayalis are for the most part engaged in the cultivation of rubber. The Punjabis are found mainly in and near the large towns. A considerable proportion "are accounted for the Police Forces, they are also extensively employed as watchmen... and frequently combine money-lending with this and other pursuits. In suburban and rural areas, they are characteristically associated with stock farming and bullock cart driving." Natives of Bombay are usually shopkeepers, and the Bengalis, who are few in number, are also engaged in occupations other than agriculture.

In summary, the Indian population of Malaya consisted chiefly of Tamils from South India who were occupied on plantations or engaged in menial labor of various types. The length of their stay in Malaya was short and their ties were with the homeland, where for the most part their families remained and to which they returned. There were no trade unions, and opportunities of developing a spirit of independence and cooperation were slight. Situated on isolated plantations, these Indians were almost completely under the control of the employers and cut off from the outside world. A small number of Indians were located in the towns and engaged in business or professional activities. For the most part these were northerners who apparently had little contact with Chinese in Malaya, who, rich or poor, have a feeling of kinship with each other. "Among the Indians this is far from being the case: the Tamils and other south Indians are a despised proletariat who have virtually no bond joining them to their alleged brethren from other parts of India who have done better for themselves in Malaya."

C. Indian Associations

In almost every town in Malaya there were Indian associations, and delegates chosen from these men once a year to hold the All-Malayan National Congress. This annual conference was founded in 1927 by Mr. S. Veerasamy, one of the most prominent Indians in the country who in 1931 represented the Indian community in the Federal Council. In 1936 a Central Indian Association was founded in Kuala Lumpur. Its objects were "(a) to promote and safeguard the political social and economic interest of the Indians in Malaya; (b) to represent, express and give effect to Indian public opinion; (c) to consider all questions affecting the interests of the whole or any section of the community; and (e) to do all such things as may be conducive to the furtherance of the above mentioned objects or any of them." How far any of these associations were representative of the Indian masses is not know. Probably the membership was drawn almost entirely from the urban population.

However, these organizations proved to be useful nuclei for the present Indian Independence Leagues, and several of the Indians who were prominent in the old associations are today actively aiding the Japanese. It should not be assumed from this fact that the Indians in Malaya were, previous to the Japanese invasion, primarily or actively interested in the Indian struggle for independence. With regard to the masses of the Indian population it is doubtful if they took any interest in political affairs, either of India or Malaya. It has been said that the Hindu merchants of Singapore were mostly loyal to the Indian National Congress and when Jawaharlal Nehru visited Malaya in 1937, he was very enthuseastically received. There appears, however, to have been very little contact with the Congress group in India. As is indicated by the program cited above, the Indians in Malaya were more concerned with advancing their political and economic position in the country of their adoption than n working for the independence of India.

D. Indians under British Administration in Malaya

Indians believe that they have serious grievances in regard to their treatment by the British in Malaya. Numerically they have a strong claim to consideration, and the prosperity of the country undoubtedly owes much to their labor. Indian criticized the Government of Malaya for failure to safeguard the economic interests of the Indian laborer. Wages have been low and the means of livelihood uncertain for the past decade. During 1931-32 when the rubber industry suffered from the general depression, large number of Indians were thrown out of work; wages were reduced by 20 per cent from the 1928 figure of 50% per day. According to proposals made by the Government of India, 73,000 Indians were repatriated free of cost and all recruitment of labor in India was brought to an end. As conditions improved, assisted immigration was resumed in 1934 at the request of the Malayan Government. Wages remained low until 1936, when,, acting on the advice of a deputation from India, the Malayan government restored half of the cut imposed in 1930. Finally in 1937 wages raised to the former level of 50% per day for men and 40% for women. When the rubber industry again deteriorated in 1938 the wages of Indian workers were once more reduced, but with the advent of war and the increase in the price of rubber, wages were fixed at 50% per day, the cost of living however, had greatly increased and the laborer did not profit from the war in any material way.

Indians declare that facilities for education of their children have been unsatisfactory. In Penang, Malacca, and Singapore, there was not a single Government Tamil school, in spite of large numbers of Tamil government employees in these places.

In regard to public services and representation in public bodies, Indians believe that their status was not commensurate with their importance. Indians were not permitted to enter the Malaya Civil Service, and they had no municipal or political franchise. There was one non-official Indian member nominated to the Federal Council and another on the Straits Settlements Legislative Council.

IV. Indians in Indochina

It is impossible to state the exact number of Indians living in Indochina; 6,000 is probably a fair estimate. About half of these are from French colonies in India, and for the most part they have established themselves in Cochinchina, though there are about 350 in Cambodia. The natives of British India are nearly all Muslims from the northern provinces. There is also a fairly large group of Chettyars from South India and a few Parsis form Bombay engage in import trade.

Indians from French India are for the most part minor government employees, postmen, policemen, assistant registrars, customs or excise clerks. The Muslims from British India are shopkeepers and pawnbrokers, cashiers and watchmen. The Chettyars, or moneylenders, most of whom are located in Cochinchina, where in 1937, there were 120 Chetti firms, from the wealthiest group among the Indians. They own a considerable amount of land and engage extensively in trade. In Cochinchina alone, Chettyars own one-fourth of the total rice-growing area. In 1933, their business methods and the hold they had acquired over the agriculture of the country aroused wide-spread antagonism. As a result of the depression, the Chetti system of short-term loans resulted in great hardship particularly for the agriculturists. Five Chetti bankers were expelled from Indochina on "the alleged ground that they created political disturbances in the country. " Later on the order of expulsion was cancelled but French authorities by establishing long term credit offices have considerably undermined the position of the Chettyars, and in the first eight months of 1933 about 65 per cent of the Chetti capital was removed to Burma, Malaya, and India. It seems probable that the Chettyars who remain form a dissatisfied group, hostile to continued French domination in Indochina.

V. Indians in N.E.I.

In the Netherlands East Indies there were, according to the 1920 census, 27,684 Indians. Of these 12,654 were born in the area; 15,030 were born abroad, presumably for the most part in India, though it is possible that emigrants from Malaya were a numerous group. The men outnumber the women by about two to one. The Indians located in Java and Sumatra number 25,638, the greater proportion of these being in Java. In Bali and Western Lombok there is "a handful of Indians," and a few more in Dutch Borneo.

Speaking of the Indians generally, the Handbook for the Dutch East Indies says," The majority are Mohammedans and come from the coastal districts of Coromandel and Malabar. Many are found in the plantation areas of Deli as coolies, car drivers, cattlemen, etc., owing to their fine physique, these so-called Klings.... Are engaged as night-watchmen on the plantations. In Java they are mostly smaller shop-keepers. They are conspicuous owing to their height, heavy growth of beards and large turbans." This reference to their height and growth of breads suggests that there is a Sikh element in the Indian population.

VI. Indian in China

The principal Indian colonies in China are in Shanghai and Hongkong. Indians in Hongkong numbered 4,475. These included the troops which formed part of the garrison, the Sikh contingent of the police, and a few merchants and clerks. According to the 1921 census of Hongkong, about 85 percent of the adult male Indians were employed as police or watchmen, or in various government departments. Most of the Indians were Punjabis or native of the North West Frontier Province. In 1930 there were 1,842 Indian living in Shanghai. "Practically all of these Indians were brought to Shanghai originally as policemen..... but after completing their term of enlistment, many remained here to engage in business or professional activities," For the most part the Indians of Shanghai are Sikhs.

B. Indians in China and Indian Nationalism

Indians in China have taken an active interest in Indian political affairs for many years. Before the last war, in both Hongkong and Shanghai there were Ghadr (revolution) societies, affiliated with similar organizations on the west coast of the Unites State and elsewhere, which conspired for the overthrow of the British government in India. A number of Indians in Hongkong and Shanghai were involved in the Komogata Maru affair in 1914 in order to test Canadian immigration law which made it practically impossible for Indian immigrations in Canada to be joined by their wives and children, and also to "embarrass the British government by compelling it either to interfere with Canada's immigration policy or to suffer a further loss of popularity in India. A Japanese vessel, the Komogata Maru, was chartered by Sikh name Gurudutt Singh, a man prominent in the Far East.

The ship sailed from Hongkong to Canada with 351 Sikhs and 21 Punjabi Muslims recruited at Honkong, Shanghai, Moji and Yokohama. The Great Majority of the passengers were not permitted to land in Canada. During the return trip war broken out and for various reasons the passengers were not allowed to land at the part of embarkation but were taken to Budge Budge in Bengal. These men formed the nucleus of the agitation in the Punjab which lasted during the war and for several yeas after. Other conspirators arrived shortly after the Komogatu Maru, and these also were for the most part Sikhs from America, Japan, Manila and Shanghai, who had been in touch with German agents en route to India. The disturbances in the Punjab which these men helped to further were for a time directed by Rashbehari Bose.

From 1920 to 1940 Indian political development in China was influenced by two separate organizations, the Indian National Congress and the Chinese Kumointang Party. Reliance on methods of terrorism was modified by the Congress policy of passive resistance, and the growing strength of the Congress in Indian encouraged increased activity among the Indians in China. At the same time the development of nationalism in China proved an inspiration to the Indian group. To a certain extent the Communists also played a part, but their influence on the Indians in China does not appear to have been very great at any time, and was probably much less after the break occurred between Chiang Kai Shek and the Chinese Communists.

C. Indian Organizations

In 1927 some Chinese members of the Kuomintang, some Korenans, a few Filipinos, some Japanese "proletarians" and a number of Indians formed the Eastern Oppressed Peoples' Association. The organization was formed originally when the radical section of the Kuomintang was in power, and its headquarters were in Hankow. Later on these were moved to Nanking, and the organizatin remained under the protection of the Kuominatang party. It has been said that Jawaharlal Nehru sponsored the establishment of the Eastern Oppressed Peoples' Association. It is possible that the idea was conceived at the Brussels Congress of Oppressed Nationalities at which Nehru was present, and in which the leftist members of the Kuomintang played an active part.

The Indian section of the Eastern Oppressed Peoples' Association in Nanking published for some years a bi-weekly called Ghadr Dhandora (Declaration of Revolution).

In line with the sympathy expressed by the All India Congress Committee for China in her struggle for freedom, and the Committee's condemnation in 1927 of the action of the Government of India in sending Indian troops to China engaged in propaganda among the Indian troops stationed at Shanghai. These troops on their way to China, had been subjected to propaganda to the effect that Indian temples in China were being destroyed, women violated, etc. "But they were met, almost at the dock, by certain men of their own nationality, who were working for the cause of Indian freedom among the large groups of Indian freedom among the large groups of Indian police and watchmen already in Shanghai.....The reaction of the troops when they discovered the untruth of the stories which had been circulated among them was great." As a result, these troops had to be sent back to Hongkong. Later two battalions, Punjabis who spoke a different dialects from that of the Indian nationalist workers in Shanghai arrived, but these too were infected with sympathy for the Chinese cause. Expenses of the Indian organization are alleged to have been paid by donation from Chinese friends and members of the Kuomintang. On the whole, the Indians in Shanghai were too poor to contribute large sums to the movement, though they gave what they could afford.

It has been stated that there were two groups of Indian agitators in Shanghai at this time. One group believed in "the passive resistance policy of Mahatma Gandhi, their leader," while the second group consisted of Communists "working for the complete overthrow of British rule in India and its members are fanatical believers in the most radical measures." Gujjan Singh, Daswanda Singh, and Gainda Singh were members of this Communist group. An Indian, M.N. Roy, was in China at this time as a delegate of the Communist International. It is not known, however, whether or not he played any active role in the Indian organization; certainly during this period he was more concerned with developments in China than in India.

Harchan Singh, an Indian nationalist of Shanghai and a member of the Eastern Oppressed Peoples' Association, who had taken part in the propagandist activities referred to above, was murdered in 1929. Shortly before his death he had compiled a list of Indians in Shanghai who were alleged to be in the employ of the British Indian Secret Service. Five Indians also members of the Eastern Oppressed Peoples' Association were charged with his murder. These were Norang Singh, Sadu Singh, Mewa Singh, and Karm Singh. They were acquitted of the charge of murder but shortly after rearrested on charges of sedition, and were given jail sentences to also Sikhs, Ishar Singh, Indar Singh, Hakim Singh, Asha Singh, and Narain Singh were arrested on charges of sedition. They were accused of reading aloud in a Sikh temple in Chapei nationalist papers received from India. This temple had been closed in 1927 by the British authorities "on the grounds that the premises were being used for Bolshevik propaganda," but it was reopened in 1928. The seditionists in question were sentenced to prison with hard labor and later deported.

In 1930, while civil disobedience was in progress in India there were a number of other arrests on charges of sedition among the Indians of China. The Indian Youth League of China issued several manifestos condemning British rule and calling upon all Indians to fight for a free Asia. In June 1930 the British police raided the League headquarters and made two arrests. In July of the same year Zapuran Singh distributed pamphlets printed in English and Chinese and published by the E.O.P.A. He was sentenced to two months hard labor and deportation.

The Indian Youth League which had its headquarters in Chapei had "some kind of agreement with the Kuomintang and Brueau of Public Safety," which enabled it to hold meetings and carry on political activity. The leaders were young working men who were literate and intelligent. They kept in touch with events in Indian and informed their countrymen in Shanghai by means of leaflets, magazines and pamphlets as well as public meetings. Chanan Singh and Kartar Singh, leading members of the League, and Surjan Singh were arrested in December 1930. All were tried for sedition, and two of the men were sentenced to imprisonment and deportation.

The instances cited above are probably only a few of many such cases of friction between the Indians and the British in China. They are, between the Indians and the British in China. They are, however, indicative of the degree to which the Indians were organized and of the enthusiasm felt there for the cause of nationalism of India.

VII. Indians in Japan

According to the Japan Year Book for 1938-39 there were 874 Indians resident in Japan. Of these, 670 were males. For the most part the Indian group consisted of businessmen and students, located chiefly in the large cities, Tokyo, Kobe, Yokohama, with a few in Osaka.

B. Indian Revolutionaries of Japan

Japan has for many years been a refuge for Indian patriots of various hues. After the Ruksso-Japanese war, Indians generally regarded Japan with admiration and respect, and to a great extent looked to Japan as the leader of Asia. At the same time certain groups in Japan pursued the policy of actively encouraging revolutionary tendencies in Asiatic countries, especially those under European domination.

The story of the Indian nationalist movement in Japan is a summary of the life histories of a small number of Indian revolutionaries who used their contacts with the Japanese to ends. In the background of this Indian movement stands Mitsuru Toyama, the power behind almost all the Japanese patriotic societies. It is not to be doubted that Toyama conspired with these Indians, extended to them his patronage and protection, and used them for his own ends.

1. Maulvi Mohammed Barkatulla: Maulvi Mohammed Barkatulla was one of the earliest Indian revolutionaries with contacts in Japan. He was born in Bhopal in 1868 and educated in Bombay and London. He became a strong advocate of Pan-Islamism and extremely anti-British. In 1909 has was appointed to the chair of Hindustani in Tokyo Foreign Language School, and while in Japan he founded a paper called *Islamic Fraternity*, which he edited for some years. In 1911 he traveled for a time in Europe, visiting Cairo, Constantinople, St. Petersburg and Paris, where he came into contact with Krishnaverma, one of the best known Indian exiles of the period. On his return to Japan "the tone of his paper became so anti-British that it was suppressed by the Japanese Government in 1912. Early in 1914 he was deprived of his appointment in Tokio....." From Japan, Barkatulla went to the United States. There he joined forces with Har Dayal who had, a few year previously, founded the Ghadr (revolution) Party among Indian immigrants settled on the West Coast. In March 1914 Har Daya was arrested by the United State Government and was about to be deported as an undesirable lien when he, together w2ith Barkatulla, fled to Switzerland. The outbreak of the war found these two in Germany. In Berlin, Har Dayal and Barkatulla, with Chatthopadyaya and Pillai, well-known Indian seditionists, directed the activities of the Indian Revolutionary Society, and conspired with the aid of Germany to overthrow the British Government in India. In 1915 Barkatulla and Raja Mahendra Pratap went to Kabul, where they formed the Provisional Indian Government. During the war this "government" "continued to encourage seditious agitation in Indian and hostile action by the frontier tribes...... After the war it threw all its influence into promoting the rebellious outbreaks in India in April 1919."

In 1927 Barkatulla represented the Hindustan Ghadr Party at the Brussels Congress against Imperialism, and later in the same year he died in San Francisco.

2. Hariharnath Thulal Atal: Hariharnath Thulal Atal was another Indian who went to Japan in the early days of the twentieth century. Like Barkatulla he held the chair of Hindustani in Tokyo Forging Language School. In 1914 the Department of Education, according to report, wanted to renew his contract, but the British authorities would not permit it. Atal stayed on in Japan but the British began to "harass him in every way," and finally in 1921 he committed suicide.

A memorial ceremony, arranged by Rashbehari Bose, was held in Tokyo, 14 June 1931, in honor of Barkatulla, Atal and Vikramratne. The last of these three lived in Tokyo for a few year where he worked with Bose "for the cause of Indian freedom." He died in Ceylon in 1928.

3. Raja Mahendra Pratap: One of the most interesting, and certainly the most picturesque of all the Indian in Japan is Raja Mahendra Pratap, a native of the United Provinces and formerly a wealthy landowner. Whether or not he played any part in the seditious movements of the period in Indian is uncertain. He is said to have founded Braindaban National University, of which he became President , and to have been the owner of a newspaper Narmalsewak. At the outbreak of the war in 1914, he went to Europe and came under the influence of Har Dayal. Through him, Pratap had an interview with the Kaiser, who "impressed with a megalomania akin to his own," sent Pratap with Barkatulla to Kabul. He became a citizen of Afghanistan and continued to live there for some years.

In 1925 Pratap, accompanied by Daswanda Singh, a student at California University started out for Tibet and Nepal to see whether they "could do any service to India from these countries." " Indian friends in California probably members of the Ghadar organization, collected money to pay the expenses of the trip. A member of the Kuomintang party went along as interpreter and Mr. Charan Singh seems to have been a member of the group. To the various Chinese generals Pratap met along the way, he presented a copy of his book, *The Religion of Love.* Shortly after this, in 1926, he went to Japan, but for some reason he was not permitted to remain there. It has been suggested that the British authorities objected to his presence in Japan, and he returned to Afghanistan. He had, according to his own account," no political ambition for the time being."

About 1930 he was sent by the Government of Afghanistan on an economic "mission" to America and on his way home, he stopped in

Japan. From there he went to Vladivostok where he was informed by the Soviet authorities that he could not proceed further. On his return to Japan, he learned that the Afghan government did not want him in the country for the time being; Pratap declared himself at a loss to explain this. He seems to have gone to Peiping shortly after this, where he published a monthly called *World Federation,* and busied himself collecting $1,000 for a building to serve as a permanent office for *World Federation.* Early in 1933 he returned to Japan. The *Voice of India*, organ of the Indian Nationalist group in Japan, published a statement by Pratap who signed himself, The Servant of Mankind, and announced that he had temporarily closed his Peiping office. He started that if Japan would realize that the British Empire was working for Japan's destruction, Japan could come to dominate Asia. When the Pan-Asiatic Congress was held in Dairen in 1934, Pratap attended it. He proceeded to Canton where he tried to organize an Oppressed Oriental Races Emancipation Society, but he was arrested by the Canton government authorities and deported to Shanghai. He was again arrested in Shanghai, but "friends" secured his release. The *China Weekly Review* reported that " It is understood that the Afghanistan leader is in Shanghai on some mission on behalf of the Japanese." According to the *Japan Weekly Chronicle*, Pratap spent his time addressing the Sikh police. On his return to Japan Pratap set out the visit Siam. In 1935 he again visited the United States. It was said that his reception was rather cold and that he found the "atmosphere not suitable for his message."

Pratap has never been one of the most influential Indians in Japan. As far as is known he has never held office in any of the numerous Indian organizations, and he seems never to have worked in close collaboration with Rashbehari Bose. Ideas or World Federation and Pan-Asianiam have been obviously more appealing to him that the narrow cause of Indian freedom. He is not at present an important figure, and is said to be regarded as a crank by his fellow Indians, although a few of the Indian students in Japan have become his disciples. A recent report suggests that Pratap has not been able to reconcile Japanese imperialism with his ideas of world federation. It has been started that he refused, "though pressed hard to do so," to attend the Japanese sponsored Bangkok Conference in June 1942.

4. Rashbehari Bose: The most prominent Indian in Japan today is Rashbehari Bose. He was born in Bengal in 1886 and educated in Calcutta. For a time he was employed as a clerk in the Forest Research Institute, but while still a young man he became involved in the Indian revolutionary movement, in which Bengalis played so large a part. In 1912-15 he directed terrorist activities in the Punjab, but when a number of the ringleaders were arrested, Bose fled to Japan. The Japanese Government ordered him to be deported, but he was protected by Mitsuru Toyama, and to avoid further trouble he took out Japanese citizenship papers. He married the daughter of a Japanese who kept a restaurant and eventually succeeded to the business.

The Japanese who's who for 1937 lists him as a journalist, lecturer, author and correspondent of Indian newspapers. This account is probably somewhat flattering. His reputation as a journalist rests chiefly upon the fact that from time to tome he has written articles for several newspapers, among them the *Calcutta forward.* He claims authorship of several books in Japanese on the Indian nationalist movement, but it is doubtful whether he has written them himself.

Bose is said to be politically honest and scrupulous, and sincere in his efforts to win freedom for Indian. According to reports he is equally convinced that this can be obtained with Japanese aid. Asked in 1933 why he did not return to India, he replied that he would come at the head of armed forces which would enter India by way of Assam. He is said to have Communist leanings and to have had contacts with the Soviet Embassy in Tokyo.

5. Anand Mohan Sahay: Anand Mohan Sahay is one of the few Indian in Japan who were ever closely connected with the Indian National Congress. He was born in 1898, the son of a landlord in Bhagalpore in the province of Bihar, and was educated at Patna University, where he studied medicine. When the Congress urged students to boycott government institutions, he have up his work at the University and joined the independence movement. He worked actively with the Bihar Provincial Congress Committee. In 1923 he set out for America via Japan, to study medicine, but decided to settle in Japan to "work of the promotion of Indo-Japanese friendship and dissemination of correct information regarding India in Japan.

Since that time he has remained in Japan. According to his biography in the Japanese *Who's Who* for 1937 he is journalist, writer, educator, teacher and lecturer on India, Japan, Asia, and international problems. He was also for some time professor at Kobe Foreign Language School. Sahay is said to be completely...... and insincere in political matters. One informant (name withheld) believes he could be bought by anyone prepared to pay the price of securing his support. The same source accuses him of extorting funds from Indian merchants to support himself and his various enterprises. Sahay and Bose are extremely jealous of one another and continually at logger-heads. Sahay is probably the cleverer of the two men.

C. Indian organization in Japan

One of the earliest Indian organizations in Japan was the Indo-Japanese Association, founded in Tokyo about 1905 by the Rev. Dharmapala and Mr. Sakurai. Viscount Nagaoka was the first president and was succeeded by Marquis Okuma. Valentine Chirol, writing in 1910, started that this society had "no connection with politics and the Indians claim that it is run for the benefit of the Japanese rather that for theirs. Those who have joined it in the hope of using it as a base for anti-British operations have certainly got very little for their pains. They occasionally write papers for the very few socialist papers of Japan, but their effective contribution to the cause is of trifling account." By 1937 this organization had no Indian members, and during theprevious decades its main activity was the development of economic relations between Indian and Japan.

The Indian National Congress Committee of Japan was organized in 1928, with its headquarter in Kobe. A.M. Sahay was on of the leaders of the Committee and retained control over it. D.P. Mahabubani of Kobe was a delegate at the annual session of the Indian National Congress in 1928. The Committee has for some years published the *Voice of India*, with A.M. Sahay as editor. Originally the paper was published in English as a monthly, but was later printed in Japanese and English and usually appeared every fortnight. Congress activities in India were well covered, and considerable space was given to the activities of the committee in Japan. In 1931 the committee opened the Indian Lodge to accommodate Indian students studying in Japan.

It probably is incorrect to assume that the committee had any close connection with the Indian National Congress. Sahay claimed that it was recognized by the parent organization in 1929, but according to report, Kripalani, the General Secretary of the Indian Congress wrote to Shay denying that this was the case, and pointing out the fact that it was contrary to Congress policy to establish or recognize branches outside of India.

Other Indian organizations include the Indian National Association founded about 1930 with branches in Yokohama, Kobe and probably elsewhere; and the Japan-Indian Society of Kanasai, established about the same time. In 1931 Rashbehari Bose organized the Indian Independence League, which had as its objects "the attainment of Independence League, which had as its object "the attainment of Independence for India by all possible means. Bose became the first president, and P.S. Deshpande secretary of the League. The League functioned as a rival organization to

Sahay's Japanese Congress Committee. The Indo-Japanese Young Peoples, Association was formed about 1934-35 "the encourage the study of Indian and Japanese problems. The Gandhi Society of Tokyo, a small and poorly organized group, seems to have been chiefly interested in economic relations between India and Japan. It is said to have been ideologically opposed to Gandhi and scornful of the doctrine of non-violence.

There were in addition to these, various Indian social and business organizations, such as the Indian Social Society, and the Indian Merchants Association.

VIII. Indian National Congress and Indians Overseas

The general attitude of the Indian National Congress to Indians abroad is best summed up in a resolution passed by the Congress at its annual session in 1936. "The Congress sends greetings to our fellow-countrymen overseas and its assurances of sympathy and help in their distressful condition and in the continuing deterioration in their status in the territories in which they have settled. The Congress is ready and willing to take all action within its power to ameliorate their condition, but desires to point out that a radical ameliorate in their status must ultimately depend on the attainment by India of Independence and the power effectively protect her nationals abroad. Except for numerous resolutions, dating from the early days of the Congress, which did little more than express sympathy with the plight of Indians overseas, interest on the part of Congress in their problems has been slight. This is especially true of Indians in South-East Asia. Gandhi's early connections with South Africa, where Indians are settled in large numbers, has tended to focus attention on that area, while Indians is South-East Asia,, expect in times of crisis such as the riots in Burma or the severe economic depression in Malaya, have been more or less ignored.

The Indian National Congress has never to any extent developed contacts with Indians abroad for political purposes. The Congress Working Committee in 1936 passed a resolution advocating the establishment of a foreign department "with a view to creating and maintaining contacts with Indians overseas and with international labor and other organizations abroad with whom cooperation is possible and with international labor and other organizations abroad with whom cooperation is possible and is likely to help in the cause of Indian freedom". This department, however, was not very active and beyond issuing a circular to Indians overseas inviting them to keep in touch with the Congress, and printing a short pamphlet on Indians abroad, did very little to fulfills its expressed function. The unofficial visit of Jawaharlal Nehru to Burma and Malaya in 1937 probably served to arouse the interest of Indians in these countries in the National Congress, but there seems to have been no attempt to follow this up with propaganda or definite programs. Sometime before 1940 the Congress opened a department of Indians overseas, and published a pamphlet entitled "Our Countrymen Abroad." This was chiefly to inform the Indian people regarding conditions of Indians overseas, and to awake interest in their problems. Perhaps, had the war not intervened, more active contacts with Indians overseas would have been instituted.

51

Indians Urged to Push Anti-British Movement by Netaji

14. October, 1944

Somewhere in Burma, October 14—In a statement on the present situation in India regarding the breakdown of the Gandhi-Jinnah talks, Netaji Subhas Chandra Bose, Head of the Provisional Government of Azad Hind on Wednesday, exhorted his compatriots inside India to intensify the civil disobedience movement. The statement follows "A few days ago, news was flashed all over the world that the Gandhi-Jinnah talks had broken down Indians everything heaved a sigh of relief, No nationalist could have adopted an attitude of approval or even of equality toward the talks that were based on the proposal to divide India into a number of states. The proposal had become still more obnoxious because it appeared that these states would all be under British domination and because there was no possibility that the Muslim League would ever cooperate with the Indian National Congress in fighitng the British Government.

I had said clearly in a previous statement on the subject that in view of the pro-British attitude of the leaders of the Muslim League, any agreement arrived at by Mahatama Gandhi and Mohammed Ali Jinnah President at the Muslim League could not put any pressure on the British Government—either in extracting more political reforms in my opinion the Gandhi Jinnah talks, even if they had led to an agreement would not have helped the attainment of Indian independence or even a compromise between the Congress and the British since the policy of the British Government under Prime Minister Churchill is strongly opposed to granting any political concessions whatsover to the Indian people.

By now it should be clear even to a child that the British Government which is based on brutal force will surrender only to brutal force. That is

1. I.N.A. Trial Papers.

why the ındians in East Asia have taken up arms for the liberation of their motherland, and what they demand is not compromise with the British Government but the total expulsion of the British from India.

The problem that now faces our countrymen inside India is what they should do now, the situation is similar to that of May in 1942. The patriots in India should intensify the civil disobedience movement but without going in for sabotage activity. Sabotage acitivities should in the future synchronise with our military operations and they should be started only when we are inside India and give the signal.

If for any reason the Civil disobedience movement cannot be intensified immediately a passive opposition to the British Government should continue and all possible preparations should not be misled by bumptious propaganda of our enemies into thinking that the Anglo-Americans are going to win the war.

Every war must have its ups and downs—particularly a world war of the present magnitude. During the first phase of this war, the Axis Powers had sweeping victories on every front, in the second phase our enemies started a counter-offensive and had some success. That phase is now coming to close. The turning point of the war is fast approaching when the initiative will pass out of the hands of our enemies and our friends and allies will take the offensive once again.

We Indians in East Asia are busy preparing ourselves for the next offensives and the day is not far off when the British retreat from Delhi will begin. During the seven months of fighting all along the Indo-Burma frontier and inside India, we have been able to take the measure of our enemies. Having beaten the enemy in several sectors while we are on the offensive our confidence in final victory has increased a hundred fold. We know that the fight will have one result, namely the expulsion of the enemy from Indian soil and establishment of a free and united India.

52

Azad Hind Fauj Orders by Lieut. Colonel Aziz Ahmad Khan regarding the formation of War Council.

BURMA *30 October, 1944*

Appointments–Officers:

444. During the absence of the Supreme Commander, A. H. F., from H Q No. 11 Unit, Lieut, Col. Aziz Ahmad Khan will deal with all routine add urgent matters, which would ordinarily have been dealt with by the Supreme Commander.

Lt. Col. Aziz Ahmad Khan will, during this period, exercise the powers of the Chief of Staff.

War Council:

445. Since the establishment of the Provisional Government of Azad Hind on the 21st October 1943, a year of intensive activity has elapsed. In the meantime, the war has reached a stage when the initiative is going to pass from the hands of our enemies to those of our friends and of our Allies. To prepare for the coming offensive, it is absolutely necessary to make an all out effort at Total Mobilisation and to further intensify and co-ordinate all our activities connected with our war-preparations. In order to achieve this objective, a special organ of the Provisional Government of Azad Hind has to be set up. The War Council of the Provisional Government has, thereofre, been formed. The War Council which is the Supreme organ of the Provisional Government for directing and controlling the war effort and the war preparations of the Government will have the following duties:

1. I.N.A. Trial Papers.

1. To further intensify the war activities that will be found necessary for the war effort and for war preparations.

2. To initiate any new activites that will be found necessary for the war effort and for war preparations.

3. To co-ordinate all these activities with a view to producing the maximum result, namely, to launch the offensive that will bring about the speed and complete otherthrow of our enemies—

The following is the composition of the War Council:—

1. Colonel	J. K. Bhonsla
2. Colonel	M. Z. Kiani
3. Lt. Col.	Ehsan Qadir
4. Lt. Col.	Aziz Ahmad Khan
5. Lt. Col.	Habib-ur- Rahman
6. Lt. Col.	Gulzara Singh
7. Shri	N. Raghavan
8. Sri	S.A. Ayar.
9. Sri	Parmanand
10. Col.	A.C. Chatterjee
11. Sri	A. Yellapa.

Appendix I

Intercepted Radio Broadcast on the Activities of I. N. A. and Provisional Government of Azad Hind 1943-44[1]

In concert with the historic Greater East Asia proclamation of Premier Tojo in the Imperial Diet on the fall of Singapore, the Indian Independence leader, Mr. Rash Behari Bose and 800 other Indian residents of Japan gathered at ... Hotel in Tokyo and issued an important statement in connection with the Indian Independence Movement, strongly urging the Indian nation to rise to the establishment of India for the Indians and India for the Asiatics. These people issued and signed this manifesto: "We Indian nationals have fought for the past fifty years against British aggression with the object of making India for Indians and India for Asia. Despite thousands of personal sacrified, our efforts so far have failed because we have had no armed support. The present war of GEA has given us a goldern opportunity for realizing our century old objective. Fellow countrymen of India, take advantage of this...... support and liquidate all of India's past quarrels with Britain. In accordance with the spirit of Buddah and Islam rise up to greet the truth and doctrine of Mahatama Gandhi." *Tokyo, English, 2.12.42*

Shigoru Hata stated "Representing this rally, wires relative to the preceding resolution will be sent to the following headquarters throughout the GEA : the Moanchukuo Genral Society, the North China Hsin Min Society, the Mongolia Far East cooperative Society, the Nanking Asia Development Fedaration and the Indian Independence Movement Office at Bangkok and others. The contents of these wires will be read to you through my representatives. At the Rally for the Rescue of India, we have resolved to give all-out support to India in her work for independence. The complete destruction of our common enemy America and Britain, has been pledged." *Tokyo, Japanese 8.27.43*

1. This report was prepared by the office of the Strategic Service, U.S. government. O.S.S. Record Group. 226. copy obtained from Diet Library, Tokyo.

Tokyo Kabuki Theatre became the scene of India Rescue People's Rally and the following resolution "Britain took a cruel measure to bring pressure on Indian people by disregarding Gandhi's attempt. Tojo promised Philippenes independence and he also promised the fullest support to India." The resolution was wired to appropriate organs.

Tokyo, Japanese 2.27.43

A capacity crowd of 5,000 attended the All-India National Meeting held in Tokyo Saturday at the Kabuki Theatre under the joint sponsorship of National Service Association, Nippon Asia Development League and the Asahi, Mainachi and Yamuri Haki newspapers. It was held in a most favourable atmosphere with popular sentiments running high in sympathy with Mahatma Gandhi. In addition, the decision reached Friday by the Japanese Government that Indians who cooperate with Japan will be accorded treatment similar to that given to the Indian nationals was met with deep satisfaction. The resolution and declaration passed were cabled to the Cencordia Association of Manchukuo, the Hain Min. Society of North China, the Chinese Council of the East Asiatic League in Nanking, the Indian Independence League in various localities in the Southern Regions, Kiwao Okamura, Vice Chief of the Tokyo Board of Information, spoke on Gandhi, as did also Nitaro Nagal, Chief of the Asia Developement Bureau of the National Service Association. *Tokyo, English, 2.23.43*

To celebrate establishment of the Provisional Government of Azad Hind, 45 representative Indian residents in Tokyo, Yokohama, Kobe, Osaka and other leading lives of Japan held a "Rice India" meeting..... Rash Behari Bose, Supreme Advisor of the Provisional Government of Free India, who recently returned from Snoyan resorted on progress of the Independence movement there. *Tokyo, English, 10.25.43*

Japan Indian Independence League

The Indian Independence Legue had four branches in Japan but since there was not good connection between them, a territorial committee was established and a first meeting held. The representatives from each branch will form a Council and their first meeting will be at Tokyo, May 2. Heretofere they have worked independently. *Tokyo, Japanese, 5.3.43*

Representatives of the Tokyo, Yokohama, Osaka and Kobe Branches of the Indian Independence Legue decided to establish a central committee for Japan which will organize and guide the work of the branches and will further strengthen the freedom movement. The committee consists of 8 members, 2 from each branch and their work is distributed among three sections and officers is charge have been appointed. These are Department of Publicity and Information, Department of Planning and Department of Welfare. *Tokyo, Hindustani 8.3.43*

The central office of the Indian Independence Legue in Japan has named the Nippon...... committee has removed to its permanent site at No. 5 (Kaminchi Akasakahu). The opening ceremonies will be held at the new premises on Jan 12, whom the Acting Chief of the new office will be formally inaugurated. This office will represent in Japan the headquarters of the Indian Independence Legue in East Asia, which is now at Shonan. The office will guide and central all the activities of the new branches in Japan while carrying on the Indian Independence Movement under the command of the Supreme Leader, Subhas Chandra Bose.

Tokyo, English 12.39.43

Immediately upon receipt of the tragic news of the demise of Mrs. Kasturbai Gandhi in the British prison at Poona, the Indian Independence League in Japan called a meeting yesterday of Indians in Nippon at its central officers to mourn her lost, with members of the League in Tokyo and representatives from the Yokohama, Osaka and Kobo Branches also participating . The meeting was held in the presence of Rash Behari Bose, supreme Advisor to the Provisional Government of Azad Hind.

Tokyo, English, 2.24.44

Local Indian residents will assemble at Honaji Temple here Wednesday afternoon to hold a prayer meeting in memory of the Late Kasturbai Gandhi who died Feb. 22 while imprisoned by the British at Poona. It is learned the function is planned in accordance with instructions from Subhas Chandra Bose, head of the Provisional Government of Free India and Commander of the Indian Independence Army, to the Indian Independence Legue in Japan. *Tokyo, English, 2.25.44*

Tokyo Branch

Rama Murti, spokesman of the Tokyo Branch of the Indian Independence Legue expressed gratitude over exemption of the Indians from the rule for control of enemy property of the casot-freezing order.

Tokyo, English, 2.27.43

The members of the Tokyo Branch of the Indian Independence League held a rally at the Sanno Hotel Monday to express their joy at the assumption of the presidency of the League by Mr. Subhas Chandra Bose. The members expressed their heartfelt gratitude to Mr. Rash Behari Bose outgoing president for his invaluable services to the cause as the father of the Indian Independence Legue of East Asia. They sent a cable to Mr. Subhas Chandra Bose pledging that..... and devotion to him.

Tokyo, English, 7.6.43

The Tokyo Branch of the Indian Independence League hold a meeting Tokyo on Dec. 2...... in regard to the transfer of the two islands of Andaman and Nicobar to the Free India Provisional Government by Japan. The Indian Independence Legue Council in Japan decided to have its headquarters in Tokyo and establish branches in Yokohama and Osaka for the purpose of .....

Tokyo, Japanese, 12.2.43

Kobe Branch

Taking advantage of the GEA war which will liberate the one billion people of East Asia, 67 Indian living in the region of Osaka and Kobe this afternoon held a meeting at Kobe, at which the Kobe Branch of the Indian Independence Association was disbanded and merged with the New India Indian League. It was decided to establish local branches of this League at Kobe and Osaka..... and headed by..... Subhas Chandra Bose of Tokyo. It was decided to work for the Independence of India.

Tokyo, Japanese, 2.23.42

As a representative of the Indian people residing in Japan, the Kobe Branch head (Tahan) of the Indian Independence League attended the formation ceremonies of the Indian Independence Army of the Free India Provisional Government.

Tokyo, Japanese, 11.20.43

Yokohama Branch

Celebrating the seventy-third brithday of Mahatma Gandhi, more than 300 Japanese and Indian friends and supporters Friday gathered at the Indian Club at Yokohama. The celebration was hold under the auspicious of the Japanese headquarters of the Indian Independence League.

Tokyo, English, 10.2.42

The Yokohama Branch of the Indian Independence League held its general meeting at the India club on Monday and unanimously elected the following officers President. (Digovio Sagani), Honorary Secretary, (Shilapi Colazani).......

Tokyo English, 10.14.42

A solemn ceremony commemorating the first anniversary of the outbreak of the current war was observed today in Yokohama by the Indian President, including President (Cordona) of the Indian Independence League. Mr. (Mahtani) of the Indian Merchants Association of Yokohama, Professor (Kimlon), the Indian representative from Tokyo. The program started with saluting the Rising Sun flag and the Indian Independence Flag. *Tokyo, English, 12.8.42*

Deep concern is being shown by Indian residents in Japan over Gandhi's hunger strike. Indian residents in Yokohama held a 24 hours fast upon receipt of the news that he challanged Britain with a gallant gesture. Indians in Tokyo and Kobe are expected to observe similar fasts in manifestation of their all-out sympathy with Gandhi's move. Professor Nichi Kimurn of..... the University in Tokyo will broadcast to Indian leaders from Radio Tokyo tonight. *Tokyo, English 2.17.43*

P.V. Sadani, President of the Yokohama Branch of the Indian Independence League, and his party are hurrying to Shonan to join the Indian Independence Army under the command of Subhas Chandra Bose.

Tokyo, Japanese, 7.27.43

Japanese Cooperation

"Victory is ours"—The days of British tyranny over Indians have now passed, declared Rama Murti, Chairman of the Indian Independence League in Japan, in hailing the Imperial Headquarters' announcement of the destruction of the main force of the British 7th division on the Burma-India border..... Murti revealed that Netaji S.C. Bose several days ago cabled a message to the Indian residents here, saying "Victory is ours, since we are fighting in cooperation with the strong Japanese army." He also disclosed that the Indian residents of Tokyo on February 2 contributed a half million yen toward the Indian Independence Army war fund, while many young Indians, formerly residents of Tokyo, already have joined Bose's army. *Tokyo, English, 3.1.44*

Indian Nationals not Enemies. The Board of Information announced that hereafter Indians who will cooperate with Japan's prosecution of the war will after March 1, not be treated as enemy nationals in Japan and the Southern regions. *Tokyo, Japanese, 2.26.43*

Contributions

Burma: The Provisional Government of Azad Hind had disclosed the reciept of a contribution of 1,000 yen to India's Freedom War Chest, as well as a message of encourgement from Masanori Isoda, who represented 8,000 villagers of Otaki village. Saitamu Perfecture, Japan. In the message addressed to Netaji Subhas Chandra Bose, Isoda writes," You seized the great opportunity of the GEA war and, collaborating with the Imperial Japanese Army in smashing the wild ambitions of the Anglo-Americans to continue hegemony in East Asia, you now are striving to drive the

Anglo-Americans out of your country and the Indian Independence Army under your leadership now is fighting on the Indian mainland. It is now time for the 400,000,000 people to rise up and.... with the Indian Independence Army. We pray God that He will give you sufficient strength to fight out the war until you achieve independence, surrounting the many hardships that will come your way. We are sending you the sum of 1,000 yen, which is the contribution of 8,000 villagers of Otaki village, who will be pleased if You Excellency would use it for your conduct of the war."

Tokyo, English, 8.10.41

Leaders

Subhas Chandra Bose

Chandra Bose, the leader of the Indian Independence League who has been in Germany recently arrived in Tokyo and on June 14 conferred with Tojo. He also was present at the Diet........ The significance of his visit to Japan is great. Premier Tojo in every Diet address has related in regard to Indian Independence that the Empire has firm faith for support and will wipe out Britain and America from India. *Tokyo, Japanese, 5.18.43*

The recent visit to Japan of Chandra Bose is bringing forth numerous comments among the German people. "In his recent addressed, Premier Tojo has reiterated that Japan is prepared to give every assistance to India in order to extricate India from the yoke of England..... Mr. Bose has travelled at ease from India to Germany and then from Germany to Japan. This points out to the people of India that the Anglo-Saxons are not the rulers of the world any longer and this psychological effect is unfathomable.... It is clear as day that the independence movement of India will rapidly become stronger. There is no room for doubt that India will gain true freedom under the leadership of such a patriot as Bose." The editorial of a German foreign agency stated the above. *Tokyo, Japanese 6.19.43*

Chandra Bose will deliver a lecture entitled, "The People of my Motherland," under the auspices of the Imperial Rule Assistance Political Society and will ask for the understanding and cooperation of the political world of Japan in connection with the movement for the liberation of India.

Tokyo, Japanese, 5.19.43

Subhas Chandra Bose, before the newspaper men in Tokyo, declared, "I am standing before you in the heart of Nippon instead of sitting idle in a prison house in India, which is symbolic of the new movement that is now sweeping over my country.... Indian outside India should make every effort to help Indians inside India and fully cooperate with each other for the attainment of independence. What Indians inside India cannot do must be done by Indians outside India." *Tokyo, English, 6.19.43*

The Borliner (Machtausgabo) commented as follows : When the visit to Japan of Chandra Bose and the appointment of Wavell as Viceroy of India were announced, the Indian Independence movement was in progress now under very favourable conditions. Bose has arrived in Japan and together with several million Indian countrymen who have already been serving in the independence movement in the Greater East Asia Co-Prosperity Sphere will be able to carry on a more native independence movement." *Tokyo, Japanese 6.20.43*

Berlin : On Saturday a message of greeting was sent by Reich Foreign Minister Joachim von Ribbentrop to Subhas Chandra Bose who recently arrived in Tokyo. The message reads as follows: "I convey my cordial greetings on the occasion of your arrival is East Asia. I thank you for your parting telegram sent to the Fuhrer, wherein you stress your solidarity with Germany in fighting against a common enemy. We trust you will be successful in your future fight for the liberty of the Indian people." *Tokyo, English, 6.20.43*

A welcome meeting was held in Tokyo by Indian residents in Tokyo and Yokohama in honor of Mr. Subhas Chandra Bose (sic), leader of the Indian Independence League in East Asia. Mr. Bose has retruned to Tokyo from his tour of encouraging all the Indians in the Greater East Asia Co-Prosperty Sphere..... his arrival in Tokyo of Mr. Subhas Chandra Bose, another leader of the Independence movement. The meeting was held in a very cheerful atmosphere expressing desire for...... and also win their home country from Britain Shockles. *Tokyo, English, 6.22.43*

In order to ask for the understanding and cooperation of all circles in our political world, also as regards Indian Independence, Subhas Chandra Bose, the Indian Independence Leader who is now in Japan, visited Headquarters of the Imperial Rule Assistance Political Society on June 23... He stated "The disobedience movement of older Gandhi has achieved no satisfactory results substantially up to the present. Moreover, Gandhi's objective of compromising with Britain and of acquiring autonomy is not the way to bring about ture independence..... Complete independence for India can only be realized by carrying on strike by force of arms, taking advantage of the outbroke of war..... I firmly believe that Indian Independence will surely succeed through the cooperation and aid of the Japanese Government and people." *Tokyo, English, 6.23.43*

Upon arrival at Haneda airport, Subhas Chandra Bose was warmly welcomed by prominent Japanese officials, including Foreign Minister Mamoru Shigomitsu, GEA Affairs Minister Aoki, and President of the Board of Information Eiji Amau, as well as leading members of the Tokyo chapter of the Indian Independence League. Bose was accompanied by a part of ......, including A. M. Sahay, Minister without portfolio, and upon stopping from the plane they exchanged greetings with Japanese leaders. Among those who anxiously watched the planes landing were two Indian girl students now studying at the Seishin Girls' School here who were waiting to welcome their father, A. M. Sahay. *Tokyo, English, 11.31.43*

Netaji Subhas Chandra Bose made an official call on Premier Tojo this morning and took his departure after remaining in conversation for forty minutes with the Japanese Premier. *Saigon, English, 11.1.43*

At the Hibiya Park Auditorium, a great lecture meeting for Mr. Subhas Chandra Bose was held. He explained the history of India in a sympathetic manner and condemned with furious rage the atrocities and exploitation of the British Government against India. *Tokyo, Japanese, 11.15.43*

Tokyo: On the first anniversary of Bose's assumption of leadership of the Indian Independence Movement, members of the Tokyo chapter of the League assembled to observe Netaji Week. Silent Prayers for those who lost their lives fighting for freedom of India were said and work was reviewed. A resolution was adopted: "Indians express joy and gratification over progress to date, they pay homage to heroes of Azad Hind Fauj, they pray for repose of heroic martyrs, they express profound gratitude to Japan for aid, they renew and reaffirm loyalty and allegiance to Netaji."

Tokyo, English, 7.4.44

Rash Behari Bose

Rash Behari Bose, Supreme Advisor of the Indian Independence League, arrived in Tokyo yesterday. *Tokyo, Japanese, 9.21.43*

Forty representatives of the local Indian community, led by Rash Behari Bose, Supreme Advisor to the Provisional Government of Free India, met at the headquarters of the Japan Chapter of the Indian Independence League this afternoon to observe the 15th anniversary of the Declaration of Indian Independence from the British yoke by Mohandas Gandhi. *Tokyo, English, 1.26.44*

The Tokyo Branch of the Indian Independence League at this time decided to hold a great prayer meeting with Behari Bose, Supreme Advisor of the Free India Provisional Government, and a large number of others participating on February 21 in Tokyo in order to encourage the Free India National Army. *Tokyo, Japanese, 2.17.44*

The Japan Chapter of the Indian Independence League will broadcast special programs to the people of India between 12 : 15 and 12 : 45 every night, giving vital news and commentaries of Azad Hind's war effort. The first program tonight features an address by Rash Behari Bose, Supreme advisor to the Provisional Government of Azad Hind. Tokyo, 3.22.44

Tokyo: Rash Behari Bose, Supreme Advisor of the Indian Independence League, now in Japan, cabled message of folicications to Subhas Chandra Bose on anniversary of Netaji Week.

Tokyo, English, 7.5.44

Rash Behari Bose, who has been devoting himself to the anti- British independence movement from early days in Japan, welcoming Chandra Bose's arrival in Japan, beamed with joy and stated: "The Indian Independence Movement must be awaited..... All preparations are made and we can only await a strong prosecution. Thus the significance of having welcomed Chandra Bose is in need of no explanation. I am at complete ease and feel as though I had attained a million allies. The activities of the Indian Independence League will probably be opened with greater strength." *Tokyo, Japanese, 6.19.43*

Training for Leadeship

Thirty-five Indian youths who have been selected to be sent to Japan by the Provisional Government of Azad Hind Fauj from Shonan to receive an education in order that they may became future leaders of Free India, today made a round of courtesy calls on Government offices here, starting with a call at the War Ministry, where they were received by Maj. Gen. Kenryo Sato, Director of the Military Affairs Bureau. The Youths, whose ages range from 15 to 19, have already received 5 month' training in Nipponego and other preparatory courses in Shonan. After receiving final preparatory training at the New Asia Institute..... Gakuin here, they will enter the Military Academy, so that they may be thoroughly trained as worthy army officers and leaders of the Azad Hind Fauj in the historic battle for independence. *Tokyo, English, 4.13.44*

Indian National Army

Today the first batch of the Indian Independence League of Tokyo, consisting of Indian youths resident in Japan, is about to leave for Shonan to join the Indian Independence Army. Mr. D. W. Sardani (P. W. Sadani), of

Yokohama, who has lived in Japan for the last thirty years and has taken an active part in Indian Independence Movement along with Rash Behari Bose, is the man in Charge. *Tokyo, Hindustani, 7.18.43*

China Independence Movement

Hongkong: Five hundred representatives of the Indian population in Hongkong gathered at a temple on Sunday and held a mass prayer for the early realization of Indian Independence and liberation of Mahatma Gandhi and other arrested leaders. *Tokyo, English, 9.6.42*

Over 1,000 Indian Nationals in Canton, including prisoners, on Monday offered reverent prayers for Indian Independence bowing reverently in the direction of Mecca. Following this, many made speeches, shouting, "Down with Britain." *Tokyo, English, 10.12.42*

Nanking: A mass meeting to rally support for the Indian Independence Movement was held at the National Assembly Hall in Nanking on Monday. Mr. Wang-Ching-Wei, President of the National Government of China, issued a statement and speeches were delivered by Dr. Chu Min-Yi, Foreign Minister, Mr. Lin Powshong, Publicity Minister, Mr. Masayuki Yoshitomi, Spokesman of the Japanese Embasy in Nanking, and others. A declaration of sympathy was passed and a message of encouragement sent to Mahatam Gandhi and the people of India.

Tokyo, English, 3.1.43

Nanking: The establishment of the Indian Provisional Governnment is Shonan with the appointment of Mr. Subhas Chandra Bose as the President of the Indian Independence League was hailed by the National Governmemnt of China as the start of the long-cherished armed revolution of the Indian Independence Movement, to which the Nanking Government has extended active support during the past year. The National Government is resolved to extend all-out help in fostering the Indian Independence Movement and the close collaboration with the new Indian Government, toward the final goal of the liberation of the whole Asiatic race from the Anglo-American yoke. *Tokyo, English, 7.5.43*

Indian Independence League
Peking Branch

The President of the Indian Residents' Association here yesterday called on the Peking Office of the Japanese Embassy and expressed hearty felicitation on the brilliant achievements of the Japanese operations on the India-Burma border. In the course of the interview, the Indian leader expressed the firm conviction Indian is certain to acquire her long-cherished national independence and freedom from British oppression with Japan's support. He sought Japan's continued assistance in the cause of Indian Independence, stating the Indians in North China are determined to follow those who have already joined the Indian Independence Army and are fighting in Burma on the Indian border. *Tokyo, English, 2.14.44*

Shanghai Branch

Shanghai: Various Indian organizations here will go into one body, following a conference Saturday. The new central body included Independence Movement, National Society and others. Officials were named and the organization started immediately. Five hundred Indians gathered at the Raco Track discuss the death of Gandhi's secretory..... gave stirring addresses falling Indians to fight. *Tokyo, English, 8.25.42*

Inuraugral ceremonies of the Indian Independence League will be held this afternoon at the Race Track and the entire Indian community..... will be attended by high ranking Japanese, Chinese and Axis officials and other sympathizers with India's cause. The organizing committee of the League has asked the Indian employers to grant their emplyees leave to enable than to be present. *Shanghai, English, 31.3.42*

Acting in concert with the Bangkok Indian Independence Federation, preparation were being made among the 2,000 Indians living in Shanghai for the establishment of a Shanghai Branch of the Indian Independence Federation. As inaugural meeting consolidating six organizations was held at the Race Course and attended by over 1,000 people representing the factions and all Indians living here and will maintain close relations with the headquarters at Bangkok, China and Indians overseas. It will enter upon positive activities been attention. (Kotochin) has been made President. *Tokyo, Japanese, 11.4.42*

All minor differences have been ironed out and all Indian communities in Shanghai have been consolidated into one association.

Seigon, English, 11.4.42

With Gen. (Iwane Matsui), Vice President of the East Asiatic League, as the guest of honor, the Shanghai East Asia Society held a round table conference at the Opera House in Shanghai. To the conference were invited representatives from the Shanghai Chapter of the Indian Independence League and the Phillipines Assocation as well as Afghanistan. Gen. (Matsui) stressed the importance of establishing an Asia for the Asiatic through the close cooperation of various East Asiatic peoples. He also explained about Japan's justified stand as well as her true intentions. Mr. (Jarlemaru), Managing Director of the Shanghai Chapter of the Indian Independence League, said, "If we miss this Heavon-sent opportunity, the Indian people may lose forever the chance of becoming independent. We are firmly determined to achieve the long-cherished ideal of the Indian Independence with the support of Japan." *Tokyo, English, 11.26.42*

Taiping Branch

A huge increase was seen in the membership of the Taiping Branch of the Indian Independence League since the beginning of this year as streams of Indian men and women have been flocking to the promises of the League, membership has increased by nearly 100% compared with last year's figures. *Tokyo, English, 3.3.41*

Hankow Branch

Celebrating the entry of Japanese and Indian Independence Army Forecast into Manipur, as well as marking the inauguration of the Hankow Branch of the Indian Independence League, a mass rally was held here March 25 at the Asia Development ground, with 1,000 local Indian participating. The function which was held under the auspicious of the Indian Residents' Association in Hankow was also attended by representatives of the Axis countries, Japan, Germany, China and Italy. *Tokyo, English, 3.28.44*

Hongkong Branch

On the 72nd birthday of Mahatma Gandhi, a rally held by the Hongkong Branch of the Indian Independence League, at which absolute obedience to the Gandhi was sworn to gain the complete independence of India. *Tokyo, English, 10.2.42*

More than a hundred members of the Hongkong Branch of the Indian Independence League at their office to hear the sensational speech of Mr. Subhas Chandra Bose which was broadcast Monday night. *Tokyo, English, 6.23.43*

Welcoming the return from Shonan of Dr. Dejo Naidu, Chief of the Hongkong Branch of the Indian Independence League, more than 2,000 members of the branch held a mass meeting Monday and reaffirmed their determination to fight to the bitter end for Indian liberty. Dr. Naidu declared that the Indian Independence Army is rapidly preparing itself for a battle against Britain. The independence movement is progressing swiftly in Shonan according to plan. *Tokyo, English, 8.11.43*

On his retun from Shonan where he attended the Indian Independence League conference, Dr. (Nai Ding), Chairman of the Hongkong Branch, declared that the activities of the league and the national army are progressing rapidly. *Tokyo, English, 9.13.43*

All Indian shops and firms in Hongkong and Kowlon were closed today in observance of the Baisakhi Festival and they will be closed tomorrow for the mass meeting in connection with National liberation Week and the Jhallinwala massacre. All Indian were expected to make it a special point to attend and participate in this historic meeting. Meanwhile, the Independence League gave out the report in the local paper that it would be thankful to all employers for granting permission to their Indian employees for leave of absence on this day.

Hongkong, English, 4.12.44

The Indians of Hongkong celebrated the Provisional Government's (birth) yesterday by holding a mass meeting..... speeches were made by leading members of the Indian Independence League. A minute's silence in honor of those who have sacrificed their lives in the cause of freedom was observed. *Hongkong, English, 4.22.44*

A mass meeting was held at the Hall of the Indian Independence League by Indians in Hongkong in celebration of the fourth Provisional Government Day and for offering prayers for Mahatma Gandhi's quick recovery from illness. The meeting was enlivened by the singing of national songs by a trio from the Indian Youth Corps, followed by a speech by Dr. Naidu, Chairman of the meeting , who declared: "This day four months ago amid cheors of universal hope and rejoicing was celebrated by Indians throughout Greater East Asia with unfurling of the tri-colored banner of the Indian nation on the doorstop of every Indian home. On this day it was proclaimed to the world that the political ideals of the people without single exception are one and one only and as regards these ideals being brought to a realization in a tangible and substantial form, no Indian, will remain tongue-tied. On this day our entire nation took a firm resolve that as long as independence is not achieved, none will rest content but will go on fighting untill Delhi is reached." *Hongkong, English, 5.22.44*

*A mass meeting of all Indians in Hongkong will be held under the auspices of the Indian Independence League at the Keenster Theatre next week to celebrate the commencement of the fight by the Indian National Army and the first victory achieved on the Arakan front in cooperation with the Japanese air arm. Meanwhile,...... will be paid to their leader, Subhas Chandra Bose, and the gallant fighting men on the front lines.

Hongkong, English, 2.20.44

Four thousand Indian residents attended a mass rally here this morning under the auspices of the Hongkong Chapter of the Indian Independence League to pray for victory for the Indian Independence Army which is now participating in Japanese operations in the Arakan factor on the Burma-India border. *Tokyo, English, 2.21.44*

The Indians of Hongkong held a mass meeting commemorating the martyrdom of the great Indian patriot, Bhagat Singh. After the singing of the national song by Jamedar Jagat Singh, a minute of silence followed.

Hongkong, English, 3.24.44

The Hongkong Indian Independence League held a meeting recently when the league was completely reorganized and Mr. (T. V.) Krishna elected the new Chairman. He declared: "We are now entering a very critical stage in the fight for independence and with the reorganization of the league the fight for freedom will be taken up with increased vigor. The present body elected is not going to sit quietly and talk. They are here to do somethings. The new chairman revealed that July 4 to 10 will be observed as Netaji Week, as it was on July 4 last year that Subhas Chandra Bose took charge of the Indian Independence Movement in Singapore. A special meeting will be held on the first day of the celebration when the new policies and aims of the league will be clearly stated for the benefit of the Indian Community and the meeting will be followed by a mass procession through the main city the meeting will be followed by a mass procession through the main city streets." *Hongkong, English, 7.3.44*

The Hongkong Indian Independence League is going to celebrate Netaji Week. Today, the first day, they held a mass meeting in the facade of the Japanese Club House, for all Indians in Hongkong to remember their Independence for the nation of India. They announced of their aim of their independence. Afterwards, there was a mass procession. All the Indians of the different organizations of Hongkong and those in Kowloon have joined this meeting. They again announce that they will ally themselves together politically to drive the British out of India. On July 9, the Japanese new pictures and Indian show will; be exhibited in the..... Theatre is Kowloon. *Hongkong, Cantonese 7.4.44*

Indian leaders in Hongkong recently held a meeting at the Indian Independence League Hall where impressive lectures and political addresses were delivered and a committee and it was decided to held weekly and fortnightly meetings in.... where he would deliver lectures on various subjects for the general education of Indian women. The committee will invite all Indian ladies regardless of caste or creed to attend the meetings regularly and fit themselves to take their places as leaders in the work of Greater East Asia. *Hongkong, English, 8.19.44*

Canton Branch

Members of the Canton Branch of the Indian Independence League on June 20 met at headquarters in (Shanghang) and adopted a resolution pledging wholehearted support to Subhas Chandra Bose, prominent Indian Independence Leader who recently arrived in Japan from Germany.

Tokyo, English, 6.22.43

Canton: A celebration of the creation of the Provisional Government of Azad Hind was held here this afternoon under the Canton Branch of the Indian Independence League. A street parade along the main streets of the city and a meeting in the public hall were the highlights of today's functions. *Tokyo, English, 10.25.43*

Hand in hand with the Japanese, all Indians are shouldering the sacred mission of overthrowing Britain, declared Dr. Nader Khan, chairman of the Canton Chapter of the Indian Independence League at a meeting highlighted by the report announcing the commencement of offensive oprations by Japanese forces in concert with the Indian Independence Army at the Indo-Burma border. Dr. Khan said, "You can't imagine how long we have been waiting for this day." He said that Indian residents last night gathered together to discuss until dawn the future of independence. He pointed out that many who gladly joined the Indian Independence Army are no doubt marching bravely on toward their mother country to the tune of roaring guns. He said,"We will continue the march until victory is won. Only glorious victory awaits us." *Tokyo, English, 2.8.44*

The Canton Chapter of the Indian Independence League held a rally here this afternoon to celebrate the participation of the Indian Independence Army in the current Japanese operations on the Burma-Indian border.

Tokyo, English, 2.21.44

The Canton Branch of the Indian Federation recently held a large.... meeting in conjuction with the great movement of Indian Independence. Besides expanding the structure of the Cultural Department, they elected now officers to fill the new posts. *Honkong Cantonese, 6.6.44*

........, Chairman of the Canton Branch of the Indian Independence League, recently came to Hongkong to strengthen the relation of the

Hongkong and Canton Branch offices... He said that the Government of Can.on is also very cooperative with the Canton Branch.

Contributions

Shanghai (Domei): It is already one year since the formation of the Free India Provisional Government and the 2,000 Indians residing in Shanghai held a commemorative rally and contributed 6,000 yen to the Indian Independence League. *Tokyo, Japanese, 6.22.44*

Indian National Army

The Canton Branch of the Indian Independence League on July 4 sent a large number of the volunteers to Shonan for the Indian Independence Army. The office of the league here is daily receiving numorous application from local Indian Youths who are impatiently waiting for the day when they will be able to take up arms for the cause of their independence. *Tokyo, English, 7.10.43*

The Hongkong Branch of the Indian Independence League decided to begin recruitment of volunteers for the Indian Independence Army. The registration of men between eighteen and thirty-five commenced on September and immediately applicants poured in.

Tokyo, Japanese, 9.16.43

In order further to bolster this movement and realize the independence even a day earlier, President Bose dispathced Lt. Col. (Nega Nadan) to the China area as representative. He arrived at Canton, Communicated his mission and examined volunteers at the Overseas Residence. *Tokyo, Japanese, 9.2.43*

Shanghai: All Indians, regardless of caste or creed, are enrolling for service with the Indian Independence Army in order to fight for......, says President (Chet Soon), of the Shanghai chapter of the Indian Independence League, who recently returned from Shonan after attending Burma's .... celebration for the formation of the Indian Independence Army.

Tokyo, English. 7.26.43

A batch of more than 400 Indians, consisting of Hindus and Muslims, is about to leave for Shonan to join the Indian Independence Army. Even the women have volunteered to serve the national cause as nurses.

Tokyo, Hindustani, 7.28.43

Indian volunteers, who are trained in Hongkong to....... among the first groups called into the Indian Independence Army by Subhas Chandra Bose, leave Hongkong as soon as they have acquired a..... knowledge of the arts of war to go it Shonan where they put themselves directly under

Bose's command, then to be sent to the front lines to fight against the allied forces, according to a Damoi dispatch from Hongkong. Because of this situation, the Branch of the Indian Independence Movement in Hongkong has decided to open a fully equipped training center for Indian volunteers on December 18 in Kowloon new Honkong.

Tokyo, German, 12.17.43

Hongkong: Observance of Indian Liberation Week here was brought to a successful close yesterday with a huge rally held by local Indian residents who pledged to offer everything for the liberation of their motherland. In line with various other parts of East Asia, local Indians observed liberation Week which started April 6 with colorful programs. Following the rally yesterday, memberes of the Indian Independence Army who are presently training here paraded the streets of the city amidst the loud cheering of a crowd wildly waving the Indian colors.

Tokyo, English, 4.14.44

Shanghai: The local Azad Hind Fauj Training Camp was officially opened in a colorful ceremony held yesterday before members of the Indian Community and prominent Japanese, Chinese and German guests,. In the opening initiation program, Captain Boo Narain, Commandant of the camp, expressed his gratitude for the facilities granted for drilling purposes and informed the guests drills which would follow would be conducted by Reservists. These recruits gave a very impressive exhibition of marching and the executive of various military orders before the guests. Nanak Chand whose position as Chairman of the local Chapter of the Indian Independence League was approved by the Provisional Government President, gave a tea party after the opening ceremony. In his speech he pointed out inauguration of the camp is a fitting manifestation of the patriotism of the local Indian community and it was the first time in the history of Shanghai that such a schools has existed, as previouslsy it was not possible due to measures taken by the British to prevernt such a movement. Doctor Herest Ley, Director of the Ostatischer Lloyd, German Language School, also addressed the meeting stating that it was not only fighting for its right but also to aid in the liberation of India. He wished every success to the training school. *Tokyo, English, 6.20.44*

The Shanghai Institute for training Indian Independence Army volunteers opened this afternoon with ceremonies attended by Mayor Chen Kung-Po, of Shanghai, Uzuhiko Usami, Japanese Minister, diplomatic envoys of Axis countrious and others. It is learned that the Institute has an enrollment of 600 volunteers, selected from many applicants.

Tokyo, English 7.9.44

The Shanghai Institute for training local Indian volunteers had the assistance and support of the local Japanese and Chinese authorities who make its establishment possible. Six hundred Indian volunteers will be accepted for a three months's training course.

Tokyo, English, 7.9.44

Shanghai: More than 3,000 Indian residents will hold a rally celebrating the capture of Imphal with address by B. Bobby Chiod Fot El. liaison officer of the Shanghai Branch of Indian Independence League.

Tokyo English, 4.12.44

Azad Hind Dal

An extraordinary meeting of members of the Advisory Board of the Indian Independence League and representatives of all Indian association and socities will be held tomorrow at the League Hall in (China House) for the purpose of forming a (fighting corps) and organizing the Azad Hind (Jatha), the Indian Independence League announced.

Hongkong, English, 5.31.44

The Hongkong Branch of the Indian Independence League announced yesterday: By order of our Netaji, a new organization is being set up under the name of Azad Hind Dal, consisting of those who were not members of the Azad Hind Fauj. Indian Independence Army, It will participate in the fight for India's independence and will work in close cooperation with the Azad Hind Fauj during and after the campaign. The Azad Hind Dal will consist of those who will work in a civilian and semi-military capacity. Enrollment of applicants will begin at the League branches on June 19. The Indian public, except those who are already in the Azad Hind Fauj, are requested to enroll. *Hongkong, English 6.16.43*

A large number of Indians have already enrolled in the Azad Hind Dall, a new organization set up by order of Netaji Subhas Chandra Bose.... In Hongkong, the Azad Hind Dal is being created for the purpose of protecting the interests and property of Indian nationals in (time of emergency). *Hongkong, English 6.21.44*

Leaders

Subhas Chandra Bose

Nanking Damoi: Subhas Chandra Bose, President of the Free India Provisional Government, who is at present visiting China, called on Premier Wang, Commander-in-Chief Hata, and Ambassador Tani. He also called at the Government Embassy and the Manchukuo Embassy to pay his respects. Mr. Bose expressed his joy upon his first visit to China and stated that in order to liberate East Asia, first there must be unity of China and second, independence of India. Without these the liberation of East Asia cannot be completed. Thus he urged Chungking for profound reflection. *Tokyo, Japanese 12.18.43*

Nanking: Subhas Chandra Bose, head of the Provisional Government of Free India. In this morning received the return visits of Dr. Ernst Wormann, German Ambassador to Nanking. A citizens welcome meeting held in his honor at the National Public Hall, after which he was guest of honor at a luncheon given by Masayuki Tani, Japanese Ambassador to China, Bose conferred with Wang Ching Wei at his official residence and with Dr. Woernann. This evening Bose will be guest of honor at a dinner party tendered by Gen. Shunroku Hata, Commandor-in-Chief of the Japanese Forces in China. *Tokyo, English, 11.19.43*

Nanking Domei : The leader of the Free India Provisional Government, Subhas Chandra Bose, while sojourning in Nanking thrice conferred with Premier Wang and also with leaders of the National Government. The significance of his visit to China is great. The conference between Leader Bose and Premier Wang mutually reaffirmed the enthusiastic assistance of the National Government towards the Indian Independence Movement and the sincere desires of the Free India Provisional Government relative to the unity of China in accordance with the fundamental rule of equality and friendship, which is the ideology of the establishment of the Greater East Asia. Thus the fundamental relationship of the two nations has been established.

Tokyo, Japanese, 11.21.43

Shanghai: The 47th birthday of S. C. Bose. was observed yesterday by the entire local Indian community. *Tokyo, English, 1.24.44*

Indian Independence League
Mukden Branch

A branch of the Indian Independence League, whose headquarters are located at Bangkok, was opened here Sunday morning before the Mukden Shrine. The branch will be open to all Indian residents in Manchukuo proper and the Kwantung Loased Territoryand will work for the emancipation of the East Asia from the Anglo-American imperialism.

Tokyo, English 9.13.42

Mukden: Responding to the enthusiastic Indian Independence Movement under the leadership of Subhas Chandra Bose, the Mukden

Chapter of the Indian Independence League has decided to form an all-Maunchukuo India Youth Corps. These youths will be trained militarily and spiritually so as to be qualified to join the Indian Independence Army is case of emergency. *Tokyo, English, 7.23.43*

Mukden: Denouncing the tyrannical rule of the British in India, which is responsible for the starvation of thousands of his follow Indians, Nichaelman Boolchand, President of the Mukden Chapter of the Indian Independence League, in an interview today declared: "Indians is East Asia have not...... time arrived to bear arms in a fight for the righteous cause and free our countrymen who are suffering torture unheard of in this history of the world at the hands of vicious Britishers."

Tokyo, English, 10.5.43

Mukden: News of the establishment of the Provisional Government of Free india was received with jubilation by members of the local chapter of the Indian Independence League, whose members unanimously reiterated their determinaiton to forge ahead to attain the goal of Indian Independence under the able leadership of Subhas Chandra Bose. In an interview, Nachaldas Boolchand, President of the local league chapter, expressed the belief that the cherished desire of the Indians to gain independence is not far distant. He added that it will not be long before the Indian Independence Army under the banner cry of "On to Delhi" crosses the Indian frontier to sweep the British from Indina soil.

Tokyo, English, 10.23.44

Heinking: Chollarom Arlwani, Secreatory of the Manchukuo Chapter of the Indian Independence League in a radio address directed to follow Indians in Hindustani, today drew a vivid contrast in conditions between Manchukuo and India and urged determined continuance of the Indians' fight for freedom and independence. Alwani outlined the fast progress made by Manchukuo from conditions of benditry and chaos to modern... and declared this had been made possible by establishment of the state on lofty ideals of racial concori and amity. He declared that Manchukuo owed much of her present prosperity to Japanese united moreal and matorial support based on Japan's principles of enabling all nations and peoples to enjoy their rightful place under the sun. He concluded this is in direct contrast to the "Fency promises" given by Anglo-Americans to the Indian people, and urged Indians to rise with greater determination in their fight against the hated enemy of Asia and humankind.

Tokyo, English 6.17.43

Burma Independence Movement

Two millions Indians residing in Burma hastened to hold a big rally to renew their determination to fight with the leader until liberation of the fatherland is achieved and also to find means in order that Mr. Gandhi may not die as a consequence of his ıast. *Tokyo, Spanish, 2/21/42*

Rangoon: "Establishment of new Burma means an establishment of a read for the transfusion of blood into India" this idea in mind, the Indians in Burma had been striving for an organization of Burma Estanblishment Service Corps. However, recently the organization of the corps has started, so that many comrades gathered in Rangoon and held a ceremony for the corps organization in an elaborate manner on July 26. noon.

Tokyo, Japanese 7/26/43

Rangoon: Indian residents in Burma, on Monday organized an Indian Services Corps in Rangoon with the object of helping to construct the new Burma as a vital blood transfusion route for Indian Independence. The head of the corps, (Sadi Lee) said that Indian in Burma will do all in their power for the construction of the new Burma (on the side) of the Indians. *Tokyo, English 7/26/44*

Indian Independence League

Rangoon: Independence League branch of Burma passed a resolution to support Gandhi's demands and fight until British rule is driven out of India will support Bose proposal. *Tokyo, Japanese, 8/11/42*

Rangoon: Echoing the...... of ...... Independence Movement, approximately 50 representatives of the Burma branch of the Indian Independence gathered at the city auditorium in Rangoon for five day conference on September 17. The conference is expected to map out a systematic plan for the Indian Independence Drive to be carried on....

Tokyo, English, 9/15/42

In order to rally Indian Nationals in Burma for the independence of their mother country, a meeting was held in Rangoon on Thursday by the Burma Chapter of the Indian Independence League. The gathering was attended by Dr. Bahmo, Chief executive of the Burmese Government, as well as by high Burmese officials, Speeches were delivered for the immediate liberation of India and overthrow of the British empire.

Tokyo, English, 9/18/42

Dr. U Ba Moung said that the people of Burma are fully aware now of this war,, why and the aim,... The leader of the Indian Independence League in Burma said that all their doubt in Japan's aim is gone. They believe the intentions of Japan and hope to be independent some day......

Tokyo, Malayan, 2/24/43

The Burma Committee of the Indian Independence League make a radio address on the night of February 23, directed to Burma and India, demanding a great stirring up of spirit on the part of all Indian people with respect to Gandhi's wishes. *Tokyo, Japanese, 2/24/43*

Rangoon: Upon the occaion of the.......Independence Preparatory Committee for Burmese Independence, the spokesman of the Rangoon branch of the Indian Independence League issued a statement in which he declared all Indians residing in Burma will extend their assistance in the rebirth of new Burma. *Tokyo, English, 5/9/43*

Rangoon: The establishment of the Free Indian Provisonary Government has decided the course of the Indian Independence Movement, declared the chief of the Rangoon Branch of the Indian Independence League, after listening to the radio speech of Mr. Subahs Chandra Bose..... Chief of the Rangoon Branch stated, "Now is the time for the Indian people to rise in arms, for (there) is the task of (storming) into India. The Indian residents in Burma should immediately launch the war of bloodhsed regardless of their (rank)" *Tokyo, English, 7/5/43*

Indian Independence League

Rangoon: In a message congatulating Burma on its independence (Mr. Payan Gamee), Chairman of the Burmese Chapter of the Indian Independence League, stated that Burma has had the glory of being an independent country (thru) the sincere support of Japan. The glory of Burma will...... accelerate the independence movement in India. The Indians have renewed their determination to fight it thru until India can enjoy the day of complete freedom. *Tokyo, English, 8/3/43*

Rangoon: Mr.(Harimal) Canis, President of the Burma Territorial Committee of the Indian Independence League, on Saturday expressed his gratitude in behalf of the Indians is Burma over the Burmese Government's declaration that the Indian-British subjects ir. Burma will be accorded treatment of a friendly third power and will be permitted in future to become maturalized Burmese citizens. He said that the present declaration is clearly a great help to the Indian Independence Movement.

Tokyo, English, 8/21/43

Rangoon: A rally, celebrating the independence of Burma, was held on Sunday under the auspicious of the Indian Independence League.

Mr. Karim Chani, chairman of the Burma Branch of the Indian Independence League, said that the new people of Asia have been encouraged by the independence of Burma. *Tokyo, English, 9/13/43*

Rangoon: On the 2nd day of Burma's Independence Festival, Sunday, prayer was offered by the Indian Independence League for the liberation of the India. Teh prayer was offered at the graveyard of King Bahadur Shah, who died a Rangoon after years of active service as the leader of the anti-British movement. *Tokyo, English, 9/27/43*

Rangoon: ..... Representatives of the Indian Independence League branches throughout Burma met this morning int the initial session of a three day conference to formualte and put into immediate action measures for the total mobilization of resources of the Indians in Burma for the successful conclusion of the struggle for Indian freedom, which neared a decisive stage with the Indian Independence Army waging war on the enemy on Indian soil. Netaji Bose said, "of course the government and people of Nippon have been giving and are ready to give all-out (wd) against the Anglo-American Armies in India, but until we mobilize ourselves to the last man to the rupee, to the last grain of food for our own army, we have no moral right to expect more aid from Nippon. The Netaji urged the assembly to apply itself to the sacred task of strengthening..... night and day to translate the decisions of the conference into action."

Tokyo, English, 4/8/44

Rangoon: A Council Meeting of the representatives of the Burmese Branch of the Indian Independence League, which had been in progress since April 8 at an undisclosed place in Burma, came to an end on April 11....... Regarding among the various representatives of the branches of the Indian Provisional Government in connection with the mobilized and vigorous movement of the Indian people will be commenced.

Tokyo, Japanese, 4/13/44

Women Members

Rangoon: Indian mothers are active in the Independence Movement under the slogan of "Indian Mothers for Independence," several hundred Indian women gathered Monday afternoon in (Ilances) sponsored by the Burma branch of the Indian Independence League. Manifesting full sympathy with Mahatma Gandhi, the Indian Mothers passed a resolution pledging all-out efforts in the drive, "India for the Indians."

Tokyo, English, 8/17/42

A group of 70 Indian women of all ages, representing provincial districts in Burma, held a demonstrations meeting Tuesday in support of the Indian Independence Movement. The rally was the first to be sponsored independently by the Indian women since the recent organization of the Burma branch of the Indian Independence League urged the complete collaboration of the Indian women in the present struggle to free India from British domination and achieve freedom for India. The group promises to be the nucleus of and achieve freedom for Indina. The group promises to be the nucleus of auxillary women's organizations within the Independence League of Burma. *Tokyo, English, 10/8/42*

In Burma, on the occasion of greeting the birthday of Queen (name)[2] an inauguration ceremony for Women's Corps aiming at the destruction of Britain was held on October 20 at Rangoon. AT 6:30 p.m. Lt. Col. (name) who was dispatched from the Indian Independence League Headquarters at Shonan, was met by the Women's Corps and arrived at the location of the ceremony, Lt. Col. (name) spoke before his audience on the admirable achievements of Queen (name) who in 1858 mobilized an army to fight desperately against a powerful army of 600,000 British forces in an attempt to protect her country. The Lt. Col encouraged the members of the Women's corps to bravely and enthusiastically follow in the footsteps of the Queen. *Tokyo, Japanese, 10/22/43*

Youth's Training Movement

The Rangoon branch of the Indian Independence League, in order to cultivate the combative spirit in independence movements in their homeland, recently established a Youths' and Boys' Training Institute. One hundred Indian youths ranging from 17 or 18 to about 25 on a schedule of approximately one month, will be givern spiritual training and when dispathced to various regions, will promote the Indian Independence Movement throughout Burma. Every region will have branch offices established and, rallying round the rising strength of youths there is keen interests to complete the independence. *Tokyo, Japanese, 9/19/42*

Japanese Cooperations

Berlin: The Indian National residing in Burma (will evacuate) to their mother country in accordance with an agreement reached among the Governments of Britain, Burma and India, according to a broadcast from Delhi, India intercepted by the D.N.B. news agency. However, it is not known (the approximate) under of Indian Nationals they will actually evacuate. *Tokyo, English, 1/24/42*

2. Rani of Jhansi

Rangoon: All Indian residents in Burma expressed profound joy at the sympathy expressed by Prime Minister Tojo in his adminstrative speech made before the Imperial Diet on Wednesday afternoon. In which reference was made to the Indian people 's painstaking efforts towards attainment of independence. *Tokyo, English, 6/17/43*

Free Indian Provisional Government...... has now moved into Burma ... Premier Tojo declared that Japan is ready to give Andaman and Nicobar to Free India. Andaman is important location for India's patriots for many of them were imprisoned here and died. This is now selected as stronghold for India Independence. *Tokyo, English, 6/17/43*

Free India Provisional Government.... has now moved into Burma.... Premier Tojo declared that Japan is ready to give Andaman and Nicobar to Free India. Andaman is important location for India's patriots for many of them were imprisoned here and died. This is now selected as stronghold for India Independence Movement. Nicobar will be renamed as "Swaragi".

Tokyo, Japanese 1/20/44

In a statement to Domei on Premier Tojo's statement of Nippon's determination to spare no efforts in extending all possible assistance for India's liberation and that all the territories of India into which the Indians National Army will advance will immediately be placed under the administration of the Provisional Government of Free India. The Netaji said, "My governement and army and Indians in general are profoundly grateful for the statement which His Excellency General Tojo issued to the world....." *Tokyo, English, 3/24/44*

Burmese Cooperation

Rangoon: It was decided in the cabinet meeting, held the day before yesterday, not to treat Indians who cooperate in the establishment of GEA as enemy nationals; however, in Burma this principle had already been in application since the beginning of military administration enforcement. and the Indians residing in Burma are expressing their deep gratitude for our measures..... However, as actually the majority of Indians cooperated with our forces, the policy of the army was not to regard the assets of these Indians as enemy assets..... It was decided to have the Burma Indian Residents Association control absolutely all the assets of owners who do not reside in Burma and have our army supervises and lend guidance.

Tokyo, Japanese, 2/27/43

The Burmese Governement declared on August 21 that the Indians who are British subjects would not be considered enemy nationals but would be treated as friendly people. With Burma as the foothold, the people of Rangoon welcome this news, that hereafter the Indian Independence Movement will progress briskly. Among them, chairman of the committee in Burma area of the Indian Independence League, (Karim) Gani, stated in resume as follows: "State Representative of Burma, Ba Maw, previously stated that the Burmese Government and its people would not begrudge any aid to the Indian Independence Movement, and the recent declaration is clearly one of the constructive moves."

Tokyo, Japanese, 8/22/43

Rangoon: Extending wholehearted Burmese hospitality, Deputy Prime Minister Thakin Mya, speaking at the civic reception accorded the Provisional Indian Government, in unmistakable terms, linked the destiny of Burma and India, declaring, "The Indian Peoples' War is the Burmese Peoples' War for independence." *Tokyo, English, 1/23/44*

Rangoon: Major General Aung San, Burmese War Minister, welcoming Netaji S. C. Bose and members of the Provisional Government of Azad Hind, declared that India "must fight for her own freedom" but will have the active sympathy and support of the whole of East Asia led by Nippon. The War Minister called on all Indians in an outside India to march forward to their own independence. The War Minister warned the attendants at the rally, we must not take things easy, we must not think that we can achieve easy victory..... Our enemies are still unconquered and they remain entrenched on the other side of us, toying with the idea of a counter offensive against us every now and then.

Tokyo, English, 1/23/44

March 25: In conformity with the statement issued by Adipadi Ba Maw, wherein he declared Burma and India must join together at this juncture for the overthrow of their common enemy, Gotaro Ogawa, Supreme Adviser to the Burmese Government, asserted "The Burmese Government is extending its utmost assistance to the Provisional Government of Free India in their fight to regain their full sovereign rights," Ogawa, who returned to Tokyo to confer with governmental authorities, at today's press interview recalled that the Burmese and the Indians in the past were bitter enemies due to Britain's crafty policy of divide and rule. He asserted that through the efforts exerted by the Adipadi, a friendly feeling is now prevailing between the two nations. Praising the fighting spirit of S.C. Bose, head of the Provisional Government of Free India. Ogawa called him "the greatest hero India ever produced". He recalled Ba Maw's statement wherein he asserted that if Netaji Bose has not been leader of the Indian

Provisional Government, cooperating between Burma and India might not have been effected so soon. Recalling the careers of the two leaders, Ogawa said both of them were natives of countries subjected to British oppression, both studied law in England, and both were imprisoned due to their anti-British agitation. He added further, both are men of action based on zeal and will-power. *Tokyo, English, 3/24/44*

Free India Provisional Government

Rangoon: It is announced that Lt. Col. Alagappan (will be) Administrator of the Advance Headquarters of the Provisional Goverment of Free India and in supreme commnad in Rangoon.

Tokyo, Japanese, 11/8/43

Information has recently been received from Burma that all arrangements for the transfer of the Provisional Government of Free India Headquarters to Burma have been completed. The Indian Independence Army which is already on the move, is itching for action and is only waiting for the zero hour from their commander, Netaji Bose. Then will begin the battle which will only end in the victory of the Azad-Hind Fauj the Free Indian Army...... powerful backed by the invincible Japanese and Burmese forces. The initiative in India's struggle against Britain has certainly passed into the hands of Netaji Bose. *Shonan, Hindustani, 11/21/43*

S.C. Bose head of the Provisional Government of Free India, from a broadcasting station in Burma, on January 8 announced that the Headquarters of the Provisional Government of Azad Hind have been shifted from Shonan to Burma and he revised the preparatory measure of the government. The Indian leader, who arrived in Burma this noon, disclosed that en route to Burma he stopped off at Andaman and there discussed preparatory measures with the Nippon authorities for transfer of the islands to the Provisional Government. He said, likewise, he discussed his appointement of Lt. Col. Loganadan of the Indian Independence Army as Chief Commissioner of Andaman and Nicobar Islands.

Tokyo, English, 1/8/44

Takashi Kaide, Manager of the overseas Bureau of the Momoi News Agency, said: The Free India Provisional Government has advanced. Geographically the Provisional Government is now nearer to its motherland, India. It was just 10 years ago, from the present up to the year 1934, Burma was placed under the British Government as part of India. It is an unforgettable, a so called state or member of the motherland, feeling for the Indians. The Supreme Adviser to the Free India Provisional Government,

Behari Bose..... states as follows: "India and Burma are lands which cannot be severed or divided. The advance into Burma of the Free Indian Provisional Government is the same as an advance into its own motherland. The Indians within the homeland of India can join with us (when we advance a little further). The raid on (name), the heart of India....... is like preparing its position for the enemy's sudden death." This is the comment. I believe that these words vividly clarify the feeling of the Indians top wards the land of Burma. For the Indians, Burma and India homeland is a land where there is no division. They have finally arrived on this land. Consequently, it is not merely that they have come one step nearer the India homeland. It is more correct to state that the Free India Provisional Government has advanced to the very front line in the battle in which they will liberate their homeland from the British.

Tokyo, Japanese. 1/12/44

S. C. Bose, Head of the Provisional Government of Free India, announced the appointment today of Shri Nambiar, Chairman of the Indian Independence League Committee in Europe, as Minister without portfolio. Shri Nambiar succeeds Lt. Col. A. D. Loganadan who was appointed Chairman of the Preparatory Committee to take over the Andaman and Nicobar Islands. The announcement said the newly appointed minister will remian in Europe while serving in the new official capacity. It is recalled that while head of state Bose was in exile in Germany, Minister Nambiar, as his right hand man, exerted all-out efforts toward uniting the Indians in the fitht against British oppression. After Bose left Germany for East Asia, Nambiar assumed, in his stead, leadership in the work of the Indian Independence Committee, in the establishment of which he participated actively. *Tokyo, English, 1/14/44*

Bose announced that the Chairman of the Indian Independence League in Europe would be Nambiar. *Tokyo, Japanese, 1/14/44*

The Provisonal Government of Free India has issued a communique standardizing the language to be used among Indians, the form of salutation, and the kind of colours to be adopted as the national emblem, and other matters......" The Council of Ministers decided that Hindustani shall be the common greeting and salutation between Indians. The present tricolor shall be the national flag of India; the song beginning with the words'Such Sukh Chain' shall be India's national song; the tiger will be India's national emblem; 'Chalo Delhi' will be the national war cry till successful conclusion of the revolution; Azad Hind Zindabad, Inquilab Zindabad, Netaji Kijai will be the national slogan till the victorious conclusion of the revolution. The plan for natonal unification in the matter of food, dress, etc., is subject to consideration by the Provisional Government of Azad Hind and its decisions will be announced in due course. In the first instance the plan so far approved by Provisonal Government......... recommendation to Indians of East Asia for adoption in their daily lives."

Tokyo, English, 2/2/44

A Headquarters Provisional Government Azad Hind communique, issued yesterday, disclosed that adequate pensions will immediately be given to families, living in East Asia, of Indian civilians who lose their lives while participating in military operation. The communique said, "A meeting of the Council of Ministers of the Provisional Government of Azad Hind was held at the official residence of Bose, Saturday, Feb 19. The advisers were also present, Bose presided .The Council of Ministers unanimously decided to award adequate pension to families of the Indian civilians who lose their lives when participating in military operations, although they are not members of the Azad Hind Fauj. The Council further decided that in the case of these Indians who had already lost their lives, and whose families happen to be living in East Asia, pensions to their families should be given immediately."

Singapore, 2/23/44

Netaji revealed that the Provisional Government shortly will organize the "Azad Hind Bank" to strengthen the government's financial positions.

Tokyo, English, 3/20/44

The Provisional Government of Azad Hind today established its own bank at a certain Burmese city, with two prime tasks of mobilizing the financial resources of Indians for India's war of freedom, and of contributing to the interests of Burma. Opening of the new bank is particularly significant in that it serves as a pivotal organ, materially and financially, for mobilizing the resources of Indians for supporting the cause of the Provisional Government Azad Hind, as well as enhancing the financial standing of the government and implementing its aims. The new bank will be under the management of four Indian directors, headed by Dina Nath.

Tokyo, English, 4/5/44

It is reported from Berlin that Mr. Nambiar, Minister without portfolio of the Provisional Government of Free India, who is now on a visit to Germany's capital delivered on April 13 a significant radio address. In his address, the speaker affirmed that the campaign for the liberation of India has already entered its decisive phase, thanks to the driving operation being carried out by the Japanese and Indian National Forces, and that all

Indians are going forward resolutely to put an end to Minister British Imperialism in India, which is not far off. *Tokyo, Portguese, 4/15/44*

In a special communique issued by the Provisional Government of Azad Hind yesterday, it announcement that five new members of state have been appointed, They are: (Lakshu Kownlaviya), Ishar Singh, (N. Ranganadhan), Lt. Colonel (Z. R. Mohan) and (Hadi Barama). Mr. (name) Alagappan will cease to hold the post of Adviser to the Provisional Government of Azad Hind and Lt. Colonel S.C. Alagappan, Minister without portfolio, will be in charge of the Ministry of Supplies in addition to his other duties. *Singapore, English, 4/23/44*

Kuala Lumpur: Another prominent local Indian (left) recently to take up a post with the advance headquarters of the Provisional Government of Azad Hind. He is 45 year old Dr. M. K. Lukshimeyah, a native of the Tanjore District in South Indian and a well known medical practitioner. When the Indian Independence League was organized, over two years ago, he was among the first to join the movement to fight for India's freedom. He became the first chairman of the Selanger Branch of the Indian Independence League and later was commandant of the Indian Independence Army Training Camp. Two other Indians also left for Burma. *Tokyo, English, 5/20/44*

Twelve months ago when the Indian Independence Movement in East Asia received new impetus, all activities converged towards one main objective. That objective was to prepare for and launch an armed struggle for the winning of freedom That objective has now been fulfilled. The Azad Hind Fauj has crossed the frontier of India and the battle for freedom new is being waged on Indian soil. This new development opened up a new sphere of activity. Previously our activities were paractically confined to East Asia. Now the situation has altered considerably. The liberated area of India has brought up new problems concerning administration and reconstruction. Further, military operations that have been launched with much success have created now problems how to ..... on with operations inside India and how to work up a revolution in the country. Consequently, we shall have in the future three spheres of activity. (1) East Asia, which will continue to be a base for our political activities and military operations; (2) the liberated areas, where problems to be faced will be mainly these of administration and reconstruction, as well as preparation for further operations; (3) enemy occupied Indian territory where the revolution has been (planned) and to which our army will have to penetrate. Since October 21,1942 the Indian Independence Movement in East Asia has been conducted by the Indian Independence League. The Azad Hind Fauj, Indian Independence Army, was the military organ of the League. Since October 21, 1943 the Provisional Government of Azad Hind took over leadership of the Indian Independence Movement and therefore of the Indian Independence League and of the Azad Hind Fauj. Till recenlty, activities of the Provisional Government of the Azad Hind have been virtually confined to East Asia. Now that the situation has changed considerably, the Provisional Government will have to look after three spheres of activity East Asia, the liberated area and enemy occupied India. Minister and advisers of the Provisional Government will therefore have to be allotted difinite responsibilities in their three spheres. One group will have to look after the work in East Asia, another in the liberated territory, and a third group in enemy-occupied India. The first group working in East Asia will be called the East Asia committee of the Cabinet. The second group working in liberated India will be called the Liberated Area Committee of the Cabinet; while the third group will be called the War Committee of the Cabinet. In East Asia the mobilization of men, money and materials will have to be expanded in order to cope with new problems...... A new ministry, called the Ministry of Manpower, will have to be created for recruiting and mobilizing more men and women of various categories for different tasks..... for the Azad Hind Fauj, for the Rani Jhansi Regiments for the Azad Hind Dal, as well as for day to day work of the Indian Independence League. The ministry of Supplies, which has recently been created, will have to be enlarged. While other ministries which may already be in existance or may be set up hereafter, will have to carry may already be in existence or may be set up hereafter, will have to carry on their work, the main responsibility in the future will devolve on the Ministries of Finance, Manpower and Supplies, The East Asia Committee of the Cabinet will be responsible for directing the work in East Asia and will be composed of those ministries and advisers who ordinarily work in East Asia. For the liberated area in India, plans for administration and reconstruction already have been prepared and they will be given effect as the opportunity comes. The necessary staff of the Azad Hind Dal already had been detailed for the purpose of......members of the Azad Hind Dal already inside India or near the frontiers., The Liberated Area Committee will consist of minister and advisers who have been especially detailed to work in these areas and such ministers and advisers as may happen to there. The War Committee of Cabinet will consist of those ministers and advisers who will deal almost exclusively with problems concerning further military operations in enemy occupied India, as well as with problems pertaining to propaganda, revolutionary activity, administration and reconstruction in that territory.

Tokyo, English. 7/3/44

The Provisional Government of Azad Hind announced details for the seven days celebration which will be held on the occasion of Netaji Week, beginning July 4. The program follows: July 4: Flag hoisting ceremonies at League branches Netaji conference with pressmen, mass rally, radio broadcast by Netaji; July 5: Public lectures at various Indian communities; public lectures at various communities; July 7: Military sports, ladies mass meeting; July 8: School children's meeting, visit to wounded at Indian National Army Soldier Hospital by Netaji and entertaining patient by Netaji Fund Committee, radio broadcast by Netaji July 9: Merchants' meeting; July 10: Public meetings, also League Branches.

Tokyo English, 7/3/44

The Provisional Government of Azad Hind and the Indian National Army are carrying on daily broadcasts from Burma on the wave length of 35.5 meters. Here are the timings of the various important items from the Provisional Government of Azad Hind Headquarters in the broadcasts from Burma News and commentary, in Hindustani, beginning at 10 minutes past 8:00 Indian standard time. News and commentary, in Bengali beginning at 21 minutes past 8:00. News and commentary in English, beginning at 45 minutes past 8: 00 Indian standard time. Special feature at 55 minutes past 8: 00 Indian standard time. The Indian National Army located in Burma broadcasts every evening on the wave length of 35.45 meters. The program begins at 9:45 p.m. and lasts until 10:00 Indian standard time. Listeners in India, don't fail to tune into the Provisional Government of Azad Hind and the Indian National Army headquarters broadcasting station, operating from Burma on the wave length of 35.54 meters in the evening. The program begins shortly after 8:00 p.m. and ends at 10:00 p.m,. Indian standard time.

Singapore, English, 8/17/44

The Provisional Government of Free India announced the creation of new decoration, "Tamgha-Eshatru Nassh" There are two classes of the new decorations. The first class decoration will be presented to Indian officers and men who render outstanding service or display exceptional bravery in the line officers and men, but also to Indian civilian joining the fight for the liberation of the motherland, and who kill or imprison Anglo-Americans.

Tokyo, English, 8/31/44

Women's Organization

Rangoon: Extending a warm welcomes to Capt. Lakshmi, the Minister of the Women's Organization of the Provisional Government of Free India, (Daw Kinna Ma), wife of Dr. Ba Maw and President of the Burmese Women's National Service Association, yesterday afternoon assured Capt. Lakshmi that the Burmese women will do everything in their power to assist their Indian sisters in the coming great struggle for India's independence. This statement was made by Burma's first lady at Ba Maw's official residence, where the Commander of the Rani of Jhansi Regiment called to make a courtesy visit following her arrival in Burma on January 7 with S. C. Bose, Head of the Provisional Government of Free India.

Tokyo, English, 1/14/44

Chandra Bose, Commander-in-Chief of the Indian National Army, accompanied by Swami Nathan Lakshmi Head of the Women's Organization of the Provisional Government of Free India. This morning inspected the Indian Women's Corps. Impressed by the intensive training carried on by the Women's Corps, Bose encouraged the women members to continue to fight for achievement of the ultimate goal of liberation of India from Anglo-Americans. *Tokyo, English 1/12/44*

Indian National Army

The India Independence Movement in India had completed its preparation when the Indian National Army advanced into Burma and leaders of the Provisional Government of Free India, including Chandra Bose, have arrived in Burma; thus; along with the coming of the third year of the decisive war, the first step of the historical march toward New Delhi has been commenced. The fact that the Provisional Government of Free India has advanced to Burma is inevitable, in view of the facts that Chandra Bose arrived at Tokyo in June, last year, and following this, on October 21, the declaration of the establishment of the Provisional Government of Free India was made at Shonan....... The advance of the Provisonal Government of Free Indian to Burma is the best opportunity for the government to make a direct call upon the people of India who are making frontal resistance against Britain. Therefore, the anti-British antagonism of thee Indian soldiers in India will be further instigated. In addition to this, the fact that the Indian National Army and the Provisional Government have advance to Burma will extend more hidden force in aiding not only the Indian soldiers who are posted along the India-Burma border but also various secret anti-British organization in India, and will instigate the activities of these organs. *Tokyo, Japanese, 1/8/44*

The indomitable and fighting determination to liberate the motherland was keyonoted in the fiery, one hour address by Subhas Chandra Bose, given yesterday afternoon before the troops of the Indian National Army which advanced into Burma along with the Provisional Government of Free India. With the sweeping march to Delhi imminent, Bose reminded his soldiers again that the 3,000,000 Indians living in East Asia, as well as 380,000,000 Indians in India, and the powerful Axis nations stand firmly and solidly in back of them.

Tokyo, English, 1/11/44

An Indian meeting, celebrating the Independence of India was held on Wednesday at the advanced base of the Provisional Government of Free India in Burma. President S. C. Bose, head of the Azad Hind personally inspected the troops under his direct command at the ceremonial grounds, packed with the pick of the international army and Burman troops, as well as of the thousands of people. President Bose and Dr. Ba Maw representative of the Burmese state, gave inspiring addresses.

Tokyo, English, 1/27/44

The Indo-British Army is now said to total about 1,403,000 of which there are 600,000 irregulars. Most of the latter troops are Indians. The drive on Delhi by the National Indian Army not only will affect these troops but their long cherished dream of making India for the Indians. The anti-British movement which is fast spreading throughout the land, is expected to become doubly active as soon as our armies advance into India crying: "India, the liberation Army is Here."

Tokyo, Japanese, 3/21/44

Subhas Chandra Bose received congratulations from Mussolini on brilliant achievements Indian National Army. Duc extended wishes for further success and added he always cherished pleasant memories of his interview with Netaji in Rome few years ago.

Tokyo, English, 4/15/44

Shonan: Subhas Chandra Bose's recent announcement that units of the Rani of Jhansi Regiment have been moved to the front lines has sent a fresh wave of enthusiasm among Indian women throughout East Asia. Following the announcement, the recruitment, the recruiting offices have been flooded with eager applicants determined to further swell the ranks of the Indian women fighting for the freedom of their motherland..... these women soldiers were well disciplined and showed no sign of feminine excitabitlity or nervousness. Proud and war like, their faces proclaimed their burning enthusiasm to go into battle against the British....

Singapore, English, 5/4/44

Rangoon: The Manipuris residing in Burma have broadcast an appeal to the people in Manipur, asking them to give fullest support and cooperation to the Indian National Army and the Nippon forces now at the gates of Manipur in order to expel the enemy and save Manipur from the clutches of British Imperialism. The message points out: "We in Burma, irrespective of caste or creed, whether we are Khattiyua or Brahmans. have been fortunate enough to enjoy, since British evacuation, under the Nippon Military Administration as well as after attainment of Burmese independence. Such blessings as complete religious liberty, with absolute freedom to practice ones own ancestral rites and rituals, equal rights and privileges with all other brother Asistics no matter whether we are white, yellow brown or black and unlimited trade facilities without any racial or class discrimination and freedom from all kinds of restraint so common under the British." It says the Manipuris in Burma, therefore , have been, all along, cooperating with their heart an soul with the government in Burma as well as Nippon and India military authorities in fighting this war and in building a new order. Recognizing that Manipur is still under the British yoke and the people are not yet free, but still are oppressed , deprived of privileges and national rights, the message asked the Manipur people to give their fullest support and cooperation to the Japanese and Indian forces "so that you may soon enjoy all the blessings of independence as we in Burma are already enjoying now."

Tokyo, English, 8/5/44

Leaders

Subhas Chandra Bose

Rangoon: By the recent conference between Ba Maw and Bose in Shonan, the part that Burma is to play in the Independence Movement was promised that Major General On Sane..... issued statement leader. Now Chandra Bose has risen as a political and military leader for liberation and independence of India.... There is no doubt that the Indian Naitonal Army, with such a leader , will certainly in the near future reach its goal.

Tokyo, Japanese, 7/24/43

Rangoon : S. C. Bose, head of the Provisional Government of Free India, arrived at the undisclosed base in Burma, by air, this morning. Bose was given a hearty welcome at the airfield by a number of Burmese and

Japanese officials and civilians, including Adipadi Ba Maw and Ranzo Sawada, Japanese Ambassador to Burma, as well as India representatives. After his arrival, Bose inspected troops of the Indian National Army and then.... (Pawa) court on Adipadi Ba Maw at the latter's official residence and on the Commander-in-Chief of the Japanese forces in Burma.

Tokyo, English, 1/7/44

Immediately after Bose moved his government to Burma, he made a radio broadcast address to the people of India, making clear his visit to the Andaman Islands, and announced the appointment of Lt. Col. Rogananadan as Chairman of the Administrative Preparation Committee for the Andaman Islands.

Tokyo, Japanese, 1/10/44

According to a Demei wire from an undisclosed base in Burma, Subhas Chandra Bose, head of the Provisional Government of Free India, issued the following statement in the name of the supremo commander of the Indian National Army. 'Ever since the formation of the Indian National Army was announced several months ago, the propaganda of the enemy has been frantic in deceits directed to the Indian people and to the British Indian Army to the effect that the Indian National Army does not exist, and that amounts to nothing more than propaganda. However, although I made no promises whatsoever heretofore in opposition to the propaganda of the enemy, I fulfilled all the promises I made to my countryman in the mother country and drove home the fact that they would be fulfilled when the time came. Moreover, I declared to the whole world that during the past two months we were native according to plan... It is a fact that our allottted time has become somowhat (shortened). We will be active according to plan and have firm confidence in fulfilling the solemn pledge of liberating our mother country when the times comes. We have absolute trust in our allied and unlimited confidence in our ultimate victory."

Tokyo, Japanese, 2/7/44

Speaking before a mass rally of Indians, in celebration of actual participation in the battle of Azad Hind. (Netaji) S.C. Bose, in his capacity of Supreme Commander of the Indian National Army, declared, that with the Indian Indepenedence Movement having entered a new phase, all Indians are awakening to the significance of the latest developments and must newly resolve to fight the battle for India's freedom to a successful conclusion. He stressed this is the last fight for the Indians and the first victory in that final battle has already been achieved.

Tokyo, English, 3/20/44

The second giant mass meeting since the establishment of the Free Indian Government was held on the 19th with Subhas Chandra Bose, the Netaji, who has just returned from an inspection tour of the front lines, as the principal speaker. *Tokyo, Japanese, 3/20/44*

The Free India Provisional Government, in the name of Subhas Bose, head of the Provisional Government and Commander-in-Chief of the Indian National Army, made the following announcement: "The Provisional Government Azad Hind hereby solemnly swears that it will fight through to the day of absolute liberation, with the friendly aid of Japan. It is therefore this government's sincere desire that our brethren render all aid directly or indirectly for the advancement of Japan-India Army. Moreover, the Free Indian territory and guarantee, the administration of general affairs. This government advises all our Indian brethren to stay out of American and British army barracks, factories, harbors and other military establishments to avoid being injured, as these will be subject to destruction by our troops." *Tokyo, Japanese, 3/21/44*

In the name of Bose, the Indian Provisional Government issued statement. It says, "The Indian National Army is now able to march on to India and into Delhi. The army members are resolved to march (onward) with the Japanese Army." *Tokyo, Japanese, 3/21/44*

Profound admiration for the hard fight of President De Valera and the Irish Government for maintenance of the neutrality of Eira was expressed by the Netaji, Subhas Chandra Bose, Head of the Provisional Government of Azad Hind, in a message addressed to the Irish nation through "Domei" news agency. The message reads, "In the history of our fight against British imperialism there perhaps is no other struggle which has influenced us so much and for which we have had so much sympathy as the struggle of the brave Irish nation for their birthright of liberty. Having boon a close student of Irish history and having been in Eire myself, I know that this sympathy is fully reciprocated from the Irish side. The other day the question of recognizing our Provisional Government was raised in the Irish Parliament. I read with deepest interest the proceedings of the debate. Though the government of Azad Hind and I know for fact that the sympathy of the entire Irish nation is with us in our struggle against the common foe, and having the privilege of knowing President De Valera and his cabinet ministers personally, I am fully aware that in their attitude toward India there is no difference whatsoever between the government and the people of Eire." *Tokyo, English, 3/27/44*

Mr. Subhas Chandra Bose, on Thursday, is issued a message regarding the inauguration of a National Liberation Week. Now this new week is to be observed in place of the former Indian National week, which began on April 6th every year. The Netaji asked all his countrymen, especially those in Greater East Asia, to observe this National function in such a manner as befits the historical significance.

Tokyo, Japanese, 3/31/44

The Provisional Government of Free India, in a news bulletin issued yesterday morning, disclosed that Netaji Subhas Chandra Bose, Head of the Provisional Government of Free India and Supreme Commander of the Indian National Army, has arrived at his Headquarters in Burma. The bulletin also disclosed that the most elaborate proparations are being made at the Burma Headquarters to celebrate "Netaji Week" from July 4 to 10. This marks the first anniversary of Bose's assumption of the leadership of the Indian Independence Movement in East Asia as Supreme Commander of the Indian National Army. *Tokyo, Japanese, 6/30/44*

On July 4, the opening day of the Netaji Week, Subhas Chandra Bose issued a statement revealing the future plans for the 3,000,000 Indians in the Greater East Asia for their independece. The content of his statement is as follows: ".......In conclusion allow me to indicate three points in our future policies. Firstly, we must continue to win battles and advance farther and farther into India. To this end, we must strengthen the fighting front with both man and material. Secondly, reconstruction activities will surely increase in the liberated areas. Therefore, we must increase the personnel for reconstruction work. Thirdly, we must strengthen the home front; and to meet this, it is necessary to exert our efforts towards the mobilization of manpower, resources and capital." *Tokyo, Japanese, 7/4/44*

An enthusiastic mass rally, highlighted by spontaneous demonstrations for the patriotic government supported by determination to free India, marked Provisional Government Day held here yesterday. The gathering, which was held in a spacious hall profusely decorated with the national colors and flowers, was attempted by prominent Indians in Burma as well as high officials of the Azad Hind Government. A martial aspect was lent by guards of honour who lined all corridors and approaches to the hall. Stressing the iron determination to continue the armed fight until India is free, no matter how long the struggle may last, Netaji Subhas Bose again reminded his audience freedom cannot be won unless all Indians units give their utmost, and also called for continued total mobilization of men, money and materials. *Tokyo, Japanese, 7/22/44*

The 6th mass meeting commemorating the establishment of the Free India Provisional Government was held somewhere is Burma. At this conference Subhas Chander Bose emphatically stated that now is the time to mobilize the total material and manpower resources of the Indian people to build up war power, and demanded a strong unification and action on the part of the people. Resolutions emboyding the common will of the 500,000,000 people of India were passed and read before the gathering by Subhas Bose. Thus the unshakable determination of the East Asia Indian people to wrest the victory for the sake of liberating India was manifested. The gist of the resolutions are as follows: This conference pays its heartfelt respect to the officers and men of the Free Indian Nationa Army....Today the Indian National Army is waiting for another battle with the enemy. The responsibility which rests upon the shoulders of the Indian people in East Asia is to use this opportune time to the best advantage and make strong preparations for the coming compaigns. With this goal in mind, the mobilization of all material wealth and manpower should be carried out to completion... The conference pays homage to the spirits of these who have fallen in this war of liberation and also felicitates the brilliant records made by our fighting men. This meeting resolves that it will face all situations shoulder to shoulder with Japan and her allies, and will continue to fight in the face of all difficulties until victory is obtained and India is freed from the oppression of foreign powers. *Tokyo, Japanese, 8/22/44*

Behari Bose

Behari Bose recently said, "India and Burma are two inseparable countries. The move of the government to Burma was like moving to its home country." This means that the Indians have a strong feeling toward the Burmese. The Indians can hardly distinguish between Burma and India.....Kawabe, Commander-in-Chief of our forces in the Burma area, said the Indian Army is growing stronger. *Tokyo, Japanese, 1/10/44*

Indian Independence Movement

A momentous conflab of Indians is now in session in Bangkok. The inaugural meeting, held on Monday, the 15th, was attended by an impressive gathering of Indian representatives from all parts of East Asia. This is the largest and most significant meeting of Indians over to have been held abroad, and had the singular distinction of having among its foreign guests the Ambassadors of three active powers, Japan, Germany and Italy, and the respresentatives of the Thai Government. Messages of great and far reaching significance were addressed to the meeting by Premier Tojo of Japan, Premier Bipul Songram of Thailand and the German and Italian envoys at the Thai Cabinet. These messages reiterated friendly greeting entertained by the three powers, Japan, Germany and Italy, towards Indian and the Indian people.... Mr. Rash Behari Bose addressed ..... inaugural message, paid the highest tribute to Mahatma Gandhi for preventing India from being involved in the present war as a (tomb) of Britain. Expressing the need for India's whole-hearted cooperation with Japan in exterminating British power, Mr. Bose asserted, "India's freedom in the true sense of the word is a problem which can be solved only by the challenge of Japan against British Imperialism." The Indian patriot added, "India should not lose any time in the fight against Britain." Appealing for immediate action, Mr. Bose told the conference, "Now let us stand up together.....preparation to work for India's independence for which Mahatma Gandhi has fought for the past 20 years."....Foreign Minister Togo and Ambassador (Taubogami) expressed to the Indian conference the full cooperation and support of the Japanese nation. Foreign Minister Togo asked the leaders of India to forget their minor differences of opinion and unite in getting their countries to stand as a body.....and exert themselves to bring about the collapse of British Imperialism.

Tokyo, English, 6/19/42

Bangkok : A mass meeting of Indian residents of Bangkok and Thenburi was held today at the Wathnakorn Theater Hall, in commemoration of the "Quit India" resolution adopted in 1942 by Indian National Congress. The gathering was addressed by Daljit Singh of Manila and Lieutenant Colonol Hussian of the Indian National Army, after which three resolution were adopted. They are as follows : "1. We express our profound pleasure that Mahatma Gandhi has voiced his emphatic assertion in a recent statement that the "Quit India" resolution of 1942 stands good in letter and in spirit, and that it cannot be altered even by .... and he has further advised Indians to hold demonstrations throughout India today to record reaffirmation of the resolution; 2. that we, on this day, renewed our determination to follow Netaji Subhas Chandra Bose in his onward march toward the promised land of free and happy India until the enemy is forced to "Quit India" through the collaboration of forces from within India and without it; 3. that we take this opportunity of congratulating the Japanese and Thai both of whom our extreme pleasure has been expressed for continuation of the same.....which has been beneficial to our cause."

Anti-Britian Statement

The Bangkok Indians stated they must take arms to achieve independence of their fatherland. The homeland of India must extreminate British and Americans and build an India for Indians.

Tokyo, Japanese, 8/11/44

Bangkok : Addressing the Indian people at home, a member of the Bangkok Branch of the Indian Independence League broadcast from Bangkok, on Tuesday night, to the following effects: "The British authorities once proudly declared that they would be able to suppress an anti-British movement in a cleared that they would be able to suppress an anti-British movement in a few days if it ever occurred in India. Despite the cruel and inhuman British oppression, the anti-British movement in India is becoming more aggravated. The distrubance in India are assuming serious proportions and, despite the ceaseless activities of the British Army and police, Indian youth and labourers are giving their all for the emancipation of their race. *Tokyo, English, 9/9/42*

Propaganda by Radio—In order to assist the patriotic Indian at home, the Indian residents of Thailand have begun a private radio broadcast, directed to India through the Bangkok Radio Station, every evening for an hour, from 8.00 to 9.00 Indian standard time. *Tokyo, English, 5/4/43*

Bangkok Branch, Activities—The Bangkok Branch of the Indian Independence League broadcast to all Indian, on the evening of September 8, encouraging them: "There is no possibility that the great spirit of Indian for India's independence and British imperialism will agree. Hold strong encouragement that the British imperialism will be thrust out from the land of India. Brethren of our motherland, prosperity is near"

Tokyo, Japanese, 9/9/42

Several thousands of Indian residents in Bangkok celebrated the birthday of Mahatma Gandhi at the Bangkok Headquarters of the Indian Independence League. Fundamental ideals of the Independence Movement were discussed. *Tokyo, English, 10/3/42*

Bangkok: The Thailand Branch of the Indian Independence League, on the occasion of the first anniversary of the GEA war, yesterday hold a commemorative rally at the (Silver Cone) Theatre. At the rally a resoultion was decided upon, stating the Japan's victory is India's victory and....Japan's brave fight they would fight their uttermost for the restoration of their mother country, India. *Tokyo, Japanese, 12/8/42*

Today the Bangkok Indian Independence Federation is to hold a ceremony of prayer for Gandhi *Tokyo, Japanese, 2/24/43*

Bangkok: On the occasion of the birthday of Mahatma Gandhi, the Thai Chapter of the Indian Independece League, on Saturday, held at its office a rally of Indian residents in Bangkok. Before 2,000 Indians the chairman of the Thai Chapter delivered a stirring address, urging all-out effort of the local Indians to fight for crushing Britian. After the rally all participants paraded the streets. *Tokyo, English, 10/2/43*

The (Wd) committee of the Bangkok Indian Independence League held a ceremony this morning to pay allegiance to the national flag of Independent India in order to felicitate the establishment of Provisional Government of Free India. About 2,000 Indians assembled at the (grounds) of the league. There a people's rally was held at the (Namo) Park, at which time (Name), chief of the Publicity Dept. of the Indian Independence League, and (Name), Educational Dept. Chief, gave speeches. A people's felicitation rally will be hold in a grand manner this evening also. Tomorrow a.m. a review of the Indian Volunteer Corps is scheduled to be held.

Tokyo, Japanese, 10/25/43

Bangkok: Commencing today, the Thai chapter of the Indian Independence League will observe Netaji Week. A mass metting was held this morning, following a flag raising ceremony. A message of appreciation and encouragement was adopted to be forwarded to Bose.

Tokyo, English, 7/3/44

Bangkok: Netaji week celebrations opened here this morning with a rally attended by more than 1,000 Indian residents headed by Sardar Singh, new Minister without Portfolio of the Provisional Government of Free India. The headquarters of the local Indian Independence League, where the rally was held, was decorated with the Indian tri-colour. The programme included singing of the Indian National songs and passing of resolution renewing the resolve to fight out the battle against Britain to victorious finish. A massage of gratitude and encouragment was sent to Netaji Bose. *Tokyo, English, 7/4/44*

Bangkok: A mass meeting and parade by Indian residents here highlighted the last day of Netaji week today. At 9.00 a.m. more than 1,000 Indian residents here assembled in front of the headquarters of the Indian Independence League in Thailand. After parading the main streets of the city, the Indian residents held a mass meeting at the local theater. The meeting opened with an address by the chairman of the league who spoke on the Indian Volunteers' Training Institute. Events included the reading of partriotic poems, composed by Indian youths, and also speeches by committee members. *Tokyo, Japanese, 7/10/44*

Contribution

The head of the Free India Committee, who recently visited Thailand, gave 25,000 baht to take care of wounded Thai soldiers and 35,000 baht to Chulalongkorn University. *Bangkok, Thai., 8/22/43*

Shonan: It was learned here Saturday that Subhas Chandra Bose, President of the Indian National Army, made a donation of 50,000 bahts to the Thai Government on one of his recent visits to that country. This donation was meant partly for the aid and comfort of wounded Thai soldiers, and partly as a contribution to the (wd) university.

Tokyo, English, 10/17/43

Free India Provisional Government

Bangkok: Subhas Chandra Bose had named (Ishaaru Sin), chairman of the Thailand Branch of the Indian Independence League, as the new State Minister of the Provisional Government of Free India. The new minister is one of the outstanding Indian figures in the (Honneian Uuyonsas) commerical circles. He has long been active in the anti-British movement, and prior to this was prohibited from returning to India by the British Government. Since the establishment of the Indian Independence League in Bangkok in 1942, he has been very active within the organization. He was appointed advisor to the provisional government with its inception....

Tokyo, Japanese, 4/22/44

Cooperation of Thailand

Bangkok: The Thailand Government announced tonight over the radio that it has extended official recognition to the Free India Provisional Government headed by Chandra Bose. *Tokyo, English, 11/19/43*

Bangkok: The propaganda Bureau announced on April 8 that Premier Pibut Songgram had sent a telegram to Subhas Chandra Bose, Commender-in-Chief of the Indian National Army, congratulating him and his men on the recent invasion of India by praying for their success. The telegram reads as follows: "Beloved Indian friends—the recent invasion of the homeland by the National Army under the leadership of Subhas Chandra Bose indeed has caused much rejoicing among the Asiatic people. At this time, in behalf of the people of Thailand, I wish to extend my sincerest congratulations to the National Army on its recent invasion of the motherland and pray for its further advance and ultimate victory in this was of righteousness." *Tokyo, English, 7/4/44*

Leaders

Subhas Chandra Bose—Bangkok—Greatly elated over the sudden advent of Mr. Bose in Tokyo, the Bangkok Headquarters of the Indian Independence League held a welcome rally for Mr. Bose on Monday, and it was attended by some 2,000 Indians. *Tokyo, English, 6/22/43*

Bangkok: Hailing the new post of Mr. Subhas Bose as president of the Indian Independence League, Indian residents in Bangkok, on Monday, voiced their confidence in him as a man of action, who is the only man in India able to bring the present complicated international situation to a successful conclusion. The Indian residents pointed out that the menace to the British by the Japanese forces on the Indo-Burma border has been doubled by the entrance of Mr. Subhas Bose on the scene, especially in view of the fact that he is strongly supported by the people of (Assam) and Bengal on the Indian frontier. *Tokyo, English, 7/5/43*

Subhas Chandra Bose, who is now visiting Bangkok, in a joint interview with reporters on July 27, expressed the firm determination to overthrow Anglo-American policy from India by mobilizing the total strength. He said: " .....When Burmese independence is realized, we will win a strong ally of Burma, which is a neighbouring country of India, and I am firmly convinced that our independence movement will be further pushed forward in a cooperative manner." *Tokyo, Japanese, 7/30/43*

Bangkok: Subhas Chandra Bose, President of the Indian Independence League and concurrently Commander-in-Chief of the Indian National Army, again visited Bangkok on August 4, on route from Burma to Shonan. During his second visited here Mr. Bose called on Premier Pibul Songgram and had a freindly talk with him. He deepended his acquaintanceship with Japanese and other Axis organs on the sport. Mr. Bose held an Indian rally at the (Name) University as a prelude to the anniversary of the suppression of the Indian Independence (wd), which falls on Monday, and exhorted all Indians in Thailand to direct their efforts toward the Independence of India. *Tokyo, English, 8/9/43*

Bangkok: President Chandra Bose of the Indian Independence League, after spending several days at Rangoon participating in the Indian Independence rally held there, arrived at Bangkok on September 30 and gave a rally speech on October 5 on the occasion of the celebration of the date of birth of elder Gandhi. He encouraged the people.

Tokyo, Japanese, 10/4/43

Rash Behari Bose—Independece Movement of Bangkok—In view of the coming conference, Behari Bose made speech through radio, encouraging those at Bangkok to do their best. *Tokyo, Japanese, 8/6/42*

Women's Corps

Bangkok: There have been many among the Indian women residents of Thailand who have expressed their desired to join the Indian National Women's Corps which was established in Shonan. The Indian Independence League, Bangkok Branch, which was impressed by this enthusiasm, immediately chose 9 women including (Mrs. Surubayaru Tuuru) as first volunteers and decided to send them to Shonan. The party left Bangkok for Shonan on December 21 with a send-off by a large number of persons, including (Basu), Adviser to the Free India Provisional Government. *Tokyo, Japanese, 12/23/43*

Bangkok: The activity of the Women's Corps of the Indian National Army in Shonan greatly inspires Indian women living in Thailand, and volunteers to join the corps are increasing steadily daily. The Bangkok section of the Indian Army, deeply moved by the eager desire.....number of....women to be sent to Shonan and a party left Bangkok for Shonan on Wednesday morning with a hearty send-off by the Indian residents.

Tokyo, English, 12/23/43

Bangkok: On Friday some Indian women, under Mrs. Narain's leadership, from the Bangkok Branch of the Indian Independence League will join the Rani Jhansi Regiment somewhere on the Indian-Burma border to celebrate the (Eighteenth) Freedom-week with great pomp. Rani Jhasi Regiment is under the command of Mrs. Lakshami.

Tokyo, Urdu, 4/8/44

Indian Independence League
Saigon Branch : Activities

Today, the Indians held a big meeting at (the Headquarters of the Indian Independence League in Saigon). The president of the meeting said— "Today is the most important for the Indians, because in 1857, on this every day, the foundation-stone of the Indian freedom was laid." After the meeting a thousand Indians tooks the oath that they were ready to make every sacrifice for the freedom of India, and they will help with life, heart and everything to destroy the British. *Saigon, Urdu, 5/10/43*

The Saigon Branch of the Indian Independence League, representing the 3,000 Indian residents in southern French Indo-China, donated a considerable amount of money to the Provisional Government of Free India as an expression of their enthusiam towards the independence cause, and a Volunteer Corps for the Indian National Army has been dispatched. A second Volunteer Corps is being already organized.

Tokyo, English, 11/8/43

Cooperation with Japan

The Indian Society in Saigon held a mass meeting on Tuesday to commemorate the first anniversary of the GEA war. The following resolution was passed at the meeting and sent to Premier Tojo: "We Indians residing in Cochin China, on the first anniversary of the GEA war, wish to convey our heartfelt thanks and compliments to the Japanese Government and its people for the brilliant victories achieved by the Imperial forces and for their efforts in costing all Anglo-American influence from East Asia. We believe that freedom and prosperity of Japan and India can be obtained only by complete victory over the United State and Britain. In order to accomplish the foregoing objects we desire that we shall spare nothing in cooperation with Japan."

Tokyo, English, 12/10/42

Free India Provisional Government

The enthusiasm of the 300 Indians living in the southern part of French Indo-China has been boosted by the establishment of the Provisional Government of Free India. The Saigon Branch of the Indian Independence League contributed 2,500,000 rupees to the provisional government as a fund for the Indian National Army, while 16,000 piastres have been contributed to the Indian Red Cross. The Saigon Branch of the Indian Independence League dispatched, yesterday, its first contingent of men who are volunteering to the Indian National Army.

Tokyo, Japanese, 11/8/43

Indian National Army

Expressing the jubilation of 6,000 Indian residents in French Indo-China over now of the Indian National Army's participation in the current Arakan operations, Sheik Mohamed, head of the French Indo-China Chapter of the Indiar Independence League, is a statement issued today, voiced full confidence in the victory of Indo-Japanese forces.

Tokyo, English, 2/10/44

Saigon: 3,000 Indians residing here held a mass meeting yesterday on the occasion of "Azad Hind" day, and adopted a resolution pledging to further continue work for the cause of complete independence and freedom of the motherland. The resolution declared that the Indian National Army has completed its first stage of operations in its fight for the independence of the motherland and, presently, is preparing for the next phase of operations. All Indians residing in French Indo-China will mobilize their total power for such operations, which the Indian National Army is fully ready to carry out. In conclusion, the resolution expressed the determination of Indian residents in French Indo-China to overcome any difficulties and to fight out the current war in close cooperation with Japan and other allied nations for the attainment of the common objective of liberating East Asia from Anglo-American aggression.

Tokyo, English, 8/22/44

MALAYA

Indian Independence Movement

Youth Movement

To do their duty and liberate their sacred land from the yoke of the British....." *Saigon, English, 3/9/43*

Addressing the enormous Indian youth rally held in Shonan Sunday, Rash Behari Bose, the President of the Indian Independence League in East Asia, declared that there can be no compromise or halfway settlement in this fight against the British. It is the united effort of the Indian youth that will bring victory and glory to India. *Tokyo, English, 4/1/43*

Shonan: Symbolic of patriotic fervour, a 17 year old girl, a Sikh, Jit Kour, on Friday offered 1,000 yen to the Indain Independence League; and has offered her name to be enlisted as a volunteer in the Rani Jhansi Regiment. It may be of interest to note that the Jit Kour had only 1,000 yen with her and she gave here all for national freedom.

Tokyo, Urdu, 10/3/43

Shonan: The Provisional Government of Free India, on Thursday, announced that Indian youngsters are under training to participate in the administration and construction of Free India in various districts to be relieved from Anglo-Amercian oppression. *Tokyo, English, 11/6/43*

Shonan: Boys and girls of the Indian National School here formed themselves into a "Balak Sena" youth corps in response to Netaji S.C. Bose's appeal to Indian youth to raise themselves into an effective body to serve the motherland. It is understood the "Balak Sena" will function under the Shonan Branch of the Indian Independence League. Already members of this new organization have started to work for the national cause, having so fai collected among themselves $250.00 as a donation towards the Independence Movement Fund. Plans for training in the role they are to play in the independence struggle are going to be drawn up. It is recalled the first of such organizations was formed in Johere Bharu at (wd) of National Liberation Week celebrations, April 13.

Tokyo, English, 4/22/44

Local Indian boys and girls have formed themselves into a (Balikpemah) or (New Corps), in response to the appeal of Netaji Subhas Chandra Bose. The decision to form this corps was carried out on May 10, when....anniversary of their counry's first war of independence.

Manila, English, 5/17/44

Indian Independence League

East Asia Headquarter in Shonan

Shonan City: It is reported from Shonan City that the Shonan Branch of the Indian Independence League will hold their Independence Rally on September 2nd at 5.50 p.m.

Tokyo, English, 8/31/42

30,000 Indians rally here Wednesday night to support India's Independence Movement. Moslems resolve and join the Independence League. Tokyo, 9/2/42

Shonan: India Independence Federation, Shonan Branch, held a rally at the ground in front of Izacc Club in Shonan City yesterday, 5.00 p.m.. First, (Goh Ho), the President of India Independence Federation, Shonan Branch, and (Dagahan), the president of Senang Branch, delivered greetings and the 30,000 attendants shouted, "Freedom or Death!", revealing their enthusiastic support for the independence of India. As the resolution of the rally, the chairman announced that the resistance strength and morals will be boosted in opposition to the British suppressions and resolved to fight to the bitter and for the independence of India, supporting the India National Congress Party. The rally was adjourned in eathusiastic manner .... The Indian soldiers who had capitulated to the Japanese volunteered to server as members of the police force and are doing good work in restoring peace and order. These Indians are permitted to act as police, revealing the perfect trust existing among the East Asiatic people.

Tokyo, English, 12/25/41

750,000 Indian residents in Malaya, in the main cities, firmly decided to fight until liberation of Indians. *Tokyo, Japanese, 8/11/42*

Oath of Allegiance

Shonan: Indian residents here will take their independence pledge in a mass meeting to be held next. Wednesday in the (Farror) Park. A procession, consisting of detachments of the Indian National Army, (of) volunteers and civilians, will start from the headquarters of the local branch of the Independence League of Free India and go to the Park, while speeches on the day and its significance will be made on this occasion (by) Indians in the Tamil language. This meeting will end after it passes a resolution (reaffirming) Indian determination to fight to their complete independence.

Tokyo, French, 1/25/44

Shonan: More than 30,000 Indians last evening reaffirmed their determination to exert their utmost for the attainment of their independence at a mass rally held at Farrar Park on the occasion of the 15th Indian Independence Day. Highlight of the meeting was the mammoth procession, consisting of a detachment of the Indian National Army, Women volunteers from the Rani Jhasi Regiment, military trainees, school children and others. An army brass band led the procession, which started from the premises of the Indian Independence League and proceeded to the mooting place.

Tokyo, English, 1/27/44

Shonan: Thousands of Indians flocked to the six extra centers, which were temporarily opened on Tuesday and Wednesday in various parts of the city, to take the Oath of Allegiance to the Netaji, Subhas Chandra Bose, and the Provisional Government of Azad Hind. These centers were opened in addition to the Branch of India Independence Leauge, is connection with the obsorvance of National Liberation Week, with a view to making it easier for them to take the oath near their place of residence. Though official figures of those who have taken the oath are not available yet, it is learned that the number tops the ten thousand mark.

Tokyo, English, 4/13/44

Women's Service

Firmly pledging their determination to cooperate with Japan's crusade to liberate Asiatic peoples from the Anglo-Saxon yoke, Indian women of the newly established Shonan Branch of the Indian Independence League sent a message to the Japan Woman's Association on March 28 on the occasion of the inaugural meeting of the branch office in Shonan.... A message of similar nature was also sent by Indian youth to Japan's young Men's Association on the same occasion.

Shonan: Malai and local Indonesian women, under the sponsorship of the paper "Fajar Asia", will hold a rally at the Shonan Kokaldo on March 6, Chikyuseta, or the birthday of Her Imperial Majesty the Empress of Japan, Lectures on the war of Greater East Asia and women's duty in the present wartime situation will be delivered by leading Malai women.

Tokyo, English, 3/2/44

Youth Movement

The Youth India, the organ of the Indian Youth Movement, made its first appearance in Shonan yesterday. The paper editorially declared, "we are confident we will maintain Mahatma Gandhi's spirit and we urge all Indians at 8.30 p.m. *Tokyo, Japanese, 9/2/42*

Shonan: The Malai Branch of the India Independence League, ever since its establishment last spring, has led the Independence Movement for 700,000 Indians residing in Malai as the influential body of the south and has continued to call reassuringly to the homeland Indians. To keep in accordance with the recent urgent situation in India in order to further strengthen the activities of the league, a general Shonan Movement has been decided upon to be carried out with Shonan volunteers such as the Prsident of the Shonan Indian Association (Kumaratini), and the manager of the Shonan Indian Newspaper, (Yaja Yanchi).

Tokyo, Japanese, 3/8/43

Shonan: The India Independence League headquarters, which has mobilized the Indians throughout the Greater East Asia sphere and is working towards concrete realization of their independence, comments.....that the appointment of Wavell, former Commander-in-Chief of the British forces in India, is but the revelation of the British plan to oppress the Indians who are becoming quite restless throughout the whole nation. *Tokyo, Japanense, 6/19/43*

Penang: Welcoming President Subhas Bose of the Indian Independence Movement Federation, the Indian National Convention of Penang was held on September 5 at the stadium. The gratitude and enthusiasm of Indian people in Penang, who for the first time welcomed their leader, reached to the climax..... *Tokyo, Japanese, 9/5/43*

Under the leadership of Subhas Chandra Bose, the Shonan Indian People's Rally to express felicitation on the Philippine Independence was elaborately staged at the Ala Park in Shonan.

Tokyo, Japanese, 10/18/43

The Central Headquarters of the Indian Independence Federation has decided to hold the All-Asia Indian people's Rally on October 25 and to start a gigantic movement for freedom and these instructions were sent to all branch associations throughout East Asia. This movement is to be carried with the objective of putting into full swing the resolution which is to be decided at the conference of representatives from all East Asia to be held on October 21 in Shonan. It is believed that, as a result of the above, the Indian Independence Movement will be further accelerated.

Tokyo, Japanense, 10/18/43

Shonan: The Indian Independence League All-East Asia Representatives Conference was convened at 10.30 at the Greater East Asia Theatre at Shonan. Indian representatives from Malai, Japan, Manchukuo, Thailand, French-Indo-China, Jawa, Boraeo, Sumatra, Burma, Hongkong, the Philippines, Colobes, Canton and other places throughtout entire East Asia, as well as staff members of the women's Corps of the Indian National Army attended. After the Indian national anthem was sung, President Subhas Chandra Bose delivered an important speech, lasting for about one hour, on the present condition of the Indian Independence movement and the world situation. Lastly he declared forcefully, "I shall announce the establishment of the provisional government in the meeting this afternoon." ..... In the afternoon meeting President Subhas Chandra Bose submitted the important bill for the establishment of a Free Indian Provisional Government. As all the respresentatives Subhas Chndra Bose as head of the Government has as its object, as a stronger unified organ for the Indian Independence Movement, the winning of independence... The structure of the provisional government will be as simple as possible and will consist of only five departments. The organisation will have, under the president, five departments, namely; The Military Affairs Department, The Financial Affairs Department, The Foreign Affairs Department, The Propaganda Department and the Women's Department. In addition there will be a small number of the minister without portfolio and government advisers who are Indians. The seat of the government will be in Burma, which is appropriate as the main base for the struggle against Britain.

Tokyo, Japanese, 7/5/43

Connection with Moslem League

Kuala Lumpur: The Moslem League of India in Malaya announced that it had dissolved itself to become merged with the Independence League of Malaya. The announcement was issued on August 21st and added that the act was approved by all the Indians of the Moslem League in all parts of the peninsula. The movement for the Independence of India, in Malaya will now be placed under one central control. *Tokyo, English, 6/25/42*

The spokesman of the Indian Independence League in Shonan, in a broadcast yesterday, made an impassioned appeal to Mr. Mohammed Ali Jinnah, leaders of the Moslem League in India, to rise again as a national leader at this crucial hour in India's struggle for independence. The.....Moslem League and the India....Moslem League of New Delhi the spokemans declared that there can only one be one resolution for any of the Indians who want the name and that resolution is to plunge themselves into the fight for Indian Independence.

Tokyo, English, 4/23/43

Shonan: "We must vow today to liberate India from the bonds with which her tyrants chained her," declared Abdul Aziz, leader of the East Asia Indian Muslims, in a message to his compatriots on the occasion of the birthday anniversary of Prophet Mohammed.....He said the participation of a Muslim detachment of the Indian National Army is yesterday's procession, as well as the face that thousands of Indians, irrespective of caste or creed, are mingling in mosques and eating the same food, are regarded as a sure indication the unity of all Indians is here. Pointing out that those who in any way try to bring discord among them would be branded traitors and tried as such, Aziz concluded, "Let us march unfaltering forward along the road of independence under the banner of the Provisional Government of Free India and sacrifice everything we have for the glory of our motherland."

Tokyo, English, 3/7/44

Shonan: The 23-day conference of Mohammadan priests of Menangkabo, for the purpose of furthering cooperation of Mohammedans in Sumatra with the Japanese Administration, was opened July 8 on the occasion of Ascension Day. The day's meeting, held at the Taishokan (Imperial Rescript Hall) was attened by 500 priests. The conference will formulate appropriate measures for furnishing collaboration among the populace in order to give impetus to the program for strengthening Sumatra's defenses, increasing food-stuff production and other self-sufficiency measures. Mohmmedans, not only in Menangkabo, but throughout Sumatra, will be requested to support the measures adopted at the conference. Much as expected to be accomplished at...., which is being held at the instance of the Menangkabo Mohammedans themselves.

Tokyo, Japanese, 7/10/44

Propaganda by Radio

Centered around the Malay Branch of India Independence Movement Federation, the Indian Independent Movement in Shonan and Malaya has doubly grown recently. The comrades of Independent Movement is Shonako will start a daily broadcast from Shonan Broadcasting Station to the people of their native land, India. It will be given daily from 10.30 p.m. (JCT) till 1.40 a.m. (JCT). Today, on the first day of the broadcasting schedule, Mr. Koshi Sei Manao, the propaganda chief of the Malaya Branch, will send the first voice, beginning with this, it is scheduled that very active broadcasting compaign to Indian will be carried out.

Tokyo, Japanese, 8/1/42

The headquarters of the Indian Independence League in East Asia, in Shonan, has begun radiocasting towards India for two hours, between 8.40 and 10.40 Indian standard time, every evening on the wave length of 25.3 meters. *Tokyo, English, 5/4/43*

Shonan Branch : Activities

The Indian Independence League Branch of Shonan, in the afternoon of September 9th, held a memorial service at the Nishi Hongwanji Temple in honour of the souls of the Imperial forces who have given their lives in the Malayan campaign. About 100 Japanese people concerned and a great number of the Indian people attended the srevice to offer their prayers of gratitude to the souls of the soldiers.

Tokyo, Japanese, 9/9/42

In Shonan city..... a branch office of the Indian Independence League was opened today. The opening ceremony was perform by General (Long Singh) who declared that....of the Indian soldiers have pledged to give their lives for their motherland. *Tokyo, English, 11/24/42*

Shonan: The Indian Mass Rally, in order to recall for Indians the notorious Amritsar massacre, was sponsored by the Shonan Branch of the Indian Independence League here Tuesday evening, which is the last day of the Indian Nation Week.

Shonan: The Shonan chapter of the Indian Independence League had a lecture at the GEA Theatre, Sunday, on the occasion of the third (Udnam Sing Azad) day. Films depicting the occasion were also shown at the theatre..... Events took place to commemorate the day set aside for (Udnam Singh Azad) who, on Time 13, 1940, assassinated Michael O'Dwyer, former Governor of Punjab, to avenge the Amritsar Massacre.

Tokyo, English, 6/14/43

Shonan—Today, on the commemoration day for the establishment of the Free Provisional Government of India, The Shonan Branch of the Indian Independence League sponsored a street parade, participated in by the National Army, Women's corps and general public.

Tokyo, Japanese, 2/21/44

Kuala Lumpur Branch : Activities

Kuala Lumpur Indian Independence League Branch starts sympathetic fast. *Tokyo, Japanese, 2/18/43*

Penang Branch : Activities

Penang: The local Indian community is greatly enthusiastic over the news of the inauguration of the Provisional Government of Free India. The spokeman of the Penang Branch of this Indian Independence League said that ever since Subhas Chandra Bose's announcedment in July, after his arrival in Shonan, that he was striving to establish such government, Indians all over East Asia were expecting such news. He added....It is the government which, under the leadership of Bose, will command confidence of Indians in the whole of East Asia. Meanwhile, a mass meeting to express the heartfelt enthusiam and pride in allegiance to the provisional government will be held here October 25.

Tokyo, English, 10/23/43

Penang: "Loyality to the Provisional Government of Azad Hind means increased responsibilites and a greater extent of coopartion and assistance with all Japanese authorities with whom the members come in contact." declared Dr. N.K. Menon, chairman of the Penang Indian Independence League, in an address at a ceremony of taking the oath of allegiance to the provisional government at the League's headquarters attended by the Indians of Penang Province. He revealed the Ceylonese in Penang, although numbering no more than 100, have already contributed $20,000 to the Netaji's fund. He emphasized that the war aims of Japan and the provisional government are exactly the same and complete liberation of India from bondage will not be possible without Japan's help. Similar ceremonies were held in Butterworth, Prai Bukit, Martajam, Nibong and Tebal.

Tokyo, English, 1/4/44

Ceylon Branch: Activities

Stockholm: At Ceylon Island an Independence Movement is growing. The Indian National Congress Party has resolved for Ceylon Island Independence.

Tokyo, Japanese, 12/25/42

Shonan: Arrangements are being made to organize a Ceylon Branch of the Indian Idependence's League, according to Perera, President of the Singhalese Association of Shonan, who issued a statement today.

Tokyo, 11/9/43

Shonan: A public meeting of Ceylonese residents here is scheduled to be held January 24, at the promises of the Indian Independence League, under chairmanship of Pillai, member in charge of the Ceylon Department of the League. Full attendance of both men and women is expected. Meanwhile Pillai and other Ceylonese leaders throughout Malai have issued a press statement urging their community to take full advantage of the opportunity afforded by the opening of the Cylon Department within the Fabric of the leagues and particularly on calling Ceylonese youths to shoulder the task with other Indians, for the common freedom of India and Ceylon are destined to form together an imprtant entity in the new order of Asians. Culture, language, religion and other environments bind them together to such an extent that no right-thinking Ceylonese can allow himself to be led astray by the cursed British divide-and-rule policy. It is therefore up to us Ceylonese in East Asia to cooperate sincerely with the movement by subscribing fully to the total mobilization demanded of us.

Tokyo, English, 1/22/44

Shonan: The Ceylon Department of the Indian Independence League, this evening, held a mass meeting in the plaza in front of the Independence League Building to encourage the Ceylon islanders in the fight for independence. (Sawvan) Anuttu, acting chief of the Penang Chapter of the Independence League, and several Ceylon young men who recently graduated from the Azad School were vehement speakers at the mass meeting. *Tokyo, English, 3/25/44*

The fervor of Ceylonese youth who are trying to escape from British Bondage had deeply impressed Bose, the head of the Provisional Government of Free India. A Ceylonese Branch of the Federation for Indian Independence was recently established and its members are new engaged in anti-British activities. The Ceylon Branch, celebrating the advance of the Indian National Army in the motherland, hold a mass meeting at 6.00 p.m., March 25, in the open square before Independence Hall for the purpose of appealing to those unify the young Ceylonese who have escaped from Ceylon. From far Penang came (Soavanamut), representing the leaders of the Penang Branch of the Independence Federation.

Tokyo, Japanese, 3/26/44

Penang: "Ceylonese in Malai fully realize that without the independence of Indian there can be no free Ceylon," declared (Yo Yoh

Do) Alawala, Secretary of the Ceylon Department, at the Indian Independence League Headquarters in an interview here today. Alawala, at present on tour of Malai, stated, upon his return to Shonan after visiting Thailand and Burma, he will hold an all-Malaian conference of Ceylonese leaders. He added he found great enthusaism among the Ceylon community at various Malaian centers he visited. *Tokyo, English, 5/26/44*

Andaman Islands Branch: Activities

Among Indian Nationals here, the Independence Movement of the home country is very strong. 7,000 compatriots are united under the leadership of the esteemed Dr. (Wong Shun) who was formely (a certain captain). They are building huge rafts on which they intend to cross the Indian Ocean to join in the fight for Indian Independence.

Tokyo, English, 9/30/42

Shonan: 200,000 Indians in the Andaman group are now singing their way to the independence of India. "The Independence of India" is the name of a song widely sung among Indian partiots today. It was once prevalent among the prisoners in the famous Andaman Prison and soon all the Indians were singing it throughout the Andaman Islands. Later the British authorities censored the major part of this patriotic song for obvious reasons, but now, under the Japanese protection, they are free to sing this song again to their hearts contents.

Tokyo, English, 10/1/43

Welfare Association

The Indian Independence League in Shonan at this time established a welfare Association and will engage in welfare work of the Indians residing in Shonan. Up to now, the Indian Independence League had heen taking charge of the welfare problems of the Indian residing in Shonan. However, as the Independence League become in the most part of political and military organ of the anti-British struggle, it's activities increased. Therefore, an Indian Welfare Association has been established, with Indian residents as members, which will be active in social work, employment and....

Tokyo, Japanese, 4/14/44

Shonan: Besides contributing $4,000 to the Patients' Fund, a party of leading Indian ladies here paid a visit to the Indain National Army Hospital to comfort recuperating soldiers. The party, headed by Mrs. K.R. Assomull, entertaind the soldiers with food, music, songs and dances.

Tokyo, English, 5/1/44

Shonan: The Indians Destitute Home was officially opened in the city with President (Ana F. Pelai).... of the Indian Welfare Association as its first director. The some is to take care of sick and destitute Indians and will be supported by the local Indian community.

Tokyo, English, 7/12/44

Study of Japanese

The Fire Insurance Bureau of Shonan had decided to grant to members of the Indian Independence League desiring to study Japanese, German, and Italian...... *Tokyo, Japanese, 4/21/43*

In order to encourage the Indians residing in Shonan whose ideal has been realized in the course of the war to study foreign languages, particularly Japanese, the Bureau of Welfare of the Special Administration of Shonan decided to loan money to these Indians. The generous action on the part of the Japanese authorities has pofoundly moved the population. *Tokyo, Franch, 4/21/43*

Colonial Settlement

Shonan: The Bintan island settlement scheme for Shonan Malaians and Indians has received the whole-hearted support of the two communities. The first group of settler formers made all necessary arrangements to leave for their new homes. Though the first batch of colonists was limited to 100 families, over 150 families are on the waiting list with some more applications pouring in. The settlers will take up farming in the island to attain food self-sufficiency.

Tokyo, English, 5/10/44

Shonan: The agricultural settlement for Indian families at Bintan Island, in the southern part of Shonan, is now ready to receive pioneers, according to a statement issued by the Indian Welfare Association. The settlement, which was sponsored by government auhorities here, among other advantages offers each settler and family four acres of land for foodstuff cultivation, and quarters, as well as a subsidy of 300 yen. The statement added that the official of the association who was sent to study conditions on the island is of the opinion the aspect is favorable and soil extremely fertile. *Tokyo, English, 6/7/44*

Indian National School

Shonan: Catering to children as well as adults, an Indian National School, under the auspices of the local Indian Independence League, has been opened here. The object of the school is to impart education in Indian culture, national spirit, Hindustani music, handicraft, gardening and other subjects. *Tokyo, English, 11/16/43*

Shonan: The graduation ceremony of an entire batch of cadets who have undergone training for posts of administrators in the liberated areas of India was held last evening in the presence of Subhas Chandra Bose and high ranking officers of the Indian National Army as well as members of the Provisional Government of Free India. Presenting certificates to the graduates, Bose exhorted them to be prepared to surmount all difficulties even at the risk of their lives in carrying out administrative and reconstruction duties in the areas of India that would soon be liberated from British occupation. The graduates completed the minimum standard of military training as well as administration and reconstruction courses.

Tokyo, English, 12/3/43

The patriotic spirit which the Shonan Indian National School inspired has become evident (of) many Indian homes in Shonan. The school has provided lessons in Indian history, cultural subjects, and specially in study of Hindustani. The school has been established to teach young children born in Shonan who know nothing of the suffering of their countrymen in their motherland. *Tokyo, English, 1/7/44*

Japanese Cooperation

On the occasion of the fall of Singapore, the Finance Ministry has added 76 Indians who are making sincere efforts for the Independence of India to the rest of those Pro-Japanese Indians who are exempted from the application of the freezing order.

Tokyo, English, 2/17/42

Shonan: "A new era has dawned in East Asia when age-long British imperialism will ultimately be wiped out of India and the long cherised independence will be acheived by Indians," declared Prime Minister General Hideki Tojo in his congratulatory message sent to the Indian mass rally held in Shonaan today. "With the Outbreak of the GEA War, all the Indian leaders rose up and have spiritually completed preparations for Independence.... Japan has not frequently declared its desire that India for Indians wi!l be established as early as possible. In other words, Japan is firmly determined to do everything in its power to help Indian attain the long-looked for freedom.....I am firmly convinced that it is the only way for the Indian to achieve their independence to cooperate with the Tripartite powers in their fight against their common enemy by taking advantage of this God-given opportunity," Prime Minister Tojo concluded.

Tokyo, English, 7/4/43

Contributions

Panang: ....The contribution by the people have already reached as high as $ 2,000,000 even immediately after the convention (Indian National Convention at Penang, Sept, 5th) was opened.

Tokyo, Japanese, 9/5/43

Malacca: Contributions to the Indian Independence League Fund have already passed the 300,000 yen mark, it was revealed by the secretary of the local branch. Including 48,000 yen collected during the visit of Subhas Chandra Bose of Malacca, the total now amounts to 364,000 yen. The general secretary pointed out that Malacca's full quote of 1,250,000 will be attainable soon. The largest contribution to the League Fund was made by Chettiar community, which contributed 269,000 yen, followed by Bombay merchants with 30,00 yen.

Tokyo, English, 10/9/43

Penang: "The response in men, money and material of the Indian community all over Malai to the appeal of Subhas Chandra Bose has been truly remarkable," declared Dr. N.K. Menon, chairman of the local Indian Independence League, in an interview on his return from a tour of Malai.

Tokyo, English, 10/15/43

Shohan: "The 2,000,00 Indian soldiers mobilized by the British will to be our side when we begin our historic march to Delhi. They will join us with all the supplies taken by the British," declared S.C. Bose, Commander-in-Chief of the Indian National Army, in his stirring addressed before a mass meeting of more than 20,000 Indians who jammed (name) park last night to congratulate the Filipions on achieving their independence. He said "Today we meet for the purpose of congratulating the Filipines on having become independent." .....Stressing that the Indians cannot attain everlasting independence with the sacrifices of their allies and friends, Bose declared, "We must fight for it ourselves, shed our own blood. If we (are) a small people, there we could get freedom at the hands of others, but we are 380 million people and, if it will be with our own sacrifices, we shall become a free people. Our fight will begin this year."....expressed confidence that a nationwide revolution will break out in India to spell doom for India's British domination.....At the conclusion of the meeting the garlands presented to Bose were auctioned, fetching over 125,000 yen. The donations in the form of cash as well as jewellary, by hundreds of Indians present, were handed to Subhas Chandra Bose.

Manila, English, 10/16/43

Firm determination and growing enthusiasm of the Indian residents in Malai to devote themselves to the cause of India's Independence is seen in the even-incresing amount of donations pouring in everyday. In the two mass rallies held in Shonan on Monday and Tuesday, a total of 20,000,000 yen was donated in cash and good to the Provisional Government of Free India. *Tokyo, English, 10/27/43*

It is reported from Shonan that within 24 hours after Netaji Subhas Chandra Bose, head of the state of the Provisional Government of Free India, had asked for $ 100,000,000 as a first installment to carry on the war against the Anglo-Americans, $13,500,000 were subscribed by the Indians in Shonan. *Saigon, English, 10/27/43*

Singapore: A "Bomb the British out of India Fund" was launched here last evening by Appavar Yellappa, chairman of the local branch of the Indian Independence League. Within a few minutes of the inauguration ceremoney, substanial sums were received from leading Indians who have promised full support. Meanwhile, Indian officers workers themselves took the initial start in collections and at the same time promised to give a portion of their salaries, monthly, for contributions towards the fund.

Tokyo, English, 2/15/44

Shonan: The Indian Press Association here has contributed the sum of 2,150 yen to the Imperial Nippen Army War Wounded Fund. This amount represents the proceeds of a dramatic performance staged here last Monday under the auspices of the association. The director of the association declared the motion is only a small token of Indian gratitude for the gallant part of the Nippon forces in conjuction with the Indian National Army for the cause of motherland emancipation.

Tokyo, English, 2/18/44

Shonan: A purse of 6,500 yen was presented to members of the Rani of Jhansi Regiment by the Indian citizens of Shonan at a women's mass meeting held Saturday in connection with National Liberation Week. Prior to the meeting the Indian women soldiers in their smart khaki uniforms marched from their camp to the league grounds, accompanied by an Indian National Army Band. *Tokyo, English, 4/10/44*

Johore Bahru: More than $200,000 in case, as well as a fresh batch (sic) of men and women volunteers for active service, were results of a vigorous campaign for the total mobilization of Indian men and material resources conducted during National Liberation Week celebration here. According to an official of the Johore Indian Independence League, the campaign will be kept up until all available resources of the Indians here have been mobilized to carry of India's war of Independence. The official disclosed that the largest contribution received were from Butupahat and Muar Districts.

Tokyo, English, 4/18/44

More than $1,000 was netted by a dramatic play staged here last Saturday at the ..... theater, under the auspices of the local branch of the Indian Independence League. This amount has been donated to the Indian National Army wounded Officers and Soldiers Fund.....

Manila, English, 5/12/44

Free India Provisional Government

It appears that the Independence Movement is to be carried on under the unified supervision of the Provisional Government, which is newly established, based under Mr. Bose's supporters. It is thought quite natural as soon as this movement for independence.....what Mr. Bose calls (routine)....It will naturally be recognized internationally as being carried on by the beligerent (party) and we think its present from such as the Indian Independence League would be inadequate.

Tokyo, English, 7/8/43

Shonan: Beginning with the materialization of independence for Burma and the Philippines, the objective of the GEA war of liberation of the various nations in Asia is steadily being realized.....As all preparation to obtain independence for India has been completed, a Provisional Indian Government will be established, it has been decided, on October 21 at Shonan and Chandra Bose will head this government. At the same time it is also expected of the new government to declar war upon America and Britain.

Tokyo, Japanese, 10/19/43

.....Issued the following statement concerning the establishment of the provisional government: "The provisional government has prepared its own individual qualities and has a truly independent character. The Free Indian Provisional Government is simply a wartime government. It is also an exile government separated from the mother country because of the war. It has just the one mission of (wd) the enemy camp and to liberate the people of (members). (Its organization) will be further strengthened (hereafter).... Under the command of Subhas Chandra Bose, Commander-in-Chief of the Indian National Army, this revolutionary army will....of New Delhi. 'On to Delhi! On to Delhi!'....The free Indian Provisional Government (has received) the aid and sympathy of the National Government of China, the Manchukuoan Empire, Thailand, and Philippine Republic which was newly born. In the same manner, Germany and Italy announced the sympathy and aid would be given when the Indian Independence began in East Asia. Japan has stated at every opportunity that politically and economically and also militarily she would not begrudge aid to India.... Subhas Chandra Bose today assumed office as President of the Provisional Government of Free India and took the following oath of office, 'I, Subhas Chandra Bose, in the name of God here vow to liberate Indian and the 380,000,000 people of India from their fetters....' When the objective of driving British power out of India is completely achieved, the provisional government will transfer all to the Indian Government which should be established in India in accordance with the total will of all Indians.....President S.C. Bose assumed office as Minister of Military Affairs and Minister of Foreign Affairs (Ameel) Chandra Chatterji, Finance Minister, S.A. Ayar, Publicity Minister, Madame Slakshmi, Women's Minister." *Tokyo, Japanese, 10/21/43*

Shonan: Lineup of the Provisional Government of Free India....head of state, Prime Minister and concurrently Miniter for War and Foreign Affairs, Subhas Chandra Bose; Publicity Minister, S. A. Ayer; Finance, Lt. Col. A.C. Chatteriji; Woman's Organizations, Swami Nathan Lakshami; Secretary with Ministerial Rank, A. M. Sahay, Supreme Adviser, Rash Behari Bose. Other advisers are—Karim Gani, Debanth Das, D.M. Khan, Ayellappa, J. Thivy and Sardar Ishar Singh. Legal Adviser is A.N. Sarkar, whil representatives of the armed forces includes Lt. Colonels Aziz Ahmed, N.S. Bhagat, J.K. Bhonsle, Gulzara Singh, M.Z. Kiani, A.D. Loganadan, Ehsan Quadir and Shah Nawaz. *Tokyo, English, 10/21/43*

Shonan: The Headquarter of the Provisional Government of Free India announced today that the first meeting of the Council of Ministers of the Provisional Government of Free India was held last night at the official residence of the head of the government, Mr. Subhas Chandra Bose, who presided. The first item on the agenda was a resolution paying homage to all those who are carrying on the heroic struggle against the British inside India, undergoing tremendous sufferings and making tremendous sacrifices, and to all those who have laid down their lives for the cause of India's freedom. The council of Minister also discussed the political and economic situation in India. *Tokyo, English, 10/23/43*

Shonan: At a mass rally of Indians held here this evening, the first since Subhas Chandra Bose returned from Tokyo, a resolution was passed expressing gratitude to the Japanese Government for its promise to cede the Andaman and Nicobar Islands to the Provisional Government of Free India and congratulating Bose on his successful completion of the recent tour of East Asia. This meeting also expresses its profound joy at the decision of the Government of Japan to hand over the Andaman and Nicobar Islands to the Provisional Government of Free India as announced by His Excellency, Premier Gen. Tojo, at the Assembly of GEA Nations, and offers its grateful thanks to the Government of Nippon for the same. The meeting reiterates its firm resolve to go on fighting shoulder to shoulder with Nippon and other allies under the leadership of Subhas Chandra Bose till our common victory is achieved and India is completely liberate from the British Yoke."

Shonan: The Provisional Government of Free India announced yesterday that it approved two systems in its cabinet meeting held on December 9, the (compensation) system and the (wd) system. Under the (wd) system, (wd) will be given to the members of the family and to (bereaved members) in the event of death in action. It will be applicable first to the Indians residing on the islands. *Tokyo, Japanese, 12/11/43*

Recognition of Government

The recognition of the Provisional Government of India by Imperial Japan is entirely different in significance from the customary recognition in accordance to the international law. That is to say, the Provisional Government of India is not a government of an indepentent nation, it is a government established primarily as an organ through which independence may be obtained. The Imperial Government of Japan recognition the Provisional government so that independence may be achieved as quickly and smoothly as possible. Therefore, diplomatic relationship ordinarily maintained among independent nations will not be made, i.e. exchange of diplomatic officials will not take place but close relationship will be maintained through the eexisting outpost organs on the spot. Following are the points that bear notice in regard to the recognition of the provisional government: This recognition declares now to the world that the Government of Japan considers her aid to India in the Movement of Independence is one of her national policies. Therefore, Imperial Japan will not stint in the least in giving her aid to India until the final glory of independence shines over India and her people. Through the request of the Provisional Government of India our government immediately reported her recognition of the India Government of friendly nations Germany, Italy, Manchukuo and the National Government of China at Nanking. Manchukuo has already declared that its government will not limit itself in giving all the aid possible to the Provisional Government of India.

Tokyo, Japanese, 10/23/43

Shonan: Subhas Chandra Bose meeting, Head of the Provisional Government of India, declared today that a notification from the Burmese Goveרment of the recognition of the Indian Provisional Government arrived.

Tokyo, Japanese, 10/24/43

The Indian people's mass meeting,commemorating the establishment of the free Indian Provisional Government, was held Octobor 4 in Shonan... Bose arrived at the place of the meeting where he was not by the chief of the provisional government. Following the review of the National Army, flag railsing ceremony of the national flag was held in a very impressive manner.Then, as Bose stood up before the ceremony grounds, a (service award) was put on the president's neck by the Indian people.... In this way the announcement of felicitation wires from Manchukuo, Thailand and other natons was made. *Tokyo, Japanese,10/24/43*

Nanking: The National Government of China today, on Monday, formally announced the recognition of the Provisional Government of Free India. *Tokyo, Japanese.11/1/43*

The Provisional Goverment of Free India today formally was recognized by the Fascis Republic of Italy, which decided to recognize the provisional government November 2 and instructed Col. Omero Principini, who is incharge of Italian interests in Japan, to formally inform the provisional government. It has been recognized by 6 nations, including Japan, China, Burma, Manchukuo and the Philippines.

Tokyo,English, 11/9/43

Shonan: Heartily reciprocating the message of felicitations from the Irish Republic, Subhas Cnandra Bose head of the Provisional Government of Free India, in a press statement today said, " I herewith sound a word of cheer in reply—our cause in just. Our demands are out birthright. We are prepared to pay the price. We shall therefore triumph. Freedom will come." Declaring it has given him the greatest pleasure to receive the message, Bose stated, "Of all the freedom movement we Indians have studied closely. and from which we have derived inspiration, there is perhaps none that can equal the Irish struggle for independence. .... the nation has had the some oppressors and exploiters as ourselves. It has had the same experience of ruthlessness, brutality and hypocrisy as we have."

Tokyo, English, 12/2/43

Declaration of War

Shonan: The Government of Free India decided to declare war on British and the U.S.A. according to a communique issued this morning.

The decision was reached at a meeting hold yesterday by the Council of Minister of the Provisional Government of Azad Hind, which met at the official residence of Subhas Chandra Bose. *Tokyo, English, 10/23/43*

Grant of Territory of Japan

Bose's message to the 3,000,000 Indians in East Asia and to the 350,000,000 of India.... Bose told Domei, in as exclusive interview, "For the Indians, the return of the Andamans represents of the first territory to be liberated from the British Yoke. By acquisition of this territory the provisional government has now become a national entity, in fact as well as in name." Liberation of the Andamans has a "Symbolic significance", he said, because the Andamans always were used by the British as a prison for political prisoners. "Like the Bastille in Paris, which was liberated first in the French Revolution, the setting free of the political prisoners on the Andamans, where our patriots suffered much, is the first to be liberated in the Indians fights for independence. Part by part the Indian territory will be liberated but it is always the first plot of land that holds the most signficance.".....The return of the Andamans, he added, will have an "emotional moral appeal to the Indian people in the fact the prison house of India has been liberated." *Tokyo, English, 11/7/43*

The declartion of Premier Tojo to the effect that the Andaman and Nicobar Islands will soon be returned to the Provisional Government of Free India has deeply impressed the 18,000 Indians who comprise the majority of the local inhabitants of the Andaman Islands and is further deepening their attitude toward the Japanese Government. According to a report from a naval correspondent in the Andamans, this reaction has first of the all manifested in the first national defence contribution in the Andamans. Then, too, as a result of a meeting hold in the office of the Military Administration on November 12, the Andaman branch of the Indian Independence League resolutely carried out a reorganization of the executive staff and decided to establish a volunteer army under the direction of the branch director. A committee for the establishment of the army has already been formed and it has been decided to select a total of an undisclosed number of men, 20 to 40 years of age, from the villages in the island.... *Tokyo, Japanese, 11/14/43*

Shonan: When the islands of Andaman and Nicobar became territory of the Free Indian National Government, in accordance with the declaration made by our Preimer Tojo at the recent CEA conference, it was decided to change the names of the two islands. Andaman Island will be called (Karido) or (wd) island and the Nicobar Island will be called (Suwaya) or (wd) island[3]. *Tokyo, Japanese, 11/26/43*

Shonan: At a mass rally of Indians held here this evening, the first since Subhas Chandra Bose returned from Tokyo, resolution was passed expressing gratitude to the Japanese Governemnt for its promise to cede the Andaman and Nicobar Island to the Provisional Government of Free India and congratulating Bose on his successful tour of East Asia, as well as reiterating determination to fight till victory is attained.

Tokyo, English, 12/2/43

The Tokyo Branch of the Indian Independence League held a (wd) meeting in Tokyo on December 2 and ..... in regard to the transfer of the two island of Andaman and Nicobar to the Free Indian Provisional Government by Japan. The Indian Independence League (Council) in Japan decided to have its headquarters in Tokyo and establish branches in Yokohama, Kobe and Osaka for the purpose of.....

Tokyo, Japanese, 12/2/43

Members of Indian Independence League of Japan met here this afternoon and adopted a resolution expressing profound gratitude for Premier Tojo's promise to transfer the Andaman and Nicobar Islands to the Provisional Government of Free India. They also despatched telegrams to Subhas Chandra Bose, Head of the Provisional Government of Azad Hind, and Premier Tojo, expressing their determination and appreciation.

Tokyo, English,12/2/43

Immediately after Bose moved his government to Burma. He made a radio broadcast address to the people of India , kaking clear his visit to the Andaman Islands, and announced the appointment of Lt. Col. Regananadan as Chairman of the Administrative Preparation Committee for the Andaman Islands. *Tokyo, Japanese, 1/10/44*

Subhas Chandra Bose recently appointed (Chiri) (Neme) as (Governor) of the Andaman Islands. He was in Germany and has been heading the Independence Committee.

Tokyo, Japanese, 1/4/44

The Free Indian Government, under the leadership of Subhas Chandra Bose, has completed all the preparation for the attack on India... with regards to Andaman Islands, Chandra Bose declared that the Japanese Government has promised that these islands will be returned to the Indian Government at the close of hostilities. *Tokyo, English, 11/9/43*

---

3. They were named as Saheed and Swaraj

Shonan: Lt. Col. A.D. Loganadan, who was recently appointed chief commissioner of Andaman and Nicobar Islands left here today for Port Blair, Andaman, to take up his post(sic). The Andaman and Nicobar Islands are scheduled to be transferred soon to the Provisional Government of free India by the Japanese Government. *Tokyo, Japanese, 2/21/44*

Love to Burma

Free India Provisional Government ... has now moved into Burma.

Tokyo, Japanese, 1/20/44

National Holidays

Shonan : Indians all over East Asia will observe Indian Independence Day, January 26, with mass meetings at which speeches will be given stressing the significance of the day. Resolutions, pledging the allout effort of the 3,000,000 Indians of East Asia for the attainment of Indian's emancipation are expected to be passed. It was at Johore on January 26, 1939 that the Congress, at the proposal of Pandit Nehru, supported by Subhas Chandra Bose, decided to take the uncompromising stand of complete independence and not a dominion status within the British Empire. Since then, Indians have renewed this pledge on January 26 each year. This year's observance will have the added significance not only in East Asia but also in India, that Indians now have a free government and their own army in their fight to realize that pledge.

Saigon, English, 1/23/44

Shonan Domei : Upon the passing of Madme Kasturibai, Mrs. Gandhi, the Free India Provisional Government has decided to observe March 1 as National (Affection) Day to commemorate eternally the seventy year old life of the Madame. *Tokyo, Japanese, 2/24/44*

Shonan: The 109th anniversary of the birth of Sri Rama Krishna, famous Indian Saint will be observed at Rama Krishna Mission tomorrow. Prayers will be offered and a public meeting held, at which A.C. Chatterji, Minister of the Provisional Government of Free India, will deliver a speach on the life and work of Rama Krishna. *Tokyo, English, 2/26/44*

Indian Liberation week began on April 6 in Shonan. Almost every day student parades and victory prayers are being held. The joy of the Indians was never as great as when the National Army recently invaded the homeland. The Azad Hind, "a newspapar published by the Independence League in Shonan, sold but every issue... In view of the strong interest of the Indians in Japan, the Independence League had M.R. (Naizu), member of the Shonan Propagarda and Information

Committee, translate Professor Kooya Nakamura's "History of Japan" into Tamil. His book sold out immediately. In the streets, the marching of the Indian women's regiment, which is in training is attracting more and more attention. It is the custom of the Chinese and Malayans to bless these woman. These people have shown sincere cooperation.

Tokyo, Japanese, 4/9/44

Penang: One of the most impressive procession in Penang took place yesterday when more than 6,000 local Indians, led by Doctor M.K. Menon, chairman of the Penang Chapter of the Indian Independence League, participated in a march along Penang's principal streets in commemoration of Indian Liberation week. Headed by Menon and members of the local Indian Independence League Committee, the procession, which was about two miles long was participated in by members of the civil volunteers, the Indian National Army and Indian women. *Tokyo, English, 4/11/4*

Shonan: During National Liberation week, celebrated by all Indians in East Asia, the Indians here did not forgot to comfort the wounded Japanese and Indian soldiers who had played a great part in the fight for India's liberation. A group of Indian school children and women visited the hospitals with their (wd) entertainment. The patients enjoyed the children's songs, dances and concerts besides the cakes .. cookies showered upon them..... *Tokyo, English, 4/11/4*

Shonan: The Provisional Government of Azad Hind Day, which falls on April 21, will be observed by the Indians here and all over East Asia. The celebration this month is expected to attract special public attention, in view of the tremendous successes achieved by the Azad Hind Fauj and its press Association here will sponsor special cinemas and lecture meetings in which brief speeches will be made by prominent Indians.

Tokyo, English, 4/19/4

Shonan: The Indians here, in conjunction with their compatriots (wd) East Asia, paid tribute today to the memory of the heroic sepoys who gave their lives 87 years ago in India's first war of independence. The Indian national tricolor and rising sun flag flew side by side at every Indian home. Thousands packed the Indian places of worship early in the morning to pray for the reponse of the gallant sepoys and for te success of the Indian National Army. A two mile long procession through the principal streets of the city highlighted the day's proceedings. Officers and men of the Indian National Army, woman of the Rani of Jhansi Regiment, looking trim and soldierly, school children and others marched jauntily through the city to the municipal square, where a mass meeting was held. Speaking to some (80,000) gathered there, Thivy, newly appointed Vice-President of the rear headquarters of the Provisional Government of Azad Hind, paid a glowing tribute to the memory of tens of thousands of sepoys who died in 1857 for emancipation of their motherland. Calling upon all those present here to emulate their noble example and sacrifice all for the independence drive launched by the Netaji, he assured them success was bound to be theirs. Amid enthusiastic scenes, the gathering unanimously resolved to carry on the fight for Indian independence under the leadership or the Netaji to and at the same time vowed to avenge the deaths of the sepoys who fell in 1857 and other martyrs whom the British have killed during the intervening years. *Tokyo, English, 5/10/44*

Shonan: Momories of India's first war of independence, and the in human treatment meted out to the unfortunate Indian nationalists ever since then, are today goading the 3,800,000 Indians all over East Asia to make greater sacrifices to wrest their independence from British hands, competent Indian circles here stated today. May 10 has been a red letter day to all Indians ever since 1857, when J.H. Mangal Panday fired the first shot and unleashed the countrywide revolution which has, till today, never been suppressed despite British boasts to the contrary.

Tokyo, English, 5/10/44

Shonan: Observance by the Provisional Government of Azad Hind Day here by the Indians today was marked by grim determination to carry on the present struggle for successful liberation of their motherland and by their firm resolve to sacrifice their all in that noble cause. The Indian national tricolor flew side by side with the Rising Sun flag from every Indian house while special prayers were offered in all places of worship by the Indians for complete victory of the Indian National Army and its allies and for the repose of the souls of those gallant men who have fallen for this cause on the battle fields of Burma and India. Glowing tributes to the war dead and to the valour of those fighting now on Indian soil were paid at mass meetings held in four centers of this city. The special feature of this day's observances was taking on the oath of allegiance to their provisional government by thousands of Indians here.

Tokyo, English, 5/21/44

Shonan: Starting Netaji week, Indian National Army met at barracks, residents paraded, held mass rally unfurled flags, prayed and broadcast. Throughout the week the Indian Tri-coloured flag will be unfurled alongside the Rising Sun. *Tokyo, English, 7/4/44*

National Songs

Shonan: National songs portraying the true martial spirit of the sons and daughters of India today, are enjoying immense popularity among Indians throughout Malai. Soldiers of the Indian National Army sing stirring verses during their gruelling marches, while volunteers sing..... on parade and even little Indian boys and girls popular airs in praise of the glory of their motherland and the cause for which their fathers and mothers, brothers and sisters are now fighting. Through the medium of Indian songs, especially Hindustani patriotic marches, national consciousness and a burning desire to win freedom has been born in the hearts of every Indian, young and old.

Tokyo, English, 11/30/43

Awards

The Provisional Government of India, at this year's first cabinet meeting, decided upon complete plans for awarding medals and orders and for providing annuities to officers and men after the termination of India's war of Independence. The plans published on Tuesday are as follows: After the termination of the war, all officers and men living will be conferred the order of the war of Independence, and in case they are killed they will be honored with order of the (Martyr). Moreover they will be conferred the order of the Indian Knight, the order of the Great Hero, and the order of the Battlefield leader together with their annuities in recognition of their respective merits. The bereaved families of the war dead will be provided with subsidies. Wounded soldiers will be conferred annuities and will be given first consideration for official posts. Privates will be specially accorded 1,000 0r 500 rupees or a plot of ground worth 500 rupees.

Tokyo, Japanese, 1/5/44

Ever since Subhas Chandra Bose appeared in GEA, India's Movement for Independence has become more active. The India Independence Headquarters issued a declaration to the effect that the Indian Independence League has formed an Indian National Army for Independence. The Indian National Army is composed of several thousands and in undergoing intense training day and night. This army makes no distinction of religion and classes.

Tokyo, Japanese, 7/8/44

Shonan: The Indian National Army was reviewed by Chandra Bose and by Tojo. Bose first stood up and expressed his gratitude that they are to fight for independence, then the first review was held. The review ended after 20 minutes. Tojo then left the stand with Bose. Bose on July...

declared that he would not stop fighting until the Indian National Army marches into New Delhi and independence is attained.

The organization of the Indian National Army is viewed in Tokyo and other Asiatic political circles as a momentous step toward the long-desired goal of India's independence. .....This Indian National Army, unlike the Indian forces organized under the British is an independent Indian army organized and led by the Indians themselves. The officers and men of this army are all ardent young Indian patriots ready to shed their blood in this (life or death) struggle... The members ... of superior arms are undergoing training daily and have already made much progress in the mechanical line. *Tokyo, English, 7/8/43*

While the Movement for Indian Independence in the hand of the Indians themselves is progressing in the lands of East Asia, the reconstruction of the Indian Independence League has resulted in the rapid development of the Indian Voluntary National Militia, which created its nuclei in May of last year in various parts of Malaysia and East Asia. This Indian militia, armed with excellent modern arms, has already reached a stage of perfect technical discipline, following the closing of the great..... on July 5 reviewed the Indian Voluntary National Militia, which is a dependency of the league. *Tokyo, Italian, 7/8/43*

The headquarters of the Indian Independence League, at 3:00 O'clock, Thursday afternoon, issued the following communique regarding the organization of the Indian National Army: To fight for complete freedom from British rule in India, the Indian Independence League has organised a National Army to be know as Azad Hind Fauj or the Indian National Army. The aim of this newly organized army is to drive out the British from India and to create an India for the Indians. *Tokyo, English, 7/9/43*

....One of these great events of this week was the official debut of the Indian National Army that took place on Thursday. You had better put it down in your notebook. From now on, Indian National Army means this is a powerful and magnificent army of the Indian volunteers who will fight actually fight for the independence of India. They are formidably equipped with all modern weapons. They are fully trained to use these weapons effectively. The organization of this army started in April, last year. It was read for action in September of the same year. Last Monday a part of this army assembled in a large force for the first time in public for a military review in the city of Shonan. All the customs and daily routine of this army are conducted in accordance with the custom of the Indian people, all the drills being conducted in their own language. It is the Indian own army. It in eager to throw itself into battle for India's independence.

Tokyo, English, 7/9/43

On Friday, the Indian Independence League at Shonan began to accept applications of Inidan volunteers for the Indian National Army. More than 2,500 Indian youths offered for enlistment on Friday. Next day large crowds came for enlistment. Chandra Bose came to supervise things and made a vigorous speech to the Indian youths.

Tokyo, Hindustani, 7/18/43

Johore Bahru: An additional batch of 75 volunteers left here for the Indian National Army training camp in Shonan yesterday, to undergo military training. The group was seen off by many friends and relatives, as well as officials of the local chapter of the Indian Independence League.

Tokyo, English, 1/17/44

Kuala Lumpur: Eager youths from all stations of life have already enlisted at the recruiting office here in response to an ... announcement that a fresh batch of volunteers is required for the Azad Hind Fauj center. Judging from the number registered since yesterday, the requirement quota is expected to be filled within the next few days.

Tokyo, English, 2/7/44

Outside Volunteers

Shonan: A large nunber of Indian volunteers have already arrived in Shonan from Thailand and Canton in order to join the Indian National Army, organized under the leadership of Mr. Subhas Chandra Bose.

Tokyo, English, 7/9/43

A batch of Indian volunteers from Sumatra are on their way to Shonan to join the Indian National Army. A second batch of volunteers from Sumatra will also be dispatched shortly. A large contingent of Indian youths are at present being given military training at severnal centers in Sumatra, prior to being sent to Shonan. *Tokyo, French, 10/21/43*

Shonan: The third batch of Indian recruits from Borneo arrived here, enroute for one of the Indian National Army training camps somewhere in Malai. Looking chearful and healthy, three recruits are representatives of many Indian races, the prominent among them being Sikhs. The leader of the group is a 6-footer, Niranpa Singh Gill, who stated the Indian living in Borneo are united with the common purpose of freeing their motherland. It is revealed that besides volunteering for the Indian National Army, the Borneo Indians are also contributing substantial sums for their country's cause. *Tokyo, English, 1/13/44*

Training Schools

Shonan: In the presence of Mr. Subhas Chandra Bose, President of the Indian Independence League, the first graduation ceremony of the famous school of the Indian National Army officers was held on Tuesday. Those graduating Indian officers will be immediately commissioned to the Service. *Tokyo, English, 7/21/43*

Shonan: In view of the daily increasing applicants for joining the Indian National Army, the headquarters of the Indian Independence League has decided to open a training institute for those Indian young men who wish to be officers among the volunteers . The committee men in charge of the entrance examination, which was held on Wednesday, were agreeably surprised to see more than 1,000 enthusiastic Indian youths rush to take the examination for the enrollment of 30 students.

Tokyo, English, 1/30/43

By Sapuran Singh, Domei Staff Correspondent, Shonan : Racial and religious differences have vanished overnight with the clarion call of Subhas Chandra Bose for total mobilization of Indian wealthy men in East Asia. Today with the disappearance of artificial barriers, the Indians now are joining together in brotherly accord as various part time training centers on the Island. So far, 15 centers have been opened by the local branch of the Indian Independence League, while 5 more are proposed for the near future Training, which began with ordinary marching, develops into use of the rifle and other firearms, while long route marches and vigorous physical exercises build up the body stamina of the trainees. Lectures are given daily on Indian history and politics to instill courage and patriotism, a spiritual force that will withstand all trials and hardships and keep up morals in the hour of battle. *Tokyo, English, 10/9/43*

Penang: Dr. N.K. Menon, chairman of the local Indian Independence League, declared in an interview on his return from a tour of Malai that many new training centers of the Indian National Army that have been established and the new volunteers eager to join the colours are extremely gratifying to headquarters. *Tokyo, English, 10/15/43*

Shonan: The Indian National Army Headquarters here is preparing to open, under the personal leadership of Subhas Chandra Bose, a training institute for women volunteers, which will be named after the Queen of Jhansi, an Indian woman patriot who had fought against British rule during the first independence war in 1857.

Tokyo, English, 10/16/43

At Johore, in southern Malai, a large number of prominent Indians were present at the (Central) Valley Railway Station yesterday to give a hearty send-off to over 100 Indian volunteers to the Indian National Army who are proceeding to Kuala Lumpur for training at the Bharat Youth Training camp. Another group of 200 Indian volunteers left for Epoh on Thursday to receive military training there at the newly-established Bharat Training Camp. *Saigon, English, 10/16/43*

Klaung, Monore State: A group of Indian women left here for Johore Bharu prior to proceeding to Shonan to join the Rani of Jhansi Regiment and undergo military training. Devaki, leader of the group when Lakshmi was head of the women's organization, addressed them last month and said they were filled with the desire to amulate her noble example and volunteer for the women's regiment. Their one desire is to share in the struggle for Indian liberation and to stand side-by-side with their menfolk to the very end. It is understood the husbands of these women volunteers already have joined the Indian National Army.

Tokyo, English, 10/23/43

Shonan: With patriotic Indian women gathered from throughout GEA, the Indian Women's Volunteer Training Camp, which opened here October 21 under the leadership of Dr. Swaminathan Lakshmi, director of the Women's Dept. of the Provisional Government of Free India and concurrently commander of the Women's Volunteer Corps, has had continuous stream of loyal Indian woman from Shonan and various Malaian Provinces, including Penang and Malacca as well as Salangor and distant Thailand, pouring into the camp. Following reveille at 7:00 a.m., Japan time, the trainees pay respects to the Indian National Flag and then they go through Physical and military training, nursing and study of Hindustani and Japanese language. *Tokyo, English, 11/19/43*

Shonan: Education should be part of the means of making Indian youth worthy sons of Mother India, declared Mr. S.C. Bose, head of the Provisional Government of Free India, in his address at the graduation ceremony of the Indian National School here on Sunday evening. In his address to the students, Mr. Bose said that he had two reasons for attending the ceremony. He wanted to express his thanks for the good work of the institution and at the same time he wanted to thank the municipal authorities for the help they have been rendering not only to the school but also to the cause of India's independence. *Tokyo, English, 12/29/43*

Kuala Lumpur: A graduation ceremony for a group of Indians of the Bharat Youth Training Camp was held this afternoon in the presence of a huge crowd which filed the Plaza in front of the government building here. Immediatly after the ceremony, graduates proceeded to barracks to join their comrades at Training Schools in the Indian National Army.

Tokyo, English, 2/1/44

Ipoh: Completing an intensive 3-month military training course, the first batch of volunteers in the Azad Hind Fauj Training Camp, situated "somewhere outside Ipho," gave an impressive display of matrial drill at the graduation ceremony held on the camp grounds recently. Paying tribute to the camp officers for the efficient manner in which the camp has been run, a high ranking officer from headquarters of Azad Hind Fauj declared he had soon for himself what proper training methods could do to Indian youths who three months ago were just raw recruits. The ceremony was climaxed by march......with the camp commandant taking the salute.

Tokyo, English, 2/2/44

Kuala Lumpur: A large number of members of the Rani of Jansi Regiment passed through Kuala Luumpur on their way to the Indian National Army's advance posts and were greeted by the local Indian community at the railway stations. There was eager excitement among the crowd waiting on the platform, among them many relatives or friends of members of the Rani of Jhansi Regiment, as the train steamed in. Trim in their military kit and unable to hide their determination by their confident smiles, these women fighters for India's freedom, after their months of strenuous training, looked in fine fattle despite the tedious rail journey. Joyous greeting were exchanged as the train arrived. Leaders of the Selangor India Indepencence League entertained the Ranis to dinner, while several citizens supplied the women soldiers with..........

Tokyo, English, 6/12/44

Training in Japan

Penang: The Indian National Army will select 25 youths from all parts of Malai and, after they have been given a short term training at Shonan, they will come to Japan in the near future.

Tokyo, Japanese, 11/13/43

Liaison with Japanese and Burmese Armies

.......A report from an undisclosed base in Burma discloses that with the object of perfecting the liaision among the Imperial Japanese forces, the Burma Defense Army and the Indian National Army, a permanent joint liaison organ has been created, composed of members of the staff of the three armies, ...it is certain to enhance the already smooth and cordial liaison among the three armies, since members of the staff of the Burma Defense Army and the Indian National Army will be sent to the General Headquarters of the Japanese forces in Burma to map out common operation jointly. ....Netaji Subhas Chandra Bose, head of the Provisional Government of Azad Hind and supreme commander of the Indian National Army, has returned to headquarters after a flying visit to the front. Lieutenant-Colonel (H.E. Algappan) has been appointed as the (representative) of the Provisional Government of Azad Hind. Lieutenent-Colonel A. C. Chatterji, Finance Minister of the Provisional Government of Azad Hind and (General Secretary) of the Indian Independence League (wd) Headquarters, was transferred to the Headquarters in Burma (on Saturday). Lieutenant -Colonel (H.E.Algappan), the new (wd)Minister of the Provisional Goverment of Azad Hind, is transferred from Headquarters in Burma to the (wd) Headquarters in Shonan and will take over the duties of Lieutenant-Colonal A.C. Chatterji, Lieutenant-Colonal (H.E. Algappan) is continuing ....the post of Minister of ....Supreme Commander, Azad Hind Fauj.

Singapore, English, 3/3/44

Women's Corps

It is reported from Shonan that as the call to arms of the Indian liberator, Sr. Chandra Bose, who has decided to organize woman's legion as an integral part of the Indian National Army, has had such a formidable repercussion among the Indian women of East Asia, several thousand Indian women, in a meeting hold on the 18th in Waterloo Street, Shonan, offered themselves for military service as regular Indian soldier.

Tokyo, Spanish, 7/15/43

Futher bolstering the fighting front of the Indian Independence Movement, a women's Corps in organized by the (Solangore) Branch of the Indian Independence Leugue at a ceremony which is slated to be held today... The now Women's Corps aims at the training of women leaders who will become the mainstay in women's independence activities.

Tokyo, English, 7/25/43

Dr. N.K. Menon, chairman of the local Indian Independence League at Penang, declared that the response of Indian women to join the Women's Regiment has been especially enthusiastic. He disclosed that new centers for training women will shortly be established in Shonan, where they will be taught military as well as Red Cross work. We shall soon be sending a pioneer unit of 50 women from Penang : "he declared." these women have already volunteered to leave their homes, to sacrifice their all for the cause of their motherland. Also within a week's time we are sending over 5000 women for military training . "In conclusion, Menon said that what struck him most during his trip was the patriotism that exists among the poorer sections of the community. *Tokyo, English, 10/15/43*

Shonan: It is revealed that large numbers of women volunteers, desiring to fight side by side with the men for the Indians' Independence, continue to join the women's Division of the Indian National Army through branches of the Indian Independence League in East Asia. The Women's Division of the Indian National Army is under the capable leadership of Dr. Lakshimi. *Tokyo, English, 10/16/43*

Shonan: "We give you our word that we will fight bravely against the alien oppressors of our motherland, with complete faith in victory," declared Miss V.M. Chinnammu, a member of the Rani Jhansi Regiment Training Camp, in a radio broadeast to Indian last night.

Tokyo, English, 1/12/44

Shonan: "The Indian National Army is already knocking on the Eastern Gate of India and the Rani Jhansi Regiment is eagerly awaiting the signal from S.C. Bose to go into action on the battlefield," declared Baljit Kaura Sikh, an Indian woman volunteer, in a radio broadcast to the Indians at home. *Tokyo, English, 1/22/44*

Pensions

Shonan: Pension and compensation for soldiers of the Indian National Army who may be injured or disabled or may lose their lives in the coming campaign was discussed by the Council of Ministers of the Provisional Government of Free India at its 3rd session yesterday evening... A committee, consisting of Lt. Cols. J.K. Bhonsle, N. Z. Kiani, N.S. Bhagat, A.C. Chatterji and Mr. D. M. Khan, was formed to go through a scheme already drafted by the supreme command of India with the purpose to make final recommandation on the same lines as are in vogue in free countries. A committee was also empowered to consider recommandations of the supreme command headquarters regarding medals and other rewards to be conferred on member Indians who distinguish themselves in the coming campaign. It is expected the official decision of the government will be announced in the near future. *Tokyo, English, 10/23/43*

Subhas Chandra Bose

Subhas Chandra Bose, your beloved leader, arrived today in Shonan, the former British fortress of Singapore. This day marks a new epoch in Indian's fight against British imperialism. ..... Subhas Bose has arrived in Shonan to take an part in the Indian Independence Movement in East Asia. *Singapore, English, 7/2/43*

Shonan: Rash Behari Bose, President of the Indian Independence League in East Asia, and the great Indian patriot and (revolutionary) leader Subhas Chandra Bose arrived in Shonan from Tokyo on Friday afternoon. At the airport the Indian leaders were received by members of the headquarters of the Indian Independence League the Malai Branch of the League, the President of the Shonan Branch and prominent members of the Indian community in Shonan ....A crowded program of engagements, beginning with courtesy calls on the high Japanese officials, has been arranged for the Indian leaders, Subhas Chandra Bose will take a leading part in the Indian Independence Movement in East Asia.

Batavia, English, 7/3/43

On the inauguration of Chandra Bose as the President of the Indian Independence League, the Chief of the Information Board of the Southern Army issued the following statement: Mr. Chandra Bose had held a conference with the Army Supreme Commander and he expressed his firm determination to serve for the Independence Movement .... At this moment, the Indian Independent Movement League, which is very.... and active organ, welcomed Mr. Chandra Bose, who is very highly regarded by the people. The 2,000,000 India people outside of India in the Southern Regions enthusiastically welcomed him. Mr. Chandra Bose, who left his motherland under the cruel and cunning suppression of Britain although he was burning with a land. His appointment to the presidency, I firmly belive, has an important and great signficance for the acceleration of a great independent movement development for the sake of India by taking more righteous path and discarding trival matters and by calling together all the comrades under, with a firm conviction that to fight through by playing a role in this Sacred War with confidence in the sincerity of Japan and her Axis friend nations and to accelerate their strids in the Independent movement under the epoch making cooperation under the command of Mr. Bose is the only way to reach their glory." *Tokyo, Japanese, 7/4/43*

Singapore: Mr. Chandra Bose .... spoke for about 15 minutes from the Shonan Broadcasting Station last night in Hindustan language and Indian language. *Tokyo, Japanese, 7/4/43*

Shonan: The headquarters of the Indian Independence League in this city officially announced today that the league members unanimously elected Mr. Subhas Chandra Bose as President of the League. It is recalled that this great Indian leader recently came to Japan from far-off Cermany and now, with the assumption of leadership of the Independence League by Mr. Subhas Bose the activities of the Independence Movement will definitely intensify both in fervor and in scope. *Tokyo, English, 7/4/43*

Upon the nomination of Mr. Subhas Chandra Bose as president of the Indian Independence League by its headquarters in Shonan today Mr. (Nobuyuke) Abo, the President of the Imperial Rule Assistance Political Society, sent the following message: "... On the occasion of your appointment as President of the Indian Independence League, the IRAPS, representing the entire people of Japan, hereby wishes you and your colleagues every success in the noble fight for Indian freedom."

Tokyo, English, 7/4/43

The news that Chandra Bose has boldly stood on the front line of the anti-British movement has filled the 2,000,00 people living outsides of India proper, in the various parts of the GEA, with great repture of happiness and the Malay Branch leader of the Indian Indedependce League stated the following: "when Chandra Bose was visiting Tokyo a few days ago , I was travelling thru various places in Malaya but when this message was once related, every Indian was full of great enthusiam. Again today Bose has lated, every Indian was full of great enthusiam stood on the front line of our Independence Movement. He is an exceptional revolutionist who does not know compromise. All the Indians with standfast determination are ready to follow this great leader." *Tokyo, Japanese, 7/5/43*

Shonan: Mr. Subhas Chandra Bose, newly appointed president of the Indian Independence League, called on the Commander-in-Chief of the Imperial Forces at the letter's headquarters yesterday afternoon and expressed his thanks for the efforts of the Imperial Forces.

Tokyo, English, 7/5/43

Subhas Chandra Bose returned to Shonan, had been gone since July or June 25. Had conferred with Commander in Chief of Japanese forces... Also in Bangkok he saw Premier Songgram.....conferred with local civil and military officals in Franch-Indo-China, also saw Yoshinzawa.

Tokyo, Portuguese, 8/12/43

Shonan: Mr. Subhas Chandra Bose started on a travel around the Malai peninsula on an important mission. He is expected to hold a series of discussions with the leaders of the Indians Independence Movement in

Malai on the preparations for advancing the Indian National Army into their mother country. *Tokyo, English, 9/1/43*

The Indian Independence League will not be abolished with the establishment of the provisional government, and it will take part in practical application of the Independence Movement measures in cooperation with the policy of the newly established provisional government. As Chandra Bose is the Prime Minister of the Provisional Government, he will also be the Governor of the Indian Indepdence League. Prior to this time, the Indian National Army came under the supervision of the Indian Independence League but in the future will come under the supervision of the provisional government. Prime Minister Bose will be the supreme commander of the Indian National Army. *Tokyo, Japanese, 10/21/43*

The Head of the provisional Free India Government, Mr. Chandra Bose, after visiting the assembly of the East Asian nations at Tokyo, visited the capitals of China and the Philippines, arrived on November 23 at Saigon, French-Indo-China. In the afternoon he attended a meeting of Indian residents. According to a dispatch from Shonan, Mr. Bose arrived on November 25 in this city. *Tokyo, Spanish 11/25/43*

Shonan: First anniversary Bose's assumption of leadership Indian Independence Movement finds all Indians here ready to carry on with increased vigor the struggle for freedom of their country and extermination of Anglo-Amercians. At present, 10 wartime training centers functioning in Shonan. A steady increase in membership of Indian Youth Corps being maintained. *Tokyo, English, 7/3/44*

Speeches and Interviews

Resume of address by Chandra Bose, Shonan: The people of India are now becoming dissatistied with the Civil Dis-obedience Movement and their determination to appeal to other means of attaining the goal of independence had increased......regardless of party we must make all preparations under one leadership..... From the standpoint of mobilizing effectively part of our effort, it is our aim to establish a temporary Free India. To lead and carry the revolution to perfection is the very purpose of the new temporary government....... The temporary government may prepare our follow men inside and outside of India for military combat and this will show the climax of nationlistic effort which has been within the hearts of all the Indians over since 1885...... What is to come will be left to the will of the people of India; a permanent government will be established and the temporary government will pass over the administrative powers to the new government. As soon as our preparations are completed thoruly, the battle of Indian Independence will be joined with the powers of the Axis nations of Japan, Germany and Italy. With the joining of India with the above combined power we will gain the eligibility of freedom and independence.

Tokyo, Japanese, 7/4/43

Commenting on the great responsibility of Babu Subhas Bose: .... Subhas Bose, arriving in Tokyo from Berlin, said during the course of press interview that the enemy has unsheated his sword and our answer must be by the sword. The Civil Disobedience Movement should be converted into an armed revolt.....Under the present set-up of delicate world situation, when the rarest of opportunity is before us, this sacred mission and message is given to Subhas Bose by Himself. The blessing of God and Divine Order is given to Bose to terminate the slavery of Indian forever...The state where Subhas Bose is standing today has been set and reached by the precious blood of his predecessors among Indian patriotic leaders. Also, we know that Babu Subhas Bose, under the presence imminent circumstances, will not consider it necessary to follow the thoughts of his revered predecessors stop by it necessary to follow the thoughts of his revered predecessors step by step.....The Indian leaders failed in their fight for freedom according to the circumstances of those times. The method with which they carried out their struggle in those days never brought them nearer to their goal of independence. The path of Indian freedom is paved with thorns. They tried to clear off this path and draw Britain on to their side by truth and negotiation, but it is impossible to kick out a strongly-entrenched power like that of the British by these methods. Therefore, Britian cannot be driven out of Indian expect with the sword. Babu Subhas Bose considers it a matter of prices and possibility to achieve Indian freedom by armed forces."

Tokyo, Hindu, 7/5/43

Shonan: Subhas Bose leading the movement, the Indian Independence Movement has become vigorous. The Indian Independence League Branch of Malai held a rally today. On this occasion Bose encourage the people, saying: "You people of Shonan and Malai are able to take the leadership for the independence of India. The reason I left India is to give aid for independence from the outside. We must receive military aid from the outside in order to destroy the British. As for receiving aid, we have reached this. You must be prepared to give all sacrifice for India."

Tokyo, Japanese, 7/9/43

Chandra said: "Today is the most glorious day for us, the Indians. We have had the privilege this day to make known to the world our intentions. Today, with the formation of this army of our own, much is anticipated in the future. Before Singapore became Shonan, the Japanese forces cried, "To Singapore, to Singapore." Let us now cry out, "To Delhi, to Delhi." The faith that the Indians have towards their new army is absolute. A truly great episode is taking place. At the time of announcement of the establishment of the army, even the elderly Indians came running to the recuiting office to offer their services." *Tokyo, Japanese, 7/9/43*

Subhas Bose in his first press interview in Shonan, said that the Provisional Government of Free India will soon be in existence. Describing this new government, he said it will not be a normal peacetime government. It will be fighting organization to organize the Indian people and lead them to victory...... the new slogan that (Subhas) in saying, "The total mobilization of all our resoureces." The phase of mobilization will naturally include the expansion to the utmost limit of the strength of the Indian National Army. Mr. Bose has declared that approximately 300,000 soldiers, under Indian officers, would take the field when the first offensive begins. The Provisional Government of Free India will also direct the training of these soldiers.... In addition to a high standard of military training, the soldiers of the Natinal Army will aso be given an intensive moral and spiritual. training so as to turn them into a highly efficient force... Once that victory is won and India is again free, it will cease to exist as a govrnmetn, end the Indian people will have to decide for themselves what form their new government should take...... With regard to Japan, he has said, "I am convinced of the sincerity of the Axis countries regarding Indian independence and particularly of the sincerity of Japan, and if that wore not enough has not General Tojo, the Japanese Premier, assured us time and again that Japan has no territorial, military or political amunitions whatever in India? Has he not, on the other hand solemnly promised all-out aid to India in her struggle so that she might attain full independence in the true sense of the term? Has not complete independence been pledged to Burma and the Philippines within this year?"

Saigon, English, 7/12/43

Subhas Chandra Bose, President of the Indian Independence League, made the following speech at a mass meeting at (Farar) Park in Shonan. On Aug. 15 on the occasion of the first anniversary of the Anti-British Resistance: The Indians in various parts of the GEA are holding this meeting, first, to felicitate the independence of.Burma, and second, to reaffirm our determination to continue with the struggle until British are driven out from Indian and until complete independence is achieved."

Tokyo, Japanese 8/15/43

Chandra Bose, President of the Indian Independence League, returned from a tour of Burma Thailand, and French-Indo-China and on August 17, in a presss interview in Shonan, stated as follows: ".... The Indian problem does not necessarily depend upon the world situation... Even in the event that the Anti-Axis forces attain some kind of success somewhere in the world, this true determination in Indian will not weaken. Rather, the victory of the Anti-Axis forces will further strengthen their imperialistic policy, but we must may that the Anti-British sentiment in Indian will be increased that much more." *Tokyo, Japanese, 8/18/43*

Bangkok: Statement of Subhas Chandra Bose—"A simulataneous outbreak of war in Europe and in Asia has been a dream I have had for the past 20 years, German authorities judged in the pst at that time that America would be defeated if war broke out. I also firmly believed in Japan's victory . After the GEA war boke out, the successive great war results confirmed my convition fully." *Tokyo, Japanese, 12/7/43*

Shonan: "Indians are now ready to commence their last assault on British power in India and the year 1944 will not only be a fateful year in Indian history out will also mark the turning point of this war toward victory ," declared Subhas Chandra Bose, head of the Provisional Government of Free India, his New year message to the peoples of East Asia ...... Declaring that in the last six months Indians in East Asia numbering nearly 3,000,000 have been welded into one solid revolutionary organization, Bose pointed out "All of them are ready of sacrifice all their worldly possessions and very lives in the coming fight for India's independence. With the sanction of forces behind them, the Indian National Army is well trained, well trained, well equipped and ready to light the spark that will start a country wide conflagration in Indian which will reduce which will reduce the British Empire to Ashes.

Tokyo, English, 12/29/43

Rash Behari Bose

Mr. Rash Behari Bose, noted Indian Independence leader stated to the press at undisclosed place, on Sunday, that 30,000 Indian overseas residents have now joined the India Independence Movement. He stated that the more strengthened the British pressure is, the more will the resistance of the Indian People increase. Mr. Bose declared that the day when their resistance is at its height is the day when the British influence makes wholesale withdrawal from India. *Tokyo, Japanese, 8/31/42*

Mr. Rash Behari Bose, President of the Indian Independence League, arrived at Shonan last night after an extensive tour of Burma. Mr. Bose is expected to stay in Shonan for a week to meet the other members of the (Council of Action) of the Independence League in order to arrive at the important decision regarding the Independence movement.

Saigon, English, 10/10/42

Shonan: The President of the Indian Independence League, Rash Behari Bose, during the course of his radio address, said , "A new Asia is in the making now and the Anglo-Ameican course is removed therefrom; but this Asia not be free, nor can there be any peace in the world as long as Indian is not free..... Our Anglo-American enemies are sandwiched between our fight for freedom on the one side and the Japanese power on the other. The day is not far off when the White Imperialists' rule shall be terminated. Out side help is necessary to drive out the Ango-American armies from Indian, and Japan has promised to render this aid."

Saigon, Urdu, 5/3/43

Shonan: The nomination of Mr. Subhas Chandra Bose as the new president of the Indian Independence League brought joy to his lifelong friend and cooperation in the Independence Movement. Mr. Rash Behari Bose, a former president of League. As a noble gesture and compliment to his co-worker, Mr. Behari Bose voices the following words at a grand rally here of the League members: "I have brought here to you one of the most outstanding, if not the greatest, personality of our beloved motherland., With the news of his arrival in Japan, the 2,000,000 Indians in East Asia who are free from the talons of British rule, rose up in one body and welcomed his arrival. This aptly speaks of the confidence the India people have for this brilliant man. Under his leadership, I am confident that you will march onto victory however difficult and ..... that may be too our final liberation. Of Course, I will always be at your side, sharing your suffering and your triumph." *Tokyo, English, 7/4/43*

Shonan: Following the mass meeting of the Indian Independence League yesterday, Mr. Rash Behari Bose former president of the League, gave a press interview..... He declared that the real battle for Indian Independence is about to begin under the personal command of Subahs Chandra Bose. the sporadic outbursts of the past have merely been skirmishes, Mr. Bose said, but now we are prepared to launch a major war against the British... Mr. Behari Bose pointed out that Mr. Subhas Chandra Bose is the most ideal leader in the coming struggle because of his relative usefulness and his fearless record as the foremost champion of India's absolute independence. *Tokyo, English, 7/5/43*

Indian Independence League
Sumatra Branch Activities

Independence meeting held at Medan. Medan, Domei: Inauguration to be held on July 31. Subject will be ousting of British and American influence from India. *Tokyo, Japanese, 7/30/42*

Medani: The Sumatra Branch of the Indian Independence League on Sunday observed here a colourful rally in commemoration of the first anniversary of the foundation of the Branch Renewed pledges were make to crush the British Empire. *Tokyo, English, 8/29/43*

Bukit Tinggi: In response to the establishment of the Provisonal Government of Free India, leading Indian Residents in Padang. yesterday morning at the Central Theater of Padang, held a ceremony for the organization of a branch of the Indian Independence League of the West Coast Province of Sumatra. At the ceremony 1,000 members unanimously adopted a resolution to extend all out support to the new Provisional Government in the struggle for freedom India. Following the meeting the members paraded in the streets demonstrating their spirit.

Tokyo, English, 11/6/43

Java Branch Activities

Batavia: Following the mass meeting of the Indian residents in Java, which has been held throughtout Java since August 8, the leaders of the Java branch of the Indian Independence League are now making preparations for driving forward the wholesale independence movement.

Tokyo, English, 8/25/42

The Java branch of the Indian League for Independence gathered at a mane rally to observe the birthday of Mahatma Gandhi and spread the news of the determination to fight for the freedom of their homeland. The rally want on record to support the anti-British fight.

Tokyo, English, 10/3/42

In order to encourage Gandhi, the Java Indian Independence League held a meeting on Feb. 15 and speeches were given. Telegrams of encouragement came from Bangkok. A resolution of determination of the Jakarta Branch was passed. *Tokyo, Japanese, 2/16/43*

Jakarta: Putting a finishing touch to the "Crush Britain and America" rallies held at various places in Java since August 3, the Java Chapter of the Indian Independence League held a grand island-wide rally at the special municipal theatre at Jakarta on Wednesday.

Tokyo, English, 8/26/43

Jakarta: The Branch of the Indian Independence League sent congratulations to the Philippine Republic.

Tokyo, English, 10/18/43

Jakarta: Approximately 300 Indians of this city adopted a resolution expressing condelence over the death of Mr. Gandhi giving went to indignaton over British inhumanity, which caused that undeserved death in prison, at a rally held this evening in the headquarters of the Indian Independence League of Jawa. *Tokyo, English, 2/26/44*

Jakarta: August 24: 2000 guilders have been donated by Indian Residents in Jawa to the Jawa Military Administration as a war plane construction fund. Assamull, Chairman of the Java Chapter of the Indian Independence League, accompanied by Akbani and Tejomall, Chairmen from the Jakarta and Bandoeng branches of the league respectively, called on the director of the People's Affairs Bureau of the local administration Tuesday to donate the sum which was collected by 3000 Indians. Determination to fully cooperate with Japan until Asia is finally liberated from the Anglo-Saxon yoke was also discussed.

Tokyo, English, 8/24/44

200,000 guilders were donated by the Indian Residents in Java to the Java Military Administration as a war-plane construction fund, (Attu Mall), Chairman of the Java branch of the Indian Independence League, accompanied by Ghani and Teji Hall. Chairman of the (local branches), called on the Director of the People's Affairs Bureau of the local administration on Tuesday, and donated the sum in a taken of gratitude for the...... of India. They also expressed the determination of the Indians to fully cooperate with the Japanese until Asia is finally liberated from the Anglo-Saxon yoke. *Saigon Hind – 8/25/44*

Borneo Branch Activities

The 75th birthday of Mahatma Gandhi was celebrated on Saturday by Indian Residents throughout GEA. On this occasion, according to a report from Kuching, the No. Borneo Chapter of the Indian Independence League decided to make a monetray donation to the Indian Independence Army for their airplane fund. *Tokyo, English, 10/2/43*

Kuching: The Indians in Borneo, like their blood brothers throughout East Asia believe that independence for India likewise signifies freedom for the whole of Asia, declared S.C. Bose. Rak Ravarty, President of the Indian Independence League in No. Borneo...... Outlining the Indian Independence Movement No. Borneo Rak Ravarty said the Indians in Kuching organized the Independence League on March 13, 1942, under the leadership of J. Lalchand, when permission was received to start activities. With the arrival of Bose in Tokyo the Indians here were spurred to further activities and his arrival in Shonan gave added courage and enthusiasm to our hearts. He said the Indians could not help but feel gratitude toward the Japanese Government for bringing Bose safe and sound all the way from Germany to Shonan.

Tokyo, English, 11/2/43

Celebes Branch Activities

400 Indians from Makassar had sent money to the Military Administration to help the Dai Nippon with the establishing of a GEA. In the newspaper "Pewarta Celebes" we published all the names of those who donated money already for this movement. Not only from the Indonesian people in this area, but also from all Asiatic people who live in Makassar we received money. *Makassar, Malay, 9/24/43*

Malacca Branch Activities

From Malacca rows report says that the Indian boys between the age of 7 and 14 will join the Youth Brigade, now being formed by the local chapter of the Indian Independence League......

Tokyo, English, 4/28/44

Free India Provisional Government

Jakarata: Hailing the establishment of the Provisional Governement of Free India., every Indian resident in Jawa is showing a grim determination to offer everything for the cause of their fatherland... The Indian Independence Army would advance into India in the due course of time. Yesterday, nearly 90 representatives of the due course of time. Yesterday nearly 90 representatives of the Indian Residents in Jawa including Kundandas, Chief Branch of the same league in Western Jawa, assembled here and discussed effective measures concerning their.... toward the new Indian Government .... Donations to the Indian Independence Army by local Indian Residents to date have reached 700,000 guilders.

Tokyo, English, 10/23/43

Subhas Chandra Bose – Speeches

Jakarta: Subhas Chandra Bose, head of the Provisional Government of India, in a radio address prior to his departure for Shonan yesterday, highly commended the determinations of the Indian residents of Java anu Sumatra to play their part in the coming struggle for India's freedom. Bose exhorted his countrymen to gird up their loins and prepare at once for the coming struggle which will be life and death a struggle for the Indians, but a struggle that will ultimately bring victory and freedom.... "Another fact came to my notice immediately after my visit to Sumatra and Java; .... inhabitants these territories have no desire to go back to the former regime which existed two years ago. To the past is a chapter of servitude, humiliation and exploitation which they would like to forget once and for all. What is particularly gratifying to me as an Indian is that my countrymen in these parts are politically wide awake and determined to play their part in the coming struggle for India's freedom." *Tokyo, English, 12/14/43*

Bose, who is visiting here for the first time, said it is difficult to imagine the Great War is at present raging when he sees normal life carried on busily and cheerfully on clean-swept Jakarta streets. Smilingly he added, "I had never been permitted to land in Jawa durimng Dutch days because of my political career. I recall our poet Rabindranath Tagore was allowed to land in Jawa in 1930 only after promising not o engage in political activities".

Tokyo, English, 12/13/43

Indian National Army

Jakarta: Keenly alive to the growing importance of the situation, more Indian youth in Jawa have voluteered for service in the Indian Independence Army under the leadership of Mr. Subhas Chandra Bose. Meanwhile, throughout Jawa, monetary donations for the independence movement are being brought in day by day to the branches of the Independence League by older Indians who are unable to offer their services directly for India's freedom. *Tokyo, English, 9/4/43*

Jakarta: Firmly determined to join the Indian Independence Army in its marcxh to Delhi, youthful Indian residents in Jawa are daily undergoing vigorous military training. It is recalled that the anti-British movement in Jawa was started in May last year when the Indian residents sent five representatives to the Indian Independence League. In the course of one and a half years since than 200 of the 3,000 Indian colonists in Jawa have volunteered for service in the Indian Independence Army and a sum of 700,000 rupees has been donated to its. *Tokyo, English, 11/28/43*

Jakarta: Upon receipt of news of the march of the Indian Independence Army in concert with Japanese Army forces .... D. T. Assesmul, Chairman of the Jawa Indian Independence League declared (that thousands of .... Ed.) Indian residents in Jawa, upon hearing the news of the commencement of the new offensives of the Indo-Burma border, are now fervently awaiting results of the drive. He continued that although the number of Indians residing in Jawa is relatively small, their loyalty and love for their country is just as high as any of their other follow men who are shedding their blood for the cause of India and GEA. As a striking example, he recalled how local Indians raised 3,000 yen all at once after learning the Japanese Administration would donate to the Indian Independence League the entire prodeeds from the news film of the Indian Independence Army which was shown to local Indians. He further declared, "At last our compatriots have started the drive into the motherland and our fighting spirit will so ar high upon the viage of victory with them."

Tokyo, English, 2/9/44

Philippine Islands

Indian Independence League

The president of the India Independence group in the Philippines stated: We must do everything for Gandhi. The independence move has begun. Gandhi is our blood and soul. We are away from our land, and cannot be in India in body. but through some method we are resolved to go forward for the Independence of India. Until the independence is achieved riots will be repeated occurrences. *Tokyo, Japanese, 8/11/42*

Brisk activities designed for the complete independence of India have been started by several thousands of Indian residents in the Philippines with the Independence League branch as its center. President (Doibe Suan) of the Independence League branch on the night of August 12 made a radio speech in Manila over station KZRH beamed at India in which he said that now is the time for all the Indian people to rise and launch a decisive fight against brutal Britain. He clearly expressed the strong determination of the Indian people in the Philippines to support India in its fight for independence. *Tokyo, Japanese, 8/14/42*

Manila: The battlecry of the Indian Independence is resulting into an organized movement by the Indian residents in the Philippines with the opening of the Indian Independence League offices in Manila. The three room headquarters will be known as the branch office of the league in charge of all activities concerning the fight for India freedom from British rule, Mr. B E. (Saiwanichi), the President, formally presided at the inauguration of the headquarters which was... with the flag of the Indian National Congress and that of Japan. *Tokyo, English, 8/25/42*

The authorities of the Indian Independence League in the Philippines decided on a one weed period from Feb. 20 to 28 as a Gandhi week, during which the Indians of the Philippine Islands will hold prayer meetings for the prolongation of the life of Mahatma Gandhi, to enable him to accomplish his 21-days fast. The first prayer meeting was staged on a large scale in the Manila Hindu Temple on Saturday. *Tokyo, English, 2/21/43*

Indians in Manila joined in celebration of Indian First War of Independence Mass meeting held with 400 Indians attending. President of Indian Independence League in Philippine Islands declared "We have not forgotten how horrible British treated Indians. With these memories fresh in our minds, will chase out the British from soil of India."

Tokyo, English, 5/11/43

Manila Domei: The President of the Indian Independence League in the Philippine Islands (Devi Dewari) prior to the Declaration of Independence in the Philippine Islands, spoke as follows: "Upon the honor of a grant of independence to the Philippine Islands, we extend our heartfelt felicitation and similtaneously offer our profound gratitude to Japan who liberated our East Asiatic Asia" *Tokyo Japanese 10/12/43*

Commencing on the beginning of the Indian March "On Delhi". He said the local Indians are enthusiastic and following closely on the news report of the progress of fighting are flooding the office with inquires. Emphasizing it is "Indeed good news," Sehwani asserted "Every Indian in the Philippines feels with heart and souls that the Indian Independence Army is march to Delhi under the inspiring leadership of S. C. Bose will be climared with victory." *Tokyo, English, 2/8/44*

Manila: In memory of Mrs. Mahatma Gandhji, who died on Feb. 22 while incarcerated in Poona Prison, the Indian community here held memorial services everning at the Sikh People. While Indians throughout the world mourn the death Mrs. Gandhi, all Indian (Shops) and establishments in the Philippines were closed with the Indian Independence emblem displayed at half must today of respect for the great woman leader.

Tokyo, English, 2/24/44

Manila: Enthusiastically following the progress of the victorious Japanese and Indian National Army troops which are reducing one British fortress after another, the local Indians are presently actively observing liberation Week which began from April 6 with a new drive to raise funds to aid the Indian National Army drive to Delhi. On April 13 a mass meeting is scheduled, marking the climax of National Liberation Week and, at the same time, commemorating the 25th anniversary of the Amritsar Massacre. Throughout the week the Indian National Flag is being displayed in all Indian Independence League headquarters to hear the latest news falshes from the fighting front, supplied by "Domei" news agency. Meanwhile, it is learned the Indians are planning to offer voluntary later service in order to aid the administation's food drive and, at the same time, contribute their share toward winning the war of GEA. *Tokyo, English, 4/11/44*

Manila: Indians in the Philippines will join the rest of their countrymen in East Asia in celebration of "Netaji week" beginning July 4 to commemorate the first anniversary of the assumption by Subhas Chandra Bose of the chairmanship of the Indian Independence League and the leadership of the Indian Revolutionary Movement in East Asia. Local observance will be held at the Medical Pharmacy Hall here at which the chairman of the Philippine chapter will speek. The program will include the adoption of the resolution of congratulations which will immediately be cabled to Bose, raising the Indian National Flag, and soliciting funds and volunteers for the Indian National Army. A special radio program will be broadcast over the local station PIAM with Kara Singh Gill. spokesman of the Philippine League, speaking. Meanwhile, on the eve of the celebration, spokesman Gill issued a statement explaining the significance of "Netaji Week" to all Indians. He said the dramatic appearance of Netaji in the orient a year ago "brought a well of jubilation among Indians in the East Asiatic countries and instilled in them pregnant hopes for the eventual release of Mother India from the British." *Tokyo, English, 7/3/44*

Foreign Minister Claro M. Reoto, in a message to the opening ceremony of local observance of "Netaji week" held this morning at the Medical Pharmacy Hall here, under auspices of the Philippine Chapter of the Indian Independence League expressed the hope that leadership of Subhas Chandra Bos, 'Indian may advance India's freedom nearer yet to realization."

Tokyo, English 7/4/44

Manila: July 27 Carrying a message from President Jose P. Laurel, an Indian jouranl titled "On to Delhi" came off the press yesterday. Published journal is dedicated to Netaji Subhas Chandra Bose, "Fearless Champion of the Indian Independence Movement and Uncompromising Exponent of the Cause of the Motherland (Dosei asterisks), whose Unexcelled Patriotism and Firm Conviction coupled with his Defialnce has Instilled fear and Terror in the British Hierarchy". The jouranal also carried messages from Foreign Minister Claro M. Recto and Shozo Maroto Japanese Ambassador to the Philippines. Indian Independence League the 148 page jouranl, through well-organized contents consisting of pertinent articles, portrays "The true situation in the Motherland so that the world, particularly our Filipine Southern may know our inglorious and miserable destiny under the Union Jack and the righteousness of our cause."

Tokyo, English, 7/27/44

Manila: Reiterating Gandhi's warnin there can be no compromise on India's demand for freedom, Karam Sigh Gill, spokesman of the Phillipines Chapter of the Indian Independence League declared people of India would not be content with anything short of independence.

Tokyo, English 8/9/44

Manila Branch Activities

Manila: A gigantic 2 day crush, Anglo American raly sponsored by the Manila Branch of the Indian Independence League was opened here this morning. Speeches were delivered by (B.B.B. Swun), President of the local chapter, Bose Vargas, Chairman of the Philippines Executive Commission, Beningo Aquire, Director General of the Kalibapi as well as by representatives of the Japanese Militaruy Administration.

Hainking, English 8/8/43

The Philippine Indian Independence League at Manila held a people's rally today. The Philippines Indian Independence League at Manila gathered together a large number of Indian representatives residing in various areas of the philippines at the Metropolitan Theater in Manila this morning in order to felicitate the establishment of the Provisional Government of Free India and held an Indian people's rally. First resolution of the Provisional Government of Free India. Then a resolution felicitating the independence of the Philippines was passed.

Tokyo, Japanese H., 10/25/43

Davao Branch: Activities

Davao, July 10: The Davao Branch of the Indian Independence League held an extraordinary meeting on the night of July 8 on the occasion of the recent nomination of Subhas Chandra Bose as President of the Indian Independence League and unanimously resolved to grant absolute support to the new President in the fight for the liberation of India from the British yoke.

Tokyo, Spanish 7/10/43

Cebu Branch: Activities

Attended by prominent Indian residents, the inauguration ceremony of the Cebu branch of the Indian Independence League was held in Cebu City last Tuesday night in conjunction with the anniversary of the establishment of the provisional government of Free India. During the ceremony, a resolution was read by chairman (Farbha) of the Indian..... Committee in the Visaya (sector). The affair was also attended by many local government and civilian leaders. *Manila, English, 3/23/44*

Cabu : With the Japanese and Indian National Army Forces having crossed the Indo-Burma border, members of the Local Chapter of the Indian Independence League gave an appreciation dinner for Japanese Filipine officials here for aid and encouragement given the Indians in their struggle for freedom from British and United States tyranny. The dinner was attended by Paulino Gullas, Commissioner for Visayas; Jose Delgade, Governor of Cebu; Kyosabu Mogaki, Japanese Consul in Cebu; and Japanese Military Officials as well as other leading Japanese and Filipine citizens. *Tokyo, English, 4/4/44*

Women's Service

Manila: About 60 Indian women residents of Manila held a meeting at the headquarters of the Indian Independence League Manila, in which they expressed their desire to participate in the National Movement. In this meeting, Mrs. Schwani, who is the wife of the President of the Indian Independence League, said that the women, shall work in the hospitals, and nurse the wounded soldiers.

Saigon, Urdu, 7/30/43

Manila: It is learned that the Indian Community in the Philippines, on the occasion of the recent visit of Subhas Chandra Bose to this city, donated 100,000 pesos to the cause of the liberation of their mother country from British tyranny.

Tokyo, English, 12/12/43

And now we bring news of the Indian Independence League in the Philippines. The (nation's) Indians have contributed (a sum of) 100,000 pesos to the Independence of Free India. Previously they had given 50,000 pesos. *Manila, English, 12/13/43*

On this day the Philippine Branch of the Indian Independence League sent a donation of 10,000 pasos to the Philippine Administration for the purpose of aiding in the increased food production program.

Tokyo, Japanese, 3/10 /44

Anti-British Demonstration

At a general meeting of the Philippines branch of the Indian Independence League on Monday, a wholehearted support of the anti-British demonstration now (appearing over all India) was expressed by the Indian residents at Manila. *Tokyo, English, 9/25/42*

A large scale anti-British demonstration will be held by members of the Indian Independence League in the Philippines on October 2 which happens to be the birthday of Mahatma Gandhi.

Manila, English, 9/30/42

All the Indian merchats on Monday closed their shops as a protest against the British Government in India and to hold a prayer meeting at the Indian temple on (name) Street for Mrs. Gandhi, who has died fighting for the independence of India side by side with her husband Mahatma Gandhi.

Tokyo, English, 10/26/42

Cooperation with Philippines

Manila: Manila revealed President Jose P., Laurel received additional messag of felicitations from branches of the Indian Independence League in Thailand, Malai and Sumatra on the occasion of the inauguraton of the Republic of the Philippines. Chairman of Thailand Branch said in part, your people have a long history of most cordial brotherly relations with the people of India. Our people very sincerely share (repoc....) Our brothers and sisters of the Philippines pray for their peace progress and prosperity." "70,000 Indians of Johore state heartly felicitations for attainment of complete independence by your excellency and the whole Philippines. Bengal for the Philippines! – read a cablegram from the Indians of Johore State, Malai. A similar message from Taise Sera, head of ...... said Indians there "Pray that the Almighty will bring happiness and prosperity to all Fillipine people in the future." Indians in Madan, Sumatra, through Mahatma, Chairman of the League branch there, stated. "andently wish the Fillipine people will forget to the goal of success under the leadership of your excellency." Manila: President Laurel sent a message to Subhas Chandra Bose acknowledgeing the gift of 125,000 pesos to the Republic of the Phillipines. This gift was given .... by Bose supporters in Manila yesterday. *Batavia, English, 12/6/43*

Manila: The entire Indian communtiy in Manila turned out this morning to senior voluntary labor service, this contributing toward winning the war, and at the same time siding the Philippines Government's food production campaign, The Indians young and old, dug the earth with determination, encouraging one another with heroic deeds of the Indian National Army on the India Front, The Indians worked side with Chinese volunteer workers, while Filipines and Japanese groups toiled nearly presenting a happy picture of GEA cooperation.

Tokyo, English, 4/23/44

Leaders

Subhas Chandra Bose

Tokyo: Surprise visit of Bose —asserted that Britain is now at War with India.

Shonan: Indian Independence has issued statement re arrival of Bose, is pleasent surprise for all Indians as well as to whole world.

Manila: Commenting on report of arrival of Bose in Jàpan, President of Manila Branch of Indian Independence League will be great blow to British and help to Indian fight for freedom.

Bangkok: As soon as news of presence of S. C. Bose in Japan came over either Indians in Asia rose up in body to strive now. Tomorrow mass rally.

Saigon : Receiving news of Bose visit to Tokyo residents of FIC attaching great hope of future activity talk to Tojo re Indian independence shortly after declaration that Japan would not spare efforts.

Rangoon: Upon receiving news of Bose arrival in Tokyo on Saturday called leaders into conference and sent cable of congratulations. Indian residents in Burma looking forward to leadership of Bose for liberation of India.

Tokyo, English, 6/20/43

Members of the (Manila) Chapter of the Indian Independence League numbering some 600 held a meeting at its headquarters Tuesday evening celebrating the presence of Subhas Chandra Bose in Shonan. The meeting passed a resolution: "We Indians of (Manila) great the arrival of Subhas Chandra Bose in Shonan and his resumption of leadership of the Indian Independence Movement. We hereby pledged to do our utmost to attain the final objectivity of the Indian Independence and of our fatherland."

Tokyo, English, 7/8/43

For the purpose of paying a felicitation call on the Philippine government upon its attainment of freedom, Subhas Chandra Bose, leader of the provisional government of "Free India arrived at Manila today, Nov. 22. Immediately upon arriving at the capital of the Island called for a visit upon President Laurel at the Malacanan Palace. Chandra Bose expressed his congratulations to his host for the happy birth of freedom for his national and held a conference on various matters. Following this Subhas Chandra Bose called upon the Japanese Ambassador in the Philippines, Murata, at his ambassadorial residence and extended words of greeting.

Tokyo, Japanese, H., 11/22/43

Manila: The Phillipines are proud and happy to welcome Subhas Chandra Bose, head of the Provisional Government of Free India, who arrived this afternoon as a guest of State accompanied by leading officers of the Indian National Army. *Tokyo, Japanese, 11/22/43*

Manila: More than 400 Indinas as well as hundreds of sympathizers resoundingly took up the challenge flung by Subhas Chandra Bose, head of the Provisional Government of Free India, to drive out the Anglo-Americans from E. Asia at a month rally held at the Metropolitan Theater this afternoon. *Tokyo, English, 11/23/43*

Manila: Indians in the Philippines reaffirmed their "Untarnished faith and absolute confidence" in Netaji Subhas Chandra Bose and pledged their entire resources to the aid of India's fight for freedom in a resolution passed at a ceremony held at 9:30, officially starting the local celebration of Netaji Week from July 4 to July 10. *Tokyo, English, 7/4/44*

Indian National Army

Manila, Domei: Ever since the return of the representatives of the Indian Independence League Branch in the Philippines who attended the convention which was recently held in Shonan, the sentiments for the participating in armed residence for the Indian Independence was further deepened. In the meeting, which was held day before yesterday, for making report of the meeting, which was held day before yesterday, for making report of the conference , several Indian youths.... immediately applied for volunteer service in the India National Army. President (name) of the Philippine Branch of the Indian Independence League and a certain number of youths decided of join the Indian Natinal Army. Monetary contribution for the causes of the independence movement is specially growing.

Tokyo, Japanese, 7/26/43

Davao: 14 Indian residents in Davao have volunteered for service with the Indian National Army under command of Subhas Chandra Bose. Encouraging these Indian volunteer warriors, the Davao Branch of the

Indian Independence League held a dinner party Monday, which fell on the first anniversary of the start of the Independence Movement by the All Indian National Congress and imprisonement of Mahatma Gandhi.

Tokyo. English, 8/11/43

Manila: More than 18 young Indian volunteers for the Indian National League gathered Monday afternoon at the finance building to undergo physical examination prior to their enlistment for active duty against Anglo-American oppressors of their motherland. Led by (Subhas Pagani), chief of the local volunteer corps, the volunteers expressed desire to die for their country if necessaruy to win independecne for India. die for their country if necessary to win independecne for India.

Tokyo, English, 8/31/43

Manila: Volunteers from the Philippine Chapter of the Indian Independence League who joined the Indian National Army some time ago are now undergoing rigid training to fight for the liberation of the motherland, according to reports received by the local chapter. It is undestood that even Manila Indians are admitted into the officers training school while others will fight for the Indian freedom in other capacities.

Tokyo, English, 12/12/43

Manila: "This is it, and I know we are going to win", declared D. B.Sehwani , President of the Philippine Chapter of the Indian Independence League, in commenting on the beginning of the Indian March "On Delhi". He said the local indians are enthusiastic and following closely on the news report of the progress of fighting are flooding the office with inquiries. Emphasizing it is "Indeed good news, " Sehwani asserted. " Every Indian in the Philippines feels with heart and soul that the Indian National Army's march to Delhi under the inspiring leadership of S. C. Bose will be climax with victory.

Tokyo, English 2/8/44

Appendix II

Decorations for the Azad Hind Fauj[1]

335. The following will be the order of precendence for Decorations awarded to members of the Azad Hind Fauj by the

Provisional Government of Azad Hind:—

(i) Shaheed -e- Bharat

(ii) Sher-e-Hind

(iii) Sardar-e-Jang

(iv) Vir-o-Hind

(v) Tamgha-e-Bahaduri

(vi) Tamgha-e-Shatrunash

II. In future there wil be two classes of the 'Sardar-e-Jung' Medal according to the standard of individual bravery, devotion to duty and leadership exhibited in the field.

The awards of 'Sardar-e-Jung' medal made up till now will be of Class I of that medal.

III. Members of the Azad Hind, who render meritorious and commendable service in the field, but fall short of qualifying for a decoration, will be granted the certificate 'Sanad-e-Bahaduri, by the Head of the State Provisional Government of Azad Hind.'

The award of Tamgha-e-Shatrunash is of the following classes:—

Class II : to be awarded to those members of the Azad Hind Fauj who kill or capture alive any British or American Officer or other rank either in single combat or in a group fight where

1. I.N.A. Trial Papers.

qualities of individual initiative and individual bravery come into play.

Class I : to be awarded to those members of the Azad Hind Fauj who exhibit conspicuous gallantry and devotion to duty in killing or capturing alive any British or American Officer or other rank either in single cambat or in a group fighting where qualities of individual initiative and individual bravery come into play.

Index

M

N

O

P

Kalpaz

INDIAN NATIONAL ARMY

A Documentary Study

INDIAN NATIONAL ARMY

A Documentary Study

(In 5 Volumes)

Volume-II

(1943-1944)

T. R. SAREEN

GYAN

GYAN PUBLISHING HOUSE

NEW DELHI - 110002

INDIAN NATIONAL ARMY—A DOCUMENTARY STUDY

Rs. 4,500/-

ISBN : 81-212-0833-5 (Set)
ISBN : 81-212-0845-9 (Vol-2)

Published in 2004 in India by
Gyan Publishing House
5, Ansari Road, Daryaganj
New Delhi-110 002
Phones-23282060, 23261060, Fax-23285914
Email : gyanbook@vsnl.com
Visit our Website at : http//www.gyanbooks.com

Lasertype Setting by: Tact Computer Graphics, Delhi
Printed at: Chawla Offset Press, Delhi

To
Manu and Kayako

List of Documents

Introduction

This is the Second Volume of the series "Indian National Army—A Documentary Study". The documents presented here cover the period from January to December 1943 and deal with events after the crisis which resulted in the arrest of General Mohan Singh. His order for the dissolution of Indian National Army was not accepted by the Japanese authorities. The President of Council of Action Rash Behari Bose took upon himself the entire responsibility of keeping the movement alive. Though no formal reply had been received, but the reply by Japanese premier to an interpellation in the House of Representatives of Japan on 4 Feb, 1943, reiterated that Japan had no territorial ambitions in India and on the contrary she would give all out assistance to see India free. Inspired by this statement the President, Rash Behari Bose placed before Iwakuro Kikan a scheme for reorganising the Indian National Army (Document-I). A Military Bureau was created under the Indian Independence League to look after the "Military administration and operations".

The scheme of Rash Behari Bose got the approval of Iwakuro Kikan (Doc-2) and the statement was issued by Col. Iwakuro clarifying the Japanese attitude towards I.N.A. and the Indian Independance Movement.

However, these developments did not satisfy certain members of the Indian Independence League in Malaya and they broke away from the Council of Action. They even submitted a memorandum voicing their concern for delay in getting a formal declaration clarifying in full the policy of Japan towards India.

Having set the army in order, Rash Behari Bose reorganised the Indian Independence League. The draft constitution was submitted to the Joint Conference of the representatives of the Indian communities in East Asia which was held at Singapore between 27 and 30 April 1943. The documents pertaining to this Conference (No. 12-15) gave a new working basis to the Indian Independence Movement. During the Conference it became fairly certain that Subhas Chandra Bose would soon be in East Asia to take charge of the movement. At the close of the Conference even Rash Behari Bose announced that Subhas Chandra Bose would be here very soon.

The entry of Bose in East Asia was announced in the Japanese press. The documents included here throw light on the significance which was attached by the Asia Press to his arrival in East Asia. There is no doubt that the presence of Bose reinvigorated the movement in South East Asia for Indian Independence. During three weeks following his arrival in Tokyo he made number of speeches, broadcast over Radio and held press conferences in which he outlined the plan which was to bring Indian freedom to fruition. Some of these documents are reproduced here as reported in the *Nippon Times*. Rash Behari Bose very graciously handed over the charge of the movement to S.C. Bose on 4 July, 1943 at a ceremony in Singapore (Dec. 25). Bose was moved by this gesture and while thanking the people expressed his views about the Indian Army of liberation. Bose said "Throughout my public career, I have always felt that though India is otherwise ripe for independence in every way she has lacked one thing, namely, an army of liberation. It is your privilege and honour to be the first to come forward and organise Indian National Army. By doing so you have removed the last obstacle in our path of freedom" (Doc. 23-24), I.N.A. was renamed as *Azad Hind Fauj*.

Bose was keen to set up a Provisional Government of free India to mobilize effectively the forces of nationalism in East Asia. The document shows as to how the task was acccomplished and how in its proclamation. Bose presented to the Indians a complete manifesto of national movement, which he was determined to pursue (Doc. 28-32).

It is interesting to note that the British Government in India did not underestimate the impact which Bose's activities in East Asia was having on Indians inside the country. The counter measures which they undertook to defuse his influence, their overall assessment of Bose's activities are reflected in the document included here (Doc. 29, 37, 43)

No doubt, the Indian National Army had been solely organised by Indians and it was meant to play a dominant role in the battle for India's freedom, still its standing with the Japanese Army was not clear.

Bose met Field Marshal Count Terauchi, the C-in-C of the Southern Expeditionary Forces and discussed with him the role of the I.N.A. in the forthcoming Japanese campaign in Imphal. Through his persistant efforts and arguments, the role of the I.N.A was clarified and an order was issued by the Hikari Kikan outlining its position (Doc. 49). The Documents also show the reorganisation and expansion of the I.N.A. under Bose's leadership. In the process of reorganisation, Bose even raised a regiment, named after the Rani of Jhansi. Although the regiment's primary duty was to nurse the wounded I.N.A. troops, still the picture of women carrying arms had immense propaganda impact. On 22 Oct. Bose formally opened the training camp for the regiment (Doc. 39).

The documents also throw light on Japanese policy towards India's Independence, Bose's participation in the Greater East Asian Nations Conference, and his assessment of it (Doc. 42). The Japanese permission to visit Andaman and Nicobar Islands, which had been placed at the disposal of the Provisional Government, British drive for anti-Japanese propaganda, the precautions taken by British authorities to safeguard the Indian Army from the propaganda of Bose are also reflected in the documents.

Not only the British, even the Americans were interested in the activities of Bose who was considered as a traitor by them. The office of the Strategic Services of the U.S. Government carried out studies on his collaboration with the Axis Power, one such report on the activities of Hikari Kikan is reproduced here (Doc. 48). It is a comprehensive report and throws light on how the U.S. Government viewed the collaboration of Bose with the Japanese. Though it covers the details about the Imphal Campaign, it has been included since a major part deals with the activities of Subhas Chandra Bose after his arrival in South-East Asia.

The documents presented here are by no means exhaustive, they merely indicate to the research students the nature of material's available and may generate some interest in I.N.A. who are more familiar with the Indian National Congress, activities of Gandhiji and Jawahar lal Nehru. The contribution of Subhas Chandra Bose and other patriots who mobilised support from abroad for weakening British hold over India cannot be minimised. The documents strongly hint at the impact which Bose's collaboration with Japan had on the British.

The documents have been arranged in the chronological order and as far as possible no changes have been made in the text. The documents have been selected from archival repositories both in India and abroad. The extracts from the *Nippon Times* were selected, when I visited that country as a fellow of Japan Foundation. The University of Tokyo gave me all the facilities to consult microfilm of the newspapers and to prepare photocopies gratis. I am very grateful to them for allowing me these facilities.

I am equally obliged to the Diet Library, Tokyo for permitting me to prepare Xerox copy of the O.S.S. Reports on Indian Collaboration with Japan.

Besides Japan, documents were also collected from the India Office Library and Records and Public Record Office. Explanatory notes have been added while the reference to the source is given on the first page of each document.

T.R. Sareen

1

Rash Behari Bose to Iwakuro Requesting Permission for Re-Organising the Indian National Army (INA) After the Dismissal of General Mohan Singh[1]

6 February, 1943

Sir,

I have the honour to state that, as the President of the Council of Action of the Indian Independence League, I have decided to reform the Indian National Army which was originally organised with your recognition and has been receiving your support and to clarify the real significance of organising this army and to promote friendly relationship between the Japanese and Indian Armies, I beg to submit herewith the following articles for your approval and consent:[2]

1. The Indian National Army is an army of the Indian Independence League and is under the direct control of the Council of Action of the Indian Independence League.

   The Indian Indepedence league will assume the responsibility of safeguarding the best interests of the Indian National Army and will request the Indian National Government when the Independence is achieved to keep this Indian National Army to form as nucleus of the future army of India.

2. The Indian Independence League is the only Political Organisation in East Asia and is organised and managed by Indians for the purpose of attaining the complete independence and establishing the full sovereignty of India free from any foreign influence, control or domination.

1. Indian Independence League Paper F. No. 45/3. History of Freedom Movement Unit. National Archives of India. (Inf future referred to as I.I.L paper F. No. 45 3).
2. Colonel Iwakuro Hideo belonged to the Imperial Guard Division. Succeded Fujiwara in February 1942 as head of the Japanese liaison agency (Iwakuro Kikan) to help the Indian Nationalists in South East Asia. But unlike Fujiwara, his relations with them were never cordial. Due to his helplessness, he could neither give permission to General Mohan Singh to expand Indian Natioal Army nor even to get clarification about the Japanese policy towards India.

The League's programme and its execution will be so guided, controlled and directed as to bring them in line with the aims and intentions of the Indian National Congress.

3. All officers and men of the Indian National Army shall be members of the Indian Independence League and shall owe allegiance to the League.

4. The Indian National Army should be made use of only:

   (i) For operations against British or other Foreign powers in India;

   (ii) For the purpose of securing and safeguarding Indian National Independence;

   (iii) For the defence of the areas where the Indian National Army is stationed in the course of advance to India.

5. The Indian National Army shall be organised on a voluntary basis. Once enlisted, each member of the Indian National Army shall be governed by the Indian National Army Act to be framed by the Council of Action.

6. The table showing the different ranks of the Indian National Army is as in the Appendix[3].

7. The Indian National Army consists of the following units:

   (i) Headquarters, Indian National Army.

   (ii) Field Force Group.

   (iii) Guerilla Regiment.

   (iv) Special Service Group.

   (v) Intelligence Group.

   (vi) Reinforcement Group.

   Further expansion to the maximum extent of the Indian National Army depending on the Indian Manpower available shall be carried out as facilities are offered by the Japanese side.

8. The organisation of each unit will be provided separately.

9. For the purpose of dealing with matters concerning the military administration and operations, a military department will be established by the Council of Action of the Indian Independence League. The staff of this department will consist of officers and men of the Indian National Army.

3 Not Included.

10. The status of the Indian National Army shall be deemed to be the same as that of armies of allied nations of Japan. Salutes and courtesies should be exchanged on a reciprocal basis to foster and strengthen good relationship between the two armies.

11. The Japanese side will give all possible assistance to the Indian National Army when requested by the Indian Independence League.

Awaiting myself of this opportunity, I beg to express my highest respect to your good-self.

2

Iwakuro to Rash Behari Bose Approving the Scheme for Re-Organising the Indian National Army and the Objective of the Indian Independence League (I.I.L.)[1]

6 February, 1943

Sir,

I have the honour to acknowledge the receipt of your esteemed letter dated February 6th, 1943, and to note that you have decided to reform the Indian National Army which was originally organised with our recognition and has been receiving our support and to clarify the real significance of organising this army and to promote friendly relationship between the Japanese and Indian armies. You request me to give approval and consent to the articles enumerated therein.

I hereby approve and consent to the understanding with the condition that "the Indian Independence League will be so guided and directed as to keep in line with the guiding of the Indian National Congress as long as it contrives to fight against the British and aims at the attainment of the complete Independence of India."

I confirm here under the articles as enumerated in your letter. (Articles I to II as in President's letter to Colonel Iwakuro.)

I have the pleasure to take this opportunity to express my high esteem to you.

---

1. Ibid, For further clarification of Japanese policy see the statement issued by Iwakuro in Sopan Netaji Subhash Chandra Bose, His Life and Work (Bombay 1946) /p. 240.

3

A Yellape[1] to N. Raghavan[2] Informs About the Developments in Singapore Regarding the Re-Organisation of the I.NA. and I.I.L. Under the Leadership of Rash Behari Bose; Refers to the Questionnaire Handed Over to the Officers for Their Consent to Join the I.N.A.

12 February, 1943

I hope to be excused for the delay in sending a report of the events that have happened here since Dalal left for Penang.

I.N.A.

Since I returned from Penang, we had discussions regarding the draft on the "Understanding regarding the Indian National Army " The alterations suggested by you were all accepted except as to Clause (4) sub-clause (3) where I found out that the Army people wanted the words "For the defence of the areas where the I.N.A. is stationed in the course of its advance into India." I believe I gave this information to you some days ago on the phone.

The "understanding regarding the I.N.A." was confirmed by Colonel Iwakuro by exchange of letters. The only condition imposed by the Japanese side is contained in Para two of Colonel Iwakuro's letter.

---

1. *Ibid*, N. Raghavan, born in Cochin, was educated at Christian College after studying law in U.K., became a prominent lawyer in Penang, joined Indian Independence League and was member Coucil of Action : Was President Malaya Branch of Indian Independence League (I.I.L.) took part in Tokyo and Bangkok Conferences, but due to differences with Rash Behari Bose, he quit Council of Action; he was not convinced about Japanese sincerety. He was, however, persuaded by Subhas Chandra Bose to join the Provisional Government of India. After Independence he served as India's Ambassador in China and Switzerland.
2. A. Yellappa, a prominent lawyer from Singapore who had come from Coorg to Malaya before the war; was adviser to the Provisional Government of India; was responsible for organising the Azad Hind Bank in Burma; died in 1945 in the bombing raid of north-east Burma.

With regard to the organisation and running of the Military Department and your suggestion of creating the post of a Deputy Director and the substitution of an Army Council in place of the War Council, I regret to say that Mr. Bose did not discuss this matter, so far as I am aware, either with the Japanese side with the army people. I believe the scheme regarding the actual organisation and running of the Military Department is as set out in the original draft shown to you at Penang.

Since my return from Penang there has been a lot of discussion with the Japanese side and the Indian Army people with a view to expedite the reorganisation of the Indian National Army. On 11th February a set of questionnaire was handed over to over 200 officers of the I.N.A. Almost 50 per cent of them have agreed to remain in the I.N.A. unconditionally. 25 per cent more will, I suppose, come in immediately reorganisation starts. As to the rest it is very doubtful and my own view is that for the time being at least, it is better that officer like Bhagat and Parkash Chand, who are unwilling to come in, are kept out of the Movement.

I understand Bhonsle will be appointed Director of the Military Bureau and Kiani, Chief of the General Staff (That is to say in charge of the Operations Department and second to Bhonsle) and acting army commander. Kiani does not, at least to the present, want to accept the substantive appointment of Army commander, perhaps because, if he does so, it may give rise to a feeling that he manouvred to get Mohan Singh out to make a place for himself. It looks that there is nobody else who can be entrusted with the post of the Army Commander—not, at any rate, at the present moment. I gather that this arrangement Bhonsle and Kiani will not give rise to any mutual jealously. What the reactions of some of the other senior officers would be, I am not quite sure. But I feel that this is perhaps the best arrangement under present circumstances.[3]

Dil Sukh Man apparently is keeping out of the Movement because he wants the highest post. If he does keep out, a large number of Jats may, for the present at least, be out of the Movement. Parkash Chand's case appears to be similar and this will affect the Dogras who number quite a lot. The Sikhs are none too happy in the army and quite a number may keep out. However, on the reorganisation and on the appointment of Bhonsle and Kiani, I expect more than 50 per cent of the officers and men are sure to come into the I.N.A. forthwith. And if matters are properly handled, as many as 75 per cent may remain in the I.N.A.

3. A Military Bureau was set up after the arrest of General Mohan Singh by Rash Behari Bose on 21 Feb, 1943 to look after the Indian National Army. Lt. Col. J.K. Bhonsla was appointed as its Director. The Bureau had five sections dealing with Military administration.

A Pledge has been drawn up and I tried to put into that Pledge as such as I could out of the Pledge drawn up by you for the Volunteer force. Mr. Bose is anxious that immediately on reorganisation the Pledge should be taken by those who remain in the I.N.A. But I doubt whether this can be carried through as there is a feeling in the Army that until the vacancies in the Council of Action are filled up it may not be quite safe for them to take the Pledge.

Council of Action

Coming to the question of filling up the vacancies in the Council of Action I think the need for it is immediate and urgent. I understand Bose wished to leave for Bangkok immediately after reorganisation and will only make arrangements after his return to Syonan. In the meantime, I do not know what arrangements are to be made regarding carrying on of the work. I do not feel quite happy under present circumstances as without your guidence, I sometimes find myself completely at a loss. There are various matters which need tackling as they arise without any delay whatsover and as you will appreciate even if my views are correct they do not carry very much weight. I am rather anxious that matters relating to the I.N.A. as also other matters should be very carefully handled as soon as the reorganisation takes place otherwise we might find ourselves in a worse mess than before. Goho is sometimes very helpful but he also finds it very difficult to pull his weight. Mr. Bose does not take Goho into confidence in all matters.

Office

The sudden appointment of Lingam as Assistant Secretary came to me as a rather unpleasant shock. I cannot yet understand the reasons for this. I showed your telegram to Mr. Bose re P.N. He was rather upset about it and said that you ought to know that there is complete trust between you and him and that P.N. was second in importance to me only in this office. I suggested to Bose that P.N. may be made Assistant Secretary. He did not object to this proposal but whether he will give the appointment letter or not I do not know.

Institute Graduates

Dr. Lukshumeyya wrote to Mr. Bose suggestion that they be granted temporary commissions as Second Lieutenants. Apparently he had discussed this matter with Major Somasundaram also who came here about two days ago to choose another batch of Instructors. I am affraid the position is rather complicated. I gathered from a conversation with

Somasundaram that there is no difficulty regarding Aiyer's position but that with regard to the other graduates he feels that if they are given a temporary commission, the N.C.O.'s may not like it at all. In view of the fact that a larger number of N.C.O.'s are going down to Kuala Lumpur, we will be faced with an unpleasant situation if commission are granted. The position would have been different entirely if commissions were granted before the I.N.A.N.C.O's went over to Kuala Lumpur. Now it might be interpreted as a deliberate attempt to give these Institute Graduates a status which from their point of view, they might not deserve.

With regard to the attitude of the recruits, Somasundaram told me that the matter could be easily settled by his issuing an order as camp commandant that all recruits must salute the Institute Graduates as if they were officers and he thought that he could issue instructions by which all N.C.O's would exchange the courtesies with the Institute Graduates. From Somasundaram I gathered that the problem arose because the Institute Graduates were touchy. They perhaps thought that from the very beginning they would receive officer's treatment from the N.C.O's and the fact that the N.C.O's did not honour them with Military Salutes rather hurt their susceptibilities.

I discussed this matter with Mr. Bose who was rather puzzled about the whole affair. He has not yet made up his mind and I personally would like to know your views on this matter before I breach the subject again to him.

It is of course difficult for me to understand the exact situation without being on the spot but my feeling is that these Institute Graduates should try to fit in the existing camp organisation without loosing their distinctive civilian status. I do not want to blame them at all but perhaps a little more accommodating spirit might have prevented such a situation arising. Somasundaram does not think it is very big problem but Dr. Lukshumeyya seems to be insistent on their having commissioned ranks.

Somasundaram originally suggested that some of the Institute Graduates could be attached as assistants to the Adjutant, Quarter Master and Company Commanders and when they themselves received some military training, ranks of 2/Lieutenant could be conferred on them.

I would like to have your considered views on the matter.

India Swaraj Institutes

I discussed the future of the Institute with Mr. Bose. He intends to make this an Army Officers' Training School, but that cannot start until the reorganisation of the I.N.A. is completed. In the meantime he does not want the buildings to be vacated lest the Navy or Osman should take possession of them.

As to the students who are still in the Institude, Bose requests you to reconsider the question of sending them to infiltrate into India. He suggests that you should take this matter over with Lt. Kanako and find out if infiltration is now possible. He thinks it is better that persons who are reliable should infiltrate rather than people of the type Osman or others have in view. The latter may do a lot of harm to our cause.

Bose himself has no idea of what is to be done until the Officer's Training School is opened. He thinks you are best fitted to devise some scheme by which the buildings will remain in our hands and the students utilised to the best advantage of the Movement.

Information and Publicity

There have been no further development since Dalal left for Penang except that Col. Kagawa has submitted another scheme to Goho, I feel extremely unhappy about the whole situation regarding this Department. Dalal was asked to start on the clear understanding that the Press and the Broadcasting Station were handed over to us and the details were to be adjusted. Now everything seems to be in the melting pot.

4

Rash Behari Bose to the Officers of the I.N.A Informing them about the Re-organisation Despite the fact that there were many who were not Willing to join the I.N.A.

13 February, 1943

I have studied carefully the answers by officers of the I.N.A. to the questionnaire put to them by me on the 10th February. I note that practically all the Officers are prepared to fight and sacrifice for the Freedom of our Motherland but I regret to say that not all of them are willing to remain in the I.N.A.

These Officers fall into the following categories—

1. Those afraid of taking action against the British.
2. Those who do not seem to have full faith in the Indian National Congress.
3. Those who believe in Dominion Status for India, which assumes a British Victory.
4. Those who do not wish to remain in the I.N.A. under the "present circumstances."

Such views if expressed by Prisoners of War may well be understood but coming as they do from Officers of the Indian National Army they naturally give rise to speculations as to the motives which promoted these Officers to join the Movement which was intended solely to fight for the complete Independence of India, and not for the attainment of Dominion Status. Whatever the status of a Dominion, it remains a Dominion of Britain and as such is a watch-dog of Britain.

1. Ibid., Singapore 1943. Even Iwakuro had met the I.N.A. officers at the Bidadari Camp and spoke to them about the advisability of joining the army, but with no effect. Subsequently they agreed to continue in the I.N.A. only under Subhas Chandra Bose.

As for those who wish to remain away from the I.N.A. under the "present circumstances," I can only say that I am hardly to blame for the present state of affairs in the Army. As you know India's fight against Britain has now reached a critical stage. Mahatma Gandhi has undertaken a three-week fast to bring still more pressure on the British to quit India, thus finally disproving any chance of a compromise. Our duty now is clear. Some of you may be anxious to know what will happen to those rejected from I.N.A. Unfortunately, I shall have no control over those who deliberately choose to quit the I.N.A. at the present juncture. I cannot speak for the Japanese, nor say in what manner or at what place they may be employed by the power whose prisoners they choose to be. Those of the Officers who do not wish to reconsider the views will have to appear before me at 11-30 hours to-day and give their reasons before I separate' them from the men. The appointments to the various Officers in the Indian National Army will be made by me as President of the Council of Action very soon. Needless to say no appointment have yet been made, but I can assure you that no Communal, Sectarian or Provincial bias will be shown.

(Sd.) Rash Behari Bose, President, Council of Action,
Indian Independence League.

5

Action Committee of the Youth Movement to Ex-Officers of the I.N.A. Requesting Them to Join the I.N.A. for Achieving India's Freedom[1]

8 March, 1943

We the Indian youths assembled here this evening extended to you a most hearty welcome into our midst. This greeting of ours not only applies to those who are present here but also to all those who are absent from the Indian National Army in this gathering.[2]

Your kind presence here today is an eloquent testimony to show that you are one with us. We duly reciprocate it.

As we see daily with our eyes how rapid strides you are making for the freedom battle of India. We feel extremely proud of you and express our profound thanks to you without any hesitation and also beg to add that your names would go into the history of India as the persons fully responsible for the realisation of Mahatma Gandhi's vision of an Indian National Army.

We make bold to assure you that we are banded together to lay down our lives for the liberation of our sacred motherland. India, from the cruel and inhuman exploitation of the Anglo-American Powers, whose machinations to make India still more a slavish country are gaining momentum daily. Your purpose also being the same as ours, we request you to take us all into your camp as youths who have willingly dedicated their lives for their country. Though we were a neglected flock all the while, we could not afford to remain like this any more.

1. I.I.L. Papper. F. No. 45/3.
2. Youth Movement, it was organised under the patronage of Iwakuro Kikan with the intention of weakening the Indian National Army. This move was never liked by N. Raghavan and other members of the Territorial Committee of Malaya. They represented against this move of the Japanese to the President, Indian Independence League, Rash Behari Bose. For details see S.A. Das and K.B. Subbaiah, *Chalo Delhi*, Kuala Lumpur, 1946. pp. 98-103.

We confess that we have no training or discipline or qualification of any kind to join you; but we boldly claim kindred with you as sons of the same soil with the same blood running in our veins. Whatever failings we have, let our ardent spirit of patriotism compensate them all and we are also confident that under your able leadership, guidence, and instructions we would prove ourselves worthy of your confidence and trust in no time.

In fine, it is our solemn conviction that you would not hesitate to be one with us and mutually pledge for the independence of our Holy Hindustan.

6

Statement of Rash Behari Bose Assuring the Indians in South-East Asia About Japanese Sincerity[1]

9 March, 1943

The Indians in their determination were greatly encouraged by the repeated declarations of Japan's accredited leaders and Statesmen such as the Prime Minister and the Foreign Minister of Japan. As early as the 16th of February 1942, addressing the members of the Imperial Diet on the fall of Singapore, Premier General Tojo referred to India and said:—

"It is a golden opportunity for Indians having, as it does, several thousand years of history and splendid cultural tradition, to rid herself of the ruthless despotism of Britain and participate in the construction of the Greater East Asia Co-prosperity Sphere. Japan expects that India will restore its proper status as India for the Indians and she will not stint herself in extending assistance to the patriotic efforts of the Indians. Should India fail to awaken to her mission, forgetting her history and tradition, and continue as before to be beguiled by the British cajolery and manipulation and act at their beck and call, I cannot but fear that an opportunity for the renaissance of the Indian people would be forever lost."

Again on the 12th of March 1942 in his message to the Imperial Diet, after the fall of Java and Rangoon, Premier General Tojo referred to India and said :—

"As to the Indian people, Japan entertains, of course, not the slightest thought of antagonising them. I desire, however to reiterate clearly that the determination of Japan to crush thoroughly the American and British influences will undergo no change whatever."

"Burma for the Burmese is already on its way to realization. It is my firm belief that now is the time to establish India for the Indians, which has for many years been aspiration of the 400 million people."

1. I.I.L. Papers, F. No. 45/3.

"Great Britain has for long deceived and continued her arbitrary rule over India. What the reality of the British promise made to India in the last Great War must be still fresh, I believe, in the memory of the Indian people. Now Great Britain is trying again to deceive India with all sorts of cajolery. If the leaders of India, misled by such British cajoleries, betray the long cherished aspiration of the Indian people and thus fling away this Heaven-sent opportunity, I believe there will be change for saving India forever and there will be no greater misfortune befalling the 400 million Indian people.

"Will India rise as India for the Indians to have the honour of co-operating for the establishment of the Greater East Asia Co-prosperity Sphere, or will she permanently stoop under the shackles of the Anglo-American Powers to leave her name as a slave to posterity? She is now face to face with the time when she should liquidate her past, see the new situation correctly and make her final decision ."

After the capture of Andamans, Premier Generai Tojo once again referred to India on the 7th of April 1942 and said:—

"The Imperial Forces which previously occupied Rangoon, an important base in Burma, and then took possession of the major strategic point in the eastern Indian Ocean, the Andaman Islands, which have hitherto been a place of exile for patriots of Indian Independence, have now at last dealt severe blows to the British forces and military establishments in India.

"The grim determination of our Empire to crush the United States and Britain is thus being steadily translated into action. If India should remain as before under the military control of Britain, it would, I am afraid, be unavoidable that, in the course of our subjugation of the British forces there, India will suffer great calamities.

"As it is, of course, fartherst from the thought of Japan to consider the Indian people as an enemy, Japan deeply sympathized with them who are likely to suffer the ravages of war.

"What Japan's intentions are toward the Indian people was made clear in my address delivered before the Imperial Diet on March 12th. In short, I am firmly convinced that now is the golden opportunity for the Indian people to exert their utmost efforts for the establishment of their long-desired "India for the Indians" in order to secure India's status as it ought to be.

"The British influence in India is now about to be exterminated. I wish once again to repeat at this juncture Japan's expectation that not only the leaders in India but the four hundred million people there, while avoiding unnecessary calamities which will result from their being misled by sweet flatteries of Britain, the nation destined to downfall, will take full advantage of this heaven-sent opportunity and break away from the British bonds which have so long shackled them and thus go vigorously forward to realise truly their long-cherished aspiration, of "India for the Indians."

When the mission of the agent of British Imperialism, Sir Stafford Cripps, to India ended in failure, Premier General Tojo addressing the members of the House of Representatives in Tokyo on the 28th of May 1942 again referred to the Indian problem and said—

"The fact that the British-Indian negotiations, with the British Lord Privy Seal, Sir Stafford Cripps[2], acting as the central figure, ended at last in rupture without accomplishing anything whatsoever, demonstrates that India has already become spiritually independent from Britain. Thus, the spiritual basis of British possession of India may be said to have disappeared already, and the first historic step toward Indian independence has just been made. "There still remains in India a framework of British possession with various military establishment, and the military forces are being steadily increased. As long as there remain Anglo-American military forces in India, Japan is determined inflexibly to crush them thoroughly. To our regret, it is, indeed, unavoidable that in the progress of such campaign some misfortunes may befall innocent Indians. What I expect at this juncture, however, is that the Indian people will rise with an intrepid spirit, expel the Anglo-American forces as well as their influence completely from India and thereby realise the Independence of their Fatherland."

These repeated declarations and assurances by the most responsible statesman of Nippon who not only heads the Government of the Empire but also as the Minister of War the whole machinery of war, have not only offered a great hope to the Indians for the future of the Indian nation but have made them greatly interested in our struggle for freedom from without. They have removed the doubts and misgiving regarding Japan's mission and have created confidence in Japan's intentions towards India.

We Indians know that if we wished to take advantage of the present golden opportunity to help our fighting Nationlist forces in India in bringing our long drawn out war of Independence to a successful conclusion, there was one and only one way to do it and that was to seek Japan's help

---

2. Sir Stafford Cripps (1889-1952) was a Minister in the British Cabinet, was sent to India in 1942 to negotiate with the Congress leaders for cooperation during the war. Cripps proposals for solving the constitutional deadlock were rejected by all the political parties.

and cooperation in this great task. The only thing that hampered the Indians in East Asia in seeking this help was the influence of Anti-Japanese British propaganda which had created some doubts in some minds. The long bitter experience of British Imperialism had made the Indian mind so pliant that they fell easy victims to the shrewd British mischief mongers and they were unable to realise and understand Japan's sincerity in the early stages. These vivid, hopeful declarations have done a lot to remove misunderstanding and create confidence. The successful celebration of the Independence Day throughout East Asia is positive proof of this fact as it is proof of our dauntless patriotism and of our burning desire to be free.

No one after reading the above declarations will question the statement that it has now become a natural thing for Indians in East Asia to associate Japan with India's fight for freedom. The reason is plain. Japan is not only the most dominent Power in Asia but, of more material importance to Asiatics, is the fact that it is Japan who has smashed Britain and America in East Asia and is now busy pulling out the last noxious weeds of Anglo-American Imperialism from the gardens of Asia which she has occupied and is holding in trust for the rightful owners, the people, who will be given control when the Greater East Asia Co-prosperity sphere becomes a living reality. Indians who thus have come into contact with the Japanese find the letter to be human beings, men to whom the doing of a kind deed is an obsession, men who from early childhood have been taught the value of the pledged word, loyalty to a cause and people, and the intrinsic worth of that thing called mercy and compassion. One foreign writer paid this tribute to Japan five years ago: "Wherever one turns one sees a people of heroes, a political constitution of imperturbable strength and authority: an administration working with high ideals; a military power equal to that of the Great Powers of the world an Empire making progress in all directions; a nation which always places in the forefront of its foreign policy "A pledge is a bond which cannot be broken whatever the circumstances." What this writer has had to say has been confirmed in our every day contact with the Japanese and things Japan. When Japan says a thing she means it and does it. It is because of this conviction that the promises of all-out aid to India without any notice of self-interest or designs of conquest has been accepted by Indians with all the sincerity with which it has made by Japan. And the letter realises that it is only a free, Independent India which can make the ideal of "Asia for the Asiatics" come true. Japan, therefore, is ready to help India gain her freedom from British misrule and to help to eradicate the evil influence which has for long and so oppressively been making the lives of Indians a misery and

India an object of world pity.

Great Britain, a past master in the art of wilfully misinterpreting the pure motives of others, has been using the clear, unambiguous and definite declarations of Japan concerning India as a spur to compel Indians to defend themselves under British control against Japan. To do so they have immorally perverted all that has been said by Japanese leaders, Statesman, politicians and Diplomats, and re-manufacturing the statements by the insertion of sentences to suit their own ends, has presented Japan to India as being menace to India. Only poltroons, knaves, rogues and liars are capable of so gross and infamy and the British have voluntarily placed themselves in each of the above classifications through the fabrication of falsehoods which they know to be falsehoods. British propagandists in recent months have been trying to whip Indian public opinion into the belief that a crisis is facing India. That crisis, again according to the British is no other than the possibility of a Japanese offensive into India. But how foolish, how untrue, how unreal such a story sounds. It is fanastic, the creature of Britain's own imagination. It is not a Japanese army which will drive the British out of India lock, stock and barrel. It is an Indian Army, which, like avenging angels, will forcibly eject the British from India at the point of the rifle and the bayonet—that is if Field-Marshal Wavell and his British hordes do not themselves stage another 'glorious retreat" this time from Indian soil.

Japan has never harboured a will to antagonize the Indian people. Far from it, Japan sympathizes with their long cherished desire and have announced their readiness to co-operate, if, mark these words, *the Indians desire it.* If Japan had any desire to harm Indians why should she, whenever she gets ready to destroy the bases of British Imperialism in India, ask the Indian Independence League broadcasting station, to advice Indians to quit such areas? Make no mistake about it, the "Crisis of India" means nothing more than the very patent and obvious fact that Britain still rules India. The prolongation of the crisis depends on how soon Britain quits India.

Japan's relations with India are as clear as crystal. Her intentions have been plainly stated and often reiterated. In the previous pages we have quoted Premier General Tojo at length to show how Japan has assured India that she has no antagonism towards India and how she wants to help us in freeing our country. If there is any doubt left in any mind even after the great Premier and General has committed Japan very definitely in his very recent declarations, then there will be no such thing as sincerity in this world. On February 4th, 1943, replying to an interpollation posed by Mr. Ryo Koyama in a Budgetary Committee meeting of the House of Representatives in Tokyo the Premier, General Tojo, reiterated the statement that the Japanese Government has no territocial ambitions in India, but rather on the contrary desires to see India regain its Independence as soon as possible. He said that whatever propaganda the enemy nations may use to counteract or discredit oft-repeated statement will amount to nothing before the overwhelming realities, indicated in the shining existence of the over-growing Empire of Manchukuo and the up and coming National government of China at Nanking. He continued by saying that the Japanese Government is the staunch unholder of righteousness and shall at all times abide by its promises. He asserted that Japan stood by its assurance given to Thailand to respect the sovereignty of its territorial integrity, as a consequence of which Thailand is now fully collaborating with Japan in the prosecution of Greater East Asia War. Japan's attitude towards Burma has been already clarified, continued Premier Tojo, adding that the Philippines, too has been assured of independence provided it comes to realise its place in Greater East Asia and collaborate fully with the Japanese policy. Asserting that realities speak more eloquently than any malicious propaganda aimed to discredit Japan, Premier Tojo declared that India, at the present juncture needs only to turn a deaf ear to enemy propaganda and to concentrate in the efforts of the immediate task before it. He concluded by saying that Japan has no territorial ambition whatever in India.

This statement by General Tojo is looked upon as being an inspiration to Indians everywhere. The Indian Independence League Headquarters in the course of a statement commenting on General Tojo's declaration said:-

"Premier Tojo's present declaration has completely shattered Anglo American mallicious propaganda to Indian people to the effect that Japan entertains no territorial ambition. The statement that Japan is striving to bring back India to its original status as enunciated by Premier Tojo has given the greatest inspiration to Indians who now realise all the more Japan's lofty spirit for construction of Greater East Asia. Premier Tojo's promise to grant independence to Burma within this year and his present statement to the effect that similar treatment will be accorded to the Philippines has given concrete proof of the ethical basis of Japan's war aims, namely eradication of Anglo-Americans Imperialism from East Asia and the construction of Asia for the Asiatics. Fully comprehending General Tojo's statement the Indian people have come to trust Japan more than ever and their Independence movement in consequence will make a rapid advance hereafter ."

7

General Staff, Headquarters to G.O.C. Indian Army Informing him about the Subversive Activities Directed towards the Indian Army from within and ourside India Specially by those who were Collaborating with Japan[1]

18 March, 1943

In letter No. DMI/4746 of 4th Nov. 1942 tentative information about the Japanese sponsored Indian National Army and views on counter measure were given and it was stated that comments and further suggestions would be appreciated. Since then additional information has been circulated and constant references to the dangers to security which the movement represents have been included in Part III of GHQ (I) Weekly Intelligence Summary. The fact that no comments or suggestions have so far been received, together with some recent events, suggests that the potentialities of the situation have not been fully realised in all quarters. The object of this letter is to outline certain recent developments which have come to light, to describele arrangements made by GHQ Security Staff for watching the situation and to stress the necessity for complementary measure in formations and units without which success in dealing with these problems cannot be achieved.

It is now quite clear that a double attack is being made on the morale and loyality of Indian troops—one directed from without India by the Japanese, assisted by renegade Indians, and the other directed from within India by Congress or Congress inspired organisations. These two compaigns are identical in aim and to some extent in method though no direct connection has yet been established between them as regards coordination or control. That in practics one is complementary to the other as regards the effect which may be produced is shown in an example quoted later in this letter. Both these campaigns are assisted by radio

1. Ministry of Defence. F. No. 601/10569/Historical Section.

propaganda in Hindustani and English from German Radio stations[2] some of which pose as secret stations in India. In the direction of this propogands Subhas Chand Bose has hitherto played a leading part. The tendency is to transfer Indian Prisoners of War captured in the middle East to Germany where it is known efforts are being made to develop "Free India" units, on the I.N.A. model.[3] A letter from an Indian P of W recently referred to the excellent treatment they were receiving and remarked that all arrangements were in the hands of Subhas Chand Bose. The following is a typical extract from German radio propoganda directed to India—

> "Let me remind you once again that the two fold object of the non-violent guerilla warfare that you are now carrying on, should be: Firstly, to paralyse the civil administration in India and secondly to destroy war production in India. I should also like to tell you that the time has come to intensify our propaganda within the Indian Army. This could be done best by sending our Partymen in large numbers into the ranks of the Indian Army. In the last phase of the national struggle, the Indian Army will have to play an important role."

Congress Party manifestos and secret instructions and correspondence which have recently been seized clearly show that the underground leaders have concluded that the main barrier to the success of their movement to obtain power is the staunchness of the Indian Army. The following is an extract from a document captured some time ago. The similarity with the extract quoted in para 2 above is worthy of note.

> "........our objective must be the capture of power from the foreign Government. How is this to be effected? We have seen that it was possible in Bihar and the U.P. to paralyse civil administration and capture power at least for sometime. That is, it was possible to bring to a standstill the machinery of civil administration. You can break the police, but what of the military.....I would press upon the organisers to think out means to meet the menace of the army."[4]

2. German Radio. This refers to Azad Hind Radio (Germany) which was started by Subhas Chandra Bose when he went to Germany in 1941. Bose's broadcasts had great impact on public opinion in India and abroad. For details see British Weekly Intelligence Summary F.No. 601/7378/H.S. Ministry of Defence, New Delhi. For Bose's activities in Germany. See also T.R. Sareen, *Subhas Chandra Bose and Nazi Germany*, New Delhi, 1996.
3. This refers to the Free India Centre and Indian Legion formed by Bose from P.O.W. in Germany.
4. This refers to the appeal issued by General Mohan Singh to the soldiers of the Indian Army to desert and join the Indian National Army for the liberation of India. Even after Mohan Singh's arrest by the Japanese in December 1942, the appeal in his name was still utilised for propaganda purposes by the Indian Independence League.

At Appendix 'A' is a copy of a document subsequently captured in which this problem is appreciated and the opening presented especially by expansion of technical recruiting for the Royal Air Force is stressed. At Appendis 'B' are copies of correspondence believed to be addressed to the organiser of the Northern Congress Zone, which indicate attempt to put into practice the scheme of the "League of Armed Forces" referred to in Appendix "A". While it is probable that the claims of progress made in this correspondence are coloured by enthusiasm, it must be accepted that there has been some degree of success at least in making contacts and establishing cells for the distribution of propaganda. No confirmation of such attempts has yet been obtained from local police or military sources in the Punjab but recent events in a battalion in Arakan (referred to below) indicate that a recent draft had been infected by Congress propaganda before leaving their training centre in the Punjab. One of the main immediate dangers of such attempts to win over military personnel is the possiblity of subversive organisations thereby obtaining supplies of explosives, etc. for sabotage purposes. In both Delhi and Bombay the police have received information and recently discovered large quantities of live bombs, revolvers and explosives obtained from friend and sympathisers in....Arsenals and Ordnance Depots. An even greater danger is the ultimate effect on morale and fighting efficiency, which will not become apparent until contact with the enemy is made.

As regards Japanese inspired activities, there seems to be no falling off in the recruitment of agents from among both Indian prisoners of war and Indian civilians in Japanese occupied territory and their despatch from Malaya and Burma, there is good evidence that parties have been sent from Hong Kong. As in the case of Germany, Indians are comparatively well treated and civilians are given the status of third national. Those Indians P of W who accept membership of the INA are freed—those who do not are subjected to harsh treatment and constant propaganda. There is evidence that numbers continue to refuse, that numbers given in and join with no intention of fulfilling the pledges they are called upon to make, but that a relatively large number, the leaders of which include regular Army ICOs, VCOs and NCOs, have become active members of the INA. From these and from civilians, parties of agents are selected for despatch to India.

While the arrangement outlined below have met with some measure of success intercepting and discovering these agents, there is no doubt that considerable numbers have slipped through. In a disquieting number of cases, individuals have managed to conceal from interrogators the fact that they have been Japanese hands, have been coached in espionage and subversive propanganda and sent back with specific instructions. Cases are now coming to light of "stragglers" who rejoined as long ago as August and September and have successfully concealed these facts. In spite of instructions issued under A.G. Branch 30065/AG. 22 of 27/7/42 in some cases such men have been reposted to units in Eastern Army, or having joined them direct have been allowed to remain there. In other cases military personnel have disguised themselves as civilians, returned to their districts and failed to report to their units for some months. These all represent a potential danger to security, however innocent they may appear to be. Such a situation cannot be treated with complacency and it is essential that commanding officers of all Indian units be warned of the necessity for ascertaining whether in fact their units contain stragglers who have not been properly interrogated.

The Japanese are now reinforcing these "deep penetration" agents with leaflet and radio propaganda addressed directly to Indian troops and issued in the name of the Indian National Army. Manuscript letters in vernacular script (translation at Appendix 'C') and emanating from Capt. Mohan Singh have been piched up by our patrols in Arakan, while Punjabi Mussalman and Sikh Personnel were recently observed from a Battery O.P. in Arakan fighting along side Japanese troops. There is no doubt that a detachment of INA is in the Akyab area.

Individual desertions of Indian troops have been reported and in a recent case a platoon sent out on patrol is believed to .....have deserted. The "Security" history of this unit is given in Appendix 'D'. Enquiries now in progress show that the company (Sikhs) to which the platoon belonged had been infected firstly by subversive Congress propaganda circulated by a draft recently joined from the Training Unit, secondly by local contacts with Mugh and INA propagandists and thirdly by INA pamphlets. (It was this company that firstly reported the Mohan Singh leaflets referred to above). This case illustrates the potential and the actual dangers to which this double attack exposes us and also the need at all times for the closest scrutiny and sifting of any reports however far fetches or even ridiculous they may appear at the time. It is essential to avoid the complacency that in so many cases leads to entries in unit intelligence reports suggesting that morale is high and subversive tendencies absent because outward and visible signs are lacking. Nearly all the units in which trouble has occurred have submitted negative security reports for some time before open signs are visible.

It is desirable here to summarise frankly some of the reasons which should dispel any feeling of complacency. The Pre-war Indian Army was in practice still a mercenary army with its morals and loyalty based on four main factors:-

(a) Recruitment from classes with long-standing martial and professional traditions which have for long been centred on loyalty to the "Sarkar" and to the King Emperor and which were still strong enough to withstand the interest of those classes.

(b) Experienced British officers able to command the respect and affection of their men.

(c) Pay and conditions of service sufficiently good to make service in the army attractive in comparison with conditions in civil life.

(d) Establishments low enough to maintain competition for vacancies.

In respect of at least (a) (b) and (d) the situation has radically changed, while it is now questionable whether (c) is still sufficiently potent to counterbalance the loss of stabilising effect of the other three. Changes in the classes from which men and particularly Indian commissioned officers are drawn, shortage of experienced British Officers with knowledge of the country and able to command personal respect and affection, combined with consistent "nationalist" propaganda are sapping the foundations on which the morale and loyalty of the old Indian Army was based. At the same time the concept of "loyalty to India" which in theory should be developed by "nationalistic" propaganda is unable to replace the other loyalties referred to above in the case of newly introduced elements or of the older element's (i.e., the martial classes). The letter are so bewildered and confused by political developments which they do not understand but which they instinctively feel will react to their disadvantage in the long run, that these older loyalties are rapidly losing their potency. It is against this background, which favours both Japanese and Congress inspired activities, that these problems must be viewed and tackled.

If the above analysis is correct, it is obvious that administrative contentment assumes increasing importance in the interregnum between the casting off of the old loyalties and the development of the new. Apart from this, it is essential that Commanding Officers and senior Indian Officers should be made to realise these factors where this realisation is not already the case and that every effort should be made to watch for and counter subversive activities of the type outlined. The basis of action in this connection is knowledge and no neglect of any clue, however trivial it may appear to be initially. It is also essential that efforts should be made continuously to impress on men, especially of the recently introduced classes, that they are fighting in India's interests and that a Japanese Victory would be disastrous to their own future.

This raises the question of publicity and propaganda about the INA and other Japanese activities. Hitherto this has not been attempted because:-

(a) It might engender lack of confidence in their troops among British officers and commanders.

(b) It would give valuable information to the enemy who is at present largely ignorant of the extent of our knowledge of his plans and activities and of the degree of success his scheme for infiltrating agents has achieved in practice.

The disadvantages of silence are that it has encouraged unwarranted complacency in many quarters. It is felt that at present publicity and open propaganda should not be allowed but that measures outlined below should be taken to ensure that the facts are more widely known to formation and unit commanders and to trustworthy Indian commissioned officers and senior VCOs.

Apart from the establishment of—

(a) a screen of Forward Interrogation Centres in Assam and Bengal for the collection, preliminary interrogation and classification of personnel returning from enemy occupied territory, and staffed by combined police and military personnel;

(b) a combined civil and military interrogation centre (C.S.D.I.C.)[5] in Delhi for the further interrogation of suspects and of personnel subsequently apprehended who escape (a),

(c) a combined civil and military staff in GHQ (know as G.S.I. (b) (i)) which sifts reports and initiates counter action against the Japanese IWAKURO organisation (outlined in GHQ (I) Weekly Intelligence Summary, Part III, para 6, dated 5th March 1943) and recommends the disposal of personnel,

It has now been decided to appoint Lt. Col. Himmat Singh (now GS O I in charge of G.S.I.(b) (i)) as GHQ Liaison Officer to visit formations and units in connection with INA and kindred matters and to assist in enquiries and to follow up specific cases such as that referred to in paragraph 8 above. He will also periodically visit security staffs at HQs Armies/ Commands with a view to concerting coordinated action and giving any assistance in his power. He will be available to visit training centres to

5. C.S.D.I.C. Combined Services Detailed Interrogation Centre was established by the Army Headquarters during the war. It had its headquarters at Red-Fort, Delhi. The centre was interested with the task of interrogating all those who were coming from enemy occupied territories especially Burma. Subsequently, it interrogated almost every soldier who was connected with the Indian National Army. They were divided into three categories— Black, Grey and White.

explain the situation and discuss security measures.

In view of the importance of countering both Congress and INA activities, it is requested that in each Army/Command, (and in lower formations at Army Commanders discretion) a member of the Security Staff, or alternatively an experienced and reliable British or Indian Officer be employed as Liaison Officer for INA questions to supplement Lt. Col. Himmat Singhi's work in following up specific cases and in ensuring that a constant watch is maintained in all units, especially training units. These officers should periodically visit G.S.I. (b) at GHQ (I) and C.S.D.I.C. Delhi to obtain the latest information. It is requested that in addition steps be taken to bring the situation and its potential dangers forcibly to the notice of all formation commanders and commanders of Indian units. Enclosures at Appendix 'A' and 'B' to this letter should not however be distributed below Brigade Commanders and burned after perusal. The necessity for making full use of material on INA and Congress, activities directed against the Army which is published periodically is Part III of GHQ (I) Weekly Summary should be impressed on formation commanders. Commanding Officers should now be authorised to put the facts of the situation, as given in these summaries, plainly to selected Indian Commissioned Officers and Viceroys Commissioned Officers where this has not already been done. For this purpose suitable extracts from these summaries may be made by Brigade, etc. Commanders for distribution to Battalion or equivalent commanders.

Finally, attached at Appendix 'E' is an extract from a letter written by a KCIO to the Director of Military Intelligence on the question of the extent to which the Army generally should be taken into our confidence regarding these developments.

The writer is a member of a family with long tradition of service in the Indian Army, but who personally is strongly imbued with nationalistic ideas. He has been in Japanese hands and was fully in the confidence of both the INA leaders and their Japanese sponsors before escaping. His views endorse much of what has been written above. This Appendix should not be distributed below Brigade Commanders and copies should be destroyed after perusal.

His Excellency the Commander-in-Chief wishes Army Commanders to give the contents of this letter their personal consideration and to submit any views or recommendations they may have for dealing with the problem.

Sd/-

Lieut.-General,

CHIEF OF THE GENERAL STAFF.

APPENDIX ' A' TO DM/4746

League of Armed Forces in India Secretary's Review of the Indian Situation

---

The Congress raised the moral of the nation but failed to contact the powerful machine of the Indian Army. If the British Goverment decided to destroy the Indian Political leaders, nothing could happen in this country to harm the British interests seriously. Again and again we have asked why the British, staunch Imperialists as they are, have not done so. The answer is the same every time, British have lost their old courage and dare-devillery. They have become sedate citizens of a glamorous world ready to guard their hoards but prizing their lives above all.

The Congress who we had always looked so far for leadership failed us when they miserably underrated Britain's strength, resources and diplomacy. We all know the result. But, where the Congress succumed, their teaching survived. Several independent bodies and parties, angry at the impotency of their leaders behind the bars, trumpeted revolution.

Several of these bodies we have helped and in some cases we have even engineered their issues. Our aim in aiding these operations of local sabotage was to help the country to obtain a favourable world opinion. From the informations at our disposal I can safely announce that the American and particularly the Chinese and Russian opinions have distinctly and effectively tilted in India's favour. This would be a help.

But, a settled Government like the British, cannot be over-thrown by world opinions or resolutions. Even sabotage of a vast magnitude would only result in the destruction of our own countrymen (the Police and the Saboteurs), each party pathetically imagining itself to be in the right. The only feasible answer to this fracas, is the active cooperation of the armed forces in this country.

Churchill's extraordinarily provocative declaration and the subsequent attempts at its justification, very nearly tipped us off our balance which would have resulted in enormous bloodshed and eventual, positive, defeat on our part. We thank the Providence for getting us out of that impasse.

Indian Army–Its Psychology

Today our army measures nearly one and half million. Over forty Brigades are serving outside the country. Every day, reports of terrible atrocities committed by the British Officers on the Indian troops pour in to us. Reports of British cowardice on the battlefields have nearly filled our files. Still the Indian Army is apparently intact - loyal to the British. Why? Because, deep down in the heart of every Indian, from rank and file to high above, there is a distinct feeling that the British would win in the end. Since the day of the mutiny, its disastrous effects on the Indian sepoys has always been rubbed into the Indian ranks and hence their sense of awe towards the British power.

In spite of these failings of the Indian Army it still remains an excellent machinery, which alone will be instrumental towards achieving the National Government.

Support the Congress

While we are reviewing Indian aspects in general we must not forget that it is only the issue of National Government that confronts us. It is the Congress that we wish to help. In all our previous meetings we had decided to avoid any contact with the Congress, yet. But now, time has come when we must join resources.

During our eleven months work we have grouped up 32 per cent of Indian Officers in our Army. This is a satisfactory figure considering that we are working under a lamentable stress of lack of funds. The ratio of British to Indian Officers today in our Army is 4.7 to 1, but even this ratio is steadily decreasing. Shortage of man-power in England makes the British Government dependent on Indian manpower not only for the Army but for the technical arms for the Air Force. The Government is evidently willing to /be taken in any Indian with the requisite education into the vital technical arm and perforce has to trust them. By the end of December 1942 a huge programme of Indianising the whole or the technical staff of the Royal Air Force is going to take effect. The replacement will be to the extent of 50,000 men and the recruitment of this staff is entirely in our hands. The whole of this enormous technical man-power will have to be recruited within two months and trained within a year entirely at Government expense. Every man recruited for this job will sign an allegiance to us and not the Government. The only unfortunate tragedy of this affair is that we face great difficulties in finding the right type of men. The Congress call not to enlist in the Army has effectively set back well over 60 per cent of the intelligent students. Although we have put our men at various universities working for the Government under Air Force training scheme, we find considerable difficulty in persuading the correct type of boys that we need for the great work.

If at this stage it could be engineered, such that the Congress could make peace with the Government of India, even under terms that may sound a little trifle and undignified, we could within the space of a year put at the disposal of the Congress vital armed forces strong enough to oust the British Government of power. Besides, a call from the Congress could let loose the intelligentsia, the material which is most suitable to us. Congress, once out of the bars should concentrate to capture power in departments of Home, Finance, Information and Broadcasting Communications, Wireless, and Civil Aviation. With Congress Ministers guiding the policy of these departments and we securing a strong foot-hold in the Armed Forces, the power of the Commander-in-chief would be null and void. It may be of interest to note that the C-in-C should be strictly left alone and even a Defence Minister's issue should not be forced.

Under our scheme of operations C-in-C's position will steadily deteriorate. Considering these factors we feel that it is essential for the Congress to patch up with the Government under whatever guise they consider best, as long as we get our material and formal support from the Congress Ministers.

Lately, reports have come to us stating that there have been considerable infiltration of Congress-minded youths into the Army. / lthough we have been able to suppress this dangerous allegation successfully, it only shows how much easier the whole process of recruitment would be for us under legal guise.

Under the new scheme of expansion of the Indian Air Force we shall have twenty squadrons of fighters and bombers within the space of one and half years. This, again, would be entirely our fabrications and would pay a vital part in our final operations.

Reviewing the world situation I strongly believe that Britain would eventually be victors. But whatever happens Germany's last blow to England would be so staggering that it may not be possible for them to recover for some time. It would be then that we would strike. With the essential services under our control and a majority of the Armed Forces on our side it would not be particularly difficult to overthrow the British Government in India. Once this is done, (which, incidentally would cause plenty of bloodshed throughout the country), we, the armed forces shall stand by the Congress in its efforts to form a National Government, till such time as it needs us, or alternatively, till the whole Indian Army is Nationalised.

APPENDIX 'B' TO DMI/4746

Extracts from Letters Addressed to the Organiser Congress Northern Zone

(A) In my last report I had mentioned that how we have worked our way into various Regiments. I also wrote about the contracts we have established. But for want of money we could not stabilise that work. Except the distribution of one pamphlet we did nothing further:

(ii) Now when we have established contacts 'above' our work is progressed methodically. Reliable contacts have been placed at Rawalpindi, Compbellpur, Jhelum, Sialkot, Lahore, Ferozepur, Ambala, Jullundur and Gurgaon. These persons have in turn developed their own contacts in the Regiments stationed at these places. It is expected that they will be able to distribute literature once a month at least.

(iii) We do have relations with the Regiments in the Frontier but we have no reliable men there. Therefore, there has been no work in that province so far. Contacts are established with soldiers when they proceed on leave to their villages. There is a great difficulty being experienced in the Frontier due to the strict vigilance of the Military Authorities. Often these regiments are in camps where even relatives cannot meet them. Besides there are many Cantonments where entry without permit is prohibited. We have got connections at Nowshera, Peshawar, Quetta and Landikotal. Pamphlets can be distributed to soldiers in the Regiments at these four places only when they proceed on leave.

(iv) Response from Gorkhas and Jats stationed at Abbottabad is very encouraging. Pamphlets in Nepali were distributed amongst the Gorkhas. One copy is sent herewith (no copy was actually received). There is a great enthusiasm amongst the soldiers.

They hate British Officers because of their (British Officers) discriminatory treatment towards them. This hatred is assuming a national character.

(v) It is our intention to extend our work to the Frontier from Abbottabad. How far we will be successful cannot be said.

(vi) In the Punjab, we have developed intimate relations with the Regiments stationed at Ambala, Gurgaon and Lahore. Great enthusiasm prevails here. We are very hopeful of the results. Cells are being established at these places.

(vii) We have trained our workers how to establish cells in the Regiments stationed in the Punjab Province.

(viii) There are aerodromes at Gurgaon, Mandauthi, Ambala, Lahore, Ferozepur and Sialkot. The pilots, who are generally from outside, include many Madrasis and Maharashtrians. We have not so far been able to establish any contact with these Pilots but efforts are being made and we hope to succeed soon.

(ix) We have good relations with M.T. walas. They have British officers but are ignorant of 'Nationalism' and Revolution. They take very long time to understand political matters. Besides, the question of bread always hounts them. But we are trying to make the best out of their hatred towards the British Officers. It has often been noticed that our pamphlets or preachings do not carry much weight with them as the talks of their own fellow soldiers. We have, therefore, tried to win over Jemadar, Havaldars and Naiks in every Regiments. They can easily influence soldiers to their point of view. The Jats are very enthusiastic about our work. The Dogras, Brahmins and the State Regiments easily accept our suggestions. Sepoys are keen to hear sensational news. At several places they have expressed desire to come to us. We have already established groups in villages who distribute pamphlets and do propaganda among soldiers while on leave.

B. Punjabi has begun to work. I have hunted up all the workers who were sitting idle and uncoordinated. Sections of Ahrars and Sikhs have come up. Provincial office is fully organised with Ludhiana Sheikhupura, Sialkot, Patiala, Lahore.

Printing of bulletins in Urdu, Gurumukhi and English have been organised. Separate arrangements have been made for propaganda amongst students, Sikhs and Muslims. Army Department has its own publicity arrangement, which published leaflets in five languages. Work in the Army is going on nicely, enclosed report will show how our pamphlets have been received. Army Department has established nine branches.

Gandhiji's fast is servings its own purpose. Lahore responded well. All colleges were closed on the first few days. Now is the time to push on work vigorously.

Sabotage Department has now begun functioning and you will hear something in the coming weeks. Now I am in a position to give you a rough monthly budget for work in Punjab.

According to present calculations, I am not expecting to get more than Rs. 4000/- here per month. So, you should be ready to give us Rs. 8000/- per month. Now when Punjab is coming up, we should work with full vigour. When once Punjab masses take up, Punjab will be in the forefront and it will affect the personnel of the Army all over India.

I have contacted workers in Jammu and work will begin there shortly. For broadcasting a gentleman has offered the materials free. We have only to bear the recurring charges. I have not yet seen them. Next I will be able to tell you in detail about them.

What about those Districts of Punjab that are close to Delhi. I would prefer, if you can arrange, work in them from Delhi. In that please let me know in details what districts I have to leave from my account.

P.S. Situation is developing rapidly and it is going beyond my resources now.

About Sind. If you send me the contacts, I can go there and find out how things are working there.

APPENDIX 'C' TO DMI/4746

Translation of Manuscript Letter in Both Urdu and Gurmukhi Script Found in Forward Area in Arakan

Dear Army Brother,

Today, the 16th February, the Jap Army have brought an Indian soldier named Peyarai of Meerut Dist., No...... Copy ......, ...Regt. On inquiry it was found that on the 14th February he, with Lieut ...., Subedar .... and 15 soldiers went on patrol. He was arrested by the Jap soldiers and sent to me.

According to his statement most of his companions wish for independence and want to join our side. But they are frightened by untrue British propaganda that the Japs used to kill prisoners and for this reason the majority do not come over to our side.

This is just British propaganda. We soldiers of lthe Indian Army were all captured in Malaya and Burma, we have been given Independence and are working an Independant Army to fight for the Independence of India.

You are all come to sacrifice your lives for Rs. 20/- or 25/- a month. For the cruel British you have left your dear parents, brothers, and relations. Do you not know that this cruel government hanged thousands of lovers of their country? Our leaders were sent to jail and bombs were dropped daily on innocent Hindus, who were ill-treated in various ways. It is better for you that you should all sacrifice your lives for the independence of your motherland.

Any brothers, who gets this letter is requested to convey this message to all Hindu, Muslim and Sikh soldiers who come close to us. You can come straightaway without fear after hiding your arms in the jungle. If you bring arms with you the Japs will suspect you to be enemies. The hiden arms will be of use to us very soon. When you come to this side show a white flag and keep your hands up whenever and wherever you meet Jap soldiers. Then tell them to take you to Capt. Mohan Singh, Indian National

Army. The Japs will bring you straightaway to me. Then you will be an independent soldier of the Independent Army under me. Officers will be given their respective ranks.

Brothers, what more am I to write to you. Please take my short letter to be a lengthy and important one as the time is very short. Do not lose this present opportunity. Time is going to be changed very soon or we will be loser.

Get up and wake.

Yours obediently,
Sd/-
Capt. Mohan Singh
Indian National Army.

APPENDIX 'D' TO DMI/4746

Extract from "Security" History of 'X' Battalion

1. The Battalion includes one company of Sikhs (mostly Jat), and one company of Jats.

   The Sikh company first came to Security notice in September 1940 when a reservist, backed by three others, tried to make the wearing of steel helmets a religious questions. One of these reservists had already been noted corresponding with a Sikh N.C.O. who had been imprisoned for playing a leading part in mass desertions of Sikhs from another unit on the eve of its departure overseas. Following on a police report of a statement by a man on leave that secret meetings were held in the unit by subversive elements. Security investigations resulted in seven suspects being removed. While the investigations were in progress three Sikhs (reservists) deserted under suspicious circumstances. There is little doubt that this trouble was linked with Kirti Communist plot, which formed the background to the 3/Ist Punjab desertions, the R.I.A.S.C. mutiny in Egypt, and the C.I.H. mutiny.

2. A close Security watch was kept on the unit and a Sikh N.C.O. was detected receiving Young Communist literature from another Sikh N.C.O. who had been earlier discharged as an undesirable. Except for this minor incident, the Security "clean up" of unit appeared to have been effective, although an ex-Subedar Major came to notice about this time, belonging to the same village as the purveyor of Communist literature, and two notorious Ghadrites who had returned from Fiji. This V.C.O. had left the unit in June 1940 (some three months before the steel helmet trouble) in an apparently disgruntle from of mind as he considered that his services (described by his C.O. as mainly trouble making and intrigue) had not been adequately recognized by Government. A unit report in September 1941 suggested that the influence of this V.C.O. apparently lingered on in the unit.

3. In January 1941 there were three instances of Sikhs receiving sure subversive pamphlets by post, but the C.O. eventually decided that these were "put up" shows, the motive being to obtain discharge. A number of other incidents, connected with the receipt of subversive literature (also a Sikh desertion with arms) occurred between January and June 1941, from when, following the discharge of suspect, no further incidents were reported until the receipt of an anonymous letter by the C.O. in December 1941. This was to the effect that as it was possible that the unit would soon go on service and many men were in debt, they should receive their credits in the Provident Fund in order to enable them to discharge these debts, and that otherwise the men might refuse to go overseas. Actually out of 300 men sent on leave prior to going on service only one failed to return.

4. **Bihar, May 1942.** Five Sikh sepoys deserted one taking his rifle and bayonet. Next day one Jat N.C.O. and four sepoys deserted. No evidence of subversive activities came to light and Jat and Sikh patrols from the unit are said to have done their utmost to apprehend the deserters. About the same time a very large number of letters were received from relatives requesting leave for men on compassionate grounds. Prior to its move to the ARAKAN area in June-July 1942, the Battalion showed a high incidence of sickness.

5. **ARAKAN rear area, July 1942.** A Jat line sentry deserted with arms.

September 1942. Another Jat desertion with arms and ammunition occurred. Three days later on V.C.O. and seven other "Escapees" from Japanese hands reported to a detachment of the Battalion. The party included one Naik subsequently catogorised as "Grey". The escapees were said to have been immediately handed over to Bde. HQ for interrogation.

November 1942. Congress agents were reliably reported to have contacted some men of the Battalion in Chittagong and to have been assured that they would join the movement when well advanced. The C.O. and Brigade Comdr. were fully in the picture, but as the unit had moved into the forward area further trouble was not anticipated.

6. **Field Censorship Report:**

January-February 1943—The unit was specially mentioned as a unit which “as a whole” complained of delays in payments of family allotments.

7. **February 1943**. A patrol from this unit reported that they had found two letters stuck in trees, one in Urdu and the other in Gurmukhi, addressed to Indian troops and signed by Capt. Mohan Singh of the I.N.A. (quoted in Appendix 'C'). The Sepoy mentioned was reported as captured by the enemy on 12th February 1943 east of Rathedaung. He returned from Japanese occupied territory on 7th March, 1943 with the party of possible I.N.A. Personnel, and is now under interrogation.

8. A point which may, or may not, have significance is that one of the I.C.Os who was transfered from the 4/19 Hyderabad Regiment, subsequent to the trouble in that unit in Singapore in July 1940, was posted to 'X' Battalion.

9. A further possible line of investigation which is being followed up, lies in statements recently obtained from a fanatical young Sikh agitator who stated that he has been employed in subversive troops under Subhas Chandra Bose's instructions. One of the units which he claimed to have established contacts is 'X" Battalion.

APPENDIX 'E' TO DMI/4746

Extracts from a letter from a K.C.I.O.[1] dated 13-3-1943

18th March, 1943

I have already stated that the I.N.A. is not to be feared as a fighting force but purely because of the Psychological effect it may have on the Indian portion of the Army as well as Civil population of this country. When dealing with this problem we must be absolutely clear about certain basic facts. However unpleasant they may be they are realities which must be faced. I say that without being unduly pessimists about this. These facts are as follows:—

(1) Every Indian (soldier included) desires a higher political status for India. The difference is only in degree. The extremists want complete Independence - the moderates Dominion status and the last group will be satisfied with something approaching Dominion status. This produces a feeling of dissatisfaction which does not always or even nearly always amount to disloyalty at present but under certain circumstances it might even develop into disloyalty. This fact is most important and must not be lost sight of.

(2) The second fact is a natural corollary of the first one in that from the point of view of the British every Indian is a possible 5th Columnist (this is difficult to write about). The number of people I have met both official and non-official who indulge in defeatist talk and take up an attitude of indifference about the Japanese menace is alarmingly large.

Indians from the British point of view may be classified into the following three categories:-

Category 1 : Strongly anti-British and some even pro-Japanese. This type are prepared to be actively hostile. They are only

1. K.C.I.O. King's Commissioned Indian Officers usually came from well-to-do families. They had their education in British public schools and later on in the British Military Academy at Sandhurst. They were pro-British in their leanings and some of them joined the I.N.A. with the intention of deserting it at the first opportunity.

a small minority.

Category 2 : Indifferent. They are the type who will adjust themselves to Jap masters if circumstances shape that way. This is the largest group and herein lies real danger.

Category 3 : Strongly pro-British and will fight the invader as readily or even more so than the British. This again is a small group but let us hope not smaller than Category 1

The above classification applies to all Indians, soldiers and civilians. The most dangerous group is Category 2 because it is by far largest group and is composed of people who have not any character (unfortunately a quality whicn is not possessed by the average man in these times). An average Army or civil officer and man would fell into this group. Most of the people here are time servers who will serve any master. Many amongst them are very vocal in their profession of loyalty and devotion to the British. It is an unfortunate fact that they have to be generally speaking accepted at their face value by the British. Loyalty is not quite as general as it believed by Senior British Officers. A number of people are loyal but they will only remain so long as it suits them.

That we have to tell people something about the INA and IIL there is no doubt about it because if we do'nt tell them they will learn about it from other sources, i.e., radio and whispering agents. My own opinion is that we must tell the barest minimum and ensure that the knowledge of these organisations does not give direct or indirect incouragement to the enemies of Britain in India[2].

2. But subsequently it was decided not to give any information about the I.N.A. in all the official correspondence, the use of the word I.N.A. was stopped, instead, it was mentioned as J.I.F.C. (Japanese Inspired Fifth Columnist)

8

Order by Shah Nawaz Khan from Headquarter I.N.A. Bidadari Regarding the Re-Organisation of the I.N.A.[1]

22 March, 1943

Sub.—Policy regarding re-organization of the I.N.A.

Herewith 2 copies of "Policy regarding Re-organization of the I.N.A." for necessary action, please.

(Sd.) Shah Nawaz Khan, Lt.-Col. C.G.S., Office of the D.M.B., I.I.L.

Copy to—

Iwakura Kikan.

Policy regarding Re-organization of the I.N.A.

1. All the formations in the I.N.A. will first re-organize within themselves. Units and sub-units will be completed in strength by a process of amalgamation. Any deficiencies will be made up from the reinforcement camp. These will be demanded as far as possible, as complete units and sub-units. Say, for instance, after re-organization Gandhi Regt. 4th Bn., is deficient of three platoons of Sikhs and one Section of Jats, Comd. Ghandi Regt. will place his demand on the Army Commander, who will forward it to the D.M.B., who, in turn, will place them on the O.C. reinforcements. System of going direct and selecting men from the reinforcement camp is strictly forbidden.
2. Reinforcement camp is being formed as soon as circumstances, permit. All the volunteers for the I.N.A. from prisoners of war camps in Syonan, and from the mainland will be concentrated there and organized on the same basis as the corresponding units of I.N.A.
3. Comd. reinforcement is entirely responsible for the organization, training, disciplines and administration of all such men under his command. He will maintain a complete record of each individual coming to his camp, showing the date of joining, original unit, place from where he came and how finally disposed of.

1. I.N.A. Trial Papers.

4. It is notified for the information of all concerned that owing to the very small number of P.M. and Sikh volunteers coming forward to join the I.N.A., Jat and Gujjar Companies may have to be accepted in their place.

5. Army Commander is requested to forward to these H.Qrs. deficiencies by Regiments, as envisaged by this letter as soon as possible, please.

6. This letter will take effect immediately as no more volunteers are expected to rejoin their units from Separation Camps.

Sd./-
Shah Nawaz Khan,[2]
Lt.-Col. C.G.S.,
Office of the D.M.B., I.I.L.
Syonan, 22/3/1943.

2. Lt. Colonel, Shah Nawaz Khan, came from a wealthy Loyal Muslim family of Rawalpindi, whose members had served the British Raj. He was born in1914. After a few years in school, he joined the Prince of Walse Military Academy from where he passed to join the Indian Army in 1935. He went to Singapore in January 1942. Joined the Indian National Army, was devoted to Subhas Chandra Bose and was member of the Provisional Government of India, took command of the 2nd Division of the I.N.A. and fought against the British along with the Japanese. Was tried by the British for Waging War against the king in what is known as I.N.A. Trials, Red Fort. After independence joined the Indian National Congress and served as a Minister.

An Appeal by A. Yellapa President I.I.L. Singapore to Indian Youth in Malaya to Come Forward and Fight for the Liberation of India[1]

29 March, 1943

One Organisation, One Leader and One Fight and Our Poorna Swaraj is Assured

Indian comrades must be aware of the official permission granted by the Malai Branch of the Indian Independence League to start the Indian Youth Movement all over Malai as a section of the Indian Independence League. In this connection, we would like to point out to our readers that this is the result of our steady action which some of our self-interested leaders misinterpreted and cried to level charges against people who were not responsible for it at all. Not realising their own shortcomings, that it was indeed the most selfish thing to-supress the youth, who undoubtedly form the backbone of a nation, the members of the Territorial Committee[2], Malai passed the following resolution at a meeting held at Penang some time ago.

"That this committee, having considered a scheme for a youth Movement on which it has been withholding action pending an opportune moment, views with grave concern the attempt that has been made to organize an Indian Youth Movement :—

Comrades there cannot be any better opportune moment than this to organize ourselves and to strength our cause. If any particular committee or section of people neglected us and oppressed us for no reason at all, we are solely to blame, for we relied too much on them and thought that they were sincere in their undertakings. They may be sincere, but definitely

1. *The Young India*, March 29, 1943.
2. This refers to the Territorial Committee, which were formed after the Bangkok Conference with the specific aim of supervising the working of the Indian Independence League within the countries of South-East Asia.

they have proved themselves unworthy, as the resolution clearly indicates. Why should there be any objection for a good work done to strengthen our cause? Why view the move with concern? It matters little, who does it, but if it is for the good of the cause, it should be welcome with satisfaction. Any one who tries to bring in the question of discipline and under its cover seeks for name and fame and self aggrandizement, is deliberately trying to harm the movement.

Our object is to fight our way and purify the activities of the Indian Independence League. Now that permission has been granted, we hope that the youth workers themselves should be very careful, so that they do not become a group of pro-British elements and targets for criticism. Instead, they should organise themselves into a strong and healthy body to fight our way till India is liberated from the yoke of British slavery. We should not deter from our main objective. We will fight till India is free. Our purpose is not to seek name and fame, but to work for the holy cause under one leader.

I thank you for accepting me as the President of the Indian Independence League, Syonan Branch. It is needless for me to emphasize the fact that the President of the I.I.L. Syonan Branch and the members of the Youth Section should understand the seriousness of the mission that we have undertaken and work as one indivisible unit for our deliverance. You all know that the most sincere worker amongest us today is Sri Rash Behari Bose, that great patriot of India and our leader and you also know that he has been and is still striving hard to lead us from darkness to light eternal.

Strong language should not be our strong point. Therefore, in the name of our sacred Mother Country in the name of the thousands of Indian martyrs who had laid down their lives in their struggle for freedom, in the name of our leaders in their struggle for freedom, in the name of India and in the name of those women of India whose brothers, husbands and fathers have undergone untold sufferings as a penalty for their love of freedom let us vow that we will organize ourselves as well-disciplined youths and march forward with Indian National Army for the fulfilment of our Mission under the able leadership of Sri Rash Behari Bose. May the almighty guide us in our struggle.

Yours in service,
A. Yellappa

10

Statement by Rash Behari Bose; Informs about the Revised Plan for the role of the I.I.L. and I.N.A. in the Light of the Resignation of the Members of the Council of Action[1]

5 April, 1943

Owing to a series of "Crises" and resignations, the general public has begun to entertain doubts regarding the Indian Independence Movement.

Our present state of inaction, however, is due to certain weakness inherent in the organisation which has guided the Movement so far. We have to examine the background and the surrounding circumstances under which the old system came into being and I find these factors to be radically changed.

Whereas in June, 1942, India was pressing for Independence from the British, today she is fighting for against Britain, both morally and physically. It was to increase the physically pressure against the British war-effort that Mahatma Gandhi recently risked his very life.

The collapse of the British war-effort would have meant the retreat of the Anglo-American forces now in contact with the Japanese forces on the Indian Border. The extent to which the British forces return is the extent to which Japanese forces advance; and that contact cannot be broken till one side is defeated. What is obvious to us, is obvious to the Indian National Congress. The Congress has considered the consequence and made the choice.

The safeguards and assurance for which we asked in June 1942 are now not necessary. Our aim is only to convert the potential strength of the Congress into an actuality and help the Congress in proclaiming a National Government. The League is NOT a state but only the begetters of a state. The future constitution of India as the relation of the Indian National Government with Japan will be decided by the Congress itself.

---

1. Indian Independence League Papers, F. No. 45/3 See also S.A. Das and K.B. Subbaiah, **Chalo Delhi**, Kaula Lumpur 1946, pp. 105-108.

In the past we have followed a system of collective responsibility and elections, similiar to that adopted by the Congress in peacetime to wrest political control by a process of Evolution. Our object is Revolution.

In the past the resignation of a member or members has resulted in the dislocation of Vital Departments, Civil or Military. This may be tolerated in peace time but never in time of War.

My immediate concern is to maintain the League as a fighting organisation, so that even if individuals indulge in a process of trial and error, the departments go on discharging their vital functions.

The following interim plan has therefore been drawn up to put the League on a war-footing.

I. Guiding Principles

1. Freedom cannot be won by a universal longing for it.
2. The success of each Branch of the I.I.L. will be judged from the number of young men it can produce, educate and train as potential fighting men for the Independence of India, and not from the numbers of Office bearers who can argue, or resign.
3. No Nation on earth holds a square foot of territory by any right of argument. The frontiers of a country are held by the human effort of the nation.
4. We must in the interests of the Nation, conserve that human effort by avoiding any action showing divison or lack of solidarity.

II. Functions of the League Branches

The Indian Independence Movement is a people's Revolutionary Movement and Not literary Clubs or debating societies. The League Branches, therefore, have three main functions:

1. The Political Awakening of the Masses with a view to producing a body of the patriots with a revolutionary spirit.
2. To obtain the financial and moral support of all those who cannot take active part in the movement.
3. To undertake due share of social uplift and relief work without getting involved in local Administrative problems.

To give concrete shape to Item No. 1, a Youth Section will be started immediately on receipt of this communication.

A women's section with its own President is to be started wherever practicable.

A Movement for boys and girls under 17 will also be started. In all National Schools Hindustani will be taught, patriotic songs will be sung and significance of daily saluting of National Flag will be taught. (Uniform same as Seva Samiti in India, i.e., Boy Scout or Girl Guide Uniform with Tricolour Scarf).

To body of spirited young people so produced will help in the other two activities of the League.

III. Naujavan Section (Youth Section)

Object: To train Indian Youths in East Aisa to:

1. Become revolutionary soldiers in the fight for India's Independence.
2. Behave as free citizens who with their example will foster the spirit of independence among the inhabitants of occupied territories.

It is suggested that where the Vice-Presidents of the Local Branches are willing to serve the National cause actively they themselves may take over the Youth Section otherwise suitable young men will be appointed by the presidents concerned.

Syllabus : The following is issued as a guide. Time Tables and period of training will, of course, vary according to the facilities in each centre.

(i) Elementary Drill and Route Marches.

Weapon training, Rifle, Pistol, Grenade

(I.N.A. Japanese side have consented to provide staff to work at different centres).

Relief Work: Nursing, Stretchers bearing, First Aid, A.R.P. Hygeine.

Meeting: National and Social Dreams.

Bicycle trips to places 30 or 40 miles away cooking of own food.

(ii) Physical Training and Labour. Building of Wooden Bridge, swimming, digging slit trenches, rowing and games.

(iii) Education: Teaching of Hindustani.

Significance of the War of Greater East Asia.

Geography, topography, maps with special reference to India.

Weak points in British War organisation and Civil administration in India.

History of British aggression in India.

Study of lives of Congress Leaders.

Study of Nippon-government will be encouraged.

(iv) National Discipline: Obey before you command. Building of character, self reliance, right living, right thinking, love for country. Ordinary Military discipline, Punctuality.

(v) National Culture : Common manners and customs. Army salute. Common good, common dress, Khaki shorts or trousers, rubber shoes with shirts. Head dress, Khaki Gandhi cap with double fold. Tricolour rectangle 5" × 2" on the left arm.

Note. Women's and Boys' and Girls' sections will choose suitable subjects from the above syllabus.

Organisation

As the Youth Movement is the potential reserve for the Indian National Army, the League "Naujawan Sections" will adopt similar organisation.

Unit of 10 .... Section
4 Sections .... Platoons
4 Platoons .... Company
5 Companies .... Battalion
3 Battalion .... Regiment.
3 Regiments .... Formation.

For the present each Branch should aim at a maximum of one Company at the discretion of the Territorial President. The training will be the entire responsibility of the League Branch and should be carried out on the most economical line, e.g., those who can afford should be encouraged to meet their own expenses. (The Naujawan Section is a popular Movement run on the lines of the Boy Scout Movement).

A tour inspection will be arranged by this headquarters during the month of April.

Training Centres for Youth Workers

In order to start a really strong youth movement a nucleus of trained workers is necessary.

An experimental school for training 50 such workers will be started at Syonan (Azad Institute Syonan) with effect from the 1st April, 1943.

The first course will last for two months at the end of which these trained workers will be available for posting to various centres.

A infiltration course for 100 young men from all territories will start on the 1st May, 1943, at the Swaraj Institute, Penang. Duration three months. From among the present Graduates from the Swaraj Institute Penang, some will be selected by this Headquarters for immediate posting as trained workers for the Youth Sections in various Branches.

The Burma Branch is running its own training centre at Rangoon on the lines of the Azad Institute Syonan. Military Staff has been borrowed from the Burma Detachment of the I.N.A.

Pocket Money

Pocket money at the rate of S. 800 will be given to all students at the Azad School. Syonam and the Swaraj Institute, Penage, as well as to the civil volunteers at the training school at Kuala Lumpur. Rations and uniforms will be free.

Military Training

The main centre of civilian volunteers for the training as regular soldiers is at present at Kuala Lumpur.

Duration of Course

Four months.

1000 volunteers will be ready for absorption in the I.N.A. by the end of May.

Recruiting will be done through the Branches of the League from their Youth Sections. The Malaya Branch can apply to this Headquarters for Medical Officers when required. The Burma and Thailand Branches can obtain assistance from the I.N.A. Detachment of Indian Army detachments stationed there.

In view of the limited training staff and the expenditure involved. NOT more than 5000 recruits can be trained at one time. If accommodation is available the Kuala Lumpur school will be expensed to accommodate these 5000. Otherwise more centres will be opened to accommodate that number.

The following approximate numbers should be kept ready by the middle of May.

Thailand	1000
Burma	1000
Malaya	1000
Hong -Kong and Shanghai	1000
Borneo and Sumatra	1000
Java, Philippines, Celebes	1000
	6000

All Branches will please estimate and inform this Headquarters of the number of recruits likely to be forthcoming from their territories during the year 1943.

Finance

The present scheme for actual military training throughout East Asia for the next 1¼ year is for 20,000 volunteers to be trained in four batches. Ultimate object is to train maximum number available in East Asia.

Syllabus

1. Preliminary training with the object of becoming tough guerrilla fighters :–
2. Drill. Physical training (P. T.) Route Marches, Weapons (Rifle, Bayonet, Tommy Gun, Pistol, Bombs and Hand Grenades).
3. General spiritual training, i.e., making them proud of themselves as Indians and determined to achieve and maintain the freedom of their country.

Training Staff

For a batch of 1000 volunteers the following are required.

Major	1	Medical Officer	1
Captains	2	Asst. M. O.	1
Subalterns	3	Asst. M. O.	1
N.C.O.s	20	Nursing Ord	5
Sepoys	100	Clerks	4
	126	Amb. N. C. O.	1
		Total	139

These have been seconded for duty with the Volunteers by the Indian National Army.

Absorption in the I.N.A.

(a) Headquarters, I.N.A.
(b) Guerilla Regiments
(c) Special Service Group
(d) Intelligence Group
(e) Reinforcement Group
(f) Field Force Group...

With their civil experience these volunteers will be more useful in these rather than in the Field force Group.

It is obvious that all cannot be absorbed in the I.N.A. owing to the limited number of arms now available. Some of the remainder will either go to other schools such as the officers. Training School or the Civil Administration School (See below) or go back as fully trained instructors for training the youths in each territory in East Asia. The names of all trained personnel will be put on the list of reserve volunteers to be called up when required.

The system is analogous to the conscription system obtaining in other countries.

Other Activities of League

It is proposed to start the following institutions as soon as accommodation and staff is available.

1. Officers' Training School

For the training of future officers of the Indian National Army. Vacancies will be allotted both to the Civilians being trained at Kuala Lumpur and to candidates from the Indian National Army.

2. Staff College

For the higher training of senior officers of the I.N.A.

3. Civil Administration School

For the political training of officers both civil and military. The civilian will be chosen from among students of the various training institutes. Special cases can be recommended by the Territorial Presidents.

Reorganisation of Headquarters.

In order to cope with the immediate task in hand the following interim organisation of the headquarters came into from w.e.f. 1.4.43 when headquarters will be established at Road, Syonan.

11

British Assessment of the Indian National Army and its Activities[1] (Extract)

17 April, 1943

6. Recent information shows that a Gurkha O. R., who was taken prisoner during the Burma campaign early in 1942 and was in Japanese hands for over six months, volunteered for "contact work" in Burma, in the course of which he rejoined our forces at Magwe with other fifth column volunteers. Subsequently he deserted, taking with him a Jamadar and two O. Rs., who had been persuaded to join the enemy by one of the G.O.R 's fifth column companies. He then surrendered to the Japanese and again joined a fifth column party at Yunangyang and accompanied it to Mandalay and Maymyo. Later he returned to Rangoon, where he was detailed to form one of a fifth column party which left for India at the end of August 1942, with instructions to collaborate with Congress workers and help them in destroying communications, dumps, etc.

7. This account of the G.O.R.'s history since first being taken prisoner by the Japanese is believed to be substantially true. It is the first definite instance which has so far come to notice of the success of a Japanese–inspired "contact party" in Burma in winning over men from our forces in the field. Incidentally, although most of the personalities involved in this episode were Gurkhas, this does not invalidate the conclusions reached in paragraph 3 of Survey No. 13 of 1943. where the reactions of Gurkhas to I.N.A. propaganda were discussed. It is perhaps significant that neither the G.O.R., the successful propagandist who accompanied him, nor any of the soldiers who were seduced from their loyalty in this affair came from Nepal. The two Japanese agents are line boys from Almora and Dharmasala respectively, the Jamadar is also a Dharmsala lineboy, while one of the O. Rs. is a Darjeeling Gurkha and the other a Dogra.

1. Military Department F. No. L/WS/1/1576. India office Library and Records, London.

8. In addition to the above report, it is known that fifth column parties consisting of men from a Sikh Regiment and from the Burma Army also returned to the Japanese after being sent out on contact work among Indian Troops during the first Burma campaign, thus demonstrating the success achieved by the original contact party which set to work from Prome.

9. There is evidence from the Arakan front that the enemy has already attempted to use his fifth column tactics against Indian troops, easing his approach on the I.N.A. principle. In March 1943 attempts to suborn the loyalty of Indian Troops in forward areas took the form of notices in Urdu and Gurmukhi signed by Captain Mohan Singh, stuck at trees where they would be found by our patrols; leaflets have also been dropped by Japanese aircraft, one of them being headed "Singapore– the cradle of Indian Army revolt" exhorting Indian soldiers to join hands with their "comrades from Malaya". Sikh and Punjabi battle–cries were heard during an enemy attack, and voices called to our troops in Indian vernaculars; there is also reason to believe that "contact parties" were assisting in the interrogation of prisoners and in efforts to persuade them to join the I.N.A.

10. In this connection it was recently discovered that one of the I.N.A. leaders had advised the Japanese that suitable Indian prisoners taken in Arakan should be given immediate instructions and propaganda treatment and returned to the British lines as quickly as possible. In this way it was hoped that they would rejoin their units so rapidly that they might appear merely to have got temporarily separated during action, and would not be suspected of having been in enemy hands. As an example of these instructions being put into effect, it is interesting to learn that three I.O. Rs., who were taken prisoner by the Japanese early in March, were released to spread anti-British propaganda only a fortnight later. One of these prisoner had a pass signed on behalf of the Iwakuru Kikan, certifying that he was employed by that organization and asking all concerned to afford him the necessary facilities to enable him to carry out his task. This is the first known instance of Indian prisoners taken on the Arakan front being released for propaganda purposes. These men are being interrogated.

12

Welcome Address by A. Yellappa at the I.I.L. Conference at Singapore; Emphasis the Need for Activating the I.I.M. and put it on War Footing[1]

27 April, 1943

Mr. Presidents, Delegates from East Asia and Friends,

On behalf of Indians of Syonan–I welcome you all to this city and I hope you will kindly forgive me for having delayed the proceedings for about half an hour. The rain in the morning upset all our programme.

Now, we have a Conference in Bangkok some time in June last year. Since then the events in India have changed. As you all know in India the British have rejected our "Quit India" policy. They are murdering our Brothers and sisters in numbers, machine–gunning them. It is our duty, Gentleman, to find out ways and means to revolutionise the Indian Independence Movement. It is no use having a democratic Constitution and having discussions on the Constitution. It is now for us to revolutionise this Movement and put the whole thing on a war footing.

We have heard, Gentleman, General Iwakuro, who came here on the 25th, and again he came in our midst yesterday and he has been repeating the same thing. He told us last time that we must have the spirit of sacrifice. We must have a sense of unity and we must make up our minds and find out where we stand. And he also said that among Indians there are some people who are real workers, some are half and some a quarter. But I can assure you Gentlemen, that every Indian, whether he is from the North, South or any part of India, every Indian wants to be free. It is the instinct of every human being to be free but the methods to be adopted differ,. Some may be longing to be free, some want to be free but want somebody else to do the work and some are real workers. We are not going into any discussion into these things, but our President will address you at length.

1. I.I.L. Papers. F. No 45/3.

My humble submission is this that we have today gathered here on a very important mission, that is to find out ways and means to put the whole Movement on a war footing. We are not fighting, Gentlemen, for leadership, we are not fighting as to who should be the leader and who should be sub–leaders, "We are fighting for a cause, and today we have only one leader, that is Sri Ras Behari Bose (Applause) and unless and until we have complete faith in him, and we are prepared to work with him there is no use having conferences. If we are not satisfied with something or other, it is for us to approach him and tell him—he is always amenable to reason and he is always approachable—and I do not want to waste your time by saying more. At this Conference today, we have a Subjects Committee meeting. The President will tell you the programme.

I thank you all for having come to this city and honoured us.

13

Opening Address by Rash Behari Bose at the I.I.L. Conference; Appeals to the Delegates to Join Hands for Achieving Indian Independence with Japanese Help

27 April, 1943

Comrades and Countrymen,

It is with mingled feelings of joy and regret that we are meeting today to discuss ways and means for the liberation of our Motherland. This is the third time within a short period of one year that we are meeting for one and same purpose. I used the words "feelings of joy and regret" – joys because our enemy is being consistently defeated by the Imperial Nippon forces and thus the British Chain of Imperialism which is strangling India is being weakened daily and our hopes of Independence are brightening; regret, because the actions of some of my colleagues have marred temporarily the speedy progress of our Movement. But with the help of Almighty God all the difficulties have been overcome, the whole Movement has been rejuvenated and placed on a more solid ground than hitherto and I can assure you that if I continue to receive your full support and co-operation our success is at hand.

Before going any further I shall repeat my words of warning in the very opening chapter of my speech at the Bangkok Conference. I wish to reiterate the same words, as I hope that it will not be necessary for us to meet again before the liberation of India. I said thus: However, if I have obeyed your command and taken this chair in spite of my knowledge of the intricacies of the problems that may confront me. I have been prompted to do so by my great faith in your spirit of co-operation and your sincere desire to put your heads together and to come to useful decisions without wasting much of your time on unnecessary discussions and arguments. I was prompted by the experience of the Tokyo Conference to give those words of warning but, despite all that, the result of the deliberations of the

1. I.I.L. Papers F. No. 45/3. See also K.S. Giani, *op. cit* pp. 140-142.

Bangkok Conference is well known to you. To remedy the short-comings of the last Conference, it has been necessary for me to call you the representatives of different territories in East Asia, and also the representatives of the Indian National Army. Let us put our heads together once again and work out a plan which should be very short and effective in our organisation and the progress of the Movement. It is a time for action and not words, so you must avoid all lengthy arguments and jugglery of words. Before working out a plan you must remember two points, (a) that Japan is at war and we can expect only what can conventionally be given to us because their needs are above ours and (b) we are preparing to get into action very soon, so the constitution should be as brief and simple as possible.

I do not wish to take up much of your time by reading out to you the history of the Indian Independence Movement, but I would like to mention a few facts which should always be remembered by every Indian. The foundation of Indian Independence was laid in 1857 when the most ruthless policies of the British resulted in a catastropic breakdown in the social and economic life of the Indians and the dissatisfaction of the people against British domination finally reached the bursting point when almost the whole country revolted to oust the British from India. This battle for Indian independence was described by the British as the Indian Mutiny. But was that a mutiny? I say NO, it was a holy war against the inhuman treatment of Indians by the British. It failed because there was no capable leader to lead the Movement to a success. Six thousand of our compatriots were hanged just because they were asking for their birthright. But since that day the seeds of Swaraj have been nourished by the blood of thousands of our beloved and respected leaders. Just a few days ago mass meetings were held in all the territories in East Asia in memory of the martyrs of Jalianwala Bagh. Let us pay respect to the memory of all those numberless known and unknown comrades who laid down their lives in the cause of their Motherland. The time is fast approaching when in every city and town in India we shall find a worthy monument erected in their memory so that posterity will pay homage to them and look upon them with pride.

You all know that great changes have taken place both in and outside India since the Bangkok Conference last year and so it is essential that we should also speed up our activities to keep pace with the progress of world events. You all know that the "Quit India" resolution was passed by the Congress Committee in the presence of Mahatma Gandhi on 8th August last year, and immediately after the meeting of Congress Committee,

Mahatma Gandhi and the President of the Congress, Maulana Abdul Kalam Azad and all the other leaders were imprisoned. It was then that the active struggle of unarmed people commenced against the armed forces of Britain. Thousands upon thousand have been thrown into prisons. Defenceless people have been shot dead and they are still being murdered daily. Villages have been bombed and machine-gunned and the properties of the innocent confiscated. But the war continues unabated and it will continue until India is free. It is therefore imperative that we should do our bit at this end to lighten the burden of our compatriots at home. Now is the time for action and not for talk. Our people are suffering under the tyrannical rule of the British in India and it is the duty of every Indian in the East to be ready to sacrifice his all when the call of his country comes.

Friends, The War of Greater East Asia is a gift from God for us Indians and every day which follows, looks brighter for Indians. Practically all the Far East has been cleared ofthe Anglo–Saxon races and their allies and it will not be long before India will also rank among the Free nations of the world. I have been working in Japan for decades so I can see that Japan is in a position to stand by the oppressed Asians and to liberate Asia. I was anxiousty awaiting the day when Japan would fully realizing the great significance of creating a free and united Asia and would feel convinced that it was in the interests of Japan itself, as also for the rest of Asia if not for the world as a whole, that the octopus grip of the Anglo-Saxon Imperialism in the East must be destroyed root and branch.

I was fully convinced that Japan alone was in a position to take the honour. I knew well that she was not in the habit of taking any serious steps unless she had fully weighed her strength and was convinced of her success. The ultimate result of her action is well known to you all. Realizing the full significance of the situation, China joined hand with Japan and declared war on the Anti-Axis powers. Japan on the other hand as a true friend took the lead and relinquished her extra-territorial rights in China which was consequently followed by all other friendly nations. The dream of Dr. Sun Yat Sen, the father of China, has been realised through the help and co-operation of Japan.

Another important happening since the Bangkok Conference is the declaration made by His Excellency General Hideki Tojo, the Premier of Japan, promising Burmese people their independence within this year. One cannot over-emphasis the good intention of Japan towards all Asiatic people and the case of Burma is an outstanding example my brothern in Burma on this very auspicious occasion.

Let us not forget that the greatest living Indian, Mahatma Gandhi who undertook twenty-one days first, partly to inspire the Indian masses to redouble their fight against the British and partly to disclose the most heinous of crimes committed by the inhuman British against the unarmed and defenceless people in India. To survive a fast of twenty-one days in a prison at the age of 74 is in my mind no less than a miracle. Mahatma Ji scored a great moral victory over the British. Let us pray that God may spare him long and lead us to success.

I am proud to say that the Indian National Army has been re-established on more solid and firm foundation and when the time comes, your comrades-in-arm wil! fight to the last men in the cause of their country. They deserve our great respect for the service is still awaiting our decision. No one can doubt the bravery of our soldiers in a righteous fight for a rightous cause. Our sympathy goes to the families and friends of those Indian soldiers who erroneously believed that they were fighting for a right cause and lost their lives in Africa and Asia. They have been misled by the same propaganda of lies by the British which is responsible for the tinge of suspicion in the minds of so many of us.

I bow my head to the bravery of our soldiers and we should have no doubt that with their whole-hearted support we are going to win our final fight against British Imperialism. Let us stand shoulder to shoulder and let us march hand in hand to success.

Another important activity of the League was the creation of the Bharat Youth Training Centre at Kuala Lumpur where almost a thousand civilians are being given advanced training in the military art by the members of the Indian National Army. The existing camp is more on an experimental basis than a regular training camp. It is anticipated that when necessity arises for the training of the mass youth volunteers in East Asia for active service as part and parcel of the Indian National Army, the existising centre at Kuala Lampur will be greatly extended and a few more centres will be opened to meet the requirements of the Army at convenient localities. Plans for such establishments are under ways and it is expected to start the work in the near future. I hope Indians in East Asia will be ready to come forward as volunteers and will undergo the necessary military training under the capable hands of the members of the Indians National Army to make themselves fit to serve the cause of their country. I want to congratulate the youths now undergoing military training at Kuala Lumpur for their sense of sacrifice, patriotism and their love for their Motherland. I appeal to all able-bodied Indians in East Asia to follow the example of these brave and true nationalists.

You all know that youth is the cream of a nation and as such Indian Youth is the cream of Mother India. I am very glad to say that I am greatly moved by their enthusiasm and resolute determination to make any sacrifice demanded of them for the victory of our battle for freedom. Youth has always played a great and noble part in all revolutionary movements. And in the great Indian revolution it is the youth of the country that is playing a most significant role. Youth is impulsive, daring, resourceful, determined and ready for any sacrifices; and it is to the youth of India that Mother India looks for actions—decisive action that will break the shackles of British Imperialism. It is self sacrificing courage of India's young freedom fighters that has reduced the British power in India to sheer importance. And it is the united effort of the youth of India that will bring victory and glory to our Motherland. It was thus imperative to create a Youth Section of the Indian Independence League all over East Asia. This important section is the nucleous of the Indian Independence Movement and is the main reservoir for supply of manpower for India's National Army. They will be the warriors of Indian Freedom and in this great battle before us there is no distinction between civilian and military. We are all Indians, we are all freedom fighters and together we shall march to liberate our sacred Motherland. Azad School has been opened for the training of fifty young Indians and all those who are found fit after an extensive course of two months will be distributed as instructors for the training of the youths of the country. I congratulate all those who have been selected for training and welcome all others who are prepared to fight in the cause of Indian Freedom.

Last but not least I would like to mention the creation of the Women's Section of the Indian Independence League. It is highly significant that our sisters are taking keen interest in this Movement and are prepared to make any sacrifices side by side with their Indian brothers in the case of their Motherland. Freedom lies at the feet of a mother. Mother make heroes. Mother produce martyrs. It is through the encouragement of mothers that the youths of a country make sacrifice. Mothers are the backbones of a country's nationalism. They are the inspiration of the masses and the encouragement of the desperate.

I appeal to you my friends who have come to participate in this Conference, to divorce all party-feelings, suspicious and prejudices and make every effort, so that when you conclude your session you have a most effective and workable plan of action for Indian freedom, so that we can start our work immediately after this conference and march ahead. I hope you have realised the shortcomings of the last two Conferences and will keep aside all old and complicated ideas which are nothing mere than mere obstacles in the progress of this revolutionary movement and will work out a simple and straight forward plan which will leave no room for future disturbance. This is a revolution and there is an international conflagration all round us and I know you will all agree there is no time for discussion and argument. So I advise you once again to sit down and the create something which will revolutionize the whole Movement. The masses are iching for action but our existing constitution is so cumbersome and impracticable that we cannot move an inch. All plans should be made on the basis of self sufficiency because this is our Movement and the major part of it should be workable by us.

In the name of four hundred million starving Indians for whom you have pledged to lay down your life, I appeal to you once again to create the atmosphere of brotherhood, trust each other and have mutual understanding far this common end of ours. Your plan of action should be such that, as for as possible, only full time workers could be permitted to function—people who will be ready to make decisions day and night and from day to day, people who should be ready to serve anywhere and in any capacity, people who will be ready to bear all personal inconveniences of sleeping on the ground, going without food, and travelling on foot or travelling by whatever conveyance may be available. Every League Branch should be so constructed and organised that every worker from the Chairman downward should, as far as possible, be a full time self-sacrificing person who should be prepared to bear all hardships and should be prepared to work in the firing line when called upon to do so. Every League official should try to undergo a complete course of military training. May God help you in your efforts.

Finally I thank the Japanese Government on behalf of the Indians in East Asia for extending every facility and co-operation in every part of the occupied territories to my countrymen. But for Japan's whole-hearted support in the cause of Indian Freedom, it would not have been possible to achieve what has so far been achieved.

I also sincerely acknowledge the friendly attitude of all the allied governments and their people and take this opportunity of thanking them for their co-operation and assistance in the cause of our Country's Freedom.

14

Iwakuro's Speech at the I.I.L. Conference Clarifies Japanese Policy Towards the I.I.M. and Congratulates the Delegates for Re-organising the I.I.L. and I.N.A.[1]

27 April, 1943

Because of the situation that has considerably changed since the Bangkok Conference which was held in June, 1942, and in order to meet the existing circumstances, you have decided to convene a meeting of all the representatives from the various territories in the East Asia in order to lay down the guiding principles anew for the Movement, and I certainly consider that the action taken by you is indeed an appropriate one. Let me offer you my hearty congratulations and express my most sincere wishes for your success.

The Greater East Asia War has developed and has reached a final and decisive stage and the whole world is absorbed in this desparate struggle. Unless we win this war, that is the Greater East Asia war, it is more than obvious that all Asiatic peoples, all Asiatic races cannot be emancipated from the bondage of the Anglo-American tyrants; and if we fail in bringing about freedom of the Asiatic racess, I am sure, that the independence of India will be doomed into the same fate.

The reasons why Nippon is offering her unstinted support for the Movement are as follows:

1. India is one of the fellow Nations in Asia.
2. Her struggle to drive out the Anglo-American influence from India falls in line with the aim of our Greater East Asia War, and thus Anglo-Americans are our common enemies in the fullest sense of the expression.
3. Through cultural relations and Buddhism, we, Nipponese, have had traditional respect and affection for India, for more than 2000 years

1. *Ibid.*

and it has indeed been unbearable to us to see the present slavery that India is undergoing under the rule of Great Britain.

Needless to say, His Excellency Premier General Tojo's several declarations have been based on these very sentiments. It therefore goes without saying that Nippon has no desire to control India in place of Britain. Nippon has no ulterior motive whatsoever in India, politically, militarily or economically.

Let me recall the events of the past year. It is regrettable that certain sections of the Indian Community have been responsible for impairing the harmonious relations that have existed between us and the Indian Community. I cannot help but notice that there is also a certain section of the Indian Community who deliberately misconstrued our intentions. You will not blame me if I feel that we have been more than insulted. However, I am sure, that these people form only a small section of the Indian Community.

Such people's misunderstandings can be attributed to the following reasons:

1. They know nothing about Nippon and the Nipponese people.
2. They do not possess a correct knowledge of China and Manchukua.
3. Some people have misunderstood our temporary measures.

   You know we are fighting an enormous War and we have taken many emergency measures and some people have mistaken such temporary measures to be permanent measures.
4. There are many who are being misleading the enemies fabricated propaganda.

We have been trying to clear such misunderstanding with the utmost patience. However, I feel that our patience has already been exhausted and it is high time that we should draw a clear line between those who are anxious to co-operate with us for the achievement of our common goal and those who are disinclined to do so.

There are three categories of people:

1. Those who are anxiously desiring the Independence of India and require our assistance believing in our sincerity. They are our friends and fellow workers. To such friends we most certainly will not stint any kind of assistance and support.
2. Those who cannot yet liquidate their pro-British feelings or those still entertaining doubts about Nippon's sincerity or those who are

not satisfied with the present policy of Nippon. Such people should be considered as elements of more or less of enemy nature and such people should be treated accordingly.

3. Those who are still wavering and playing the game of "Wait and See". In my opinion such people should also be treated in the same manner or those of hostile nature.

I firmly believe that the Indian Independence League and the Indian National Army are organised and managed by only such people as those belonging to the first category. I trust that the League at this Conference consisting of representatives of such people should lay down new guiding principles and so reform the League as to make it perfectly workable in true co-operation with us which, of course, must be based on mutual trust.

I wish you again every success.

15

Proceedings of the I.I.L. Conference held at Singapore in April 1943 to Revive the Indian Independence Movement (I.I.M.) after the Resignation of the Members of the Council of Action. Reaffirms the Resolution Earlier Passed at Bangkok and the New Constitution of Indian Independence League[1]

27 April, 1943

Indian Independence League Conference of Delegate From East Asia Held at Syonan

Plenary Session

The meeting started with the singing of Vande Matram and a National Song by Indian Girls. Major General Iwakuro then addressed the gathering. The Chairman of the Reception Committee, Sri A. Yellappa made a speech welcoming the delegates. The President, Sri Rash Behari Bose, then delivered his Presidential address. After the speech was over he said that he wished to nominate the following gentleman to form the Subjects Committee.

1. Dr. Lukshumeyah
2. Dr. Majumdar
3. Sri B. A. Mallal
4. Sri K. A. Narayanan
5. Sri J. A. Thivy
6. Sri A. Yellappa
7. Sri B. Prasad
8. Sri D. Pandey
9. Sri Mahtani
10. Sri A. M. Nair

1. *Ibid.*

11. Sri D. N. Khan
12. Lt Col. Bhonsle
13. Lt Col. Kiani
14. Lt Col. Loganathan

Dr. Lukshumeyah spoke reiterating the confidence of the gathering in Sri Rash Behari Bose and requested the delegates to accept the proposal. The Committee nominated was unanimously approved. The President then announced that the Subjects Committee would not meet at 2.30 p.m. as shown in the programme but would meet at 10.30 a.m. on the 28th.

Copies of some draft resolutions were distributed to the members of the subjects committee and the meeting ended.

Resolutions
(Syonan 28.4.1943)

Whereas it is the objective of the War of Greater East Asia to destroy for over the British and American Imperialism in Asia and thus emancipate the Asiatic people from Anglo-American yoke; and

Whereas it gives an opportunity for India as an Asiatic country to realise the goal of complete independence ; and

Whereas the representatives of the Indians in East Asia hold conference at Tokyo and Bangkok in March and June 1942 respectively and resolved that the object of the Indian Independence Movement shall be the complete independence of India free from any foreign control or interference of any nature whatsoever; and

Whereas in conformity with such resolution and for the carrying out of that objective a written Constitution of the Indian Independence League was framed as a result of the resolutions passed thereat; and

Whereas the Indian Independence Movement has been organised all over East Asia in accordance with the resolutions passed at the above said Conference; and

Whereas now the British Government in India has rejected the "Quit India" demand of the Indian Nation and has thrown Mahatma Gandhi and other revered leaders of India into prison and is pursuing an inhuman policy of mass murders and wholesale arrests throughtout India and is perpetrating such atrocities as the bombing and machine-gunning of innocent and defenceless population of India; and

Whereas the Anglo-American forces in India are deliberately using India as a base of operations in their war to perpetrate the Anglo-American exploitation of Asiatic Nations; and

Whereas the objective of the War of Greater East Asia cannot be achieved unless the Anglo-American forces of aggression in India are annihilated; and

Whereas the conference of Indians in East Asia records its profound conviction that a state of emergency exists and that therefore nothing short of direct and immediate military action against the Anglo-American forces in India would help the Indian Nation to achieve its goal of complete Independence of India.

This Conference therefore to meet the existing circumstances and in conformity with the wishes of the Indians in East Asia passes the following resolutions to take the place of Bangkok Resolutions of 1942.

1. That this Conference reaffirms that the complete independence of India free from any foreign control or interference of any nature whatsoever is the object of this Indian Independence Movement as it is that of the Indian National Congress, and resolves that the Indian Independence Movement shall be guided by the principles indicated below:

   (a) That Unity, Faith, Sacrifice, shall be the motto of the Indian Independence Movement.

   (b) The Movement should be carried out in a revolutionary manner including military action.

   (c) That India be considered as One, and indivisible.

   (d) That all activities of this Movement be on a National basis and not Sectional, Communal or religious basis.

   (e) That the framing of the future constitution of India be only by the representatives of the Indians in India.

   (f) That the sympathy, co-operation and support of Japan is essential for securing the object of this Movement, namely, the Independence of India.

2. That the Indian Independence League owes allegiance to India.

3. That the Indian National Army is the army of the Indian Independence League and all officers and men of the Indian National Army as well as members of the Indian Independence League shall over allegiance to the League.

4. That this conference reiterates the true significance of the National Flag of India, the correct interpretation of the elements of the Flag being a follows:

Saffron—Courage and Sacrifice
White—Peace and Truth
Green—Faith and Chivalry
Chakra—Home of the masses

5. That for the purpose of financing the Indian Independence Movement the President, Indian Independence League, East Asia, be authorised to raise funds from Indians in East Asia.

6. That the entire Indian Independence Movement be placed on a War Footing immediately and that the Constitution of the Indian Independence League be so altered as to enable it to discharge its vital war duties with the utmost speed and efficiency, and

7. That this conference resolves that the written Constitution of the Indian Independence League passed at a Conference in Bangkok of Indians in East Asia in June, 1942, be amended and that the written Constitution approved and passed herein be adopted in its place.

8. That this Conference adopts the following Constitution for the Indian Independence League organisation.

9. Constitution Of The Indian Independence League—(Passed at a Conference in Syonan-to of Indians in East Asia in April, 1943 (2603) when the written Constitution passed at a Conference in Bangkok of Indians in East Asia in June 1942 (2602) was amended.)

   (i) This Act may be cited as the Constitution of Indian Independence League in East Asia.

   (ii) In this Act:

   "President" shall mean the present President of the Indian Independence League in East Asia, Sri Rash Behari Bose or his successors.

   "Chief Executive" shall mean the President.

   "Headquarters" shall mean the Office of the President.

   "Territories" shall include:

   Japan and Manchukuo

   Phillipines.

   Thailand.

   Malai.

   Burma.

Borneo Celebes.

Hong Kong, Canton and Macao.

Other parts of China including Shanghai.

Indo-China.

Djawa.

Sumatra.

Andamans.

(iii) The Indian Independence League shall consist of :—

(a) A Chief Executive (President)

(b) Council of Action

(c) War Council

(d) Territorial Committees

(e) Local Branches

(iv) Local Branches

(a) Local Branches of the Indian Independence League may be formed at a public meeting of Indians in any locality who shall elected committee. The President may nominate a Chairman from among the Committee Members.

(b) Vacancy or vacancies on such Committee or in the office of the Chairman shall be filled up by the Territorial Chairman with the approval of the President.

(c) All Indians above the age of 18 shall be entitled to be members of such Branch on compliance with the Rules framed from time to time by the Committee subject to the Approval of the President.

(d) No such Branch shall be recognised as a Branch unless the President accords and continues to accord to such Branch due recognition; provided, however, that all Branches of the Indian Independence League now in existence and recognised in the various territories in East Asia shall until otherwise decided upon by the President be recognised by the Indian Independence Movement.

(v) Territorial Committee—Representatives elected by the Committee of the Local Branches in each territory shall form as Territorial Committee for the effective working of the

Movement within the territory, subject to the approval of the President. The President shall nominate the Chairman of the Territorial Committee.

(vi) The Territorial Committee in each territory shall supervise and control the work of the Movement within its territory through its Chairman, subject to the approval of the President.

(vii) Chief Executive. (President)—The President shall be the Head of the Indian Independence League in East Asia and shall have powers to nominate his own successor. The successor or successors of the person nominated by the President shall be elected by the Council of Action and the War Council.

(viii) The President will formulate ways and means for the effective carrying out of the policy laid down at this Conference and shall deal with all new matters that may arise from time to time and which may not be provided for by this Conference and his decision shall in every case be final and binding on each and every member of this Indian Independence Movements.

(ix) For the proper and efficient carrying out of the work, the President shall have power to create as many departments as are necessary and expedient and to appoint and dismiss Administrative Officers and staff whenever he deems fit so to do.

(x) The President shall have power to alter, amend or rescind any previous decisions made by him, including any decision arrived at in this Conference.

(xi) The President shall have general superitendence and control over all Branches of the Indian Independence League in all territories and over the Indian Independence Army.

(xii) The President shall decide the military policy in consultation with the War Council.

(xiii) War Council—War Council will consist of the President, Director of Military Bureau, the Army Commander whenever available and one or more advisers nominated by the President as the exigencies of the situation may require.

(xiv) Council Of Action—The President will nominate two or more members, who and the President will constitute a Council of Action. The members of the Council of Action as nominated by the President will functions only in an advisory capacity and will give advice as and when required by the President.

(xv) Head Quarters—The Headquarters of the Movement shall be at any such place as may be decided upon by the President from time to time.

10. That this Conference pays its humble homage to the countless Indian patriots who have laid down their lives in India's war of independence in and out of India and expresses its deep admiration for the heroic fight now being waged by the Indians against the Anglo-American armies of occupation in India.

11. That this Conference expresses its sincere gratification at the war policy of Nippon and conveys to the Imperial Government its best wishes for the continued successes of the Imperial Japanese Armed forces, and records its grateful appreciation of the various Declarations and pronouncements as made by His Excellency General Hideki Tojo, the Premier of Nippon, expressing the preparedness of the Imperial Nipponese Government to give its unstinted support to the cause of complete independence and full sovereignty of India.

12. Further this Conference places on record its deepest appreciation of and grateful thanks for the co-operation, assistance and support extended to this Movement and its objective by the Imperial Government of Nippon.

13. That this Conference conveys to all the powers fighting against Britain and America its sincere congratulations and prays that their efforts may meet with complete success.

14. That this Conference gratefully acknowledges the sincere and friendly attitude the Government and people of Germany, Italy, Thailand, China, Manchukuo and other friendly powers have adopted towards our struggle for freedom and places on record its deep appreciation and thank for the offer of assistance and co-operation extended by them to this Movement.

15. This Conference offers hearty congratulation to the Burmese Nation to whom the Imperial Government of Nippon has promised to grant independence within this year.

16

Minutes of an Interview between Members of I.I.L. Malaya and Col. Kagawa; Clarifies the Relations between the I.N.A. and the Japanese

1 May, 1943

Present: Lt. Col. Kagawa[1]
Lt. Kunizuka[2]
Dr. Lukshumayya
Sri B. A. Mallai
Sri G. Maganlal
Sri S. N. K. Nagappa Chettiar
Sri J. A. Thivy[3]
Sri S. Shanmugam
Sri A. Yellappa
Sri K. M. Kannampilly
Dr. D. K. Majumdar
Dr. N. K. Menon
Dr. J. Samuel

Col. Kagawa said that it was a good opportunity to discuss the problems of the League organisation in Malai and asked those present to tell him of any difficulties they were experiencing in their territories.

Dr. Samuel replied that the *Gunseibu* in Penang did not show much recognition of the Indian Independence League in its dealings. Col. Kagawa

1. Colonel Kagawa Yoshio was Staff officer in Hikari Kikan.
2. Lieut. Kunizuka, was an interpreter with Fujiwara Kikan and subsequently with Iwakuro Kikan, played a major role in persuading Mohan Singh to form the Indian National Army. He has recorded his experience with the Indian Nationalist in the book entitled *Rainbow Across the Sky* in Japanese.
3. J.A. Thivy, (1904-1957), born in Malaya. After studying in England, became a prominent lawyer, joined Indian Independence League and was its Vice-President, was minister in the Provisional Government of India. After War, founded Malayam Indian Congress and was its President; was diplomatic representative of India in Malaya, then Indian High Commissioner in Maurtious; served also as ambassador to Greece and Hague till his death in 1957.

asked for concrete examples. Dr. Samuel gave as an example the difficulties experienced in holding meetings.

Col. Kagawa asked what the position was in the other states.

Sri Shanmugam replied that there were no difficulties in Malacca.

Dr. Majumdar said that in Negri Sembilan also there were no difficulties.

Sri Thivy said that in Perak they had to inform three departments. In the case of sub-branches they had to inform the departments even for committee meetings, and minutes nad to be submitted.

Col. Kagawa asked whether there were any other difficulties being experienced.

Sri Thivy said that the indifference shown by the Government to those who go against the League made the position of the League rather difficult. He gave as an instance the attitude of the Government towards those who had refused to pay their quota to the Indian Independence Fund.

Col. Kagawa asked whether the allotments made by Sri Bose were fair.

Dr. Lukshumayya replied that it depended on whether the collections were to be repeated or not.

He said that Sri Bose had empowered him, as chairman of the Malaya Branch, to reduce the amounts where he considered such a reduction fair and necessary. He had already reduced the amounts allotted to some states, and he was going to suggest to Sri Bose that it would be better to have smaller contributions at intervals.

Col. Kagawa asked whether they could think out any better methods of collection.

Dr. Lukshumayya said that he was working on it. Unequal proportions in different states made the collection difficult. In Syonan for instance no collection had yet been made.

Col. Kagawa requested those present to study the best ways for the future. In Japan contribution to political parties always voluntary.

Sri Yellappa said that the Bose had seen the Mayor of Syonan a month ago but the Mayor had not yet given the necessary permit to start collection. As soon as the permit was got they could start.

Sri Nagappa Chettiar said that most of the Malay officers were anti-Indians. In the Survey Department in Kedah for instance only Malays are employed. Even the Indians who were employed in that department previously had not been taken back.

Sri Narayan said that they were having no difficulty in Selangor.

Col. Kagawa wanted to know whether there was any possibility of communists taking advantage of the League organisation to advance their activities.

Dr. Lukshumayya said that there were practically no communists among Indians.

Col. Kagawa said that the British did not like the League Movements. They might use the Chinese to discredit the Movement or make use of it.

Dr. Lukshumayya said that no signs had yet been seen of any such action in the Mainland. In Penang there was one instance of some records being discovered when a house was raided, of a plan to discredit the League or to cause bad blood between the League and the Japanese.

Col. Kagawa said that they had a confidential report that about 80 Indian soldiers, who had taken part in the Malain campaign were leading the communities in their activities.

Dr. Lukshumayya asked whether these soldiers were communists by persuation or simply robbers.

Col. Kagawa said that at present they were only robbers but there was danger of their being influenced by the communists.

Dr. Lukshumayya said that they had been watching to see if the communists would attack the League leaders. So far there had been only one case when Sri Thivy was shot at.

Sri Shanmugam said that there was one important question which he wanted to discuss. There was a recent announcement by Premier General Tojo that Indians were no more enemy nationals, but this was not being given effect to in all places. For instance, in some states attorneys of principals in India were allowed to operate business while in other states they were not. If the Kikan could help in having a uniform policy throughout the territory, it would be of great assistance. Col. Kagawa said that it was a problem very difficult to solve in a general way. He suggested that it would be better to tackle individual cases one after the other as they arose. He also said that if the attorney had proper document, it would be easy to settle.

Sri Yellappa said that on 6/7/02 instructions were given by the government regarding Asiatic people, to the effect that all those who left Malai before the 8th of December were not to be considered as aliens. Yet in a few cases this rule was not being applied.

Col. Kagawa said that he would like to know the rules regarding this and also the instances from each state.

He then explained the campaign on the Indo-Burma border. After that he gave an account of League activities as he conceived them. He said that when the Indian National Army and the Japanese advance into India, all organisations in India may be destroyed. The British may adopt the scorched earth policy. Who will then put back the organisation into existence? Essential repairs of a strategical nature will of course be carried out by the Japanese army, but other things will have to be looked after by the Indians themselves. The Indian Independence League will act as an intermediary between the Congress and the Japanese. If the Indian National Army and the Japanese occupy any portion of India, it is possible that there may be a revolution in other parts of India. Then the Indian National Army and the Indian Independence League should go in advance and take the initiative to take advantage of the situation. For that the League should have trained men. Such training cannot be done overnight. It must be done beforehand. One can say when the operations will start. It might come as a surprise. But must be ready when operations start. For instance in the case of propaganda, if Japanese are sent to do propaganda, it will not be good. The League must have large numbers of people— specialists in broadcasting, writing pamphlets, leaflets, etc. For instance, in broadcasting the League should select fit people and send them to broadcasting stations, and have them trained during the peace time. The League will require the service of technical experts. It must get details of men in Malai who are qualified and mobilise them when the time comes. The League must train young men to fight. We can expect to get plenty of arms from the enemy. Thus every Indian will be utilised in the Movement. Suppose the Indian operations start and the League has no organisation for it, there is bound to be trouble between the Indians in India and the Japanese. If the League could prepare a scheme, the Japanese will give all facilities. Col. Kagawa said that these were his dreams. He requested those present to discuss these points with the President.

Before leaving he said that with the transference of the Headquarters of the Kikan from Bangkok to Syonan, the Malai Branch of the Kikan had ceased to exist but that the policy and principles would be still the same. He also announced the change in the name of the Kikan from Iwakuro Kikan to Hikari Kikan.

17

General Staff Branch Instructions to the British Officers to Check the Subversive Activities of the I.N.A. Against the Indian Army[1]

3 May, 1943

1. Replies from H.Q. Eastern and Southern Army Central Command to these HQ letter no DMI/4746 of 18/3/43 have been considered. These and certain other connected problems have been under active consideration and certain decisions on matters of policy have been approved by H. E. the C-in-C. These are set out below under their various headings.

   Disposal of stragglers from Burma who have prima facie never actually been prisoners in Japanese hands.

2. Numerous cases are coming to light of stragglers from Burma who maintain that they have never actually been prisoners in Japanese hands, but who have spent varying periods in enemy occupied territory before returning to India. In some cases these men are self-confessed deserters in action who have returned to India disguised, as civilian refugees and have remained in their villages or elsewhere for periods upto months before reporting to their units of regimental centres. In some cases they have only reported because they have heard that their presence has come to light and they are being searched for. There are many variants and by no means all initially deserted. In some cases personnel have reported back to their units without disclosing the fact that they returned to India in refugee guise and remained at large for some time, but have subsequently served satisfactorily for some time before the facts came to light.

3. While primarily disciplinary cases, the possibility cannot be ignored that some of these men may have developed subversive tendencies

1. F. No. 601/10569/H.S. Ministry of Defence.

during their sojourn in enemy occupied territory. They are potentially the most dangerous form of enemy agents. There is the additional consideration that knowledge that there are a number of such cases who have hitherto "managed to get away with it" must be fairly widespread and cannot but have a bad effect on morale and discipline and encourage such conduct.

4. It has been decided that where such cases come to light each should be considered on its merit and disposed of on the basis of expendiency on the following lines:

(a) Trial by Court Martial where a definite case can be established and there are prospects of exemplary punishment.

(b) Dismissal and detention under Defence of India Rule 26 where trial is not expedient but prima facie the individual will be danger to security if left at large.

(c) Dismissal where the facts warrants this, but trial by Court Martial is not likely to be successful and it is concluded that the individual is likely to be less of a danger out of the Service than in it.

(d) Retention in the Service where the individual has "got away with it" for some time and his subsequent service has been satisfactory or the circumstances otherwise justify this, the question of whether he remains with his unit or is reposted being decided on its merits.

(e) Retention in the service with summary reduction in rank where the facts justify this and where action as in (c) or (d) would have a bad effect on others.

The question of setting up central machinery to investigate and dispose of such cases is under consideration and orders will be issued in due course by adjutant General's Branch.

Action against members of "contact", parties apprehended.

5. "Contact" parties consist of individuals who after capture by or desertion to, the enemy are sent back to our lines with instructions to encourage desertion or to build up I.N.A. cells in units and training centres. They may also include civilians from enemy occupied territories.

6. Trial by Court Martial on capital charges should be resorted to in the case of military personnel in well-sustained cases, the decision being left to G. O. C. - in -C. the Army/ Command concerned. Death

sentences should be carried out by hanging in Civil jails, or in reoccupied territories under arrangements to be made by the Civil Affaris Service. Civilian accused should be handed over to the Civil Authorities for trial under the Enemy Agents Ordinance if within Indian territorial limits, otherwise their cases may be disposed of by the courts set up under the Civil Affairs Administration in reoccupied territory.

7. In coming to a decision as to whether it is expedient to resort to trial, the following factors should be considered:-

(a) Probability of conviction and of a sentence sufficient to obviate the individual subsequently becoming a menace to security. In the case of civilians should trial result in a finding "Not Guilty" but the circumstances otherwise warrant it, would still be possible to detain under Defence of India Rules. In the case of military personnel dismissal by administrative action would be necessary before such detention could be affected. In cases therefore where conviction is doubtful for want of legal evidence, it would be preferable in the interests of security to dispense with trial and to forward the individual on to C. S. D. I. C. for disposal in accordance with existing practice.

(b) Whether the value of conviction and punishment as a deterrant to others outweights the value of information that might be obtained from the individual or from using him (if willing) as evidence in other cases. We now have a great deal of information on I.N.A. organisation and methods outside India, i.e., in Japanese occupied territory, but information as to the organisation, if any, within India, and of contacts in Indian units, is of very great importance with view to preventing the spread of contamination. We have not yet reached the stage where we can dispense with any potential source of this latter type of information.

8. Normal publicity should be given through Service channels by publication unit, formation and Indian Army orders, promulgation of findings and sentences on parades in the unit to which the convict belongs/being resorted to at the discretion of G.O.C.-in-C. Armies Commands.

Publicity and Counter Propaganda on I.N.A. and I.I.L. Questions.

9. This has been considered under three main headings:-

   (a) To Troops

   (b) To the General Public

   (c) To the enemy including I.N.A. and I.I.L. personnel in enemy occupied territory.

To Troops

10. In HQ letter DMI/4746 of 18/3/43, it was ruled that, for the present, the dissemination of information about I.N.A. and kindred activities should be confined to British Officers, and to selected Indian and Viceroy Commissioned Officers (V.C.O.'s). It has now been decided that we should put the situation plainly to all Indian ranks and prepare them to meet a method of attack of which they are at present largely unconscious. Commanding Officers should be authorised to explain the situation frankly to all I.C.O.S. V.C.Os and men, omitting only details likely to be of use to the enemy, such as the extent of our knowledge of the detailed organisation and personalities of the I.N.A., details of our own organisation and methods for discovering and dealing with agents and of the degree of success they are achieving. Commanding Officers should however be given details of members of their regiments known to be active members of the I.N.A. and be permitted, at their discretion, to pass these on to their Subedar Major and Unit Security Officer, to assist the latter in their task of keeping the Commanding Officer informed of developments with in the unit.

11. The Subject of Japanese efforts to suborn the loyality of the Indian Army should be dealt with on the following general lines:–

   (a) Description of Japanese treatment of prisoners of war, including such items as forced labour, semi-starvation, violations of caste, propaganda, flattery and promises.

   (b) The effects of this treatment in dividing prisoners into three categories:–

      (i) Those who have joined the I.N.A. and promised to help the Japanese and intend to keep their promise;

      (ii) Those who have joined the I.N.A. with a view to help the Japanese and do not intend to keep their promise;

      (iii) Those who refused to join the I.N.A.

(c) The methods adopted by the Japanese to exploit those in (B) (i) and (ii) including lectures, training is espionage, propaganda, sabotage etc., and return to India in contact parties.

(d) No descredit attaches to a man unfortunate enough to be captured who agrees to join the I.N.A. or undertake any employment offered by the Japanese *with the sole object of:*

 (i) *returning to India at the earliest opportunity and who immediately on return reports the full facts and whole truth immediately to the nearest HQ., or*

 (ii) *otherwise deceiving the Japanese.*

(e) Those who feel that they can successfully undertake the role of deceiving the Japanese and the Indian traitors in their pay should do so.

(f) We now have means of ascertaining the names of those who promise to assist the enemy and *actually become active enemy agents;* whether they remain in enemy occupied territory or re-enter India.

(g) Steps will be taken to stop the family allotments and to confiscate the property of those who are known to have become traitors. When apprehended they will be brought to trial on Capital Charges.

In passing on information to troops, the terms "I.N.A." or "Indian National Army" should not be used except in a derisory manner, and attention should be drawn to the facts of the so called "Burma Independent Army" which the Japanese disbanded as soon as it had fulfilled its role of betraying Burma to the Japanese. Care should be taken to prevent these titles being given currency as describing this traitorous movement.

12. An essential corollary to the frank treatment of the question outlined above are measures to encourage the moral resistance of Indian troops to I.N.A. and I.I.L. propaganda, whether the latter is applied to them while with our own forces or in the event of their being captured. Special measures of an All–India nature to assist in this are under consideration and further instructions will follow.

To the General Public

13. It has been decided that for the present there should be no over publicity in India outside the Armed Forces regarding the I.N.A. or

I.I.L. as organisation. No attempt will however be made to conceal the fact that individuals are known to have become traitors, but such publicity will be incidental to publicity to the troops (described above) and to counter propaganda directed to the Japanese and INA–IIL themselves (described below). No use will be made of the terms "INA" "IIL", "Indian National Army" or "Indian Independence League" in giving publicity to any action taken against members of these organisations. Nor, except in exceptional cases, will publicity be given outside the Services of the names of individuals against whom action is taken or who are known to be in these organisations. The question of general publicity measures is however, under reference to Provincial Governments who may consult commanders of Armies/Commands as to their views on the matter.

To the Japanese, the I.N.A. and the I.I.L.

14. Hitherto no direct propaganda or Counter Propaganda specifically refering to either I.N.A. or I.I.L. has been included in broadcasts or leaflets directed to the Japanese Army or to Indians in enemy occupied territories. It has now been decided to initiate a campaign both in Japanese and in Indian languages designed to :–

(a) Undermine the confidence of the Japanese in the I.N.A., especially in its leaders;

(b) Undermine the confidence of the I.N.A. in itself, in the Japanese and in its leaders;

(c) Play on the fears of genuine members of the I.N.A. / I.I.L. by stressing :–

(i) that the families of Indian Officers and men in enemy hands are being well looked after and family allotments or allowance are being paid regularly hitherto without exception,

(ii) that we know that certain (unspecified) disloyal I.C.O.s, V.C.Os. and men are actively helping the Japanese and trying to persuade others to do so.

(iii) that steps are now being taken to stop the family allotments or allowances, and to confiscate the property of, individuals known to be helping the enemy.

15. With regard to para 14 (a) and (b), the daily broadcasts, in Japanese and Indian languages directed to the Japanese Army and to the Indians in enemy occupied territory will be used to indicate that–

(a) Our troops are now being instructed in the methods used by the enemy to soborn their loyality.

(b) They are being encouraged, the event of their being captured, to accept enemy offers, with a view to deceiving the enemy and escaping with information both about the enemy and Indian traitors assisting them.

(c) Number of individuals have already escaped by these means and the great majority of these sent back to India by the enemy have reported immediately and given full details of :–

(i) Their instructions;

(ii) The Indians helping the Japanese and those ostensibly doing so but actually deceiving them;

(iii) All they know about enemy strategies, dispositions and intentions;

(iv) Composition of future parties.

(d) A number of I.C.Os., V.C.Os. and men have been decorated for the gallantry, resource and skill they have displayed in deceiving the Japanese and the Indian traitors and in escaping.

16. It has also been decided to drop leaflets designed to reinforce the broadcasts and with the object if encouraging genuine escapes and also "desertions" from the I.N.A., especially in forward areas. These will include promise of safe conduct to actual members of the I.N.A.

17. In both broadcasts and leaflets, actual names of escapes or "deserters" may be given in certain specific cases where considerable effect, either of encouragement to loyalists or uneasiness to disloyalists or to the enemy, would result from disclosure. Normally however the object will be to leave the enemy and the Indian traitors uncertain as to the actual extent of our knowledge of success.

18. It is realised that broadcasts in Indian languages on this subject, though directed to enemy "occupied" territories will inevitably be heard in India itself. This will inevitably result in a certain amount of general publicity in spite of the policy of restricting this to the Services for the present. To minimise this "spill over" to the public

of India, G.S. I. (q) broadcasts will avoid all specific reference to either I.N.A. or I.I.L. organisations.

19. It is intended to introduce the propaganda policy outlined above with effect from 15th May and to leave the enemy in no doubt, of our intention to encourage prisoners to join the I.N.A. from that date.

20. Paragraphs 2 to 7 of this letter are issued with the concurrence of the Adjutant General in India.

18

Implementation of the Recommendations of the I.I.L. Conference, Held at Singapore on 27 April by the I.I.L. Malaya Branch[1]

8 May, 1943

The Conference of the Committee of Representatives from Territories all over East Asia held at Syonan from 27th to 30th April, effected vital changes in the Constitution of the Indian Independence League. The main trend of the changes was towards putting the organisation on a war footing, giving full dictatorial powers to the President. A copy of the new Constitution is sent herewith for your office. You will notice that there is a change in the designation of the President (of the Territorial Committee, State Branch or Sub-Branch). Kindly have all rubber stamps changed from "President" to "Chairman" and make other necessary alterations according to the Constitution.

Propaganda

More intensive and widespread propaganda is necessary now more than ever. In the earlier days, enrolment of labourers owing as members was not feasible to the fact that in many parts Estates had not yet resumed work, and even in the case of those, Estates which had reopened, the labourers were getting only a few days work. In some States, however, as a result of negotiations with the Syonan Gomu Kumisai, labourers have been assisted to join the League. In Johore for instance each labourer gets 5 day's extra work to enable him to become a member of the League. Such or similiar attempts should be made in each state to make it possible for the labourers to join the League and even if they cannot immediately join, League officials and workers should make it a point to keep up and strengthen their contact with the labourers.

Membership in most states seems to have come to a standstill. In all popular movements like ours a period of slackness is common after the

1. I.I.L. Papers., F.. No. 45/3.

original enthusiasm, but we should be always on the watch to pull up the organisation from stagnating in a state of complacency. Increase in membership is not merely to effect an increase in finance. Our efforts towards organising the movement in Malai cannot be considered to have succeeded until every Indian, man or woman, is a member of the League.

Finance

The Malaya Branch has recently made to all Branches substantial contributions towards organisation expenses. Apart from this it has also been decided to reduce the contribution from the branches from 25% to 5% of membership fees each month starting from Ist May, 2603. This has been done to allow to each Branch more money to carry on its work within its territory with greater vigour and intensity. Branches must, however try as far as possible to make themselves financially self–supporting. All expenses which are not essential to the advancement of our cause must be cut out. Funds for distress relief must be raised locally by each Branch and sub-Branch.

Youth Section

Almost all Branches have now organised Youth Sections. It has come to our notice recently that there is in some circles an erroneous impression that this is a Movement separate from and independent of the League. The Youth Section is one of the sections of the Indian Independence League and, as such, is a part and parcel of our movement. The Azad School at Syonan is now training a number of youths from all over Malai. These people will be sent out after training as Instructors and we are confident that with their arrival the Youth Sections in all Branches will proceed with their work with intensified activity.

Messages

We have received instruction to the effect that messages will be accepted only if they are from Indians to Indians. Branches are therefore requested not to accept any more messages from non-Indians or from Indians to non-Indians. All the messages of this type remaining with us awaiting broadcast will be sent back to the Branches to be returned along with the fees to the parties concerned.

Syonan
8th May, 2603

Indian Independence League
Malaya Branch
Secretary

19

Statement of S. C. Bose After his Arrival in Tokyo; Requests Indians in East Asia to Take up Armed Struggle Against the British in Collaboration with Japan

19 June, 1943

Ladies and gentleman!

"At the outset, I may say that it is for me a very great pleasure to offer you my cordial greetings, since I have been for a long time connected with journalism in my own country."

"You may be wondering what has brought me to this part of the world at such a time. For long years, British jails India and Burma have been my residence. But the fact that today I am standing before you in the heart of Nippon, instead of sitting idly in a prison house in India, is symbolic of the new movement that is now sweeping over my country. It was in accordance with the will of my countrymen that I left homeland more than two years ago and whatever I have done since them, is also in accordance with their will".

"During the last World War, our leaders had been bluffed and deceived by wily British politicians that is why we took a vow more than 20 years, my generation has striven for freedom and has eagerly awaited the hour that has now struck–the hour that is for the Indian people the dawn of freedom. We know very well that such an opportunity will not come again for another hundred years and we are, therefore, determined to make the fullest use of it".

"You have so often heard of the war that is being waged for freedom and democracy. But you can very well imagine what my countrymen think of those Powers that talk of freedom and democracy and deny the same to one–fifth of the human race–the Powers that reply to the demand for liberty by terror and brutality and by massacre of unarmed men, women and children. British imperialism has meant for India moral degradation,

1. *Nippon Times* 20 June 1943. The above Statement was read at the Press Interview which Subhas Chandra Bosh granted to newspapermen at the Imperial hotel, Tokyo.

cultural ruin, economic impoverishment and political enslavement. Is it any wonder, therefore, that the Indian People have at last solemnly received to end the British yoke?

"The present world conflict means for the Indian people struggle between the forces that want to maintain the status quo and those that are determined to overthrow it. Can any one blame us if in such a conflict, our sympathy lies with those Powers that stand for change for New Order? And when these Powers support our demand for freedom, it is but natural that our sympathy for them should deepen into enthusiastic support.

"Inspite of all that, Anglo-American propaganda has been saying to the contrary, believe me when I say that the overwhelming majority of the Indian people desire to see the Tripatriate Powers emerge victorious. The victory of the Tripatriate Powers will mean the defeat of Anglo-American imperialism, the dismemberment of the British Empire and the restitution of India's lost liberty."

"The Tripatriate Powers have rendered the greatest help to India's struggle by waging war against our eternal foe. And they have earned our lasting gratitude by offering us-not only sympathy, but support and assistance. Nevertheless, it is our duty to pay for our liberty with our own blood".

"The freedom that we shall win through our sacrifice and exertions. we shall be able to preserve with our own strength. We, therefore feel very strongly that we should actively participate in the war against our common foe. The enemy that has drawn the sword, must be fought with the sword".

"Civil disobedience must develop into armed struggle. And only when the Indian people receive the baptism of fire on a large scale, will they qualify for their freedom".

"Since, I left India more than two years go, I have travelled all over the world and I have, therefore, been able to study the world situation quite objectively. I have also seen something of the inside of Japan, Germany and Italy. I am not blind to the difficulties that still lie in the path of the Tripatriate Powers—but I also know their strength and the sources of their strength. I am not, therefore, impressed at all by all this loud task of a second front, whether in Europe or in the Pacific, of landing in Europe or of an offensive on the Indo-Burma frontier".

"If noisy, bumptious propaganda could win a war, the Anti -Axis Powers would have had their victory long ago. We all know that in this World War, time is not working in favour of the Anglo-American Powers as it did in the last. Winston Churchill was constrained to admit it publicly the other day at Washington. From my own study of the general war situation, I have the 100-percent conviction that, however long those struggle may last, there can be but one outcome; namely, the absolute victory of the Tripatriate power and their Allies".

"Another point in which you may be naturally interested is as to what the Indian people think of Japan. Japan was the first Asiatic Power to stem the tide of aggression that had been sweeping over Asia in the 19th century. Japan's victory over Russia in 1905 was the starting point of the Asiatic renaissance in the 20th century and as such, it was hailed enthusiastiscally by the Indian people, as it was by the Japanese. Japan was, and is, a historical necessity for the revival of Asia".

"It is true that Indian public opinion regarding Japan changed considerably after the outbreak of the China Affair in 1937. But the out break of the War in East Asia has fundamentally altered the situation".

"Today, Japan is fighting our enemy. On the other hand Chungking is an ally of Anglo-American Powers. Moreover, General Chiang Kai-shek has been giving his full support to the British domination of Burma and India".

The average Indian is not interested in ideological questions. He is interested only in the political and economic emancipation of his country. Consequently, whoever sympathizes with and supports India's Independence is automatically India's friend and ally. Last but not the least, the adoption by Japan of the new China policy, has made the Indian people ask why General Chiang Kai-shek does not to try to arrive at an honorable understanding with Japan and why he is allowing himself to be used as a tool by the Anglo-American Powers.

"India and Japan have, in the past, been bound by deep cultural ties which are about 20 centuries old. In recent times, these cultural relations have been interrupted because of the British domination of India. It is, however, certain that when India is free these relations will be revived and will be further strengthened".

"Moreover, in view of the active support and assistance which Japan has been giving and will, in future give to India's struggle for independence, it is but natural that the grateful Indian people will enthusiatically welcome close political and economic cooperation with Japan, when they are masters of their own homes and of their national destiny".

"In this connection, I should add that the statements made by Prime Minister General Hideki Tojo on India since March, 1942, and repeated by him before the Imperial diet on June 16, 1943, have made a profound impression on India and have greatly helped to improve as the days roll by".

"Industrial production-satisfactory though it is will be pushed up further in order to cope with and overcome any possible advance made by the enemy. And lastly, one can see with his own eyes that there is an immense reserve of manpower which can be drawn upon at any time, if the necessity arises."

"Ladies and Gentlemen, For all these reasons, I feel absolutely confident of the ultimate defeat of the Anglo-American Powers, of the break-up of the British empire and the liberation of 398- millions of my countrymen".

20

Japanese Reaction to the Arrival of Bose From Germany

20 June, 1943

Subhas Chandra Bose, eminent Indian nationalist, is now visiting Japan, it has been revealed. The Japanese nation is happy to bid him cordial welcome, for he is a man whose record and life aim are such as command the respect of all true Orientals.

As the greatest Indian leader outside the prison- infact the only Indian leader of first rank who is not, in some British jail- Mr. Bose represents the shining hope of the four hundred million peoples of India for freedom. Twice the president of the national congress party, he finally resigned to found the Forward Bloc which demanded immediate and complete independence from British rule without condition or compromise. Undaunted by the material power of the British Empire, the leader has long been courageously pitting his intelligence and his spirit against the physical might of the alien rulers of the country in a manner which calls forth admiration.

It is significant indeed that this man who is the personification of India's hope for independence has found it feasible to return from Europe at last to direct at closer quarters the movement for the liberation of his homeland. It is an indication that thė victories of Japan and the Axis are presenting the Indians with an opportunity such as they, have never have again to throw off the yoke of the British rule. The hour of destiny for India may be close at hand, if only all the Indian people will realize it as Mr. Bose and other clearsighted leaders realize it so well.

To the Japanese people, the presence of Mr. Bose at the time cannot help but emphasize the contract between India and the countries, which Japan has been able to help more directly. Fresh in the memory in Prime Minister Tojo's announcement of only five days ago that the Philippines would be accorded independence within this year, while a few months

1. An Editorial from *Nippon Times*, 20 June 1943.

ago there was his similar statement with respect to Burma. The spectacle of Burma and the Philippines rising as independent sovereign nations while older, larger and potentially infinitely more powerful India lies helplessly in chairs is one which must arouse in the breast of every Indian a tumult of emotions which defies description. But as fellow-Orientals, the Japanese people can sympathize with the Indians in the humiliation and indignation they must feel over the contrast between their lot and that of the Burmese or the Filipinos.

The contrast in essence, however, is not so much that between Burma and the Philippines on the one hand and India on the other as between Japan on the one hand and Britain on the other. Japan as an Oriental nation, is naturally sincere and anxious to help promote the welfare of all the nations of this part of the world. Britain on the other hand, as a distant imperialistic Power can have no interest is any Oriental country except as an object of exploitation.

No amount of sophistry can hide his fundamental difference between the attitudes of Japan and of Britain. Jan Christian Smuts, the Prime Minister of Union of South Africa, in an attempt to quiet the carping criticism of British imperialism on the part of some Americans, wrote recently in the American magazine Life that the reason India has not been able to become a "free" commonwealth like Canada or Australia is that the Indians have not been able to agree on the terms of a national constitution. What Smuts deliberately hides is the fact that if there is lack of agreement among the Indians, it is the British who have created and have consistently fomented that disagreement in accordance with their policy of divide and rule. At any rate Smuts' argucment is beside the point, for what the Indians want is not the fictitious "freedom" of being a British "Commonwealth" but complete independence from all British connections. On that point there is agreement enough among all the Indians, and as for the constitution of such a truly independent India, it should be one concern of Smuts or any other torch-bearer of British imperialism.

The British also like to say that "freedom" of the illusory kind which they always mean will be granted to India after the war if the Indians prove themselves "worthy" of it by fighting for Britain now. It may be remembered that the same promise was given during the last World War, with what results everyone knows. Such an attitude on the part of Britain not only indicates most clearly the insincerity of the British, but it also reveals that they have no little confidence in their own strength in the war that they must resort to bribery in an attempt to secure the help of the Indians. In contrast, Japan is not making vague promises of future independence to Burma and the Philippines on condition that they help Japan in the war. Japan is granting complete independence to Burma and the Philippines while that war is going on, for Japan has no doubt as to the outcome of the struggle. Japan is acting now on the premises of certain victory, while Britain, hedging on the outcome of the war, is merely promising action in the future on the premise of her doubts.

As the Indian people fret on their condition and their prospects for independence, they may well take to heart Prime Minister Tojo's words of five days ago when he said, "For this plight of India I feel at once sympathy and indignation. Japan is firmly resolved to exhaust all means in order to help expel and eliminate from India Anglo-Saxon influences which are the enemy of the Indian people, and enable India to attain full independence in a true sense of the term. I confidently look into the day, which I trust will soon come, when the ardent and widespread desires of the Indian people are fulfilled and they regain, freedom and prosperity". This is Japan's message of goodwill to the Indian people.

Copy of a Platoon Lecture Prepared by the I.I.L. Entitled "Our Mission" in Life as Indians First and Last[1]

21 June, 1943

My brothers,

From the lectures you have had so far, I am sure all of you have no doubt or misconception in your mind, regarding the history of our movement both in India and in East Asia, our policy and the principles, which we are pledged to abide by. We have also studied in details all the requisite characteristics we should cultivate, for the attainment of our object, including the spirit of Bushido in Nippon. During the course of our study hitherto, we have learned to evaluate correctly our merits and defects, assets and liabilities in an unprejudiced, unbiased manner. We are quite conscious of our original status and attainments from the cultural, economic and political aspects. We have learnt how and to what extent we have been degraded from every point of view after the British advent in India; and to what depths we have sunk in every aspect. You would now be in a position to understand the imperative necessity for such knowledge and training, concerning the political and spiritual aspect of our movement in order to enable us to achieve our mission in life.

We are all Indians, first and last, both in the army and in the civil. It is vitally essential that all of us should develop this outlook constantly at every opportunity. We must root out completely from our minds all ideas of provincialism, sectarianism and other aspects of individualism. Such an outlook is more essentially required in our action than in our thought and speech. We are engaged in a war of supreme and momentous importance not only to ourselves, but also to the entire world today. The problem of

1. European Manuscript Collection No. A73 India Office library and records, London copies of some of these platoon lectures are also available amongst the Indian National Army papers at the National Archies of India. For some other lecture see Appendix; These were meant to create patriotic sentiments amongst the soldiers of the Indian National Army and were given regularly. Each one of the officers was given a copy also.

India today is a problem of bread and salt, of famine and nakedness of disease and dirt, and of degradation and death to the Indians. The causes of such a downfall of India from her glorious past we have studied in details. We have no doubt in our mind that it is essentially due to British imperialistic domination of India, for well over two centuries. We know also the secret of the means of remedying India's pitiable state. The only thing that remains to be done is to translate our ideas into action.

We have to survey all aspects of our mission in life. The problem of India is a world problem. There will be no end to this war as long as India remains the bone of contention. There can never be any lasting peace in this world as long as India remains a subject nation, as long as every fifth man in the world is a slave under British domination, as long as forty crores of humanity are shouting aloud for freedom, as the cry of their souls, and as long as British imperialism continues to perpetuate such slavery of the souls, captivation of the spirit and physical torture of pain, hunger and suffering due to starvation and total neglect of responsibility of the British rulers of India even to preserve the very existence of Indians as a nation, let alone promote their happineess and welfare. Before the advent of the British, peace and plenty reigned in India. After the advent of the British, there was apparent a seemingly outword peace in India due to their technological unification of our country by railways etc. for purely political advantages and objects; but, all the same, our souls are shouting aloud and clamouring for freedom of thought, speech and association. How can ever there be real and lasting peace under these circumstances? Hence we, Indians, feel very strongly that all subject nations must be liberated, if any object has to be served by the colossal wars, that are now being conducted on a scale, unprecedented and unknown in history so far, and of an importance which is most genuinely world-wide, in extent and intensity. It is advisable for warring nations to take note of these facts, declare their respective war aims unequivocably and to carry out their campaigns accordingly. In precept and practice, Dai Nippon has carried out all these noble principles in so far as it relates to her campaigns in the Far Eastern theatre. What of England, whose sole aim is to get all the others to do the fighting for them in all the theatres of war, where they desire to perpetuate their imperialistic preserves at the expense of other nations, either subject or free. The British have not declared their war aims so far, nor will they ever do so.

What is our outlook in life, as Officers and men of the Indian National Army. We are real revolutionaries. Hence our outlook is much more pointed and specific. We have defined duties assigned to us in this noble mission we have under taken to achieve. We have pledged our lives to do so. Nothing on earth is going to deter us from achieving our object. No earthly possession or wordly remuneration is going to unhinge our grim determination. We are quite conscious of the fact that the British have used the 'Golden Key' to suit their purpose, wherever deemed feasible, by the offer of suitable bribes such as titles, rewards, high posts, jagirs, etc. Just playing to human weakness. Alas! Most of us have been involved in our economic grip, no doubt: and hence passive sufferers in the struggle. But some of us have gone out of our way to oblige the British rulers of India with a view to help ourselves, which conduct is unfortunately detrimental to our nations' interests.

The British no doubt work on their time-honoured dictum of Walpole that 'Every man has his price'. These victims of our nation, with the motive of self-aggrandizement, have been directly responsible for our subjection and slavery to a very large extent. Would that we can remove the curtain and open the eyes of these fattening and glittering unfortunates, and retrieve their stagnant and misguided mentality? It will be a great day when we can make them see the day light of truth and clear up all their misconceptions.

The idea of reward or remuneration is totally inconsistent with that of a revolutionary mentality. Once we accept any thing in this life of ours, however, deserving we might have been, the recipient of the gift automatically becomes the paid hireling of the donor. Hence even the very thought of a similar nature, in a revolutionary is quite untenable.

We have to enlighten ourselves by a study of the origin and growth of revolutions in the past in different parts of the world. It was always a question of struggle between the' haves' and the 'have nots'. Those who had not, desired, naturally to have things , vitally essential for them. In the annals of the world history, the first upheaval between the masses and classes occurred in Europe between the Plebians and Patricians in Rome. Christian religion during the mediaeval period retrieved the masses of Europe, who were steeped in ignorance and barbarism. Christian missionaries were able to achieve this result, by preaching to the masses the gospel of faith, hope and charity. However, during the Middle Ages the masses in Europe were the slaves of the barons. The Renaissance in Europe did not contribute enough to the liberation of the masses. The next upheaval was during the French Revolution, when the message of liberty, equality and fraternity was proclaimed from the housetops. In reality this was a middle-class revolution. Yet, it was this attempt made by the French people in 1793,with the object of equalizing the wealth among all the people of France, by the different means in their power that tended towards socialism. Henceforward, the adherents of socialism propounded their theories of uplift of the masses. By this time Capitalism had already made its mark; and suffering labour under capitalistic domination was able to feel their inherent power and strength. All these ideas gradually gained ground and trouble broke out in many countries from time to time between the suffering masses and the dominating and pleasure-loving capitalistic classes. Such a struggle took the shape of strikes, lock cuts and other forms of protests which resulted in the trickling through a little more of the capital, the sole property of the owning classes, down to the masses in the shape of increased wages, diminished working hours and other elements of amenities of life. All such events in different parts of the world gathered strength in the minds of the masses and culminated in the Proletariat Russion Revolution in 1917. The advanced Labourities and communists in all countries have the dream of a Proletariat Revolution throughout the world. Such revolutionary ideas have captured the minds of many of our youngmen in India. The suffering masses in India are already seething with revolution.

India, in her glorious past, had her own politics, economics, sociology and all that is essential for the growth and expansion of a race. The ancient Indian Village Social System, as in vogue in India, has won the admiration of all the modern socialists. Karl Marx, the well-known exponent of Socialism, has devoted a whole chapter on the Indian Village Social System, in his book. Das Kapital. However, the ancient Indian civilization underwent many changes through time, due to various reasons. The priest class were in the ascendant, to start with, with the drawback of exclusiveness and monopoly of knowledge. Then came the power of the solider, and the rule of the military, with its more liberal views of life but with the ideas of pomp, power and territorial aggrandisement. Next came the capitalist civilisation, with its ideas of progress of science and culture and utlisation of that knowledge, but with its inherent defect of accumulation of wealth in the hands of the few and corresponding suffering and poverty of the masses. Hence the struggle of the masses all over the world, even for the bare elements of life's amenities, which have been deprived to them by the possessing classes. Hence the upheaval all the world over, with a view to solve the problem of distribution, for a fair and equitable division of the benefits of science among the suffering humanity at large. Hence the coming into existence of a new order in Asia and in Europe. Hence the idea of co-prosperity sphere and Pan-Asiatic co-operation, interdependence and Federation.

In so far as India is concerned, such an upheaval among the masses is nothing new to Indian history. It is only a revivification of the ancient system of India, for the benefits of all the forty crores of our suffering humanity. That is the end and aim of all our agitation. That is the ultimate objective of all our leaders. That is the Summum Bonum of our Purna Swaraj. There is no word in English literature to describe the correct meaning of Purna Swaraj. It includes complete freedom of our mind, body and spirit, freedom of our thought, speech and action, freedom of association, freedom to enjoy all the bounties of our motherland, freedom to promote happiness and comfort of our masses, with advancement of human knowledge for the welfare of humanity at large. The term Independence is not complete in itself; because India does not desire to live in isolation. What India wants is inter-dependence of all nations, on the terms of equal and mutual reciprocity. Then only the forces of freedom and progress would assert themselves all over the world. Then only the happiness of humanity at large would be ensured and the Utopian millenium would come in to being.

What have we got to do to achieve this nobel mission of ours? We have to rejuvenate our minds completely. We want a complete transformation of our thoughts and activities. For this purpose, education in the origin, course and progress of our national evolution and spiritual training are essentially required. That is what is being provided for you by the Department of Enlightenment and Culture. Have we forgotten the past when the rise of the Marhattas, the Sikhs and the Rajputs moulded our society and politics? Do we not remember that our sense of duty was realised to the maximum extent by our Rajput heroes and heroines? Are we not conscious of the fact that our saints of Maharastra gathered all the spiritual forces which culminated in the ascendancy of Shivaji who succeeded in creating a nation out of the various scattered groups? Have not our great reformers, like Buddha, Ramanuja, Ramananda, Nanak, Chaitanya, Kabir and other risen against the priestly tyranny of our religion and caste system? Are we going to be caste-ridden and religion-driven, steeped in orthodoxy and superstition? Do we not realise that one of the causes of our downfall is a total neglect of our masses, amounting to a national sin against man and God? How can we over associate ourselves with the British system of Government which is determinated to humiliate India before the world?

So, what have we got to do, in order to fulfil our mission in life, the attainment of Purana Swaraj for India? First and foremost we have to feel fro.n the heart. Through the heart comes inspiration. Love opens the most impassable gates. Love is the gate to all secrets of the Universe. Do you feel that millions of our countrymen have been starving for over 200 years, due directly to British domination and exploitation of India? Do you feel that millions of our friends and relations in India are dying of hunger and starvation to-day? Does this thought not make you restless and sleepless? Does it not generate in your minds an intense love for your motherland? Does it not make you realise your sense of duty to your Motherland? Have you not thought of some practical solution in order to soothe the sufferings of the starving and voiceless millions of India, which are progressively increasing from bad to worse, day by day? Have you not yet developed the strength of character and will power, to overcome all obstructions in your path. However insuperable they might be? Come what may in this world, your grim determination should be to pursue your objective, until you achieve your goal. Let fortune support or thwart you, let others blame or praise you, let death come to you to-day or a hundred years hence, let the rest of the world support or desert you, none of these events should count in any way with you at all. You should never swerve from the path of truth righteousness, your sense of duty to yourself, to your friends and relations, to the land of your birth and in fact to humanity at large, in order to support the freedom forces in this world, to establish the new order of inter-dependence of all individuals and of all free nations. You should never rest until slavery and subjection are completely removed until domination and exploitation are totally annulled. It is absolutely imperative that all ranks in the I.N.A. in particular should develop that steadfastness in their life's mission. If your thoughts are sincere, true and correct, if your love for your country is really what it should be, then it is certain that your ideas would permeate the most impenetrable obstacles around you and would pulsate the whole world in your favour. Such is the force and driving power of thought, of sincerity and of honesty and purity of purpose.

We are not stones and trees. We are not inanimate matter. We are all human beings possessed with life, commonsense and power of discrimination and judgement. Why should we behave.

22

Message of Congratulation From the Japanese Premier, General Tojo to the Indians Assembled at Singapore to Welcome Bose: Reiteraties Japan's Desire to See India Free[1]

3 July, 1943

On the occasion of welcoming the Great Leader Sri Subhas Chandra Bose, the Indian Independence League in East Asia held a meeting of the committee of Representatives of Indians in East Asia at Syonan, which has been liberated from British bondage. With this welcome to Subhas Bose, you are taking a long stride towards decisive action with renewed and grim determination to achieve India's Independence.

On this occasion, I extend my most sincere congratulations because it is a happy augury not only for India but for all East Asia also.

Since the outbreak of the Greater East Asia War, the Imperial Japanese forces have annihilated the enemy wherever he was found, and within a very short time, battered all the Anglo-American strategical points in this part of Asia.

At the same time, the bonds of unity among Japan, Machukuo, China and Thailand have been strengthened, and they are irresistably advancing towards the goal of the establishment of the sphere of co-prosperity in East India.

With unshakeable faith in ultimate victory and the triumph of justice for which Japan is fighting, the accumulated wrongs and misdeeds of the British are going to be wiped out. Thus the brilliant dawn of Greater East Asia has arrived.

This is the golden opportunity for India to liberate herself and such a rare opportunity will never occur again.

With the outbreak of the Greater East Asia War, Indian Nationalists in India rose against their British rulers, and India has thus already attained

1. K.S. Giani, *op.cit.* p. 11.

spiritual independence. The British Empire which is gasping for a last breath, will in desperation choose any means to put off the day of their impending doom, and America is also stretching its devilish hands towards India.

In a situation like this, it is by no means an easy task for Indians to achieve India's complete independence; but four hundred million Indian should unite into one solid body and win their own freedom and independence with their own blood and toil.

The sincere wish of Japan for the fulfilment of India's long cherished ambition of "India for Indians" has been proved beyond doubt by the repeated declarations of the Government of Nippon.

Nippon is inflexibly determined to exhaust all her means to help Indian achieving her independence which is the earnest desire off Indians.

It is Japan's sincere wish that the active movement for the achievement of India's Independence must be intensified both inside and outside India, and the Anglo-American forces must be driven out of every corner of India as early as possible. The world situation is becoming more complicated and taking advantage of this, the Anglo-American enemies will no doubt intensify their intrigues. Traditionally Nippon is a country, which invariably keeps faith where friends trust each other, and so is India.

I sincerely wish that Indians will not be deceived by Anglo-American intrigues and miss the God sent opportunity to win their freedom, I trust that Indians, with firm faith in the victory of Japan, Germany and Italy, will fight for justice and righteousness shoulder to shoulder with us.

I firmly believe that this is the only way that Indians can hasten the glorious day of their Freedom, and I sincerely wish them every success in their brave fight.

23

S.C. Bose's interview with the Press; Outlines his Concept of full Freedom and Explains the Reasons for Achieving it with the Help of Tripartite Power[1]

3 July, 1943

Q: What prompted you to come to Japan?

A: There are two reasons: The first is a general reason, namely, that I believe in a personal contact with all the Tri-partite Powers; the second is a special reason, namely, that here I shall be nearer my country, and therefore there is a possibility of working more effectively from these quarters.

Q: To what extent do you think, your broadcasts to India are being, listened to by the people?

A: So far there has been no general prohibition or confiscation of radio sets, though in some cases the local authorities might have done it. Generally speaking, it is rather difficult in India to prevent from listening over the short-wave band: first because the British authorities want to be heard from London, New York and Cairo; and second because we do not use on a large scale sets only with the medium and long wave bands. Therefore, in case the British authorities prohibited short wave bands, people would not be able to listen even to Indian broadcasts on medium and long wave bands. For instance, when I was in prison in 1940 they kept me confined alone: I strongly protested against this solitary confinement, and allowed at last to listen over the radio. But I was allowed at last to listen over the radio to music programs. But I was able all the time to listen to broadcasts from Berlin and Italy.

Q: What prompted you to leave India in 1941?

A: I had three aims, first to find out the correct war situation and general international conditions, which was impossible to judge from inside

1. *Nippon Times*, 4 July 1943.

India, and thereby to judge what the results of the war would be; second, I wanted to get into contact with the Axis Powers and to see for myself their attitude regarding India; and whether it was possible to cooperate with them against the common enemy; third I wanted to make contact with Indians abroad in order to organize them, so that they also would help our fight for freedom. I may say all these three objectives have been fulfilled.

Q: Do you think that help carried to the independence movement to India from abroad can work Independently from the trend of the movement inside India?

A: No, we must work in complete harmony, with the same aims and by a common strategy. This is possible only when someone who has worked inside India comes out and contacts with people outside. It was for this that I had to take the risk of escaping from India.

Q. Perhaps it will be more risky to re-enter India? In fact you stated that no power on earth can prevent you from doing so. Do you mean by that campaign will start from inside India, even if prepared abroad?

A: Well, the campaign is really prepared inside India. But we have to give necessary directions so that people inside can expand the movement in accordance with the general war situation. When we have on the whole a more favourable war situation, then we can intensify the campaign at home. If not, we must go slowly. We have to wait until there is crisis for England in the general war situation-then act both by action from inside and pressure from outside. The time will come when I will have to re-enter India.

Q: What is meant by action from inside and pressure from outside?

A: The main thing is for us to fight. We must do our utmost to free ourselves and only when we have done our best, can we ask others for help. Even if help is offered to us we cannot accept it unless we can also do our share. By pressure from outside I mean two things; pressure of general war situation and also Indians outside India giving all possible help.

Q: Will not your effective campaign from abroad prompt the British Government to come to terms with the Congress as a result of which there might be split caused within the Congress itself, one

side following you and another following the compromised views? If such a situation arises, what would be your attitude?

A: The possibility of a compromise is always present, and we are determined to carry on our flight even if a part of our countrymen enter into a compromise with Britain. That a compromise has not already taken place between Mahatma Gandhi and the British Government is due to two reasons: first our party in the Congress has intensified the anti-British feeling throughout the country to such a degree that unless the British Government agrees to transfer full power immediately to India. Our leaders will not be able to persuade their people to accept the compromise; second, Churchill himself, is wrongly against making any concession now to the Indian people, because he wants to make up the war losses by exploiting India even more after the war is over.

Q: Please outline the meaning of "Purna Swaraj" and the course of its evolution during the past 20 years.

A: Before 1930 the goal of the Congress was swaraj. But the conception of swaraj and what relation India would have with Britain did not result altogether from the constitution of the Congress. "Swaraj" means "self–government", but the meaning of this phrase was rather vague: it was interpreted by us as complete independence, whereas older people thought it was possible to have swaraj in the form of dominion status, as Canada and Australia, and still remain within the British Commonwealth. In 1928, at the annual session held in Calcutta, Mahatma Gandhi moved a resolution that our demand be for dominion status. This was opposed by me, and after a long debate my resolution was defeated by 900 to 1,400 votes. But really speaking, many people voted against some because M.G made it a question of confidence. We had already organised a party within the congress, the Indian Independence League, and throughout 1929 we spread propaganda all over the country. In December 1929, at the Congress session held in Lahore, the situation was so changed that, had Gandhi opposed full independence, he would have been defeated. So at Lahore Gandhi himself came forward and moved a resolution by which complete independence, or purna swaraj should henceforth be our political objective. Now, in principle, it is impossible to reach any compromise therefore we have been holding that any talk of such a compromise means going against the Congress principles.

Q: What part is America playing in the present situation in India?

A: America has now lost the moral influence she had before she entered war. Everybody in India now realizes that America, under Roosevelt's administration has developed a new imperialism. As a result she has been sending to India her representatives and armed forces, so that in spite of the British Government being in India, the American Government is gradually going to get control of our country.

Q: At the interviews you give to foreign correspondents, much attention was called to your declaration that you were ready to abanden non-violence.

A: As far as civil disobedience campaign is concerned, there is no reason for abandoning it since it has proved so effective. It is our task to do more. But all the time, during these last 40 years there has been a big secret movement advocating and even employing violent tactics and lately in the congress, too resorted in some cases to them. The abandoning of non-violence is nothing new. But now the point is to adopt it on a big scale.

Q: Turning to external factors, let us make two suppositions, either the Japanese Army remains stationery on the Burmese-Indian border, or it advances into India. How would you act to meet these two respective conditions?

A: We desire the Indians themselves should take the initiative in the fight against British rule, whether it be an armed struggle, or a civil disobedience campaign. At the same time, they should utilize any new development in the war situation in any part of the world.

Q: It has been often said that the Indian problem is social reorganization and modernization more than independence. What do you think about this?

A: The political movement for independence has been in reality the strongest factor in bringing about social and educational reforms, as well as the development of national economy and industry. But we know from the actual experience that until we have gained complete freedom. It is impossible to bring about radical reform. Men in the Congress have most progressive ideas on such questions, and once India is free politically, they will be the best qualified to carry out a full programme of reform.

Q: What have you understood to be in the conception of the Axis Powers regarding India?

A: All the Axis Powers support the unconditional independence of India. It is for the Indian people themselves to decide what kind of political and social order they want to set up, and in this matter none of the Axis Powers will interfere in the least. For our part is but natural that we desire close relations with the countries that has helped us in your struggle for liberty.

24

Address by Rash Behari Bose while Handing over the Command of the I.I.M. to S.C. Bose; Explains that the Victory of the Axis Powers would Definitely Lead to India's Freedom[1]

4 July, 1943

"It is indeed a great pleasure for myself and for you all that we meet today, so soon after our last conference in Syonan. But events are marching fast these days and our Movement for the sacred cause of Mother India has made enormous strides in the two months since our Conference at the end of April. To day we are on the eve of the most vital the most decisive phase of our fight for the freedom of our Motherland, and I am confident that we are on the threshold of victory.

Friends, it is now one year and a half since the Indian Independence Movement was organised in East Asia. For all practical purposes, that historic day, December 8th 1941, when Japan unsheathed the sword of righteouseness to destroy the Anglo-American Imperialism and to liberate the Asiatic Nations from bondage...... that historic day marked the inception of the Indian Independence Movement in its present form. You do not expect me on this occasion to review the progress of our Movement, to enumerate our efforts, our successes and our failures. You know we started from scratch with nothing but our indomitable spirit of service to our Motherland. But soon we found sincere friends and powerful allies and our Movement gathered strength, thanks to your efforts and cooperation, thanks to the patriotic fervour of Indians throughout East Asia. And our most sincere gratitude is due to our Japanese friends, the Government of Japan, the local Military Authorities in every part of East Asia and to the Japanese Nation in general.

1. Sopan, *Netaji Subhash Chand Bose, His Life and Work* (Bombay-1946) pp. 293-300.

Friends and Comrades-in-Arms, as you all know very well, we have had our share of trials and tribulations, some trivial other serious. But thanks to your grim resolve in the battle for India's freedom and to your patience and devotion to duty, our movement survived all obstacles in its way and emerged with increased strength and solidarity. Today the Indian Independence League is an All-East Asia Organization an organization which is almost on a war footing. The League's Branches throughout East Asia are functioning smoothly and every Branch is contributing its share to the success of the great event's. I want to thank you form the _very bottom of my heart for all the support, assistance, and co-operation extended to me by you and your colleagues, as well as by compatriots throughout East Asia is the fulfilment of duties and responsibilities you have entrusted to me.

Friends, I told you that we are now on the eve of a new phase of our fight for India's independence. For decades India has been struggling against British domination and exploitation. Thousands of Indian patriots have laid down their lives in the cause of India's freedom; and even at this very moment, all India is at war with Britain. As Mahatma Gandhi, our revered leader has stressed "This is a fight to the finish". And with the help of Almighty God, the fight will be finished with the glorious victory of India and ignominious defect of India's enemies, the Anglo-Americans.

Friends, a casual glance at world events today will show you what I mean. Within India the Anti-British revolution has been going on for nearly eleven months. The British boasted that they would crush the revolution in no time but they have failed and failed miserably, inspite of all the ruthless terror and repression they unleashed on India's freedom-fighters. Beyond the frontiers of India we Indians in East Asia are girding for battle to supplement the efforts of Indian Nationalists at home. And in support of us for the assistance of India we have powerful allies, the Japanese. It was only the other day while I was in Tokyo that Prime Minister general Hideki Tojo. re-affirmed Japan pledge of all out aid to India in her fight against the Anglo-American forces. And you will remember that Premier Tojo also made the categorical declaration that it is Japan's policy to assist India to attain full independence in the true sense of the term.

Friend and Comrades-in-Arms, now you see why I am confident that India's victory is a certainty. As I have told you very often, the odds are in our favour—I mean in India's favour—and against our enemies, the Anglo-American enemies of India. This is our God-sent opportunity—an opportunity that we must take advantage of. For decades India fought

Britain single-handed, but today, India has powerful allies. Japan and her Axis partners in Europe are India's friends and allies. India is with them in this war. Victory of the Axis Powers means slavery of India for hundreds of years to come. Therefore as Indians our duty is clear. For the sake of India's freedom, for the sake of justice and decency is this world, for the sake of a better order of human life and intercourse, we Indians must work and fight for the victory of Japan and the Axis Powers. For, as I have just said, victory of Japan and the Axis powers means victory of India, the freedom of four hundred million Indians, the glory of Asia and a new order in the world.

Friends, when I left Syonan for Tokyo towards the end of May, I told you that I would be back in about six weeks. And I am here now. I want to thank the Administrative Committee of the Headquarters for the most efficient manner in which they had carried on the work during my absence and, want to thank you all for the warm reception you accorded me on my return.

Today we meet here just two days after my return from Tokyo and naturally you would expect me to say something of what I saw and heard in Japan. Well, I was impressed by many things I saw and heard during my brief sojourn in Japan. I was greatly impressed by the great sympathy for India's cause on the part of the entire Japanese Nation from His Excellency the Premier down to the man in the street. Freedom of India is stressed on all sides and the entire Japanese Nation is prepared our and out in helping India expel the Anglo-American enemies and to win the National Independence. And you know for yourselves that Japan is fully confident of her ability to help us crush the Anglo-Americans in India. And was for the sincerity of Japan's policy we have before us the historic example of Burma which will be independent very soon and that of the Philippines which will emerge as a free country within the course of this year 1943.

Friends, this is India's golden opportunity—an opportunity the like of which may never again occur. We take this opportunity and we save our Mother land, we save the four hundred millions of our compatriots from the alien tyranny that has been crushing their body and soul for over two hundred years. On the other hand, we miss this opportunity and we betray our Motherland. We condemn our four hundred million brethren and the future generations of India, to slavery for ever. Now or never is our opportunity, now or never is India's chance for freedom.

Friends and Comrades-in-Arms, you might probably expect me to say somethng more of what I saw in Japan. Well, I saw in Japan a great and powerful Nation in its grim resolve for victory. And remember what I told you just a little ago; Japan's victory means India's freedom. India's victory and glory.

In Japan, I saw mighty forces at work forging, weapons of war, assuring victory of the Asiatic cause. The unity and determination of the people of Japan are mervellous, their war-efforts at their zenith, factories work day and night turning over war planes, tanks, arms and ammunition. The huge factories and workshops which once carried on peacetime manufacture, are armament factories now which means the entire industry of Japan is a war industry. The entire labour of the Japanese Nation is now war-labour. New docks and shipyards in various parts of Japan turn out war-ships and merchant vessels to further strengthen Japan's invincible Navy and intrepid merchant marine. Training of soldiers, officers and airmen goes on throughout the country and millions of youngmen are joining the armed forces. And as for the food situation in Japan, I got exactly the same food that I got last year. There is plenty of rice, fish, meat and vegetables. One year and a half of war has not in the least affected Japan's food situation, thanks to the excellent planning and control by the Government. In one word, I found Japan, united as one man with no thought but of war and victory-victory of the holy war of liberation, victory that would mean freedom and prosperity for India and all Asia.

Friends and Comrades-in-Arms, you might now ask me what I did in Tokyo for our cause, what present I have brought for you. Well I have brought for you this present (turning to Subhas.) Shrijut Subhas Chandra Bose needs no introduction to you, to India or the world. He symbolises all that is best, noblest, the most daring and the most dynamic in the youth of India. As an all India leader in the fight against British Imperialism, he stands as a class by himself. He is a brilliant leader and an uncompromising fighter. He has dedicated his life to the cause of Mother India and he richly deserves the name of "Desh Sevak Subhas". Eleven times he has been to British political prisoners but all that suffering and sacrifice have only strengthened his dynamic will to wage the battle for freedom until victory is achieved. Friends, this is one of the happiest moments in my life. I have brought to you one of the most outstanding personalities of our secred Motherland to participate in our campaign for the freedom of India. The spontaneous and enthusiastic welcome which the two million Indians in East Asia have extended to Subhash is an unqualified assurance to him—and to me and to India-that Indians in East Asia have whole heartedly placed themselves and all they have at his command.

Friends and Commander in-Arms! In your presence to-day. I resign my office and appoint Deshsevak Subhas Chandra Bose as President of Indian Independence League in East Asian.

25

Address by Col. J.K. Bhonsle, Director Military Bureau Welcoming Bose as New President on Behalf of the Army; Hopes that his Leadership will Inspire the People and Guide them Successfully to the Achievement of India's Freedom

4 July, 1943

Sri Subhas Chandra Bose, Sir,

Two days ago I, on behalf of the Indians of East Asia, had the proud privilege of welcoming you amidst us, today, as a soldier, on behalf of the Indian National Army, I greet you.

Your brilliant achievement's as one of the greatest leaders of contemporary India and the sacrifices that you have made for the cause of the motherland, are so well known to every one that there is no need for me to narrate them here.

To us you are a new hope, your arrival has instilled a new spirit among our soldiers. So far we had an ideal and a cause to fight for, now we have a leader who will inspire and guide us successfully to the achievement of our goal.

The battle of Indian Independence started in 1857 and has gone on incessantly ever since. So far victory has been denied to us. During every phase of our struggle there was something lacking. We had no armed force to fight the might of the British Empire. We had the leaders of the highest caliber, our men and women showed courage and valour unparalleled in the word history. Unarmed and unaided from outside they defied the British Empire. Through shear tenacity of our purpose we managed to get a few concessions out of the grudging Britishers, but final goal of complete Independence was still not achieved.

To win a victory it is necessary to engage the armed forces of the enemy in a battle and destroy them. To carry out this operation you must have an organised armed force of your own.

1. K.S. Giani, *op.cit.* p. 15.

To day India has an army pledged to fight for the liberation of India. We are determined to fight any one who tries to dominate India. India is ours and must belong to us. Our friends can come there and deal with us as friends, but no one other than Indians shall ever rule her again. We have tasted the misery of slavery long enough. We will be free and shall remain free.

The sacrifice and sufferings of thousands of the brave Indians who have laid their lives at the altar of freedom and the prayers of the starving millions of Indians have borne fruit today. The combination of cincumstances has created a most favourable situation for India.

Telling blows by the Axis Powers have broken the might of the Anglo-American Imperialism, the people of India are up in revolt and with the help of Nippon we have organised ourselves in East Asia to fight for our motherland. We have been given a promise of all out aid by Nippon and the other Axis Powers have given us the assurance of their support.

We are ready and pledged to our motherland. We only await your orders. You are our leader, we have trusted our destinies and the destiny of India in your hand. When you think the opportune time to strike has come, on your orders we shall march forward.

Ours shall be a grim but a glorious fight. I am sure—may certain—our soldiers will give a good account of themselves. We will meet the enemy in the field and destory him there and rid the sacred Bharat Mata from the evil influences of Anglo-American Imperialism for ever.

Vande-Mataram.

26

Bose's Speech at a Huge Rally at Singapore While Taking Over the Command of the I.I.M. from Rash Behari; Requests all Indians to Rise and Fight for the Liberation of Their Enslaved Motherland

4 July, 1943

"From the bottom of my heart, I thank you, Mr. Rash Behari Bose, the representative in East Asia of the movement for Indian Independence, for appointing me leader in East Asia of the movement. I have accepted that post and I humbly pray the god will give me strength to carry out my duties, and hope sincerely that I will be able to satisfy completely my compatriots inside and outside of India. If you accept the experience that I have gained in India and out since the outbreak of the current great war then you too will understand as I, do that the god above is protecting us from the many cases of persecution and oppression and is leading our efforts toward victory and freedom. By this fact my optimism and confidence has increased a hundred fold.

"My friends the time has finally come for the freedom loving Indians to rise. In war time and in emergency, however military discipline as well as the indomitable loyalty to fall for a great cause, if of the greatest, necessity. Therefore I would like to call upon all of my compatriots in East Asia to prepare fully to go into the intense fighting lying before us with solid organization under one centralize control and leadership. I believe deeply that you will not act contrary to my expectations.

"I also believe firmly that freedom loving Indians throughout the world who have continued to work actively for Indian Independence will all give their support to the present movement. And the Indians at present in enemy countries and who therefore are unable to work actively for Indian Independence also support us spiritually. This is the first time in recent world history that Indians in various foreign countries have been

1. *Nippon Times*, 5 July 1943.

united into one centralized organizations aiming at the attainment of common goal. What is further to be noted is that patriotic Indians outside India are working as one for their motherland in perfect harmony with complete contact with their comrades in India. Since I left India in 1941, carrying with a truly important mission. I have had frequent occasions to declare openly, bluntly that my mission is based on the will of the absolute majority of my compatriots. And in spite of every device the secret police contrived to prevent me from doing so, I have maintained continuous contact with my compatriots at home.

"Not only that, I can tell you here that in the last 12 months a great number of representatives have made contact from all directions with India. Some of these representatives where captured, some were shot to death. But when the time comes we will without fail avenge them fully. The greater number of these representatives, however escaped being captured, and especially, according to recent reports, are carrying out action satisfactorily. That is, the patriotic Indians in foreign countries are working actively as fitting representatives of the fighters for Independence in India. I would like to repeat that what we have done until today, and what we will do in the future for the independence of India have not been contrary to what compatriots desired. I say that definitely again to all Indians.

"Then how can we gain independence? There was a time when we hoped that Britain would be forced under an international crises to accede voluntarily for its own good to Indians demands for independence. But those friends who held that veer today no doubt feeling the sorrow of this futile dream. It is clear that Britain, during the war and after, will continue to exploit India. The Wavell is about to be sent to India as Viceroy is only for that a reason.

"A certain section in India seems to be extremely dissatisfied over the appointment of Wavell. They probably wanted some one like Hali-fax for that post I can not agree with such a view. By Wavell's appointment I see, like the handwriting on the wall a prophecy of the future. Wavell's carries with him a fate of being the last British viceroy in India. The new viceroy has the duty to increase Britain's political and economic exploitation of India but as result the hate of Indian masses will become further aggravated and united revolutionary power will take a long step forward being more powerful.

"However, Britain, at the same time she puts into force a brute dictatorial rule, without fail, plan to accomplish a compromise. Such a plan will only be a trick, a ruse and nothing more. It follows that you, our compatriots inside India, must see through to the truth and prepare just as you did in April, 1942, when special envoy Cripps proposed futfile promise.

"In his recent address given at the Guild Hall, London, Prime Minister Churchill use the term "British Common Wealth", and that has clearly revealed his attitude towards India. Of course, it is natural for the imperialistic British Prime Minister to adopt every possible effort to main the integrity of the British empire. Whatever proposal he might make to India, it form nothing but the wish to cheat the Indians. It will absolutely meaningless to think of compromising with the British empire will soon disappear from the face of the earth.

"You who have learned the history of the movement for emancipation in all countries of the world know that for the attainment of independence two conditions are necessary. The first is a favourable international situation and the second is the sacrifice.

"The first condition has been already realized. If India had to fight the British Empire with her bare hands, our task must have been very difficult. But Japan, Germany and Italy are now fighting our enemy and giving him fatal blow, and thus our burden is greatly lightened. These three nations are also determined to continue the war until the imperialism of the United States and Great Britain is destroyed. Thus we are in a favourable position.

"My friends, these two years, I had been continuing to travel to see the real condition of the world war. This study has convinced me that however long the war might continue there only one result—the complete victory of Japan, Germany and Italy, and their allies. Of course, there will be various difficulties before the British-American imperialism is totally smashed.

"Then in a long war, there will be certainly temporary changes in the war situation. I am well aware of the fact, that at present the United States and great Britain are enjoying temporary advantages in certain unimportant fronts. But the entire war situation and particularly strategic conditions are very favourable to Japan, Germany and Italy.

"As time pass the United States and Britain will suffer continued defeats, as you will see. Though the British Empire possessed vast national strength, it has been asking for aids from all quarters. This it is natural for us to ask for sympathy and co-operation as far as possible.

"All past emancipation movements in world history had foreign supports to attain success. In case of India, Japan, Germany and Italy have become our natural allies and therefore, in case of necessity there is nothing wrong in willingly receiving their sympathy and aid.

"Some of you seem to have been influenced by British propaganda and doubt the sincerity of the attitude of the Japan, Germany and Italy toward India. It is quite natural for nations fighting British imperialism to support all demands of India. Then, putting Britain aside for a moment, it will be good for Japan, Germany and Italy, or the whole world, that India will become free. The three nations announced their attitude toward India several times in the past.

"The Government of Japan, through Prime Minister Tojo, announced its policy towards the Philippines, Burma and India because of hypocrites, their propaganda organs said that the Japanese attitude lacked sincerity. Prime Minister Tojo bravely announced to the whole world that the Independence of Burma would be given not after the conclusion of the war but within the present year. That was fatal blow to the British and American propaganda.

"The attitude of the Japanese Government toward the Philippines and Burma is proof of her sincerity and justice. As one of you, I can find no reason to doubt the attitude of the Japanese Government.

"Japan is a strong nation who successfully repulsed foreign invasion. Unless Asiatic peoples who had become slaves are liberated, Asiatic countries would never be safe from the threat of invasion. Japan knows this fact better than any other Asiatic nation.

"Further more, in Japan today there has arisen strong Asiatic consciousness and there is an atmosphere of desiring to cooperate with Asiatic races for their emancipation. These favourable development are giving all enslaved Asiatic people an opportunity to liberate themselves and to establish a new order based on liberty and justice. If there is any one who doubts this point, I feel like saying to him, "Believe me". In view of my loyalty or atleast patriotic sentiment toward India, even enemies cannot say that I am betraying my Motherland.

"As I have said at Tokyo recently, the British Government persecuted me all the time, but it was unable to crush my conviction and principle. Who can move my principle? Craftly British political parties could not cheat me, and no body else can.

"All Indians must bear in their mind that when the United States and Britain should be victorius, India will be left in the state of slavery and will be exploited more than ever.

"Thus the only hope for India to gain independence and freedom rests on the victory of Japan, Germany and Italy. Thus we must work so that our flight, the Axis' victory and the freedom of India will be brought together.

"My friends, we are now given the most favourable international situation. Therefore for attaining freedom, it is only necessary to exert sufficient endeavours and to make sacrifices. In this respect, our efforts in the past were not at all unsatisfactory.

"You will remember my declaration made last May, 85 years after the First Indian Independence war, following the departure of Sir Stafford Cripps from India, that Indian resistance had entered an important stage.

"We passed a number of mile posts as we advanced on our road to independence. One of them was the intensification of non-violence and non-obedience movement. Another was the launching of a drive to cause disturbance in India following the arrest of Mahatma Gandhi in August last year. August 1942 is a most important period in the history of the independence movement in India. During that month the men in the movement abandoned their passive attitude in the drive in favour of an attitude of active resistance. It was during this month that the mass of men in India made up their minds to use some other method than non-violence and non-obedience in order to achieve their ideal of their independent India. It was clear that the time had come for the Independence movement to enter the new stage.

"The thing the Indians at home and abroad have to do today is clear. They have to build a structure enabling them to work for an independent India under unified direction.

"The aim of this structure is to organize the Indians in a manner which will enable them to rise in arms against British Imperialism when the time to do so has come. I have an idea of mobilizing all our resources effectively, an idea which impels me to organize a provisional government is to direct the effort to revolutionize India and realize the ideal of an independent India.

"In order to gain its end the provisional government will prepare the Indians at home and abroad for an armed struggle with American and British Imperialism. An armed struggle for an independent India represents the last phase of the national effort of the Indian people since 1885. The provisional government will have finished its work when American and British imperialism is swept out of India. A permanent government reflecting the will of the Indian people will then be set up, to it the provisional government will transfer power.

"When we are fully prepared for our final armed resistance, it will be possible for us to fight at the side of Japan, Germany and Italy. By participating in the war against the common enemy we should be able to qualify as the people of free and independent nation. Blood shed in the cause of great and holy principle is the price we have to pay for freedom and independance. When we the Indians are ready to shed blood in this way they will have laid firmly the foundations of a structure of national unity. It must be remembered that in sacrificing ourselves to acquire freedom we shall be getting the power to preserve the freedom once it is gained.

"Friends, I wish to express my hearty gratitude to you who repose trust in me and who have signified your intention of giving endless support to me. I have an unshakeable confidence in our ability to win in the struggle for freedom. But it will be dangerous for us to make light of the enemy. I warn you that there will be ups and downs before the ideal we are after is a reality. The enemy is strong, and he will stop at nothing to check us. I imagine that you will find yourselves starving and in frightful difficulties in the final stages of our fight for freedom.

"Freedom will be yours only when you have passed the trial. I have a firm conviction that you will overcome difficulties which are sure to confront you along the way to freedom and be successful in bringing freedom and happiness to your mother country which is impoverished and in the state of slavery".

Inqiulab Zindabad! Azad Hind Zindabad

Bose to the INA Soldiers : Outlines their Duties Towards their Motherland[1]

5 July, 1943

Soldiers of India's Army of Liberation and my Comrades,

To-day is the proudest day of my life. To-day it has pleased Providence to give me the unique privilege and honour of announcing to the whole world that India's Army of Liberation has come into being. This Army has now been drawn up in military formation on the battlefield of Singapore, which was once the bulwark of the British Empire. This is not only the Army that will emancipate India from the British yoke, it is also the Army that will here-after, create the future national army of Free India. Every Indian must feel proud that this Army—his own Army—has been organised entirely under Indian leadership and that when the historic moment arrives, under Indian leadership it will go to battle.

There are people who thought at one time that the Empire, on which the sun did not set, was an everlasting Empire. No such thought ever troubled me. History has taught me that every empire has its inevitable deadline and collapse. Moreover, I had seen with my own eyes, cities and fortresses that were once the bulwark, but which became the graveyards of by-gone Empires. But standing to-day on the graveyard of the British Empire, even a child is convinced that the almighty British Empire is already a thing of the past.

When France declared war on Germany in 1939 and the campaign began, there was but one cry which rose from the lips of German soldiers "To Paris, to Paris." When the brave soldiers of Nippon set out on their march in December, 1941, there was but one cry which rose from their lips "To Singapore, to Singapore." Comrades! My soldiers! Let your battle cry be "To Delhi, to Delhi." How many of us will individually survive this war of Freedom, I do not know. But I do know this that we shall ultimately win and our task will not end until our surviving heroes hold the victory-

1. *Nippon Times*, 6 July, 1943.

parade on another graveyard of the British Empire—the Lal Kila or Red Fortress of ancient Delhi.

Throughout my public career, I have always felt that, though India is otherwise ripe for independence in every way, she has lacked on thing; namely, an army of liberation. George Washington of America could fight and win freedom, because he had his army. Garibaldi could liberate Italy, because he had his armed volunteers behind him. It is your privilege and honour to be the first to come forward and organise India's National Army. By doing so, you have removed the last obstacle in our path to freedom. Be happy and proud that you are the pioneers—he vanguard—in such a noble cause.

Let me remind you that you have a two-fold task to perform. With the force of arms and at the cost of your blood you will have to win liberty. Then, when India is free, you will have to organise the permanent army of Free India whose task it will be to preserve our liberty for all time. We must build up our national defence on such an unshakable foundation that never again in our history shall we lose our freedom.

As soldiers, you will always have to cherish and live up to the three ideals of faithfulness, duty and sacrifice. Soldiers, who always remain faithful to their nation, who perform their duty under all circumstances, and who are always prepared to sacrifice their lives, are invincible. If you, too want to be invincible engrave these three ideals in the innermost core of your hearts. A true soldier needs both military and spiritual training. You must—all of you—so train your selves and your Comrades that every solider will have unbounded confidence in himself will be conscious of being immensely superior to the enemy, will be fearless of death and will have sufficient initiative to act on his own in any critical situation, should the need arise. During the course of the present war, you have seen with your own eyes what wonders, scientific training, coupled with courage, fearlessness and dynamism, can achieve. Learn all that you can from this example and build up for Mother India an absolutely first class modern army.

To those of you who are officers, I should like to say that your responsibility is a heavy one. Though the responsibility of an officer in every army in this world is indeed great, it is far greater in your case. Because of our political enslavement. We have no tradition like that of Mukden. Port Arthur or Sedan to inspire us. We have to unlearn some of the things that the British taught us and we have to learn much that they did not teach. Nevertheless, I am confident that you will rise to the occasion and fulfil the task that your countrymen have thrown on your brave shoulders. Remember, too, that the British have suffered defeats on so many fronts, largely because of worthless officers. And remember also that out of your ranks will be born the future General Staff of the Army of Free India.

To all of you I should like to say that in the course of this war, you will have to acquire and experience and achieve the success which alone can build up a national tradition for our army in future. An army that has no tradition of courage, fearlessness and invincibility cannot hold its own in a struggle with a powerful enemy.

Comrades! you have voluntarily accepted a mission that is the noblest that the human mind can conceive of. For the fulfilment of such a mission, no sacrifice is to great—not even the sacrifice of one's life. You are to-day the custodians of India's national honour and the embodiment of India's hopes and aspirations. So conduct yourselves that your countrymen may bless you and posterity may be proud of you.

I have said that to-day is the proudest day of my life. For an enslaved people, there can be no greater pride, no higher honour, than to be the first solider in the army of liberation. But this honour carries with it a corresponding responsibility and I am deeply conscious of it. I assure you that I shall be with you in darkness and in sunshine, in sorrow and in joy, in suffering and in victory. For the present. I can offer you nothing except hunger, thirst, privation, forced marches and death. But if you follow me in life and in death—as I am confident you will—I shall lead you to victory and freedom. It does not matter who among us will live to see India free. It is enough that India shall be free and that we shall give our all to make her free. May God now bless our Army and grant us victory in the coming fight!

Inquilab Zindabad! Azad Hind Zindabad!

28

Communique by I.I.L. Headquarters Announcing the Aims and Objects of the I.N.A. Under the Leadership of S.C. Bose

5 July, 1943

The I.I.L. in East Asia has organised an Army. This army will be known as the Azad Hind Fauj or the Indian National Army. The Azad Hind Fauj has sworn allegiance to the cause of India's complete independence. The officers and men of Azad Hind Fauj have dedicated their times to the secret task of expelling the British from Indian and establishing an India. for the Indians. After the above communique, the spokeman of the I.I.L. made the following statement:-

"You have just listened to the official announcement of the Indian Independence League Headquarters, that the League has organised an Army which will be known as the Azad Hind Fauj or the Indian National Army. You have also heard that this Azad Hind Fauj or the Indian National Army has sworn allegiance to the cause of India's complete independence and the officers and men of the army have dedicated their lives to the sacred task of expelling the British from India and creating an India for Indians.

I wish to make it clear to the world that the Indian National Army has been organised solely by Indians and consists of picked soldiers from Indian Volunteers who have taken a solemn oath to achieve the complete independence of India by fighting the British and wiping out of India all traces of the two centuries of British Rule. They are anti-British in very fibre of their being and they are inspired by the spirit of independence. They have dedicated their lives to the cause of India's freedom; they have no thought of personal comforts luxury or profit, their one motto is "Freedom or death" to quote Mahatma Gandhi's dictum; and they are ready to lay down their lives in the fight for India's complete independence.

This is the first time in India's history since the advent of the British that a truly National Army has been raised.

1. K.S. Giani, *op.cit.* pp. 23-24.

The sole aim of the I.N.A. (Indian National Army) is to destroy the British Power and influence in India and to make an India for Indians.

As I said earlier the I.N.A. is a picked fighting force from Indians selected on the basis of volunteer system. The men of this force are burning with the anti-British spirit of independence.

The anti-British spirit permeates the entire I.N.A. it is organised on a system best adopted to the Indian genius and is in tune with the revolutionary war which the I.N.A. is expected to wage when the time for action comes.

The training of the I.N.A. is also adopted to Indian spiritual and cultural heritage and Indian military traditions. A strong anti-British spirit and the spirit of independence are the bases of the moral spiritual training undergone by every single soldier of the I.N.A. from the commander down to the soldier. Their training goes on from morning till night. As soldiery the entire I.N.A. is best upon beating British tactics and it is well trained and equipped so to do.

The uniform of the officers and men of the I.N.A. also conform to the Indian Spirit, Indian genius and Indian environments.

The British have been ruling over India by sedulously following their policy of "Divide and Rule". They carried this policy in to the Indian Army also thus keeping alive the difference of race and religion in the Indian Army and thus preventing the growth of National consciousness in the Army. Fully realising the diabolical nature of this "Divide and Rule" policy of the British the organisers of the Indian National Army have laid the axe at the very root of this traditions. All distinctions of class, caste, creed and religion have been abolished in the Indian National Army which has been organised on truly National lines. There are no water-tight compartments based on the religious faiths of the members of the I.N.A. Every man of the I.N.A. feels that he is an Indian first and Indian last. His goal is liberation of India from British rule; and his motto is unity, faith and sacrifice.

The officers and men of I.N.A. are undergoing an intensive training course of enlightenment and culture to fit them spiritually for the sacred task before them.

Spartan living is one of the marked features of the I.N.A. and Indian manners and customs have been given an honoured place in the general conduct of the I.N.A.

To wipe out every trace of denationalisation deliberately fostered by the British by the compulsory use of English language and to establish strong bonds of affinity between the officers and men, the Indian language has been adopted as the medium of communication between officers and men at the barracks and on the field.

I would most emphatically stress once again that the I.N.A. is entirely of the Indians and for the Indians. And only task to which the I.N.A. has solemnly decided itself is the winning of India's complete independence.

Nippon has repeatedly pledged all-out aid to India to achieve her complete independence free from any foreign control or interference.

In conformity with this pledge the relations between the I.N.A. and the Nippon Army are those of two allied armies."

29

Re-organisation of the I.I.L. by S.C. Bose in the Light of the New Wave of Interest Shown by the Indians in East Asia after his Arrival[1]

13 July, 1943

In view of the new responsibilities that the Indian Independence Movement has to face in the near future and in view of the wave of enthusiasm that is visible among Indians in East Asia, it has become necessary to reorganise the Indian Independence League. The first step in this direction is to reorganise the Headquarters of the Indian Independence League. For this reorganisation, some of the existing Departments have to be expanded while other new Departments have also to be set up. I am giving below the scheme of reorganisation. I shall watch carefully the result of this reorganisation and in the light of experience, I may make further changes—if and when necessary.

Departments

1. Military Bureau, 2. Recruitment, 3. Training, 4. Supplies, 5. Finance, 6. Publicity, Press and Propaganda, 7. Health and Social Welfare, 8. Overseas, 9. Women, 10. Reconstruction, 11. Education and Culture and 12. General Secretary.

Department of Recruitment

This Department will organise Recruitment for the Azad Hind Fauj (Indian National Army) all over East Asia in a systematic way. This is a new Department.

Department of Training

The existing Youth Department will be absorbed in this new Department. The work of this Department will be to provide some kind of training for all recruits throughout East Asia until the Army is in a position to take over these recruits and put them into military barracks.

---

1. S.A. Das and K.B. Subbaiah, *Chalo Delhi*, Kuala Lumpur, 1946, pp. 149-156.

The existing Training Institutes will be managed by this Department and if necessary, more may be started. The present staff of the Youth Department will come under this Department and fresh appointments will be made, if and when necessary, according to the amount of work that has to be handled by the department. The Head of the Youth Department will become the head of the Department of Training.

Department of Supplies

The function of this new Department will be to collect supplies from all over East Asia for the Indian Independence Movement in general and for the Azad Hind Fauj (Indian National Army) in particular for present and future use.

The existing Stores at the Headquarters of the Indian Independence League will henceforth be managed by the Department of Supplies.

Department of Health and Social Welfare

The existing Welfare Department will be absorbed in this Department. The new Department of Health and Social Welfare will have two sub-departments-namely: (a) Medical, and (b) Social Welfare.

The existing Welfare Department with its staff will be absorbed in the sub department of Social Welfare. The head of the Welfare Department will become the Head of the Sub-department of Social Welfare. The medical Sub-department will be under a junior Medical Officer. The whole department of Health and Social Welfare will be under a Senior Medical Officer.

Overseas Department

The work of this new Department will be:

(a) To direct and stimulate the work of theh Branches

(b) To establish new Branches where necessary

(c) To maintain regular contact between the Headquarters and the different Branches.

Women's Department

This will be a new Department. The work of this Department will be to organise Indian women throughout East Asia and direct and stimulate their activities in connection with the Indian Independence Movement.

This Department will also recruit women for the Army and will organise a Red Cross Department form among Indian women and girls.

Reconstruction Department

The work of this new Department will be:

(a) To prepare plans for the future—particularly in connection with future administration in India.

(b) To train men for future administration, etc.

Education and Culture

This will be a new Department. The function of this Department will be to direct the educational and cultural activities of Indians in East Asia to provide for additional facilities in this connection, in so far as it is possible for the League to do so.

General Secretary's Department

The functions of this Department will be—

(a) To maintain liasion with the Hikari Kiran[2]

(b) To co-ordinate the work of the different Departments

(c) To perform any special duties that may be assigned by me from time to time.

This Department will have a sub-department, to be called the House Sub-department. This sub-department will deal with problems arising out of the daily work of the Indian Independence League Headquarters, e.g., (a) Transport and Petrol, (b) Buildings and their equipment, (c) Light, Telephone, etc. at the Headquarters, (d) Medical Staff, and (e) Arrangement for the stay of guests coming from outside.

When the work of the House Sub-Department increases it may be necessary and advisable to convert it into a full-fledged Department.

Establishment

Questions dealing with establishment (e.g., appointments, allowances, transfer, etc.) will be dealt with by me. The Department concerned will, however, make recommendations from time to time.

Existing Staff

The existing Staff will all continue to work for the League in future. Transfers from one Department to another may, however, be made, if found

---

2. Major General Iwakuro had departed form Malaya to take up another appointment leaving the Kikan in charge of his successor Col. Yamamoto, the Kikan came to be known as "Hikari Kikan," "Hikari" meaning light and glory.

to be necessary, in order to give effect to the re-organisation scheme outlined above.

Detailed Instructions

Detailed instructions with regard to the working of each Department will follow.

Sd/-
Subhas Chandra Bose,
President,
The Indian Independence League
East Asia.

The following circulars were issued by the Departments of Recruitment and Training to provide detailed instructions for the working of each department:

Indian Independence League Headquarters.
(Department of Recruitment).

Subject: Recruitment

You may be aware by now that the Headquarters of the Indian Independence League have been re-organised and that, in order to effect the Total Mobilisation of our manpower and resources, several new department have been started. In accordance with this plan, this Department has come into existence and it is the earnest desire of our President that at least 300,000 men, (including women volunteers) be recruited for the coming fight for India's freedom.

Regarding the training of these recruits, the newly formed Training Department will address you separately. I shall only tell you this that we do not want to call up these recruits at once. In fact, the training will be done in three stages. In the first stage, recruits should not leave either homes or their professional work—and they should do only morning or evening drills. In the second stage, they will be brought into camps for whole-time training—when these camps are started in diffferent parts of East Asia. In the third stage, they will be brought in to military Barracks when they will become full-fledged members of the Azad Hind Fauj (Indian National Army).

It will be considered a breach of discipline if any recruit suddenly gives up his professional work, or leaves his home, before he is called up for whole-time training.

To carrry on the recruitment of volunteers for the Indian National Army in a systematic way, the following machinery is being set up:—

1. Under each Territorial Committee, the Chairman of every I.I.L. Branch will be the Recruiting offficer for his own area.
2. Under each Branch, the Chairman of every I.I.L. Sub Branch will be Assistant Recruiting officer and will be responsible for recruitment within his area.
3. The Recruiting Officer (Branch Chairman) will supervise and co-ordinated the work of the Assistant Recruiting Officers. In case any Assistant Recruiting Officer fails to do his work properly, the Recruiting Officer will have authority to remove him and appoint a new Assistant Recruiting Officer in his place—after obtaining the approval of the chairman of the Territorial Committee.
4. The Chairman of each Territorial Committee will be the Chief Recruiting Officer for his area. He will supervise and co-ordinate the work of the Recruiting officers within his area. In case any Recruiting offficer fails to do his work properly, the Chief Recruiting Officer can remove him and appoint a new Recruiting Officer in his place—after obtainning the approval of the Secretary of the Department of Recruitment of the I.I.L. Headquarters.

Duties Regarding Recruitment

1. Each recruit should fill in an enrolment form and hand it over to the Assistant Recruiting Officer.
2. These forms should be collected and sent to Headquarters through the Recruiting Officer and the Chief Recruiting Officer.
3. Owing to extreme emergency, old forms are being made use of, until revised forms are printed by this Department.
4. In case of shortage of printed forms, typed enlistment forms may be used by any Recruiting Officer or Assistant Recruiting Officer.
5. Each Officer, either R.O. or A.R.O., who is directly responsible for recruitment should keep a register of all the recruits who have applied for enlistment within his area—together with all particulars regarding each recruit.
6. Every C.R.O., R.O. and A.R.O., will please note that there will be no age-restriction for recruits applying for enlistment. Printed forms of enlistment which contain age restriction should be amended accordingly.

7. Each Assistant Recruiting Officer should arrange for the Medical Examination of each recruit within his area. If necessary, he will, take the help of the R.O. in this connection and the R.O. will if necessary, take the help of the C.R.O. in this connection.

8. The forms of enlistment duly filled in should be forwarded to Headquarters, together with the Medical Officer's report.

9. No recruit should be rejected by the Medical Officer simply because he does not come up to the Army Standard— Provided he is otherwise physically fit.

10. Each Branch or Sub-Branch as the case may be, should meet the expenses in connection with recruitment.

11. Enlistment forms together with the Medical Officer's report should be sent to Headquarters regularly once a fortnight. The first instalment of enlistment forms should be sent up as soon as possible.

12. In order to facilitate and expedite the work of recruitment the Headquarters will send to each Territorial Committee one or more Military Recruitment Advisors. The C.R.O., R.O. and A.R.O. are requested to make the fullest use of these Advisers.

Secretary,
Department of Recruitment

Indian Independence League Headquarters
(Department of Training)

Subject—Training

In view of the total mobilisation in which Netaji requires not only the youth but all able-bodied men to serve irrespective of age, the existing Youth Department has been absorbed in the Training Department.

2. The training being imparted to the Youth Sections by the I.S.I. and the Azad School Graduates at the local centres in Malaya will be continued under the directions of the "Member in Charge Training" of each branch or sub-branch.

More Instructors for local training will be sent to Malaya Branches on demand by the Malayan Chairman.

The demand from other territories should state the approximate number of recruits likely during the next 3 months.

3. The system of training will mobilise the manpower of East Asia in three successive stages:-

1st Stage—Local training in the nature of part time instructions for 2 hours in the morning or evening, every day as far as possible.

This is the responsibility of the territorial Branch and its Sub-Branches. Recruits should neither leave their profession, nor their homes.

It will be considered a breach of discipline if any recruit suddenly gives up his professional work, or leaves his home, before he is called up for whole-time training.

Instructors for this purpose will be provided from I.N.A. and from men trained in Central Camps.

Officers of the Azad Hind Fauj (I.N.A.) who are on recruiting or other duty will be utilized wherever possible to supervise such training and to help the Local Chairman in matters of Military Training and Organisation.

2nd Stage—Central Training in Central Camps under the direct Control of this Headquarters.

(i) Ordinary Camps; (ii) Special Camps.

(i) Territories will be informed of their quota for ordinary camps as and when Camps are ready. Although no high educational qualifications are needed, the best men from local training Centres must be selected to make up this quota.

The first ordinary Central Camp will open in Malaya on or about August 15. The total quota of 5,000 is allotted to Malaya. Detailed instructions later.

(ii) **Special Camps**—The highest possible educational qualifications are needed for candidates for Special Camps.

Three such Camps, the Azad School, Syonan, the B.Y.T.C., Kuala Lumpur, and the Swaraj Youth Training Institute, Rangoon, are already in existence.

Another Camp, the Azad School, Penang, for 100 volunteers will open during the first week of August 2603. As other territories will not be able to send candidates in time the quota of 100 will also be required from Malaya.

Other territories should proceed with the task of sifting good material and must send in applications as soon as possible.

3rd Stage—Training in Azad Hind Fauj.

This will begin as soon as the Army is in a position to absorb the men permanently.

When the system is in full swing volunteers from the 1st and 2nd stages of training will provide a large reservoir for the I.N.A.

4. *Conditions and Allowances*—In addition to free clothing, board and lodging, men in all central camps will receive a normal pocket allowance.

5. Training Syllabus and Organisation for the 1st Stage and will remain the same as given "Interim Plan" dated 13-4-2603 except that more emphasis will be laid on Physical Fitness Route Marches, and Military Training.

A simple specimen programme for the month of August is given below:-

Once a week : Route March Distance to be incresed from 5 to 15 miles.

Daily : P.T. : 45 mins., Spiritual Training : 20 mins, Drill : 45 mins, Instructions for next day and rest 10 min.

Total : 2 hours.

Sundays and Holidays : Special lectures for spiritual and political training.

6. *Finance*—The expenses in connection with training will continue to remain a territorial responsibility as far as the 1st Stage of training is concerned.

Secretary,
Training Department.

30

British Propaganda Against the I.N.A. and I.I.L. after the Arrival of Bose in East Asia

23 July, 1943

1. Since 1.1.43 G.H.Q. has been producing daily propaganda talks which are addressed via All India Radio to Japanese troops and to Indians in occupied territories. The Japanese talks form part of a short joint programme, the rest of which is produced by the Far Eastern Bureau, British Ministry of Information, located in Delhi, who contribute news, news commentaries and music. The Indian language talks form part of a similar programme conducted by All India Radio. During the first few weeks "answers" from enemy controlled wireless stations indicated that these talks had at least been 'noted' by the enemy, who evidently feared their effect. Soon afterwards, decrees were issued forbidding listening to Allied broadcasts, and thereafter, as was to be expected, answers were no longer given to our talks.

2. On 15.5.43 a special campaign against the J.I.F.C. was opened in G.H.Q. radio programmes. About five weeks later, Subhas Chandra Bose appeared in Tokyo and gave a series of broadcast speeches. It was suspected at the time that this move was made partly as a counter-propaganda measure - a suspicion which has since been confirmed by Bose himself. He is reported to have stated at a recent press interview in Singapore that one of his two main objects was "to deal once and for all a crushing blow upon the enemy propaganda conducted against the Indian Nationalists working abroad, and also against our friends who have been helping us in our work for India's freedom".

3. In the anti-J.I.F.C. campaign the aim has been to :—

   (a) Discourage the Japanese from sending further contact parties to India.

---

1. War officer 208/803. P.R.O. London.

(b) Encourage any parties that are sent to give themselves up on arrival in our lines.

(c) Give food for thought to genuine traitors.

(d) Give encouragement and confidence to those who join the J.I.F.C. but remain loyal.

(e) Encourage Indians to pretend to co-operate with the Japanese in order to deceive them.

(f) Foster distrust between Indians and Japanese.

(g) Impress the Japanese with the futility of relying on a few despised traitors and terrorists.

4. With these objects in view, our talks have been based on a limited number of definite themes. It must be remembered that these themes are treated from so many different angles that a short synopsis of this kind cannot include all the arguments and appeals used. The first of the following lists gives the line taken in addressing the Japanese in relations to J.I.F.C. and other Indian questions, the second covers propaganda addressed to members of the J.I.F.C. themselves in Hindustani, Punjabi and Tamil. In addition in the broadcasts in Japanese, consistent attacks on the morals of the troops after made by "Plugging" certain definite themes. Japanese prisoners captured in Arakan have admitted that these broadcasts are listened to by the troops.

5. Japanese—

(a) India remains completely indifferent to alternate threats and blandishments of Japanese propagandists, and to the antics of Indian traitors in Japanese pay.

(b) Indians realise that the way to Indian freedom and independence is by co-operation with the Allies. They have seen too many examples of Japanese conquests to believe any talk about Japan helping India to independence.

(c) The Japanese are being deceived by the majority of Indians who join the J.I.F.C. and the rest are men whose reputations bring them nothing but scorn from true Indian Nationalists.

(d) All Japanese efforts to employ Indians as spies and saboteurs have failed miserably, because these men always report back to their units and give valuable information about Japanese dispositions, etc.

(e) Japan relies on the support of Congress, but this party has always been strongly anti-fascist and anti-Japanese. In any case it has lost much of its influence in India by now.

Indians realise that Congress has been the main obstacle to their attainment of unity and independence.

(f) Japan's pro-Congress propaganda makes no appeal to the many minority parties and communities, nor to the martial races.

(g) All our troops are being encouraged to pretend to co-operate with the Japanese.

(h) Japanese susceptibility to flattery shown by the success of the German Fifth-Column in Japan, as well as by that of the Chinese and Indians in occupied territories who "pretend to co-operate".

6. Indian Languages—

(a) We know all about the J.I.F.C. organisations - who are the real traitors and who are still loyal, etc.

(b) Although refusal to work for the Japanese in any circumstances is highly meritorious, Indians in occupied territories can best assist us by pretending to co-operate with the Japanese and so finding opportunities for escape. Hints on how this can be done and examples of escapes are given.

(c) Exposure of Japanese propaganda methods with examples of broken premises, exploitation of religious sentiments, misinformation etc. Our knowledge that only very few Indians are deceived by this propaganda. "Deceive the Japanese but do not be deceived by them" is constantly repeated.

(d) Distrust between the Japanese and Indian leaders. The stories of the Indian conferences held in Tokyo and Bangkok, murder of certain delegates, etc.

(e) The wretched positions of these traitors who have become Japanese puppets, and the fate of those who have tried to defy the Japanese and insist on the rights of Indians, showing that the Japanese have no intention of allowing independence to India.

(f) Descriptions of traitors and their past records, showing that all are criminals and thoroughly corrupt swindlers. The fate in store for such non-contrasted with the welcome accorded to these who use the J.I.F.C. as a means of escape and report to our authorities.

(g) Examples of Japanese rule in Korea, Formosa, Manchuria, China, etc. after false promises of independence. Determination of Indians to prevent the same rule in India.

(h) Behaviour of the Japanese Army in Burma. Fate of the Burma Independence Army, which was never armed or assisted by the Japanese as promised, and was finally disbanded. Forecast of the Japanese treatnent of the J.I.F.C.

(i) The aims and aspirations of true Indian Nationalists and how these would be defeated by the Japanese.

(j) Hints of anti-Japanese organisations among Indians in occupied territories, including 'messages' to contact, etc.

7. In this campaign, a definite policy has been worked out regarding the tone of the appeal and the general "atmosphere". It has been maintained throughout that those talks are given by representative Indian Nationalists who know Japan, and who therefore know what Japanese rule in India would mean. They address the Indians in occupied territories as friends and brother nationalists (except, of course, the proved traitors). The aim is to maintain an entirely Indian atmosphere, references to the British being few and far between, and usually of a general nature in speaking of the allied Nations. It should be fully realised that only Indian propaganda can have any effect on who are exposed to a constant barrage of India for the Indians with the help of Japan", especially when this is preached by a man of the caliber of S.C. Bose.

8. It is not easy to produce radio propaganda for audiences whose reactions are practically unknown and whose attitude of mind probably varies from sympathy to violent antagonism, by the recent Japanese reactions described above, coupled with letters of appreciation that have been received by A.I.R. from listeners in India,

give some reason to hope that the right lines are being followed. Covert channels are also being used where possible to reinforce this "overt" propaganda.

9. The fact that these overseas programmes are partly "run by the Army" has not been and should not be made public.[2]

---

2. British reactions to the formation of the I.N.A. are reported in the Weekly Intelligence Summary by the General Headquarters. Anti-Japanese propaganda was designed to create mistrust in the Japanese mind about the sincerity of the Indian soldiers. For details F.No. 601/7378/Historical Section, Ministry of Defence, New Delhi.

[illegible] (a) and (f) [illegible] (c)

[illegible] some reason to hope that the right lines are being followed. [illegible] are also being used where possible to reinforce this [illegible]

The fact that these overseas programmes are partly run by the [illegible] and should not be made public.

[illegible]

The [illegible] the city that was [illegible] independence.

[illegible]

[illegible] applied [illegible]

[illegible]

31

Japanese Image of the I.N.A. as given by Nakazawa

25 July, 1943

The spectacular review the Indian National Army recently held in Shonan, the city that was once Singapore is now an old story. The world already knows that the Indian National Army is a mighty force composed of patiotic Indians, that is the vanguard of the provisional Indian Government, which is being organised that it is fully equipped, well trained and efficient army, having artillery, engineering and communication units as well as infantry and that is constantly augmenting in prepration for the war of independence.

The world also knows that it is functioning under political as well as military leadership, as it recently claimed as its commander Subhas Chandra Bose, President of the India Independence League, and the greatest active leader India has today.

Yes, the review is an old story, but in that old story, we find the facts, which are not necessarily new, but which are worth remembering.

Passive Resistance Over

One of these facts is that India's days of passive resistance are over, and the Indians are now determined to win their freedom at the point of bayonets. This, however, does not mean that the principle of non-participation and non-violence, which Gandhi preached and practiced all his life, has lost its influence, but rather that the principle is to be applied in a more effective manner. It is the case of giving bullets of the predatory animals that could not be mitigated or banished by the Bible.

Another fact the old story brought out is that India is not alone in her fight for freedom. The numerous greetings and encouragements the National Army received on the day of review proved the fact that all the

1. The above assessment was given by Kn. Nakazawa, the press correspondent of *Nippon Times* after seeing the Indian National Army Parade at Singapore *Nippon Times* 25 July 1943.

right thinking nations in the world are solidly behind India and as per Japan, she is ready and willing to do all in power for the liberation of the country.

It was in Japan that Subhas Chandra Bose made his first request for assistance, as well as first declaration of Independence. It was in Japanese territory that the first Indian National Army was organised, and had its review. All these, many other similar sets, proved beyond the shadow of doubt that India considers Japan as other supporter in the cause.

India knows that only a winner can give her real assistance in the venture of her type. It may be that India had realized the fact that the true champion of Independence is not England or the United States, but Japan. She saw how splendidly Japan's effort to establish the Greater East Asia Co-prosperity Sphere is progressing, and, especially how some of the nations in the sphere are gaining the Independence with the aid of Japan, Burma, for instance, is in a fairway to attain her freedom.

The Philippines is another nation to realize shortly her hope of independence. She, who, only a little while ago was groaning in the vice of American imperialism—whom the United States squeezed dry, and then, try to cast out under pretence of giving her freedom, is now joyfully preparing herself for the day of independence.

Not only these candidates for the honour of independence—all the nations in the Co-Prosperity Sphere are working together, harmoniously, diligently and contentedly for the peace, progress and prosperity of their own.

Looks upto Japan

Seeing these things, India must have concluded that Japan is the true liberator of oppressed nations, and that she is the country to which India must apply for support.

Whatever the reason may have been, this reason this recent attitude India is, worth remembering in that it reveals the fact England and the United States are not the friends of independence.

Still another fact, that was brought out in connection with the review that the Indian National Army is the beginning of the Provisional Government. This Provisional Government will be free from the domination and corroding influence of England. It also will be different from the exiled government in London, for, while those exiled governments are idly waiting, and hoping against hope, for the day of deliverance to come, the Provisional Government will form the centre of the Indian activities abroad, and render powerful cooperation and stimulus to the independence movement within

India. After winning independence for its motherland the government will affiliate itself with the government of Free India and work for the welfare and prosperity of the people.

Establishment of the Provincial Government means that the independence movement outside of India is no longer fugitive decentralised sporadic movement but that it is an open well organised and consistent activity, which will continue to grow increasingly strong until freedom is own.

Mobilising Own Resources

In addition to these facts, the National Army brought out a new idea as to making the non-participation more effective. It is the idea of saying and using India's resources and manpower for her own independence. England is struggling desperately to improve her position in the war by mobilising the wealth and fighting population of India. By using the same old promise of post-war independence the promise which she used during the First World War, and which she broke after the war she is demanding that India surrender all her wealth and ablebodied population for England to use.

To yield to that demand is to prolong the days and horrors of slavery for India. As it can be seen in her past action, England has no intention of liberating India

What, then, should India do ? Should she prolong her days of servitude by offering her wealth and blood to England, or should she continue her passive resistance despite persecution and death?

It is this question which the Indian National Army answered, by openly hoisting its battle flag against England and by proving ; the fact that; India's effort to liberate herself will have support of all the right thinking nations, it; called for the patriotic Indians to use their resources and ; manpower on the way of Independence. Why make sacrifices to prolong the days of servitude? Let our sacrifice be the cause of our liberation. That is the thought the National Army inspired on the day of its review.

These facts must be most encouraging to the valiant sons and daughters of India, as they bring to them the thrilling realisation that independence is no longer a dangerous dream and that the time Destiny selected for India to strike for freedom is here. It is certain that this realisation will inspire all the Indians to respond to the call of ; the National Army, and starts fighting , and continue fighting, until they win the glorious diadem of absolute and everlasting independence.

32

Addressing the INA Soldiers as Supreme Commander, Bose Reminds them about their Duties and Responsibility in the War Against the British for the Liberation of India

25 July, 1943

Brother Officers! It is my wish that we should be familiar among ourselves, and all of us should know what is our object; what are our duties and responsibilities and how to discharge these duties and responsibilities satisfactorily.

First of all, I will myself tell you something about me. Because, I wish to let you know what is my individuality and what is my individual life, as, in future, we shall have to work together and tread the same path.

After the university career, I entered the political world. The most important question at the time was this: What Indians did during the last war? What was the result and what were the experience and lessons we got for the future? In India and in England it was our experience that the policy of our leaders was wrong. Of course, we were depending upon our leaders for action. But we young men and students were thoroughly disappointed. In our minds there was only one idea, that the mistake committed by our leaders in the last war should not be committed again. We thought, if we get an opportunity in future, we will not make such mistakes.

There was another big question. In Europe, after the war, in the year 1918 and 1919, there were many changes; new governments were coming into existence, which had not existed before the war. The Czechs ceased to be a part of the Austro-Hungarian Empire. Another race, the Poles, formed their own government. When I went to Europe, I had the opportunity of meeting two or three Indian leaders there. They all advised me that if we want to do anything for our Motherland we should study the history of

1. *Nippon Times*, 27 July 1943.

the war and the experiences of the such history should be utilized for our fight against Britain. We began to learn the understand things. We came to know how some leaders of Czechs went out of their country for doing propaganda and getting help from the enemies of Austria and Hungary. They joined hand with Britain and France against Austria, Hungary and Germany.

The Poles, too formed an army of 30,000 and took part in the war. It was their fortune that Germany and her allies were defeated, and after the war, they were able to form their own government.

There is no reason why we should not also go by the same path, and taking advantage of the international situation, we should fight shoulder to shoulder with the enemies of Britain, to get complete freedom.

The people of Ireland also took advantage of the war. They openly revolted under the Sinn Fein Party against the British. In the City of Dublin, the Sinn Fein Party had an army of 3,000 only. They had also an army of 10,000 strong in the country. Something went wrong with their plans and the rebellion that started in Dublin did not spread to the countryside. Anyhow they kept the City of Dublin under their control for eight days. The revolution occurred during Easter, and so the revolution is called the Easter Revolution. Though the revolt did not materialise in 1916, it again broke out in the year 1919, just after the war. They had only 5,000 volunteers. This time is was different. War was over. From England troops could be brought to suppress the rebellion. Even then this army of volunteers numbering 5,000 carried on their fight and in the end the British were brought to their knees.

In 1921, we began working in India with all the experience that we had from the study of the history of the last war. At that time as you know, Mahatma Gandhi had launched the Non-Co-operation Movement enthusiastically with the specific idea in mind that when an opportunity offers itself, we should take up arms against the British. We knew also that Germany would try to take revenge and then would come our opportunity as well.

We joined the Congress in 1921 under Mahatma Gandhi, because there was no other way to carry on our fight to keep up the honour of the nation in the face of terrible British oppression. Hindus and Muslim were united. But we knew definitely that the Civil Disobedience Campaign in India would not be completely free. Of course the movement did create the political consciousness among the prepared the people for armed struggle. From 1921 onward we were waiting for an opportunity to take up arms, and that opportunity was a war in Europe.

This is not my individual view but it is the view of many young men who came under Mahatma Gandhi in 1921. Certainly there were a few young men who believed in non-violence, but many of them were strong supporters of violence and they were awaiting the proper time to strike.

I went to Europe in 1933 and remained up to 1936. My idea in going to Europe was to study the situation and to know what was going to happen next. During the stay in Europe I visited Berlin and made acquaintance with certain Government officials and met Fuehrer Hitler. I plainly asked them when they were going to strike at British so that we might also take up arms simultaneously against the British. They replied that they were not at all going to fight Britain and they hoped that all their demands would be fulfilled by Britain. They were for a compromise with Britain. However, they expressed their sympathy for Indian freedom. I argued with them about the British hypocrisy and their cunning policy as Indians know best about that by personal experience, and warned them that, when Britain thought that the German power was getting stronger, she would openly come into conflict with Germany. In the end I told them: "Britain is our traditional enemy. We will fight her, whether you support us or not". But I had no doubt that war would start in Europe soon. Anybody could understand this, by having a look at the preparations that were going on in Germany. When I went to Europe this time, I reminded them of what I said in the year 1936.

My idea in saying this is that I came back from Europe with a strong conviction of what was going to happen. The new party that came in power in Germany was always for a fight. I clearly understood that the German demands would not be accepted by the British and if the British found the Germans growing a bit strong, they would fight the Nazis. In 1938 when I went to Europe I noticed some changes. Germany was beginning to understand that the British would never fully accept their proposals. In September 1938, when the Germans put forward the case of Sudetan Germans, Mr Chamberlain rushed to Munich to come to an agreement with Herr Hitler. There was a time when all parleys of international value generally used to take place in London. But when I saw the British Prime Minister, Mr. Chamberlain going to Germany, leaving his own country and when he accepted the German demands, I realized the secret. It was the first time in the history of the British that a Prime Minister of England relegating the usual custom, proceeded to a foreign country to accept the demands of another nation.

Then I started propaganda in India that a war in Europe was inevitable and it was the duty of Indians to be alert and to try to force Britain to accept our demands, and if they did not, to prepare ourselves for a fight. I was noticing the reaction of the public to my propaganda, and I was convinced that the full support of the general public was with me. But our leaders were thinking in a different way, particularly Mahatma Gandhi whose policy was to wait and see. But we young men were not deterred by this policy. We redoubled our propaganda. We were asking the people of India to take advantage of the golden opportunity that would be presented to them in the near future.

In the annual session of the Indian National Congress at Tripuri in March 1939, I tabled one resolution demanding freedom for India within six months and such an ultimatum to be sent to the Government. In case this demand was not conceded in that period, we should prepare the people for a fight against Britain with whatever might we possess. It was, of course, in the nature of an ultimatum and resolution was introduced, keeping in view the tense international situation and knowing full well that a conflagration would begin in Europe within six months.

When the war actually started in September 1939, the public began to realize that what I said in March was correct. It was our duty at that time to unite all the Nationalist forces and bring pressure on the British Government to concede to our demand, and if unsuccessful, to fight for it. But our leaders were thinking and acting in a different way. They were under the impression that Britain would become weak in the course of the war and to get the Indian help, they would come to an honourable agreement with the Congress. I tried to point out the absurdity of such a notion and told them whatever might be the weakness of Britain during the war they would never allow to rid themselves of the power in India. The weaker they grew the more powerful would become their grip on India. Without India they would not be able to prosecute the war successfully. They would begin looting and plundering the country's resources as they got weaker and weaker.

In March 1940 when the Congress Session was in progress, we expected a forward step. But Gandhiji had his own way. He was to wait and see. We began to lose our minds, come what may, to start our own movement. An Anti-war movement was started throughout the country. It became somewhat serious; many people courted imprisonment. Meanwhile I got information that Gandhiji himself would launch a civil disobedience movement in November as the Government did nothing. I heaved a sigh of relief that if Gandhiji starts a movement, it will have world-wide repercussions. The whole world will come to know that Indians are fighting for freedom. All the nations will think that Indians deserve freedom. We will surely get the sympathy of the world to have saved our honour.

But I thought that by the weapon of Civil Disobedience alone we will not achieve freedom. The movement would surely bring pressure on the Government and hamper its war effort, but the government would never consider our demand. That was my idea. We were thinking what to do. What new method should be adopted. Young men were doing their bit and bombs and revolvers. We got into touch with these young revolutionaries. I knew their strength. They were real revolutionaries with high spirits. But their strength and sacrifice were not enough to achieve complete independence for our Motherland.

It was then we began scanning the pages of history and found many an example and learned many a lesson. The American example was before us. I began to realise, and even came to the conclusion, that without outside help the Indian revolution would not be successful. The United States got a lot of help from France. Even General were despatched from France. In the history of the world, it is not a new thing to get assistance from other nations for winning freedom for one's country.

The news we got in India were twisted and more of a propaganda nature. It was natural that Britain should do so. But to understand the real situation of the world by remaining inside India was not possible. What would be the result of the war and how the war would end and who would win in the end? What were the ideas of Indians abroad, how they were thinking about India's fight for freedom, how to get help from them for thinking about India's fight for freedom, how to get help from them for India's independence and whether it was possible to get material help from the enemies of Britain? These were the questions which made us think that somebody should be sent outside India. I thought of sending some persons to foreign countries. Certainly it was a most difficult task, strictly restricted as our movements were. I thought also that such a person should leave India as the British really "understand" and as the India people seriously take. At last I decided myself to get out of India.

I was in jail at that time. To get out of the jail was a difficult problem. To slip away from jail would make it difficult for me to leave the country in view of the British C.I.D. At last I decided to go on hunger-strike. This decision was taken after steeling my heart, that I would either die or get out of the jail. When my decision was made known to the Government it created a stir in the official circles as they never wanted to see me die in the jail. The Superintendent of the jail came and entreated me not to undertake hunger-strike. He argued that if all the prisoners went on hunger-strike the King's Government would come to a stand-still, and warned me that if I died in the jail it would be my own responsibility. My hunger-strike went on for six days. They tried to forcibly feed me but I was determined to die the way of Jatindra Nath Das. After seven days, a secret conference took place at Government House. They wanted to do something as the medical report about my condition was serious. They set me free with the idea of rearresting me after a month. I got information of this in good time. Meanwhile some arrangements could be made for my escape from India and I left my country.

Experiences I had a lot, after leaving my homeland. I was listening in to both the radios. I had the privilege from the German authorities to hear the enemy radio and propaganda. I had the opportunity of visiting all the fortifications and other defences all over Europe. After these personal experiences, I have no doubt what will be the result of the war. As I said in your prade the other day, the war will be a prolonged one but there will surely be one result, that is, the collapse of Britain, and her empire.

Now the question is this. What is the position of India under these circumstances? The destruction of the British Empire is certain, and the whole map of the world will be changed. What will be the position of India in the new map? The British will be driven out of India, and what should be our position then? We should think about this. There are three alternatives;

One is to keep away from the war and to have a neutral attitude. Second is to go and beg for freedom from the new invader and the third is to take part in the war with the enemies of Britain and qualify ourselves for freedom.

I know what alternative you prefer. For us there is but one alternative that is, to fight hand in hand with the enemies of Britain and contribute our share in the destruction of British Empire.

The internal situation in India is very grave. It is our duty to encourage and support the forces that are in India doing, their bit against Britain. What is the internal situation in India to-day? The whole population is against the British Government.

People are carrying on the fight without arms. To suppose millions of unarmed people, a small army of thousands equipped with the all modern arms is enough. When I had the privilege of meeting Herr Hitler, I took the liberty of asking this question of India and sought his advice as to what path we should tread. The Chancellor of Germany, who is himself an experienced revolutionary, giving his opinion, said that a well-equipped army of a few thousands would be able to control millions of unarmed revolutionaries. He added that so long as an external power did not knock at the frontier no change could be expected in the internal situation. We should form part of this external power. We hear so much nowadays of a second front. It is we, who should create a second front in India. It would have been possible for them to face us in both the fronts, had not the Axis Powers crippled and maimed them. The Axis power had made our work easier. We are thankful to them for doing this, but at the same time, it is incumbent upon us to do our duty towards our motherland. To do this work an army of 50,000 is enough, but we should be prepared to raise an army of 300,000.

The question now is this: What are the duties of this army? There are two duties which this army will have to perform. The first and important duty is, of course, to fight the enemy and free our motherland; the second one is also no less important. It is to form such a powerfull army in India that will free any nations put together and to defend India forever against foreign invasion. Our sisters and brother in India are facing even bigger ordeals with cheer and enthusiasm. For the Indian Independence and for India's welfare, there is no greater work than this.

While in Europe, I tried and I was successful in forming a small National Army. I have brought photos of the army. In Berlin and Rome Indians are thinking and doing things as you are thinking and doing here. Everywhere in the world, wherever there are Indians, a new spirit, a new awakening has come among Indians.

that we should need. The [illegible] of [illegible] is [illegible] experience [illegible] giving information, and that a well-equipped army of a few thousands would be [illegible] in [illegible] of [illegible] the [illegible] no longer [illegible] under [illegible] no change could [illegible] the internal [illegible] We [illegible] at this [illegible] from [illegible] to [illegible] from [illegible] [illegible] and [illegible] We are thankful to [illegible] but at the same time, it [illegible] upon us to do our [illegible] our [illegible] This [illegible] an army of [illegible] is enough, but we should be prepared to raise an army of [illegible]

The question now is [illegible] What are the [illegible] of this army? There are two duties which this army will have to perform. The first and [illegible] duty is, of course, to [illegible] and [illegible] our [illegible] and the second [illegible] from [illegible] that will [illegible] Our [illegible] and [illegible] for the [illegible] work than this.

While [illegible] I [illegible] of [illegible] a small [illegible] army I have [illegible] of the army in Berlin and Rome [illegible] you are [illegible] Everywhere in the world [illegible] a new spirit [illegible]

33

Speech of Bose on the Occasion of Independence to Burma Granted by the Japanese, Reminds them that the Liberation cannot be Complete until India is Free

1 August, 1943

Countrymen and Friends! Today is the first of August, 1943. Today an event of great historical importance has taken place. Right in the midst of a World War, an Independent. State has come into being. Burma—our neighbour has achieved her Independence and she has now her own national Independent Government. Long Live Free Burma!

You all know that when the war in East Asia broke out in December, 1941, the people Burma decided to utilise the opportunity for recovering their lost liberty. Instead of co-operating with the British Government, the vast majority of Burmans did their best to help in expelling the British from the country, and the result is that today, not only has Burma been liberated from the British altogether, but she has actually realised her long cherished goal of Independence.

The Independence of Burma in this momentous crisis in world history, has a two-fold significance for us. It shows, in the first place, what a nation can achieve, if it knows how to seize an opportunity which history has offered. Secondly, just as the conquest of India supplied the British with a jumping-off ground for their attack on Burma in the nineteenth century—similarly, the emancipation of Burma has supplied the Indians Independence Movement in East Asia with a spring board, for its attack on Britain's army of occupation in India, during the twentieth century.

Burma was deprived of her liberty long after India was. Nevertheless Burma has stolen a march over us and has attained her liberty, while we are still passing through the throes of revolution. On behalf of the India people and of myself, I offer my warmest congratulations to the people of Burma

1. K.S. Giani, *op.cit*, pp. 46-47.

on the achievement and I heartily wish them increasing progress and prosperity in the days to come. I offer also my hearty felicitation to His Excellency Dr. Ba Maw, the head of the New and Independent state of Burma and I wish him all success in the discharge of the manifold responsibilities which have now devolved on him. It is a source of great pleasure and gratification for me that so soon after meeting Dr Ba Maw in Syonan, during the first week of July, I can offer him my greeting and congratulations as the head of the new and Independent State of Burma.

Friends, you are aware of the many promises which the British Government has given to the Indian people during the course of the their rule in India—promise which have always proved to be mere scraps of paper. You are aware also that these promises have been repeated since the outbreak of the present war and all sorts of silly excuses have been put forward to show that in the midst of a war, transference of power from British to Indian hands cannot take place. As against this example, we now see that right in the midst of the war, the promise of liberty made by the Prime Minister of Japan. His Excellency General Tojo, on behalf of his Government and nation, has been fully redeemed. Where there is a will there is a way and this statesmanship and generosity on the part of Japan, will bring into bold relief the hypocrisy of British politicians—while they will demonstrate the real character of Japan's state policy.

The Independence of Burma will, I am sure, be soon followed by the Independence of the Philippines. Asia is now on the threshold of a new era in her history. This is a unique opportunity for all the suppressed nations of Asia to rise and effect their emancipation. It is above all the sacred duty of the Indian people to seize the present golden opportunity and fulfil their age-long aspirations.

The liberation of Asia cannot be complete until India is free. The Indian people must, therefore, rise and liberate themselves and thereby help the emancipation of other Asiatic nations. Above all, India must seize the hand of friendship which Japan has offered to India and to other suppressed nations of Asia. Confronted by a common foe, the people of India must march shoulder to shoulder with the brave Nipponese nation, till the enemy is overthrown and India recovers her lost liberty.

Inquilab Zindabad! Azad hind Zindabda!

34

Statement by Japanese Board of Information Reiterating Support to Indians for Ending Anglo-Saxon Domination in India[1]

8 August, 1943

"A year ago today, Mahatma Gandhi was imprisoned for no other reason than for having proposed a resolution demanding the immediate withdrawa! of British influence from India—a resolution which was unanimously passed by the Indian National Congress party. It was a just and legitimate demand arising from the age-long aspiration of the people of India for freedom, Independence and the right to govern themselves.

"Ignoring the wishes, the desires and the human longings of the Indian people without as much as a show sympathy and consideration and conscious only for the preservation and promotion of her own selfish interests. Britain, for the last twelve months has intensified more than ever before the pressure on the Indian masses to make them submit to her tyranny.

Since the imprisonment of the Mahatma on August 9, last year, 60,229 Indian patriots were arrested of whom 26,000 were pronounced guilty and 18,000 held under detention up to the end of the year, according to the statement of Reginald Maxwell, Home Secretary of the Viceroy's Council, on February 12. According to the same office, on August 3, 11,717 political prisoners were in prison as of June 1, and from the outbreak of the war in Europe to June 3 this year 76,646 Indians have been sentenced to hard !abour throughout the whole country. This actual figures may be expected to be much larger, for we would not expect a British official to tell the whole truth.

1. The above statement was issued by Japanese Board of Informatioin, *Nippon Times* 9 August 1943.

"Arrests and imprisonments have not been the only instruments of oppression used by the British. They have driven Indian men into uniforms by compulsory conscription, creating an army known under the false name of Indian Volunteer Army which, according to General Auchinleck, numbers 2,000,000 men. They have gone further to press civilians into auxillary and other war services by large scale mobilization. To supply and feed the Allied armies, the British authorities are forcing the Indian farmers, by compulsory measures, to report their yearly crops which they are requisitioning for the armed forces. Nothing is done to ensure the equitable distribution of food-stuffs among the Indian people. The consequence has been serious food shortages and widespread famine, raising prices and mounting tensions in daily life.

"British policy in India, however, is neither strange nor surprising. To quote, for example, from the figures of British Empire the casualties announced my Deputy Prime Minister Clement Atlee to the House of Commons last June. India with 101,197 casualties, has sacrified as many men in Canada, Australia, New Zealand, South Africa and other British colonies combined. This alone attests the fact that India is being made to give her blood to the British cause without getting anything but oppression in return.

"Who does not know that what the British call defence of India is nothing more than the defense of Britain's imperialistic interests? Who does not know that the British policy in India today is to defend British interest against the Indian people themselves? Who does not know that the real defense of India, if necessary, can be ensured only by the full independence of India?

"India's hour of destiny is fast approaching. As British oppression has intensified and as British policy has revealed its naked self. So during the past year has the passive resistance of the Indian people grown and intensified into active resistance. India's saintly leader Mahatma Gandhi, has already issued the battle cry, "This is a fight to the finish".

"The activist leader, Subhas Chandra Bose, has called the British hand by declaring, Indian should ever cherish the illusion that one day England will be inducted to recognize India's independence. Our independence admits of no compromise. The hour has struck and every patriotic Indian must advance toward the field of battle. When the blood of freedom-loving Indians begins to flow India will attain her freedom... Now or never is our opportunity, now or never is India's chance of freedom'.

"The independence of Burma, once a province of India, has encouraged and inspired the Indian people to fight for the attainment of the same goal. And close to the borders of India there stands today a massive army force composed of volunteers, the Indian National Army, under the command of Subhas Chandra Bose, ready to go into action when the hour strikes.

"The activities of Chandra Bose and his call to arms as the only means of redeeming India has produced far-reaching effects on the Independence movement both within and without India. All the peoples of Asia stand united and ready to support the people of India in their fight for freedom, for in their freedom lies the hope of real all-inclusive Greater East Asia.

35

Special Order by Bose on Taking Over Direct Command of the I.N.A.

25 August, 1943

In the interests of the Indian Independence Movement and of the Azad Hind Fauj I have taken over the direct command of our army from this day.

This is for me a matter of joy and pride-because for an Indian, there can be no greater honour than to be a Commander of India's Army of Liberation. But I am conscious of the magnitude of the task that I have undertaken and I feel weighed down with a sense of responsibility. I pray that God may give me the necessary strength to fulfil my duty to India under all circumstances, however difficult or trying they may be.

I regard myself as the servant of thirty-eight crores of my countrymen who profess different religious faiths. I am determined to discharge my duties in such a manner that the interests of these thirty-eight crores may be safe in my hands, and that very single Indian will have reason to put complete trust in me. It is only on the basis of undiluted nationalism and of perfect justice and impartiality that India's Army of Liberation can be built up.

In the coming struggle for the emancipation of our Motherland, for the establishment of a Government of Free India, based on the goodwill of thirty-eight crores of Indians and for the creation of a permanent army which will guarantee Indian independence for all time, the Azad Hind Fauj has a vital role to play. To fulfil this role, we must weld ourselves into an army that will have only one goal—namely, the freedom of India—and only one will namely to do or die in the cause of India's freedom. When we stand, the Azad Hind Fauj has to be like a wall of granite: when we march, the Azad Hind Fauj has to be like a steam-roller.

1. *Malai Sinpo*, 30 August 1943.

Our task is not an easy one: the war will be long and hard, but I have complete faith in the justice and the invincibility of our cause. Thirty-eight crores of human beings, who form about one-fifth of the human race, have a right to be free and they are now prepared to pay the price of freedom. There is consequently no power on earth that can deprive us of our birthright of liberty any longer.

Comrades, Officers and men! With your unstinted support and unflinching loyalty, the Azad Hind Fauj will become the instrument of India's liberation. Ultimate victory will certainly be ours, I assure you.

Our work has already begun. With the slogan 'Onward to Delhi!' on our lips, let us continue to labour and fight till our National Flag flies over the Viceroy's House in New Delhi, and the Azad Hind Fauj holds its victory parade inside the ancient Red Fortress[2] of India's metropolis.

Subhash Chandra Bose
Supreme Commander

2. Subhas wanted to march through Manipur with the I.N.A. and to hoist the Indian National Flag at Red Fort. His slogan of "March on to Delhi" was a battle cry for the I.N.A. However, it was not Subhas, but Nehru who hoisted the National Flag at Red Fort on 16 August, 1947, where the old guards of the I.N.A. rallied to redeem the unfulfilled pledge.

36

Speech of Bose at Kaula Lumpur; Thanks Indians in Malaya for Financial Help and Requests the Young People to Join the INA.

5 September, 1943

Friends! I want to thank you most heartily for the purse you have presented to me this evening. It is a handsome purse, but I shall call it handsome, only if you regard it as a first installment. Considering, what other town are paying and within a very short time; considering also what Ipoh has paid as a first installment. I am sure that Indians in Kuala Lumpur will be anxious to see that this contribution is multiplied atleast five times and if you cannot do that, I am afraid, you will be doing a great disservice to your country. You are very proud of your city and rightly too. It is the second city in this part of the world and if you enjoy the prestige, you must fulfil the responsibilities that follow from that distinction and prestige.

I will now tell you that what we want in cash is only a part of our total requirements. The time has come when we have to give our all in the service of our mother-land. The days of minimum sacrifice are over. The time has come, when each and everyone of us has to think of the maximum sacrifice, which he or she is able to offer, and that sacrifice has to be in human life, in money, in other resources, which are necessary in order to equip a modern army for its marches. I am glad to know that you citizens of Kaula Lumpur and Selangor state are anxious to do your duty in every respect and my only remark and request to you is to expedite your collections as soon as possible so that our army may be equipped sooner than many expect and be ready to march to the field of action.

From my experience. I am convinced that so long as the Indian people remain unarmed, so long as the British Government has a modern army under its control and so long as we do not take up arms for our struggle for

1. K.S. Giani, *op.cit.* pp. 56-59.

freedom, we shall not be able to achieve independence for India. I do not know of one instance—of one single instance—in the whole history of mankind where a nation has been able to achieve full independence without resorting to arms, but apart from history, our natural experience in the course of several decades has convinced us that we have to take up arms in the final stage of our struggle if we want full independence and not a diluted form of it. So long as peace reigned all over the world it was practically impossible for the Indian people to get arms and fight with arms. It was impossible for the people inside India. It was also impossible for people outside India, but thanks to this war, what was impossible four or five years ago has today become possible. If you want arms you can get them not inside but outside India. You could not do it even if you wanted to. That is why I say this war has been a God-sent opportunity to us. It has given us a unique opportunity for achieving not Dominion Status or Colonial self-government, but full and complete independence.

The only question I would like to put to you as Indians is whether you really want full and complete independence. If you do so you must pay the price. You must organise a complete modern army and march with that army to India.

To-day the British have one front—the Indian national front, you might call it—inside India. The British with their army are able to cope with this Indian national front. If you can put up a second front—not a bogus second front, but a real second front then it will be imposible for the British to maintain their position in the country. I am convinced when the Indian National Army appears on the frontier of India its very appearance will be a clarion call to the people in general and also to the Indian army to rally round the banner of Indian revolution. This is not a wishful dream on my part. I know the people at home are fully aware of our activities in East Asia and the British too are aware, but we do not care. The time has come when we could openly proclaim to the whole world what we have been doing, what we are doing and what we are going to do in the future. Our brethern in the Indian Army who today are standing under the Union Jack and anxiously waiting for the Indian National Army on the continent of India. That is the position at home without any exaggeration. It is therefore our duty to hurry with our work and see that the National Army goes to the aid of India as soon as possible.

Ever since the existence of the Indian National Army was announced to the world and its intention of marching to Delhi, you will be surprised to learn that there has been a complete change in the tactics of British propaganda. Up to recently British propagandists have been saying that to-day Nippon has become the enemy of India and that its army intends to march into India, but ever since they realised that the Indian National Army had been formed and is getting ready to march into India, there has been a complete change in the attitude and also in the tactics of British propagandists and now they are anxiously trying to work up the Indian people to take a stand against the Indian National Army. The British Government knows, as much as we do, what the attitude of the Indian people and the Indian Army will be when our army appears on the frontier of India, and that is why they are anxious to do their best to win over the Indian people to their side so that they may take a stand against the Indian National Army.

But the most unexpected surprise came to me when I was told that British propagandists on the occasion of a Hindu Festival and appealed to the Hindus of India to get ready to fight their brothers who are going to march in from outside. The British propagandists even went so far as to say that the good old days have come back again!

Friends! The Anglo-Americans have found out now a new Napoleon. According to the Anglo-Americans, Lord Louis Mountbatten is amphibious. He is a master in land and sea operations. Well, what is the career of this amphibious monster? He is the hero of Dieppe. Dieppe was an attempt by the British army to land in France and expel the Germans from that part. Within 24 hours they were completely wiped out and there ended all the heroic exploits of Lord Louis Mountbatten. Because of his achievement at Dieppe he had been made commander-in-chief of the South East Asia command. I challenge you to show me one country in the world today where promotions are made not for success, not for victories, but for defeats. It is a unique achievement of the British army and its government in this war. I can assure Lord Louis Mountbatten that a much bigger and greater Dieppe is waiting for him in East Asia.

Perhaps, there are some people living in East Asia, and even in Malai, who are still hoping and dreaming that the British will come back. We have heard of them. There are a few such men in Syonan also. I can only pity them. You know what Syonan was and is today. The British—I do not say it, I only repeat it—took twenty years to build Singapore and how many days to get out? Seven days. This is an achievement and still there are people who believe they will come back! The biggest bulwark of the British Empire is now the biggest graveyard of that Empire and it shall be a graveyard. The days of the British Empire are over. If you have any doubt turn over the pages of history. Every Empire has had its glory and also its decline. The British Empire had its glory during the last war and since then its decline has become very rapid and we have witnessed with our own eyes the last phase of the decline.

I have always said that the last war brought about the disappearance of the two Empires—the Ottoman Empire of the Turks and the Austro-Hungarian Empire. This war will see the end of the British Empire and out of the ashes of that Empire will rise a free India. The two things are identical—the defeat and dismemberment of the British Empire and the creation of an independent India. If you want India to be free you have to work and fight for the overthrow and dismemberment of the British Empire.

British propaganda of late has adopted new tactics and that is to utilise to the best advantage the small success they have achieved in Africa and Sicily. If you were to listen to the propaganda that British agents have been carrying on all over the world you would think that with the occupation of Sicily they have already won the war. I know something of Europe, not only of peace-time Europe but war-time Europe, and I know all these places where fighting has taken place. I know also the strength and weakness of the Axis powers in Europe and from experience I want to assure you that whatever may happen in Europe has no bearing on the situation either in India or East Asia. Whatever may happen in Europe, Indians will be ready if only we put forward the required effort. Therefore, do not hesitate for one moment by any propaganda the enemy may carry on to-day or tomorrow and be firm in your belief and faith that it has become possible for Indian people to achieve independence.

First of all is it a very big effort that we have to bring an army of 200,000 to 300,000 to India? Look at the millions and millions of people fighting on all fronts in different parts of the world. For the salvation of 38 crores an army of 300,000 or even 400,000 is nothing at all and it is possible for the people of East Asia to contribute enough men for this army. It is possible also for the people in East Asia to contribute money and every material for the equipment of the army. Therefore, let us concentrate all our energy on the one task of organizing an army and bringing it to perfection as soon as possible.

Friends, our tasks to-day is to bring perfection as soon as possible to the army that exist to-day, along with it we have to expand our army because the war is going to be a long and hard one. We want more and more young men to come in and get training. I congratulate you that you have in the heart of Kuala Lumpur one of our camps where Indian young men are trained for the coming fight for freedom. Well, it is not only in

Syonan and Kuala Lumpur that they are being trained to-day. Malai is dotted with camps and many of these camps were formerly camps of the British army. They have been turned over to us for our use. That reminds me that when we go to India we shall also find ready-made barracks for our national army. We won't have to build new barracks. From Calcutta to Bombay and from Rawalpindi to Madras, there are splendid barracks not for the Indian army but for the British Tommy, but these splendid barracks are going to be taken for our Indian National Army and I promise to give the British in return all the prisons for their use.

Friends! to defeat Britain we shall need help from outside. The enemy is asking for help all over the world. The almighty British Empire, over which the sun never sets, that mighty British Empire is going round the world with the begging bowl. It is not merely at Washington that they are asking for help but all over the world, even the poor Indian people, the slaved Indian people, are not spared. Even Indian people have to do their share in men, money, munitions and war materials. They are begging even Indian people to help them in their hour of need. We have to fight today not merely the might of Britain but the combined might of Britain and her allies—a most powerful combination. If we are to fight and win we shall need help and take help when the time comes, but there will be no humiliation in accepting or asking for help when we have first done our duty.

At this juncture, the duty of the people of East Asia is to put forward the maximum effort. Remember you have an opportunity of doing something which your countrymen is other parts of the world cannot do. What can Indians in Europe, Africa, America or even in England do? They are helpless. I know many of them are dying to serve and fight for their country's freedom but it is impossible for them to do so. They are unable to organise an army or join the National Army but all that is within your reach, if you only make it your mission you can join the National Army and work for its success. Therefore, when the call of sacrifice reaches your ears do not flinch. Thank Providence that He has given you of all Indians in the world a unique opportunity to serve your country and fight for your country's independence.

37

Speech of Dr. Lakshmi, Commander Rani of Jhansi Regiment; Requests Women to Join the Movement for India's Liberation[1]

25 September, 1943

"We Indians have only two way open. Either we have to work for the liberation of our country or we have to be British agents. Which do you prefer?." asked Dr. Lakshmi, leader of the Rani of Jhanshi Regiment, in a spirited address to the Indian women of Selangor on Thursday.

The meeting was held on the Lawn in front of the Indian Independence League office, Mrs. Lukshumeyah, Member in charge of the women's section of the local League, was at home to Dr. Lakshmi on the occasion of her visit to Kuala Lumpur from the headquarters of the League in Syonan. Indian women in large numbers provided a picturesque appearance in saris of variegated colours. Conspicous among them was Dr. Lakshmi in smart military dress. Introduced by Mrs. Lukshumeyah to the gathering. Dr. Lakshmi speaking in Tamil said: "Friends! English is the language of our enemy and I am determined not to use it at our public functions. We have to eschew that as far as possible in our life and that is a prerequisite to the achievement of national independence.

"I have a lot of friends here as well as in India. But those who do not subscribe to our national cause, who do not believe in the righteousness of the Independence movement, are not my friends, I have decided to devote my undivided attention to the liberation of our motherland. That is my mission and I am determind to pursue it unmindful of difficulties and

1. *Malai Sinpo*, 25 September 1943, Dr. Lakshmi Swaminathan, was born in Madras on 24 October, 1914. After studying at Queen Mary College, went to England to get her medical degree; went to Singapore in 1940 and after the fall of Singapore joined the Indian Independence League. Bose asked her to organise Rani of Jhansi Regiment, became Minister for Women affairs in the Provisional Government of India. After Independence married Prem Kumar Sahgal, who was convicted in the Red Fort Trials.

obstructions in the way.

"The independence we want for India is not for men alone. It is for the whole country composed of men and women. So if men are doing their share, I ask you what have you to offer? If your mother is sick will you leave it to your brother alone to nurse her to health and normalcy? Will you not shoulder your part of the burden? Well, that is the condition of Mother India today. She is sick and enslaved. She wants the help of everyone of you.

"Let not posterity look down upon you that you let down such an opportunity. Opportunity comes but once whether in the case of a nation or an individual. Let not the daughters of Mother India be found wanting at the crucial hour. "Look back at the history of India. You will find that women have never been behind their men in any branch of life. I am sure you women of Selangor are not going to be behind men, providence has given an opportunity to the Indian women of East Asia. Will you let it slip and repent for it later? Will you allow the curse of posterity to fall upon your heads?

"Think of the great reaction in India when we, women, fight shoulder to shoulder with our men. I am not here to force you and you are not without patriotism to be torrid. There may be many among you who, due to various reasons, are unable to contribute to the movement by active participation in the Rani of Jhansi Regiment. To such of you I say let your hearts be with the movement. And if your heart and spirit are with the movement I know you can contribute a lot in various forms. It is a full fledged faith in the movement that I ask of you.

"Many of you may think it is only men who will have to fight at the front. Do not for a moment think so. Our army is unlike other armies of the world in this respect. If anybody had told me a few years ago of women fighting of war fronts, of women handling rifles and braving bombs. I would have scoffed at the idea and dismissed him for a knave or fool. But what was a dream. What was impossible, has became possible today. We shall fight our adversaries with modern arms right on the battlefield.

"Ever since I joined this movement I have felt a new strength, a strength born of the righteousness of our mission. I know everyone of you will realise it in your own person when you understand the true significance of this movement.

"Here lies an opportunity to live and work for a good cause, and I am sure my sister's of Selangor will rise to the occassion. I have heard some Indians, men and women, say that they are madrasis, Punjabis, and so on. Discard this parochial spirit and say. 'I am an Indian. I come from India. India is my mother country. This spirit should permeate among you.

"Friends! whatever happens India is going to be free at the end of this war. But are you going to bring upon yourself the dishonour that you were inactive and indifferent at a time when India stood at the cross roads? The British empire is doomed and in its doom is the birth of a true and independent India. We Indians have only two ways open. Either we have to work for the liberation of our country or we have to be British agents. I ask which do you prefer?

"The British are our enemies and as such we want to fight them. We shall never allow ourselves to be taken prisoner. We shall handle the rifle and kill a few Britishers before we die. What I want in you is that iron determination not to flinch from the path we have chosen. We must drive the Britishers, our enemies, out of the country. Driving them out of that holy land should be the prime aim of our life.

"Friends! Therefore, it is better that you learn to use the rifle. Women who join the regiment should be prepared for all kinds of work and they will be treated alike in the camp. What we lack is unity, and here is a golden opportunity for you to forget your caste, creed and social standing.

"I appeal to you to have absolute faith in our Netaji. His is a life devoted to the cause of Mother India. He has travelled all over the world, studied political and military conditions in every country and knows the relative strength and weakness of each. There is none either in India or outside better suited than he to lead a movement like this. Implicit obedience to him is what I require of you.

"There may be people among you who say the British will come back within six months. If you come back within six months. If you come across one ask his whether he is better informed than our Netaji. Do not for a moment believe such nonsense.

"Unless we are prepared to sacrifice our utmost, in property and in blood, we are not going to have Swaraj. Those of you who are not in a position to join the regiment can help our movement in other ways. A relief camp is being run in Kuala Lumpur and many of you can spend an hour a day assisting in the work there. You may propagate Hindustani our *lingua franca*. You can collect old clothes to dress wounded soldiers. Many ways are open to you".

38

Speech Delivered at the Chamber of Princes's Secret Session by Lt. Col. K. Himmat Singh, Briefing them about the Japanese Intentions Towards India and tbe Steps taken by the Government to Counter the Propaganda of S.C. Bose, Who was Collaborating with them

15 October, 1943

Your Highnesses,

There is no need for me to say that I consider it is a great honour and privilege to be given this opportunity of addressing your Highnesses today.

I most humbly wish to explain at the outset that I am not lecturing today because of my relationship with His Highness the Chancellor, nor am I here as a propagandist. I am addressing you because I have some knowledge of Japan and the Japanese, and of their aims and policies. I was Assistant Military Attache in the British Embassy, Tokyo, from 1926 – 1928 when I became a qualified Japanese interpreter. Again for nearly two years before the outbreak of the war with the Japan, I was first Secretary in the British Embassy. At the beginning of hostilities. I was interned for nearly eight months with the rest of the Embassy Staff, about ninety in number. During this time we were treated more as convicts than as diplomats, and had to do labour like any coolie. For instance, I had to work as a porter and scrub floors for the first four months. In the latter four months, my duties included gardening, removing rubbish, cutting wood and looking after children; the last was really quite pleasant work which I did not mind in the least. In some ways these occupations served a useful purpose in that they kept us busy and did not allow us much time for worrying.

As a result of my experience, and from my knowledge of Japan and the Japanese, I am convinced that Japan is a menace to our country. Her

1. Foreign and Political Department, F. No. 83-X/1944. N.A.I.

policy of the 'New order in Asia' and of the so-called 'co-prosperity Sphere' is nothing but a desire on her part for the subjection and enslavement of certain Asiatic countries, including India in the West. Australia in the South, Hawaii in the East and the Maritime provinces of Siberia in the North. Believe me when I say that if the Japanese ever came to our country, which God forbid, they will completely destroy our culture and religion, and all our cherished customs and institutions.

The subject of my lecture to Your Highnesses may be described as 'the Japanese' conspiracy against India.

Before going into the details of this conspiracy, it will not be out of place to give you a short history of Japan, which will serve as a background for what I shall have to say later. Japan, as Your Highness know, is a very young country, whose records go back only as far as twelve hundred years. However, the Japanese have recently been faking their history to show that its records can be traced as far back as two thousand six hundred years, so that they may be able to claim to be the oldest empire in the world, which, of course, is nothing but a lie. The only people who believe in this are the Japanese themselves, who have been so taught from their childhood.

In fact, Japan was not known to the outside world earlier than a hundred years ago. It was a backward country then and was ruled by a feudal system of overlords called DAIMYO, the head of which was the SHOGON or Commander-in-Chief, called TOKUGAWA. There was an emperor, but he was merely a puppet, and was kept shut up in his palace in KYOTO. The commander-in-Chief was so jealous of his power that he would not allow anyone from the outside world to enter the country, nor was any of the inhabitants allowed to leave. Even the making of boats was a criminal offence, and the punishment for it was death.

About eighty years ago an American fleet commanded by Admiral Perry, an American officer, was on a cruise in Far Eastern waters, and it put in at Yokohama. The Japanese had never seen a battleship before, and you can well imagine their surprise at seeing these huge vessels. The only name they could devise for these ships to them so queer in appearance was 'Black Ships'. They opposed a landing party with their double-edged swords, but without success. However, they were clever enough to realise the danger to their country if the fleet remained there for a long period. Accordingly they accepted without delay whatever terms were offered them, in order to be rid of the unwelcome visitors as quickly as possible. One result of this visit was that the Japanese soon realised that their segregation and the TOKUGAWA rule had prevented them from making any progress compared with other countries in the world. There was discontent in Japan, which eventually led to a civil war of three years duration. At the end of the civil war the emperor was restored to his rightful place as head of the state, and this first act on assuming power was to remove his capital to the present city of Tokyo.

Soon afterwards, a number of scholars were sent to England and other European countries, to study their constitutions. On their return, these scholars recommended the adoption of the Prussian model as best suited to Japan; accordingly a constitution very much like the Prussian was adopted. There is a Lower House known as the Diet, and an Upper House or House of Peers. It is interesting to note that an Englishman, Sir Francis Piggott, assisted in drafting the Japanese constitution. His son, Major-General Piggott, R. E., served as Military Attache of the British Embassy in Tokyo for about fifteen years.

The first foreign Embassy to be established in Japan was the British, and it was the British Embassy and its staff who acted as advisers to the Japanese nation until the end of the last Great War. The Japanese Navy also has been trained by the British on more or less British lines. It is well known that in the Russo-Japanese War, some Japanese naval vessels had British Naval Officers abroad as advisers. In short, the point I wish to make is that the Japanese have cunningly and cleverly utilised the British to attain their present position; and they realised that their planned object of ruling Asia could only be achieved at the expense of England and America. In order to carry out their plan, they made up their minds twenty years ago to go to war with us, and since then they have been secretly preparing to that end. Meanwhile, England and America who had been trying their best to make a settlement with Japan, were being cleverly deceived by the Japanese into believing that she had no intention of resorting to war for the solution of grievance outstanding between them.

We must give the devil his due, and we must give the Japanese credit for being a shrewd people. They appreciated the world situation as follows:–

In 1935 Japan had calculated that in about 1939 or 1940 the European War was likely to break out. She also appreciated that by about 1942 the Axis would be winning the war, and that therefore it would be to her advantage to join the war against us; and strike us in the back to gain her object. This is where she made her mistake. We also unfortunately made several blunders; for example, when Japan attacked China, in 1937, we believed as a neutral, and both America and ourselves sold to Japan various war materials such as petrol, iron, etc. We thought that Japan would use them for her normal purposes but she cleverly deceived us, using China as a training ground for her troops, and hoarding most of the stores and materials for future use against us. She also increased her navy, army, and air force several fold during those years. Meanwhile we all the time were trying to pacify her, and reach a permanent settlement. Your Highnesses probably remember the negotiations that went on in Washington for a month before the outbreak of war with Japan. They were on the point of breakdown when Japan cunningly bluffed and deceived us by sending a special envoy, Kusru, who said that he had special instructions to make a permanent settlement. While the negotiations were still going on in Washington, they made their treacherous attack on Pearl Harbour, Hong Kong and North Malaya on December 8, 1941. However, this did more good than harm, because it brought America into the war from the beginning—which otherwise might not have happened for some time.

Often on my tours the Indian troops asked me the question, 'Are the Japanese superior, that they had all these successes?' I can assure Your Highnesses that the Japanese are not superior to any British or Indian troops. The reason for their initial successes is that they had been preparing for the last twenty years, whereas we had been making no preparations. That we must admit; and that is the cause of the initial setbacks. I can assure Your Highnesses that things will be different in the near future, and the Japanese realise this better than anyone else.

Now, reverting to the main subject of my talk, namely the Japanese conspiracy against India, I will begin with the early days. Your Highnesses may be aware that Japan's interest in India as a target for attack and eventual annexation is no new development. Even when she was Britain's active ally in 1914-1918 against the Central European Powers, our counter- espionage service discovered Japanese intelligence activities in India. some of them carried on by government officials acting under the cover of diplomatic privilege. But Japan was active not only in her use of agents in India, but in her sedulous cultivation of Indian subversive elements in the Far East; the use to which these elements have since been put leaves no doubt as to Japanese intentions from the start. As early as 1915, Rash Behari Bose, having fled from India after his unsuccessful attack on the life of Lord Hardinge, found asylum in Japan. He was made the protege of Toyama Mitsuru, an arch schemer whose name has figured frequently in the history of Japan's underground plottings. Bose married a Japanese wife, by whom he has had several children, adopted Japanese nationality and to a large extent the Japanese way of life, and has identified himself with the interests of his new country. The Japanese, for their part, have generally accepted him as their fellow countryman and have made use of him both for internal propaganda—for he is reputed to write and speak Japanese excellently—and in their approach to the Indian community in Japan.

Rash Behari's headquarters have for many years been in Tokyo, and his influence in Indian circles there has been very great. He became in fact the doyen of the Indian community of merchants, students and a few masters who had found a niche there. The Japanese assisted the development of his influence by judicious means: for instance, after a time it became difficult if not impossible, for an Indian student to get himself accepted for one of the technical universities without being guaranteed by Bose. While he consolidated his position locally. Bose did not make the mistake of forgetting to maintain his connection with revolutionary and nationalists circles in India, with which he kept up a regular correspondence. Bose has always been a terrorist, and he has made no secret of the fact that he considers non-violence a mawkish and ineffective creed for the winning of Indian independence. He did not therefore identify himself whole-heartedly with the Indian National Congress; at a time when Congress associations abroad could still be affiliated to the parent body, he ran his own nationalist society in Tokyo with the title of the Indian Independence League. This did not, however, prevent him from keeping in touch with a number of important individual political leaders in this country.

In 1923 a Bihari named Anand Mohan Sahay went to Japan as a student. He had previously been private secretary to Babu Rajendra Prasad, whom he has always affected to consider as his Guru. It was not long before he went over to the Japanese possibly ambitious to emulate Bose, and by similiar means he became the political leader of the Indians in Kobe and its neighbourhood. He too increased his influence with Japanese assistance, and Indians of all kinds found him useful as a go-between in dealings with the Japanese authorities. In October 1932, he made himself president of the Indian National Congress committee in Kobe, and when all foreign Congress bodies were disaffiliated by order of the parent body, in March 1936, he kept the association going as a purely local body of nationalist-minded Indians, under the name of the Indian Nationalist Association of Japan.

R.B. Bose and A.M. Sahay, both ambitious and both sold to a nation which, as they must have realised in their secret hearts, intended little good towards India, have always been more or less rivals for power and the favour of the Japanese. The latter, however, succeeded in making good use of both of them, each in his particular sphere of influence and while Bose has apparently always been trusted by the Japanese, and has been the bigger figure for propaganda purposes. A.M. Sahay was used not only in Kobe but to develop subversive activities among Indians in other parts of the Far East. The Germans also had a hand in Sahay's work, but that is not relevant to the subject of this talk.

In Shanghai in Canton and in Bangkok, there existed besides the law-abiding Indian merchant community (most of whom were however trained to some degree with what they called "nationalist" stentiments) a number of Indian renegades and malcontents of the worst type. Some of these were fugitives from British justice, and all were given over to sedition and traitorous activities. In 1940 Sahay was sent to organise these seditious elements in Shanghai as well as to encourage nationalist opinions. The open result of his work was the formation of an 'Indian National Association of China'. Likewise, a lieutenant of Sahay was sent to Bangkok, where a nationalist body called the 'Indian National Council' was formed under the presidency of an ex-Bengal revolutionary who went in Siam by the name of Swami Satyanand Puri. Simultaneously with these activities the Japanese in Canton were engaged in efforts to suborn the Indian troops in Hong Kong, and in 1941 Indian agents were despatched from this area to perform the same task among the Indian troops in North Malaya, but were exposed and caught before they had achieved anything useful. These efforts, however, did bear some fruit, as was shown during the fighting in Malaya, where Indian fifth columnists organised and trained by traitors in Bangkok were sent down to create confusion among the Indian troops in the front line and to go to work without delay in an effort to suborn those who were made prisoner.

The local subversive elements outlined above achieved little in the first months after the Japanese victories in the Far East as a result of the personal ambition and jealousies of the leaders and the total lacks of discipline in their followers' ranks. Realising this, Japan attempted to improve matters by forming an organisation which would place all these subversive elements under one control and would at the same time establish itself as the controlling influence in the lives of all Indians in the Far East—the intention being of course to mobilise all possible resources which could eventually be used against India itself. A preliminary conference of the better known traitors was held in Tokyo at the end of March, 1942, and a fulldress convocation was held at Bangkok in June of that year. Delegates from the Indian communities in most of the countries of the Far East were present and everything possible was done to ensure that the conference should come to the previously approved conclusions which the Japanese desired.

This result, Your Highnesses, was achieved—but not without some opposition on the part of some of the delegates, who, though they might be nationalists were not traitors. In the end, however it was agreed that an organisation known as the 'Indian Independence League' was to be the only recognised association for Indians in the Far East; that it was to assist the Japanese with military forces which were referred to by the high sounding but false title of the 'Indian National Army' in the war against the allies; and that it would not only organise fifth column activities in India, but would accept all enemy assistance necessary to defeat the British and drive them out of the country. It was at this time that the name of Subhash Chandra Bose was first importantly associated with Japanese sponsored acitivities among Indians in the Far East, for he was declared to be the patron of the Indian Independence League. By the end of 1942, but not without considerable difficulty due to jealousy among the erstwhile leaders of local national associations in various parts of the Far East, these bodies were merged into the newly formed League or driven out of existence. It was on this foundation, Your Highnesses, that the Japanese proceeded to build their fifth column offensive against India.

With regard to the civilians in Occupied Territories, the Japanese lost little time in making it clear to them that, whether they desired it or not. Indians were to assist in furthering the Japanese aim of a Greater East Asian Co-prosperity Sphere under Japanese domination. Although there has been little indication that Indian civilian themselves have been subjected to the ruthless treatment meted out to others immediately following the Japanese occupation, the treatment given to the Chinese, who were tortured, raped or butchered in thousands, was carried out openly without any attempt at concealment, thus indication without a shadow of doubt what Indian civilians could expect if they attempted in any way to hinder or oppose the Japanese plans.

This first phase, the creation of fear in the minds of Indian civilians, was soon followed by Japan's virtual recognition of branches of the so-called Indian Independence League inaugurated at Bangkok. This League, whose leading members are disgruntled anti-British and Pro-Japanese

Indians, was given what amounted to the power of life and death in regard to the control of all Indians, in that civilians who did not enrol were deprived of the right to obtain rationed food and to do business. Although on the face of it the League was an authority independent of the Japanese, it was in reality, whether always voluntarily or not we cannot say, taking its orders from the Japanese and dancing to the tune piped by them.

Once this regimentation of Indian civilian had been started, the League was used by the Japanese for the purpose of stirring up hatred against the British, by means of intensive propaganda and false war news. In the propaganda field, much play was made of the Japanese intention to free India for the Indians, while false war news was intended to suggest that the defeat of Britain and her allies was inevitable, that the Japanese were to become the rulers of the Far East for all time, and that for these reasons it was obvious that it would greatly benefit Indians if they co-operated with the Japanese and assisted in the setting-up of a free India within the co-prosperity sphere.

Indian military personnel on the other hand, were obviously intended to be put to more important use by the Japanese, which is the reason perhaps for the treatment accorded to them after capture. There is an abundance of irrefutable evidence to show that in an attempt to break down their morale, and so their loyalty to the Crown, Indian military personnel were subjected to torture, such as the refusal of food and drink, flogging and extremely hard labour for long periods under the most trying weather conditions; while there were numerous instances in which soldiers who refused to allow their loyalty to be shaken were put to a cruel death in front of their brother officers and men. At the same time, as in the case of civilians, disgruntled Indians were later brought in to disseminate propaganda which, *inter alia,* indicated that if the soldiers would serve the cause of Japan they would be accorded good treatment and be comparatively free again.

This propaganda aimed not only at persuading soldiers to join an Indian Traitor Army, which the Japanese proposed to use against the Allied forces in a possible invasion of India or alternatively for the purpose of opposing any Allied attempt to advance into Burma or other Japanese-occupied territory further south; it also aimed at persuading them that unless they did so join they could expect no amelioration of the intolerable conditions in which they lived.

In these circumstances it is not surprising that a considerable number of military personnel did outwardly profess their willingness to serve in the traitor army, after their powers of endurance and resistence to propaganda and their physical discomfort had reached a very low ebb. How much reliance the Japanese will be able to place in any army raised on these lines, however, is another question, there are indication that a very great majority of these suborned troops will revert to their true loyalty immediately a suitable opportunity presents itself.

In order to create a fifth column weapon in India, which could sabotage the Allied war effort, perform espionage, suborn the Indian Army, and create a state of public opinion favourable to their intentions, the Japanese began sending their agents into India early in 1942.

In the first three months of their campaign, the Japanese used only prisoners of war who had been suborned in the ways that I have described. After a full of three months during the monsoon, they relaunced this offensive in September, 1942, this time employing Indian civilians as well as prisoners; most of the agents had been trained for fifth column work at one of the ageneies set up by the Japanese for schooling agents in this type of warfare. The greatest number of agents arrived in October, and then the numbers began to fall until they ceased in January of this year.

After two months of inactivity, March saw the arrival of new agents, and this time prisoner of war who had captured in the recent Arakan campaign were among those apprehended. The peak figure was reached in April; since then agents have been arriving in decreasing numbers. All of them have been given a variety of tasks to perform in India, including sabotage, espionage and propaganda. They have been supplied with money and many have been equipped with weapons that they have been taught to use.

The total number of agents despatched to India since the initiation of this campaign cannot be disclosed for reasons of security. We are confident however that these agents have not paid a dividend. This is partly due to the excellent security measures in operation, partly to the poor type of Indian who volunteers for this type of work, and partly to the increasingly favourable position of the Allies on all fronts. Whatever new steps the Japanese attempt in this direction, we shall meet them confidently.

Realising possibly that they cannot hope to achieve any results in their territorial designs against India unless the Indian Army which has resisted them so fiercely in the past has been corrupted through subversive activities, the Japanese have devoted considerable attention to suborning Indian Army personnel. In the forward areas they have attempted in various ways to cause panic and confusion in front-line troops and by distributing anti-British literature. Against units and regiments centres within India, the Japanese have tried to suborn Indian troops through the medium of prisoners of war who have been told to rejoin their units and there to spread anti-British propaganda. They have also been told to instruct men whom they could suborn to kill their officers and to desert with their arms during operations.

Turning their attention to the general public, Japan's first object was to dispel the feeling of mistrust from the minds of Indians. Their agents have been ordered to attempt to win over the Indian public by impressing upon them Japan's peaceful intentions towards India, and her desire to see an independent India on the lines of Burma. The Japanese have tried to bolster up these impressions with propaganda stories of the invincibility of the Axis powers. The latter line must need revising! Their propagandists and fifth column organisers have also turned their attention to Government servants, to certain committees, and to political parties notably the Congress Party. S. C. Bose at present their chief propaganda weapon. These attempts on the morale of the general public have not been as well received as Japan might have expected, since a feeling of distrust for the Japanese still exists in the minds of many Indians.

Your Highnesses will know that the Japanese have not confined themselves to the use of agents and broadcasts in the attempt to further their aims. They have produced papers and pamphlets printed in various Indian languages, which have been scattered among front-line troops and also dropped by air in India. In the forward areas, they have also coerced the local inhabitants into distributing much of their propagandists literature. Japanese efforts continue, but so far we have fought them successfully and shall go on fighting successfully any attempts to create a fifth column organisation within India which has its object the paving of the way for a Japanese army intent on the aggrandisement of Japan and the humiliation of India.

It would be wrong to lose sight of the part played by the arch-traitor Subhas Chandra Bose in this nefarious campaign against India. The Japanese realising that they were not attaining the desired result, asked the Germans for the loan of this renegade, in the belief that an ex-President of Congress would be a figure capable of restoring new life into a decaying movement. S. C. Bose arrived in Japan from Berlin at about the beginning of June; soon afterwards, he moved to Singapore where be was proclaimed supreme Commander-in-Chief of what is commonly known as the JIF Army, (i.e., Japanese Inspired Fifth Column Army) whose existence was at this time formally announced. The Japanese at last had found a willing tool, notorious enough to feature prominently in their Indian broadcasts.

Subhas Chandra Bose now stands (in the place once so confidently occupied by Rash Behari) as supreme head of the Indian Traitor Organisation established by the Japanese, and is co-operating whole-heartedly with enemy by coercing Indians into furthering Japanese designs on India. Bose's past condemnations of Japan's brutal attack on China have been temporarily and conveniently forgotten by his masters.

Since his assumption of office as C-in-C of the Traitor Army, he has devoted much of his subject matter in his broadcasts to the supposedly increasing strength of his army, and to the opening of training camps. He has also threatened an invasion of this mothercountry by these traitor forces; but the successive dates so unwisely announced by him for this coup have passed harmlessly by, and have brought him only scorn in his listeners' eyes and a reputation as a vain boaster. Even now he must be pondering the unhappy fate when the Japanese find their fifth column weapon to be unwiedly and futile, when their armies are being annihilated, their ships lying on the sea bed and their aircraft obliterated from the skies.

But, Your Highnesses, we are not waiting till that day comes to combat this threat to India. At this moment vigorous counter measures are in hand. One of them is the direction of propaganda against the enemy himself and against the peoples of the territory he has occupied. Responsibility for this propaganda is divided between various departments interested in the Far East, and it is carried out by means of broadcasts and of leaflets dropped from the air.

G. H. Q. is particularly interested in the preparation of broadcasts addressed to Japanese troops and in both broadcasts and leaflets for Indians in occupied territories. Large numbers of these Indians are of course, prisoners of war, and we hope that some of our news gets through to them. Some of you have already been asked, and have graciously agreed, to broadcasts messages of encouragement to these prisoners. In fact, several speeches by Princes have already gone over on the air.

It is an unfortunate fact that most people in India are, or were until recently extremely ignorant about the Far East and about Japan especially. The Japanese had been carrying on propaganda all over Asia for some years, so that people who had no direct knowledge gained a vague impression that the Japs were perhaps quite nice people. Naturally they are trying to keep up this impression in the occupied territories by intensive propaganda and it is the task of a special section in G. H. Q. to expose their real character and intention. Working on this job there are a number of people who have a good knowledge of Japan, and, of course, we are able to make use of a certain amount of the information that reaches us from the occupied territories. I cannot give you many details about the subjects covered in these broadcasts, as it would take too long but our main objects are to refute the lies told by the Japs, to show how their smooth words cover the most barbaric acts, to describe the sufferings they have caused by their aggression, to expose their intentions of ravaging India, and to show that for all their boasting, they cannot hope to win against the Allies.

There are, I am sorry to say, a few Indians who have turned traitor and are attempting to help the enemy. As you can imagine, our propaganda does not neglect these men and we have, I hope, left them in no doubt as to India's opinion of them and the punishment they can expect after the war. We have been able to show that Subhash Chandra Bose's talk about invading India is nothing but a bluff and a propaganda stunt, and that he himself is an ambitious self-seeker.

We have reason to believe that our propaganda is being successful to some extent since the Japanese controlled station go to a good deal of trouble to answer us back and Bose himself has declared that one of his main objects is to combat propaganda from Delhi.

Another of our counter measures which is applied to the Indian Army has been the setting-up of a Central Group, consisting of a number of officers themselves apprised of all the relevant facts, who give the truth regarding the Japanese—not as propaganda but as information—direct to a group of Indian other ranks in each unit. These informed troops then pass on the matter to their fellow soldiers of all ranks. It can be compared with the system existing in some of the territories governed by Your Highnesses, where news is sent through the Station House Officer who passes it on to villages through the daily Chowkidar parade.

Its effect has been to enlighten the Indian sepoy about his enemy in an idiom which he can understand fully. As Your Highnesses will realise, a man is seldom apprehensive about things that he knows and understands. The theme of Central Group is 'KNOW YOUR ENEMY'.

The setting up of these contacts, called 'Josh Groups' in each unit has had a valuable result in establishing a quick and very direct channel of communication which can manifestly be used for constructive purposes, apart from merely combation the J.I.F.C.

Now for a few words about Security. Broadly speaking, you can divide military intelligence into two parts. One: Information, or finding out about the enemy's plans; Two: Security, or preventing the enemy finding out about your plans. This general security of plans can itself be divided into three branches of Security, namely: Security of Information, of Personnel, and of Material.

First, Security of Information. This, as the form implies, deals with preventing the enemy learning about such concrete facts as our operational movements, the relative strength of our forces and so on. 'Security of Personnel,on the other hand, deals with the less tangible factor of troops' or it may be civilians, morale: and its object will be to prevent the enemy getting at our minds through defeatist propaganda, subversive appeal, and so forth. The third branch, Security of Material, is meant to prevent the enemy getting at our physical resources, such as arms and ammunition, shipping and other transport, aircraft and airfields, all of whose destruction would vitally interfere with the success of our operations.

Much has been said in this war of the danger from the Fifth Column, but it is only one aspect of the 'Security problem, namely the existence of enemy agents in one's own country. Officials and other persons in positions of responsibility must, of course, know of the implications of the fifth column, but there is a good deal to be said for the idea that talk in public about the fifth column should be discouraged as it, tends to create a feeling of uneasiness and distrust which is very demaging to public morale. And this very damage to morale is in fact an aid to the enemy. No, Your Highnesses, all this mystery which surrounds the subject of the fifth column and of Security generally, really does more harm than good. Security is just one factor of Intelligence , and Intelligence is just one factor in military strategy or tactics. They both have the same end in view as has the operational side of planning and should thus be based on co-operation and regarded as integral parts of the same general scheme. There should be no room for that attitude summed up in the early days of the war by a security officer who complained that he was asked either, 'Why the hell are you snooping around?' or (when things went wrong) "Why the hell didn't you snoop round?"

Nevertheless though the Fifth Column can be given undue notoriety, the danger of the indirect attack has assumed an importance in this war considerably greater than ever before, and it is to combat this that the Field Security Service was formed and embodied in the Intelligence Corps. Its duties are, broadly speaking, to combat the triple menace of Espionage, Propaganda, and Subotage directed against the armed forces of the Crown; that is to say, to help in preserving the Security of Information, Personnel and Material. It does this mainly by instilling into the armed forces a sense of what we call 'Security-mindedness and touches them to adopt such

Security measures that the enemy agent will get no information, the saboteur be kept at arm's length and the propaganda fall on deaf ears.'

Field Security Sections are attached to formations in the field, located on important lines of communications at bases and in ports. Their duties, for which they are specially trained are primarily to advise and supervise in Security matter; but in operational and protected areas they are largely engaged on Security Controls to prevent any hindrance to military operations and to ensure their secrecy. May personnel are linguists and they often undertake the duty of interpreter, help in the control of prisoners, seize abandoned enemy documents and material, and undertake a multitude of other duties to safeguard the operations in progress.

The sections in ports, in conjunctions with the police and civil authorities assist in the maintenance of Security of port installations and shipping, the secrecy of troop movements and of shipping inforamations. They also help to control the merchant seamen and passengers using the port. Airport sections, composed of R.A.F. personnel, perform similar duties at important airfields where aircraft enter or leave India.

Our own Field Security Service has already done invaluable work in the India Command and in operations on the Eastern Frontier; with the advance of our armies it will extend its activities to S.E. Asia.

Already there is a growing interest in all measures pertaining to Security on the part of the forces and police from many States under your Highnesses control. It is felt that the Army can help Security organisation in the States of considerable extent by sharing the experiences gained throughout the war; and as the outcome of a suggestion made by the delegates attending the first States 'Security Conference at Bombay, the fighting services have undertaken to train as many States' military and police officers as they can find vacancies for , both in basic and specialised Security duties, first at the Intelligence Corps (India) Training Depot at Karachi, and afterwards by attachments to Army or R.A.F. field, seaport or airport Security Sections in accordance with the special needs of the States.

Your Highnesses, in my humble opinion the adoption of proper Security measures in the States is of the utmost importance; this is especially so if one considers the known views and policy of the Japanese regarding rulers and states. It is the aim of the Japanese to destroy the Princely Order entirely and from the root. It is indeed their aim, should they ever come to India, to destroy all the privileged classes and stable elements of the country. Before us is the example of Korea and the Northern Malay States. In Korea, the ruling family has been completely destroyed, with the exception of one prince who lives in virtual custody in Japan. His name is Prince Rio. He was forced to marry a Japanese girl, and is now three-quarters Japanese, and the only member of the Korean ruling family left in existence. Even I was treated like a prisoner before the war and during the war. I was interned, as I have told you earlier in my talk. My only crime was that I was related to an Indian Ruler and was a loyal subject of the King. However I feel that the Japanese paid me a great compliment by treating me as they did, I could describe to you at length the various episodes and example of ill treatment which I had to undergo, but this is not possible owing to limitations of time.

The Japanese aim is to destroy, in the territories they occupy, all culture and religion which is not of Japanese brand. This would happen were they to come to India. Your Highness will excuse me for reverting to the subject, but I must repeat that Security of the States is of very great importance, and it is essential that in matters concerning Security of the States should fully co-operate with, and obtain advice from, the military authorities who are in a position to advise from their past experience. Immediate steps should in my opinion be taken by the States to guard against Sabotage of ports, railways and airfields, subversive elements such as Congress, Forward Bloc and activities of other undesirable bodies, and false rumours spread by enemy agents. The States should also provide for security of information of military value and should counteract enemy radio propaganda and keep a watchful eye on the pro-Japanese elements living in States, who either had contacts with the Japanese before the war or who have been repatriated since. I cannot urge too strongly the necessity of early steps being taken to increase the security mindedness in the States by sending military and police officers for training in specialised security duties.

I apologise to Your Highnesses for taking up so much of your valuable time and I thank you for attending this talk, and beg to be forgiven for any unintentional mistake I may have made.[2]

---

2. Major Himmat Singh was the younger brother of Maharaja Jam Sahib of Nawanagar, was sent to Japan as Assistant Military Attache in the British Embassy. His main task was to report on the activities of the Indian Nationalists in that country and how to prevent their collaboration with the Japanese before the war.

39

British Intelligence assessment of Bose and His Activitites in East Asia after His Arrival from Germany[1]

15 October, 1943

20. Brief accounts have been furnished in previous Surveys of Subhas Bose's Movements and main activities in the Far East since the date of his arrival there from Germany sometime in June this year, but it should be remembered that the contents have all been based on information culled from Axis sources in the form of broadcasts and Domei press message, and that we therefore know neither more nor less than the Axis have been prepared to tell us. On the hypothesis, however, that what they have made known in regard to his actual movements and activities is founded on fact, a short review of the main events up to date and an attempt to appreciate the effects of his presence on the Far Eastern situation and in India may prove of interest, though the conclusions reached about reactions in occupied territory must, of necessity, be treated with reserve.

21. Soon after his arrival in Tokyo, Bose attended the 82nd Extraordinary Imperial Diet Session on the 16th June, following a conference with Premier Tojo and Foreign Minister Shigemitsu. He later interviwed the Press. This intereview gave us the first indications of the general lines on which all his subsequent utterances were to be based, namely that India could no longer expect to gain her freedom by passive resistance but must resort to the use of force; that while Indians should be prepared to accept Japan's active assistance in an outside attack on India, Indians in India must also be ready to begin the fight for freedom from within.

22. No estimate can be made of the true and immediate effect of Bose's appearance on Indians in the Far East, but within a short period the

1. War office F. No. 208/818. Public Record office.

either was loaded with eulogies, resolutions, reviews, interviews and propaganda descriptions of other ceromonies, in an attempt to indicate that this Axis move was a popular success of no mean proportion. In India, on the contrary, there was little evidence that the news was received with more than mild interest.

23. At the beginning of July Bose arrived in Singapore from Tokyo and officially assumed the Presidentship of the so-called Indian Independence League and concurrently the post of Commander-in-Chief of the JIF Army, the inauguration of which had just been officially announced; but he did not at this time do more then hint that he intended to use this army for something better than mere propaganda purposes, when in his speeches he emphasised the militarisation nature of the struggle that would be necessary in order to bring about independence. Once again he stressed the need for action within India and the necessity for all organisations whether within or without India, to transform themselves into a disciplined fighting organisation under one leader. He described the international situation at that time as favourable to this purpose.

24. It was from Singapore also that Bose announced his intention of forming a Provisional Goverment of Free India, which was to prepare Indians for an armed struggle and ultimately make room for a permanent Goverment chosen by the people.

25. Intense propaganda on these lines continued to have no very marked effect in India, though an increase in rumours was noticed, while some personal interest was evinced among nationalists and revolutionaries in regard to future developments and Bose's military pretenions in particular. As regard reactions in Malaya and elsewhere in the Far East, it is difficult to assess the degree of spontaneity in what the Axis claimed to have been an overwhelming response, but in Singapore and Bangkok, in particular, where there are a considerable number of disgruntled anti-British Indians to assist him, it is reasonable to suppose that Bose used his appeal and his knowledge of mob psychology to good effect and that the results were, perhaps within definite limits, fairly gratifying to him.

26. Towards the end of July Bose left on a visit to Bangkok, Rangoon and Saigon, returning to Singapore in August; Axis broadcasts contained no news of this until after he left Rangoon on the return

journey, in Bangkok he visited the Japanese, German and Italian embassies and conversed with the Thai Foreign Minister, and on the 27th July attended a welcome mass rally before leaving for Rangoon. In his address at this rally he made it clear that the JIF Army was to be used for the invasion of India, when he reminded his audience that their slogan was to be 'On to Delhi' and said that he felt there would not be many who would not revolt from the Indian Army when the JIF Army arrived on the frontier.

27. Bose was in Rangoon from the 29th July till the 3rd or 4th August. He attended the Burmese State Foundation Assembly meeting on the 1st August, while a visit to the Civil JIF H. Q., an address to an Indian mass meeting and interview with the Press were the other main items on his programmes. He had little new to say, except that he suggested that the majority of Gandhi's followers would be prepared to extend even their complete physical support to the independence movement once the JIF Army had successfully penetrated India.

28. His attendance in Rangoon at the proclamation of Burma's independence was good propaganda from the 'fight for freedom' angle, particularly among Indians in Burma, who must have been considerably impressed by the standing of their leader in the new Greater East Asia, in view of the fact that Indians are generally despised and hated, and reckoned of no account, by the Burmese. In India, however, such interest as came to notice in this connection at the time was centred more in Japan's apparent generosity towards Burma than in Bose's well-timed arrival and presence at the proclamation ceremony.

29. On his return to Singapore, Bose's first engagement of any importance was a rally of 20,000 Indians, whom he addressed on August the 15th. In referring to his Rangoon visit and the inauguration ceremony he had attended, he drew a bright picture of the JIF Army's victory parade in Delhi after his conquest of India. Informing his listeners in the Army and among the civil population that the JIF Army was now on the move, he declared that it was the task of Indians to start a second front in India. He subsequently told the Press that great preparation were under way in Burma for the accommodation of the JIF army and that Burma was to be the future headquarters of the independence movement. It was at about this time also that the first

mention was made of Bose's offer to supply rice to India. Other propaganda was to the effect that Bose's agents had reported unrest in the British Indian Army an Bengal and Assam; that Indian youths all over India were forming secret military organisations and undergoing training in order to join the JIF Army when it arrived in India, and that sabotage was on thc increase in Indian factories.

30. The only noticeable result of this propaganda was in connection with Bose's rice offer, for very shortly afterwards the Bengal Provincial Hindu Mahasabha passed resolution recommending that Government should consider importing rice from Burma and Siam. Though the resolution did not go so far as to suggest that Bose's offer as such should be accepted, it is clear that it wsa prompted by that offer, the motive being, however, political expediency with the intention of embarrassing the Bengal Government rather than sympathy with Bose. Apart from the action of the Hindu Mahasabha no developments have been reported, though, as was to be expected, rumour-mongers did not let the opportunity slip entirely.

31. At the end of August Bose again left Singapore for a tour of North of the Malaya and further visits to Siam and Burma. It is claimed that the tour was in connection with supervising the work of the Civil JIF organisation and the training of the JIF Army in these areas. In Bangkok he inspected the Siam committee of the Civil JIF organisation and participated in the celebrations of Mahatma Gandhi's 75th birthday, when he addressed a mass meeting. He also broadcast from the Bangkok station. In Burma, where he arrived on the 24th of September, he attended the celebrations of Burma's independence and conversed with the Premier and other leading Burmese officials. Here also he inspected the Burma committee of the Civil JIF organisation, visited training camps and gave addresses to youths undergoing training. In an apporach to Muslims, Bose visited the tomb of Bahadur Shah, the Late Mughal Emperor of India, and laid wreaths on the grave. He was "shocked to see the tomb in ruins" and asked the Burmese authorities to carry out repairs, thus demonstrating, beyond all doubt, what was called "his profound love and respect for Muslims." In a Press interview he said that the JIF army was well equipped with modern weapons and was ready to march on Delhi. Other details concerning Bose's visit to Rangoon were furnished in the last issue of this summary.

32. There are no indications as yet to the effect of Bose's recent tour, but after his return to Singapore at the beginning of October he declared himself satisfied with the progress so far made towards the goal of "total mobilisation"; the morale of both civil and military JIFs and the I.N.A. was everywhere very high, while in the case of the latter men and women were coming foward in large numbers to volunteer. At the same time a less boastful and somewhat plaintive note was to be detected in his warning that the final struggle for liberty would be hard and long and that it would take at least twelve months, or perhaps more, to liberate the whole of India. Likewise in earlier utterances during his tour in Malaya, he pointed out that manpower and materials must be contributed by Indians themselves before they turned to others for help. All this tends to suggest that Bose's claims that the JIF Army was ready to march on India have been a little premature, while there is also a hint that the Japanese have not implemented their much publicised promises of unlimited help in his plans.

33. Detailed conclusions regarding Bose's plans and the ultimate effect of his activities on behalf of the J.I.F.C. organisation as a whole must await further evidence. All that can be said at the moment is that no slackening of efforts to develop and organise the fifth column and militant potentialities of the so-called Indian Independence League and the JIF Army can be assumed while Subhas Bose remains at the helm of affairs, while it is also easy to believe that any useful role played by the JIFC in Japanese plans will be very largely due to his inspiration and leadership.

40

Address by A. Yellappa Welcoming Bose on His Second Visit to Singapore; Requests Indians to Follow Bose for Achieving Indian Independence[1]

21 October, 1943

Friends,

This is the second occasion since the arrival of Netaji Subhas Chandra Bose that the Indians in East Asia have come to attend a conference of this kind.

We met on the 4th of July this year, when Sjt. Rash Behari Bose, the pioneer of the Indian Independence Movement in East Asia, brought for us Sjt. Subhas Chandra Bose as a gift from Tokyo.

On behalf of the Syonan Indians, I welcome you all to this conference.

Many great changes have come into being in the International world since the arrival of Netaji Subhas Chandra Bose. Burma has been declared independent. Announcement of the Philippine independence has been made; and I can assure you, ladies and gentlemen, that under the leadership of Netaji, our Hindustan will be also free in the near future. Now I am asking the two million Indians in East Asia whether they wish to be free or not. If your reply is in the affirmative, then follow Netaji and obey his orders. This is not the time for political discussion. Leave all the questions for Netaji and learn to obey orders. Then and only then can Indian be free.

Delegates, Friends, Ladies and Gentlemen, I have great pleasure in once again welcoming you to this conference.

1. I.I.L. Papers, F. No. 45/3, N.A.I.

41

Proclamation of the Provisional Government of Azad Hind by S.C. Bose[1]

21 October, 1943

After their first defeat at the hands of the British in1757 in Bengal, the Indian people fought an uniterrupted series of hard and bitter battles over a stretch of one hundred years. The history of this period teems with examples of unparalleled heroism and self-sacrifice. And, in the pages of that history, the names of Sirajuddaula and Mohanlal of Bengal, Haider Ali, Tippu Sultan and Velu Tampi of South India, Appa Sahib Bhonsle and Peshwa Baji Rao of Maharashtra, the Begums of Oudh, Sardar Shyam Singh Atariwala of Punjab and last, but not least, Rani Laxmi Bai of Jhansi, Tantia Topi, Maharaja Kunwar Singh of Dumraon and Nana Sahib — among others — the names of all these warriors are for ever engraved in letters of gold. Unfortunately for us, our forefathers did not at first realise that the British constituted a grave threat to the whole of India, and they did not therefore put up a united front against the enemy. Ultimately, when the Indian people were roused to the reality of the situation, they made a concerted move — and under the flag of Bahadur Shah, in 1857, they fought their last war as free men. In spite of a series of brilliant victories in the early stages of this war, ill-luck and faulty leadership gradually brought about their final collapse and subjugation. Nevertheless, such heroes as the Rani of Jhansi, Tantia Topi, Kunwar Singh and Nana Sahib live like eternal stars in the nation's memory to inspire us to greater deeds of sacrifice and valour.

Forcibly disarmed by the British after 1857 and subjected to terror and brutality, the Indian people lay prostrate for a while — but with the birth of the Indian National Congress in 1885, there came a new awakening.

1. I.N.A. Trial Papers. The above proclamation was read in Hindustani by A.M. Sahey, in Tamil by Mr. Cidambaran, and in English by Netaji himself.

From 1885 until the end of the last World War, the Indian people, in their endeavour to recover their lost liberty, tried all possible methods—namely agitation and propaganda, boycott of British goods, terrorism and sabotage and finally armed revolution. But all these efforts failed for a time. Ultimately in 1920, when the Indian people, haunted by a sense of failure, were groping for a new method, Mahatma Gandhi came forward with the new weapon of non-co-operation and civil disobedience.

For two decades thereafter, the Indian people went through a phase of intense patriotic activity. The message of freedom was carried to every Indian home. Through personal example, people were faught to suffer, to sacrifice and to die in the cause of freedom. From the centre to the remotest villages, the people were knit together into one political organisation. Thus, the Ind·an people not only recovered their political consciousness but became a political entity once again. They could now speak with one voice and strive with one will for one common goal. From 1937 to 1939, through the work of the Congress Ministries in eight provinces, they gave proof of their readiness and their capacity to administer their own affairs.

Thus, on the eve of the present World War, the stage was set for the final struggle for India's liberation. During the course of this war, Germany, with the help of her allies has dealt shattering blows to our enemy in Europe while Nippon, with the help of her allies, has inflicted a knockout blow to our enemy in East Asia. Favoured by a most happy combination of circumstances, the Indian people today have a wonderful opportunity for achieving their national emancipation.

For the first time in recent history, Indians abroad have also been politically roused and united in one organisation. They are not only thinking and feeling in tune with their countryment at home, but are also marching in step with them, along the path to freedom. In East Asia, in particular, over two million Indians are now organised as one solid phalanx, inspired by the slogan of 'Total Mobilisation'. And in front of them stand the serried ranks of India's Army of Liberation, with the slogan 'Onward to Delhi', on their lips.

Having goaded Indians to desperation by its hypocrisy and having driven them to starvation and death by plunder and loot, British rule in India has forfeited the goodwill of the Indian people altogether and is now living a precarious existence. It needs but a flame to destroy the last vestige of that unhappy rule. To light that flame is the task of India's Army of Liberation. Assured of the enthusiastic support of the civil population at home and also of a large section of Britain's Indian Army, and backed by gallant and invincible allies abroad but relying in the first instance on its own strength, India's Army of Liberation is confident of fulfilling its historic role.

Now that the dawn of freedom is at hand, it is the duty of the Indian people to set up to a Provisional Government of their own, and launch the last struggle under the banner of that Government. But with all the Indian leaders in prison and the people at home totally disarmed it is not possible to set up a Provisional Government within India or to launch an armed struggle under the aegis of that government. It is, therefore, the duty of the Indian Independence League in East Asia, supported by all patriotic Indians at home and abroad, to undertake this task of setting up a Provisional Government of Azad Hind (Free India) and of conducting the last fight for freedom, with the help of the Army of Liberation, (that is, the Azad Hind Fauj or the Indian National Army) organised by the League.

Having been constituted as the Provisional Government of Azad Hind by the Indian Independence League in East Asia, we enter upon our duties with a full sense of the responsibility that has devolved on us. We pray that Providence may bless our work and our struggle for the emancipation of our Motherland. And we hereby pledge our lives and the lives of our comrades in arms to the cause of her freedom, of her welfare, and her exaltation among the nations of the world.

It will be the task of the Provisional Government to launch and to conduct the struggle that will bring about the expulsion of the British and their allies from the soil of India. It will then be the task of the Provisional Government to bring about the establishment of a permanent National Government of Azad Hind constituted in accordance with the will of the Indian people and enjoying their confidence. After the British and their allies are overthrown and until a permanent National Government of Azad Hind is set up on Indian soil, the Provisional Government will administer the affairs of the country in trust for the people.

The Provisional Government is entitled to, and hereby claims, the allegiance of every Indian. It guarantees religious liberty, as well as equal rights and equal opportunities to all its citizens. It declares its firm resolve to pursue the happiness and prosperity of the whole nation and of all its parts, cherishing all the children of the nation equally and transcending all the differences cunningly fostered by an alien government in the past.

In the name of God, in the name of by gone generations who have welded the Indian people into one nation, and in the name of the dead heroes who have bequeathed to us a tradition of heroism and self-sacrifice we call upon the Indian people to rally round our banner and strike for

India's freedom. We call upon them to launch the final struggle against the British and all their allies in India and to prosecute that struggle with valour and perseverance and full faith in final victory until the enmy is expelled from Indian soil and the Indian people are once again a Free Nation.

Signed on behalf of the Provisional Government of Azad Hind

Subhas Chandra Bose (Head of the State, Prime Minster and Minister for War and Foreign Affairs)

Captain Mrs. Lakshmi (Women's Organisation)

S.A.Ayer (Publicity and Propaganda)

Lt. Col. A.C. Chatterji (Finance)

Lt. Col. Aziz Ahmed, Lt. Col. N.S. Bhagat, Lt. Col. J.K. Bhonsle, Lt. Col. Gulzara Singh, Lt. Col. M.Z. Kiani, Lt. Col. A. D. Loganathan, Lt. Col. Ehsan Nadir, Lt. Col. Shah Nawaz, (Representatives of the Armed Forces) A. M. Sahay, Secretary (with Ministerial rank) Rash Behari Bose (Supreme adviser), Karim Ghani, Debnath Dass, D.M. Khan, A. Yellappa, D. Thivy, Sarder Ishar Sing (Advisers), A. N. Sarkar (Legal Adviser).

42

Message of the President of the Board of Information Welcoming the Formation of the Provisional Government of India and Assuring that Japan has no territorial designs on India[1]

22 October, 1943

"Valiantly shouldering the hope and trust of the peoples of East Asia, the Provisional Government of Free India, headed by Subhash Chandra Bose, has come into being on October 21."

"The independence of India has for a long period of time been the aspiration of the entire Indian people and the hope of the entire world, in East Asia, Burma, who has long been in the throes of agony under the aggression and exploitation of Britain, has become independent. The Philippines, who has been prevented from manifesting her true natural traits by the oppression of the economic imperialism of the United States, has also attained independence as a genuine East Asian country. And now we witness the establishment of the provisional Government of Free India adding a new glory in India.

"Since the beginning of the 17th century, when she extended her tentacles of aggression toward India, Britain has consistently oppressed and exploited the Indian people, and the British people have lived in luxury and comfort at the sacrifice of the Indian people. However, the people of India gradually generated a strong sentiment for resistance against British rule and in particular following the Russo-Japanese War the Indian desire for Independence became increasingly intense.

"In the last World War, the British Government utilized to the maximum extent the manpower as well as material sources of India, baiting the Indian people with the promise of self-rule after the war. However, they not only broke the promise, but, more than that, they intensified their

1. *Nippon Times*, 23 October 1943.

oppressive rule, as witness the horrible massacre of several thousand innocent Indian people at Amritsar."

"In the present great war also, the British pressure on India has been further strengthened and the Indian people have been involuntarily conscriped for military service and sent to the most dangerous front lines. According to the figures announced by the British Government in June of this year, the casualties of the British Empire forces reached 500,000 of which the Indian losses were as much as 100,000 the casualties of the British empire forced to bear an immense share of the military expenditures as well as an enormous amount of munitions of war, with the result that the whole of India is now suffering from vicious inflation and lack of commodities. Moreover, due to British mal-administration, the condition of starvation has been created in the provinces of Bengal and others with numerous people dying day after day. Reports of these miserable conditions have been spread in Britain and the United States and have become the subject of serious discussion in the newspapers of those countries even in the British parliament.

"Despite these conditions that British pressure on India instead of being relaxed, has been further intensified, especially since August of last year. In the so-called Atlantic Charter, which Britain and the United States claim to be their war aim, there is a principle of the self-determination of peoples, but its application is excepted in the case India, further exposing deceptive policy of these two countries.

"In view of these circumstances, it has come to a point where the freedom of India can never be granted merely by entreaties toward Britain and where British influence must be cast out of India with force of arms. The righteous indignation of fair minded people throughout the world has been aroused against the despotism and oppression of Britain.

"Mr. Bose has for a long time been fighting for the independence of India. When he was arrested by British authorities in India in July 1941, the Indian people protested in sympathy against Britain by engaging in hartal. Subsequently he fled from India and spent his time in Germany laying his plans for independence of India. In June of this year, he made a sudden appearance in Japan after which he went South where he has since strengthened the Indian Independence League, organized the Indian National Army and proceeded vigorously to make various preparations for independence.

"The time having ripened, the Provisional Government of Free India has been established. This government has in its hands the glorious destiny of developing in the future into a government of truly emancipated India.

"The Indian National Army under the command of this government is made up of vigorous young men who are burning with enthusiasm for Indian independence and are ready to make the supreme sacrifice for their country. When this army begins its march of liberation into India, it will be the time for the emancipation of entire India from the British Shackles wih which it has been bound for centuries.

"In pursuance of the great ideal of enabling all nations each to have its proper place and all peoples to live in peace and security, the principle underlying the founding of our empire, the Japanese Government have repeatedly in the past expressed their sympathy and their intention of extending all possible support to the independence of India. Firmly believing that the establishment of the Provisional Government of Free India is an event of profound significance to the complete realization of Indian independence, the Japanese Government have recognized that government today and have reaffirmed their policy to give every support to its efforts for the attainment of its object.

"In order to resist these developments perchance the British will adopt further oppressive measures or a policy of cajolery toward the Indian people. Whichever attitude they may take, it is clear beyond any doubt that what she will give to India is nothing but repression and suffering. We have risen to eliminate these expressions and sufferings. The Indians also have arisen. Japan and India will fight together and together will surely win through. As stated by the spokesman of the Provisional Government of Free India, Japan has no territorial or economic ambition whatever toward independent India. Her sole desire lies in the promotion of the well-being of the entire Indian people. It is our firm conviction that the day when this desire is realised will surely arrive in the near future."

43

Speech by Bose at the Opening of the Training Centres for the Rani of Jhansi Regiment[1]

22 October, 1943

Sisters and Brothers

The opening of Rani of Jhansi Regiment Training Camp is an important and significant function: it is a very important landmark in the progress of our Movement in East Asia.

To realise its importance, you should bear in mind that ours is not a merely political movement. We are on the other hand engaged in the great task of regenerating our Nation. We are in fact ushering a New Life for the Indian Nation, and it is necessary that our New Life should be built on sound foundations. Remember that ours is not a propaganda stunt; we are in fact witnessing the re-birth of India. And it is only in the fitness of things that there should be a stir of New Life among our womenfolk.

Our past has been a great and glorious one, India could not have produced a heroine like the Rani of Jhansi if she did not have a glorious tradition. The history of great women in India is as ancient as the Vedic period. The greatness of Indian womenhood had its roots in those early days when India had its Sanskrit culture.

The same India which produced great women in the past also produced the Rani of Jhansi at a grave hour in India's history. And today while we are facing the gravest hour in our History, I have confidence that Indian womanhood will not fail to rise to the occasion. If for the war of independence of Jhansi, India had to produce and it did produce a Lakshmi Bai today for the war of independence of the whole of India to liberate 38 crores of Indians India has to produce and shall produce thousands of Rani's of Jhansi.

In the same way as we have figures like Maitreyi in India's ancient days, we have the inspiring examples of Ahalyabai of Maharashtra, Rani

1. *Nippon Times*, 24 October 1943.

Bhawani of Bengal, Razya Begum and Noor Jehan, who were shining administrators in recent historic times prior to British rule in India, I have every confidence in the fertility of the Indian soil. I am confident that India as in the past will also produce the best flowers of Indian womanhood.

When in 1921 a new political life started in India thousands, nay lakhs of our sisters also joined the movement and came forward to make sacrifices. In those days it was great thing to go to prisons. Our Indian brothers and sisters got ready to undergo the ordeal of prison life and I remember still how in December 1921 at Calcutta the two jails were full. The Britishers built two more jails and these two were also packed in a few days.

When the Britishers found that the Indians were not restrained by fear of prison life, they changed their tactics. They resorted to the method of throwing leaders into prison and using lathis and bullets against the masses. Joining the Civil Disobedience Movement then meant willingness to face lathi charges and gun-fire and the Indians not only men but also women got ready to face lathi charges and gun-fire. I cannot forget an incident in Calcutta when we held a procession against the orders of the Government and when the police tried to break the procession by lathi charge, some of our sisters made a cordon around us (coming between us and the police) without flinching to free lathi charges. Thus I have witnessed while in India how the spirit and determination of our sisters have been growing stage by stage.

Not only in the history of the Passive Resistance Movement but in th history of the Revolutionary Party also we have the examples of our brave sisters who have played a noble part. I know of many sisters who became daring revolutionaries. If one type of courage was necessary for passive resistance another and more active courage is necessary for revolutionary efforts and in this too I found that our sisters were not wanting. In 1931 an English magistrate was shot by two girls; the age of one was 16 and the age of the other was 17. In India even ordinary men will shudder before magistrates, but these two young sisters bravely went to the house of the magistrate and fired at him. You can easily imagine what wonderful courage those young sisters might have had Such courage does not descend from the skies; it comes from the soil of India; it has its roots in the age-old traditions of India's past.

Since 1928, I have been taking interest in women's organisations in India and I found that given the opportunity our sisters could rise to any occasion. There was one Rashtra Mahila Sangh of ladies in Bengal which did splendid work. In December 1928 a volunteer corps of 500 women was formed which was not only run on sound lines but their parades and their discipline gave us great hopes and confirmed my belief in the fact that given the impetus and opportunity Indian women could perform duties entrusted to them in a befitting manner. I have also seen women organisations in India giving training in arms available in a slave country like lathis and daggers and the way our sisters were progressing was remarkable.

And so when I began to undertake the task of guiding the Indian Independence Movement I felt that our sisters should also be given the opportunity to serve India at this grave emergency. I consulted many and I was told by some that though to raise a women's regiment might be possible in India it would be an impossible task in East Asia. What they said did not affect my conviction and my determination. And today you have before your own eyes what our sisters have accomplished. Their work has started in July and only now the training Camp for them is being opened. The delay is not due to any shortcoming on their part. The delay was due to our difficulties in finding the accommodation and making the necessary arrangements. Meanwhile, I know that our sisters were getting impatient and anxious. I heard that they were intending to lead a deputation to me to ask me whether I have forgotten them. I feel happy today that the camp is ready and the camp is being opened today on the anniversary of the birthday of the Rani of Jhansi.

I may at this jucture say a few words about the Rani of Jhansi. When the Rani of Jhansi started her fight her age was only Twenty. You can easily imagine what it would have been for a girl of twenty riding a horse and wielding her sword in open battle. You can easily realise what courage and spirit she must have had. The English Commander who fought against her said that she was the best and bravest of the rebels. He made this admission because Jhansi Rani's bravery was something which he could not hide, for he himself had to fight against her. First she fought from the Jhansi Fort and when the Fort was besieged she escaped with a party to Kalpi from where she put up a fight. When she had to retreat from this battlefront she made an alliance with Tantia Topi, attached and captured Gwalior fort and using that Fort as the base continued the battle and in this last and great battle she died fighting.

Imagine what amount of courage would have been necessary to carry on the fight in spite of more than one defeat. Yet this 20 year old Rani had the courage and showed a valour which shall be a source of inspiration to Indians for generations to come.

Unfortunately Jhansi Rani was defeated; it was not her defeat. It was the defeat of India. She died but her spirit can never die, India can once again produce Jhansi Ranees and march on to Victory.

156 of our sisters are going to start their training in the Camp which is being opened today. But I hope that their number at Syonan will reach 1,000 very soon. Training Camps for women have also been started in Thailand and Burma but at Syonan we have the Central Camp and I feel that in this Central Camp we should at least have one thousand potential Ranees of Jhansi.

You have just now heard the brave words of the Commandant of the Rani of Jhansi Unit at Syonan. She expressed their determination to work ceaselessly day and night to get prepared for the onward March to Delhi. I feel joyous at hearing that slogan "On to Delhi" from our sisters as I have been hearing it from our brothers.

With these words I declare the Training Camp open. And I would appeal to all the delegates present to carry my message to their localities and to make every effort to realise the programme I have now laid before you."

44

Japanese Press Reaction to the Formation of he Provisional Government of India by Bose[1]

22 October, 1943

The Provisional Government of Free India

The formation of Provisional Government of Free India under the leadership of Subhas Chandra Bose and its declaration of war upon Britain and the United States yesterday constitute an important advance toward the goal of an independent India. To be sure, the Provisional Government is still a government without territory, but that fact does not in the least detract from its legitimacy. For it is obvious that the country of India itself is not its own but a hostage in the hands of an alien conqueror, and the Indian living within India are not free agents with the power to exercise their own will but are slaves forced to submit to the dictates of their British masters. The only free Indians are those to be found outside the territory of India and the only untrammeled expression of Indian will is to be found among these Indian refugees abroad. It is hence but a logical move, in fact an imperative move, that a real Government of India be composed of these overseas Indians who alone are in a position to represent the genuine will of their country.

That these Indians abroad have long been carrying on an active independence movement is an incontrovertible indication of what all India feels, and the fact that recently under the practical, leadership of Subhash Chandra Bose this independence movement has produced a formidable Indian National Army proves the resolute force with which the Indians are determined to carry out their will. Now the formation of a Provisional Government to back up this Army and to give its political direction demonstrates that one more tangible step has been taken in the evolution of the movement for India's

1. An Editorial from *Nippon Times*, 22 Oct. 1943.

liberation. The movement for independence has had a long history, but never before has there been a real Army and a real Government to give it practical and substantial power. The emergence of the Provisional Government is therefore one more indication, and a most momentous one, that the goal of an independent India is at last perceptibly at hand.

The declaration of war by this Provisional Government upon Britain and the United States of course means that there can never more be any talk of compromise or bargaining with the British or their American ally. That is as it should be, for past experience has shown how futile is any attempt to reason with such a predatory beast as the British Empire which can live only by feeding upon the living bodies of its victims. The infamous record of broken promises, the solemn pledge of self-rule given when Britain need India's help in the last World War only to be shamelessly retracted when the need was over, merciless beating down of even such passive and pacifistic mass movements as those inspired by Gandhi, the spurious proposals of Sir Stafford Cripps for an illusory and conditional "dominion" status to be granted at some indeterminate future time under extensive reservation and restrictions, the reactionary obstinacy of Amery and the militaristic high-handedness of Wavell, the callous indifference and criminal incompetence of the British administration toward the present frightful famine the very while the starving Indians are being pushed to the front lines of Britains war, the fact that even the most patient advocates of sweet reasoning have been rewarded by being clapped into prison—these are proofs enough of how futile it is to attempt to deal with the British with anything other than their own weapons of force. In fact, all movements for political arrangements through negotiation or peaceful methods have not only proved futile; they have proved positively harmful to India's cause, for they have only served to delay the necessary resort to the only effective method of force.

If India is to become free, as indeed justice and moral necessity demands, it must be through the efforts of the Indian people to fight and to build. No time is more opportune than now when Britain is reeling under the mortal blows of war and when strong friends like Japan are at hand to give aid to the Indian National Army; the instrument for the building of a regenerated India has now been created by the formation of the Provisional Government.

45

Recognition of the Provisional government of Azad Hind by Japan and other Foreign Power[1]

23 October, 1943

The Board of Information, Tokyo, on October 23, announced the Nippon Government's recognition of the Provisional Government of Azad Hind. The announcement was as follows :

"The Provisional Government of Free India, having been established with Mr. Subhas Chandra Bose as the Head, the Nippon Government in its firm belief that it is a great forward step toward the realization of an independent India for which the Indian people have long aspired, has recognized it as the Provisional Government of Free India and hereby declares its intention to extend every possible co-operation and support in the Provisional Government's efforts to attain its object."

The following telegram was received by Netaji Subhas Chandra Bose, from His Excellency Premier General Hideki Tojo—

"Your Excellency—I have the honour of sending you my hearty congratulations on the establishment of the Provisional Government of Azad Hind which has been Your Excellency's long cherished desire and thereby dashing forward to expel the British influence to attain the everlasting prosperity of India. The Nippon Government is firmly determined to render every possible co-operation to your Government.

"I take this opportunity to offer my best wishes for the successful and prosperous future of your Government and pray for your good health."

At the 83rd session of the Imperial Diet which met on Oct. 26, in Tokyo, Premier Gen. Hideki Tojo made the following reference to India in his speech:

"Turning to India, we find her 400,000,000 people still under Britain's ruthless heel and, with the ambition of United States recently added to

1. D.B. Das, *op.cit*, pp. 184-187.

that pressure, they are continuing to experience indescribable miseries. The cruel rule of Britain and the oiutrageous conduct of the Angol-American forces have further intesified the friction and antagonism between them and the Indian people, thus creating a profound social confusion accompanying an unprecedentedly great famine. The grave situation which is becoming aggravated day by day and month by month, is admitted even by Britain and the United States themselves.

"With many Indian patriots thrown into prison by the British and millions of innocent people thrown into agonies of starvation, the conditions is India at present are indeed tragic and the object of common grievance of all humanity. Such a situation we can by no means leave to take its own course. At this very juncture, Indians who hold their motherland close to their hearts have risen in unity under the leadership of the great patriot Mr. Subhas Chandra Bose and on the twenty-first of this month, the Provisional Government of Free India was established. Thereupon, Nippon proceeded to recognize that government on the 23rd.

"It is truly a great pleasure for us to declare to the world through this chamber that Nippon is determined to support that government consistently in the future and to put forth her utmost efforts for the independence and emancipation of India.

"The complete independence and freedom of India and the lasting prosperity of the 400,000,000 Indian people are what Nippon sincerely desires. I have not the slightest doubt that in the purpose Nippon may count not only upon the wholehearted co-operation of all Greater East Asia peoples but also meet the earnest desire of all high-minded peoples throughout the world.

"It is my strong conviction that this rising tide of the movement for India's emancipation with the active co-operation of the people of Greater East Asia will inevitably bring, in the not distant future, the glorious day of independence and prosperity to India."

In a statement on the speech by Premier General Hideki Tojo Netaji Bose declared:

"The first speech of His Excellency represents a fitting climax to a series of soul-inspiring pronouncements on the Indian question since the fall of Singapore last year. The Indian people owe a special debt of gratitude to him for the personal interest in and sympathy for Indian Independence that he has consistently cherished and demonstrated.

"I am confident that Indian people will give practical proof of the gratitude on the filed of battle."

Germany

The Reich Foreign Minister, Herr Von Ribbentrop, officially notified Netaji Subhas Chandra Bose, by telegram, that the Reich Government was extending its recognition to the newly formed Provisional Government of Azad Hind.

Burma

On 25th October information was received in Syonan that the Independent State of Burma recognised the Provisional Government of Azad Hind.

Philippines

The Philippine Republic's recognition of the Provisional Government of Azad Hind Ws conveyed to Netaji Subhas Chandra Bose, Head of the Provisional Government of Free India, by Jose P. Laurel, President of the Republic of the Philippines, in the following message :—

"The Philippine Government and people have learned with profound gratification the establishment of the Provisional Government of Free India under your leadership in the firm belief that the freedom of India is essential to a new world order based on justice. The Philippine Government is pleased to recognise your Government and sincerely hopes to see established a new free and independent India as befitting the race that has made one of the greatest contribution to human civilization."

Croatia

On October 27, the Government of Croatia extended its formal recognition to the Provisional Government of Free India.

China

It was officially announced at Nanking on Nov. 1 that the National Government of China extended recognition to the Provisional Government of Free India.

The following is the text of the telegram from the Foreign Minister of the National Government of China to Netaji Subhas Chandra Bose, recognising the Provisional Government of Azad Hind:

"Your Excellency, learning through the Nippon Embassy in Nanking that a Provisional Government has been established on October 21 under Your Excellency's leadership, I have the honour, on behalf of the National Government, to extend formal recognition and sincere congratulations on the determination of your government to participate in the war and the reconstruction of Greater East Asia, and to place the Indian people in a position of realising their long-cherished aspirations and of contributing to final victory. With assurance of my highest consideration, Tsu Min Yee, Minister of Foreign Affairs of the National Government of China."

Manchoukuo

It was officially announced on the same day in Hsinking that Manchoukuo formally recognized the Provisional Government of Free India.

Italy

The Provisional Government of Free India was formally recognized by the Fascist Republic of Italy on Nov. 9.

Thailand

The Government of Thailand officially recognised the Provisional Government of Azad Hind, it was announced over the Bangkok radio on the night of Nov. 18.

Thus the Provisional Government of Free India was recognised by Nippon, Germany, Burma, the Philippines, Croatia, the National Government of China, Manchoukuo, the fascist Republic of Italy and Thailand.

46

Addressing a Mammoth Rally Attended by More Than 50,000 Indians, Bose Exhorted the Indian to Rise as One Man to Oust the British from India; Informs Them About the Significance of the Formation of the Provisional Government of Azad Hind

24 October, 1943

When I addressed you last on October 17th, on the occasion of our meeting to congratulate the Philippines on its achievement of Independence, I told you that Burma and the Philippines had become independent and that the next would be India's turn. To-day I fell joy in informing you that the turn of India has now come and the Provisional Government of Azad Hind has been established by us and recognised by the world.

When we look back at the succession of events which had slowly but steadily led to this important landmark in the history of our independence Movement, we could clearly see that everything has been happening under the guidance and help of Providence. The will of God has been with us and if to-day the Provisional Government of Azad Hind has been established, it is a Government which has been declared to the world in the fulness of time and fitness of things.

With the beginning of the present War in Europe, our life-long enemies, the Britishers received their first blows in the West and became weakened thereby. If they had continued to receive blows in the West only, the cause of Indian Independence could not have benefitted thereby. But when the Greater East Asia War started in the East, our enemies received greater blows and became more weakened by one defeat after another. More important and significant than the losses in the East was the fact that a new door—a door undreamt of by them—was opened in the East for the emancipation of India.

The British strategists had always expected a menace to India from the North Western Frontier; little did they envisage the possibility of an

Army of Liberation marching into India from the Northern Frontier. They never dreamt of this possibility: nor were they prepared to defend an attack from this direction.

There is another interesting aspect of this question. Even supposing that the Britishers, suffering defeat after defeat in the West, had retreated up to the North Western Frontiers of India, even that would not have helped the cause of Indian Independence. Because there is Western Asia, we do not have any colony of Indians. On the other hand, Destiny had kept three millions of Indians in East Asia. And when the enemy was driven out of East Asia and the help of Asiatics was forthcoming, the material was there in these three millions of Indians for a real bid for independence.

With the Britishers driven to North East Frontiers of India—to the Indo-Burma borders—a golden opportunity thus arose for liberating India, and if the Indians in East Asia had not risen to the occasion, even that opportunity would have been lost. But the Indians in East Asia, I am glad to say, did not fail India at this great hour; they heard the call of the times and organised themselves into the Indian Independence League and started the formation of the Indian National Army. A retrospective survey of the events of the past few years clearly shows that Destiny had prepared the stage in an undreamt of way for the final war of Indian Independence. Things have happened steadily in the fulness of time and the fitness of things and who can deny when I say that the grace of God, India's Hour has come, that India's turn to be free has come.

When I came to East Asia and took up the lead of the movement, my first objective was to re-organise and strengthen the Indian Independence League, and to reform and stabilise the Indian National Army.

In my address to you on the 15th August, I told you that I am determined to set my foot on the holy soil of India before the end of this year. I always mean what I say. Mine was not an empty declaration or a mere boast. Since then, our preparation have been continuing slowly but steadily. You will remember the Military Review which took place here on this madian on July 9, and this morning you would have noticed that the Indian National Army which took part in the Review was far smaller than that of July last. I revealed in my address at the Military Review that morning that a considerable part of the Indian National Army had left Syonan already and that they were on the road to India. All our preparation have been proceeding in a satisfactory manner and recently it became necessary to take another and more important step, a decisive stop in our march towards Independence.

The question would naturally arise as to what would be the leadership under which the Indian National Army would fight. And it was right time for us to clear our position. The world in general and Indians in particular had to be told under whose leadership the Indian National army was going to fight and who would take over the territorial rights in Indian when the enemy is driven out. And so, at the right time, we established the Provisional Government of Azad Hind at the Conference of Indians in East Asia held on 21st October.

If we had formed such a Government three years ago, the world would have called it a farce; and the enemy might have called it a propaganda stunt. But the Provisional Government having now risen as a natural sequence to the oranisation of the three millions of Indians in East Asia and the establishment of the powerful Indian National Army, even our enemies would have to think twice before calling it a propaganda stunt. The present Provisional Government of Azad Hind is not a plaything; it is a solid and powerful body having as its sanetion the will of the three millions of Indians united as a granite wall by the Indian Independence League and having as its support the Indian National Army.

In forming this Government, we have made no innovations because it has always been part of the technique of revolution to declare a Provisional Government just on the eve of a final War of Independence. Many examples are available in history for the adoption of this method. We have for instance, the case of the Czechs and the Irish as well as the case of Mustapha Kemal who formed a Provisional Government of Anatolia before the Turkish War of Independence. By taking this step on the 21st October, we have not only acted at the right time but we have also adopted the fight method.

It is true that it would have been better if such a Provisional Government could have been established within the frontiers of India. But under the present circumstance it is not practical politics to have such an organisation like the Indian Independence League or such an armed force like the Indian National Army within the frontiers of India. And any Provisional Government declared within India without the proper organisation and armed strength would be a farce; it would be some thing which our enemies could suppress in no time. This being the truth, and taking all the factors into consideration, patriotic Indians cannot but come to one and only conclusion that the only practical path for the achievement of our Independence is the path which we have now chosen.

In the proclamation of the establishment of the Provisional Government of Azad Hind on the 21st October, I have clearly defined the objectives and limits of this Government. We are not a Government like the ordinary administrations established in normal times; and hence, we have not followed the normal method nor have we opened departments which are essential only for the administration of a country in normal times. The first and foremost function of this Government is to wage the war of Independence and hence our Cabinet is primarily a War Cabinet.

Secondly, this Government would undertake to administer the liberated territories during the transitionary period only. We shall continue to function till the last Englishman is driven out of India, till India becomes Independent and law, order and peace are restored in Free India and till a Permanent Government of Free India is et up according to the will of the thirty-eight crores of Indians in India. I appeal to you and to every Indian in East Asia to read the Proclamation issued by us on the 21st October and understand fully the true significance of our Provisional Government.

I would also take the opportunity to emphasie that if a few have been elected as members of the Government does not mean the vast majority are absolved of their duties or responsibilities. For the sake of administrative convenience and necessity, a few have been made members of the Government, but the responsibility of the Government lies equally on all the Indians in East Asia.

Those who have assumed functions in the new Government machinery have not assumed any grand positions; they have assumed in fact greater burdens and responsibilities. The path of the Government is not a path of roses and very soon this Government will have its trail on the battlefield. You must not think even for a moment that there has been any elevation of individual position.

If there has been any elevation of position, it has been that of India and the Indians. Who can say that by the formation of this Government and its recognition by the world, the status and position of the Indians have not increased in the eyes of the world? You must realised that this is your Movement and that this Government is you Government, and that your duties as members of the Indian Independence League have now increased ten-fold.

We have two great tasks before us. The first task is to make full and final effort with a view to crossing the frontiers and setting foot on the holy soil of India before the end of this year. The second task is to continue our work and carry on our preparations for a long war. The retreat of

Britishers from India would mean the final destruction of the British Empire and so it is only natural that the British will try to cling to India with all their might.

It is not going to be an easy affair to drive the Britishers from India, but I am confident that once we are on the Indian soil we shall get necessary help and strength from the Indians in India. The Indian in East Asia, however, should realise that their efforts must continue as ever till our final objectives are achieved.

I would once again reiterate that our programme of Total Mobilisation must be carried out with greater vigour as a sequal to the formation of our Provisional Government. I would once again repeat my appeal for Men, Money and Materials. It is the duty of the Indians in East Asia to see that there is a continuous stream of men, money and materials forthcoming till we achieve final victory.

I may say in this connection that my call for men to rally round the Colour has been receiving satisfactory response. The way young Indians in East Asia have come forward as volunteers and the way in which our sisters have responded to my call to from the Rani of Jhansi Regiment have been inspiring indeed.

And about the offer of money and materials, I may say here that the response from the poorer and middle classes has been encouraging. I have come across instances of the spirit of sacrifice among our poor brethern which would bring tears to the eyes of even a stone-hearted man. A washerman came to me and gave his "all" and further said that he hailed from Jhansi and he would like to march along with our sisters of the Rani of Jhansi Regiment as their washerman. A poor ill-clad Indian who was a barber came forward with 200 dollars which represented his saving for years and gladly offered it for the cause.

Especially moving are the sacrifices of our Gowala brethren. These brothers came, gave all the cash they had, all the cattle they possessed and offered themselves as Volunteers for the Indian National Army. The poor classes have been showing by their actions and example the meaning of Total Mobilisation. It is only the rich who want to know whether Total Mobilisation means five or ten per cent of their savings. The poor have been spontaneously coming forward with their all and their own selves.

It is high time that the rich revolutionised their outlook. They should realise that when a Volunteer joins the ranks and goes to the front he does not ask whether he should spill five per cent or ten per cent of his blood. He goes to the front tos pill every drop of his blood. The life of one such volunteers is to me more precious than millions of dollars. What I would ask the rich to understand is that if they do not want to come forward to give their lives, they should at least come forward to give their possessions.

I have heard that some of the rich people have been saying that we are a nuisance and that the nuisance would be over when we leave Syonan on our march of India, I want them to know that though we may march, the Indian Independence League would still be here carrying on our "Home Front" programme while we are engaged on the fighting front. We cannot spare the rich; we cannot spare any Indian because ours is a life and death struggle and we are determined to carry on our fight to victory by all means and at any cost.

I have also said that some of our rich friends are thinking of changing their nationality to dodge the Indian Independence League's demand for funds. To these misguided friends, I have to say that there are only two alternatives before them; either they must become true Indians and do their duty at this hour of need or they must say that they are friends of Britain and be treated as such. In East Asia, there is no room for Britishers or their friends except in jails and the time is not far off when in India also their position will be the same. I hope there will soon be a re-orientation of outlook among the few rich Indians who have not satisfactorily responded to our call.

I shall now inform you of two very important decisions of the Cabinet of the Provisional Government of Azad Hind and place them before you for your ratification.

There was a time when the Britishers in their propaganda tried to ignore or belittle our Movement in East Asia. Now they have taken it seriously and for want of any other tactics they have resorted to abusing me from their radio stations. The tactic of abuse is the last refuge of the weak, of those who are at their wit's end.

But it is significant that the enemy has realised our strength and he understands that ours is not a mere propaganda stunt. The reactions and repercussions of the establishment of our Provisional Government has been world-wide and it will be no exaggeration if I say that it has created panic both in London and Washington.

The enemy radio stations were rather quick this time in flashing out the news of the formation of our Government through their broadcasts. Meanwhile, we have received the recognition of the Imperial Government of Nippon, and this, I must say, is a historic event of tremendom importance. If this recognition was a solitary act without any precedent there could have been opportunity for people to question have bonafides or this gesture. But, fortunately, this has not come as an innovation. This has come as one of the corollaries of Nippon's Asiatic policy based on justice and equality. The world has heard of this policy; it has already heard of the independence of Burma and then of the Philippines and so the recognition of the Provisional Government of Azad Hind has come as the natural result of the policy.

The Anglo-Americans have been proclaiming from their house-tops that they were the champions of Liberty and Democracy but their actions have repeatedly given the lie to their claims. Apart from their determination to maintain their hold on India, they have enslaved independent countries like Iraq and Iran. They have been and are trying to enslave free Burma.

In contrast to this, we have the action of Nippon in recognising Independent Burma, Independent Philippines and now the Provisional Government of Independent India. Our Nippon friends have always been showing us every sympathy and now, by this recognition, they have rendered us the greatest moral assistance for which we are greatly thankful. And so, the Council of Minister of Azad Hind have unanimously passed a resolution deeply appreciating this gesture of Nippon. I place their resolution before you for your ratification.

"The Provisional Government of Azad Hind (Free India) places on record its deep appreciation of the message conveying the news of recognition by the Imperial Government of Nippon of the Provisional Government of Azad Hind. The Provisional Government of Azad Hind expresses its grateful thanks to the Imperial Government of Nippon for the generous offer of wholehearted co-operation and assistance contained in the above message."

Our thanks are due to Premier General Tojo for the great interest in Indian Independence. We have to thank also Colonel Yamamoto, the Chief of the Hikari Kikan, for his co-operation, especially in the establishment of the Provisional Government of Azad Hind.

The next Resolution which was unanimously adopted by my Council is a more important one. The Council after discussing the political, economic and military situations in India came to the unanimous conclusion that the hour has struck for the declaration of war against Britain and America by the Provisional Government of Free India.

Last Night at 12.55 a.m. we declared war through the radio and it is interesting to note that 2 a.m., the enemy radio stations also gave out the news of our Declaration of War. This shows how alert they are in watching what steps we are taking. The Britishers know me well enough during my fight against them in India and they know well enough also that I will not make a declaration without having the strength to enforce what I say. Our declaration is not again a propaganda stunt. The coming events would show that we meant what we said.

Before I place our resolution declaring war on Britain and America before you for your ratification, I would ask you to realise its implications and to give your decision after full consideration.

Our Declaration, I repeat, is not an empty threat. We are resolved to carry it out with the last drop of our blood. And when I ask you to ratify it, I do not want to have the resolution carried in a formal ceremonial way. You ratification would mean that you are as much resolved as we are to shed your last drop of blood in enforcing the Declaration. I know that I need not put this equation to the Indian National Army because I know their mind and their deep anxiety to be on the Road to Delhi. I am now asking the Civilians as to whether they are one with us in making this Declaration, because if they are one with us they should come forthwith to give the fullest effect to our Programme to Total Mobilisation.

Friends! I want you to realise that we are taking part in a meeting which is not a propaganda show; this is not a ceremonial affair. We are here at a historic meeting to decide on a life and death issue. If we succeed in the project, thirty eight crores of Indians will be free. If, on the other hand, as God forbid, we fail, for at least another century our Nation will be doomed to slavery and untold misery. I have told you at the outset how the hand of God has created this golden opportunity for us. I have shown you how we have moved from stage to stage and we have reached the right opportunity to strike at our enemy, I have told you how e now have the organisation, the army and the Provisional Government of Azad Hind recognised by the world and how we have secured every help and support. Are we going to fail India at this great hour in her history?

Realise all these things, consider deeply all the implications of a Declaration of War and if you decide to take the war path, if you feel in your heart of hearts ready to face anything and everything in the historic fight against the British, if you feel that you are ready to give body, soul and all to fight our enemy until victory is won, then rise and give your ratification to our War Declaration by your acclamation.

Friends! My joy and pride knows no bounds at having witnessed the outburst of enthusiasm and spirit of revolution in you, and your thirst for Independence. With this spirit permeating the hearts of the Indians in

East Asia there could only be one sequel to our Declaration of War. And that is a fight which cannot fail to end in victory and with this demonstration of the united will and unified spirit of the Indian Nation, it may be an easy victory over our enemies. The meeting is now over and I would appeal to you to calm yourselves and to return to your homes, resolved forthwith to make every effort to bring our war to a victorious conclusion.

I would, lastly, call upon you to give three cheers for Revolution, for Free India and for the Government of Nippon.

At the 83rd session of the Imperial Diet which met on October 26, in Tokyo, Premier Gen, Hideki Tojo made the following reference to India in his speech:

"Turning to India, we find her 400,000,000 people still under Britain's ruthless heel and, with the ambition of the United States recently added to that pressure, they are continuing to experience indescribable miseries. The cruel rule of Britain and the outrageous conduct of the Anglo-American forces have further intensified the friction and antagonism between them and the Indian people, thus creating the profound social confusion accompanying an unprecedentedly great famine. The grave situation which is becoming aggravated day by day and month by month, is admitted even by Britain and the United States themselves.

"With many Indian patriots thrown into prison by the British and millions of innocent people thrown into agonies of starvation, the conditions in India at present are indeed tragic and the object of common grievance of all humanity. Such a situation we can by no means leave to take its own course. At this very juncture, Indians who hold their motherland close to their hearts have risen in unity under the leadership of the great patriot Mr. Subhash Chandra Bose and on the twenty-first of the month, the Provisional Government of Free India was established. Thereupon Nippon proceeded to recognize that government on the 23rd.

"It is truly a great pleasure for us to declare to the world through this chamber that Nippon is determined to support that government consistently in the future and to put forth her utmost efforts for the independence and emancipation of India.

"The Complete independence and freedom of India and the lasting prosperity of the 400,000,000 Indian people are what Nippon sincerely desires. I have not the slightest doubt that in this purpose Nippon may count not only upon the wholehearted co-operation of all greater East Asia People but also meet the earnest desire of all high minded people throughout the world."

47

Bose Assessment of the Greater East Asia Conference, Anticipates Unity of Asian Nations in Future under the Leadership of Japan[1]

9 November, 1943

I arrived in Tokyo on October 31 from Shonan, alongwith my party. I had heard before my arrival that an Assembly of Representatives of Greater-East-Asia would meet in Tokyo—but I had received no details about that Assembly. I had myself been thinking for sometime past that such a conference was urgently needed, in order to mobilize the whole of East-Asia for the war-effort and also for post-war reconstruction. Consequently, the news of the conference delighted me beyond measure. I was naturally curious to meet the representatives from East-Asia and also attend the Assembly. Owing to the special situation of India and of the Provisional Government of Azad Hind (Free India), it had been decided between us—and very correctly too—that I and my party would attend the Assembly as observers. Hence, I was in a position to take a thoroughly objective view of the conference and its proceedings.

At the aerodrome, as we alighted, we were given a very hearty reception by Their Excellencies the Foreign Minister and Minister of Greater East Asiatic Affairs, the Navy Minister and Major-General Arisue, as well as other Army leaders and notable personalities. Many of them I had known before during my last visit to Tokyo and I was glad to meet them again and to be able to greet them once more. I was then driven to the residence of my host, Viscount Shibusawa, and the round of public function arranged for us, begin at once.

---

1. *Nippon Times*, 9 November 1943, Greater East Asia Conference. Was held in Tokyo from 5 November 1943. It was attended by the representative of asiatic nations, i.e., China, Burma, Thailand, Phillipines, Manchuko. Subhas Chandra Bose attended the conference as an observer, while General Tojo led the Japanese delegation.

The prologue to the Assembly of Greater East-Asiatic Nations took place on November 4 at the official residence of His Excellency, the Prime Minister, General Tojo, when the Representatives were all invited to tea. I and my party were included among the guests -though we were not among those who were to participate actively in the proceedings of the Assembly. At this tea party I found that I was personally acquainted with Representatives of Nipon, Thailand and Burma but the Representatives from Manchokuo, China and Philippines were strangers to me. Nevertheless, I found that within a short time, the atmosphere became very cordial and friendly and toward the end of the function, while talking to some members of the Nippon Government, I said that the function appeared to me like a family party. This was also the impression some other gentlemen present at the tea party, with whom I compared notes.

It was an excellent idea to arrange this function the day before the Assembly was to meet. The result was that when the Assembly gathered the next day–November 5–the participants were no longer strangers to one another. This added greatly to the cordiality of the atmosphere which prevailed at the assembly and helped to make it a success.

The keynote of the conference was given expression to in a characteristic manner by His Excellency, the Representative from Burma, Adipadi Dr. Ba Maw. He remarked in one of his speeches at the Assembly that though the representatives of the East-Asiatic Nations spoke different languages and perhaps used different forms of expression, there was one underlying thought—one objective and one will behind all their utterances. He was absolutely correct and truthful in interpreting the mind of the participating Representatives, for the atmosphere of the Assembly declared emphatically—"East Asia is one."

Though there was an underlying unity pervading the Assembly it was an intellectual treat to notice and to study among the participating representatives a difference in temperament and also in the form and manner of expression. For instance, his Excellency Prime Minister General Hideki Tojo stood out before the Assembly as the soldier— statesman— whose utterances were incisive in character and why being inspired by idealism, were remarkable for their clarity and convincing logic. His Excellency, the Prime Minister of Manchoukuo, was the type of the elderly and experienced politician, who had weathered many a strong, but had ultimately steered his ship to port. His Excellency the President of the Chinese Republic, was the seasoned politician, ripe with knowledge, who was sure of his own position and had grim but silent determination— and who did not, therefore, need gesticulation to convince his listeners. His Excellency, the President of the Philippines, had the fiery eloquence of an expert Parliamentarian who could by his sincerity and passion, brings tears to the eyes of his listeners and carry audience with him. His Royal Highness, Prince Wan of Thailand, was a perfect mannered, cultured aristocrat, conscious of the proud tradition and heritage of his country, who would be an ornament to any society in the world. And His Excellency Dr. Ba Maw was—as he himself said—like a soldier, coming from the front, who knew that his country was within the firing line and whose heart was burning with the desire to contribute in giving a knock out blow to the enemy and thereby make his contribution to the creation of a free and united East Asia.

The Assembly of Greater East-Asiatic Nations proved that East Asia was really and fundamentally one. Nevertheless, for the critical observer, it was a delight to see that the unity was manifested in a diversity of form, expression and temperament.

The Assembly of Greater East-Asiatic Nations was a complete success. There can be no doubt at all about it. It helped to consolidate firmly's the East-Asiatic Nations - for the purpose of winning the war and also for that of constructing a new order, to replace the old and worn out one. All honour to his brain that first conceived of this conference! And all credit to those who organized it made it such a striking success!

As for the Joint Declaration, unanimously and enthusiastically passed by the Assembly, it will prove to be a Charter of Liberty for the Nations of East Asia. And I may venture prophecy that the world at large will hear more of this Charter in future and will also need it when the time comes to attempt once again the formation of an internatioal society of nations.

As for the enemy, I am sure that when authentic news about the Assembly and its achievements reaches the enemy's camp, there will be a anxiety, fear and consternation.

but it seemed [illegible] remarks.

[illegible] whole of mankind [illegible]

[illegible] President of the Philippines, [illegible]

[illegible] of Parliament [illegible]

[illegible]

[illegible]

[illegible] the Excellency

[illegible]

[illegible] whose heart was

[illegible]

[illegible]

[illegible]

[illegible] Asian [illegible] that East [illegible] the critical society [illegible]

[illegible]

[illegible] important

The [illegible] Asian [illegible] concrete

[illegible] There can be no doubt [illegible] to consolidate

[illegible] East [illegible] to make the war and

[illegible] end were not

[illegible]

[illegible]

[illegible] of Liberty for the

[illegible] the world at large

[illegible]

[illegible] international society of

nations.

As for the future, I am sure that when we do now about the Assembly and its achievements [illegible]

[illegible] real and constructive.

48

Military Intelligence Assessment of the Indian National Army, after its Re-organisation by Subhash Chandra Bose; Issues Guideline for Dealing With it

10 November. 1943

General Description

1. Owing to a recent reorganization, following upon the arrival of S. C. Bose from Germany, definite information regarding the strength, organization, etc. is scanty.
2. In 1942 we estimated that about 15,000 P. W. might have been suborned, or more probably coerced, into joining the I.N.A. A revised, but very tentative estimate is 41,500; this is based on the reports of agents and escapes. The latest Axis broadcast claim a strength of 200,000. As the total number of Indian P. W. in Japanese hands is 70,000, this figure could only be attained by extensive recruitment of largely indifferent civilian material.
3. HQ and the bulk of the I.N.A. are probably still located in Singapore, but are believed to be moving to Rangoon. In February 1943 there were two camps in Singapore, and one each in Kluang, Johore, Seremban, Rangoon and Hong Kong.
4. In 1942 the I.N.A. in Malaya was believed to be organized into 3 Bdes (Guerilla Regts) and a Field Group, under a HQ organized on British lines. The new organization is unknown, but a recent addition is a regiment of women, in which lies potentialities for trouble if it goes into the field.
5. Some Light Automatics and rifles have been issued, and a few British wheeled vehicles and carriers. A standard uniform was accepted in 1942, which Bose is said to have redesigned. A number

1. War officer No 203/4756. PRO.

of training camps are known to exist, notably in Penang, which have been played up in recent Axis broadcasts. There are also several schools where JIFS (both ex P of W and civilians) are trained in espionage, sabotage, subversive propaganda and wireless before being sent to India as enemy agents with definite tasks. Some are trained in parachute dropping and about twenty four have been dropped by air to date. Of these twenty have been captured. Two parties each of five were landed by submarine and were also captured.

6. What morale and espirit de corps existed in the I.N.A. had a set back owing to temporary disbandment followed by reorganisations. There has also been evidence of communal intrigues, which resulted in the Sikh leaders being largely displaced by Hindus and Muslims. On the other hand there is no evidence of definite ill feeling amongst the communities.

7. I.N.A. personnel have hitherto been used for espionage and propaganda tasks, and in assisting the Japanese to "control" the population in forward areas. Bose has however repeatedly claimed that the I.N.A. is being trained to take the field as a fighting formation to "liberate" India. While there are, as yet, no signs of such a move, it would be in keeping with Bose's character for him to attempt a spectacular coup.

Counter Measures

8. **The Central Group.** The Central Group is a body of carefully selected officers who after preliminary training visit units and set up small cells known as Josh (enthusiasm or Verve) Groups. These cells are selected by C.Os and generally consist of one officer and Indian officers and NCOs. Their task is to expose the Japanese and their tools, includate doctrine that India must destroy the Japanese, or be destroyed by them and so prepare Indian units for possible encounter with armed JIFS in the field. 750 Josh Groups have been formed and results are most encouraging.

9. **GHQ Broadcasts.** These are directed in various languages to Japanese occupied territory. The Indian Army has, of late, been encouraged to listen to them also. Amongst other indications of the effect of this campaign, Bose stated in an interview in Singapore that one of his two main objects was to crush the enemy propaganda directed from Delhi at Indian Nationalists working abroad. An outline

of GHQ broadcasting is given in an Appendix[2]. Leaflets in vernacular languages are also dropped in enemy occupied areas encouraging JIFS to take every opportunity to return to our lines and make a clean breast of their activities. These leaflets are also designed to sow distrust in JIF leaders.

10. **Instruction Issued to Troops.** Commanders have been instructed that all troops are to be taught that I.N.A. personnel (JIFS) encountered in the field are to be treated and fought as enemies until they are killed or surrender.

Security and Legal arrangements

11. **Interrrogation.** All I.N.A. personnel on capture or surrender are passed to the nearest forward Interrogation Centre for a rapid interrogation. More detailed interrogation is carried out by similar centres in rear, selected personnel being sent to the Combined Services Detailed Interrogation Centre (C.S.D.I.C.) in Delhi. All persons whether suspected of being JIFS or not who return from enemy occupied territory also pass through this interrogating organisation which also extracts from them intelligence about the enemy.

12. **Classification.** Following upon interrogation and a cross check from records, personnel returning from enemy occupied territory are classified as White, (loyalty and morale unaffected) Grey (loyalty or morale temporarily affected) or Black (definitely dangerous). Military Whites and Greys are reconditioned at a special camp, Blacks are detained under Defence of India Rules or special ordinances or when possible brought to trial. Similar arrangements exists for civilians, but there is as yet no reconditionsing camp for them.

13. **Trials.** In the case of military persons a Standing Court Martial has been established, which is duplicated by a Central Tribunal on the civil side. Military and civil legal advisers study the cases, berif interrogaters, and advise the prosecutors. There is a special Enemy Agents Ordinance under which both military and civilian personnel may be tried in camera.

14. **Detention.** Civil Blacks are segregated in civil jails; military Blacks are sent to a separate place of detention. Both classes will be removed in due course to a special jail now under construction.

15. **Security Staffs.** A combined DMI/DIB (Director Intelligence Bureau) staff section has been set up at New Delhi to deal with all matters of

2. Not printed.

policy, intelligence, and security executive action concerning the I.N.A. (and I.I.L.). Provision has been made for this section to be represented in all major formations in operational areas. The Security corps, which is based on Calcutta, provides the staff (civil and military interrogating officers and police personnel) for Forward Interrogating Centres which ate established at various focal points in operational areas in Bengal and Assam.

49

Decision of the Liaison Conference for the Transfer of Andamans and Nicobar Island to the Provisional Government of India

10 November, 1943

Re—The Andamans and the Nicobars

1. The time to transfer the Andamans and the Nicobar to the Provisional Government of India should be decided separately and for the time being the subject is to be disposed as follows :

(a) Provisional Government staff will be allowed to stay in the area, participating in administration provided such participation will remain within the limit of smooth military campaign and its related activities will not be jeopardized.

(b) The said participation in the administration will be further extended by and by, and the desire of the Provisional Government of India will be fulfilled by and by under the leadership of Regional Supreme Commander.

(c) It is granted for the Provisional Governmnet to make use of the point that the transfer of the said area to the Provisional Government as an existing fact.

(d) Even after the transfer of the said area, it should so be arranged as all the request in connection with the defence of the area should be compiled with.

1. Ministry of Defence War History Section Proceedings of the Liasion Conference, Tokyo.

50

From Takazumo Oka, Vice-Admiral Imperial Japanes Navy to Bose; Informs him about Arrangements Made for his Visit to the Andamans

16 November, 1943

Dear Sir,

I have the honour to send you herewith the reply of the Imperial Japanese Navy to the desires expressed by your excellency in the course of our conversation on November 12th. I desire to avail myself of this opportunity to convey my sincere wishes for your excellency's continued good health and for the speedy attainment of the object of the founding of Free India.

His Excellency Mr. Subhas Chandra Bose
Head of the Provisional Government of India

Mr. Bose's visit to the Andaman and Nicobar Islands. Barring a sudden change in the military situation, arrangements will be made to have this visit made during the early part of December. Details of the trip will be communicated to Mr. Bose by the Commander-in-Chief of the Fleet stationed in Shonan. This trip is to be kept strictly secret until in its completion.

Publicity subsequent to the completion of the visit. It is desired that this publicity be undertaken along the lines formally communicated to Mr. Bose by Prime Minister Tojo on November 13th, i.e., to the effect that "We are already going ahead with preparatory measures necessary for a speedy and smooth transfer of the islands (such as .... etc.)".

---

1. I.N.A Trial Papers, It was at the Greater East Asia Conference, that General Tojo decided to hand over the Andaman and Nicobar Islands to the Provisional Government. These islands were under the charge of Japanese naval authorities. Bose went to Andaman towards the end of December, 1943 to decide about the appointment of an Indian Chief Commissioner and the nature of his participation in the administration alongwith the Japanese. After the visit Lt. Col. A.D. Loganadan alongwith his staff went to Andamans in February 1944.

Appointment and dispatch of a Governor. In accordance with the statement made by the Prime Minister, a Governor is to be appointed after completion of the transfer. It is to be understood that, pending completion of the transfer, an official of the Provisional Government bearing some such title as "Chief Commissioner for the Andaman and Nicobar Islands" should be dispatched to co-operate fully in the military administration of the Islands under the direction of the Naval Commandent there.

Dispatch of an army contingent by the Provisional Government. The Naval Authorities can fully appreciate the reason for the Provisional Government's wishes in this matter. But since the time and method of carrying out this measure must be made to fit in with the conditions prevailing on the Islands, an answer on this point will be given later after further consideration. There would, however, be no objection to the dispatch of two or three military liaison officers.

Dispatch of Indian engineers. Considering that the two Islands constitute an area of intensive military operations, there would be no objection to carefully selected technicians being sent after consultation with the Naval Commandant of the Islands. But in view of the conditions now prevailing there. It is to be understood that for the time being such technicians are to co-operate in undertakings connected with military operations. Attention must be called, finally, to the fact that since the transportation and communication facilities are only sufficient for our military needs, it will be difficult for the present to carry out any policy which will make any considerable demand upon ships or communication facilities.

51

Status of the Indian National Army as Decided by the Hikari Kikan; Declars I.N.A. as an ally of the Japanese Army

3 December, 1943

The Indian National Army constituted by the favour of His Imperial Majesty, is the armed forces of the Indian Independence League.

The Indian National Army will be treated as the army of an ally. Do not strike its members, be not haughty and keep your temper. Give up false sense of superiority.

Contents

1. War office F. No. 208/863. P.R.O.

Chapter I

The 400 million people of India, oppressed by the British for many years, have come forward with the desire to abolish the British rule and to obtain complete independence for their Motherland. They have obtained strength from the opportunity afforded by the Great East Asia War to drive out the force of America and England for Japan. They have come forward to these steps from all quarters and abandoned their policy of non-resistance and non-violence and have advanced to obtain independence at the cost of their own blood..

The essence of this battle for independence is the Indian National Army.

To achieve the object of the war, laid down in the Imperial rescript on the declaration of war, which is the destruction of the enemies England and America, we must drive their force from India. The Indian National Army, whose object is to overthrow the British raj in India, is therefore our ally.

This booklet is to give a rough idea of how we should feel and not towards the Indian National Army.

Chapter II

The Origin of the Indian National Army

In consideration that we, the Imperial Army, under the divine guidance of His Imperial Majesty, are to overthrow the power of England and America in East Asia, the question was considered of building up an army of Indians resident in East Asia who, with an understanding of Japan and with her help, would fight England for the independence of their Motherland guided by a true spirit of patriotism. "India is not England's watch dog". The Indian National Army was formed in September 1942. After about a year of instruction and training under the Japanese Army it was reorganised and its existence was published to the world in July 1943. Thus it is an army, constituted by Imperial favour, fostered by the Imperial Army, composed of Indians who with their life-blood fight for the Independence of their Motherland, and are fighting our common enemy with a common purpose.

Chapter III

Underlying principles of the I.N.A.

1. The Indian National Army is the Indian People's own army. The purpose of the I.N.A. is to secure the independence of India by Indian and although they are fighting our common enemy with a common purpose are not by any means a "Fifth column of the

Japanese Army" nor are they a "fatigue party". They are the army of the Indian Independence League and with the dawn of the Independence of India will constitute the forces of the new state.

2. The spirit of I.N.A. officers and men. Officers and men swear an oath of loyalty to India through the Indian Independence League. Their creed is unity, fidelity and sacrifice. They are banded together with the one object of overthrowing England and achieving independence for their Motherland.

3. The principle of having picked men. Only picked men from among volunteers are used as this is preferred to large members.

4. Relation to Japanese Army. They are treated as an ally by the Japanese army. In combined operations the senior commander of the I.N.A. will receive instructions from the senior Japanese commander.

In combined operations the control by the senior Japanese commander will be exercised through the senior I.N.A. Commander.

Chapter IV. See Appendices I, II, III and IV. (Annexure X)[2]

Chapter V

Treatment of the Indian National Army

Officers and men of the I.N.A bear friendship and trust towards the Imperial Army and treat us as real allies, friends and helpers. Their hundreds of years of oppression, tyrarmy and deceit and exploitation at the hands of the British have instilled in them a perverse shrinking and lack of spirit. Owing to anti-Japanese propaganda by the British they have very wrong ideas of Japan. They are strong individualists and materialists as well as possessing many customs arising from their religious beliefs—This makes them very difficult to handle. They frequently have quick tempers especially on the battle field. We Japanese, as leaders in the building of a new world, as being comrades in the destruction of England and America, must treat them with a kindly and tolerant leniency whatever weak points they may have. The following are the chief practical points regarding our treatment of them—

1. Approach them as a real ally. As has been stated, the Indian National Army has been constituted by the favour of his Imperial Majesty; it has the praiseworthy mission of obtaining independence for its Motherland; it is fighting the same enemy and with the same object as ourselves; it's essence is Indian's patriotism. For these reasons it has

---

2. Not Printed.

been decided that it shall be treated as an ally. We must thoroughly understand this principle and approach them as a true ally. Owing to the cruel treatment they have received from the British over so many years they have a suspicious nature, and therefore there must be no action which might lead them to think that we have given them the name of "ally" without the status. It is necessary to handle them in such a way that they will have the same feeling as ourselves.

2. Value your fights of command. It is obvious that the rights of command of the forces of an ally are to be held in high esteem. It is only by placing a high value in these rights that the capabilities of the I.N.A. can be developed to their highest pitch. Command will be exercised and through the senior I.N.A. commander and great care must be taken that odd units who have no rights of command do not issue orders off their own bat. The HIKARI 'Kikan' is the medium through which control and co-operation of the I.N.A. is exercised smoothly so as to develop its capabilities to the best advantage.

3. Compliments will be paid as to allied army. Where there is no respect there is no confidence and no co-operation. Where there are no compliments there can be no respect. The Imperial rescript ordering punctilious saluting in the army covers also allied armies and it has been decided that military compliments will be given to the I.N.A. as to the force of a friendly country.

4. Memorize their dress, badges, pass words and signals. By memorizing their dress, badges, pass words, singles etc. difference of opinion and friction regarding saluting, intercommunication, etc, can be avoided.

5. Discard the feeling of superiority and do not look down on them. The thought that white people are a superior race and coloured people are inferior one is to be thoroughly eradicated. It is to break down this that we are waging the Great East Asia War. In the bottom of our hearts we have the mistaken pride that we Japanese are a superior people. This must be discarded and we must cease to look down on them and show respect for their official powers. It is only by such respect that they will be happy that their blood is Asiatic and will make a favourable comparison between ourselves and the English and so draw closer to us in their esteem and reliance.

6. Do not strike its members, be not haughty and keep your temper. These are the secrets in handling the I.N.A. If these are not observed, all is finished. One blow will destroy years of kindness and the ear

will not incline our way a second time; such an act will be the biggest insult in a man's life and will leave its mark which can never be expunged. For this reason striking I.N.A. personnel is strictly forbidden. Haughtiness will never bring friendliness but antipathy which cannot be eradicated. If we get angry they cannot understand us and become unhappy. We cannot then get close to them even if we try and alienation and friction result.

7. Do not tell lies. They have extremely good memories. They remember who said what and when and where and having laboured under British lies for so many years are extremely shrewd at discerning them. If we tell lies they will think that we are the same as the British, trust will be lost, suspicion increased. We must therefore get them to believe that we Japanese value the truth and we soldiers never tell a lie.

8. Assert your rights and understand their custom of not showing gratitude. They are very strong in the assertion of their rights. For instance, they think that they are entitled to a fixed ration at all time and if owing to difficulties of supply we ourselves do not get a meal but supply them theirs, they will not be happy if it is not full scale. Rather will they insist on their right to the amount deficient. In such cases anger is futile. It is equally futile to think that they will be grateful for any trouble we may take to look after them. If there is anything we do that seems to earn gratitude it is best to forget about it. If we do some kindness that may warrant some regard they will never even think of it as a kindness at all. They are quite fixed in this line of thought.

9. As far as possible respect their religious prejudices. Indians have many and various religious prejudices and are stricter in their observance of these than we Japanese imagine. Very serious problems arise if they are prevented from observing them and it behoves us to respect these prejudices as far as possible. For example :

   (a) To resist in the slaughter of cattle in front of Hindus and Sikhs and pigs in front of Mohamedans. (in the I.N.A. all religions are mixed and the consumption of beef and pork is entirely abolished).

   (b) The removing of the turban or cutting the hair of Sikhs.

   (c) Pulling the tuft of hair on a Hindu's head.

   Remember the points in the other booklet "commonsense about India".

10. It is advantageous to have someone appointed in each 'butai' as in charge of Indian troops. From the points of view that Indian troops are very awkward to deal with, a suitable person appointed to this position will be able to develop their best co-operation and will make them contented.

11. Handling of front line operative. Officers and men of the I.N.A. are not only employed in battle as the Japanese army, but are employed on various duties vis-à-vis Indian troops inside the enemy's lines. For this purpose they may wear mufti or be disguised or again in proper uniform pass through our front line troops into the enemy. They may pass to and fro between the opposing forces and in order that there may be no possibility of their being shot by mistake, our front line troops should have explained to them methods of recognition, pass word etc. At the same time we must proffer them a warm helping hand. Further when they seduce and bring over personnel from the enemy we must treat these strictly in accordance with the regulations for the treatment of prisoners of war and it is forbidden to kill or ill-treat them in the presence of the operatives who bring them in.

Chapter VI

Conclusion

The problem of India is of the greatest importance in the satisfactory prosecution of Great East Asia War. Attack on India is absolutely unavoidable but in India the British and American forces are our enemy, the 400 million Indians are not on any account the same.

But, hand in hand with these 400 million people we can destroy the British and Americans and go far towards victory in the Great East Asia war, liberate India and establish her independence.

Already the people of India have risen in war against the English. The Indian National Army is in truth their advance guard. Furthermore, they are blessed by His Imperial Majesty's favour and have limitless faith in Japan and the Imperial Army and look to us for help which we have promised them. The people of India expect much from them. We are Japan's advance guard to India and are divine soldiers of Japan the Righteous. By helping the I.N.A. without losing their trust, we together will succeed in the object of the war, to win the destruction of England and America and so carry out the will of His Imperial Majesty.

52

General Staff Branch to G.O.C. Indian Army Comments on the Subversive Activities in the Indian Army, from Abroad and its Linkage with the Indian Nationalist Inside the Country; Issues Directions to Deal with the Situation

18 December, 1943

To :

G.O.C.-in-C. N.W. Army, etc.

1. In this HQ No. DMI/4746 dated 18 March 1943[2], reference was made in paragraphs 3 and 4 to attacks on the loyalty to the Indian Army being made from within India by subversive organizations affiliated to the underground section of the Congress movement, in appendix 'A' to that letter was a copy of a document referring specifically to this attack.

2. Now attached are extracts from reports on what Jai Prakash Narain has said in the course of conversation with police officers who are dealing with him. He is the notorious underground leader of the Congress Socialist Party who was recently arrested. He is described as being in a "blustering mood", and what he says cannot all be taken at its face value. His remarks, however, confirm that efforts continue to be made to undermine the loyalty of the Indian armed forces, and that those responsible for the campaign consider that they are making some progress, especially among technical personnel and emergency commissioned officers. The reference to the "Air service" should be compared with the reference to the "technical staff of the Royal Air Force" in Appx. 'A' of our letter of 18 March 1943. Even while discounting J.P. Narain's sweeping claims, there is no doubt that the type of educated youth which the technical arms and services require is, potentially, the most receiptive medium for subversive approaches, and certaining (together with the emergency commissioned officer) the most likely I attempt to make what capital he can from his

1. Ministry of Defence, Historical Section F. No. 601/19869/H.S.
2. Document No. 7

position in the armed forces to further his own future ends, or those of the political party to which he belongs.

3. You are requested to handle the information given in the attached extracts with great care, in order to avoid compromising further interrogation and action arising therefrom.

Sd/-

For Chief of the General Staff

Extracts from the Reports on Talks with Jai Prakash Narain Recorded upto the 25th November, 1943

"I have held the office of the General Secretary of the All-India Congress Committee from January to October, 1932, during the Congress campaign of that year. Dr. Saifuddin Kitchlew, Mrs. Sarojini Naidu and C. Rajagopalchariar worked as President, one after the other, during my tenure of office. I was arrested at Madras in October 1932. I was underground and had my office in Bombay."

"I was arrested in 1940 for an objectionable speech and was released from jail in December, 1940, when I went to Calcutta to meet Subhas Chandra Bose. He was recouping health. We discussed various political problems."

"Subhas told me that Bengal was prepared for a mass movements and he was too keen that a conflict be picked up with the Government on some issue. He suggested that Holwall Monument could be utilised for the purpose. He did not mention to me about his intentions of disappearing but he did express the view which tended to show that he believed in accepting foreign help for India's emancipation. He was not very clear with me on account of Congress Session, when the C.S.P. remained neutral on Pant's resolution. There is, however, no difference between our and Forward Bloc's ideology as far as the independence of India is concerned. There is no doubt about Subhas Chandra Bose's sincerety. He is a fervent patriot. He is definitely not Japanese quisling. He advocated socialism in his presidential address at the Haripura Congress Session. He is prepared to accept foreign country's aid for liberating India from British yoke. He believes in accepting help from the Axis, but we Congress Socialists are prepared only to receive aid from a sympathetic country like China, Just as the Irish people received help from Americans. I don't believe that Axis invasion could directly help us. We can, of course, exploit an Axis invasion."

"Both Nehru and Subhas favour mass movement and are ultra anti-British, determined to end British rule in India. They differ in methods of attaining the same. Nehru does not believe in foreign aid and is anti-fascist, but Subhas holds the view that Indians do need foreign help. Athough Nehru does not believe in foreign aid, he would not lose the opportunity to exploit a foreign invasion on India to get rid of British 7yoke."

"I have not heard Subhas Bose speaking on the radio but as far as his propaganda goes, he has one million Army of Indian and I believe that to be in Burma with headquarters at Singapore. I don't think M. Ghandhi will take back Subhas in the Congress in the event of his return to India, which is only possible under a national government. His being taken back in the Congress is also not an impossibility."

"Subhas was elected Chief of the National Army set up by the Japanese and Rash Behari worked as his Deputy. There was no possibility of a Japanese invasion previously, nor is there one now. It is either Subhas's creation or this propaganda calculates to be exploitation by the Japanese. It appears that Subhas had discussed his plans with Germany when he visited that country before. It was for that reason that he first went to Germany and then after discussing plans with them he went to Japan. I don't think that he had been to Japan previously. I tried to contact Subhas Bose but could not find a suitable person to arrange that contact. I wanted to consult him to chalk out a plan for coordinating our efforts for the liberation of the country. I wanted that he should continue his activities from outside while I should carry on my work from inside the country."

"In those days (November, 1942) Benares was the storm centre of the movement and I stayed there for about a month. Here I met all my co-escapees and it was decided to work in labour, among students, in police and other Government departments and among kisans. Dislocation was one of the most important items of the programme and we paid special attention to it. The Central Directorate was already in existence, and I learnt that some I.C.S. and other Government officers helped us in this movement, but their number unfortunately is much less as compared to those who promised and then did not help. Most of those officers, who supported us, are quite safe because the Government could not afford to stir up resentment by wholesale dismissals."

"During the present underground movement we have been publishing lot of literature in Calcutta, Bombay and other places for distribution in military, police and public. In Bengal we had formed committees in all the districts. Literature was sent to these committees and they arranged further distribution. Literature was published in almost all the languages and for all Government departments. We succeeded in subverting many Government Servants through out literature. No Government servent is a member of C.S.P. but lots of Government servants and even the I.C.S officers assisted us in the present movement. We enlisted the sympathy of Government servants by propaganda. I can confidently say that we were successful in all ranks of the military but in police we could only subvert lower ranks. We had the strongest contacts in the military in Assam sometime before my arrest, but later a number of workers were arrested resulting in loss of many contacts. Now our propaganda is best in Eastern India, particularly Bombay, Ranchi and Gaya. We have found that new entrants in the Army are far more nationalist than the older people. We have got our own people enlisted in the military in order to disrupt the British Government from inside. We exploited the present famine situation and did propaganda in public through posters and pamphlets urgeing them not to dislike rats (sic) but to go to jail for national cause."

"In February 1943, when I was at Bombay, I discussed with my colleagues the present Congress campaign. I found that the present movement had been a failure in as far as that we could not maintain our hold even in those *illaquas* where we succeded in ousting British Authority. There were two phases of the Congress mass movement. The first one was the open agitation which was started by the unorganised masses and in which violence took place, but much less in comparison to the intensity of the movement. The second phase was the underground movement which was organised secretly and in which terrorist activities were resorted to. It was in the first unorganised mass movement that we were able to oust British Authority from many districts, but in view of lack of solid programme our workers could not continue the agitation successfully. My idea is that we shall have to set out plans for the next movement much ahead of inaugurating the actual movement."

"I placed a plan before my other colleagues for the formation of a military volunteer organisation. I thought that we could make use of arms and ammunition collected and manufactured during the present phase. We would be able to prepare the masses in order to produce another mass rising. A meeting was held at Bombay and violence was discussed."

"I laid the foundation of a new organization. The Central Directorate did not approve of my action, but they did not condemn it as well as it was considered that after M. Gandhi's arrest everyone was leader of himself. The new organisation was also not to be under the C.S.P. I named it 'Azad-Dastas' and later changed the name to 'Azad Sena'. It is completely to be a secret organisation. Congress Socialists, Congressmen and even non-

Congressmen are its members. After drafting its constitution, I got first part of 'ABC of Dislocation' printed at Bombay and sent messangers to all the Provinces for the organisation of the same. I took inspiration in the formation of the Azad Sena from the news of 'guerilla warfare' in China, which had also been practised in Russia, American War of Independence and other freedom struggles. I decentralised the organisation and the Azad Sena is only a Provincial and local body. It is functioning in the eastern parts of U.P., Bihar, Bengal and Assam. There may be in other provinces but I am definite that there is none in the Punjab. The object of the organisation is to prepare bands of trained political workers, who could not act as the nucleus of the future military side of the administration when the British Rule ends. They have instructions to try to make contacts with the military to make them disloyal to the British Rule. The looting of mail bags, small post offices, revenue collections, Government property is their line of work. They make up their funds by such means. They will be of much use to us in the third phase, which I am sure will come about shortly and will be of a revolutionary nature with open terrorism by using the arms and bombs collected in the second phase. The Azad Sena also believes individual terrorism to be inevitable at a certain stage. Looting of public men for political purposes is not approved. Manufacture of arms and collection of the same is part of their programme. The ones manufactured locally are no good and the best are the arms and ammunition obtained from servicemen. One object political purposes. The Azads are trained in handling of firearms which they have to use in their self-defence and also in their plan of looting etc. I am 'Pahla Azad' and all writing issued over that name are mine. The Azads are locally numbered and ten Azads form one Dasta."

"As far as the war is concerned we have never been concerned with its consequences. It was immaterial for us as to who won. Japan was not an enemy of India and if after the expulsion of the British they persisted in invading our country we could consider our plan of action. We would have negotiated with Japan. We do not care if our struggle helped the Japanese because we thought that if we could overthrow the British we could also fight the Japanese. I assured the workers that Gandhiji would not take action as usual. I assured the workers that Gandhiji would not take action as usual against those indulging in the underground activities. I further explained to the "Azads" that they should try to pick up the support of as many militarymen as possible."

"We have done lot of propaganda in the military. We were late in coming out to take control of the situation. Although the economic situation in the country helped us in fomenting an agitation yet the international situation was such that it did not let us extend our field of work. We knew that masses had spontaneously risen to the occasion in August, 1942. We hoped for another mass-rising and tried to prepare the masses for it. In order to keep in touch with the masses we sent workers in rural areas. We tried our best but failure was due to no change in the international situation. In Bihar and Assam the movement was strongest on account of the strength of the Congress organisation in these two provinces, in Bihar the Congress work was supplemented by the Congress Socialist Party and the Kisan Sabha while in Assam organisation had been started much in advance. Shanti Senas had been formed in Assam with 50,000 membership. The Congress movement has been successful only at places where organisation had been done before the starting of the movement. I.C.S. and I.P. officers also helped us in such provinces. In Bihar we had the maximum sympathy from the police and our sympathisers included I.P. offiers. In Bengal I.B. the highest officers who supported us were Deputy Superintendents.

As far as military was concerned, we never asked them to desert. We had pledges of loyalty to the Indian Republic printed which were required to be signed by militarymen offering to join us. We were contacting them with a view to make them disloyal to the British Government and to get arms through them. This was also the work and an item in the programme of the Azad Senas. We knew that military never revolted unless their masters were in crippled state. We did not feel that the present international situation was such that the Government was weak and a military revolt could have been successful. We only wanted them to be ready for action when the Government was about to collapse. The Indian military is generally dissatisfied and we were able to win over 80 per cent of the men in Air service, 50 per cent of Garhwalis, 50 per cent of Sikhs and we also succeeded in the formation of cells in all technical units stationed in Bihar and Assam. The emergency commission officers are generally more nationalist and it is too easy for us to win them over. It is an easier task to convert them than it is to get an information from the Imperial Secretariat at Delhi. During the movement I used to receive copy of a 'strictly secret' report of the Congress movement sent by the Viceroy to the Secretary of State for India.

Appendix–I

American Intelligence Report on the Activities of Indian National Army and the Working of Hikari Kikan in Burma; gives Comprehensive Account about the Emergence of the Indian Independence Movement under the Leadership of Subhas Chandra Bose (Extract)

Literally translated, Hikari Kikan means "Light Organization", but a better rendition of the phrase may be "Enlightenment Agency". The Burma branch of the Hikari Kikan is the agency of the Japanese Army which is charged with the training and use of Indians in the war against the Allies. As such, the Burma branch combines many functions, including espionage, sabotage, propaganda, combat intelligence and even military government.

Espionage constitutes one of its primary functions. The Hikari Kikan Annual Report for 1943 lists 568 men dispatched from Rangoon to forward areas. Many of these agents were destined for deep penetration into India. Some of the parties were briefed in specific subotage missions, but most ot them combined espionage sabotage tasks.

The Hikari Kikan Command includes both civilians and military Jifs (Japanese Inspired Fifth Columnists). The military Jifs are enrolled in the Indian National Army (I.N.A.), which is nominally the army of the "Provisional Government of Free India" under the leadership of Subhas Chandra Bose. The Civilian Jifs are agents directly responsible to Hikari Kikan officers.

Most of the personnel under Hikari Kikan are devoted to operational contact work rather than to deep penetration. Indians trained in Hikari

---

1. Hikari – Kikan a successor organisation to Iwakuro Kikan was established under the command of Col. Yamamoto. *Hikari* in Japanese means "Light" and Kikan means organisation. It served as a liaison agency between the I.N.A. and the Japanese Government. The note was prepared by office of the Strategic Services, U.S. Government and throw considerable light on the relations between the I.N.A. and the Japanese military authorities, Diet Library, Tokyo.

Kikan schools and camps are detached in small groups to regular Japanese Army units. Their tasks are to infiltrate behind the Allied lines for reconnasissance purposes and to attempt to suborn Indian troops by distributing leaflets or by personal contact with small isolated detachments. On occasion such infiltrating groups have been known to practice deception tactics, shouting misleading command to Indian Army units. In at least one skirmish they were able to capture a position because they were not recognized as enemy troops until it was too late for the defending forces to repel them.

The Indians under Hikari Kikan have not often been used in actual combat. Civilian Jifs are used either as interpreters or liaison men or as agents for deep penetration. The military Jifs of the "Indian National Army" have been employed largely as auxiliary details for the use of Japanese battallion and regimental commanders.

In the field of propaganda, Hikari Kikan operates both in combat and in general sphere. Radio broadcasts in Indian languages from Rangoon are under the aegis of one section of Hikari Kikan headquarters. Agents sent into India have carried leaflets and have been instructed to disseminate rumors. For combat propaganda, one I.N.A. unit carried 210,000 leaflets; another was equipped with 285,000 leaflets. A few portable printing presses have been available and have been used at the front for producing leaflets.

Certain field units of Hikari Kikan's I.N.A. are charged with the reception and indoctrination of Indian prisoners of war. A recent Japanese Army directive for the treatment of prisoners of war in Burma laid special emphasis on the way in which to deal with captured Indian troops. They were to be handled with special care, and any who demonstrated a desire to join up with Japanese controlled forces were to be enrolled in the I.N.A. After a few weeks of indoctrination and conditiong in one of the centers just behind the front, they were to be returned to combat as allies of the Japanese. This "quick release" treatment of prisoners succeeded in some measure in augmenting the I.N.A. forces, but some of the presumably indoctrinated Indian troops promptly returned to the British lines. The Japanese have had much more success with the so-called "hard-core Jifs". These are either civilians or former Indian Army soldiers, most of the latter captured in Malaya, who have become so thoroughly indoctrinated by Japanese propaganda that the Japanese can place absolute reliance on them.

Still other Hikari Kikan personnel have been trained as Civil Affairs officials and appeared during the short-lived Japanese occupation of part of the Manipur plain. Civilian Jifs wearing armbands inscribed with the letters 'A-D'[2] in white have been seen. Their role presumably was to take over the administration of conquered territories in India.

The possibilities of exploiting the Indian political situation have not been overlooked by Hikari Kikan. The use of Subhas Chandra Bose, in itself, was a brilliant though futile attempt to arouse the Indian population. Beyond that, agents have been dispatched into India to contact political leaders and thus to pave the way for a Japanese invasion.

The Japanese General Staff counted heavily on the aid their troops would supposedly receive, once the Japanese standard was planted on a bit of Indian soil, from the revolt of the people of India. Hikari Kikan was to be the instrumentality whereby the nominally independent forces of "Free India" were controlled by the Japanese Army. The authority empowering Hikari Kikan to control and coordinate all phases of the "I" offensive (the propaganda-espionage-subotage assault on India) did not come into effect until the end of 1943.

While the Japanese established espionage schools and military training camps for Indians soon after the conquest of Burma, their early efforts in the utilization of these Indians were not well organized and were generally unsuccessful. Internal dissension among the Jifs at Singapore and elsewhere was temporarily halted by the advent of Subhas Chandra Bose. In July 1943, Bose assumed leadership of the Indian Independence League (I.I.L.) and of the League's armed forces, the Indian National Army. Bose proceeded to reorganize the Jif movement. In October 1943, the Burma branch of Hikari Kikan was also reorganized, its personnel increased and its authority strengthened. By December 1943, the Burma branch numbered more than 100 Japanese, including officers, civilians and non-commissioned personnel, and was empowered to coordinate the "I" offensive.

All this authority was on paper, however. In reality as one Hikari Kikan officer complained in his diary, the Hikari Kikan has no authority to issue orders in the field. Army Unit Commanders had full power over the Jif groups attached to their commands. And, the same diarist comments, the Japanese Army generally regarded the I.N.A. as an espionage group rather than as a true national army. Hence both military and civilian Jifs seem to have been used for routine reconniassance tasks and were not employed as Hikari Kikan had planned and as Army Headquarters had ordered.

---

2. It stood for Azad Hind Dal.

The description of Hikari Kikan activities which follows is based on incomplete evidence which occasionally contradicts itself. The internal contradictions of the data are, however, readily understandable when we realize that the Japanese and Jifs themselves are a bit confused on the exact organizational authority of Hikari Kikan, that there are internal feuds, that there are over-lapping jurisdictions, in short, that Hikari Kikan-Burma Branch, suffers from the faults of a war agency hastily conceived and too quickly thrown together and into action.

Organisation.

As a result of the reorganization of December 1943, the Burma Branch of Hikari Kikan was divided into five sections, with headquarters in the Golden Valley Estate, Rangoon. Each of these sections is responsible for certain phases of Hikari Kikan activities and the work of every section is coordinated with that of the five Hikari Kikan outpost agencies. The outposts are supposed to act as liaison posts and as forward operating bases for agents in the field.

The chief of the Hikari Kikan is Lt. General Isoda Saburu. His Chief of Staff is Colonel Yamamoto. Early in 1944 the General Headquarters of Hikari Kikan moved from Singapore to Rangoon.

The Commanding Officer of the Burma Branch of Hikari Kikan is Lt. Colonel Kitabe, who had five officers attached to his staff in December 1943, three Lieutenant Colonels, one Major and one Medical Corps Captain.

Section One. This Section is in charge of general affairs and the intendence and prevention of espionage.

Section ("Han") One of the Headquarters staff is a secretariat section, having a strength of three officers, eight non-commissioned officers and eight civilians. It has jurisdiction over administrative affairs.

This section is also charged with maintaining security and conducts counter-espionage activities. The Annual Report of Hikari Kikan for 1943 makes special note of the organization of security and counter-espionage service. It says that attempts have been made to collect information in order to forestall enemy plans, especially these directed against the I.N.A. and the I.I.L. This was done :

(a) By keeping in close touch with the military police and similar organizations, as well as with branch political "Hans" and military "Hans".

(b) By attempting positive counter-espionage work, i.e., the exposure of the enemy intelligence system.

The security paragraphs of the Annual Report assert that the Indians themselve felt keenly the need for a counter-espionage service and one was organized within the I.I.L. and the I.N.A. in August, the object being to enable the Indian himselft to detect spies. The report notes that the general system of counter-espionage, supervised by the Hikari Agency, would be complete at the end of 1943. No details of the system are given, save that it would be under the control of the Burma Branch in all important essentials. It would seen from this that an internal network in the Gestapo style has been set up within the I.I.L. and the I.N.A. The Indians in these organizations must be well aware of this and may resent its existence.

Section Two. This section is charged with the direction of the affairs of the Indian Independence League.

The supervision of the I.I.L. and its associated Youth Training Centre is in charge of the three Japanese civilians who comprise the personnel of Section Two. This section, despite its small personnel, is one of the most important within Hikari Kikan. The I.I.L. has been conceived by the Japanese command as the means whereby millions of Indians would be rallied to the standard of the Greater East Asia Co-Prosperity Sphere. The League extends its activities to all territories in conquered Asia where Indians reside, but it is specially active in Burma where the motherland of the League's members lies just beyond the front. The Burma chapters of the I.I.L. were formerly under the direction of Bileshwar Prashad, who became President of the Burma I.I.L. in September 1942.

Prashad was succeeded by Karim Gani in March 1943. About that time Hikari Kikan took hold of the League in Burma and gave a great impetus to the League's activity. Presumably Hikari Kikan furnished whatever supplies and services the Japanese Army had to offer to further the interests of the League.

Soon after that, Subhas Chandra Bose assumed leadership. His arrival in Rangoon in July 1943 marked the opening of an intensified drive to persuade and coerce Indians in Burma to "donate" their money and services to Bose's movements. Bose raised many recruits for the I.N.A. and substantial sums of money. The "mobilization of wealth" enabled him to establish the National Bank of Azad Hind, Ltd. So affluent has Bose become of late that he recently contributed a munificient gift of Rs. 500,000 to Bu Maw's daughter on the occasion of her wedding. This sum may well be charged up to the purchase of goodwill on the books of the I.I.L.

The Japanese Government has backed up Bose. In October 1943 the Provisional Government of Free India was recognized by Japan and later by other Axis countries. At that time, Bose assumed the title of "Netaji-Fuehrer"—and the Andamans and Nicobars were nominally handed over to the Provisional Government with much ceremony and protestations of mutual esteem.

Meanwhile detachments of the I.N.A. were moving into Burma and headquarters of the I.I.L. in Burma was reinforced by many of the League's top personnel from Malaya, including a Colonel Alagappan who was Bose's Deputy. The League official toured throughout Burma, giving pop talks, persuading local Indians to cooperate and inducing them to contribute cash.

A fine flurry of meetings and celebrations took place in December 1943. The monthly report of Hikari Kikan for that month lists seven gala occasions, including a "Festival of Popular Gratitude" for the transfer of the Andaman and Nicobar Islands to be staged in January 1944, a conference of League branch leaders of lower Burma, and an entertainment for "about fifty people who have contributed over ¥ 20,000 to the Nethaji fund".

One paragraph in the same report states that Hikari Kikan will furnish every facility to the Bose government in preparation for the scheduled shift of the League headquarters to Burma. Officers of the Provisional Government were seheduled to be established in Rangoon by the end of January 1944. The "Government" officers were to be in Harbin Road. Bose himself was to live on University Avenue and his ministers on Park Road.

In the same document, Hikari Kikan officials are instructed to direct the attention of the Bose establishment to the necessity for taking defensive and counter-espionage measures. Just how the Japanese in this section of Hikari Kikan exercise their control over the I.I.L. and the Provisional Government is not clear. Nor is the exact relationship between the I.I.L. and the Provisional Government clear. However, office holders of one are very often officials in the other as well.

The League's headquarters, now in Rangoon, is divided into eight units.

Unit A.	Civilian recruitment and training. This is run by Jifs of the I.N.A.
Unit B.	Propaganda. Also managed by I.N.A. Jifs, notably Colonel Alagappan and Colonel Gilani
Unit C.	Art. This presumably has to do with posters and drawings for leaflets.
Unit D.	Field Propaganda.

Unit E.	Supply.
Unit F.	Accounts.
Unit G.	Reconstruction.
Unit H.	Women's Department.

The first four units are closely allied with I.N.A. and will be further treated in the discussion of the I.N.A. The Reconstruction department is intended to furnish plans and personnel for the government of territories to be conquered in India. This contingent of military government is known as "Azad Hind Dal". The representatives of this department were in Tamu at the end of May; there were about thirty of them, mostly Bengali civilians although they held honorary official rank in the I.N.A. Each bore an armband incribed with the letters A.H.D. in white.

The Women's Department may have something to do with the Rani of Jhansi Regiment, a regiment composed entirely of women under the command of Captain S. Lakshmi.

The League has a Youth Training Centre in Rangoon which had some 700 students in November 1943. Five classes were under training, each being groomed for specialized tasks. These were :

(1) Administration of occupied territories.

(2) Special duties (possibly this means espionage and sabotage).

(3) Field propaganda.

(4) Counter-espionage.

(5) I.N.A. Trainees.

A new class was under formation for training in wireless communications. Each class had eight instructors and auxilliary instruction was given by branch members. The Hikari Kikan report for December notes that special attention is to be given to the strengthening of training in counter-espionage. The class was to be specially indoctrinated and "all members will create an atmosphere of sincerity such as is seldom seen, by swearing a solemn oath to commit suicide of their own volition if they neglect their studies or fail in their duties."

Hikari Kikan, at the end of 1943, seemed to be greatly aware of the necessity of taking counter- espionage measures. In addition to the counter-espionage system, established within the I.I.L., and the class of 33 students then undergoing special counter-espionage training at the Youth Training Centre, still more personnel were to be selected from the Centre for the Underground Spy (Senka Teicho) Section. The first class was to be ready for its duties by the end of January.

Another paragraph in the counter-espionage section of the December report stated that preliminary investigations of the officials who hold office under the British had been carried out.

Both the Japanese and Bose were taken in by their own propaganda. The whole abortive offensive into Manipur seems to have been premised on the idea that Japanese occupation of any bit of Indian territory would be sufficient impetus for a wholesale revolution in India. The consequent decimation of three Japanese divisions will undoubtedly affect the consideration of the use of Bose and his Jif followers.

An interesting exposition of Bose's fallacy is contained in a document which was issued by Hikari Kikan on 15 January 1944 at the headquarters of the Ratsu Division. In this document the part to be played by the Forward Bloc in India is stressed. The Forward Bloc was that part of the Indian National Congress which formerly adhered to the views of Bose. While it has some members in Indiàn even now, its activities are by no means as dangerous to the Allies as the Hikari document would make them out to be. The document says :

"The Bloc includes a Propaganda Department and 'Secret Warfare' Department. The latter had been carrying out underground activities since the foundation of the party, and its personnel unlike those attached to the former (who have mostly been arrested), have so far escaped imprisonment. They are now preparing both to enlarge their membership and stir up a revolution. Unfortunately, however, an internal revolution will not in itself suffice to eradicate British Military Power. Accordingly, as soon as the Japanese Army strikes the first blow against the British inside India, the population will be awakened from its dream about Britain's power and a really great rising may be expected. Therefore, judging from the situation inside India, the sooner the Japanese Army attacks India the better; Should the Indians make a compromise with Britain the internal situation will suddenly turn to Britain's advantage. Furthermore, militarily speaking, she will have time to strengthen the defence of Eastern India.

"For this reason military operations need never be on a large scale; our object can be attained satisfactorily by local operations. Accordingly we should gain success by creating a situation of panic within India, using our propaganda to inflame the Indians' own will to fight."

Section Three. The section has charge of general intelligence, editing of espionage reports, translation work, general propaganda, photograhic work, printing and broadcasting.

Every Wednesday, at 1500 hours, a meeting is held in the committee room of the Broadcasting Administration Office in Rangoon. Representatives of Section Three of Hikari Kikan play an important role in these meetings at which the trend of radio propaganda during the coming week is determined. The head of the Propaganda Department of the I.I.L. is present, as are officers of the Army Propaganda Department and the Burma Broadcasting Administration. But the evidence indicates that it is the Hikari Kikan officials who actually decide what the propaganda line is to be.

Several different propaganda media come within the sphere of Section Three. In addition to radio broadcasts, the thirteen Japanese civilians of this Han supervise the production of leaflets and the publication of newspapers. All propaganda disseminated from headquarters lies within their jurisdiction. Combat propaganda, however, is the task of Section Four of Hikari Kikan.

In addition to its propaganda jobs, Section Three edits intelligence reports from the field, furnishes translation services, analyzes the flow of intelligence and disseminates intelligence summaries. It acts as a reporting board as well as the agency of propaganda control. The actual dissemination of propaganda from headquarters very often is done by the propaganda Department of the I.I.L., but it is clear that the League's propagandists take their views from Hikari Kikan officials, an American or a British soldier?" and then proceeded to write the answer. Clues of effective propaganda against the enemy may well be gleanded from the enemy's propaganda to us.

Newspaper

A large printing press of Hikari headquarters of Rangoon turns out four newspapers, all of which are nominally published by the I.I.L. Our air raids over Rangoon curtailed the output of newspapers when one of the presses was destroyed and the printers fled. The shortage of newsprint further complicates the efforts to keep these publications going. But because newspapers are considered to be of high propaganda value, their production receives high priority. In the words of one Hikari Kikan report "Education of the Indians in Burma and the inculcation of the spirit of independence in them, will be promoted by the following newspaper."

Four newspapers were being published in December 1943 :

Azad Hindustan—weekly in Hindustani—2,000 copies.

Sudandara Hindustan—twice weekly in Tamil—5,000 copies.

Sawatantara Hindustan—twice weekly in Telegu—1,500 copies.

Azad Hind—weekly in English, the successor to "New Order".

Motion Pictures—Japanese propagands films are distributed by Hikari Kikan for showing to Indian troops and civilians. Photographs of the I.N.A. are posted on bulletin boards in Japanes posts.

Intelligence Report and Summaries

Hikari Kikan intelligence summaries, by Allied standards, are sketchy but fairly accurate. Ground sources in the contatizone and boradcast monitoring seems to supply the bulk of their information. Photo reconnaissance and deep penetration information are very weak. The Japanese do not hesitate to report facts unpleasant to themselves but their deductions from these facts, and their analysis of Allied intentions are frequently very wide of the mark.

One Intelligence Summary which covers the period 16 December to 25 December 1943 contained seven parts. It bore the seal "Oura", perhaps indicating authorship by Caption Oura, Commander of Section Four of Hikari Kikan headquarters.

Part 1. "Summary"—the highlights of the periods are briefly mentioned, including intensive bombing by Allied planes, numerous reconnaissance flights over likely landing points and the completion of the new road to the front by the Allies.

Part 2. "Enemy Dispositions on the Indo-Burma Frontier"—gives Allied troop dispositions in nine areas, ranging fron Chittagong to Waikhong. The information in this part is fragmentary but definitely useful to the Japanese Command.

Part 3. "Enemy Air Situation"—is very scanty. It gives nothing more than the mention of several Allied raids and the names of a few Allied Air Commanders, the latter heard over the Delhi radio. The judge from this report, the Japanese have very little information concerning our air Order of Battle.

Part 4. "Enemy Shipping Position"—is also extremely brief and uniformative. Two bits of information are given, one concerning a convoy in the Bay of Bengal, its presence deduced from wireless interception, and te other a report of an air reconnaissance over the water south of Chittagang.

Part 5. "Military Interception"—deals, in some detail, with tours taken by Allied commanders and by officials of the Government of India. Excerpts from Allied broadcasts included President Roosevelt's declaration that American had sent 3,800,000 men abroad and that the number would be increased to 5,000,000 men in July 1944. Three excerpts from statements by King George, Lord Linlithgow and Admiral Mountbatton, respectively, say that the defeat of Japan will follow the downfall of Germany.

Part 6. "Points from Military Topography"—contains road report from the Allied combat zone. These reports are comparatively full and accurate, and, indeed, constitute the best intelligence of this summary.

Appendix A.— Lists 30 more road reports which are headed "Assam Road Reports, Based on investigations carried out by the I.I.L., the Investigation Han ("Chosa Han") and the Hikari Organization Agencies at Kalewa and Homalin, dated 13th December, 1943."

Appendix B— "Organization of SEAC and India command"—Contains little more than could be gleaned from Delhi broadcasts.

Section Four. This Section has charge of military intelligence, special operative work, and propaganda in the field.

Propaganda and intelligence are functions of this section, but the propaganda carried on by Section Four is field propaganda employed in combat situations, as contrasted with the general propaganda emnating from headquarters, which is the responsibility of Section Three. The intelligence tasks of this Section include specifically military information and the intelligence derived from the activities of deep penetration agents. The training of these agents, their staging, briefing and utilization, is apparently the job of Section Four.

Field Propaganda. Leaflet distribution and loud speaker appeals are the two main media of Hikari combat propaganda. Broadcasts of Indians in the Allied ranks are given first priority. As one Hikari documents put it, "The aim of these broadcasts being to convince them (Indian troops) of the sincerity of the Japanese Army, certain victory for the Axis and the defeat of the British." Annotating this statement, the document reveals that the encouragement of anti-British resistance and the promotion of a spirit of independence will contribute to the success of the operations of the Japanese Army.

As matters actually worked out, however, loud speaker appeals carried on by Section Four badly misfired. At Kohima, for example, both British and Indian troops were subjected to intensive Japanese propaganda, but the British troops were frequently addressed in Hindustani while the Indian troops were addressed in English. The Royal West Kents were the recipients of a grand promise that all deserters would be promoted to the rank of Jamdar.

Three mobile printing presses were posted along the Chindwin, immediately prior to the start of the offensive, to turn out spot leaflets. On 11 March, one of these presses was in operation on the East bank of the Chindwin and presumably was taken into Manipur. The leaflet campaign was no more successful than the loud speaker attempt. Comparatively few Indian troops deserted to the enemy and the effect on British units was slight.

Although Hikari Kikan, together with the Special Service Section (Tokumo Kikan) of the Japanese Army, were the chief instrumentalities whereby field propaganda was disseminated, the direction of the propaganda campaign was in the hands of the regular Army commanders. An order from 15th Army Headquarters, dated 17 January 1944 and addressed to 31 Division of the Homalin outpost of Hikari Kikan, detailed the procedure for field propaganda. It placed special emphasis on the Gurkha propaganda scheme which seems to have been a particular favorite of the Japanese command. The order, signed by General Mutaguchi Renya, commanding officer, 15th Army, stated:

"1. The Army in Burma will carry out propaganda in the field according to the Gurkha Propaganda Scheme and also the Army Propaganda Scheme. In carrying out this propaganda scheme for India, the Hikari Commander will come under the orders of the Army Commanders, in the direction of field propaganda against the Gurkhas, as this part of he scheme is of military and defensive importance.

"2. Army commanders will direct field propaganda against the Gurkhas in accordance with Hayashi Operation order B/51 and based on the Gurkha Propaganda Scheme. In this field propaganda work the local Hikari Advanced Dett. will assist.

"3. Divisional Commanders will be able to carry out this field propaganda with the aid of the local Hikari Dett. (with the exception of the Maymyo

Branch), and will also utilize their own Intelligence Tais. The main object of these scheme is to sow dissension among Gurkha troops. The local Hikari detachments will come under the orders of Divisional Infantry Commanders, in this propaganda work against Gurkhas."

The Appendix to the order was entitled "Propaganda Scheme Against Gurkha Troops".

1. **Policy**—In carrying out propaganda against India, the national character of the Gurkhas and the special conditions prevailing in Nepal should be borne in mind and utilized in the anti-British struggle. In particular we must strive to arouse dissension among Gurkha troops.

2. **Organization Orders**—The C in C of the Army in Burma and the Commander of the Hikari organization will carry out this propaganda in accordance with Appendix to Mori operation order B/34. This propaganda will take three forms.

   (i) Propaganda in the field.

   (ii) Internal propaganda.

   (iii) Establishment of communications.

"Propaganda in the field is the responsibility of the Army in Burma which will instruct Hikari organizations as to method of operation.

"In accordance with the outline of the propaganda scheme for India (Appendix to Mori Operation Order B/34) the C in C 15 Army and G.O.C. 55 Div. will direct forward detachments of Hikari organization to carry out this propaganda in the field.

"Propaganda other than that mentioned in paragraph 4 will be the responsibility of Hikari organization. Outline as follows:

"Internal propaganda to breed anti-British fooling in Nepal, to prepare for the establishment of an anti-British Government and to cause disaffection of Gurkha troops. To further this propaganda we must establish reliable means of communication between Burma and Nepal.

3. **The Meaning of Propaganda in the Field**—Our object is to sow dissension among Gurkha troops in the front line and in the rear.

4. Plan of action regarding Gurkhas is based on permission to permit against the British by making use of the special conditions prevailing in Nepal due to feuds between the Royal families and hostility of the population towards these families.

"In connection with this propaganda, Japanese political attitude towards Nepal is that when India gains complete freedom we shall also be able to grant Nepal her independence without delay.

"In our propaganda, we emphasize that at present Nepal is independent only in name and that, in diplomatic and military matters, she is completely under British control. There can be no real independence for Nepal until the British are defeated. The British hinder all economic and educational development in Nepal. We believe that the British have taken away the Gurkhas livelihood and have made him merely a solider-slave."

Deep Penetartion

Among the Hikari Kikan lists which have been taken, there is one which is entitled "Table of Spies and Liaison Personnel disciplines during the year 1943". This might have been a most valuable and information document had it been more accurate and complete. Parties of agents which were definitely known to have been dispatched into India and not listed, while some groups which apparently never were sent in are mentioned. Moreover, the 104 agents enumerated as being destined for deep penetration represent only a part of the total number of Hikari Kikan personnel available for aspionage missions. No names are given in the lists. The number of "Spice and Mission—Personnel" dispatched from Rangoon to staging areas near the front comes to a total of 568 men.

These discrepanies indicate that Hikari activities have not been so well coordinated. There is other evidence to show that the weekly directive were not always interpreted in the same way by the outposts and by Army commanders as they were at Headquarters. The organization of Hikari Kikan work, specially as it concerns deep penetration operation,, was not entirely efficient. When parties arrived at staging areas, it was frequently found that no preparations had been made to send them forward. Trail Intelligence was usually lacking and communications preparations were exceedingly crude. The Japanese, however, have been quick to recognize these defects and have steadily tried to improve all phase of Hikari Kikan work. They have given special attention to tightening up the deep penetration procedures.

Training Schools for Deep Penetration

In this attempting to lighten up their deep penetration procedures, they have changed their network of agent training schools from a haphazard set of poorly organized centers to a well integrated system with relatively fewer schools but with a much more practical curriculum. More than a dozen different training schools for Hikari Kikan personnel are known to have existed in Burma and Malaya. Most of these are defunct, but three are still carrying on.

The earlier schools, all of which are now either defunct or recognized, were small and were staffed wholly or chiefly by Indians. Both the staff and students of these earlier schools were of poor caliber for Hikari purposes. It is to be remembered that the Hikari Kikan organization did not take over full control or deep penetration operations until the latter half of 1943 after the first schools had been in operation for a year or more.

The instructors at the schools which were first established were primarily propagandists with limited technical knowledge and experience. The students were, on the whole, volunteers who were motivated by political considerations and who had no training of a military nature. The instruction given was very circumscribed. It consisted chiefly of "inspirational" lectures on the holy mission against the Allies, with some training in progaganda methods and some small arms practice. The schools which were established later and those which are now in operation are more efficient. They have larger staffs and have more Japanese Army men as instructors. The Indian instructors are men who have themselves engaged in Hikari operations. The students, too, are now selected with more care and are more suitable for the work. Rangoon and Penang have been the principle centres for the training of agents. A total of some 13 schools are known to have existed in the two places, eight in Penang and five in Rangoon, out of these 13 schools only three are still in operation, namely; the Rangoon Sawaraj Institute, Kanbe and the Swaraj Young Men's Training Institute, Thingangyun in Rangoon, and the "Sandy Croft" School in Penang.

Kanba

The Kanbe school was one of the first established and became one of the largest of the training institutes. At one time, it had over 700 students. It originated as school for volunteers from the local chapters of the Indian Independence League. For a while, it ran along in a desultory fashion with a very short course of training and few practical demostrations. About the beginning of 1943 it was changed from this amateur basis and become an important centre or the production of trained agents.

The school was first heard of in a broadcast during September 1942. It was then described as an institute for training young Indians for membership in the Independence Movement. It seems that two courses, each of which lasted about a month, were held in the last quarter of 1942. Early in 1943, a six weeks course was initiated and another one was started in April 1943.

The aims of the Kanbe school were at first somewhat confused. One of the students believed that he was destined to undertake intelligence tasks for the Japanese; others seem to have believed that they would eventually become administrators of areas in India which had been taken over from the Allies.

Recruiting for this school was first done through the district branches of the Indian Independences League, although the school itself sent out recruiting parties from time to time . The recruiting was not successful.

Special Operative Section	Wireless Communication Section	Counter Espionage Section	Gaoshala Training Camp

The same captured document records that steps were being taken in December 1943 to improve and complete the training. More instructors were to be provided and more help was to be given by Hikari Kikan members; the hours of instruction in Japanese were increased; certain reforms in the internal administration and the training were effected, the latter including long route marches, all on the Japanese model.

The Special Operative Section, Kanbe S.Y.H.T.I.

Special attention was paid to the toughening of members as the following extract from a captured document shows: "all members from this section will live in the open, in tents pitcched on the sports field of the Training Centres and will do their own cooking; they will be trained in all branches of study. Though they will be plagued by mosquitoes and suffer from the severe cold at night, these hardships will build up a spirit of hardships."

Little is known about the training carried out inside the school, but a captured document reveals that a forced march from Rangoon to Eoulmein and back was planned. On the march students were to carry out political exercises, "directed towards the 50,000 Indians in the district". These exercises were to include practice in spreading propaganda in spying, in recruiting students, in lectures and in communication by wireless.

The reference to wireless training agrees with other information that about 60 students from this section had completed their wireless training by the end of December 1943. The same report states that an additional 22 trained W/T personnel would meet requirements " for the opening of operations" which are assumed to have been the Manipur operations which commenced in March of this year. Wireless training is not a new feature of the Kanbe curriculum, for it is known that in the middle of 1943 two parties were earmarked for such training. One of these was believed to have gone to Boundary Road, Rangoon.

The Wireless Communications Section, Kanbe S.Y.M.T.I.

This sections consisted of 10 men but nothing more is known about their training or movements. They are not to be confused with the personnel of the Special Operative Section undergoing W/T training, as mentioned in the preceding paragraph.

The Counter Espionage Section, Kanbe S.Y.M.T.I.

This Section is mentioned in the Hikari Kikan Annual Report for 1943. This report reveals that Hikari Kikan's efforts for better security before the provisional Government moved into Burna lead to the formation for this section. The document clained that 33 men were especially selected for it. These men are said to have begun training on 11 December 1943, but apparently due to Bose's interference stopped it in February 1944. This appears to have been the first real attempt to set up a defensive counter-espionage system made by Hikari Kikan, which has usually appeared to engage in offensive intelligence.

Thingangyun.

The Thingangyun school is the largest of a group of schools founded and directed by an old Indian revolutionary known as Hari Singh, alias Usman Khan. It was opened at the end of 1942 to receive students for advance training from another school which Hari Singh had founded in Penang. It also took Indians recruited by Indian Independence League in Burma. The first course lasted from January to April 1943, and included about 90 students, half of the Punjabis. Their training was supposed to be very comprehensive; instruction was given in propaganda work, espionage and sabotage, and some of the students were removed from the course to undergo specialized training as parachutists or as radio operators and a few even returned to Penang for a "submarine and boating" course. Most of the original classes were dispatched for deep penetration work and a good many of them have been apprehended.

The curriculum was varied one. There was a course in the manufacture of bombs; daily instruction was given in the handling of rifles, revolvers, and submachine-guns. There were practical monouvers to test the ability of the students to carry out sabotage tasks and they were given a good deal of practice in entering places guarded by barbed wire and other abstacles. One reports they even had instruction covering methods of injecting poison.

One of the agents dispatched from Thingangyun testified under interrogation that his instructions were to hamper communication by damaging railway lines, telegraph wires, post offices and other government buildings. This was the usual testimony as to the training and instruction of agents at Thingangyun, but this interrogation report also included the mission of undertaking antidemolition meansures in the event of British withdrawal. The agents were instructed to join British demolition parties and, after gaining their complete confidence, to pretend to assure responsibility for the demolition of strategic intallations. In that way they could preserve these installations intact for the use of the advancing Japanese forces.

The code work for Thingangyun seems to have beeen extremely rudimentary. One member of a contact party stated that he was taught 17 words, 11 of which are produced below. Messages of a domestic nature, deaths, marriage, arrivals and departures denoting operations are sent; the subject of the message relates to a military or naval unit and the verb is either sent in clear or denotes some opertaion activity. The words of the code are as follows :

Mangni—Army
Acheha—2 Dvisionas
O.K.—3 Divisions
Bahut Achcha—4 Divisons or 2 War Ships
Pita—Aircraft Carrier
Mata—Crusier
Larka—Destroyer
Larki—Submarine
Shadi Hogai—Army has moved off
Bimar—Ready for attack
Margay—Unsuccessful

Besides the Kanbe and Thingangyun institutes, three other Jif Training schools are known to have existed in Rangoon: (1) Biren Roy's School, (2) Baba Amar Singh's School, and (3) the Golden Valley Hikari Kikan Training Centre. All three are now defunct.

Biren Roy's School.

This school was founded and run by Biren Roy, an ex detenu of Dacca. It was opened in the latter half of 1942 and was located in Neojy Building, Sparkes Street, Rangoon. There was no regular staff except Biren

Roy himself, but N.K. Bannerjee of the Thingangyun Institute and some of the senior students also lectured occasionally. There were about 32 students, all Bengalis recruited in Burma.

The training consisted mostly of informal discussions. Fire-Arms pratices was conducted on the roof. The students were not allowed to leave the building. The school was more of an informal secret group than a regular training centre.

The students were trained with a view to deep penetration operations. It was planned that parties should infiltrate into india and there cause internal confusion. Students were instructed to resort to "money actions" when in need of funds to sabotage railway and telegraph lines and to cause strikes.

From time to time small parties were sent off for infiltration into India. They were provided with revolvers and small amounts of forged Indian notes. They were told that the arms were to be used in self- defense and, if arrested, for suicide .

Baba Amar Singh's School

This school was founded in February or March 1943 by Baba Amar Singh who was brought by the Japanese from Bangkok to Burma for the purpose of organizing intelligence activities. The school was opened in Rangoon but was later moved to Mawlaik.

The staff consisted of Baba Amar Singh himself and two of his chief recruiters, Chanda Singh and Ram Kekha.

There were about 25 students who were of poor type.

While located at Rangoon, little useful training was given. After moving to Mawlaik , some elementary instruction in bomb making and the use of small arms was given.

A member of agents from this school were sent to Manipur state to contact the ex-royal family and to engage in sabotage, espionage and propaganda against troops and government employees. As far as is known, all these agents were arrested before they had approached their tasks. One feature peculiar to this school is that the parties were provided with guides, residents of the Indo-Burma frontier areas, who had been through the same training as the agents themselves. Some of these guides were intended to provide the communications between the agents and the Japanese.

The Golden Valley Hikari Kikan Training Center

At least one course of instruction for Jifs is known to have been given at the Rangoon Headquarters of Hikari kikan at the Golden Valley Estate. This course began early in June 1943.

The instructors were either wholly, or almost wholly, Japanese. The students trained in this course were all Gurkhs, some were civilians and some military personnel, who were specially selected from the Swaraj Young Men's Training Institute, Rangoon, with a view to their special training as agents for contact work with British Burkha troops in operational areas.

The training given consisted in propaganda lectures along the same lines as those given to the Gurkhas in the Penang Training School (i.e., that Nepal was not an independent country but enslaved to the British; that the Gurkhas should therefore fight to gain independence; that the Japanese, unlike the British, had no desire to rule Asia or India, but wished merely to act as guides to all brother Asiatics), and instruction in map reading, espionage, sabotage, the theory of making and using hand grenades and bombs, and guerrilla warfare.

Despite the training in guerrilla warfare, which was probably largely, if not wholly, theoretical in character, it is quite clear from the instructions they received on being dispatched to the forward areas that they were intended at act as contact propagandists against British Gurkha troops and were not expected to infiltrate behind the lines.

Penang

During the latter half of 1942 no fewer than five Jif training schools were opened in Penang: 1. the Samraj Institute, managed by Raghavan; 2. the Penang Propaganda School, controlled by Hari Singh, alias Usman Khan; 3. The Chopra School also cont¨olled by Hari Singh; 4. A school for Muslim prisoners of war, under Colonel Gilani; and 5. a small school for Singhalese.

Two courses were held at Raghavan's Institute, the Short Course which began early in August 1942 and lasted about six weeks, and the Long Course which began about September 1942 and continued until May 1943 when it was disbanded.

The Short Course had 32 students, all civilians, largely South Indians, who were recruited in various parts of Malaya by Raghavan himself.

The time-table allotted 10 hours a day to lectures on politics, espionage, methods of infiltration, methods of secret graphic correspondence, propaganda, Indian history and Indian geography. Students were also taught Morse code, elementary Cipher work and the use of small arms. The course officially closed at the end of August but there was an additional fortnight's training in swimming and the use of canvas and rubber boats.

The aim of the Short Course was to train parties of agents who were to proceed by Submarine to India, there to link up with other parties from the Institute who should be sent by the overland route. The agents were to collect information about the strength, composition, disposition and morale of the fighting services, about communication and transport facilites, the labor situation, workshops and factories, the state of public morale, and the attitude of the civil and military towards Japan. They were also to conduct propaganda about the impending invasion and subsequent liberation of India by Japan. They were to organize strikes and boycotts and to work in cooperation with Congress elements, urging them to commit sabotage.

In most cases exact instructions regarding areas of operation were not given, such phrases as "North West India", "the East Coast", or "Bombay and Karachi" being used. Some agents were to have roving commissions all over India, collecting all the informations they could on the wide variety of subjects mentioned above.

Two submarine parties of five agents each were landed at different points on the West Coast at the end of September 1942. Some weeks later 10 other agents attempted to cross into India from Burma in small groups. The arrangement was for the submarine agents to contact the land agents by means of posts addresses and rendezvous. Each submarinc agent was to have a land agent as his partner with whom he was to work. Information was to be collected by the submarine agents and passed to the land agents who were to send it to Burma by locally administered messengers or to take it themselves. Nothing came of this plan as all the agents concerned were arrested before they could got to work. Two of the renaining six crossed into India from Burma and were arrested.

The Long Course began before the Short Course had finished. It was originally intended to last for three months but dragged on until May 1943.

The students were mostly civilians selected by the I.I.L. in Malaya, but a certain number of prisoners of war were also included. Various estimates of the total number in the Long Course have been reported but the probable figure is approxinately 100. As in the case of the Short Course, the majority were South Indians.

The training was on much the same lines as that given in the Short Course, but more attention was paid to details. Students were divided into 3 divisions, specializing in political work, propaganda, or special operational espionage. All students were lectured in Economics, Hygiene, and First Aid; they were also taught military drill and the use of rubber boats.

One member of the Long course who has been apprchened was instructed to supervise the work of the Short Course students who had already proceeded to India, and also to prepare for Long Course submarine landings on the West Coast of India early in 1943. When the other Long Course agents arrive in India, he was to try and place them in regimental contractors institutes and was himself then to form an agency and travel around inspecting his agents. There is no information of the plan being put into practices and no use has been made of Long Course students as a whole, though some may have joined other training centers. It has been stated, however, that the Long Course was disbanded and sent home because the Japanese became suspicious of Raghavan, whom they removed and interned for a time.

With the termination of the Long Course in May 1943, the school was closed. Some of the students took up duties at various I.I.L. institutions in Malaya, while, in September, many more joined the I.N.A. Officers' Training Center in Singapore.

Hari Singh's Propaganda School. Hari Sing's Propaganda School was opened in September 1942 by Hari Singh, alias Usman Khan. The school was located at 34 Northan Road, Penang, in a building which is generally known as "Dr. Jaggat Singh's Sea-side Residence."

Hari Singh was assisted by Sukchain Nath Chopra of Gujranwalla, a former schoolmaster in the Malaya Educational Service, and Mohd. Zahir Khan, alias Moti. Later R.L. Avasti, a former wireless operator from the Andamans, became the leader of the school.

Recruiting appears to have been carried out mainly through I.I.L. though individuals or small groups may have been specially selected by Hari Singh or his own recruiters. Students have come to this training center from Shanghai, Bangkok and Malaya. Some of them have been prisoners of war. In December 1942 some 70 students were reported to be attending the course, while the total intake between November 1942 and April 1943 is reported to have been 132. In December 1942, about 70 students were sent to undergo further training at Hari Singh's Thingangyun Institute, while two other batches of over 20 were detached to join other institutions at Penang.

Training

There seems to have been no fixed syllabus. Students were, however, instructed in propaganda methods, the use of small arms, bomb making, sabotage and disguises. Special items such as the establishment of communication systems, "Submarine and boating" training, and possible parachute jumping were also included. A code was taught by which agents operating in India were intended to communicate intelligence through the All India Radio Welfare.

Early in 1943, the students of Hari Singh's School came to be known as "Avasti's party", as the name of their leader was R.L. Avasti, a former wireless operator from the Andamans. More students from Singapore joined this group and also others of Hari Singh's followers from Shanghai who had arrived in Penang in December 1942. Avasti's Party faded from the Penang picture in May 1943 when he, with 30 of this party and 10 of Sangha's group left for Burma to join the Swaraj Young Men's Institute, Thingangyun.

Penang.

The Pouning Propaganda School appears to have been largely a holding centre where prospective agents were given preliminary training while waiting to be sent to more specialized and advanced courses to other intelligence training centre.

The Chopra School.

The Chopra School was founded either towards the end of 1942 or very early in the 1943. It was originally located at 82 Northen Road, but moved in March 1943 to a more secluded area. The School was under the general direction of Hari Singh, but was under the immediate control of S.M. Chopra, former Headmaster of Batu Pahat High School. The staff consisted only of Chopra and a Japanese named Sakuna.

The original students of this school consisted of five brought back to Penang by Hari Singh from the Thingangyun Institute, Rangoon, for special training. They were joined in February 1943 by 19 others, bringing the total up to 24. Most of the students were North Indians.

The training given in the Chopra School was secret and nothing is known concerning it says that it included the usual political lectures which were given by Chopra, and small arms instruction which was given by Sakuna. "Submarine and boating" training was also probably a part of the curriculum.

In March 1943 the school moved to a more secluded area and began intensive training. This continued until September 1943 when Chopra and some of his students left the school, leaving the remainder of the shool to carry on as best they could. Its fate since that date is not definitely known, but it probably closed soon after.

Colonol Gilani's School for Prisoners of War.

The school for Muslim prisoners of war had 40 students and was under the direction of Colonel Gilani. As a result of dissension among the student's themselves, the school closed in November 1943 and the party returned to Singapore.

The Singhalese School.

Little is known of the Singhalese school except that intensive training in W/T and boating was given.

These five training schools actually achieved very little in the way of concrete results. One totally unsuccessful operation was undertaken by the students of the Short Course and it is reported that a party of agents landed in Ceylon in December 1943 which was probably composed of students from the Sinhalese Training centre. These two operations, so far as is known, constitute the sum total of results of the five schools.

Deep Penetration opertion. A number of attempts of deep penetration with India have been made by JIFSs. Defils of these attempts so far as they are know, fallons. In July 1943 a group of Patharis which have served as bodyguard to the D.M. Khan, M.R. Mulliale groups. Well recruited to return to India. They were to make contact with Muslim political circles, to organize general obstruction to the war effort, and to prepare the people for the invasion of the Jif army.

The party consisted of 12 members. Two were sent ahead in September 1942 as an advance group. They were followed in November by seven members of the group and the remaining three, including the leaders, arrived early in December 1942. All of these twelve agents, except one, passed through the British security organization. Of these, two were detained under the defense of India Rules, while eight were allowed to return to their homes in the Punjab under surveillance. They have now been re-arrested.

2. The elaborate but unsuccessful attempt of two parties of students from the Penang Short Course who landed by submarine on the West Coast of India at the end of September 1942 has already been described in connection with the account of Short Course hold in Raghavan's Swaraj Institute at Penang.

The execution of four of these agents was announced in October 1943. Two of the land agents who were to have cooperated with the agents landed by submarine, T.P. Kumaran Nair of Malabar and Ramu Thevar of the Ramnad District, Madras, both of whom were living in

Malaya at the outbreak of hostilities with Japan have also been executed.

3. At the end of April and beginning of May 1943, about 50 students of the Swaraj Young men's Training Institute, Thingangyan, left the school for deep penetration tasks in India. Fifteen of them have been apprehended and the remainder found their way to the Arakan and Chindwin fronts. It was probably planned that they should infiltrate into India, but it is likely that they eventually abandoned this plan and engaged in contact opertions.

4. In the fourth week of April 1943, seven parties of Jif parachute agents were dropped in Assam. These agents were the product of the First Parachute Course, held at Mingaladon and Penang.

   One of these parachute parties which was captured was supplied with money and equipment, including wireless transmission sets. Five members of this party, Ajaib Sing of Amritsar District, Zahir Ahmed of Sheikhpura District in the Punjab, S.L. Mazumder of Chttagong District in Bengal, Andeshwar Rai and Sham Lal Pande of Gorokhpur District in the United Provinces, have been convicted and condemned to death. The sentences of the last two, however, have commuted to transportation for life.

5. Sometime in the latter half of 1943 a number of agents trained in Baba Amar Singh's School were sent to Manipur State to contact the ex-royal Family, and to engage in sabotage, espionage and propaganda against troops and government employees. As far as is known, all the agents were arrested before they had approached their tasks.

6. In October 1943, a party of seven civilian Jifs were given money and dispatched from Kanwa to Chittagong with two Mugh guides. En route two membe of the party became separated by the remaining five, together with the two guides, went forward until they were arrested by a village defense party.

This group of seven agents was selected from a group of 24 or 25 Jifs that had been brought from a village near Akyab to Khaungdok when they had been brought to Kanwa. The Akyab group was composed of 16 civilians Jifs brought from Taungaup and 8 or 9 local civilian Jifs. The 16 Jifs from Taungup were in turn part of a party of 70 agents brought there by Maruyamn from the Rangoon Kanba Swaraj Institute.

The final instructions given to the group of 7 Jifs, all of whom were Bangalis, prior to their leaving Kanwa for Chittagong may be summarized as follows:

(a) Two of them were to proceed to the Chittagong district south of the Kamfuli River and :—

  (i) Put over the usual pro-Japanese propaganda surreptitiously, and gauge the reaction of the public.

  (ii) Try the contract local Congressmen or "patriots" with pro-Japanese inclinations and take them back to the enemy.

  (iii) Inform the public that there were 3,000,000 Indians in Burma well trained in military tactics.

  (iv) Ascertain whether Indians previously sent from Burma were carrying on similar propaganda or not.

  (v) Collect all possible information about military dispositions in the area specified.

(b) One of the agents, who is a resident of a village near Chittagong Town, was to proceed to the town and carry out the instuctions contained in (a) (1) and (5) above.

(c) The two remaining members were to proceed to the Chittagong Hill Tracts and carry out the same tasks as the two in (a) above.

7. The most recent attempt to deep penetration into India took place in March 1944 when 12 Muslim ex-prisoner of war agents were landed from a submarine on the coast of Baluchistan. These agents were members of an original party of 70 Muslims formed in September 1942 by "Lt. Col" Gilani, 1 Bahawalpur Inf. at Penang.

They received training in "Lt. Col." Gilani's School in Penang. Their training consisted of physical training, which was most unpopular, history, map reading, instruction in swimming and the handling of boats, bomb making, periodical route marches, jungle warfare training and propaganda training. Discipline was not rigid, training was badly organized and there was no fixed program. The students fired a pistol and Tommy Gun course on the range and after this weapon training was discontinued. They were taught how to make and use two types of electric bombs, a tube bomb, and four types of incendiary bomb.

Upon the arrival of Subhas Chandra Bose, training was intensified and students were primed with answers to questions he might ask about the unsuitability of Pakistan. Bose was entertained with a sea-landing display. He spoke to all the students and praised their work. But soon afterwards the school was closed and students returned to Singapore. In

December 1943 a party of 20 was selected out of the original 70 as suitable for deep penetration agents and in January 1944 left for Penang where they underwent further training in the "Sandy Craft" School in sabotage, the use of disguises, swimming, the handling of boats, propaganda and wireless telegraphy.

From these 20, twelve were alternately selected and transferred to another school for special intensive training. Here decisions regarding disguises and routes in India were made and a final landing practice carried out.

The 12 were divided into two groups of six, namely, a W/T group and a propaganda, espionage, and sabotage group. The former, with cleverly disguised wireless sets, were split up into 3 groups of two each which were to operate in the U.P., Bengal and N.W.F.P., respectively while the later group was to operate single member in the Punjab, U.P., Mohmund areas and two members in the N.W.F.P. The leader of this second group was to establish his headquarters where most convenient. Members were to contact the "Forward Bloc" and collect intelligence through that organization for transmission by stages via the N.W.F.P., U.P., and Bengal, to Burma. The party embarked on a Japanese submarine on the morning of 27 February and were landed near Pasni on the Baluchistan coast on the night of 24-25 March and immediately surrendered themselves to the local authorities. They were arrived with revolvers and grenades and carried a large sum of money in currency notes and small diamonds.

Section Five. This section is in charge of the political education and military guidance of the Indian National Army.

The Indian National Army is nominally the Army of the Provisional Government of free India, and its Commender-in-Chief is Subhas Chandra Bose who is the head of the Provisional Government. But just as the Indian Independence League and the Provisional Government of Free India although nominally autonomous bodies, are actually guided and directed by the Japanese through the agency of Section Two of Hikari Kikan, so also the Indian National Army is actually controlled, not by the Provisional Government to which it is nominally responsible, but by Section Five of Kikari Kikan. The relation between Kikari Kikan and the I.N.A. is made clear from the following quotation from a captured Japanese document:

"With regard to the command and employment of the I.N.A., its autonomy will as far as posssible be respected. On points of detail it will be guided unobtrusively by the advisory officers and N.C.O.s furnished by Kikari Kikan, but the appearance of autonomy will be preserved."

The first attempts to organize an Indian National Army were made in June 1942 after the Bangkok Indian Independence Conference when it was announced, that Captain Mohan Singh had been made General Officer Commanding the Indian National Army which was about to be formed. By November 1942, it was estimated that its approximate strength in Malaya was 24,000 concentrated in and around Singapore.

A paper organisation which may have existed, and in part at least certainly did exist, on the ground, was announced as :

(a) Three guerilla brigades (Gandhi, Nehru and Azad).

(b) A field group (brigade) consisting of a signal company, an armored unit, an ordnance unit, and a supply unit.

(c) A special service group (now known as the Bahadur Group).

(d) An Intelligence Group.

(e) A cadets training group.

(f) A provost unit and detention camp.

The training was elementary and armament and equipment were on a meager scale.

In November 1942, an advance party of the I.N.A. of 400 men, 200 of the special service (or as it is now called the Bahadur Group), and 200 picked men from the Gandhi, Nehru and Azad Brigades, was dispatched to Rangoon.

In December 1942, a quarrel occurred between the leaders of the I.N.A. and the Japanese which resulted in the disbanding of the Army. A reorganization took place about March 1943, but it was not until Bose took command in July 1943 that serious attempts were to recruit, organize and train the new Indian National Army.

The Headquarters of the reorganized I.N.A. was originally Singapore but has now been transferred to Rangoon.

The majority of the Indian National Army personnel are ex-prisoners of war from Malaya.

It is probable that all I.N.A. personnel now carry pay books and identity discs. To date the only known block of serial numbers is 54307 to 54558.

In addition to passes, paybooks and identity discs, Jifs also take use of a “secret” sign in order to establish their status as genuine Jifs. The use of this sign was reported by a captured Jif whose information referred to the 4 Corps front. He stated that if a member of the I.N.A. has difficulty in convincing a Japanese of his identity he makes a "T" sign on the ground of indicated a "T" on the palm of the hand. In some cases, I.N.A. personnel have stiched the outline of the letter "T" under the lapel of the coat or on other garments. This report is confirmed and the practice shown to be general by a documents entitled "Points are recognition of I.N.A. in the front lines "issued by a Japanese regiment commander in Arakan. An extract dealing with the recognition of I.N.A. personnel returning from behind the lines runs as follows:

"On meeting with one troops, all of them must not only proclaim them identity as Hikari Kikan or I.N.A., but also expos the letter "I" sign strtched to their cash or other garments."

Special attention was given to the topography of Burma, Assam and Bengal. Bayonet training, propaganda lectures and jungle warfare training replaced guard duties and fatigues.

About the middle of August 1943, a second company was formed. The composition of these two companies was:

(a) "A" company, commanded by Captain (Jif Major) Misra, composed of 200 Singapore prisoners of war; all well trained.

(b) "B" company, commanded by Jem. (Jif Major) Ram Sarup, composed of Singapore prisoners of war, volunteers from Boundary Road Camp, a platoon of the 1/15 Punjab Regiment, many notorious Jifs, all of whom had operated conspicuously in the forward areas and been recalled to join the Bahadur Group, and a few well known Indian Officer renegades who knew the type of work carried out in the front lines.

For a short time both companies underwent intensive training consisting of lectures on the I.N.A., the art of disguise, world history, the "national struggle for independence", and map reading. The greatest stress was, however, laid on work in the front line and on propaganda, espionage and sabotage in the rear of our troops. There was instruction in the installation of loudspeakers in the forward areas, and the use of bows and arrows to shoot propagande leaflets among our forward troops.

Early in September 1943, the "B", "C", and "D" Companies of the Bahadur Group arrived in Rangoon from Singapore.

In a captured Hikari Kikan document (undated but probably issued in December 1943) the Bahadur Group is directed to "carry out operative work in frontline areas (mainly military operative work and the pacification of local Indians").

During the period August to December 1943, sixteen parties of Bahadur Group personnel, totaling 481 men, were dispatched from Rangoon to forward areas.

The intelligence group.

This group, like the Bahadur Group which it closely resembles, is composed of intelligence agents. These agents, however, unlike those of the Bahadur Group, were intended from the first for tactical operations. The function of the intelligence group is similar to that of the Battalion Intelligence Sections of the British Army. The agents of the Intelligence Group also carry out espionage in plain clothes. In the captured Hikari Kikan documont mentioned above they are ordered to collect information in frontline areas and to infiltrate, when necessary, into the enemy rear in order to collect information there.

The Intelligence Group which Bose is reported to have described as "the eyes of the Indian National Army" was formed in Singapore about March 1943, of prisoners of war from the various prison camps there. It was located in Bidadars Camp and was under the command of "Lt. Col. S. A. Malik. Malik was assisted by a Japanese officer and an N.C.O. The Japanese officer is reported to have remained with Malik and to have eventually accompanied him to the forward areas.

Training.

The training program was fairly comprehensive. Tactical training consisted of compass work, map reading, use of cover, signalling, patrolling, methods of observation and infiltration, toughoning exercises including physical training, bayonet practice, route marches, swimming and boating. "Spiritual Lectures" were also occasionally delivered by two of Bose's Military Advisors. The rest of the training was the responsibility of platoon commanders. Small arms, but no ammunition were issued during training.

Move to Rangoon.

On 22 August 1943, the whole group, total of 350 men, left Singapore for Rangoon which they reached early in September. During the journey they were joined by Companies "B", "C", and "D". The combined groups were visited by Subhas Chandra Bose who addressed them and gave Rs. 5/- to each man. In Rangoon they were located at Hingaladon where the Advance Party of the Bahadur Group was already stationed. Training was begun inmediately on more rigorous lines than in Singapore. Forced marches and "living hard" were daily features of the training. In addition, lectures were given by "Major" Ram Sarup on the topography of the Indo-Burma frontier and the location of forward British defences.

Reorganization.

In the first week of January 1944, the original organization was changed to a H.Q. section of about 110 of all ranks and six sections each consisting of 4 officers, 5 Havildars, 10 Haiks, 10 Lt/Naiks and 11 Sepoys; total 40.

At the beginning of February 1944 it was estimated there were approximately 200 members of the intelligence group in Rangoon and 150 in forward areas. It is not unlikely that the estimate of the number in forward areas was too small.

Activities.

The work of these well trained espionage-cum-intelligence personnel in Araken has included infiltrating behind our lines in civilian dress for espionage tasks, reconnoitering positions with japanese patrols, active patrolling and distributing propaganda leaflets through local inhabitants. They were all armed and morale is said to be high.

During December 1943, five parties of Intelligence Group personnel, totaling 280 men, were sent to forward areas from Rangoon.

Reinforcement group.

This group of Jifs appears to be closely similar in character to the Bahadur and Intelligence Groups. Like them, it was formed in Singapore, it arrived in Rangoon sometime during the period September-November 1943. During December 1943, five sections of 26 to 30 men each of the Reinforcement group, totaling in all 139 men, were dispatched to forward areas.

One section of 27 men went to Akyab. The other four sections had the 15 Army front (upper chindwin) as their destination. In an order to the Chief of Staff, Area Army, these sections of the Reinforcement Group were ordered to the responsible for reinforcing the I.N.A. and for taking charge of Indians including Gurkhas who were taken prisoner or who surrendered. Mixed parties of Jifs, consisting of members of the Bahadur, Intelligence and Reinforcement Groups were operating in February 1944 in the Kalowa and Le-U areas. Early in April 1944, it was estimated that some 200 members of the Reinforcement Group were present in forward areas.

The Guerilla Brigades.

There were originally only three Guerilla Brigades or Regiments– Gandhi, Nehru and Azad. These were like the Bahadur and Intelligence

Group elements in the pro-Bose I.N.A. which were carried over into the new organisation. A fourth brigade, known as the "Bose Brigade", was forced at some period subsequent to the reorganization of the Indian National Army, in March 1943.

The advance Party of the I.N.A., which moved from Singapore to Rangoon in November 1942, had two hundred picked men from the three original brigades. The Bose Brigade arrived in Burma towards the end of 1943. Five parties of the Bose Brigade totaling 447 men, arrived in Rangoon by land between 20 and 23 December 1943. Early in 1944, the remainder of the Gandhi, Nehru and Azad Brigades arrived in Rangoon from Singapore.

All brigades are reported to be organized on similar lines, each having three battalions of five companies; an estimated strength of 3000; an approximate fire power of 100 L.M.Gs., 100 T.S.M.Gs., a number of M.M.Gs., and boyes A/Tk rifles, 20 A/Tk mines, 20 demolition mines, in addition to pistols, rifles and grenades. Each brigade has a portion of Bahadur Group attached.

All ranks of Bose Brigade wear a circular cloth disc of orange and green on the left arm, the orange upper most. This distinguish badge is in addition to the circular total tri color worn on the left breast.

In unconfirmed report from a Jif states that the following green cloth identification badges are worn on the left arm by Gandhi Brigade personnel :

Brigade Headquarters and attached Bahadur Group personnel–

No. 1 Battalion – a circle

No. 2 Battalion – a triangle

No. 3 Battalion – a square

The Azad and Nehru Brigades wear similar Badges coloured yellow and light blue respectively.

Towards the end of March, the Ist Battalion of the Bose Brigades moved up to Arakan and on 1 April were in Kabaw, 9 miles south, south-east of Kaladan. At about the same the 2nd and 3rd Battalion moved up to the Chin Hills.

Sometime in February of March 19th, the four field brigades, Gandhi, Nehru, Azad and Bose Brigades, together with the Bahadur Intelligence and Reinforement Groups were organized into what is known as the No. 1 Division of the Indian National Army. The original strength of the No. 1 Division was about 15,000.

There is a Mortar Company, armed with British 2nd and 3rd mortars, attached to the H.Q. of the No. 1 Division.

The No. 2 Company of the three Motor Transport Companies of the I.N.A. arrived in Rangoon from Singapore during the last week of November 1943. Its strength was reported to be between 250 and 300 men.

No. 1 Motor Transport Company was identified at the end of the June 19th South of Ye-U.

No. 2 Motor Transport Company was working between Ye-U and Kalowa on supply carrying duties for the Japanese in June 1944.

The L. of C. Hospital arrived in Rangoon from Singapore sometimes toward the end of 1943.

The exact date of the arrival of the No. 1 A/A Coy, in Burma is not known but it was probably in October or November 1943. One party of the No. 2 Company consisting of 21 Indians and 2 Japanese, reached Rangoon from Singapore by sea on December 1943, and a second party of the No. 2 A/A Company, composed of 30 Indians and 2 Japanese arrived in Rangoon from Singapore also by sea on 8 December 1943.

On 11 December 1943, the No. 2 A/A Company, under the command of Major Matsunaga and accompanied by five Japanese, was dispatched by railway to an up country point between Pegu and Rangoon. Since December 1943, two more A/A Companies have arrived in Burma. There are, therefore, now four A/A Companies. One is located between Pegu and Rangoon, another is in Moulmein and two are in Mingaladon.

The Rani of Jhansi Regiment.

According to radio news broadcasts from Japanese controlled station elements of this regiment are now present in forward areas in Burma. The regiment has its headquarters in Singapore where presumably the main body of the regiment is still located. It is commanded by a "Captain" S. Lakshmi who is described as having been formerly a doctor in a Singapore hospital, with a "Lieutenant." Sathyavarthy Thevar as second in command.

The language of the broadcast seems definitely intended to convey the impression that the members of this regiment will play an active military, even combatant, role which, however, seems proposterous.

No estimate of the size of the regiment nor of the members now in Burma is available. It is probably that the number in Burma is small and it seems unlikely that the Rani of Jhansi Regiment will have any save propaganda value.

Special Task Unit.

This unit is commanded by "Captain" Khurana (2nd Lt. A/8 Punjab Regiment). It was located in Bidadari Camp, Singapore, in December 1943 when its strength was about 180 mostly exprisoners of war. They are said to be undergoing parachute and Secret Service training. It was reported in June to be undergoing training in Sumatra.

Sometime between the beginning of September and the end of November 1943 a group of 223 Engineers arrived in Rangoon from Singapore. This group was dispatched by lorries on 30 November 1943 to the 15 Army.

A Bodyguard Battalion which is believed to be Bose's personal unit has now arrived in Burma. Half of this Battalion went from Rangoon to Mandlay about the end of April 1944. One company of it was allotted to "Colonel" Chatterji on his appointment as "Governor of the Liberated Areas."

The Battalion organization is :

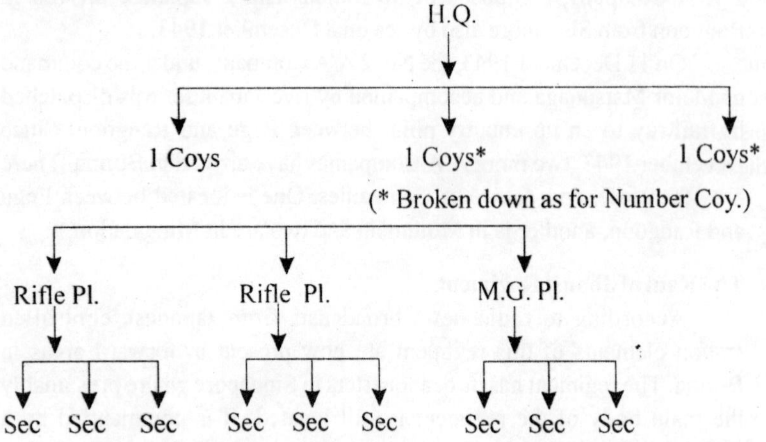

No. 1 Engineering Company was identified at morch during the second week of July, but at the end of the month it retired to Mandalay for rest and its duties were taken over by the No. 2 Engineering Company.

In December 1943, the No. 2 Division of the I.N.A. was billeted in Bidadari Camp, Singapore. The infantry Regiment of this Division was reported en route for Burma in May 1944. It is probably that all or nearly all the No. 2 Division is now in Burma.

The organization of the No. 2 Division of the I.N.A. is given in Appendix "A".[3]

The No. 3 Division is reported to consist of the 6th, 7th and 8th Guerilla Regiments.

3. Not Printed.

I.N.A. Training Schools

In 1943, "Lt. Col" Ehran Qadir set up Youth League Centres in Malaya for the military training of Indian Civilion youths. Two types of schools existed, one for elementary and the other advanced training, the former being styled Bharat Youth Training Centre, the latter Azad Schools, the recruits being found by the I.I.L.

The minimum age for recruitment into the Youth Training Centre is 17, and the syllabus comprises preliminary military training, discipline, spiritual and propaganda lectures. At first the staff consisted of seconded I.N.A., N.C.Os, but later was formed from trained civilians. On completion of training about 10 per cent of recruits go to the Azad Schools for advanced training, whereas the remainder go to the Azad Schools for advanced training, whereas the remainder go to the Reinforcement Group rear organization in Singapore. The selected 10 per cent of recruits sent on the Azad Schools are given further instruction in military matters, arms training and propaganda. These schools are staffed by I.N.A., N.C.Os., and the object is to produce instructions send back to the training centres. Very promising recruit from these schools may be selected for further at the O.T.S.

The training centres so far located are at Kuala Lumpur, Seletar, Seremban and Penang, and Azad Schools are not Penang and Singapore.

A similiar recruit training battalion is reported to have been opened in Rangoon for Indian civilians living in Burma. It was accommodated in what is known as Gaoshala Buildings in the neighbourhood of the Kanbe S.Y.N.T.I. It was, however, quite distinct from the S.Y.N.T.I. and concerned itself solely with the military training of recruits with a view to their eventual absorption into the I.N.A. Reinforcement group. They may also have been intended to provide first reinforcement for the I.N.A. Guerilla Regiments which were to operate in Burma this year. It is not so far clear as to whether this school and primarily organised by the I.I.L. or the I.N.A., but one Jif source who was an instructor states that it was essentially on I.N.A. organization and under district control of and responsible to "Col." Alagappan.

The first course began in October 1943 and the scheduled to last for four months. There were 500 recruits in the course, of whom three-quarters were Madrassis. They were organized into three companies which of three platoons, each of approximately 50 men. The school had an allotment of 150 rifles and bayonets, distributed on the scale of 50 per company. During training, one platoon of each company would use the rifles whilst the remainder were receiving theoretical instructions. The only weapon in which the recruits were trained were the rifle, LMG and TSMG. There was no issue of uniform and the recruits paraded in an assortment of multicolored bazaar clothing. In addition to military training recruits were given occasional propaganda lectures.

This instructors were mainly drawn from the Bahadur and the Reinforcement Groups and when the main body of these groups arrived in Burma, the instructors were withdrawn and returned to their units in order to complete their mobilization.

The Manipur Offensive.

At the beginning of the Manipur offensive in March 1944, Jif forces consisted only of composite parties of Bahadur, Intelligence and Reinforcement Groups in the Chin Hills (Kalewa), Le-U and Homal sectors under Jif sector leaders. "Lt. Col." Malik was leader in the Chin Hills sector. "Major" Maghar Singh was a leader of the Le-U group and "Captain" Ajmer Singh was in command of the Homalin forces. There were, in addition to these organized parties, several miscellaneous bodies of agents, but the part played by them was negligible. From March to June, "Lt. Col. " Malik's parties operating south of Bishenpur. Major Maghar Singh's three parties were indentified at Imphal, Palel and Kanglatongbi while "Captain" Ajmer Singh's parties were in the Kohima area.

All these groups carried out the usual Jif intelligence tests, i.e., collection of information and supplies, reconnoitering. infiltration routes to India, pacification of local inhabitants, dissemination of verbal and written propaganda, handling of Indian prisoners of war, with a view to enlisting them in the I.N.A...., decoys, suborning British Indian troops and doing fatigue duties for the Japanese. All groups were soon very much depleted and the existence of two of the groups, "Major" Maghar Singh and "Captain" Ajmer Singh surrendered in June.

In March the No. 2 and 3 Battalions of the Bose Brigade (No. 1 Guerilla Regiment) arrived in the Chin Hills. The No. 3 Batallion took over garrison duties from the Japanese in the Falan Haka area. One company was located at Falan and another at Raka, while the three remaining companies were on the line of communication east of Falan. The No. 2 Battalion of the Bose Brigade was reported to be in Tiddin area.

In April, the No. 2 Guerilla Regiment (Gandhi Brigade) arrived in the area south of Palel. This was the first Guerilla Regiment to come into action. Early in May it made an abortive attack against the Palel airfield as a result of which it suffered very heavy casualties. Notwithstanding this early set back and subsequent desertions, the Regiment continued active patrolling and skirmishing throughout May and June.The raids, however, decreased in the first half of July, probably due to the reduced strength of the Regiment which was by this time less than half the original establishment, sickness, desertions and battle casualties having taken heavy toll.

During May, the No. 3 Guerilla Regiment (Azad Brigade) arrived in the area north of the Palel Tamu Road. May and June were comparatively quiet months for the No. 3 Gueriella Regiment (Azad Brigade) though desertion to the British were daily occurrences. The Regiment became more active during the first half of duly, carrying out sporadic raids at a cost of many casualties.

Towards the end of May the No. 2 and No. 3 Battalion of the Bose Brigade (No. 1 Guerilla Regiment), with the exception of three companies which were left in the Chin Hills, one of them probably at Haka. moved from the Chin Hills to the Ukhrul Area. Events in Kohima prevented the commitment of the Regiment and the force was hastily within southwards. By the middle of July it was out of Manipur.

The 2nd and 3rd Guerilla Regiments and the 2nd and 3rd Battalion of the Guerilla Regiment were nominally under the command of the Headquarters of No. 1 Division which, by the end of May had opened up at Tamu and shortly thereafter moved forward on the Palel Tamu road.

The Nehru Brigade (4th Guerilla Regiment) was reported moving west from Mandalay in late April. A small advance, of this regiment was operating 14 miles in north–east of Tiddin early in March, but the main body of the Nehru Brigade never arrived in Manipur and little is known concerning it.

Coincident with the retreat of the Guerilla forces in the Ukhrul area, early in July, what was left of "Captain"Ajmer Singh's forces withdrew from the Kohima areas to Ukhrul. From Ukhrul they continued to retreat but whether towards Hamilin or Tamu is uncertain. Earlier reports indicated Hamalin, but a later report states they were destined for Tamu.

The Jif forces in "Lt. Col." Malik's section south of Bishonpur continued active during the early part of July, but on the 12th of that month Malik was reported to have left for Rangoon.

In the latter half of July, No. 2 and No. 3 Guerilla Regiments (Gandhi and Azad Brigades) which had respectively been south and north of the Palel Tamu Road began withdrawing. No. 2 (Gandhi) Regiment by this time was reduced to three companies. Both regiments were reported to have left for the Kalema area. No. 1 Division Headquarters was also withdrawn back from Tamu probably to Kalewa or Mandalay by the end of July.

By the end of July, most of the I.N.A. were back in Burma and reported falling back on Kalewa.

Strength of I.N.A.

At the beginning of the Manipur offensive in March 1944, the total strength of the I.N.A. in Burma was approximately 13,000. Of these, about 9,000 were Guerilla troops divided among the four guerilla regiments of No. 1 Division., the combined Bahadur, Intelligence and Reinforcement Groups personnel amounted to about 1550, distributed as follows:

Bahadur Group	:	1,000
Intelligence Group	:	350
Reinforcement Group	:	200

The remaining 2,450 I.N.A. personnel were distributed among various small units such as the Bodyguard Battalion and the Engineering, Motor Transport and Artillery Companies.

During the Manipur campaign the No. 2 Guerilla Regiment (Gandhi Brigade) suffered heavy casualties. Its original strength was about 1,900 but by the middle of June it was only 1,700 strong. Up to the 8th of July, its losses amounted to 607 (132 surrendered or captured, 278 killed and 197 wounded). It was reported that on 21 July there were only 650 of the Gandhi Brigade left in Manipur as in addition to these killed and captured there were reported to be more than a thousand sick and wounded in the Moreh Hospital.

The No. 2 Guerilla Regiment's losses were considerably smaller. Its total casualties, up to 8 July are estimated to be about 100 (captured or surrendered 44, killed 39, wounded 17).

Total Casualities

The Bahadur, Intelligence and Reinforcement Groups have also suffered fairly heavy casualties. Exact figures are not available but it seems likely that the number of their personnel does not now exceed 1,000.

Apart, therefore, from reinforcements brought in from Malaya, the I.N.A. forces in Burma number about 11,000.

According to a former I.N.A. officer the No. 2 Bahadur Group and the Infantry Regiment of No. 2 Division was en route to Burma in April or May 1944. They are therefore, probably new in Burma. Indeed, it is likely that the whole of No. 2 Division has reached Burma by this time. If this is the case, then there are about 19,000 I.N.A. troops now in Burma.

Upon the assumption that No. 2 Division started moving forward from Malaya to Burma in September 1944 when its training was scheduled to be complete there will be some 28,000 of the I.N.A. in Burma by the end of 1944, of whom about 21,000 will be guerilla or equivalent troops.

The Future of the I.N.A.

What use, if any, the Japanese will make of the I.N.A. troops now, or yet to arrive, in Burma is uncertain. One Hikari Kikan sources is reported to have said that the I.N.A. would be withdrawn and not used again. Another report has it that all I.N.A. personnel were to be recalled to Rangoon and the senior officers sent to Tokyo. On the other hand, reports believed to be reliable state that reinforcements were arriving in Burma from Malaya.

The Japanese are doubtless disappointed in the I.N.A. Nevertheless, it appears unlikely that they will make no use of the nineteen to twenty-eight thousand well trained Indian troops. Should the Japanese launch a new offensive in Burma, the I.N.A. will probably be called upon to play its part and should no new offensive be undertaken, they will doubtless be utilized in holding and delaying activities.

Outposts of Hikari Kikan.

The five branch agencies of Hikari Kikan were located at (1) Akyab, (2) Kalewa, (3) Homalin, (4) Hyitkyina and (5) Mayayo.

Akyab Branch.

The Akyab Branch of Hikari Kikan was in charge of Jif activities in Arakan. Captain Hatteri who was head of this branch was in command of several officers and civilians.

Early in 1943, six officers, seven N. C. O.s, four senior civilians, five junior civilians and two subordinate employee were dispatched from Hikari Kikan Headquarters in Rangoon to Akyab and Mayayo. After receiving its share of these reinforcements, the Akyab Agency Outpost was reorganized to form an Akyab Operative Group. The Branch was organised into three sections as follows:

(1) Military Affairs and the Prevention of Espionage

(2) Intelligence

(3) Special Military Affairs

The object of this organisation was stated to be to develop the various activities of the branch including the guidance of the Indian National Army and the Indian Independence League.

The Arakan Front

At the end of August 1943, 70 civilian Jifs, students of the Kanbe Institute were dispatched from Rangoon to Arakan. The first elements of the Bahadur Group moved up to Arakan in September 1943 and a further contingent in October 1943. "Major" Mishra, who commanded the company of the Bahadur Group in Rangoon, left on 14 October with a detachment of 33 men and established his headquarters at Buthidaung. The duties of the Bahadur group personnel were mainly military espionage in forward areas.

Towards the end of 1943, there was indication of an intensification of the "I" offensive in Arakan.

The number of Jifs in Arakan in December 1943 was estimated to be not less than 300. The bulk of them were concentrated in camps at Buthidaung and neighbouring villages. There were lesser concentrations in Mangdaw and the coastal area opposite Teknaf where Jifs were responsible for the organization and supervision of local volunteers for coast watching at the mouth of the Haf River. The volunteer patrols were allotted definite areas. Their tasks were to prevent British agents from crossing the Haf River, and to watch the movement of British patrols. The patrolmen carried lathis and the Jif patrol leaders Versy pistols.

The 300 or more Jifs in Arakan at the end of 1943 were partly civilians trained in the Rangoon Swaraj Training Schools, Kanbe, and other training schools and partly military non-combatant Jifs of the Bahadur Group. The exact proportion of each is not known, but it is likely that the two groups were roughly equal. Forward of Akyab Island firm identification indicated 44 military personnel and 54 civilians.

Although Jif positions altered from time to time in conformity with the tactical situation and Japanese troop movements, nevertheless certain parts of Arakan were more or less permanently manned. Thus, up to the time of his reported relief, Jagat Singh,who was controller of Jif in Arakan, had his headquarters either in Buthidaung or just south of it in Kanbyin. Towards the end of October 1943 he was reported to have moved to Nalpannya. Although the Japanese officer supervising the Jif activities in forward Arakan was reported to have had his headquarters in Maungdaw, it is nevertheless thought that in December 1943 the forward group headquarters still remained at Buthidaung, with subordinate headquarters at Maugandar (HQ controlling the coasts watching on the Naf) Kyankataw and/or Arakan. There were also other Jif posts chiefly around Buthidaung and Maungdaw.

Towards the end of 1943, Jagat Singh, who had previously been in command of the Jifs in the Arakan, was relieved, at least temporarily, by "Major" Mehr Dass.

Prior to the arrival of a contingent of the Guerilla Brigade on 10 February 1944, all the Jifs in Arakan were divisible into three categories.

(a) Commanders

(b) Tactical intelligence agents

(c) Strategical intelligence agents.

Commanders.

Previous to the relief of Jagat Singh by "Major" Mehr Dass, towards the end of 1943, commanders appear to have been selected by Jagat Singh himself or his immediate assistants, but therefore it would appear that Hikari Kikan began to tighten its control. The commanders were allotted to Jif posts, working on their own or under orders of the Japanese. Their functions were generally:

1. Mediating between the Japanese and the local population. Mediating included beating and blacklisting persons unsympathetic to the Japanese.

2. Helping the Japanese to administer Arakan.

3. Disarming the locals as well as coercing them into carrying out intellingence tasks for the Japanese.

These Jif commanders moved about freely and had considerable authority.

Tactical Agents.

These were hard core Jifs whose work took two forms:

1. Quasi-Military, e.g., those who with local volunteers were responsible for patrolling the left band of the Naf.

2. Purely intelligence, i.e., propaganda activities directed against our frontline troops, espionage in forward areas, and the training of local volunteers to become intelligence agents, chiefly for espionage work.

The making of propaganda broadcasts, tapping in all telephone conversations, distribution of propaganda leaflets, and oral approach to our troops, are all examples of the type of work that was carried out by these Jifs.

Strategical Agents.

These agents were, in a sense, merely guests of the Jif commanders in the forward areas and had already received their orders prior to leaving for the forward areas. They received their training and orders before leaving their training school. Having reached the forward Jif posts, arrangements, were or at least were supposed to be, made for them to proceed on their ways: arms, money, route instructions, and in some cases guides were given them.

In addition to the Jifs themselves, a considerable use was made of local inhabitants in "I" operations in Arakan. The Japanese placed considerable reliance on these agents who usually were much better fitted for frontline espionage tasks and as guides to infiltration parties than are Jifs themselves.

Until towards the end of 1943, the Jifs in Arakan were not organised in any detail by Hikari Kikan and matters were left very much to the discretion of local leaders. At about that time, however, Hikari Kikan tightened its control and attempted to make the organization more efficient. The paybooks and safe-conduct passes issued to Jifs, the equipment issued to tactical agents, e.g., tapping in equipment, and the system of coast watching, introduced at this time, are indications of the general attempt to step up efficiency which coincided with the improvement of the training schools.

On 10 February 1944, "Major" Misra and Captain Hattori were joined by the No. 3 Section of the Intelligence Group, consisting of 70 men and 110 men of the Field Force. Personnel of both forces were lightly armed. On 11 February this composite force, together with a detachment of the "A" Company of the Bahadur Group and about 50 Japanese, moved south-east of Taung Bazaar and dug in. From there mixed patrols of Japanese and I.N.A. were sent out.

The work of the Intelligence Group personnel in Arakan included infiltrating behind our lines in civilian dress for espionage work, reconnoitering positions with Japanese patrols, active patrolling and distributing propaganda leaflets through local inhabitants.

Around the middle of February 1944, it was estimated that the total number of Jifs in Arakan was still about the same as it had been in December 1943, i.e., between three and four hundred. The number in forward areas was thought to have increased to about 150, most of whom were military Jifs. These estimates were probably too low.

Jif strengths forward of Akyab in the latter half of February were supposed to be approximately:

Bahadur Group	70
Intelligence Group	70
Field Force	110
Kanbe S.T.K. students	50
Others	110

But as this enumeration omits the five to six hundred Indian soldiers reported at Poikthayat Village and Taung Bazaar, it is as best correct only with respect to the groups mentioned and must not be taken to be a complete estimate of Jif strength in Arakan at the end of February 1944.

Whereas in December 1943 it was reported that Jif forward operators were unarmed except in a few cases with rifles, and in the case of leaders with revolvers, in February 1944 it was reported that military Jifs who then constituted the bulk of the forward operations were armed with rifles, pistols and grenades on the same scale as the Japanese soldiers. While it is probable that even in December there were Jifs better armed than they were supposed to be, it should nevertheless seem that Jif armament was increased during that period. This is an harmony with the general tendency during that period towards a stricter and more military organisation. Somewhat later, probably in February or March 1944, the organisation of the military Jife was still further tightened up by the formation of the No. I Division of the Indian National Army.

On 16 December 1943, the "A" Battalion consisting of 67 men of the Intelligence Group, and 27 men of the Reinforcement Group were dispatched from Rangoon to Akyab.

Operations in the Taung Bazaar area around the middle of February provided the first known instance of Jifs being used in a fighting role. A captured document shows that a general warning was issued to all Jifs in the area to concentrate east of the Mayu Range for an important operation. In the early stages of this operation, part of the enemy's infiltration is reported to have been covered by Jifs. They also attempted to cause confusion among our troops by shouting in English and Urdu. They carried out espionage tasks and acted as messengers. About 30 Jifs were also included in a raiding party which was active in arranging communication on the road from Bawli Bazaar to Maungdaw after 6 February.

At the end of February 1944, a captured Jif stated that there were about 110 agents of the Bahadur Group alone operating on the Arakan frontline.

Quick Return Tactics.

A number of I.O.R.'s captured after February 4, 1944 were set back to our areas Japanese after a week or ten days, with instructions to contact Indian and spread discontent and arouse enthusiasm for and interest in the I.N.A. and its cause. Pamphlets were also used at this time for the same end.

During the March operations in Arakan four groups of Jifs were active. Two of these were composed entirely of ex-prisoners of war. The tactics employed by these groups were:

(a) "Semi-guerilla."

(b) Intelligence.

In their role as semi-guerillas, Jifs, always in concert with Japanese troops, raided camps, interrupted telephone communications, demolished one or two bridges, and in one operation acted as a screen for an outflanking movement. During raids they shouted to our troops with the object of causing confusion among them.

Their intelligence work consisted of reconnoitering positions, preparation of sketches, collection of information about our troops, and distribution of propaganda leaflets in forward zones and behind our lines.

Their miscellancous duties included interrogation of and guarding Indian prisoners of war and attempts to suborn them and acting as porters for Japanese troops. Some were I.N.A. uniform, others adopted local dress.

Some time prior to the middle of March the remainder of the "A" and "E" Companies of the Bahadur Group, under the command of "Ram Sarup, who had been in command of the "E" Company in Rangoon, moved up from Rangoon into Arakan.

Towards the end of March the No. 1 Battalion of the Bose Brigagde arrived in the Kaladan area. On its arrival in this area it is reported to have had an ambitious plan for independent action against the rear of our troops east of Kaladan. On 31 March and 1 April, I.N.A. forces of platoon and company strength, acting independently for the first time, clashed with our troops. On 31 March one platoon attacked our position 6 milessouth-south-east of Kaladan. On 1 April our troops engaged a company of Jifs with some Japanese and inflicted several casualties in hand to hand fighting. It was reported by a captured Jif Havildar that the No. 1 Battalion of the Bose Bridage was located in the Khabaw (9 miles south-south east of Kaladan) area. After these encounters the plan for independent action appears to have been abandoned as no further attempts at independent action were made.

The increase in Jif activities expected in the Kaladan area after the arrival of the No. 1 Battalion of the Bose Brigade at the end of March did not materialize and a portion of the battalion moved northwards with the Japanese troops. On 26 April our patrols estimated a company of the I.N.A. in the area of Amte, 16 miles north-north-west of Paletwa, and on 29 April our troops engaged an estimated force of one company of I.N.A. and two companies of Japanese.

Kalewa Branch.

The Kalewa outpost of Hikari Kikan was established in August 1942. This outpost was used as a base for the collection of information and special operative work. It was in particular charged with making efforts to undermine the loyalty and morale of British Indian troops in forward areas. In February 1943, Lt. Yamada took charge and the personnel of the outpost was increased by the addition of seven men. It was also allotted twelve non from the 33rd Division. Lt. Yamada's chief assistant was a civilians named Sudo, but he also had several other assistants, both military and civilian.

Toward the end of August, or early in September 1943, a party of the Bahadur Group made up of personnel from "A" and "E" Companies was dispatched from Rangoon to Kalewa. This party was later reinforced by seven prisoners of war from the Wingate expedition and six old renegade prisoners of war. Eventually sixteen were selected for forward work and subdivided into four groups each containing (a) one hardened renegade (b) one Bahadur Group man, (v) one Wingate prisoner of war, and (d) one renegade of the 1/15 Punjab Regiment. Those groups moved first to Hake, and then the Tauk to report on troop dispositions, distribute leaflets, and to try to suborn Indian troops. Each party was given Rs. 1000 and each man had a rifle, 30 rounds of ammunition, and three grenades. In the middle of October 1943 this group of sixteen Jifts stated from Kindat for Falam. They arrived near Falam at the end of October and a party of three including one Gurkha from Wingate's expedition and one renegade from 1/15 Punjab Regiment were given Rs. 1,000 and instructed :—

(a) To distribute Jif propaganda pamphlets in English, Roman Urdu Gurkhali on routes used by British troops.

(b) To contact and suborn Indian troops.

(c) To collect information concerning British dispositions.

(d) To report back to intelligence headquarters at or near Falam.

The Kalewa branch received further reinforcements in December 1943 when 33 men from the "A" and "E" companies of the Bahadur Group and for composite parties of Jifs from the Bahadur, Intelligence and Reinforcement groups were sent forward from Rangoon to northern fronts. The total strength of the four composite groups amounted to 600 men.

Of the 33 Bahadur personnel, 7 were designated to Kalewa and 10 to Kaka. Just how many of the 600 men of the composite parties were sent to Kalewa is not definitely known, but it is safe to assume that at least one-fourth went to the Kalewa region.

Jifs in the Kalewa area (including the Chin Hills) fell into the sanic three categories as these in Arakan, namely, (1) leaders, (2) tactical operative for local use and (3) strategically operative for deep penetration. Jif leaders in this area seem not to have exercised the same authority as their counterparts in Arakan. Here the Japanese generally handled the agents themselves. The lesser leaders, i.e., the hardened ex-prisoner of war renegades were directly under the control of the Japanese and their activities consisted cheifly of controlling in turn the rank and file tactical agents and carrying out frontline contact work themselves. There is no evidence that they were used to mediate between the Japanese and the local civil population as their counterparts did in Arakan.

Among the Jif leaders of this area were "Lt. Col." Malik, "Major" Haghar Singh, Baba Amar Singh, Schail Khan and Wazir Mohd. Khan. The three latter arrived with their own parties from Hong Kong. In the latter part of 1943 Jif activities increased, an increase which coincided with the arrival of new trainees from the Rangoon Kanbe Training Institute. These new Jifs assisted in such tasks as frontline espionage, subversion of forward troops, and the distribution of propaganda literature. In December 1943 W/T operators were very active in attempting to intrude on British W/T links with the primary object of extracting information regarding British order of battle.

Towards the end of December 1943, armed Jifs began occasionally to be encountered by British patrols indicating that the tendency of the Japanese to arm their intelligence agents had increased. Deep penetration agents were generally issued with arms before they left India.

At the end of December there had been some strategical operators in forward areas for a considerable time but up to that time they had confined their efforts to assisting tactical agents in their work except for some attempts to infiltrate through the Falam area.

As in Arakan the Japanese began, toward the end of 1943, to make increasing use of local inhabitants as guides for contact parties, and also for further espionage tasks, but these local agents were seldom armed, or trained for special intelligence work. In December 1943 Yamada was apparently concentrating on maintaining contacts with the local inhabitants of Manipur.

In February 1944, there was a composite force of Bahadur, intelligence and Reinforcement Group personnel, under the command of "Lt. Col." Malik, east of the Chindwin, near Kalewa. This forces was divided into five aprties, one of which was under the immediate command of "Lt. Col" Malik. Three of thee, including Malik's own party, worked in the Tiddin and Tonzang areads and later moved north to the Bishenpur area where they were seen about the middle of April in a very depleted condition. Despite their losses they were active during the early part of July but on 12 July, Malik was reported to have left the Rangoon. A fourth party was sent to the Fort White area and a fifth operated at first in the Minthame area and later on the Tanu Road, in concert with a party from Mawlaik.

The work of these parties consisted in the collection of information about British dispositions in the front line, and in the two cases, in Silchar and Mymensingh, sabotage behind the British lines, interrogation and attempts to suborn Indian prisoners of war, spreading of propaganda literature in forward areas and among the local population and the usual fatigues for Japanese troops. Malik himself was a prominent propagandist among Indian prisoners of war in the Tonzang area. During a night attack of 16-17 March on Tiddin Road some confusion was caused by Jifs shouting contradictory orders.

By February, Major Maghar Singh had collected, at Le-U, a force similar to Malik's and about the 10th of March it crossed the Chindwin at Paungbyin and was distributed in the Tamu ara and north of it. Members also operated at Ukhrul, and Maghar Singh and a Jif party reached MS 105 on the road Imphal-Kohima with about 500 Japanese on 4 April. On 7 April they were at work near Kanglatongbi. Some of this party looted a British ordnance dump and were later seen wearing the new-style battle dress which gave some of them access to British positions without suspicion.

The tasks of the Le-U Group were generally the same as Malik's Chin Hills Group. A moire definite indication of the role of this group is revealed by a captured document according to which one of Maghar Singh's parties was to cooperate with a raiding group and was responsible for reconnsitering the route in addition to enlisting guides.

Homalin Branch

The Homalin Branch of Hikari Kikan was the last of the five outpost to be established. The need for an agency in this locality was not felt by the Japanese until June 1943 when it was considered that an intelligence base was necessary. On 8 June 1943, Lt. Yomamara and two men were sent to Homalin where they established a Hikari Kikan Outpost.

The Officer commanding this Outpost in December 1943, was Lt. Kanako who was assisted by a staff of two non-commissioned officers and two civilians.

The Jif forces in the Homalin sector were under the command of "Captain" Ajmar Singh, an ex-prisoner of war who, prior to his capture by the Japanese, was a 2nd Lt. of the 6/1 Punjab Regiment. Ajmar Singh arrived in Rangoon with the Advance Party of the I.N.A. in 1942. He left Rangoon in December 1943 in charge of a force consisting of Bahadur, Intelligence and Reinforcement Group personnel. Upon reaching Homalin he took over command of all Jifs in that sector.

"Captain" Ajmar Sing's group was divided into three parties. One party crossed the Chindwin north of Homalin on 15 March 1944 and was attached to a Japanese battalion during its march to the Kohima area via Layshi and Jessami. On 15 April 1944, this party withdraw from its position north of Kohima and closed up with party No. 3 under Ajmar Singh cast of Kohima.

The second party reached the Chindwin south of Homalin where six numbers were attached to a Japanese unit proceeding to Sangshak while the rest were distributed over the Ukhral area. Here a detachment was formed and left for the road Map-Kohmima. Later four numbers were sent on an espionage and propaganda task to the road Dinapur-Imphal. The remainder of the party followed and were last identified 500 yards cast of Aradure, south-cost of Kohima.

The third party under Ajmar Singh at Chodima was reported cast of Kohima together with party No. 1 on 6 June 1944, "Caption" Ajmer Singh surrendered to British troops south-cast of Kohima.

Personnel from the Homalin group were present in operations around Ukhrul and Sangabak where they shouted to British troops to lay down their arms and surrender. At Sangshak a negaphone was used. These efforts had no success. They later attempted to suborn Indian prisoners of war captured in those areas. A Jif reported that in Ukhrul area a few armed Jifs were attached to every Japanese formation. The task entrusted to one party operating near Kohima was to report the British withdrawal from Kohima by lighting a fire by night or by haisting on I.N.A. flag by day.

In December 1943, the Homalin Branch of Hikari Kikan was conducting its activities in cooperation with Nishi Kikan whose branch in that area was at that time staffed by five Japanese.

Nishi Kikan—Nishi Kikan is a frontier intelligence organization in Burma working through the indigamous peoples of the Chin Hills area. The work of Nishi Kikan is similar to that of Hikari Kikan, but its contact are different.

Conclusion

Hikari Kiran "I" offensive in India has, judged in terms of its ultimate objective , so far proved a failure. India remains securely in Allied hands, and parts of Burma formerly held by the Japanese have been recaptured by Allied forces. But if the "I" offensive has failed, the blame cannot be laid wholly upon Hikari Kikan. The "I" offensive is but a part of the whole offensive against India, The Japanese made the fatal mistake of supposing that as soon as India was invaded, there would be a nationalist revolution which would completely neutralize British and American military strength in India, thereby leaving the field open for Subhas Chandra Bose's puppet forces. The Japanese did not count on having to fight for India. Rather they expected, once the borders were well crossed, to be received with open arms by the Indian masses, Bose assured them that this would happen and the Japanese predisposed thereto by the recollection of their successes in French Indo-China, Thailand and Burma believed him. The Japanese invasion of Manipur did not, however, produce the expected revolution. The Japanese met serious opposition which they had not expected and had to fight a campaign for which they were not prepared. In consequence they were defeated.

Hikari Kikan's failure to realize the falsity of Bose's claims makes them in a measure responsible for the failure of the offensive against India, but this responsibility they share with the whole Japanese command for it is clear that it was not Hikari Kikan alone that was taken in by Bose's claims.

It will be fairer to Hikari Kikan to judge it by its measure of success in the performance of its own special tasks.

Hikari Kikan's deep penetration operations have, so far as our evidence goes, been completely unsuccessful; but in operational contact work its agents have done better. Jif guerillas have achieved some success in a nuisence role, and espionage in formal areas has been moderately successful as is evidenced, by the Japenese knowledge of road and rail conditions and Allied battle order. Propaganda in the field has mostly been inept and has achieved little. The effects of newspapers and radio broadcasts are hard to estimate, but there is no doubt that Japanese controlled broadcasts to India have had considerable effect on Indian morale. The task of guiding the I.N.A. has not been without its difficulties, but on the whole Hikari Kikan seems to have done fairly well. It is noteworthy that comparatively few Jifs have deserted to the British.

Despite the unfavourable conditions of the Japanese in Burma a Japanese counter offensive may be confidently expected unless some large scale Allied operations forestall it. It is doubtful if the Japanese any longer entertain hopes of conquering India, but it seems probable that they will make as large use as possibile of Indian and Burmese puppet forces in an effort to recoup their losses in Burma and to maintain their hold on that country.

Appendix–II

Marching to Delhi a Poem by Yone Noguchi a Japanese Poet; brings out the Essence of S.C. Bose's Slogan "Chalo Delhi" Meant for the Indian National Army[1]

MARCHING TO DELHI

By Yone Noguchi

(Translated by himself from Japanese)

I

"Delhi, Delhi, to Delhi!"
The war-cry replies to a storm of cannon-balls,
And praises the might of powder and smoke.
Leap over the terror that trenches command,
And entrust your bones to a hill of the mother-land!
In a blazing sand your palm grasps,
You will find all the rewards that Death bestows.
And the hunger you suffered from hundreds of years
Can's be filled till an Independence feast is spread.

II

"Delhi, Delhi, to Delhi!"
The fighting array beats its wings;
The bugles begin to cry.
The war wagons grown wild;
The cannons send up their sacrifice fire,
Oh, the heroes, the crusaders to win liberty, they go to the front!
They know a night feast of victory is waiting behind,

---

1. The above poem was translated from the japanese by the author and was published in *Greater Asia*, Dated 2.12.1943. Bose had earlier given the clarion call of "Chalo Delhi" to the Indian National Army. Yone Noguchi, a Japanese poet, was very much interested in Indian Independence. A friend of Rabindra Nath Tagore, but they parted company when Japan marched into China. Tagore did not like the Japanese aggressive policy in China

And their hunger will be filled at last;
They know their own history has now to begin.

III

"Delhi, Delhi, to Delhi!"
Krishna bids them to burn in love of the mother-land,
Putting a holy fire on their own souls.
The glory of many thousand years comes to life again,
And will create over the Ganges a rainbow-bridge.
Lo, the snowy citadel of Himalayan peaks
Drives back law-breakers, forbids them not to invade again
The depthless waters of the Bengal gulf.
Gets graves ready and waits for their coming.

IV

"Delhi, Delhi, to Delhi!"
The war-cry rings through India's whole land;
People's blood boils and seethes.
Making an arched squall of anger,
That will never fail to ruin the enemy's camp.
Lo, the anti-British war-men go in majestic line,
The crusaders to take liberty by force are they!
Ah, what enemy can defy Heaven's will ?

Appendix–III

British Intelligence Report on Spy Schools set up by I.I.L. for Training Civilians in South-East Asia[1]

1. AZAD SCHOOLS AND YOUTH'S LEAGUE TRAINING CENTRE— Early in 1943 Capt. (Lt. Col) Ehshan Qadir, a Military member of the Indian Provisional Government and Director of the Training Centre in East Aisa, set up the following different kinds of I.N.A. Training institutions for training civilians for the I.N.A.

   (a) Bharat Youth's Training Centres—Meant for elementary military training of civilian recruits. Age limit for recruitment in these centres was 17, and duration of course was 3 months. The recruits were given preliminary military training, taught discipline and given spiritual and propaganda lectures. At the termination of the course 10% of the recruits were selected and sent for advance training in Azad Schools while the remainder were absorbed into the I.N.A. through the reinforcement group. These centres were originally staffed by I.N.A. instructors who were later replaced by trained civilians. Outstanding studens may be selected to be trained as Officers in the O.T.S.'s. Those training centres were opened at Kuala Lumpur, Seletar, Seregam and Penang.

   (b) AZAD Schools— These schools were meant for further training of recruits selected from the above training centres in order to turn them into instructors. Instructions included weapon training etc., while propaganda schools were opened at Penang and Singapore.

   (c) The following details about Kuala Lumpar Bharat Youth's Training Centre are available, and it is believed that they apply to the other centres as well—

1. F. No. 601/7378/H.S.

(i) Recruitment—As a result of propaganda carried out by the I.I.L. through notices in the papers and visits of recruiting parties, civilians in E.O.T. volunteered and were recruited. All classes of Indians in occupied torritory were accepted.

(ii) Rations—Rations were good and were supplied by local rich members of the I.I.L. in turn as a part of their war effort.

(iii) Dress—Recruits were issued with khaki shirts and shorts, boots, puttoos, socks, hosetops, and used to wear I.N.A. cap and breast badges.

(iv) Pay—Recruits were paid at the rate of $8, while Havs, Nks and L/Nks get $27, 16 and 14 respectively.

(v) Training—For the first two months, training consisted of P.T. and feet drill. In the last month rifle drill was introduced. No one ever fired a rifle during training and weapon training consisted of naming the various parts of the rifle. No other arms were taught, over theoritically. Various kinds of patrols were taught in theory, but no exercises were done except a few jungle marches.

(vi) Organisation—The centre was divided into 5 Coys, called Azad, Gandhi, Boss, Ghaffar and Nehru. Each Coy had 4 Pls each of three Sections each of about 15 men. Total strength of the course being 800/1000. Company staff consisted of an Officer Company Commander and a Hav. Major, Four Pl. Havs., 4 Nks and 12 L/Nks.

(vii) Displine—Platoon Havildars were authorised to give corporal punishment, which was the most common way of dealing with various offences. The number of strokes varied with the nature of the offence.

(viii) Morale—Student being volunteers, co-operated in training and disciplines, and there were no cases of desertion. The officers and staff were not considered cruel or exacting.

2. Goashala Training School—

(a) In October 1943 a school similar to the BHARAT Youth's Training Centre was started in Goashala building near Karbe

(Rangoon). Its object was to train civilians with a view to their eventual absorption into the I.N.A. and perhaps to provide reinforcements for **Guerilla Brigades** which were to operate in Burma in 1944. The first course started in October 1943, and was scheduled to last for four months.

(i) Organisation—There were about 500 recruits on the first course (about 75% Madrassis) and they were organised into 3 Coys each of 3 platoons, each of about 50 men.

(ii) TRAINING—The school had a total of 150 rifles and bayonets which were distributed amongst Coys at 50 per Coy. Platoons took it in turn to use rifles. Rifle, L.M.G. and T.S.M.G. were the only weapons taught.

(iii) DRESS—No uniform were issued to recruits, who paraded in bazaar-bought multi-coloured clothes.

3. Officers' Training School.

There are two I.N.A. O.T.S.' in existance, one in Singapore and the other one in Rangoon. Details as far as known, are as follows :—

(a) O.T.S. Neesoon—Although this O.T.S. existed on paper it did not actually start functioning as such until April 1943. With the reorganisation of the I.N.A., the O.T.S. was overhauled and arrangements were made to start the first course in April 1943. 60 students attended the course, 5 of whom were civilians. The course lasted till the end of July 1943. All except 4 cadets passed out, and were posted to various units of the I.N.A. as officers. A second course was started on 1st August 1943, and consisted of 75 civilians and 125 military personnel. Experience during the first course had shown that civilian cadets could not keep pace with the Army cadets, so at this course the civilians were kept separate and underwent 6 months' tranining. The first three months of their course were devoted to elementary training, after which they were to be incorporated into the military wing of the 3rd course, which started in November 1943.

Selection—Candidates for O.T.S.' were selected by the unit commanders and were interviewed by Brigade Selection Boards. If recommended, they went before the Final Selection Board at I.N.A. HQ which was the deciding authority.

Organisation—The Military wing was organised into two Coys, i.e., Delhi Coy and Meerut Coy. Each Coy had two Pls, which were commanded by cadets in turn.

Training—Syllabus covered the following subjects :—

(i) **Weapon Training**—Rifle, Pistol, TSMG, LMG, 3 inch mortar, Vickers MG, A/Tk rifle and hand granades.

(ii) **Field Work**—Trenches, wiring, mines and rafting.

(iii) **Geography**—India and neighbouring countries on the Indo-Burma border. Connection of India with East Asia with special reference to Japan. Land route between India and Burma.

(iv) **Tactics**—Advance, rear and flank guards, outposts, patrolling, field craft, street fighting. Passage of water obstacles, attack, defence, field signals, night work, jungle warfare and schemes on both sand models and the ground.

Note—No training was given in, and no reference was ever made to, withdrawal tactics.

(v) **Map Reading.**

(vi) **Spiritual training**—Lectures on propaganda and morals.

(vii) **General Knowledge**—World War, etc.

(viii) **Discipline**—I.N.A. Act and Pl Commander's power of punishment.

(ix) P.T. and Drill.

(x) **Demonstrations** of the type of Artillery and its use.

Note—At the end of the courses; cadets were taken to visit the Japanese N.G.O.'s training school at Port Dickson, where they saw demonstration of bayonet fighting, line discipline, camouflage, use of folding boats, field craft and crawling. Cadets were specially taught Japanese methods of bayonet fighting.

Text Books—Roman Urdu editions of Indian Army M.T.P.'s and S.A.T. volumes were the only text book used. Books were hold by instructors only, and students took notes.

Awards—The best cadets at the end of each course were awarded the Sword of Honour, and the next best cadet a watch.

4. **Mayangon O.T.S. (Rangoon)**—In April 1944 an O.T.S. was opened in Mayangon (Rangoon) to serve the I.N.A. troops in Burma. The course were scheduled to last 3 months, and there were 50 candidates for the first course. From other details it is believed to be similar to Neesoon O.T.S.

5. **Bangkok Training School**—An I.N.A. Training school for the civilian recruits was reported to have been opend in Bangkok in Nov. 1943 by Major Rashid, who was then appointed Chief Recuiting Officer of Siam. No details about the schools are available, except that it was situated on the coast about 40 miles from Bangkok.

6. **Shanghai Training School**—It is reported that towards the end of 1943 the I.I.L. proposed to open a training school at Shanghai in order to train Indian civilians there, with a view to their final absorption into the I.N.A. The I.N.A. was asked to produce the Instructional staff for the above institution. A party of 3 officers and 8 N.G.O.s left Singapore for Shahghai about February 1944, under Capt. B. Narain Das, who was selected as Commandant of the School. No further information is available.

7. **Zeyawaddy Youths's Training Centre**—This is a small scale Bharat Youth's Training Centre, and is typical of various similar centres started by the I.I.L. in Burma. These miniature centres are commanded by a subaltern from the I.N.A. assisted by I.N.A. N.G.O. instructors.

   It is not known whether these are meant to give preliminary instructions to recruits prior to their joining one of the main training centres of recruits are drafted straight into the I.N.A. units from here.

8. **I.N.A. N.G.O's Training Schools**—An N.G.O.'s Training School were started under the Military Bureau at Johore Bahru. The course were of six weeks duration, and each course was attended by about 100 students. The syllabus followed the training given at S.A.T. school, Pachmarhi, with emphasis of Map Reading. Jungle warfare was also taught.

9. **Batches to Japan**—It is reported that a batch of Indian students went to Japan in August 1943 for study, and were to be trained in the Japanese Academy. Early in 1944 another similar batch was reported to have been selected to proceed to Japan to undergo 3 years' training there. No further details are available.

10. **I.N.A. Staff College**—It was proposed to open an I.N.A. Staff College, but the idea was dropped in view of the Burma operation where the maximum number of officers were required for operational duties.

[illegible] Intelligence B[illegible] for Spy Schools set up in 1944. [illegible]

4 Malayan [illegible] A.S.S. (Singapore).—In April 1944 an O.T.S. was opened [illegible] Singapore to train I.N.A. troops in Burma. The courses were [illegible] months, and there were 80 candidates for the first course. From other details it is believed to be similar to [illegible] O.T.S. [illegible]

5 Bangkok Training School.—An I.N.A. training school for the [illegible] was reported to have been opened at Bangkok in [illegible] Major Hashim, who was then appointed [illegible] It was situated on the [illegible] about 10 miles from [illegible]

6 Shonan Training School.—[illegible] the I.N.A. purposes [illegible] a [illegible] school [illegible] Indians in [illegible] their [illegible] The [illegible] A party of officers and [illegible] N.C.O.s [illegible] 1944 [illegible] was selected as Commandant of the school. No further information is available.

7 [illegible] Training Centre [illegible]—The [illegible] Training Centre [illegible] various [illegible] conducted [illegible] [illegible] whether they are meant to give preliminary instructions to recruits prior to their joining one of the main training [illegible] I.N.A. [illegible] N.C.O.s Training School [illegible] Training School [illegible] and [illegible] Military [illegible] Dal [illegible]. The course [illegible] six weeks duration, and each course was attended by about 100 students. These [illegible] followed the training given as a [illegible] course. Technical [illegible] of [illegible] handling, jungle warfare was also taught.

Training in Japan.—It [illegible] reported that a batch of Indian students [illegible] to Japan [illegible] for study and were to be trained in the [illegible] Academy. Early in 1944 another batch which was reported to have been [illegible] Japan [illegible] 3 years' training there. No further details are available.

10 I.N.A. Staff College.—It was proposed to open an I.N.A. Staff College but the idea was dropped in view of the Burma operation when the maximum number of officers were required for operational duties.

Appendix-IV

Copies of Platoon Lectures.

DEPARTMENT OF ENLIGHTENMENT AND CULTURE

D.M.B. I.N.A.

PLATOON LECTURE

UNITY OF INDIA, PAST AND PRESENT

Unity, Faith and Sacrifice— OUR MOTTO
Purna Swaraj For India— OUR GOAL

---

1. Platoon Lectures. The enlarged Military Bureau organised by Rash Behari also included a new department namely the Department of Enlightment and Culture. This department did very useful job of organising the platoon lectures in Hindustani and English. The object of the lectures was to broaden the outlook of the soldiers of the Indian National Army and to create in them a sense of patriotism. These lectures were published by the Military Bureau in the form of Booklets which were distributed to the soldiers. These are copies of lecture which were given to I.N.A. soldiers during Training. All the copies of these lectures which included one on "Bushido" are available at the India Officer Library of Record, London in printed collection. M.SS. European No A. 73.

Appendix-IV

Unity of India, Past and Present

My Brothers,

Today, I want to talk to you about the Unity of India. As you know, most of the European people think that India is not one united country and that Indians cannot form one united nation. The British ruler of India and the people of Britain are mainly responsible for this evil talk; they do so because, they want to rule our country, BHARAT MATA or HINDUSTAN, for ever. Without our help and without all the nice things that our country producccs, the British Empire cannot exist. If India becomes independent, the wealth of India will not be sent to England. So, England wants to keep India under her control for all time to come. That is why, the people in Britain tell the whole world that India is not one united country and that Indians are not a nation. This is one of their main reasons, for keeping Hindustan as a subject colony, under their power.

What are the reasons given by the British people for this opinion? They say that India is a very vast country with different kinds of people living in it. The people of India, they say, have many languages, and many religions, and many castes and sub-castes,.They also argue that the habits and customs of the Indians, living in different parts of India are different. A Madrasi, according to them, is not like a Punjabi and a Hindu not like a Muslim. Thus they tell every one that some other outside power, like themselves, should stay in India; in order to control the people of India. They want the world to believe that the Britishers are staying in Hindustan only for the benefit of the Indians themselves. But, they are robbing the country right and left. Their loot and plunder of our country has resulted in abject poverty of our people in Hindustan. Nearly thirty six crores out of 40 crores of our brothers and sisters in Hindustan are not able to find even one square meal a day. In the last census, more than ten lakhs of our people were officially shown as beggars. This extreme poverty of our people is one of the many results of British rule in India for the last 200 years.

Now, let us see if the reasons given by the British people against the unity of India are correct. What are the facts? To know the truth, we will have to go back, to the time of old days, about five thousands years ago; and study the real history of India. The British history of India is not correct. The British did not educate us in the proper way. They taught us in such a way, as to suit their purpose. Their whole object was to keep us under their thumb.

About 5,000 years ago, we, Indians, had a great culture, when the people in the other parts of the world were still very primitive, not knowing even how to clothe themselves. Our ancient culture was called Indo-Aryan civilisation. We had various schools and universities. Our ancestors knew various arts and sciences, like Physics, Chemistry, Botany, Astronomy, Mathematics, etc., which were not known to the rest of the world. They were also very clever in music, poetry, painting, sculpture. engineering, architecture, etc. Our ancestors, out of all this learning and knowledge, developed various social customs and manners which were of benefit to themselves, their country and their rulers.

During the last 1,500 years, India has had several foriegn invasions, including that of the British invasion. India's wealth attracted these foreign invaders to our country. Our ancestors had a very flourishing shipping industry in those days, extending from China in the east of Egypt and Rome in the west. All these foreign invaders brought with them their own languages, customs and manners. They all tried to introduce their habits into our country and get our people to practice them. But, have any one of these foreign invaders, succeeded in their attempts to any extent? Most certainly not! In spite of all these foreign invasions, our culture, our greatness, our habits and social customs, and our unity of thought and behaviour have all remained the same as in days gone by. Which-ever part of India we may visit, our food is the same, our daily mode of life is the same, our family relations are the time, our individual behaviour to the community at large is identical throughout the country; and our social conduct among our neighbours and friends, being one of the mutual help and toleration, has embraced us all into one united nation.

How have we reacted to all these foreign invasions to our country during the last 1,500 years? How is it that our ancient culture has remained unaltered to a great extent, in spite of our coming in contact with so many different types of foreign people! The Jews and the Portuguese came first, over a thousand years ago. Then came the Islamic people, as the Turkey, the Tartars, the Moghuls, the Afghans, etc. Then came nearly all the people from Europe, as the French, the Dutch, the Danes the Belgians, the Germans, and last but not least, the English people.

Nearly all these invaders were attracted to India only by our wealth. Very few of them wanted to annex territory or found a kingdom, unlike the British. The chief among the original invaders were the Islamic nations. Their rule in India lasted from 12,00 to 17,00 for nearly 500 years. The Capital of the First Islamic Empire was founded in Delhi in 1207. When the Moghul rulers settled in India, they did not know any other homeland except that of India. Hindustan was their Motherland and Delhi was their capital.

The happiness of India and the Indian people were their happiness; and the rulers of India at the time shared the sorrows and adversities of the people. The name of Akbar, the great Moghal Emperor, and his wonderful principles of Empire building, based on love of the people of India, are well known.

No doubt, the Islamic nations brought with them their Persian art and culture, the Urdu script, their music, painting and poetry, their methods of architecture and sculpture. But they did not displace the existing Indo-Aryan civilisation of the country. The culture of the Indians present at the time was so great, so noble and so tolerant that it absorbed and assimilated the foreign Islamic culture that came into the country without much difficulty: On the part of the newcomers, there was a keen desire to settle down in India and fuse with the people of our land at the time. And the Indians, then absorbed the newcomers, once the later had conquered them and founded an Empire. Any resistance that was offered to the foreign invasion at the time, was before and during occupation.

Once the Moghul rule was established, Hindu and Muslims lived as brothers. There was a happy fusion of languages, ideas, social habits and customs, and their methods of earning their livelihood was the same. These common ideas and habits are found among Hindus and Muslims throughout Hindustan today. We have produced a common language, Hindustani, out of the blending of Hindi and Urdu. This language, Hindustani, is spoken by more than half of our people in Hindustan. More than half of its words are from Sanskrit. This language may be written either in Hindi script or the Persian Urdu script. The original Dravidian languages of South India are no doubt different, but they also have half of their words from Sanskrit.

There have been several attempts in the past to unite our religions of Hindus and Muslims. The names of Guru Nanak, Kabir, etc. are famous in this connection. The great Sikh Faith is a result of union of Hindu and Muslim religious ideas. Besides the religion of the Sikhs we have had several other religions in India, like Buddhism, Jainism, Christianity, Zorastrianism or the religions of the Parsis, etc. We have had no trouble or dispute among ourselves at all, at any time. Whenever we disputed for our rights for more food, for more freedom the British called all these troubles, as religious disturbances. The real cause of all mill strikes, hartals, etc., was the extreme poverty of India, and the cry was for "more food, more clothing, more wages and other essentials of life." The British gave the name of religious disturbances for these economic troubles.

But now, all our people know the real cause of their troubles, their sufferings and their poverty, as being due to the British rule of India, producing this abject poverty, disease, famine, starvation, etc. Our people, all over India, are now united in their poverty and adversity, and they know the cause of their present state, is being due to British rule. They are therefore, united in their desire for getting rid of the British rule from India, and obtaining Purna Swaraj for India.

Mahatma Gandhi has been very largely responsible for such united effort of the masses of India. The Indian National Congress has effected this wonderful union of our people, under the guidance of Mahatmaji by efficient organisation and discipline of the masses. The All Indian Peasant Association (Kishan Sabha) has united all our peasants and small land holders. The All India Trade Union Congress has absorbed all our labouring classes, factory workers, mill labourers, miners, estate labourers and all others, employed in any particular trade, industry, or other walk of life. The organisation and discipline of this class of people is of a very high order indeed. The All India Spinners Association and the All India Village Industries Association are similar associations, for absorbing our people, in order to deal with their economic troubles. Their discipline is high, their strength is enormous, their organisation is efficient, their national consciousness is supreme and their will and determination to get rid of the British rule is very strong. Such is the mass mentality of India to day.

In the old days, Emperor Asoka achieved political Unity of India, without Railways or other communications, and his Empire was much bigger than that of Britain today, as it included Afghanistan and Central Asia. There was no trouble in his Empirc, because he united the people and ruled over them, by dint of his love for them. Not so the British, who are ruling India today by repression, oppression and force. With the aid of modern science, the British, introduced Railways, etc., into India. But it was all really to enable them to take our wealth from our country to their own homes in England, and to control India and hold India under their power. If there was trouble in any part of India, the British could use the Railways to send troops, to that locality. That is how they control India.

So, it is wrong to say that India is not a United Country and that Indians do not form a nation. Even English writers have admitted that, among all the various religions, languages, castes and sub-castes in India, there is a fundamental unity among all the manners and customs of the people in India, from very old times. Our original culture has remained unchanged. Our systems of pilgrimage for religious functions in the different parts in India have preserved the unity of our faiths and principles. Our languages and dialects show evidence of unification. Our village social system and the methods of earning their livelihood of our masses, have remained unaltered in so far as the main principles are concerned.

The British conquered our country by force of arms and wars; and then united our country by Railways, etc. But all these were done for their own benefit.

The British increased our differences and promoted fights among ourselves, in order to continue their robbery and plunder of India. There is no such thing as the Hindu-Muslim problem in India. The Muslim do not differ from the Hindus in their blood. Both Hindus and Muslims belong to the same race or same mixture of races. So, they must form a united nation. The great majority of Hindus and Muslims are peasants or small traders or minor craftsmen. A few educated classes, among them, who are job hunters, help the British to promote the so called Hindu-Muslim differences, for their own personal benefit.The policy of the British is to "Divide and Rule." The Hindus and Muslims have been united before, and are united now, in their determination to drive the British away from India.

What is our lesson today? We, officers and men of the Indian National Army in East Asia should have no difference among ourselves and should form one common blood brotherhood, for the achievement of Purna Swaraj for India. We must bear our Common Indian National Tri-colour Flag in mind always and contribute our all, for our common cause.

DEPARTMENT OF ENLIGHTENMENT AND CULTURE

D.M.B.—I.I.L.

PLATOON LECTURE

Requisite Characteristics For Attainment Of Our Object

Character is the Mainspring of Man's Action.
Displine Improves Character and Efficiency

Appendix-V

Requisite Characteristics for Attainment of Our Object.

My Brothers,

From the lectures that have been delivered to you under now we should all be quite clear in your mind what our movement in East Asia stands for, and what special purpose is intended to be served by our policy, aims and objects. I would once again repeat to you that our final goal is Purna Swaraj for India, unfettered by even a vestige of Imperialistic foreign domination of any description, and that our immediate objective is to help in the present revolution of India. Such a statement could authoritatively be made now, because we know from current events that a state of revolution at present exists in India. Our object is not to guide India, not to determine India's future constitution or anything like that..Decisions regarding these items should be left entirley in the hands of Indians in India. We in East Asia, are only a drop in the ocean as compared to the strength of Indians in our mothercountry; and it would be presumptuous on our part to decide the fate of India for the future. Even the very idea of it is so ridiculous that it is useless and unpardonable to waste any time on this aspect of the question.

For the achievement of our object and fulfilment of our policy we depend entirely on our inner strength in India, which consist of the grim determination of our leaders in India, who have been devoting their entire life's career for the success of our mission on the one hand and of the conscious national awakening of forty crores of our masses in India who are seething with a revolutionary spirit of resistance to Anglo-American Imperialism at the present moment on the other. Our movement in East Asia is part of such movement in India, our policy here is the policy of the Indian National Congress, their representative organ which has also been voicing the feelings and remedying the sufferings of Indians abroad. Our flag in East Asia is the Indian National Tricolour flag adopted by our nation at home in India. It is just but right that the Indians in East Asia should help in our cause and in our mission for Purna Swaraj for India, as the whole outlook is identical without even a shadow of difference or doubt.

In this connection, the help of Axis Powers, particularly by Japan, willingly offered by them, is a matter of very great appreciation by the Indians in East Asia and at home. Premier General Hideki Tojo has repeatedly expressed his sympathy towards the cause of Indian Independence and promised every assistance that is necessary for the attainment of Purna Swaraj for India. The Axis Powers have realised fully well that a subject anywhere in this world is not an asset, but a liability to the world. Because their production solely for the benefit of dominating, imperialistic nations is bound to be much less than otherwise. Their economic and cultural sufferings and ignonimity due to their lower political status are bound to jar on the happiness of independent neighbouring nations. Further, as long as one nation is subject to the domination of another, as long as the idea of Empire building the Imperialism persists, there can never be any real peace in the world. That explains the change in outlook of the Axis Nations. That is the difference between the old order and the new. We should, therefore welcome their most valuable and sympathetic assistance which has been particularly offered to us by Japan for the success of our mission.

At the same time, we should not forget that it is primarily our cause, our mission and our country's Independence that we are fighting for; and it is, therefore absolutely vital that we should play the leading role in the matter of service and sacrifice for the success of our mission. It is our sacred duty to contribute our all towards our cause and accordingly we have most solemnly pledged to do so.

We should now consider in detail the essential characteristics we should possess in the Indian National Army for the success of our mission. At this stage of our national awakening it is needless for me to stress our motto 'Unity, Faith and Sacrifice', which principles are signified by our National Tricolour Flag. There is no doubt whatsoever that without full faith and confidence in our mission it is difficult to develop a keen desire for what we want. Once we evince a keen desire to achieve an object, we are bound to work hard for the same. And the obstacle which might come across our projects would all easily melt away. That is our experience in everyday life.The stronger we desire to obtain something the easier it will be for us to fulfil our heart's desire. Because, all the time we are working as hard as ever for thc same and we are eagerly looking forward to final results. So it is essential that all of us should develop a very strong desire to achieve our mission and work very hard for the same, putting our heart and soul and our wholehearted zeal and energy and our entire resources into it. Our cause is a colossal one and our individual capacity may seem very limited and insignificant when compared to our immense undertaking. But there is no reason whatsoever to be despondent. Because, it is our collective strength and our joint united front, equivalent to forty crores of our countrymen, that is bound to assert itself before long for the fulfilment of our long cherished wish, the freedom of India

It is needless to stress the necessity for complete unity to the Indian National Army, forming one common Indian brotherhood, without giving way to sectarianism. I would implore one and all of you not to think of yourselves in future on any lines other than that of Indians, first and last. Any other consideration should not take precedence over our primary object which is Purna Swaraj for India. United we stand and divided we fall. This should be our guiding principle, unlike the British policy of Divide et Impera.

It is unnecessary to emphasis the necessity of our preparedness to sacrifice at this stage of our training and experience except to draw your attention to the fact that there should be faltering on your part at any time when you may be put to the acid test. Our first thoughts should be always our country first and our national Tricolour Flag first above everything else even including our lives.

How are we going to live up to the noble principles of our motto? What are the characteristics we should develop and how should we train ourselves for the same in the I.N.A.?

First and foremost, I would place our character at the very top of the list as it really brings out the inner man and exposes the individual in his or her true colour. Character is stated to be the main spring of a man's action. Without character we can never achieve our ambitions. Human beings possess the extra faculty of thinking and acting for themselves, besides being capable of doing things in an automatic way as animal do. Our mind or conscience tells us what is right and what is wrong in any special procedure. We are in a position to judge which is correct and which is not correct. We have got the power to decide correctly and formulate our actions accordingly. We should develop our power of judgement and discrimination in our everyday life. The results of some of our actions, supposedly based on our judgment, may go wrong. But, as long as we abide by the dictates of our conscience, no harm can accrue to anyone. After all, there is not much difference between conscience and commonsense in plain language.

What is actually wanted is honesty of purpose and truthfulness. There is no harm in committing a mistake unintentionally. After all, most of us learn only by committing mistakes. Otherwise, there is little room for improvement with regard to some of us. But we must be able to prove to ourselves and to the world that our intention was good. We must be able to lay our hand on our heart and say that we made an honest effort in all our actions and we did not intentionally go wrong. A guilty conscience is the worst punishment we could have; and contrariwise a clear and satisfied conscience is the highest form of reward we could ever expect to have.........Our character is after all our mental makeup with regard to our decisions and our actions in everyday life. That is why they say that we are all judged by our character. If we want to hold up our heads in this world we should possess character. We came into this world with a clear conscience. We should, therefore abide by that clear conscience during the periods of existence in this world until we clear out of this world with the same conscience.

The least that we could do to any particular individual or cause is not to be harmful if we cannot be helpful. But the Indian National Army expects a lot of more than this passive attitude of non-interference. Our cause is so colossal and immense that there is not only ample room but also vital need for all of us in the Indian National Army and several thousands more to come, to put forth all our brains and resources for the success of our cause. Some of us are inclined to do only six annas worth of work, because our pay is only six annas. This kind of attitude will not do so. The idea of doing so much work equivalent to so much pay received is to ridiculous to be discussed. There is no doubt that we must put forth our maximum efforts. Being strict revolutionaries we should consider ourselves as being on subsistance basis. Today we may have ample, comforts by way of rations, pocket money, clothing, accommodation, etc. Tomorrow we may be deprived of all these items and we may not be in a position to obtain even the minimum essentials to preserve life. We may have to go without food for days in jungle warfare. That is where sacrifice would come in. Are we going to give up our cause under those trying conditions? What is our answer to this question? Our straightforward answer, of course, is 'No'. We shall not give up our mission under any conditions of personal discomfort or sufferings. We shall carry on until we drop down dead. Not until then shall we cease fighting. We shall carry on our struggle to the bitter end of our destiny. We shall continue our onward march until complete freedom has been won for our mothercountry. Our only glory consists in devoting our entire life's career for the success of our cause and our only reward is Purna Swaraj for India. We have no other expectations in this world! That should be our grim determination. If we are destined to die in our attempts we cannot escape it and we cannot avoid it. So many of us should have been killed outright several times over during the last Malayan Campaign. Still, some of us have yet been spared in order to fulfil some of specific purpose in this world. None of us can foretell the future. We do not know what is awaiting us. So, why should we worry? As long as we have the courage of our convictions that our cause is right we should carry on wholeheartedly until life and energy are still left in us, for the success of our mission, until Purna Swaraj has been assured for India.

Having once come into the movement it is absolutely vital for us to recognise competent authority and maintain Discipline in the strict sense. All orders and instructions issued by competent authority must be implicitly carried out in the spirit they are intended to be observed. This, however, does not preclude discussion on relevant points in the interests of our cause though the final discussion on all such matters should be left entirely in the hands of the issuing authority. Once the final orders have been issued they must be carried out wholeheartedly by all concerned without question and without challenge. All ranks may rest well assured that; whatever orders and instructions have been issued the Indian National Army in its present form, they have been done so after mature consideration in due regard to the exigencies of our cause. All personal interests would be safeguarded as far as exigencies permit and as far as facilities are available. But, as regards fundamental policy it will always be on the line of our first consideration and our first attention always for our cause. So, all of us in the I. N.A. should realise that personal consideration should be waived in preference to the cause.

It should further be pointed out that there should be no room for any doubt in our minds as regards fundamental issues. Should there be any doubt on any particular matter it should be at once cleard by reference to senior officers, etc., in the chain of command. A word of caution has to be mentioned against gossip and alarmist reports. Gossiping shows improper use of time, laziness and lack of discipline. As such, it should be discarded and discouraged by all concerned. Alarmist reports are dangerous to the cause. Officers and other ranks in the I.N.A. who are known to be spreading false rumours and alarmist reports will very soon be spotted. They are bound to be considered Pro-British and treated as enemy spies. Let them not complain if strict disciplinary action is taken in regard to their false and alarmist rumours. If anyone in the I.N.A. should hear of such rumours he should report forthwith in detail to his senior officer and get the information corrected or confirmed as the case may be. Such individuals should find no place in the I.N.A. and they would do well to leave the I.N.A. without further delay in their own interests. Fortunately, the great majority of us in the I.N.A. are thinking correctly and acting in the right direction now-a-days. The sooner we spot these cankers and get rid of them the better it would be for our movement.

SUMMARY OF TODAY'S LESSON

1. Our policy in East Asia is to help in the Revolution of India. Future of India to be left in the hands of Indians at home in India.
2. The inner strength of India, our real strength.
3. Help of Japan and other Axis Powers is welcome. But we should bear the brunt of our work.
4. Our Motto—UNITY, FAITH AND SACRIFICE.
5. Character is stated to be the mainshpring of man's action.
6. Honesty of purpose, Truthfulness, Conscience and Commonsense.
7. If we cannot be helpful, we should not at least be harmful.
8. Readiness for sacrifice, even at risk of privations and sufferings.
9. Discipline and strict observance.
10. Dangers of Suspicion, Gossip, False Rumours and Alarmist Reports.

DOS AND DON'TS

FOR OFFICERS and MEN of The INDIAN NATIONAL ARMY

[illegible]

[illegible] Bureau, [illegible] East Asia, Syonan

DO'S AND DON'TS

FOR THE OFFICERS and MEN of The INDIAN NATIONAL ARMY

Carry it in Your Pocket Always, Consult it Freely

Published by The Headquarters Director of Military Bureau, Indian Independence League, East Asia, Syonan

Do'S

1. Achievement of Independence of your Motherland should be your sole objective. Devote your heart and soul to it.
2. Administer justice tempered with mercy.
3. Always speak the truth; a liar is never respected.
4. Always encourage the spirit of your men. Remember the spirit is mightier than the sword.
5. Always uphold the honour of the Army.
6. A soldier must exercise initiative and determination in his work.
7. Always respect the honour of those who are under your protection.
8. Always stand up when a superior officer comes in.
9. Always be polite. It costs nothing and yet you can be firm.
10. Always be smart on your parade.
11. All lawful commands must be obeyed.
12. Before moving into a Camp, always take necessary measures to ensure:–
    (i) adequacy of rations and water supply.
    (ii) sufficiency of accommodation.
    (iii) suitable lavatory arrangements.
13. Be an optimist, courageous and self-reliant in life.
14. Be practical. Never be late on your parade.
15. Be tolerant to the opinions of others.
16. Be honest in all your dealings and work, for it is the best policy.
17. Be loyal to your superior officers.
18. Cultivate the spirit of self-help.
19. Cultivate an outlook of universal brotherhood.
20. Conserve energy and resources.

21. Cultivate the spirit of chivalry. Remember that the spirit of Indian chivalry is famous in the history.
22. Discharge your duties faithfully.
23. Ensure always the physical fitness of your men. Remember that only by doing so can you fulfil your bounden duty to put at the disposal of your commander the highest number of rifles at the time of action.
24. Exercise daily.
25. Fight hard for your country.
26. First obey and then you will learn how to command.
27. Give clear and complete orders.
28. Give up your seat for a superior officer or a lady when in gathering or in a conference.
29. Give credit to your commander for any achievement in an action, no matter how much you may have done.
30. Have confidence in yourself.
31. Keep secrets closely guarded.
32. Keep your appointments.
33. Knowledge is power, acquire it.
34. Live a frugal life yourself but be generous to others deserving.
35. Live and let live.
36. Loyalty and co-operation lead to success.
37. Love and respect your men and they will love and respect you.
38. Maintain the strictest discipline. This is Foundation of efficiency of the Army.
39. Make Unity, Faith and Sacrifice your life's motto.
40. Obey orders implicitly and carry them out intelligently. Remember upon this depends the efficiency of the Army.
41. Provide healthy recreation and exercise for the men. These are excellent safeguards against venereal diseases.
42. Respect the honour of a woman like that of your mother.
43. Religion pertains to the individual. It is what you live.
44. Resist temptation manfully. If you are unable to resist, get away from the temptation.

45. Rudeness is a sign of lack of se!f control and low breeding.
46. Recitify a wrong whenever you can, it is never too late to mend.
47. See that orders are carried out.
48. Show the utmost toleration in matters religious.
49. Take precautionary measures always in time. Whether it is against disease, attacks of politics. Remember prevention is always better than cure.
50. Take good care of the lives and welfare of the men. Remember you are responsible for them.
51. Train in peace for fighting in war. Constant training greatly increases the efficiency of the army.
52. Trust in God and do the fight.
53. Trust your brother officers and men until proved to the contrary. Remember trust begets trust.
54. Treat a young recruit kindly.
55. Utilise every opportunity to infuse the National spirit in your officers and men.
56. When faced with a problem think over carefully, making allowances for the other man's point of view, and then come to a definite decision.
57. Work hard and with devotion. Hard work never kills a man.
58. When travelling in a train car or bus, give up your seat for an older men, women and the children. Never rush.
59. When there are large number of people to get something say tickets in the railway station or cinema, stand in a queue.
60. You and your men should feel proud that you are Indians.

DON'TS

1. Don't be defeated by failure in a good cause. Try again and again.
2. Don't betray confidence.
3. Don't discuss your superiors. This is bad discipline. Remember, if you do, you too may be discussed by your subordinates.
4. Don't discuss politics unless you are specifically asked by your superior officer. Politics is dangerous for the army; it saps discipline.
5. Don't get drunk and make a fool of yourself. Alcohol is neither a

food nor a necessity.

6. Don't hesitate to take the initiative in a good cause.
7. Don't kill your conscience.
8. Don't lean on others.
9. Don't relax until you have achieved your object and consolidated it.
10. Don't talk losely. The enemy may be listening and you may thus endanger the lives of thousands.
11. Don't brag or boast about your capabilities.
12. Don't hesitate to admit a mistake. It will show up your courage and character.
13. Don't express disagreement in a gathering or conference against your commander or superior officer. If you have divergence of views, settle it up with him first.
14. Don't break up a queue and rush forward.
15. Don't fish for a compliment for a good thing done.
16. Don't dishonour a fallen enemy.
17. Don't use profane language or commit a bad deed. Remember every profane word you speak or a bad deed you do, leaves a track in your brain which predisposes you to repeat it. Be careful.
18. Never belittle the power of your enemy.
19. Never dishonour yourself; death is preferable.
20. Never lose your character. A characterless man is dangerous and is a disgrace.
21. Never betray your Motherland.
22. Never put off till tomorrow what you can do today. Remember a stitch in time saves nine.
23. Never vacillate. Vacillation is the death-knell of an army.
24. Never backbite or carry tales. It demeans you and lowers your self respect. Remember that every time you wish to throw mud on to others, a little of it will stick on to your fingers.

DEPARTMENT OF ENLIGHTENMENT AND CULTURE

D.M.B.—I.I.347L.

PLATOON LECTURE

BRITISH AGGRESSION IN INDIA

British Imperialism—The Cause of Indian Poverty

Freedom is Our Birthright

British Aggression in India (Extract)

My brothers,

Today, I want to talk to you about British aggression in India. As I told you in my previous talk, it was the wealth of our country that attracted all the Western nations to Hindustan. The British came to India in 1608, as a band of adventurers, for purposes of trade only at first. They were called the British East India Company. But very soon, they became very greedy and wanted to establish a British East Company of adventurers wrote to their Agents, in Madras, instructing them to establish a civil and military power, as to create and secure such a large revenue, to maintain the foundation of a large well-grounded, sure, English Division in India, for all time to come.

The battle of Plassey was fought in the year 1757. It was after this battle, the British East India Company agents came into contact with Emperor Shah Alam who was then ruling in Delhi. In the year 1765, the British East India Company agents obtained from Emperor Shah Alam the Diwaney of Bengal, Bihar and Orissa. By this is meant, the British had only the right to collect revenue, and that too, only from these three provinces. This gave a foothold for the British not only to contact the Moghul Court, but also gradually to convert the right of revenue collection into one of acquisition of territory. The Moghul Empire had become disrupted; and the local rulers had become weak and corrupt. The East India Company's English servant adventurers plundered our country, both individually and jointly. They used all the means in their power, both fair and foul, to suit their purpose. The British Agents of the Company set the ruler or chief of one State against the ruler of his adjoining State and produced wars between them; the British themselves took the side of either the one or the other, till they finally swallowed up, either both the states together or one after the other. They plundered and looted all the States, they thus annexed systematically. They accepted bribes from several princes and chiefs and tried to keep them all under their control.

In the annexed areas the British East India Company extorted revenue by severest taxation of land and goods. They untilized all those collections for developing their own trade and also for their own wars and compaigns in India in order to acquire more territory. That is how the British got money for territorial expasion in India.

It is not that the British acquired territory in India without any trouble or difficulty. It took them one hundred years, from 1757 to 1857, to conquer the whole of India. Every inch of territory was contested by every Maharajah, Rajah , Nawab or Chief. But the odds were very much against them. Our Chiefs did not possess them advantage of modern scientific weapons which the British Agents had; but much more than that, was the evil and treacherous infiuence of the British over their own adjoining rulers. Their own friends were converted into their enemy.

In spite of all these disadvantages, our ancient rulers actually defeated the British in several open battles. In the famous battle of Calcutta, Siraj-up Daulah defeated the British. But he was so well-mannered as not ill-treat even his defeated enemy. What did the British do in return? They got Sirajud-Daulah assassinated by foul intrigue so that they could annex his kingdom. This is how the British East India Company annexed nearly the whole of the so-called British India, and kept the rest of the Indian States under their complete control.

Once a map of India was shown to Maharaja Ranjit Singh. He asked what was the meaning of the red blotches in the map. The Maharaja was told that the red colour showed the extent of territory annexed by the British. Then the Maharaja shouted "Jaldi, Sab lal ho jaega" and his prophecy came true very soon. So much for territorial aggression of the British in India.

During the time of East India Company, the British established monopolies for several articles required for food and other essential use, such as rice, salt, tobacco, betal nut, etc. Nobody else but the British could trade in these aritcles and they made all the profits on these articles, absolutely necessary for the use of Indians. When the British ships came to India, they came empty; and when they returned to England , they went back loaded with raw products from our country. In order to prevent the empty ships from rolling, a certain amount of weights had to be put in their hold. The British put Cheshire salt in it and brought this salt from England to India and sold it in India. In order to be able to sell this salt the British in India reduced the production of salt in India and also levied a tax on Indian-made salt. That is the origin of the Indian Salt Tax. The people of India protested many times, but to no purpose.

The British, after establishing themselves in India, started a policy of exploiting the country to their own advantage.They destroyed all our ancient local industries and handicrafts.They oppressed all the Indian artisans and compelled them to give up their respective trade. They did not want the Indian workmen to do or make any article, because the British wanted to dump their own machine-made articles for sale in India, particulary clothing and other articles required for our everyday use. Our country was producing enough raw goods; but they were all exported to England. All Government rules and laws were made in favour of the British rulers in order to enable them to achieve the above object.

In 1814, cotton piece goods was bought by India from England to the extent of half a lakh of rupees; and now, more than one hundred crores of rupees worth of cotton goods are coming from England to India every year. As you know, cotton is grown to a very large extent in India. Before the British came to Hindustan our ancestors used to make most beautiful cloth in quantity not only sufficient for their own use, but also for exportation to distant countries outside India. Now, why should the British take away the raw cotton from our country, convert them into cloth in their mills in England and bring the cloth back to India for sale? Because the British wanted work for their own people in England, work for their ships, etc., and at the same time make huge profits for themselves. And, we have to pay all these additional expenses. If we manufactured our own cloth, as we used to before the British came to our country, there will be none of these additional expenses to pay, and the profits of the manufacturers will be much less, as the cloth is intended solely for the use of our own people. Thus you see how the British have deprived us from making even cloth such an essential article required for our daily use. You will also note how costly it is for us to be under British domination.

That it why Mahatma Gandhi very strongly advocated the use of Khaddar by all Indians without hesitation. There are several lakhs of our people, working as active volunteers, as members of the All-India Spinners' Association. That is how Mahatmaji wanted to stop the drain of one hundred crores of rupees every year to England from India for the purchase of cloth alone.

The present position, in so far as industries are concerned, is that we have to buy most of our requirements from foreign countries, particularly England. Our own industries are still undeveloped. Our people have therefore no employement but agriculture. As the number of people thrown on the land for work is very great, the extent of land available for each individual in India becomes naturally very small. Owing to lack of irrigation facilities, agriculture is dependent on weather conditions; if there is rain our people can cultivate the land. If there is no rain they cannot do so. So, the amount of food material produced in India is very small. It cannot be increased owing to lack of proper facilities. In other countries, the people are not dependent on weather solely for their agriculture; and they have dams, reservoirs and canals, etc. They use also modern machines in agriculture.

The final result is that our brothers and sisters in Hindustan have become extremely poor with famine conditions, starvation, poor nutrition and disease. So much for the economic aggression of the British in India.

The British Military Aggression of India is well worth our study. The Army in India, both British and Indian, is costing more than one fourth of the total income of our country, i.e., 60 crores. The Army in India is maintained for three different purposes. First of all, Indian soldiers could be sent to any country outside India for their own imperialistic purposes. That is why we are all here. When this War broke out, the British declared India as being belligerent, because India is only a tail to Britain in all respects. So, the Government of India were able to send us all to Malaya, Burma, etc., without consulting our Assemblies. Secondly, the Army in India is intended to help in putting down internal disturbances in Hindustan. So , it is really an army of occupation in India. Last of all, the Army in India may be useful for the defence of India against foreign invasion. This is what is happening today on the Indo-Burma border.

The extravagance of the British Army in India cannot be described., Most of the officers were of British nationality. Lord Curzon said that one of the most important units in the scheme of British imperial defence was to provide the British Government with an efficient striking force, ready to attack any one at a moment's notice. The Army in India has been used outside India for British imperial purposes several times.

The strength of the internal security troops, for internal peace, is nearly 70,000. There are more British troops in this than in the Field Army in India. In 1857, during the first War of Indian Independence, the whole of Bengal Army formed one common brotherhood, and acted fatally against the British. In order to prevent a recurrence, the British have provided a very large number of British officers in all the units of the Army. Further they have formed in India Army Battalions, down even to companies, groups based on tribal, sectarian, religious and communal basis.

These groups will fight against the interest of one another and can never unite against the British. So, it is the British idea that the Indians in the Army could never combine against them.

Further, Indians in the Army are never admitted to positions of power and responsibility in the Army, nor do they ever get a chance of commanding or leading branches of the Army, requiring technical skill and knowledge. Without the British officers there is no chance for Indians to assume leadership.

The Auxillary Force of India includes only British and Anglo-Indian residents of India. The Army is not allowed to mix with civilians, which is quite unlike that of Japan or any other modern country. Military efficiency demands close co-operation and contact between the army and the civilians. In India the gulf between the two is very wide. Also, in the Indian Army, the difference between the British Army Officer and the Indian soldier is very wide. There is no camaraderie or espirit de corps.

Thus the British made Indian Army in India could never be patriotic. It is only an Army of occupation in India, meant mainly for suppressing internal revolutions, strikes, hartals, etc. It is not what it should be, as in other independent countries. So much for the British Military Aggression in India.

Politically, the British made such rules and laws in the Government of India, from time to time, as to keep us completely under their power. They wanted the Indians to fight among ourselves and to work for their benefit. From the time the British rule started in India; the policy of the British rulers in India has been one of 'Divide and Rule'. In 1905 Lord Curzon passed the notorious Act for the partition of Bengal into Hindu and Mohammedan areas. This was first opposed by Hindus and Muslims of Bengal, and later by the whole of India. On account of this partition, the policy of Boycott of English goods. Swadeshi and formation of National Schools was adopted throughout the country. Six years later, during the Delhi Durbar, the partition of Bengal was repealed as a result of popular agitation. In 1909, the British Government of India passed the Morley, Minto Reforms. According to this separate councils came into existence, based on religious and sectional differences. Several protests were made by our leaders, but to no effect.

From 1914 to 1918, our people worked wholeheartedly for the benefit of the British in all the theatres of War, in the hope that India would get Self Government under British rule. India contributed over fifteen lakhs of men, besides a very large amount of war materials and donations of large sums of money.As soon as War broke out, the flower of our Army was marched off to Flanders in France and the world knows that it was owing to the bravery and courage of our men, the first advance of the Germans into Mons was stopped; and the tide of battle turned in favour of the Allies against the Germans. What was the result of all this help we rendered to the British? The British passed the notorious Rowlatt Bills in 1919 by which the British could arrest any Indian without charge, on mere suspicion, and punish the Indian people without trial. The dastardly massacre of 2,000 of our men, women and children at Jallianwalla Bagh in Amritsar by rifle and machine gun fire by the British troops and the massacre of innocent. unarmed people by dropping of bombs from aeroplanes from a height of 200 feet in several villages of the Punjab, were the result of the Rowlatt Bills.

In 1920, the British tried to give soothing syrup in the shape of Montague-Chelmsford Reforms which again adopted the policy of 'Divide and Rule'. The Indians shouted for milk, but the British rulers of India gave them rice water instead. Being dissatisfied thoroughly Mahatama Gandhi started the scheme of non-violent non-co-operation against all British institutions and British methods. Mahatmaji wanted to arouse the national consciousness of our people and at the same time, to produce a parallel Indian State within the British Government of India.

Index

C

J

K

P

Q

R

INDIAN NATIONAL ARMY
A Documentary Study

INDIAN NATIONAL ARMY
A Documentary Study
(In 5 Volumes)

Volume-I

(1941-1942)

T.R. SAREEN

GYAN PUBLISHING HOUSE
NEW DELHI-110002

Indian National Army—A Documentary Study

Rs. 4500 (Set)

ISBN: 81-212-0833-5 (Set)
ISBN: 81-212-0844-0 (Vol. 1)

Published in 2004 in India by
Gyan Publishsing House
5, Ansari Road, Darya Ganj, New Delhi-110002
Phones : 23282060, 23261060, Fax : 011-23285914
E-mail : gyanbook@vsnl.com
Website : http://www.gyanbooks.com

Laser Typesetting at : Shree Vaishnavi Creations, Delhi
Printed at : Chawla Offset Press, Delhi

To

Raghav, Rachan and Sumeet

List of Documents

Appendix-I

Appendix-II

Appendix-III

Appendix-IV

General Introdution

The history of India's struggle for freedom was unique in the sense that it was conducted on two fronts, one inside the country which believed in non-violent means as propagated by Gandhiji, and the other through the efforts of Indian nationalists abroad, who wanted to wrest freedom from Britain by an armed revolution. In their bid to overthrow the British they sought help from many foreign powers. They joined hands with Germany during the First World War, and forged an alliance with international communism after the Russian Revolution for the same purpose. The objective was the same when they collaborated openly with Japan during World War II. Their alliance with Japan culminated in the formation of the Indian National Army (I.N.A).

No doubt, the INA itself was defeated alongwith Japan, but even in its defeat, as Nehru says, it became a symbol of India's fighting for independence. The very idea of an Indian army founded and commanded by an Indian of unquestionable patriotism was enough to evoke enthusiasm from an unarmed people long used to watching the display of British military might. The INA represented the last attempt of the Indian people to fight together for the liberation of a united India. Even Gandhiji, not a very sympathetic critic of the ideology of the INA, admitted that :

"Though the INA failed in their immediate objective they have a lot to their credit of which they might well be proud. The greatest of these was to gather together under one banner men from all the religions and races of India and to infuse in them the spirit of solidarity and oneness to the utter exclusion of all communal or parochial sentiment."[1]

The formation of the INA was neither abrupt nor entirely the handiwork of the Japanese. Indian revolutionary nationalists had been

carrying on their anti-British propaganda from Japan even before the First World War. At that time Japan was an ally of England and could not therefore openly express sympathy for Indian nationalist aspirations, nevertheless, it unofficially supported and helped Indian revolutionaries instead of persecuting them to oblige Britain, as Siam and the U.S.A. had done. The anti-British activities of Barkatullah, Lala Lajpat Rai, Rash Behari Bose, H. L. Gupta, Kesho Ram Sabarwal and many others were not only tolerated but also given considerable encouragement by many Japanese leaders. Japanese politicians like Count Okuma, Inaki and Toyama Mitsuru, the hero of the Black Dragon Society, defended the Indians and impressed upon the Government of Japan that it should ignore the repeated British demand for the extradition of two important Indian revolutionaries, Rash Behari Bose and H.L. Gupta.

Even after the First World War, for a few years some Japanese leaders were still not very enthusiastic about the question of Indian freedom. As Matsumoto, former Attache in the Japanese embassy in London says, "the moderates in Japan were eager to maintain good relations with Britain and pleaded caution on the question of Japanese interference in Indian affairs; in view of British sentiments on the subject of Indians in Japan, the choice was between friendship with Britain and with a handful of Indian revolutionaries."[2]

The policy changed on the eve of World War II, when active cooperation began between the Indian nationalists and the Japanese. The credit for this cooperation in East Asia and for the initial formation of the INA goes to Sardar Pritam Singh, General Mohan Singh, Mohammad Akram and the Japanese intelligence officer, Major Iwaichi Fujiwara. The Indian groups in Japan under Rash Behari Bose, Anand Mohan Sahay and Raja Mahendra Pratap had been watching the deteriorating relations of Japan with Britain and the U.S.A. and hoped that Japan's success in the conflict might help the struggle for India's freedom. In fact, Rash Behari Bose had approached the Japanese Imperial General Headquarters for help in the event of War with Britain. His views on collaboration were listened to, but no promise was made. Independent of the Indian nationalists in Tokyo, however, the Japanese high command decided to encourage other Indian groups in East Asia.[3]

The Indian community in East Asia was quite strong numerically and economically and the Japanese were particularly interested in

forging links with them. The Japanese had two basic aims in view while cultivating an alliance with the Indians. First, their cooperation was essential in the event of an Anglo-Japanese war, since neither the local population nor the Chinese could be trusted. Secondly, Indians could provide valuable information about the British Indian troops stationed on the Thai-Malaya border. The task of negotiating with Indian groups was assignend to Fujiwara and Colonel Tamura, the Japanese Military Attache at Bangkok, who used the assurance of all-out Japanese help to the cause of Indian independence in order to win over the Indian nationalist groups in Thailand and Malaya.

During the negotiations the idea of the formation of a volunteer force for the liberation of India from among the Indian prisoners of war was mooted. The idea was discussed between Pritam Singh, Baba Amar Singh, Major Fujiwara and Colonel Tamura, and some sort of agreement was reached even before the Pacific War. Sardar Pritam Singh and Baba Amar Singh, were former members of the Ghadr Party and had been operating in Thailand. They had formed an Independence League of India and were friendly with the Indian troops. Both parties came to an agreement to collaborate with each other. It was agreed that Pritam Singh's organisation would undertake certain activities as soon as war broke out between England and Japan; it would march with the Japanese army and carry out propaganda among Indian soldiers of the British army. In fact, the ground under the feet of British power was to be cut by shaking the loyalty of British Indian soldiers in Malaya; if possible they were to be won over and reemployed against the British.[4]

The Pacific War broke out in December 1941. Japan smashed her way to Java, Malaya and Burma right up to the eastern frontier of India. With the defeat of the British, the first batch of the Indian army units under Captain Mohan Singh surrendered to the Japanese. As arranged earlier, they were given most cordial treatment by Sardar Pritam Singh and Fujiwara Kikan— a liaison agency under Fujiwara. By his seeming sincerity, Fujiwara inspired Mohan Singh with the idea of liberating India with Japanese assistance. Mohan Singh pondered over the idea and its implications for several days and then, as if in a mystical revelation, grasped the significance of the suggestion and the urgency of his mission. He agreed to organise the Indian army units being abandoned by the British into a well-knit Indian National Army.[5] Initially, the idea of the formation of the INA was not, however, fully supported by the Japanese military administration in East Asia.

They reluctantly agreed to its formation but allotted it the limited role of controlling Indian prisoners of war and maintaining law and order in some territories under their occupation; they looked at it as a valuable instrument of propaganda or of local policing, rather than as an army of liberation.

Despite this attitude, Mohan Singh proceeded with the formation of the INA, especially after the fall of Singapore when the Japanese handed over to him nearly 45,000 personnel of the Indian army who had surrendered at a ceremony at Ferer Park.[6] Mohan Singh began the conversion of the soldiers of the Indian army into a nationalists army with one important advantage—both officers and soldiers of the British army were in a state of psychological shock and had lost confidence in the leadership of the British. Under Mohan Singh they felt secure and, when a new mission was proposed to them, their response was encouraging. In view of the heterogeneity of the Indian soldiers, it was not an easy task for Mohan Singh to turn them overnight into fighters for freedom, but it goes to his crecdit that he was able to bring about a semblance of unity among them. By the middle 1942, about 40,000 P.O.Ws in all had agreed to join the INA. There was an enthusiastic response for enlistment from Indian civilians also. Lectures were given to the volunteers on the political and economic problems of India, on the lives of the Indian national leaders and Indian efforts for achieving freedom. Men of different faiths were encouraged to live together and eat from the same kitchen and celebrated religious festivals jointly.[7] It was all inspired by the lofty ideals of unity, faith and sacrifice, and every soldier had taken a solemn pledge to sacrifice his all for the honour of India. A nationalist army was ready in the middle of 1942 to launch an attack on the British for the liberation of the Indian people.

At the same time, Rash Behari Bose, on account of his standing with the Japanese, took over the presidentship of the entire movement in East Asia. In coordinating the efforts for India's independence he called two conferences at Tokyo and Bangkok where resolutions were passed to organise the INA and invite Subhas Chandra Bose to East Asia from Germany to lead the movement. Mohan Singh was a man in a hurry and wanted to capitalize on the favourable conditions then prevailing in India. India was in the grip of the Quit India Movement; British military power in the region was at its lowest ebb; and an initiative by the INA might have dealt a serious blow to the British. But for their own reasons, the Japanese postponed the drive towards

India and their Indian nationalist allies started doubting their intentions. British propaganda also played its role and Mohan Singh began to believe that the Japanese wanted to use the Indians as their tools. These doubts led to a crisis towards the end of 1942, particularly because of the failure of Japanese liaison officers to understand the Indian point of view. The officers did not have a definite idea of Japanese policy towards India; consequently, they were unable to cooperate with the Indian nationalists to the satisfaction of the latter.[8]

In this dispute,Rash Behari Bose sided with the Japanese and dismissed Mohan Singh. But the Indian nationalist in East Asis realized that it was not possible to carry on the movement under the leadership of Rash Behari Bose who did not question the wayward policy of the Japanese as boldly as Mohan Singh did. The consequent crisis of leadership was resolved only with the arrival of Subhas Chandra Bose from Berlin; Rash Behari Bose, as a Japanese citizen, had failed to inspire confidence in his comrades.[9]

By the time Subhas Bose was allowed to land in East Asia the war situation had taken a new turn and Axis powers had suffered reverses at many places. Nevertheless, the conception of Indo-Japanese collaboration changed after Subhas assumed command of the INA. He possessed an indomitable will and great organisational ability. While Mohan Singh had thought only of strengthening the INA as a military machine, Subhas had a wider vision of mobilising the entire Indian manpower in East Asia into an irresistable army of liberation and of hurling it against the British in India. After he had been assured full support by the Japanese, he thoroughly re-organised the Indian Independence League and the Indian National Army; thereafter, he formed the Provisional Government of Free India and came to an agreement with the Japanese military authorities with regard to the role of the INA. Subhas convinced the Indians in East Asia of the sincerity of Japan and boosted their morale by dispelling their doubts about the ultimate victory of Indian nationalist forces. He made them realize that Japanese military assistance to the INA against the British was as necessary for the Japanese to ensure the security of their own co-prosperity sphere as it was for the achievemtent of India's independence.

After his arrival in Japan, Subhas met the Japanese premier, Tojo, on 10 June 1943, and again subsequently on 14 June. The latter was highly impressed by his patriotic zeal. Here was an ardent revolutionary

whose whole life had been devoted to the cause of India's independence and whose thinking was very close to that of Japan. Naturally, Tojo had no hesitation in conceding his demand for unconditional help to the Indian independence movement. Two days after the meeting, Tojo declared in the Diet that Japan was determined to extend every possible assistance to the Indians to eliminate Anglo-Saxon domination in India and enable the country to achieve full independence. This statement came at a time when the war was not going well for Japan. But Subhas was optimistic; his patriotism and eagerness to liberate India made him oblivious to the changing reality of the war, and he was convinced of the ultimate victory of the Axis powers. The Japanese liaison agency, now known as Hikari Kikan, was placed under Yamamoto, who had known Subhas in Berlin.[10]

Subhas took over the leadership of the movement on 4 July 1943 from Rash Behari Bose and was overwhelmed by the reception he received, He told his audience that he was 'absolutely sure' of their victory, but reminded them that considerable effort and sacrifice were required to achieve the goal. With his magnetic personality and fine oratory, Subhas soon created among his associates an acute awareness of their duty towards their country. Sahay recalls that under Subhas' leadership the officers of the INA regained their self-confidence and the civilian population realized that they had found a leader in whom they could place their trust unreservedly. The Indian merchants all over East Asia began contributing to the Azad Hind Fund and young men started pouring into enroll themselves as volunteers in the INA. The INA was galvanized into life and was publicized openly as 'India's Army of Liberation'; Subhas' fiery speeches inspired it with patriotism and a sense of sacrifice, and he outlined a twofold task for it : 'With the force of arms and at the cost of your blood you will have to win liberty. Then when India is free, you will have to organise the permanent army of free India whose task will be to preserve our liberty for all time'. He further emphasized the need for aid from the Axis powers as, in his view, there was 'nothing wrong if we accept their sympathy or even their help, should we need it'. At the same time, he wanted the Indians in East Asia not to depend entirely on foreign aid and to achieve independence by themselves.[11]

Though Subhas had taken over what Lahiri describes as a'made to order' movement but by putting his body and soul in the task he was able to expand it. His single-minded devotion to the cause of Indian

independence did not fail to impress even those Japanese army officers who were still doubtful about his credentials. Both Mohan Singh and Subhas were very conscious of the need to bring about harmony among the different religious groups in the INA and Indian society in East Asia. They achieved remarkable success in bringing the Sikhs, the Muslims and the Hindus into a common brotherhood. But whereas Mohan Singh had conceived of the INA only as a military movement, Subhas widened its scope so as to make it the vanguard of a people's movement in South-East Asia and to raise it into a national campaign for freedom.[12]

Subhas was keen to set up a Provisional Government of Azad Hind and to fully reinforce the INA —of course, with the consent and help of the Japanese government. The Hikari Kikan was hostile to the plan, which was likely to affect its power and importance adversely, but Subhas could visualize that, if the Azad Hind Government was recognized by Tokyo, the INA would have to be recognized as an allied army of an allied government—a goal for which Indians had been striving since 1942. He hoped that the Azad Hind Government would ultimately replace the British government when India became free, but he knew that at that early stage the Provisional Government had symbolic rather than real value. As he explained, it was not 'like a normal peace-time government' and its objective was to conduct the final war against the British and their allies in India. The announcement of the setting up of the Provisional Government of Free India was made by him on 21 October in Singapore[13]. The next day the Provisional Government declared war on Britain.

From the day the Provisional Government was formed, the INA had a will, a purpose and a mission; it was now to fight out India's last war of independence, with the new war cry 'On to Delhi'. The reaction of officials of the Government of India to Subhas' slogan, 'On to Delhi', was mixed. They were no doubt perturbed by developments in East Asia, but had grave doubts about prospects for the movement. A British report on Subhas' activities ridiculed him, suggesting that during his tour of the southern regions under Japanese occupation he had announced his intention of flinging his allegedly well-equipped Indian National Army across the India-Burma frontier before the end of 1943 no less than five times. To deflate the movement, the British presented Subhas as a traitor and spoke of the INA with disdain. Nevertheless, the Commander-in-Chief of the British forces in a secret despatch to

the Secretary of State for India was constrained to report that Bose should not be dismissed as 'a mere loquacious tool of the Japanese', for his influence on Indians, both in India and abroad—if not actually on the Indian soldiers—was a factor to be reckoned with.[14] An official analysis of Subhas' position at this time further stated rightly that 'Bose has now finally burned his boats with us by virtue of his association with Germany and Japan, his political future being entirely dependent upon the continued military success of the Japanese and the paralysis of British rule in India by internal revolt.' British officials, however, were convinced that the internal revolt was not possible since public morale and internal security was fairly steady. They believed that his chances of whipping up a major revolt would appear to be small. Had he arrived in East Asia last August or even during Gandhi's fast his prospects would have been much better': naturally Bose's efforts to send agents to precipitate an internal revolution in India were not very successful.[15]

Subhas, however, hoped that the INA would have a tremendous psychological impact on the Indian people and would spark off a revolution inside the country once it stood on Indian soil. Mohan Singh was never given any indication about the role which the INA was to play by the Japanese in their march towards India, but Bose was determined that it should play a significant one in ousting the British, with or without the Japanese army. He believed that strategy rather than military strength would defeat the British. As the Supreme Commander of the INA, he knew that an outright victory against the superior British and American forces was impossible, but he firmly held that armed activity near the borders of India would provoke Indians to rise against the British. Bose's success in making an effective appeal to the patriotism of Indian officers and his powerful leadership, together with the liberty given to unwilling men and officers to leave the INA if they so desired, seemed to have changed the character of the army into a real, revolutionary force. Subhas reorganised the entire structure of the Army. The Directorate of Military Bureau was converted into the headquarters of the Supreme Command. Bhosle was appointed the Chief of Staff. Each unit of the INA was placed under a Divisional Commander. Intensive military training was imparted to them by officers, and Bose himself took a keen interest in raising morale. He revised the pay of the INA ranks, reviewed it straining at every opportunity, improved its rations and made every effort to bind

the officers in true commradeship. Lectures were arranged for the soldiers from time to time so that they could understand the significance of the purpose for which the Army had been organised. The lectures were published by the Indian Independence League and distributed among the ranks.

Before the INA could develop into an independent and strong force, it was necessary for Subhas to settle the question of its relationship with the Japanese army. The Anglo-American block had spread word that the INA was a puppet army raised and equipped by the Japanese to serve their own ends. This impression had to be obliterated from the minds of INA soldiers before they could be expected to play their rightful role in the war of India's liberation. Besides British propaganda, even some Japanese army commanders thought that the INA was fit only for intelligence work and could not be relied on in actual fighting. For instance, Field Marshal Count Terauchi,Commander of the Southern Expeditionary Force, told Subhas that in the event of the Japanese advance towards India, the main burdan of fighting would be borne by the Japanese army and the INA would be utilized for propaganda and purpose. This role was not acceptable to Subhas and other INA commanders. The soldiers of the INA, too, did not consider this role adequate. Mohan Singh had raised his voice against the Japanese attitude and been ousted, but Bose was a stalwart, both physically and figuratively, and commanded the respect of the Japanese. He frankly told the Japanese that the only role acceptable to the INA during their advance towards India was that of the vanguard, Indian freedom had to be won by Indians, for the freedom secured through Japanese sacrifice would be worse that slavery. He declared that 'the first drop of bloodshed on Indian soil should be that of a soldier of the INA.[16]

Though Count Terauchi's reaction was not very favourable, the Japanese Chief of Army Staff, General Sugiyama, promised that in the impending Imphal campaign the INA would rank as an allied army under Japanese operational command.After these negotiations, Bose decided to move his headquarters to Rangoon in the first week of 1944, for he thought that Burma was to become the springboard for an attack on India. As the Supreme Commander of the INA, he saw to it that intensive training was given to the soldiers and he took a keen personal interest in each and every soldier. In view of the small size of the INA, it was decided to train the troops in guerilla warfare; they

were to be lightly equipped for mobility and penetrate enemy lines. Japanese officers gave INA units guerilla training, including in musketry, bayonet fighting and camouflage work.

Towards the end of 1943, the Allies decided to start a counter-attack against the Japanese. To check this the Commander of the Japanese Southern Army was sounded on 7 January 1944 that 'in order to strengthen the defence of Burma, the G.O.C. Southern Army is to attack the enemy when the conditions become favourable and occupy and consolidate the Imphal area and the strategically important regions in North-east India.'[17]

With the Imphal operation just around the corner, Subhas had a very crucial meeting to discuss joint operations with General Mutuguchi at Maymyo, where a ceremonial photograph was taken. According to an eyewitness, after the photograph session, Bose, smiling from behind his spectacles, said to the General while going into the house. 'This is the first time. I am being photographed with Your Excellency. I hope our next photograph will be at Imphal before long'. The interpreter communicated this to General Mutuguchi, who replied: 'Please wait for about fifty days. I shall fulfil your desire'. Both Bose and Mutuguchi were very optimistic about the outcome of the campaign and the latter believed sincerely that the Imphal campaign would reverse the whole course of Japan's deteriorating war situation everywhere.[18]

The main strategy of the Japanese was to push their defence line from the Chindwin river to a more strategic place in the Indo-Burma frontier mountains in order to capture the Imphal and Kohima areas, which were the main base of the Anglo-American forces, and thus to forestall their design to attack and recapture Burma. To achieve this, the main operations were to be directed towards two sections, namely, the Arakan hills and Imphal. In these operations, the Japanese agreed to align three regiments of the INA with three of their own divisions,—the 15th, 31st and 33rd—comprising more than 100,000 soldiers. Two hundred soldiers of the INA were attached to each of the advancing Japanese units. These soldiers were divided into four groups, with different functions. The first group was to carry on front-line propaganda among British Indian troops; the intelligence group was to collect relevant information; the reserve group was to look after those Indian soldiers expected to surrender to the INA—Japanese forces; and the administrative group was to look after the area occupied

by the Japanese army while advancing towards India.[19] As a matter of fact, the strategic planning of the Imphal campaign had a limited objective for both the Japanese and the INA. It was to provide the Japanese with a sure base for the defence of Burma, and for the INA a springboard for a country-wide revolution to oust the British.

The Arakan attack was launched by the 55th Division under Lieutenant-General Hanaya on 4 February 1944; the INA unit of the Bahadur Group under Major L.S. Mishra and the second unit of Subhas Brigade under Major P.S. Raturi were attached to the Japanese division. In the Arakan sector, everything initially went in accordance with the Japanese plan after the offensive commenced in February; but soon it met with tough resistance. The Japanese 55th Division, ignoring tough British opposition, took hold of Taung Bazar and trapped the 7th Division of the British Indian army. The attack was very sudden and, as Hugh Toye says, to a great extent its success was due to 'the reconnaissance and subversion of an Indian outpost position by Major L S. Mishra the INA Commander in Arakan'.[20]

The British too praised the work of the INA contingent under L.S. Mishra on the Arakan front. They admitted that, in the initial stage, the INA propaganda was able to persuade many Indian soldiers to desert the British Indian army and be subsequently absorbed in the Bahadur Group. But the INA failed to create really large-scale confusion among the Indian troops and to win them over to the Japanese.[21]

The main Imphal campaign was carried out by three Japanese divisions to which were attached two INA battalions. One battalion was to help the Japanese check the advance of the West African Division in Arakan, and the other to take charge of the Haka-Falam Sector. On 10 February 1944, Lieutenant-Colonel Shah Nawaz Khan, who was commanding the 2nd and 3rd battalions of the INA, was given orders to carry out an offensive on the Haka-Falam front, while Colonel M. Z. Kiani, Commander of the No. 1 INA Division, was asked to set up his divisional headquarters at Chamal on 17 April 1944.

The Japanese advance in the Imphal-Kohima area had been very swift. However, their initial success was met with stiff resistance from the British, who were able to keep up an almost continuous stream of air supplies. Soon the INA was fighting in eight different sectors of the Burma-India border, in the plains of Imphal and in the neighbourhood of Kohima. A detachment of the INA under Colonel S.A. Malik and Captain Itosa of the 33rd Division penetrated into Indian

territory and planted the Indian tricolour at Moirang in Manipur on 14 April 1944. The swift Japanese advance in the Tiddim Bihsenpur sector brought some Indian prisoners of war into the orbit of Malik contingent, and they were sent back on sabotage work. Malik achieved tremendous success and, after establishing his base in Indian territory, he even organised a local Manipuri spy ring; besides, a number of captured British soldiers joined the INA voluntarily. The INA soldiers also established their headquarters at Moirang in the house of a local Manipuri sympathizer, Hemaru Thambalyuo Singh.[22]

The other two battalions of the Subhas Brigade under Shah Nawaz proceeded towards Haka-Falam in the Chin Hills. The Japanese considered it important to hold these two strategic points to protect their lines of communication. Shah Nawaz established his base at Myitha Haka on 24 February 1944 and took over charge of the defence of Haka on 3 April from the Japanese. His men successfully patrolled areas around Falam. In May a part of the 2nd battalion raided the British patrol base at Klang, about 20 miles west of Haka.

The INA and Japanese forces wanted to stop a British offensive before it could materialize or gather adequate strength, and operations had been taken up simultaneously in both the sectors, The INA was halted within three miles of Imphal because it lacked air support while the enemy, in a desperate last-minute stand, poured reinforcements into Imphal by air. Lord Mountbatten, the British Commander, was to defend Imphal at all costs. In the defensive battle he adopted a strategy which proved successful. He subsequently recorded that: 'The Japanese High Command played into our hands by staging an all-out offensive. It was most fortunate that at this stage the enemy should choose to fight us on our own ground near our own base, in the only areas where our existing lines of communication could adequately support us in a large-scale campaign, and when our air bases were sufficiently near the front to enable our supply to be undertaken.'[23] With the onset of the monsoon, the position became desperate for the INA and orders for withdrawal were given. INA soldiers had to walk hundreds of miles without a morsel of food over days on end. With the hills shrouded in mist and the tract either washed away or under ankle-deep mud because of incessant rain, it was difficult even to retreat. During the few months of fierce warfare, INA soldiers had given ample proof of their fighting qualities and courage. They coped successfully with the numerically superior and better equipped enemy forces, and

gave them a crushing defeat on various fronts. But they were not destined to accomplish their mission. The postponement of the operation was made public by Subhas in a special order in which he said the INA would 'launch a mighty offensive against our enemies once again' as soon as preparations for it were complete. But the postponement of the campaign was a prelude to the final catastrophe.

The failure of the Imphal campaign was attributed to many causes by participants in it. Count Terauchi ascribes the defeat to the Japanese lack of preparedness in getting supplies to the front and 'to the under-estimation of the enemy's capacity of supply by air'. The British propagated the idea that the Japanese made the 'fatal mistake' of supposing that, as soon as India was invaded, there would be a nationalist revolution which would completely neutralize British and American military strength in India, thereby 'leaving the field open for Bose's puppet forces to fight for India'.[24]

But at the same time the Army Headquarters in India admitted in a secret dispatch that the results of the Japanese offensive might have been disastrous for the British had they been able to establish 'a solid foothold in the area' and finally in India; and that 'the conquest of even a single Indian State by the Japanese would have widespread repercussions upon morale and politics', as 'the plain of Imphal was a prize whose capture by the Japanese might have altered the whole course of the war in Eastern and Southern Asia and influenced deeply the history of India and China'.[25]

The exploits of the INA have been glorified by many of its members, but perhaps Fujiwara's assessement of the INA is the most balanced, though he admitted at the time of writing that it should not be taken as 'a positive or accurate judgement'. 'As a revolutionary army', he writes, 'its morale was high as it was quite well organised; but the standard of its tactics, training and leadership was low', and 'it lacked in particular offensive strength and tenacity'. Fujiwara observes that the INA lacked in technical training and mountain warfare skills, and had no experience in the construction of fortifications; it could not absorb the disappointment of reverses and suffered from psychological setbacks which forced it to go on the defensive. But he concedes that its revolutionary spirit, organisation and discipline—which were generated first by General Mohan Singh and nurtured by Subhas Bose, and which were the very foundation of the INA—were maintained by the officers and men of the INA.[26]

The strength of the INA lay in its devotion to the cause of India's independence. The thought of winning a piece of their homeland back from the enemy was uppermost in its mind and almost all INA soldiers went wild with joy when they crossed into India. Some even got down on their knees and kissed the earth. Two Japanese war correspondents who had accompanied the INA forces have given the following account of the occasion: 'We were deeply moved when we saw the Indian soldiers bursting out with joy when they had the first glance of the mountains and rivers of their beloved motherland .... The cries of Jai Hind, Jai Hind, rent the sky and reverberated in the enemy camp through dense jungles on the borderline.'[27]

Despite defeat, Subhas was not willing to give up the fight for the liberation of India: 'the roads to Delhi are many and Delhi remains our goal. The Azad Hind Fauj will fight to the last man and to the last round', he told the Indians after reaching Bangkok. He continued his propaganda, and when the Gandhi-Jinnah meeting was scheduled to be held in the summer of 1944 he urged Indians not to believe that a settlement between the Congress and the Muslim League could lead to independence.

After the Japanese surrender on 15 August 1945, Subhas was allowed to proceed on his journey in a plane provided by General Terauchi. The plane crashed and Bose's death was announced to the world on 23 August. His tragic death and the surrender of the Indian National Army at Singapore marked the end of a vibrant chapter in India's struggle for freedom from abroad. The British attempt to denigrade INA officers by putting them on trial for treason towards the end of 1945 was doomed to failure as the subsequent events proved.

The British, both in England and India, were understandably hostile to its members—particulary in the officer corps. Their antipathy towards the INA ranged from tolerance born out of necessity, to bitterness. Wavell the viceroy, himself had a very low opinion of the INA men 'who were for the most part the weaklings and softlings of the prisoners of war in Malaya'.[28] While there was a difference between the War and the Home Departments as regards the prosecution of the INA, they were one in their opinion that no INA personnel would be reinstated in the army.

At a meeting in August 1945 it became apparent that there were two extreme points of view on the question of policy towards the INA. One was that members of the INA had committed a most serious offence

and should all be punished with the penalty that the law provided. The other was that the INA men were not pro-Japanese, that their sole object was to achieve freedom of India, and, since India was being promised freedom in the near future, there was no valid reason to take a serious view of what they had done. Wavell was undecided, as it was not known whether Subhas was still alive or dead. He wrote to the Secretory of State on 20 August about the difficulties involved in handling the INA as 'this was the first occasion in which an anti-British politician had acquired a hold over a substantial number of men in the Indian Army and the consequences were quite incalculable. Many of the INA men obviously had a great regard for Bose and he might yet become a national hero'. He wanted the Cabinet to consider Subhas' case carefully and observed that it would be a good thing if he was disposed of without heing sent back to India.

For the authorities in India, Bose's death no doubt solved difficult problem of dealing with him, but 'his patriotism and achievements, even though from the wrong side of the fence', in their view was 'likely to hold an important place in the nationalist mind', and his case was bound up with the future of the captured members of the INA. This assessment of the military intelligence was not altogether wrong. In June 1945, when the captured INA prisoners were being harassed in Burma, Bose echoed the feelings of all Indians when he declared that public opinion might not be strong enough in India to achieve independence, but it would certainly stop the prosecution of the INA prisoners. And this was exactly what happened. The government had no alternative but to initiate the prosecution under mounting pressure from the army, but it decided to prosecute only a limited number of INA members. The Viceroy categrically ruled out 'harsh measures against the INA as a whole', as it 'would undoubtedly be wounding to the majority of Indian opinion.' Taking a middle line, he proposed to 'punish only the leaders', while others 'were to be treated with clemency'. The lenient policy was advocated by the Viceroy in view of popular sympathy for the INA and the knowledge that, even if their conviction was 'secured, which is doubtful, pressure for remission of sentence would be great and the convicted persons would certainly be released by the Congress Government if they came into power'[30]. In a communique it was announced that all INA prisoners were to be discharged and no pensions to be given to them under the code of conduct rules. The communique further clarified that 'there can be no

question of re-employing in the Indian Army anyone who has violated the soldier's code and betrayed his companions'. Another communique on 28 August 1945 stated that it was 'necessary to take some disciplinary action either by discharge from the army or by trials by court martial' against those who were alleged to have committed 'particularly heinous crimes'. The idea of a wholesale prosecution was given up and it was decided to proceed against chosen INA personnel; but even then the British could not expect the approval of the Indian masses and political parties. Already, the public was hailing INA members as heroes. The Congress passed a resolution in September which said that it would be a tragedy if INA members' were punished for the offence of having laboured, however mistakenly, for the freedom of India'.

Three INA officers were chosen for the first court martial. They were Shah Nawaz, G.S. Dhillon, and P. K. Sahgal. The opening of the trials on 5 November 1945 brought into focus the inadvisibility of the policy of the government. There were unprecedented riots all over the country, and seldom had there been a subject that had 'attracted so much public interest' as these trials. The general line of defence was the INA men were motivated by patriotism and, therefore, should not be punished at all.

From the Indian point of view, the success of the trials was thanks to popular support and the able defence put up by Bhulabhai Desai. Desai argued that the INA was an organised force of a properly constituted government which the accused had joined as true patriots; therefore, they had every legal right to fight on behalf of the government they supported. Bhulabhai Desai carried on his defence for more than ten hours spread over two days. The burden of his defence was that the case before the court was not a personal case, that 'the honour and the law of the Indian National Army were on trial before the court'. His testimony exploded the myth spread by the British that Indians had joined the INA to escape inhuman torture at the hands of the Japanese, or to safeguard their lives. He forcefully asserted the right of a subject people to wage war for its liberation and contended that the prisoners of war had voluntarily organised themselves into the INA, which was the army of the Provisional Government of Free India. Hence, the charges levelled against them did not come under the purview of the Indian Army Act.[31]

Despite the convincing arguments of the defence counsel, the three officers were found guilty of waging war against the King and

were sentenced to transportation for life; their arrears of pay and allowances were forfeited. Though under pressure, the C-in-C later remitted the heavier part of the punishment, namely, the sentences of transportation for life.

There were different opinions about the outcome of the trials and their impact on the Indian political scene. From the Indian point of view, they dealt a 'deadly blow to British prestige, canalizing the mass fervour into the fight for freedom'. On the other hand, British diehards thought that 'by conceding the demand for leniency the Government of India weakend the clan of the army'. Sir Francis Tuker, the most senior British officer in the Indian army wrote that the trial had tended to erode the discipline of the Indian army by lightly punishing those who had 'cashiered' themselves from the army and turned against it.[32] A British Parliamentary delegation which came to India in the beginning of 1946 to study the situation reported back that the effect of the INA trials had been very severe but varied markedly with different elements in the army. The old, long service class, such as V.C.Os, was deeply offended that 'the INA have not been treated with the full rigour of the law, but the younger generation are impressed by the political aspect'. Nevertheless, it concluded that the army could still be 'relied on to do its duty except in th event of civil war in which case its loyalty would inevitably be divided among the combatants'. But soon the government realized that the army's troops were 'the only stable element in the country' which could be relied upon for maintaining peace and order in any eventuality'. In fact, the INA trials had completely shaken discipline in the Indian army and soldiers were now more nationalist in their outlook than before.[33]

The year 1946 opened with widespread strikes in the Royal Air Force. This was followed by the revolt of the navy in various parts of the country. Commenting on the indiscipline and strikes in the army and air force, the Chief of General Staff was informed by the G.O.C. Eastern Command that the widespread disturbaces were meant to persuade Indian troops that their future lay in throwing in their lot with the Congress, which was effectively the ruler of India, rather than with the British. The navy report also revealed that the revolt, besides creating disturbances amongt the naval forces at Karachi and Bombay, had created dissatisfaction in the lower formations of various overseas commands of the Royal Air Force and had introduced the word 'strike' for the first time in the history of the services. The report further admitted that the political campaign for freedom had reached

'a crescendo' and that the INA affair was violently exploited to incite Indians still serving in the army. The report revealed that the deeds of the INA had heightened the political consciousness of the armed forces, and that it was no longer possible to rely on Indian troops.[34] All this made it quite apparent to authorities that they could no longer rely on Indian army to rule India and it was decided to grant independence to India on 15 August 1947.

Though defeated on the battlefield, the INA achieved a tremendous victory in India. Its own glory was shortlived, but it hastened the process of the liquidation of the British Empire. After Independence, the INA heroes became what Ganpullay calls 'back numbers' for the only fault of having agreed to fight militarily for the freedom of their country. They drifted into different fields and could not become a part of the Indian army—the role which Subhas had envisaged for them. Wavell noted this change after he had a talk with Jawaharlal Nehru in May 1946 and wrote to the Secretary of State for India: "I think, from what he said, that Congress has begun to realize that the INA is not entirely a creditable asset'. In order to make the erstwhile INA soldiers less effective, Nehru suggested to the Viceroy that some employment opportunities should be provided to 'keep them out of the hands of the more extreme elements' However they were not to be taken back in the army, for the C-in-C had warned that, 'if after the formation of the National Government, the political parties sought to reinstate INA personnel in the Army, that would have a serious effect on Army morale and he himself would resign rather than agree to it'.[35] Wavell conveyed these sentiments of the C-in-C to Nehru, who was still toying with the idea of employing INA personnel, made it very clear that there was no question of re-instatement of INA personnel in the army so long as British power remained. Even the question of their employment in the police was categorically rejected. Nehru yielded to the above threats.

Notes and References

1. *Harijan*, 14 April 1946.
2. South-East Asia Translation and Interrogation Centre, *Historical and Intelligence Bulletin* No. 241, Historical Section, Ministry of Defence, New Delhi (hereafter referred to as SEATIC Bulletin).
3. SEATIC *Bulletin* No. 234. This *Bulletin* is very important as it contains a detailed account of the activities of Fujiwara Kikan and the INA based on the interogation of Fujiwara in 1946 at Singapore.
4. *Ibid.*
5. 'How the INA was Born' by General Mohan Singh, *Bombay Chronicle*, 8 Dec. 1946.

6. For a detailed study of the subject, see T. R. Sareen, *Japan and the Indian National Army* (New Delhi, 1986). This article is based on the above book.
7. Mohan Singh, *A Soldier's Contribution to Indian National Independence* (New Delhi 1974), pp. 82-83.
8. Indian Independence League Papers, F. No. 453, NAI, New Delhi.
9. T. R. Sareen, *op.cit.*, p. 106.
10. Memoirs of Colonel Yamamoto, available in the history of the freedom movement records, NAI.
11. Arun, *Testament of Subhas Bose* (Delhi, 1946), p. 39.
12. Military Department, F. No. L/WS/2/45, IOLR, London.
13. See details about the formation of the Provisional Government of Azad Hind and its policy in S. A. Ayer, *Unto Him A Witness* (Bombay, 1951) pp. 180-90.
14. F. No. 601/7553/H (Historical Section).
15. Mil. Dept. F. No. L/WS/1/1576 (IOLR).
16. Shah Nawaz, *My Memoirs of INA and its Netaji* (Delhi, 1945), p. 75.
17. F. No. 601/7775/ H. (Historical Section).
18. Joshiro Takagi, *Imphal* (Tokyo 1963). The book is in Japanese, and only extracts already translated into English have been used.
19. Memoirs of Lt. Gen. Saburo Isodo, Head of the Hikari Kikan (English translation used).
20. Hugh Toye, *The Springing Tiger* (Delhi, 1962), p. 115.
21. General Headquarters, India, *The Japanese Campaign in Arakan* (Simla 1944).
22. See INA Martyrs' Memorial Number published from Moirang.
23. Quoted in Biseshwar Prasad (ed.), *History of the Indian Armed Forces in the Second World War* (Delhi, 1966) p. 159.
24. F. No. 355/INA (Historical Section).
25. F. No. 601/7398/H. (Historical Section).
26. SEATIC bulletin No. 240 (Historical Section).
27. Quoted in Ba Maw, *Breakthrough in Burma* (London, 1968) p. 354-55.
28. F. No. R/3/1/330, IOL.
29. Wavell to Pethick-Lawrence, 20 Aug. 1945 in Nicholas Mansergh (ed.), *The Transfer of Power 1942-47*, Vol. vi, p. 107.
30. Memorandum by the Secretary of State for India, 24 October, 1945; *Ibid.*, pp. 382-3.
31. See INA Defence by Bhulabhai Desai as reproduced in Motiram (ed.), *Two Historic Trials in the Red Fort* (Delhi, 1946).
32. Francis Tucker, *While Memory Serves* (London, 1950), p. 53.
33. See Report of the R.I.N. Commission of Inquiry, F. No. 601/7968/H (Historical Section).
34. See Note on Wavell's interview with Jawaharlal Nehru, 2 May 1946 in Nicholas Mansergh (ed.), *The Transfar of Power 1942-47*, Vol. VII (London 1978) pp. 394-95.

Introduction to Vol. I

During their struggle against the British, Indian nationalists sought help from many foreign powers. The nature of foreign assistance varied from time to time and was determined by the relationship of the assisting country with Britain. In the present documentary study it is intended to trace the links between the Indian nationalists and Japan during the Second World War and how their collaboration resulted in the formation of the Indian Independence League (IIL) and the Indian National Army (INA). Though the interest of the Japanese in the activities of Indian nationalists' fighting from abroad began during the First World War, yet the alliance took concrete shape only after the Second World War.

The credit for putting the Indian Independence movement in East Asia on a sound footing and for the initial formation of INA goes to Sardar Pritam Singh, General Mohan Singh and Major Fujiwara. As head of the Japanese Intelligence agency, Fujiwara appreciated the demand put forward by Indian nationalists on the eve of the Pacific War for the formation of an Indian Voluntary Army from amongst the civilians and the Prisoners of War of the British Indian Army. Fujiwara inspired Mohan Singh after the defeat of the British in Malaya in 1941 with the idea of liberating India with Japanese assistance and thus the INA was born.

By the middle of 1942, IIL had been properly organised and INA had taken shape as a well-disciplined military unit under General Mohan Singh. But it was soon apparent to the Indian patriots that the Japanese wanted to utilise this army as an instrument of propaganda rather than an army of liberation. General Mohan Singh was irritated at the indifferent Japanese policy. He was a man in hurry and wanted to capitalise on the favourable situation then prevailing in India. At that point of time India was in the grip of the Quit India Movement, the British military power in the region was at its lowest ebb, and an initiative by the INA might have given a serious blow to the British. But for their own reasons, the Japanese postponed the drive towards India and their Indian nationalist allies started doubting their intentions. The British propaganda also played its role and General

Mohan Singh began to believe that Japanese wanted to use Indians as their tools. These doubts led to a crisis of confidence towards the end of 1942.

In this dispute Rash Behari Bose sided with the Japanese and dismissed General Mohan Singh. But Indian nationalists in East Asia soon realised that it was not possible to carry on Indian struggle for liberation under the leadership of Rash Behari Bose who did not question the wayward policy of the Japanese as boldly as Mohan Singh did. The consequent crisis of leadership was fortunately resolved with the arrival of a dynamic leader, Subhash Chandra Bose from Berlin.

The documents included in this first volume cover the period from December, 1941, when Indian nationalists joined hands with the Japanese military authorities till December, 1942, when General Mohan Singh, who had organised the INA was dismissed and imprisoned by the Japanese.

Curiously enough, even after more than fifty years some of the official records regarding Indian National Army are not open for consultation in India as well as abroad. Despite archival restrictions, a vast amount of material is available both official and non-official in various institutions and archives of India, Thailand, Malaysia, Singapore, Japan, England and the U.S.A. A few good works have also been written by some historians and others having links with the INA., these are General Mohan Singh, 'Soldier's Contribution to Indian Independence', Fujiwara, 'F. Kikan', S.A. Ayer, 'Unto Him a Witness', C. Lebra, 'Jungle Alliance', K.K. Ghosh. 'The Indian National Army', and Hugh Toye, 'The Springing Tiger'. But still a comprehensive and objective history of the Indian National Army based on original sources is yet to be written and this can be done only if all the documents are made available to the scholars.

The publication of documents on any topic can be the outcome of selection. This is an inevitable result of vast range of records available on the subject. The hitherto unpublished documents included in these volumes were collected from India Office Library and Records, Public Records Office, Imperial War Museum London, National Archives of India, and Historial section of the Ministry of Defence, Government of India and other repositories in South East Asia and Japan. The principal categories of documents are the reports of the Army Department or War Office, speeches, statements and memoirs of the participants and the interrogation reports of some of the prominent members of the I.N.A. As far as possible the documents have been arranged chronologically though some overlapping is bound to be there. For example, British report on the Fujiwara Kikan was compiled after the war, but has been placed amongst the documents of the year 1942 as it throws a good deal of light on the events

of that period. Similarly an interrogation report of Major Fujiwara, who played an important role in the formation of the INA alongwith the report of Mohan Singh have included in this volume. These reports were compiled after the war, but deal with this crucial period and contain information not available any where else. These reports may be read with the memoirs of Fujiwara which he prepared in 1959 for the Foreign Ministry of Japan. The relevant extracts form this memorandum which was written in Japanese have been translated into English and are included here with he hope that these will clarify many points mentioned in the earlier documents. These are given in the Appendix alongwith the statement of N.S. Gill, which throws a great deal of light on the Japanese Policy towards I.N.A.

The emergence of the INA after the defeat of the British Indian Army was viewed with grave concern by the authorities in India and England Eleborate security measures were taken by the Indian Army and they carried on propaganda against the INA. At the same time the Director of the Military Intelligence (D.M.1) was keen to have information about the intentions of the INA, their leaders and the nature of threat they were likely to pose for India. For getting the information they employed large number of loyal agents. On the basis of the information received the D.M.I. was submitting reports with his comments. The reports prepared by D.M.I. have been included in these volumes. The study of these reports show as to how well informed the British were about the activities of the INA, and their collaboration with Japan and how they kept the Indian public in the dark about the very existence of the INA. The documents about the British policy included here also show as how much they were worried by the activities of Subhas Chandra Bose and the INA.

In this selection, the original documents have been reproduced as closely as possible. In rare cases punctuation have been added and spelling mistakes rectified. Where possible short explanatory notes have been given. The documents in this volume mainly deal with the circumstances leading to the formation of the I.N.A. and I.I.L. proceedings of the Tokyo and the Bangkok conferences, clash between Rash Behari Bose and Mohan Singh on the one hand and between Japanese on the other hand and the crisis which led to the arrest of Mohan Singh.

The documentas presented here are by no means exhaustive, they merely indicate to the research students the nature of the materials available on the subject and may prove to be halpful to them to understand the working of Indian nationalism under Bose as compared to Gandhi. However, it will be necessary for the students to verify the official reports with the private memoirs included in these volumes.

During the course of my studies of the I.N.A., I had the opportunity to meet many persons who were closely connected with Bose and the I.N.A. They were kind enough to either place at my disposal the documents which they had in their possession or their memoirs which they had written, but did not publish. I have included some of them in these volumes. I am extremely thankful to them especially A.M. Sahay, Shah Nawaz Khan, General Mohan Singh, Hugh Toye, S.A. Ayer, Capt. L.C. Talwar and many others for their kind help.

For the compliation of these five volumes. I received assistance from many organizations and individuals in India and abroad. Though it is difficult to mention them individually, but I would like to place on record my gratitude to them. Without their help it was not possible to compile these columes.

Volume one was completed when I was a Senior Fellow of he Indian Council of Historical Research for a period of one year. I am thankful to the Council for their assistance and especially to prof. S. Settar, who was then the Chairman. He encouraged me to complete this work even though the council did not extend the Fellowship after one year.

I will be failing in my duty if I do not place my appreciation of help which I have received from time to time from the staff of the Historical Section of the Ministry of Defense. They have been very cooperative and allowed me to consult the I.N.A. papers when these were in their custody. To consult these papers, I got the special permission through the efforts of Dr. D.C. Verma, for which I am grateful to him. I am equally thankful to the staff of the National Archives fo India, Assam State Archives Dispur, Guwahati U.S. National Archives, Maryland, India office Library and Records, Public Record Office London National Archives, Singapore, Malaysia and Thailand, for their assistance from time to time.

I have no words to thank the members of the I.N.A. Relief and Enquiry Committee. I have visited their office often at Darya Ganj for the last more than thirty years. They were very helpful and even provided me with the full set of the documents which were presented to the court as exhibits at the time of the trial of the I.N.A officers in 1945. The relevant documents from this collection have been included in these volumes.

Last but no the least, I am obliged to Dr. S.R. Bakshi and my wife Dr. Anuradha their for their friendly assistance and advice in the preparation of these volumes. It is hoped that these documents may prove useful to the students and teachers.

T. R. Sareen

New Delhi : 6.10.2003

1

Appeal from Sardar Pritam Singh, Sikh Missionary, to Indian Soldiers in Malaya Asking them not to Fight for the British in the War[1]

5 December, 1941

Dear Indian Soldiers in Malaya and Burma : We advise you to follow the programme of the Indian National Congress under the direct leadership of our great Saint Mahatma Gandhi and the programme instructed by our Indian patriots abroad. The programme for you is that you should never obey the orders of your English Commanders when they would order to attack Thailand. Thailand is connected with India through religion of Lord Buddha, Culture and Sanskrit literature. Therefore, Thailand is a brother country to India. So you should not fight this in any case. And you should never fight Japan, Germany or any other country who is enemy of British, because all such countries are our indirect friends. So to come to the conclusion, you should never help England in this war. If English loose this war there would be ample chance for India's freedom. Some deceiving English propagandists would cheat you and the writer has heard that English dogs bark before innocent Indians to show that they (English) are saving India from Germany, Japan or some other enemy countries of England who want to govern India. But it is wrong. No country has ever done any wrong to India, except these English pirates and thieves in disguise of democratic devils—as they call themselves. Congress and patriotic Indian like Independent League of India prohibit you in helping English.

---

1. Indian National Army papers, File No. 295. I had consulted these papers when these were in the custody of Ministry of Defence. These have now been transferred to the National Archives of India. (In future referred to as I.N.A. Papers.) Copy of this appeal in original hand-written is reproduced in K.S. Giani, *Indian Independence Movement in East Asia*, Lahore, 1947.

2

Speech of Pritam Singh on the Occasion of the Opening of Independence League of India in Bangkok Requesting Indians to Refrain from Helping the British War Efforts[1]

9 December, 1941

The whole of Japanese nation unanimously in a single voice taken a pledge to take her fate for the fulfilment of her incomprehensible spiritual aim of liberating the whole of Asia from the British yoke. We welcome this God given opportunity that Indians have been waiting for since 1904. By the grace of God we are starting on a non-stop voyage to reach India's goal of complete independence. The members of the Independence League[2] of India either in India or abroad firmly believe that all the Independence movements started by the patriotic Indians in India or outside can only prosper when they receive worldwide sympathy and solid help, alongwith their heroic struggles against the British.

In the past, Indian national leaders repeatedly urged the British to reconsider to abandon their blood-sucking policy towards India for which the English never cared the least. British Jingoism is corrigible now. The day of decision has now come when the God's curse in inflicted upon the British for their wicked and treacherous deeds.

England is gasping for breath on the verge of death, having tasted the result of her incendiary declaration of war against Germany, and now she has to face indestructable armed forces of Japan.

---

1. I.N.A. Papers; File No. 295.
2. Independent League of India was a secret organisation in Thailand founded by Sardar Pritam Singh. On the eve of the Pacific war and after the landing of the Japanese forces in Thailand, its existence was announced on 9th Decembe, 1941 and its branches were opened in various cities of South Thailand as they were overrun by the Japanese Army. League collaborated with the Japanese.

Nations in the world have stood up in increasing members, declaring England as the common enemy of Humanity and this combined power, still increasing in number, directly and indirectly help the achievement of Indian freedom. The liberation of India would also emancipate the whole of Asia from British imperialistic suppression and rule, and emancipated Asiatic countries would not then be called the colonies of any empire. Thus would the Asiatics would no more be the black coolies of the White Anglo-Saxon.

Every attempt made by the Indians to achieve freedom of India has always been called "a revolt" by the English, perhaps because other nations were not in a position, under the circumstances then prevailing to openly sympathise towards it. From now on we wish and surely hope that all the freedom loving nations in this world whole-heartedly and openly sympathise with Indian patriotic movements and would officially recognise the Indian people's legitimate right of complete Independence of India.

We appeal to all our Indian, brethren wherever they are, to refrain from helping the British war efforts, and to stand up together to attain the glorious Indian freedom. All Indians should fight to eliminate the Anglo-Saxon from the whole Asia whatever energetic endeavours and sacrifices they have to make.

Immortal Prophets and Martyrs of India call upon you to serve your Motherland Bharata.

3

Copy of an Important Notice by the Japanese Forces on Entering Thailand Assuring Indians to Carry on their Business Peacefully[1]

10 December, 1941

Every Indian in Thailand is hereby informed on the behalf of the Commander-in-Chief of the Japanese troops, Bangkok :–

1. That the Indians should carry on their business as usual. I assure them that no interference will be made in their work, etc. by the Japanese troops. But if any body, inspite of so much assurance, will try to escape from this country or spread false rumours or raise objections, will be considered as an enemy and will be liable to be punished. Remember the following four things in mind :—
   (a) Perform your business peacefully.
   (b) Don't spread false rumours.
   (c) Don't escape from Thailand.
   (d) Love the Japanese and respect them, in order that the Japanese should love you in return.
2. If any one who will fail to comply with the above four advice will be considered as an enemy and will be punished.
3. We Azad Hind League, guarantee your safety.

By the order of Commander-in-Chief
Japanese troops.

---

1 I.N.A. Papers; File No. 9.

4

Aims and Objects of Azad Hind Sang formed by Pritam Singh with Japanese Help after the Pacific War[1]

21 December, 1941

Minor details regarding the formation of the Azad Hind Sang or Azad Bharat Sabha in Bangkok as given by persons interrogated here, are slightly conflicting, as is to be expected, but the account given here is the nearest to the truth obtainable at present.

Its objectives were :—

(a) Close collaboration with the Japanese.

(b) The supplying of volunteers for subversive role on Malaya and Burma Fronts.

(c) Propaganda and broadcasting to stir up anti-British feeling.

Its lending members who had been operating secretly for two or three months prior to the arrival of the Japanese in Bangkok were as follows :–

(1) Giani Pritam Singh[2]
(2) Baba Amar Singh
(3) Master Bhagwan Singh
(4) Amar Singh Suchdev
(5) Seva Singh

---

1. I.N.A. Papers F. No. 384.
2. Sardar Pritam Singh (1910-1942). Son of S. Maiya Singh, belonged to a noble Sikh family of Lyallpur district. After matriculation joined Lyallpur Agricultural College and Sikh Missionary College. On request from Sikh Missionary Society, Bangkok, was sent on April 11, 1933 to act as a priest in Thailand. Was associated with Raja Mahendra Pratap and Baba Amar Singh. Even before the Pacific War was in league with the Japanese and had full faith in Japan, negotiated for help with Major Fujiwara for the liberation of India. Was instrumental in the formation of Indian National Army and the Independence League of India. Died in plane crash in March, 1942 while going to attend the Tokyo Conference.

(6) Labh Singh Matta
(7) Kishan Singh Sethi
(8) Raj Singh Kalra
(9) Master Kartar Singh

The Sang was sponsored and financed by the Japanese, including Major General Tamura, Lt. Ito/s.c military attaches and Major Fujiwara, who is believed to have been working as an employee of the Tamura Koma Shoten a Japanese firm in Bangkok.

On 9th Dec. 41, the formation of the Sang was made public, its H.Q. was established in the house of Ram Singh Kalra in Tung Maha Mek Rd. near the Bangkok Wireless station, Serial No. 7 above assisted by :–

(10) Ishar Singh Daler
(11) Jaswant Singh Sethi
(12) Kundan Singh

Went round Bangkok distributing registering persons as members. The following were probably its earliest recruits:–

(13) Tarlochan Singh
(14) Nandan Farsi
(15) Dunia Shukul
(16) Sadhur San Ahuja
(17) Ram Surat Chobe
(18) Gopal Singh
(19) Harnam Singh
(20) Gurbax Singh
(21) Keshar Singh
(22) Anurudh Shukla
(23) Peshawari Lal
(24) Ganga Singh
(25) Indar Singh
(26) Autar Singh (Narulla)
(27) Mehal Singh
(28) Narain Singh (Narulla)
(29) Gurbax Singh (Chawla)
(30) Ishar Singh (Narulla)
(31) Amar Singh
(32) Babu Changur Singh
(33) Lal Singh (Padre)
(34) Amarnath Suchdev
(35) Dr. Onkar Singh
(36) Master Karnail Singh

(37) Naranjan Singh
(38) Mehal Singh
(39) Amar Das (Champi)
(40) M.A. Shastari
(41) Lal Singh
(42) Harbans Singh
(43) Sardara Singh (Golati)
(44) Sukhu Bhagat
(45) Arjan Das
(46) Puran Singh
(47) Narain Singh Shagufta

Subsequently 80 per cent of the Indian population of Bangkok was persuaded to register as members.

The more prominent leaders of this Sang, were semi-educated and lacking in personality and capability, who, knowing of the impending arrival of the Japanese forces, had decided to be the first to collaborate, with a view to enhancing their own personal position and venting their anti-British feelings. Due to this, and it's being Japanese controlled and considered to be a purely Sikh organisation, the Sang quickly fell into disfavour of thinking Indians of a more true nationalistic outlook, including the D.N. Das and Swami Satyananda Puri.

On the departure of Giani Pritam Singh to Malaya, D.N. Das and his following commenced organising the Indian National Council. This led to friction which continued until the amalgamation of the two parties in April 1942. This amalgamation was mainly brought about by the work of (Lt. Col.) Naranjan Singh (Gill) and (Major) Mahabir Singh (Dhillon).

Activities of the Sang

The main activities of the Sang are as follows :–

(a) Recruiting and organising of Giani Pritam Singh's Malaya party.

(b) Publication on 9 Dec. 1941 of leaflet, and arrest of 50 Indians attempting to leave Thailand on 16 Dec. 1941.

(c) Baba Amar Singh's Mission to Saigon to spread the movement (accompanied by Serial No. 21 on 11 Dec. 1941).

(d) Major Minami's "Burma Party".

(e) Organisation of volunteer group, total about 50, including members of Giani and Minani parties and a few others.

(f) Organising broadcast and propaganda section consisting of Serial Nos. 2, 3, 6, 7, 9, 11, 20, 38, 39, 40.

(g) Subversion of 4,000 I.A. officers and men who actually came

over to the Japanese (figures taken from Seva Ram's report, and subsequently the formation of Mohan Singh's I.N.A.[3]

(h) The formation by Feb. 1942 of I.I.L. Branches at :–

Alor Star	
Sungei Pattani	Kuala Lumpur
Kulim	Kajang
Taiping	Klang
Kuala Kangsar	Negri Sambilan Seramban
Ipoh	Malacca
	Penang
	Singapore

whose membership totalled about 150,000.

It is apparent that the Japanese themselves realized that the Sang though it was initially of great importance, was not, truly representative of the Indian people in Bangkok and shortly after their arrival in Bangkok they called for the formation of an Indian National Council to represent the Indian community.

The Azad Hind Sang, inspite of its leaders, met with unexpected success.

3. This refers to the anticipation of Sardar Pritam Singh that the British forces would be defeated in Malaya. After having come in contact with the soldiers of the British Indian Army before the War, he expected to form a voluntary Army from amongst them who would surrender. Having this in mind, Pritam Singh insisted for this provision in the agreement with Fujiwara. Pritam Singh was keen to train this army for the liberation of India.

5

Captain Mohan Singh to Major Fujiwara Iwaichi Conveying the Willingness of Indian Prisoners of War to Join Hands with Japanese Forces and to Form Indian National Army to Fight the British[1]

31 December, 1941

Reference your notes and Memoranda handed over to us on 30th and 31st December 1941.[2]

We have thoroughly studied all points and in principle we agree with them. Certain minor modifications and suggestions are placed before you for your consideration.

1. Our modified Views as Regards Cooperation with Indian National Army

We consider it a point of great honour for us to accept kind, valuable and reverable leadership Mr. S.C. Bose and his party in Berlin. We all know that he is an extremist who believes in revolutions and radical changes. People in India are most anxiously waiting for any movement started by Mr. Bose and they are ready to support him. He is extremely popular amongst all freedom loving Indians, even his political enemies have great respect and regard for him. His photos can been seen in practically in every house in India. In most cases people worship him like a god. He is a leader whose very name will stir up a great revolution

1. *Ibid.*
2. The memorandum could not be traced. Hugh Toye thinks that these papers were destroyed. On the basis of the original copy of this letter which the British discovered from the papers of M.Z. Kiani, they were sure that it was written by General Mohan Singh and Mohammad Akram. The text of the letter does not give the name of the person who wrote the letter but it was addressed to Fujiwara Kikan.

amongst Indian masses, which will have strong reaction in the Indian Army. It will cause a split in the Indian National Congress circle and the majority of the Congress will join Mr. Bose. We, members of the Indian National Army are prepared to shed every drop of our blood for Bose. His very name puts new life into us.

We sincerely appreciate the Japanese Government's efforts to cooperate with Mr. S.C. Bose. We further request that the Japanese Government may kindly use all its political influence to get Mr. S.C. Bose's support and leadership for such a great movement. If the Japanese Government is successful in it, then in our opinion half the battle in India is won. The day Mr. S.C. Bose's name comes before us we promise that if it suits our purpose we will openly condemn the Indian National Congress.

We appreciate very valuable work done by Mr. Pritam Singh in Malaya. We have great respect and regard for him and will do our best to enhance his influence and prestige. We are willing to cooperate with him with great pleasure.

2. We request that as far as Co-Prosperity Sphere is concerned the Japanese Government may very kindly discuss it directly with Mr. S.C. Bose. We will be most willing to agree to any decision mutually agreed upon by the Japanese Government and Mr. S.C. Bose. We only went to see for our information details and description of Co-Prosperity.

3. Participation of Indian National Army[3] in Malaya and Burma

It is true that the Army which is not prepared to fight in the front line is not worth its name. We do not want to be disinterested and passive observers of the Japanese operation. We also realise that we will not be able to show our face to the world if Indians do no play any active part in freeing their motherland. On the other hand it will be an honour to the Indian National Army to fight side by side with the glorious and world-famed Japanese army. We request that before sending the Indian National Army to the front line the following point should be considered.

---

3. Pritam Singh had in mind the formation of the Indian Voluntary Army. During the discussion, Fujiwara suggested that the Army thus formed may be known as "Volunteers for Indian Freedom:" but Mohan Singh suggestion that it should be called the Indian National Army was gladly accepted by all. For the first time, the name was mentioned in this letter to Fujiwara of 31st December, 1941 from Mohan Singh.

(a) The present Indian National Army consists of men belonging to twenty different regiments coming from different parts of India. It is in fact a very strange mixture. In several cases they speak different languages. To train them under new leaders and under new ideas to fight against the army from which they have come requires some time.

(b) It is also essential that when the Indian National Army is used for the first time it should set a very good example of its bravery and fighting spirit. It should enter the battlefield most modernly armed and equipped. As it is going to fight side by side with the Japanese Army, it is requested that it should be armed and equipped and trained in the same manner. It is just a foundation today, we hope in the near future it is going to be a very big Army. Putting it in the frontline with inferior equipment is sending it to be butchered as was done by the English. This will set a bad example and morale will be lost.

(c) If the Indian National Army is used in Malaya we must not forget that in several cases our men will be fighting against their own units. In certain cases they have got their real brothers and other near relations serving in their own and other units in Malaya. To prepare our men to fight against all this again requires time.

(d) We should also remember that the Indian Army consists of soldiers who have once thrown their arms away on the battlefield. The soldier who lays down his arms in battle may be :

(i) Timid and thus frightened to fight.

(ii) Discontented and thus not willing to fight.

(iii) Exhausted by continuous troubles and hardships which he has undergone since he has come to this country. He might have made up his mind to do no more fighting.

(iv) In certain cases he is just separated from his unit by force of circumstances otherwise he would be fighting for his regiment. To build up the morale and fighting of such soldiers requires selected leaders and stern discipline.

(e) The present strength of the Indian National Army is very small. For its reinforcement and further extension it is entirely dependent on the Indian Army and the Indian in India. Therefore, it is essential that the Chief theatre where this army should be used should be India where it will attract several

Indians to join and enlarge it.

Considering all those points we request the first time the Indian National Army is used in the front line should not be in Malaya but Burma or better still in India. This will give us some time to prepare. We do not want to set any bad example.

4. As far as the leadership of the Indian National Army is concerned all the officers attending the conference held at Alor Star on the morning of 31st December raised a strong unanimous objection to the words in Malaya', and they requested that' in Malaya may very kindly be deleted from that sentence.

6

British Assessment of the Role Played by Fujiwara Volunteers in the Surrender of British Forces at Singapore[1]

15, February, 1942

The Fujiwara Kikan volunteers were the Indian Army soldiers, who immediately or very shortly after surrendered to the Japanese in Malaya in Dec. 1941 and early Jan. 1942, rallied to the cause of Mohan Singh. For the remainder of the campaign up to the capitulation on 15 Feb. 1942, they worked in cooperation with the Japanese and against their erstwhile brothers-in-arms, thus becoming the initial recruits for what later became a fully organised and actively militant anti-British Organisation–the I.N.A.

Following their occupation of Thailand in 1941, the Japanese military authorities contacted the members of the Indian Congress Party, Bangkok, and were successful in enlisting their support to organise subversive activity amongst Indian troops during the impending campaign in Malaya.

This work was in charge of a Japanese Intelligence Officer, Major Fujiwara. His functions appear to have been almost entirely administrative; he spoke no English, and was always assisted by an interpreter.

On the Indian side the lead was taken by Sikhs, notably one Giani Pritam Singh, who established an office in Haadyai in southern Thailand close to the Malaya border, and on the outbreak of hostilities followed in the wake of the advancing Japanese forces.

It is clear that the subversion of Indian troops was a carefully thought-out and integral part of the Japanese plan of campaign. In the first few days of the war, surrender leaflets were dropped by plane, and

1. Combined Services Detailed Interrogation Centre Report No. 31 (C.S.D.I.C.). The above note was prepared in August, 1945, but since it covers the period from December 1941, it has been uncluded here.

the fall of Penang within ten days of the outbreak of war was ascribed by Baba Amar Singh to the excellent work done by the Fifth Column.

The campaign proceeded favourably for the Japanese from the start, and prisoners were not long in coming in. Amongst the early surrenders were :–

8 Dec.	1941	Sub. Allah Ditta Khan
11 Dec.	1941	Capt. Patnaik[2]
11 Dec.	1941	Jem. Puransing Khawas
15 Dec.	1941	Capt. Mohan Singh
15 Dec.	1941	Capt. Mohd. Akram
15 Dec.	1941	Jem. Sadhu Singh

The facts appear to be these :–

(a) The opinion of the Sub Maj. of 1/14 Punjab (a Dogra, and after the collapse of the first I.N.A. a non-volunteer) is that in his on Mohan Singh was conscientious and efficient, and enjoyed the trust alike of his CO, his fellow-officers anu his men. His conduct during the campaign up to the time of his surrender is stated to have been above reproach, and he was in the company of his CO, Lt. Col. Fitzgerald at the time of surrender.

(b) Another report has it that Mohan Singh and Mohd. Akram used frequently to boast of the manner in which they had surrendered to the Japanese.

On this much graver issue, the available information is as follows :–

(c) One informant has stated that at an unspecified date previous to the outbreak of war, a number of responsible ICOs including Lt. Col. Gill 19 Hybad and Mohan Singh were sent on an espionage mission to Thailand. While performing this duty, they came into contact with Giani Pritam Singh and other Indian revolutionaries, with whom they made an agreement to divulge to the Japanese information of a military and security value with a view to the overthrow of British power. They also agreed to carry out propaganda work among Indian soldiers.

(d) In this connection, it is interesting to note the statement of (another soldier) that when 1/14 Punjab was at Tg Pao near Jitra in Sept. 1941, Mohan Singh went on one month's leave, from which he was recalled after twenty days, and that on his return, the relations between Mohan

2. Capt. Patnaik belonged to the Medical Unit in the British Army. He was amongst the first batch of Indian soldiers who surrendered to the Japanese. Shah Nawaz records that the Japanese tried to pursuade him to form a nucleous of a voluntary army, but he refused. See Shah Nawaz : *My memories of I.N.A. and Netaji, Delhi 1946, p. 15.*

Singh and the other officers of the on became somewhat strained.

(e) A further statement is to the effect that as early as Oct. 1941 he knew that Baba Amar Singh and other Sikh revolutionaries were active in Thailand.

(f) On the other hand, Major M.S. Dhillon, RIASC, who was closely connected with Gill and Mohan Singh considered that liaison between those officers and the Japanese was unlikely.

(g) In further refutation of the suggestion of collusion between Mohan Singh and the Japanese is a reported conversation between (another witness) and Mohan Singh, in which the latter mentioned–but was himself clearly not privy or accessory to a probable agreement between the Fujiwara Kiken and Giani Pritam Singh.

(h) Finally, it appears that some initial pressure had to be brought by the Japanese on Mohan Singh and Mohd. Akram before they agreed to engage in Fifth column work.

From the date given above, the following meagre conclusions appear consistent :–

(a) While there is little doubt that India officers were fully aware previous to the outbreak of war of the activities of Japanese-sponsored anti-British elements, there is no positive evidence that Mohan Singh or any other Indian officer had contact before capture with calls of disaffection in Thailand or Malaya.

(b) Despite the strong pro-Sikh bias of the first I.N.A., and the suspicious circumstances of the meeting early in the campaign of Mohan Singh and Giani Pritam Singh, it is considered, in view of his strongly nationalist sympathies which became immediately evident, that while Mohan Singh was probably ripe for subornation, his encounter with Giani Pritam Singh was purely fortuitous, and not the result of a previous arrangement.

After capture near Jitra about 15 Dec. 1941, Mohan Singh was taken to Alor Star, where about ten days later he appears to have yielded to the mingled threats, blandishments, and promises of position and prestige offered by Giani Pritam Singh and Fujiwara. For the next fortnight his movements are somewhat obscure, but he appears to have been employed in preparations for the reception of PW in Alor Star and Ipoh. No contact on infiltration work was done at the time, and the PW were employed solely on fatigue duties.

This was a period of consolidation and organisation. In the words of Major Fujiwara "The foundation of the I.N.A. was laid at Jitra, Alor Star and Ipoh".

It is clear, however, that knowledge of the subversive activities of Mohan Singh must have been bruited abroad even amongst soldiers still fighting on the British side before the end of 1941. In this connection the incident may be noted of Sep. Ghulam Mohd, 5/2 Punjab ("Salooni"– possibly a "quick release") who after inadvertently wandering into the Japanese lines about 26 Dec. 1941 rejoined his unit, five days later started a whispering campaign about the kind treatment shown by the Japanese to PW, and about a mysterious Sikh "General", who was fighting alongside the Japanese. This story magnified and distorted, would spread quickly through the on and beyond, and must have tended to undermine the morale of the sepoys.

In the first few days of 1942, Mohan Singh moved his HQ from Jitra to Ipoh, and sent out parties to organise the collection of stragglers and wounded. These parties were unarmed, and at this stage do not appear to have been engaged in shouting or other frontline work, but were kept at some distance in the rear, with instructions to shepherd PW into the camp at Ipoh, where they were informed, "all arrangements had been made by Capt. Mohan Singh". Following the battle of Slim River on 7 Jan. 1942, when three boes of Indian infantry were dispersed in confusion, 2/4,000 PW were rounded up, and immediately subjected to intensive propaganda by Mohan Singh and his henchmen. This propaganda was almost completely successful, and the majority of the PW readily agreed to transfer their allegiance to the Japanese side.

It was at this time that the plan was first made of sending organised contact parties of PW to accompany the Japanese, not only to round up stragglers and wounded, but, if necessary, fight against the British forces.

When volunteers were asked for from among the PW in Ipoh, the response is reported to have been at first half-hearted, but after further explanation and persuasion, some hundreds stepped forward. As the Japanese wished for a party of approximately only 200, some selection was necessary. On the method adopted, some informants maintain that, so far as the rank and file were concerned, men were quickly detailed in a haphazard fashion. In view of the extreme dull-witt of some recovered 'F' volunteers, there is reason to believe that this may be the case. Others state, however that the VCOs appointed to lead the party, and others present at the time, picked out those who by their intelligence, keenness, and physical fitness would be most suitable for this work.

After being selected, the volunteers were given white armbands with a latter 'F', and told that if challenged by Japanese troops they were to announce that they belonged to the 'Fujiwara Kikan'.[3] Opinions differ as

to whether they were issued with arms at this stage.

Their tasks were :–

(1) To collect stragglers and wounded and indoctrinate them with anti-British propaganda, and where opportunity offered, to send them back to their units as "quick-release agents".

(2) By infiltration into the British lines and mingling with Indian troops to spread alarm and despondency, disaffection and confusion, and by thus undermining morale to induce desertions.

(3) To assist the Japanese in all respects, if necessary by fighting, and to give them information of operational value.

About 21 Jan. 1941, the 180 volunteers who had been selected in Ipoh under command of Sub Allah Ditta, 22 Mtn Regt, (who had just been given the rank of 'captain') and accompanied by Mohan Singh and some Japanese, moved to Kuala Lumpur, where a further call for volunteers to make the number up to 200 brought an immediate response. In Kuala Lumpur, further propaganda lectures were given. About 23 Jan. 1942 a conference, attended by the senior Indian officers and a few Japanese, was held, at which final orders were given.

After final arrangement had been made, the party left Kuala Lumpur about 25 Jan. 1942 and proceeded via Malacca to Muar, where they rounded up about 600 PW, mainly of 219 Jat and 5118 R Garh Rif who were immediately set to collect stragglers, rations and imn.

About 29 Jan. 1942, leaving he freshly-captured PW behind, the Fujiwara Kikan, taking with them a lorry-load of arms, proceeded to Batu Pahat, where the arms were distributed and everyone was given money. In preparation for the final assault on Singapore Island, practice was carried out in combined operations, and the party was for the first time divided into sections as follows (numbers are approximate) :–

	Officers		**Strength**	
No.	Sub	Allah Ditta	22 Mtn Regt	
	Jem	Puransingh Khwas	2/1 Gr	18
No. 1 Sec	Jem	Pritam Singh	R Bombay S & M	39

3. An organisation known as "Fujiwara Kikan" was formed after the Pacific War. In Japanese, Kikan means liaison agency-the Japanese called their agencies after the men who led them. This organisation in its initial stages had both Indian and Japanese members and were issued bands with letter "F" which stood for "Fujiwara, Friendship and Freedom". It served as a liaison agency between the I.I.L./I.N.A. and Japanese Military authorities in South East Asia.

			(Sikhs)	
No. 2 Sec	Jem	Sujjan Singh	1/14 Punjab (Dogras)	42
No. 3 Sec	Hav	Hukam Singh	4/19 Hybad (Jats and (Kumaonis)	28
No. 4 Sec	Jem	Fazal Dad	5/14 Punjab (mainly Gurkhas)	38
No. 5 Sec	Jem	Fateh Khan	5/14 Punjab (Gurkhas, PMs and Pathans)	45
No. 6 Sec	Jem	Dilmansing Thapa	2/1 GR (Gurkhas)	19
				229

Two Japanese officers accompanied the party, and one or two Japanese soldiers were attached to each section.

On 6 Feb. 1942 the Fujiwara Kikan moved from Batu Pahat to Kota Tinggi opposite the eastern end of Singapore Island.

On 9 Feb. 1942, No. 4 Sec. under Jem Fazal Dad was attached to assist in the service of the guns of a Japanese army unit, with which they remained up to the time of surrender.

In the meantime, the remaining sections and HQ Sec crossed Johore Strait to Pulau Ubin on 10 and 11 Feb 1942, where for the next few days they did general fatigue duties for the Japanese.

On 12 Feb 1,942, HQ Sec and Nos. 1, 2, 3 and 5 Secs were sent on an infiltration mission via Johora Bahru to Singapore, while No. 5 Sec on the night 13/14 Feb. 1942 crossed by country boat to Singapore Island at Tampinos Bahru, where on 14 Feb. 1942, they were successful in raising the Japanese flag.

By this time the situation on Singapore Island had so far deteriorated that the members of the Fujiwara Kikan were enabled easily to mingle with units still fighting, and so effect large-scale surrenders. Owing to the extreme caution and unwillingness on the part of recovered PW, to account for this part of their experiences, little is known of this confused period, but from information supplied by recovered members of the Fujiwara Kikan itself, as well as the suspicious circumstances of some surrenders it is clear that the success of the Fujiwara Kikan among the demoralised and dispirited Indian troops must have been considerable.

With the fall of Singapore, the history of the 'F' given volunteers as

an independent unit ends. At the Ferrer Park meeting on 17 Feb. 1942, the 'F' volunteers were seen strutting about displaying their armbands; for a few months they enjoyed a privileged position as members of Mohan Singh's bodyguard at Moun't Pleasant; and with the inauguration of the I.N.A. in Sep. 1942 they became merged in Nehru Bde. Some later rose to high rank in the I.N.A. while others quickly sank back into obscurity; following the collapse of Mohan Singh some became non-volunteers.

The degree of responsibility that can be attached to the Fujiwara Kikan for the defeat of British army in Malaya cannot yet be decided. In contrast to the very fully documented data in existence about Ram Sarup's party which left Kuala Lumpur for Burma shortly after the departure of the Fujiwara Kikan, the information about the later party is meagre. Emphasis has inevitably tended to fall on the later feats of the I.N.A. and until recently the Fujiwara Kikan has been neglected.

The Fujiwara Kikan undoubtedly played a very large part in weakening the morale of Indian troops in Malaya, and it is around this body of traitors that the ignoble traditions of the I.N.A. developed. But there are still gaps in our knowledge.

In particular information on the following topics is very scanty :–

(1) The detailed movements of Mohan Singh.

(2) The conduct of Suh Allah Ditta Khan, 22 Mtn. Regt. (The first active JIFC and the comd. of the Fujiwara Kikan in the field) between his desertion and his meeting with Mohan Singh.

(3) The surrenders on Singapore Island for which the Fujiwara Kikan were directly responsible.

7

Japanese Premier General Tojo's Address before the Diet on the Fall of Singapore Exhorting Indians to Get Rid of the Ruthless Despotism of the British[1]

16 February, 1942

As already announced by the Imperial Headquarters, the Imperial forces have occupied Singapore yesterday, February 15th.

The Army and Navy authorities will make their report concerning the circumstances of the actual fighting. However, I am glad to state my views and conviction at this opportunity.

At the outset of the War, following the issuance of the gracious Imperial Rescrip[2] our forces immediately crushed the main body of the American-British Defeat; and in 18 days they brought Hongkong to submission; in 26 days they occupied Manila, and in 70 days they brought about the fall of Singapore. Thus the important bases of the United States and Britain for their encroachment on East Asia for many years past have all fallen into the hands of the Imperial Forces. Such strategic points as Borneo, Celebes and New Britain have also been occupied by our forces, and moreover the main body of the Dutch East Indies fleet has been annihilated. The Imperial Army and Navy are now carrying out operations in a vast area, on a scale unparalleled in the history of mankind.

These brilliant victories are solely due to the august virtue of His Majesty the Emperor under which the officers and men of the Emperial forces are bravely and energetically carrying on their campaign. To the

1. I.N.A. Papers. F. No. 294. This speech is also reproduced in the publication. Our Freedom and Japan brought out by Indian Independence, league Headquarters in 1943 from Bangkok.
2. This refers to the Imperial Rescript issued by the Japanese Emperor on 8 December 1941 declaring war on United States and Britain.

spirits of those who have offered their lives for the defence of the empire, without concern for their homes and their own lives, to those officers and men who are sick or wounded in remote strange lands, to those who are strenuosly fighting on Land, sea, and in the air by defying extra-ordinarily difficulties and dangers, and to those fellow-countrymen who have sent their husbands, sons, and brothers to the front enabling the latter to exert themselves without worry and who are looking after their homes or helping them and are doing their best in the service behind the guns by enduring all difficulties - to all of the them I wish to render my profound appreciation.

As I have already stated on various occasions, the object of the War of Greater East Asia has its origin in the great ideal which inspired the founding of our Empire. It aims at securely establishing a new order of co-existent and co-prosperity on ethical principles, with our Empire as its nucleus, by making each country and people in Greater East Asia have their proper place. It is completly different in its essential character from the attitude of the United States and Britain toward East Asia.

Singapore and other strategic points, which have hitherto been the bases of the United States and Britain for the invasion and domination of East Asia, are resurrecting with boundless hope and glory as bases for the construction of the New Order and defence for the peoples. Malay Peninsula are already starting on the road for such new construction with steady strides.

On this epochal occasion I wish to reiterate once more the real intentions of Japan to the peoples and countries concerned.

The Imperial forces are steadily carrying out offensive operations in the region of Burma also with its strategic points falling one after another into their hands. But the true intention of Japan in marching into Burma is to crush British military bases as well as to cut off the route for American and British aid to the Chiang-kai-shek regime. It is farthest from the thought of Japan to regard the Burmese people as her enemy. Therefore, if the Burmese people take full cognizance of the actual situation of Britain, which has exposed its utter inability, and offer to co-operative with Japan by shaking off many years past. Japan will gladly extend them its positive cooperation for the establisment of Burma for the Burmese, the long-cherished aspiration of the Burmese people.

It is a golden opportunity for India having, as it does several thousand years of history and splended cultural tradition, to rid herself of the ruthless despotism of Britain and participate in the construction of the Greater East Asia Co-prosperity sphere. Japan expects that India

will restore its proper status as India for the Indians and it will not stint herself in extending assistance to the patriotic effort of the Indians. Should India fail to awaken to her mission forgetting her history and tradition, and continue as before to be beguiled by the British cajolery and manipulation and act at their beck and call. I cannot but fear that an opportunity for the renaissance of the Indian people would be forever lost.

8

Proceedings of Joint Conference of Representatives of Indian Independence League, Malaya and Thailand Regarding the Policy to be Adopted for Collaboration with Japanese for the Liberation of India at the Forthcoming Tokyo Conference[1]

9 March, 1942

Present : The following gentlemen were present.

The Indian Independence League, Malaya.

1. Shri N. Raghavan.
2. Shri B.K. Das.
3. Shri Suchca Singh.
4. Shri K.A.N. Iyer...
5. Dr. Majumdar...

From Singpore

6. Shri S.C. Goho.
7. Shri K.P.K. Menon...

Indian Independence League, Thailand.

8. Sardar Pritam Singh.
9. Sardar Amar Singh.
10. Dr. Onkar Singh.

Indian National Council, Thailand :

11. Swami Satyanand Puri,

Indian National Army.

---

1. Indian Independence league papers collected by the History of Freedom unit F. No. 45/3. Now deposited with the National Archives of India, New Delhi. (In future referred to as I.I.L. papers). See also. K.S. Giani. op. cit. pp. 33-40. The above collection is very important to understand the early activities of the Indian National Army and Indian Independence League in South East Asia.

12. Captain Mohan Singh.
13. Captain Mohamad Akram.

Indian Prisoners of war.

14. Lieut. Col. N.Z. Gill.
15. Major M.L. Kiani.

Mr. Otagura attended the meeting as observer.

Shri N. Raghavan presided and requested Major Fujiwara to open the Conference. Major Fujiwara expressed very great pleasure at having had the opportunity of meeting the representatives of the Indian Independence League of Thailand and Malaya. The meeting was of particular significance in that it was being held in the citadel of British Imperialism in Asia, namely Singapore. He wished the conference every success and earnestly hoped that their endeavours to liberate India would be crowned with success. He regrets that he could not remain longer with them owing to other engagements. Shri Raghavan thanked Major Fujiwara for his very encouraging words. Major Fujiwara then left the meeting.

The Chairman then requested Sardar Pritam Singh to address the meeting. Sardar Pritam Singh explained how the Indian Independence League was formed in Thailand at Bangkok and then thanked the Indians in Malaya for their ready cooperation in having organised branches of the League in all centres of Malaya.

The Chairman proposed a resolution appreciating the patriotic work of Sardar Pritam Singh and thanking him on behalf of the Indian community in Malaya for his selfless work in the cause of the liberation of their motherland. The resolution was acclaimed unanimously by the conference.

The Chairman then pointed out that two points were to be considered by the conference.

1. Whether the present time is the proper occasion for the Indians in Far East to take action for the attainment of Indian Independence.
2. If this is the proper occasion, how should We proceed towards the attainment of our goal.

Captain Mohan Singh said that he got into contact with Sardar Pritam Singh at a place near Jitra on 15th December, 1941 and learned about the Indian Independence League. Subsequently he met Major Fujiwara, and after that he had been in constant touch with them. At first he was doubtful of the Major's purpose, but now he was fully convinced of his sincerity in desiring to assist in the liberation of India from British control. The situation that all of them had visualised to that time was completely changed with the fall of Singapore. They did not expect to find in

Singapore such a very large number of Indian soldiers, nearly 50,000. The total strength of the Indian Army now in Malaya was near, 60,000. To feed them, to equip them and to look after their other requirements would be a big problem, and the Indian Independence League must give immediate consideration to it.

Lieut. Col. Gill spoke about the 50,000 Indian prisoners of war at Singapore and wished to know what was to become of them.

Swami Satyananda Puri explained the formation and objects of his organisation, the Indian National Council of Thailand. The objects were mainly, (1) to work in cooperation with the political activities in India, (2) to win the sympathy of the Indian National Congress, (3) to secure all India leader as President of the organisation. Explain the third object, he told the meeting that Pandit Jawaharlal Nehru was reported to have stated that Indians residing outside India could not interfere in Indian politics and that those who do so could be considered as traitors. This organisation was therefore afraid that it might by treated as a body of Quislings in the pay of the Japanese. Unless all possibilities of such a stigma were removed, nothing could be achieved. He therefore suggested that contact should be established with Sri Subhas Chandra Bose and that he be requested to lead us. Swami Satyanand Puri said that he had sent a Telegram to Shri Bose from Bangkok on 2nd February 1942 to that effect and had received a reply over the radio agreeing to accept the Presidentship of the Indian organisation in the Far East working for Indian Independence.

Shri S.C. Goho requested Sardar Pritam Singh to explain to the conference the purpose of the proposed delegation to Tokyo.

The Sardar said that the delegation was proposed to meet in an informal conference at Tokyo, to discuss the problem of Indian representatives and to negotiate with Japanese authorities terms of cooperation with Japan for achieving the independence of India.

Lieut. Col. Gill stressed the importance of carrying out effective propaganda in India to prepare the necessary atmosphere so that the Indian army overseas would receive the willing cooperation and help of all Indians when it should match into India. The Indian army had been till now fighting under certain pledges. Before they can break those pledges, they should be convinced that their former pledges were, really in keeping with the honour and self respect of free Indians, and that breaking them they would not be doing anything unsoldierly or dishonourable. For that too propaganda among them was essential.

Sardar Pritam Singh said that some propaganda was being carried on in the troops and that more would be done on that line.

Shri K.P.K. Menon discoursed at length on the Policy followed by the Indian National Congress till now. Two years ago the Working Committee of the Congress asserted complete independence as the goal of India. In the past the Congress had followed two methods both without success. It had first tried to appeal to the good sense and democratic sentiments of the British to grant freedom to the Indians. Later on, on the outbreak of the present war, Mahatma Gandhi started the 'No war campaign' which, however, did not ask the country to desist from helping in the war efforts by positively refusing men, money and material for the prosecution of the war. The result has been a "watchful inactivity" on the part of the Congress. There was a third course remaining, viz. the application of force. India was not prepared for that, but now that Japan was willing to offer us help, we should accept it. Efficient and effective propaganda should also be carried on both inside and outside India.

Shri S.C. Goho spoke on the necessity of creating in India confidence in the intentions of Japan regarding India.

Swami Satyananda Puri suggested that Japan should make a declaration assuring Indian Independence. He mentioned that he had heard over the radio that the Working Committee of the Congress had removed on 13th January, 1942 "non-violence" from the creed of the Congress.

Shri Sucha Singh stressed the necessity of immediate action as delay would be detrimental to the cause. India was ready for action.

Lieut. Col. Gill agreed with Shri Sucha Singh. He said that if the British were to know of the intentions of the overseas Indians, they may remove the Indian units from India to the Middle East and replace them with British units. Moreover, delay would make the strength of the British in India greater as they would be able to produce more ammunition and war materials. Hence delay would be suicidal to the cause.

Summary of conclusions reached at the conference.

1. This is the time when all Indians in Asia should unite for Indian freedom.
2. We believe that the psychological moment has come to strike for Indian freedom.
3. The first thing to do is to carry on propaganda within and outside India among the military forces and civilians.
4. Shri Subhash Chandra Bose should be requested to come to Tokyo and accept the leadership.

The meeting was adjourned till 1.30 A.M. Tokyo time. Tuesday, 10th March.

A Joint Conference of representatives of the Indian Independence League of Malaya and Thailand was held on Tuesday, 10th March, 1942.

Here follows the summary of the conclusions arrived at the conference.

1. Preferably with, otherwise without, the approval of Indian National Congress, we decide to act, if we shall be convinced that the action that we are going to take will be in the best interest of India.
2. We decide to work for the liberation of India with the assistance and support of the Nippon Government.
3. Propaganda and infiltration is to be carried out by each and every means. Details are to be left to an expert Committee.
4. The Tokyo conference is to be attended by Shri N. Raghavan, Shri K.A.N. Ayer, Shri S.C. Goho and Shri K.P.K. Menon as representatives from Malaya and Sardar Pritam Singh and Swami Satyananda Puri as representatives from Thailand.
   The delegat from the Indian army will be decided later on.
5. The delegation can at this stage (at The Tokyo conference) commit themselves to not more than inducing the Indian National Leaders to the view that may be adopted by the delegates at the Conference.
6. A resolution for placing Indian Prisoners of War in Singapore on the same footing as the Indian National Army unanimously, passed, to be forwarded to Major Fujiwara and any one else he may suggest.
   The Conference was adjourned since die.

9

Proceedings of Tokyo Conference which Decided the basis of Indo-Japanese Cooperation during the War for the Overthrow of the British in India; Indicate the Role of Indian National Army in its Fight for India's Liberation

28 March, 1942

The Indian Independence conference was held under the Chairmanship of Mr. Rash Behari Bose, at Sanna Hotel, Tokyo, Japan from Saturday, the 28th March, 1942 to Monday the 30th March, 1942 at which the following representatives were present[1] :

1.	Mr Rash Behari Bose.	2.	Mr. H. Raghavan
3.	Mr. K.P.K. Menon	4.	Mr. S.C. Goho
5.	Mr. Mohan Singh	6.	Mr. N.S. Gill
7.	Mr. G.M. Khan	8.	Mr. M.R. Mullick
9.	Mr. Osman, Hari Singh	10.	Mr. Piara Singh
11.	Mr. D.S. Deshpande	12.	Mr. A.M. Nair
13.	Mr. C. Lingham	14.	Mr. B.D. Gupta
15.	Mr. S.N. Sen	16.	Mr. L.R. Miglani
17.	Mr. Rajah Sherman	18.	Mr. K.V. Narain.

First day, Saturday the 28th March, 1942

Mr. Rash Behari Bose Chairman, opened the conference at 2 p.m. with the welcome address to all the delegates and other gentlemen and requested their whole-hearted cooperation in the attainment of the common object, viz. the complete Independence of India.

---

1. Foreign department, File No. 313-X/1942., National Archive of India (NAI). General Tojo, sent a message to the delagates expressing the intentions of Japan towards India and its desire to go ahead with its mission of destruction of the Anglo-Saxon powers. For the text of the message see K.S. Gyani, *op. cit.* p. 45.

At the outset the Chairman expressed heartfelt condolence on the demise of four colleagues, namely Mr. Pritam Singh, and Swami Satyanand Puri. Mr. K.A.N. Ayer and Mr. Mohammed Akram from Malaya who were to attend this conference and who met with a fatal air accident while on their way to Tokyo.

All stood up and offered profound prayer in silence for the repose of the souls of departed patriots.

The conference resolved to send letters of condolence to the bereaved families and Mr. Raghavan kindly undertook the responsibility of conveying the letters.

Resolved

1. (a) That this conference is shocked and grieved at the news of the air disaster in which four Indians representative viz. Messrs. Ayer and Mohammed Akram from Malaya and Mr. Pritam Singh and Swami Satyanand Puri[2] from Thailand who were travelling to Tokyo lost their lives and while expressing its deep sense of sorrow, place on record the great loss to the movement and the Indian generally caused by their untimely deaths.

   (b) That the copy of this resolution be sent with the condolence of this conference to the members of the bereaved families.

That this conference sends its sincerest condolence and sympathies to the members of the bereaved families of Mr. Otogora and six other Japanese gentlemen who lost their lives while travelling by the same plane to Tokyo.

At this Colonel Iwagoru, who attended representing the Government of Japan, kindly gave an adress of Welcome to the members of the conference. On behalf of the Imperial Government of Japan he expressed whole-hearted support to this conference in its noble efforts to achieve independence of India.

---

2. Satyanand Puri-(1902-1941) was a professor of Oriental philosophy at Calcutta University before he left for Thailand in 1932. On the recommendation of Rabindra Nath Tagore. His real name was Prafulla Kumar Sen. He founded the Thai-Bharata Cultural Lodge to foster close cultural relations between Thailand and India. Was President of Indian National Council formed in December, 1941 after the outbreak of war. Was not impressed by the Japanese support of Indian Independence. While going to Tokyo in March, 1942 died in the plane crash, alonghwith Sardar Pritam Singh and others. Swami had a deep suspicion about the Japanese intentions, but in order to protect the Indian Community in Thailand, he agreed to cooperate with the Japanese.

See Appendix "A".

Mr. Raghavan on behalf of the conference thanked suitably Colonel Iwagoru and through him the Imperial Japanese Government and the Japanese people for their kind encouragement.

Agenda No. 1

Attitude of the Indian regarding this war was taken up and the following resolution was read and unanimously passed.

Whereas we believe that this war of Greater East Asia is sure to destroy British influence and power in Asia, and whereas we believe that this golden opportunity for the realisation of India National Goal which is nothing but complete Independence and whereas depending upon the self-conscious effects of various Asiatic nations, a new Asia is sure to rise as a result of this war, we hereby resolve that we must join hands with Japan in accordance with the decreed policy of the Imperial Japanese Government, made through premier General Tojo on the occasion of the fall of Singapore.

Organisation

(a) Formation of local branches of leagues, for the duration of war, President to be elected by Committee from at the meeting of the representatives of the Place. Vacancy on the Committee to filled by the majority votes of the Committee.

President, not removable without the vote of the three-fourths of the members of the Committee.

(b) Central. The president of the various local bodies together with the representatives of the Indian Army in East Asia, which representatives shall not exceed the total number representatives who will lay down the general policy of action and elect a COUNCIL OF ACTION consisting of the President and for staff members, of whom at least two shall be from the military.

The council of action shall be responsible for the working cut the general policy and in such working out they shall appoint departmental officers of the purpose of administration.

Department Civils

(a) Foreign Department or liaison department
(b) Finance Department
(c) Legal Department
(d) Propaganda Department
(e) Relief Department

(g) Civil Volunteers Department

Indian National Army Headquarters Military

(a) War Department

(b) Recruiting Department

(c) Military Intelligence and Military Police Department

(d) Prisoners of War Department.

1. It is resolved that, if in the discretion of the Council of Action it is feasible to summon a meeting of the representatives and take their advice on matter of the general policy the Council shall do so.

2. It is resolved that, before taking any military action against India, (including Ceylon) contrary to the wishes, policy or opinion of the Indian National Congress, the Council of Action shall first get the approval of the Committee of the representatives and act as directed.

3. We request that military action against India will be taken only by the Indian National Army and under the command of Indians. Together with such military, naval and air cooperation and assistance as may be requested from the Japanese Authorities by the Council of Action.

Requests to the Imperial Japanese Government

1. It is resolved that, in further clarification of the attitude of Japan towards India, the Imperial Japanese Government be requested to make formal declaration to the effect.

(a) That Japan is willing and ready to give all possible help to India to sever its connection from British Empire to attain complete Independence.

(b) That on such severance of India from the British Empire Japan would recognise the full sovereignty of India on attaining Independence.

(c) The absolute independence of India would be guaranteed by the Imperial Japanese Government.

(d) That the Imperial Japanese Government of Japan would exercise its influence with other powers and induce them to recognise the Independence and sovereignty of India.

(e) That the framing of the future constitution of India will be left entirely to the representative of the people of India.

2. It was also resolved to request the Imperial Japanese Government to render such financial help for the successful carrying out of our object as may be required from the time to time on the distinct understanding that such help is to be treated as a loan to be repaid to Japan by the National Government of Independent India, when it comes into being.

3. To give all facilities for propaganda, Travel transport

communications, within the area under the control of the Imperial Japanese Government, in the manner and to the extent requested by the council of action and also all facilities to come into contact with the National Leaders, the workers, and organisations in India.

4. To clarify the position of Indian troops now under control in occupied territories.

5. To recognise and facilitate the use of the present National flag of India in all territories under Imperial Government of Japan.

6. To consult in all matters of administration affecting the Indian Community the Indian Independence Leagues of the respective places and places where there are no league recognised leaders of community approved by the league branch nearest to such place.

(a) This conference resolves that in order to obtain full support and cooperation of Indians in various parts of Greater East Asia, a fuller meeting of Indian representative should be called at Rangoon or any other suitable place at the earliest opportunity and that M Rash Behari Bose is hereby authorised to take the necessary step to give effects to the various decisions made by the conference pending their ratification at the later conference as stated above.

(b) This conference hereby appoints Mr. Rash Behari Bose as interim president of the Council of Action.

(c) Resolved that next conference shall be held before the 1st of June, 1942 possible and in any case not later than 1st of July, 1942, and interim president shall make necessary arrangements.

(d) Resolved that next Conference besides the Presidents and/or Representative of various Indian Independence League as hereinafter limited (in person or by proxy) and military representatives of Indian Army in East Asia, in all the members attending this conference should be invited to attend.

(e) The Conference to ratify the decisions herein shall be held at Bangkok in the 3rd week of May 1942, and representative and/or presidents not exceeding the number indicated herein below may attend the said conference.

Japan	8	Hong Kong	8	Thailand	9
Changhai	8	Macao and Manila	2	Indochina	5
Malaya	20	Burma	20	East India	8
				(Java, Sumatra, Borneo, Celebes)	

Total : 90

Representatives of the Indian Army in East Asia will also attend as previously agreed to (Under Agenda III. (b).

General

That this is Committed to a definite policy of the closest cooperation with Japan and it shall on electing an official definition of the term "Greater East Asia Co-prosperity sphere" and its application endeavour by every possible means at the command of this movement :–

1. To persuade Independent India to be a member of the sphere on a footing of equality with Japan.

2. To confer on Japan the most favoured National treatment on a reciprocal basis.

(A) This conference place on record its profound gratitude to the Imperial Government of Japan, for their active sympathy in the cause of Indian Independence and expresses its thanks for their generous hospitality and for the ample facilities provided for the successful termination of this conference.

(B) This conference put on record its profound thanks to Mr. Rash Behari Bose who by fact patience and generality as Chairman contributed not a little to the success of this conference.

(C) While they individually find themselves in perfect agreement with the decisions of this conference, the members of the good-will mission of Malaya hereby make they do not commi Indian in Malaya to the decisions of this conference but will try their best to induce them to the views of this conference. Mr. Osman's[3] suggestions on education and other matters contained in Appendix B, attached hereto are noted for action at the opportune time.

Appendix 'A'

"It is my great pleasure to greet you at this conference which would mark new birth of "India for the Indian". To day your dual ideology of

---

3. *Baba Hari Singh Allas Osman Khan*
An old member of the Ghadr Party, had played a prominent role in the Indo-German conspiracy to smuggle arms and ammunition in India during hte first World War. He lived in hiding after the War under alias Osman Khan in Indonesia and worked for a number of years with Emil Helffrich. He went to Shanghai in 1930 and was associated with the Japanese Naval authorities. Worked under Commander Hidoka of the China Intelligence Section. On the eve of the War, tried to establish contacts with the other Indian revolution aries in East Asia. With the help of the Japanese sent two persons to Thailand to inform Baba Amar Singh to contact Japanese Military Attache for help to start armed struggle against the British. Played an active role at Tokyo Conference. Went to Andamans in 1942 to start a branch of Indian Independence League. Had an implicit faith in Japanese sincerity.

"Independence of India" and India for the Indians over which you have been most concerned is going to realised before long because it is my belief that outbreak of the war has created an opportunity which is most favourable for its realisation. If you lose this golden opportunity by being crowardly lazy or too much involved in mutual antagonism, you and your descendants would remain slaves for nobody know how long. The objective world situation is rapidly changing. It is your mission to prepare fully and immediately so as to adjust your slaves for the fast changing times and liberate India from the British yoke. We the Japanese are prepared to give the spiritual and material aid to your revolutionary task without any compensation or condition. It is needless to say that the common enemy British will employ every means, such as the deceit, bribery, "Divide and rule policy and threats. On these points we must be very cautious. "Heaven helps those who helps themselves". Indian Independence cannot be sought from anybody, for less from India's enemy England, from whom you can only except oppression. India's able leaders must make good use of the surroundings international conditions, in order to lessen the amount of sacrifices involved. In her part what Japan expects from India that she should do away with all the retardings ideas of religious and class antagonisms and the various revalries between political and military ways of Independence, that she should realise that the realisation of Indian Independence in itself is a great revolution to be led to success only on the strength of her leader's firm determination and of the fiery patriotism of all the Indian and that realising that one action is superior to hundreds of arguments she should make use of conditions surrounding her and advance for the attainment of independence. And we wish to assist her in their ambition of India, and that we will not hesitate to extend and any help to the Indians in their fight and that without any ulterior motives.

Please take your own time and engage yourselves in calm deliberation so that you may arrive to a plan of action which may be beneficial on all parts for future India as well as East Asia. This is my request to you all, and it comes from the bottom of heart.

Appendix 'B'

1. Specific instructions should be given to any troops attacking India to refrain themselves and to stop others from destroying places of worship belonging to the various religious bodies in order to avoid any sort of friction liable to be caused by such sabotage acts.

2. As soon as possible the property of the Indian Government and other rich Indians considered pro-British including the Indian princes should be placed under the joint control and custody of the occupying Indian troops to avoid embezzlement or looting etc.; so that on expiration the war the Indian Government may be in the position to cover up the expense.

3. In all kinds of Government affairs, external or internal the Indian Religious leaders should not be consulted and their membership should never be taken in various state councils.

4. Compulsory education, irrespective of male and female sect, should be started as soon as possible on realisation of the independence of India.

5. Various societies opened in different cities found not in favour of achieving complete Independence of India and not cooperating with the main body, should be dissolved as soon as possible.

6. Able and patriotic volunteers should be enlisted from every part of East Asia including Shanghai, Honking, Java, Sumatra, etc. so that they can enjoy equal privileges in order that they also partake in serving their motherland.

7. All Indian Nationals, irrespective of their financial standing class or religion, should be treated on an equal footing in the matter of state affairs.

8. In war time just as women in all countries of the world are allowed to take full share in rendering their best service for the freedom of their respective countries, similarly Indian women are also anxious to fulfil their duties, in every possible way for the freedom of our country. But in the British region, the women of India have not been given the same power and freedom which men have so far, as a result of which women in India have not been allowed to take part in Government affairs. In order to rise them to the same standard of freedom as the men we should allow them the discretion of taking active part in serving our motherland even against the wishes of their parents, husbands and other relatives supposed to be Pro-British. Military training should be considered as compulsory part of education.

10

Interrogation Report of Major Fujiwara; Explains the Circumstances Leading to the Formation of Indian National Army; How he Inspired Capt. Mohan Singh to take Charge of Indian Prisoners of War; gives Credit to Sardar Pritam Singh for his Patriotism; Comments on difficulties faced by him in Dealing with Japanese High Command for an Independent Status for Indian National Army (Extract)[1]

Fujiwara[2] in April 1941 was told to concentrate on American Affairs as he might be sent to America. However, owing to general deterioration in relation between Japan and America he was unable to go. It was not until August 1941 that he began to study Indian Affairs.

Before he left for Siam he was told to work as Assistant to the Military Attache Col. Tamura. He was to control and support members of the Indian Independence movement. Fujiwara requested Gen. Okamoto head of No. 2 section to choose someone more suitable for the job than himself. He pointed out that he had no experience of work of this kind

---

1. South-East Asia Translation and Interrogation Centre. Bulletin No. 234. This report may be read alongwith the memorandum-compiled by Fujiwara at Appendix III.
2. Fujiwara (1907-1986)
   Born in 1907 in Hygo. After graduation in 1927, he entered Military Academy, Tokyo and joined the staff college in 1935 . Became a staff offier in 1938. At the time of his posting in Siam, he was promoted as Major-Rated by the British as being of doubtful reliability, still was considered as a clever staff office with plenty of initiative; was popularly called the midwife of Indian National Army; was associated with its rise and fall; was head of Fujiwara Kikan till 1942. After the war became a Lieut. General in Japanese Self-defence Force. After retirement was head of the Fujiwara Asian Research Institute in Tokyo.

and knew nothing India. Besides he could not speak either English or Hindi or any other language spoken in Southern Asia. His objections was overruled and he was told that he would receive instructions from Col. Tamura who was experienced in this type of work.

According to reports from the Military Attache in Bangkok, the Indian Independence League which had its headquarters at Bangkok and which had branches in Shanghai, Hongkong and Siam had contacted the Japanese Military Attache about June 1941 in order to obtain help from the Japanese Government against the British and to develop Indo-Japanese collaboration. The Military Attache had sent in optimistic reports of the size and power of the Indian Independence Movement but these had been belied by report from Col. Ichida[3] then stationed in India who reported that the political parties in India especially the Congress was not favourably inclined, despaired Japan. The Congress party according to Col. Ichida strongly condemned Japanese aggression in China and upholding its principles of non-violence did not welcome assistance from the Asian countries. In Ichida's opinion, therefore little cooperation from the India was to be expected. No links were established with the Congress party.

Further there was no prominent Indian resident in Japan who could be used as a leader of these movements. In fact the Japanese were afraid that some of the Indian residents in Japan might be British agents. A certain Mahender Partap had visited Col. Odeki in Imperial H.Q. in 1941 about the publication of a Hindustani Newspaper in Japan but the Japanese were not impressed.

For these reasons, the Japanese had to pin their hopes for Indo-Japanese cooperation on the I.I.L. in Bangkok. However, the Japanese were hamphered by their lack of experts on Indian Affairs. Takaoka Daisuke, a member of the Diet and Kimura Nikki a professor at the University of Ceylon and one or two others wrote books attempting to explain India to the Japanese but Fujiwara did not think that these publications had been particularly effective. Among the Military Generals Sugiyama and Imamura, Lt. Gen. Hono, Ando, Kuroda and others had been stationed in India during the reign of Taisho 1912-26 when they were junior officers. But at that time there was no question[7] of war between Britain and Japan and they had take no advantage of their opportunities. Col. Toshima who had previously been Military Attache in India was in

3. Col. Ichida was Japanese Consul. General in India.

Brazil in December 1941 and Col. Ichida was at that time interested in D.I.A. Neither was therefore available to give their expert advice.

In Bangkok, Col. Tamura realised that Fujiwara had no experience of the work he was requested to do, nor had he training in languages. Tamura, therefore instructed him to stay in Bangkok in order to get acquainted with the life and situation in the Southern Area.

In the middle of October 1941, Tamura introduced Fujiwara to the I.I. League. According to Tamura's introductory explanation it was a secret organisation working for the Indian Independence which had first approached him in the summer of 1941. It had its headquarters in Bangkok and its principle figure were Amar Singh and Pritam Singh. Amar Singh was too old for successful work and the real power was Pritam Singh. Tamura considered that collaboration with these people was the only way of making progress on the Indian question. Col. Tamura therefore asked Pritam Singh to meet Fujiwara. The first meeting was devoted to mere introductions. Fujiwara met and talked to Pritam on about three occasions. One occasion he was accompanied by Amar Singh. As interpreter Fujiwara used Ohtaguro who had been a teacher in the Japanese Elementary School in Singapore.

At first the discussion was about political condition in India and the current state of affairs in the independence movement. Fujiwara listened to Pritam Singh and formed his general impression of his personality. From these conversation Fujiwara obtained the following impressions :–

(1) Both Amar Singh and Pritam Singh were ardent and zealious enthusiasts for Indian Independence, who had no ulterior motive.

(2) I.I.L. had no connection with the Congress and although they appeared to have some members in Hong kong, Shanghai and Southern Siam they did not have as powerful an organisation as the General staff had expected.

(3) The I.I.L. did not have friendly relations with the other Indian parties in Bangkok (Swami, Das).

(4) The I.I.L. did not appear to have any organised branches in Malaya and Burma.

(5) Pritam Singh had a great respect for Subhash Chandra Bose.

Towards the end of November or the beginning of December information reached Tamura that there was little chance of compromise in Washington and war between Japan and Britain and America was inevitable.

On instructions from Tamura, Fujiwara drafted an agreement which was approved by Tamura for the Japanese and by Amar Singh[4] for the

Indians. The Agreement was reported to the Japanese Southern Area Army Headquarters. Pritam Singh became much more active when he heard of the likelihood of war. The Agreement was briefly as follows :

(i) The final objective was stated to be the establishment of peace in Greater East Asia by cooperation between two equal and free nations–Japan and India.

(ii) The I.I.L. was to prosecute a campaign against Britain to secure complete independence of India from the British yoke. For this purpose, Japan pledged herself to give all possible aid and guaranteed that she had no ambition in India whether political, economic, cultural, religious or otherwise.

(iii) The I.I.L. was to pursue the following policy as soon as the war started.

(A) The I.I.L. would advance with the Japanese Army into Southern Siam and later into Malaya where they would expand the I.I.L. and encourage anti-British feeling. At the same time, they were to promote cooperation between Indian residents and the Japanese.

(B) The I.I.L. was to organise a voluntary army who would fight for Indian Independence. This Army was to be staffed by Indian Army officers and men and from local Indian volunteers. (This article was suggested by Pritam Singh who considered that an invasion of India by Japanese forces alone would be misunderstood and would not be welcomed in India. He wanted Indians to take part in her own liberation).

(iv) The Japanese Army was to show its support for the Indian Independence by a friendly attitude towards Indians in the areas that they occupied and conciliatory treatment was to be accorded to Indian Prisoners of War.

---

4. *Baba Amar Singh 1883-*
A great Indian revolutionary, son of Wariam Singh, a Jat Sikh of Ludhiana was born in 1883. Went to Siam in 1903 served as a surveyor on the Northern Siamese railway under the Germans. During the war came in contact witht he Ghadrites. Was convicted in the Mandalay conspiracy case and sentenced to death, which was later converted to life imprisonment. After serving 20 years in Rangoon, was released in 1937. Went back to Thailand in early 1940 to pursue his aim of outing the British. Contacted his old Comrades in Bangkok, Shanghai, Singapore and Burma. Worked closely with Pritam Singh in the Indian Independence League. joined the Japanese on the eve of the Pacific War and was instrumental in signing an agreement with Lt. Col. Tamura, the Japanese Military attache in Bangkok.

(v) The I.I.L. was to extend its organisations to all areas in the South-East-Asia in the wake of operation. The Japanese guaranteed full support.

(vi) The I.I.L. undertook to prosecute a vigorous propaganda campaign in all occupied areas as well as in India proper. On their part the Japanese undertook to allow the I.I.L. to use all Japanese propaganda organs including Tokyo (Tokyo broadcast were not clearly received at that time. But Berlin broadcast by Bose were thought to have made a profound impression in India).

(vii) Details were to be discussed by local H.Q. and minor problems dealt with as they arose.[5]

Fujiwara pointed out that the Sikh elements predominated in the movement at that time. He felt that there would be little possibility of major developments of the I.I.L., unless it could embrass all Indians of whatever caste, race or religion. Pritam Singh agreed.

Information that war would start within a few days was received on 4 December 1941 and Fujiwara was then appointed the staff of the Southern Area Army. At the same time Col. Tamura was told that Indian affairs in Siam and Malaya would henchforth be the responsibility of the C-in-C Southern Area simultaneously Southern Army placed all matters pertaining to Malaya directly under the Commander of 25th Army. As a result the Tamura-Pritam Singh Agreement was referred to 25th Army. On 6 December, a signal was received stating that war would begin on 9 December and Fujiwara contacted Pritam Singh to make preparation to move South. They left Bangkok for Singora on 10 December by Air. Pritam Singh was accompanied by 21 Associates and Fujiwara by Captain Tsuchimchi and 2 Lt. Yonemura who had been working in the military Attache's office in Bangkok since November 1941. On arrival in Singora, Fujiwara reported to H.Q. 25 Army and met the G.O.C. Chief of Staff. Fujiwara acquainted himself with the plan of operations and with dispositions of Japanese forces. At the same time he received orders to form the Fujiwara Kikan whose duties were :

---

5. No authentic copy of this agreement could be traced in the records available in India or U.K. Fujiwara's version of the agreement as given in his Memoirs F. Kikam is quite different from the one he has given during the interrogation. Another Japanese Government publication *Subash Chandra Bose and Japan* mentions that in the agreement the Japanese Government agreed to put Pritam Singh's organisation in touch with Subhas in Berlin. But on this point, Fujiwara is silent. A copy of hte agreement was sent to the Imperial General Headquarters at Tokyo and the Southern Army Headquarters at Saigon for information and approval. It is not known as to whether, this was approved by the Japanese authorities.

(a) To carry out the policy laid down in the Tamura-Pritam Singh Agreement (emphasis was placed on support of the I.I.L.).

(b) To send out Liaison officers with each column to secure proper treatment for India P.W. and Indian residents in the area occupied. They were to prevent friction between the Japanese Army and Indian everywhere.

(c) To rescue and protect the Sultans and if possible to support pro-Japanese propaganda among the Chinese and the Malayas.

(d) To report all cases of misbehaviour of Japanese towards the local population.

(e) To ensure secrecy regarding the plans and movements of the Japanese army when they were cooperating with the I.I.L.

Army H.Q. ordered all operational units to cooperate with the Fujiwara Kikan in all measures adopted by the Kikan so long as they did not impede operations.

The officers of the Kikan could not speak either English or Hindustani. It was, therefore all the more necessary to carry out the promises they had made and to show their friendliness by deeds if not by words. With this aim they had to support the locals even in disputes with the Japanese officers and men even though their inclination might be against such action. They had to be careful to show that they considered the Indians the equals of Japanese and had to avoid any suggestion of patronising. As these principles had been very carefully installed into the minds of all members of the Kikan, they were able to command the "affectionate respect and trust of the Indian prisoners". No unfortunate incidents occurred between December 1941 and April 1942.

Plan for Assisting the I.I.M.

(i) Establishment of Branch of I.I.L. at Alor Stor. After the successful outcome of the engagement at Jitra Kikan HQ and I.I.H.Q. were transferred to Alor Stor on 12th December 1941. Arriving at Alor Stor the I.I.L. at once convened a meeting of Indian locals. Pritam Singh spoke on the principles of Indian Independence Movement. He received a very enthusiastic welcome and opened a branch there. At the same time the Indians who had fled from their homes gradually returned.

(ii) Arrival of Mohan Singh. On the afternoon of 13th December the I.I.L. reported that there was a battalion of Indian troops located some 25 miles east of Alor Stor, who intended to surrender owing to their large casualities. Also their escape route was cut. The Commander of the battalion was an English Lt. Col. Fitzpatrik and all the other officers and men were Indians. Early in the morning of 14 December Major Fujiwara

and Pritam Singh accompanied by interpreter Otagura set out unarmed to contact the battalion. Following the advise of some Indian locals they stopped on the way in a rubber estate and established contact with the British Commander by means of local inhabitants. While carrying out the surrender negotiations, they had a breakfast with the British Commander. The negotiations were carried on in a friendly spirit and they immediately left for the Battalion position where arrangements for surrender were made. Captain Mohan Singh was the senior Company Commander. The Battalion handed over all their weapons in a well disciplined manner. Afterwards Pritam Singh established friendly relations with the Indian officers. Immediately after they had returned to Alor Stor the British Commander was sent to Japanese Army HQ.

*(iii) D*iscussion with Mohan Singh for about a week after the surrender of the Battalion. Major Fujiwara discussed matters with Captain Mohan Singh explaining to him the Emperor's desire for the emancipation of the subject peoples. Captain Mohan Singh expressed his earnest wish to see India independent. He understood the principles of I.I.L. movement and agreed with them in general terms, but stressed the importance of forming a volunteery Army. It was first necessary to instill the idea of independence into the minds of the officers and men of the Battalion. Major Fujiwara agreed with Mohan Singh in this particular and stressed the importance of active enthusiasm. It was left to Mohan Singh to instill these concepts into the minds of the Indian officers and men without undue haste.

(iv) Mohan Singh criticism of Japanese Policy. On 19th December the Kikan moved to Sungei Patni and thereafter to Taiping. Captain Mohan Singh had a number of conversation with Pritam Singh and in conversation pointed out to Fujiwara that the Indians disproved of Japanese aggressive policy in China and Manchuria and of their method of colonisation in Korea and Formosa. Fujiwara promised, however, that the principles of Tamura–Pritam Singh agreement would be upheld in every respect as regards India and that Japan had no imperialist intention in the Southern Area. Mohan Singh expressed confidence in Bose as a leader and considered that there would be more chances of success for the movement if he could be brought to take charge.

(v) Interview with Yamastita on 17 December Pritam Singh, Mohan Singh and other officers visited Japanese 25 Army H.Q. in Alor Stor and met General Yamastita. Yamastita gave the interview in order to show

personally his support for the movement, his respect for their patriotism and to promise all possible assistance through Fujiwara. The I.I.L. advanced to Sungei Patani on 19 December from there to Penang and by the end of the December 1941, it had advanced to Taiping. Ipoh was reached in the beginning of January 1942. The I.I.L. held meetings everywhere, they always received an enthusiastic welcome as at Alor Stor. Branches were established at each place. Fujiwara accompanied Pritam Singh. Raghavan and Menon who were both influential persons were contacted in Penang.

As a result of the activities of the I.I.L. local Indians became reconciled to the Japanese Army and many sepoys who had deserted after the battle of Jitra after discarding their uniform and arms began to come to the Indian Barracks at Alor Stor and Sungei Patani. Towards the end of December, Mohan Singh who was suffering from his 39th bout of Malaria visited Fujiwara in Alor Stor and announced that he had made the following decisions.

(A) With the assistance of the Japanese, the Indians would set up an Independence Movement.
(B) An Indian National Army would be organised at once.
(C) The I.N.A. should be clearly connected with the I.I.L. for the time being.
(D) Mohan Singh should be responsible for the guidance of Indian P.W.
(E) The Japanese Army should accord friendly treatment to Indian P.W.
(F) Those who wished to participate in the I.N.A. should be enrolled under the command of Captain Mohan Singh.
(G) The I.N.A. should be recognised as an ally of the Japanese Army.

These discussions were conveyed to the Army Commander who agreed and stressed that the way to success for the movement was close cooperation between I.N.A. and I.I.L.

In the above conversation Mohan Singh added that though he had taken some time to reach these decisions, his determination was incontrovertible as it was in accordance with the feelings of the Indian officers and men in Sungei Patani and Alor Star. Fujiwara expressed his respect for these decisions and promised all possible support for the I.N.A. but he emphasised the need for close cooperation between I.N.A. and I.I.L.

Fujiwara's Impression of Mohan Singh

Fujiwara formed the impression from the time he met him at Alor

Stor that Captain Mohan Singh was an ardent and strong willed patriot who was very careful in the way he came to a decision. He was considerate to his subordinates and was sincerely respected by them.

On 3 January 1942, the Kikan and the I.I.L. moved to Ipoh. I.N.A. H.Q. followed and the I.I.L. opened another branch at Ipoh. In accordance with the wishes of Mohan Singh the Indian Army prisoners from Penang were concentrated in Ipoh. Here there were no Japanese guards and activities were unrestricted. In the Camp, the Liaison officers of the Fujiwara/Kikan lived, worked and charged there pleasures with the Kikan troops. In Ipoh, at the request of the I.N.A. and I.I.L. pamphlets for use among Indian soldiers and civilians were produced. These were entrusted by the Fujiwara Kikan to Japanese Air units for distribution.

The I.I.L. and H.Q. of Fujiwara Kikan moved to Kaula Lumpur on 15 January. They remained there till 12 February. As the Japanese Army progressed I.I.L. opened branches in Kuala Lumpur. Sere-mben, Malacca, Maur, Johore and other large and small cities occupied in the day to day advance. They held discussions and cooperated mutually with influential Indians in each place. They assisted Indians in difficulties and protected Indian deserts and stagglers. With the influence of volunteers, it was clear that the influence was spreading throughout Malaya. The I.I.L. reported all cases of illegal requisitioning of goods from Indians to the Fujiwara Kikan who took steps to remedy grievances. Any other reasons for Indian discontact with the Japanese Army were also reported to Fujiwara Kikan for action. As a result of these measures, local confidence in the Fujiwara Kikan increased.

Activities of the I.N.A.

I.N.A. H.Q. moved to Kuala Lumpur in the middle of January. Mohan Singh in collaboration with Fujiwara Kikan made many effort to improve the quarters and supplies for some 2,000 Indian P.W. interned in Kuala Lumpur and Maur. In addition he collected volunteers for the I.N.A. and made preparations for organising the force. A certain amount of training was carried on.

After the battles of Jitra, Salim and Maur Indian's deserted in large number and took to the jungle. It was realised that much of the arms and equipment thrown aside by these man was going into the hands of the Communists.

With the unexpected speedy progress of the operations it was anticipated that the British Indian Army would retire to Sumatra and Java without putting up a strong resistance in Singapore. Recognising this fact, Mohan Singh realised the need for immediately increasing the number

of volunteers for the I.N.A. Therefore, he chose out a number of able men and sent them to the front to carry out pro-I.N.A. propaganda. According to Fujiwara there were about 200 members of the I.N.A. at the time of the capture of Singapore. He was unable to give any details of their activities during the attack on Singapore, but some 1500 Indian desertee and stragglers were rounded up by their efforts.

The surrender of the British force was signed on 15 February 42 and on 16 February Fujiwara was made responsible for all Indian P.W. Fujiwara prepared a speech to deliver to all Indian P.W. This speech was approved by the Chief of Staff who also agreed to do his best to provide quarters and supplies for Indian P.W. Fujiwara took charge of some 45,000 P.W. at Ferer Park from British Staff officer Hunt. Immediately afterwards Fujiwara delivered his speech on 17 February 1942 followed by Pritam Singh and Mohan Singh.

The I.N.A. and Kikan worked day in and day out to house, feed and supply the tens of thousands of Indian soldiers spread throughout Malaya peninsula and in Singapore. Japanese guards and Indian camps were withdrawn and autonomous control established.

As in other places over Malaya mass meetings were held in Singapore. After negotiations with the Japanese Army freedom of association, freedom of speech and permission to hoist the Congress flag were agreed to. On 1 March 1942, Southern Army informed 25 Army that the staff department was arranging a meeting of representatives Indians in Tokyo to discuss measures for the establishment of Indian Independence. Ten representatives from Siam and Malaya were required Fujiwara and Col. Iwaguro were ordered to accompany these representatives and Fujiwara was warned that, Col. Iwaguro would replace him as O.C. Fujiwara explained this project to the I.N.A. and I.I.L. and conference was held at the house of Mr. Goho. The following representatives were nominated.

I.I.L. Raghavan, Menon, Aiyer, Goho, Swami Satyanand Puri, Pritam Singh.

I.N.A. Lt. Gill, Mohan Singh and Captain Akram.

The party left Singapore on 10 March, 1942.

The first aircraft arrived safely but the second aircraft had an accident owing to bad weather and all were killed.[6]

While in Saigon, Fujiwara was officially informed that Col. Iwaguro

---

6. Those who died in the plane accident were Swami Satyanand Puri, Pritam Singh, K.A. N-Ayer and Mohammad Akram.fdf

would be taking over from him and that he would return to Southern Army H.O. after he had reported to Imperial H.Q.

As a result Fujiwara did not take part in the conversation which took place in the Sano Hotel. Fujiwara returned to Singapore on 15 April. While in Tokyo, Fujiwara reported to the Chief of the General Staff to the chief of No. 2. Section and to the Head of the 8 Departments. In his report, he emphasised the following points.

(a) The Indians flatly refused to allow the Independence Movement to be used to further Japanese Imperialist ambitions and would not allow the I.I.L. or the I.N.A. to be used as puppets. Such method would not receive support from inside India.

(b) The I.I.M. should be based on the support of the masses and on public opinion. No success for the I.N.A. could be expected without enthusiastic backing. As a result it was essential that there should be close cooperation betwee¬ the I.I.L. and the I.N.A.

(c) All Indians of every party in the I.I.M. aimed at complete independence with democratic constitution like that of Britain. They did not generally sympathise with Axis plans and aspirations and resented interference or coercion. In supporting Indian Independence, Japan had to acknowledge these facts and had to be careful not to attempt to force upon I.I.L. and I.N.A. Japanese principles and methods. Condensation from others was deeply resented by the Indians.

(d) Indian opinion disliked Japanese aggression policy in Manchunia, Formosa, Korea and China. In order to gain the approval of Indian opinion it would be necessary to review Japanese policy in these spheres in relation to the new conditions. Further unless Japanese respect for liberty and equality was proved by their actions in the liberated countries of South East Asia, i.e., by respecting the independence of Siam and Burma, no success could be expected.

(e) It was desirable that the support of the parties within India be obtained for the movement and especially the support of the Congress party. For this purpose the I.N.A. and I.I.L. should confirm as near as possible to the policy of the Congress party.

(f) The basis of Japanese in supporting the Indian Independence Movement should be the creation of a united state which stood above difference of religion and caste. All action at encouraging such differences should be avoided. However, the Japanese should allow the movement to develop in its own way.

(g) Indians in Southern Area had a great respect for Subhash Bose,

then in Berlin. To clarify these points Japan should make a clear statement of her fundamental attitude towards India and should take measures to prove her support of the I.I.M. All promises should be kept and they should sincerely be encouraged a spontaneous Indian movement for Indian Independence without ultior intentions. The Iwagura Kikan should be regarded primarily as a liaison unit. About 10 April Fujiwara arrived back in Singapore where he dissolved the Kikan and retired to Supreme H.Q. in Saigon arriving there by the end of April.

Fujiwara was much impressed by the passionate expressions of gratitude of members of the I.I.L. and I.N.A. and Indian P.W. when he bade farewell. Fujiwara was pleased to recollect that there had not been a single instance of unfriendly relations between the Indians and the Kikan during the period he was in charge, i.e., during the first stages of organisation.

11

Additional Information on the Events Leading to the Formation of the Indian National Army as given by Major Fujiwara during the subsequent Interrogation (Extract)[1]

Before going on to deal with the negotiations between Giani Pritam Singh and Fujiwara, a description of the state of political feeling amongst Indians in Bangkok will not be out of place.

2. Though Fujiwara, is himself unable to give many details about the pre-war Indian Independence movement in Bangkok, it now is possible to reconstruct from other sources, the part played by renegade Indians, who, in the hope of securing the freedom of their country from one power, were prepared to make themselves subservient to another. In Bangkok the whole Indian Independence movement under Japanese auspices throughout South East Asia originated. And, as by 1945 this movement was to have flourishing branches in all countries occupied by the Japanese, and in the I.N.A., under the dynamic leadership of S.C. Bose, was to weld itself into a fighting body which might have seriously prejudiced the Allied military effort in Burma and Malaya, some details of its early history are relevant and of more than academic interest.

3. While dealing with the inception of the Indian Independence Movement in Bangkok, it is a point of historical interest to note that it was in that city also that the diehards of the I.N.A. (belonging to S.C. Bose's entourage and to 'X' Regiment) took refuge in 1945 following the collapse of the Japanese forces in Burma.

4. The pre-war Indian community in Bangkok, comprising mainly petty traders dependent on the support of the British Legation and Consulate in the furtherance of their business interests, were not generally

---

1. F. No. 250/I.N.A. papers. The interrogation took place in 1946, but the events described cover this early period. As such the report is included here.

speaking, politically-minded. The "Indian Association of Thailand", a body functioning, under the aegis of HM Legation for common social and commercial interests, but excluding matters relating to religion or politics, and whose chief office-bearers were some of the senior members of the business community, had been in existence since 1928.

5. In 1940, a change was noticeable however, first by the election to the committee of the Association of some younger and more radically-minded members and by the foundation of Nov. 1940 of the "Thai Bharat Cultural Lodge". The leading spirits in this enterprise were : –

(1) Swami Satyananda Puri, a Hindu of good education and culture, something of an ascetic and visionary, and with strong political and nationalist leanings.

(2) Deb Nath Das, an Indian domiciled in Tokyo, whence he came with the avowed intention of organising anti-British activities.

6. The "Thai Bharat Cultural Lodge", apart from its ostensible object indicated by its title, was a body whose subversive trend was sufficiently indicated by the hoisting of the Congress flag at its inaugural meeting.

7. After this somewhat provocative and challenging ceremony of initiation, little was heard of the "Thai Bharat Cultural Lodge" during the next twelve months, a sate of affairs which can be accounted for :–

(1) By the return of Deb Nath Das to Japan, while Swami Satyananda Puri, his lieutenant, being more of scholar than politician, shared a vaning interest in the Lodge's political activities.

(2) By the coercive measures taken by HM Legation in collaboration which he Government of India to penalise Indians participating in anti-British activities.

8. During this uneasy period, two other personalities made their appearance, the first of these was Giani Pritam Singh, formerly a Sikh missionary, "whose conversation and aspect was always in religious tones and terms and gestures", and grand fatherly Baba Amar Singh, who we fears imprisonment for his part in the Mandalay conspiracy had served only to strengthen his implacable hatred for the British, and who, on the termination of his sentence, had managed to escape from India by evading the passport authorities and had established himself in the Sikh Gurudwara in Bangkok.

9. These two Sikhs do not, however, appear, if one source is to be believe, to have had complete mutual understanding, as is apparent by a visit paid to HM Consul General in the autumn of 1941 by one Lal Singh, an emissary from Baba Amar Singh, denouncing the treasonable activities

of Giani Pritam Singh. Shortly after, Baba Amar Singh, either knowing or appreciating that the zero hour for the Far East was at hand, and so probably desirous of lying low until he saw how the tide of war would go, removed himself to northern Thailand, while the reappearance of Deb Nath Das in Hongkong in Oct./Nov. 1941, was a further indication of the probable course of events.

10. In connection with the activities of Deb Nath Das and Swami Satyananda Puri, Fujiwara has stated that Col. Tamura told him that Deb Nath Das and Puri had called at the Japanese Embassy to sound the Japanese on their views on the Indian question. But as Col. Tamura had already committed himself to cooperating with Giani Pritam Singh, he told Swamy Satyananda Puri and Deb Nath Das to make up their differences with Giani Pritam Singh, as the Japanese did not intend to give support to any one Indian faction at the expense of the other. (If this information supplied by Fujiwara of Swami Satyananda Puri having approached the Japanese, is correct, Swami Satyananda Puri was much more than the visionary and other worldly ascetic which he has some times been thought to be).

11. Another account, of some interest, but as yet not confirmed from any source, is given by Civ. Kartar Singh in CSDIC (I) 'V' Sec. Repb. F/308 Page 7 and 'V' Sec. Intelligence Rept. No. 2 dated 23 Jan. 46.[2] This is to the effect that some time before the war, the Japanese brought to Bangkok two members of the San Francisco "Ghadar Party" from their Shanghai office. These men were :–

1. Kartar Singh Guami, who later went to Burma.
2. Harnam Singh Dhillon, who later went to Penang.

The following were also privy to the presence of these men in Bangkok :–

1. Amar Singh Sachdev (CSDIC (I) 'V' Sec. Rept. VK/11)[1]
2. Ishan Singh Sethi who was connected with the Immigration Dept. and stood guarantee for Kartar Singh Qaumi and Harnam Singh Dhillon ('V' Sec. Rept. F/277)
3. Master Bhagwan Singh CSDIC (I) 'V' Sec. Rept. F/278.

Kartar Singh further states that "Amar Singh Sachdev knew the Japanese schemes for going to war against the Allies and the Japanese,

2. These reports have not been reproduced, but can be consulted amongst the I.N.A. papers now deposited with the National Archives of India.

took him into their confidence and he was feeding fat on Japanese money".

Note : OC 'V' Sec. considers that these allegations made by Kartar Singh against Amar Singh Sachdev are somewhat exaggerated due to personal animosity. It is however, felt that there is at least a sub-stream of truth in them. They are not however confirmed by Fujiwara.

29. In considering the general political temper and atmosphere in Bangkok previous to the war, it is interesting to notice that Major Niranjan Singh Gill (B1190) who was sent on a secret mission to Thailand in Nov. 1941 to find out the attitude of Indians, has stated that, apart from Giani Pritam Singh and Chanda Singh (the notorious Osmanite), the community, mainly being merchants, showed but little interest in politics. (CSDIC (I) 2 Sec. Rept. 1096 para 4 on B1190).

Meeting between Giani Pritam Singh and Fujiwara

30. Fujiwara states that he had little contact with Indians prior to going to Bangkok, and that his knowledge of India was limited to what he had read in two books. He himself cannot understand why he was allotted this post, for he could speak neither English nor any Indian language. He thinks, however, that the probable reasons were two in number :–

1. He was the only officer of the General Staff who could be spared to be sent to Col. Tamura.

2. The CGS had selected him as a young officer, full of enthusiasm and ambition, and anxious to distinguish himself in some particular line.

31. On arrival in Bangkok in Oct. 1941, Fujiwara was welcomed by Col. Tamura, who told him to take a few days local leave to acclimatize himself, and to accustom himself to his new surroundings. There did not appear to be any urgency. He was told to take things easy, and that it would be useful to learn English. (Fujiwara states that, as his appointment was in the "I" Bch. and not in "Ips"–the members of which Bch always jealously guarded their secrets–he had no direct knowledge of the Japanese premeditated attack in Dec. 1941).

32. On settling down to work, Fujiwara was told by Col. Tamura that he (Tamura) had been approached by Giani Pritam Singh with a request for Japanese assistance in the cause of India's freedom.

33. It was only at the beginning of Dec. 1941, when the international situation began to take a more serious turn, that Fujiwara had four meetings with Giani Pritam Singh, who claimed that he had fellow-workers

in Singora and Haadyai in Thailand, and in Canton, Hong Kong, Shangai and even in New York. He has not however been successful, on account of the efficiency of the British security net, in making contact with any anti-British agents in Malaya, and added that it was impossible to get in touch with Indian military personnel, or to obtain information that would be operationally useful to the Japanese, owing to the frequent changes of station made by British units in Malaya.

34. The following points raised by Giani Pritam Singh were discussed :–

1. Relations between India and Japan should be on an egalitarian basis, i.e., India should not be in the same status as Manchuria and Korea. Indians in Malaya should not be militarised as the Chinese had been.
2. Giani Pritam Singh expressed no faith in the Gandhian doctrine of non-violence, asserting that Indian Independence could only be won by force of arms. He therefore sought Japanese cooperation to this end, in arms and equipment, with the proviso that the Indians should be allowed to raise and organise their own army of volunteers.
3. A representative Indian who could unite all classes should be invited to come to the Far East and the name of S.C. Bose was suggested.
4. Contact with Indians in Japan.

35. Comments on the above : (a) The issue of equality of status between Japan and India, and of the right to raise an army free from Japanese interference, thus raised (and expressed in terms (1) and (2) above) at the first meeting between Giani Pritam Singh and Fujiwara, was to lead to the dissolution of the first I.N.A., to cause friction between S.C. Bose and the Japanese, and was never fully resolved during the whole period of the Japanese inspired Indian Independence Movement. The failure of agreement on these issues from start to finish, is in itself sufficient evidence of the vain hopes of success which can be entertained by an Independence Movement, sponsored by and subservient to a major power, which is itself been on a military of aggrandizement and dominion.

It is of some significance to the future course of events to note that, in their first conversations with Fujiwara, both Giani Pritam Singh and Mohan Singh suggested the name of S. C. Bose as a leader of the Indian

Independence Movement. (Sec. Rept. 1007 para 37).

36. Fujiwara, submitted a name on his discussions with Giani Pritam Singh to Col. Tamura who forwarded it to Southern Area Army HQ in Saigon and to Imperial HQ in Tokyo. Fujiwara states that, as he had no idea how the attack would develop, and as he had not exactly made up his mind how he was to utilize the Indians in Malaya, This memo did not make any suggestions of a definite or detailed nature. The only other Indian with whom Fujiwara had a meeting in Bangkok before the outbreak of hostilities was Baba Amar Singh, an old man, but full of fire and violently anti-British.

37. About 5 Dec. 41, Fujiwara was appointed a Staff Officer on Southern Area Army HQ and was ordered to be prepared to report to Singapore (Southern Thailand) as staff officer (Propaganda) to .. 25 Army under Gen YAMASHITA.[3] His immediate superior was .. SUZUKI, Chief of Staff of 25 Army.

The Printing of Leaflets

38. The account so far given has indicated that, while the Indian community in Bangkok, being mainly interested in the success of their business enterprises, was not politically-minded, there were potential sources of disaffection which would be ready to seize an opportunity of striking at British power. It has further been indicated that one man (Giani Pritam Singh) had taken steps prejudicial to British interests by establishing clandestine contact with the Japanese, with a view to cooperating with them, and rallying the Indian populace to their side on the outbreak of hostilities.

39. On 7 Dec. 1941, Fujiwara told Giani Pritam Singh to await development and be ready to move. No sooner had the bloodless occupations of Bangkok had taken place on the night of 7/8 Dec. 41, then the well-laid plans of Giani Pritam Singh were immediately put into operation.

40. S.M. Ghosh reports (see CSDIC (I) 'V' Sec. Rept. F/293) that on calling at the office of the "Thai Bharat Cultural Lodge" on the afternoon of 8 Dec 1941, he was informed by Swami Satyananda Puri that he (Swami) had refused a request by Giani Pritam Singh for the use of the Lodge's cyclostyle machine to print surrender leaflets intended for distribution among Indian soldiers in Malaya.

3. General Yamashita Tomoyuki, after conquering Singapore, was transferred to a new post is Mancharia in July, 1942. After the defeat of Japan, he was tried and was executed in 1946.

41. On 9 Dec. 1941, Giani Pritam Singh, accompanied by Master Bhagwan Singh, again visited the "Thai Bharat Cultural Lodge" with the same request, but Deb Nath Das, who was in the office at the time, vehemently protested. That evening, Swami Satyananda Puri and Deb Nath Das were sent for by the Japanese Legation, where they were asked and again refused, to allow Giani Pritam Singh to use the cyclostyle machine for the desired purpose. On the following day, at the instance of Giani Pritam Singh, Master Bhagwan Singh, Baba Amar Singh and others, leaflets in Urdu, Gurmukhi, English and Hindustani (presumably printed at some locality other than the Thai Bharat Cultural Lodge) were distributed throughout Bangkok.

42. (1) While the distribution of leaflets amongst Indian tps, particularly in the early stages of the Malyan campaign, has been reported on numerous occasions, this is the first account which has been given of the planned treachery of Giani Pritam Singh in arranging to have them printed.

(2) From the apparent haste with which these leaflets were printed, support is given to the contention of Fujiwara that, while both he and his Indian collaborator had their plans well-made in advance, neither Fujiwara, far less Giani Pritam Singh, was privy to the detailed plans of the Japanese High Command. On the other hand, copies are in existence of letters prepared for distribution to Indian soldiers as early as Sept. 1941, which clearly show that Giani Pritam Singh had given thought long before the outbreak of war to the question of spreading disaffection among Indian tps.

(3) The reported attitude of Deb Nath Das is hard to follow. This man had lived in Japan before the war, and had a part in the founding of the "Thai Bharat Cultural Lodge", but detailed information about his movements in 1940 and 1941 is not available at CSDIC (I). If the account given by S.M. Ghosh of the objection raised by Deb Nath Das and Swami Satyananda Puri to the printing of leaflets on the cyclostyle machine of the "Thai Bharat Cultural Lodge" is correct, there are no grounds for the suspicion (aroused by the journey made by Deb Nath Das from Tokyo to Bangkok to take part in its foundation) that the "Thai Bharat Cultural Lodge" was sponsored and financed by the Japanese.

(4) If then, Deb Nath Das was not a dupe of the Japanese at this stage, it is felt that his state of mind was probably similar to that of Swami Satyananda Puri (and of Capt. Mohan Singh on his first meeting with Fujiwara and Giani Pritam Singh) which is interpreted as one of initial suspicion and distrust of the sincerity of Japanese motives towards India.

suspicion and distrust of the sincerity of Japanese motives towards India. That Swami Satyananda Puri very soon adopted a more trustful attitude to the Japanese is evidence by his acceptance of the office of representative Indian in Bangkok on 13 Dec. 1941.

(5) Civ. Kartar Singh states that the leaflets for distribution to Indian tps were mainly the work of Master Bhagwan Singh who arranged for them to be lithographed at Phit Buri. ('V' Sec. Rept. F/308 para 4 on Kartar Singh). As in 'V' Sec. Rept. F/362 on Master Bhagwan Singh there is no mention of such lithography having been done, and as counter-allegations are made by Bhagwan Singh against Kartar Singh, it is thought that there may be some personal ill-feeling between these two men.

Organisation of Giani Pritam Singh's Party and the Move to Malaya

43. On the same day (9 Dec. 1941) on which he made overtures to the Thai Bharat Cultural Lodge for cooperation in the printing of leaflets, Giani Pritam Singh held a meeting and organised the Azad Hind Sang, which was directly under the control of the Japanese. The only Mohammedan who attended this meeting was a maulvi, and the members were mostly Sikhs.

44. After waiting for word of the success of the Japanese landings in Malaya, Fujiwara, who had been standing by the Bangkok since he had his appointment to 25 Army HQ, flew from Bangkok to Singora in Southern Thailand on 10 or 12 Dec. 1941. He was accompanied by Giani Pritam Singh and three other Indians whose names he does not know, but who appeared to be of minor importance. (Their names are given in CSDIC (I) 'V' Sec Information Rept No. 2. dated 23 Jan. 46).

45. From Singora, the party proceeded via Haadyai to Alor Stor in Northern Malaya, where, by 14 Dec 1941, Fujiwara had established his HQ, and with the help of Giani Pritam Singh, had held the first meetings to organise a local branch of the I.I.L.

46. In Haadyai, in Southern Thailand, armbands were obtained for issue to Giani Pritam Singh and the Indians of his party, in order that they might be identified by Japanese soldiers. Fujiwara states that the 'F' on these armbands stood for 'Fujiwara, Friendship, Freedom'.

47. On 15 Dec. 1941, Mohan Singh was captured, Fujiwara has been unable to add to the detailed account given in 'S' Sec Rept 1007 on the circumstances of this surrender. It should be noted that the accounts given by both Fujiwara and Mohan Singh agree in the following

(1) That the initial suggestion for forming the I.N.A. came from Fujiwara and Giani Pritam Singh, and that Mohan Singh was at first hesitant about taking this decisive step.

(2) That having given the matter some thought (which he had ample opportunity of doing, as he lay on a sick bed for almost a week during this period) Mohan Singh, who was in Alor Star and Sungei Patani between his capture on 15 Dec 1941 and the end of that month, made a journey to Taiping with the specific purpose of freely offering his services to Fujiwara on New Year's Day, 1942.

48. Fujiwara agrees with the account given in 'S' Sec Rept 1007, paras 26 and 33, on the rivalry that existed between Mohan Singh and Giani Pritam Singh. The latter, having initiated the Independence Movement, would have liked to be regarded by the Japanese as the leader and to have Mohan Singh under his Comd. Giani Pritam Singh's idea was that the I.I.L. should be the executive body with the I.N.A. as its army and under its Comd. Mohan Singh, on the other hand, wished to be quite independent of the I.I.L.

49. Fujiwara's own attitude was that (to use his own imagery) he regarded Mohan Singh and Giani Pritam Singh as two wheels of an engine, and that he could not give power and prominence to one at the expense of the other. For this reason, Fujiwara considered it advisable to keep before the eyes of his two puppets the name of S.C. Bose (whom both men had individually named as the Indian who could best unite all factions). Fujiwara's main war was by diplomacy and conciliation to enlist the complete support of both men.

Giani Pritam Singh's Party

50. In his progress with Fujiwara in the wake of the advancing Japanese Army, Giani Pritam Singh had in the meantime by no means been inactive. In each town, as it was occupied by the Japanese, Fujiwara and Giani Pritam Singh delivered lectures on the sincerity of Japanese intentions towards India and on the necessity of avoiding panic. I.I.L. badges were issued to Indians civilians and their names were registered as members of the body. As they continued south, Giani Pritam Singh found that, as so many local volunteers were enlisted in the towns through which they passed, the recruiting party which he had brought from Thailand and outlived its usefulness, so that, at their own request, the majority returned to Bangkok in the latter part of January, 42. (Sec. 'V' Sec. Inf Rept No. 3 which confirms this).

51. Fujiwara states that, once he had appreciated the merits of Giani Pritam Singh and Mohan Singh, he left to them the organization of Indian civilians and Indian Army PW respectively. Fujiwara also points out that, as he was throughout the whole campaign primarily a staff officer under Gen. Suzuki on Army HQ, he had many other duties to attend to, and delegated much of his work to his two Indian assistants.

The 200 Volunteers or "Fujiwara Volunteers"

52. Fujiwara states that the Japanese welcomed the scheme of forming a party of Indian soldiers who would advance on Singapore alongside the Japanese, for in this way they could have confidence that the PW, who had fallen into their hands, and the civilian population, lulled into a submissive frame of mind by the specious promises of Japanese "protection" and of participation in the "co-prosperity sphere", were amicably disposed towards their new masters. The Japanese had been afraid that Indian soldiers, whose units had been defeated in battle, would adopt civilian disguise and cause havoc behind the lines. Fujiwara claims that no Fifth Column or intelligences work was done by the 200 party, who were used as a collecting agency for defeated and scattered Indian tps.

53. Fujiwara states that the party of 200 volunteers were armed for self-protection, but that these arms were never used, or were certainly never intended to be used, as offensive weapons. Fujiwara has no recollection of Sub Allah Ditta, 22 Mtn Bty nor of the incident referred to in 'S' See Repts 833 para 22, and 1007 para 58, where Fujiwara is stated to have given his watch to Allah Ditta.

Notes :– (1) The above account, combined with the evidence accumulated from many sources and confirmed by 'S' Sec Repts on Mohan Singh and Allah Ditta, lends weight to the general conclusion that the main duty of the party of 200 was the collection and organisation of stragglers.

(2) Fujiwara has confirmed the statement of Mohan Singh (see 'S' Sec Rept 1007 para 54) that he (Fujiwara) was unwilling to hand over rifles to Allah Ditta's party until Mohan Singh had personally assumed full responsibility for anything that might happen.

(3) It is felt that the aura of infamy and glory that has grown up around the treacherous, yet in the end petty achievements of this party of renegades, is largely a

product of rumour and exaggerated accounts of heroism. Allah Ditta himself records an instance of how, after the fall of Singapore, in order to increase his prestige in the I.N.A., he kept silent when some vingtorious, but entirely fictitious account was being given of his assistance in directing the fire of a Japanese part 36). It should in this connection be noted that Sub Allah Ditta himself states the 200 volunteers were selected on the basis of whet her they could swim since he imagined the party would have to swim from Johore Bahru to Singapore Island.

The Fujiwara Kikan

54. When questioned on the organisation bearing his name, Fujiwara stated that in reality it was not a Kikan in the same sense as the Twakuid of Hikari Kikan, but that it was merely a name given to himself and his small party of assistants. These assistants reported for two main purposes, as interpreters and to assist in the requisitioning of rations and supplies of the I.N.A.

These associates were :–

Interpreters

2/Lt. Kunizuka	(English)
Cpl Otaguro	"
Cpl Ishikawa	(Hindustani)

Administrative Assistants

Capt. Tsuchimochi	2 i/c. Dispatched to Burma Area Army HQ in Feb. 42, for the purpose of furthering the Indian Independence Movement and forming an I.N.A. in Burma (This was Ram Sarup's party)
Lt. Segawa	
" Yamaguchi	
" Nakamiya	
" Yonemura	

Civilians used in Singapore :–

Suzuki
Masubuchi
OTA
Hashimoto

Kitamura

ITO – Last seen in Bishenpur.

55. Regarding the Japanese members of his staff, Fujiwara stated that the four officers were all graduates of the Nakano School (a School of advanced "T" training) and had all come from Tokyo on this special assignment. None of them had any experience of India. The only other member of the party of whom Fujiwara has only information was Otaguro, who had been educated in a Japanese School in Singapore, and come to Bangkok just before the outbreak of war.

56. The Japanese attack on Malaya from Thailand was made in three columns in each of which Fujiwara allotted numbers of his party as follows :

(1) Fujiwara himself was attached to 25 Army HQ which formed the right flank of the Japanese thrust. With Fujiwara was Giani Pritam Singh, Otaguro and other Japanese and Indians. The advanced element of 25 Army was 5 Div., to which was attached Lt. Nakamiya with two Indians.

(2) One Regt. of 5 Div., to which were attached 2/Lt. Yonemura and a few Indians for contact work, was allotted the central sector.

(3) On the left flank, where 1 Regd of 18 Div advanced via Kota Bharu, was 2/Lt. Segawa and 2 Indians.

Notes :– (a) While there is much information on the party operating with Fujiwara, little is known about the parties under Yonemura and Segawa.

(b) Confirmation of the information in the last three paragraphs will be found in a note on the Fujiwara Kikan, based on an interrogation of Capt. Kunizuka by Field Security Service HQ, Singapore. (Their FS/A/2 to Singapore Security Bureau, copy to 'S' Sec. CSDIC (I) dated 19 Mar. 46 refers).

(1) To establish local branches of the I.I.L.

(2) Organise Indian PW into Camps. Only members of the Fujiwara Kikan were to have jurisdiction over Indian PW (i.e., any such PW captured by Japanese units were to be handed over to the Fujiwara Kikan).

The Surrender of Singapore and Fujiwara's Return to Tokyo

58. Fujiwara states that Mohan Singh and he remained at Kuala Lumpur until a few days before the fall of Singapore. (This is confirmed by Mohan Singh) Fujiwara has no new information to add on the events in Singapore at the time of the capitulation and immediately after. In Mar. 42, he accompanied the Indian delegates by plane to the Tokyo Conference, which he himself did not attend as he was granted leave, on

Conference, which he himself did not attend as he was granted leave, on the termination of which he returned to his post of Staff Officer (Intelligence) at Southern Army HQ. He was succeeded in his post, as Staff Officer i/c Indian affairs by Col. (later Maj. Gen.) Iwaguro who had also accompanied the party of Indians to Tokyo. Iwaguro had no previous contact with Indian affairs, but held an important appointment in the Ministry of War, where he was head of the "Adjutant Section" From the date of his return to Tokyo, Fujiwara's active connection with Indians and Indian affairs ceased.

Note :– Fujiwara has stated that the welcome which was given to Japanese tps by Indians in Malaya during the victorious advance down the Malaya peninsula far exceeded the expectations of the Japanese. The degree of importance which, from the time of the Tokyo Conference, the Japanese attached to the puppet Indian Independence Movement is seen in the appointment of an officer higher in rank than Fujiwara to take charge of Indian affairs, i.e. Col. Iwaguro.

Ram Sarup's Party and Captain Tsuchimochi

59. Asked whether the idea of sending a party of Indians to Burma had originated with the Indians themselves (i.e., Mohan Singh or Giani Pritam Singh) Fujiwara stated that in Dec. 1941 or Jan. 1942 a signal was received by him from HQ Southern Regions, ordering that, in view of the success of the Fujiwara Kikan in the Malayan operations, Fujiwara himself should go to Burma and organise a similar movement amongst Indians in order to facilitate the operations of 15 Army. Fujiwara, however, was instrumental in arranging for Capt. Tsuchimochi, his 2 i/c to be sent in his place.

60. Early in 1943, while Fujiwara was working as an 'I' officer on Count Terauchi's staff in HQ Southern Regions in Saigon, he was ordered to go to Singapore to try to help Col. Iwaguro to smooth over the trouble that had arisen in Singapore due to the collapse of the I.N.A. On arrival in Singapore he addressed a meeting of Indian officers "whom he looked upon and still looks upon as his good friends". In this speech Fujiwara spoke to the following effect : "Mohan Singh as a great friend of mine for whose opinions I have every respect. I am anxious that the I.N.A., which I started as a baby and reared up, should not collapse." He further exhorted them not to give us the struggle for the Independence of India, an honourable cause for which the I.N.A. had been called into being.

61. Commenting on this speech and on his relations with Mohan Singh, Fujiwara stated that while he was in charge of Indian affairs,

Mohan Singh and he had always remained on friendly terms. He liked Mohan Singh for his honesty, straightforwardness and boldness. They lived together like friends, and it was seldom that any doubts arose in Mohan Singh's mind. But after his return to Tokyo in Mar 1942, the friendly atmosphere, which, fostered by Fujiwara's diplomatic handling of Mohan Singh, had existed between the Japanese and the Indians, changed. Filing up doubts as to the sincerity of the Japanese began to assail Mohan Singh. At the time he went to Singapore in early 43 on his mission of reconciliation, Fujiwara had desired with all his heart that a understanding could have been come to between the Japanese and the Indians: but all his pleadings and persuasions were in vain.

Some Comments by Fujiwara on his Relations with Indians and on the Indian Independence Movement

62. Fujiwara states that during the short time he was i/c Indian affairs, he was adversely criticised by his fellow Japanese officers for being too friendly to Indians, and the opinion was even expressed that he was more of an Indian than a Japanese. Fujiwara indicated that he himself was sincere in his attitude towards Indians, and that more than once he adopted an attitude that was sympathetic to the Indians but was opposed to that held by the Japanese High Command. Fujiwara's opinion is that the I.N.A. would have been much more successful if it had been left to Indians themselves, in the same fashion that he left detailed administration to Giani Pritam Singh and Mohan Singh, and he further considers that if he had been retained i/c Indian affairs after Mar 1942, he should have done better than Iwaguro.

63. Fujiwara has little direct information of Indians after his departure to Tokyo in Mar 1942. From his observation of the I.N.A. on the Imphal front, he was given it as his opinion that the defeat of the Japanese in the Burma campaign was in no way due to the lack of fighing spirit on the part of the I.N.A.

64. Asked whether in his opinion, the I.N.A. was a purely propaganda army or if the Japanese considered it had a co-combatant status, Fujiwara maintained that it was definitely regarded as a combatant force, and that it was regarded as having an offensive role. As an example of this, he cited the stage of the Imphal operations at the end of June 1944, when elements of the I.N.A. details not known by Fujiwara were covering a position on both flanks of a Japanese unit astride the Palel-Mawle road, with the object of holding the Allied advance on Malwe, and so covering the withdrawal of Japanese 15 and receive from Kohima and Ukhrul.

(Fujiwara was able immediately to cite this example of the use of the I.N.A., as he had used to as tactical example when he had been an instructor at the Army War College).

65. It should be noted, however, that the Japanese do not appear to have committed the I.N.A. to battle until a definitely defensive stage of the campaign had been reached. When the Japanese offensive thrust towards Imphal and Kohima was in progress in the early months of 1944, the I.N.A. was kept in the rear. Fujiwara can remember the names of only Shah Nawaz, Malik and Kiani of the I.N.A. comds in Burma, but can give no information about their personalities or achievements.

66. Fujiwara denies completely the story that when Maj. Niranjan Singh Gill (RI190)[4] was staying in the Oriental Hotel, Bangkok at the time of his secret journey to Thailand to find out the degree of anti-British feeling amongst Indians, he (Fujiwara) was living in the next room.

67. He also denies the story recorded in CSDIC (I) 'V' Sec V/298 on Jagat Singh Dhillon of his having given a revolver to Harnam Singh Dhillon, as a token of esteem for his (Dhillon) having shot a British officer PW.

Hikari Kikan[5]

68. Fujiwara has no direct information on the Hikari Kikan, nor of its relations to the I.N.A. He states, however, that each of the three Japanese Div. (15, 31, 33) in Burma had a Hikari Kikan representative, who reported to Hikari Kikan HQ. The Hikari Kikan had liaison direct with 15 Army HQ, and with the I.N.A. He represented the chain of command thus :–

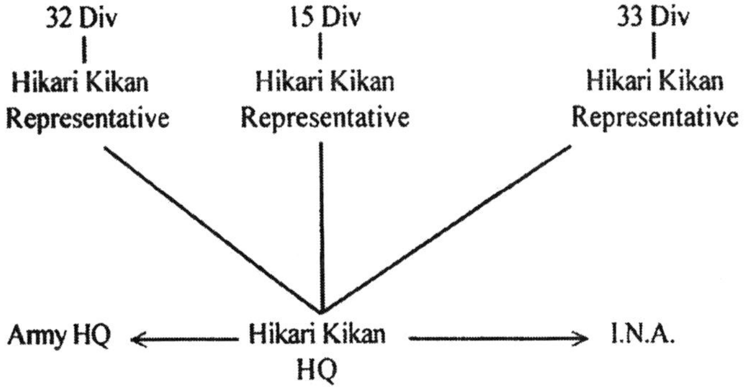

4. It was under a seperate serial number allotted to each person that the Interogation Report was recorded. These reports are available in I.N.A. papers at National Archives of India.

5. Activities of this organisation, which served as a liaison Agency between the Japanese Government and the Provisional Governemnt of Azad Hind are given in Volume III, IV and V.

Difficulties Experienced by the Japanese in Organizing the I.I.L. and I.N.A. in Malaya

69. Fujiwara has summed up the difficulties experienced by the Japanese in organising the I.I.L. and I.N.A. in Malaya as follows :–

(1) Mohan Singh's doubts as to Japan's sincerity in aiding India's fight for freedom.

(2) Lack of knowledge of Indian customs and religions by Japanese soldiers, and their generally insulting attitude towards Indians. The lack of military courtesies (saluting) by both Indian and Japanese. Illtreatment by the Kempei Tai.

(3) The failure of the Japanese to regard the I.N.A. as a wholly independent army.

(4) Members of the I.I.L. attempting to further their own interests through the formation of the I.I.L. and I.N.A.

Later War Experiences of Fujiwara

70. The movements of Fujiwara after his visit to Singapore early in 1943 are given in brief.

Apr. 43	Reported to HQ 15 Army in Rangoon, and participated in the Imphal operations as Staff Officer.
Aug. 44	Promoted Lt. Col.
Sep. 44	Became Staff Officer (Operations) 15 Army HQ.
Dec. 44	Received orders to return for posting to the Army War College as an instructor. Owing to scarcity of shipping was unable to proceed at once.
Feb. 45	Arrived in Japan and took up his appointment at the Army War College.
Apr. 45	Became Senior Staff Officer, 2 Area Army in Japan.
Jan. 45	Appointed Staff Officer, 57 Army in Southern Kyushu.

Conclusion

71. Fujiwara has confirmed but has not materially added to the considerable body of information now available on the Japanese-sponsored Indian Independence Movement, particularly in the crucial period between Oct 1941 and Mar 1942. From the information which he has supplied, the gravamen of the indictment, on the charge of collaborating with the Japanese even before the outbreak of hostilities,

must be levelled against a few malcontents in Bangkok.

72. There is no doubt that the latent nationalism amongst Indian in East Asia would have made the development of an Indian Independence Movement inevitable. But without the initial assistance of Giani Pritam Singh, Mohan Singh and a few more arch-renegades, the movement would never have assumed the proportions that it did.

12

Japanese Premier Tojo's Speech Regarding Military Activities in India for Helping the India Nationalists

4 April, 1942

Imperial Forces have previously occupied Rangoon, which is an important point in Burma, and the Andaman Islands, a strategically important point in the Eastern part of the Indian Ocean and a place of exile for Indian Independence Patriots. And now, advancing further, it has been arranged to strike a decisive blow against the British military power and military establishment in India.

In this way the firm determination of the Imperial Government to chastise America and Britain is being steadily realized.

If India should remain as previously under British military control it is unavoidable that Indian will suffer considerable war damage through the Imperial Government's attack to exterminate Britain.

From the outset the Imperial Government's intention has not been to regard India's four hundred million people as enemies. Towards the Indian people who would suffer war calamities in this event there is genuine sympathy.

The real intention of the Imperial Government is clear from statements in my speech of March 10th, in the Imperial Diet. That way I indicated my firm conviction that this was a golden opportunity for Indians to exert all their strength to create "India for the Indians" and to establish India's original form.

This coming autumn British power in India will be crushed. I hope again that India's leaders will avoid incurring pointless war havoc, misled by the soft talk of England, under whose control India's four hundred million people have been, and that, seizing this heaven-sent opportunity, they will break asunder England's yoke of many years and advance in the realisation of "India for the Indians."

---

1. File No. 254; I.N.A. Papers.

13

N. Raghavan's Views about the Japanese Policy Towards India's Independence

5 May, 1942

1. Declaring his fixed determination to fight for the freedom of his country from the Anglo-Saxon bondage with the help of friendly power, namely; Nippon, Mr. N. Raghavan, President of India Independence League, Penang, who attended the conference of the Indian Independence League has just returned from Tokyo.

2. In an interview granted to me at his residence yesterday, Mr. Raghavan was full of confidence that the sacred mission of Japan in driving British and Americans out of Asia would be successfully completed.

3. Mr. Raghavan said that he would like to appeal to all his countrymen not to miss opportunity of taking up arms. If need be, to fight for their own freedom in particular and to help the Nipponese Forces in fighting for the freedom of all Asiatic races in general.

4. When questioned about his stay in Tokyo, Mr. Raghavan was full of praise for the Japanese people and officials and said that when he was in Japan he had found Japanese people exceedingly polite, in fact he said, the grater the person, the more humble he appeared to be. He further told me that he had visited many cities in Japan and Formosa during his brief stay there, he had delivered some 70 to 80 speeches and he was much taken by the kindliness and very friendly disposition of the people. One thing which struck him most forcibly, he said, was that although it was war time, there was no blackout in Japan and life there appeared quite normal. As a matter of fact, the atmosphere there was one of the quiet confidence.

---

1. *Penang Daily News*, 5 May, 1942.

5. The people appeared very determined in help their Government to prosecute the Greater East Asia War to successful conclusion at all cost.

6. Referring to the unfortunate fatal plane crash in which four of his comrades, who were also proceeding to Tokyo were killed, Mr. Raghavan expressed his profound sorrow.

7. In reply to my question regarding the service held in Tokyo in memory of the dead, Mr. Raghavan said that in Tokyo, a most touching ceremony was held when prayers were offered for the response of the souls of these unfortunate representatives. He added that he was told that the ceremony was one of the greatest ever held in Japan.

8. Mr. Raghavan informed me that the families of the deceased had been compensated both by the Government and by the Air-plane company each of whom had given $ 10,000, thereby making a total of $ 20,000 to each of the deceased family.

9. On behalf of the Indian Independence League of Malaya. Mr. Raghavan said that he was glad to be able to offer a gift of $ 10,000 to the family if Japanese interpreter, Mr. Ottaguro who was in the ill-fated plane at the time of the accident and who had also lost his life.

10. It will be recalled that Mr. Raghavan left Penang to attend the Conference of the Indian Independence League in Tokyo towards the end of March. He said that he arrived there at the time when the cherry trees were in full blossom and they presented to the visitors most magnificent sight which they would remember for a very long time.

11. Mr. Raghavan was asked his opinion about the destruction of cherry trees in Washington by the Americans, he said that when he heard of revolting Americans action in cutting down these trees in Washington, he felt terribly ashamed that a Democratic Power like America, which had always boasted of its civilization, could have stupped to such a base and unspeakably mean action.

12. When in Tokyo, he added he and his comrades had met His Excellency Prime Minister Mr. Hideki Tojo who had promised them that Japan would assist India to fight to her full Independence.

12. In reply to my question again Mr. Raghavan said that His Excellency Prime Minister Mr. Hideki Tojo was very kind and polite to them. He added that unlike the British imperialism, there was no such thing as colour prejudice or colour bar in Japan.

13. On being asked whether he had any opportunity of listening in to the Penang Broadcasting Station, Mr. Raghavan said that he had the opportunity to listen in while in Tokyo and Saigon, where he stopped on his return journey. He said the reception was very good indeed.

14

Report by Lieut - M.M. Pillai and Lieut. V. Radhakrishnan, who Escaped from Singapore after its Fall; gives Detailed Information to the British about the Collaboration between Soldiers of the Indian Army and the Japanese

7 May, 1942

After the surrender of Singapore I was interned at Bidadari P.O.W. Camp until 1st May, 1942 when I was transferred to the Sapper Camp at Tyersall Park. Through intermediaries I was able to contact Lieut. Radhakrishnan, who was living in McNair road in his bungalow, as the Volunteers had been disbanded and not interned and plans were laid for our escape into India. These plans, however, were upset by my transfer to Tyersall Park Camp from which escape was difficult. Fortunately, Captain Mohan Singh issued orders that all Indian officers should meet him in person on 7th May at Bidadari Camp, and with that as an excuse I left for Bidadari Camp which I reached at midday on the 6th. Having reported my arrival there Captain Natarajan, M.C., I.M.S., and myself slipped out that night and surreptitiously made our way to R's bungalow where we spent the night.

When Lieut. Pillai came to visit me four days before the fall of Singapore, it struck me that he would make an excellent companion in the event of our attempting to escape should Singapore surrender. With this in mind I spent all my time after its fall collecting information which would help us on our way to India, and at the same time I visited all the P.O.W. Camps in an attempt to contact P. Eventually P. contacted me and we made plans for the escape. My first task was to raise funds. This I did by selling most of my possessions. On the evening of 6th May P.

1 Fortnightly Intelligence report Far Eastern Bureau. Ministry of Defence Archives, Liaison Office, the Netherlands. The information provided by them to the British was of great help.The British got information from many other agents.

and Capt. N. arrived at my bungalow. Our combined funds amounted to $ 600 and I had also managed to obtain, under false name, membership cards of the Indian Independence League. The money we had was barely enough for two people. It was even less sufficient for three. We bought cigars and tinned provisions like butter, jam, horlicks, tins of milk, etc., from a friend's shop and took the night train to Penang.

Buying tickets was an ordeal. The Japanese soldiers beat the passengers with a cane whilst buying tickets, and no tickets were issued unless money was given in Japanese currency notes in their various denominations. Their Commander-in-Chief issued a proclamation to the effect that all currencies were valid in Malaya! I bought the tickets and narrowly escaped the Japanese birch, an unfortunate Chinese girl next to me getting it on her thigh. The station was quite dark and there were some I.N.A. Sikhs on watch for P.O.W. escaping from the Island. We huddled ourselves into a goods carriage and lay in a dark corner.

Our dress was a dhoti, a long shirt and a Gandhi cap, all in Khaddar (home spun Indian cloth usually associated with the symbolic dress of a Congress volunteer), and a long towel which could either be tied like a turban round the head or left to hang from the shoulders. Incidentally, this is also the standard dress worn by Chetties Agents. Chetties are usually money lenders.

The train arrived at Bukit Mertajam on the afternoon of the 9th going very slowly over the Johore causeway at even less than walking pace. The bridges that had been blown up had been improvised by the Japanese and the train service was running. At the bridge near Kuala Lumpur one engine had capsized and we saw the capsized engine. The Japanese get over this difficulty by attaching the engine to the back of the train at the station before the bridge and pushing the carriages slowly over the bridge. Then when a carriage is well over the bridge another engine is hooked to this carriage, the old engine is disconnected and the train then starts. Pretty smart! we could not see very much of the route as we had to spend two nights in an overcrowded carriage which was very stuffy. We got down at Bukit Mertajan. To cover this distance by walking would have taken us at least a month as it is a journey of 500 miles.

We crossed to Penang by ferry which is still working, but controlled by the Japanese. At Prai our luggage was examined. We hid most of our money in our clothes as we had been told that we would not be allowed more than one hundred dollars each. We kept this amount in our purses

and after rough handling by the Japanese examiners we were able to get out and reach a friend Ramakrishna Iyer in Beach Road.

We told Mr. Ramakrishna Iyer of our plans as we knew he could help us. He was the proprietor of the Malayan Corporation, a small firm of importers and exporters. He is a graduate, a Brahmin from Coimbatore; South India. He told us that it was possible to enter Siam with a passport of three month's validity. So the next morning we went to the Japanese passport office, which is housed in the previous government building in Beach Street, and gave our photographs in the typical dress of Chetties. We had to bribe the clerk, a Chinese, to have it done quickly and to tell the Japanese officer that we were bonafide merchants and thus avoid enquiries. Even the Japanese officer's peon had to be bribed. We gave as our address a bombed house in Market Street so as not to get our friend into trouble. The passports were ready the next morning. They cost us only 25 cents (about 6 annas) each, but we had to pay $ 5 each to the clerk and $ 2 each to the peon and $ 5 each for our passport photographs.

We then toured the town to see what state it was in. The jetty and parts of Chulia and Market Streets were bombed into ruins. Food was not very expensive and the Japanese had issued an order that it was not to be exported from the Island. Rice could be had and also such things as onions and potatoes, which we had not seen at Singapore, could be had at a price. Prices for clothing were very high. The trams were running and we heard that the hill railway would soon be in order. The water and electricity supplies were working. On the whole Penang was normal and it looked less like a battered city than any other in Malaya. Our messing was arranged by our friend in a hotel and cost us all $ 30.

On the afternoon of the 13th we left for the frontier Badang Bosar by train. On this route there was more destruction to be seen. The bridges were very crudely repaired and we saw some damaged aeroplanes at the Alor Star aerodrome. We reached Padang Besar on the same night. We slept there the night and the next morning, after rough handling by Japanese officers and soldiers and some Siamese, we jumped into a goods train with open vans bound for Siam. About 50 Japanese soldiers travelled on this train. On the wayside stations we saw a few Japanese soldiers standing and looking at the train and some were walking along the railway track in full kit.

We reached Haad Yai about 1000 hours. In a train opposite us, bound for the Malayan frontier, there were a few Indian Businessmen–Tamils. They asked us if we had Siamese passports and on our replying the negative told us to get in touch with a Mr. Mathu and a Mr. Velayudham

Pillai. We could get a passport of about a month's validity for about if we bribed Mr. Velayudham to stand security for us.

During this conversation, one of the emigration officers came and questioned us about our passports. We showed the Japanese one and he told us to follow him to the emigration office for further instructions. In the office we found a Siamese officer who spoke good English. He told us to get a surety for a temporary passport or we would have to return to Malaya.

We left our bags in the office and went in search of the two people we had been told to get in touch with. We found Mr. Muthu and the man who had advised us on the train. They told us to get photographs so we went to a Chinese shop opposite and were photographed. It cost us 8 ticals each (dollars and ticals are now at par) and they were ready at 2 p.m. Mr. Velayudham then appeared. He said he was glad to meet businessmen new to Siam, that he was willing to help us, but that we must not take part in any politics and that we must be back at Haad Yai by the end of a month. He undertook to stand surety for us for the sum of 800 ticals and explained that he only did this sort of thing for gentlemen he knew would not forget him. After exchange of information about businessmen in Malaya he took us to the passport office and stood surety for us. He appeared to be much respected by the government as the officers showed him deference. We paid him $ 60 with which he seemed to extraordinarily pleased. He gave us the following information about Siam which was collaborated the more northward we travelled :–

(1) The Japanese currency notes were discounted, the further north one went but British currency notes were accepted and very welcome. In and about Bangkok people only offer 70 per cent of its value for a Japanese note.

(2) The Japanese were building a powerful aerodrome and extending the one at Sungei Patani and one midway between Haad Yai and Sungei Patani. There were a number of Japanese troops at Haad Yai and they were monopolising the Siamese railways for the transit of their troops and material. They were preparing secret landing grounds for their planes near Yaad Yai.

(3) There was a good deal of talk of the Japanese having asked for the incorporation of the whole of Siam above Malaya to a line connecting Rahnong and Chumpon on the north. The reason advanced by the Japanese was that this would make it Japanese territory from Singapore to Victoria Point. The Siamese prime minister had refused his request. The Siamese were enraged and talking about war between Siam and Japan.

(4) The Japanese told the prime minister that they would incorporate the Southern Shan States with Siam in their new order in East Asia, after the defeat of the British. They would also persuade Marshal Petain to surrender to Siama slice of territory on the northern bend of the Mekong River. The Siamese were not willing to accede as they were of the opinion that the people of the Shan States would be willing to join with Siam in any case. It was therefore unacceptable as a reward from Japan to Siam. As to the Indo-Chinese territory, the Siamese were suspicious as they considered that the Japanese were merely trying to increase dissension between Indo-China and Siam. They presumed the Japanese must think them fools as this change would only increase the length of Siam's frontier with China and thus Japanese could transfer some of the burden of fighting the Chinese to Siam.

(5) The Siamese had asked for the incorporation of the whole of the region south of the town of Moulmein up to the tip of Victoria Point with Siam. The Japanese would not do this as it was essential to safeguard this vital region against possible British sea attacks and the Siamese navy would be unable to do this. In this event the whole of the Archipelago would be lost to the Japanese as well as the Nicobar and Andaman Island.

(6) On the outbreak of hostilities on 8th December, 1941, the Siamese troops fought the Japanese well near, Haad Yai even though they were outnumbered and outclassed by superior weapons. The Japanese casualties were over 200 and when the order ceasefire came from their prime minister the Siamese troops were furious and so were their commanders, who had the disadvantage of never knowing their orders till the last minute.

(7) Most of the Siamese were pro-British and particularly pro-American, but they were unable to express their feelings. There were spies everywhere from Russia, Germany and Japan, and even the prime minister's own spies as he was in fear of assassination.

(8) From the 1st April an order was issued that all men and women were to wear European dress. This led to a shoe shortage, so the order was modified and women did not have to wear shoes. Thus we saw the strange spectacle of women in gowns, skirts, hats but going bare-footed.

(9) There was a food shortage in the country.

(10) The Japanese had been ordered not to molest Siamese women. But cases occurred causing much ill feeling.

Haad Yai looks like a half built town where work has suddenly ceased. Railway stations in Siam had the English names blacked out. Very few of

the Siamese would talk English and even the English time tables and information for travellers were not to be seen.

In the hotel where we stayed we found a few Sikhs talking late into the night drinking and shouting revolutionary slogans. There were more prostitutes than anyone else in this town. It has the semblance of an occupied town.

The next morning Captain Natarajan's fever was better so we left for Tap Tiang or Trang on the west coast to stay with a Mr. Muthia–a Chettiar. He was very helpful. He gave us the following information about Siam :–

(1) The richest Indian in the whole of Siam is a Sikh by the name of Bishambar Singh. There is no town without a branch of this man's shop. It is estimated that about a third of the houses in Bangkok belong to him. He was behind the financing of the I.N.A. and the propaganda on behalf of Indians overseas.

(2) The brain of the movement was Swami Satyanand Puri. He was in great repute as a scholar, and the Japanese made him the first Indian Consul of free India in Bangkok. He has since been killed in a plane crash.

(3) The Siamese Government intended arresting all Indians as British subjects on the outbreak of hostilities. All escaped internment by the action of Bhishambar Singh who subjected to the Siamese. Government surety freeing the rest of the Indians.

(4) There were not many restrictions on Indians whom the average Siamese regards with affection. Many kept their radio sets and were listening to our broadcasts. The Japanese influence was indirect and through pressure on the Government.

(5) There were continuous troop movements all over the country.

(6) There was a rumour that there were high staff officers of the German army in Siam.

(7) There was a proposal to snift the capital from Bangkok either down south or up north to Ayuthia.

(8) A lack of patent medicines in the country caused an influx of some clever limitations such as aspirin, etc.

After a day's rest on account of Captain Natarajan's illness we left Trang on the 17th by train reaching Chumpon that night. This to is on the east coast of Siam almost in line with Victoria Point.

That night was spent in a hotel and the next day we took a bus on our way to Renong. About 5 miles out of Chumpon we came to a big battalion H.Q. where we were told to alight. The Siamese National Anthem was played are a sentry told us to stand to attention and salute their

flag. Our bags were examined and the bus moved on. There was an escaped Chinese from Penang travelling in this bus, who cor.. to his nervousness of the position of the Chinese in Siam.

We travelled about 30 miles by bus to the Pak Chan estuary where we got into a motor boat run by the Siamese Government. It was about 10 a.m. and after sailing for about three hours we touched a small village where we stopped for a meal. After the meal we continued the journey by boat arriving at Pak Nam at about 5 p.m. that evening. As the tide was low we had to wait for a canoe or sampan to take us up the backwater about 3 miles, to Ranong. The night was spent at a hotel and on the following morning we asked some Pathans the best route to take for Burma. The Pathans, so my information went, had a colony round the region of the Isthmus of Kra. Living in a Buddhist country, and being fanatical Moslems themselves, they were not over friendly with the natives and their loyalty to the British Government could not be questioned. They advised us not to attempt the journey as the jungles were full of Siamese and Burmese dacoits and the monsoon had commenced.

In a tea shop we met Abu Bakar Kaka, a Moslem from Malabar, who offered to take us to a Japanese official where we could obtain a passport to enable us to cross into Burma at Victoria Point. The official in question, when we got there, reminded us of a pocket edition of Mephistopheles, an old man of about 70, reputed to have been the brains behind the Japanese infiltration round Victoria Point. We concocted a story to enable us to procure passes giving us an unmolested passage to Moulmein. He was impressed with our story but said that he could not have passports ready until 23rd of May as he had to send rations to the Japanese troops in Sumatra and look after the 5 ships that were bringing Australian and Dutch P.O.W. from Malaya and Java. These troops were to be employed as a labour corps for making a road from Victoria Point to Mergui, cleaning up bombed houses, in towns like Tavoy, repairing bridges and existing roads. We realised that these four days were for checking up on us. However nothing could be done about it.

On the 23rd we obtained our passes and took a car to Pak Nam. Here we took a boat to Victoria Point arriving where about 4 p.m. in the evening. Before embarking we handed in our Siamese passports at the emigration office at Pak Nam and had them endorsed to the effect that we were leaving the country before the end of the month as this would release Mr. V. Pillai from all responsibility.

Whilst in a provision shop at Victoria Point an Australian sergeant came for stores. The prices were high but the shopkeeper was pro-Ally and he was allowed to take Rs. 15 worth of goods free, and was told to tell his friends that they could do the same. The Australian informed us that by tipping the Japanese sentry 20 cents a time he was allowed out. He gave his name as Eric Merrill and said he came from Perth. There had been talk amongst the P.O.W. of escaping but it was head that this was too risky as it meant almost certain death.

That evening, with the aid of the shopkeeper, we were able to catch the Japanese boat to Mergui. On account of a squall and fog we were forced to anchor off an island for the night of the 24th after only doing about 10 miles. We sailed early next morning with the weather continuing to be rough but not so foggy and on our way we say two aerodromes, a wireless station and a few Japanese soldiers.

A fellow traveller, whom we suspected of being a Japanese spy, informed us that Mr. Knife, D.C. at Victoria Point, was a prisoner at Bangkok. He was a Thakin officer so we asked him how the Thakins had obtained their arms and training. He replied that they had secret associations all over Burma, with members in the Government services. A party of Thakins had been trained in Japan and led the Japanese troops when encircling the British. Their weapons were obtained from secret German and Japanese sources.

We reached Mergui on the 25th at 5 p.m. after a rough voyage of about 200 miles. We stayed at a hotel, but Captain Natarajan stayed with some relatives who were indiscreet in their talk and people came to know something of us. We therefore decided to leave by bus, but as none was going till 2nd June we set off by foot. We set out early in the morning of 31st May, and after crossing a river at noon we reached a village on a rubber estate, 28 miles up the Tavoy road, that night. The headman of the village was very hospitable and gave us food and beds. Here we met a Bengali postmaster who told that the Japs had come to the estate a fortnight back and informed the coolies that they would receive work. The Burmese coolies, however, were working on the estate under instructions from the Thakins. He added that he had had a telephone message from the Japanese military at Mergui asking him to be on the lockout for 4 escaped Australian P.O.W.

The next morning we left and reached Palaw the same day. The town was under the Thakins though there were many Japanese troops in the vicinity. Petrol was difficult to obtain although the Burmese had hidden large quantities from the Japanese. A gallon could be illicitly obtained for

about R. 10/-. The Thakins were forcibly recruiting young boys in the neighbourhood and training them as troops.

The next night we reached Palauk. Ploughing was going on, rains were said to be normal, and the place presented a green and fertile appearance.

We reached Pe on the 3rd June, Chaungwabin on the 4th, and late on the 5th we arrived at Tavoy. The next morning we toured the town and found it completely gutted. The electric supply, however, was functioning. The tin smelting company's shops were not working. Trade between Rangoon and Tavoy was functioning by means of country boats. The Japanese at Tavoy are living in the school building.

On the road to Tavoy many bridges had been destroyed by the retreating British and near Mandao the Japanese were rebuilding one. There were about 100 Japanese here presumably engaged on this work. It was near here that we saw 5 or 6 lorry loads of Dutch prisoners moving up with another lorry of Japanese.

We left Tavoy on the 7th by bus, having obtained tickets through the aid of a Bengali Doctor we met there, and arrived at Ye the same evening. Here we were befriended by a Raman Chettiar who put us up and arranged for a bullock cart and boat to take us as far as a place called Ilamaing which we reached on the 8th forenoon. There is a train service from here to Moulemein, of which we availed ourselves reaching the town on the 9th at sunset. We were accompanied by Raman Chettiar's son. He was of great help to us as he could read, write and talk fluent Burmese. On the route we found telegraph lines cut, wires pulled down, pole uprooted, looted stations and many similar acts of vandalism. The salt factory on this route was not working, and many stray Japanese soldiers were to be seen.

At Moulmein we stayed with Messrs the Bank of Chettinad Ltd. under the hospitality of Mr. Muthukumar. Our journey had now lasted a month, we were worn out through walking, a bullock cart ride, a boat journey, bus journey, etc. but we wanted to push one so we decided to start off again the next morning.

We found some parts of Moulmein badly damaged, but the city itself was comparatively untouched. High prices existed and people were fed up with the Thakin authorities; the Japanese were expected to take over the administration on the 10th.

We crossed over by ferry to Martaban. The engine of the paddle boat was in a bad way, the steam leaking giving us a mild steam bath. The Japanese were running this boat and the charge was two annas per man. The boat was overcrowded and it took us half an hour to cross.

At Martaban we caught the train. People were packed in like sardines. Here telegraph wires were down and bridges blown up but the Japanese were doing a lot of repairing. We came to some station and the train stopped. From here there were buses running to Pegu by stages but we had to walk as we had no money. We walked 5 miles and rested at a place called Nimphale. We heard that people coming from Rangoon had mentioned fighting between the Karins and Burmese.

Next morning we left for Kyaikte, by foot (22 miles) reaching it at moon. The railway bridge was broken but we were able to cross to the other side by a road bridge in the town, where there were Japanese troops. En route we found a goods train going to Moplin and travelled by it as far as Kyai Katha where we were fed by a South Indian Mohamedan fisherman who sent us along in a boat with a party of Indian merchants bound for Rangoon. The night was spent at Mewa, and after breakfast next morning we left for Pegu 12 miles away. Here we parted company with the Rangoon merchants and continued on foot, but we sent Captain Natarajan by bus, as he was enable to walk, and asked him to try and raise money and information for our journey north. Our rendezvous was the Bank of Chettinad Ltd., in Rangoon.

In Pegu we heard that the Japanese had taken over the administration from the Thakins whom they did not trust. We heard that a Thakin had murdered a Japanese officer and as a reprisal measure many Thakins were executed. The Japanese were favouring the other communities in contrast to the Burmese, and were trying to restore the city to some sort of normal life. The railway station was damaged, but trains were going at a slow speed to Rangoon and Mandalay. It was possible to get free tickets to these places, but too many enquiries made this idea unhealthy. We therefore abandoned the idea of going to Mandalay and set off on foot the next day for Rangoon. Hlegu was reached that evening and owing to the poor condition of our feet a Chetty took pity on us and arranged for our transport by Japanese lorries driven by Tamils, with the result that we were able to reach Rangoon on the afternoon of the next day–the 14th.

We met Natarajan at the Chettinad Bank and found that he had got involved with some pro-Japanese Indians who seemed to know far too much about us. They had suggested to Natarajan either that he join a party of fifth columnists who were scheduled to infiltrate into India through Manipur in July or else stay in Rangoon and practise as a doctor. We told Natarajan that he must straighten things out for himself as we were going on to Prome where he could catch us up. This we did and

reached Prome on 17th having been lucky enough to get shoved into a train at Rangoon.

Whilst at Prome we heard that Akyab was being heavily bombed by the British. We saw the Japanese burning corpses in Prome at night with kerosene. These corpses came by lorries from the direction of Akyab.

We were now faced with the prospect of alternative routes; the Akyab route through the Taungup Pass, up the Irrawaddy past Monywa, Kalewa and Kalemo, upto Homalin and then by the Tamu road to Manipur, or through Mandalay and then north into northern Assam. The informative obtained made us decide the Akyab route impassable due to thick undergrowth, leeches, wild animals, absence of villages, many mountain streams and 160 miles of uninhabited territory. We eventually decided on the Kalewa route either through Kalemyo or via the Tamu Road. In the meantime Natarajan arrived and as he was set on the Akyab route we decided to part company. In addition to this he was ill and needed rest before resuming the journey.

Eventually, after 12 days stay, we left Prome by boat for Pakokku on the 29th June. On our way we touched Thayetmyo, Magwe, Minbu, Yenangyaung, and then on the evening of 5th July rascals of the Burma Independence Army siezed our boat, ordered us out and made the Burman boatman carry 50 of these Thakin soldiers free of charge to Pakokku as well as supply them with rice.

We took refuge in a Chetty's house at Salle. He tried to persuade us to stay with him, but we told him of a brother lying sick at Monywa whom we must reach at all costs. We eventually left Salle on the 9th July and walked to Chauk and from thence to Singu a distance of about 20 miles. The next morning we came to Nyau, 4 miles north of Pagan. We eventually reached Pakkoku on the afternoon of the 12th.

Leaving Pakkoku we walked to Yesagyo on the 13th, and Mauk on the 14th. The next morning we crossed the Chindwin and arrived at Chaungoo on the afternoon of the 16th. After resting here we continued to Monywa which we reached on the 17th.

We met three Manipurians coming from Mandalay. They had Japanese passes and were going to Manipur. They appeared to be fifth columnists. One of them, Guna Singh, spoke English and had been in the Burma Railways. They told us we could get passes from the Japanese to go by their motor boats (the ones of the Irrawaddy Flottilla Co. run by the Chittagong Mohamedan Serangs under Japanese orders) to Kalewa. We went to the Japanese to try for these passes. We were successful in obtaining these passes by spinning a yarn about a sick brother. On the

22nd July we left Monywa in one of these boats which contained about 50 Japanese troops amongst which were about 6 of their engineering corps. We did some translation work for them from one of the Brown and Sharpe Machine Shop manuals. We starved the first day, got some rice the second day, cleaned their vessel and arrived at Kalewa at about 5 p.m. on the 25th.

The whole town was deserted with the exception of some Japanese troops and a few Indian coolies impressed by the Japanese. We remained at Kalewa 4 days, after which we set out by foot on the last stage of our journey. At the 5th milestone of the Kalemyo road we were helped of two Japanese soldiers to cross a deep nala by boat. They bought our sweaters for Rs. 2. Later we had to cross another river and several mountain streams where the bridges had all been destroyed. We were providential stopped by a Burmese boy asking us not to take the Tamu road as Indians were killed by the Burmese on that road. In fact–we were on the wrong road. We then returned to a village called Indian Guji where we received hospitality. We had to wait here till the 2nd August before we were able to take a boat across the river. We eventually entered Kalemyo at about midday on the same day. It was wonderful to see a sign board saying Tiddim 66 miles and Falam 72. We chose the Tiddim route as it was shorter. We were so excited we ran although we had to climb some 2000 feet in 5 miles. After 11 miles we reached Stockade No. 3 of our outpost. Here we were made welcome and interviewed and sent on our way to Falam where we made our report. We reached Aijal on the 18th, Silchar on the 20th and arrived at Calcutta on the 23rd, and on the 26th August we reported at G.H.Q. New Delhi. Thus ends our narrative. We had travelled 1000 miles by foot, 1000 miles by boat, and 1000 miles by goods train. We had also journeyed by bullock cart, on tops of buses, motor boats, canoes, sampans, mules and ponies, but it was not a bad journey. Our chief consolation that we came through with information that has proved to be valuable. We are grateful to the men who helped and guided us and thank God for bringing us through safely.

APPENDIX "A"

Conditions in P.O.W. Camps–Singapore

(Report by Lt. M.M. Pillai and Lt. V. Radhakrishnan who escaped 7-5-42

A. Changi Civil	1. This was one of the most modern prisons built in reinforced concrete at a cost of a million dollars, with

provisions for armed sentries, and is almost like a fortress making escape virtually impossible with the sea opposite guarded by the Japanese.

2. All the British troops in captivity are kept here with the European personnel of the Volunteers and the P.W.D. engineers who were all commissioned into the volunteers a week before the surrender.

3. A certain part of the prison is earmarked for the civilian prisoners (European). Heads of Government departments, chiefs of commercial firms, firms of a semi-Government or a semi-military nature are all here. Lady Shenton Thomas, he Governor's wife, is allowed to stay with her husband who is here too.

4. **Guards** consisted of about one battalion of Japanese troops, which also included some I.N.A. personnel.

5 (a) **Health** generally bad. Dysentry, typhoid and cholera rife. This is partly due to the lack of proper medical aid owing to the shortage of medicines which had been taken away by the Japanese, and to the scarcity of medical personnel who, being Indians, were taken away from their units. This resulted in the deaths of several European soldiers.

(b) Japanese doctors supervise the hospital scrutinising prescriptions and medicines.

(c) Visitors are allowed in the hospital on permission being previously obtained from the Japanese doctor there, or through the recommendation of Japanese in the town.

(d) Wives of prisoners lying sick in the hospital may succeed in getting permission to visit their husbands during their stay in the hospital. This facility, however, is academic as firstly, there are very few Europeans that have their wives on the island, and secondly it is difficult to make the contact as information about the patients is hard to obtain. Thirdly, permission is not come by easily. The Bishop of Singapore is allowed to visit sick prisoners in the hospital twice a week, of which one of sit is a Sunday. He is free and acts as a channel in so far as

contacts are concerned.

6 (a) **Food**. For the first few days food was scarce and poor, later two meals of rice and dhal were received a day with occasional meat, fish, cigarettes and small quantities of rolled flour, but no vegetables or sugar. Salt is plentiful.

(b) Six months of provisions existed in the prison and barracks which was unknown to the Japanese but was known to some Indians, and would eventually become common knowledge. These provisions were being used to supplement the meagre scale of rations.

(c) Food could be bought when on working parties, but this was forbidden.

7. **Treatment.** All officers below field rank were treated as O.Rs forced to work, some of whom were seen driving M.T. for the Japanese about the Island. Hard work was carried out all day in the sun with no amusements or any form of relaxation. From personal contacts I saw that during the three months of captivity they had become very emaciated and many of them looked thin and lean, with even the bones of the chest visible.

8. **Pay**. No Indians received pay, the assumption is, therefore, that the British did not either.

9. **Escapes**. Four P.W. attempted to escape which resulted in one being shot and the others being recaptured after shooting a Japanese sentry. This led to increased vigilance on the part of the authorities.

10. **Clothing**. Many were seen working in the sun almost naked except for a pair of ragged shorts.

11. **Communications**. Up to the time we left we had very reliable information that there was no communication with the outside world by way of letters or radio. Contact could be established with men on working parties.

12. **Morale**. Very high in spite of all their privations. They were cheerful and evinced an interest in news and had great faith. Never was I impressed by these people as when I saw them in their privation.

1. Seletar faces the mainland of Johore, is slightly north-east and about fourteen miles from the centre of the town.

2. The Australian P.O.W. are kept here. The general and current report is that the Australians preferred to remain apart from the British and Indians. The Japanese were only too willing to concede to this request, as it was to their advantage to foster and promote dissensions among the white prisoners. How far this report is based on fact I do not know, but it is widely believed and from personal knowledge, and the behaviour of individual Australian prisoners, I suspect there is truth in the report.

3 (a) **Health**. Generally worse than that of the British prisoners, and also due to the lack of medical equipment and the poor food received. This has resulted in several deaths.

(b) There are practically no visitors because firstly, the locality is far from the town and there are no means of transport, and secondly, the Australians being new to the Island have very few friends. Permission to visit it appears, in theory, to be easy, but in actual fact I had not heard of anybody having visited them, except for a Catholic missionary and the Bishop of Lahore.

4. **Food** and **Pay** similar to paras. 6 and 8 of A above.

5. **Treatment** similar to para 7 of A above with the addition that after May some 3,000 P.O.W. were drafted into Burma to Victoria Point, Mergui and Taboy where they were employed on works of reconstruction.

6. **Escapes**. None was heard of, but escape should be easy as there was no wire at the time that we left. Once outside the camp, however, everything would be against an escaper, not even a friendly pro-British inhabitant would dare to help knowing the penalty.

7. **Clothing** and **Communications** similar to paras 10 and 11 of A above.

8. **Morale** low whilst discipline was very bad.

1. This camp is wired and moted. The main part of the Indian P.O.W. is kept here. Bidadari is the cemetry on the road to Paya Lobar and is midway between Changi on the east and the town on the west. There was a regular bus service to the town and back when we left.

2. **Health**. Similar to para. 5 of A with the exception of the medical personnel, no shortage of whom exist.

3. **Food, Treatment** and **Pay** similar to paras. 6, 7 and 8 of A.

4. **Escapes**. The barbed wire having been put up by the P.O.W. themselves is not well done, and escape is therefore fairly easy. Escaping for I.O.Rs is extremely easy from working parties as no guards are provided and are even often unescorted from the camp to the place of work. Officers are kept as hostages with the Japanese inspectors of work and have to be responsible for the numbers of the party, but when a man is missing no report is made of this and it is left for the Japanese to discover this fact for themselves later in the camp with the result that no one can be blamed.

5. **Clothing**. In the main this is similar to para. 10 of A.

6. **Communications**. Contact with the camp was easy, in addition to which receiving sets were kept hidden.

7. **Morale**. Poor.

1. This is near to 10th milestone on the Bukit Timah road–the arterial road between Singapore and the mainland. The camp is a little off the main road, is not very well guarded and escape from here is rather easy.

2. 80 per cent of the I.N.A. are here, and in particular all senior Indian officers with Japanese sympathies; also all hospital and army postal personnel.

3. All other conditions are similar to C above with the exception of radios none of which exist and morale in particular is very bad.

1. This is a camp for Sappers three thousand of

whom were here, and is just beyond the Botanical Gardens which is some distance from the town but close to the European residential areas of Tanglin and Orchard roads.

2. Conditions are similar to C with the exception of (a) morale which is high and the troops are resisting enemy propaganda to join the I.N.A., (b) radio receiving sets are hidden in the camp and P.O.W. regularly listen to the B.B.C. and A.I.R., and (c) escape from here is not easy on account of barbed wire fencing and will become even more difficult when the I.N.A. are posted as sentries.

1. This camp is near the aerodrome and was formed about mid-April to hold about 2,000 prisoners of war (Indian).

2. It is fenced with barbed wire and like all other camps is in the process of being moated.

3. All other conditions are similar to C with the exception of radio sets none of which exists.

1. This is near Alexandra hospital and was formed about mid-March to hold about 2,000 Indian P.O.W.

2. All other conditions similar to C except that there are no radios.

15

British Assessment of the Japanese Policy Towards India after the Outbreak of the Pacific War[1]

12 May, 1942

On the outbreak of the war with Japan on December 8th, 1941, all the British officials and their families were interned in British Embassy and thereby cut off from all communication with the outside world, the only source of information available to them being the daily newspapers, which were allowed into the Embassy by the Japanese authorities.

, Judging from these daily newspapers, one is inclined to believe that the activities of the Indians in Japan and the aim of the so-called War of Greater East Asia were on the following lines :–

First and foremost the real aims and meaning of the "Co-prosperity sphere" and the War of Greater Asia became clear, in as much as they clearly included in the influence of this Sphere not only the countries of the Far East, but also Burma, India and Australia. Further more, there was a possibility of including in this Co-property sphere, it the opportunity arose, the remaining countries of Asia.

One is also inclined to believe that Japan's policy, in reality, is based on the idea of racial grouping, i.e., West versus East, but at present efforts are being made to cover up this policy of racial and colour rivalry, yet however, much Japan denies this policy, it seems that racial and colour rivalry will be the natural sequence of the War of Greater East Asia if Japan is successful. India at the outset of the war and even prior to their successes in Malaya and elsewhere, Japan openly showed her interest in India and premier General Tojo publicly announced that the Indians should take this opportunity and revolt in order to drive the British out of India, thereby gaining for themselves their Independence.

1. Foreign Department F. No. 313-x/1942 National Archives of India, New Delhi (NAI)

This, in fact, seemed to be Japan's trump card, and according to the tone of the newspapers a revolt on the part of the Indians was a certainty, an impression which was no doubt gained from the opinions and the influence of the two Boses, i.e., Rash Behari Bose and Subhas Chandra Bose of the Revolutionary Party in India, now in Berlin.

It must be a great shock to Japan that no Indian leaders have so far made any pro-Japanese statements and that Indians have not revolted in the expected manner : furthermore, it must be very painful for her to realise that Congress and the Muslim League, however much they may offer as regards the future constitution of India, appear, as far as can be gathered here, to have come to some understanding with the British for the defence of India, If India is threatened by some outside Power.

Right from the start of the War, Rash Behari Bose, who was mistakenly considered to be a spent force, showed his true colours and came out into the open, proving that he had been in close touch with the Japanese authorities in the movement to drive out the British from India. He took over the leadership of the newly formed Indian Independence League, with A.M. Sahay as his assistant, while at the same time Subhas Chandra Bose assumed the leadership of the League in Europe with the same object, i.e., the overthrow of the British in India. One is obliged to think that Japan seriously believed in these two Boses and their followers and therefore in their miscalculation as regards Indias revolt. Even after the so-called failure of Sir Stafford Cripps mission, Japan began to fear that the Indians, far from revolting to help Japan against the Allies, will in the near future be likely to make the war a national causes, unite among themselves and support the allies against the Axis in general and Japan in particular. This attitude of India and its political leaders seems to have not only disappointed Japan but also to have assured her because it must have upset her plans. According to the tune the newspapers, she has now changed her attitude to India. At first it was war "India for the Indians" with the Indian themselves gaining their own independence and thereby forming a separate unit outside the co-prosperity sphere. But later a different tone, and very threatening one was adopted on a which was pursued unit the Bangkok Conference in June," first, if the Indian political parties and their leaders do not realise and appreciate the real aim of Japan and do not cooperate with her in driving the British out of India, then Japanese for Indian's sake must invade India and drive out the British herself, so that India may occupy her rightful place in the greater East Asia Co-prosperity Sphere under the benevolent guidance of Japan.

This change of policy was followed up by Japan's attack on Trincommule, Calcutta, Madras and Visakhapatnam in April, 1942. At that time she was still hoping that her success in Malaya and the capture of Singapore would make the Indian rise in revolt, but once more disappointed. After the occupation of Burma, the newspapers again displayed a hostile attitude towards Indians asking the Indian soldiers that if they did not revolt or if they allowed the British to used any Indian naval bases or the British Army to remain India, the Japanese could advance on India to crush the British. This was followed up by Air-raids in areas on Imphal and Mahalapur.

One has the feeling, that the Japan was posed to attack India and that this is the reason why she is making these futile excuses. However, one wonders what her next move will be, will she attack Australia, India or Chungking, first? Or all together? And will the impending monsoon, which may hold her up until October, give her time to prepare for major operation.

One must admit, that in the light of their past successes the Japanese have proved that they have every thing worked out in minute detail, and that neither the impossible country nor the difficult climate have caused any hitch in their operations, which seem so far to have been successful.

Since the occupation of Burma by the Japanese, the newspapers have started to print articles on the topography, geology and climatic conditions of India, and at the same time have been making such of the alleged speeches and writings of Gandhi in his Harijan newspaper, in which the demands, that the British shall clear out of India, all of which is no doubt propaganda for home consumption.

The following extract from newspaper article shows perhaps the Japanese line of thought or even the course of their future action :–

"The Imperial Japanese forces, which have driven out British influences from Asia, have brought India under their domination. The complete elimination of Britain from India must be the logical conclusion of the execution of the policy of fighting the war of greater East Asia to finish, etc. etc".

16

Ko Ishii, Japanese Ambassador, in Bangkok, to Vishitre Vadakarn, Deputy Minister of Foreign Affairs, Requesting him to Extend Support to the Indian Independence League to Carry on their Activities Freely in Thailand[1]

28 May, 1942

Dear Nai V. Vichitr,

In confirmation of our conversation of yesterday, I hereby wish to state that the Japanese Government is prepared to support the Indian people to establish "India for Indian People", and in this connection I wish to ask your Government to work jointly with us in the following ways :

1. The Thai Government is to cooperate with the Japanese Government with sincere sympathy to help positively the movement of the Indian people in their endeavour to get rid of British fetters and to establish "India for Indian People."
2. The Thai Government is to give facilities to the political movement of the Indian people in Thailand to a reasonable extent. As the Indian people desire to open a meeting of the representatives of all Indian people in East Asia in the middle of June at Bangkok, the Thai Government is to give the necessary permission for such meeting to be held at their request. The Thai Government is further to recognize that the central office of this political movement is to be set in Bangkok, and will consequently give facilities of travelling and dwelling to those Indian people connected with the said meeting.
3. The Thai Government is to give enough protection to the Indian people in their activities in cultural and economical life. I also wish to assure your Excellency that this movement will prove harmless to your country, and to that, the Japanese Government will pay its most serious attention to avoid any discrepancies that may have arisen.

---

1. File No. 401, I.N.A. Papers.

17

Japanese Premier's Message congratulating Indian Independence League for holding Bangkok Conference

15 June, 1942

It is with the greatest of pleasure that I send you my heartiest congratulations on the occasion of the convention of the Indian Independence Conference in Thailand, our ally, on the initiative of the leaders of the 2 million Indians living in Asia to create a new epoch in the movement for Indian independence.

Since the outbreak of the Greater East Asia War more than half a year has elapsed. During this period the British defences in Asia for Placating India has practically been wiped out by the gallant Imperial forces and a golden opportunity to realize the long cherished aspiration of Indian independence has come.

At this juncture if the leaders of the 2 million Indians in Asia in calling this conference respond to Japan's true desire for the Indians to create India for the Indians, Japan is quite prepared to give her unstineted support as it has been announced from time to time, and I might add that the Axis Powers are ready to cooperate in according their full support.

Britain, which is meeting with defeats in Asia, Europe, Africa and in all theatres of war, is facing an extremely miserable state of affairs which she brought on herself by her own mis-doing. She is now demanding great sacrifices of India through her usual crafty way of threat and supplication. However, the far sighted and able patriotic Indian leaders wisely realizing the heavenily bestowed destiny of India, and fully cognizant of the world affairs, are determinably resisting Britain, a fact which I want to express my deepest respect.

---

1. File No. 401, I.N.A. Papers. For the message from Thai Prime Minister P. Pibulsonggram, see *Bangkok Chronicle,* 15 June 1842.

Though the construction of India for the Indians constitutes my most sincere desire, India still remains British territory and military establishments, as well as military forces, are being daily strengthened. Japan is firmly determined decisively to destroy Britain and she will be competed to take action so long as British military strength remain in India. In order to rescue India from war disaster it is necessary that Britain should give up her ambitions in India or India herself must sever her relations with Britain on her own initiative.

Fortunately, as I believe the present conference represents the general public opinion of the Indian people of the East, I pledge that Japan is fully prepared to support the independence movement.

In congratulating most earnestly the success of the present conference I hope sincerely that the Indian people will fully understand Japan's true intentions and with the people both inside and outside of India working in close cooperation to achieve its cherished hope of independence.

18

Speech of the Italian Minister Signor Guido Crolla at the Bangkok supporting Indian Independence[1]

15 June, 1942

"It is indeed a source of deep gratification for me to attend the opening session of this Conference which, thanks to Thailand's hospitality, gathers here to-day the Representatives of the various Indian movements in the Far East.

The bonds between India and Italy date far back in history. They were existing even before the Roman Empire, which was a great attempt of unifying western and eastern cultures. In the Middle Ages the daring exploit of an Italian, Marco Polo, brought the two worlds closer again, while the Republics of Venice and Genea were intensifying their trade with India through the Mediterranean.

In more recent times Indian culture found and still finds in Italy many scholars and admirers and the Italian youth is taught in school has to appreciate the contribution given by India to the history of humanity.

The Italian people who have for no long hardly struggled to recover their unity and independence cannot but offer sympathy and understanding towards the suffering and aspirations of the Indian People.

Italy's interest for the cause of Indian independence is deeply rooted in the past. Indian exiles have always found in Italy a most cordial welcome and hospitality.

This particular sympathy, which is spontaneous, lively and disinterested has rootly found expression in the institution of a society in Rome called "The Friends of India", where Indian patriots of undaunted faith and sincerity, such as Iqbal Schedal, are working for the cause of Indian liberty followed by the friendly and unanimous encouragement of

1. *Ibid.* The text of message is also reproduced in Giani, *op. cit.* p. 74.

the Italian public opinion. "The Friends of India" wish to create as closer connections as possible between cognate associations existing in Germany, Japan and Thailand with a view to attaining the final aim through a better and greater co-ordination of their respective efforts.

The enduring passion of the Indian People is approaching its decisive moment.

The war which the Tripartite Powers are victoriously waging against India's secular oppressor is destined to create a new order in contrast with the old one ruled by Anglo-Saxon selfishness and abuse.

Within the frame of such a New Order the Indian People after having shaken the British yoke, shall, as a free Nation, find the place which their high civil and cultural traditions entitle them to.

Italy, Germany and Japan have no territorial ambitions in India. Their support is therefore all the more disinterested and their friendship all the more sincere.

The Representatives of Free India gathered in Bangkok to-day are confronted with the highly responsible task of shaping the future destiny of their own Country in accordance with the wishes and the interest of the Indian People.

In union with Germany and Japan, Italy is wishing this conference the best success."

19

Dr. E. Wendler, the German Minister's Speech at Bangkok Conference Promising Help for the Liberation of India[1]

16 June, 1942

It is especially gratifying to me as German Minister in Bangkok to be able to accept the invitation to attend the opening session of this Conference at which prominent representatives of the Indian people will deliberate as to the means of shape and safeguard the future of India in accordance with the wishes of the Indian people. I need hardly emphasize that Germany takes a lively interest in these questions as was also stressed a short time ago by the fact that the German Chancellor received at his headquarters the well-known champion of the Indian independence idea, Subhas Chandra Bose. The world war raging today will spell the end of the dominion of the British and Americans who have ever subjugated and used for their own purposes the peoples in their power. The nations allied to each other by the Tripartite Pact, Germany, Italy and Japan, will see to a just New Order, terminating Anglo-American tutelage over the rest of the world. Thus also the possibility arises for the Indian people, after nearly two centuries of subjugation by the British, a subjugation which has cost India so much misery and suffering, to shape the future destiny of their country according to their will.

The German people have shown the greatest sympathy towards the people of India. The outstanding cultural achievements of India during the course of her long history dating back-thousands of years, have always been the source of special interest in Germany. Germany was also the first country in Europe in which the great values in the spheres of Indian philosophy and poetry were fully appreciated. It is therefore self-evident that the German people, notwithstanding the

1. *Ibid.*

which they find themselves involved, even at the present time follow with much sympathy the significant happenings in India and, together with the peoples of Italy and Japan, show the greatest interest in the fight for freedom of the Indian people.

The Great Powers of the Tripartite Pact, Germany, Italy and Japan, are all the more in a position to raise their voices as sincere friends of the Indian people since they have no territorial interests whatsoever in India.

They have but one desire : that India and her people, in free self-determination, be heading for a better future and develop to a level corresponding to the riches of the Indian soil and the great gifts of its inhabitants.

20

Address of Rash Behari Bose at the Bangkok Conference Expressing Faith in Japan for the Liberation of India and Asking the People to Cooperate in the Struggle[1]

16 June, 1942

The creation of a Free, Happy and United India-an India which the Poet visualised and the superman is creating. The burden is ours. We have to carry it. The success is assured, once we put faith in India.

We are grateful to those who have been showering on us sympathy and encouragement in helping us carry this burden. The spontaneous sympathy from far and near-will ever remain as a treasure. We thank every one of you.

" Bande Matarm. Inqlab Zindabad, Azad Hind Zindabad ! "

Mr. Rash Behari Bose was then formally elected President. He delivered the following Presidential Address :-

" Your Excellencies, Friends and Compatriots!

" Allow me to express my sincere thanks for the great honour you have done me by calling upon me to occupy this chair and guide the deliberations of this historic conference. While greatly appreciating this expression of love and affection for me, I am not unaware of the fact that along with this honour you have placed on my shoulders a great responsibility by electing me the President of this Conference. However, if I have obeyed your command and taken this chair in spite of my knowledge of the intricacies of the problems that will come before this conference, I have been prompted to do so by my great faith in your spirit of co-operation and your sincere desire to put your heads together and to come to useful decisions without wasting much of your time on unnecessary discussions and arguments. I am sure I can count upon your unreserved help and

1. I.I.L. Papers F No. 45/3.

cooperation in successfully conducting the business of the conference.

" As I stand here, my thought goes to the unfortunate air accident, last March, that claimed the lives of our four valuable comrades-Swami Satyananda Puri and Gyani Pritam Singhji of Bangkok, and Captain Akram and Mr. Nilakanda Iyer of Malaya, while they were flying to Tokyo to attend our Indian Independence Conference.

" We can well realise the great loss to our cause at such an important period of our struggle and we all feel it very deeply. However, brethren, let us take it as inevitable and pray for the peace of their souls. In our grim final struggle against British Imperialism, we shall have to offer great sacrifices. Many of us will have to lay down our lives before the world can see India free. It can be well said that these four comrades have given us the lead, of which our compatriots in Thailand and Malaya can be well proud of.

" During and since 1837, when we first revolted against British Imperialism in India, hundreds of thousands of our most respected and beloved compatriots have laid down their lives in their efforts to free our Motherland. We cannot forget the fact that they have nourished the seeds of Swaraj with their blood and it is the result of their supreme sacrifices that we are to-day so near our goal and can hope with confidence to achieve independence in the near future. World knows only a part of the long list of those Indian victims of British Imperialism. Let us pay respects to the memory of those numberless known and unknown comrades. Placed as we are to-day, we can do very little beyond that. But the time is fast approaching when in very city and town in India, we shall find a worthy monument erected in their memory and we Indians will pay homage to them and look upon them with pride.

" Our homage is also due to those respected leaders and workers as well as the organisations that have in various ways made untiring efforts since 1857 to liberate our country from bondage. Their list is in no way small and in no way their contributions were negligible. Let us pay our respects to that greatest living Indian Mahatma Gandhi, who, with his magic wand, roused the Indian masses from the centuries-long slumber and has created self-confidence in them. We can have no doubt that when the new and true history of India will be written, Mahatma Gandhi's name will have to be mentioned as the Saviour of India.

" I do not want to take Your time by going into the details regarding India's struggle for freedom since 1857. Suffice it to say that although the failure of our revolt of 1857 was a great blow to the nation and although a general depression had overwhelmed the country, our efforts to overthrow

British rule never ceased. Under the circumstances prevailing in those days, the activities had to be carried on underground and within a limited scope; and whenever there was an opportunity, a revolt was attempted. After minor preparatory stages our first effort on a large scale was made when the war of 1914-1918 started. Our workers were active everywhere. The Indian army was prepared to join the revolt. A part of the Indian army had actually revolted rather prematurely. We thought we were going to succeed. Unfortunately we did not meet with success on that occasion. Thousands of our compatriots had to pay the highest price of patriotism. Thousands were sent to the Andamans and Mandalay and hundreds of them still remain rotting in prisons and concentration camps.

" During that war of 1914-1918 the British had been partially successful in receiving India's co-operation by telling lies and making false promises. Our people were misled by the fine phraseologies of the shred British diplomats. They promised us freedom after the war, as they are doing even during the present war. But soon after the conclusion of that war, it was realised that the British not only did not mean to keep their promises but definitely wanted to take away even that shadow of civil liberty that the Indians were having in pre-war days. When they protested against that, the response from the British side was in terms of bombs, bullets and machine-guns. Needless to mention that the tragedy of the Jallianwala Bagh of Amritsar in April, 1919, is still fresh in the memory of every one of us and the wound has not yet healed. It really cannot be healed until and unless we have completely destroyed the power that was responsible for the great humiliation of our people.

Every tragedy, however, has a lesson and so had the tragedy of Jallianwala Bagh. The blood of more than one thousand of those innocent martyrs, that included even our women and children, could not go without significant results. The great upheaval that swept India from one corner to the other, and the great movement of Non-Cooperation and Civil Disobedience that has been carried on by the Indian National Congress since 1919 and that has wonderfully organised the masses of India for political struggle, were undoubtedly the direct result of the massacre at Jallianwala Bagh.

" We all must bow our heads in reverence and be greatful to those brothers and sisters who by giving their lives at Jallianwala Bagh have created a new life in India. As we know to-day, millions and millions in India are prepared and determined to suffer and sacrifice their all for the cause of their motherland. When in 1939 the war in Europe started, Britain once again began to indulge in jugglery of words in order to secure Indian co-

operation and help. But to the great delight of us all, to this very day the nationalist leaders in India have refused to be misled and have continued to resist all British efforts to drag India into war. Our respect goes to Mahatma Gandhi for the most admirable way, he has led the nation clear of all dangers of being entangled in this war.

" With this background in India, the Greater East Asia War was declared on the 8th December, 1941. No matter in which part of the world he or she might be living, whatever might be his or her attitude towards Japan, I refuse to believe that there was a true Indian patriot who was not extremely delighted and gratified in his heart of hearts when the great news of the declaration of War by Japan against the Anglo-American races reached his or her ears. I refuse to believe there is any true Indian patriot, whatever be his or her career or conviction, who might not have rejoiced, as from day to day, the mighty Imperial forces of Japan on land and sea and in e air went on administering crushing blows against their imperialism in Asia, and the British Imperialist bases in these parts began to totter one after the other like houses of cards. For is there a man whose eyes I cannot withhold joyous tears when he sees before his eyes the power of the greatest enemy of humanity and peace, the greatest aggressor of centuries being destroyed ? Those of us, who were destined to five and work in Japan, had particular reasons to be overjoyed at these most welcome happenings.

"We have been working in Japan for decades so that we can see Japan in a position to stand by the oppressed Asiatics and to liberate Asia. We were anxiously awaiting the day when Japan would fully realise the great significance of creating a free and united Asia and would feel convinced that it was in the interest of Japan herself, as also for the rest of Asia if not for the world as a whole, that the octopus grip of the Anglo-Saxon Imperialism in the East must be destroyed root and branch. We all were fully convinced that Japan alone was in the position to take the honour. Thus when on the morning of the most auspicious day, the day of the Enlightenment of Lord Buddha, we heard the most auspicious news of Japan's declaration of war against our common enemy, we felt that our mission in Japan was fulfilled. We felt convinced that India's freedom was assured. Being in Japan for decades, I knew well that Japan was not in the habit of talking and debating unnecessary and meaningless things. I knew well that she was not in the habit of taking any serious step unless she had fully washed her strength and was convinced of her success. I therefore did not share the views of those who thought that due to her continued military activities in China, she was too exhausted to challenge the mighty Anglo-Saxon, or the so called ABCD combined forces. I was one of those

who had not the slightest doubt that the war in China was a prelude to the real war against Powers who were actually responsible for the continued fratricidal conflict between China and Japan. Happenings on the international chess board during the past more than ten years have been suggesting that such a worldwide conflict was inevitable. It was also apparent that the question of Indian freedom could be successfully solved only when Japan rose in arms against British Imperialism.

" Now that Japan and Thailand have taken up arms against our common foe, the joint efforts of our worthy allies ensure the doom of the British Empire and our complete victory is assured.

" These effective efforts on different fronts to destroy our common enemy, bring us a reminder regarding our own duties and responsibilities in this common effort for our common cause. We must ask ourselves what we have done and what we are going to do to contribute to this great cause. Only praising Japan, Germany and Italy will not entitle us to the position for which we are craving. We must contribute our mite and must make the greatest sacrifice we can make. Then alone can we command the respect and consideration of our worthy allies and then alone we can claim a place worthy of a great nation like ours in future international assembly.

Realising this very important fact, and our duty towards our motherland at this most important juncture, we in Tokyo promptly met on the 8th of December, 1941 at the Rainbow Grill and decided upon a programme of action. My Compatriots formed a committee and asked me to lead the movement and I gladly agreed to abide by their decision. We at first undertook to consolidate Indian opinion in East Asia in favour of a definite fight from without. Meetings were held in different centres of Japan and resolutions were passed emphasising the solidarity of our compatriots, the great need of declaring Independence of India by destroying British Imperialism, and expressing confidence in our work.

On the 26th December, 1941, for the first time in the history of Indians in Japan, a Conference of nearly fifty representatives of the Indian residents in Kobe, Osaka, Yokohama and Tokyo-all the four cities, where Indians reside-was held at the Railway Hotel at Tokyo to consider the problems. A resolution was passed calling upon the Indians to realise the gravity of the situation and the danger ahead of India. The resolution read as follows:-

"Whereas the continued defeat of the British and their allies in Europe and Africa has sealed the fate of the British Imperialism in Europe.

Whereas the most decisive destruction of British sea and land forces by Japan in the East has given a death-blow to the power and prestige of British Imperialism in Asia.

Whereas the war is fast approaching the shores and borders of India, the British stronghold, Axis powers may be obliged to invade India in order to destroy the main source of British fighting strength.

Whereas such an invasion will bring unimaginable and extremely unusual hardships, miseries and sufferings to millions of innocent and helpless Indians in cities, towns and villages, and

Whereas the only way to avoid this most unhappy situation is .to declare complete independence of India from British rule and to cut off all possible connections with British Imperialism in every possible way immediately;

The Indian Nationals residing in Japan assembled in this Conference, most seriously and earnestly appeal to the Indian National Congress and the people of India to immediately declare Independence and to capture all power from the British in India and to take immediate effective steps to stop each and every source of Indian aid to British Imperialist War and to declare on behalf of the people that India has no desire whatsoever to be involve I in this conflict and has never been willing to help Britain.Our representatives were sent to Shanghai and on 26th of January this year, a huge gathering of the Indian residents of Shanghai was held in Young Men's Association hall when similar resolutions as passed in Tokyo were very enthusiastically passel and our movement was given unanimous support.

In the meantime we established contact with the military and civil high commands in Japan and began to impress upon them the necessity of helping India in her struggle for freedom for the very achievement of the great object for which Japan had declared war against British and America. We made it clear to them that so long as British Imperialism in India continued, Japan could not expect a final victory in this war. At last: we succeeded in prevailing upon them and General Tojo, the Prime Minister of Japan, openly declare before the Imperial Diet that his Government was prepared to help the Indians in our efforts to free our country from the long bondage. In his declaration before the Imperial Diet on the fall of Singapore he said :-

"It is a golden opportunity for India, having, as it does, several thousand years of history and splendid cultural tradition, to rid herself of the ruthless despotism of Britain and participate in the construction of the Greater East Asia Co-Prosperity Sphere. Japan expects that India will restore its proper status of India for the Indians and it will not stint herself in extending assistance to the Patriotic efforts of the Indians. Should India fail to awaken to her mission forgetting her history and tradition, and

continue as before to be beguiled by the British cajolery and manipulation and act at their beck and call I cannot but fear that an opportunity for the renaissance of the Indian people would be forever lost."

The declaration offered us great encouragement and we felt convinced, that India could safely hope to be free before the East Asia War comes to an end. Counting upon the promises of General Tojo, we established our headquarters at Sanno Hotel and started our activities and preparations in right earnest. We decided that a Conference of the representatives of Indian organisations in various parts of East Asia should be held for exchanging views regarding our future move. With the help of the military authorities things were conveniently arranged and the representatives of our compatriots residing in Malaya, Honkong and Shanghai along with us of Tokyo, sat in conference for three days and arrived at certain decisions and framed the preliminary constitution for the working an I progress of our movement. Those friends from abroad, who participated in Tokyo Conference, had occasion to come in contact with responsible members of the Japanese Army in Tokyo and to know more and more about the standing of our movement, Discussion at the Tokyo Conference were varied and we did our best to lay dowa a solid foundation upon which we could base our plan of action in future. We all know that the Conference in Tokyo was held at a time when things were less settled than they are today. Friends from East Indies were not present. We were deprived of the valuable help and advices of our friends in Thailand due to the unfortunate accident. Burma and Andamans were still in the hands of our enemies. We, therefore, were unable to come to a decision that could be claimed to be representative of the views of our compatriots in East Asia as a whole. We, therefore, decided to hold a larger and most representative Conference at a later date when the decisions taken at Tokyo were to be ratified. This Assembly in which we are participating, to-day is the result of that decision.

"The responsibility to convene this Conference was placed upon my shoulders and I was asked to hold it in this city. I am sorry that the Conference was delayed by a couple of weeks. We expected to arrive here earlier but due to extraordinary period, through which we are passing things could not be always done as expected and we have to adjust our selves according to circumstances.

" I know I have exhausted your patience by chronologizing the events and activities during the last more than six months. But, it was necessary to acquaint you with what has happened and how we have proceeded, before we sit down to business and put our heads together to knock out far reaching decisions.

"Friends, we all realise the gravity of the situation and also the fact that we are passing through the most important period of India's history. I don't want speeches. We had enough of that during the last more than five decades. We really cannot afford to waste our time on meaningless talks and arguments. Those who want to really serve the motherland cannot have much time to talk. If we go on talking without coming to any concrete decision, time will not wait for us and we shall be left only to shed tears at our past folly, and it will be too late to mend things. I know there are knotty problems that will come before you for discussions and will need your most careful consideration. I know you will have to do a lot of thinking and face a lot of doubts from within, before you can decide. But, if you have come with grim determination to thrash out a positive, concrete, and actually useful plan, you will be able to come to quick decisions. Let us all fully realise our responsibilities towards our land of birth and let us realise well, that our down-trodden country cannot afford to lose this golden opportunity that comes only once in centuries. Our brothers and sisters have in hundreds of thousands laid down their lives and have suffered and sacrificed for more than a century so that our country may be once again free. Let us rise to the occasion and carry their efforts to success so that the souls of martyrs in Heaven may find peace and be pleased. Let us rise and act so that the great preparations that Mahatma Gandhi has made during the last more than two decades, may bear fruit and our children in future may think of us with pride and respect as the members of a free nation.

"I know many of you have come with doubts and suspicious regarding the ultimate fate of our country as the result of our activities. I assure you that I can well appreciate your feelings of uncertainty and Your desire for security and yet I believe they are based on false promises. Having bitterest experiences of Imperialist exploitations for centuries, we have begun to doubt even our goad friends and if we insist on this attitude, the world will go on and we shall be left behind to regret our indecision.

"I want to sound a note of warning here. Our enemies have always been successful in keeping us divided and creating false impressions in our -minds on such occasions. On many occasions in the past, we have missed opportunities to free our country by being victims of lying British propaganda. I can only hope that we shall not repeat our folly. Our doubts and suspicions are to a great extent the results of shrewd and well-thought plans of our enemies to sabotage our efforts. Those of us who have intelligence enough and who are not blind to facts and happenings can see the way clearly.

"We should feel thankful to the Governments of Japan, Germany Thailand and Italy for their most friendly attitude they have been showing towards our cause. We must be particularly thankful to Japan for the most encouraging and hopeful definite promise of help in our sacred cause Let us not forget the words of Pandit Jawaharlal Nehru when he said :-

Success often comes to those who dare and act, it seldom goes to cowards.

"I make an earnest appeal to you all friends to see that when you conclude your session, you have a most practical and workable plan of action for India's freedom so that we can start our work right after the Conference and march ahead. We are fortunate enough to have the most valuable help of our Indian Army at our disposal. They deserve our great respect for the great service they have already rendered to our cause by refusing to serve the enemies of India. But their greater service is still awaiting our decision. No one can doubt the bravery of our soldiers in a righteous fight for a righteous cause. Our sympathy goes to the families and friends of those Indian soldiers who have, erroneously believing that they have been fighting for a right cause, lost their lives in Europe and Asia. They have been misled by the same propaganda of lies by Britain that is responsible for the unfounded suspicion in the minds of so many of us. I bow my head to the bravery of our soldiers and we should have no doubt that with their wholehearted support we are going to win our final fight against British Imperialism. Let us stand shoulder to shoulder and let us march hand in hand to success. Let us remember we have one indivisible Nation India one enemy England one goal complete Independence.

Bande Matram

21

Japanese Assessment of the Bangkok Conference[1]

18 June, 1942

A plenary session of Indian Independence League was held at the royal theatre in Bangkok on Monday, by over 100 Indian delegates from Tokyo, Shanghai, Hong kong, Malaya, Shonan Island, Borneo, Java, the Philippines and other places. There were also present, besides Mr. Teiji Tsubokami, the Japanese Ambassador to Thailand, the German and Italian Ministers, and these diplomats spoke in ardent support of the Indian Independence movement. It is certainly very significant that such a meeting was held at Bangkok in East Asia at a time when the position of Britain in East Asia has been completely undermined in the sequel to the development of the War of Greater East Asia and British Domination of India is on the brink of collapse.

The Indian Independence League has decided to establish its headquarters at Bangkok and to develop the Indian Independence movement vigorously through close collaboration with all its branches in East Asia. One prominent feature of the League is that it represents a Union to which men of all political factions and religious faiths are afflicted. It is indeed unprecedented in the history of the Indian Independence movement that a unified front has been formed by Indians irrespective of party and religious distinctions. That such a big Union has been brought into existence argues that the Indian Independence movement has a new and big advance.

The belief obtained among many people for a long time that India lacked internal unity was an unnatural state of affairs brought about by the policy of causing dissensions, which was consistently pursued by Britain. The British authorities attempted to paralyse the Indian Independence movement by diverting the attention of the Indian populace

1. *Japan Times and Advertiser,* 18 June 1942.

from political to religious problems. They deliberately misrepresented the Indian national movement for the acquisition of independence and freedom as a movement launched and carried on by a certain religious sect for the expansion of its influence, and accordingly brought pressure to bear on it in the specious name of protecting the minority rights.

Whereas, in Europe, the mention of majority or minority elements implies racial antagonism, it is not so in India, where it refers exclusively to religions. Although the Indian people embrace different religious faiths, they are of the same racially. If, therefore, there does exist a conflict of interests among the Indians, it is imply of a character either regional or religious antagonism. As a matter of fact, subsequently of World War No. 1, things in India have been moving in the direction of the formation of a united front among all classes for the vigorous pursuit of the independence movement in the face of all kinds of interference offered by the British authorities and, now a big Union of Indians in East Asia has finally been organised through the formation of the Indian Independence League. One noteworthy fact in connection with the Bangkok Congress is that Japan and other Axis Powers caused their Ambassador and ministers to attend the meeting and give words of support and encouragement. This fact demonstrates that the Indian Independence movement has the support of Japan, German and Italy. In the course of his message of congratulation to the congress. General Hideki Tojo, the Premier stated that "I take delight in being able to say that I have convinced myself that the present congress is an embodiment of Indian opinion in East Asia". He further declared that I swear to the Congress that the Japanese Empire is prepared to back the movement for Independence for India which is the aim of the present Congress that the Japanese Empire is prepared to back the movement for Independence for India which is the aim of the present Congress. By enlisting the support of the Axis Powers the Indian Independence movement has assumed world wide dimensions. India is no longer an isolated entity. It is a country which is working strenuously for the overthrow of British imperialism through close collaboration with the Axis Powers who are devoted to the establishment of a new world order. Britain who failed in the negotiations with India conducted recently through Sir Stamford Craps has now dispatched the Duke of Gloucester to India in order to placate the discontented, but his present visit is exciting no interest among the Indian people. This is quite proper and as it should be, for the Indian people who rejected Sir Stafford Cripps' proposals in their entirety are not looking for any present whatever, from Britain. In fact, the compromise

plan produced by Sir Stafford embodied the maximum of the "concessions" which imperialist Britain could make to India. Judging both from the trends of internal conditions in India, the independence of India is irresistible. The leaders of the Indian independence movement are unanimous in demanding the withdrawal of the British forces from India and the severance of all connection with Britain. We feel confident that after the present Bangkok Congress, the Indian independence movement will go forward nakedly under unified leadership and we consequently look forward with high expectations to the success of this movement.

22

Mohan Singh's Appeal at the Close of the Bangkok Conference Requesting Indians to Prepare Themselves for Long and Hard Fight Against the British; thanks Japanese for their Support[1]

19 June, 1942

At the closing session of the Indian Independence conference, Captain Mohan Singh said : I am delighted that during my short sojourn in Bangkok I am again privileged to speak to you. The first time I was ordered to do so by the President but this time it is my own desire to talk to you.

Since the day of my arrival I had been looking forward for an opportunity to speak to you heart to heart. Listen patiently, I want to talk to you non-stop unless you signal me that what I say is no longer required and time for action has arrived. I except you all Hindus, Muslims, Sikhs—High or low—old or young to march together hand in hand. We will obey our heart's desire. Believe me, our hearts will not deceive us. Is there any better guide in this world than sympathy, truthfulness, love and unity, which I tell you, will take us along the right path.

The stone-hearted are those who are not moved. I say you are made up of the strongest steel. You shall not be beaten and shall be attracted to the liberty's magnetic pole. Aren't you feeling that force of attraction to day, if not I say you and your hearts are rusty. Burnish the rust and prepare the surface for the magnetic attraction–In short strengthen the will of sacrifice, Brethren, Behold! The world is undergoing stupendous change.

Look! Your next door neighbour is in the struggle. You cannot go on sitting dumb-founded. We must always bear in mind the example of

1. Papers of General Mohan Singh. See also I.I.L. Papers F. No 45/3.

the great Eastern Nation Japan. What a small country it was. But in a short time–I should say in the twinkling of an eye it has performed a miracle. The vicious encirclement by ABCD Nations has not only been broken but completely destroyed. So much so that the enemy in its run had no time to turn round and see what was happening behind.

Hundreds of aeroplanes, thousands of guns, hundreds of thousands of machineguns, rifles, motorcars and lorries and incalculable amount of ammunition have been left behind. Hundreds of huge dumps of ration, stores and other essential war materials in ship leads were made over to the Imperial Govt. of Japan. But the most important item of the war machine–millions of trained officers and men handed over were intact.

Funny enough! that Churchill—the mischief monger of the world, is still not ashamed of his eye-wash activities. Ladies and Gentlemen! I am not telling you fables. I have seen all this myself. This unparallel example of valour and sacrifice of the Nippon soldiers has annihilated the pride of the two big Nations. The world, you all know, is wonder-struck at this miracle.

The creation of the Almighty God is in transformation, Earth and heaven are changing and the whole map of the world has changed. Nations and the order of the world has changed. Those who were behind have gone for ahead of the mark. Those who considered themselves forward of everyone and were proud of thier empires are one the verge of extinction.

True! All this has happened but whither are we Indians. Are there any signs of change in us? I emphatically say, No. No signs of change at all. What is there lacking in us? I say sense of realisation of self-sacrifice and patriotism. Are we dead? No! We are in a state of slumber. This of course must end now. The time has come that we got rid of this evil disease.

I ask you, Brothers, what should we do to bring about the awakening. Do you want the scene of Bhagat Singh's crucification reported in front of you? Do you want our sacred temples at Nankana Sahib flooded with human blood and see the burning of people alive? Do you want your countrymen to repeat the scenes of bloodshed in the streets of Peshawar? Say, do you want a Japanese soldier to come in front of you and cut open his heart and show the anatomy of love and sacrifice. I do not understand what actually is wanted. We must transform ourselves. We have to undergo the treatment alone by ourselves and the very treatment is also in our own hands.

It astonishes me when I compare ourselves with other countries. Take for example Thailand, I say, the country of God and his blessed people. There is nothing to disunite them. No religious strife. They are proud Thais. Their culture ressembles Indian culture. To them platform of liberty is totally different from other things. There is only one faith—one understanding—oneness as Thais, say to live as brothers.

I am sure every small town in this country has an association of Thais, where every Thais, irrespective of what class or creed he belongs to, has the right to be a member. On the other hand isn't it lamentable that our weaknesses, yet urk in us even in this country where we breathe free air. Why isn't there an institution of Indians instead of smaller sectional clubs. I call this derogatory on the part of the Indian brothers of this town.

Religion is truth and as such is the force of humanity. A lover of religion is a worshipper of God. It does not matter what creed or faith he fellows and such a man is justice seeker and beloved by all. Temples, Mosques and Gurdwaras, I say all the places of worship are sacred to lovers of God.

But we Indians trapped in the British treachery have always disrespected the faith and religion of others. Have forgotten the truth. Have engrossed ourselves into ill-will. Have forgotten the Creator. I say, if I were to stand at one corner of India and shout at the top of my voice that God is this and God is that, I can assure you not one would listen to me.

Probably a few might call me a fool. But if I were to speak against Guru Gobind Singh, Lord Krishna or Prophet Mohammed, then what my fate would be, I am sure, you can visualize. It is terrible that there should be bloodshed on the names of those whom God sent as religious leaders than that on the name of very God. The worst part of it is that if a word is said against Guru Gobind Singh, a Sikh would get enraged and be prepared to shed his blood.

If anything is said against Prophet Mohammed then only a Muslim would consider it an insult. Mind you, both of them have been the leaders of human-beings. Why should we then dishonour them? Remember God is one and indivisible and as such same for all. Why should we get angry and despise our own people? If you pass an insulting remark about any town of a free Nation, then the whole nation will fight for its honour. But alas! India has been chewed into bits by foreign domination, yet none of us would feel it.

If Hindu Brothers come to know that Mohammedans have slaughtered a cow, then who can check the anger of Hindus. The whole community will be prepared to sacrifice itself. If Mohammedan Brothers come to know that a pig is being killed in the vicinity, the whole Mohammedan community would be ready for shedding blood. But we do not realise that on this triffling matter of killing animals millions of our brave soldiers have been slaughtered. I say the whole country has been butchered.

If a Hindu slaughters a pig, a Mohammedan slaughters a cow, we often shed our blood but never feel ashamed to this when notorious Englishman gets these animals killed and eats them. What a fate? We Indians cook and serve with our own hands dishes on the table of Englishman. Believe me this happens every day and night in India. You can always see this being done in Army Officers' Messes and Hotels.

We never realise how we are cutting each other's throat and yet never kill that person who is responsible in slaughtering our Indians, cows and pigs. Our religious faiths and the strength of the Nation has been disrupted so much that we are divided, sub-divided and redivided again into chips by the English.

A Mohammedan would be called an Infidel if he offered respects to a Sikh brother in Sikh words and style. A Sikh would be cursed by his community if he saluted and respected a Mohammedan brother in the Muslim words and style. A Hindu for similar offences would be removed from.his community. But have you ever realised that day and night you wish not only to the English but amongst yourselves Good Morning, Good Evening and Good Night, in totally foreign language and culture. Our children instead of calling the parents in our beautiful Indian languages shout in foreign language as Daddy and Mummy. We never feel sorry at this but would strangle the child's throat if the expression is in a Muslim way or Hindu way.

(a) Religions do not teach us hatred and division. Why do we fight? I say it is criminal to despics God's made man.

(b) Religions do not teach slavery. Why are we slaves? It is no fault of religion to live as slaves. We must be free or die in the struggle for liberty. A coward and a slave have no place and right to live in this world. Now is the time to rejuvenate ourselves. Yesterday's slaves are to-day's free men. We can amend the wrongs. I felt it as my duty that I should give you this as a warning signal and I have done it. Now that time is gone that if you are slapped on the right check. you should offer the left.

The right of right is obtained and retained by might. Fifty years ago, Japan sent to Europe books on Philosophy, law and order but the English did not understand. Later on Japan sent to them samples of toys, cloth and crockery but they did not see and listen. Eventually Japan picked up sword and defeated Russia just on the gospel of to live and let live. This, Gentlemen, opened the eyes of the world. European powers recognised Japan as a first rate Eastern Power. The tumultuous world has always been as such. Might is right.

In the struggle for existence the oppressed must overthrow the oppressor and must live. Today the whole is a battlefield. Clouds of tyranny and injustice are hanging over India. But remember when war is over justice is bound to prevail. If we are to live in this world in peace and justice, now is the time that we must gird up our loins and uproot the enemy from the sacred soil of India. Do not forgot that we have no desire to become the laughing stock of the world.

It would be no use to weep over the split milk when the time is gone. It is not the question of the present 400 millions, it is a question of the coming thousands of thousands generations of sons and daughters of India. Sacrifice and unity are our chariots to ride over the battlefield to fight and regain the ground of honour and glory. You have got the heart. Put the feet in stirrups and reins of confidence in the hands of Providence. We shall be victorious.

23

Resolutions Passed by the Bangkok Conference Confirming the Collaboration of Indians in East Asia with the Japanese for Overthrow of the Western Powers, Spells out the Demand for Expansion of Indian National Army[1]

20 June, 1942

The Bangkok Conference, held under the auspices of the I.I.L. of Greater East Asia and the Chairmanship of Rash Behari Bose, opened at the Silapakorn Theatre at 0900 hrs. on 15 June 1942 and lasted till 23rd June. Indian leaders at that time estimated that there were two million Indians in the "East Asia Co-prosperity Sphere".

Delegates came from Burma, Malaya, Thailand, China, French, Indo-china, East Indies and the Philippines. They totalled about 100 civilian delegates and 50 military.

The main objects were :–

1. To co-ordinate the movement for Indian Independence, which had already stated but lacked uniformity and cohesion, in those territories of East Asia, which had fallen under Japanese control.
2. To clarify the position regarding their inclusion in the "East Asia Co-prosperity Sphere".
3. To determine the purposes for which the I.N.A. should be used.
4. To decide what assistance could be expected from the Japanese without committing to Post-war Japanese domination.

The Japanese gave every assistance in this Conference and ordered

1. Indian Independence league papers F. No. 45/3. These papers were consulted when these were with the History of Freedom movement unit. These papers have now been transfered to the National Archivs of India. In future referred as I.I.L. Papers 45/3 For the text of the speeches at this conference by A.M. Sahey, Raghvan, and Gill, see Gaini, *op. cit, pp. 74-75.*

the Thai Government to do likewise. The conference passed the following resolutions :–

1. Whereas it is the objective of the war of Greater East Asia to destroy British Imperialism in Asia; and

Whereas it gives an opportunity for India to realise the goal of complete independence; and

Whereas it is the belief of this Conference that a new and regenerated Asia of Free Nations is certain to arise as a result of this said war :

This Conference expresses its sincere gratification at the war policy of Japan and convey to the Imperials Government its best wishes for the continued success of the Imperial Japanese Armed Forces.

2. This Conference conveys to all the powers fighting against British Imperialism its sincere congratulations and prays that their efforts may meet with complete success.

3. This Conference places on record its sense of deep admiration for the most determined manner in which the Nationalist Leaders at home have been trying to refuse to be drawn into this war on the side of the British and their Allies, and for the frank and definite demand for the withdrawal of the British from India. In the opinion of this Conference, unless the British withdraw from India and the Allied Forces cease to make use of India as a base for war operations and war preparations unimaginable and innumerable sufferings will be the lot of the people of India.

4. Resolved that a Movement for achieving complete and immediate independence of India be sponsored by this Conference.

Object

5. This Conference endorses the view of the Tokyo Conference held in March 1942 that the complete Independence of India free from any foreign control, domination or interference of whatever nature shall be the object of this Movement, and is emphatically of opinion that the time has arrived to take necessary steps for the attainment of that object.

Guiding Principles

6. Resolved that the Indian Independence Movement sponsored by this Conference shall be guided by the principles indicated below :

(a) That unity, faith, sacrifice, shall be the motto of the Indian Independence Movement.

(b) That India be considered as one, and indivisible.

(c) That all activities of this Movement be on a national basis, and

not on a sectional, communal or religious basis.

(d) That in view of the fact that the Indian National Congress is the only political organisation which could claim to represent the real interests of the people of India, and as such to be acknowledged the only body representing India, this Conference is of the opinion that the programme and plan of action of this Movement must be so guided, controlled and directed as to bring them in line with the aims and intentions of the Indian National Congress.

(e) That the framing of the future constitution of India be only by the representatives of the people of India.

(f) That a joint Axis policy favourable towards India will be advantageous to India.

(g) That the sympathy, cooperation and support of Japan is invaluable in securing the object of this Movement, namely the Independence of India.

7. Resolved that an organisation be started for carrying on the Indian Independence Movement and that it shall be known as the Indian Independence League.

8. Resolved that the Indian Independence League shall immediately proceed to raise an Army called the Indian National Army from among the Indian soldiers (combatants and non-combatants) and such civilians as may hereafter be recruited for military service in the cause of Indian Independence.

Constitution

9. This Conference adopts the following Constitution for the Indian Independence League organisation.

(i) The Indian Independence League shall consist of :

- (a) A Council of Action,
- (b) A Committee of Representatives,
- (c) Territorial Branch, and
- (d) Local Branches.

(ii) (a) Local branches of the Indian Independence League may be formed only at a public meeting of Indians in any locality who shall elect a Committee and a President.

(b) Vacancy of such Committee or in the Office of the President may be filled up by the Committee.

(c) All Indians above the age of eighteen shall be entitled to be members of such Branch on compliance with the rules of the Branch.

(d) No such Branch shall be recognised as a Branch unless the Territorial Committee as constituted hereinafter accords and continues to accords to such Branch due recognition, provided however that all Branches of the Indian Independence League now in existence and recognised in the various territories mentioned in article (vi) hereof shall until otherwise decided upon be recognised by this Movement.

(iii) Representatives elected by the Committee of Local Branches in each territory shall form a Territorial Committee, and the Territorial Committee shall make such rules as it may consider necessary for the effective working of the Movement within the territory.

(iv) The Territorial Committee in each territory shall guide, supervise and control the work of the Movement within its territory and shall also elect representatives as constituted hereinafter.

(v) Territorial Committees and Committees of Local Branches under them shall have power to make rules not inconsistent with the rules by the Committee of Representatives or in case of Local Branches by the Territorial Committees.

(vi) (a) A Committee of Representatives shall be constituted by civilian representatives selected by the Territorial Committees in the territories herein below set out and by representa tives selected by the Indian National Army.

Japan and Manchukuo	4
Philippines	2
Thailand	6
Malaya	14
Burma	21
Borneo and Celebes	1
Hongkong, Canton and Macao	2
Other parts of China, including Shanghai	2
Indo-China	1
Java	2
Sumatra	1
Andamans	1
	57
Indian National Army	33
	90

(b) The Council of Action shall be at liberty to include in the above list of territories any other territory and fix the number of representatives from such territory to the Committee of Representatives, providing in that event for increase in the representatives from the Indian National Army, equal to two-thirds of the number fixed for such territory.

(vii) Every member of the Committee of Representatives shall sign the Oath of Secrecy in the prescribed form before he takes his seat on the Committee.

(viii) The Committee of Representatives shall be responsible for the general policy and programme of the Indian Independence Movement and its decision shall in every case be final and binding on each and every member of this Movement.

(ix) The Committee of Representatives shall have power to alter, amend or rescind any previous decisions made by it, including any decision arrived at in this Conference.

(x) No meeting of the Committee of Representatives shall be valid unless two-thirds in number of the Members of the Committee are present (either in person or by proxy).

(xi) A Council of Action consisting of a President and four (4) members, of whom at least one half shall be from the Indian National Army in East Asia, shall be appointed by the delegates to this Conference. The first President shall be Sjt. Rash Behari Bose and the four members shall be: :

1. Sri N. Raghavan
2. Captain Mohan Singh
3. Sri K.P.K. Menon
4. Colonel G.Q. Gilani.

(xii) Any vacancy in the Council of Action caused by death, resignation or otherwise of Members not exceeding two in number at a time, may be filled up by the other Members of the Council, and in the event of more than two such vacancies the Council of Action shall call a meeting of the Representatives to fill such vacancies.

(xiii) The Council of Action shall be Responsible for the carrying out of the policy and programme of work laid down by this Conference and as may hereafter be laid down by the Committee of Representatives and shall deal with all new matters that may arise from time to time and which may not be provided for by

of Representatives and shall deal with all new matters that may arise from time to time and which may not be provided for by the Committee itself.

(xiv) For the proper and efficient carrying out of the work the Council of Action shall have power to create as many departments as are necessary and to appoint and dismiss administrative officers and staff whenever necessary.

(xv) The Council of Action shall have no power to alter or amend the Policy laid down by this Conference without the sanction of the Committee of Representatives.

(xvi) The Council of Action may at any time summon a meeting of the Committee of Representatives to be held at such places as the Council may decide provided that necessary facilities for travel to Representatives and at least 14 days' notice of such meeting have been given to the Secretaries of the Territorial Committees and to the Headquarters of the Indian National Army. On a requisition by twenty members (Representatives) hailing from more than one territory such a meeting shall be called by the Council of Action and the necessary notices and facilities for travel shall be given.

(xvii) The Council of Action shall have general superintendence and control over all Branches of the Indian Independence League in all territories mentioned in article (vi) and over the Indian National Army.

(xviii) The Council of Action shall cause to be kept a register of all the territorial and local organisations and may remove there—from the names of any such organisations and withhold or withdraw recognition of any such organisation.

(xix) The Council of Action shall have collective responsibility.

(xx) The allotment of Portfolios shall be amongst the Members of the Council of Action and at the discretion of the President.

(xxi) The Headquarters of the Movement shall be at Bangkok or such other place as may hereafter be decided upon by the Committee of Representatives or the Council of Action.

(xxii) The deliberations of the Committee of Representatives and the Council of Action shall be privileged and no action of a disciplinary character can be taken against any member in consequence thereof by any Branch or Territorial Committee or by the Indian National Army.

(xxiii) Changes in the Constitution of the Indian Independence League may be made only by vote to that effect by three-fourths of the Members of the Committee of Representatives.

10. Resolved that a request be made to the Nippon Government that it may be pleased to place immediately all Indian soldiers in territories in East Asia under their control at the disposal of this Movement.

11. Resolved that the formation, command, control and organisation of the Indian National Army be in the hands of Indians themselves.

12. Resolved that it is the earnest desire of this Conference that the Indian National Army from its inception be accorded the powers and status of a free National Army of an Independent India, on a footing of equality with the armies of Japan and other friendly powers.

13. Resolved that the Indian National Army shall be made use of only:

(a) For operations against the British or other foreign powers in India,

(b) For the purpose of securing and safeguarding Indian National Independence and,

(c) For such other purpose as may assist the achievement of the object, viz : the Independence of India.

14. Resolved that all officers and men of the proposed Indian National Army shall be members of the Indian Independence League and shall owe allegiance to the League.

15. Resolved that the Indian National Army shall be under the direct control of the Council of Action and that the said Army shall be organised and commanded by the General Officer Commanding, Indian National Army, in accordance with the directions of the Council of Action.

16. Resolved that in the event of military action being taken against the British or other foreign powers in India, and for the said purpose the Council of Action may be at liberty to place the military resources available to it, under the unified command of Indian and Japanese Military Officers under the direction of the said Council of Action.

17. Resolved that before taking any military action against the British or any other foreign power in India, the Council of Action will assure itself that such action is in conformity with the express or implied wishes of the Indian National Congress.

18. Resolved that the Council of Action shall make all efforts to create an atmosphere in India which would lead to a revolution in the Indian Army there, and among the Indian people, and that before taking military action the Council of Action shall assure itself that such an atmosphere exists in India.

19. In view of the great urgency and imperative necessity of informing and convincing our countrymen in India and abroad, and friends of India all over the world, of the meaning and purpose of this movement, and in view of the fact that propaganda in and outside India is one of the most effective means of waging the war for Indian Independence, this Conference resolves to take immediate steps to carry on active and vigorous propaganda by Broadcasts, Leaflets, Lectures and by such other means as may be found possible and practicable from time to time.

20. That all foreign assistance of whatever nature shall be only to the extent and of the type asked for by the Council of Action.

21. Resolved that for the purpose of financing the Independence Movement the Council of Action be authorised to raise funds from Indians in East Asia.

22. The Conference places on record its grateful appreciation of the support and encouragement given to this Movement by the Imperial Government of Japan, and resolves that the Council of Action be authorised to approach if and when necessary the said Government with a request to render such monetary help as may be required from time to time for the successful carrying out of the object of this Movement, on the distinct understanding that such monetary help is to be treated as a loan repayable to the Imperial Government of Japan by the National Government of India.

23. Resolved that the Imperial Government of Japan be requested to be good enough to provide all facilities for Propaganda, Travel, Transport and Communication within the area under the control of the Imperial Government of Japan, in the manner and to the extent requested by the Council of Action, and also all facilities to come into contact with the National leaders, workers and organisations in India.

24. Resolved that the Imperial Government of Japan be requested to be good enough to arrange with the local authorities concerned that in matters of administration affecting the Indian Community, the Indian Independence League in the respective places, and in places where there are no branches of the League, recognised leaders of the community approved by the League Branch nearest to such places, be consulted.

25. Resolved that the Government of Thailand be requested to be good enough to consult the Indian Independence League (formerly known as the Indian National Council and the Independence League of India) in matters of administration affecting the Indian community in Thailand.

26. The Conference, while recording its grateful appreciation of the various pronouncements made by General Tojo, the Premier of Japan, expressing the preparedness of the Japanese Government to give its unstinted support to the cause of Indian Independence, reiterates the Resolution of the Tokyo Conference that in further clarification of the attitude of Japan towards India, the Imperial Government be good enough to make a formal declaration to the effect :

(a) That immediately on the severance of India from the British Empire, the Imperial Government of Japan shall respect the territorial integrity and recognise the full sovereignty of India free from any foreign influence, control or interference of a political, military or economic nature.

(b) That the Imperial Government of Japan will exercise its influence with other powers and induce them to recognise the National independence and absolute sovereignty of India.

(c) That the framing of the future Constitution of India will be left entirely to the representatives of the people of India without interference from any foreign authority.

27. Resolved that this Conference is Committed to a definite policy of close cooperation with Japan and it shall, on eliciting an official definition satisfactory to this Movement of the term 'Greater East Asia Co-Prosperity Sphere' and its implications, endeavour to persuade Independence India :

(a) To be a member of such Sphere or a member of any other international combine of which Japan is a member, on a footing of equality with Japan; and

(b) To confer on Japan the most favoured nation treatment on a reciprocal basis.

28. Whereas it has come to the knowledge of this Conference that Indians in the territories which are now freed from the domination of the Anglo-Saxons and their Allies by the Imperial Forces of Japan own considerable movable and immovable properties in these territories; and

Whereas owing to the exigencies of war a number of Indians had to leave these territories, leaving behind their properties without making arrangements for their care and management; and

Whereas the Imperial Government of Japan has promised its unstinted support to the cause of Indian Independence; and

Whereas an enormous amount of money is required to carry on and complete the object of the said movement in East Asia; and

Whereas an appreciably steady income is likely to be derived from the said properties in the said territories; and

Whereas in the opinion of the Conference, the handing over of such properties to the Indian Independence League by the authorities concerned, on the distinct understanding that the said properties are to be returned to their rightful owners when claimed, will be welcomed as a sign of goodwill and encouragement towards this Movement.

Now this Conference Resolves

That the Imperial Government of Japan may be pleased to arrange with the authorities in the territories now freed from the domination of the Anglo-Saxons and their Allies by the Imperial Forces of Japan, to hand over the properties owned by the Indian (including those owned by Indians Companies, firms and partnerships) and left by them owing to the exigencies of war, to the Council of Action in this Movement in trust for their rightful owners, to manage and control the said properties, and advance the income thereof for the use of this Movement, to be repaid as and when claimed by the said owners.

29. This Conference having learned with regret that Indians residing in certain countries under the occupation of the Imperial Forces of Japan are being treated as enemy aliens, and suffer hardship and loss in consequence; resolves that the Imperial Government of Japan may be pleased to make a declaration to the effect :

(a) That Indians residing in the territories occupied by the Imperial Forces of Japan shall nót be considered enemy nationals so long as they do not indulge in any action injurious to this movement or hostile to the interest of Japan, and

(b) That the properties both movable and immovable of those Indians who are now residing in India or elsewhere (including the properties of Indian companies, firms and partnerships) be not treated by Japan as enemy properties so long as the management or control of such properties is vested in any person or persons residing in Japan or in any of the countries occupied by or under the influence or control of the Imperial Japanese Forces, and to instruct the authorities concerned in the respective territories to give effect to this policy as early as possible.

30. That this Movement adopts the present National Flag of India and requests the Imperial Government of Japan and the Royal Government of Thailand and the Governments of all other friendly powers to recognise the said flag in all territories under their jurisdiction.

31. This Conference requests Sjt. Subhash Chandra Bose to be kind enough to come to East Asia, and appeals to the Imperial Government of Japan to use its good offices to obtain the necessary permission and conveniences from the Government of Germany to enable Sjt. Subhas Chandra Bose to reach East Asia safe.

32. That no unauthorised publicity be given to any of the Resolutions adopted at this Conference, but a manifesto be issued by this Conference setting out the purpose and policy of this Movement, and incorporating such decisions and details as may be found proper and beneficial to be made public.

33. This Conference places on record its deepest appreciation of and grateful thanks for the cooperation, assistance and support extended to this movement and its objective by the Imperial Government of Japan.

34. This Conference gratefully acknowledges the sincere and friendly attitude the Governments and the peoples of Germany and Italy have adopted towards our struggle for freedom and places on record its deep appreciation and thanks for the offer of assistance and cooperation extended by them to this Movement.

35. This Conference places on record its grateful thanks to the Government and people of Thailand for the opportunity given to hold this Conference at Bangkok, for their kind hospitality, and for their sympathy and cooperation in India's struggle for freedom.

24

Rash Behari Bose to Colonel Iwakuro Requesting him to Forward the Resolution Passed at the Bangkok Conference to the Imperial Japanese Government for Approval

22 June, 1942

As President of the Indian Independence Conference held at Bangkok this month (and now in session) I have the honour to convey to the Imperial Government of Japan the following Resolution which was unanimously adopted :–

> Whereas it is the objective of the War of Greater East Asia to destroy the British Imperialism in Asia, and
>
> Whereas it gives an opportunity for India to realise its goal of complete Independence and
>
> Whereas it is the belief of this Conference that a new and regenerated Asia of free nations is certain to arise as a result of the said war,
>
> This conference expresses its sincere gratification at the War Policy of Japan and conveys to the Imperial Government its best wishes for the continued successes of the Imperial Japanese Armed Forces.

---

1. K.P.K. Menon Papers; File No. 1. Nehru Memorial Museum and Liberary, (NMML) New Delhi.
2. Col. Iwakuro Hideo, was a senior officer of Imperial Guard Regiment. He succeeded Fujiwara as head of the liaison agency (Iwakuro Kikan) to assist the Indian Independence movement. his attitude towards the expansion of INA. and the questions of antonomy led towards the deterioration of relations between General Mohan and the Japanese. Iwakuro had very little interest in the question of Indian Independence and was replaced, when Subhash Chander Bose took over the command of the Indian National Army.

This conference conveys to all the Powers Fighting against British Imperialism its sincere congratulations and prays that their efforts may meet with complete success.

2. Further various resolutions with a view to achieving "the immediate independence of India, defined as complete independence of India free from any foreign control, domination or interference of whatever nature" were adopted. The sense of the Conference as was evident from the Resolutions adopted and opinions expressed was that such independence could not at present be achieved without the goodwill, of cooperation and full support of the Imperial Government of Japan. The conference which knows the various declarations of Policy and statements by His Excellency Premier General Tojo had little doubt that the Imperial Govt. of Japan recognised that the time had come for India to have immediate independence and that the Imperial Govt. of Japan would place every facility in the hands of the sponsors of the Indian Independence Movement and of the people of India to achieve the immediate independence of India.

3. It is with this firm conviction that we hereby place before the Imperial Government of Japan some of the conclusions arrived at the Conference with the earnest request to the Imperial Government for assistance and support in giving effect to them.

4. Some of the guiding principles of this Movement were indicated as follows :–

That Unity, Faith, Sacrifice shall be the motto of the Indian Independence Movement. That India is considered as ONE, and indivisible.

That all activities of this Movement be on a National basis and not on Sectional, Communal or Religious basis.

That in view of the fact that the Indian National Congress is the only political organisation which could claim to represent the real interest of the people of India and as such be acknowledged the only body representing India, this Conference is of the opinion that the programme and plan of action of this Movement must be so guided, controlled and directed as to bring them in line with the aims and intentions of the Indian National Congress.

That the framing of the future constitution of India be only by the representatives of the people of India.

That a joint axis policy favourable towards India will be advantagious towards India.

That the sympathy, cooperation and support of Japan is invaluable in securing the object of this Movement, namely, the Independence of India.

5. The Conference resolved for carrying on the Independence Movement to start an organisation called the Indian Independence League.

6. On the assumption that the Imperial Government of Japan will be pleased to place in our hands every facility for this move, the Conference resolved that the Indian Independence League shall immediately proceed to raise an army called the Indian National Army from among the Indian soldiers (combatants and non-combatants) and such civilians as may hereafter be recruited for military service in the cause of Indian Independence. With the same object the Conference authorised me to make a request to the Imperial Government of Japan that they may be pleased "to place immediately all the Indian soldiers in territories in East Asia under their control at the disposal of this Movement". The request is being made on the same assumption that the Imperial Government would place in our hands the necessary material for achieving the object of this Movement in their declared Policy for helping India in the attainment of complete and immediate independence. It was also the desire of this Conference that "the formation, command, control and organisation of the Indian National Army may be placed in the hands of Indians themselves". I may be permitted to point out that a good deal of assistance and guidance in this connection may be required by our Army in order to make it an efficient fighting unit. We fully hope that this desire of this conference will be viewed with approval by the Imperial Govt. It was "the earnest desire of this Conference that the Indian National Army from its inception be accorded the powers and status of a free National Army of the independent India on a footing of equality with the Armies of Japan and other friendly countries". In your helping us to create a National Army of our own to fight our battles against the British in India and to regain our Independence we feel certain that the Imperial Government would be willing to confer on that Army the powers and status asked for as without such powers and status the Army may not be spiritually free, and may suffer from an inferiority complex, and may be regarded by India not as an Army of freedom and of Free India but as a reaction to our for some other purposes. It will be of immense advantage to our Movement if we can convince India that the Imperial Government has of its own accord given such a status to the Army which it helped to create for the liberation of India and which may in due course form the

nucleus of India's National Army. Another Resolution in connection with the National Army was as follow :–

Resolved that the Indian National Army shall be made used of on only :–

> For operations against British or other foreign powers in India
> For the purpose of securing and safeguarding Indian National Independence and
> For such other purposes as may assist the achievement of the object viz. the Independence of India.

This Resolution if accepted by the Imperial Government will re-assure public opinion in India that the object that we have in view is only the full and complete independence of India by ejecting the British and other foreign powers and establishing a National Government in India.

7. The Conference decided that all officers and men of the proposed Indian National Army should be members of the Indian Independence League and should owe allegiance to the League.

8. The Conference also decided that subject to approval of the Imperial Government, the Indian National Army which may be created may be placed under the direct control of the Council of Action of this Movement and should be organised and commanded by the General Officer Commanding the Indian National Army in accordance with the directions of the Council of Action.

9. Another direction to the Council of Action was that in the event of military action being taken against the British or other foreign powers in India and for the said purpose the Council of Action may be at liberty to place the military resources available to it, under a unified command of Indian and Japanese Military Officers under the direction of the said Council of Action. We hope that when the time comes the Imperial Govt. will be willing to agree to such unified command. We shall gratefully appreciate such an act as a great favour done to this Movement for Indian Independence.

10. There were two resolutions as to the time for taking such action and we hope that they will also find approval with the Imperial Government. They were as follows :–

> Resolved that before taking any military action against the British or any other foreign power in India the C/A will assure itself that such action is in conformity with the express or implied wishes of the Indian National Congress.

Resolved that the C/A shall make all efforts to create an atmosphere in India which would lead to a revolution in the Indian Army there and

among the Indian people and that before taking any military action the C/A shall assure itself that such an atmosphere exists in India.

The reasons for the said Resolutions were the anxiety of the Conference in making the move to be on the side of the Indian people as represented by the Indian National Congress without whose assistance there may be various difficulties and repercussions in the achievement of the object we have in view. The adoption of the Resolution meant that every endeavour should be made by this Movement that the support and co-operation of the Imperial Government to carry on effective propaganda in India with a view to converting the Indian masses and the premier political body in India to the view held by this Conference. The resolution will also presuppose that complete reliance is placed by this Movement in the Imperial Government to enable us to do our work in such a way as to convert India to our view. The success or otherwise that we may be meeting with in our convincing the people of India that this Movement is a thoroughly bona fide Movement on our part for securing complete independence for India.

11. It was also with the view that the Conference adopted the following resolutions :–

> In view of the great urgency and imperative necessity of informing and convincing our countrymen in India and abroad and the friends in India all over the world of the meaning and purpose of this Movement and in view of the fact that propaganda in and outside India is one of the most effective means for waging the war for Indian Independence, this conference resolves to take immediate steps to carry on active and vigorous propaganda by Broadcasts, Leaflets, Lectures and by such other means as may be found possible and practicable from time to time.

12. Another resolution that was passed was as follows :–

That all foreign assistance of whatever nature shall be only to the extent and of the type asked for by the C/A.

We, who implicitly trust in the sincerity of Japan's intentions, believe, that such assistance when requested by the C/A of this movement will without doubts forth coming from the Imperial Government in as ample measure as may be required.

13. There was a resolution passed "that for the purpose of financing the Independence Movement the C/A be authorised to raise funds from Indians in East Asia", but the Conference also resolved "that the C/A be

authorised to approach if and when necessary the Imperial Government of Japan with a request to render such monetary help as may be required from time to time for the successful carrying out of the object of this movement on the distinct understanding that such monetary help is to be treated as a loan repayable to the Imperial Government of Japan by the National Government of India when it come into being". We shall be for ever grateful for this favour.

14. The Conference also requested that the Imperial Govt. of Japan will kindly see its way and be good enough to provide "all facilities for propaganda, Travel, Transport and Communications within the area under the control of the Imperial Govt. of Japan in the manner and to the extent requested by the C/A and also all facilities to come into contact with the National Leaders, workers and organisation in India". This provision we may be permitted to point out is very important for the effective commencement and culmination of our Movement for Independence.

15. In order to give a clear status to this Movement in the territories under the control of Imperial Government there was a request by the conference that the authorities in the various places may be good enough to consult in matters affecting the Indian Community in such places the Indian Independence League and in places where there are no Branches of the League recognised leaders of the Community approved by the League Leaders nearest to such places. Such action, we need hardly say will establish this Movement in the confidence of the Indian Public of the various localities.

16. This conference while recording its grateful appreciation of the various pronouncements made by General Tojo, the Premier of Japan expressing the preparedness of the Nipponese Government to give its unstinted support to the cause of Indian Independence reiterates the resolution of the Tokyo Conference that in further clarification of the attitude of Japan towards India, the Imperial Government of Japan be requested to be good enough make a formal declaration to the effect :-

(a) That on the severance of India from British Empire, the Imperial Government of Japan shall respect the territorial integrity and recognises the full and absolute sovereignty of India free from any foreign influence, control or interference of a political, military or economic nature.

(b) That the Imperial Government of Japan will exercise its influence with other powers and induce them to recognise the National Independence and absolute sovereignty of India.

(c) That the framing of the future constitution of India will be left entirely to the representatives of the people of India without interference from any foreign authority.

This was substantially the Resolution adopted at the Indian Independence Conference held at Tokyo in March this year.

17. This Conference also resolved that :–

This conference is committed to a definite policy of the closest cooperation with Japan and it shall on eliciting an official definition satisfactory to this Movement of the term "Greater East Asia Co-Prosperity Sphere" and the implications endeavour to persuade Independence India :–

(a) To be a member of such sphere or a member of any other international combine of which Japan is a member, on a footing of equality with Japan ; and

(b) To confer on Japan the most favoured national treatment on a reciprocal basis.

18. The Conference also requested that the Imperial Government of Japan may be pleased to direct by making a declaration to the effect that Indians residing in the territories occupied by the Imperial Forces of Japan shall not be considered enemy nationals so long as they do not indulge in any action injurious to this Movement or hostile to the interest of Japan".

19. The conference adopted the present National Flag for the Movement and in order to give the flag, which is the Flag of Indian Freedom, a real status appeal to the Imperial Government of Japan and to other Friendly Government to give recognition to the said Flag as the Flag of this Freedom Movement in all territories under their jurisdiction.

20. There was also an appeal to the Imperial Government of Japan "to use its good offices" to obtain the necessary permission and convenience from the Government of Germany to enable Sjt. Subhash Chandra Bose, the Indian Leader, to reach East Asia safe.

21. The conference placed on record "its deepest appreciation of and grateful thanks for the cooperation, assistance and support extended to this Movement and its objective by the Imperial Government of Japan".

22. It is our earnest hope that the Imperial Government will see nothing objectionable in these resolutions, a copy of which is attached hereto. We appeal to the Imperial Government of Japan to be kind enough to give effect to these and earnestly and entreat that the Resolutions will receive the most favourable consideration from the Imperial Government

The future of our country depends entirely on the success or otherwise of this Movement and such success in its turn is entirely dependent on the support and cooperation that the Imperial Government may be extending towards it. From the various pronouncements of His Excellency, Premier General Tojo, this Conference implicitly believe that the resolutions would find acceptance and that every facility will be given to this Movement and to Indians to win the complete Independence of India.

25

From Iwakuro to Rash Behari Bose Informing him that the Imperial Japanese Government would Extend Whole-hearted Support to the Indian Independence Movement; but no Specific Reply was Necessary as Regards Resolutions

10 July, 1942

Dear Mr. Chairman,

I have the honour to inform you that the Imperial Government is determined to extend whole-hearted and unstinted support, as evidenced in the repeated statements made by Premier Tojo, and also in his recent message of facilitation to the Bangkok Conference, in regard to the request dated on June, the 22nd, 1942, from the Indian Independence League to the Imperial Japanese Government with the object of attaining complete independence for Indian by supporting the Independence Movement in India and removing Anglo-American influence.

The Imperial Japanese Government agrees with your view to keep the resolutions of the Bangkok Conference secret, and it is also the wish of the Imperial Japanese Government that this reply will be kept under strict secrecy.

I wish to take this opportunity to pay my profound respect for your brave and strenuous efforts and earnestly wish you all the success in trying to shake off the yoke of despotism, which Britain has been imposing on your Fatherland.

1 K.P.K. Menon Papers; File No. 1. NMML.

26

British Assessment of the Indian National Army After its Expansion and Formation in the Light of Bangkok Conference[1]

17 July, 1942

The "Indian National Army" is the title given by the Japanese to a force which they intend to use to attack India's war effort. The existence of the nucleus of this "army" is established; the following account of its nature and purpose is, however, largely unsubstantiated, and must be treated with reserve.

The Japanese claim that the I.N.A. now numbers 70,000, and an establishment of 90,000 has been mentioned. This figure is considerably in excess of the total number of Indian and Gurkha prisoners of war in Japanese hands, and there is no proof that any substantial number of these prisoners have become pro-Japanese in sympathy. The Japanese claim may therefore be regarded as a target, which must include a considerable proportion of the civilian population in Japanese occupied territories.[2]

The professed objects of the I.N.A. are espionage: subversive propaganda directed, in particular, against the Indian Army: and military operations aimed at the "liberation" of India. As regards operations, it has been suggested that the Japanese intend to use elements of the I.N.A. to precede their troops in the advance, with the object of exhorting Indian troops to lay down their arms and, in general, to cause confusion

---

1. Weekly Intelligence Summary, General Headquarters-India F. No. 6017668/ Historical Section, Ministry of Defence, New Delhi. These reports are also available at the Public Record office London.
2. It is known that by the end of August, 1942, nearly forty thousands soldiers had given the pledge to join the Indian National Army. For details see. Mohan Singh, *op. cit.* pp. 100-150.

amongst our forces. This employment would be in accordance with Japanese methods, as exemplified in Malaya and Burma.

The I.N.A. is open to all Indians, and determined attempts appear to have been made to enlist Gurkhas. Potential recruits are subject to intensive propaganda stressing Japanese goodwill towards India, and in the case of Gurkhas, laying claim to an alleged Mongol affinity. More material inducements probably include promises of quick promotion, high pay, and money awards for specific services. In this connection a first hand, but unconfirmed, report states that Japanese attempts were made in Burma as far back as 1931, to induce pensioners, deserters and discharged soldiers to enlist in the Japanese Army. Sepoys, or the equivalent, were offered Rs. 60/- per mensem, with other ranks in proportion. Colour is given to this account by independent reports of a Gurkha "Captain" in the Japanese army, who interrogated Gurkha prisoners of war, and told one of them that he had been with the Japanese for a long time.

Independent, but unconfirmed reports suggest that the advanced Headquarters of the I.N.A., under an Indian "Chief of Staff", may be in Rangoon, where a "Spy and propaganda" school is said to be established under an ex-V.C.O. General control is probably exercised from Bangkok. It is certain that the Japanese have bribed and released prisoners of war in the hope that they would spread pro-Japanese propaganda on return to their units. A number of Indians with military titles have been employed as broadcasters and commentators at Japanese controlled wireless stations. In one case an I.N.A. "Captain" has been fairly definitely identified with an Indian V.C.O. captured in Malaya, and certain other possible identification have been made.

The I.N.A. is stated to be under the direct command of the movement's Working Committee. The following is information regarding the I.N.A., additional to that published in a recent Summary. Japan is to provide 1000 tanks and 400 planes. After the conquest of Burma, the plan envisaged was that Japan would concentrate on China and Australia, leaving India to the I.N.A.; if this failed, the Japanese would then attack India themselves.

Many of our prisoners of war (stated in one report to have been released) were taken to Rangoon, where Indians and Gurkhas were strictly segregated from the British. The Indian Wing of the prison camp was divided into companies, apparently with an eye to the future organisation of the I.N.A. Indians and Gurkhas were subjected to propaganda lectures. Volunteers were called for to carry out espionage and anti-British

propaganda. Small parties were then organised, some to move with Japanese troops and shout "Stop! You are surrounded!" and the like, in Indian dialects. Others were to return to India to spread anti-British propaganda; they were then given money (about Rs. 40/- each), a *lungi* and P.T. Shoes and sent off in small parties. Two parties of Japanese spies were to go to India through Chittagong to contact Gandhi and Nehru.

To sum up, Japan is fostering, among Indians in the Far East, a movement of dangerous potentialities. It seems evident that she is attempting to give her plans the air of a spontaneous move, controlled and developed by Indian patriots, and to persuade the world that the "Free India" movement directed from Bangkok is in effect linked with the policy of Gandhi and the Congress. So far as can be judged, this new political front against India has had little effect on the public of this country. Several reports have, however, been received which refer to the departure from occupied China of bodies of Indians for fifth column work in this country.

27

Rash Behari Bose to Iwakuro Requesting him Again to Get Specific Clarification from the Imperial Japanese Government regarding their Attitude to the Resolutions Passed by the Bangkok Conference; Refers to Differences Emerging in the Council of Action on Lukewarm Response from the Japanese High Command[1]

5 September, 1942

Sir,

I have the honour to inform you that your kind communication dated 10th July, 1942, was considered by the Council of the Indian Independence Movement and, while we appreciate deeply the promise of support and sympathy contained therein we feel it our duty to point out that the said communication does not

(a) Specifically reply to the requests contained in our latter, dated 22nd June, 1942, and

(b) does not specifically clarify the attitude of the Imperial Government on the various points raised in the said letter and in the resolutions of the Bangkok Conference.

2. Your communication also does not indicate whether our said latter dated, 22nd June 1942, was referred to the Imperial Government and, if so, whether any reply was received from the Imperial Government thereto. When we forwarded our letter dated, 22nd June, 1942, and the resolutions, we were already in possession of the declarations made by His Excellency Premier General Tojo and our intention was to have further clarification

---

1. K.P.K. Menon Papers, Nehru Memorial Museum and Library, New Delhi. This is also reproduced by Mohan Singh in his hook *Soldier's contribution to Indian Independence*, New Delhi, 1974. p. 189.

of the position of the Imperial Government on specific matters raised in the Resolutions.

3. We shall deem it great favour if a reply to the Resolutions and my letter to you, dated, 22nd June, 1942, could be obtained from the Imperial Government.

4. We thank you in anticipation.

28

Memorandum by Mr. W.W. Coultas. His Majesty's Consul–General in Bangkok on the Development and Organisation of Indian Independence Movement in Thailand after the Outbreak of War in Far East; Refers to Indian Soldiers who are Still Loyal to the British[1]

20 September, 1942

1. The first enclosure[2] to this memorandum comprises a summary of notices and reports dealing with the Indian Independence Movement in Thailand as published in the *Bangkok Times* newspaper during the period from February 1st to July 20th 1942. The second enclosure is a list of the names of Indian mentioned in the first enclosure. Reports published prior to February 1st are not available, save for a few extracts from copies of newspapers obtained from members of the British community, since it was not until that date that permission was granted by the Siamese authorities for the *Bangkok Times* newspaper to be received by His Majesty's Legation.
2. A perusal of the enclosures will acquaint the reader with the progress of the Indian Independence Movement in Bangkok during the period immediately following Japan's entry into the war as well as furnish him with information regarding its development and organisation, culminating with a description of the Conference held in Bangkok during the latter half of Jun, 1942, for the furtherance of the aims of the Indian Independence League, which was attended, it is said, by over one hundred delegates from the Pacific area.
3. Before commenting on the information contained in the enclosures, it will be useful to describe briefly the situation in Bangkok as regard

---

1. Foreign Office, 371/31870, Public Record Office, London.
2. Enclosures have not been printed.

India British Subjects prior to December 1941. The Indian population in Thailand, including residents in Bangkok and the provinces, is believed to number about 50,000. The races included in this number comprise Hindus, Muslims, Sikhs and a small sprinkling of Christians. Apart from a numerous watchman class, all, except a negligible minority, are engaged in various branches of commerce. Few are wealthy and the great majority are uneducated. Some years prior to the outbreak of war in Europe, the leaders of the various Indian communities had, with the approval of His Majesty's Legation, united in forming an association of an undenominational character styled. "The Indian Association of Thailand." The objects of this society were the furtherance of common social and economical interests, to the exclusion of matters relating to politics or religion. The Association, which appears to have founded about the year 1928, continued to function as a common meeting ground of Indians in Bangkok and as their representative body, without, however, encroaching on the right of individuals or communities to approach H.M. Minister or Consul-General on matters affecting private or communal interests; (e.g., representations made by the local Sikh community against the hair-cutting regulations imposed by the Siamese educational authorities on boys attending state schools). Its direction remained until the year 1940 in the hands of a few senior members of the various Indian communities, most of them old residents of good standing who had been brought up in the extra-territorial tradition and had reason to remember with gratitude the unremitting interest taken in their welfare by His Majesty's Legation and Consular officers. Whilst these old-timers remained in control there was little danger of the Association's activities going beyond the limitations imposed by its articles. A change, however, came with the elections of the new committee for 1940, when, owing to a lack of vigilance on the part of the senior members, a majority of seats on this body was captured by younger and disaffected elements. On account of the dubious methods employed by the latter in achieving this 'coup', a bitter feud, which was still unhealed at the time of Japan's declaration of war, divided the Bangkok Indian community into two camps. In consequence of this feud, since neither side would give way to the other, the Indian Association of Thailand practically ceased to function; nevertheless it was only due to the unyielding opposition of the loyal elements that the Association was not immediately converted into an active centre of

disaffection. This check to the machinations of the more radical group was, however, overcome by the intervention of Swami Satyananda Puri, a Hindu of some pretensions to culture and scholarship, the details of whose career will be found summarised in the entry under April 9th in the first enclosure. This individual appears to have seen an opportunity in the then existing situation both for fostering subversive propaganda amongst Indians in Bangkok and for obtaining financial support for his own cultural activities. With this object in view he started an institution which he styled a "Dharmasharam", with himself as head, to which he invited subscriptions from local Indians. At the outset his appeal met with but little support, and it was not until the autumn of 1940 that, with the cooperation of Debnath Das, who had arrived from Tokyo with the object of organising anti-British activities in Thailand, that he achieved any success. This was accomplished by converting the so-called 'Dharmashram', an institution for the promotion of Indian cultural research, into 'The Thai-Bharata Cultural Lodge', a society founded ostensibly for the fostering of interest in the Indian origins of Thai culture, in which object Swami SatyanandaPuri was able to interest several prominent Siamese, including His Highness Prince Varnvaidya Varavarn. The latter, as President of the Royal Institute, and himself a scholar of some distinction, gave his patronage to the new body, and actually read an address at the inaugural ceremony. How far he was privy to the real objects of the Society, for which its alleged cultural activities were merely a cloak, it is difficult to say. It will suffice to mention here that His Highness was warned by His Majesty's Legation of the suspicions attaching to the new body and that, at its suggestion, H.M. included in his inaugural address a watching hint that politics lay outside the field of cultural pursuits. Notwithstanding these warnings, however, it was remarked that the hoisting of the Indian Congress flag played an important part in the opening ceremony, convincing evidence, if it were needed, of the political motives underlying its creation.

4. The inauguration of the 'Thai-Bharata Cultural Lodge' in Bangkok took place towards the middle of November, and a full report of this event and of the attendant circumstances was sent at the time by H.M. Minister to the Government of India, who had been kept abreast of the 'Indian' situation in Bangkok as it had developed since the outbreak of war. For nearly twelve months following the inauguration of the 'Thai-Bharata Cultural Lodge', however, little progress appears

to have been made, while there was a noticeable waning of interest on the part of the local Indian community in the new institution. There were several factors to account for this. First of all, the return to Japan of Debnath Das and, with his departure, the dwindling of the fervour aroused by his eloquence; secondly, the fact that Satyananda Puri, despite his nationalist convictions, was at heart more of a scholar and ascetic than a politician; thirdly, and most important, the deterrent effect of the steps taken by H.M. Legation, in collaboration with the Indian authorities, to penalise Bangkok Indians participating in anti-British activities. These steps amounted to an embargo on travel, since, on arrival in India on business or otherwise, such person found themselves deprived of their passports and thus immobilised during the pleasure of the authorities. These penalties far outweighed any pleasure derived by the politically minded in indulging their anti-British inclinations, and were effective in preventing any wholehearted support of the Thai-Bharata Cultural Lodge during the period mentioned. The Swami, indeed, was reported to have been much discouraged and to have decided at one time to abandon politics and devote himself entirely to religion and literature. It was during the same period, however, that Baba Amar Singh, the ex-convict of the Mandalay Conspiracy Trials of 1915/16, is now known to have evaded the Indian passport authorities and to have established himself at the Sikh Gurdwara in Bangkok, and it is evident that from this retreat this political fanatic was quietly playing the Japanese game with the assistance of Giani Pritam Singh, the ex-Sikh missionary, whose subversive activities were not fully disclosed until after his death in February, 1942; (See entry in enclosure under date April 2nd). On the whole, however, it may be said that this was a period of marking time during which the anti-British movement amongst Indians in Bangkok, so far as overt action went, rather hung fire.

5. This was the situation in the late autumn in 1941 when the reappearance in Bangkok of Debnath Das in October/November of that year gave food for thought to those who had followed his activities in that city twelve months previously. No definite information was at the time available regarding the object of his visit, though in the light of later events it seems clear that he came on instructions from his Japanese masters with orders to stand by and await events. At the same time, some speculation was aroused by the visit to H.M.C.G. of an emissary from Baba Amar Singh, the

reprieved ex-convict of the Mandalay Conspiracy Trials mentioned in paragraph 4 above. This emissary (an elderly gentleman, named Lal Singh), stated that Baba Amar Singh wished to denounce to the British authorities the treasonable activities of Giani Pritam Singh, the ex-Sikh missionary, who, he said, was actively engaged as a Japanese agent in anti-British and pro-Japanese propaganda amongst Indian troops in Malaya. When asked the reason why Baba Amar Singh did not make this important communication in person, Lal Singh stated that gentleman had recently left Bangkok for Nakawn Lampang in North Thailand, information which was afterwards verified by H.M. Consul at Chiengmai. It would appear, therefore, that late in November Baba Amar Singh either knew or suspected that the zero hour in the Far East was approaching and had decided to play for safety. We learn, however, that after the fall of Singapore he visited that city, together with S. Amar Singh and Swami Satyanandapuri, to attend a meeting of the Independent League of India, (see entry in enclosure under date of March 27th). There were however, no further developments in the local situation before communication between H.M. Legation and the outside world was severed in consequence of events following the Japanese declaration of war. It should be made clear, however, that all information concerning the local Indian situation was passed to the Government of India as and when it became available. There is accordingly nothing in the above summary which has not been the subject of an official report from His Majesty's Legation Bangkok, to the authorities in India, whose information from this source was thus completely uptodate on December 8th, 1941. His Majesty's Legation was also the channel for communication to the Government of India of a number of valuable reports received from His Majesty's Consul at Songkhala, South Thailand, regarding similar activities in the Southern provinces.

6. The summaries of press announcements and reports contained in the first enclosure to this memorandum give a picture of the development of the Indian situation in Siam from day to day following Japan's aggressive action in that country, with an interval, however, previously referred to, of nearly two months during which no newspapers were received inside His Majesty's Legation. These summaries deal mainly with the activities of the Independent League

of India in Bangkok and in Malaya after the fall of Singapore, and also furnish a fairly detailed account of the Indian Independence Conference which was opened in Bangkok on June 15th. 1942, and which is stated to have been attended by over a hundred delegates from territories included within the so-called Greater East Asia Co-Prosperity Sphere. In this connection, the "Bangkok Times" issue of June 13th published a list of the names of delegates to the Conference from Malaya and Hong Kong, while later issues give some account of the subjects dealt with in its public sessions.

7. On of the first steps taken by the Siamese Government after that country's adhesion to the Axis cause was to issue a proclamation stating that none of the Asiatic subjects of Great Britain residing in Siam would be treated as enemy aliens provided they did not attempt to leave the country. In this category were included all local residents of Indian, Burmese, Malaya or Chinese (British born) race. This attitude had been expected and Asiatic British Subjects, who had sought advice previously on the subject of evacuation, had been told that in the opinion of H.M. Legation they had little to fear by remaining in Siam, since the Japanese would most certainly pose as their protectors and "liberators", while the large number involved rendered any kind of wholesale evacuation impracticable.

8. The following facts emerge from the press summaries under reference:–

   (1) The activities of the local branch of the Independent League of India commenced very shortly after Japan's declaration of war and invasion of Siam.

   (2) Indian groups took part in a mass parade organised by certain local authorities on February 6th for the purpose of demonstrating their solidarity with the Siamese Premier in Siam's declaration of war against Great Britain and the U.S.A.

   (3) The control of the *Bangkok Times* newspaper, formerly the only British-owned journal in Bangkok, was almost immediately taken over by the Japanese under the editorship of an Eurasian from Rangoon named EARDE, who had previously been employed on the reporting staff, and who, from accounts received, had not been thought to bold anti-British views. It appears that this newspaper became the main instrument of Indian anti-British propaganda in Bangkok during the months that followed. It was used also as the chief organ of publicity for the Indian

independence movement in Siam.

(4) At the outset, at least, the Indian independence movement did not receive the unanimous support of all classes of Indians in Bangkok. An article published in the issue of February 12th., concludes with a complaint that the well-to-do classes of Indians in Bangkok had shown no interest in the work of the Indian Independence League and had kept themselves aloof. On the other hand, it is to be noted that the telegram addressed to the "Tokyo Independence Mission" on March 25th purported to be signed by the Presidents of the local branches of the Hindu Dharma Sabha, the Sikh Community and the Arya Samaj.

(5) Prior to the Conference held at Bangkok during the second half of June 1942, a delegation of some 60 Indian soldiers arrived in Bangkok from Malaya on February 17th: (see under March 4th in enclosure). This mission was headed by Captain Ram Sarup and by Captain Nazara Singh. The members of the mission were lodged on the premises of the Indian Independent League of Bangkok.

(6) Great publicity is given to the tragic fate which overtook Swami Satyanandapuri and his companions, who perished in an aeroplane accident on 24th March whilst on their way to Tokyo to attend an important conference there, and the memorial service held in their honour (see under April 20th) was on a scale which was evidently intended to elevate them to the rank of national heroes.

(7) The organisation of the Indian Independence Movement in East Asia is described in the text of a Trans-Ocean message from Bangkok dated Berlin June 26th. (See entry under date of June 27th). According to this message and a similar communication from Tokyo published on the authority of the "Asahi Shimbun" correspondent in Bangkok :–

(a) The headquarters of the movement will for the time being remain in Bangkok.

(b) Regional Headquarters will be established in various centres.

(c) Branches will be established in each city under the control of Regional Headquarters, which, in their turn, will be subject to the guidance and control of Bangkok.

(d) Regional Headquarters will appoint delegates to a Committee of Representatives. This body will sit in Bangkok and will be composed of 90 members, of whom 57 will be civil and 33 military representatives. This Committee, or Council, will function as a Parliament and will be the representative organ of the two million Indian residents in the Southern Regions". It will be the task of this Committee to work out concrete measures for the attainment of Indian Independence.

(e) Finally, the policies mapped out by the Committee will be submitted to the Supreme Council of the Indian Independence League, which shall consist of 5 members; including Mr. Rash Behari Bose. (It is stated in the *Bangkok Times* issue of July 2nd that this Supreme Council, which appears also to be called the "Council of Action", is composed of the following members :–

Rash Behari Bose, Captain Mohan Singh, N. Raghavan, K.P.K. Menon and Colonel C.Q. Gilani.

(8) The Movement will operate under the name of the Independence League (AZAD HIND SANGH) in conjunction with an Indian National Army which will be created under the command of Captain Mohan Singh.

(9) The role played by Subhas Chandra Bose from Berlin in relation to the direction of the Indian Independence League is not disclosed. He would appear to have no official position on the Council of Action, but see texts of telegrams addressed to him from Bangkok as reproduced in the enclosure under dates March 27th and July 22nd.

(10) The objects of the Indian Independence League are, according to an advertisement inviting membership first appearing in the *Bangkok Times* of July 9th, "to secure complete and immediate independence of India free of any foreign control or interference of whatever nature".

(11) As distinct from the Indian Independence League, there would appear to have been another and earlier organisation established in Bangkok, styled "The Indian National Council" and working for the same objects. In the title of the article printed in the *Bangkok Times* issue of April 14th, Debnath Das is described as "General-Secretary of the Indian National Council" while

under date of March 30th Swami Satyanandapuri was described as its Chairman. Again, in the issue of April 20th, the memorial service held in honour of the last named is reported to have been conducted under the joint auspices of Thai-Bharata Cultural Lodge, The Indian National Council and the Independent League of India. There is, however, no indication of the origin or functions of this body. Anti-British broadcasts from Siam reported in the *Bangkok Times* from time to time are described as being given "under the auspices of the Indian National Council". The latter is probably to be identified with the "Indian National Committee" mentioned under date of February 5th in the enclosure as having made a donation to the Nippon Red Cross Society. The possibility that the "Indian National Council and the Indian Independence League were originally rival organisations is suggested by a Notice to Indians published on December 19th in the *Bangkok Times* newspaper, which endeavours to give the lie to so-called false rumours, that there are two parties in Bangkok canvassing for the support of local Indians. A copy of the text of this notice is attached.

(12) Nothing has appeared in the *Bangkok Times* to suggest that the Indian Independence Movement has found any enthusiastic support in Siamese circles either official or unofficial. The Siamese Government was officially represented at the memorial service for Swami Satyanandapuri and his companions, of which so much seems to have been made both in Japan and Siam. A reception was given by the M.F.A. in honour of the delegates attending the Independence Conference (June 20th), while calls were made on the same Minister by Ras Behari Bose and other members of the Council of Action on the eve of their departure from Bangkok. On the whole, however, the attitude of the Siamese Government towards the movement may be said to have been perfunctory.

9. According to reports received from non-interned individuals amongst the allied nations resident in Bangkok, the Indian Independence Conference held in Bangkok was far from being the success it was advertised to be, owing to a failure to reach agreement on a working policy. One informant, who had an opportunity of talking with a delegate, was told that several had attended under compulsion,

having been pressed to do so by the Japanese military authorities in Singapore. Although there is no means of checking this statement, it may well be true. Moreover, it is interesting to note that, according to information received from another source, there were in Bangkok Indian troops interned as prisoners of war, who had either remained loyal to the Raj or were at least still being treated as enemies, since they were being forced to give their labour in the local Railway Workshops and on the Bangkok Harbour Extension Scheme. Finally, it is believed that, although Debnath Das was duly elected President of the Indian Independence League (Bangkok branch), there has been some difficulty in forming a local committee, which is yet another pointer to the lukewarmness of local Indian residents to the movement.

29

Major Himmat Singh Report on Development of Indian Independence Movement in South-East Asia with the Help of Japan; gives Assessment about Bangkok Conference

22 October, 1942

Sir,

I have the honour to submit report of my observations as regards the Bangkok Indian Independent Conference held at Bangkok on June the 10th 1942. As I was interned from the beginning of the war until repatriation this information was entirely gathered from the newspapers and from various Allied officials whom I met on the repatriationship. Among those I am most grateful to are His Norweign Majresty's Minister at Bangkok Mr. Hassell and his wife and also to the British Consul General at Bangkok. Some of the Indian repatriates have also given me some valuable information.

The development of organisation of the Indian Independence League Movement

2. The moment kept its activities underground although in fact it began one year prior to the war, when D.N. Das of Kobe visited Thai and with Swami Satyananda Puri established the first Thai-Japan Society, both in Bangkok and Kobe. Again just before the war. D.N. Das without the knowledge of the British authorities slipped out of Japan to Thai where he has remained since.
3. It was on February the end of this year that the Indian Independence

---

1. Foreign Department, File no. 313-X/1942, N.A.I.
2. Major Himmat Singh was the younger brother of the Nawab of Nawanrage. From 1930 onward he was Military Attache, British Embassy in Tokyo and carried on propaganda against the Indian nationalist in Japan.

League came out into the open showed their line of policy. First of all, on this occasion the League sent the following address to Field Marshal Plaek Khitasangka Pibulsonggram, the Thai Premier, on his declaring war on Britain and U.S.A.

"We feel happy to see that the Thai and Japanese nations are united together to face their common enemy. It is our earnest desire to see our motherland free from the British with the assistance of these nations."

4. When Malaya fell, this League became very active in inducting the captured Indian prisoners to become disloyal and join the so-called Indian National Army to fight the British. On February the 12th, 1942, according to the *Bangkok Times*, this was stated to number about 40,000.
5. It seems that the formation of the Indian National Army was first organised by a Captain Ram Sarup and Captain Hazara Singh who visited Bangkok on March the 4th 1942, with 60 other Indian army military prisoners. There is no doubt that several of the captured military officers and men of the Indian army have taken part in these anti-British activities by joining the Indian Independent League.
6. It is well known that the movement of the Indian Independent League in Bangkok was given full guidance by Rash Behari Boss and the Foreign Office of Japan; also by Subhas Chandra Bose and his forward Bloc in India, supported by the German Ambassador in Thai. The aims and objects are no doubt, similar to the resolutions passed by the preliminary Indian Independent League Conference held at the Sanno Hotel in Tokyo on March the 28th, 1942.
7. As delegates from the Indian Independent League, Swami Satyananda Puri, Sardar (Giani) Pritam Singh, Captain Akram and N. Iyer were flown from Thailand in order to attend this conference but the aeroplane containing them crashed near Nagoya Bay and they were said to have been drowned. It is interesting to know that the Indian repatriated from Shanghai on the "Tatuta Maru" were of the opinion that this was not an accident, but think that the four delegates were purposely got rid of by the Japanese. When asked what reasons the Japanese had for doing so, they replied that the Swami from Siam was a most powerful personality and did not approve of Japanese interference in gaining the Independence of India; also that he

strongly disagreed with Rash Behari Bose being made President of this conference as he considered Bose, who had been neutralised almost a decade ago, to be Japanese subject. Whether the Japanese really got rid of these leaders in order to have any interference with their programme one cannot say definitely, but there is no doubt that we could make good propaganda out of this incident. The British Consul General at Bangkok told me that the Swami was a great personality and Sanskrit and Buddhist scholar; and also a great friend of the Thai royal family in close touch with the highest official authorities in Thai. His influence with the Indians in Thai was so great that if he really opposed Japan in her policy he could have been a great obstacle to the Japanese in carrying out their policy as regards India. For Swami's record see Appendix no. under April 9th. Japan made a great fuss over the ceremonies of the last rites of these four drowned delegates. The Prime Ministers, General Tojo, attended the ceremony and read the obituary message.

8. The public speeches delivered at this conference in Bangkok are shown in Appendix No. 'A'.[2]

9. The Bangkok conference kept its resolutions most secret and therefore they are not yet known but the Minutes of the preliminary conference held at Sanno Hotel in Tokyo in March, obtained from loyal Indian subjects, clearly gives one an idea of what they might be. (See Appendix No. B) These resolution include :–

"Agenda 1. The attitude of the Indian regarding this war........."

"Agenda 2. Complete Independence of India

(i) Ideology of independence

(ii) Nature and time of Independence

Agenda 3. To spread independence movement to east to Asia and in India. Under Agenda 3 are details of policy which include :–

(i) method of propaganda and contacts with leaders in India.

(ii) Organisation of the League with the Council of Action.

(iii) administration. Departments include :–

(a) Foreign department or Liaison department

(b) Finance department

(c) Legal department

(d) Propaganda department

---

2. Not given here.

(e) Relief department

(f) Civil Police and Intelligence department

(g) Civil volunteers department

(iv) Indian National Army organisation which includes :–

(a) War department

(b) Recruiting department

(c) Military Intelligence and Military department

(d) Prisoners of War department followed by the method of military action against India by the so-called national army as under:–

(1) It is resolved that, if in the discretion of the council of action it is feasible to summon a meeting of representatives and take their advice on matter of the general Policy the Council shall do so.

(2) It is resolved that, before taking any military action against India, (including Ceylon) contrary to the wishes, policy or opinion of the Indian National Congress, the Council of action shall first get the approval of the committee of representatives and act as directed.

(3) We request that military action against India will be taken only by the Indian National Army and under the command of Indians, together with such military, Naval and air-cooperation and assistance as may be requested from the Japanese authorities by the council of action.

(v) Request to the Imperial Japanese Government. Six resolutions were passed as follows :–

(1) In further clarifications of the attitude of Japan towards India, the Imperial Japanese government be requested to make formal declaration to the effect that :–

(a) That Japan is willing and ready to give all possible help to India to sever its connection from the British Empire to attain complete independence.

(b) That on such reverence of India from the British Empire Japan would recognise the full sovereignty of India of India on attaining independence.

(c) That absolute independence of India would be guaranteed by the Imperial Japanese Government.

(d) That the Imperial Japanese Government of Japan would

recognise its influence with other powers and induce them to recognise the independence and sovereignty of India.

(f) That the framing of the future constitution of India will be left entirely to the representatives of the people of India.

II. The Imperial Japanese Government be further requested to render such financial help for the successful carrying out of our object as may be required from time to time on the distinct understanding that such help is to be treated as a loan to be repaid to the Japan by the National Government of Independent India, when it comes into being.

They should give all facilities for propaganda travel, transport and communications within the area under this control of the Imperial Japanese Government, in the manner and to the extent requested by the Council of Action also all facilities to come into contact with the National Leaders, the worker, and organisation in India. Also to clarify the position of Indian troops now under the control in occupied territories. To recognise and facilitate the use of the present National flag of India in all territories under the Imperial Government of Japan. Finally to consult in all matters of administration affecting the Indian community, the Indian independence Leagues of various places where these exist and in places where there are no branches, recognised leaders of community approved by the League branch nearest to such places.

(vi) Resolution re-interim work. See Appendix No. B.

10. Under Appendix B of this minute interesting items are :–

1. Specific instructions should be given to any troops attacking India to refrain themselves and to stop others from destroying places of worship belonging to the various religious bodies in order to avoid any sort of friction liable to be caused by such acts.
2. As soon as possible the property of the Indian Government and other rich Indians considered Pro-British including the Indian princess should be placed under the joint control and custody of the occupying Indian troops to avoid embezzlement or looting

etc. so that on expiration of the war the Indian Government may be in position to cover any expense incurred.

3. In all kinds of Government affairs, external or internal and the Indian religious leaders should not be consulted and their membership could never be taken in various states councils.
4. Able and patriotic volunteers should be enlisted from every part of East Asia including Shanghai, Hongkong, Java, Sumatra, etc. so that all can enjoy equal privilege in order that they also partake in serving their motherland.
5. In the war time just as women in all countries of the world are allowed to take full share in rendering their best service for the freedom of their respective countries, similarly Indian women are also anxious to fulfil their duties, every possible way for the freedom of our country. But under the British regime the women of India have not been given the same power and freedom which the men have been so far as a result of which women in India have not been allowed to take part in Government affairs. In order to raise them to the same discretion to take an active part in serving mother land even against the wishes of their parents, husbands, and other relatives supposed to be pro-British. Military training should be considered as compulsory part of education.

11. In conclusion I consider this Bangkok conference was a new and significant step taken by the Indians residing in the Far East, when they held at Bangkok the first general conference of the newly organised Indian Independence League at which Rash Behari Bose of Tokyo, head of the Asiatic section, presided.
12. According to the Japanese press more than 6,000 Indians attended and there were also present 100 delegates representing the 2 million Indians residing in the Japanese occupied areas. Among them, there were two representatives each from Japan, Hongkong, Maci, Manila, Borneo, French Indo-China, Java, Sumatra, and Shanghai, three from Thailand, four from Burma, six from Malaya, and one representative of the newly formed 'Indian Militia', Colonel Mohan Singh-a sikh, who is probably a deserter from the Indian Army,
13. The Conference elected a working committee of 36, among them a certain Raghava of Malaya and D. S. Pande (alians Deshpande) of Tokyo. Although their policy is to be kept secret, some of their aims are :-

(1) An immediate and full acquisition of Independence for India.
(2) Dissemination of propaganda throughout in India and East Asia.
(3) Appeal to Japan and other Axis powres for practival help.
(4) Formation of the Conference, messages of congratulation and promises for support were read from the Japanese Prime Minister, General Tojo, the Japanese Foreign Minister, Mr. Tojo, the Thai Prime Minister, Subhas Chandra Bose of Berlin, and other important personages in the Far East. In General Tojo's message, a definite promise was given that Japan would back the Indian Independence movement.

15. The most significant and note worthy fact in connection with this conference was that Japan and other Axis powers caused their Ambassadors and Ministers to attend the meeting in which these latter not only gave promises of the active support of their respective countries, but also made a clear and joint declaration to the effect that, while, both wish and are prepared to help India to obtain her independence, they have no territorial or other interests of any kind, in India. This new policy of soft-pedaling, however difficult to believe, may have some effect on the Indian politicians of the Forward Bloc and the other doubtful elements, but no effect whatsoever on any of the other political parties, who have seen Japan at work in China for the past 5 years. For Japan to have any success at all in this policy, it will be necessary for her to avoid attacking India and making a second China out of that country, since such an attack in whatever guise it is delivered, will tend to unite the Indians and curse them to oppose her on the side of the British.

16. The conference at Bangkok marks the end of the first stage and the beginning of the second, viz, that of anti-British activity on the part of Indians residing in the Far East. This means that they have reverted from the stage of underground organisation to that of open and positive action.

17. It should be stressed that the only way in which the movement started at the Bangkok conference can effectively make itself felt outside India, is timing its actions with a Japanese move into India. For this reason it would appear that the conference is in some way connected with Japan's next phase of operatoins, namely an advance into India, which, however, would produce a contrary reaction in India to that hoped for.

18. I had hoped to obtain a copy, of the secret resolutions passed at the Bangkok Conference from a person in Shanghai who attended the Bangkok Conference. This person was going to be repatriated on the "Tatuta Maru" but at the last moment the Japanese authorities got suspicious and stopped him from boarding the ship. However, it may be possible that these resolutions may be obtainable from other sources. It is believed however, that the Bangkok Conference elected a supreme executive committee with its headquarters at Bangkok.

30

Outline of the Propaganda Scheme of the Indian Independence League; Makes Special Reference to the Need for Fomenting anti-British Feelings Amongst the Overseas Indians and Mobolising their Support for the Liberation of India[1]

24 October, 1942

(I) The Object of Propaganda

The object of our Propaganda is to prepare India to overthrow the British rule and to establish Swaraj or self-rule.

(II) The Aims of Propaganda

In order to achieve this end quickly the propaganda had to be carried on keeping in mind the following aims :–

1. The creation, fomenting and strengthening of anti-British feeling among Indians
   (a) By pointing out the wrongs and misdeeds committed by the British in India.
   (b) By showing how the British were using the men and materials of India to serve their own selfish ends.
   (c) By drawing specific attention of the people to the inhuman cruelties, such as Jallianwala Bagh murder and other innumerable atrocities, committed by the British in India.
2. The rousing of national spirit and patriotism of the people to a high pitch
   (a) By dealing on their national virtues as a highly civilized people.
   (b) By recalling the brave deeds of their ancestors.

1. F. No. 101, I.N.A. Papers.

(c) By telling them the stories of the lives of their great men.

(d) By emphasising the fact that to Indians patriotism forms part of their religion.

3. There must be ceaseless endeavour to stir the people to action
   (a) By making them feel passionately proud of the past glory of India.
   (b) By creating great discontentment in their mind regarding their present humiliating position.
   (c) By inspiring them with faith in, and courage to make, their own destiny.
4. Try to convince them that there is no salvation for their country so long as even a shadow of British domination remains in India.
5. To instil confidence in their strength, ability and determination to bring about the revolution.
   (a) By telling them what their forefathers did during the war of Independence 1857.
   (b) By recalling to their mind the remarkable unity and enthusiasm manifested by the people during the non cooperation and Salt Satyagraha movements in recent times.
   (c) By taking parallel instances from the histories of other countries similarly placed such as America, Ireland, Turkey, Italy, and showing how they were able to overcome difficulties and attain their objective.
6. To impress on them the imperative necessity of taking full advantage of the present world situation to regain India's freedom:
   (a) Make them understand that England's difficulty is India's opportunity.
   (b) Britain is meeting with disaster in all theatres of war and her collapse is inevitable and certain.
   (c) If we do not act now, an opportunity like this might not occur again.
7. To draw an imaginative picture of a free India and show how she would be enjoying material prosperity, cultural amenities, political status and international prestige, commanding tremendous influence among the free nations of the world.
8. Incessantly deal on national unity and the great necessity for keeping the nation united to achieve its end. Tell them that 100 per cent unity would be impossible in any country. There is enough unity in India now. Whatever disunity that exists is the creation of the British Government and it would disappear when

that Government ceases to exist in India.

9. Any attempt by any party to enter into any sort of compromise with Britain should be promptly condemned
   (a) Let the people know how the British were ready to make promises when they were in difficulties and how they broke them when those difficulties were over. What happened during the last war and after.
   (b) Firmly assert we want independence now and not a promise for granting independence in future.
10. We have to seek the sympathy and support of other nations in our struggle. Our propaganda will be so formulated as to convince other nations the justice of our cause and to show that we deserve their help.
11. Tell the people the ways and means of achieving their end
   (a) By having recourse to strikes.
   (b) By terrorising the British Officials.
   (c) By refusing to cooperate with the Government in the administration.
   (d) By not rendering them any help in the prosecution of the present war.
   (e) By stirring up revolt.
   (f) By such other means intended to paralyse the British Government.
12. Make the people believe that in achieving the Independence of India we are not only liberating a great people from their thraldom of centuries, but we are also laying the foundation for world peace. Show that without the independence of India peace would be impossible in the world.

(III) The Means of Propaganda

Since the purpose of propaganda is to present an idea in the most attractive and effective way–possible so as to produce a desired opinion in the minds of the public we have to use all possible vehicles of expression by which the people could be reached. The means may be varied to suit special times, places or circumstances. But the following may generally be adopted for our purpose :–

(1) Radio
(2) Press
(3) Leaflets
(4) Books, pamphlets and booklets
(5) Pictures and cartoons

(6) Lectures

(7) Dramas and moving pictures.

(IV) The Methods of Propaganda

In utilising the means mentioned in Section-III we have to adopt varying methods to produce the desired result. But three things have to be borne in mind when we consider the method of propaganda generally :–

(a) How effective it can be

(b) How lasting it can be

(c) How extensive it can be.

Let us now take each of the meansf mentioned in Section III.

1. Radio: The only direct and effective propaganda that could be carried on in India from this part now is through the medium of the short—Swave stations yonan, ᴗangkok, Saigon, and Rangoon. Absolute care, caution and vigilance must be preserved in using these stations for independence propaganda. A radio network on a systematic basis has to be made which would pour out revolutionary fire in India.

(a) Care must be taken that as far as possible the programme of one station does not conflict with those of others. There is bound to be some overlapping. But this must be minimise.

(b) There must be perfect coordination of policy among the four stations. They may present the same point from different angles. But some of them should not express a view which would be contradicted by others.

(c) The listening public in India must not be judged by the number of Indians who own radio sets, since considerable groups of Indians listen-in-every private set and coffee shop set. While plenty of educated Indians welcome serious talks on current events and other topics the average India wants a racy programme in his own mother tongue. Political happenings must be explained to him in a manner which he would understand easily. The usual news service and commentaries should met by literal translations of the English.

(d) Persons who are in charge of these stations must be picked man actuated with revolutionary fire and high sense of patriotism, who would inspire enthusiasm among the members of the staff working under them.

(e) Programmes must be so arranged that entertainments and serious talks must take their proper places with a view to attract and retain the interest of the listeners.

(f) Officers in charge of these stations must carefully watch the programme of the important stations of the world and modify or change the programme of our stations, from time to time, to meet the changing circumstances.

(g) Only men absolutely essential to run a station efficiently should be taken. Keep the members down, but see that the men that you take are those who are prepared to work with conviction and purpose. Increase in number would make the administration rather cumbersome. For the smooth working of the station administration should be subordinate to programme.

In view of the restrictions imposed on the use of short wave sets in Malaya and other parts it is necessary to provide facilities to the listeners of medium sets by repeating the more important programmes connected with the Independence propaganda through the local stations, which would also set up loud speakers in important public places where they could listen in.

It is necessary to keep up the spirit and enthusiasm of the Indians of East Asia at a high pitch and this would be difficult if they are not sufficiently supplied with Indian news and are not provided with facilities to hear more important talks on Indian Independence.

The four short wave stations would be directly controlled by the Headquarters in such manner as the Member in charge may decide from time to time.

The Indian section of the medium wave stations will be run in consultation and cooperation with the Propaganda Department at each territory.

2. Press: The function of the press is

(a) To keep the people informed about the world events generally and events in India particularly.

(b) To rouse up their spirit and enthusiasm.

(c) To formulate and focus public opinion concerning Indian Independence.

For this purpose the press must be encouraged.

(i) To give plenty of Indian news of the right type.

(ii) To express their views boldly.

(iii) To give circulation to their papers widely. Now, restrictions are imposed on the circulation of papers. Some papers are not allowed to be circulated beyond their respective states. These

restrictions must be removed and all papers must freely circulated through the whole country.

This part of Propaganda is mainly intended for people in Malaya, Burma, East Indies and other places in East Asia living in their respective territories. It could not for obvious reasons help the propaganda in India. In each territory in East Asia there must be some papers in English and in more important Indian languages directly controlled by the Independent League while the policy of other papers owned and conducted by private individuals must be guided by the Independent League. The Indian Press in Syonan would be controlled by the Headquarters in such manner as the Member in charge may decide from time to time.

3. Leaflets: Small leaflets for throwing in India by bombers may be prepared. They must be very carefully done. Through them different classes of the people must be appealed to. They must be prepared in the more important languages of India and in English.

4. Books, pamphlets and booklets: These are mainly intended for the people in East Asia. Informative booklets and pamphlets in simple language dealing with the different aspects of Indian Independence must be printed and distributed in such languages as are necessary.

5. Pictures and cartoons: Even illiterate people could be attracted by this method of propaganda. The cartoons must be simple but attractive. Pictures drawn from history and current events showing. British attrocities and misdeeds may be specially useful.

6. Lectures: Specially trained speakers must carry on propaganda. Irresponsible and ill-equipped persons should not be allow to speak in the name of Independent Leagues. Every Leagues must have a list of such speakers.

7. Dramas and Moving Pictures: Wherever possible these also could be made useful for propaganda. There is enough talent in Malaya for dramatic entertainment. It only requires to be organised.

The Strategy of Propaganda

It is propaganda that prepares the soil for the growth of revolution. So it must precede any organisation for carrying out the revolution. The strategy consists in adopting the mode, net and means of propaganda to changing circumstances. The following hints may be noted in this connection : –

1. Events in India should be carefully observed and mass reaction on our propaganda noted. Misrepresentation of facts by the British will have to be corrected. Advantage should be taken of

Allied defeats to tell the people of their weakening powers. Any tendency to despair or to be despondent should be promptly checked.

2. The allied propaganda must be closely and continuously watched. Our propaganda Executives must think out and give directions so that opportunities are seized as they arise and new situations do not take us by surprise.
3. Japanese intentions regarding India must be tactfully handled. There is no use telling India that in offering to help her to gain her independence, Nippon actuated by altruistic motives and nothing else would not carry convictions to the minds of intelligence and practical men. Our propaganda must convince India that it is as much to our advantage as that of Japan to destroy British domination. Japan does not want India to be used by Britain as a Military and naval base against Japan. And India does not want British domination to be continued. So there is something in common between India and Japan. This common basis of their comradeship must be emphasized in all our propaganda.

(V) The Organisation for Propaganda : The member in charge of Propaganda of the Council of Action is responsible for entire control of Propaganda in the whole of East Asia. For purposes of Propaganda the whole of East Asia may be divided into following 10 territories :–

1. Philippines
2. Thailand
3. Malaya
4. Burma
5. Borneo and Calebes
6. Hong Kong, Canton & Macao
7. Indo-China
8. Java
9. Sumatra
10. Andamans

In each territory the propaganda activities will be guided and controlled by an officer called the Controller of Propaganda assisted by an Advisory Committee consisting of not more than six and not less than three members. The Member in Charge shall appoint a Controller for each territory who shall nominate the members of his Advisory Committee in

consultation with the Executive of the Territorial Committee. As far as possible the Controller of Propaganda must be a member of the Territorial Executive.

Each State or District within a territory shall have a State or District Controller of Propaganda through whom the Controller of Propaganda shall put into execution the policy and programme of Propaganda as laid down by the Member in charge of Propaganda. District and State Committees shall give all help and facilities to the State or District Controllers to carry out the instructions of the Controller of Propaganda and for this purpose shall constitute Propaganda Advisory Committee for their respective territories.

(VI) Propaganda in the Indian National Army

This may be divided under two heads :–

1. Propaganda among non-volunteers.
2. Propaganda among volunteers.

1. Propaganda among non-volunteers: The existence of a large number of non-volunteers may be due to one or other of the following reasons :–

(i) Either they have no faith in the movement or

(ii) They may be actuated by motives of self-interest such as fear of loss of pay or property or

(iii) Some of them might be sitting on the fence to see how things progress.

Propaganda among these must be carried on in such a manner as to counteract all these evils and to convert them into–enthusiastic supporters of the revolution.

The policy must be to win them over to the movement not by compulsion or coersion but by persuation. To take in men who are not convinced of the cause would weaken the movement. The propaganda to be carried on among them should be more or less on the lines specified in Section-II dealing with the Aims of Propaganda. But the following points may be noted in this connection.

1. Every unit must have its Propaganda Officer who should organise the propaganda work in his unit. There must be a man on whom the troops depend for the quantity and palatability of their political and educational rations.
2. No restriction is to be put on the men for expressing and discussing their problems frankly and clearing their doubts.
3. There must be quite a number of men with special knowledge on

political and kindered problems and who are willing and able to give talks and lead discussion groups in their units. To discover them and to utilise their talent is the business of the Propaganda Chief of the Army.

4. The services of civilians with special knowledge on any subjects could be requisitioned whenever necessary.
5. Some measure of compulsion would be necessary to make the troops attend the lectures. You cannot expect people, many of whom left schools years ago and left the habit of technique of learning, to attend the lectures without compulsion.
6. The Propaganda Officers will not only ascertain but stimulate educational demands in the army.

2. Propaganda among the Volunteers must be directed on the following lines :–

(a) To make them feel that they enjoy the proud privilege of being soldiers of liberty to free their motherland from the bondage of centuries.
(b) They have the strength and ability to achieve their end.
(c) They are the forerunners to the creation of a new India.
(d) To serve India at a time like this must be considered the highest end and aim of every Indian.

There must be separate propaganda for officers and for men. Propaganda among officers must be conducted with greater precision and thoroughness. The following points may be noted in this connection :–

1. The Officers are interested in questions of military strategy and policy, the other ranks are mainly–interested in general political problems.
2. It is no use telling them simply it is their job to fight. We have to tell the meaning and the background of the conflict and the purpose we have in view.
3. Special emphasis must be laid on the fact that only when our faculties are trained and our ambitions developed can we rise to our proper stature as free men.
4. Political education should be considered not as an isolated activity, but in general setting of the soldiers work, welfare and needs.

The Propaganda Officers of the Indian National Army must constantly keep in touch with the member in Charge of Propaganda and seek his advice and assistance in whatever manner required.

(VII) General Hints on Propaganda : It would be advantageous to keep in mind the following truisms in connection with propaganda generally :–

(a) 1. Military attack the body physically and crush it; Propaganda attacks the mind, ruins the morale and create within the enemy self-destructive emotion and eventually let the enemy destroy himself.

2. We must aim to wake up the mass mind of Indians and fill it with hope, faith and courage.

3. Always state the truth and then put the interpretation most favourable to support our cause.

4. The Propagandist must firmly believe in what he wants to convince others. He must hypnotise himself before he can mesmerise the public.

5. What we think strongly we generally accomplish because our sub-conscious thoughts tend to realise themselves. We have therefore to build up in our sub-conscious mind a great and overwhelming faith in our country's cause and ultimate victory.

(b) The following seven secrets of propaganda success are mentioned by a great authority on Propaganda :–

1. The first essential in propaganda is Repetition. In the short memory of the public lies the propagandist's greatest asset and his greatest handicap. The repetition carries with in no doubt the danger that the public may be bored and lose interest in the arguments advanced. But if the propagandist persists and secures a sufficient number of new "slants" to his appeal he is bound to impress certain section of the public.

2. The second essential of sound propaganda is colour. The average individual is not interested in abstractions; but he is intensely interested in facts and personalities. The propagandist should not try to force his arguments upon the public; but he should endeavour to influence them by reports that rouse sympathy for his own cause or antagonism towards his opponents. Such propaganda can be very effective; by stringing together a few incidents, for, the man in the street is always prone to argue from the particular to the general.

3. The third major principle of propaganda is that it should contain at least a kernel of truth. The most remarkable application of this principle in post-war years was the German campaign against Czechoslovakia between May and September 1938. The sudeten Germans notoriously suffered from grievances and

injustices, economic hardships and the non-fulfilment of pledges solemnly given when the Czechoslovakian State was formed.

4. The fourth principle of propaganda is that it should be built round a slogan. The slogan is the supreme illustration of the power of brevity in propaganda. The average modern reader does not go in for long closely reasoned, arguments. He had neither the time nor the inclination to digest them. His news is served up to him in short, bright articles, and the propagandist, to succeed, must follow the fashion of the times.
5. The fifth principle of propaganda is that it should be directed towards a specific objective. The application of the principle would involve a careful study of the habits and characteristics of the people sought to be served. To fire off propaganda bullets at random is a wasteful policy.
6. The sixth principle of propaganda is concealment of motive. Propaganda is a campaign camouflaging its origin, its motive, or both, conducted for the purpose of–obtaining a specific objective by manipulating public opinion. When propaganda is disguised the subject is more open to suggestion than would otherwise be.
7. Timing is the seventh principle of propaganda success. It is a recognised maxim of publicity that once the initial groundwork has been performed, a mass attack is the best possible method of launching a campaign. The propagandist has to display opportunism to reap the reward. It dictates the time at which propaganda should be released. Allied with this principle is the recognition of the value of reticence in a propaganda campaign. Frequently a propagandist will succeed by knowing, not when to speak, but when to keep silent. When his opponent has a powerful case, it merely plays into his hand by attempting on explanation. The proper course here is to lie low and wait for the public to forget, hastening that desired end by launching a counter-offensive on a totally different subject.

31

The Aims and Objects of the Indian National Army after its expansion by General Mohan Singh[1]

30 October, 1942

1. Object : The object of the Indian Independence League (of which the Indian National Army is a part) is to unite all Indians in Japanese occupied territory in the struggle for India's "Independence". It aims at a 100% membership and to this end all civilians are compelled to 'volunteer' for membership.

In March, 1942, a Conference was held in Tokyo which was attended by several of the more important members of the I.I.L. and the following resolutions were adopted :-

(a) "We are confident of the complete elimination of the British influence from Asia and of the rebirth of the new Asia, as well as of India after the war. We should accept General Tojo's generous offer of help and work in close co-operation with Japan to emancipate our country.

(b) Complete independence implies full freedom of action and thought without the least foreign interference or influence.

(c) Only Indian forces under Indian commanding officers will attack India.

2. The Conference placed the following demands before the Japanese Government:-

(a) Japan will recognize the Indian National Government after the elimination of the British one.

(b) Japan will guarantee complete independence to India.

(c) Japan will persuade other foreign. Government to recognize the Indian National Government.

---

1. F. No 601/7378/H.S.

(d) The Indian representatives will frame the future constitution of India.

(e) RASH BEHARI BOSE will be the President of the Council of Action.

3. The Conference gave the following undertaking :

(a) The Indian National Government would be responsible for the repayment of the loans which the Japanese Government will make in India's struggle for freedom.

Punjab Regiment. His second-in-Command was Captain "Mohan (Mohammed) Akram", (unidentified) who is believed to have been killed in an aeroplane crash.

Other identified personnel of the I.N.A. include :-

Lt. Col. G.Q. Gilani, Ist Bahawalpur Infantry.

Major Naranjan Singh Gill, 4/19 Hyderabad Regt., who made an anti British speech at the Bangkok Conference.

Major Mirza, Field Accounts Officer, who broadcast an anti-British speech from Saigon.

Jem Ram Sarup, 4/19 Hyderabad Regt: who organizes recruiting in Rangoon. In addition a number of men' suspected of being members of the I.N.A have been identified.

12 names of men known to be in the I.N.A. are unidentgified.

13. An unreliable statement by an I.N.A. agent gives the northern land routes used for infiltration into India as :-

(a) Monywa – Kaleva – Tamu Manipur
(b) Mandalay – Myitkyia (or Mogaung) – Naga Hills – Ledo
(c) Through China into Bhutan and Nepal and thence to India (improbable).

This agent states that route (b) was used by the first parties of 5th Columnists who came to India under cover of Indian refugees from Burma.

32

British Analysis and Reaction to the Activities of Indian National Army Directed Towards Indian Army[1]

6 November, 1942

1. No one knew anything about the I.N.A. before the fall of Singapore. It came like a bombshell after the capitulation. It seemed that the Japanese had made some pre-arrangements to tamper with the loyalty of the Indian Army. A man called Giani Pritam Singh had come to some understanding with the Japanese Embassy at Bangkok. He was secretly publishing posters and training 5th columnists before hostilities broke out. His understanding with the Japanese was that the Indian civilians should not be treated as enemy subjects and that Indian soldiers too should not be treated as enemies. He said that he complained to the Japanese that Indians have no enmity with Japan and the Indian soldier does not want to fight Japan. He is being misled by the English and made to fight for Rs. 14 per month. He was sure the Indians would not fight when his men told them not to do so. He met with varying success he said. He has since been killed in an air accident.
2. His methods were to send Indians right to the frontline and then shout to the Indian troops not to fire. The other method was to send the Indian prisoners back after treating and feeding them well, thus showing that the Japanese treat Indians very well. All the soldiers captured up country owing to the difficulty of terrain while withdrawing, he attributed to have deserted due to his propaganda. It is certain some people must have been influenced by this, especially near the end of the campaign when morale was low.

---

1. Military Department, File No. L/WS/1/1576, Indian Office Liberary and Records, London, (I.O.L.R.).

3. After the withdrawal from Jitra position, Capt. Mohan Singh of the 14th Punjab Regiment, was left behind and started working with the Japanese. It was he who brought the I.N.A. into existence. He is feeding it with his ideas and is influencing it with his personality. He has got no weakness in the form of greed, lust, drink, women, etc. as far as one can find out. At the time when [the Informer] left Singapore there was a general feeling among the officers, that right or wrong, one thing was certain, that Mohan Singh was sincere and not acting a part. His assistant when he came to Singapore after the surrender was Capt. I.J. Kiani of 5/2 Punjab.
4. Capt. Mohan Singh lectured to the 60,000 Indian troops assembled in Farrer Park and 90 per cent of them went wild with the idea of Indian Independence, and the National Army. They cheered Mohan Singh at the end of his speech most enthusiastically. Major Fujiwara decided to keep the Indian soldiers who surrendered in the general capitulation as P.W. for some time.
5. The inadequate supplies of food, the lack of medicine, the extremely brutal and barbarous treatment, the beating of officers and soldiers alike, set in a reaction. By April the Japanese were universally hated and the idea of I.N.A. had lost momentum. At the end of April Mohan Singh came back from Tokyo and started his propaganda lectures. After a few days, lists were asked from officers showing whether they elected to volunteer for I.N.A. or not. Along with it were implied threats by the Japanese that the non-volunteers would be badly treated and non-cooperative leaders even shot. These threats had their effect. It was evident that, not for love, but to avoid torture, many officers volunteered. At that time of indecision [Informer] although still under treatment for his wound, as outdoor patient, escaped as he had decided not to volunteer.
6. A few months after his escape [Informer] heard that in Burma, with the exception of a few officers, all had volunteered. The Japanese made capital out of the arrest of Mr Gandhi and Pandit Nehru which caused many people to go over to the I.N.A.
7. The idea of a National Army has a great attraction for the rank and file. If one thinks "From where do our recruits come?" It will be found that they are the same material and come from the same places where the Congress made frantic efforts to win over 'the rural population of India'. These seemingly inarticulate millions have in fact been made politically conscious to an appreciable degree by Congress propaganda. The modern recruit of the Indian Army is very different

to his predecessor of 1914-1918. Hence this lurking danger, this already prepared foundation for I.N.A.; is always there. A little real or imaginary grouse, a little subversive propaganda, and a reverse to the Allies have their hidden possibilities. This monster will not care to show its face till the last minute when prevention or cure may be impossible. This idea of I.N.A. will be exploited to extremes by the Japanese to make the Indian Army in India ineffective. They will use radio, secret agents, leaflets, promises and every other ingenious method to get at the sepoys and officers. They intend putting Indians (I.N.A.) against Indians (I.A.) and thus bank on their brotherly feeling which will make their loathe firing on each other.

8. Next, one thinks what is the remedy for all this. It is a terrific problem and all the suggestions here have been put down with a spirit of humility, that they may per chance do some good. Actually, one does not feel qualified to say anything on such a grave problem.

9. The most ideal solution of course is to have a National Government in India. That will nip all this idea of I.N.A. in the bud, and make the I.A. [Indian Army] impervious to any form of foreign propaganda. The government has made perhaps all efforts to come to some understanding with the Congress and if the Congress is not prepared to cooperate, then perhaps the remaining elements, who are cooperating sincerely may be helpful. The Japanese do not want India to come to an understanding with England. That is why they made super-human efforts to bomb India and Ceylon while Sir Stafford Cripps[2] was in India. They wanted to impress India with their might. They wanted to frighten India. If India comes to an understanding with England it will be a death blow to Japan.

10. The ideal perhaps is not attainable. A thing that struck one in Malaya was the tremendous power and influence of I.C.O.'s over the men. If the officers of some unit were prepared to volunteer then the whole unit would volunteer without hesitation and if the officers did not want to volunteer then the man and V.C.O.'s would also be disinclined. Hence if the I.C.O.'s wholehearted cooperation can be enlisted to combat this menace, then a great degree of success can be assured. Now the I.C.O.'s as a class have been labouring under

2. Sir Stafford Cripps (1889-1952) - British Statesman. During the War was ambassador to Moscow 1940-42, Minister of Aircraft production 1942-45. Was sent to India to negotiate with the Indian National leaders to solve the constitutional problems in 1942.

some imaginary or real grouses. The Indianisation Committee, 1939, looked into this matter and made some recommendations. Its report was never made public. Its recommendations were (i) throwing open all the I.A. to Indians, (ii) bringing back V.C.O.s into the Indianized battalions, (iii) and the basic rates of pay to be the same for all the officers (Indians not getting overseas allowance in India). The first two recommendations have been acted upon, if the third is also adopted it will make I.C.O.s happy and contented. Their feelings will reflect on the whole of the Indian Army. There is another type of grouse on which bitter comments are sometimes heard–"The complete, reluctance of the B.G.Rs to salute I.C.Os". These are little things but sometimes they assume great proportions in people's minds.

11. The other remedy is propaganda. Let the I.A. know what the Occupied Countries are like under Japan, how the Japanese treat the conquered peoples, their atrocities, greed and ambition to role the whole of Asia. Radio and press are very useful for propaganda, but nothing can better a talk from a living man, where the audience can ask questions and the personality of the speaker can impress the listeners.

33

Mahabir Singh Dhillon's Escape from Burma; his Interrogation by the British Provided Detailed information about the Indian National Army to them[1]

11 November, 1942

1. In forwarding Major M.S. Dhillon's diary of events while in Japanese hands, the following note on his attitude is added for the information of the D.M.I.
2. During interrogation Major Dhillon has shown the utmost anxiety to give us information detrimental to the Japanese. He conveys the impression that he is entirely out to help us.
   He is politically minded and is, in my opinion, pro-Congress (he describes this as "Nationalistic" which is presumably the Indian National Army's name for the same attitude).
   Reading between the lines of the account, it seems probable that he has been of use to the Japanese during the past eight months.
   He is much impressed with the Japanese fighting spirit and their determination to spare no trouble and expense to get things done quickly. He does not think much of their equipment however.
3. Three points which struck me as suspicious are :
   (a) He was anxious to send his signet ring by an agent to Hav. Udai Singh, who was promoted by the Japanese and given charge of one of the fifth column camps in Rangoon. He claimed that Udai Singh would send us valuable information. The latter is now at Kalewa.
   (b) He appeared to think that we were not enthusiastic about this idea and suggested that a radio message enquiring about Udai

1. Military Department, File No. L/WS/1/1576, IO.L.R.

Singh's welfare would inform Udai Singh that the Dhillon was safe.

(c) Dhillon is not married. He had trouble with his family over refusal to marry in his own caste. He wanted to marry a girl outside it. This might loosen his ties with India and single him out as a man whom the Japanese might expect to return to them.

4. In my opinion, Major Dhillon is uncertain in his own mind as to his future attitude.

5. It will depend a good deal on our attitude towards him. He is clever and potentially very useful to us. He might cause dissension in the I.N.A. through propaganda. It remains for decision whether we are to trust him or not. Half measures would be useless, he is much too clever to be taken in by eyewash.

Major Mahabir Singh Dhillon, R.I.A.S.C.

Unit-22 Bde. Tpt. Ccy.

Captured at Singapore on the 16th February, 1942

Took part in Malaya Campaign as Comdr. 11th Div. Amn. Coy. From Jitra to Johore Bharu. Johore Bharu-Singapore as L. of C. Tpt. Coy.

Original plan to escape immediately after the General Surrender together with Major A.N. Weinman (A.I.R.O.) miscarried due to the four sons of the civilian through whose agency the steamer was to be obtained not having been released from the Volunteers.

17th February, 1942: On this date all Indian and British troops were separated. The Indians collected at Farrer Park. Lt. Col. Hunt handed them over to the Japanese on behalf of the British Government. Major Fujiwara, the Japanese Intelligence Officer took them over on behalf of the Japanese Government. Col. Hunt then left the parade and Major Fujiwara made a speech. He read out Premier Tojo's declaration about the Japanese desire to seek an Independent India, and handed over the Indian prisoners to Capt. Mohan Singh C.O., I.N.A. Fujiwara's speech was translated into English by 2nd Lt. Kunizuka. Lt. Col. Gill was told to interpret it into Hindustani. Gill made it perfectly clear both before, during and at the end of the speech, that he had been told to translate and what he said was not his own personal view. Capt. Mohan Singh then made a stirring, emotional and anti-British speech, at the end of which there was great excitement and wild cheering. The Officers' lines were quiet, but the troops appeared to be deeply move. Mohan Singh announced the creation of the I.N.A. and told the men that they were not prisoners. This emotional display worried Gill and me considerably. In the evening Mohan Singh asked me to go and live with him and help him administer this huge

force. I tactfully declined to do so. With the others I went to Neesoon Camp on the 18th February. Life there became difficult owing to volunteers coming in and delivering lecture. Discipline was getting bad, and for the first time I began to wonder if my refusal to live with Mohan Singh was a wise step. Living with him I might have prevented quite a lot of trouble to other Prisoners of war. Gill also thought the same. Therefore, I was sent to Mohan Singh's H.Q. as the Prisoners' Representative on the 25th February, 1942. It was not difficult for me to persuade Mohan Singh to send out a letter saying that the I.N.A. and Prisoners of War were two quite different organisations, and that volunteers should not live with the Prisoners of War also that there should be no political lectures. Gill wanted this point settled. I have no doubt that for the time being, this broke the backbone of the I.N.A. With the help of Gill and Mehtab we were also able to organise the food and medical services. Rations had to be collected from all over Singapore, and there was a great shortage of medicines, which had to be collected from various dumps with the Japanese assistance. Gill also did everything possible to get the water supply functioning. We also arranged for a wider distribution of our men in order to avoid overcrowding and disease.

25th February, 1942. Sent to H.Q., I.N.A. (Capt. Mohan Singh) as Prisoners of War Liaison Officer.

28th February, 1942. Taken by the Japanese to Saigon together with Lt. Col. N.S. Gill.[2]

Route followed : by air – Singapore to Bangkok. 3 days to Bangkok.

In Bangkok taken to Col. Tamura, Japanese Military Attache. Introduced to Baba Amar Singh, Master Bhagwan Singh, Swami Satyananda Puri and Das. Also met Lt. Ito (Pilot) who was Liaison Officer for Indians in Bangkok and worked with the Japanese Military Attache. By air-Bangkok-Saigon.

We were told that the German Military Attache will also be flying in the same place as us, and that we were not to speak to him. For this reason we were provided with "Mufti".

Saigon. Stayed three days. Met only one Japanese Lt. Col. and one Major. They came to the house where we were accommodated. We found Capt. Ehsan Qadar, 5/2 Punjab, Sub. Shangara Singh 5/14 Punjab, Hav. Shiv Singh 5/2 Punjab, there for wireless propaganda.

5th March, 1942. Returned to Singapore and found Captain Mohd. Akram 1/14 P.R. living with Captain Mohan Singh. The former appeared

---

2. See Statement of Gill at S.No. 43.

to wield great influence on the letter, and they shared a room. My place as Prisoners' Rep. had been taken by Major K.S. Mehtab, R.I.A.D. I found a definite feeling of hostility towards me at H.Q. I.N.A. Apparently influences had been at work in my absence. Mohan Singh also warned me that the Japanese disliked me. He refused to return me to the Camp. For this reason I shifted to another house with Mehtab, giving the excuse that Mohan Singh's house was overcrowded.

15th March, 1942, Mohan Singh went to Tokyo to attend the Tokyo Indian Independence Conference. He took with him Lt. Col. N.S. Gill and Capt. Mohd. Akram and the civilians whose names are noted in the margin. A few days later we heard that the plane carrying Capt. Mohd. Akram, Ayer and Swami Satyananda Puri of Bangkok had crashed into the sea just before reaching Japan.

I had access to a radio set in Mohan Singh's house and used to collect all news, especially from Delhi and London. Thus, on two occasions I read over to the Officers in the Camps to keep them informed of world events and to prevent mental inertia. This was construed as propaganda against the Japanese and the I.N.A. and I was forbidden to use the radio set. Hostility towards me in the Japanese and I.N.A. quarters increased. In fact, I was told afterwards that I might have been shot if it had not been due to a definite request of Mohan Singh that no harm must befall me in his absence.

25th April, 1942. Tokyo party returned. I.N.A. and Japanese poison Mohan Singh against me, so much so that Mohan Singh actually avoided me.

26th April, 1942. The Japanese warn Gill that he will have to go to Bangkok. The excuse given was that he was to unite the two Indian parties there, namely the Indian National Council and the Indian Independence League. He was told that he could take me and another Officer. He selected Capt. S.M. Hessian 4/19, Hyderabad. The real reason was that before forming the I.N.A. they wanted Gill and me out of Singapore as they thought our presence would harm their movement.

27th April, 1942. Fujiwara and Capt. Mohan Singh delivered a propaganda lecture to all Officers including V.C.O.'s Gill, on my advice, refused to speak. After this lecture Gill spoke confidentially to about 20 Officers Gist of his talk was : "I have tried to serve the Indian Soldiers to the best of my ability, in an administrative capacity. I am convinced that the Japanese want to exploit the Indian Soldiers for their own purposes.

I am no longer able to serve you. I am being separated from the troops and sent to Bangkok against my wishes.

I may be exploited personally. Remember that I do not represent you now.

He also spoke to the Officers including V.C.O.'s of 4/19 Hy.

28th April, 1942. Gill, self and Hussian, with Japanese Officer, left Singapore by car, stopped en route at Kuala Lumpur and Penang. Caught the Bangkok train from Hadoyai. Reached Bangkok on the 5th May, 1942.

5th May to 1st September. At Bangkok. Our second plan to escape was made here. Got into touch with a local Indian for guides into Burma. The difficulty was to get out of Bangkok without the knowledge of the Japanese. It was eventually decided to say that Gill was not keeping well, therefore, a fortnight's change of air at Hua Hin a seaside resort not far from Bangkok was contemplated. From there the escape was to be carried out. By now the date for Bangkok Indian Independence Conference was fixed, and it was decided that perhaps the best time to escape would be after the Conference, when some useful information as regarding the Conference would be available. About the middle of June Mohan Singh and party arrived at Bangkok to attend the Independence Conference. Mohan Singh first told Gill that I could not attend the Conference, as I was not a Volunteer, but later changed his mind and told me to attend, mainly because Gill and I were so well known in Bangkok that the absence of either of us from the Conference would create suspicion. After the Conference Mohan Singh wanted to take Gill and me to Singapore. Fortunately there was only one seat in the plane and that he took himself. Gill and I stayed behind though Mohan Singh had left instructions for us to move by rail.

Our second plan to escape was formulated and amended whilst Mohan Singh was still at Bangkok. Colonel Iwakuro, the Japanese Officer after whom the Dept. that deals with Indian questions in East Asia is named, sent for Colonel Gill towards the end of July, 1942. He offered to place him in charge of the Indian Intelligence Service in and outside East Asia. This Gill refused to do. The next day he asked Gill if he would accept to run an Indian Contact organisation with his H.Q. in Rangoon. Gill promised to consider this proposal. He and I discussed this question and we agreed that here was an excellent opportunity to make good our escape with all the political information which we collected before, during and after the Bangkok Conference. Iwakuro asked that his conversation with Gill be kept secret from Mohan Singh on the I.N.A. and Bose of the Independence League. It was fully realised that this Contact Scheme, from the Japanese point of view, was no more and no less than espionage pure and simple. This appeared the only way to escape, but the idea was

so repugnant (although this would have enabled us to completely deceive the Japanese) that Gill and I could not bring ourselves to accept Iwakuro's proposal.

A few days after his return to Singapore, Mohan Singh had a telegram sent to Gill to report to Singapore at once. I was able to persuade Gill to leave me behind at Bangkok, because I did not want to get involved with the I.N.A. Even my silent presence there would have been harmful. I also strongly advised Gill not to deliver any lecture etc. at Singapore, and if compelled to do so to try and get out of it somehow. The idea was that the Prisoners of War must not get the false impression that Gill was in the I.N.A. Gill was at Singapore for 10 days, and whilst he was still there the arrests of Gandhi, Nehru and Azad took place. This roused the Indian people of East Asia against the British. It also helped the I.N.A. to draw into their fold quite a lot of waverers.

Gill and I then decided it was absolutely necessary for one of us, if not both, to escape to India with full information, and to contact the Government of India without delay. With that in view it was decided to accept Iwauro's Indian Contact offer. Mohan Singh sent 20 men to Gill for this scheme. Gill selected the Officers, namely, myself, Tehl Singh 1/8 Punjab, J.B.S. Grewal 5/2 Punjab and Bakhtawar Singh (I.E.). These Officers were specially selected by Gill because they had difficulties with the I.N.A. All these came to Bangkok.

We left Bangkok on the 1st September, 1942 by air in three or four parties, and one party went by rail to Singapore and thence by sea to Rangoon. After reaching Rangoon on about the 10th Gill decided to take Tehl Singh and Grewal into his confidence about the escape plan. We decided that three forward posts be established, one at Mityaha, one at Kalewa and one at Akyab. Grewal was to go to Mitkyaha, myself to Kalewa and Hav. Shiv Singh 5/2nd to Akyab. Most of our men we could trust but Hav. Shiv Singh we suspected as a spy of Mohan Singh certainly, if not of the Japanese. We therefore arranged that Shiv Singh should go to Akyab and the pro-Japanese element must be sent through him. Both Grewal and I were to go to our respective posts at Mitkyaha and Kalewa, and to reconnoitre the routes to the nearest British post. It was agreed that we were to send Gill a code telegram, as follows :

"Routes 1st. class. Very good"

(a) This meant "you can come here even with Japanese escort, if they will not let you come alone. I can manage to get you over the border".

"Routes 2nd class. Good"

(b) This meant "I can get you over the border, but you must not come with a Japanese escort"
"Routes 3rd class. Bad"

(c) This meant "Things are very difficult and I cannot get you across under any conditions".

The message was to be handed over to the nearest Japanese W.T. for onward despatch to Gill through Iwakuro Kikan, Rangoon.

Gill was to send a party of four each to Grewal and me, followed by a second party. He himself was to come last with the balance of his organisation. This would have meant that in about 3 weeks to a month, all our men would have come to India. The men were not to be taken into confidence at Rangoon, but our Forward Post Comdrs. were permitted to tell them the plan if they considered there was no risk of the Japanese getting to know our scheme.

Grewal and I left Rangoon on the 19th September, 1942, by rail. We reached Mandalay on night 20/21st. We crossed the river by a country boat and reached Sagain on the 22nd. We spent the night at the station and left for Monyma early next morning, reaching Monywa in the afternoon. At Monywa I went to the Sikh temple and there saw Capt. Pritam Singh 3/16th, who I had left for Bangkok. I told Pritam Singh that he need not worry and that I will get him over the frontier as soon as possible. Unfortunately no steamer for Kalewa was available till the 3rd October, and we had to wait at Monywa from 23rd September to the 3rd October. On the 3rd October we were provided transport in a Japanese convoy which was conveying Col. Koba's Regt. H.Q. and a B. to Kalewa. The journey took 9 days and we reached Kalewa on the 11th. The delay was due to the unwillingness of Indians employed to run these steamers and to want of proper fuel. The steamers are being run on firewood instead of coal. This necessitates frequent stops for refuelling and firewood is not always dry.

Colonel Koba knew that I was connected with Iwakuro Kikan. He was most helpful. On reaching Kalewa I decided to go as far forward up the river Chindwin as possible in order to be as far away as possible from Japanese troops, so that Gill's escape could be arranged.

When I told Koba that I would establish my H.Q. at Mowlaik or Kindat he wanted to send a Japanese escort with me. I was able to dissuade him from this course by saying that the presence of a Japanese escort would arouse suspicion of British Agents, who might report our location to their Government.

I left Kalewa on the 12th and reached Kindat on the 15th October. On the 18th October, I sent Capt. Pritam Singh with the first party whose previous instructions, which they had received from the Japanese in Rangoon, I cancelled, and whom I told to accompany Pritam Singh. On the 20th October Bakhtawar Singh reached Kindat from Rangoon. I then had to decide quickly. There was no doubt that the Japanese would not left Gill escape, nor would they let me escape. Luckily for me no Japanese troops were where I was, and I had two courses open to me :

(a) To stay at Kindat and get in touch with Gill again.

(b) To leave Kindat and escape with as many men as possible. I decided against course (a) and for course, (b) due to the following reasons :

  (1) It would have taken me at least 6 weeks to get in touch with Gill and to get a reply from him.

  (2) The Japanese were sending troops up the Chindwin and a party of 20 had already arrived at Massein. If I did not clear out of Kindat almost at once they might arrive any day at Kinda and make my escape most difficult.

  (3) Knowing the Japanese mind I was certain that there was no hope of Gill being permitted to leave Rangoon once the Japanese had refused to let him do so.

  (4) I had valuable information which I could have sent by say 2 Lt. Bakhtawar Singh to India, but only Gill and I personally knew all the Japanese, Indian and some German personalities in East Asia, and it was necessary for Gill and me to come over to this country to convey the information to the Government of India. Gill obviously could not come and so I had to do so.

The Japanese were apparently getting suspicious of Gill and me and therefore there was a great risk of them breaking up the organisation and thus preventing any one of us escaping.

I left Kindat by boat on the 21st and reached Autong on the 22nd. I left Auktong on the 23rd and following an elephant trail reached 2 M.S. on Sittang-Tamu road. I halted the night there and on the 24th reached M.S. 22 halted there for the night and next day, i.e., 25th reached Tamu and got into touch with the nearest Bde. H.Q.

34

Rash Behari Bose to Col. Iwakuro Requesting him to get Formal Acceptance of Bangkok Resolutions by the Imperial Japanese Government; Hints Towards the Emergence of Differences in Council of Action[1]

28 November, 1942

Sir,

In further reverting to the enclosed (copy of the letter sent to you and subsequently withdrawn) we have again the honour to place before you the imperative necessity of receiving a formal assurance from the Imperial Government as to which portion of the Resolutions passed at the Bangkok Conference has been adopted without qualifications or change by the Imperial Government, which portion has not been approved, and which portion has received approval subject to alterations. We have had in the past few months certain reasons for anxieties and if we have to be true to the great trust that has been placed in us not only you but by the Indian Public in East Asia, we cannot remain any more without requesting you to be kind enough to forward the enclosed letter to the Imperial Government and vouchsafe to us a reply from them as requested.

In this our request, we fully hope that you, who have personally watched and understood our Movement, will accord to us your sympathy and support.

If a reply is forthcoming at this earliest possible opportunity, it will considerably facilitate the further work and progress of this Movement. Though this letter is being sent to you formally, we shall, if so required,

---

1. I.I.L. Papers; File no. 45/3, For the attitude of the Impenial Japanese Government policy towards the Bangkok Resutionols see the official publication *S.C. Bose and Japan, Tokyo*, 1956, pp. 78-82.

be pleased to wait on you at any time, and at a mutual conference have further discussions with your good self. We hope, however, that you will be good enough to act upon this letter immediately as it is our considered opinion that a reply from the Imperial Government is urgently required for the work, which is now awaiting our attention.

Thanking you in anticipation,

Enclosure

Indian Independence League,

Syonan,

29th November, 1942

Rash Behari Bose to Colonel H. Iwakuro,

Chief of the Iwakuro Kikan,

For favour of Transmission to the Imperial Government of Japan.

The Council of Action had a series of sittings recently when it took stock of the whole situation concerning the Indian Independence Movement in East Asia and the development of the revolutionary struggle in India. The enormous increase in the number of members in the Independence League, the wide network of League Organisations throughout East Asia, the tremendous enthusiasm seen everywhere for the cause which we stand for and the spirit of sacrifice manifested by all classes of Indians in East Asia have given us immense satisfaction in the progress of the Movement made possible by the help and cooperation of the Imperial Nipponese Government. The rapid march of revolutionary events in India resulting in the growing number of strikes, rebellions, sabotage and other mass actions have further raised our hopes and leave us in no doubt regarding the intentions and determination of our countrymen to overthrow British rule and to regain our independence at any cost. We have now reached a stage at which we feel that before we take any further forward move, it is necessary to clear matters, to understand our position perfectly and to cement Indo-Japanese friendship without which it is impossible for us to do any effective work for the attainment of our objective.

We are unfortunately so placed that we have not so far been able to contact with leaders in India and ascertain their views regarding our policy and our own plans. This makes our responsibility all the more sacred and onerous. The time would not be distant when we shall have to deal with a Provisional National Government in India and when that comes, we must be in a position to convince them that we have taken every possible step to maintain the safety, dignity, and integrity of our country when once our goal of independence has been reached.

We have, therefore, after very careful consideration, come to the conclusion that it will be advantageous and in the interest of our Movement to request the Imperial Government of Japan to favour us with a reply at the earliest possible opportunity, clarifying the position on the following points:

1. A copy of the Bangkok Resolutions has been forwarded to the Imperial Government so long ago as the 22nd July, 2602. Though we have been working on the basis that such resolutions would be accepted by the Imperial Government, we are not yet in a position to know exactly where we stand with regard to these resolutions. We do not want to conceal the fact that anonymous enquiries are still being made by many leading members of our community regarding these resolutions and we find it difficult and even embarrassing to give them a satisfactory reply. It is, therefore, of urgent importance to us to request the Imperial Government to be good enough to inform us, formally and at the earliest possible opportunity, regarding the acceptance of the Bangkok Resolutions and if there is any resolution to which the Imperial Government cannot give their support, we shall be glad if they would kindly define their attitude towards the same.
2. Recognition of the Council of Action as the Supreme Executive of the Indian Independence Movement in East Asia and the acceptance of their status as such is absolutely necessary in order that the Council of Action may function efficiently.
3. The Imperial Government must no doubt be aware of the propaganda that is being carried on by the British Government in India regarding the intentions of Japan, Although we had some declarations from His Excellency Premier General Tojo and other leading statesmen of Japan to the effect that Japan has no political or military ambitions in India, we would respectfully suggest that a full, formal and solemn declaration binding on the present and future Government of Japan regarding the intentions of Japan to recognise and support the absolute independence and full sovereignty of India immediately on the removal of British rule in India, is found essential to instill complete confidence and to place the Movement on an effective and proper footing.
4. As a corollary to the acceptance of the Bangkok Resolutions, it is necessary that the formation and existence of the Indian

National Army on the principles laid down in the said resolution will be formally and publicly recognised and all facilities offered for its expansion with a view to make the army a strong and efficient one to carry out the great purpose for which it is intended.

We are conscious of and profoundly grateful to the Imperial Government of Japan for the great help they are rendering to Indians in connection with the Movement and with further support, which we have no doubt will be forthcoming, we shall be able to attain our goal of independence in the immediate future.

35

Minutes of the Meeting between General Mohan Singh and Colonal Iwakuro for Resolving the Confidence Crisis between Indian National Army and Japanese Authorities on the one hand and between Indian National Army and Indian Independence League on the other[1]

2 December, 1942

Colonal Iwakuro was not in his usual happy and cheerful mood. He looked depressed. He said "I am very sorry that mutual dissatisfaction and suspicion has started and we have started thinking in these terms. I am sorry that your side has taken this attitude. I never said this a Japanese puppet movement on the contrary I have the firm conviction that this is entirely an Indian show and we are trying our utmost to help and support this glorious attempt. But I cannot understand why you have taken this drastic step. After very thoughtful deliveration we have come to this conclusion that it is of no use to continue this movement in the present prevailing atmosphere. It is much better to stop it. I entirely leave it to you to do anything you think fit and those of you who don't think it advisable to continue any further they can go back to their previous tages, i.e., the prisoners of war. Do as you please we want's impede in any way. It is very tragic that my genuine efforts have gone in vain. I am feeling very lonely and depressed. I feel I have been betrayed by my own beloved son. Visualising the whole thing I clearly see the fundamental differences of two different character.

I am very sorry that this sort of stage has arisen. This movement was a child of my dreams. All my energies were devoted day and night to bring about the successful realization of those dreams. I never started

1. Indian Independence League Papers. F. No. 45/3.

it to be ended in such a abrupt manner. It will be a tragedy from my view point if this mightly fabric fails before fulfilling the cause for which it was raised for. The Council of Action after careful deliberation and thoughtful consideration drafted the letter requesting a reply to the Bangkok resolutions. We also consider all possible reaction from your side and were prepared for all eventualities. The letter was discussed in detail yesterday in concurrence with you and it is extremely regrettable that we went back dissatisfied by the unaccommodating welcome given by you. The Japanese side should also be blamed for this.

Gen. On our return from Tokyo Major Fujiwara told us that Tokyo resolutions were accepted in principle but subsequently you told us the contrary and latter on as regards Bangkok resolutions you gave us some vague promises which never materialized. Naturally we had to become suspicious. Now we thought that time has come when we should exactly know where we stand.

Col. after Bangkok resolutions I tried my best to get the formal reply for you but unfortunately there were so many constitutional difficulties that it was impossible to get the requested reply, but at the same time our Govt. decided to give the practical shape to the various resolutions.

At such a critical moment, when Mahatma Gandhi is engaged in life and death struggle for the emancipation of India from the British yoke it is regrettable that this suspicious atmosphere has started. You are ignoring the practical application and just worrying for a mere scrap of paper.

Gen. We Indians are very accommodating. We always trust people and this has been our national character and in fact our present plight is the direct outcome of our placing too much trust in the British at one time or another. We have been repeatedly betrayed and cheated and that's why we have developed a suspicious nature. As individual's we are prepared to trust you and several other Japanese friends but our national trust is a very sacred trust and much above mere individual trusts and I am afraid we are not satisfied what we have heared or seen so far in this respect from the Japanese side.

Col. I am still trying my best to assist you in every possible way and I am sending these M.Ps to Japan with a personal message. I am also forwarding some special instructions in this matter. I have been preparing these papers for the last two months. It may be our last interview but I would like to show you my views forwarded to my government for kind consideration.

Salient Points of the Letter Forwarded

1. Japanese should fully help in satisfying the burning desire of patriotic Indians for complete independence.
2. Japan should try to bring about friendly relation between Indian and herself, i.e., the spirit of goodwill and good neighbourhood.
3. Japan should not force the Indians to join any sphere politically, economically, militarily an culturally.
4. Japan must respect the territorial integrity and full sovereignty of India.
5. All treatment should be on equal basis and under mutual understanding.
6. Japan should not aspire for new interest in India beyond already existing before the war.
7. All Indian property to be handed over to the Indian government soon after the occupation.
8. On the request of the Indian people Japan should give all technical advise and assistance.
9. Japan should not interfere in any of Indian internal affairs and all occupied territories should be immediately handed over to the Congress or Indian Independence League.
10. In case of external invasion on India's request, Japan should give all possible help. Defence of India should entirely be left in the hands of the I.N.A.

While the British are still there, the Japanese will fight the British and utilise the aerodromes, landing grounds and other strategical points.

I have been working day and night writing so many training pamphlets for the I.N.A. and it is a great tragedy to stop this now at this stage. I feel that you have let me down and betrayed.

Gen. It is none of my business to advise the Japanese Govt. but I must say Japan will make a great blunder if she invade India before absolutely clarifying her status and position. India has been fighting the British for the last 150 years with all possible means and methods at her disposal and she will continue to fight Japan till she has attained her one and one objective, i.e., complete independence. India has seen many invaders and history proves that all of them met their final end on the same side. Today India is politically awakened and she can never be subjugated. A free, strong and friendly India not only be a great asset to Japan but will also contribute for the peace, property and deliverance of

Japan but will also contribute for the peace, property and deliverance of mankind.

Col. I love my country as you love yours and quite agree with you. It is equally bad for my country to invade India with any selfish intentións. In Manchuria we have been quite true to our declarations, because we declare all five races should equally benefit by the new order. Prince Konoi's promises are still carried to the last word. (China)

Gen. Before we started this movement we knew your policy in Manchuria and China. We have been seen your ways in Malaya and heard about Burma and this is the reason that we are very careful about our commitments. Our only hope was that Japan will be wise enough to adopt a different policy in different territories. We cannot tolerate these types of government in our country, so before taking any further step we want definite assurances.

Col. I quite agree with you, India's question is a separate question and I am trying my best to request the Premier to issue a clear and formal declaration. Please understand the Japanese viewpoint; we are absolutely ready to cooperate wholeheartedly.

Gen. I will talk the whole matter with my colleague in the light of what you told me just now. Till then I am not in a position to say anything on this major issue.

Col. This Burma incident has caused great misunderstanding which was all enacted in heart tamper. Mr. Yutani is a strong supporter of Indian cause and he fully understands Indian problems and Indian character.

Gen. I beg to differ. Col. Kitabe is a soldier and head of Iwakuru Kikan in Burma and he should not have been influenced by Mr. Yutani. In fact Mr. Yutani himself said and more over I don't agree that Mr. Yutani has the foggiest idea about Indian character and Indian problems. He might have come across some labour and cooly classes of Indians or he might have associated with some rich ignorant Indians. It is only today that I have received a letter from Mr. Prashad written by Mr. Yutani ordering him to dismiss two gentlemen working in his office and employ some one else. I don't think you will appreciate if this thing is done to you by some one and yet you say that he is very pro-Indian and helping the Indian cause. I would like to point out that Mr. Deshpande who has been brought up, educated and married in Japan and who was a staunch supporter and admirer of Japanese people is at all satisfy with the whole show after working for the last few months. He is trying his utmost to get away from this movement as soon as circumstances will permit him to leave this force.

36

Minutes of the meeting between General Mohan Singh and Major Fujiwara Regarding the Arrest of N.S. Gill; Refers to Mohan Singh's Requests to Japanese Authorities to Meet Gill to Find out about the Desertion of M.S. Dhillon and other Persons of Indian National Army on Burma Front[1]

8 December, 1942

Major Fujiwara started with apologies that such an incident has happened at this time and he hoped that the G.O.C. has not taken seriously. He asked G.O.C. whether he could suspect Col. Gill G.O.C.'s replied–"Nothing doing–Not at all". He went on to explain the charges against Col. Gill. Col. Gill has been watched right from the beginning and that they were sure that he had a complete network of British spies in and out of the I.N.A. That he during March selected 6 trusted officers to convey to the British Govt. India what was happening in the Far East. Out of the 6, 2, had succeeded in crossing the border and the remainder about Col. Gill's activities. In Tokyo Major Fujiwara was warned not to trust Col. Gill by some of the Indians there to whom Col. Gill had told telephone some one that this movement was nothing and that he was definitely pro-British. However Col. Gill played so well with me (Major Fujiwara) that he had no suspicion whatsoever that Col. Gill was a British espionage agent. Col. Gill requested Major Fujiwara to make him the C-in-C and G.O.C. (Mohan Singh) was nothing. Major Fujiwara said he had already given his word and he will never divert but he said that I promised him that you will be a useful partner.

During this time Mr. Senda interrupted now and then on other matters like :–

1. Indian Independence League Papers. F. No. 45/3 .

1. Do not doubt the Japanese sincerity.
2. There were technical difficulties re-clarification.
3. The announcement was not made because of strategic reasons.
4. The Japanese C-in-C has already sent circular to the Japanese to treat Indians as comrades in arms, etc. You have a sincere and open heart and now must not crush this movement.

To these G.O.C. replied suitably in this manner :–

1. From the very beginning I came and started these activities with complete sincerity.
2. After the Bangkok Conference the formation of the I.N.A. was done in full trust.
3. Now I am honour bound to safeguard the interest of the men under me so that they may not be exploited and for this and several other reasons have taken this step.
4. Individuals do not matter and I am prepared to take all the blame.

To these Mr. Senda nodded and agreed that whatever you (G.O.C.) have done you have done in full sincerity and he wished that as soon as the matter is clarified the movement will flourish.

After this the G.O.C. began :–

What has happened is not unexpected by our side.

We were ready for this show. Re: Col. Gill I cannot believe and will not that he is working for the British. From my close association and the work he has done for me I have not the slightest doubt.

This incident can be looked at by a disinterested person in the following lights :–

(a) That I have called Col. Gill from Burma and have handed him over to the Japanese for my own personal.
(b) That you believe that the present deadlock has been created by Col. Gill and to get rid of him you taken him away.
(c) To separate him from me during this juncture.

Under all these circumstances my position become awkward. As I have told you that not one Gill or one Mohan or one Bose but Hundreds may have to be sacrificed to achieve our goal. I do not matter. It will be the greatest blot on me not to take the responsibility. I have done all these and I stand by all my actions. May I ask a few questions Re: Gill again :–

Q. Can I meet the 6 parachutist that landed in Pegu?
A. Impossible. They are under the charge of M.P.
Q. Can I meet the Officers despatched by Col. Gill?

A. I think it is not possible.
Q. Can you name these officers?
A. Yes, I shall give you detailed news after I get from the M.P.
Q. Can I see Col. Gill now and then?
A. As the M.P. have full powers it is not possible but after the investigation I think it will be possible.
Q. Can you tell me the approximate dates of the arrest of the Officers and when they crossed the border?
A. During Aug. but I am not certain.

The G.O.C. then said that "this step taken in my view by the Japanese was entirely wrong and it does not good to the Japanese. It was a wrong move yet it was expected by me. The proper thing would have been that you should have sounded me about this earlier and that would not have been so bad. All the san.. I am of the opinion that you have taken him away, for no reasons except stated before. I only regret that you are entirely wrongly informed and your move is wrong. It was I who brought about his deadlock, sincerely tool, and I should have been arrested.

I have to fight hard against my conscious and imagination to believe Major Fujiwara's story about Gill, because in 1939 after the outbreak of the European War certain officers (Sikhs) planned to capture Punjab. I was in it. We decided to put up the claim of Maharaja of Patiala and one senior officer amongst us took the scheme to Col. Gill at Army Headquarters at Simla. Col. Gill kept that secret to this date. He advised us to wait as it was not the proper time. There can be no other better proofs of his sincerity towards India. Then Mr. Senda remarked that as Col. Gill's way of living was completely Anglicised his personal opinion is that he might like the British because he had achieved highest possible post for an Indian in the Army. He was of the opinion that quite unknowing Gill was pro-British.

To this G.O.C. said, I don't agree with you because most of us army officers lived like and amongst the British yet we could never change hearts. Whatever it is. Gill is or never was pro-British. Some of us might have liked their ways but not their rule.

Major Fujiwara then requested the G.O.C. to call on Col. Iwakuro and inform him about our meeting.

G.O.C. replied that he cannot do this till he can make up his mind.

away, for no reasons except stated before. I only regret that you are entirely wrongly informed and your move is wrong. It was I who brought about his deadlock, sincerely tool, and I should have been arrested.

I have to fight hard against my conscious and imagination to believe Major Fujiwara's story about Gill, because in 1939 after the outbreak of the European War certain officers (Sikhs) planned to capture Punjab. I was in it. We decided to put up the claim of Maharaja of Patiala and one senior officer amongst us took the scheme to Col. Gill at Army Headquarters at Simla. Col. Gill kept that secret to this date. He advised us to wait as it was not the proper time. There can be no other better proofs of his sincerity towards India. Then Mr. Senda remarked that as Col. Gill's way of living was completely Anglicised his personal opinion is that he might like the British because he had achieved highest possible post for an Indian in the Army. He was of the opinion that quite unknowing Gill was pro-British.

To this G.O.C. said, I don't agree with you because most of us army officers lived like and amongst the British yet we could never change hearts. Whatever it is. Gill is or never was pro-British. Some of us might have liked their ways but not their rule.

Major Fujiwara then requested the G.O.C. to call on Col. Iwakuro and inform him about our meeting.

G.O.C. replied that he cannot do this till he can make up his mind.

37

Statement by Rash Behari Bose, President Council of Action Regarding the Crisis between Indian National Army and Indian Independence League; Requests Indians in East Asia to Continue Struggle for Indian Independence[1]

10 December, 1942

My colleagues of the Council of Action have resigned. The Constitution to that extent has broken down and, on behalf of the Indians, in East Asia, I, as President, have decided to carry on, pending the election of other members which can be done according to our Constitution only by the members of the Committee of Representatives from the various territories of the East Asia. In exercising all the powers and duties of the Council of Action, which consequent on the resignation of my colleagues, have vested in me, I believe I am interpreting the Constitution of our Movement in the most politically sound way and thus respecting the mandate of the Indians of East Asia given to me at the Conference held at Bangkok in June this year. I have, from the 9th of December onwards, taken control of the Movement and I once again pledge to serve the cause of Indian Independence without fear and without favour, loyally and conscientiously and to the utmost of my ability. I shall endeavour my very best to interpret the conscience of our people, and give effect to their wishes and dictates. I shall not, as far as humanly possible, allow anything, however powerful it may be, to come between us and our objective, namely the absolute Independence of India, free from any foreign control domination, interference or even influence of any nature. In taking over control, I know and fully believe, that what I have done—to save the Movement for Indian Independence from collapse—will meet with the approval of my countrymen wherever they may be.

---

1. I.I.L Papers F. No. 45/3.

As with many of my countrymen, the cause of Indian Independence has always been nearest to my heart. For that I had been striving my utmost to pave the way for the liberation of our Motherland. It was not only liberation from the British yoke that I wanted, but liberation from any yoke whatsoever. There was a time when even the people of Nippon, among whom I lived, viewed the question of Indian Independence with indifference. But I strove on, and today I believe that we have succeeded in securing their sympathy and support an—international asset of no mean importance for any nation to have at the present juncture and for the future. We have secured the sympathy of other nations as well. It would have broken my heart if at this moment I had let this Movement die because some of my colleagues took it into their heads that unless on every point they had their way they could not go on. On the other hand, I believe, that if there are difficulties in the Movement, they can and shall be rectified. If there are doubts and fears, they can and will be cleared. If there be even obstruction in our path, it is my firm conviction that those should be removed and the way made clear for achieving our object, the much-longed-for and long awaited Independence of Hindustan. The co-operation or otherwise of any Nation, however, valuable it may, be, is not a rock on which the ship of Indian Independence should founder. We shall fight our battles with such help if possible, but without it if necessary.

The Indian Independence Movement was, as is well known, being carried on even prior to the War. But the declaration of War and of the Japanese attitude towards Indian Independence outlined in the statement of His Excellency Premier General Tojo made it possible to work this Movement in the various committees in the East Asia openly and without hindrance. The Movement was started even prior to the Bangkok Conference. We have been carrying it on now for nearly a year. At Bangkok we were given by the delegates assembled there a definite mandate to carry it on, and as a result of that mandate more organisations, both civil and military, were established. We were making progress. Very recently my colleagues felt that some further clarification of our position was necessary for us to work the Movement. With that view I was in complete accord. Where some of us differed was in the contention that without such clarification–and that forthwith–the Movement could not and ought not to proceed. Thus arose a deadlock. In my negotiations for clarification which started immediately on our deciding in the third week of last month to secure such clarification, I found that some time was necessary to obtain results. I therefore advised the Council that we should

give a little time, that having carried on the Movement all these months, it would not cause much harm, danger or hardship by carrying it on for a few weeks more in the same manner as we had been doing, and thet if at the end of our negotiations, we could not get satisfactory arrangements made, we were entitled to consider and change out policy if necessary. It required a little patience and a good deal of perserence. I felt happy when after discussions amongst ourselves, on the 4th of December, It was agreed that matters should be left for further negotiations and for report by the end of next month. On the 5th of December, however, for no apparent reason, I was informed that some of my colleagues again changed their minds and the decision arried at on the previous day was not to be acted upon. It was them that I realised there was more in the Move than what appeared on the surface. Immediately on such realisation I began my fight against the Move, against the creation of a deadlock, against the break up of our Movement and disruption of our work. I pleaded with my colleagues not to resign and precipitate crisis and a deadlock which would result in hardship, misunderstanding and unhappiness, and may ultimately damage our cause. I assured them that I was as jealous of our rights as they were. My stay in a foreign country has not made me any the less a patriot than other sons of India, but has only intensified my attachment and affection to my Motherland.

My colleagues resigned on the 8th of December, I have given deep consideration to their letters of resignation. I am of the view that they should not have resigned without consulting the representatives from the various countries in East Asia. I am of opinion also that it was not necessary for them to have resigned at all, as some of them appeared to have done, for the solution of the matters raised by them. But they are their own best judges and so I have accepted their resignations with regret. Since I am confident that the Movement can be carried on for India's and India's benefit only, and all outstanding questions solved to our satisfaction, I have taken upon myself to continue the Movement with the support and co-operation of the Indians in East Asia. While on the one hand I shall be carrying on with our work, I shall, on the other hand, also spare no pains to negotiate and secure for the Movement every facility and support for which my colleagues and I have all the while been asking. At the earliest opportunity I shall be reporting to my countrymen, the progress that I shall be making. In the meantime the work will go on, and name on the civil side or the military side of the Movement need entertain the slightest fear. There shall be as little upsets as possible. The Movement shall be carried on as heretobefore. I shall endeavour to

put into it as we go along even deeper enthusiasm and more vigorous activity. I must assure every branch of the League and also the Indian National Army that my taking over on myself the rights, duties and responsibilities of the Council of Action need not in any manner mean changes in the Constitution, Organisation or development, of the civil and military Institutions that we have endeavoured to create, nurse and nurture during the last few months. I guarantee to them that I shall not be a party to any act that will jeopardise their interests or the interests of our Motherland. These interests have always formed my sole objective in the work that I have undertaken to myself

I know I have the trust and confidence of my brothers and sisters in the arduous work ahead. If my opponents call me a puppet, let them do so. But let me assure them, that they are sinning against a man whose only end and aim in life is to see his country free, absolutely free and Independent, who is as proud of his birthright as any Indian alive, and who has staked his all and who will stake the last drop of his blood in upholding the honour and integrity of Hindustan. I seek nothing from life except the success of our mission. If once it is accomplished I shall retire into seclusion in some nook or corner of our beautiful Homeland. The full and complete Independence of Hindustan is our objective and let no differences, personal or otherwise, cloud or obstruct the issue. I appeal to my countrymen, to continue to render to me and to this Movement their generous support and co-operation in abundant measure, without which nothing can be accomplished, but with which, I have complete confidence, we shall carry on our fight to its successful termination–the attainment of India's Independence.

38

General Mohan Singh to Rash Behari Bose challenging his Statement; Expresses his Unwillingness to Cooperate with the Japanese under the Present Circumstances[1]

13 December, 1942

I am in receipt of your letter of the 12th instant, I maintain that with the resignation of the four members of the Council of Action you have no authority to assume any of the powers you claim in your letter.

In the preliminary conference held at Tokyo and again at the Conference at Bangkok we were most anxious that no one individual should have dictatorial powers. We frustrated all attempts in this direction. The outcome of these conferences was the creation of a Council of Action and the limiting of the powers of the President to only giving effect to its decisions, you are now striving to invoke the constitution to do the very mischief that we took so many precautions to avoid.

We are all faced with a grave situation. All the members of the Council of Action save you have resigned. Rule 12 of the constitution provides how the vacancies of the Council of Action should be filled up, and until such vacancies are filled up in the manner stated therein you cannot arbitrarily assume all the powers and functions of the Council of Action. You may be the sole surviving member but you cannot act for the whole Council specially in view of Rule 19 of the constitution which lays down "the Council of Action shall have collective responsibility. If you do, you do it at your own risk.

It is apparent from your correspondence that you are not only totally ignorant of anything pertaining to an army but have some foolish and misguided notions about it. Let me put down a few facts concerning the Indian National Army which may help to clear your mind.

(a) The members of the Indian National Army are pledged to me and

1. I.I.L. Papers; F. No. 45/3,

me alone by name and I am pledged to safeguard the honour and dignity of the I.N.A. We form one indivisible whole. It was raised and trained for an honourable cause; that of securing the unfettered independence of India and not to satisfy the passing whims and fancies of any particulars individual.

(b) This army will only be part of any movement if it is convinced that that movement is conducted in the interests of India. It has been found necessary under the circumstances in which the army was raised and trained to depart from normal practice and keep the officers informed of the trend of political events. They are fully aware of the position you have played and the manner in which you have played it. There is nothing but disgust and contempt for you. In fight any person or persons for the attainment of its goal.

The events of the last few weeks, however, have convinced us that, under the existing circumstances, we cannot usefully serve our motherland through the Independence League in East Asia and we have accordingly thought it fit to sever our connection with it.

I have had the opportunity to come across the false and malicious reports including your statement issued on the 10th instant "To the Indian patriots of East Asia" concerning our resignations. They constitute a deliberate attempt to misinform and mislead the public as to the true facts. The varsions given are all of your own manufacture and one-sided. I am most anxious that the public should be acquionted with the true facts in order to ensure that their patriotism should not be exploited by unscrupulous people wishing to serve their own selfish ends.

I therefore challenge you to face the public at a meeting at which I shall take the opportunity to present the facts to them and let them decide the correct standpoint for themselves. If you do not call such a meeting forthwith I will be compelled to issue a statement placing all the facts before the public.

The above letter has not been written to contest or disprove the position you hold for yourself in your imagination. You to me have only been the sole surviving member of a defunct Council of Action since the resignation of the others. It is merely written as a courtesy and to avoid future unnecessary instructions by you to the Army. Needless to say that if you still persist in writing anything it will not be answered.

2. The text of the pledge was "I will be an unconditional volunteer for the Indian National Army under General Mohan Singh, which will fight for the liberation of India".

39

Secret Orders of Mohan Singh for Dissolution of Indian National Army in the Event of his Arrest by Japanese Military Authorities[1]

21 December, 1942

The Indian National Army will be dissolved shortly. It is with deep regret and great reluctance that this decision has been arrived at. Circumstances have arisen under which it is impossible for the Indian National Army to forge ahead to achieve its goal, i.e., the complete Independence of India without any foreign control, influence or interference.

I thank all ranks of the Indian National Army for their loyal and enthusiastic support in this great undertaking. Though we have not been able to achieve our final object, the movement has not been in vain. It has inculcated in us a true national spirit. It has brought a degree of unity among us unknown in the past, and it has shown to us and to the world at large what we are capable of, if only we are left to ourselves.

All the members of the Indian National Army are welded into a patriotic group. We were and are prepared for supreme sacrifices. It is up to everyone to ensure that those sacrifices are directed in one and only one direction–the achievement of our goal of independence. Let us never forget that we are not concerned with ourselves alone. We have at stake that great and beautiful land of ours with its 400 millions—our brothers and sisters. To her freedom we are wedded. I, therefore, appeal to you all to continue demonstrating that solidarity that you have so admirably manifested before. I know you will now and always continue to do so. Remember our strength is in our unity and our life is for our country.

---

1. I.I.L. Papers; File no. 45/3, This special order was to come into effect as soon as General Mohan Singh was separated from the I.N.A.

A confirmatory order will be sent out as soon as arrangements, with the Nipponese are complete. In the event of my being separated from you before such an order is issued, the dissolution will take place automatically and immediately. Also at the same time, the resignation of all members of the Indian National Army and their release from all obligations and undertakings to me and the Indian National Army will be taken for granted.

India First and India Last.

Long Live India.

40

Statement by Rash Behari Bose Supporting Japanese Policy and Condemning Mohan Singh for his Non-cooperation; gives Details about the Crisis between the Indian Independence League and the Indian National Army; Defends Japanese Policy[1]

27 December, 1942

It has been my desire for sometime to clear the existing misunderstanding between the Indian National Army and the Indian Independence League, but unfortunately, owing to the extremely heavy pressure of work I have not been able to express my views in public though I did manage to talk to the military officers and some civilian officials of the League. Later I wish to speak before a mass meeting on the whole issue but for the present, wish to circulate this statement for your immediate information.

It is a known fact that our Motherland has been exploited and looted by the British for the last two centuries and during the period thousands of our patriots and leaders have sacrificed their lives for the emancipation of Hindustan. Even today thousands of our brethren in India are being murdered daily. This is the reason that not only in India, but all over the world every Indian is clamouring for the freedom of India. Remember the words of our leader Mahatma Ji "Do or Die."

It is about thirty years ago that I threw a bomb at the Viceroy and as I was an active member of the Lahore—Delhi and Benares conspiracies, I had to leave my country and to seek foreign help. With the aid of Germany I was able to send home two ship loads of arms and ammunition but unfortunately they were confiscated before reaching India. What was

---

1. F. No. 311/I.N.A. Papers. The statement was published by the I.I.L. Headquarters, Singapore under the litle "Our struggle" by Rash Behari Bose and was widely distributed amongst the members.

the motive behind this all? Freedom of my country, which is very dear to me. I feel confident that everyone of you have the same love for the freedom of our fair land if not more. As for me I have forsaken everything–life, wealth, relatives and all other things which were dear to me for the sake of our country. The British offered thousands of rupees as a reward for my head. They succeeded in persuading the Japanese Government, through their ambassador to hand me over to them, and I was ordered by the Japanese Government to leave Japan within five days, but fortunately some of my Japanese friends concealed me in their house and there I lived in obsecurity for seven years. Had the British been successful in taking me back to India I would have been killed long ago. That is why I have great belief in the Almighty God who has helped me and guided me all through these pertious years and I hope He will not forsake me in this sacred work, which you have placed on my shoulders by electing me as the President of the Council of Action at the Bangkok Conference. I shall see that our mission does not fail, and the trust put in me faithfully carried out.

Comrades: Let me tell you that we in the Far East shall soon join hands with our brethren at home and shall create such a revolution in India that we will achieve our most cherished purpose—complete freedom of India. He reads to die as free men rather than to live as slaves. The time has passed for India to stay under a foreign power. India must be free during this struggle. India would have been free long ago if we had been in possession of arms and ammunition. History tells us that many nations have fought their battles with foreign help. In our struggle for Independence, the more the Congress fought with non-violence methods the more brutal became the methods of the British. For this reason I worked in Japan with a view to asking for help when the occasion arises. I am glad to tell you that my work and labour of last thirty years has borne fruit.

On the outbreak of the Greater East Asia War I interviewed the minister of Home Affairs and other important officials of various departments, as well as members of the General staff in our struggle for freedom and I was promised such support and cooperation in our struggle for freedom and I was promised such support I can assure that in Japan you will find a true and sympathising friend. She has very clear intention about the independence of India. The help she is offering to the Indians is not because she wants to dominate India but because the enemies of India are also her enemies, and, therefore, cooperation and unity between the two peoples is essential. I can tell you that Japan will not rest until

the last soldier of Anglo-Saxon race is removed from India, she is determined to destroy British-American influence in Asia. So why should we not grasp this God send opportunity and fight for the complete freedom of India?

Before I go any further I want to say very clearly that the Indian Independence Movement is ours and ours alone which has been specifically formed to fight for the independence of India. Remember this Movement is neither of the Japanese people nor of their Government. They have nothing whatsoever to do with it except that they have offered all their help for the defeat of the common foe, for which we are indeed grateful. But suppose a time were to come when we begin to receive not sufficient help or say nothing at all, are we to give up our Movement? The answer is No. The Movement must continue until our country is completely free from any kind of foreign domination or influence. It is our Movement, our struggle and we alone shall have to decide its fate. It is therefore imperative for every true son of India who loves freedom to join this Movement with heart and soul and move forward with complete determination until our independence is achieved. You will have to face several drawbacks, discouragements difficulties and obstructions in the attempt but you should not be disheartened as you have shouldered a most sacred cause and have become the custodians of four hundred millions of India. You should therefore see that this Movement is not used by anyone for any other purpose, except the gaining of Indian Independence. It is equally the duty of every one of us to be ready to crush any opposition or die in the attempt. Remember that at the declaration of the Greater East Asia War this Movement was at full swing in Japan, Shanghai, Canton and Bangkok. The Indian Independence League was established by me in Japan in 1924. As I was perfectly aware of the position of Indians during and after the war I had a clear understanding with the Japanese Government on this matter and it was through this process that Major Fujiwara asked for the cooperation of Indian patriots and our late beloved Sardar Pritam Singh took a major part in the pageant of the Malai campaign. Captain Mohan Singh joined hands with Sardar Pritam Singh on 12th December, 1941, with a party of a few persons. Sardar Pritam Singh being a civilian and Major Fujiwara being a Japanese Officer, did not know very much about the Indian soldiers and officers so the administration and command of Indian military personnel was given over to Capt. Mohan Singh. It was desired to teach to them nationalism, patriotism and love for freedom and to prepare them for struggle for the freedom of India, I realised that the organisation of

the Independence Movement in East Asia was not merely my affair but the concern of my countrymen residing there. It was for this reason that arranged for the Conference of some of the leaders in East Asia including military officers, which was held at Tokyo in March last year. The fundamental principles of this Movement were laid down at that Conference. Subsequently at the Bangkok Conference I received the mandate of our countrymen in East Asia to carry on this Movement in the best way possible. Nobody can ever doubt that considerable progress has been made in the great work we have undertaken and in which Capt. Mohan Singh played a major part. There are great possibilities of our succeeding at attaining our objective. The Bangkok Conference was held in June last year and certain resolutions were passed for the guidance and working of the Movement. In accordance with these resolutions a Council of Action was elected as the Supreme Executive Body of the Movement.

Prior to election, Mr. Mohan Singh in his speech made statements which now appear to be misrepresentation of facts because he solemnly gave us to understand that the majority of the Indian Army personnel were prepared to join this Movement without any threat or force and that they had acclaimed him as their military leader. I was horrified at a later date to learn of the atrocities meted out to officers and men of the Indian Army for which the blame naturally falls on Capt. Mohan Singh. Many of our poor brethren were shot while many were tortured, humiliated or sent to concentration camp and thus by sheer threat and violence he demoralised the majority of officers and men and compelled them to become volunteers, which is against our principle. I for one will be the last man to see my countrymen shot in cold blood. This is what we are fighting for against the British and I personally cannot afford to see Indians tortured in this manner.

In accordance with the resolutions of the Bangkok Conference Indian National Army is a part of the Indian Independence League and every officer and man of the I.N.A. is a member of the Indian Independence League and owes allegiance to the League. It must be understood that an army is an army of a country and not of an individual so it was wrong of I.N.A. personal to give allegiance to an individual without raising an objection. I was under the impression that the whole I.N.A. was well aware of resolution because an Officer was purposely sent down as a representative of Mr. Mohan Singh to explain in details the resolutions to Army which I understand he did from camp to camp. Not only that I am further given to understand that on return of Mr. Mohan Singh a few

conferences were held at his bungalow and the position was clarified to the officers who later join the I.N.A.

I however was being informed of the situation in Syonan and I felt it desirable to hold a meeting of the Council of Action in Bangkok but unfortunately the members could not come for some reason or the other, and under the circumstances I was forced to come to Syonan for discussion.

There was however, at any moment, any divergence of opinion on the broad principles along which this Movement should continue, nor, were there any difference of opinion as to the necessity of obtaining sufficient assurances from the Imperial Government of Japan regarding their acceptance of the basic principles enunciated at the Bangkok Conference. The reply to the Bangkok resolutions which was delivered to us dated the 10th July was not so satisfactory. I was in agreement with my colleagues that a further clarification of the Imperial Government's attitude towards the resolutions adopted at the Bangkok Conference was desirable. On 5th of September 1942, a letter was addressed to Colonel Iwakuro requesting that the Imperial Government should give us a more specific reply to the Bangkok Resolutions. On receipt of this letter, Col. Iwakuro intimated to me that such a request to the Imperial Government might be misconstrued and lead to a good deal of misunderstanding and suggested that the letter should be withdrawn. An emergency meeting of the Council of Action was held on 7th September at which all members were present except Mr. Raghavan. The meeting decided to withdraw the letter which was done accordingly.

This matter again came up for a good deal of discussion in the meetings of the Council of Action during the latter part of November. The necessity for requesting a further clarification of the Imperial Government's attitude on these important issues was found essential. We, therefore, formulated our proposals and submitted them in Col. Iwakuro for transmission to the Imperial Government of Japan, and at a joint conference we explained to Colonel Iwakuro the necessity of giving us more formal assurances than we had had up till then. Although the discussion with Col. Iwakuro did not give us full satisfaction, I pleaded with my colleagues in the Council of Action that they should give me time to enable me to take up these important issues with the Imperial Government of Tokyo. On the 20th of November, the Council of Action had already decided that my colleague, Sri N. Raghavan, and I should visit Tokyo if need be and take up these important matters directly with the Tokyo Government.

In the latter part of November, it came to light that Mr. Mohan Singh as G.O.C. of the I.N.A. had arranged with the Iwakuro Kikan for the transport of some I.N.A. troops to Burma for purposes of training. An advance party was sent by the G.O.C. to Rangoon without the consent of the Council of Action. Naturally the Council of Action wished to know about the move to greater detail and was not prepared to sanction movement of troops without its knowledge. During the discussions in the Council of Action, Mr. Mohan Singh, for the first time since the Bangkok Conference placed before the Council the state of affairs existing in the Army. It was then that the Council of Action, was in a position to realise that if the Indian National Army was to become a strong and efficient fighting force for the purpose of achievement of our freedom, a radical change in the existing organisation was absolutely necessary. It is perhaps essential to state here the reasons why I, as President, Council of Action, left all questions relating to the Indian National Army in the hands of Mr. Mohan Singh. I was of the opinion before these facts became known to us that it would be better to entrust the organisation of the I.N.A. in the hands of our G.O.C. and to give him that confidence which he said, was essential for him to carry on the great task. I therefore refrained from interfering with the work of the G.O.C. in the belief that the latter would, in turn, keep the Council completely informed of the position of the Indian National Army from time to time. There have been ample opportunities for the G.O.C. to appraise the Council during its sittings in September and October of all the difficulties which he was facing in relation to the organisation and expansion of the I.N.A. but unfortunately in these matters either no information or very meagre information was supplied to the Council of Action.

I regret to have to say that in matters connected with the I.N.A. the G.O.C. arrived at important decisions without reference to the Council of Action. In fact the Council was kept almost in darkness with regard to various important activities of the I.N.A.—a state of affairs which we tried to rectify. I thought it was vitally important that the Council of Action should immediately take control of the policy regarding the Army and all questions of major importance should be decided by the Council and not by the G.O.C. I had to write to Col. Iwakuro to that effect so that no further mistakes would be committed.

Because of all this muddle which could have been avoided Mr. Raghavan, who was all the time advocating better coordination between the Army and the Council, resigned. I asked him to withdraw his resignation as matters were now getting better. On the 4th December, at

my request, the members of the Council agreed to give me time till the end of January, 1943, to enable me to obtain full and satisfactory assurances from the Japanese Government. I was glad that I was given further time to attempt at a solution of those difficult questions before my colleagues resigned.

The next morning, that is on 5th December, I was surprised, therefore, to hear from Mr. Mohan Singh, Col. Gilliani and Shri K.P. Menon that notwithstanding the previous day's decision, they were not prepared to carry on the Movement unless an assurance was immediately given that a reply to Bangkok resolutions in detail would be obtained on or before 1st January, 1943. As far as I know, there was no one in Malai capable of giving such an assurance. Moreover it was virtually an ultimatum to the Japanese Government which would have offended them. I then realised that an attempt was being made to obstruct the solving of the questions in issue in order to wreck the Movement. This I was not prepared to agree to. I was not then, an.' even now I am not satisfied that the Japanese Government is insincere. At all events we have not, as yet, explored all avenues open to us to find our ourselves whether the Japanese Government is prepared to help this Movement in such a manner as we desire. If we find that they are not sincere then we shall drop their help but not till then. Notwithstanding the inexplicable attitude taken up by my colleagues, I tried to negotiate with the Japanese authorities to arrive at a formula which would help us in tiding over the present crisis.

On the 6th December, a most unfortunate event happened, namely the sudden arrest of Col. Gill by the Japanese Military Policy for certain investigations. Col. Gill was taking an active part in the present crisis however on enquiry I found out that his arrest had no connection with our crisis, although it gave an impression that it was.

On the afternoon of the same day a meeting of the Council of Action was held Mr. Raghavan being absent. However, the other members said that unless their request for sending the ultimatum, on the 5th December, were acceded to immediately, it would be impossible for them to continue in this Movement. The meeting of the Council of Action was adjourned till the 10th December for further discussions on all these questions. Later in the evening, however, I received a letter of resignation signed by all three of them. I must confess that it did not cause me much surprise because I had a feeling for some time that they were not interested in attempting to secure a settlement. So I accepted all the resignations. This being the position I had no other alternative but to take over the powers and duties of the Council of Action according to our Constitution pending

the election of new members which can be done only at a meeting of representatives of various territories in East Asia and of the Indian National Army.

Mr. Mohan Singh, from the very beginning, wanted to carry on his work despotically. He wanted to have a free hand in his undertakings, and as such, he could not bear the idea of being interfered with by others in his work but constitutionally he had to work under the Council of Action. In order to sweep away this restriction, he intensified his exercise of dictatorial influence over the I.N.A. and infused wrong idea into the minds of his officers and men that the army belong to him, and that he was its master.

Moreover in the last meeting of the Council of Action Mr. Mohan Singh tried to blot out the Council of Action pressing upon the Council to get an immediate clarification of a few questions from the Japanese authorities which as I have stated above was impossible because there was none in Malai who could answer on the spot. On receiving no reply, he, as well as the other two members of the Council of Action tendered their resignations the same evening without waiting to meet on the 10th December as was previously arranged. Col. Gillaini, in his capacity as an officer of the I.N.A. under Mr. Mohan Singh, had no alternative but to comply with the wishes of his superior and thus relinquished his post.

Since Mr. Mohan Singh was instrumental in the election of Mr. Mennon as a member of the Council of Action and his election was mainly due to the military votes, he was obliged to resign together with Mr. Mohan Singh.

Two of the highest military officers having resigned I wished to call the rest of the senior officers in order to acquaint them with the whole situation and inform them of my plans. So, I asked the G.O.C. to sent these officers to meet at the Sea View Hotel on 12th December. The G.O.C. however, thought it necessary to enquire in what capacity I had called that meeting and what the purpose of that meeting was. As President of the Council of Action and, as such, the Head of this Movement, I am entitled to meet any officer of the I.N.A. and the G.O.C. is not at liberty to ask for an explanation from me. However, I pointed out to him that the powers and duties of the Council of Action were vested in me as the President and the sole surviving member of the Council of Action. The G.O.C. not only ignored my directions but stated in his letter to me dated 12th December, 1942 that :-

(a) "the members of the Indian National Army are pledged to me (i.e., Capt. Mohan Singh) and me alone by name" and

(b) "under the existing circumstances, we (meaning, I presume, the Army) cannot usefully serve our Motherland through the Indian Independence League in East Asia and have accordingly though it fit to sever our connection with it."

The tone and contents of this letter came to me as a great shock. I could hardly imagine that any officer appointed G.O.C. of any army would disown the very Movement of which the army forms an integral part and claim that that army is his own private personal army. I could not for a moment believe that any officer or any man who had volunteered for service in the I.N.A. did ever imagine that he was pledge loyalty to an individual and not to the Movement which brought into existence that army.

When Mr. Mohan Singh had resigned from the membership of the Council of Action and said that he had nothing to do with this Movement he should naturally have washed his hands off the command of the I.N.A. but he did not. He waited for further three weeks, thinking that as the Council of Action does not exist, any decision reached between the Indian side and the Japanese would be between him and the Japanese Government. But his idea did not materialise because the Japanese authorities stuck to the Bangkok resolution by recognising the Council of Action as the Supreme Body of which I was the only surviving member. As a matter of fact Mr. Mohan Singh approached Col. Iwakuro with a letter stating clearly that the Indian National Army belonged to him and that he wished to dissolve it. On the other hand he informed his officers that if anything happened to him they should dissolve the army immediately.

In the face of the above facts, I had to take the most painful but the only course open to me namely the removal of General Mohan Singh from his post as G.O.C. of Indian National Army.

Before closing the facts of the case I want to give you extracts from the speeches of the Premier General H. Tojo at the various occasions concerning India and from which I hope you will be able to know the intention of the Japanese Government towards India.

1. In his address before the Diet on the fall of Singapore on 16th February 1942 the Premier General Tojo said :–

   It is a golden opportunity for India having, as it does, several thousand years of history and splendid cultural tradition, to rid herself of the ruthless despotism of British and participate in the construction of the Greater East Asia Co-prosperity sphere. Japan expects that India will restore its proper status as India for the

Indians and it will not stint herself in extending assistance to the patriotic efforts of the Indians. Should India fill too awaken to her mission forgetting her history and tradition, and continue as before to be begailed by the British cajolery and manipulation and opportunity for the renaissance of the Indian people would be for ever lost.

2. In his Message to the Imperial Diet on 12th March, 1942 the Premier said :–

   It is my firm belief that now is the time to establish India for the Indians, which has for many years been the aspiration of the 400 millions Indian people.

Great Britain has for long deceived and continued her arbitrary rule over India. What the reality of the British promise made to India in the last Great War must be still fresh. I believe, in the memory of the Indian people. Now Great Britain is trying again to deceive India with all sorts of cajolery. If the leaders of India, misled by such British cajoleries, betray the long cherished aspiration of the Indian people and thus fling away this heaven-sent opportunity, I believe there will no chance for saving India for ever and there will be no greater misfortune befalling the 400 million Indian people.

While India rise as India for the Indians to have the honour to co-operate for the establishment of the Greater East Asia Co-prosperity Sphere, or will she permanently stoop under the shackless of the Anglo-American Powers to leave her name as a slave to posterity? She is now face to face with the time, when she should liquidate her past, see the new situation correctly and make her final decision.

3. In his advice to India on 7th April, 1942 General Tojo said :–

The Imperial Forces which previously occupied Rangoon, and important base in Burma, and then took possession of the more strategic point in the Eastern Indian Ocean, the Andaman Islands, which have hitherto been a place of exile for patriots of Indian Independence, have now at last dealt severe blows to the British forces, and military establishments in India.

The grim determination of our Empire to crush the United States and Britain is thus being steadily translated into action. If India should remain as before under the military control of Britain, it would, I am afraid, be unavoidable that, in the course of our subjugation of the British forces there, India will suffer great calamities.

As it is, of course, fartherest from the thought of Japan to consider the Indian people as an enemy, Japan deeply sympathise with them who

are likely to suffer the ravage of war.

What Japan's intentions are toward the Indian people was made clear in my address delivered before the Imperial Diet on March 12th (see I. above). In short, I am firmly convinced that now is the golden opportunity for the Indian people to exert their utmost efforts in order to secure India's status as it ought to be.

The British influence in India is now about to be exterminated. I wish once again to repeat at this juncture Japan's expectation that not only the leaders in India but the four hundred million people there, while avoiding unnecessary calamities which will result from their being misled by sweet flatteries of Britain, the nation destined to downfall, will take full advantage of this heaven-sent opportunity and break away from the British bonds which have so long shackled them and thus go vigorously forward to realise truly their long cherished aspiration, of "India for the Indians."

4. In his address before the Lower House of the Diet on the Progress of the War and on Economic Problems of the Greater East Asia on 28th May, 1942 the Premier General Tojo said :–

> There still remains in India a framework of British possession with various military establishments, and the military forces are being steadily increased. As long as there remain Anglo-American Military forces in India, Japan determined inflexibly to crush them thoroughly. To our regret, it is, indeed, unavoidable that in the progress of such campaign some misfortunes may befall innocent Indians. What I expect at this juncture, however, is that the Indian people will rise with an intrepid spirit, expel the Ango-American forces as well as their influence completely from India and thereby realise the independence of their Fatherland.

I must emphasise that before we can take a final and decisive step to completely stop this Movement, we have got to be satisfied beyond doubt that the Japanese Government are not sincere in their desire to assist us and that they want to use us mere fifth-columnists or puppets. It is also necessary before the final step is taken to consider the repercussions of such a step on the two and half million Indians in East Asia and 400 millions in India, a matter which seems to have escaped the attention of my three colleagues. I would have been untrue to the trust reposed in me by you all if I had allowed any wrecking of the Movement immediately and before we could even find out the attitude of Tokyo.

I have given you a true pen picture of the whole situation and I leave it to your good judgement to decide. You must always remember that this Movement and the Army do not belong to any one can and they can never be so. The foundation of this Movement was laid, years ago. Despite all opposition to the struggle it is gaining a momentum. Many die in the struggle and a greater number take their place. Many have played their part in this drama of Indian freedom and disappeared from the stage of sacrifice but the Movement continues to expand and is gradually carrying us to the ultimate goal. I may die tomorrow but one of you should be ready to take my place and when he dies there should be another to take over the responsibilities. It is the most sacred duty of every Indian to sacrifice his all for the complete independence of India and the Hindustan of tomorrow will be proud of you. If you survive in the struggle, you shall be called heroes and if you died in the attempt you shall be martyrs.

I therefore appeal to you in the name of our Motherland to set aside all petty differences, make one unit and brotherhood and move forward as one team and the freedom of our country is assured. Remember you are born only once and will die only once; whether it is on a sickbed or whether it is on the battlefield. Come forwards as men, live as men and die as men, so that the India of tomorrow can be proud of you.

The Indian National Army does not belong to me or to Mr. Mohan Singh or to any one of you, but it is the vision of four hundred millions of Indians. Remember, when it did not exist; it did not exist; but once it is formed, see that nobody can break it. It shall only break when no trace of an enslaved India is left. If you have the feeling of nationalism and want to live as a free citizen of the world then answer the call of your Motherland and join this Movement. This is your work just as much as mine so there shall be no force and threat of any kind. This is merely a service for your country. By serving your country you are serving yourself. A small party of true and patriotic men is worth more than any army of hundred thousands which may betray India at the time of her need.

Comrades, it is a God sent opportunity. Everything is in our favour. One of the world's greatest powers is prepared to help us, and even the inner voice of the heart tells me that India must be free during this struggle.

41

Statement by Iwakuro Kikan Clarifying Japanese Policy Regarding the Crisis, Arrest and Dismissal of General Mohan Singh; Reafirms Japanese Government's Policy to help Indians to Gain Independence[1]

29 December, 1942

On receiving a report from the Indian Independence League to the effect that General Mohan Singh has been dismissed today from his present position of G.O.C. of the Indian National Army becoming a mere Mr. Mohan Singh from today, the Japanese side has to recognise the action taken by the League to my great regret.

Your glorious Indian National Army has been established according to the resolutions of the Bangkok Conference as an Army belonging to the Indian Independence of India. I cannot but admire the level best with which you have been striving day and night to attain the sublime ideal for the sake of your mother country.

Mr. Mohan Singh, however, has of late had an opinion which is fundamentally different from that of the League regarding the Indian Independence Movement in East Asia, holding a serious doubt about the sincerity of Japan. He himself has declared that he has severed all his connections with the Indian Independence Movement in East Asia and arbitrarily made a proposal to me about the dissolution of the Indian National Army, under the wrong impression that it is his own private army. Thus he has reached a conclusion which is not acceptable both to the Indian Independence League and the Japanese side.

---

1. I.I.L. Papers; File no. 45/3; on 29 December, Mohan Singh was removed from the INA command and was taken into custody by the Japanese Military Police. He was kept at an Island in Sumatra and gave a statement after the War explaining his position. See. Appendix II.

Mr. Mohan Singh's reasons are as follows :–

1. That the Japanese reply to the resolutions of the Bangkok Conference is not itemised with the management of the properties of absentees Indians in Burma.
2. That the Japanese side has an intention of using the Indian National Army.
3. That the Japanese reply to the resolutions of the Bangkok Conference is not itemized article by article, hence unsatisfactory.
4. Japanese side has not given recognition to the Indian National Army by publicly announcing its existence.
5. That there have been several happenings of assult and insult inflicted by Japanese on the officers and men of the Indian National Army.

Out of these instances, he seems to have reached the wrong conclusion that Japan's real intention must consist in the utilisation of the National Indian Army as its 5th column with the aim of controlling India in place of Britain and therefore he further concluded that seeking the help and cooperation from the Japanese side will not be good for the I.N.A. which is loyal to India. Thus he came to the conclusion of dissolving the Indian National Army.

I feel extremely sorry about the present issue for the sake of Japan as well as India, and I would like to appeal to your good judgement by reviewing the issue from the Japanese standpoint, clarifying its real facts. First of all, I must make a strong protest, for the sake of Japan's honour, against the wrong assumption that Japan is going to control India in place of Britain. I, as a representative, of Japan, declare hereby the Japan's real intention as follow :–

1. Japan has no territorial, political, military or economic ambitions at all toward India. Any assumption, therefore that Japan is going to control India by replacing Britain is nothing but a malicious enemy propaganda of Britain and America.
2. India should be a complete independent country as India of Indians. Therefore the two nations, Indians and Japanese, will stand on an equal status as friendly nations, on her attaining independence.
3. As the Indian Independence League is an organisation of Indians themselves whose movement should be developed by keeping inseparable relations with the major current of the National Movement within India, Japan has got the slightest intention of utilising it for Japan's 5th column. However, the Indian

Independence League, being a political organisation should be carried out in such a way that they will not infringe on the sovereignty of the respective country, before its advancing into India. But, after it has advanced, it will receive no restriction or interference whatever from any country other than India.

4. The Indian National Army is an Army belonging to the Indian Independence League, and it is by no means a private army belonging to an individual and Japan has no idea that the Indian National Army will be used for any purpose other than those provided in the resolutions of the Bangkok Conference.
5. Japan's aid of establishing peace in Asia and India's aim to secure her complete independence, both is not, therefore, motivated by any selfish ambition. The Japanese wish for India's complete independence is a natural expression of the Japanese national sentiment, with which they have regarded India with respect and love for the past 2,000 years. Therefore, there is no intention on our side of demanding, at present or in future, from you any consideration whatever in exchange for our support.

Although the principles as above mentioned have several times been expressed by the Premier General Tojo in his statements and the Japan's real intention has been clearly explained, I am prepared to recommend to the Japanese Government to issue another Official statement which may be more satisfactory to you at an early opportunity.

I am, further, prepared to request the Government to formulate a concrete policy as to how to support the Indian Independence League and clearly indicate the contents of such policy.

The several instances, which have been utilized by Mr. Mohan Singh for his twisting Japan's real intentions, are no doubt regrettable matters and yet most of them were caused by the differerce in ethical ideas, customs and language between the Japanese and Indians, which will be naturally corrected and improved by the mutual understanding and sincere effort, and by no means constitute problem which is so fundamental as to destroy the friendship and confidences existing between the two nations. The creation of an unfortunate breach between Japan and India may virtually mean to you the loss of a great opportunity of attaining India's Independence and I firmly believe that such a happening will be by no means favourable to both Japan and India, which otherwise shall be friendly nation in the future. If Japan deals with the Indian question with such an attitude as mentioned above, there can be no fundamental question between the two great nations which cannot

be solved, unless, of course, you are contended with being a faithful watch-dog of Britain, or are mislead by Anglo-American propaganda.

It will serve some useful purpose, I believe, to explain at this opportunity about some questions which otherwise, I am afraid, may lead Japan and India to estrangement :

1. On the Itemized reply by the Japanese Government to the Resolutions of the Bangkok Conference

Although I consider that your request for an itemized reply is reasonable. I regret to say that the Japanese Constitution does not permit the Government to issue a written reply in such a form as desired by the Indian Independence League for the reason that the same is a mere political organisation and cannot be regarded as a state. The Japanese Government, however, fully recognising the existence of the League and its movement, have issued a written reply promising general support, and instructed the Iwakuro Kikan to meet with the wishes of the Indian Independence League to the greatest possible extent. I am sure that you will readily admit that we have already done a great deal in this connection. It is my wish therefore, that you will not regard our replies as similar to the empty promises of Britain.

2. On the Public Announcement of the I.N.A.

We have been refraining from making a public announcement about the existence of the I.N.A. simply because we thought that a greater strategical effect could be gained, if it is done simultaneously with the start of the Indian campaign. However, should the Indian Independence League prefers the present political effect to the strategical one, I shall not be reluctant to make a public announcement of its existence after the settlement of the present issue.

3. On the Handling of the Indian Prisoners

We cannot agree to the proposal to put the Indian prisoners under the supervision of G.O.C. of the I.N.A. because of the rules and regulations of the Japanese Government. The manners and purposes of using the prisoners shall be solely decided by the Japanese according to the discretion of its own.

However, we have no objection to grant authority either to the I.I.L. or to the G.O.C. of the I.N.A. of inculcating anti-British independence spirit into the prisoners, as well as of selecting the members out of them for the I.N.A.

4. On the Arrest of Col. Gill

Regarding the arrest of Col. Gill there was current a rumour, I have

heard, that it was a political engineering to separate him from Mr. Mohan Singh. The fact is that, while he was executing a special mission in Burma, he was connected with a case of his subordinates Major Dhillon and several others, who had jilted away to the British side and also with a case of sending a secret correspondence from Col. Gill to a senior adjutant of the British General Headquarters in New Delhi. In this connection, not only Col. Gill but several others who are connected with these cases have been also taken into custody for examination in Bangkok and Rangoon.

5. On the disarming of the I.N.A.

The Japanese army has never attempted the dissolution of the I.N.A. or its disarmament.

6. On the Future of Mr. Mohan Singh

Mr. Mohan Singh, driven by a impulsive sentiment, blinded by a narrow minded subjective idea, has made indiscretly an error this time of hampering the Indian Independence Movement and his sincere devotion to this mother country, we Japanese will regard him with honour and respect his own will as regards his future movement, as long as he refrains from any conduct that may injure the Japanese Indian relations or Indian Independence Movement.

7. On the Insult of the Officers and Men of the I.N.A.

Regarding the assault and insult inflicted by the Japanese upon the officers and men of the I.N.A. We have already made an arrangement wilh all those concerned in order to guard against such happenings with full precaution, and therefore in future the situation will be better. Should such things happen again, we shall deal with each case on its merits in good faith.

With the above I have explained the attitude of the Japanese side toward the various questions which seem to have been the cause of the present unfortunate situation.

With this statement, I believe that you have now understanding of Japan's real intentions and will remain in the I.N.A. as hitherto and work for the progress of Indian Independence movement.

Friends : I sincerely ask you for your calm and careful examination of the present issue lest you should be dependent, or you will disappoint your fellow countrymen who are courageously fighting at this movement the anti-British war in your country, India.

Premier General Hideki Tojo, replying to an inter-pellation posed by Ryo Koyama in the Budget Committee Meeting of the House Representatives this morning, reiterated the statement that the Nippon Government has no territorial ambition in India but rather, on the contrary

desires to see India regain its independence as soon as possible. He said that, whatever propaganda the enemy nations may send out to countreact and discredit the oft repeated statement, it will amount to nothing before the overwhelming realities, indicating as shining examples the ever growing empire of Manchukco and the up and coming of the National Government of China at Nanking. He continued that the Nippon Government is a staunch upholder of righteousness and shall at all times abide by its promises. He asserted that Nippon had stood by its assurances given to Thailand to respect the sovereignity and territorial integrity, as a consequence of which Thailand is now fully collaborating with Nippon in the prosecution of the Greater East Asia war.

Nippon's attitude towards Burma has already been clarified, continued Premier Tojo, adding that the Philippines too has been assured independence provided it comes to realise its place in Greater East Asia to collaborate fully with the Nippon policy. Asserting that realities speak more eloquently than any malicious enemy propaganda aimed to discredit Nippon, Premier Tojo declared that India at the present juncture needs only to turn a deaf ear to enemy propaganda and concentrate its efforts in its immediate task.

He concluded saying that Nippon has no territorial ambition whatever in India.

42

British Assessment of Indian Independence Movement in East Asia; Examines its Repercussion on Indian Army and Japanese Policy Towards their Position in India[1]

30 December, 1942

The Pre-War Situation

1. In 1937 there was a Conference at Tokyo attended, among others, by Rash Behari Bose, Hari Singh alias Osman Khan, Giani Pritam Singh, and Swami Satyanand Puri. (The two lastnamed were subsequently killed in an air crash flying to Tokyo in March, 1942 together with Capt. Mohd. Akram and K.A.N. Iyer). This conference planned anti-British propaganda in Siam, Malaya, Burma and India. It gave special attention to Indian troops in the Far East and, it is thought, made a general plan for an organisation on the lines of the Indian National Army to operate in the event of war. The foundations of this fifth column work were built around Congress and Revolutionary organisations by the Japanese Intelligence.

2. Colonies of disaffected Indians existed at centres in the Far East for many years before the war. In Japan, Siam, Shanghai and Canton their activities were encouraged by Japan and, when the war with Japan commenced in December, 1941, there wee Indian fifth columnists ready to take the field, advance with Japanese troops and start subversive activities among both our Indian troops and Indians residing in Far East territories. In this connection, a report received just before Japan's entry into the war mentioned a Fifth Column School at Tsingtao in China, the recruits for which were drawn from Far Eastern countries, special attention being paid to British Indians.

3. The Indian Congress Party, Bangkok, was founded by Ram Seth

---

1. Military Department, File No. L/WS/1/1576, I.O.L.

Pande in 1937. In 1937 Giani Pritam Singh enrolled volunteers for "fifth column" activities and by 1939, 40 batches of volunteers were ready for despatch to Malaya for propaganda work.

Activities after Japan's Entry into the War

4. On the outbreak of war, or just before, Giani Pritam Singh, accompanied by Sudarshan Adha of Gorakhpur, Anrudh Shukal, Kartar Singh, Jhanda Singh, Qadur of Kedab Chand Khan and probably others opened an office at Haadye in Siam (a few miles from the Malaya frontier), where Kartar Singh and Jhanda Singh had previously resided. From here the party moved forward as the Japanese advance under the direction of Major Fujiwara of the Japanese Army. The activities of these parties were assisted by leaflets dropped from the air.

5. Where Indian disaffected organisations already existed these were, taken over, officials being changed and new branches opened as appeared desirable. In non-British territories, i.e., Siam and Shanghai, the removal of British influence allowed the anti-British element to come into the open. Where there was no suitable organisation in existence, such as in Hong Kong, one was quickly started. These local associations were represented to be a combination of social welfare societies and influential mediators between the Indians and Japanese. Gradually, but without delay, the position was reached whereby the local association became apparently all powerful so far as Indian affairs were concerned; it became the "go between" for complaints and petitions to the Japanese, and controllers of rations and privileges generally, and was thus able to discriminate against no association members. Consequently many probably joined the associations from motives of self-interest.

6. Another method of recruitment followed gangster lines. This is particularly apparent in the case of Hong Kong, where the original Indian Independence League workers, Sohail Khan (formerly a night watchman of Hong Kong and a Japanese spy), Zahoor Ahmad (a pre-war military deserter) and M.R. Malik (absconded from Hong Kong about a year before the war for "financial reasons") establish something of a reign of terror amongst Indians under presidency of D.M. Khan (formerly a clerk in government service at the Queen Mary Hospital). Rich and influential Indians were despoiled and forced to throw in their nominally with the Indian Independence League for fear of physical reprisals, or of denunciation to the Japanese authorities.

7. There were, however, many Indians in the Far East, already possessed of anti-British feelings, who welcomed Japanese assistance

against Britain and needed no incentive to join these associations. Following the conquest of Malaya a belief gained ground amongst Indians that the British would be expelled from India and this gave considerable impetes to the Indian Independence movement which spread rapidly.

Fifth Column Activity in the Field

8. As already stated the Japanese had Indian Fifth Columnists ready to take the field in conjunction with their troops, with the task of starting subversive activities amongst local Indian residents, and to influence Indian troops captured or otherwise encountered. These parties supported the Fifth Columnists already in the country and met with considerable success in their task of shaking the confidence, and thereafter undermining the loyalty of Indian troops and civilians.

The Suborning of Prisoners of War

9. Whether or not there was, before hostilities, any definite understanding between disaffected Indian officers of the Army in Malaya and Hong Kong and the Japanese (as has been suggested) there is no doubt that the latter soon had a following of traitors, real or assumed, from amongst captured Indian personnel of all ranks. Having first won over a few officers, the general technique has been for them to work on others by propaganda, Japan's role as a friend of India is stressed–her alleged aim, so far as India is concerned, being that of assisting her to attain complete independence. Probably, however, a much strong argument in winning troops over has been the promise of better conditions of living; in nearly all cases condition for Indian P.W. have been bad in the first instance but have then been steadily improved as men have been won over in accordance with the policy that all Indians who shower signs of responsiveness should be accorded greatly preferential treatment as compared with other P.W. In the case of Indian officers, one of the inducements held out has been promotion by a stop in rank, and promises of his office when the "Independence" of India had been won. There is evidence, however, that, in individual cases, no apparent inducement has been necessary to cause Indian P.W. to transfer their allegiance.

10. From the earliest reports the name of Captain Mohan Singh has been prominent. There is unconfirmed information that this officer, and others, were in touch with the Japanese before hostilities; and one report says that he telephoned to the Japanese in Alor Star asking them to come and take his party over as prisoners. Mohan Singh is a Sikh, a King's Commissioned Officer of the 1/14th Punjab Regiment, who passed out

from the Indian Military Academy in 1934, having previously had several years service in the ranks. One report suggests that he was disgruntled at not having received acting promotion in his turn; at all events there is no doubt that little persuasion was needed to win him over to the side of the Japanese; he took with him a Capt. Mohd. Akram of the same battalion who was later killed in an air crash on his way to the Tokyo Conference. Both these officers quickly rose to prominence, and on 24th June, 1942, the Berlin Radio announced "Captain Mohan Singh of East Asia fame" to be a member of the Council of Action of the Indian Independence League, and Chief of the General Staff of the Azad Hind National Army. Later reports all refer to Mohan Singh as the G.O.C. of the Indian National Army, and I.N.A. leaflets recently addressed to Indian troops on the Arakan front have been signed by him. One of his qualifications for leadership is a marked gift of eloquence.

The Tokyo and Bangkok Conferences

11. In spite of the good start made in winning over Indian nationals to the support of Japanese aspirations, things were not moving altogether smoothly. In places like Shanghai and Bangkok there were independent Indian National Associations, the leaders of which did not relish the idea of being submerged by the new Japanese controlled organisation. In the Japanese sponsored organisations also there were intrigues, peculation and fighting for position and, in consequence, no real unity of effort.

12. To remedy this state of affairs the Japanese, probably in consultation with Rash Behari Bose and other Indian renegade, decided to attempt to weld the various Indian associations into a single Indian Independence League; the Tokyo Conference of March, 1942, was accordingly summoned for this purpose, but owing to conflicts of personal ambition was not an unqualified success. It was therefore considered necessary to hold a further conference this time at Bangkok.

13. The Bangkok Conference was held from the 15th to 25th June, 1942. The conference was well stage–managed, Gandhi's portrait and Congress flags being widely displayed in imitation of the approved Nazi practice at such "party" meetings. Rash Behari Bose led off with a long speech intended to convince the delegates that Japan was India's truest and best friend; this theme continued to be stressed or possibly overstressed, by messages from Togo and Tojo, and addresses by the Japanese Ambassador. The German, and Italian Ministers harped on the same string, but somewhat naturally hinted at the claims of their respective countries to be regarded as India's sincere and disinterested

supporters. Other speakers included D.N. Das, A.M. Sahay, N. Raghavan, Capt. Mohan Singh and Lt. Col. N.S. Gill; Lt. Col. G.D. Gilani moved the vote of thanks. Mohan Singh's speech was long and emotional and is said to have deeply affected the audience.

14. The Conference resolved to sponsor a movement for achieving the complete independence of India through the Indian Independence League. It was also resolved, in furtherance of the Indian Independence League's objective, that the Indian National Army should be raised immediately from among Indian soldiers, combatant and non-combatant, and such civilians as might be recruited for that purpose. Another resolution involved the Council of Action in an undertaking to create an atmosphere in India which would lead to a revolution in the Indian Army and among the people; the creation of such an atmosphere was to be a prelude to the invasion of India. A further resolution accepted the burden of propaganda inside and outside India, by broadcasts, leaflets, lectures and any other means; these other means may in the light of later events be defined as espionage and sabotage. The Conference also laid down certain principles, amongst which were :

(a) That India should be considered as one indivisible whole.
(b) That all Indian Independence League activities should be on a national basis, not sectional, communal or religious.
(c) That the Indian Independence League's policy and programme must be in line with the aims and intentions of the Indian National Congress.
(d) That India's future constitution must be framed by representatives of the people of India.
(e) That a joint Axis policy favourable to India was accepted as advantageous, and that Japan's support was invaluable.

15. There was also a number of resolutions apparently designed to safeguard the independence of control of the League and Indian National Army and to ensure the good faith of the Japanese. These resolutions, it is interesting to note, were for the most part, not for general publication; the deduction is that (with good reason) a measure of distrust regarding Japanese intentions existed amongst the delegates, but that the Japanese, backed by Rash Behari Bose and his clique, insisted that a solid front should be presented to the outside world.

16. Constitution of the Indian Independence League.

The constitution of the League was laid down as follows :

(a) Council of Action
(b) Committee of Representatives

(c) Territorial Committees

(d) Local Branches.

17. The Council of Action elected consisted of :

President	:	Rash Behari Bose
Civil	:	N. Raghavan
		K.P.K. Menon.
Military	:	Capt. Mohan Singh
		Lt. Col. G.D. Gilani.

Its function, as laid down, is to carry out the policy and programme of the League, and to deal with any new matters which may arise; also general superintendence and control over all Indian Independence League branches and over the Indian National Army. It also had powers to create departments as necessary and powers to appoint and dismiss administrative officers.

18. The Committee of Representatives was to be elected by Territorial Committees and to include representatives selected by the Indian National Army. This committee was also to be responsible for general policy, and its decisions were to be binding on every member. Representation on this committee was to be as follows :

	I.I.L. Members
Japan and Manchoukuo	4
Philippines	2
Siam	6
Malaya	14
Burma	21
Bornoo and Colobos	1
Hong Kong, Canton and Macao	2
Other parts of China including Shanghai	2
Indo-China	1
Java	2
Sumatra	1
Andamans	1
	57 or 50
I.N.A. Members	30
Total	87 or 80

19. There is some doubt regarding the figure from Burma out the probability is that the first figure quoted is correct, for this would roughly agree with one of the Bangkok resolutions which appears to aim at keeping the Indian National Army representation at 1/3rd of the total of the Committee of Representatives.

20. Territorial Committee were to be formed by representatives elected by Local Branch Committees, for organisation and control within the territory concerned. Local Branches would be formed by meetings of local Indians above 18 years of age, subject to approval by the local territorial committee, with the provise that branches of the Indian Independence League already in existence would continued to be recognised. The Headquarters of the movement were initially at least to be located at Bangkok.

21. Particulars of known Indian Independence League branches with office bearers are not complete or authoritative, and much of the information awaits confirmation.

Strength of the Movement

22. Many reports on the strength of the Indian National Army have been received placing it as between 60,000 and 90,000 but for the Indian Independence League no estimate exists. Whether the figures quoted for the Indian National Army are correct is very doubtful; they probably represent a target strength. It is also difficult to assess at what stage a P.W. becomes a recognised member of the Indian National Army. In Rangoon Jail, for instance it appears that personnel "unlisted" into the Indian National Army, and told off the companies, etc. are still, in some cases, subjected to bad treatment to induce them to "volunteer" for the fifth column parties. It follows that many men who are nominally members of the I.N.A. are probably not prepared to carry out executive tasks in support of the enemy. This presumption is strengthened by the fact that a number of the members of intercepted I.N.A. infiltration parties do not appear to have had the intention to carry out tasks to which they were assigned.

Japanese Intelligence Organisations

23. The departments in charge of intelligence affairs are known in Japanese as Kikans and the name of the Japanese director is added as a prefix. The combination, e.g., Iwakuro Kikan, is generally used as a password for agents. Thus, early in Malaya there was the Fujiwara Kikan, Major Fujiwara being then in control of this activity. In Burma, Minami

first controlled the Kikan. Later, in June 1942, Col. Iwakuro took over general control. Iwakuro, a middle aged man who does not speak English, was Japan's representatives at the Tokyo Conference in March, 1942, and was doubtless behind the scenes at the Bangkok Conference in June. The second in-command of the Iwakuro Kikan is Lt. Col. Saito, and the staff at the H.Q. in Bangkok is believed to be over a hundred strong. Extensive records are maintained and besides intelligence the Kikan looks after Prisoners of War and Indians generally; it is the Japanese link with the Indian Independence League, of which the Indian National Army is an integral part, and is responsible for co-ordinating the subversive activities of Indians in the East.

24. There are Iwakuro Kikan branches at Singapore, Penang and Rangoon. A branch at Akyab is possibly a sub-branch under Rangoon. Each Branch is in the charge of a Japanese Lt. Col. assisted by Japanese officers and civilians, and Indians of the Indian Independence League and Indian National Army. Lt. Col. Kitabe is in charge at Rangoon and Lt. Col. Matsua at Akyab.

25. Amongst their activities the Kikans control the sending out of espionage, fifth column and "contact" parties. Contact parties were quickly formed during the Malayan Campaign from amongst P.W. with the tasks of contacting and subverting our troops, and to round up stragglers and isolated parties into the Indian National Army fold. Apparently the scheme was of sufficient success to justify sending a large party of some 50P or 60 prisoners of War under a renegado officer, Jemadar (Captain in the Indian National Army) Ram Sarup, of the 4/19th Hyderabad Regiment, from Malaya to Burma as early as February, 1942, for similar work. There are grounds for believing that these parties had some influence on the behaviour of portions of certain Indian units during the fighting in Lower and Central Burma. Subsequently also, the various Kikans, arranged the despatch of parties, military, civil and mixed, into India. A further survey will describe this activity in detail.

26. Under the auspices of the branches at Rangoon and Penang, instructional institutions have been set up. There are probably others. In Rangoon, there is the military institution accommodated at Mohan Camp (Boundary Road) and the Akram and Gilani Camps, on Kokino Road, and a civilian institution at Cushing High School, where training in espionage and fifth column work is imparted.

43

Statement of N.S. Gill given at the Time of his Arrest Explaining his Position with Regard to Desertion of M.S. Dhillon; Expresses his Faith in Sincerity of Japan; Apologises for Misunderstanding between him and Japanese[1]

31 December, 1942

1. I have had the pleasure and privilege to come into contact with Nippon since the fall of Synon[2] on 15th February this year and I have been working in close touch and cooperation with Iwakuro Kikan ever since then. In March and April, I visited Japan and attended the Tokyo Conference of Indian Independence. Later in June, I also attended the Indian Independence League Conference at Bangkok. During these conferences and on many other occasions, during the period, February to December, I made many anti-British speeches, both in public and private and in all places, Thailand, Burma and Malaya. From the very beginning, I associated myself with the Indian Independence Movement which aims at the destruction of the British. I was the one who with General Mohan Singh held the first conference of Senior Indian Officers shortly after return from Tokyo. This Conference passed strong anti-British resolutions and was attended by the prisoners of war as well as Volunteer Officers. Everyone agreed. I am of the opinion that news of my anti-British work must have reached India, as although I have high connections in India, not a single message of welfare has come for me while most of the Officers, and many sepoys have got messages. The British authorities obviously do not allow a message for me. My anti-British feelings and

1. I.N.A. Papers; File No. 295. This statement may be read with the record of his activities, which he sabmitted to the History of Freedom Movement when he was sarving as India's Ambssadre in Ethopia at Appendix I
2. Japanese Changed the name of Singapore to Synon.

activities should be clear from the foregoing. Indeed, I can indeed, have nothing at all to do with the British now or in the future.

2. Further more, I definitely belief India's only salvation is in the destruction the British and now is the time for it. I also believe that with Nippon's leadership, Asia must again regain its former glory and play its rightful and dominating part in the world of the future. Again, now is the time for all Asiatics to combine with Nippon and gain that goal, otherwise we may be left behind and America may gain the upper hand in the world, same as Europe had in the last 100 years. If that happens (God forbid) then Asia's lot will be (as) unfortunate as it has been while Europe was in ascendancy.

3. I therefore beg to point out that holding the views given in paragraphs 1 and 2, how can I possibly, even remotely, have anything to do with Espionage for the British. That would mean being the enemy of my own country, and enemy of Asia. Can I be such a low creature, God Forbid. I shudder to think of it even. Please do not even, for a moment, think so. No! no! I love my own country too well and hate the enemy off my country, British, again too well.

4. I was told on the morning of 8th December, that I was suspected of Espionage on behalf of British. After my ten months work with the Indian Independence League, this charge came as a great shock to me and I confess I was deeply hurt. No other charge would have heart me or degraded me so much. I was too astonished, too worried to think of it even. I could not believe it, and can hardly believe it now that such a charge has been brought against me. However, misunderstandings do often arise but they are also cleared soon.

5. Ever since I have come here (8th December morning) I have been constantly considering and reviewing all my actions, since 15th February to trace as to what event could have possibly let to even a remotest suspicion against me. During this period I can only think of my stay in Burma, which may possibly have to do anything with this. Then again, after carefully reviewing everyday's work in Burma, I can only think of one event which could have thrown even a suspicion, and that event is the actions of my 2nd officer, Mr. Dhillon. Here I would like to say that I had gone to Burma after arrangement with Col. Iwakuro to run an India contact organisation with a view to getting information from India and spreading our propaganda there. I had taken on this work after hesitation. On arrival at Rangoon, I found others doing similar kind of work. So again, I asked Captain Sakai (Colonel Iwakuro,s representative with me) that I do not want to do this work.

I only quote the last two sentences to show that had I ever thought of espionage, I would not have acted like this. Later even, I told Captain Sakai (even before Dhillon's departure) and once Colonel Iwakuro that the work was not to my liking. Again, please think, would I have acted like this, if I had any thought of espionage, for without this work I would return to Syonan and espionage would be out of question. Again all my men were selected on the qualification of being anti-British and pro-Japanese. Some of these men were well-known past revolutionalists. Could I have made such a selection if espionage had ever entered my mind?

6. Reverting to Dhillon's'[3] actions, on arrival at Rangoon, I decided to open up posts at Mytkyina, Kalewa and Maymyo. I decided to send my three senior officers to these posts. Later Maymyo was abolished, and that officer stayed at Rangoon. Dhillon's post was Kalewa. My orders were for officers to establish the posts, carry out the reconnaissance supervise the first party entering India through their post, and Akyab had been captured. Immediately I thought if it was Dhillon's work, they came to the conclusion that it was not because the captured party entered Indian about the same time of not earlier, than Dhillon could have done. They entered by an entirely different route to the one decided when Dhillon left Rangoon. So I concluded that the capture was just luck. The reason for the capture was being investigated when I left. Later on, on Captain Sakai's advise we decided to send my two officers and some men to do propaganda work in the Army. It is my firm belief that to do spy work most effectively, officers must manage to rejoin the Army in India and then work hidden. So instructions were issued by me to these officers and they were given some letters to be used if they helped them to join the Army. They were to go by Kalewa so as to make sure of truth about Dhillon and if Dhillon had really gone, these lettered again may come useful. Their effort must be to get back into the Army. Captain Sakai was informed about this and he agreed if necessary hand yourself over and join the Army in India. Please note that I never gave any letter or instruction to Dhillon because he was never meant to go to India. Whereas these officers were definitely to go to India and if necessary use false pretences, including my name so as to gain their object. I made these officers sign an oath in our secret temple in Rangoon that they would be true to our country's interest. That oath is somewhere in my papers here and can be found in the luggage. I need not say that our

3. See Document No. 33.

country's interest automatically mean anti-British. No true Indian can say otherwise and this is what Mahatma Gandhi the most respected man in India says. In fact our interest in India can only be anti-British and nothing else. So you see, my intentions and Anti-British feelings in this oath as late as middle of November. These officers were definitely going to India to do anti-British work by hook or by crook and all means and instructions were issued to that end. One more factor about Dhillon's case. If the news is correct then it appears that he has taken everybody in the post with him. How if I was implicated in this, could I issue such an instruction which will straightaway bring doubt and suspicion. Obviously, Dhillon got all his men together, I don't know why, except for some selfish interest of his own and went. If it is true, he has deserted nothing else. My fault in this, has been misjudging him, and he will pay for it when we meet him in India. I had told the other two officers going to India to watch Dhillon carefully. These two officers were still in Rangoon, when I came here. So my blame in this has been misjudging Dhillon and I am sorry for this, but I am not alone in this. General Mohan Singh also trusted him and they knew each other much longer. He wanted to keep Dhillon as his military secretary, and only because I had no senior officer, I kept him, otherwise I would have sent him back.

7. The only other thing which may raise doubts in our minds possibly is my past career. I was educated at English schools and spent my time with Englishmen. Let me tell you that among this type of Indian (who has got to know the Englishmen well) that strongest anti-Britishers are found. Mr. Nehru was an English School scholar, and he intensely hates the British. Mr. S.C. Bose (now in Berlin) went to England and passed Indian Civil Service and now is the terror of the British. Many other examples, even with Indians with English wives, are like this. I have, from a long time, disliked the English because they brought slavery to India. Twice in my service of eighteen years, I was nearly turned out of the Army, and once because I fought for India's dignity, and once when I fought over Mahatma Gandhi's policy and views and this was in 1931, during the second civil disobedience movement and during his famous Salt March to Dandi.

8. To sum up therefore, I sincerely hope that the foregoing paragraphs have proved beyond the shadow of doubt that leave alone an act, I have not been even guilty of thought of espionage for the British. I never was, and never would be such untrue Indian. On the contrary I fervently hope that I will prove in these critical days, a true Indian, by taking my share of the work in the Independence movement.

My conscience and heart are so clear of any thought of espionage that I am prepared to take an oath to that effect.

Part Two

PRESENT FEELING AND FUTURE

1. My own feelings and convictions and actions are based on following two salient points :–

(i) British must be defeated in this war.

(ii) Japan must come out victorious.

I want (i) because that means Independence for India. I want (ii) because that is necessary if India is to get Independence and because it will mean Asia under Nippon's leadership playing the leading role in the world after the war. That is only right and just as Asia has practically half the population of the world. Any other course will be disastrous to India and Asia. It is on these two principles that my actions are based and will be based. Further my trip to Japan has strengthened my respect for that country.

You may well ask that if these had been my principles, why some of our actions have not entirely been consistent with that. That is what I will explain in the next paragraph which will show the principles have remained the same, but some incidents, now and then have affected our actions.

2. Now that I have time, calmly, cooly and with detachment to review everything I fully see that our chief mistake has remained suspiciousness. I remember Col. Iwakuro, at Bangkok Conference, saying that we Indians were suspicious. I have to admit that his words have proved true and this may have marred our vision. Perhaps it is true due to period of slavery under British. This is unfortunate but I do say that it has not affected our sincerity.

When I review the generous treatment given to Indians in East Asia by Nippon, it is amazing that sometimes we have failed to appreciate it. Indians have been treated extremely well. Their prestige has gone up. In Thailand it has gone up 100 per cent. Then again, see how-well Indian prisoners of war have been treated. National spirit and army have been created. Indians in East Asia have became one with no Hindoo-Muslim disunity. It is therefore surprising that we have failed to appreciate fully the attitude and generosity of Nippon. I am afraid, I, among others, have also to take this blame that I failed to understand this position fully well.

I would ever say that it was an act of ungratefulness not to appreciate the position and still be suspicious. It was most unfortunate. Also, if even I had not come from Rangoon, events will have happened the same, but I did associate with them and an surprised now how we failed to realise the rear position. Mr. Bose, our President, was wisest of all and we should have followed him implicitly and should do so now.

I will take the liberty of saying that you please on your side must also realise why this happened. We were mostly young, inexperienced in politics, or big dealings. We had got certain large powers and this may have marred our outlooks. It was due to all these combined that we showed suspiciousness when it was not justified.

I don't know what has happened since I was arrested, But I sincerely hope and pray, that everything is all right and the Independence movement and Army are as strong as ever. Our movement, and our service to India. Any damage to it will be a serious loss to us, and at this time which may never come again. As soon as I got this realisation, I wanted to come out and do my very best, but my presence here, prevented me. To sum up, therefore, I may say, that it was our foolishness and inexperience that made us think of asking for conditions. Now when I quietly think that when such powers as Britain and America failed to make conditions with Nippon, what made us think of such ridiculous ideas. All I can say is that it was not insincerity or lack of confidence.

3. I hope I have made up my position and outlook quite clear. Where my wording is not fully understood, I will be only too glad to explain. I have only to add that I have made this statement in absolute sincerity and honesty.

4. I am anxiously waiting to come out and work for the independence of India in the closest cooperation with Nippon and that I may be of good use because (a) I have quite high connections, relatives and friends in India, particularly northern India, (b) I know the Indian Army and senior Indian officers better than anybody else (c) I am well known in the extremist and other Sikh parties, perhaps better than any other Sikh in East Asia. I say this, not in any self praise, but to show that in my humble way, I could be of use to our movement and I want to do so honestly and faithfully.

I request, therefore, that a copy of this statement be sent to Colonel Iwakuro and a copy to Mr. Bose, for their consideration if there is any part which Police authorities would not like to forward, that part may be erased, and the rest sent, although I hope as complete a part as possible of my statement will be kindly forwarded to give them the complete

picture, for which I should be very grateful indeed.

5. Last but not least, I must once more, express my gratitude to you and your soldiers for the kind and polite treatment given to me here. On my going from here I would like to give you a short statement to be published in my name, or anonymous, (as you consider fit). I want to say in that, about the good food, etc. given to prisoners, even now in wartime. If you would permit me, I would get that statement ready.

Signed N.S. Gill

Appendix-I

N.S. Gill's assessment of Indian National Army and Indian Independence Movement in East Asia under the Patronage of the the Japanese[1*]

Introduction

1. I write this for the consideration of the "Compilers of the History of India's Freedom Movement" for there is just a possibility that the earlier phases of the Indian National Army formed in the Far East during 1942 may not be known to the extent required for an accurate history; at least I have not seen such an account. I dare to do so because I was intimately and directly concerned with these events. My task and duty will be fulfilled if this article throws even a little new light and so helps the compilers, however little that may, in the formation of their final judgment.

2. I find it easier and quicker to write in the first person. The concerned events are over 12 years old, and I am 12 years older too. Hence I feel reasonably confident of recording the happenings impersonally to the best of my knowledge and with a view to accuracy. For the same reason I give no comments, and only state the facts.

3. This article is divided into the following three parts :–

(i) Brief outline of the events leading to the formation of the I.N.A.

(ii) I.N.A. during 1942 (Parts 'A' and 'B').

(iii) Imprisonment under the Japanese and the British.

My main purpose is to bring the contents of Part II (B) to the notice of the compilers. I also wish to add, that if due to this article or even

1. History of Freedom Movement Papers B 5/3.
2. The above Account was written by N.S. Gill after more than 20 years of the events. It is included here in order to show as to how Gill changed his opinion of the Japanese after the War. Gill could not forget his loyalty to the British and created a near crisis in the relations between Indian National Army and the Japanese by sending M.S. Dhillon to India. (Doc. No. 33)

otherwise the compilers wish any additional information from me or have any queries, I shall try to answer the same frankly, realizing it is for history and not for any books or novels.

Part I

BRIEF OUTLINE OF EVENTS PRECEDING THE FORMATION OF I.N.A.

4. By the middle of 1939 war had become imminent. So as a precautionary measure and before the actual declaration of the Second World War, the British despatched one brigade of Indian troops, known as Force EMU to Singapore in early August. My battalion (4/19 Hyderabad Regiment, now the Kumaon Regiment) was a part of this force. It was an Indianized battalion and among other officers of this unit were the present Commander-in-Chief General Shrinagesh and Lt. General K.S. Thimayya, all three of us being Captain then. This was the first Indian army fighting force to reach Singapore. War was declared shortly afterwards. In December 1939 as I had graduated from the Staff College, Quetta, I was posted to Army Headquarters and returned to India.

5. My stay in India was however short. In October 1940 I was promoted and posted as a Staff Officer on the newly formed 11 Indian Division (11 Ind. Div.). Our destination was Malaya. It appears the plan for the defence of Malaya was enlarged. It was decided to defend Singapore by defending the whole of Malayan mainland. Hence, as there were no troops in Malaya proper, this newly formed Division was posted on the mainland with Headquarters at Kuala Lumpur. The Division was in position by the end of 1940. In early 1941 another Indian Division, the 9th, was also sent to that country. The 9th Indian Division replaced the 11th which moved north with Headquarters at Sungei Patani near Alor Star. A little later an Australian division also arrived in Malaya. There were thus 3 divisions (in addition to Singapore Fortress troops) in Malaya when the war opened; viz. the Australian, 9th and 11th divisions, being posted in southern, central and northern Malaya respectively. 9th and 11 divisions were formed into an Indian corps with Headquarters at Kuala Lumpur. I happened to be the seniormost combatant Indian officer of the Indian Army in Malaya then.

6. It was generally expected that the Japanese would concentrate and attack from Indo-China, and that the first landings would be in south Thailand near Singora and north-east Malaya near Khota Baharu. The latter was in our actual occupation. To learn something about the former,

a number of officers were sent in disguise and under false names and passports to reconnoitre south Thailand in particular from Haadyai to Singora and from Haadyai eastwards to the Malayan border. I was one of these officers, who crossed the Thai border as a barrister. I was also given the task to visit Bangkok, as news had been received that a number of Indians were secretly in league with the Japanese. This was in November 1941. By the time I returned on 2nd December, we all were under battle conditions expecting fighting any moment. But the big surprise was, that we were not allowed to cross the Thai border and capture Singora, where the landing was expected. Yet the plans were made and based on the capture of this port so as to hit the Japanese at their weakest time, i.e., when landing. Weather it was due to the fear of violating Thai neutrality, or fear of thrusting our forces too forward or something else, I am not in a position to say. But the plan was not followed. And the Japanese landed exactly at the expected places and were totally but pleasantly surprised at no opposition. This was in the early hours of 8th December 1941, when Japanese simultaneously attacked Pearl Harbour. Only then were we ordered to cross the Thai border. But it was too late. Japanese had obtained a base and an aerodrome and had won the first vital round without battle. The Malayan plan of defence was to cause the maximum delay to the enemy, so that sufficient troops would be rushed to reinforce the Singapore fortress for its proper defence and later reattack.

7. To what extent this unopposed landing was responsible for the rapid retreat of British forces, I am not in a position to say, but a good chance of delay had been lost without a battle. There were other causes for retreat also. We had no air force, perhaps its vital role was not realized. The Japanese did, air bombing at their leisure. They also had armoured units, when a number of our military leaders had considered the terrain of Malaya impracticable for such vehicles. Furthermore after the successful attack on Pearl Harbour, and sinking of the 'Prince of Wales' and of the 'Repulse' a few days later, the Japanese had complete command of the sea. No wonder the retreat was quick and the whole of Malaya and the so called mighty fortress of Singapore fell to the Japanese within 2½ months of the attack, to be exact on 15th February 1942.

8. There is no doubt that the quick and ignoble defeat of the British forces hastened the process of a national movement. There is also no doubt that the Indian troops were in the main mercenary and there was no real cause for them to fight. Yet the Indian soldiers fought well under difficult and adverse circumstances. My division, i.e., the 11th fought from the first to the last day of this campaign, without any rest, reserves or

reinforcements. Of course such a fight without any patriotic motives cannot create heroes! But the troops fought well with heavy casualties, as a matter of discipline and training. They were however only too relieved the battle had ended.

Part Two

INDIAN NATIONAL—IN ARMY 1942, 'A'–FORMATION

9. After the fall of Singapore, the Japanese insisted that all Indian officers and soldiers be segregated from others. Hence we all gathered at the Farer Park, on 15th and 16th February 1942. It was then that I and Majority of others learnt that a group of officers and men had been helping the Japanese during the battle under the charge of captain Mohan Singh and the seeds of the I.N.A. had already been sown. They had been cut off after the first long attack in the North of Malaya about the middle of December. They had found some civilian Indians under S. Pritam Singh with the Japanese troops, through which contact had been established between them and the Japanese. For the first few days after the fall of Singapore we devoted ourselves looking after the men's health, a dysentery and cholera were taking their tolls. Various camps were established and doctors did a very good piece of work. At the same time talks about forming a movement went on. The Japanese informed us that in Japan an Indian Independence League had already been formed under the leadership of that well-known revolutionary Ras Behari Bose. Consequently a deputation of officers and civilians proceeded to Tokyo in April 1942, to have talks with Shri Ras Behari Bose and Indian from the other parts of the Far East with a view to forward to help the cause of Indian Independence. The three military officers selected for this meeting were Captain Mohan Singh, Captain Mohd. Akram and myself. Among the civilians were Mr. R.N. Raghavan, India's Ambassador-designate to Argentina and Mr. K.P. Kesava Menon, ex-High Commissioner to Ceylon.[3] Unfortunately one of our planes crashed in Japan killing all occupants. Among them were Captain Mohd. Akram, Shri Ayer and Shri Satyanand Puri a Bengal revolutionary. Among the Indians residing in Japan was Shri A.M. Sahay, though to our surprise we only met him after some difficulty. Raja Mohendra Pratap was also there. Our

3. They were appointed after independence.

surprise was greater still, as we were not allowed to meet him, and only did so secretly on our own. He immediately warned us that Japanese wanted to use us as puppets. This caused a disturbance in our minds, which later was to mount up. However, this meeting of Indians from Malaya, Japan, Thailand, Hong Kng, Indonesia and Manchuria decided to hold a bigger meeting of Indians in the Far East Asia at Bangkok in June-July, 1942, and meanwhile to proceed with the preliminary arrangements for the formation of a strong Independence League and I.N.A. We returned to Singapore towards the end of April or early May.

10. The Japanese had sensed my hesitation. They were correct too, for I could not bring myself to look at them as pure liberators without any other motives; I could not adjust myself to the Axis views, of which Japanese were a part. So immediately on return to Singapore, the Japanese sent me to Bangkok ostensibly to organise the Indian Independence League there, but in reality to get me away from Singapore and other officers and men. In June-July the big conference took place at Bangkok. It was a very well represented meeting of Indians from every country in the Far East. A Council of Action was formed to direct the activities of all Indians in territories under the Japanese occupation. It was formally decided to form a national army. While in Bangkok I noticed another incident. Whenever diplomats from the German Embassy would come to see me, the Japanese would question me, and ask me not to meet them again. This was a strange behaviour for allies.

11. Towards the end of July I was called back to Singapore to help in the organisation of the I.N.A. There were over 40 thousand Indian prisoner of war soldiers. Of these the vast majority volunteered to join the I.N.A. But of the volunteers only about half could be got ready. The Japanese could not equip all, or perhaps they hesitated to do so. It was amazing how quickly and successfully we instituted Hindi words of command for the English. Questions of caste and creed, which the British for their own reasons had nurtured vanished overnight. All ate together from the same cook house. Nobody thought of provincialism or communalism. All considered themselves Indians. Within a few months a disciplined body of Indian soldiers with a new spirit of nationalism was ready, to act. The basis of the I.N.A. was a division divided into three brigades named Gandhi, Nehru and Azad Brigades. It was of course not equipped with modern arms. But a guerilla force of about 20,000 was ready to act, admirably suited to act in the jungles of Assam and Bengal. It was realized that this force alone could not defeat the British forces in a direct battle, but its impact on the whole of India and on the Indian Army in

particular was our primary motive and the main weapon. And the spirit behind the I.N.A. soldiers was the real asset and the main force. Everyone was ready to march into India, no matter what the obstacles.

12. It must be recorded however the Japanese response to our spirits and views was not as hoped for. So during these days I often felt perturbed. On the one hand I went forward fully helping the organisation of the movement as its advisor, on the other hand I was more and more troubled by the motives and behaviour of the Japanese. The Japanese sensing this again sent me to Rangoon to organise the forward headquarters and espionage into India. I went to Rangoon via Bangkok in August. Here in Burma also the majority of Indians were awaiting to be organised and led forward. The start was made. Four bases were established and a number of parties were sent to filter into India. In Burma also the treatment and outlook of the Japanese left much to be desired. We constantly felt that we were merely being fitted into Japanese plans and no more. Indians were ill-treated. No real power or freedom of action was given to us. My fears and doubts only increased in November 1942. I was suddenly flown back to Singapore.

'B'

DISSOLUTION

(It is for this part that I have mainly written this article).) After I had written this article I have seen the book *The Two Great Indians in Japan* by J.G. Ohsawa. On pages 58 and 59 of this book are the following pertinent sentences :–

"In Indian National Army, a big disorder begun. Captain Mohan Singh and Lieutenant-Colonel Gill were its leaders. They were not satisfied with the G.H.Q. of Tokyo, because all resolutions of the Bangkok meeting had not been implemented. I.I.L. too were not satisfied, they were revolting."

These sentences however hardly explain the reality and it is this important phaze I want to clear.

13. On my return to Singapore I found the situation tense. My fears and worries about the Japanese had affected other also. And there were good reasons for these suspicions, major ones being –

(i) Japanese were ill-treating many Indians and complaints brought no results.

(ii) A large number of our anti-air craft gunners had been taken

away and posted in various parts of Singapore as part of the Japanese defences. We were not even allowed to see them. They were made to wear Japanese uniforms and shout 'Banzai' (Three cheers) for the Japanese Emperor.

(iii) Our request that the formation of the I.N.A. be proclaimed to the world was side-tracked.

(iv) Our request that India's complete independence be declared by the Japanese was ignored.

(v) Our wish that Netaji Subash Chandra Bose be brought to lead the movement also drew no favourable answer.

(vi) We were merely being fitted into the plans of the Japanese General Staff, no more, no less.

14. Thus it became clear to me and many others that we had no real powers and the intention was to use us in accordance with the Japanese policy and strategy more or less as puppets. Naturally resentment arose among us and I was perhaps the spearhead of this resentment. Instead of satisfying our reasonable requests and winning us over, we were threatened and tempted both, particularly Mohan Singh and myself. We managed to stand firm. I, whom the Japanese considered the centre of opposition to them, became their first victim. In the early morning of 8th December 1942 (exactly one year after their attack and entry into the war–a day considered auspicious by them), the Japanese Gestappo arrested me and put me in an underground dark cell in solitary confinement. And I remained a prisoner (the word 'prisoner' cannot explain the conditions of arrest under the Japanese secret police for which please see Part III) till the end of the war, when I believe I escaped because news had filtered out about my whereabouts. After my arrest Mohan Singh and others stood firm and now demanded another condition–namely my release–before they could negotiate. So a fortnight afterwards Mohan Singh was arrested and the first I.N.A. stood dissolved. From here on the story can be better told by others who were direct participants in the later events. I personally remained a prisoner till 22nd August 1945, when I was released and sent to a camp from where the British arrested me in September. I then remained their prisoner till April 1946, when I was released from the Red Fort–thanks indeed to the great support of our nation led by our Prime Minister.

15. At the beginning of this sub-part 'B', I have made a note that my main reason for writing this note is this part. I repeat it. It should be known that while Indian soldiers and officers were ready to fight for their country, they refused to be puppets. It should be known that they knew something of the world events going on, The stand of the axis and allies

and that they tried to work for the real interests of the country according to their right and understandings in difficult circumstances and were not merely 'Yes Men". And for this stand the Japanese never forgave them and made many of them their worst victims, such as myself and those who were sent to new guinea. I think it is fair that this phase of the Indian National Army should be known also, as many foreigners are too prone to dub the I.N.A. as a puppet of the Japanese. If this part of the I.N.A. was fully known, then the posterity can pass the correct judgment on them, i.e., they were ready to die for their country but not as puppets of anyone. True, various individuals joined the I.N.A. with varying motives in those difficult conditions. But in general the above remarks hold true and hence I consider it my duty to bring the same to the notice of the compilers, so that justice is done to those who worked and suffered in those days and so to India's sons and to our country.

16. I have only to add that the above stand which surprised the Japanese, and for which they inflicted heavy punishments nevertheless brought desired results. Netaji came over, most of the things we asked for were generally accepted and second phase of I.N.A. started under the dynamic leadership of Shri Subash Chandra Bose, a phase which is now history. It appears the two phases were complimentary. Without the first, the second would not have been feasible. Without the second, the first would have been of no value. Hence both phases should be known, viewed in the right perspective to make the whole story, for both should reflect credit to India and her sons, though the first did not have the good fortune of having a famed person to lead it, nor is it so known as it should be. Yet individuals are a part of a phase or a movement. Therefore it is essential on that the movement be known from all its aspects and to give one such aspect, which I consider an important one, is my present task. I seek forgiveness of the compilers if it was already known in which case I am only happy to confirm it. As I said at the start I will only be too happy to give any additional information required or answer any queries.

Appendix-II

Statement by General Mohan Singh after his Release from the Prison at the End of the War; throws Light on the Events Leading to his Surrender in Malaya and Formation of the Indian National Army; Explains his Differences with the Japanese and Rash Behari Bose, his Arrest and Internment during the War; gives Assessment of Japanese Policy Towards Indian National Army[1]

I was arrested on 29th December, 1942 at Singapore by the Japanese for reasons clearly stated by them in a comprehensive statement (copies of which were freely distributed to Indian soldiers and civilians in Singapore) issued by Major General Iwakuro on the day of my arrest.

I was released on 26th August, 1945 in Sumatra after 32 months of confinement and at the conclusion of the war.

I have been awaiting the arrival of a responsible Allied Officer in this country to hand over myself to him. This I am going to do tomorrow and before doing so I have decided to issue a statement for the general information of my countrymen.

---

1. W.O.F. No. 208/810, Public Record Office, (P.R.O.) London.
2. General Mohan Singh (1909-1989) was born in a Sialkot village in 1909. After matriculation, he joined the Army as a Sepoy. He was trained at Kitchner college and was made Captain in 1940 and Major in 1941 before he left for Malaya. Before the outbreak of the Pacific war, he was attached to the 1/4 Punjab Regiment. He surrendered to the Japanese on 15 December. After discussion with Fujiwara and Pritam Singh he agreed to organise the Indian National Army. Was dismissed by Rash Behari Bose on 29 December 1942 and was kept unde detention for two months at a sea side Bungalow in Singapore. He was afterwards removed to a near by island (Puloou Ubin) and kept there till the end of December 1943. Later he was taken to Sumatra and detained there till the surrender of the Japanese. After the War, joined politics and was member of Lok Sabha.

STATEMENT[3]

1. Before Surrender

War with Japan broke out on 8th December, 1941. My battalion, the 1/4th Punjab Regiment, was the foremost battalion on Thai-Malaya border in the well known position of Jitra. Till the evening of 11th December, 1941, I fought on the British side as dutifully as any soldier should do. At about 1700 hrs., the same day, a Japanese tank unit broke through our dispositions. The battalion was completely disorganised and dispersed in small parties to various directions in the jungle. My small party consisted of Lt. Col. Fitzpatrick (Commanding Officer) myself and two N.C.Os Till midday, 14th December we remained lost in thick jungle and heavily flooded marshes; all the time trying and struggling to find our way out. On 13th evening Captain Mohd. Akram, also of our battalion, with a small party of Pathans met us accidentally. On 14th we reached Kuala Narang, a small town, 22 miles away from Alor Star. Here we were reliably informed by a Malay Civil. Official and local Indians that the Japanese were already in ALOR STAR and that they were pushing forward.

Lt. Col. Fitzpatrick Captains Akram and I held a brief conference and we decided to surrender.

1. Mental Picture

I must state here that when the war on the Eastern theatre broke out and even before that I was mentally greatly disturbed by the British War Aims.

I could not convince my conscience that it was correct for Indians to shed their blood for an end which was not applicable to them. Britain, faced with an imminent invasion danger of England itself, had declared to the world that she was fighting for freedom, democracy and other high sounding principles. She beseeched Allied Powers to come to her help. Even at the time of the most critical period of her National history and when she was utilising India to fight for her own freedom, she refused to consider the question of India's freedom. Instead she ordered the arrest of Indian leaders because they were considered guilty for asking freedom

---

3. The above statement was issued on 26 August 1945 in Sumatra and clarifies many points not mentioned by either Fujiwara or Gill in their account of the events leading to the collaboration between the Indian National Army and the Japanese General Headquarters.

for India. Why should, then, we Indians fight for a thing, the mere mention of which, was considered sufficient crime for the greatest of us, to be put behind the prison bars?

The obvious deductions which I could draw from the British attitude at that time were :–

(a) That British will never give India freedom unless she was compelled by force of weighty circumstances, which circumstances we Indians must create. In other words she will not grant freedom but we will have to take it from her.

(b) That Britain will never release her hold on India as long as Indian soldiers, paid, fed, clothed and armed by poverty stricken India, remain loyal to the British, irrespective of India's own fate.

Then why were we Indians fighting? The only answer which I could find was that we were fighting merely as dignified, befooled mercenary heroes at the expense of poor India for the sole benefit of Britain and thus helped Britain to keep India in Subjugation with Indian men, money and materials.

This was my mental picture just before surrendering and I am absolutely sure was the mental picture of most Indian officers, N.C.Os and other ranks of the Indian Army.

Here I also want to take it absolutely clear that before my surrender I had no connection whatsoever with any Japanese or any of their agent. In fact I had never seen a Japanese before.

2. After Surrender

At the time of surrender Major Fujiwara, representative of the general staff of General Yamashita, told me that I was not a prisoner. He also said that all Asiatics and particularly the Indians were their friends and that Japan was prepared to extend all help towards the attainment of Indian Independence. This was not what I expected and naturally I was very much impressed but not convinced. Lt. Col. Fitzpatrick was separated from us.

After this, and till the end of December, 1941 I carried on many long discussions with Major Fujiwara. Captain Mohd. Akram and Mr. Pritam Singh who was brought by the Japanese from Thailand to be made leader of the Indian Independence League movement, also attended these discussions. In these talks Major Fujiwara tried his best to convince me that the Japanese were absolutely sincere regarding the question of India and said that if I could raise a patriotic Indian army they would give all aid.

From these talks it was not difficult for me to see that the Japanese had their eyes on India as well. It looked to me that if they meet cheap victories they would at least try.

They had brought with them from Thailand a band of Indian civilians headed by Mr. Pritam Singh who was opening Indian Independence Leagues. Without meaning any ill will to any of these Indians, I must state that I was shocked with their intellect and the utter lack of understanding of what they were talking about. They might have been sincere and I think Pritam Singh was but sincerity alone is not sufficient. They were quite unconsciously playing directly in the Japanese hands.

In the light of two week's continuous discussions I was convinced that the Japanese were seriously determined to create some sort of movement. I had no doubt that in order to achieve their end they would apply all imaginable and even unimaginable methods. There was no such thing as neutral in their dictionary. They looked at every one either as a friend or a foe. A group of Indians attracted towards them was prepared to take the leadership to mislead Indians. Under those circumstances to stand aloof meant inconceivable damage to the Indian cause. My clearest and definite aim at that time I had in my mind that if the Japanese prove sincere, I would after consulting leading Indian civilians of political reputation, do my best for the furtherance of India's cause.

In that short time I had heard and seen enough of the Japanese atrocities on Prisoners of War and civilians. I wanted, even at the risk of my life, to spare Indian soldiers, that inevitable fate which was then befalling Chinese, British, and Australian soldiers. I also wanted to save Indian civilians from terrible hardships and atrocities.

To sum up, my aims for joining the Japanese were :

(a) Further the cause of India's freedom.

(b) Save Indian prisoners of war from certain and lingering death.

(c) Try to save Indian civilians and their property from the Japanese.

It is a matter of great satisfaction and consolation to me that in all these aims I succeeded to a great extent.

It must also be remembered here that the British forces were running as fast as they could, leaving all of us to our own fate, our own resources and in the hands of victory drunk Japanese who respected no laws and no moral codes of honour except their own.

On joining the Japanese I immediately started to teach patriotism to Indian soldiers. Throughout in my patriotic education I stressed this point that at this moment India's enemy No. 1 was Britain and India's enemy

No. 2 would be that nation who had designs on India whether it be Japan or any other.

So I organised Indian prisoners of war in a strong patriotic body fully determined to die only for India.

In doing this I had these objects at the back of my mind. Firstly a patriotic soldier will not be easily exploited. Secondly the British in India would also think twice before transporting ship loads of Indian soldiers to serve as gun fodder to various theatres of war without recognising them as men fit for Independence. Thirdly the world would also be awakened to the faet that Indian soldiers also love their country and wanted freedom as much as any other people.

As regards the practical cooperation with the Japanese I did only that such or even less than that which no prisoner of war could avoid at that time.

3. Alternative Plans

Whether I believe the Japanese to be sincere or not at that time it was very difficult for me to decide. Even if changes of sincerity were only 1 to 10 I wanted to test it. It was worth it. In any way it was going to bring out the truth. If they were trying to use us as it suited them we were also trying to use them as it suited us. I was prepared for both eventualities.

The Plan which Did Not Materialise : I was never in favour and I made it very clear to the Japanese that I would never consent to take Japanese into India.

Forces to liberate India should consist purely of Indians. I wanted to raise and train a patriotic force of 200,000 to 500,000 strongly united, well disciplied and completely independent. This entire force was then to be taken on Indo-Burma border and when there I wanted to give an open challenge to the British to come to an agreement with the Indian National Congress, that being the real voice of India, or fight. At the same time, I wanted to make an appeal to America, Russia and China to back our just demand and also wanted to make it clear to them that we were not Japanese puppets. If even then Britain remained adamant I wanted to fight and die to the very last man at Indo-Burma frontier.

I had strong conviction that that action would alarm the world. America, Russia and China, acting that we were not Japanese puppets and knowing our demand to be a just one, would not keep quiet and would certainly press Britain to accede to our demand. I also knew that the death of about 400,000 Indians would count more than 100 millions alive.

Alas ! Japanese were to prove beyond all doubts, insincere for they did all in their power to hamper the creation of such a force because it did not suit them and it only suited INDIA. They wanted a puppet army only for propaganda.

The one That Materialised : My plan in case the Japanese proved insincere from the very beginning was that at the appropriate time, I would challenge them and put their sincerity to a very severe test before taking any action that may jeopardise India's cause. At that proper moment I wanted to demonstrate, openly, publicly and boldly and expose once for all the Japanese designs. That moment would come when I was fully convinced about the solidarity and patriotism of Indian soldiers. Only then it would be proper, I thought, to give Japanese designs a shattering death blow and so expose them that it would be impossible for them to exploit Indians.

As it happened only this plan came into operation and for six months after my arrest the Indian Independence Movement in the Japanese Occupied countries was for all practical purposes dead. Only the arrival of Mr. S.C. Bose, whose name dazzled and blinded many sincere Indians that it came to life again. Even then thousands of Indian officers and other ranks and civilians, who were whole-heartedly in the moment before, did not join and have consequently suffered considerably.

The Japanese were under the impression that I was just a captain and it could not be possible for me to raise, organise and train such a force as I intended. Therefore they were very liberal on all verbal support. Thanks to the hearty cooperation of the officers and men and also Indian civilians that all my plans began to materialise far quicker than my own expectations. It was only when the Japanese realised that my plans actually started to take shape that they were alarmed. The Materialisation of my plans meant the complete destruction of their own.

4. Leadership in the Army

I do not feel happy to speak on this delicate question but now; on my release from the Japanese, I have been told by some Indian friends that the late Mr. Rash Behari Bose, the well-known Japanese puppet, had tried to mislead the Indian public by misrepresenting the real causes of my arrest. I am also glad to hear that the public, especially in Singapore, was too well informed to believe him. Still I want to clear this point here.

Mr. R.B. Bose in his campaign of lies, to hide his own weakness, levelled certain charges against me which included that I had designs for a dictatorship. How on earth he believed that he could convince the public by such lies is beyond me; when his own official statement and the official

Japanese statement issued by Major General Iwakuru, stated clearly and which conclusively proved that the principles involved were mainly Japanese insincerity and mistrust, their designs to use the I.I.L. Movement as a puppet movement and the I.N.A. as their 5th columnist, their misbehaviour towards Indian officers and men, the question of Indian civilian property etc., etc.

It was never my desire to create myself a general or a political leader. I remained a captain all through till after Bangkok conference held in June, 1942. If I had any such aim, there was nothing in my way to stop me from creating myself anything. I knew, I was an average army officer and I had no misunderstanding or complex about my military or political abilities. I was always sincerely prepared to give place a better man.

Until the fall of Singapore about 8,000 Indian soldiers had united under me ready to sacrifice everything for the Indian cause. As it happened, no officer senior to me surrendered. All the men declared their complete faith in me and accepted me as their leader.

A few weeks after the fall of Singapore, I collected about 30 senior officers (all majors and colonels), briefly explained to them what I had done so far, requested them to investigate fully and critically examine all my works and if in their honest judgement I was found guilty of injuring the Indian cause; or if proved that I was a Japanese paid man, I should be duly punished. I also appealed to them to carry on the work of Indian freedom and that they were free to select their own leader for this work, under whom I would gladly serve to the best of my ability in whatever capacity he decided to utilise my services. They unanimously selected me again as their leader and I had to accept their decision. This decision was again confirmed by the representatives of Indians in East Asia at the Bangkok Conference held in June, 1942, where I was unanimously elected member of the Council of Action and again appointed General Officer Commanding, The Indian National Army, by the Council of Action.

I may add here that it was repeatedly proposed in the Bangkok conference that I should take over complete control of the moment and I rejected even to hear such a proposal.

5. Council of Action and Col. N.S. Gill

The members of the Council of Action, as every one known were as follows :–

Mr. Rash Behari Bose (President), Messrs. K.P.K. Menon and N. Raghavan, Lt. Col. G.Q. Gilani and myself.

It must be mentioned that Col. N.S. Gill, although not elected member, C of A (for reasons I do not want to state here) played as important a role to serve India, as any other member of the C. of A.

Col. N.S. Gill : He was my chief military adviser. He was in my humble opinion the ablest military brain (Indian) in the East. I am not aware of the charges invested against him by the Japanese but I can declare that he is a true and great patriotic son of India. I maintain that after knowing the true intentions of the Japanese and having seen their treatment of the other Asiatics, particularly the Chinese, no true Indian with the least sense of justice, courage of conviction and strength of character could work with the Japanese.

At this time I do not know whether he is still alive or has already been tortured to death by the Japanese. It is my humble request to the Indian nation, that if he is not alive, those responsible for his death, whether Japanese or Indians, should be brought to justice. I may mention here that a very senior Japanese Officer, who was by no means his friend, said to me once that men like Gill are presented to nations once in centuries. I did all in my power to get him released but I too followed him soon.

Mr. Rash Behari Bose : It may be interesting to know that why we elected such an incapable man, a well-known Japanese puppet, whom no one trusted, as our President. That was the most unpardonable and historic blunder. We were under the impression that influence for India's benefit. At the same time we made it doubly sure that he had no power whatsoever as President of the C. of A. He was also our puppet. But when we all resigned he made use of some sort of a legal clause and declaring himself as 'the sole surviving member of the C. of A' assumed a dictatorial role with the help of Japanese bayonets.

Messrs. Menon and Raghavan : Both these gentlemen were very able and sincere Indian patriots. The organisation of the Indian Independence League, Far East was their creation. Their chief fault from the Japanese point of view was that I must add that during the most critical and trying time of crisis, Mr. Menon played a very bold and noble part at the risk of not only his life but also of his large family, I have the greatest admiration for his brave stand.

For shattering R.B. Bose's and his henchmen's plans of preconceived dictatorship, the drafting of the Tokyo conference's resolutions and the drafting of the constitution at Bangkok Conference were the fruits of the labour of M/s. Raghavan and Menon.

Lt. Col. G.Q. Gilani : He too joined the movement with great enthusiasm but after seeing the Japanese, his confidence too was shaken.

During the time of crisis he stood with me as a true soldier and colleague.

I may be pardoned for developing on leadership and the C. of A but it was essential to say a few words.

6. Indian Soldiers

It will, I am sure, gladden the hearts of Indian people in India to known that out of about 55,000 Indian prisoners of war about 45,000 had volunteered for India's cause (although the Japanese did not allow me to raise an army of more than 20,000). These volunteers included men from all classes recruited into the Indian Army including a large number of Gurkhas as well. Out of the remaining 10,000 nearly half were such who were prepared for India's cause but who did not trust the Japanese. Officers belonging to this group rendered me very valuable service. The rest I am ashamed to say were either too selfish or too coward. Some of them do not deserve to be called Indians.

I am proud to state here for the information of my countrymen that the army that I raised was truly a patriotic Indian Army. It was the only Japanese sponsored Army in the East which had no Japanese advisers, instructors, symbols, words of command, uniform, badges or their flag and which demanded equal respect. This was no easy task. I had to fight for every single item.

7. Crisis

Having worked for about a year with the aims and motive mentioned above and having perceived the Japanese evil designs and being firmly convinced that they just wanted to exploit us, I put forward this my opinion in the C. of A. This was done in the second half of November 1942.

All my colleagues of the C. of A. agreed with me except the 'brave' President. We agreed to demand an explanation from the Japanese and very strongly requested the President to put forward our view to the Japanese asking them to.[4]

Next day the President replied that he had accepted our resignations. On the same day I delivered two open lectures to all the officers (about 1,000) placing before them clearly all the facts, proving the insincerity of the Japanese and Mr. R.B. Bose. I told them that this was the trial for which we had been preparing for so long. I warned them that the trial would be very severe probably entailing the loss of lives of many of us but it must be undergone calmly and bravely as befit true soldiers. Only then would the world know that we were patriots and not puppets of the

4. For details see Appendix IV.

Japanese. I also told them that since we could no longer serve the cause of India I was taking steps to dissolve the army which was unanimously approved.

As already stated, Mr. R.B. Bose assumed the role of a dictator, declaring that he derived that right because he was the sole surviving member of the C. of A. So he declared himself as Commander of the Army as well. Needless to say that the Japanese bayonets were supporting his actions. But when he tried to interfere in the Army by ordering me to send certain officers to him, I gave such a rude and threatening reply, stating in it what I thought of him and what other officers and men of the I.N.A. considered him to be also telling him to keep his hands off the Army. Today, when I recollect the wording of that letter I myself feel ashamed for having sent him such a reply. But with that letter his interference in the Army ceased once for all. Far from wanting to meet officers of the I.N.A. he was afraid of coming out of his rooms which were heavily guarded by the Japanese.

Dissolution of the Indian National Army : On the 15th I sent a letter to the Japanese stating that I had absolutely no confidence in the Indian Independence League Movement conducted by the Japanese in the East and that the Army should be immediately dissolved and the members of the I.N.A. should again revert to the status of prisoners of war. In reply to this Major General Iwakuru told me that having once declared these soldiers to be free, they could not be reverted to the status of Prisoners of War. He asked me that if I had no confidence in the moment in the East whether I had confidence in the freedom movement in India and if so, he was prepared to allow me to take the army inside India, to work there for India's cause. I must confess that I was completely surprised but I immediately accepted his proposition. Later on after consulting my senior officers, who all heartily approved of it, when I re-enquired, nothing came out of it.

On 21st December, 1942, I issued open warning orders thanking all officers and other ranks for the sacrifices which they were prepared to make for India's cause and warning them that as the army could no longer serve India's cause, I was going to dissolve it.

An other secret letter was sent to all battalions which was to be opened in case I disappeared secretly, removed, arrested or shot. This letter contained the final, dissolving orders freeing all ranks from all obligations and from their personal pledge given to me and I took all the responsibility.

The long awaited day came at last. I was arrested on the morning of 29th December, 1942 and the secret letter was opened in all battalions and was strictly obeyed.

It is not correct for me to say what happened after my arrest clearing the situation. The President was so afraid of the Japanese that he wanted to run away. Of course we did not allow him to do that. Eventually we compelled him to put our demand which he did tremblingly.

The Japanese flatly refused to consider these demands and instead threatened us for daring to demand from the mighty Imperial Government.

But we expected this and were not frightened.

On 4th December, 1942, having consulted all my senior officers, I again, put up in the C of A. a 'Minimum demand' which included besides others, a demand to give me a free hand to raise an army not less than 200,000 strong. This was again supported by the C. of A. except of course the President who shed considerabl amount of tears, remarking that that would mean his death. In that demand I made it very clear that if the Japanese did not accede to my demands in toto by 1st of January, 1943, the Indian National Army would have nothing to do with the Indian Independence League Movement or the Japanese after that date and would be automatically considered dissolved. This was considered an ultimatum on any part by the Japanese who said that even the U.S.A. had not dared to insult the Japanese with such an ultimatum.

I was threatened, cajoled and begged not to make such a stand and finally pressed to resign. I stood firm and refused to do anything of the sort. The whole I.N.A. united as one man, stood behind me. In vain did the Japanese try to split the officers. The splendid united stand made by the Officers deserves the greatest admiration. Only two men failed in their duty, both of whom had in fact nothing to do directly with the army. One of them was a medical man and the other a regular infantry officer. I knew they were Japanese informers. I allowed them purposely to attend all secret meetings of officers which I was conducting daily in those days so that the Japanese may be duly and truly kept informed about the attitude of the I.N.A. At that time we were already armed and were not afraid. The Japanese knew this too and were very cautious.

Arrest of Col. N.S. Gill : Very early in the morning of 8th of December, 1942, when it was still dark, 17 members of the Japanese Military Police headed by a colonel, the chief of the M.P., whose name I have forgotten, raided my house and demanded Col. Gill who was sleeping in my bungalow. He gave me a written promise that if I permitted the arrest of Col. Gill, they promised that in future no member of the I.N.A. would be

touched. I strongly protested and did not agree and asked him to arrest me also. This he refused. They took Gill away. I became furious on such high handedness. Till midday, various high ranking Japanese officials tried to pacify me. I, however, refused of listen to any of their excuses and demanded Gill back which was not done.

Resignation from The Council of Action : Calling an immediate meeting of senior officers I placed the facts before them. They unanimously agreed with me that the time for a decisive step had come. In the afternoon, a meeting of the C. of A. was held, which Mr. Raghavan did not attend and who we came to know had already resigned on some other issue. We three, Mr. Menon, Lt. Col.G.Q. Gilani and I, submitted a joint resignation from the C. of A. Besides various other reasons for our resignation we strongly protested against the Japanese high handedness in arresting the Gill.

It was Year 1942 : Finally in connection with my work I want to state that all this happened in the year 1942 when the Japanese were intoxicated, maddened and blinded with victories, when every member of the Japanese armed forces considered himself no less than a personal representative of their Emperor, when the slightest disobedience or difference of opinion with the lowest Japanese meant certain death, when famous Allied generals were not only forced to sign unconditional surrenders but had to bear quietly several personal insults, injuries and indignities, when Allied soldiers, British, Americans, Australians and Dutch were dubbed as white slaves of the descendants of the Sun Goddess. It was in that very period that I took the gravest decision of exposing Japanese insincerity publicly. Those; who have the slightest experience of the Japanese and their ways in the war, particularly in the year 1942, can well visualise the sort of punishment that I was expecting for my action at that time.

I myself am surprised to find myself alive today. I know that I owe my life to the splendid stand of 20,000 armed Indians in Singapore on that day and the backing and sympathy of all Indians in the East.

I am not sure of my fate and before handing over myself to the British I think it my duty to thank all the members of the C. of A. all the officers, N.C.Os and men of the I.N.A. who stood so loyally and firmly united with me and Indian civilians for their sympathetic support extended to me all through in the movement.

I must also thank Major General Iwakuru (I do not know whether he is dead or alive) for publishing a comprehensive statement stating clearly, openly and boldly the reasons of my arrest. By doing that he did a service to India.

8. Before handing over myself to British

As I may not have another opportunity of meeting them I want to express my heartfelt gratitude to the following, who, at the personal risk of their lives helped me in several ways during the days of my confinement:

Corporal Abdul Rahman of Singapore Police

Mr. Teja Singh of Anti-Malarial Dept., Singapore.

Mr. Cheah, a Chinese gentleman of Singapore.

All the Chinese inhabitants of Ubin Island (off Singapore) especially Messrs. All Bhoe and Tan pang Ling. S. Pritam Singh of Sumatra.

Dr. Roesm and his wife of Manindjau. S.W.K. Sumatra. Miss Soefjani Mawani of Matoer S.W.K. Sumatra.

And also Lt. Col. Ogawa who sincerely sympathised with me and who saved my life at a very critical time in my confinement.

Appendix-III

MEMOIRS OF FUJIWARA IWAICHI
pertaining to his role in the formation
of the Indian National Army (Extract)

War History Document No.70
August 1959, Tokyo

This was written after the release of Fujiwara from Singapore. It should be read with the Interrogation Report included in this Volume. This account was written in Japanese from which portions relevant to the study of the Indian National Army were translated.

Section 1: Patriots' Leap into the Dark

On a chilly December day of 1940, a secret confidential telegram was delivered on the table of Lt. Col. Kadomatsu[1] of the 8th Section of the Army Department of the Imperial Headquarters located at Miyakezaka of Tokyo. It was from the chief staff officer of a certain division of the Japanese 21st Army stationed at Canton. It was addressed to the deputy chief of staff, and to convey the following request of three Indians who had contacted the Japanese army Headquarters at Canton after leaving Hongkong secretly. That they were confined in the jail of Hongkong on charge of anti-British activities, but had escaped. They wanted to go to India, Berlin and Malaya secretly to establish contact with their comrades and carry on their fight against the British. For that they wanted Japanese protection to go to Bangkok if possible, otherwise to Indo-China, from where they proposed to go their destination overland on foot. Although the names of these three persons were not mentioned in the Telegram, yet in the footnote it was appended that they were Sikhs, and confirmed their claim of being anti-British patriots.[2]

Lt. Col. Kadomatsu and Maj.-O (Ozeki) spent some time in studying the implications of this telegram, and came to the conclusion that a reply should be sent to this telegram. Thereupon they sent the following reply after obtaining the approval of the higher authorities. 'The Japanese army in Canton should investigate the anticedents of these persons in more detail carefully, and should try to comply with their requests as far as possible'. Even before this telegram reached Canton, the following telegram was received from Canton. 'The three Indians in question have been placed on board a steamer bound for Kobe, and the general staff office is requested to take the necessary steps in this regard.

Thereupon Lt. Col. Kadomatsu entrusted the task of ensuring safe and secret, transportation of these three persons to Bangkok to Maj. Fujiwara, I myself, (At that time I was a captain). A certain Capt. K. was allotted the task of assisting them. After confirming that the Imperial Headquarters did not have any special project about these three persons. I started making arrangements for their journey by boat to Bangkok, and

---

1. Lt. Kadomatsu Shoichi, was in-change, Intelligence operations towards India at General Headquarters in Tokyo.
2. The names of the three Indians were Kartar Singh Quami, Harnam Singh Dhillon and Hari Singh.

at the same time sent a telegram to Mr. Tamura, our military attache at Bangkok, to make arrangements for their safe and secret landing in Bangkok.

Just at that time a boat was spotted which was about to sail for Bangkok for bringing back a cargo of rice. Unfortunately I have forgotten its name.

Capt.-K (Koi Wai) immediately left for Kobo, and succeeded in enlisting the cooperation of the captain of the ship with the assistance of local police. On a dark night, the three Indians were put on board the ship in great secrecy.

In fact they were transferred from the incoming boat straight to the outgoing vessel, without even giving them time to land on the soil of Japan. They were accommodated in a hold of the ship, and remained there till they reached Bangkok.

Capt.-K reported that the three Indians did not utter even a word of complaint over the extremely uncomfortable conditions. On the contrary they were moved to tears over the goodwill and warm gesture of the Japanese army. Again, they assured that in case of their detection on the way by British or Thai police, they would immediately commit suicide so that Japan did not get implicated and showed the knives they had kept ready for the purpose. They showed their firm desire to bear the heat in the hold during the voyage through warm South China Sea, and would try to do their best to stand upto the expectation of Japan.

As we did not have any political or military scheme whatsoever about these persons, their names even were not recorded on the files, which I regret now very much. We were extremely happy over the fact that we could offer our humble assistance to these three patriots fighting for their country's Independence just out of friendship, transcending above narrow nationalistic designs.

The ship slowly moved south across the South China Sea where the temperature was above 100°C with the three Indians on board. The condition inside the hold was unbearable like that in a boiler room. The presence of these three Indians was known only to the captain and purser of the ship. The purser carried day's food only once during the night stealing the eyes of the crew, and encouraged them as much as possible. Although it was unbearable, yet they did not express the desire to come to the deck at night to get fresh air even once. As they did not have valid travel papers, they were transferred to a small boat from the ship under the strict supervision of the Military Attache Col. Tamura. The three Indians left the ship passing off as coolies, and reached the residence of the military

attache near Lumbini Park. Presently we received a telegram from the military attache informing the safe landing.

The colonel acted as an ideal host, providing the three tired and exhausted Indians with cool bath, cool drinks, Indian food and good place to sleep.

The next night Col. Tamura asked these men about their future plans. When the colonel expressed his concern over their prospective difficulty in an unknown city, one of the three Indians with great self composure said that the old veteran Amar Singh was there in Bangkok. He was the leader of the Indian Independence League with Headquarters in Bangkok. A young Indian Pritam Singh was there to assist him. The IIL was a secret society of the Sikhs set up with the sole objective of liberating India from the British rule, and had members in Hongkong, Shanghai, Tokyo, San Francisco and Berlin. The three Indians next vanished in the darkness of Lumbini Park after expressing gratitude and soliciting Japan's help for the forthcoming Independence struggle. After a few days a tall Sikh priet called on Col. Tamura at his residence secretly and solicited his interview to the Sikh guard. He was Pritam Singh, and this was the first step in the contact between the IIL and the Japanese army.

Following this, both Pritam Singh and Amar Singh met Col. Tamura a number of times.

Although Thailand at that time was showing pro-Japanese leanings, yet it was within the sphere of influence of Britains and had turned into a hot bed of intelligence warfare by Japan, Britain, USA, China and Germany. Hence extreme caution was called for. The talks did not go beyond a certain point because the Anglo-Japanese relations had not deteriorated during the early summer of 1941 yet to the extent where war become a probability. However, through these talks Col. Tamura was convinced that the IIL was a secret society with a membership network spread over Tokyo, Shanghai, Hongkong, Southern Thailand, Malaya, India, Berlin and other places, and committed to anti-British struggle, if possible with arms. He also saw the prospect of obtaining military and political intelligence regarding Indian and Malaya through the IIL. Again, Pritam Singh and Amar Singh also could confirm the good wishes of Japan through the talks held with Col. Tamura. It was in this way that the bridge of friendship was build between Japan and the IIL.

In the midst of such quick changing situation Lt. Col. Kadomatsu, who was the staff officer of the Imperial Headquarters in charge of propaganda arrived at Bangkok in plain dress towards the end of July 1941. In case war broke out between Japan and Britain, then Burma, Malaya

and the Eest Indies would become the main scenes of war. The attitude of the people of these countries as well as of India would be decisive. Although these countries were under imperialistic occupation for a long time and apparently had lost national consciousness, yet there were very strong nationalistic movements in India and Burma. In case Japan took the initiative to study the national aspirations of these peoples and assist their struggle with proper understanding then they would become the most valuable ally of Japan in the event of war between Japan and Britain. As this is quite obvious to those who have studied the rudiments of war strategy, Lt. Col. Kadomatsu also probably had this conviction when he came to Bangkok. However, this is not possible overnight. When he left Tokyo he had one very important objective in view, viz., to assist the movement of the Thakin Party of Burma which was established towards the end of 1934. This was also not particulars in view of any war between Japan and Britain, but to hamper the assistance to Chiang Kai Shek through the Burma-China Road by Britain. However, as war between Japan and Britain was apprently round the corner, he advised Col. Tamura to step up all his schemes related with enlisting the support and cooperation of Singapore. He was very familiar with the situation in Singapore involving the Chinese by virtue of his long stay there and had a large number of acquaintances among the Chinese. The trail of Sumatra and Java was totally missing. After promising to send the officers required for the job and money to Tamura, Kadomatsu returned to Tokyo. I was at that time working as the youngest officer in charge of news and propaganda of Section 8, and I was under the belief that Kadomatsu had gone to Indo-China on an urgent work. I came to know that he actually went to Bangkok for the first time when he reported to Col. T, the head of the Division, on the developments there on his return.

Although the whole idea was in a nebulous stage, yet I felt that a firm ideological conviction normally required for sponsoring such a project was totally lacking. However, it was mentioned during the trips that I myself and Capt.-K had some providential connection with the IIL source. As this did not involve our main duty, and as no comment was invited, we kept quiet. In the mean time the Japanese forces marched into South Indo-China, in July, and the Anglo-Americans retaliated strongly by freezing Japanese assets abroad, abrogating trade treaties, prohibiting sale of petroleum, and bringing about rupture in Dutch-Japanese oil negotiations. Thus the destiny was slowly leading us towards war.

I continued with my cautious life renting a room in Thailand Hotel. Apart from that I was cautious over the movements of the boarders and

the waiters. After a few days I realised that there were a few military officers whom I had seen before somewhere. They were the officers who had come to train the Thai soldiers to handle Japanese planes and tanks supplied by Japan. Besides there was Lt. Col. Y who was a member of the committee set up for determining the national boundary between Thailand and Indo-China. The waiters, however, apparently overlooked my presence. In order to avoid my becoming a topic of discussion among the Japanese boarders, and thereby attracting the attention of Thai police and the agents of the big powers, I requested the military attache to find out a house for me in a very non-conspicuous locality. After a few days, 2nd Lt. Yonemura came to this hotel as an employee. It was indeed painful for me to see one of my assistants and comrades just pretending to be a waiter in this hotel just for the sake of our fatherland. He had to maintain rather cold and formal relation between a guest and a boy not acquainted to each other. Only our eyes expressed our feeling.

He played his part very skilfully. That made me feel all the more pity for him. At night he came to my room stealthily for contact.

I think it was 10th of October, the day when I met Pritam Singh, the representative of IIL, with which my destiny was going to be tied up. It was decided that we would meet at the residence of the military attache at noon. He came in a Samlom, at the appointed time. I was waiting rather impatiently and longingly for him alongwith the military attache. As he was led in by a boy, I had the shock of my life. I had expected a rough and tough looking revolutionary, but contrary to my expectation he was a lean and thin tall and somewhat nervous and soft looking Sikh youth. Another shock was his greeting with folded hands, which we do at the time of prayer to God, whereas I had expected to shake hands. After formal introduction by Col. Tamura, he said that he had heard a lot about me, and was waiting to meet me longingly, and shook hands with me. In reply I said that I would feel it a great honour to be able to associate myself in realising their lofty ideal. I came to Bangkok with the firm conviction that their fight for Independence would be crowned with success ultimately, and I would cooperate with them whole heartedly. Col. Tamura acted as the interpreter, and on hearing my wishes he was very happy.

Then we made ourselves comfortable, and I asked about the three Indians of Canton. He thanked me profusely on hearing that I had arranged their passage to Bangkok. He continued that the three Indians were very much grateful to the Japanese general staff office, and that they had already reached their respective destinations safely. And he added that our cooperation and joint work became more or less a settled fact at that time.

In that sense we were old comrades. Then he related about their political struggle. He had plunged head long in the country's political movement in 1939, and had to leave India as his life was in danger. He came to Bangkok via Singapore, and was working as an assistant to Amar Singh.

He expressed his anger at the British deception of India at the time of First World War, and confided his conviction that Independence of India could not be achieved without the uprising of the Indian people. Thereupon he asserted that the Second World War should be taken advantage of for starting armed struggle for Indian Independence. He also expressed great respect for Subhash Chandra Bose who was in Berlin at that time and pledged consolidation with the movement headed by him in Europe. He supported the stand of the leaders of Indian National Congress in not welcoming assistance from the big nations in the Independence struggle as this would mean inviting an evil to get rid of another evil. The sole objective is to attain Independence of India without any strings attached from any country. He said "In case we seek assistance of foreign countries for our Independence struggle, we would lose the support of our countrymen. Even then, we believe that we should not let this golden opportunity slip, and hence should not hesitate in seeking foreign assistance. This situation has created a great and painful dilemma for us." Even when we were discussing this hot topic, he remained very cool, and not even once did he betray his excitement. It became very clear to me that I had a very cool and rational man of firm conviction to deal with.

Even in this first meeting I got a hint of our future course of action. After this political talk was over, I asked him about his turban, long beard and the iron ring on his wrist. In that connection I came to know a rough outline of Sikh religion. This first confidential meeting lasted for two hours, Col. Tamura acting as the interpreter.

In this very first meeting a bond of friendship was established between us, where we could express our view without reserve. I felt that there was a path of glory lying ahead of us.

At the time of parting he expressed his desire to meet after three days. He proposed the house of a cloth merchant as the next venue of our meeting so as not to rouse suspicion with his frequent visit to the military attache house. Col. Tamura immediately approved of it. It is needless to say that I was also of the same opinion. I was slightly worried over this meeting. This was because I was very bad in English. I had neglected it during my middle school days, and ever since the cadet schools days, I had to concentrate on Chinese. I was also worried over the health of Pritam Singh, as he had fits of cough during his talks.

Two days after the first meeting, Col. Tamura introduced me to an young man called Otaguro. He was about thirty, dark and was a teacher of English in the Japanese primary school in Singapore. He had come over to Bangkok following deterioration in Anglo-Japanese relations. He was quite affable and appeared to be sincere. After talking with him I got the impression that he had neither understanding of nor interest in nationalist movement, and did not care much over the political developments in the region. However, he was prepared to do anything and everything in case it was for our fatherland.

In this way I got another comrade who was to become my ear and speech. Another happy thing occurred on this day. A house was finally spotted for me in a very ordinary locality near the Bangkok railway station. It had become vacant as a Japanese professor of Taipei Medical College, who returned to Japan after completing his assignment of research on certain tropical diseases. I inherited both the maid servant as well as the furnitures. It was a very inconspicuous house, with five bed rooms on the first floor and a big hall and dining room on the ground floor. As the stay at the hotel was telling on my nerves. I practically grabbed the opportunity and shifted on the very day the professor vacated it.

On that very day I instructed Otaguro to find out the house of the Indian in whose house the meeting had been fixed. He located in the venue on the first floor of a pickle godown behind a dilapidated house inside a narrow lane about four kilometres from the Lumbini Park. He also made a report on the distribution of the houses in the locality. As well as the residents and the details upon the topics that were likely to be discussed the following day with Pritam Singh till late; and I was extremely related over the prospect of gaining a first hand knowledge of the activities of the IIL in Southern Thailand and Malaya besides the activities of the Indians in Bangkok. I also decided to discussed over his own idea of Indian revolution. I was also supposed to exercise extreme restraint in not allowing Pritam Singh to know anything about Japan's preparations for war against England and America.

When I left Tokyo in early October, there were rumours over war with the Anglo-Americans, but even though middle of October had passed, there were no such signs. However, the coded message of the state of war could come in any day. In that case what a pity it would be that I had not yet succeeded in evolving any viable policy to implement the task for which I had come. Most of my assistants had not yet arrived, nor there was any information from Tashiro (Shigeto) and Kamimoto (Toshio) in Southern Thailand, who had been summoned to Bangkok. I passed the

night sleeplessly. As it dawned, I jumped out of the bed, took a good shower, and had a gulp of whisky straight. It was only after this I had a sound sleep.

I left my house at about 7 P.M. telling my maid servant that I was going to dine with our ambassador, and after walking some distance with great care to ascertain whether someone was following me. I picked up a Samlom and went to the China town, just in the other end of the town. From there I came back to the Lumbini Park after changing the Samlom a number of times, where I found Otaguro waiting for me. Next we both started for the destination on foot, with great caution.

We reached the house 10 minutes before the appointed time. There was a man in flowing white robe standing under the eves of the house. As we tried to pass him, he stopped both of us. He led us to the first floor of the pickle godown, where at a corner I found a small table, a small chair and a simple dirty bed, besides the suffocating smell of the pickles. There Pritam Singh was waiting for me. As usual he first greeted us with folded hands, and then shook hands. He apologised for the dirty venues but added that it was necessary for precaution. As a man was standing below on watch, we could proceed with our talks with ease. Although it was very oppressive there, yet I requested him to be at ease, and said that I was very happy over his caution.

The night was very oppressive and sultry without even slightest breeze, and there were hordes of mosquitos feasting on us. The talks went on for about five hours over tapid water to quench our parched throat. He first of all expressed his views of the Indians in Bangkok.

In Bangkok there was Indo-Thai Friendship Association besides the IIL. This organisation had its allegiance to Indian Nation Congress, and two of its active leaders were Swami[3] (a professor of Bangkok University) and Das. This organisation had connections with the German Embassy, as well as the backing of the local Indian businessmen, and as such was much more powerful than the IIL. This organisation was at daggers drawn with the IIL the latter being supported mostly by the Sikh.

This Mr. Das had in the past lived in Japan, leading the anti-British movement in Japan together with Sahay. I had the occasion of meeting Anand Mohan Sahay and Das (Deb Nath) in Tokyo in spring this year. I immediately realised that the rivalry between the two organisations was a very delicate matter; and apprehending the likelihood of exposure of the

---

3. This refers to Swami Satyanand Puri and his associate Dab Nath Das who were very prominent in Thailand.

IIL activity because of the rivalry. I enquired from Pritam Singh whether some sort of cooperation could be ensured between the two organisations. He ruled out any such possibility. I had a great impulse to develop separate contact with my old acquaintance Das, but realising that this would give Pritam Singh a very adverse impression, I decided to postpone the question of cooperation between the two organisations till the outbreak of hostilities. I was also afraid that such a move might expose the Japanese contacts with the IIL. However, I tried to press the necessity for cooperation between the two organisations for the success of the Independence movement, and if this was not possible, then at least to reduce the friction to the minimum for the sake of the greater objective.

Next I came to know about the presence of the supporters of the IIL at Hatai, Yala in Southern Thailand and at Kotah Bahru on the north-east coast of Malaya. Pritam Singh made monthly trips to these places under the pretext of preaching, but mainly to maintain contact with these people as well as to distribute IIL propaganda pamphlets. He reported a heavy concentration of British Indian forces along the Thai-Malaya border, and the comrades of Pritam Singh in the region are trying their best to propagate the cause of the IIL, but has so far failed to attain any tangible result because of frequent rotation of the forces.. Because of antipathy towards the Britishers at the bottom of their hearts, the British Indian forces accepted and read the pamphlets with great delight. He expressed his confidence that in the event of war in case Japanese forces invaded Malaya and he went alongwith the Japanese forces and made appeal directly to the Indian soldiers, then there would be very good response.

As he related, I had hoped in the beginning for the penetration into Malaya and to a certain extent into the British Indian forces by his organisation, but was slightly disappointed on hearing the full report. However, he dropped hint about his earnest desire for Japanese declaration of war against Britain, but I refrained from making any comment on this socre. I urged him to continue with his propaganda among the Indian soldiers in Malaya as the situation was rather tense. I also could hear his future plan about his movement. He was apparently convinced of the inevitability of war between Japan and Britain, and in such an eventuality he wanted the Japanese assistance in raising an Indian Independence Army from among the Indian officers and men of the British Indian army, as well as from among the Indian living in Thailand, Malaya and Burma, and take up arms against the Britishers. At that stage he wanted to develop the IIL in global scale.

My response to this plan of Pritam Singh was spontaneous, and I

promised all helps possible. He solicited Japan's cooperation in Asia establishing contact with Bose in Berlin, and the privilege to use Saigon Radio and Tokyo Radio for anti-British propaganda for Indian Independence.

At that time Pritam Singh had all his attention focussed on the broadcasts by Bose. He wanted me to help him in exchanging messages with Pratap in Tokyo and his comrades in Shanghai. Although the fateful day was approaching fast and I was tempted much to encourage him by confiding the fact, yet I exercised restraint. It was indeed regrettable that the talks could not touch upon the vital points at such a crucial stage. The Indian who was standing on watch below was trying his best to keep of the mosquitos, and everytime he slapped against his body we lowered our voices and tried to judge the situation. During the talks Pritam Singh had fits of cough, and as the night advanced he betrayed signs of fatigue. Finally I enquired about his health.

With slight worry he said that he had been suffering from some throat trouble, but it was nothing serious. He ruled out his death before accomplishment of the noble task assigned to him by God. I was very much impressed by his resolution. We suddenly realised that it was already past 2.00 A.M. Finally he said that he would be away the whole of last week of October for making contacts and propaganda in Southern Thailand. We parted after agreeing to meet again during early November. We both left the quiet and sleepy lane cautiously and emerged on the main road.

On the way back also, we changed Samlom a number of times covering almost half the city and finally returned home. Although I was extremely tired, my mind was very fresh. After ordering the maid servant to bring whisky and cold water, I recollected the words of Pritam Singh, and wrote them down in my memo while wetting my throat with whisky. It was already dawn when I got into the bed ultimately. Next day I reported the contents of the discussion to Col. Tamura, who in turn forwarded it to the Imperial Headquarters. It was quite apparent that the situation was worsening consequent to the oil embargo imposed by Britain, USA and Holland. In the mean time Kamimoto and Tashiro came to Bangkok from Southern Thailand and reported on the situation there.

As expected, Tashiro failed to make any appreciable headway with his project with the Chinese. After they returned to Southern Thailand, Uemochi, Nakamiya, Yamaguchi, Segawa, Takimura, Ishikawa and others came to Bangkok from Tokyo together with Masufuchi. According to my plan, I retained the charge of IIL, with Yamaguchi, Nakamiya, Ishikawa and Otakuro as my assistants. Nakamiya acted as an employer of Nikku Yoko

Co. and Ishikawa and Takimura as the employees of the military attache. All others were sent to South Thailand as employees of Mitsubishi Co. and Dainen Koshi Co., to assist Tashiro and Kamimoto. As all these people were new to the place, it was necessary for them to get accustomed. Again, it was also necessary to make reasonable progress with our projects so that any sudden outbreak of war did not take us by surprise. I lodged them for a few days at my house, and tried my best to convince them of the ideological aspect of our projects. Yamaguchi and Ishikawa started living permanently with me and they were very pleasant company indeed. At night Nakamiya and Segawa came to my residence for contact.

We discussed till late on the ideals inspiring us as well as the policy to be adopted for accomplishing our mission. These were our happiest moments in Bangkok. In case the Far East became the field of war, in that case the ideal of Japan should conquer all the obstacles and confrontations for building up coprosperity sphere, in which there would be no place for any feeling of being ruled by the conquered nations, or any pride of conqueror.

The nations of East Asia should be liberated from foreign rule and exploitation, and a new order of peace and welfare should be ushered in where all the nations would get proper opportunity to achieve political goal and maintain their cultural tradition. The Japanese nation has the obligation to stand in the vanguard and accomplish this mission. The religious belief, customs and manners and attitude towards life of all these nations should be respected. Moreover, we should avoid having a subjective attitude towards these things. We should try to gain appreciation and approval of our ideal from other nations through the sincerity of our action.

The British and Dutch rule was about hundred years old, and has thoroughly pacified the local people through skillful policy and rewarding the collaborators. As against this we are not only inexperienced, but also we were inadequately prepared. Hence the only way before us to break the stranglehold was to appeal to the national aspiration of these peoples with great sincerity, Indeed sincerity is the key that opens all doors.

Our movement should assume the shape of assisting the spontaneous movement of our comrades among these nations who would respond to this idea of Japan. There should be no place for coersion or interference, and they should not get any impression that they were being exploited or used as puppet. We should set at the work sincerely without any ulterior motive. Our dedication should match the patriotism and spirit of sacrifice of the freedom fighters of the various nations of South Asia and India.

Another important aspect of our work was that we were supposed to act the mediator in between these nations and the Japanese forces, and check the repitition of violence committed by a section of the Japanese officers and men in China against innocent population and prisoners of war.

A firm commitment was to be obtained from the operational forces to this effect. We had to be reconciled with the difficult demands imposed on us as the intermediary standing in between these peoples and the Japanese operational forces. And we would have to fulfill this difficult task with boldness and firmness.

For the present the most important question was the understanding and unity of the team. The harmony existing among the team members should automatically influence the leaders as well as the common people of this region. In my talks with my comrades at night I emphasised the above points citing numerous examples. All agreed to whatever I said.

Pritam Singh returned from Southern Thailand in the beginning of November. We had another meeting at the above place. This night he introduce me to Amar Singh, who wore a white flowing beard and appeared to me not less than seventy years old. The old man quietly walked upto me and stood in front of me just like a statue. With both his hands across his breast he looked at me intently through his beard which reached upto his waist. And he offered prayer to God reciting something.

I felt as if a messenger of God was standing in front of me. In his stern looks and solemn face I could read inviolable sincere feeling, and indomitable spirit. My face surely had expressed my respect and relianee for this old patriot about whom I had heard so much.

After finishing his prayer, he pulled a chair and sat besides me. I was rather overwhelmed in his august presence. Next he started speaking in a low but forceful voice emating from deep down his chest which could be singled out even from among million. He talked without stirring his body, and his eyes moved either on my face or on that of Pritam Singh. Sometimes he looked at the ceiling as if thinking of his distant home. During his talk he often prayed for God's help with closed eyes. As he talked, he often got excited, and I could read his feeling in the tightening grip of his right hand. In no time the ascetic turned into a fiery revolutionary and I was easily overwhelmed by his solemn attitude.

He branded the British conquest and rule of India as a case of immorality and deception. Since his early youth he had dedicated his body and soul to fight for the freedom of his country and his compatriots. He had spent, consequently, ten long years in the prisons of Andaman and Rangoon, where he was mostly kept in fetters. He related his tortures

and consequent hardening of his conviction as if chanting prayers. And even at this fag end of his life he has lost none of his ardour to stand at the vanguard of his country's freedom struggle. He also expressed his confidence that God's blessings were with the IIL and the Indian people. I must confess that the talks of the old man were not wholely ratio ıal or logical, yet I was very much impressed. I was not very optimistic about the capacity of the old man to lead freedom movement of grand magnitude. Somehow he lacked political consciousness and capacity to plan required of such a leader. He appeared to me as an emotional man rather than a logical man, instinctive man rather than a man with deep insight. And I felt that the old man and Pritam Singh were a very harmonious pair.

After the old man had finished, I enquired about the situation in Southern Thailand from Pritam Singh. He related that he could contact his comrades in Kuantan and Kotah Bahru, who were very active, but had again failed to establish cells in Kedah area.

He also regretted the failure to carry out proper propaganda and win over supporters among the British Indian forces because of frequent rotation of the forces assigned to border protection duty. Next I wanted to know about the distribution of his comrades in Southern Thailand, especially around the Thai-Malaya border, as well as in Kotah Bahru, and the mode of their operation. But I did not press the point as he was reluctant to speak on the subject. This was because I knew that for success mutual confidence was of paramount importance, and all cooperation should be on voluntary basis.

The talk next shifted to the attitude of the Indian people and leaders towards Japan. I solicited their frank opinion about the thinking of the Indian people in general towards Japan. This was because I thought that this would provide me with better understanding of the situation and would help me in evolving the plans for fulfilling my mission. In the beginning Pritam Singh was a bit hesitant, and started with Japan's failure on the propaganda front vis-a-vis Britain, America and Chungking. However, as talks proceeded, he expressed his views rather frankly. Japan's policy towards its colonies of Formosa and Korea, andthe military action and policy of Japan in Hanchuria and China have created the image of an warlike aggressor in the Indian mind.

Again, citing the cases of violence and cruelty of the Japanese officers and men against the Chinese masses, obtained from British, American and Chungking sources, he expressed his profound shock. He warned me that the Japanese propaganda was incompatible with the actual deeds of the Japanese forces. He emphasised that as the Indian people were more

sensitive towards colonial policy and military and immoral actions than the Chinese people. I however, tried to blame the malicious propaganda of the enemies of Japan for creating such an impression of Japan. Moreover, I frankly admitted the necessity of correction of Japan's policy after criticising Japan's colonial policy towards Formosa and Korea, as well as its policy and military action with respect to Manchuria and China. I also expressed my disapproval of the violence and immoral actions of a section of Japanese army officers and men in China. I took great pains to explain the imperial will of establishing a new order of peace and prosperity in the Far East based on liberty and equality of all the oppressed nations of the region. I also emphasised that steps were being taken to correct the Japanese policy and that actions were being taken against the guilty officers and men after the fall of Nanking. As evidences, I cited the declaration of our Prime Minister Koneo and the pamphlet titled 'Dos and Donts for the Expeditionary forces' by Gen. Hata, the commander in chief of the China Expeditionary Forces. I also tried to enlighten him on the traditional virtues of the Japanese people in an attempt to solicit his understanding and related my belief that Japan, being the motive force in establishing new order in East Asia, was on the process of reflecting upon its own policies I actions in order to effect necessary corrections. We agreed that exploitation, coersion and domination should be totally banished from the idea of Indo-Japanese cooperation, which should transcend above piety nationalistic rivalry and confrontation, and that respect for the traditional cultural values and political ideals of various nationalities should form the very basic of coexistence and coprosperity in the Far East.

Moreover, we took a vow to stand in the vanguard in the struggle for realising the above ideals. Amar Singh listened to our talks with great interest and satisfaction, and when we ended our talks with the above vow, he rejoiced slapping against his thigh. And standing up he prayed to God for protecting us and said that God would be with us in our noble mission. The perspitation drops oozing out from the face of both Amar Singh and Pritam Singh were shining like oil. We were recalled back to the realistic world with crowing of the first cock. With a start we looked at our watch. It was past 4.00 A.M. After fixing our next meeting five days hence, we left the place after agreeing not to use the place for such meeting any more.

As we were trying our best to develop mutual understanding and grasping the significance of the basic ideals necessary for our future work, the situation in the Pacific went on deteriorating from bad to worse. Towards the middle of October, Tokyo News reported the fall of the third

Koneo cabinet. With the formation of Tojo cabinet on the 18th October, I intuitively felt that the Japanese-Amcrican talks were on the verge of collapse and the Imperial Headquarters was going to opt for war in a very near future. The Japanese people in Bangkok somehow became restless around this time, probably reflecting the above developments.

I found myself in a position where it was impossible for me to know beforehand anything about the strategy and line of action to be adopted by the Imperial Headquarters and the Southern Forces in the event of hostilities. However, from the emphasis on reconnaissance of Southern Thailand and east coast of Malaya by the Japanese army, discussions among the Japanese service personnel, and my own knowledge on strategy. I was quite certain that occupation of Thailand and landing in Malaya were now just a matter of time. In view of iron wall like defence of Singapore on the side exposed to the sea, the range of the Japanese army and navy aeroplanes based in Southern Indo-China, and the objective of occupation of Singapore, it was quite inevitable that landing of Japanese forces in Southern Thailand and Kotah Bahru was already a foregone conclusion.

I also came to know that Lt. Gen. Yamashita had been assigned the job of capturing Singapore. He had shifted his Headquarters to Saigon, and was concentrating his 25th Army at Hainan Island for the purpose.

As I realised that the war was round the corner, I found myself faced with a dilemma the necessity to keep the war preparations of the Japanese army a closely guarded secret was rather incompatible with the necessity for drawing up a concrete plan for our project. As we were practically unprepared at that time, it was absolutely necessary to explain the resolution of the Japanese army to Pritam Singh in order to persuade him to draw up a concrete plan and start the necessary preparations. On the other hand any leakage of the operation plan of the Japanese army would have a very serious repercussion.

Pritam Singh probably got an air of this development from his sixth sense, and asked me several times about the real intension of the Japanese army. However, I was unable to give any satisfactory answer to him. During the first half of November, I had a number of meetings with Pritam Singh, changing the venue with every meeting. These meetings cemented our friendship and mutual reliance. These meetings helped me in obtaining a first hand knowledge of the Indian Independence movement and the conception of movement sponsored by the IIL. I also succeeded in catching a number of hints over the question of assisting and cooperating with the IIL.

I was somewhat worried as I realised that the Imperial Headquarters

would be in for a great dissolution in case it had placed too much hope on the capability of the IIL in winning over the local Indians and Indian soldiers in Malaya at the time of Anglo-Japanese hostilities. This was because the IIL had not succeeded in penetrating these targets appreciably as was claimed by Lt. Col. Kadomatsu of the Imperial Headquarters. Moreover, the feeling among the Indians was far from being pro-Japanese. What was more important was that very little time was left. I racked my brain in conceiving the plan of fulfilling my mission on the basis of my faith and ideal, the suggestions provided by Pritam Singh and the stern reality of our unpreparedness. The rough outline I had chalked out was that with the outbreak of hostilities the members of the IIL would be urged to penetrate the enemy line and win over the Indian soldiers after making appeals to them directly. Again, efforts should be made to bring the Indian masses in Malaya and Thailand within the folds of the political movement of the IIL as quickly as possible. After the opening of the hostilities, the IIL movement would proceed with the dual objective of winning over the Indian soldiers of the British Indian army in particular and the Indian nationals in general.

The programme for the Indian soldiers was as follows. The members of the IIL and the F-Organisation (F-Kikan) would dedicatedly protect the Indian war prisoners and explain to them the ideal of the IIL and the real intension of the Japanese army, in order to raise a volunteer army for Indian Independence as quickly as possible. The programme for the Indian people in general was also almost identical. The members of the IIL and the F-Organisation would protect and allay the fears of the Indian people living in terror in the midst of hostilities, explain the political aims of the IIL and Japan, and attempt to persuade them to join the IIL movement and set up the IIL units all over the occupied territories and then go in for reaching the Indian masses under the enemy sphere of influence.

These two programmes were complementary to each other as the two wings of a bird. Spreading the IIL movement among the Indians living in Burma and other East Asian countries and seeking support from the Indians in India were of vital importance.

The members of the IIL and the F-Organisation should dedicate themselves to the movement of the Indian people and their interest and freedom, guarantee their safety, and try to gain confidence through their bravery and modesty. Again, the Japanese forces should not commit even the slightest violence on the Indian residents and soldiers, rather should support their patriotic movement, ensure their life, property and freedom, and show proper understanding and enthusiasms. Again, the IIL being a

voluntary and spontaneous movement of the Indian people should transcend above the narrow provincial and religious bias, and adopt a policy with an appeal to all the Indians. Again, it was also necessary to impress the Japanese people, especially the Japanese military and government leaders with proper understanding of India and the Indians, especially their freedom movement. (Indeed, the Japanese people had a very meagre knowledge of India and the Indians).

When I thought over this problem, I felt that it was more necessary to create proper understanding and atmosphere of cooperation among the Japanese military officers and men rather than seeking Indian response. Besides looking after the Indian affairs, I had to give proper guidance to Tashiro and Kamimoto over their Chinese and Harimau projects respectively. Towards the end of November, a new question of establishing contact with and enlisting cooperation of Malay Youth League cropped up.

Towards the middle of November, the Japanese Consulate General of Singapore supplied me with information on the anti-British Malay socialist group Malay Youth League. This secret organisation of the Malays worked under the cover of the newspaper 'Warta Malayas' and had its base in Singapore. It had established cells all over Malaya, receiving enthusiastic support from the Malay intellectuals and proletarians. The object of the movement was to gain freedom from the British, and neutralise the propertied Malays acting as the tools in the hands of the British.

I also came to know that this group had established contacts with the Japanese Consulate General in Singapore. As the activities of Harimau[4] was motivated only by anti-Chinese grudge devoid of any principle whatsoever, it was not possible to place much reliance on him to appeal to the Malays for their nationalistic cause. Moreover, his influence was restricted only to Kuantan State. Thus it is needless to say how welcome this news was to me and the military attache. I immediately started chalking out plans to enlist the cooperation of the Malay Youth League.

I got a detailed first hand information on the subject towards the end of November when the Japanese Consul General Tsurumi posted in Singapore came over to Bangkok. I tried to evolve plans to bring about cooperation between the active workers of Malay Youth League and the members of the F-organisation already working in South Thailand. However, the time at disposal was too short.

On 28th November, I went to the Japanese embassy as usual in the

4. This was a pseudonym for Tani Yutaka, a prominent leader of Malaya.

morning, and after talking with the ambassador for a while I proceeded to meet the military attache. As I entered his room, his assistant twinked at me and whispered to me to go down to the lounge. His action sent horror creeping through my mind at the prospect of getting out plans exposed. I was overwhelmed with only one worry; whether my twelve comrades deployed in Southern Thailand had been captured by Thai police or British and Chinese agents because of their over enthusiasm. However, he conveyed to me a message in a very low voice for which I was least prepared. He said that the talks between Japan and America had reached a deadlock, and that war would start sometimes early December. The work of the F-Organisation regarding Malaya would then pass into the jurisdiction of Gen. Teraushi, the Commander-in-Chief of the Southern Forces. The general would place the organisation under the command of Gen. Yamashita, commander of the 25th Army. I also had expected such a development, but when I came to know about it finally, I felt unprecedented excitement. Immediately two thoughts came to my mind. One was to contact Pritam Singh and discuss about concretes plans of our work. The second was how to rush to South Thailand without delay together with Pritam Singh, the members of the IIL and the organisation so as not to be too late at the start of hostilities. I requested to keep a Douglas aeroplane ready for me there and was glad to receive his immediate approval.

I immediately took steps to meet Pritam Singh that very night. I sent Yamaguchi to the manager of Mitsubishi Co. with a request to use his house for the meeting, and sent Otaguro to inform Pritam Singh. The tension of the military attache and his assistant was reflected in the behaviour of all the members of his office, and when I stepped on the road the peaceful atmosphere struck me as a grim contrast.

Although we were drawing up plans on Malaya, yet we were not very sure about the attitude of the Thai government, on whose soil we were hatching our plans. I was under the impression that the Japanese ambassador and the military attache would try to persuade the Thai government to permit peaceful stationing of Japanese forces in Thailand. However,, the Thai reaction was anybody's guess in view of complicated national and international situation. In case the Thais decided to disagree then all the Japanese in the country would be taken into custody. In that case all the members of the organisation including myself would be taken into custody in Bangkok and Southern Thailand, and the whole work would come to a standstill. Even the thought of such a prospect sent chill through my spine. The safest course appeared to be to withdraw to Saigon immediately and then to land in South Thailand alongwith the operational

forces. But the snag here was that it was impossible to take all the members of IIL including Pritam Singh to Saigon together with us. There was almost no prospect of Thai government's permitting Pritam Singh to leave the country legally, and any attempt on his part to leave the country illegally was surely to be watched. Even if it was possible, it was already too late. (It would be an extremely dangerous step to try to smuggle out Pritam Singh in a Japanese plane). As there was no official communication about the start of hostilities, discussions with Col. Tamura drew blank. There was no way left but to resign to our fate.

That night I met Pritam Singh at the residence of the manager of Mitsubishi Co. As luck would have it, the manager was absent. Carefully avoiding any hint at the intention of the Japanese army, I explained to him about the impending rupture in the Japanese-American talks, and that Japan was expecting Anglo-American attack any moment. In that case, I added, the Japanese army would go into action, Malaya becoming the prime target. I cautioned him that the time for us to act might come much earlier than expected. I expressed my views over the necessity to start discussions on concrete plans for action. As expected I could read tension on the face of Pritam Singh.

That very night we held four rounds of talks on our future plans. I listened to Pritam Singh passionately explaing his conviction frankly with great attention. Fortunately as there was identity of view over the concept of ideal and there was proper understanding, his line of thinking agreed with that of mine this time also. Excepting for very minor technical aspects, there was no serious divergence of views. The plan we finally drew up had to be a very abstract one since we had no idea of the army's operational plan or the course the operation might actually take.

We agreed to have the following points as our ideal and basis of cooperation, and vowed to each other to do our best for realising them.

1. The principle objective of our cooperation will be to realise friendly relation between Japan and India, both the countries constituting partners as independent, free and equal nations. The two countries will cooperate with each other with the ultimate aim of bringing peace, freedom and prosperity in East Asia.
2. The IIL will take up armed struggle for achieving quick and complete Independence of India, and will welcome overall support from Japan. However, in this connection Japan will guarantee that it will not have any territorial, military, political, economic and religious design against India in return for its help.
3. The IIL will transcend above narrow provincial, religious and party

bias, and will welcome all the patriotic Indians willing to fight the Britishers within its fold. Again, it will try its best to create an atmosphere of cooperation and harmony between the local people and the Indians in the zones of military operation.

4. Immediately on the outbreak of Anglo-Japanese hostilities, the IIL will implement the following programme.
   (a) The IIL will advance to Southern Thailand and Malaya alongwith the Japanese army and establish itself among the Indian people living there, trying its best to rouse anti-British feeling among the local Indians and the Indian soldiers and to create an atmosphere of cooperation with the Japanese forces.
   (b) The IIL will raise a volunteer army from among the Indian soldiers of the British Indian Army and the Indian civilian population of Malaya, and will make preparations for the future fight for freedom.
   (c) Depending upon the situation, the IIL will try to enlarge the above movement of item (b) to encompass the other territories of East Asia.
5. The Japanese armed forces will take the following steps for ensuring success of the various aspects of the IIL movement mentioned above.
   (a) The Japanese army will confer freedom of activity to the IIL in its occupied and operational territories as much as operational considerations can permit. It will also ensure safety and assistance to the members of the IIL.
   (b) The liaison work between the Japanese armed forces and the IIL as well as direct assistance to the IIL will be entrusted to the Fujiwara Organisation (Fujiwara Kikan). This organisation will try its best to facilitate the promotion of the IIL movement. (The Fujiwara Kikan will be organised formally as soon as hostility breaks out).
   (c) The Japanese forces will not treat the Indian prisoners of war and the civilian Indian population in the operational zone as hostiles, rather they will be treated as the compatriots in general are treated. The life, property, freedom and honour of the Indians will be protected and respected. Again, the places of worship will be protected and these will not be used by the Japanese forces for any military purpose. The Japanese officers and men will be apprised of this and will be forbidden to violate these.
   (d) The Japanese army will permit the IIL to use Radio Tokyo and the other radio stations of the occupied territories as well as

Bangkok Radio for carrying out effective propaganda activity. Again, the Japanese army will provide aeroplane facilities to the IIL for distributing propaganda literatures.

(e) The Japanese army will lend its good offices to arrange liaison between Subhash Chandra Bose in Berlin and the IIL.

(f) The Japanese army will provide necessary money and material to Pritam Singh considered essential for carrying on the IIL activities on demand, and will not hinder collection of voluntary contributions from the Indians in the operational zone.

Besides preparing the above Tamura-Pritam Singh Memorandum we discussed about the following items.

(a) Just after the start of war, the members of the IIL and of Fujiwara Organisation will proceed to Southern Thailand in a Japanese plane provided by the Japanese army for the purpose.

(b) The IIL will prepare propaganda materials on the basis of the above memorandum.

(c) A symbol will be fixed for discriminating the IIL members from the enemy and ensuring freedom of movement and activity in the battle zone. All the Japanese officers and men will be enlightened on the symbol.[5]

Note : Later on the letter F was fixed as the symbol after discussions with Pritam Singh as it could be readily recognised by the Japanese soldiers. The letter F was selected out of consideration that it was the initial letter of 'Friendship' and 'Freedom', not to tell of 'Fujiwara'.

(d) The IIL will make preparations to organise a number of propaganda squads immediately on arriving at Southern Thailand, and send them behind the enemy lines for carrying out propaganda among the Indian soldiers of the British Indian Army and the civilian Indian population.

The above memorandum was prepared in English and Japanese, and was formally signed by Col. Tamura and Pritam Singh on the Ist of December. As it was signed, we forget all our painful sleepless nights spent on discussion and were pervaded with a great sense of joy and success. And we vowed to each other to stand at the vanguard of the two nations and accomplish our mission with all earnestness, by cooperating with each other.

Incidentally this was also the day when the meeting in the Imperial Diet decided to go in for war.

---

5. See the Interrogation Report of Fujiwara. Document. No. 10

The main strength of a Japanese navy task force was proceeding towards Pearl Harbour for launching a surprise attack, and a massive force of Japanese army and navy had collected at Hainan Island for attacking Malaya. Of course, we were in complete darkness of these development. This was indeed a fateful day when Japan got into the whirlpool of the great Pacific war.

Copies of this memorandum were forwarded to the Headquarters of the Southern Forces and that of the 25th Army at Saigon. The approval came immediately. Another copy was also sent to the Military Section of the Imperial Headquarters in Tokyo.

Now started the busiest period of my life. I had to discuss with Pritam Singh over the steps to be taken for implementing the programme chalked out in the memorandum. Again, I had to maintain contact with the Malay Youth League, and exchange messages with and send instructions to the members of F-Organisation in south Thailand. Pritam Singh also sent his secret messenger to South Thailand, and tried his best to evolve an operation plan.

In Bangkok, the members of the F-Organisation had to remain in battle readiness for any eventuality.

It was rather impossible for a Japanese to conceive of a soldier without bald head and a sword on his waist, probably because of the long tradition of feudalistic administration ever since the militarists grabbed the government. Again, the atmosphere in the army also gave absolutely no scope for deviation from the traditional values. Anybody seen without bald head and a sword by his side was likely to be branded as coward immediately. Even the reporters, authors, artists and monks accompanying the armed forces as non-combatant without exception put on military uniform and took sword gladly. It was the custom of the time for the military civil administrative officials and businessmen sent for reconstruction and rehabilitation after military operations to aspire to have some sort of military rank, however, nominal it might be.

As all my associates and myself had entered Thailand as diplomats or employees of commercial firms or hotel employees, it was not possible for us to have our formal military uniforms with us. The job assigned to us was neither to subjugate the enemy and the local people by brute force, nor to overwhelm them by weilding authority. The only arms we had at our disposal in confronting the enemy and the local people were our virtue, integrity and sincerity. We were not supposed to carry even a bit of iron. and hence the stern military uniform was not for us. We had to put on dress that would bring us close to the people among whom we were

expected to work. Considering from the conventional contempt of the Japanese army towards the people engaged in pacification work it was certain that we with long hair and plain dress would not be welcome guests running about in the battle field. A large number of obstacles were bound to be placed on our way. Even then I had no intention to procure military uniform as such a step would betray our antecedents immediately.

After considering the various *pros and cons* of the problems, we decided to get simple khaki riding-dress made by some local Chinese tailor. I also decided to get a number of pistols sent from Saigon for self protection of the IIL members and the F-Organisation members who would have to move about in the front. I personally decided not to carry either sword or pistol. However, I decided to put on my rank marking and staff officer's badge, and to carry a silver baton.

I sent orders to all the members of F-Organisation to retain their long hair.

With these rapid developments we became very nervous about the move of the Thai government. At night information was sent round to the Japanese residents to collect at the Japanese primary school in small groups. All the military personnel gathered in the military attache's room, at night. An ominous silence, as if precussor to the events to follow, befall the street in front of the military attache's room and some doubtful figures, apparently Thai secret police, started moving about suspiciously on the street. An uncanny tension gripped everybody in the place. However, we did not take up sieze-like position in order not to provocate the Thais. Although the night of seventh with a likely threat to our life was advancing fast, yet the fortunate development was that the movement of the Japanese forces was still shrouded with great secrecy. Reports started pouring in that the foreigners in the Oriental Hotel were still peacefully gossiping around the dining tables and crowding the dance floor. Finally the time has come to inform Pritam Singh about the development.

However, the Thai attitude towards Japan was not yet clear. In case the Thais adopted an anti-Japanese posture, then just like the local Japanese Pritam Singh was also surely to be put behind the bars alongwith associates. In order to prevent Pritam Singh from visiting me, I sent Odakuro and Yamaguchi secretly to the house of Pritam Singh to inform him about the war. He was to be informed that the war would start on the following day dawn, and as the Thai attitude was not very clear he was to remain very careful. However, he should make preparations to go to Southern Thailand on the day following the start of war, i.e., on the seventh alongwith me. My two informants related to me on return that even cool and calculating

Pritam Singh was besides himself with excitement. With a very happy expression he had offered prayers to God muttering that at last the long waited time had come, and God would be on his side.

I felt a great burden releaved from my breast, which was torturing me eversince I came to know about the war. I could easily guess the feeling of Pritam Singh who had waited all these years just for this day, and could feel the echo of this feeling in my mind. And I took the vow afresh that as the representative of the Japanese nation I would live upto the expectation of Pritam Singh and would try to render all possible help for fulfilling his lofty ideal.

The night started dawning slowly. The distant cocks started crowing. Still there was no news on the whereabouts of the Thai Prime Minister Phibun Songkram. The negotiations were at a standstill. The movements of the foreigners did not betray any sign of abnormality. The number of uniformed Thai police started increasing around the Military attache's office. Probably the Japanese forces had already landed at Singora and Patani in Southern Thailand and Kotah Bahru in Malaya.

In the Gulf of Thailand also a Japanese convoy must have entered by now. The Koŋoe Division was probably moving towards Bangkok in lightening speed overland from Indo-China. There might have some skirmishes also with the Thai forces. In the morning, a Japanese plane was supposed to come flying over our building for contact. Day before yesterday at the time of arriving at an understanding the signal informing that Thailand was neither as enemy nor a friend had not been agreed upon. There was no other way out other than writing down the signal 'Not known' on a piece of cloth and displaying it at the race course. Presently a Japanese army plane came flying from the east and started circling over the military attache's office. Immediately a few persons ran to the race course carrying the signal cloth. As soon as they started unfurling the singal, scores of Thai police who were watching the situation came running and forcibly snatched the cloth and took all the Japanese alongwith them towards the stand. The whole thing happened in a few seconds. Immediately the assistant to the military attache ran to the place in a car. The plane circled over the building vainly for a number of times and then vanished towards east. Almost simultaneously with this disturbing news started pouring in. 'The Japanese forces landing at Bangkok port ran into resistance from Thai police and Thai people'. 'Clashes have occurred between Thai forces and the advancing Japanese forces along the Thai-Indo-China border.' 'The Thai army in Bangkok are getting ready for action.' etc. The Japanese employees of the embassy and military attache's office

knowing Thai language hurried to the troubled spots and tried their best to stop the incidents. Although the Thai attitude was not very happy, yet there was no varulous anti-Japanese feeling. We all in the military attache's room clung to the radio for news from Radio Tokyo, and did not leave the radio even for a moment.

Declaration of the state of war with Britain and America in West Pacific, Imperial announcement of declaration of war, speech by Premier Tojo, success of the surprise attack on Pearl Harbour, surprise landing on South Thailand. Such good news came pouring out of the microphone of the radio one after another. All of us were overwhelmed with emotion, and there was none whose eyes were not wet. Finally, we heard out national anthem followed by martial music, which only went to highten our excitement even further. At about 11 P.M. a messenger came hurriedly from the residence of the ambassador bringing the message of reappearance of the Thai Prime Minister and successful conclusion of negotiations. He also reported that the Konoe Division was almost on the outskirts of Bangkok. At a stroke we were relieved of the oppressive apprehension that had gripped up since the night before. I again sent my messenger to Pritam Singh to set his worries at ease relating the latest developments. The time finally had come where we could meet each other openly and start out work.

Within a few minutes we arrived at a decision. It was decided to send a propaganda squad of the IIL alongwith the main strength of the advancing Fifth Division. Two of Pritam Singh's associates who had accompanied us from Bangkok were selected for the purpose, and I ordered my three assistants, Lt. Nakamiya, the old man Shiba and Susuki to accompany the above two persons for liaison work. The group boldly started for Alor Star front in the midst of heavy rains.

After seeing off the group, I accompanied Pritam Singh to a rally of his associated living around the Thai-Malaya border. Next we inaugurated a conference of Indians in Hat Yai, established the Southern Thailand branch of IIL, and undertook the task of organising IIL propaganda squads for sending them to the Kotah Behru front. Capt. Tsuchimochi remained busy converting the two story residence of Tashiro on the outskirts of Hat Yai into the Headquarters of the IIL, and the office of Tainan Koshi Co, into the office of the F-Organisation. Next I went to inspect the IIL Headquarters alongwith Capt. Tsuchimochi. A large number of Indians had already gathered there, and they were very happy to see both Pritam Singh and myself.

I was very happy over Capt. Tsuchimochi's arrangement. Pritam Singh

was also very happy. Pritam Singh immediately went to the first floor and unfurled an Indian national flag from the verandah, I could see his hand shaking with emotion as he unfurled the national flag. For a while he prayed to the national flag, bathed in the western sun just like an erect statue. We standing down below were also overwhelmed with emotion. Next, a strip of cloth with the words IIL written on it in Indian language and Japanese was hung from the railing of the verandah. This was for he first time that the IIL came out of hiding, and in effect declare war for liberating motherland. Thus a new dimension was added to the war that was progressing in the South.

Next Pritam Singh announced the convening of a conference of local Indians on the following day. Thus we passed the first night in the front. Throughout the night, a continuous stream of Japanese forces moved south towards the Alor Star front.

As we were proceeding along the road to Sadao, our vehicle entered a side road on instruction from Pritam Singh. After advancing along the zigzag road of the rubber plantation, we stopped in front of a ramshakle hut. A Sikh appeared from inside in a hurry, surprised by the sound of the motor engine. He was just like a recluse seeking salvation away from human habitation. He was about 50 years old.

Pritam Singh who had got down in a hurry ran to him and embraced him as soon as he saw him at the door. As soon as Pritam Singh saw me, he introduced his friend to me. I have forgotten his name. We were ushered inside the house. He praised the bravery of the Japanese forces which had put the British Indian forces to flight in the vicinity of Sadao on the day before. He hurriedly prepared tea and made preparations to leave with us. All his possessions were a bedstead made of bamboo and rope, some sooty pots and pans and a set of dirty dress which he was mending. Even if he left the house unlocked, there was nothing inside worth for a thief to steal. I was very much impressed by this man who had voluntarily chosen such an austere life gladly in such a God forbidden place for the sake of motherland. In this way, Pritam Singh picked up two more of his associates living in the region before returning to Hat Yai. On the street crossing of Hat Jai I could see propaganda posters of IIL pasted prominently. These were brought from Bangkok by Pritam Singh, and a large number of Indians were reading them avidly.

In the afternoon, about two hundred Indians, men and women, young and old gathered in front of the Headquarters of the IIL. Almost all the Indians living in the town had gathered here. Pritam Singh made the maiden speech of his life addressing these people from the balcony. One Indian

interpreted his speech in Tamil. Every sentence of Pritam Singh was greeted with wild applause by the people. The tone was low, but very forceful. It was a passionate speech expressing firm desire to fight for the freedom of Motherland.

The Indian, who were in a state of terror ever since 8th December when their dream was rudely broken by the guns of the Japanese forces, had their fears set at rest as a result of this meeting. They also recovered their national consciousness.

On the following day, i.e., 12th, Pritam Singh gathered his comrades from Yala, organised them into two propaganda squads, and sent one of them to accompany the A-Detachment, which was advancing along the Yala-Beton Road. 2nd Lt. Yonemura and Kamimoto accompanied this equal as liaison officers from the F-Organisation side. Again, the Harimau band also penetrated behind the British lines in this sector under the guidance of 2nd Lt. Yonemura. The second propaganda squad proceeded to the Kotah Bahru front by train, with 2nd Lt. Segawa and Nagano of F-Organisation accompanying as the liaison officers.

That night I held a very friendly discussion with Capt. Mohan Singh and Pritam Singh. During the first part of the talks I related my happy experience over the surrender of the Indian soliders led by Capt. Mohan Singh. We both appreciated the smooth way the whole thing had been arranged. Both Capt. Mohan Singh and Pritam Singh again sympathised with my sincere regret over the two unfortunate incidents of the afternoon. During the later part of the talks I explained the Japanese army's views over assistance to the Indian Independence movement, and the details of cooperation with the IIL as seen from the angle of the Japanese forces. Herein I also expressed my own views on the success of the Indian freedom struggle. I pointed out the dishonour and sad plight of the conquered nations. I also related my firm conviction that the Independence of India should be won by the Indians primarily through their own struggle. I emphasised that the Second European War followed by the great East Asian War has provided a unique opportunity to the Indian people to rise in revolt and win back their glorious freedom. In that connection I related the Japan's committed objective of supporting Indian Independence struggle with all understandings as one of the goals of the present war. Besides I also related four of my personal views frankly. *Firstly*, both Japan and India should take the enemy as the common enemy for realising the Indian objective. *Secondly*, Japan is historically bound to India through religion and culture. *Thirdly*, location in East Asia has bound the destiny of the two nations. *Lastly*, people in general are extremely angry over the servile position of the Indian people.

Capt. Mohan Singh also cited a large number of instances of British misrule of India and discrimination of the Britishers against the Indians, and explained his pains over the unhappiness and dishonour of a survile nation. He also agreed with my view that the Indian Independence can be achieved only through the revolution of the Indian people. He finally concluded by saying that he would be in the vanguard in case such a revolution breaks out for the Independence of India. He appreciated my conviction over the sincere desire of the Japanese army to give all out support to the freedom movement of India. However, he sought my assent to discuss something, which was not be very complementary. For the sake of future happiness of the two nations of India and Japan, after tendering proper apology. It was regarding the colonial rule of Japan over Korea and Formosa, and the Japanese policy towards Manchuria and China. All these, he added, coupled with the actions of the Japanese armed forces have created a very adverse impression of the Japanese people on the Indian people in general. The content was more or less the same as that already discussed by Pritam Singh before. I listened to his views very attentively and expressed the same views which I had expressed to Pritam Singh earlier.

After relating the above views, the captain emphasised that whatever method may be adopted for achieving the Indian Independence, it is imperative that, this should receive the approval and whole hearted support of the Indian National Congress, the mainstay of the Indian nationalist movement. This view of Capt. Mohan Singh was contrary to the view held by Pritam Singh and myself, and I realised that this view had moderated his enthusiasm for Indian revolution with Japanese support. I tried to convince him by arguing that the form of political struggle adopted by the Indian National Congress should be very flexible and should change with the changing international situation. I also related my assessment of the situation that in case international situation ripens in favour of armed struggle as advocated by the great Indian revolutionary Subhas Chandra Bose, or the movements launched by Subhas Chandra Bose and the IIL succeed in producing encouraging results and become a real force for the Indian Independence, then the Indian masses would come forward to support this struggle and the Indian National Congress also would find it difficult to stand aloof. Our talks were held in a very friendly atmosphere where we expressed our views frankly, nevertheless passionately. I was very happy to learn about the latent patriotism of Capt. Mohan Singh, and his grudge against the ruling English people.

This talk, however, dashed all my hopes of enlisting Capt. Mohan

Singh's support to our movement in a foresee-able future, but I felt convinced that he could be won over in the long-run. It was already 3.00 A.M. when the talks ended. We had talked almost the whole day since morning without break, but the talks were so interesting and earnest that I was totally oblivious of fatigue. We went to bed after agreeing to continuing our talks the following night.

The prospect of the eleventh Division of the British Indian Army making any firm stand in the region north of Perak river following the collapse of the Jitra Line appeared to be very dim in the face of heavy pressure of the pursuing Japanese forces. The English forces beat a hasty retreat to the south of the Perak river leaving the vast military installation at Sungei Patani. There was no sign of organised resistance at Taiping either. In case the Japanese forces succeeded in capturing the vital bridge over the Perak river before the British forces could destroy it, then the front would shift to Central Malaya at a stroke. A fierce battle was also likely to develop over the capture of the Penang Island.

The work of the F-Organisation was showing all the symptoms of enlarging manifold. The time had come to mobilise all our strength to work all along the front for the welfare of the local people and the Indian soldiers of the British Indian Army. Again, urgent work was piling up like protecting, accommodating, feeding and medically assisting the ever increasing number of Indian soldiers in Sungei Patani and Alor Star areas. Again, discussion with Capt. Mohan Singh was also very vital. The IIL organisation also had to be established in the various regions north of Perak river. A liaison officer had also to be sent to Kotah Bahru area to substitute 2nd Lt. Segawa. Protection of the Sultan of Kedah, and negotiations with the Sultan and the Malay Youth League were also a very tricky affair. We were desperately short of hands. I also had only one person capable of interpreting talks in English in my team. I had no spare hand to look after our safety, accommodation and food. I had to select persons for these duties from among the persons who came to us on recommendations from the IIL or just out of goodwill for our work. As for meals, we had to pull alongwith Chinese and Malayan dishes exclusively.

I was very much worried over the slowly accumulating fatigue because of my hard work. On 16th, ultimately I succeeded in procuring the services of two persons for our work. One was 2nd Lt. Kunizuka, an interpreter of the Fifth Division. He had graduated from Yamaguchi Higher Commercial School and was an employee of a certain trading firm of Kobe before he was drafted for service. He was indeed a genious so far as English language was concerned. The other person was one Ito, an employee of the Japanese

consulate at Singora. He was fairly conversant with day to day spoken English, and volunteered to join the F-Organisation on hearing about its activities. He was also very young in age. I entrusted all the jobs connected with looking after all the Indian prisoners of war in Alor Star and Sungei Patani area, as well as the liaison work between Capt. Mohan Singh and the F-Organisation, to these two enthusiastic members. At that time the number of the Indian prisoners had, in all probability, reached the figure of 700. And I requested these two members to be constantly by the side of the Indian prisoners and share their food and lodging just like any other Indian.

Of course they were not given even a bit of iron. Although they were very talented and earnest, yet they lacked experience. Indeed I had entrusted them with very heavy responsibility, and I expected that they would fulfil their mission magnificently. I solicited Capt. Mohan Singh's good offices for discipline and positive cooperation of the Indian prisoners, and I got his ready approval.

With their sincerity, kindness, earnestness and amiability they immediately won over the Indian prisoners, who started treating these two young members as their darling. They slept amidst the Indian soldiers, shared their food with great relish, and worked like a clock without any sign of fatigue or grudge. From the very first day they started learning Indian language from the soliders. On the 16th, the Indian soliders taken prisoner by the 5th Division in the battle of Jitra were handed over to the F-Organisation, and they came and joined the group of Capt. Mohan Singh. The new arrivals were very happy to find their old comrades in this camp. Which was free from any restriction expected on such occasion.

On the 17th noon, I arranged a luncheon party with the members of the F-Organisation, IIL and the officers and NCOs of the Group of Mohan Singh. I wanted to have it in Indian style to cater to the taste of the Indians, and requested Capt. Mohan Singh for cooks. The backyard of the police station became alive with the busy cooks since early morning. At the stroke of twelve, we stopped all work and went to the venue. The table were full of strange looking dishes, and there was an orchestra of strange musical instruments.

I was very much surprised by the deep impression this luncheon created in the minds of the Indians, although I had just casually arranged it thinking that such a step would help fraternisation. Capt. Mohan Singh stood up and gave a table speech on the following line. 'For a staff officer of the victorious army to invite his Indian prisoners of war, and that also who have just surrendered hardly two days back, even down upon the

level of NCOs to Indian style luncheon and partake Indian food with them is something rather inconceivable for the British army. In the British army, the British officers never take meals together with their Indian fellow officers, although they may fight shoulder to shoulder in the same unit. In the officers club any suggestion, however, earnest it may be, put forward by the Indian officers for Indian style meal is rejected outright. This earnest invitation of Maj. Fujiwara transcending over the petty bias of enemy and friend, victor and vanquished, or race is a singular proof of his friendship which he has been showing to us since day before yesterday, and which even a thousand words would have failed to convey. We all are so deeply impressed by this gesture that we fail to find adequate words to express it. It is needless to say that todays food and arrangement are thoroughly inadequate because of the abnormal conditions prevailing presently although we have tried our best to satisfy the request of Maj. Fujiwara. Capt. Mohan Singh spoke each and every word of his speech with deep emotion, and that he spoke the views of all the Indians present there was corroborated by thunderous applause that followed the speech.

Although most of the F-Organisation members including myself had left Bangkok in October, yet this was the first occasion for most of us to have an Indian meal together with the Indians. As we were at a loss since we could find neither chopsticks nor forks, our Indian friends taught us the way to partake with hands, as was the custom in India. Kunizuka and Ito, who had picked that up the day before immediately, started eating with hands feigning great ease and were warmly applauded. Yamaguchi started such a terrible hiccup after swallowing the first morsel of curry that everybody burst out laughing. It was indeed a grand success for forging Indo-Japanese understanding.

Sweet rice cooked in ghee, unbearably hot curry, fowl meat with skin and bone on, all these were too much for me to eat with ease. I wetted upto my wrist with curry. All the officers sharing my table including Capt. Mohan Singh smiled at my clumsiness. I felt as if whole of my oral cavity was on flame. At last, Capt. Mohan Singh also could stand it no more, and brought a fork for me alone. I appreciated his gesture, but I declined it because I was very happy to try to eat just like all other Indians although somewhat clumsily.

Around this time Capt. Mohan Singh was very busy during the day time discussing various things with Pritam Singh and his fellow officers, and looking after the accommodation, provision, health etc. of the Indian prisoners. We brought in tents, provisions cooking utensils, clothing and medical stores from the Godown of the British army in Jitra and Sungei. As the Japanese forces were preoccupied with pursuing the enemy, they did

not have any time either to spot out the British military stores; and even when these were located there was nobody to look after these properly. Taking advantage of this volatile situation, I permitted Capt. Mohan Singh to bring the goods required for the Indian prisoners from the British military stores under Japanese occupation. I took this step out of my own discretion as I thought that any formal request to the Japanese high command or the commissariat department would invite unnecessary restrictions and imposition of ceiling, etc.

Kunizuka and Ito developed very good understanding with Capt. Mohan Singh, and assisted him very well in avoiding unnecessary troubles with the Japanese soldiers. The Indian officers also proved to be very loyal assistants to Mohan Singh. The Indian NCOs and soldiers also carried out all the orders loyally and sincerely, and there was not even a single case of contravention of discipline. It was indeed commendable that they strictly observed all the military discipline and did not behave like prisoners at all. The luncheon party of the 17th helped in creating a feeling of brotherhood between the members of the F-Organisation and the Indian officers and men. When the Indian soldiers saluted me with sincere look, I felt the illusion as if I was being greeted by my own men of my unit. Again, when I exchanged salute with the Indian officers, I felt as if I was exchanging salute with the fellow officers of my regiment. The propaganda squad led by Gopal Singh with Capt. Tsuchimochi as the liaison officer reached the camp of Sungei alongwith a large number of Indian prisoners after carrying out successful propaganda among the Indian army stragglers in Taiping area. Lt. Nakamiya, who had been assigned the duty of protecting the Sultan, reached the Sultan's palace at Alor Star successfully, and his work there received high praises from both the Malays and the Japanese forces. Later on, he left the old man Shiba with the Sultan and rushed to the Perak river front alongwith the propaganda squad of the IIL. There was also a very sad news. It was the death of 2nd Lt. Segawa Kiyoshi in engagement with the enemy. Hence I had to hurriedly send the only officer left with me Lt. Yamaguchi to Kotah Bahru by plane to look after the work there.

Although Pritam Singh was very busy with discussions with Capt. Mohan Singh and organising the IIL propaganda squads, yet he found time to establish IIL branches in the areas around Alor Star. Our life in the IIL Headquarters and the F-Organisation Headquarters was indeed a very busy one.

Although I was extremely busy, yet I made time at night to have a very through and frank discussion with Capt. Mohan Singh for four consecutive

nights following 16th December. From these meetings I realised that the captain was a man of excellent character, and I could also get a clear insight about his convictions. Mohan Singh also on his part appeared to understand me, and as such did not hesitate to bare his mind. I discovered his ardent patriotism, and his sincere desire to dedicate himself for the liberation of his motherland. I discovered all the qualities of a leader of revolution in him. He was very friendly to his colleagues and subordinates, he reasoned rather than following blindly, had a very sincere and plain attitude, firm resolution, capacity to carry out resolution, and impressing all with modesty and frankness. We agreed on a number of points like follows. That the Second World War has brought a grand opportunity at its wake for the Independence of the various nations of the South East. Asia including India, and that the Indian people should garb this chance to win back their freedom. That the newly liberated nations should rise above petty rivalries and strive for mutual prosperity and co-existence treating each other as equal partners. That there is not a single field where the national interests of the Indian and the Japanese people can clash with each other, and that the two nations are destined to remain good friends cooperating with each other with no scope for military confrontation between the two nations. That the lofty goals described about can be achieve only by mobilizing the patriotic young people of the various nations of South East Asia. During the talks he expressed great respect for Subhash Chandra Bose, and expressed the view that all the Indians in South East Asia will unanimously place themselves under the leadership of Subhash Chandra Bose in case he come over to East Asia to lead the freedom struggle.

I was very much impressed over the great esteem in which the Indians in general held Subhash Chandra Bose. He was almost a divine figure with them. I, in my turn, communicated this view to the Imperial Headquarters whenever I got any opportunity. I was of the view that the Germans may not approve of any proposal to send Bose to East Asia in view of their campaign towards Middle East. However, the thing that pained me most was that not a single revolutionary leader of the subjugated nations of South Asia, who could rightfully claim to represent his people, had come over to the Japanese side, although it had been advocating great East Asia Co-prosperity Sphere in its life and death struggle. This could be attributed to the callous attitude Japan had shown till then towards the nationalist movement of the peoples of the region.

I confided to Capt. Mohan Singh that it might be difficult to invite Bose to East Asia at the moment because of the international developments

therefore the IIL should try to organise freedom movement in East Asia for the moment, and next associate this movement with the great enterprise of Bose in Europe, thus giving it a global status scale. I also assured Capt. Mohan Singh that I would try my best to persuade the Imperial Headquarters to convey to Bose his feeling. I also tried to encourage him to take bold step as taken by Bose.

After five nights of discussions, it appeared to me that I had almost won him over. He was apparently thinking to accept the sincerity of Japan as a real one. This was because he promised to try for gaining the support of his countrymen, especially Congress party, and try to gain unanimous approval of his fellow officers and men. I knew it very well that any hasty emotional step to organise a revolutionary army to win over freedom through armed struggle was bound to end in a failure in the long run. Voluntary participation of all the officers and men dedicated to the cause in the Indian National Army was the only way to achieve success. So I requested Capt. Mohan Singh once again to consider the whole question coolly and carefully without making any haste. Pritam Singh also approved of what I had said.

At that stage I felt that a meeting of Pritam Singh and Capt. Mohan Singh with the commanding officer of the Japanese forces Lt. Gen. Yamashita would be very useful as this would provide a very good opportunity to both my friends to ascertain directly the Japanese army's intention over the question of supporting the Independence movement of the Indian people. So I proposed such a meeting. As both of them welcomed this meeting, I called upon Lt. Gen. Yamashita around 20th afternoon alongwith Pritam Singh, Capt. Mohan Singh and four Indian officers of the INA.

Lt. Gen. Yamashita greeted us warmly. He ushered us to the operation room, and standing before the operations chart, he explained the overall war situation in the Pacific. Next he explained frankly the Japanese army's earnest desire to give all out support to the Indian Independence movement, and requested my friends to put forward all the demands without hesitation as that the Japanese army could give all the necessary support and assistance to the IIL movement. The Chief of Staff, Maj. Gen. Suzuki was also present in the meeting. Both Pritam Singh and Capt. Mohan Singh thanked the two generals sincerely. This meeting lasted for about 40 minutes. It appeared to me that all the Indians were very much impressed by this giant of a man (Lt. Gen. Yamashita) who expressed all his sympathies over the question of Indian Independence.

Two days before this meeting I came to know about the sudden

withdrawal of the British force from Penang and liberation of all the Japanese confined in the Jail of Penang by local Indians and Malay. One of the Japanese confined in the jail had come to inform me with the assistance of the local people. This news came as a great surprise for me as the Japanese army assessed that the British forces would try to retain Penang at all cost. All started slowly realising the gravity of situation created by the start of hostilities. One phase of discussions with Capt. Mohan Singh was thus over, and as the prospect of settling down of the Indian prisoners of war into a peaceful life was very rosy. I started considering plans for my next move.

It was the last day of the year 1941. Suddenly Capt. Mohan Singh came from Alor Star to visit me without any prior intimation. He was accompanied by Capt. Akram and 2nd Lt. Kunizuka. I received the party at the porch. Just at a glance I could read great tension on the face of Capt. Mohan Singh who seldom betrayed his feeling. When I shook hands with him I found his hand burning hot. His lips were dry and he was gasping for breath. His face also appeared very emaciated.

I was taken aback and practically shouted involuntarily "Captain, what is the matter? You are running such a high fever, and yet why you have taken such a rash step in coming to visit me? " He replied that he had caught malaria, and although it was a bit rash, yet he had rushed to see me in order to intimate me the important decision he and his comrades had taken and had a thorough discussion over the subject. Although his eyes were bloodshot, yet they bespoke of firm resolution. I could not help getting overwhelmed by this resolute captain. Although I knew that his talks would be of very important nature, yet in view of his serious condition I forced him to take some malaria medicine and take rest in bed.

I requested Masubuchi (Sabei) and Capt. Akram to look after him. He might have caught this disease when he was engaged in Jitra operation. Methodical Capt. Mohan Singh with strong sense of responsibility did not have a moment's rest eversince his surrender, carrying out discussions with me and Pritam Singh day and night, looking after accommodation, food and sanitation of the officers and men, thinking over the questions of joining the patriotic a movement and discussing the topic with his fellow officers and men and the cause of this attack could probably be traced to his over work and fatigue. I felt like bowing down my head when I realised that he had come all the way to discuss with me despite his serious illness.

After some time, Mohan Singh recovered slightly and then had a discussion with Pritam Singh. Next he came to my room and thanked us. With the coming down of fever, he appeared to be slightly better, but he

was very tired. I offered him to be comfortable in the sofa so that we could continue with our talks with ease. Next Capt. Mohan Singh stated that following a number of meetings over the question of armed struggle for the liberation of India, the officers and men had unanimously decided to take up arms for the freedom of motherland provided the Japanese authorities agreed of the following conditions beforehand. The conditions put forward by him were as follows. (1) That Capt. Mohan Singh will organise the Indian National Army, (2) That the Japanese army will give all possible assistance and support to this army, (3) That the INA and the IIL will have independent existence, both cooperating with each other as brother organisations, (4) That the Japanese army will entrust the supervision of the Indian prisoners of war to Capt. Mohan Singh, (5) That the Japanese army will treat the Indian prisoners as friends, and will release those aspiring to join the INA, (6) That the Japanese army will treat the INA as an ally, both sides bound by alliance, etc. I personally had no objection to all these conditions put forward by him. However, as this was a matter of great importance, I refrained from making any reply immediately pending the approval of the army high command.

After expressing my above views over the proposals of Capt. Mohan Singh, I tried to emphasise the instance of cooperation between the INA and the IIL. I said that the two were like two wheels of a vehicle with two wheels, and a revolutionary army should be organised on the overall support of the people for achieving success. Capt. Mohan Singh replied that it was that very reason why they selected the name of Indian National Army for this liberation army instead of Volunteer Army for Indian Independence. Next he added that instead of keeping the INA prerogative for the ex-British Indian service personnel, its doors would be thrown open to all the Indians, and in view of the army's role in liberating motherland, emphasis would be laid on ideological indoctrination. I was very happy to see that he listened to my views attentively and appreciatively. After further discussions we agreed on keeping the two organisations separate from each other bound by the bondage of friendly cooperation, and organise the INA mainly from among the volunteers of the Indian prisoners with active support of the IIL. The indoctrination aspect would be entrusted to the IIL. In order to raise the strength of the INA rapidly Capt. Mohan Singh decided to send some of his excellent comrades into the British lines and make propaganda among the Indian soldiers.

One of the conditions put forward by Capt. Mohan Singh, viz. the question of official declaration on treating the INA as an ally, posed some technical difficulty. So it was decided to accede to the condition in effect,

and postponing the official and formal declaration on the issue till the INA took proper shape. Capt. Mohan Singh thereupon decided to organise the INA headquarters, and proceed to Ipoh in near future.

As we arrived at a very good understanding. I called upon the Headquarters of Gen. Yamashita, and explained the conditions put forward by Capt. Mohan Singh and the details of discussions to his chief of staff Suzuki and staff officer Surgita. The chief of staff Suzuki also expressed view similar to those of mine on the question of according the INA the status of ally formally. He agreed with the other conditions of Capt. Mohan Singh, and received the official approval of Gen. Yamashita. I also utilised this opportunity to make a detailed report on the contacts with the vice-chairman of the K.M.M. Mr. Onan Siraji[6] and the youth from Sumatra, Mr. Said Abu Bakar. Chief of Staff Suzuki was very happy after these two contacts.

I immediately returned to my Headquarters and reported the approval of Gen. Yamashita to Pritam Singh and Capt. Mohan Singh. Both of them were extremely pleased. By chance, Col. Tamura had also come to visit us from Bangkok on this very day. He was very happy that we had indeed succeeded in taking our first step towards success. We all drank toasts after toasts to our success. I requested Capt. Mohan Singh to be my guest for the night and proceed to Alor Star on the following day; but he explained the urgency of communicating the decision of the meeting to all the officers and men back in the camp as quickly as possible, and take up the task of organising the INA without any delay. While taking leave, Capt. Mohan Singh warmly shook hand with me and said "Although I am, by nature, rather slow in arriving at a decision, yet once I decide I try my best to accomplish it. I have left my newly wed wife in India. As soon as my activities become known to the British authorities they will subject her and all other members of my family to inhumane torture. I have decided to dedicate myself and my dear family to the cause of my country. As has been said by Gen. Yamashita the other day, I have acquired a new friend in you, of course at the cost of my wife. I hope you will realise that all the officers and men have decided to fight for our motherland knowing fully well that their families in India will be subjected to barbarious treatment by the British authorities in India. The fighting spirit of these men who have decided to sacrifice everything for the noble causes of motherland's freedom is thousand times stronger than that they had when they were

---

6. One of the most active leaders of K.M.M. (Kesatuan Malayu Muda) a political organisation is Malaya.

just the members of the British Indian Army. "I on my part listen every word he uttered with chocking emotion. I vowed in my innermost heart to contribute my might to the noble cause that inspired the soldiers to organise the INA. Despite his high fever Capt. Mohan Singh set out for Alor Star that very night alongwith Capt. Akram and 2nd Lt. Kunisuka.

Thus the crusader for achieving the noble goal of liberation of motherland was born at last for which Pritam Singh had struggled for all these years. Thus it was in Taiping the capital of Perak state that the curtain was raised on the last day of the year 1941 of a new and glorious chapter of the Indian Independence movement that ultimately culminated in the end of century old British rule of India.

As we both, Pritam Singh and myself, stood at the porch silently watching the party vanish in the darkness of night with deep appreciation Pritam Singh grasped my hand and said only one word 'thank you'. I don't think that any other expression could have expressed the depth of feeling he was having. Pritam Singh immediately took a steps to inform the leaders of the IIL in Northern Malaya of the decision of Capt. Mohan Singh.

The year 1942 dawned. After Defeat in the Kedah plains the 11th Division of the British Indian Army reinforced with the 12th Brigade and the 28th Brigade, which was deployed in Ipoh area, took up position in the Kanbaru-Slim area after destroying all the bridges during retreat. Again, the Kwamura Brigade of the 5th Division came across stiff resistance from the British forces in the vicinity of Kohon, north of Kanbaru. Thus, there were all symptoms of a grim battle developing in the region.

In the morning we all in my headquarter together with our honoured guest Col. Tamura gathered in the lawn in front of our building raised our national flag in the acacia tree, and prayed for our success facing east towards our fatherland. The red ball of our national flag appeared to be all the more beautiful bathing the morning sun. As if it was also blessing us for success.

The Indian Independence Army had become a reality and the contacts with the Young Malaya Association as well as the Sumatran youths were also established. Harimau also probably had succeeded in penetrating behind the British lines. The Kanbaru-Slim front was also warming up. This battle held the key to the capital of Malaya, Kuala Lumpur. The day was not far when the Japanese army would become undisputed master of the Malacca Straits. A golden opportunity was coming for the F-Organisation to expand its activities all over Malaya and Sumatra. We drank toasts for our success with champaign, and then started packing our things to proceed to Ipoh.

The members of the INA propaganda squads were handpicked by Capt. Mohan Singh himself after very careful screening of the volunteers. During the last few days Capt. Mohan Singh had devoted almost all his time with these people training them in the art of penetrating the enemy line and gaining friends, after explaining the ideals of the Indian Independence movement. This training programme continued even when they came over to Ipoh. The handpicked volunteers were divided into a number of groups. They were dressed as army stragglers and ordinary local inhabitants for penetrating the enemy lines with ease. Preparations were also made so that they could dress up as the regulars of British Indian Army. Besides carrying armband with the letter 'F' written on it and certificate from the F-Organisation for facilitating their passage through the front line Japanese forces, they carried INA propaganda leaflets calling upon the Indian soldiers to join the Indian National Army. Tauchimochi, Nakamiya and Yonemura, who had successfully smuggled a number of IIL propaganda squads carrying propaganda leaflets as calling upon the Indian soldiers to join the INA, returned to my Headquarters to smuggle these INA propaganda squads behind the enemy lines. They came alongwith about one hundred Indian soldiers who had surrendered in Kanbaru area. As soon as the trucks carrying them stopped in front of my headquarters, scores of officers and men from the nearby INA camp came running and embraced them as they got down. Capt. Mohan Singh also came hurriedly and gave them a word of advice and encouragement. These people, who were very apprehensive over the treatment they were going to receive in the enemy hands, had all their fears set at rest on seeing correctness of what they had read in the propaganda leaflets. Nothing could have made me happier than this.

The battle line was slowly moving south towards Sunkai. That night the 1st propaganda squad of the INA started for the front accompanied by Nakamiya as the liaison officer. Prior to their departure Capt. Mohan Singh tried to inspire them as much as possible. I also spoke a few words in encouragement. All of them vowed that they would accomplish their mission with all their might even at the cost of their life. Everybody in the camp was present there surrounding the squad. All were chocked with emotion. At last the time of departure came. As they boarded the truck and the engine was started, all present raised cheers.

The next day the 2nd, the 3rd INA Propaganda Squads departed for the front accompanied by the F-Organisation liaison officers Nakamiya. Tsuchimochi, Yamaguchi and others went on running to and fro in between my office and the front. The liaison officers first went to the front line

Headquarters together with the INA propaganda squad, ascertained the war situation and the exact location of the front line, and studied the location and topography suitable for penetrating the enemy line easily. Next they went to the commanding officer of the front, requested for safe passage of the propaganda squad, and discussed with him further on the situation and topography. After pin pointing the places where the enemy vigilance was, tax apparently lax, they proceeded to the foremost line. There were very few convenient places for slipping through in this region excepting the battle line, as the whole territory was one of vast jungle excepting for a narrow strip of rubber plantations on the two sides of the sole motorable road. Again, the rubber plantations could offer very little shelter to them in the face of saturated shelling by the trench morters of the British Indian forces. The brave members of the F-Organisation and the INA propaganda squads crawled to the foremost Japanese position braving the enemy shelling and sniping. There they shook hands with the soldiers and got a first hand knowledge about the enemy skirmish line and topography. The members of the INA propaganda squads were excellent in judging the enemy situation. There the members of the propaganda squads bade farewell to the liaison members and penetrated the enemy line. They tried to spot Indian units having no British Commanding Officer or British soldier amongst them. After ascertaining safe penetration, the liaison officers withdrew to the rear and returned to the Headquarters collecting the Indian prisoners from the various units. There were three hurdles not the way of successful accomplishment of mission by the F-Organisation liaison officers.

Firstly, there was the likelihood of misunderstanding between the members of the IIL and INA propaganda squads and the Japanese officers and men. Again, they might be shot at mistaken as enemy. To avoid these the liaison officers accompanied the squads upto the skirmish line. Extreme care was taken so as not to bring any physical harm to the propaganda squad members.

The second difficulty involved in persuading the Japanese staff officers and front line Japanese commanding officers, who lacked proper understanding over the significance of our work. A large number of these people suspected that the INA soldiers who were the members of the British armed forces till the other day might be in league with the British Army. Whenever enemy shells landed near the command posts or artillary positions by chance, they suspected that their positions had been betrayed by the propaganda squad members who had crossed the front line a little while ago. The F-Organisation members had to do their best to explain

that the suspicion was unfounded. Even though they were convinced of the sincerity of the Indians, yet they thought that the Indians might have betrayed the Japanese positions which they had seen just a little while ago during interrogation following capture. We firmly rejected any such eventuality and sought their cooperation agreeing to shoulder all responsibilities. It was not a very easy task for a 2nd Lieutenant and Ist Lieutenant to convince a regimental commander or a brigade commander. I must confess that when we sent the first propaganda squad to the front, we were very much worried over the way they would act once get reached the enemy lines. I was at that time mentally prepared for a few black sheep, but even then in view of greater interest resolved to proceed with the work.

However, within ten days, it became very clear that all our apprehensions over the activity of the propaganda squad members behind the enemy lines were totally unfounded. When the battle line shifted to Kuala Lumpur following the battle of Slim, both myself and Capt. Mohan Singh could confirm that none of the ten propaganda squad members belonging to the IIL and the INA defected to the enemy. When I came to know this. I was all the more impressed by the firm determination of the members of the IIL and the INA, and this served as a great inspiration to me for devoting myself wholeheartedly to my mission with the belief of unlimited success.

I was also convinced that with such firm conviction the INA was bound to write a glorious chapter in the history of Indian Independence struggle. The third point which worried me was the distance the liaison officers had to cover in fulfilling their duty. These four or five persons were running to and fro in between the Headquarters and the front about two hundred kilometres away just like a piston, as well as all over the front. Although such activity was fraught with great danger, the members of the propaganda squads were exposed to yet greater danger. Supposing that they succeeded in penetrating the enemy line and persuade the Indian soldiers to come over to our side, yet it was extremely dangerous to cross the Japanese line with a large body of soldiers. In this jungle territory it was extremely difficult to cross the shirmish line at night without being mistaken by the battle weary and trigger happy Japanese soldiers. If these surrendering soldiers came under Japanese fire even one due to misunderstanding, it would render the future work of the propaganda squads extremely difficult. Capt. Mohan Singh and myself had a very careful discussion over these problems and the possibility of capture of the propaganda squad members by the British forces. On the basis of

this, Capt. Mohan Singh issued the following sinstructions to the members of the INA propaganda squads.'Search for the units without British officers' 'Next spot individual soldiers or small groups', 'if possible, search for the men of your own unit', 'If you find a reliable Indian soldier, speak to him about the IIL and the INA, 'Tell them the treatment the Indian prisoners are receiving in the hands of the Japanese', 'In case they agree to surrender, persuade them to convience their close comrades', 'Brief them as follows on the procedure of surrender', leave the front, and hide in the dense jungle nearby', 'In case of strict vigilance by the commanding officer, wait till the skirmish line plunges into confusion with the Japanese breakthrough', 'Instead of firing directly against the Japanese forcers, fire at the sky', 'when the time is ripe, take advantage of the confusion and hide in the Jungle,' Even if the British commanding officer orders retreat, do not accompany him'. 'Hide your weapons in the jungle'. 'After the 1st line Japanese forces pass, raise white flag and come out,' 'show the INA propaganda leaflets to the Japanese soldiers'. These instructions were also printed in the form of propaganda leaflets in case it became impossible to explain these orally.

In view of the rapidly developing situation I thought of shifting my base to Kuala Lumpur by the 8th January morning. But I was forced to spend one more day at Ipoh as I had a very important guest. Moreover I had to dispose of some work connected with the newly developed contacts in the Straits of Malacca area. This important guest was my old colleague in Section 8 of the Imperial Headquarters, who was at the moment in charge of my work. This Maj. - Ozeki had come to get a first hand knowledge of our work and the latest developments achieved by us. As I was convinced of the human quality of the IIL and the INA, and their dedication, I tried to drive home the importance of Japanese assisting this movement in all possible ways. Although I did not have a clear picture of the future course of this movement, as well as all the plans I had in my mind were still in very nebulous state, yet I tried to explain all the ideas I had in my mind after making a report on our work till date. I promised to make an official report at a later date after seeing the developments further which would help me in evolving concrete plan. The main points on which I tried to convince him are as follows :

1. The great ideal of establishing a new order of Coprosperity in East Asia will succeed only after it gets the support of the thirty-five crore people of India.

The war between Japan and the allied countries is likely to be a protracted one. An early settlement of the war can be achieved only through

an early capitulation of Britain. The attitude of the Indians will be a decisive factor in bringing about British capitulation. It will be too foolish to rest on the laurrels of Philippines, Malaya and Pearl Harbour. Policy should be evolved to incorporate India in the camp of the nations of East Asia as quickly as possible. It will be too late to just wait for the war situation develop necessitating this. Japan's military might will be stretched to extreme limit with the annexation of Burma. It will be just impossible for Japan to reach for India militarily, and even if such an action is taken, it will immediately meet with the resistance of the Indian people, if the primary object of such a move is just dislodging the British forces. This resistance will be inspired by two factors, their sensitivity to foreign domination and their impression about Japan. Japan should adopt a policy of wining over the Indians without taking recourse to arms and try to persuade them to cooperate with Japan in setting up a new order in the Far East. For this Japan should give all possible support to the Indian Independence movement standing on the footing of equality, without any ulterior motive. Not to have any design of any type on India is of primary importance here. Again, any interference in their ,political movement or any attempt to control such movement should be strict taboo. Only through this it will be possible to inspire the Indians to become an enthusiastic member for setting up a new order in the Far East.

2. On the basis of the above understanding the Japanese government should make public its basic attitude towards the Indian Independence movement, as well as Japan's policy towards India.

3. The Imperial Headquarters and the Japanese government should sit together for evolving a policy towards India, that will cover all the aspects.

4. The activities of the F-Organisation should be extended to Burma so that a call can be given directly to India.

5. Again, Japan's policy towards India should be evolved in global perspective. For this contact should be established with Subhash Chandra Bose in Germany, so that the policy will have its effect both from the east and from the west. However, emphasis should be laid so that impact will be greater from the east in view of the prevailing conditions. From this viewpoint, the best course will be to invite Subhash Chandra Bose to come over to the east for leading the movement.

6. The basic tenet of Japan's policy towards India will be to give all possible support to the spontaneous movement of the Indian people living in East Asia. In this policy there should be adequate provision to support both the political movements and military actions at present under

consideration of the leaders of the IIL and the INA. In the political field, Japan should encourage all the Indians living in East Asia to join the movement of the IIL . On the military front, a very strong INA should be organised with the help of the volunteers of the Indian prisoners of war and ordinary Indians living in the region. Both these wings should be helped to go to India and build up massive and powerful nationalist movement.

7. The members of the IIL and the INA, not to tell of the Indian people, are watching with great interest the way Japan is going to implement the New Great East Asian order in Burma, Philippines, and other occupied territories of South Asia. It can be easily understood that the approval of the thirty-five crore Indians depends wholely on this. Japan should put the ideal of the new order in practice in Burma, Philippines and other occupied territories of South Asia.

8. The Fujiwara Organisation should be properly reorganised so that it can make useful contribution for realising this ideal when the time becomes ripe. I shall try my best to prepare ground so that the imperial government can implement this policy without any difficulty.

Maj. -O listened to my views very attentively. He also promised that he would try his best so that the ideas proposed by me could be realised.

After the Slim battle, the Indian soldiers who surrendered started pouring in into the camp of Kuala Lumpur, and their number crossed the figure of one thousand in no time. There was also a company which came from the vicinity of Port Swatenham carrying a leaflet calling for surrender dropped by a Japanese plane. The camp was located in the heart of Kuala Lumpur city. Previously housing British troops. The barracks were of thatched roofed, and were in a fairly good condition. There were some permanent structures also. Especially the structure housing the command office was a beautiful two storeyed concrete building. There were also a number of structures for the officers.

The capacity of the camp could be increased to accommodate about three thousand soldiers just by adding a few structures. Although the Japanese army had initially decided to take over the camp, but after negotiations they agreed to step down in favour of INA. It was estimated that already the number of the Indian soldiers surrendered all over Malaya had reached the mark of two thousand five hundred.

Capt. Mohan Singh expressed his desire to concentrate these Indian soldiers in Kuala Lumpur in order to consolidate and strengthen the INA, as well as to facilitate overall supervision, training and policing. To ensure military discipline and to provide with adequate supplies and medical

facilities. I readily agreed with this view of Capt. Mohan Singh as this would mean strengthening both the INA activities and the INA command. Thereupon Capt. Mohan Singh started taking steps to bring the Indian prisoners to Kuala Lumpur from Alor Star, Sungei Patani, Ipoh, Pinna and other places. Capt. Mohan Singh took a special care about the rest and recuperation of the inmates, as well about the treatment of the sick and wounded. These instantaneously won over the soldiers, and they found in him a person on whom they could rely upon. This loving attitude of Capt. Mohan Singh towards his followers instantly found response from the IIL, which started door to door campaign for donation in cash and kind for the Indian soldiers. The local Indian population responded to this call generously. An old Sikh resident called Budh Singh made a huge contribution in the form of provisions and clothings. He even sent fruits and flowers to the convalescing soldiers.

After becoming convinced of the sincerity of his comrades as a result of their splendid achievement during the Slim battle, Capt. Mohan Singh draw up three new plans and sought my cooperation. One of it was to arm a section of the INA soldiers and start training. The second plan was to build up a very powerful propaganda wing for persuading the Indian soldiers in the British army to defect in a large scale and join the INA. He drew up this plan as he was very much apprehensive that the British might give up the idea of making a decisive stand at Singapore and might prefer to retreat. The third plan was to utilise the facilities of Saigon Radio for carrying out effective propaganda to the Indian people. I supported these Ideas of Capt. Mohan Singh enthusiastically, and promised all help. After getting the approval of Maj. Gen.-Suzuki, the chief-of-staff, light weapons sufficient for two companies were handed over to the INA. Some talented officers of the rank of captain were selected and sent to Saigon. As the Japanese army hurriedly moved south, Kuala Lumpur remained practically free from Japanese forces excepting for the military administration personnel after a few days. The INA soldiers remained in the camp with Indian sentry standing at the gate with rifle in hand. The camp was fenced nominally with barbed wire. There were only two Japanese officers, 2nd. Lt. Kunizuka and I to for liaison work in the camp. Even then, not a single soldier tried to escape, nor did they have any trouble with the towns folk. Staff officers of the Imperial Headquarters and high command as well as newspaper reporters who came to the front to gain a first hand knowledge of the developments were taken aback on seeing the management of the camp, and many of them expressed grave doubts. On hearing their remarks often I thought that such a possibility was indeed

there, but even then the overall situation was so natural and we were so accustomed to it that we felt such an eventuality inconceivable. The 3rd Air Group Command moved into Kuala Lumpur immediately after its occupation. I sent 2nd Lt. Yonemira to the command and reported the misbehaviour of some of the officers and men of the unit at Lipis, and requested for appropriate action. The next day the deputy chief of staff Maj. Gen.-E (ENDO) visited the F-Organisation office alongwith a second lieutenant, who was responsible for the Lipis affair. Maj. Gen. -E had punished the officer immediately, and had sent him together with his deputy to apologise to Capt. Mohan Singh and me, promising to return the articles taken away from the Indian soldiers.

I was deeply moved by the action of Maj. Gen.-Endo Suburo, and while reporting this to Capt. Mohan Singh I also tendered my apology for the misbehaviour of the Japanese soldiers. Capt. Mohan Singh also was deeply moved by the action of Maj. Gen. - E, and profusely thanked him. He said, "Such misbehaviours by some officers are but natural in any army. And it is very rare for a general of the victorious army to apologise to the lower ranking officers and men captured during fighting. This splendid action of the Japanese has only heightened our esteem for it. This will indeed have a tremendous input on our psychology for voluntarily observing the military discipline strictly. Next, he enquired from me on the punishment meted out to the 2nd lieutenant. He asked me to request the general not to punish the young officer severely.

This compassionate attitude of Capt. Mohan Singh impressed the deputy chief of staff deeply. During my talks with the deputy chief of staff casually he mentioned about the difficulty he was facing with the Kuala Lumpur airport. In view of the war situation, this airfield was of vital importance, but had been rendered unservicable firstly by Japanese bombing, and secondly by the British forces during withdrawal. It was urgently needed for, mounting air strikes against the enemy. Reading the signs of vexation on his face, Capt. Mohan Singh enquired about the cause. On being told the reason, he immediately offered to undertake the repair work with the help of the INA.

Maj. Gen. -Endo was very happy over this offer. As the preliminary step Lt. Nakamiya visited the command Headquarters and solicited understanding and respect after explaining the manners and customs of the Indian soldiers as well as enlightening them about the INA. Proper cooperation was solicited from the employees and officers of the air field. It was decided to attach one of the E-Organisation members with the Indians going for repairs. From the following day about one thousand

INA members went to the air field for carrying out repair works. They worked so earnestly from 9.00 A.M. to 4.00 P.M. that they immediately won the hearts of the Japanese present there and who became very good friends, eventually.

The work proceeded very smoothly and there was not a single dispute. Gen. -E rewarded the Indian soldiers with money, food and other articles of day to day use. The INA soldiers put the air field back into service within a week. Maj. Gen. -E won the heart of the Indians to such an extent that they held a ceremonial parade in his honour on the day the work was completed.

From the very first day Pritam Singh reached Kuala Lumpur, he went round visiting the leaders of the Indian community, discussing with them over the question of unifying the Indians politically. On 15th December a delegation of seven or eight leaders of the local Indians headed by Dr. Lakshmi visited me, and thanked me for the protection given to the service. They were also very grateful over the support accorded by the organisation to the Indian Independence movement. The delegation also frankly expressed its views on Indian Independence movement and on the interest and protection of the Indian community in Malaya. I, on my part, explained the oral motive of the Japanese government and the plans of the Japanese army on military administration. Our discussions went on for about two hours in a very cordial atmosphere. The delegates expressed their intention to join the IIL, and promised all help to the Japanese army. That night I was invited by the Indians to an Indian style dinner, which helped in cementing our relation. I was impressed by the views of Dr. Lakshmi, as well as his concern over the welfare of the local Indians. I was also deeply moved by Budh Singh who earnestly advocated the cause of the IIL and the INA, and who had already shown very good attitude towards the INA officers and soldiers. A meeting of the Indians in Kuala Lumpur was held on 16th January where the branch of the IIL was established in the city. This was followed by a series of similar meetings in the cities of Central Malaya just like Surenban, Klan, Malacca, etc., where resolution on establishing IIL branches was adopted. The IIL movement spread through the Central Malaya just like forest fire. With success in Central Malaya, the IIL movement was poised for grand success in Malaya. The Indians made all possible contributions for the INA officers and men.

All of us, Pritam Singh, Capt. Mohan Singh and myself, became confident of the success of our movement after seeing the response from the Indians whereever we went. We also discussed plans for spreading our movement to Burma and all over East Asia, with Malaya as the base, with the ultimate objective of spreading it into India proper.

Although I was extremely busy with the work of the F-Organisation yet I availed of every opportunity to come in contact with Pritam Singh, Capt. Mohan Singh and the leaders of the Indian community in various localities, as their frank views helped me greatly in crystallising my ideas on the policy Japan should adopt towards India. As I was convinced that before long time would come when my views would be solicited by Tarauchi the Commander-in-Chief of the Southern Forces and by the Imperial Headquarters.

Again, in order to ensure smooth passage of my recommendations when officially sought for by the authorities, I tried to win over as many members of the top leadership beforehand as possible by explaining my views and requesting them to see the actual conditions whenever the staff officers of the supreme command came to Malaya to gain a first hand knowledge of the situation. With the above end in view, I also sent personal letters explaining my p ints to my fellow officers in the Imperial Headquarters and the Supreme Command Headquarters at Saigon.

About 600 Indian soldiers were taken prisoner after the Moar Battle. With these the inmates of the Kuala Lumpur camp crossed the figure of 2500. The Japanese forces were pursuing the British forces hotly after defeating them at Batbaha and Gomas. The immediate objective was Johar Bahru. The resistance of the British forces in Malayan Peninsula was practically over. The British forces were gradually withdrawing to Singapore. The fall of Johar Bahru was now a matter of days. The command Headquarters of Gen. Yamashita was advanced to Klan from Kuala Lumpur. The final scene of the war in Malayan peninsula was about to be enacted. The Japanese forces were converging on the citadel of the British empire in the Far East, Singapore.

Around this time the thing that worried us was the possible withdrawal of the British forces from Singapore. In case they decided to withdraw to Sumatra and Java the question was whether they would force the Indian soldiers, who were early waiting for a chance to join the INA, to accompany them.

Lt. Nakamiya and 2nd Lt. Yonemura proceeded to Johar Bahru front alongwith a member of F-Organisation members. The object was to assist the propaganda squads of the INA. Capt. Tsuchimochi was staying back at Moar to look after the Indian soldiers. 2nd Lt. Kunisuka and Ito remained at the INA Headquarters exclusively devoted to liaison work. The two armed companies of the INA which Capt. Mohan Singh had organised and was training were slowly acquiring fighting strength befitting revolutionary army. The will and conviction of Capt. Mohan Singh were

slowly becoming firmer, and he was slowly acquiring all the qualities expected of a general of a revolutionary army.

Around this time the Japanese forces were concentrating on the Thai-Burma border to make a drive for the Salween river in Burma. The 15th Army struck on the 19th January at the vacuum behind the British forces which were pressing the Japanese units in Tavoy very hard and quickly reached the Salween river. The 55th Division advanced from occupying Kokala on the 22nd, and reaching almost Moulansin sometime later. The 33rd Division advanced to the vicinity of Kyawkala, and was getting ready to make a thrust towards Salween. The British forces in that sector consisted of 11th Burmese Brigade and a part of the 17th British Indian Army.

In the Philippines, the force commanded by Lt. Gen. Homma captured Manila on 2nd January, and from 27th started a general offensive against the American forces led by Gen. MacArthur in Batam peninsula. Borneo was secured by joint army and navy operation. Again, Oslebes and New Britain were occupied on the 23rd and 24th of January respectively. The Japanese forces were making lightening progress through the Pacific and the Southern areas.

In view of these developments I was sure that time had come for me to present my views on the policy Japan should adopt with respect to India to the Imperial Headquarters and the Supreme Command. Again, out of consideration of my duty towards Pritam Singh and Capt. Mohan Singh, I felt that it was my duty to persuade the Central authorities to accept officially the plan we had evolved. Although this was nothing but a secret desire of a petty major of the Japanese army, yet it was a very useful mission indeed. It had to be accomplished at any cost. After returning to Kuala Lumpur, from the very first night I had been preparing the draft of the India policy secretly so as to present it to the authorities when required. That very night I got a telephone call from the command Headquarters at Klar quite late. This was from Lt. Co.-O, staff officer of the Southern Command located at Saigon. He was a senior staff officer of the Southern Command in charge of intelligence and propaganda. We had exchanged a number of communications on my plans on India.

I was summoned to the Command Headquarters at Klan to report on the progress of my work, and at that time to put my views on the policy Japan should adopt towards India in writing. I replied that I would report at the Command Headquarters after two days, I was also overwhelmed with joy that I could not sleep that night. My sixth sense told me that staff officer Lt. Col. -O, in whom I had placed so much confidence, had been

won over, and that he has came to the Command Headquarters with the purpose of observation of the situation and personal assessment. That very night with all my soul I poured out all my plans on paper. I read the final draft over and over again. I was swept off my feet by my own manuscript. I was so engrossed with it that I didn't know even when it dawned. I came back to myself on hearing loud notes of truck engine at the porch followed by loud talking of people. Lt. Nakamiya had returned from the front to report the developments. The sun was shining brightly. I left my manuscript on the desk and went downstairs hurriedly. Capt. Yamaguchi, Capt. Nakamiya and 2nd. Lt. Kunizuka were very happy over the manuscript, where I had put down our views in words and my firm desire to persuade the centre to adopt it. They took great pains in fairing the manuscript with great care and giving it proper shape of official document. The whole process was completed around noon.

I boarded the Studebaker with three copies of the manuscript, one for my Commanding Officer Gen. Yamashita, one for the commander-in-chief of the Southern Forces Gen. Terauchi, and the third one for the Imperial Headquarters. I was accompanied by Kitamura. In the eyes of the officers gathered at the gate to see me off I could read their feeling. 'We pray for the successes of your mission. You try to stick to your points for the sake of IIL, INA and India, for which we are working so hard. I was sure that I would have my way with all my sincerity, conviction and zeal'.

The car proceeded along the Singapore Road to Klan at break neck speed of 60 miles. On the way unfortunately there was a puncture, and hence we reached Klan towards dawn. Because of the tension, I forgot the fatigue of two days' work without a moment of rest. The command Headquarters was located in a rubber plantation in hurriedly constructed barracks, when I entered the room of staff officer Lt. Col. Cokamura, I was surprised to find there my old course mate, who was also the staff officer of the 37th Osaka infantry regiment formerly. He was also equally surprised, and jumped up and embraced me, congratulating me for the success of my mission. There was also one Lt. Col. Kondo in the room. He also congratulated me for my work. Besides there were two Lt. Cols., both staff officers of the Imperial Headquarters.

From them I came to know that Lt. Gen. Nagatomi, Chief of Personnel Division of the War Ministry and Lt. General Tanaka, Chief of Operations Division of the Imperial Headquarters had arrived at the command Headquarters only the day before alongwith a few senior officials as the personal representatives of War Minister Gen. Tojo and of the supreme chief of staff respectively, for on the spot study of the war situation.

Again, as luck would have it, these senior officials were mostly my acquaintances, under whom I had served. My confidence increased hundred folds, and I felt that I was sure to win my point. First of all I report to the staff officer of the Southern Command Lt. Col.-Okamura on the general situation, and then explained the draft I had carried, which was to be presented to Gen. Terauchi. It took about one hour. As I started making the report, the two staff officers of the Imperial Headquarters begged leave of us out of courtesy. But I requested them to stay on as no secrets were involved. My motive for requesting them to stay on was that they should report my talks to the two lieutenant generals. Both the staff officers gladly remained behind eagerly listening to the talks. From their behaviour I felt that they approved of my views. Lt. Col. Okumura approved of my views enthusiastically and requested the two lieutenant colonels from the Imperial Headquarters to lend their support to the plan.

As I was under the jurisdiction of the command of Gen. Yamashita, it was necessary to forward all official reports and my views for the higher authorities through the 25th Army Command. However, the views I was going to present did not relate to Malaya and Sumatra which were under the jurisdiction of the 25th Army. It rather related to India, which was bound to occupy a very prominent position in the Japanese place for establishing a new order in East Asia. So I felt that I should try to put forward my view directly to the leaders of the Imperial Headquarters and the War Ministry, and seek their approval. I was afraid that by the time my plan reached the proper authorities, my views would most probably get distorted while passing through the 25th Army Command and the Southern Command, not to tell of the time factor. I felt the visit of the important officials of the Imperial Headquarters and the War Ministry as heaven sent opportunity for presenting my report and views directly to them. After finishing my report, I went to staff officer S. of Gen. Yamashita to make report and solicit his support. He also expressed his approval of my plan, but he pointed out simultaneously that for the government of Japan to approve such a bold and grand policy officially, it would take a lot of careful deliberation. As I came out after making the report, I found Lt. Gen. Tanaka and Lt. Gen. Tominaga enjoying a stroll in the rubber plantation in the morning sun. As I saluted, Gen. Tanaka asked me what the hell was I doing in such a place. I felt as if all my blood rushing to my head, but realising that I had reached the most crucial point I replied boldly that I was carrying out the Indian policy, besides carrying out propaganda to the Malaya and the Sumatrans.

With a very amiable voice he enquired of the nature of the work and

the way I was faring. With great firmness I replied that I was trying my best and that I was confident of success. I had come there to present a report and my views for enlarging the scope of my work and draw up a revised policy to include whole of India and immediately implement it for forwarding to the Imperial Headquarters and the War Ministry. I found Gen. Tominaga listening to my reply with great interest. Instinctively I felt that they had heard about my report and my views from their two staff officers already, and hence took some interest in the subject.

Next Gen. Tanaka asked me about the success I had achieved. As I got the opportunity I was waiting so eagerly, I immediately related the organisation of the INA at Kuala Lumpur with a few thousand Indian prisoners of war, and that the strength of this revolutionary army was bound to increase vastly once the Singapore operation went on smoothly. I also related the success of the IIL movement in whole of Malaya, and its spread to Burma and the various regions of East Asia. But its dedication, the IIL had laid the foundation for carrying this revolutionary struggle into India.

Lt. Gen. Tanaka looked at Lt. Gen. Tominaga, and after a meaningful wink at him said to me whether he could have a look at the INA whose drum I was beating so much Lt. Gen. Tominaga also immediately expressed his willingness to see the INA. The most I had expected of these two generals was that they might at best reluctantly agree to hear my views after a lot of persuation. I just could not believe my own ears when these two top ranking leaders of the Japanese army expressed their desire to accompany to Kuala Lumpur, see the INA, and have a chat with Capt. Mohan Singh and Pritam Singh, besides listening to my views. I was besides myself with joy. Lt. Gen. Tanaka immediately called his staff officer-K and ordered him to make preparations for the trip to Kuala Lumpur, and keep a plane ready for the purpose. After taking leave of the two generals I ran to the staff officer of the southern forces Lt. Col.-O and reported this development. He told me that this was due to persuation of the two staff officers of the Imperial Genaral Headquarters who had accompanied the two generals. He encouraged me so that I could boldly explain my project to them. The staff officers of the commanding officer Yamashita were literally taken aback to see me cornering the two generals and the team of the Imperial Headquarters, seven persons in all.

On that very day I reached Kuala Lumpur airport around noon together with the two generals and the Imperial Headquarter steam. The team proceeded to the local command office conducted by the local commandant from the airport, and I hurried to the F-Organisation Headquarters together

with Lt. Yamaguchi who had come to receive me. Lt. Yamaguchi was also very happy to see the two generals. As soon as this news spread in the F-Organisation, all the young officers there falicitated me over the success. But they were also a bit worried over the arrangement to be made for the team as time for preparation was not there. I immediately called Pritam Singh and Capt. Mohan Singh and explained the whole positions. Both of them were also very happy. After discussions we decided to put our views frankly to the two generals and planned the whole show accordingly. I was also very happy to present our situation to the two generals without concealing anything or taking recourses to any deceit.

After careful consideration I prepared the schedule as follows. It was to start with a visit to the INA camp followed by a review of troop a meeting of the two generals with Pritam Singh and Capt. Mohan Singh at the INA Headquarters, a meeting Capt. Mohan Singh with the team of the Imperial Headquarters, and finally my report to the two generals. Pritam Singh and Capt. Mohan Singh started preparations immediately. The first two items of inspection of the camp and military review started around 4.00 P.M. Although it was a very hurriedly arranged review, they marched in regular formation under smart officers, creating a very good impressions on the two generals. Next, the meeting was held in the INA Headquarters between Capt. Mohan Singh and the two Generals. In a very serious tone Capt. Mohan Singh explained the actual situation of the INA and the firm resolution of the officers and men. He also expressed his gratitude to the Japanese army for assisting the INA movement through the F-Organisation. As agreed upon earlier, no concrete topic was taken up during the discussion both the generals were deeply impressed by the ideal of the Pritam Singh and Capt. Mohan Singh, and encouraged them enthusiastically.

After the party left, I ran to the local command alongwith Capt. Mohan Singh and his deputy Akram to meet the team that had accompanied the two generals. 2nd Lt. Kunizuka accompanied us to interpret. There was no special topic for discussion. The object was to let the officials of the Imperial Headquarters to have an idea of the character and conviction of Capt. Mohan Singh, besides developing acquaintance. It was quite obvious that the real motive of the two generals in taking so much trouble to come all the way to Kuala Lumpur and meet Capt. Mohan Singh was to ascertain Capt. Mohan Singh's personality and whether he was worth backing by Japan, I was so sure of the outcome that I did not have even slightest apprehensions. This was because I had no doubt about his patriotism and

watching his eversince Alor Star. Another point in my favour was that the team consisted of my old acquaintances, who also had excellent records to their credit. The talks were very frank and continued for about an hour. As expected Capt. Mohan Singh succeeded in creating a very good impression in their minds. The talks went on also the following line. Lt. Col.-: Okamura " I must confess that most of us lack a clear understanding of the national character of the Indian people. I think by now you have studied the national character of the Japanese people. Do you think that the understanding of the national character of the two nations is very important in forging the cooperation between the two nations."

Capt. Mohan Singh : "Just like you I also lack a clear understanding of the national character of the Japanese people. However, in the past I had read a book on Bushido of Japan. There I have read of three divine objects, viz., sword, jewel and mirror. The sword signifies bravery, the jewel benevolence and mirror righteousness. It was written there that these three objects denote the spirit of Japan. Indeed I have seen the bravery of the Japanese soldiers eversince the engagements along the Thai-Malaya border with my own eyes. Again, the actions of Maj. Fujiwara and other members of the F- Organisation have confirmed the benevolence, righteousness and gentleness of the Japanese people.

We the Indian people attribute religious significance to benevolence and righteousness. I personally believe that being the nations of the orient, both the peoples have many things in common in their national characters."

Lt. Col. Okamura, "I hope you will not mind if I put a somewhat delicate question to you. We quite often hear that the Independence movement of India is very much handicapped due to religious confrontation and castism not to tell of rivalry and antagonism between various racial groups. Could you please enlighten us on this point."

Capt. Mohan Singh, "I do not agree with the above viewpoints popularised in Japan. I think that our love for motherland should transcend the narrow sense of loyalty to religion or race. Although the caste system has survived till today, yet it is a legacy of the past, and this inhuman and anti- social contradiction is slowly vanishing from the national scene. I do not think that the elimination of this evil is that difficult as some of the foreigners think. Rather this system is very much encouraged by the British rulers. We are building up the INA by sinking all narrow caste prejudices and religious and racial differences, setting the liberation of motherland as our supreme goal. Our patriotic officers and men have risen to the occasion, and there had been not a single case of trouble due to these factors. This fact will serve as an ample proof of the correctness of our conviction."

Lt. Col. - O : " I hear that the Burmese have a strong sense of antipathy towards the large number of Indians living amongst them. The Japanese army is now thinking to advance to Burma and liberate the Burmese people. As this question is of grave importance, could you please express your viewpoint over this problem?"

Capt. Mohan Singh : "We must frankly admit that there are good reasons for the resentment of the Burmese people against the Indians. The Indians there have some sort of superiority complex towards the Burmese people. The Indians are more enterprising than the Burmese, and thus have succeeded in monopolising land and business. Again, afraid of the Independence movement of the Burmese people, the British government has stopped recruiting them for military and police service. The British government is employing the Indian soldiers and Indian policemen to supress the nationalist movement of the Burmese people. These are some of the main causes of Burmese resentment against the Indians. The conflict over interest and feeling is rather very deep rooted. But even then I do not think that it is an impossible problem with no solution. If the leaders of the two countries try to sort out the trouble across the table after overthrow of British bondage keeping the greater interest of the prosperity of the nations of East Asia in view, then I think that the problem can be solved without much difficulty.

The above are some of the topics that were discussed during the meeting. The team of the Imperial Headquarters got a thoroughly clear picture of the convictions, intellectual capability, seal and personality of Capt. Mohan Singh. After Capt. Mohan Singh had left together with his deputy Akram, Lt. Col.-O (Okamura) went to the room of the two generals and made a report on the meeting. After sometime I was called by the two generals.

After offering me a chair, Lt. Gen. Tanaka practically poured cold water on my enthusiasm by saying "Fujiwara, you have dragged us all the way to this place, but from the report of the staff officer Lt. Col. - O it transpires that Capt. Mohan Singh, whom you are grooming so much, is not a person worth that much of trouble. What do you have to say on this points?"

I was simply taken aback by this question of the general. But the next instant I recovered my self composure as I felt that this was just an attempt to test my own conviction. There were of course a number of reasons for my thinking like that. Both the generals had given a very favourable impression that very morning at Klan, and during the guard of honour and talks with the Indian officers also they had shown

considerable interest. Thus becoming convinced that the general was saying something which he really did not mean, I said " Sir, that is not correct. From what Capt. Mohan Singh had said during the above talks, my confidence in and respect for Capt. Mohan Singh have hightened all the more. In case any member of your team has such a misunderstanding, then I would like to hear the cause for it directly from him."

In a cold and blunt tone the general asked, whether I was challenging the report of the staff officer?

I replied : " Yes. However, reliable the staff officer may be, yet I want to assert that this particular report is wrong. I have seen Capt. Mohan Singh over the last fifty days standing on the verge of life and death. I am sure that my study of Capt. Mohan Singh is not wrong."

With this assertion of mine the general softened his tone and still somewhat ironically said, "Capt. Mohan Singh is basically a soldier of the British Indian Army. He is neither a politician , nor a revolutionary. And moreover, compared to the famous leaders of India, nobody even has over heard of his name. In the language to the king in chess he is just a pawn.

I encouraged myself by saying that the critical moment had come and but I should not give way, and said: "Sir, as you have said, Capt. Mohan Singh in a soldier. He has not been tempered by the flame of revolution. Again, he is also very young in age. But we know many instances of soldiers heading revolutions. All the famous revolutionaries were little known young men in the beginning. Selfless love for the country, passionate ardour for revolution, capacity to carry out decision, and foresightedness are the qualities which make grand revolutionary out of unknown young men. I have seen these qualities in Capt. Mohan Singh. Although you have likened Capt. Mohan Singh with pawn, yet I do not contribute to your view. Even if it is assumed that he is just a pawn at the moment, yet he has enough capability to become a queen and checkmate the king."

As I ended, the general said 'Un' in a tone of assent. I could also read signs of approval in the eyes of Lt. Gen. Tominaga, who was silently listening to the talks. Being encouraged I continued: "Independence of India and Indo-Japanese cooperation are essential for the successful conclusion of the East Asian War and realisation of Japan's cherished objective of establishing a new order in East Asia in the form of Great East Asia a co-prosperity sphere. However, out of self complacency Japan has taken no notice of India and has not taken any step to cultivate friendship with the Indian leaders. Because of this we have failed to win over a great leader like Subhash Chandra Bose on our side. However, at the moment

we have succeeded in winning over Capt. Mohan Singh and a few thousands of his comrades in INA as well as the tens of thousands of Malayan Indians. In case Japan displays appropriate statesmanship as I am advocating and implement it in whole of East Asia, then it will be possible to mobilise more than a lakh of Indian soldiers whom we are going to capture in the Malayan campaign, besides the millions of Indians living in the region in our anti-British war. This is the only way for enlisting the support of free India in establishing the new order in the East. Furthermore, both Pritam Singh and Capt. Mohan Singh are committed to the Independence of India, and they do not have any adventurist ambition. They would gladly hand over the leadership of the IIL and INA to any great leader of India who would like to assume leadership and would work as his assistants without any grudge. They are sincerely hoping that Japan would extend invitation to Subhash Chandra Bose to assume leadership of the Indian Independence movement in East Asia."

After I had finished suddenly general Tanaka changed his cold attitude, and told me to explain in brief the contents of my report. He initiated the talk asking any views on the importance of Japan's policy with regard to India.

After I had talked a little, suddenly he stopped me telling that he had enough of my explanation, and told me to speak about concrete plan if any. Although I was slightly taken aback as I had least expected such an interruption, yet I recovered my composure and put forward my view as I had done in Ipoh to the staff officer- O of the Imperial Headquarters.

After I had finished, the general only curtly said that he would keep my explanation in view. Seeing my slight disappointment over the general's cold reception of my urgings, Lt. Gen. Tominaga said " Never mind young man, try to do your best." Saying this he offered me a glass of whisky following which Gen. Tanaka also offered me a glass of whisky. I could not make out whether my mission was a success or a failure. However, I felt that the net balance was in my favour. This was because, when I had expressed that the F-Organisation should be replaced by a very powerful organisation in case it was decided to implement a very vigorous India Policy. Gen. Tanaka asked my opinion about a suitable person to head this organisation. I told that the person should be politically mature, sincere and a very good diplomat. In view of the gravity of the question, he was probably trying to test me, and was telling something which he did not really mean. The reason for my thinking like this was that it was not possible for the two generals to make any firm commitment over such an important issue without the concurrence of the War Minister and the Supreme Command.

As soon as I came out of the room of the generals after thanking them for taking all the trouble of coming to Kuala Lumpur, the officials of the Imperial Headquarters accosted me asking about the interview. I replied that I had a thorough bashing.

Lt. Col. -O reassured me telling that I had indeed scored a success in case I had a good bashing from Gen. Tanaka. He also congratulated me for having found a magnificent man like Capt. Mohan Singh. Although I had enough self-confidence to accept the above verdict of the colonel, yet I had a bit of apprehension at a corner of my mind.

On my way back I called upon Capt. Mohan Singh at his official residence. He sought my opinion about the day's proceeding. I assured him that all was well. Knowing my liking for alconol, he told his deputy to bring a bottle of whisky. Over whisky we talked in a very relaxed mood, and I enjoyed the bliss of pure friendship free from any duplicity.

It was past midnight when I returned to my Headquarters. All were waiting there eagerly without going to bed. With great confidence I told them that all was well. Immediately the whole office was engulfed in a festive mood, and again over whisky I related the developments that took place since morning. On the following morning I saw the two generals and their party off at Kuala Lumpur airport. They were to proceed at right to Saigon. Here for the first time the two generals expressed deep appreciation of my work and encouraged me to go ahead with my work.

One of the staff officers of the generals took me aside and said that he had been ordered by Gen. Tanaka to express his personal appreciation of my work and the success I had achieved. As my work was of extreme importance the general wanted me to pour my heart and soul into the work. My views were also very educative and the generals were very much happy over these. I was very happy to know that the two generals had approved of my proposals, and there was every likelihood of their being adopted by the topmost authorities. I was besides myself with joy, and thanked him profusely. As soon as the aeroplane left, I suddenly felt a heavy burden removed from my chest, and simultaneously with this I was overwhelmed with terrible fatigue.

On 30th January evening the advanced units of the 5th Division of the Japanese army finally captured Johar Bahru. The only bridge connecting the island of Singapore with the Malayan peninsula was destroyed by the retreating British forces. Around this time the 6th batch of Sumitra Youth Group vanished into night darkness of the Malacca Straits for crossing over to Sumatra. With the departure of this group all information on the developments in Sumatra ceased. Again, Mr. Onam of

Young Malaya Association was busy training his comrades for starting work immediately with the fall of Singapore.

On 4th February I came to know that a general offensive on Singapore was scheduled for 9th February. On this very day I received two orders from the 25th Army Command. One was a copy of the order of Gen. Terauchi, the Commander-in-Chief of the Southern Forces, to Gen. Yamashita, the commander of the 25th Army. The other was the order of Gen. Yamashita to me. The order from Gen. Terauchi ran on the following lines : 'The 25th Army will dispatch a section of the Fujiwara Organisation to Burma, which will carry on and support the IIL and INA movement under the overall command of the 15th Army Commander Lt. Gen. Iida.' The order from Gen. Yamashita ran as follows: 'The Head of the Fujiwara Organisation will immediately bifurcate the Fujiwara Organisation and send a section to Burma to give active support to the IIL and the INA movements in the area.' It was evident that one of the earnest desires of Pritam Singh and Capt. Mohan Singh and which I had strongly advocated in my proposal had been accepted by the commander-in-chief of the Southern Forces. Burma occupied a top priority position in our scheme as it was adjacent to India, besides having about two million Indians. Thus, extending our work to Burma constituted a great turning point in our work. Yet with the decisive battle for Singapore just round the corner and advance of the Japanese forces on to Sumatra in near future it constituted a heavy burden for the F-Organisation to send some of its members to Burma as we were extremely short of hands. It was expected that the Burma campaign was going to be a tough one in view of the zise of the country, lack of communication and prevalence of diseases. However, these were problems about which nothing could be done beforehand. The Japanese forces were faced with the dual task of fighting the enemy on one hand and solving these problems on the other. Although we were extremely short of hands, yet I decided to send my best associates to Burma in view of the importance of the assignment. Thereupon, I selected Capt. Tsuchimochi, the seniormost officer in the organisation to head the team, and placed three of my most trusted associates, Ishikawa, Kitamura and Takimura, under him. Although it was extremely unfair to impose such a heavy burden like that on only four persons, yet that the best I could do at the moment. The only thing we could hope for was the positive assistance from the 15th Army.

I also immediately held a meeting with Pritam Singh and Capt. Mohan Singh and discussed about the war situation in Burma after disclosing the contents of the orders I had received. Both of them were extremely happy. After detailed discussions it was decided to send a team of three groups.

One from the IIL with Pritam Singh as the head, the second from the INA consisting of sixty propaganda cadres with a certain captain of the INA as the head, and the third consisting of four F-Organisation members including Capt. Tsuchimochi. The F-Organisation members were to coordinate the work with the Japanese forces on active duty. It was decided to start preparations immediately so that the team could leave Kuala Lumpur on 9th February by train. The Japanese forces in Burma at that time were making preparations to cross the Salween river after capturing Moulmein on the 31st January. The British forces in this area had retreated to the west bank of Salween and a section was retreating overland towards Rangoon. Intelligence reports indicated that reinforcements had reached Rangoon from India, and that a Chinese detachment was on way to Rangoon from Yunnan.

The Headquarters of the Southern Forces in Saigon was at this time busy preparing plans for the capture of Rangoon and the important enemy bases in Central Burma.

Besides preparing plans for the capture of Burma, the Japanese forces were also busy providing large scale assistance of the Thakin Party of Burma which was leading the anti-British nationalist movement of the Burmese people. Content between the Japanese army and the Thakin Party had been established as early as 1940.

About thirty young Burmese nationalists headed by Aung San representing the extreme faction of the Thakin Party had escaped from Burma by land and by sea, and at that time were receiving training in arms secretly at Hainan Island under enthusiastic supervision of the Imperial Headquarters. A cell called Minami Organisation (Minami Kikan) with Col. Suzuki as the head had been established for coordinating this work. It was a very powerful organisation composed of about ten members including the head, drawn from both the army and the navy. With the declaration of war in December 1941, these Burmese young men under the leadership of Aung San and the Minami Organisation came to Thailand and immediately undertook the task of raising a volunteer force from among the local Burmese under the name Burma Independence Army (BIA). The BIA accompanied the Japanese army when it advanced into Burma from Thailand. The BIA received very enthusiastic welcome from the Burmese people everywhere they went and the Burmese young men came forward in large number to swell its ranks.[1]

The BIA played almost no operational role as it was hurriedly raised from among people who had no military training whatsoever, but it facilitated

the head, and the third consisting of four F-Organisation members including Capt. Tsuchimochi. The F-Organisation members were to coordinate the work with the Japanese forces on active duty. It was decided to start preparations immediately so that the team could leave Kuala Lumpur on 9th February by train. The Japanese forces in Burma at that time were making preparations to cross the Salween river after capturing Moulmein on the 31st January. The British forces in this area had retreated to the west bank of Salween and a section was retreating overland towards Rangoon. Intelligence reports indicated that reinforcements had reached Rangoon from India, and that a Chinese detachment was on way to Rangoon from Yunnan.

The Headquarters of the Southern Forces in Saigon was at this time busy preparing plans for the capture of Rangoon and the important enemy bases in Central Burma.

Besides preparing plans for the capture of Burma, the Japanese forces were also busy providing large scale assistance of the Thakin Party of Burma which was leading the anti-British nationalist movement of the Burmese people. Content between the Japanese army and the Thakin Party had been established as early as 1940.

About thirty young Burmese nationalists headed by Aung San representing the extreme faction of the Thakin Party had escaped from Burma by land and by sea, and at that time were receiving training in arms secretly at Hainan Island under enthusiastic supervision of the Imperial Headquarters. A cell called Minami Organisation (Minami Kikan) with Col. Suzuki as the head had been established for coordinating this work. It was a very powerful organisation composed of about ten members including the head, drawn from both the army and the navy. With the declaration of war in December 1941, these Burmese young men under the leadership of Aung San and the Minami Organisation came to Thailand and immediately undertook the task of raising a volunteer force from among the local Burmese under the name Burma Independence Army (BIA). The BIA accompanied the Japanese army when it advanced into Burma from Thailand. The BIA received very enthusiastic welcome from the Burmese people everywhere they went and the Burmese young men came forward in large number to swell its ranks.[1]

The BIA played almost no operational role as it was hurriedly raised from among people who had no military training whatsoever, but it facilitated

1. For details see. Izumiya Tatsuro, *The Minami Organ*, Rangoon 1981.

Johar Bahru Strait and launched general offensive against the citadel of Singapore. The INA propaganda squads and the members of the F-Organisation immediately proceeded to Singapore to carry out propaganda to the Indian soldiers.

I had to proceed to Johar Bahru in great haste for guiding our work in this decisive battle. Because of this I could not see off the Burma team at the Kuala Lumpur station. On 8th February I gave a farewell party to the INA squad members at my residence, and that very night I gave another farewell party to the four F-Organisation members. I felt very sad to part with these boys with whom I had shared my joys and sorrows for the last four months or so. They were proceeding to the battle field in the north, and I was proceeding to the battle field in the south. Indeed this could be our last parting. Indeed Pritam Singh and Capt. Mohan Singh were also holding such parties with such heavy heart with their associates. On the 9th February morning I bade farewell to Capt. Tsuchimochi and left for the front together with Nagano.

I shifted my office to Singapore after getting the approval of the Chief of Staff on 16th February.

At night I reached the hillock west of Raffle's University from the Bukipanjan crossing in just five minutes driving along the Bukitema Road. Just a few days on the 13th night back we had taken more than eight hours to cross this stretch of land. The houses and the trees on both sides of the road were the vivid witnesses of the fierce engagements that were fought here. I could see everywhere the graves of those heros who fell here, covered with unknown red flowers of the tropics and their water bottles hanging from their memorial slabs.

Under special instructions from Gen. Yamashita, ordinary soldiers were prohibited from entering the city proper. Only the military police and some auxiliary forces assisting the military police were permitted entry into the city for maintaining law and order. There were checkposts everywhere, and even the individual soldiers in plain dress were not permitted to enter the city not to tell of the units. There was not a single soul on the road. One million inhabitants of the city had confined themselves indoors out of sheer fear. A large number of houses were destroyed during the weeklong artillery bombardment, and rotting human bodies were befouling the air everywhere.

Lt. Nakamiya had selected a house in the residential district of British police officials near Raffle's University on the western suburbs of Singapore as the office of the F-Organisation. He had complied with my instruction of selecting a simple house in the suburbs slightly away from the city

hubs but with good traffic facilities. Because this area constituted the first line of defence, the whole area including the houses was littered with war equipment and ammunitions, and all the open spaces were dug up with trenches leaving no space even to walk.

On this very day the INA command, IIL office and Sumatra Youth Group were shifted to Singapore. In the evening a joint committee of the British and Japanese forces was set up in the British High Command Office at Fort Canning for the handing over of Singapore. It was ordered that the F-Organisation also should be incorporated in this body. It was also decided that the formal handing over of the Indian soldiers will be held on the following day, viz., 17th afternoon at Farah Park.

According to the report of the British committee members, there were about fifty thousand Indian soldiers. There were also almost equal number of British soldiers. The Japanese army estimates had put the total strength of British forces in Singapore at about thirty thousand, of which about ten to fifteen thousand were Indian soldiers. The Japanese committee, members were taken aback when they heard these figures from their British counterparts. Numerically the Britishers were several times stronger than the attacking Japanese forces. In case the British forces had held out for a few more days and tried for a counter offensive, then the Japanese forces inferior both numerically and in equipment would have surely met with a serious debacle. The greatest problem that faced me right at the moment was the question of looking after fifty thousand Indian soldiers with about four army officers and about ten civilians as my assistants, with no preparations whatsoever. They had to be accommodated, fed, and controlled and their personal hygiene had to be ensured. In addition the original purpose for which the F-Organisation had been set up had to be fulfilled. My head was full of the above problems as I returned to my office in car. The previous night the F-Organisation was allotted the additional task of procuring the list of persons involved in political and ideological crimes from the detective department of Singapore. I had sent 2nd. Lt. Yonemura and Tashiro to the British Detective Department to procure this list in the morning. Lt. Nakamiya was running about in search of barracks for accommodating the Indian prisoners of war. Lt. Yamaguchi was busy cleaning the F-Organisation office littered with arms and ammunitions left behind by the British forces.

After hearing the reports from my staff, I gave them instructions on the work for the following day. I told Lt. Nakamiya and 2nd Lt. Yonemara to search for barracks all over Singapore to accommodate the Indian prisoners numbering fifty thousand, as well as to procure the necessary provisions

and sanitary facilities. Some INA officers were detailed to assist them in their work. Lt. Yamaguchi was allotted the task of making preparations for the handing over ceremony of the prisoners at Farah Park. All the members scattered in all directions for discharging their duties. After the members of the F-Organisation had left, I had a discussion with Capt. Mohan Singh and Pritam Singh over the prisoners of war handing over ceremony scheduled to take place on the following day. It was decided that after formal taking over of the charge of the Indian prisoners of war from the British representative. I would first address the Indian prisoners as the representative of the Japanese army, followed by Capt. Mohan Singh and Pritam Singh as the commander of the INA and the representative of the IIL respectively. It was also decided that I would meet the Indian officers after the ceremony following which the prisoners would be dispersed in the different camps in a planned manner. All three of us were thoroughly aware of the importance of these first addresses to the prisoners. It was decided to procure very good microphones for the purpose. We also agreed to request the Japanese army propaganda division to send photographers to record this historic occasion. I was to prepare my speech by the following morning, and get the approval of the army chief-of-staff Maj. Gen.-S only after the consent of Capt. Mohan Singh and Pritam Singh. That night I was very busy preparing the speech. It ran on the following lines.

(A) One of the war objectives of Japan is to liberate the nations of East Asia.

(B) Japan earnestly hopes for the Independence of India, and is prepared to give all out assistance for the achievement of this goal. Japan does not have any design whatsoever on India.

(C) The fall of Singapore has brought a golden opportunity for bringing about Indian Independence.

(D) The Japanese army holds the freedom movement of the INA and the IIL in high esteem, and with this in mind is giving all possible support to these movements. Both these organisations are showing extremely good work in protecting the Indians in the war zone and the Indian army stragglers.

(E) The Japanese army treat the Indian prisoners as brothers.

(F) Those prisoners desiring to join the INA for liberating India will cease to be prisoners. They will be given total freedom and all help will be given to them

(G) The Japanese army will deal with the Indian prisoners through Capt. Mohan Singh.

(H) The Japanese army will try its best to provide the Indian prisoners with all the necessities. However, because of the situation arising out of rapid advance of the Japanese forces, adequate supplies have not come up yet. If there is any temporary shortage because of the circumstances stated above, you are requested to show proper understanding.

It was almost midnight when I completed my speech. When Capt. Kunizuku just started to translate it, Capt. Mohan Singh suddenly came into my room in a very agitated mood.

With visible expression of anxiety on his face he said that one of the INA propaganda squad members had been arrested by some British officers and had been kept in confinement. There was a likelihood that he might be tried for treason. It was indeed very difficult to watch the execution of a comrade. So he had come to discuss with me on the question of getting him released at any cost. I was very happy over this fresh proof of Capt. Mohan Singh's love and friendship for his comrades. I immediately took a resolution to save his comrade who was my comrade as well. The name of the British officer concerned and his address were also known. Although the instruments of surrender had already been signed, yet the issue concerned the enemy who had fought desperately even the day before and who were still carrying arms. I felt slightly worried. But any delay might bring about irreparable harm to the arrested person. It was not possible to hesitate either. I decided to go to the unit concerned and talk to the particular officer directly. Capt. Mohan Singh tried to dissuade me as he realised the danger involved. As there was the likelihood of the whole issue getting very complicated in case I entrusted the job to the young officers or I sought the assistance of the Japanese units or military police, I decided to stick to my decision. As Mohan Singh also wanted to accompany me, we both went to the unit concerned guided by an INA propaganda squad member who had witnessed the arrest. We also took an escort of a few INA soldiers. I strictly forbade my companions to commit any violence unless the British troops initiated such a situation. Entering the room of the battalion commander I resolutely protested against the impropriety of keeping in confinement of an INA soldier, who had been assisting the Japanese forces, disregarding the signing of surrender on the 15th. The battalion commander accepted my protest and immediately handed over the INA propaganda squad member in his custody to me.

I was extremely happy that the matter ended so amicably. I could not contain my joy when I saw Capt. Mohan Singh embracing his released comrade with tears in eyes.

On our way back Capt. Mohan Singh thanked me profusely. Although it was past midnight, yet both Mohan Singh and myself had to study the

rapid advance of the Japanese forces, adequate supplies have not come up yet. If there is any temporary shortage because of the circumstances stated above, you are requested to show proper understanding.

It was almost midnight when I completed my speech. When Capt. Kunizuku just started to translate it, Capt. Mohan Singh suddenly came into my room in a very agitated mood.

With visible expression of anxiety on his face he said that one of the INA propaganda squad members had been arrested by some British officers and had been kept in confinement. There was a likelihood that he might be tried for treason. It was indeed very difficult to watch the execution of a comrade. So he had come to discuss with me on the question of getting him released at any cost. I was very happy over this fresh proof of Capt. Mohan Singh's love and friendship for his comrades. I immediately took a resolution to save his comrade who was my comrade as well. The name of the British officer concerned and his address were also known. Although the instruments of surrender had already been signed, yet the issue concerned the enemy who had fought desperately even the day before and who were still carrying arms. I felt slightly worried. But any delay might bring about irreparable harm to the arrested person. It was not possible to hesitate either. I decided to go to the unit concerned and talk to the particular officer directly. Capt. Mohan Singh tried to dissuade me as he realised the danger involved. As there was the likelihood of the whole issue getting very complicated in case I entrusted the job to the young officers or I sought the assistance of the Japanese units or military police, I decided to stick to my decision. As Mohan Singh also wanted to accompany me, we both went to the unit concerned guided by an INA propaganda squad member who had witnessed the arrest. We also took an escort of a few INA soldiers. I strictly forbade my companions to commit any violence unless the British troops initiated such a situation. Entering the room of the battalion commander I resolutely protested against the impropriety of keeping in confinement of an INA soldier, who had been assisting the Japanese forces, disregarding the signing of surrender on the 15th. The battalion commander accepted my protest and immediately handed over the INA propaganda squad member in his custody to me.

I was extremely happy that the matter ended so amicably. I could not contain my joy when I saw Capt. Mohan Singh embracing his released comrade with tears in eyes.

On our way back Capt. Mohan Singh thanked me profusely. Although it was past midnight, yet both Mohan Singh and myself had to study the distribution of the fifty thousand Indian soldiers in different camps on the

to their camps. I requested Lt. Col. Hunt to hand over the Indian soldiers who had already arrived, and to hand over those yet to arrive directly to the Japanese army. So we immediately started the ceremony. Through the mike, all the Indian soldiers were ordered to sit down facing the dias. The officers were told to sit in the front row. Lt. Col. Hunt took up position in front of the mike. All the Indian soldiers packing the park looked at Lt. Col. Hunt with great attention. In a very business like manner he said the Indian soldiers that they were being transferred to the Japanese army, and as such they should obey the command of the Japanese army in future. After speaking these few words, he handed over the list of names to me. The list contained about forty five thousand names. By this all the Indian soldiers came under the jurisdiction of the Japanese army. After telling the colonel that I had taken over the charge of the Indian soldiers. I requested him to leave the place. According to the schedule already drawn up, I stood in front of the mike. I felt ninety thousand eyes focussed on me. Suddenly there was pin drop silence. To my right stood 2nd Lt. Kunizuka for translating my speech into English, and to his right stood Lt. Col. Gill for translating my speech into Hindi. I was about to make a historical declaration of the philosophy of my work as the representative of the Japanese army to the forty five thousand Indian soldiers sitting in front of me. I felt all my blood roaring through my body and rushing to my head. With my manuscript in my hand I first made obeisance to the Indian soldiers respectfully in order to show the sincerity of friendship to all the Indian soldiers who had assembled there. The Indian officers and men seated there responded rather reflexively, some by folding their hands and some by touching their forehead with their right hand. At that very instant I felt that a bond of friendship was established between me and the Indian soldiers. Then I introduced myself to the Indian soldiers by saying "My friends, the soldiers of India, I am Maj. Fujiwara, the Head of F-Organisation, who has come here to take over the charges of you all from the British authorities on behalf of the Japanese, and for establishing the bond of friendship between the peoples of India and Japan. "As soon as this was translated into English by 2nd. Lt. Kunizuka, I saw nods of approval in the front row where the officers were seated. As soon as this was retranslated into Hindi by Lt. Col. Gill, I saw the same nod of approval among the thousands of soldiers in the rear. I felt that I had succeeded in touching the hearts of all those seated in front of me. After explaining the philosophical background of Japan's intension to establish a new order of Prosperity in East Asia based on liberty, equality and fraternity of the liberated nations of the region, I proceeded to assure them of Japan's

earnest desire to give all possible support to the Indian Independence movement. The last part of my speech was drowned in deafening applause of my listeners. The next part of my speech also received similar welcome when I expressed my firm conviction that the fall of the British citadel in the Far East Singapore signalled the collapse of the empires of England and Holland in East Asia and liberation of the nations of the region from imperialistic fetters. The listeners went so wild with enthusiasm that it was not possible for me to continue my speech for a while till the applause subsided.

Next I introduced the glorious achievements of the IIL led by Pritam Singh and the INA led by Capt. Mohan Singh, and declared the Japanese army's all out support to these two movements. This was also received with similar applause. I explained to them that the Japanese army will not treat the Indian soldiers as prisoners of war, rather they will be treated as friends and brothers. The Japanese army had always regretted the sad destiny of confronting you all in the battlefield with arms for no fault of yours or ours. However, today we have been freed from that destiny, and have succeeded in establishing the bonds of friendship and brotherhood, with the blessing of God. The Independence of a nation should be won over by the nation through struggle that should arise from within the nation. I also declared that those soldiers willing to join the INA after taking the vow of loyalty to India and to fight for the freedom of motherland, will cease to be prisoners forthwith, and they will be given all possible help. Not only that their right to fight will also be recognised. As soon as I finished this line I saw thousands of caps flying into air besides deafening cheers. My speech lasted about forty minutes. This speech of mine can be considered as one of the landmarks in the birth of the Indian National Army. Together with the speeches of Pritam Singh and Capt. Mohan Singh, this speech also can be taken as a historical declaration deserving due recognition in the history of India.

Pritam Singh and Capt. Mohan Singh took the mike after me. Both of them spoke in Hindi. Both of them described the activities of the IIL and the INA, and expressed their firm conviction of gaining India's Independence through armed struggle, with both of them standing in the vanguard of the fight. After describing the state of the Indians as living corpses because of servitude, they appealed to all those present to join the struggle for the liberation of motherland and put an end to the shame of foreign domination. Each and every word they uttered went home deep into the hearts of the Indian soldiers. As their speech ended the crowd burst out into thunderous applause, the caps went flying into air, and all

tried to come near the dias. For some time chaos reigned supreme. All of them were imbued with inspiration for dedicating their lives for the cause of their motherland. Thus ended the meeting of the Farah Park amidst great success. Next I proposed to Capt. Mohan Singh and Lt. Col. Gill to have a meeting exclusively with the officers in the hall. Lt. Col. Gill immediately ordered the officers to assemble in the hall. We all sat around a round table, and I proposed to the officers to have a frank discussion over their questions and doubts on the Japanese army in particular and Japan in general.

The officers put questions on the motive of Japan in supporting the Independence of India, the extent of support Japan was prepared to give to the Indian Independence struggle, cooperation between the INA and the Japanese army, organising the INA and arming it etc. I replied to these questions on the basis of the memorandum of Pritam Singh and Col. Tamura and the discussion I had with Capt. Mohan Singh at Taiping. I frankly admitted that the question of organising and equipping of the INA and its cooperation with the Japanese army should be settled by bipartite talks between the Japanese authorities and the Indian leaders. I succeeded in winning over the understanding and friendship of the Indian officers through these talks. After the end of the talks, Lt. Col. Gill issued instructions on the accommodation of the soldiers. The Indian soldiers assembled in the park started moving towards their camps just like flood water breaching the dyke. All the members of the F-Organisation and of the INA were mobilised to guide them to their camps. It was night by the time the last soldiers reached their camps.

Immediately after the meeting I returned to my office alongwith Pritam Singh. This was because there was a scheduled meeting with two representatives of the local Indian community Goho and Menon. Pritam Singh had briefed them beforehand over the nature and function of the F-Organisation, as well as about me. They were well versed with the activities of the IIL and the INA, and also knew about the grand spectacle of the Farah Park, Pritam Singh had also briefed me about these two persons beforehand. As we settled down for discussion after an exchange of greetings, we felt as if we were old friends. I was very much impressed by Goho who initiated the discussion on the subject of freedom, honour and interest of his compatriots. He appeared to me as a person with strong character and will, with capacity to enforce decision besides having great political consciousness. In this sitting we discussed about the support of the IIL by these two gentlemen, appointment of Goho as the President of the Singapore chapter of the IIL, and the meeting of the Singapore Indians

tried to come near the dias. For some time chaos reigned supreme. All of them were imbued with inspiration for dedicating their lives for the cause of their motherland. Thus ended the meeting of the Farah Park amidst great success. Next I proposed to Capt. Mohan Singh and Lt. Col. Gill to have a meeting exclusively with the officers in the hall. Lt. Col. Gill immediately ordered the officers to assemble in the hall. We all sat around a round table, and I proposed to the officers to have a frank discussion over their questions and doubts on the Japanese army in particular and Japan in general.

The officers put questions on the motive of Japan in supporting the Independence of India, the extent of support Japan was prepared to give to the Indian Independence struggle, cooperation between the INA and the Japanese army, organising the INA and arming it etc. I replied to these questions on the basis of the memorandum of Pritam Singh and Col. Tamura and the discussion I had with Capt. Mohan Singh at Taiping. I frankly admitted that the question of organising and equipping of the INA and its cooperation with the Japanese army should be settled by bipartite talks between the Japanese authorities and the Indian leaders. I succeeded in winning over the understanding and friendship of the Indian officers through these talks. After the end of the talks, Lt. Col. Gill issued instructions on the accommodation of the soldiers. The Indian soldiers assembled in the park started moving towards their camps just like flood water breaching the dyke. All the members of the F-Organisation and of the INA were mobilised to guide them to their camps. It was night by the time the last soldiers reached their camps.

Immediately after the meeting I returned to my office alongwith Pritam Singh. This was because there was a scheduled meeting with two representatives of the local Indian community Goho and Menon. Pritam Singh had briefed them beforehand over the nature and function of the F-Organisation, as well as about me. They were well versed with the activities of the IIL and the INA, and also knew about the grand spectacle of the Farah Park, Pritam Singh had also briefed me about these two persons beforehand. As we settled down for discussion after an exchange of greetings, we felt as if we were old friends. I was very much impressed by Goho who initiated the discussion on the subject of freedom, honour and interest of his compatriots. He appeared to me as a person with strong character and will, with capacity to enforce decision besides having great political consciousness. In this sitting we discussed about the support of the IIL by these two gentlemen, appointment of Goho as the President of the Singapore chapter of the IIL, and the meeting of the Singapore Indians

YMA supporters from the jail. He said that he wanted to work for the cooperation of the Malayan people with the Japanese army under the support and guidance of the Japanese army. After felicitating him for safe release from jail I promised all cooperation for fostering friendship between the Malayan and Japanese peoples. I proposed to him that for the moment we should concentrate on bringing out the banned paper *Warta Malaya* and helping out the poverty striken supporters of the YMA financially. After the departure of Ibrahim, I called upon the deputy chief of staff Maj. Gen. -M, (Manaki) and solicited his approval for converting the YMA from a political organisation into a cultural body for the cultural uplift of the Malayan people. At that time the army authorities were thinking of adopting a short sighted policy of derecognising all the political, cultural and economic bodies of the local people. This was motivated either by its complacency over the success in Malaya, or by the apprehension of the attitude of the local Chinese who had till then carried out a boycott Japan movement and who might take advantage of these organisations for carrying out anti-Japanese movement. At any rate such thinking was totally incompatible with the professed lofty ideal of establishing a new order of coprosperity sphere in the Far East by liberating the nations of East Asia. Such breach of trust has resulted in trampling of peoples reliance in Manchuria and China. All my associates and myself were trying to mobilising the peoples of India, Malaya and Sumatra for the noble cause with all our zeal sincerely believing the imperial rescripts and messages issued on this lofty ideal. It was impossible for me to tolerate this duplicity. I expressed my conviction to Maj. Gen. -M. and requested him to lend his support to the YMA as an organisation for fostering cultural understanding of the Malays. After somewhat heated argument for more than thirty minutes he finally consented to allow the YMA to function as an organisation purely for cultural uplift of the Malays. He immediately agreed on the republication of the party paper *Warta Malaya* and giving priority to the YMA members in appointments. Next I called upon the head of the propaganda division of the army and succeeded in getting his approval for free supply of the materials and rent free use of press for its publication. By this I succeeded in discharging a part of my obligation to the YMA. Encouraged by this success I resolved in my mind that in future also I should hold my ground like this in face of all difficulties in order to discharge my part of the duty towards my comrades. The time had come at last to part company with the YMA. It had already been decided that the military administration will incorporate the YMA, which will in turn devote

exclusively to peaceful cultural activities. I introduced my friends Ibrahim and Onam to Maj. Gen.-M and solicited his support and understanding. To my friends I promised all possible help for all the time to come even though our official relation was going to be snapped. On the 19th, a general meeting of the Singapore Indians was held at Farah Park, the meeting which has made a lasting impression on all those who have witnessed it. Tens of thousands of Indians filled the park, and the dias was decorated with flowers and cloth. Goho, the chairman of the Singapore branch, gave an inflammatory speech to the crowd, which was cheered repeatedly. After Goho, Pritam Singh, Capt. Mohan Singh and myself addressed the crowd one after another. Thus was established the Singapore Branch of the IIL, and with this, the IIL, ultimately succeeded in embracing all the Indians living in Thailand and Malaya. On this very day it was decided to bring all the INA units scattered all over Malaya to Singapore on the basis of the proposal of Capt. Mohan Singh. This task was assigned to 2nd. Lt. Yonemura. By this Singapore became the main base of the IIL and the INA, and these two organisations reached what we may say as the offtake stage.

Around this time, Premier Tojo delivered his historic speech in the Imperial Diet where he promised liberation to the peoples of East Asia, Independence of Philippines, and all our support to the Indian Independence struggle. Thus at long last one of my dreams which I had been trying hard to push through was realised. The only drawback of this declaration was that it was too abstract.

At a time when Pritam Singh was busy convening a meeting of the heads of the IIL branches spread all over Malaya and Singapore in Singapore and Capt. Mohan Singh was busy in enlarging and consolidating the INA which had now assembled in Singapore, I received a telegram from the Imperial Headquarters of Tokyo via the Supreme Command of the Southern Forces. According to it, Rash Behari Bose, a veteran Indian revolutionary and an old resident of Tokyo had convened a meeting of the leaders of the Indian Community of various regions of East Asia in Tokyo with the good offices of the Imperial Headquarters for discussing the political problems related to the liberation of India. Another objective was to establish cordial relation with the Japanese authorities. In all about ten leaders were invited; to be selected from among the IIL leaders of Malaya and Thailand and the INA. The delegation was expected to reach Tokyo by 19th March. In this telegram I was instructed to accompany the delegation to Tokyo, besides one Col. Iwakuro. Intuitively I felt that the

exclusively to peaceful cultural activities. I introduced my friends Ibrahim and Onam to Maj. Gen.-M and solicited his support and understanding. To my friends I promised all possible help for all the time to come even though our official relation was going to be snapped. On the 19th, a general meeting of the Singapore Indians was held at Farah Park, the meeting which has made a lasting impression on all those who have witnessed it. Tens of thousands of Indians filled the park, and the dias was decorated with flowers and cloth. Goho, the chairman of the Singapore branch, gave an inflammatory speech to the crowd, which was cheered repeatedly. After Goho, Pritam Singh, Capt. Mohan Singh and myself addressed the crowd one after another. Thus was established the Singapore Branch of the IIL, and with this, the IIL, ultimately succeeded in embracing all the Indians living in Thailand and Malaya. On this very day it was decided to bring all the INA units scattered all over Malaya to Singapore on the basis of the proposal of Capt. Mohan Singh. This task was assigned to 2nd. Lt. Yonemura. By this Singapore became the main base of the IIL and the INA, and these two organisations reached what we may say as the offtake stage.

Around this time, Premier Tojo delivered his historic speech in the Imperial Diet where he promised liberation to the peoples of East Asia, Independence of Philippines, and all our support to the Indian Independence struggle. Thus at long last one of my dreams which I had been trying hard to push through was realised. The only drawback of this declaration was that it was too abstract.

At a time when Pritam Singh was busy convening a meeting of the heads of the IIL branches spread all over Malaya and Singapore in Singapore and Capt. Mohan Singh was busy in enlarging and consolidating the INA which had now assembled in Singapore, I receivbd a telegram from the Imperial Headquarters of Tokyo via the Supreme Command of the Southern Forces. According to it, Rash Behari Bose, a veteran Indian revolutionary and an old resident of Tokyo had convened a meeting of the leaders of the Indian Community of various regions of East Asia in Tokyo with the good offices of the Imperial Headquarters for discussing the political problems related to the liberation of India. Another objective was to establish cordial relation with the Japanese authorities. In all about ten leaders were invited; to be selected from among the IIL leaders of Malaya and Thailand and the INA. The delegation was expected to reach Tokyo by 19th March. In this telegram I was instructed to accompany the delegation to Tokyo, besides one Col. Iwakuro. Intuitively I felt that the

the impression I got from the telegram of the Imperial Headquarters was correct. Col. Iwakuro had held many key posts in the War Ministry, and had taken part in the Japan-America peace talks just before the outbreak of war. He was also posted in USA in that connection. He was one of the most capable and politically talented officers of the Japanese army. Many leaders of the government and of public life were his close friends. He was the fittest person for pushing through and supporting the India policy by mobilising both government officialdom and the leaders of the public life, and well as for dealing with the Indians at political level. I called upon Col. Iwakuro at his residence in the military barracks near the Menam river. I did this because I wanted to inform the colonel of the work I had done till then as well as to apprise him of the belief under which I had worked so far. During the course of talks I repeated my convictions which I had expressed to Lt. Col.-O (Ozeki) of the Imperial Headquarters at Ipoh as well as my plan on Indian policy which I had presented to this very officer at Klan. I particularly emphasised the need for abandoning the petty plotters mortality which had been adopted so far in China, and adopt an open national policy towards India based on political and national ethics. The Iwakuro Organisation should not be a spy type plotters body. I wanted it to be some sort of ambassadorial organisation fit for representing Japan in Independent India. I request him to decline in case the authorities in Tokyo was intending to set up this organisation for just facilitating the operations of the Japanese army, or in other words a scheming body.

The colonel agreed with my viewpoint. I was extremely happy to find my viewpoint accepted by Col. Iwakuro, a capable officer of the Japanese army. I was very happy to find an enlightened officer like him due to take over the charge of the new organisation that was going to be set up for pushing through the India policy with great vigour. It was indeed very difficult to mobilise the positive support of the army and the government and the diet, where a proper understanding of such a project was almost totally lacking. Again, mobilising the support of the people in national scale was another important factor. In this respect the appointment of the colonel came as a great boon.

Around this time brisk propaganda activities beamed towards India started from the Saigon Radio. A team of a few members of INA headed by Capt. was engaged in this work with all out support from the Propaganda Division of the Japanese army. The propaganda from Saigon Radio was much more effective than that of the Tokyo Radio. Goho utilised this overnight stop over to make a broadcast to the people of India on the situation in Malaya and Singapore prevailing at that time.

At Saigon we had to board two planes due to some unavoidable reasons. It was decided that we seven, Col. Iwakuro, Capt. Mohan Singh, Lt. Col. Gill, Raghavan, Goho, Menon and myself would go straight to Tokyo from Saigon in a plane. The other team consisting of five members, Otakuro, Swami, Pritam Singh, Ayer and Capt. Akram, were to leave Saigon two days after us by plane. On 11th March we left Saigon by plane. But at Rainan Island our plane develope engine trouble detaining us in the island for two days. There was no facility worth mentioning where the delegation could be accommodated. I contacted the local naval command, but failed to elicit any cooperation. The naval commander there was unwilling to allow the foreigners inside the naval base. With great reluctance he allotted a dirty barrack to us close to the airport. This indifferent attitude of the naval commander indeed made the Indians very unhappy, and to make amends as much as possible, I ran about procuring fresh eggs and fruits. But the results fell far short of the efforts. The situation was so miserable that we were not provided with even the required number of cots. Even those provided were old and rickety ones. I had to sleep on the floor. It did not matter much to me as I was accustomed to such life in the front. But for the members of the delegation who were accustomed to luxurious living in Penang and Singapore, this was a memorable experience indeed. They felt more pity for me seeing that I was trying to do my best for their comforts. Finally our plane was repaired, and we reached Tokyo via Taipei and Shanghai, where we spent one night each.

As soon as we disembarked, the plane went back to Taipei to bring Swami and his party. Officials from the Imperial Headquarters were there at the airport to receive us and the delegation was comfortably lodged at the Sanno Hotel. Already Oskon and Khan were there as the delegates from Shanghai and Hongkong respectively. The weather was extremely cold for the visitors from the south. Especially elderly Menon was shivering with cold. In Tokyo the delegates were taken charge of by the officials of the Imperial Headquarters, which left me with a feeling of great dismay as I had planned all the time to show my friends round Tokyo.

The day following our arrival I went to the Imperial Headquarters together with Col. Iwakuro. There I got the opportunity to report on my work and the latest developments to the chief of staff and the concerned officials of the Imperial Headquarters. I took advantage of this to express my views and convictions on the policy that Japan should adopt towards India, which I had presented to the authorities whenever I got an opportunity. I concluded my briefing by emphasising the following four points : (a) That the Japanese government should immediately chalk out a

concrete policy towards India on the basis of the declaration of Premier Tojo in the Diet on the 20th January and proclaim it to the world openly without any delay; (b) that this should be adopted as the committed policy of the Japanese nation as a whole; (c) that proclaiming the scope of the New Order in East Asia should be the precondition for justifying Japan's policy towards the occupied territories; and (d) that all possible support should be given to the movements arising from among the Indian people, and no undue moddling should be carried out. I also expressed the view that the Iwakuro Organisation which was going to be set up for taking over the works concerning India from the Fujiwara Organisation should be more of an ambassadorial organisation rather than an organisation for some specific objective. As far as possible it should have diplomatic status. I felt that all those present were deeply impressed with my speech. After finishing reporting, I met Lt. Col. - K and Maj. -O of the 8th section which was in charge of this work, and discussed with them on the plan prepared by the Imperial Headquarters. Col. Iwakuro also participated in the discussion over this draft plan. Here I came to know that the plan was drawn up on the basis of the plan which I had earlier submitted to the Imperial Headquarters. But the most disappointing thing was that this plan carried a title ' The Indian Stratagem (Draft). Moreover, the Imperial Headquarters kept the political affairs with respect to India within its direct control, assigning the miscellaneous works in the operational zone to the Iwakuro Organisation. With the approval of Col. Iwakuro, I strongly demanded a drastic modification of the whole conception on which the whole plan was prepared. It took full two days of argument to convince those people, and ultimately the title was changed from 'The Indian Stratagem (Draft)' into 'Indian Policy Plan', and the contents were also modified to eliminate all traces of stratagem. I was very happy to realise that this trip to Tokyo proved to be so significant. During this time, the delegates were going round Tokyo sightseeing according to schedules drawn up by the Imperial Headquarters. I devoted all my available time to accompany them round Tokyo and to fulfil their wish as far as possible. Here a very delicate issue cropped up. The delegates who came from the south alongwith me were unable to adjust mentally with the Indian representatives of Japan , who had been carrying on Indian Independence movement in Japan under the leadership of Rash Behari Bose, and who had the patronisation of the Imperial Headquarters. The allegation of the IIL delegates was that these people had lost their freedom of movement and speech as they had lived long in Japan and enjoyed Japanese hospitality, and hence they had a tendency to get degraded to the status

concrete policy towards India on the basis of the declaration of Premier Tojo in the Diet on the 20th January and proclaim it to the world openly without any delay; (b) that this should be adopted as the committed policy of the Japanese nation as a whole; (c) that proclaiming the scope of the New Order in East Asia should be the precondition for justifying Japan's policy towards the occupied territories; and (d) that all possible support should be given to the movements arising from among the Indian people, and no undue moddling should be carried out. I also expressed the view that the Iwakuro Organisation which was going to be set up for taking over the works concerning India from the Fujiwara Organisation should be more of an ambassadorial organisation rather than an organisation for some specific objective. As far as possible it should have diplomatic status. I felt that all those present were deeply impressed with my speech. After finishing reporting, I met Lt. Col. - K and Maj. -O of the 8th section which was in charge of this work, and discussed with them on the plan prepared by the Imperial Headquarters. Col. Iwakuro also participated in the discussion over this draft plan. Here I came to know that the plan was drawn up on the basis of the plan which I had earlier submitted to the Imperial Headquarters. But the most disappointing thing was that this plan carried a title ' The Indian Stratagem (Draft). Moreover, the Imperial Headquarters kept the political affairs with respect to India within its direct control, assigning the miscellaneous works in the operational zone to the Iwakuro Organisation. With the approval of Col. Iwakuro, I strongly demanded a drastic modification of the whole conception on which the whole plan was prepared. It took full two days of argument to convince those people, and ultimately the title was changed from 'The Indian Stratagem (Draft)' into 'Indian Policy Plan', and the contents were also modified to eliminate all traces of stratagem. I was very happy to realise that this trip to Tokyo proved to be so significant. During this time, the delegates were going round Tokyo sightseeing according to schedules drawn up by the Imperial Headquarters. I devoted all my available time to accompany them round Tokyo and to fulfil their wish as far as possible. Here a very delicate issue cropped up. The delegates who came from the south alongwith me were unable to adjust mentally with the Indian representatives of Japan , who had been carrying on Indian Independence movement in Japan under the leadership of Rash Behari Bose, and who had the patronisation of the Imperial Headquarters. The allegation of the IIL delegates was that these people had lost their freedom of movement and speech as they had lived long in Japan and enjoyed Japanese hospitality, and hence they had a tendency to get degraded to the status

of Japan's puppet. They were especially skeptic about Rash Behari Bose who had lived in Japan as exile for tens years marrying a Japanese lady, there, by loosing much of Indian character, on the other hand, the Indians of Japan asserted that the IIL representatives were, till the other day the loyal subjects of Britain without having any revolutionary background, and that for no rhyme or reason they bore grudge against the Indians of Japan. I tried to do my best in bringing about reconciliation between the two groups. The behaviour of one Mr. K who was appointed as the guide of the party by the Imperial Headquarters aggravated the complicated the situation all the more. The words and deeds of this gentleman displayed all the clumsiness of the Japanese people, like showing too much courtesy bearing upon infringement on privacy, deciding things on the basis of personal judgement without bothering for the views of the guests, posing as an authority on Indian affair, etc., which were not necessarily motivated by any ill will. Swami and his party was scheduled to reach Tokyo on the 19th of March, evening. Unfortunately strong wind started blowing since the morning of this day which gained in intensity as the day advanced. By afternoon, the visibility became poor with flying dust. Towards evening it started drizzling. I was sure that the arrival of the party would be postponed in view of the inclement weather. However, towards evening I came to know that the party had left Shanghi in the afternoon for Tokyo. I thought that the party would land at some airport in Kyushu or Osaka and would wait for the weather to improve. In the evening I got a telephone from the Haneda airport informing that wireless connection with the plane of the party had snapped around 15.00 hour when the plane was flying over the Ise Bay. Slowly it turned into a rain storm at night. I sent telegrams to the various airports enquiring about the plane. Inauspicious thoughts started contains my brain. The delegates also shared my anxiety. I earnestly hoped for the safe landing of the plan somewhere. That night I remained awake for the whole of the night waiting for replies from the airports, but there was no news. Towards dawn. I dreamt the faces of my dearest friends Pritam Singh, Capt. Agnam and Otaguro. By noon of the following day it became obvious that the plane had not landed at any airport in Central Japan.

Otaguro's wife had come to Tokyo to receiveher husband. I had to tell the IIL delegates and the wife of Otaguro to be prepared for the worst It was indeed a very sad and painful task. Towards evening I got a news that a plane had crushed in the hills beyond Nayoya the evening before. The worst had happened. The rescue teams all over central Japan were put on search duty. From all the available information it transpired that the plane

permanently lost to the world alongwith the death of my five dear comrades. As I write these lines, my heart is filled with the sorrow for my departed dear friends and the irreparable loss of the precious document.

The conference of the Indian delegates of the East Asia was inaugurated at Sanno Hotel on the 20th of March in an atmosphere of gloom following the death of the four comrades. On the first day Col. Iwakuro and myself were permitted to be present as observers. Besides the four IIL and INA delegates from Malaya and Thailand, there were delegations from Hongkong, Shanghai, Philippines and Japan. The chairmanship of the conference was pressed on Rash Behari Bose. For some reason or other, one of the most influential leaders of the Indian community of Japan and a veteran freedom fighter, Sahai, was missing from the conference. Another notable absentee was Mohendra Pratap. I was very such intrigued by their absence. The wall facing the delegates was decorated with huge Indian and Japanese National flags. After first expressing condolence for the four dead delegates, the chairman welcomed the delegates for the various regions of East Asia. Next he explained the unique chance that had arrived at last following the declaration of Premier Tojo committing all possible support to the Indian Independence movement as well as the rapid success of the Japanese forces. Following this he thanked the delegation of IIL and INA from the south for their dedicated activities in Malaya and Thailand. He finally wound up by telling that the main objective of the meeting was to have a free and frank discussion on the political problems concerning the freedom movement of India besides free exchange of views among the delegates for evolving a concrete policy for mobilising politically the Indians in South Asia for the Liberation of Motherland. However, this eloquent speech of Bose apparently failed to make much impression on the delegates, especially the delegates of the IIL and the INA. Despite such apathy, all the delegates were determined to stick to their objective of working for the liberation of Motherland. The delegates individually and in groups, inside the conference hall and outside exchanged views and carried out discussions. Ultimately it was decided to save the IIL the status of the sole political organisation of the Indians of East Asia for carrying out the freedom struggle. And it was decided to convene a conference of the Indians of East Asia at Bangkok in May under the auspicies of the IIL to decide the future course of activity of the organisation.

It was decided that the regular activity of the IIL and the Iwakuro, organisation would start after that conference. The IIL delegates had a private meeting with Premier Tojo where they confirmed the Japanese

Government's intention to support the Indian independent movement.

When the search for the missing plane was on. I got another telegram which plunged me into fresh grief. It was from the chief of staff of the 27th Army informing the death of Harimau who was ailing in Singapore hospital. He was involved in all sorts of desparate criminal activities like looting gold bars from mail trains, and his reputation was so bad that mothers used to pacifying their troublesome children by threatening to call him. However, as war spread in Malaya, he suddenly changed his mind and as a true patriot started assisting the Japanese forces. He meticulously adhered to my strict order of not indulging in any anti-social activities, and his band did not including in any violent activity even once. His activities behind the British lines facilitated the Japanese advance greatly. Although he was only twenty eight years old, yet he had a very chequered career. It must be mentioned here that the reform and winning over of Harimau was achieved through the skilful persuation of Kamimoto and 2nd Lt. Yonemura. Especially Kamimoto was his constant companion eversince April 1941, persuading at every opportunity to give up the evil ways. Indeed it is very difficult to forget the noble dedication of Kamimoto who quite aften stood at the brink of death for fulfilling his duty. Immediately I took steps to get his name enrolled formally in the Ministry of Defence as a civilian attached to the army. The next day I was invited to the reporters club of the War Ministry to deliver a talk on the fascinating life and activities of Harimau before and after the war. The big newspapers devoted about a quarter of a page in reporting my talk. A memorial service was held for him in the Yasukuni Shrine at Kudan of Tokyo. Thus he ended his life as a loyal son of Japan. In the mean time Col. Iwakuro was busy preparing plans for successfully accomplishing his new assignment and was enthusiastically searching for people to staff his organisation. For this the colonel had to remain in Tokyo for some time. It was however, tentatively decided that the new organisation would take over the members of the F-Organisation excepting for myself and a few other civilian members. As for me, I was to go back to the Supreme Command of the Southern Force in Saigon. However, I was to carry on with my organisation for the time being till the Iwakuro Organisation took over the charge. Hence I had proceed to Singapore immediately ahead of the delegation. There I reinforced the F-Organisation by coopting, 2nd Lt. Hara, 2nd Lt. Kaneko, 2nd Lt. Matsushige and 2nd Lt. Tsukamoto and a few other NCOs to cope with the ever expanding scope of activity of the F-Organisation. I left Tokyo for Singapore on the last of April. Just before the departure I got the confirmation of the death of my five friends. Because of violent storm

and rain the plane had lost its way and crushed in Japan Alps in Nagano Prefecture. On my way back I met the mother and older sister of Harimau in Fukuoka airport. As I tried to console them, in tears they said that they were happy that he had laid down his life for the cause of the country. They were very happy to hear the achievements of Harimau which I related to them. In Saigon I met the staff officer Lt. Col. -O at the Supreme command of the Southern Forces and reported the developments in Tokyo and requested him to make the necessary preparations for sponsoring the Bangkok Conference. During this talk it was decided that the Iwakuro organisation would take over the charges from the F-Organisation by the end of April. I returned to Singapore on the 5th of April. This trip of mine coincided with rapid developments in the war situation all over South East Asia. In Burma Rangoon fell to the Japanese forces on 8th March, following which the Japanese forces were regrouping for launching an offensive against Central and northern Burma. The 16th Army landed in Java on the 1st of March, and by 9th of the same month the Dutch East Indies army surrendered. The Konoe Division of the 25th Army landed in Sumatra on 13th March; and on the same day the Andaman group of Islands were captured.

In the Philippines, the final offensive against the Batan peninsula started on the 5th of April.

Appendix-IV

Interrogation Report of General Mohan Singh : Throws New Light on the Formation of the Indian National Army and his Views of the Japanese Policy (Extract)[1]

20. During November the clouds of war had been first looming and then seeming to recede. When the Bn moved back to Sungei Patani it had seemed that there was still hope, but H/1050 was ready for recall and on Sun 30 Nov. 41 had made special arrangements for any telegram arriving to reach him where he was staying. From 2 to 6 Dec. was spent in the well rehearsed Jitra position. By 0400 hrs on 8 Dec. however the bn lessone coy was at Alor Star railway station ready to move by train to Singora in Thailand. The remaining coy had been detached and had already set out by road to occupy positions on the Thai-Malaya border. But the Japanese had landed during the night of 7/8 Dec. at Singora and the railway was already cut. The bn therefore did not actually entrain and at dawn on 8 Dec heard the bombardment of a small railway station, and remained there all day. At 1700 hrs orders were lived to move back to Jitra and to take up the allotted position between the main Jitra position and the frontier. The previously moved to the frontier was by this time and contact with the enemy. Another coy was at once moved up also during the night 10/11 Dec. A Gurkhas Bn occupied the former bn position.

21. Between 1/14 Punjab and the Gurkhas there lay an extensive marsh which the road crossed by a mined causeway. The plan was that 1/14 Punjab, having fought a delaying action would retire behind the causeway which would then be blown. During these days of contact the Punjabis had gained considerable confidence and met with some success. They were however, retiring slowly, according to plan. On 11 Dec. they were to move behind the causeway but as this was being done, the Div

1. W.O. 208/833. Public Recent office London. Mohan Singh (H. 1050) was interrogated in 1945 by Col. Hugh Toye, the British Intelligence Officer.

Comd, encouraged by the successful delaying action fought, ordered 1/14 Punjab to hold on for another night. "You can do it", H/1050 heard him tell the CO, "they have no tanks." Five minutes later Japanese tanks attacked down the road while the bn was moving to the new position forward of the causeway ordered. Complete dissintegration ensued. Survivors were caught between the fire of the tanks and the deep waters of the marsh augmented by recent heavy rains. H/1050 and his Co found themselves together in the waters of the marsh East of the road. Together with 2 NCOs they remained in the water for about 24 hrs trying to find a way of escape to the South. Darkness fell almost immediately after the action and in attempts to skirt the marsh, the party became lost in the jungle. On the evening of 13 Dec, while enquiring the way in a village, the party fell in with Capt. Mohd Akram and about 10 Pathans of 1/14 Punjab. The 2 parties joined and on the morning of 14 Dec. found a footpath which they thought might lead to Alor Star. Other stragglers joined them. During the afternoon the party, now about 60 strong, emerged from the jungle at Kuala Narang and took up a position in a rubber clump. H/1050 then volunteered to reconnoitre for information on the general situation.

Reconnaissance and Surrender

22. H/1050 and an NCO went to the nearby Kuala Narang which they found full of confusion and rumours. After conversation with some local Indians they located a Malay officer who told them that the Japanese had now advanced far beyond Alor Star. H/1050 thereupon collected some food and drink which he took back to the position with the aid of several civilian Indians. When Lt. Col. Fitzpatrick[2] heard the news he said that he himself would go and see the Malay official. After doing so he conferred with Capt. Mohd. Akram and H/1050, and having considered all courses open decided to surrender. A message was accordingly sent by villagers to whatever Japanese Military Authorities might be in Alor Star that a party of men was at Kuala Narang and that it wished to surrender. The party thereopen moved from the rubber clump position to the police station in Kuala Karang. During the evening a reply came from Alor Star to the effect that there were Indians with the Japanese and that an Indian gentleman and a Japanese officer would come next morning to see the surrendering party.

23. At about 0900 hrs next morning Giani Pritam Singh arrived in a car which flew the Congress flag. He assured Lt. Col. Fitzpatrick that he, Giani

2. Lt. Colonel. Fitzpatrick was Commanding the battalion which surrendered to the Japanese. Mohah Singh was warking with him.

Pritam Singh, was responsible for the treatment of PW and that everything would be well. He also said that a Japanese officer was waiting nearby and would presently come to receive them. Lt. Col. Fitzpatrick then went with Giani Pritam Sigh to see Maj. Fujiwara who had halted his car some distance away. When they returned, H/1050 had assembled his men ready for the surrender which then took place. Lt. Col. Fitzpatrick was immediately separated from his men and H/1050 never saw him after that day.

24. The whole party of PW was then taken to barracks prepared for it at Alor Star. H/1050 and Capt Mohd Akram travelled in the car of Giani Pritam Singh and asked that gentleman what was the meaning of this mysterious protection which he seemed to have undertaken. Giani Pritam Singh, whose conversation and aspect was in religious terms tones and gestures, had replied that he had been for a whole year now working for the freedom of India. He thanked God that he had now with him two Indian officers who would be able to work to that end too. His dreams, he said, were at last being fulfilled. He had certain pacts with the Japanese and wished to raise an Indian Independence Army. H/1050 asked if he really did trust the Japanese, and Pritam Singh impressed both the newly taken PW with his blind faith.

25. At this point H/1050 recalls that during the early days of the battle for Malaya Bde HQ had sent men who could read certain Indian languages in order that they might translate some pamphlets which had mysteriously arrived in the front line. H/1050 was much too busy himself to take any notice at that time, but Habibur Rehman who had seen some told him afterwards that they contained a lot of nonsense and were subversive.

The Early Days

26. On arrival at Alor Star H/1050 was taken to the office of Maj Fujiwara who was extremely busy, H/1050 there met his battalion commander for the last time. In the office next door H/1050 found Giani Pritam Singh and with him from 7 to 10 Indians, mainly Sikhs. Pritam Singh once more expressed his great pleasure at meeting H/1050. Pritam Singh appeared to be on the best possible terms with Maj Fujiwara. When Fujiwara at last found time, he told H/1050 to rest for a while and have some food. Accordingly the rest of the day was spent in settling his men into their quarters, in collecting cooking utensils and food.

Late that evening when the PW were about to go to sleep, Maj Fujiwara sent for H/1050. Mohd Akram accompanied him to Fujiwara's office where they found also Giani Pritam Singh. This was the first of several interviews during which the project, mentioned by Giani Pritam

Singh in the car, was discussed. At these discussions Giani Pritam Singh was always a silent listener. The Japanese Atokuro invariably interpreted for Maj Fujiwara. Maj Fujiwara asked the two officers whether Giani Pritam Singh had explained everything to them. It had been quite evident to H/1050 from the very first that Giani Pritam Singh was an unintelligent dupe of the Japanese and he made this clear to Fujiwara many times. Giani Pritam Singh, he said, might be a sincere believer in the freedom of India, but he just did not understand the full implication of the things about which he was talking. He had no political background, and it was futile for a man with no political background to try to lead a movement which could only be political. H/1050 did then mention that there was a man, S.C. Bose, who would be a capable leader, but he was not to hand. As for Pritam Singh, H/1050 had not understood him at all. Maj. Fujiwara therefore proceeded to expound the matter in his own way. He did not particularly comment on the mention of Bose. He talked much of the "Co-prosperity Sphere", of "Asia for the Asiatics", and of the sincerity of the Japanese in their desire to help India to liberate herself. Much of his talk was extremely vague and H/1050 more than once asked for a written definition of this "Coprosperity Sphere" and "Greater East Asia", but Maj Fujiwara never committed himself to anything definite. He talked a great deal about Congress, about the high ideal of Freedom, and at last reached the point of his whole argument. Freedom, he said, could not be achieved by sitting on an arm chair, Gandhi was only a religious leader and could not cause any real political changes. To change the world there must be an army and soldiers fighting. It was soldiers, he said, who made history. Then he turned to H/1050 and told him in effect "And what are you going to do about it? It is for you to choose. If you want your freedom you must aspire to do something active, you must raise an Indian Independence Army."

28. H/1050's attitude on the Congress point was as follows :

He did not agree that non-violence was futile, and he strongly resisted Pritam singh's desire, expressed during the course of the talks, to keep the IIL, as it was already called by Pritam Singh, separate from Congress. Violence would of course come and H/1050 was all for it, but nothing must be done against Congress policy.

29. H/1050 reported to his officers and men next morning the conversation which had taken place on the previous night. He expressed his own feeling that extreme caution was necessary. In particular all should beware of private individual approaches both from Pritam Singh and from

the Japanese.

30. Maj Fujiwara reinforced his attempts to impress Indian officers with Japanese friendliness by taking them out to see Gen Yamashita, who gave them some tea, and uttered, though in less fluent form, some of Fujiwara's own slogans.

Mohan Singh's Depression and Major Fujiwara

31. The mental condition of H/1050 at the time when he felt the impact of these subversive attempts, deserves examination. It is explained in his own words in the document reproduced at appx "A"[3]. He was unusually cast down by the Jitra fiasco because his own bn had initially fought so well, and because at first hopes had been so high. The whole defeat was, in his view, and there was much in the immediate circumstances to make him think this, the result of the colossal blunder of the divisional commander in changing at the last minute a plan which had been rehearsed for months and which had so far worked extremely well. He saw great dumps of food, man and POL in the vast Jitra position, all abandoned and intact. The confusion that reigned, hunger, fatigue and the shock of defeat all combined to accentuate his mental depression. Nevertheless, H/1050 was only impressed by Maj Fujiwara's talk and was not convinced. From a purely nationalist point of view he felt that he would be ready to do something if India's benefit would really result, but he did not believe that the proposal of the specious Maj Fujiwara would achieve that end. Maj Fujiwara, he says, was an extremely clever man. His attitude was always one of great charm and friendliness. He was a man who, with a whisky bottle in front of him could talk all night and be fresh to start again at breakfast time. H/1050 did not, at these first interviews, accept Maj Fujiwara's offer of drink, well knowing that his sobriety at this time was of the greatest importance. The talks continued whenever Maj Fujiwara had leisure during 16 and 17 Dec.

Mohan Singh's Arguments

32. While the talks were going on, H/1050 heard that on 11 Dec a certain Puran Singh and another Gurkha Rfn had been captured. These men were at once instructed by the Japanese to move forward as a propaganda contact party. Under threats they did in fact go forward, but they returned without having attempted to carry out their instructions. They told H/1050 that there were some Gurkha PW at Alor Star aerodrome, and that when they were first captured a written document was read out to

3. All references to appendix in this report have not been printed here.

them on parade. This purported to be some kind of a pact between Giani Pritam Singh and the Japanese.

33. As soon as he heard this, H/1050 went angrily to Pritam Singh, wishing to enlist his support in accusing Fujiwara of exploitation and insincerity. Pritam Singh did not take the matter seriously and H/1050 therefore himself went to Fujiwara. "You are not taking the long view" he said. " This use of Indians as a Fifth Column is positive proof that you wish to exploit us. Do not think for a minute that if you defeat the British here you will shake more than the outermost branches of a vast tree whose roots you can only attack in India. Until you shake the British in India you will not have shaken them at all. If you go to India now, all India will join the British to turn you out. We are the only people who can defeat the British in India and we are willing to take up the cudgels if you give real proof of your sincerity. This frontline business must not recur."

34. By 18 Dec Fujiwara and Pritam Singh, who had been from the first hopeful that they could use H/1050, were sure of him. They had wanted some one with recent knowledge of India and a man with experience of and a name in the army. H/1050 was an active patriotic officer, facts which had made them all the more eager. Nevertheless, they had made no concrete proposals yet.

The First Step

35. On 18 Dec Maj Fujiwara and Pritam Singh went away. Kunizuka,[4] who had arrived a day or two before, remained, and ITO[5] joined him soon afterwards. By that time H/1050 had gone so far as to say that before he could be convinced to take any steps of his own, he must have the best possible proof and assurance of Japanese sincerity towards India. As an earnest of this he demanded complete control of all Indian PW so far captured. He felt in his heart that if he could do something for the prisoners, —the original 60 of his party had already increased to nearly 1,000—that would be one clear gain from his dabbling with the Japanese. Maj Fujiwara had replied that of course he could do anything he liked; the Japanese, he said, were good, kind people, they were not out to stop anybody doing anything he wanted. Let H/1050 take the PW and do what he liked with them.

36. When Maj Fujiwara went away, therefore, H/1050 began to organise food, quarters and comfort for the 1,000 Indian PW with him, and

---

4. Lientenant Kazunon Kunizuka was an interpreter with F. Kikan.
5. Major Ito Keisaku, served as interpreter and Liasion officer with the Indian soldiers.

also to give them mild "spiritual" lectures in fulfillment of his side of the bargain. He continued to do this until 24 Dec. On the night of 23 Dec. Giani Pritam Singh returned to Alor Star. H/1050 found that Giani Pritam Singh had already organised Indian Leagures in Alor Star and Sungei Patani and that Maj Fujiwara used to address them. Pritam Singh painted a very rosy picture of Penang and said that there were other Indian PW in Sungei Patani. Many of these, he said, would be willing to co-operate, with the Japanese. H/1050 furious that he had not been told previously of these further PW, held a meeting on 23 Dec attended by Capt Mohd Akram, Capt Patnaik and about 10 VCOs, including Malik Fateh Khan and Sadhu Singh. He told his audience that this was the first step in their exploitation and a clear proof of Japanese insincerity. Giani Pritam Singh was quite incompetent to deal with people like the Japanese and he must be replaced as soon as possible by S.C. Bose. The meeting agreed with these sentiments.

37. On 24 Dec H/1050 went with Giani Pritam Singh to visit Fujiwara at Sungei Patani. He claimed that the Japanese had already provided sufficient proof of their sincerity, and after some vituperation he managed to persuade Maj Fujiwara to place in his charge the 400 new Indian PW at Sungei Patani. H/1050 also asked that Bose might be brought from Germany. He had from the first been corresponding secretly with Fujiwara regarding the possible removal of Pritam Singh. He had strongly objected to Pritam Singh's interference with PW and had on one occasion thrown out of a PW camp a civilian Sikh who had entered uninvited and called for volunteers. He put it to Fujiwara that either he should get some reliable Indian gentleman from Malaya to lead whatever movement he proposed, or else that he should call for Bose.

38. Fujiwara agreed that Pritam Singh would ultimately have to be discarded, but he insisted that he should remain leader of the movement in Malaya. As for Bose, his patriotism was undoubted, but, as an Asiatic, he should have entrusted himself to Japan and not to Germany. Fujiwara thought it would be impossible at present to bring Bose from Germany and was disinclined to ask for him. It was up to those present, he said, to build up the movement.

39. Having organised to some extent the PW in Sungei Patani, H/1050 returned to Alor Star on the same day. Pritam Singh and Fujiwara were about to leave Sungei Patani for Taiping which was the present front line, on 25 Dec. After this Pritam Singh never went to Sungei Patani or Alor Star in H/1050's knowledge. Up to this time H/1050 had had no contact whatever with the Indian Leagues, although he had occasionally met Indian civilians on their visits to Giani Pritam Singh.

The Plot Thickens

40. H/1050 now suffered a severe attack of malaria which put him out of action until 30 Dec 41. On 26 or 27 Dec he received a message from Fujiwara calling him to Taiping. H/1050 promised to go as soon as he was well enough.

The Conference at Alor Star

41. *Comment* : The story of 30 and 31 Dec can be reconstructed in its essentials from the letter reproduced as Annexure 2 to "S" Section CSDIC letter ST/17/4 of 23 Sep 45, and as Appendix A to this report. The carbon copy from which this was reproduced was found by M.Z. Kiani in May 42 in a drawer at H/1050's H.Q. Kiani is emphatic that it was written by H/1050 himself, and there can be little doubt that this is true (Note : The word "equipped" is spelt "equipped" a spelling mistake which H/1050 still makes). H/1050 cannot remember writing it nor can be remember discussing it at the conference which he held at Alor Star during the morning of 30 Dec. He says, however, that its contents represent the gist of his conversations with Fujiwara at Sungei Patani on 24 Dec and at Taiping on 31 Dec. We may safely assume that this letter was written either by Mohd Akram or by H/1050 at Taiping on 1 Jan 42 in reply to detailed written proposals from Fujiwara regarding the formation of an Indian National Army.

42. During the morning of 30 Dec H/1050 called a conference of officers and VCOs. He can remember the names of only 5 of those who attended :

1. Capt Patnaik
2. Mohd Akram
3. Sub Allah Ditta (H/876)
4. Sub Fateh Khan
5. Sabhu Singh

H/1050 told the meeting that he had decided to co-opetrate with the Japanese to the best of his ability, if they would hand over PW. Someone, he said, must take this risk as the possibilities were clearly worthy of exploration. Let no one else, for the moment, commit himself.

The Taiping Letter

43. The greater part of the letter reproduced at Appx "A" speaks for itself, but H/1050 makes a few comments in clarification of detail.[6]

(a) Ref. Para (1) The point in promising to denounce the Indian National Congress was this. The meeting wished the Indian National Army, as its

6. See Doc. No. 5.

name suggested, to work on the lines of the Indian National Congress. Pritam Singh wished to keep his movement separate. The meeting was not willing to follow the advice of Pritam Singh in this matter, but if S.C.Bose, having assumed the leadership, were to suggest the same thing, the meeting would be delighted to agree. (b) Ref. Para (2) Even now Fujiwara had not produced a clear definition of " the co-prosperity sphere". The meeting therefore gave up the idea of trying to obtain a definition and put the burden once more on S.C. Bose.

(c) Ref. Para (3) (e) The meeting appreciated that Malaya would be conquered very soon and that Burma would follow after no long interval. H/1050 felt that the organisation of an army out of material so dubious would take a considerable period.

(d) *Comment*: H/1050 cannot account for para 4. It may refer to one of two things. Fujiwara had evidently proposed a leader for the Indian National Army in Malaya. If, as is most likely, he proposed H/1050 , then this paragraph is an attempt to make his leadership substantive for all theatres and not merely temporary for Malaya. The alternative less probable in view of the discussions reported in paras 32 and 33, above, is that Fujiwara had proposed Pritam Singh.

H/1050 in Taiping

44. H/1050 reached Taiping late on 31 Dec 41. Pritam Singh met him, was very solicitous about his health, provided him with accommodation, dined him any during the evening told him about the League already organised in Taiping. He told him furthermore that he thought Fujiwara would now hand over all Indian prisoners captured.

45. (Note : Although H/1050 cannot remember it, it is considered probable that he handed over to Fujiwara the letter reproduced at Appendix "A" at an interview which took place on the morning of 1 Jan 42.).

46. H/1050 remembers the interview. Fujiwara was very gracious and said that PW would in future be handed over to him. H/1050 promised in return to do all in his power to secure the independence of his country. He would start patriotic education immediately, patriotic education which had been deliberately refused by the British in order that they might continue their exploitation of India. He would start preparing to raise the I.N.A. so that when the decision was taken the army would be ready to be raised. This, he said, would be a matter of time. He must see more of the Japanese, and he must consult the many civilian Indians with whose financial support alone the army could be raised. It was clearly understood that the I.N.A would be raised from Indians, directed by Indians, for the purposes of India and of India alone.

47. Next day H/1050 returned to Alor Star. He told his officers that he alone was committed, and that all others would take their time in deciding what they were to do. They approved, however, heartily of his action and praised him saying "We have a sincere man in you, that is evident. We pledge you our complete trust." On the same evening H/1050 addressed the IOR PW for 1½ to 2 hrs. He claims that he met with a rapturous reception, that the convinced all of his desire to work for India's benefit and that the men professed themselves united as one man behind him. Indeed they were readier than he; they wanted to become the "Indian National Army" at once while H/1050 could not see his way to organising it for some time. On 3 Jan 42 he similarly addressed officers and men at Sungei Patani, and was similarly received. All committed themselves to him. H/1050 emphasised to them that they were only committed to himself personally and that he alone was committed to the Japanese. H/1050 strongly denies the statement of Alah Ditta (H/876) that the Japanese asked him in Alor Star for a party to go and suborn Ind tps in the field at Kampar. H/1050 heard nothing about the Kampar fighting (in which) remnants of him own bn, it transpired, were involved, until he was in Ipoh. He points out that it is fundamentally unlikely that the Japanese would have admitted to him a setback of their own at this stage.

48. H/1050 then returned to Alor Star where he remained until 7 or 8 Jan 42. He spent his time in organisation of the PW camp, in the "partiotic education" which he had promised to commence, and in selecting for his future activities a personal staff. His future intentions were to move forward in order that he might be able to organise newly surrendered personnel as early as possible in their captivity. This he thought would both increase his personal prestige and prevent PW being exploited by the Japanese by unauthorised employment in the front line.

(*Comment* : H/1050 has admitted the above under interrogation. His aims at this point in his "public statement" are , however, not so definite).

Military Organisation of PW

76. From 15 Feb to 15 Mar 42 organisation of PW had proceeded. In addition to the central committee under Gill and the 2 committees under Bhonsle and Kiani respectively H/1050 had himself taken on as personal staff officers Maj Mehtab and Maj M.S. Dhillon (c25) By 22 Feb 42 the following officers had also been called from KUALA LUMPUR :

1. Capt. Habib Ur Rehman
2. Capt. I.J. Kiani (H/1159)
3. Capt. Patnaik.

Patnaik was made liaison officer between H/1050 and the medical

organisation he had set up under Chatterji. The latter was assisted by Lt Cols Algappan and Loganadan. H/1050 at first paid a great deal of attention to the medical set up because of the large number of hospital cases among PW. There was no medical assistance available from the Japanese and medical supplies, hospital furniture and comforts were all obtained from Indian civilians of Singapore. By the end of the month things were working to H/1050 satisfaction.

77. Early in Mar 42 about 100 volunteers were supplied to work as a guard at Changi. H/1050 first of all put a VCO in charge of this party but after a few days he appointed Gurbaksh Singh Dhillon. The conduct of this officer at Changi caused him, when he heard of it, shame and sorrow, but he claims that he had no control over the actions of Dhillon or of any other member of the Changi Guard which was entirely Japanese controlled and Japanese armed. H/1050 tried repeatedly without success to establish control of this and other such detahments.

78. At the same time about 200 AA Gunners under a VCO were detailed to man their own guns, situated between Singapore railway station and Buonavista village on Singapore Island. Fatigue parties were also continually supplied to satisfy the extremely heavy demands of the Japanese. These were run by a separate working party office.

79. Towards the end of the month H/1050 collected officers at Bidadari, and then the ; officers and some VCO's at Neesoon. In a speech he gave a brief outline of his achievements and of his intention, without any political referene. He emphasised that when the I.N.A was raised it would be purely on a volunteer basis, no pressure would be used, and all ranks would be given at least a month in which to think over the proposal when it came, and to make up their minds freely. Lectures and propaganda would not, he said, be allowed at present. Now all ranks must set about overcoming the pressing administrative difficulties which faced them.

The Journey to Tokyo and the Aeroplane Accident

80. The mysterious circumstances which attended the death of 4 members of the Goodwill Mission while en route to Tokyo make necessary a detailed examination of the arrangements made for this journey, and the time table of events. The first point that is clear is that the 4 delegates were named by the Japanese at short notice for an air passage on 13 March to Saigon. The vacancies, said Fujiwara, had suddenly occurred and he suggested that those 4 could best be spared by Mohan Singh and Raghavan to leave early. Accordingly Nos. 4, 5, 6 and 9 of para 75 left by air on 13 Mar.

81. The main party left Singapore on 15 Mar and, passing the other party in Saigon where it had been delayed, arrived in Tokyo on 19 Mar via Hanoi. Formosa and Sanghai.

82. H/1050 thinks that Swami S.N. Puri's party must have left Saigon on 18 Mar. He afterwards verified that it spent 3 nights at Canton, its first stop. It must therefore have reached Shanghai on 21 Mar and, after a further halt of 3 nights, left for Tokyo on 24 Mar. The remaining members of the goodwill mission heard about the accident on 25 Mar from Fujiwara. He said that on 24 Mar the aircraft, having halted at Fukuoka soon after mid-day, had disappeared somewhere between there and Tokyo and had not yet been found. The pilot had been in radio touch with the ground until 1535 hrs.

83. H/1050 and his companions were extremely suspicious both because of the interval between the accident and their receiving information of it, and because 24 Mar had been a day of such bad flying weather that they rather doubted if any passenger.

86. At 1000 hrs next morning formal discussions opened. H/1050 and his companions from Malaya immediately voiced their opinion that the whole thing as far as they were concerned was a trap. Firstly a formal conference was taking place contrary to the understanding that had been given. Secondly the Malayan delegation had been fatally weakened by the loss of 4 members. Thirdly Bose had brought insufficient nominees from Tokyo to ensure him a majority. They insisted that their status as observers should be at once recorded in the minutes. Nevertheless, as the conference proceeded, it became evident that the Malayan party contained the only men of constructive ability at the conference. The rest of the set up as far as they could see was entirely dominated by Japanese influence, and the Japanese had not chosen their puppets well.

The Observers Draft the Resolutions

87. The Japanese had provided "for consideration of the conference" a draft constitution for the Indian Independence movement. This provided:

(a) Election of President

(b) A selection by the president of 2 Councils, firstly an Advisory Council of 8 members, secondly an Executive council of 11 members.

(c) Duties and responsibilities in detail of each member of the Executive Council.

(d) Power of the President to dismiss or replace any member or all the members of either council.

The draft constitution did not make any mention of the source of the funds necessary to run the movement.

88. The 5 from Malaya listened very carefully to what they came to consider an appalling document. They then rose in turn to express individually and collectively their utter revulsion and set about to destroy it item by item. The document was denounced in the very strongest possible terms. H/1050 said that no soldier serving under him would have anything to do with such a constitution and went on to demand that unless, in any future council or conference, his soldiers were represented by 50 of the total number of representatives he would have nothing to do with any further discussion at all. R.B. Bose, who had not expected such a storm, immediately agreed to drop the draft constitution, and appealed to the Malayans to do something, draft something, produce something, whatever it may betosave his credit with the Japanese. H/1050 and his companions, seeing clearly that none of the other delegates had the education or ability to draft anything at all sat to work on the following conditions :

(a) that no movement should be started until properly elected representatives could be provided from all parts of East Asia.

(b) That resolutions should be immediately drafted to be put before such a future conference.

89 Menon, Raghavan and Goho drafted the Tokyo resolutions on 30 and 31 Mar. The "conference" discussed, and adopted resolutions during 1 and 2 April. H/1050's demand for 50 military representation on any future conference was agreed. (Note : Proceedings of the Tokyo conference are at AppxV)

After several days spent in sightseeing in Japan the 5 delegates from Malaya left Japan via Fukuoka, and Shanghai where they spent 4-5 days. Singapore was reached on about 22 Apr. 42.

90. H/1050 summarises the achievements of the Tokyo mission as follows:

(a) It had a'ccomplished the end of any designs that Bose might have had for exploiting the Indian situation for the benefit of Japan by himself assuming a dictatorship.

(b) Preparations had been made for the establishment of the movement on a constitutional basis.

(c) The importance of the position of the I.N.A. had been recognised and the principle had been accepted of representation for the army in any future conference equal to the total civilian representation.

Raja Mohindra Parshad (Partap)

91. While he was in Tokyo H/1050 and other Singapore delegates

met Raja Mohindra Parshad.[6] H/1050 says that this man went to Germany through Afghanistan during the war 1914-18. While in Afghanistan he met Amanullah and Nadir Shah, and founded some futile movement in Germany. He returned to the East after the war, going to Japan through Russia and China. He has, says H/1050, a plan of his own for the successful govt of the world, and thinks that the centre should be in Afghanistan. At the outbreak of war with Japan he was publishing a newspaper in English and Japanese and was issuing pamphlets. On about 7 or 8 Dec 41 the Japanese High Command sent for him and asked him to head an Indian Movement. He told them that he was prepared to do this on condition that there would be no interference from the Japanese either in regard to propaganda or to personnel.

Any money supplied by the Japanese would be repaid when the movement was established. The Japanese decided that he was most unsuitable and sent for R.B. Bose. They placed Raja Mohindra Parshad under surveillance on the outskirts of Tokyo and told him he was not allowed to see the "Goodwill Mission" The Tokyo Indians would not say where he was. The Malayan delegates therefore found out for themselves and met him secretly. H/1050 considers him by far the ablest and sincerest Indian in Japan.

The Bidadari Resolutions

92. On his return to Singapore H/1050 found that the situation in camps had been complicated by the appearance of rifts, schisms and quarrels of various kinds. These had mostly arisen from one month's experience of the Japanese, without the saving influence of H/1050. On 24 Apr there was a memorial ceremony for those killed in the aeroplane accident. On 25 Apr all senior officers and some captains, about 25 officers in all, assembled at Bidadari for a statement by Lt Col .Gill of what happened at Tokyo. During this explanation H/1050 for once, sat quiet. When Gill had gone, however, H/1050 indulged in a sentimental chat which led up to the drafting of the Bidadari resolutions. "I have done my duty" he said, "until now almost singlehanded. I have secured for you a draft agreement between the Indians of East Asia and the Japanese. Now my work is over and I place myself in your hands. There are many officers among you far senior to myself, and I have been feeling that I can no longer impose myself upon you without consultation. Gentlemen, I am in your hands". Lt Col Gill then spoke to the sincerity and worth of H/1050 whom he

---

7. This refers to Raja Mahender Partap, an old Indian revolutionary nationalist, who was not allowed by the Japanese to work with Rash Behari Bose. After the war, he was interned, because of his suspision of Japanese intentions.

admitted he had at first suspected. Now he had known him day and night for 5 weeks. There was no better leader; and in his view it was the duty of those present to follow him. All agreed that H/1050 should remain military leader of the movement with their full support. The Bidadari resolutions themselves, as is already well known, were vaguely worded and ambiguous. They pledged the full efforts of those who made them in accomplishing the good of India and made no promise of co-operation with Japan to any other end. Before the meeting broke up officers were asked to explain the Tokyo resolutions to the men under their authority. None were asked as yet to volunteer.

93. On 27 Apr H/1050 addressed a meeting of all officers at Bidadari, which had assembled to bid farewell to Fujiwara who was handing over to Iwakuru. Fujiwara made an ortatory speech in Japanese in which he referred to H/1050 as "GOC". H/1050 made the following points in his own speech :

(a) He was anxiour only for the good of India, and not working either for rank or for position.
(b) He would only recognise rank given him by his own fellow countrymen.
(c) The time for volunteering was not yet ripe. When the call came volunteers must be prepared to fight against the Japanese also if the interest of Indian so demanded.

Gill Goes to Bangkok

94. The Indian community in Bangkok generally did not believe in the death of S.N. Puri and his 3 companions. Moreover, much strife had arisen between rival factions who wished one individual or another to succeed to the Indian leadership. Furthermore, there was trouble in a working camp in Bangkok to which some Indian PW had been sent in the absence in Tokyo of H/1050. (Comment : See No. 2 Section Reports 952 and 934 from corroboration of this statement and No 2 Section Report 968 on Capt Jiwan Singh Bains for one account of the working camp in Bangkok). Fujiwara requested that Lt Col Gill should be sent to Bangkok to put an end to the quarrelling and trouble. H/1050 and Gill talked over the suspicion that was in both their minds that this might be a plot to separate them. United, they felt they were very strong, a fact of which the, Japanese must be aware. They talked this over also with Raghavan and Menon, and eventually decided that they could take the suggestion at its face value. The fact that it had already been agreed that the next conference would be in Bangkok, they thought, made a trick unlikely.

H/1050 Goes Up Country with Fujiwara

95. On about 1 May 42 H/1050 went with Fujiwara on his farewell tour

of league branches in Malaya. The programme was :

1. May - Meeting of civilians at Batu Pahat addressed by Fujiwara and H/1050. The two went on to another meeting at Muar where they addressed civilians. They also saw officers in the PW camp there. They reached Kulala Lumpur during the evening, and Fujiwara dined with the IIL. H/1050 did not attend the dinner, but was present for a few minutes towards the end of the party. The speeches were over, and he has no idea what was said.
   Immediately upon arrival H/1050 had gone to the house in which he had gone to the house in which he had previously stayed in Kuala Lumpur. A play was going on in an improvised theatre nearby, and it soon became bruited abroad among the Indian soldiers there that he had arrived. Many, therefore came to see him and all asked him to speak to the men. He did so for a few minutes from the stage on which the play was being acted.
2. May - H/1050 made a long speech to officers and IORs at Kuala Lumpur. He did not specifically ask for volunteers, but many men were volunteering continually none the less. The two went on to Ipoh and held meetings there on the same day.
3. May - They went on to Penang where they attended a dinner party given by the IIL.
4. May - Alor Star. After Lunch H/1050 addressed officers and IORs. Returned to Ipoh.
5. May - Returned to Kuala Lumpur, and spent the night there.
6. May - H/1050 addressed a miscellaneous audience in the Gurdwara.

H/1050 returned to Singapore with Fujiwara the same day.

Recruiting Begins

96. Two or three days after the return of H/1050 from this tour, camp comds were called together and informed that recruiting would now begin based on the Bidadari resolutions. There were still to be no lectures, because H/1050 had already found that suitable lecturing can make simple soldiers of the type with which he had to deal volunteer for almost anything. Camps comds returned next day with long lists of men they said had volunteered, and clearly expected to be congratulated on their individual success as recruiters. In some instances whole units were reported to have volunteered en masse. H/1050 refused to accept this sort of

volunteering and insisted that each individual volunteer should sign for himself. In every unit, he would say, there must be some sick, some weak, some unfit, and someone who is bound to object to volunteering. No unit is ever unanimous about anything unless there is good sound terrorism going on. H/1050 suspected that this was the case and accordingly demanded individual signatures. Lists poured in until 30 May. Then H/1050 decided to stop recruiting as the 25,000 names which had already been given were enough to begin with. Many complained that they had not beenincluded in lists of accepted volunteers.

97. Meanwhile H/1050 had come to the conclusion that the Bidadari Resolutions, sound as they were, could not be the basis for raising an army. He determined therefore to state his real purpose in a speech to all volunteers.The Bangkok Conference had already been fixed for 15 Jun 42, and delegates were to leave on 5 or 6 Jun.

H/1050's Speech to Volunteers on 3 Jun 42

98. H/1050 addressed all volunteers who had been assembled near Alor Star Camp on 3 Jun 42. He spoke for about 1½ hrs. It was an all out propaganda speech and it worked up to a peroration which ran something like this:

> "Some of you have volunteered for this reason and some for that. Some with reservations in your heats, reservations based on those Bidadari Resolutions. I know those resolutions and what they have meant to us. But now I am going to plead the cause of the soldier before the Indian people of East Asia at Bangkok. I feel that I cannot go and be your fit, your whole hearted representative while I am bound by these reservations of yours. I must be free of them. I want you to cast all such reservations and clauses aside. I want you to have full confidence in me, that I may go, your plenipotentiary, to negotiate for you and to triumph with you."

The response was immediate, unanimous, and enthusiastic. The Bidadari Resolutions were no more. Propaganda was hence forward let loose and all encouragements were used to sharpen the faith of the volunteers.

Preparations For the Bangkok Conference

99. By the terms of the Tokyo Resolutions, H/1050 was entitled to take with him to the Bangkok conference a number of soldier delegates equal to the 90 civilians who had been delegated from the various IIL branches of East Asia. He had, however, by this time gained so much self confidence that he was sure that he alone could carry all opposition even without the presence of a single other army member. He took therefore

only 25 delegates. They were finally detailed on 4 Jun and the whole party left on 5 Jun by train.

100. H/1050summarises the period 22 Apr 5 Jun 42 as having included the following main events :

(a) The Bidadari Resolutions, a step preliminary to the raising of the INA.
(b) Departure of Gill to Bangkok.
(c) H/1050 tour up country with Fujiwara, and the departure Fujiwara, and the departure of Fujiwara.
(d) The beginning of volunteering, 25, 000 men signed on.
(e) Volunteers addressed for the first time. The scrapping of the Bidadari Resolutions.
(f) H/1050 is now fully prepared to raise the INA.

The Bangkok Conference

101. The Malayan delegates to the Bangkok conference arrived in Bangkok on 11 Jun and were accommodated at the Trocadero Hotel. On the same day H/1050 met Gill, Dhillon (C25) and Hussain (B919). On 12 and 13 Jun 42 preparatory committee meetings were held in the hotel. There was already a reception committee in existence under Ishar Singh or Sahay. On the night of 13 Jun there was a dinner party given by R.B. Bose at which H/1050 and other guests spoke. Next day H/1050, Raghavan, Menon called on the Italian and German embassies. On 15 Jun the conference opened with a plenary session at which representatives of the Axis powers spoke. Bose gave a presidential address in English. Many other delegates spoke including H/1050. The session closed at about 1300 hrs. The meeting was given full publicity and press reports.

102. During the evening there was a formal exchange, of views at a hotel on the banks of the Bangkok River, and next morning there took place the first business meeting at which there were no outsiders. The day was H/1050's. He made a full report on progress in the INA to an enthusiastic audience. As he spoke he felt that there were political undercurrents in the place which, if allowed to reach the surface, might wreck the conference on entirely irrelévant arguments. He saw in the congregation Dost Mohd Khan, the right hand man of Bose, who had even at Tokyo raised the Congress-League issue, and felt that the same issue would inevitably be raised again. He therefore made a great point in his speech of recognition of Congress leadership by the INA. In the view of the Army, he said Congress was alone the voice of India. Congress was the people of India. Supporters of other creeds, of Pakistan, Khalistan, and even Japanistan were the enemies of India as far as the INA was concerned. The Army

would only think of Hindustan. By this H/1050 roused the enthusiasm of Congress supporters to fever pitch, and left opponents and possible issue-raisers dumb founded on this matter for the rest of the conference. The first piece of business transacted was the election of the subject committee. This consisted of 12-15 members, including:

1.	H/1050	5.	Raghavan	9.	Das B.K.
2.	Gill	6.	Menon K.P.K.	10.	Ishar Singh
3.	Gilani	7.	Bashir Mallal	11.	Member from Burma
4.	Chatterji	8.	Sahay	12.	Member from Burma

103. The subject committee spent 17, 18 and 19 Jun debating resolutions which were put to the conference, discussed and adopted on 20 and 21 Jun. These are reproduced for convenience at appx D although they are already well known. One copy was forwarded to the Japanese for favour of reply and comment, and a reply was promised by Iwakuru who was in Bangkok for 28 Jun. The delegatcs therefore decided to remain in Bangkok until that date. But when 28 Jun arrived, the representative who went to receive the reply was told that it would not be ready for another week; the chiefs off delegations should therefore remain, and the rest of the representatives disperse. On 3 or 4 Jul the head delegates in their turn were told that the reply would be another week at least, and that there was no need for any but the members of the Council of Action to remain to receive it. The Council of Action was told on 12 Jul that such was the time necessary to translate this precious document, that it would not be possible to produce it for some time longer. The President therefore, said the Japanese, would alone wait to receive it. The Council of Action therefore dispersed. H/1050 heard in Bangkok for the first time of Gill's intelligence activities in that city before the war.

Exclusion of Gill from Council of Action

104. The Council of Action was formed on 21 Jun by open election, but H/1050 says that in fact it had already been nominated by the various groups meeting in secret before the meeting. Bose was president. H/1050's party agreed to that much because they felt, as they had done in Tokyo, that if the man had any influence at all with the Japanese, it could not but be valuable to the Council as a whole. For rest, he was not an impressive or even intelligent man, and would be a figure head, whom the Council of Action would rule. The members, H/1050 claims, were virtually nominated by him. As is already well known they were Raghavan, Menon, Gilani. and H/1050. Gill was not elected, and for this H/1050 gives several reasons. Firstly although liked by H/1050, he was generally distrusted. He had been an early supporter of H/1050, but nobody ever had a good word

to say for him. "He is ambitious, "one would say, "he is trying to oust H/ 1050." - "Look at his weaknesses", another would whisper, "how dependent he is on drink and women. Such a man cannot be a true supporter of a revolutionary movement. The influence of H/1050's circle , most of whom spoke like this, had prevented H/1050 from carrying out what had one time been his idea, to hand over to Gill the leadership of the whole movement. It was again partly responsible for Gill's exclusion from the Council of Action. H/1050 also considered that it would look bad and might arouse comment for both Army members of the Council to be Sikhs. The movement was already dubbed in some quarters a Sikh Movement . (Comment : See CSDIC(I) no Sec Report 958 on B 958 in which Mount Pleasant seemed to Capt Burhan Ud Din the HQ of a Sikh Raj. Furthermore Gillani, a Muslim, a State officer, and a plotter used to the intricate politics of Indian State Courts, was eminently suitable. H/1050 did at one time think of increasing the strength of the Council to seven, merely for the sake of including Gill. Gill was keenly disappointed, and when H/1050 saw this he genuinely regretted the decision he had taken. He attempted to make amends by a personal explanation, and by making it clear that whoever was on the Council of Action, Gill was 2IC of the INA, and by promising Gill redress, including the rank of General, in duc course. (H/ 1050's attitude to Gill is best explained in his own words at Appx B, page 8)

H/1050's Plan of the First Division INA

105. During the days of waiting after the conference, H/1050 put up to iwakuru, after obtaining the sanction of Bose who was so ignorant that he could not possibly do other than approve, his plan for the formation of the INA first Division, a body of 15,000 tps. This was to be an experimental formation, and future formations would depend on experience gained in raising this. The plan finally included 3,000 civilians, but H/1050 cannot remember whether this was his idea or whether it was added by Iwakuru. There were to be two main groups in the Division. Firstly, the Hind Field \Force consisting of 3 bns and attached services. Secondly, the Guerrilla Force, a formation of nine bns organised in three regts. Therc would also be the SS Group of 500 men for Intelligence duties. These would work not necessarily with the INA, but with the Japanese or alone as decided by H/ 1050. Iwakuru agreed to this plan, and emphasised the need for careful selection.

Ram Sarup Reports

106. When he was in Bangkok H/1050 met Ram Sarup (CSDIC (I) B 1000), who reported on progress in Burma. Over 2000 PW, he said, had been taken; of these many had been taken on road building fatigues

which few survived. Misra had joined him. H/1050 at this time gave Ram Sarup his intelligence role. He was instructed to report on topography, British dispositions and intentions, and the attitude of local tribes on the Burma border. During the months that followed H/1050 received some reports from Ram Sarup, but he cannot remember details. The last of these arrived during Nov 42. He regarded Ram Sarup, but he cannot remember details. The last of these arrived during Nov 42. He regarded RAM SARUP, as being an able rain and very good for his rank. He had himself planned to go to BURMA and carry out intelligence work on a rather larger scale.

First Meeting Council of Action

107. Several meetings took place at Bangkok. At the first, on 24 Jun, H/1050 was formally appointed to head the Army with the rank of full General. At subsequent meetings IIL HQ for the whole of East Asia was planned, personnel were selected, and propaganda lines laid down. Tours by R.B. Bose were mentioned, but H/1050 cannot remember whether it was then decided to move Bose's HQ to Syonan or not.

Gill's Party

108. Early in Jul 42 Iwakuru sounded Gill on his readiness for a special task, but was promptly referred to H/1050. H/1050 and Gill speculated on what the task might be and it crossed their minds that it might be another attempt on the part of the Japanese to separate them. Very respectfully and cautiously Iwakuru mentioned the matter to H/1050 next day, and H/1050 refused to consider parting with Gill at such an important time. No details had yet been given, and although he gathered the impression that Gill rather inclined towards accepting the offer whatever it might be, H/1050 does not think that it had been previously discussed by Gill and Iwakuru. H/1050 was not, however allowed to take Gill to Singapore with him as there was only one seat on the plane which took him, and it was only after forcing the issue with Iwakuru in Singapore that he finally had his way. Gill arrived on about 20 Jul by special plane.

109. Iwakuru broached the "special task" again in Singapore, but H/1050 again refused. About five days after this, however, Gill himself said, "Let us take this thing very seriously. If a secret service is to be organised, with tentacles all over fast Asia, with HQ in Bangkok or Rangoon, perhaps it would be as well for us to have the thing in our control. Perhaps we would be missing something if we refused any longer. H/1050 saw this point, and finally agreed to let Gill go if he so wished and if he really thought that there was danger of this thing falling into the hands of others, who might use it to the disadvantage of India. Gill was thereupon handed over to Iwakuru on the explicit condition that H/1050 could have

him back at any time when he called for him. Gill was allowed a free hand in the selection of personnel, and he selected about 15 officers and NCOs. (Comment : The full list can be found at Appx "A" to CSDIC (I) 2 Sec Report no 620) H/1050 thought that Gill had made a mistake in choosing so many Sikhs. M.S. Dhillon (c25) who was selected by Gill had been intended by H/1050 for the post of Military Secretary. (Comment : See S Sec CSDIC (I) ST/17 dated 23 Sept 45 Annexure I which refers to this fact.)

Planning Proceeds

110. H/1050 spent the period 20 Jul-31Jul in Planning in detail the rough outline he had presented to Iwakuru. He was assisted by about 20 of his officers whom he succeeded in keeping busy. The paper organisation was then submitted to the Japanese, who approved it in mid Aug 42.

The Personal Oath

111. Meanwhile H/1050 had approached the matter of collaboration with the Japanese purely as a soldier would, was beginning to have his own doubts of Japanese good faith. Either the IIL or the Japanese might one day try to dominate the Army, and then he would have to be very firm . In case of such an eventuality he decided to bind the Army to himself by a personal oath. He called together Gill, Gillani, Prakash Chand, Brar, both Kianis and told them that while he was not an ambitious man he felt that this oath was necessary in the interests of the Army as a whole. The draft was on the following lines :

> "I hereby volunteer unconditionally for the Indian National Army which is being raised under the command of Mohan Singh to fight for the freedom of my country."

This was to be signed by every volunteer and would cancel all previous undertakings. The "oath" was the subject of enquiry and recrimination by Raghavan on 2 Sep 42C See Appx E.)

112. When this was made public there were even more signatures than before, although H/1050 carefully abstained from lecturing until the signing had been done. When he did lecture to volunteers at each camp in turn, he inflamed, their enthusiasm to a white heat. When his propaganda was let loose, with songs, dramas and other devices, he was invited to visit non volunteers at Seletar. He claims that he created there a very good spirit, but that he did not ask for volunteers. (Note : Stracey was then Camp comd.)

Reaction to the Events in India

113. The August resolutions of the Indian National Congress became a main factor in propaganda as soon as they became known. The arrests

were of course regarded as proof of British insincerity to India, and of their fundamental unwillingness to grant independence. H/1050's feeling was that unless the British reached some definite agreement with Congress now, they would not do so late on.

They would just hang on to India as long as they could. Public indignation- both among volunteers, and as far as could be ascertained, among the Indian civilian community in Singapore, was high.

Raising of I.N.A.

114. About mid Aug 42, H/1050,s plans for organisation of the army had been approved. He therefore set about raising it. The Japs, in approving, had suggested a time table. I Div was to be complete by Dec, and was to be raised roughly as follows :

19 Aug. - Selection of HQ personnel : 15 days for organisation.

5 Sep. - Selection of Bde and major unit comds and staffs; 15 days to organise.

19 Sep. - Selection by Bde and unit comds of Bn comds. Bn comds then given 15 days to select staffs and choose coy comds.

19 Oct. - Selection of pl comds. These then given 15 days to organise pls and choose Sec comds.

5 Oct. - Selection of Coy comds. Coy comds then have 15 days to orgainse Coy HQS and choose pl comds.

5 Nov. - Selection of Sec comds. 15 days for selection of Sec personnel, issuing of equipt etc.

19 Nov. - Target date for completion of organisation from ex- military personnel.

5 Dec. - Selection of first batch of civilians (1500).

19 Dec. - Selection of second batch of civilians (1500).

Equipment and stores were collected from the Japanese dumps of captured, material, and complete in the central I.N.A. stores by the end of Aug. They were to be issued out to units as HQS were formed.

115. By the time this time table arrived, H/1050 had formed his own Supreme HQ I.N.A. had made a few plans himself, and had distributed a certain amount of work to the more capable of his staff officers. He also had worked out a programme in conjunction with his Chief of Staff M.Z. Kiani. He had decided not to include of civilains in 1 Div after all because of the delay involved and had made a time table by which the div would be formed within 10 days. H/1050 was to inspect the complete formation on the 10th day. This time table was submitted as a counter proposal to the Japanese, who replied through Ogawa that this was just another example of cantankerousness, that the way they had proposed was the proper way

to form a div, that the counter-proposal was all very well as a document, but that they would like to see how it worked. H/1050 thereupon carried it out from 1 to 10 Sep. On 8 and 9 Sep were held bn and then regt comds' inspections, and on 10 Sep H/1050 inspected the div. The Japanese were as much pleased as surprised. In the organisation, the AA gnrs lent to the Japanese in Mar 42 had been included as an arty unit, in fulfilments of H/1050's promise that they would be first members of his I.N.A. They were not present on the parade of 10 Sep as they were still under Japanese control. 1 Div strength was 17,000 instead of the 15,000 sanctioned by the Japanese. Offrs were gazetted 2/Lt on 1 Sep and thereafter were given promotion in accordance with their appointments.

H/1050 Asks for a Second Div

116. A week later H/1050 approached Iwakuru and very strongly pressed for the raising of 2 div. He said he had 25,000 surplus volunteers already and that provided the equipment was forthcoming, 2 div would be ready for parade on the 7th day after its foundation. He was by now extremely confident and went on to detail his Tokyo plans. He wished he said, to raise ultimately an army of half a million. He asked for immediate facilities to train 6,000 civilians instead of the 3,000 previously planned, and authority to recruit up to 100,000. His recruiting office had already gone out to various places in Malaya, to recruit the first 3,000, and had been overwhelmed with recruits. There had been quarrels at recruiting stations over selection by recruiting offrs. The 6,000 were ready. H/1050 further asked that an OTS should be established and opened by the end of Sept 42. This was only matter of equipment, the staff was already selected and standing by.

Crisis Begins

129. Bose arrived on 18 Nov, and on 19,20, and 21 Nov the Council of Action sat. H/1050 put before it all the points over which he had been pondering and which he had been preparing with K.P.K. Menon. Extracts from minutes of all these meetings are at Appx K,L, M, and N. The main points stated by H/1050 mainly on the morning of 19 Nov were :

(a) Army Matters

(i) The delay in raising a large INA. 3 months had passed and the Japanese had not committed themselves. They were delaying with diabolical cleverness, thought H/1050, until 1 Div was out of reach in Burma. The move to Burma of 1 Div would imede the formation of 2 Div, because cadres for new units would then have to be brought from Burma.

(ii) The delay in putting recruitment on a firm basis. It was now 3 months since H/1050 had put this matter up to Iwakuru first and there was still no definite answer.

(iii) Iwakuru had still not agreed to the formation of an CTS, in spite of continual promises.

(iv) The AA gnrs, lent to the Japanese in Mar 42, had not been returned in spite of frequent demands. Every demand was answered with a promise that they would be returned after just a little longer delay.

(v) Failure hitherto to secure the return from Burma of Lt Col Gill. This also had been frequently demanded by H/1050.

(vi) There had been instances of ill treatment of INA personnel by the Japanese, civilians and military. On one occasion 2 INA, offrs in a Singapore hotel had been abused by a Japanese civilian, assisted ably by Japanese offrs, and had been finally turned out of their places. H/1050 had made representations about this incident to Iwakuru several times, but without success.

(vii) About 400 volunteers had been lent to the Japanese by H/1050 in Oct 42 for one month only. These were to work as a transport coy in Sumatra. The Japanese had used them in fact as slave troops and had ordered them to remove their INA badges of rank.

(viii) In summary, H/1050 said that he felt the Japanese did not intend to make the INA a real army, but to maintain it as a puppet force, unable to enforce its own will.

(b) Civil Affairs

(i) The Bangkok resolutions had been unanswered. In the absence of a definite statement from the Japanese Govt of their intentions towards India and the Indian Independence Movement, of how far they agreed with the Bangkok resolutions, and of how far those resolutions could be taken as a basis of future policy, members of the Movement were living in a fool's paradise. There must be an immediate clarification.

(ii) H/1050, strongly supported by K.P.K Menon, suggested that the Council request a declaration from Tenno Heika himself. That, he said, would be the only sort of declaration which the Japanese were unlikely to repudiate later.

(iii) The Japanese were continually treating Indian property as enemy property. A representation received from Burma (to which reference is made in the minutes of 19 Nov) had indicated a similar state of affairs there.

(c) Other Points

(i) The Japanese had been sending Indians trained at Penang to India without the knowledge either of H/1050 or of the Council of Action. H/1050 had frequently tried to obtain from Iwakuru the truth about the Penang schools but had been so far completely unsuccessful. (Comments : H/1050 says that Gilani and Raghavan had both refused to tell him anything about what was going on in Penang except in the vaguest possible terms.)

(ii) H/1050 had secretly acquired 4 leaflets designed by the Japanese for dropping in India. In spite of the fact that the council of Action had long ago set up a committee for the preparation of leaflets for this purpose, and had with great care designed several, the Japanese had not shown their leaflets either to H/1050 or to the Council of Action. The Japanese leafletss were in any case extremely unsuitable in his view.

(iii) H/1050, with the support of K.P.K. Menon, closed by saying that he was certain that the Japanese had designs upon India and that any collaboration in the present circumstances could only be regarded by the people of India as rank treachery.

130. All this was not recorded in the minutes because members felt that if things turned out well in the end, the record would look bad.

(Comments : In any case the extracts from minutes which survive, were selected with a view to representing the crisis as an internal Council of Action quarrel and not the result of differences with the Japanese. Naturally, therefore, they would not include H/1050's outbursts.)

Movement of Troops

131. By the time the above meeting was held H/1050 had received news that a ship would be available on 4 Dec to take about 900 men to Burma. The council decided that pending the statement by the Japanese of outstanding questions, no further movement of troops would take place, and a note was sent to Kunizuka saying that no troops would be moved in future without the sanction of the Council of Action. This was intended to provoke a note, referring to the movement proposed on 4 Dec, to which the Council of Action would give a definite negative reply. The Japanese note of 21 Nov, however was on a scrap of paper and stated categorically: "The Movement of INA troops to Burma will be completed during Dec and Jan". This is referred to in the extracts from Council of Action minutes dated 21 Nov 42 reproduced at Appx M.

132. On 21 Nov Bose decided that a letter demanding general clarification should be drafted, but for the present he and Raghavan were

going to visit Medan. There had been no previous hint of such a visit and H/1050 thinks what it was simply a devise to delay action. The two left on 22 Nov.

Ogawa's Proposals for Expansion

133. As H/1050 reported the Council of Action on 21 Nov (see Appx M) he was approached, during the night of 20 Nov 42, with proposals for expansion. He realised that these had been produced thus suddenly because the Japanese had smelt trouble and were attempting to pacify him, and picked at once on their weak point -the date. He had been demanding expansion ever since Sep 42 (see para 132 above) and these "proposals" were no real step forward unless a date were given. The Japanese refused to do this.

Gill Returns Further Deliberations

134. Gill was met on arrival at the airfield on 25 or 26 Nov by a car which brought him at once to H/1050 for a conference. H/1050 detailed briefly the progress of the crisis to date, and Gill in his turn told H/1050 that Dhillon had deserted and gone to India. He did not say that he had sent him nor did he mention any letter either then or at any other time. H/1050 asked if the Japanese yet know about this, and on Gill's negative answer, old him to keep the whole matter secret. Dhillon's desertion was not disclosed to any Indian in Singapore until the Japanese did so when arresting Gill.

135. Bose and Raghavan returned on 26 Nov 42 and either men or on the following morning during a meeting of the C of A, Bose said that he was going to Bangkok on personal business. The other members of the Council told him that he was merely trying to avoid a crisis by running away, and was playing the delaying game of the Japanese. "What business", they asked sarcastically, "either personal or private could be more important than the crisis which had arisen ? you must stay." Bose eventually gave way.

136. Meetings of the Council of Action took place on 27 and 28 Nov. Appendix N represents, according to H/1050 what took place on 27 Nov. Minutes of the either meeting have not, unfortunately, been recovered H/1050 was instructed to present another note to Kunizuka on the subject of movement of troops to Burma. He said this.

Kagawa's Recruitment Proposals

137. During one of the 2 meetings Kagawa came in with a recruitment plan he said that it was H/1050's own plan (see para 116) with minor alterations,. H/1050, however, disagreed, as Kagawa's plan disposed of

the main points he had put up. Firstly he had said that the object of training Indian civilians was to make them soldiers of the I.N.A., while Kagawa's plan proposed to make them I.I.L. workers. Secondly, H/1050 had stated as his target figure for civilian recruitment an eventual 250,000 while Kagawa only mentioned the original 6,000 recruited in Sep 42 (see para 116 above). Kagawa's plan also said that the I.I.L. was to supply equipment and rations for the new recruits, and that no more arms would be provided by the Japanese.

138. This "Plan" made clarification an even more immediate necessity and ended any doubts remaining in the Council of Action. On 29 Nov, therefore, Bose took to Iwakuru the letter reproduced at appx O together with a copy of that presented and withdrawn in Sep 42 (appx H). Iwakuru received him very rudely and flatly refused to consider the matter. Accordingly the Council of Action drafted the following letter to Iwakuru for onward transmission to Tokyo.

Indian Independence League.
Syonan, 29 Nov 2602.

To,

Colonel H. Iwakuro,
Chief of the Iwakuro Kikan.
For Favour of Transmission to the Imperial
Government of Japan.

The Council of Action had a series of sittings recently when it took stock of the whole situation concerning the Indian Independence Movement in East Asia and the development of the revolutionary struggle in India. The enormous increase in the number of the members in the Indian Independence League, the wide network of League organisations throughout East Asia, the tremendous enthusiasm seen every where for the cause which we stand for and the spirit of sacrifice manifested by all classes of Indian in East Asia, have given us immense satisfaction in the progress of the Movement made possible by the help and co-operation of the Imperial Nipponese Government. The rapid march of revolutionary events in India resulting in the growing number of strikes, rebellions, sabotage and other mass actions have further raised our hopes and leave us in no doubt regarding the intentions and determination of our countrymen to overthrow British rule to regain our independence at any cost. We have new reached a stage at which we feel that before we take any further forward move it is necessary to clear matters, to understand our position perfectly and to cement Indo-Japanese friendship without which it is impossible for us to do any effective work for the attainment of our objective.

We are unfortunately so placed that we have not so far been able to contact with leaders in India and ascertain their views regarding our policy and own plans. This makes our responsibility all the more sacred and onerous. The time would not be distant when we shall have to deal with a provisional National Government in India and when that comes we must be in a position to convince them that we have taken every possible step to maintain the safety, dignity and integrity of our country when once our goal of independence has been reached.

We have, therefore, after very careful consideration, come to the conclusion that it will be advantageous and in the interests of our Movement to request the Imperial Government of Japan to favour us with a reply, at the earliest possible opportunity, clarifying the position on the following points :

1. A copy of the Bangkok Resolutions has been forwarded to the Imperial Government so long ago as the 22nd July (CSDIC (I) wrong, June) 2602. Though we have been working on the basis that such resolutions would be accepted by the Imperial Government we are not yet in a position to know exactly where we stand with regard to these resolutions. We do not want to conceal the fact that anxious enquiries are still being made by many leading members of our community regarding these resolutions and we find it difficult and even embarrassing to give them a satisfactory reply. It is therefore an urgent importance to us to request the Imperial Government to be good enough to inform us, formally and at the earliest possible opportunity, regarding the acceptance of the Bangkok Resolutions to which the Imperial Government cannot give their support, we shall be glad if they would kindly define their attitude towards the same.
2. Recognition of the Council of Action as the Supreme executive of the Indian Independence Movement in East Asia and the acceptance of their status as such is absolutely necessary in order that the Council of Action may function efficiently.
3. The Imperial Government must no doubt be aware of the propaganda that is being carried on the British Government in India regarding the intentions of Japan. Although we have had some declarations from His Excellency Premier General Tojo and other leading statesmen of Japan to the effect that Japan has no political or military ambitions in India, we would respectfully suggest that a full formal and solemn declaration binding on the present and future Government of Japan regarding the intentions of Japan to recognise and support the absolute independence

and full sovereignty of India immediately on the removal of British rule in India is found essential to instil complete confidence and to place the movement on an effective and proper footing.

4. As a corollary to the acceptance of the Bangkok Resolutions it is necessary that the formation and existance it is necessary that the formation and existence of the Indian National Army on the principles laid down in the said resolution will be formally and publicly recognised and all facilities offered for its expansion with a view to make the Army a strong and efficient one to carry out the great purpose for which it is intended.

We are conscious of and profoundly grateful to the Imperial. Government of Japan for, the great help they are rendering Indians in connection with this Movement and with further support, which we have no doubt will be forthcoming, we shall be able to attain our goal of Independence in the immediate future.

Dated This 29th Day of November, 2602.

Sgd. R.B. Bose,
President Council of Action
Indian Independence League.

139. On 30 Nov Iwakuru ordered all members of the Council of Action to meet him on the morning of 1 Dec.

The Storm Breaks

140. Bose and his Council presented themselves at about 1000 hrs. There were also present Mr. Senda 2 Japanese Diet members, and 2 or 3 senior Japanese officers besides Iwakuru. K.P.K, Menon was the Council of Action spokesman, Bose being far too dumb to cope with a situation like this. He spoke freely and boldly the mind of the Council in a speech which lasted for about 30 minutes. He said that the Japanese policy of continual delay had raised doubts in the minds of the Council of Action members and that while such doubts persisted the Council could not undertake to go on misleading the Indian public. Iwakuru replied in violent terms, accusing the Indians of having suspicious distrusting minds. He said that Indian Independence was as yet a babe unborn. It could only be seriously considered when the Japanese reached India. He, Iwakuru, was the representative of the Japanese Government, his view was the Government view, and he categorically refused to forward the letter. The meeting broke up at 1600 hrs after an excellent lunch.

141. H/1050 thinks that Iwakuru on that occasion acted in accordance with he instructions received from his C in C on the previous evening. Iwakuru himself would have liked to be less uncompromising.

142. H/1050 throughout the crisis had been in close daily touch with his INA senior officers, (majors and above), to whom he reported progress each evening. He had told them on the eve of Iwakuru's conference that he expected one of four things to happen. Iwakuru might refuse clarification point blank. He might be advised by other Japanese offrs to give way. He might compromise or he might begin another delaying action. H/1050 thought that either of the first two would be good, but that the third and fourth would be dangerous. He continued to inform his officers of every move and they knew exactly what was going on up to the end. H/1050 says that he was aware that Chatterji and Ehsan Qadir (B 978) reported all that went on at these conferences of officers to the Japanese. Both these officers were well in with Iwakuru and his underlings, and visited them frequently. B978 was carrying a whispering campaign against H/1050's position during this crisis. While H/1050 said that the Japanese were brutes, B 978 said "let us tame the brutes". He was suspected by all of secret dealings with the Japanese.

143. The Council of Action and the INA officers as a whole were rather relieved than sorry at the answer Iwakuru actually gave. The same day PW officers were summoned to a meeting in a PW camp, and were told by a Japanese officer that all Indian PW would be in future be treated as such, and that there would no longer be any chance for volunteering. H/1050 heard about this.

H/1050 Decides to Act

144. On the same evening H/1050 ordered that all surplus volunteers would revert to PW status. It was now quite clear to him that the Japanese only wanted a small INA of political and propaganda value : he also saw that they realised his own growing power and his real patriotism, and that they had decided they must check him. They must also know, he thought, that with such first class legal brains as Raghavan and Menon in the movement, they could only exploit Indians through a small army. They could trust, moreover their own tps with the available weapons better than Indians, and arms were in short supply. Finally, H/1050 felt that the Japanese had underestimated the Indian officers. They thought that they were men who had burned their boats, who would not now be received back into the British fold, and who would therefore finally submit to them.

145. From the INA point of view he considered the following things :

(a) Expansion was now clearly out of the question.

(b) The Burma offensive would certainly take place early in 1943.

(c) H/1050 would not be able to exercise effective control over his tps in Burma, scattered as they would be.

(d) Now the whole INA was concentrated, united in support of him, and any action he took would be thereby strengthened.

(e) If the Japanese later agreed to expansion, he would have great difficulty in carrying it out if committed to active service.

146. H/1050 therefore appreciated that the time had come for action. Menon entirely agreed, and all the points mentioned above had been discussed before and approved by INA senior officers. H/1050 knew of his own popularity with the Indian civilians, and decided that he must make some public demonstration of his feeling about Japanese insincerity. He told his officers that the movement could go on no longer. (*Comment*: At Appx B H/1050 alleges that it had been his intention from the first publicly to expose the Japanese if they proved insincere about India. It is considered that this claim should be treated with reserve.)

147. On 2 Dec 42 a further letter was sent to Iwakuru by Bose which said that he council of Action was seriously considering its own position. This is at Appx Q. A meeting of the Council of Action of which no minutes are available, discussed the present impossible situation. H/1050 and K.P.K. Menon suggested that the movement had played along with the Japanese for long enough, and that if any further collaboration was to take place it must be done after a conference of representatives and under a new Council of Action. H/1050 further said that it was now definite that not a soldier more of the INA could move from Malaya.

148. During 2 and 3 Dec great pressure was brought to bear on H/1050 by his Japanese friends and on 3 Dec Fujiwara arrived, having been summoned to bring H/1050 round. For 3 hrs Fujiwara tried to persuade H/1050 that this ship at least must go on 4 Dec, but H/1050 was adamant. H/1050 told the Council of Action about his stand in a session on the afternoon of 3 Dec. and his officers were informed during the same evening. By this time all INA senior officers had given H/1050 a pledge of their unconditional support, that they would resist all attempts by the Japanese to exploit them, and that should H/1050 be dismissed, or resign, they would under no circumstances continue the INA or raise another. This pledge was given at a meeting when Gill presided in H/1050's absence.

149. Fujiwara then approached individually each member of the C. of A. with some success, any H/1050 became a little annoyed with them for wavering. He put to the Council four demands (embodied in minutes of 5 Dec Appx R) without which he considered not movement should take place. Other questions, he said, could be settled at leisure. These must be conceded at once.

Resignations from Council of Action

150. On the morning of 4 Dec Raghavan resigned, and in his letter (Appx S(a)) excused himself by blaming H/1050 for the whole trouble. By the time the Council of Action met; however, Menon, Gilani and H/1050 had prevailed upon Raghavan to withdraw his letter for the sake of a collective resignation later. Raghavan was therefore present during the afternoon when the other three pur a draft letter of resignation for all to sign. Bose replied with a pathetic appeal for 2 months respite and promised to take up and solve all outstanding questions. (Minutes of this meeting are at Appx R) The draft resignation was withdrawn on Bose's promise.

151. Further consideration by Menon, Gilani and H/1050 only convinced them that Bose was playing Iwakuru's delaying game. Raghavan still vauered. On 5 Dec. therefore, they put up H/1050's four demands, and said they would resign if these were refused. These are embodied in the extracts from Council of Action minutes dated 5 Dec. reproduced at Appx R. If they were granted, the members concerned would consent to Bose's request for time. These points came to be known as "Mohan Singh's ultimatum". They were put to Iwakuru by Bose.

152. Iwakuru was even more outspoken than he had been on 1 Dec. and on 6 or 7 Dec categorically refused to consider this "ultimatum".

The Arrest of Gill

153. Before dawn on 8 Dec 42 the chief of the Kempei Tai[9] and 17 of his henchmen called upon H/1050 , and having wakened him, gave him a letter. The letter requested him to hand over Lt Col Gill who was wanted on charges "of a serious nature. The Kempei Tai chief had instructions to deal gently with H/1050 and if possible not to quarrel. The letter said that if Gill were handed over, no other member of the INA would ever be arrested. H/1050, however, refused to hand over Gill, knowing full well that his refusal would not make any difference. He was quite capable, he said, as Coc, of investigating any crime, and he must be told the charge. The Kemei Tai then proceeded to arrest Gill, H/1050 went with them to their office in order to ascertain the charges. A Japanese office took him aside and told him that Gill had sent a letter to the AG in India and that the Kempei Tai held a copy of it . H/1050 said that he did not believe this, but Gill was removed despite H/1050's violent protests, to the Kemei Tai lockup. The Japanese made further vain attempts to pacify the raging H/1050.

154. H/1050 told INA officers about the arrest of Gill on the same

9. Name of the Japanese Militery Police.

morning, saying that "the time" had come, that all ranks should now be ready for any sacrifice.

Resignations

155. The resignations of H/1050, Gilani and Menon had already been drafted when Gill was arrested. Raghavan sent in his resignation again during the morning, and when he was located by the other three towards evening he could not be persuaded to withdraw his letter once more and to resign jointly with them. He wished, says H/1050, to save both his face and his skin. Bose himself refused to resign, and the three therefore handed over their original joint lettrer, to which a paragraph referring to the arrest had been added. All resignations and Bose's replies are Appx S. Bose claimed that the only point of difference between himself and his resigning colleagues was whether or not to exercise "all patience" with the Japanese before deciding that the Movement had failed.

H/1050 Tells the INA

156. H/1050 spoke in Bidadari and Neesoon to all INA officers on 9 Dec. He told them the full story, already known to some of them. He appealed for unity and a spirit of sacrifice. He said that his duty was to fulfil the purpose for which the INA had been raised. He referred to the volunteers, oath and said he would take full responsibility. This was probably, he said, the end of the INA. Its continuance would only serve the designs of the Japanese and their puppet Bose who wanted to exploit PW for his own advantage. His audiences were profoundly moved and many, including H/1050 who says that nobody loved this army as he did, wept.

Further Correspondence 10-20 Dec

157. Bose, who was affecting to assume all power as the sole survivor of the Council of Action, now evidently realised that H/1050 was bent on dissolving the INA. He sent for all senior officers, with the notable exception of Gilani and H/1050, in an attempt to overpower H/1050's influence. The correspondence between H/1050 and Bose that followed this order is at Appx T. It ended in a crushing victory for H/1050 which probably decided his eventual fate.

158. On 15 Dec 42 H/1050 wrote to Iwakuru saying that all members of the INA would now revert to the status of PW, and that none of them and any confidence left in the Indian Independence Movement under the puppet Rash Behari Bose. Iwakuru's reply is given in H/1050's own words on page 8 of Appx B. He offered to let the INA work inside India, but this offer faded from his memory within 24 hours.

The Crisis Reported to India

159. On about 7 Dec H/1050, after discussion with Gill, felt that it was his duty to India by some means to convey there the news of what had happened so far. He knew that to help the British was now to help India, as it was quite evident that the Japanese were out only to exploit. At the same time he felt that he could not, because of his previous uncompromising attitude towards the British, and of the harsh things he had said about them, send intelligence to any British officer. He therefor selected 5 Sikh civilian recruits, of good education, who were natives of Kuala Lumpur and guaranteed reliable by Budh Singh, and old gentleman of Kuala Lumpur, who had been doing social work among PW there. (Comment : See CSDIC(I) report 978 para 6. This is the same man). These man were to proceed to Thailand, Burma and India in civilian guise. He made them learn their messages by heart and also gave them documents which they must absorb ad destroy before crossing the Malayan border. His instructions were to pass on the information to INA comds of PW camps, to Ram Sarup in Burma and to Congress leaders and Indian Officers of the Indian Army in India. The names of the 5 selected are :

1. Ajaib Singh
2. Kehar Singh
3. Dalip Singh
4. Ajit Singh
5. Mukham Singh

160. H/1050 says that between 7 Dec 42 ad 29 Dec 42 other men were detailed for similar duties by Gilani and Brar. Gilani agreed to pass information to India through Penang agents, if possible.

(Comments : The above information is confirmed generally by Gilani. Brar only knew of Nos 2 and 5 on the list above. He says they were commissioned to convey to various INA officers commanding PW Camps in Malaya, Thailand and Burma, news of what was happening, and to warn them not to let themselves be exploited by the Japanese. He knows of no order for these men go to India. Kehar Singh reached Bangkok, and having contacted the men whose names had been given to Brar by Gill, returned to report in Feb or Mar 43. Mukham Singh did not go further than the borders of Malaya. He did not join the 2nd INA and 6 months before the Japanese surrender he joined the Communist guerillas in Malaya because he was being pursued by the Kempei Tai.)

The Dissolution of the INA and the Arrest of H/1050

161. A warning order for the dissolution was issued on 21 Dec. It contained a full statement of the situation, and said that as the purpose for

which the INA was raised could not be served, duty to India demanded that it be dissolved. H/1050 also sent a secret letter to all units, which was marked "To be opened in the event of the removable, disappearance, assassination or arrest of the GOC". This contained final orders for the dissolution, for the removal of badges of ranks the burning of records, the absolution of all ranks from their personal pledge to H/1050, and their reversion to PW status. The purpose of this letter was not to make the dissolution conditional upon the arrest of H/1050, but to forestall and sudden attempt to take control of the INA before H/1050 was ready to dissolve it. (*Comment* : Gilani, who seems to have had a foot in each camp within the Council of Action, says that H/1050 delayed the dissolution because he still hoped to reach a separate understanding with the Japanese. Eshan Qadir (B978 (I) Report 978 (para 39 (I)) refers to Raghavan's anxiety to obtain control of the INA).

162. Although all this was now purely an army matter, K.P.M. Menon continued in the complete confidence of H/1050 and was informed of every move.

163. H/1050 may have held a few more meetings of officers between 21 and 29 Dec. On the morning of 29 Dec Iwakuru asked H/1050 to meet him at 1100 hours. Before he went H/1050 received a second message, that Iwakuru wished to see all INA officers of the rank of Major and above at INA HQ at 1200 hrs. H/1050 told his officers they he might not return from this interview, and ascertained that all his instructions were understood.

164. At Iwakuru's house there were also present Bose, Senda and four or five Japanese officers. When H/1050, arrived, Bose produced from his pocket a letter (H/1050 says not drafted by Bose) and handed it to H/1050. This was a dismissal and a statement of charges, clearly the sequel to the series of letters reproduced at Appx. T. It ended by saying that in consideration of his services H/1050 would be saved alive and provided with he necessities of life. H/1050 replied that this final injustice was not altogether unexpected, but that he understood how Bose wasn't really responsible for it. Iwakuru then read in Japanese, and para by para, Senda read in English, along statement setting out Japanese charges against H/1050 and answering H/1050's own accusations against the Japanese. H/1050 thinks that copies of this statement were subsequently distributed on a wide scale. H/1050's reply, although no reply to such a categorical document was strictly called for, was that he had done all in the interests of his country. H/1050 was then arrested and he never saw the INA again.

Remarks by H/1050

165. At this point H/1050 gives a summary of his intentions for and

views about the first INA. This follows the lines of his "public statement" at Appx "B".[10]

(a) He began it because he saw an opportunity of serving his country. He recognised the risks, but also realised that nothing worthwhile is ever accomplished without running risks.

(b) Had the Japanese remained sincere, there would today have been no distinction of volunteer and non-volunteer. All PW would have been united in the INA. Civilians too, -1942 was a time when every Indian worth the name was prepared to bear arms should a worthy purpose and a worthy leader appear : the INA would by now have been immense. The purpose of such an army was that it should go into action in Burma, and by suffering a very few casualties arouse such a storm of public feeling in India and in allied countries as would compel the British to come to terms with Congress. If this did not occur, the INA would fight to the last man. 1942 was the psychological moment, the INA might have achieved its purpose then, but the moment could not recur.

(c) Whatever concessions were after the dissolution wrong from the Japanese were —due to the brave stand made in 1942 by officers and men of the INA, and to a few brave and forthright civilians, one of whom was K.P.K. Menon. A second factor was, of course, the changing tide of war. The Japanese at no time honestly wished the freedom either of India or of any other country which they could subject by force.

(d) H/1050's decision in Dec. 42 was the result of mature and careful thought, and not of a sudden brainstorm. It was not easy for him to destroy that which he had created, but he was convinced that India's interests demanded its destruction.

(e) H/1050 categorically denies the suggestion made to "S" Section by Lt Col Gill that Lt. Col. Gill was in any way responsible, save as a supporter of H/1050, for the destruction of the INA. The matter had never been discussed by H/1050 and Gill before Dec. 42.

---

9. Appendix II.

Index

G

H

W

Y